Women in Scripture

Women in Scripture

A Dictionary of
Named and Unnamed Women in the
Hebrew Bible, the Apocryphal/Deuterocanonical Books,
and the New Testament

Carol Meyers,

General Editor

Toni Craven and Ross S. Kraemer,

Associate Editors

WILLIAM B. EERDMANS PUBLISHING COMPANY
GRAND RAPIDS, MICHIGAN / CAMBRIDGE, U.K.

This edition published 2001 by Wm. B. Eerdmans Publishing Co.
255 Jefferson Ave. S.E., Grand Rapids, Michigan 49503 /
P.O. Box 163, Cambridge CB3 9PU U.K.
www.eerdmans.com

Printed in the United States of America

06 05 04 03 02 01   7 6 5 4 3 2 1

Library of Congress Cataloging-in-Publication Data

Women in scripture: a dictionary of named and unnamed women in the
Hebrew Bible, the Apocryphal/Deuterocanonical books, and the New Testament /
Carol Meyers, general editor; Toni Craven and Ross S. Kraemer, associate editors.
                    p.   cm.
Includes bibliographical references and index.
ISBN 0-8028-4962-8
1. Meyers, Carol L.   II. Craven, Toni.   III. Kraemer, Ross Shepard, 1948-
                BS575.W593   2000
            220.9′2′082 — dc21
                99-089577

JACKET ILLUSTRATION: *Women at the Nile.* The five women depicted on the jacket are part of the paintings on the west wall of the third-century C.E. synagogue at Dura Europos in Mesopotamia. The two figures at left probably represent two of the women walking along the Nile with Pharaoh's daughter in Exodus 2:5. The two women at right, who face the unseen Pharaoh, may be the two midwives of the exodus story, Shiphrah and Puah. The kneeling figure defies identification. She may be the Egyptian princess discovering the infant Moses or the baby's mother putting him into the river.

FOR OUR DAUGHTERS

✛

Kathryn Ruth Craven
Jordan Harriet Kraemer
Dina Elisa Meyers
Julie Kaete Meyers

Contents

—◦◦◦—

CONTRIBUTORS

VALERIE ABRAHAMSEN, Boston, Massachusetts

SUSAN ACKERMAN, Dartmouth College

HUGH ANDERSON, University of Edinburgh, Scotland

JOUETTE M. BASSLER, Perkins School of Theology, Southern Methodist University

ANGELA BAUER, Episcopal Divinity School

LYN M. BECHTEL, Drew Theological School

ALICE OGDEN BELLIS, Howard School of Divinity

ADELE BERLIN, University of Maryland

CHANA BLOCH, Mills College

KARLA G. BOHMBACH, Susquehanna University

BEVERLY BOW, Cleveland State University

ATHALYA BRENNER, University of Amsterdam, Netherlands

MARC ZVI BRETTLER, Brandeis University

SHEILA BRIGGS, University of Southern California

BERNADETTE J. BROOTEN, Brandeis University

LUCINDA A. BROWN, Wilmington, Delaware

RHONDA BURNETTE-BLETSCH, Greensboro College

CLAUDIA V. CAMP, Texas Christian University

TONY W. CARTLEDGE, Apex, North Carolina

JOHN J. COLLINS, University of Chicago

TONI CRAVEN, Brite Divinity School, Texas Christian University

SIDNIE WHITE CRAWFORD, University of Nebraska, Lincoln

MARY ROSE D'ANGELO, University of Notre Dame

KATHERYN PFISTERER DARR, Boston University School of Theology

DIANA VIKANDER EDELMAN, James Madison University

TAMARA COHN ESKENAZI, Hebrew Union College

J. CHERYL EXUM, University of Sheffield, England

CAROLE R. FONTAINE, Andover Newton Theological School

FRANK S. FRICK, Albion College

TIKVA FRYMER-KENSKY, University of Chicago

JENNIFER A. GLANCY, LeMoyne College

BETH GLAZIER-MCDONALD, Centre College

ELAINE ADLER GOODFRIEND, California State University

WILLIAM R. GOODMAN, JR., Lynchburg College

SANDRA L. GRAVETT, Appalachian State University

MAYER I. GRUBER, Ben-Gurion University, Israel

JO ANN HACKETT, Harvard University

WALTER J. HARRELSON, Wake Forest University Divinity School

SUSAN TOWER HOLLIS, Western New York Center of State University of New York, Empire State College

LILLIAN R. KLEIN, Bethesda, Maryland

RONALD S. KLINE, Arlington, Texas

ROSS S. KRAEMER, Brown University

ALICE L. LAFFEY, College of the Holy Cross

ELIZABETH C. LaROCCA-PITTS, Duke Divinity School

AMY-JILL LEVINE, Vanderbilt Divinity School

LYNN LiDONNICI, Vassar College

VASILIKI LIMBERIS, Temple University

ELIZABETH STRUTHERS MALBON, Virginia Polytechnic Institute and State University

MADELINE GAY MCCLENNEY-SADLER, Duke University

ANNE McGUIRE, Haverford College

CAROL MEYERS, Duke University

ERIC M. MEYERS, Duke University

MARGARET M. MITCHELL, McCormick Theological Seminary

CAREY A. MOORE, Gettysburg College

JULIA MYERS O'BRIEN, Lancaster Theological Seminary

CAROLYN OSIEK, Catholic Theological Union, Chicago

THOMAS W. OVERHOLT, University of Wisconsin, Stevens Point

ILANA PARDES, Hebrew University of Jerusalem, Israel

RICHARD I. PERVO, University of Minnesota

TINA PIPPIN, Agnes Scott College

CAROLYN PRESSLER, United Theological Seminary of the Twin Cities

ADELE REINHARTZ, McMaster University, Canada

KATHARINE DOOB SAKENFELD, Princeton Theological Seminary

JUDITH E. SANDERSON, Seattle University

LINDA S. SCHEARING, Gonzaga University

NAOMI STEINBERG, DePaul University

KEN STONE, Chicago Theological Seminary

SARAH J. TANZER, McCormick Theological Seminary

PHYLLIS TRIBLE, Wake Forest University Divinity School

PIETER W. van der HORST, Utrecht University, Netherlands

GALE A. YEE, Episcopal Divinity School

Preface

Over the past three decades, biblical scholarship has given unprecedented attention to the women portrayed in the Bible, as well as to various biblical passages that have direct or indirect relationship to women's lives. That scholarship has produced a voluminous literature, which explores the status and role of women in biblical texts and in the ancient world that produced them. In academic institutions, the study of women, or more broadly of gender, in the Bible has become an accepted component of several disciplines — religion, literature, ancient history, women's studies, and so on. Yet the results of scholarly attention to female figures in the Bible have not yet become fully integrated into introductory textbooks and other general books about the Bible. Nor have they yet become widely discussed in pulpit and pew.

This new academic interest in biblical women was motivated in part by broader political and social issues. Despite the theoretical separation of government and religion in the United States and many Western countries, attitudes and policies that affect women's lives are often determined by biblical materials, either in explicit reference to certain texts or in the general way in which Western culture has incorporated biblical ideas. Certainly people within most Jewish and Christian denominations, whose beliefs and customs are rooted in biblical tradition, are often affected by the Bible in matters of gender, that is, cultural ideas about female and male.

The enduring political and religious impact of the Bible on Western society is colored by the many ways in which biblical figures, men as well as women, have been portrayed in postbiblical culture. Many works of Western literature, art, music, and theology elaborate on biblical characters and themes. Indeed, creative interpretation and expansion of biblical materials can become powerful and prominent enough to obscure the fact that female figures in their "afterlife" — the way they appear in postbiblical cultural productions — may diverge significantly from their biblical depictions. Milton's *Paradise Lost*, for example, mentions an apple as the forbidden fruit in the Garden of Eden; and Michelangelo and many other artists paint apples into their "temptation" scenes. Yet the biblical account makes no mention of an apple but rather says "fruit." The literary and artistic interpretation of fruit as apple may have no negative consequences, but other similar interpretations and interpolations that change or distort the biblical text definitely do. From antiquity to the present, for example, Eve has been referred to as a temptress or sinner, yet those terms are nowhere to be found in the Genesis 2–3 narrative. Think of the consequences of such interpretive labeling.

How can consumers of Western culture, with its varied representations of biblical women, sort out the biblical origins of those images? How can those concerned with the way the Bible affects the political, economic, social, and religious lives of women evaluate the biblical foundations of such influence? Biblical scholarship, of course, provides important information for these quests. Some of the academic work on women and the Bible has been published in forms accessible to nonspecialist readers. Yet that work is often narrowly focused, and none of it claims to be comprehensive. *Women in Scripture* was conceived as a way to collect the best and most up-to-date scholarship — feminist biblical scholarship — in a single, user-friendly book. To do so, we have drawn upon the expertise of more than seventy experts, both women and men, from America, Europe, and Israel.

In *Women in Scripture* the combined effort of these contributors summarizes much of the new knowledge, generated since the late 1960s, on women in biblical texts. At the same time, it has produced new scholarship. In our attempt to be comprehensive, we came upon scores of passages mentioning women that had never before been studied from a feminist perspective. Such a perspective seeks to understand a text specifically for the way it functions as a representation of women's lives and experiences and also to evaluate whether sexism is encoded in the text, its traditional interpretations, or both.

In designing this project, we decided at the very outset that it ought to include biblical materials about women that are found in the authoritative Scripture — the canon — of both Jews and Christians. The female figures and the texts mentioning females thus come from three "scriptures." *Scripture* is a term that designates a document or set of documents that is deemed highly important or authoritative in a religious community. In this case, Jews and Christians are the scriptural communities, and the entries in this dictionary are taken from (1) the books of the Hebrew Bible (known to Christians as the Old Testament), which *is* the Bible for Jews; (2) the Apocryphal/Deuterocanonical Books (ancient Jewish writings not included in the Hebrew Bible), which are considered canonical by Roman Catholics and, with several additions, by the Eastern and Russian Orthodox Churches; and (3) the New Testament, which, along with the Hebrew Bible, is authoritative for all Christians.

Deciding to include those three sets of Scripture was the easy part. Identifying and organizing the material represented in them proved challenging. The obvious place to begin was with the women, whether historical or literary figures, whose names

are mentioned in the Bible. Entries based on those 205 names comprise Part I of this volume. The 205 entries, however, do not represent 205 different women. Ten women are known by two different names (for example, Naomi is also called Mara; Esther is also known as Hadassah; Dorcas and Tabitha are the same woman; Zosara is the same woman as Zeresh), and one has three alternative names. Of course, only one article has been written for each woman. The reader will simply look up any one of the names in the alphabetical arrangement to be directed to the article's location.

Those 205 names also include twenty-seven instances in which several biblical figures bear the same name. These have individual entries. In most cases (nineteen of them), two different women are called by a particular name (for example, the well-known Miriam of the exodus story, and an obscure Miriam who appears in the listing of the Calebites in 1 Chr 4:17). But several names are found more often. Three names appear three times, and one name is used for four women. The most popular name in the Hebrew Bible is Maacah, which refers to seven different women; and Mary in the New Testament refers to at least six and possibly seven separate individuals. It should be noted that the second Salome entry is about the dancer who brought about the death of John the Baptist; because she is not actually named in the New Testament, the name Salome is conjectural.

Also, eleven of the entries in Part I are composite ones, having two or, in several cases, three parts. That is, when a single biblical woman appears in more than one section of the full Jewish-Christian canon, the entry for her consists of separate discussions related to each section. The most obvious example is Eve, whose entry comprises three parts because she is mentioned in the Apocryphal/Deuterocanonical Books and in the New Testament as well as in the Hebrew Bible. But there are anomalies. Rebekah of the Genesis narratives appears in the New Testament; however, because her name is spelled differently (Rebecca) in Romans, her entry is titled Rebecca, with a reference to it at the composite Rebekah entry. Another anomaly is the entry for Bathsheba; after the discussion of the Hebrew Bible figure, the reader is directed to the discussion of her appearance in the New Testament in Part II because her name is not mentioned in Matt 1:6, where she is simply called the "wife of Uriah." Similarly, the unnamed woman in Dan 11:17 presumed to be Cleopatra is discussed in an entry, entitled "Wife of the King of the South," in Part II.

These 205 entries for named women include several names that are also found in the Bible as men's names. Nahash, for example, denotes the king of the Ammonites in 1 Samuel 10–12. It is therefore often supposed that the Nahash in 2 Sam 12:25 is also a man. Yet the syntax in the 2 Samuel text is ambiguous, and it is just as likely that the name there denotes a female. In all such cases, we have given women the benefit of the doubt and provided an entry that explains the difficulty in the language and allows for the possibility that a woman is indicated. In some cases, names that can be used for both women and men are present in genealogies and other lists of names. Without a narrative context, it is virtually impossible to identify whether women or men are being mentioned. We may have unavoidably missed several such named women, though every effort has been made to be comprehensive.

Identifying all the named women and women's names in the Bible was only the first step in accomplishing our goal of listing all biblical females. Even the casual reader of the Bible will notice that many important figures as well as minor characters, both female and male, remain nameless. In the tragic story in Judges 11, for example, the offering of a young woman's life becomes part of her father's desperate vow on the eve of battle, and she ultimately dies because of that vow. She is known only as the "daughter of Jephthah"; her name is not included in the tale. Similarly, the woman who anoints Jesus in the Gospels of Matthew, Mark, and Luke, and the Samaritan woman in John 4, both significant figures in the New Testament, remain anonymous (interestingly, however, the Gospel of John identifies Mary the sister of Lazarus as the anointing woman). Such is also the case for the unnamed martyr-mother who witnesses the persecution and death of her seven sons in 2 Maccabees 7 and 4 Maccabees 8.

The omission of women's names may result from literary strategy, biblical androcentrism, concern with patrilineality (tracing descent through the male line), or some other reason. Because many male characters also remain anonymous, the absence of women's names cannot be simply attributed to biblical sexism. Whatever the reason for the many nameless women (and men) in the Bible, we are not the first to wonder about them. Since antiquity, both Jewish and Christian tradition has given them names. Noah's wife (Gen 6:18; 7:7, 13; 8:18), for example, has been assigned more than 103 names in postbiblical discussions of the Genesis flood story. For the New Testament, people such as the Canaanite (or Syrophoenician) woman and her daughter (Matt 15:21–28; Mark 7:24–30) are given names in ancient Christian sources.

Because of the plethora of anonymous women, we added Part II to this project. This, the largest section of *Women in Scripture*, contains entries for all unnamed biblical women in the order in which they appear, book by book, in the Hebrew Bible, the Apocryphal/Deuterocanonical Books, and the New Testament, following the New Revised Standard Version (NRSV) sequence. Part II begins with the first female created, according to Gen 1:26–28 (and also mentioned in Gen 5:1–2); and it ends with the bride (and bridegroom) of Rev 18:23.

The books of the Hebrew Bible are ordered differently in Jewish Bibles than in Christian ones. To arrange the entries in Part II of this book, we decided to follow the ordering found in the NRSV, one of the most up-to-date and widely used translations into English of the original Hebrew, Aramaic, and Greek of the Bible. Following the NRSV order appears to privilege the Christian community. That order concludes the Hebrew Bible with the prophetic books, which can be interpreted as pointing toward a fulfillment of prophecy in the New Testament. The Hebrew Bible, however, in its original languages and in Jewish translations, such as the New Jewish Publication Society (NJPS) version, ends with the books of Chronicles. We hope that our readers will understand that we have used the NRSV ordering simply to provide a point of reference available to the widest group possible and not to point to the Christian canon as the only authoritative arrangement.

The fact that Part II of *Women in Scripture* is the largest section may seem puzzling at first. Are there really more than 600 unnamed women in the three sections of the Bible? The numerous entries in Part II result from our experience in forming the list of entries of anonymous women. Because we could find no way to search for female characters electronically, we looked for them by the painstaking method of scrutinizing each biblical book, chapter by chapter and verse by verse. During this task we discovered that, in addition to mention of historic and literary figures, general and generic references to women abound in biblical legislation, as part of the populace in biblical prophecy, as various groupings of women in the New Testament Epistles, and so on. Because the distinction between specific female characters and generic female figures or collective female groupings is often blurred, we decided to be as inclusive as possible. Part II thus provides entries for all unnamed biblical females, whether they be individuals or groups, and whether they have narrative or generic roles.

To avoid being repetitious, in some instances we have combined the discussion of certain "types" of women in a single entry. The term *widow,* for example, appears in many legal, prophetic, and other kinds of biblical texts. The major entry on widows is found at their earliest mention in the Bible (Exod 22:22, 24) and discusses most other passages in which the word appears. Subsequent passages that mention widows are cited in the book, referring the reader back to the entry at Exodus 22. In this way, someone who comes across a reference to a widow while reading Ezekiel, for example, and wants to know about the status or role of such a woman, can look up the chapter and verse in Ezekiel in Part II and be referred to the Exodus entry on widows. Such an entry for the Hebrew Bible does not, however, include New Testament

widows; such entries do not span the three sections of the canon.

Certain unnamed women who appear in several New Testament books have an entry for each book. In most cases, this is because the authors of the Synoptic Gospels (Matthew, Mark, and Luke) share much material (see the introduction to the New Testament); less often it is because a narrative about a woman appears in the Synoptics and also in the Gospel of John. Generally, we have provided the major discussion for all of these narratives in one Gospel and additional entries focus on the distinctive elements in other Gospels.

Although we are reasonably certain that Part I is a complete listing — that we have identified *all* named women — we are less confident that we have located every unnamed one. Many entries in Part II were created well after we began the editing process. In reading the work of various contributors, we noticed allusions to or mention of other females that were not on our original entry list. Of course, we immediately wrote entries for them as they came to our attention.

The problem of identifying unnamed women was exacerbated by some of the translation decisions made by those responsible for the NRSV. Because of linguistic differences between English and the original languages of the Bible, in some places the translated version masks the presence of women. At the end of the Book of Ecclesiastes, for example, a verse refers to certain women as "women who grind." Those three English words translate a single Hebrew word, a feminine plural participle; and the reference to women is clear. However, a parallel feminine plural participle in that text, denoting "women who look through windows," is translated "those who look through windows." Those gazing out of windows are explicitly female in the Hebrew, but their gender identity is ambiguous in the English version. Clearly, reading through the Bible in English obscures such references to women, and we have done our best to locate them by studying the Hebrew, Aramaic, and Greek texts of the Bible.

Although we have tried to be comprehensive, we

have refrained from including every kind of text that involves females. For example, we have not provided entries on female animals, even when those animals may be used symbolically to indicate something about human female character or behavior. For example, the term translated "ostriches" in the NRSV is literally, in Hebrew, "daughter(s) of wailing" in nine places in the Hebrew Bible (for example, Lev 11:16; Isa 3:21). This figurative terminology may allude to the role of women as mourners, but we have not included it in this book. Nor have we included botanical imagery that uses human terms; we haven't provided an entry, for example, for the description in Gen 49:22 of vine branches as "daughters" of the vine stock. Nor, with one exception, have we assigned entries to inclusive terms, such as "people" or "families," for groups that would certainly have included women. The exception is the entry "Person (Female or Male) Presenting an Offering" (Lev 2:1, etc.); we thought it was important to identify this case of female participation in religious ritual. On the other hand, such groups are sometimes indicated by "gender pairs," mixed-sex groups identified by phrases such as "men and women," "boys and girls," "sons and daughters," and "male slaves and female slaves." The females in these pairs have been assigned entries; in such cases, we do note that the mention of a female is accompanied by the mention of an equivalent male.

In giving titles to entries for women without names in Part II, we wanted to identify the women without using the name of the man with whom a woman might be associated by birth, marriage, or other relationship. In many cases that has not been possible; the reader will find entries such as "*Wife* of Samson" (Judg 14:1–15:6) and "*Sister* of Paul" (Acts 23:16). Wherever possible, we used other kinds of identification. Some entry titles indicate a woman's geographical location, such as "Women of Thebez" (Judg 9:51). Others, such as "Women with Hand-Drums, Dancing" (Exod 15:20) and "Women Praying and Prophesying" (1 Cor 11:2–16), signify women's professions or activities. Sometimes a woman's sexual or marital status provides the most

relevant title, such as "Woman Who Miscarries or Is Barren" (Exod 25:26) and "Divorced Wife" (Matt 5:31–32). In identifying each person or figure, we have tried, wherever possible, to use the Bible's own words.

The last section of *Women in Scripture* presents another category of biblical females. All the named and unnamed women in the Bible in Parts I and II are humans. Although we excluded female imagery contained in references to flora and fauna, we decided to include another kind of nonhuman female — female deities, abstract qualities personified as females, and females as symbols of political and geographical entities (cities, countries). Some of these nonhuman females appearing in the Bible have names, as do goddesses such as Asherah, mentioned more than a dozen times in the Hebrew Bible. Others are abstractions, such as Wisdom or Wickedness portrayed as a woman. Cities and other territories, both in ancient Israel and elsewhere, are called daughters or women; such depictions are included. Finally, several entries in Part III may be of special interest to readers concerned with the gender of God in the Bible. One explores female imagery for God in the Hebrew Bible, another examines such imagery in the Apocryphal/Deuterocanonical Books, and a third deals with Woman Wisdom in the New Testament.

Each entry begins with a listing of the biblical chapters and verses in which the subject of the entry is found. For the Hebrew Bible, the versification in the NRSV in some places diverges from that of the Hebrew text. In such cases, we use the chapter and verse numbers of the English rather than the Hebrew. Then, for the named women of Part I and the named nonhuman females of Part III, an etymology presenting the meaning of the name is provided in quotation marks (for example, for Deborah, "bee"; for Abital, "my father is dew"; for Phoebe, "bright, radiant"; for Susanna, "lily"). If the etymology is uncertain, possible meanings are suggested.

The body of each entry combines a recounting or summary of the biblical materials with a discussion of the historical or literary context. The longer entries, which deal with figures for whom there is extensive or otherwise significant biblical information, draw upon the approaches and methodologies employed by the best biblical scholarship concerned with gender. We have sought to make each entry stand on its own; but in many cases consulting one or more related entries will enhance the reader's understanding.

Most entries conclude with several cross-references, alerting the reader to other relevant entries. For most, a brief bibliography is also provided. These references, which are not meant to be comprehensive but rather to indicate materials accessible to the general reader, appear in abbreviated form. Full bibliographical information is listed at the end of the book.

Although we have avoided the use of abbreviations, some terms are used so frequently that designating them with initials seemed appropriate. A case in point is the use of NRSV for the New Revised Standard Version, a translation of the Hebrew Bible, the Apocryphal/Deuterocanonical Books, and the New Testament published in 1989. There are also abbreviated references to several other English versions, such as the NAB (New American Bible), the NEB (New English Bible), and the NJPS (New Jewish Publication Society Bible). References to biblical books use the book abbreviations established by the Society of Biblical Literature.

At the end of the book we have also provided a listing of the ancient extrabiblical sources that are mentioned in many of the entries. The list identifies each work and, if possible, indicates its approximate date.

A number of entries, particularly those dealing with female figures in the Hebrew Bible, mention dates. The entry on Jecoliah, for example, tells us that she was the consort of Amaziah, the ninth king of Judah, who reigned from 798 to 769 B.C.E.; and the entry on Prisca mentions the date, 56 or 57 C.E., of Paul's letter to the Romans. These absolute dates represent one of several options that have been suggested by scholars attempting to establish chronologies for biblical antiquity. Absolute chronologies can be established only by correlation with extra-

biblical materials, and the precision of those correlations varies with the reliability of the sources. In *Women in Scripture,* the absolute dates follow the chronology suggested in the *Anchor Bible Dictionary'*s article on chronology. Similarly, the dates mentioned in many entries on female figures in prophetic books follow scholarly consensus reflected in standard reference works such as the *Anchor Bible Dictionary* and *Harper's Bible Commentary.*

For all dates, the abbreviations B.C.E. (before the common era) and C.E. (common era), rather than B.C. and A.D. respectively, are used. This pattern, which avoids privileging Christian tradition over Jewish usage, is common in many scholarly publications dealing with the Bible.

Another abbreviation in this book may be unfamiliar to some readers. In the Hebrew Bible, God has a proper name that appears in Hebrew as four consonantal letters, YHWH, known as the Tetragrammaton. The vocalization of that designation for God is difficult to determine. The name of God was deemed so holy that the scribes who developed vowels for the biblical text — until sometime in the sixth to eighth centuries C.E. it had had only consonants — chose not to vocalize God's name, which should not be uttered aloud lest it be taken in vain, in violation of the Fourth Commandment (Exod 20:7). English translations of the Hebrew Bible thus render God's name with the capital letters LORD, in recognition of the fact that in Jewish tradition the term *lord* was substituted for God's name, so as not to risk profaning it. Some scholars accept the possibility that God's name would have been pronounced "Yahweh"; others are less certain. We have opted to present God's name by the transliteration of the four Hebrew consonants YHWH.

Finally, in designating the various ethnic and political groups mentioned in many entries, we have used the Bible's own terms wherever possible. Some confusion, however, surrounds the matter of how best to refer to the inhabitants of the Persian province of Yehud, which was established after the Babylonian exile in the late sixth century B.C.E., in approximation of the territory of the southern kingdom of Judah. (Judah, taking the name of the tribe of Judah, had existed as a monarchic state for some three and a half centuries after the breakup of the united monarchy when King Solomon died, c. 928 B.C.E.). The Judeans, or preexilic inhabitants of Judah, are called "people" or "children" of Judah in the Bible. The postexilic residents of Yehud are sometimes designated by the Hebrew term *yĕhûdîm*, usually translated "Jews" (see Neh 4:1). That designation, however, does not fit with our understanding of the emergence of the term "Jews," used in the religious sense, several centuries later. The use of the Greek term *Ioudaioi* (masculine plural), to designate a community ("Jews") sharing religious beliefs and practices (rather than to refer to residents of a geographical area), is not attested until the third century B.C.E. Thus we use the term Judahites rather than Jews for the residents of Ye-hud (sometimes also called Yehudites by scholars) in entries dealing with the Persian period (sixth to fourth centuries B.C.E.) unless the reference is more general, as to former Judeans exiled to Egypt, Babylon, or Persia.

This preface has provided an overview of the project, its goals, its organization, and its conventions. In addition, we urge the reader to consult our three introductory essays. In the first, because the entries on texts from each of the Bible's canonical sections draw upon the methods of critical biblical scholarship, we explain how such scholarship emerged, as distinct from traditional religious readings of the Bible, and how it understands the nature of the diverse materials that comprise the canon. Then we offer brief descriptions of the three parts of the full canon and some observations about the location of passages mentioning women in each. The second essay is an overview of feminist biblical scholarship, from its nineteenth-century origins to its contemporary complexity. And the third essay, because this is a book organized by women's names or the lack thereof, considers names and naming practices in the biblical world. After each essay, we have included bibliographical references so that those who wish to go beyond these introductory treatments can consult appropriate sources.

CAROL MEYERS
TONI CRAVEN
ROSS S. KRAEMER

An Introduction to the Bible

Critical Biblical Scholarship

Carol Meyers

The Bible is arguably the world's best-known book. Ironically, perhaps because it is so familiar — directly and indirectly — to so many, it also may be one of the world's least understood literary productions. Biblical scholarship, which seeks to understand the origin, content, historical context, and literary strategies of the Bible, is a well-developed, centuries-old discipline. Yet the discoveries of biblical scholarship over the past two centuries, which may constitute as revolutionary a contribution to Western intellectual history as have the theories of Marx, Darwin, and Freud, have had relatively no impact on the general public. Most people today approach scriptural texts precritically, in much the same way that they have for the past two millennia.

The entries in *Women in Scripture* have been written by professionals working under certain assumptions about the Bible that have emerged from the historical-critical revolution in biblical studies. Because those assumptions are not widely known, the following comments are meant to introduce modern biblical scholarship and how it has shaped the contributions to this volume.

Perhaps the most important issue to be raised and examined by modern biblical scholars concerns the unity and authorship of the Bible, which traditionally had been considered a unique, unified, consistent, error-free, and authoritative expression of God's word and will. The text itself, along with rabbinic or ecclesiastical interpretations, was the basis of belief and practice for virtually all Jews and Christians. For scholars, this ready acceptance of the inviolate sanctity of the existing text changed dramatically in the wake of the Reformation. Influenced by the critical thinking of European humanism and rationalism, they used common sense and logic to read the Bible as they would any other cultural document. This trend began in the seventeenth century and was widespread by the end of the nineteenth.

Three other developments affected the new, post-Enlightenment readings of Scripture. First, the scientific revolution of roughly the same era produced new perspectives on the natural world and its origins. Second, explorations and excavations in Bible lands were beginning to uncover texts with remarkable similarities to many biblical passages. Third, the critical readers themselves, even though most of them were ordained Christian (largely Protestant) clergy, were largely free of dogmatic constraints because of the relative freedom of post-Reformation biblical religion.

It became increasingly clear to scholars that the traditional views about authorship, unity, scientific veracity, and function of biblical texts needed to be reevaluated. Neither the full Christian canon (Hebrew Bible, Apocryphal/Deuterocanonical Books, and New Testament) nor any one of its three component Scriptures is a single-author book, they realized, but rather a complex anthology, a skillfully organized blend of many literary genres (songs, letters, laments, aphorisms, laws, history, prayers, legends, and so on) composed by countless authors over a long period of time. The date of the earliest parts of the Hebrew Bible, though still disputed, may be the twelfth century B.C.E.; the "youngest" texts of the New Testament date to the first half of the second century C.E. The Bible itself, with a number of books bearing the names of individuals (for example, Jeremiah, Mark, Tobit), indicates some multiple authorship. But virtually all biblical books, scholars could now see, were the result of various hands, writing with different levels of skill and for different purposes, and — tellingly — with different points of view, over extended periods of time. In particular the Pentateuchal books (the first five books of the Bible), with their repetitions and conflicting details, seemed to result from redactional activity that combined any number of discrete sources. Even some prophetic books, notably Isaiah and Zechariah, were recognized to have separate components (known as First Isaiah, Second Isaiah, and probably Third Isaiah; and as First Zechariah and Second Zechariah), combined into one longer work perhaps because of thematic connections or for some other reasons that cannot be determined with surety. And the Gospels were understood to have been composed in stages, incorporating materials from various sources — some used by two or more Gospels, some unique to each Gospel. Recognition of this complexity of authorship meant discarding the traditional ascription of the first five biblical books to Moses, of the Psalter to David, of Ecclesiastes and the Song of Solomon (also known as Canticles or the Song of Songs) as well as the Wisdom of Solomon to Solomon, of the full text of all prophetic books and many New Testament and Apocryphal/Deuterocanonical ones to the men whose names they bear.

Scholars in the twentieth century developed increasingly sophisticated understandings of how and why the different kinds of literature represented in the Bible took shape. Furthermore, as more and more ancient manuscripts have been discovered in Old World libraries and through excavations, they were able to recover the long and fascinating process by which the various parts of the Bible were collected in a canonical whole by the early centuries C.E. They also began to understand how biblical manuscripts were carefully preserved and faithfully transmitted. For example, the earliest manuscripts of the entire Hebrew Bible — early medieval copies that may postdate by as much as a thousand years a posited "original" version of some parts of the Hebrew Bible — are highly reliable traditions.

Recent trends in biblical scholarship do not necessarily view all the contradictions and differences among various passages of the Bible as reliable indicators of separate compositions, as earlier analyses did. Nonetheless, the acceptance of multiple authorship and divergent beliefs within the Bible as a whole is fundamental to all biblical scholarship except that of the most conservative, literalist groups. Individual scholars may differ greatly in their understanding of whether or not, or to what degree, God played a role in inspiring the creation of biblical texts; but they converge in their awareness of the complexity and diversity of the composite scriptural product. That is, biblical scholars now assume that the Bible consists of countless combined documents that reflect the biases and backgrounds of its many authors. So skillfully have the pieces been assembled, however, that attempts to identify them and account for their individual histories have not led to the same kind of consensus.

The developments of modern science influenced biblical scholarship most strongly in its understandings of biblical cosmologies. (Note the plural: the early chapters of Genesis are not the only scriptural references to the beginning and the structure of the cosmos.) The ancient Ptolemaic concept of the universe could be reconciled with the biblical accounts. Not so for the astronomical and scientific observations of Copernicus, Kepler, Galileo, and Newton. Biblical interpreters could no longer claim that the Bible was scientifically accurate; they could not approach biblical cosmogonies as if they were scientific treatises. Eventually, as other creation accounts of equal or greater antiquity became available to biblical scholars, they understood the biblical accounts of creation to be poetic expressions of the struggle of ancient Israelites, like that of other ancient peoples, to understand their own place in the created realm. The truths of biblical texts dealing with the cosmos are best evaluated in terms of their portrayal of the relationship between God and humanity within the world and not in terms of scientific veracity. Those texts convey ideas about the meaning of creation and not about how and when the world came to exist. Similarly, critical biblical scholars do not look to the Book of Revelation for a description of how the world will end any more than they look to Genesis for an understanding of how the world began.

By the end of the nineteenth century, biblical scholars had also recognized that the narratives in the New Testament and Apocryphal/Deuterocanonical Books as well as the Hebrew Bible that read as if they were history cannot be taken as factual records. The stories of the ancestors in Genesis, for example, were understood to be highly legendary if not fictional accounts of the pre-Israelite world. Like the beginnings and endings stories, they contain important messages but are not themselves literally true or historically accurate. Similarly, the divergent accounts of Jesus in the Gospels often say more about the meaning of Christ to different groups of early Christians than about the exact details of his life on earth. More blatant departure from historical veracity is characteristic of biblical "novellas" such as the books of Esther, Judith, and Susanna.

The crafting of the books of the Bible, like the writing of other documents known from the ancient Semitic and Greco-Roman worlds, was never intended to record the past in a way that fits our modern conceptions of historiography, conditioned by Western intellectual traditions. The compelling literary productions collected in Hebrew and Greek Scripture have blurred forever the boundaries between historical event and cultural expression. The formative events and formidable personalities of the biblical period are available to us now only in narratives and poetry, often brilliantly constructed, that frequently tell us more about the world of the narrators and poets than about the past they alternately celebrate and decry. In some quarters of biblical scholarship today, there is great skepticism about the ability of researchers to recover from the scriptural legacy much of the history of ancient Israel, early Judaism, and nascent Christianity. But for most people working in this discipline, the biblical record does contain valid and authentic clues about the biblical period and its timeless cast of characters and depictions of communal life.

The contributors to this volume accept the concept of the Bible as a historically conditioned anthology of books produced by many writers over a long period of time — more than a millennium. They thus avoid taking the biblical record naively at face value. They are, for example, more apt to say that the text says that something happened rather than to report it as having occurred. And they are more likely to focus on the literary presentation and function of biblical women, be they generic types or figures in narratives, than on their role in Israelite history. Yet, at the same time, passages with female characters, like most biblical texts, often are invaluable sources of information about the general social world, with its own conventions and values, in which the anonymous composers of biblical literature lived. Many entries thus provide information about the social dynamics of women's lives in biblical antiquity. The women and men who have written the entries for *Women in Scripture* are well trained in ancient biblical languages and in Near Eastern or Greco-Roman history. Their approach to the female figures in the Bible both respects and contributes to modern critical scholarship; it also speaks to the interests and concerns of Bible readers outside the academy.

The Hebrew Bible

Carol Meyers

The first, largest, and oldest part of the combined Jewish and Christian Scripture is the Hebrew Bible, known in Christian tradition as the Old Testament. Because it is so much a part of the religious and cultural life of the contemporary world, its antiquity and complexity are not often recognized by Bible readers. Biblically based liturgy and theology and also biblical allusions in Western culture are so familiar that the long passage of biblical texts from their often unrecoverable origin to their role as sacred Scripture is obscured. It is beyond the scope of this work for the individual entries to indicate the place of various passages or persons within the overall shape and story of the Hebrew Bible. The following description is thus meant to provide rudimentary information about the organization, age, contents, and authorship of the Hebrew Bible.

In its original languages (Hebrew and Aramaic) and in modern Jewish translations, the Hebrew Bible is an anthology of twenty-four books. Those books are organized into three major divisions, which probably reflect the order in which they became selected and collected. That process, whereby certain writings became important in the community and were considered sacred and authoritative, is called canonization. The word *canon* is derived from a Greek word that goes back to the Hebrew word *qāneh* and eventually to a Sumerian word denoting a reed that served as a measuring rod. The concept of physical measurement came by extension to mean a standard by which something is evaluated. Biblical literature was considered canonical when it "measured up" to some standards, which cannot be clearly recovered, about what was authentic revelation and should be included in a collection of holy texts.

The formation of the canon of the Hebrew Bible represents an ongoing process rather than a single decree by an individual leader or a religious council. The status of certain sacred works was apparently discussed from about 90 to 100 C.E. by a group of rabbinic sages meeting at a center of ancient Jewish learning called Jamnia, near the Mediterranean coast west of Jerusalem. Most scholars reject the notion that the Jamnian sages made any official decisions about the canonical whole. Rather, they apparently were concerned with a group of texts, or biblical "books," that were already widely accepted as sacred. They may have consolidated some texts and debated the sanctity of others; but they were working with a set of works that was already close to its final canonical form. Indeed, long before Jamnia, several late Hebrew Bible passages refer to parts of the three major sections, to be described next, of the Hebrew Bible. Ezra 3:2 (late fifth or early fourth century B.C.E.) refers to the "torah [NRSV, law] of Moses"; Dan 9:2 (second century B.C.E.) alludes to "books" that seem to be a set of biblical prophets. Somewhat later, Luke 24:44 (late first century C.E.) mentions the "teaching [NRSV, law] of Moses, the prophets, and the psalms." It seems safe to say that twenty-two of the books of the Jewish canon had been accepted as sacred by the end of the first century C.E. (some of them having achieved that status many centuries earlier) and that the full Jewish canon of twenty-four books was fixed somewhat later, perhaps not until the end of the next century.

The first of the major divisions of the Hebrew Bible is the *Pentateuch* or *Torah* (from Hebrew *tôrâ*), composed of the first five books of the Bible (Genesis, Exodus, Leviticus, Numbers, Deuteronomy). This group of books is sometimes called the Five Books of Moses because of the traditional ascription, as in the Ezra and Luke passages just mentioned, of these works to Moses, who was considered the transmitter of God's teachings to Israel. The designation Torah for the Pentateuch — and sometimes for the entirety of Jewish Scripture — is often misunderstood. The word means "teaching" or "instruction," and by extension in its canonical setting, "revelation." A more narrow meaning, "law," is sometimes used in translations (as in the NRSV of the Ezra and Luke passages quoted earlier) and gives the erroneous impression that the Pentateuch and even the legal materials it contains are primarily laws when in fact they are conceptually teachings, some of which are expressed in the form of prescriptive regulations.

The material contained in the Pentateuch represents a wide chronological range. No one knows how old the earliest passages are or how ancient are the events they purport to describe. As our discussion of critical biblical scholarship indicates, it is now deemed unlikely that the ancestral narratives of Genesis, believed for a long time to reflect Semitic migrations of the early to middle second millennium B.C.E., are authentic historical documents. Even if they do contain vestiges of social customs of life in the second millennium B.C.E. or references to sites occupied in that epoch, the form in which they have come to us bears signs of the writing style and spelling of the tenth century B.C.E. or later. Similarly, the story of the exodus and the wanderings in the wilderness, which may reflect thirteenth-century B.C.E. movements of peoples out of Egypt, is the product of much later literary activity. Embedded in those narratives of Israelite beginnings, however, are several archaic poems, such as the so-called Song of the Sea and the Song of Miriam in Exodus 15, which many scholars date to the period of earliest Israel (thirteenth–twelfth centuries B.C.E.).

The legal and cultic materials that comprise the rest of the Pentateuch contain sections of various ages and probably reached their final form at some point in the mid–first millennium B.C.E. Scholars vary widely in assigning dates to the completion of the Pentateuch, offering possibilities from the sixth to the fourth centuries B.C.E. However, because Ezra apparently considered the "torah [NRSV, law] of Moses" an authoritative document and is said to have read it out loud to an assembly of all the people (see Neh 8:1–3) by the late fourth century B.C.E., most scholars accept that the Pentateuch had

achieved something close to its final form by that time, if not earlier.

The second and largest division of the Hebrew Bible is known as the *Prophets* (*Nevi'im* in Hebrew). That designation is somewhat misleading in that the Prophets consists of two major sections, the Former Prophets and the Latter Prophets, the first of these being a collection of "historical" rather than prophetic books. The Former Prophets consists of four books — Joshua, Judges, 1–2 Samuel, and 1–2 Kings — which relate the tribal beginnings of Israel in the "promised land" and its subsequent existence as one and then two monarchic states. The ancient designation of the Joshua–Kings set as prophetic probably reflects the fact that these books have what might be termed a prophetic worldview in which, simply stated, God blesses those who obey the divine word and punishes those who are disobedient. It may also stem from the way in which a series of early prophets, such as Samuel, Nathan, Elijah, and Elisha, figure in the narratives, particularly in the books of Samuel and Kings. In any case, these works are quite different from the Latter Prophets, which consists of the books of the three Major (that is, large) Prophets (Isaiah, Jeremiah, and Ezekiel) and a fourth book, itself a collection: the twelve Minor (that is, small, or short) Prophets, sometimes called the Book of the Twelve.

The historical material that begins in Joshua and ends in Kings is a continuation of the story of the people Israel that begins in the Book of Exodus. Although not long ago critical biblical scholarship had understood the pre-Israelite narratives of the ancestors to be highly legendary, it had viewed the biblical books that comprise the Former Prophets as a collection of historical records, albeit ones with impressive folkloristic and literary embellishments. The biblical books that read as history were taken to be just that.

Contemporary biblical scholarship has revised this notion. Because of disparities between the past "recorded" in the Bible and the past recovered by archaeological work that is far more sophisticated and accurate than the prove-the-Bible type of projects carried out earlier in this century, most biblical scholars now recognize that these narratives about

Israel, from its twelfth-century B.C.E. beginnings in the land until its defeat by the Babylonians in 586 B.C.E. and the subsequent exile of its leadership and many of its people, were not written as a historical record by eyewitness observers of a series of Iron Age events. Rather, much of the Former Prophets, especially those portions dealing with the premonarchic and early monarchic period — the united monarchy of Saul, David, and Solomon (c. 1025–928 B.C.E.) — was probably composed to express emotions as well as ideas and values, using the vehicles of story and of poetry. The biblical materials mix creative imagination, historical memory, and probably some information from written sources; they were brought together for ideological purposes, decades if not centuries after the events they purport to describe. Even the materials about the later monarchic states, the northern kingdom of Israel and the southern kingdom of Judah (formed after the death of Solomon and the breakup of the united monarchy), although probably drawn from archival records, are selected and framed by editors to express their views about past events.

The process that cast the Former Prophets in its preserved form may have been initiated as early as the beginning of the monarchy in the late eleventh–early tenth century B.C.E. However, many scholars believe that a major impetus for collecting the historical narratives was the late-seventh-century B.C.E. nationalist reform of King Josiah, as reported in 2 Kings 22–23. A subsequent updating, to account for the latest event mentioned in 2 Kings (the release of the exiled King Jehoiachin from Babylonian prison c. 562 B.C.E.; see 2 Kgs 25:27), would then have occurred during the exile. These two spurts of compilation and editing together produced the four books of the Former Prophets, a work that many scholars link with the Book of Deuteronomy, calling the resulting five books the Deuteronomic History because the ideology of the Former Prophets seems to be based on that of Deuteronomy.

The origin and dates of the Latter Prophets have been somewhat easier for scholars to identify. In some cases, the prophetic books themselves are replete with chronological data. The superscriptions of many of them link the ensuing prophecies to the reigns of certain kings, whose regnal years have been established quite reliably. For example, the first book of the Major Prophets, Isaiah, opens (1:1) by declaring that Isaiah's visions are from the epoch of four specific kings of Judah, whose reigns all date to the eighth century B.C.E.; and two of the Minor Prophets, Hosea and Amos, can similarly be dated to that century. These three prophetic books mark the beginning of what is known as the era of "classical prophets" — those who produced books that are called by their names and are included in the canon of the Hebrew Bible.

Although there are fifteen canonical prophets (three major and twelve minor), at least some of these prophetic works, as pointed out earlier, represent the work of more than one prophetic hand. References to several eighth-century B.C.E. kings at the beginning of Isaiah would seem to make that book an eighth-century work. Yet the oracles of comfort and restoration beginning in Isaiah 40, along with specific references to Cyrus, the late-sixth-century B.C.E. Persian emperor (Isa 44:28; 45:1), make it certain that parts of Isaiah, probably chaps. 40–55, come from an unnamed sixth-century prophet known by scholars as Second Isaiah; and the rest of the book (chaps. 56–65, called Third Isaiah) was probably authored by yet another anonymous prophet or prophets. The Book of Jeremiah, although quite certainly spanning the reigns of the last five kings of Judah — the prophecies begin in 627 B.C.E. and end a few years after the 586 B.C.E. conquest of Jerusalem — contains more than the oracles of Jeremiah. Some of the prophetic sections may be the work of one or more of Jeremiah's disciples, and certainly the prose narratives that contain biographical data about Jeremiah were penned by someone other than the prophet — probably his scribe, a man named Baruch (see Jer 36:4).

The last of the canonical prophets are associated with the restoration, in the late sixth century B.C.E., of a political community that approximated the preexilic kingdom of Judah. The Babylonians had not only conquered Judah and deported its rulers and leading citizenry, but also demolished its chief national symbol, the temple in Jerusalem. When the Persians replaced the Babylonians as imperial rulers of the east Mediterranean lands, their policies of dominion meant limited self-rule for subject territories, including that of the Judeans, which now became a province called Yehud. Granted considerable local autonomy, the people of Yehud rebuilt their temple with the encouragement of the postexilic prophet Haggai and his contemporary Zechariah (whose oracles appear in Zechariah 1–8; the rest of the Book of Zechariah contains the words of one or more slightly later prophetic figures). Finally, the last postexilic prophetic work is the Book of Malachi. This book has no direct chronological information, but most scholars place it in the mid–fifth century B.C.E. Like Haggai and much of Zechariah, Malachi is a prose work, differing from the soaring oracular poetry of the preexilic and exilic prophets. The emotional force of poetic prophecy was apparently an important ingredient of prophetic communication to the ancient Israelites and their leaders; and the shift to prose in the latest biblical prophetic works, which some scholars call proto-rabbinic, indicates a transition to other forms of literature that would emerge in nascent Judaism.

The third division of the Hebrew Bible, called the *Writings* (*Ketuvim* in Hebrew) or Hagiographa (Holy Writings), contains the remaining books of Jewish Scripture and was the last to assume its canonical shape. Its component books are largely a product of the postexilic and Hellenistic periods (late sixth to second centuries B.C.E.). Some of the Writings, however, such as the Book of Psalms, contain materials that are similar to second-millennium B.C.E. Canaanite poetry and thus may be as old as other early parts of the Hebrew Bible. Similarly, some parts of Proverbs show a clear dependence on Egyptian wisdom literature of the early first millennium B.C.E.

The books that comprise the Writings are grouped in several miscellaneous collections. Five of the short books (Ruth, Esther, Song of Solomon, Lamentations, and Ecclesiastes) are known as the five *megillot* (scrolls), or festival scrolls, because they are read aloud as part of Jewish liturgy for

certain holy days. Two other of the Writings are themselves compilations: Psalms and Proverbs. Two more, Job and Daniel, are in a class by themselves. Finally, the Writings division — and thus the entire Hebrew Bible — ends with two historical books that were perhaps originally one continuous work: Ezra-Nehemiah, the account of the postexilic organization of the province of Yehud under the leadership of two returning exiles whose names the book bears, and 1–2 Chronicles, which recapitulates the historical narrative of parts of Samuel and Kings but with special attention to priestly matters and the reign of King David. The Hebrew Bible thus ends with a quotation from the Persian ruler Cyrus, urging the rebuilding of the temple and the return of the people to their land. This final message of renewal was pointedly appropriate to the period in which the canon was nearing completion — immediately following the destruction of the second temple by the Romans in 70 C.E. and the concomitant departure of many Jews from Jerusalem.

Some of the books that form the Writings section of the Hebrew Bible were not recognized as canon-worthy by at least some groups of first-century Jews. The Book of Esther, for example, was a contested part of the Writings because it never once mentions God, nor does it refer to basic biblical concepts such as covenant and temple. Similarly, the Song of Solomon does not seem to contribute to Jewish piety; and its explicit sexual language may have been troublesome to some. Yet there was apparently enough popular support for these books to ensure their inclusion in the canon. But other late-first-millennium Jewish writings, some of which are found in the Apocryphal/Deuterocanonical Books, were ultimately excluded from the Jewish canon for reasons that can no longer be determined.

Probably many ancient Israelite texts did not achieve either the canonical or deuterocanonical sanctity that would have ensured their preservation. The Hebrew Bible contains references to a number of works that are no longer extant, such as the Book of Jashar (Josh 10:13), the "records" of the seers Samuel and Gad and of the prophet Nathan (1 Chr 29:29), the Book of the Acts of Solomon (1 Kgs

11:41), and the frequently mentioned Book of the Annals of the Kings of Judah (for example, 1 Kgs 15:7, 23) and Book of the Annals of the Kings of Israel (for example, 2 Kgs 15:11, 15, 21, 26, 31). The disappearance of works that lacked popular appeal or religious value was probably commonplace in the ancient world; some books may even have been deliberately destroyed or suppressed. The names of more than a hundred dramatists from the ancient Greek world, for example, are mentioned in other sources, but the plays of only a few of them have survived; and not all the plays of much-celebrated playwrights are extant — of the eighty plays attributed to Aeschylus, only seven have survived.

The organization and sequence of the ancient Israelite works preserved in the Hebrew Bible, which is also sometimes called the Tanak or TaNaK (an acronym using the first letters of the Hebrew names of the three major divisions of Jewish Scripture: *Torah, Nevi'im, Ketuvim*), are probably not familiar to most Bible readers. Except for the NJPS version, most English translations use an arrangement that obscures the organization of the Hebrew Bible. The sequence of books in the Pentateuch is identical in Jewish, Catholic, Orthodox, and Protestant Bibles. However, the number and order of the books in Prophets and Writings are changed. The four composite "historical" books (1–2 Samuel, 1–2 Kings, Ezra-Nehemiah, 1–2 Chronicles) of Jewish Scripture are separated into two books each and are grouped together; Ezra, Nehemiah, and the two books of Chronicles follow the two Samuel and two Kings books, which themselves come after Joshua and Judges. A long historical sequence, augmented by the two scrolls (Ruth and Esther) purporting to contain historical narratives, thus constitutes the second part of Christian Bibles. A group of poetic and wisdom books, excluding prophecy, comes next; and the last grouping is that of prophecy, with the Minor Prophets counting as twelve individual books and with Lamentations, often attributed to Jeremiah, coming immediately after the book named for that prophet.

This arrangement yields thirty-nine separate books and is found in Protestant translations, such as the NRSV, which is the version used as the basis for all the entries in *Women in Scripture*. The organization of the NRSV and other Protestant Bibles is not, however, a decision of Christian translators. Rather, it is based on the order of books in the earliest translation of the Hebrew and Aramaic texts of Jewish Scripture into another language. In the last centuries B.C.E. and the early centuries C.E., increasingly large numbers of Jews lived outside the land of their ancestors; they spoke Greek, the vernacular of the east Mediterranean world of the period, as their first language. Even in their ancestral land itself, Jews became proficient in Greek. In the third century B.C.E., Jews in Egypt began to translate Hebrew Scripture into Greek, thus starting the translation of the Hebrew Bible conventionally known as the Septuagint (or LXX, meaning "seventy") because of a legendary account that the translation was completed by seventy-two scholars in seventy-two days. Other Greek translations were also made. The Septuagint reflects a different tradition about the arrangement and also the contents of the Hebrew Bible. It includes, for example, the collection known as the Apocryphal/Deuterocanonical Books. And, because the Septuagint was the Bible of the Greek-speaking early Christians as well as of certain Jewish communities, Christian translations are based on it. Furthermore, Catholic and Orthodox Bibles, like the Septuagint, contain the Apocryphal/Deuterocanonical Books.

Not only are there differences in arrangement and contents between the Septuagint and the earliest complete manuscript of the Hebrew Bible (the Leningrad Codex, dated to 1009), but also variants exist in the style, spelling, wording, and even the contents of certain books. The LXX version of the Book of Jeremiah, for example, is about one eighth shorter than the Hebrew version; and its series of oracles against the nations is placed in the middle of the book in the Greek instead of at the end, as in the Hebrew. Job is also considerably shorter in the Greek.

Such differences in the Greek and Hebrew texts indicate that there is virtually no possibility of reconstructing an "original" Hebrew Bible. Clearly, a number of versions of the Hebrew Bible were in circulation during the period in which it achieved its final canonical form. Because of the variants among the earliest texts, it is impossible to cite the Bible as the "exact" word of God; the various textual traditions record "God's word" in differing ways, and some of those variants are theologically significant.

Whatever the differences in the earliest traditions, it is clear that once the Hebrew Bible as a whole became the sacred Scripture of the Jews, enormous effort was made to preserve and transmit biblical manuscripts as carefully as possible. The Leningrad Codex mentioned earlier comes at the end of a long series of copies, yet it bears striking resemblance to fragments of biblical manuscripts dating to the last few centuries B.C.E. and the first century C.E., discovered at Qumran near the Dead Sea. Parts of every book of the Hebrew Bible, except Esther, are represented among the Dead Sea Scrolls. Some of them are virtually the same as the medieval Hebrew Bible, attesting to the care of repeated copying. Some few, however, bear a stronger similarity to the Septuagint. Again, evidence for distinct textual traditions of the Hebrew Bible makes the notion of an "original" Bible untenable.

The complexity of diverse Greek and Hebrew textual traditions is compounded by the fact that translations into other ancient languages, such as Latin (the Vulgate), Aramaic (the Targums), and Syriac (the Peshitta), sometimes contain variants that seem to be more reliable — that is, produce a text that makes more sense and has fewer inconsistencies — than do the older Greek and Hebrew manuscripts. Text scholars struggle to sort out these divergent traditions. Their work allows translating committees, such as those that produced the NRSV, the NJPS, the NAB, and other modern English versions, to use the most trustworthy texts possible so that they can render translations that might approximate an "original" text.

‿

With the exception of the writers of the Latter Prophets (books designated with the names of prophets) and passages traditionally ascribed to

Moses, David, and Solomon, very little is known about the authors of biblical writings. Until recently, biblical scholars have assumed that virtually all of the Hebrew Bible was produced by men: by priests, scribes, sages, prophets, courtiers, and other elite males. Perhaps the few poems attributed to women — the Songs of Miriam, Deborah, and Hannah — indeed had female authors. But the rest of Jewish Scripture, including the two books with women's names (Ruth and Esther), was understood to be the product of male authors.

Recently, however, scholars have begun to realize that it may be a grave and unjust error to assume that women were excluded from the domain of literary creativity that produced works included in the canon. There is no reason to believe that ancient Israelite women did not share in the nearly universal role of women as composers of genres such as love songs, lullabies, and laments. Such compositions, probably originating as oral literature, are likely to be found in the Hebrew Bible, even if they were written down by men or embedded in texts edited by men. Part of the Book of Lamentations, for example, may have been composed by professional women mourners (see 2 Chr 35:25); and many see women's love poetry, especially the sections attributed to the female lover, in the Song of Solomon.

Beyond these more obvious cases of probable female authorship, the question has been raised about whether other biblical writings might be the work of a female author or authors. For example, significant sections of Pentateuchal writings have been attributed for centuries to the highly skilled literary hand of an anonymous person called "J," the first initial of the name of God, Jahveh (YHWH), in German, because the theory that such a person, who favored the use of the name YHWH for God, was first proposed in German scholarship. That hypothetical writer has been referred to as a man by generations of biblical scholars. But about ten years ago, several scholars independently proposed that J might in fact have been a woman. They argued that, because of the strong female characters in the materials attributed to J and because of the presumed sensitivity of J to women's issues, one cannot be certain that the skilled storyteller of the so-called J narratives was a man.

The attribution of large sections of the Pentateuch, especially many of the family tales in Genesis, to a woman can never be more than theoretical. Yet the fact that stories of family and children are often considered by ethnographers to be women's compositions means that such a theory cannot be easily turned aside. Even if the total set of narratives thought to be the work of J was compiled by a male writer or editor, the likelihood remains that he drew upon traditional family stories, some of which were composed, probably orally, by women.

In considering written compositions, the common assumption that Israelite women were not literate and could not have produced documents is also being contested. Unlike their neighbors in Mesopotamia and Egypt, the Israelites used an alphabetic script, which made writing and reading much easier and thus more widely accessible than in other parts of the ancient Near East. To be sure, most people, if they learned the alphabet, would have used it for little more than simple record keeping or messages. More developed literary skills were probably the prerogative of wealthier families; and there is no reason not to assume that some elite women, along with elite men, were quite literate. Queen Jezebel, for example, writes letters in her husband's name (1 Kgs 21:8). And Queen Esther writes an authoritative letter establishing a national festival (Esth 9:29). Consequently, as for literature originating in oral tradition, some biblical literature composed in writing may also be the product of female creativity. Professional female prophets, wise women, royal women, and other such figures, who were conceivably literate, perhaps contributed to the literature of the Hebrew Bible. Recent feminist scholarship, for example, has tentatively identified a female "voice," if not a female hand, in certain parts of the Book of Proverbs, traditionally considered the teaching of a father to his son. And the presence of female discourse has been proposed for a variety of other biblical texts. Perhaps the material gathered in *Women in Scripture* will enable scholars to make further assessments about the presence of female voices.

The process of locating and investigating hundreds of named and unnamed women for this book allows us to add another kind of information to our understanding of the role of women in Hebrew-Aramaic Scripture — the distribution of named and unnamed women in the various books and divisions of the Hebrew Bible. The following comments about where and how often women appear in the Hebrew Bible are based on approximate counts. As we have indicated in the Preface, the list of named women in Part I of this book is reasonably accurate. The list in Part II (unnamed women) does not lend itself to determining precise numbers; some entries are collective, discussing types of women found in multiple books or presenting miscellaneous women mentioned in several of the longer prophetic books. Nonetheless, there is some value in looking at the distribution in even an approximate form.

The two greatest concentrations of female figures occur in Genesis (thirty-two named and forty-six unnamed women) and in 1 Chronicles (forty-four named women and fifteen unnamed women). The relatively large number of women in the first book of the Bible, compared with the rest of the Pentateuch (with only eighteen total named women in the other four Pentateuchal books) as well as other parts of the Hebrew Bible, must certainly be a function of two features of Genesis. First, it has several genealogies that include daughters as well as sons (see the entries "Daughters [and Sons] of Adam, etc." [Gen 5:4, etc.] and "Daughters [and Sons] of Shem, etc." [Gen 11:10, etc.]); the ancient Israelites reckoned descent patrilineally yet still sometimes listed women in their lineages. Second, Genesis differs from most of the rest of the Hebrew Bible in being a series of family stories rather than narratives of national history; whatever their role in domestic life may have been, women could hardly be omitted from such accounts.

The presence of women in 1 Chronicles is also a function of genealogical activity. Except for Michal, King David's wife and a major figure in the David narratives, all forty-three other named women and all but three of the fifteen unnamed ones appear in the first nine chapters of 1 Chronicles. These chapters consist largely of genealogical materials and include women at certain points, perhaps to highlight particularly important clans or families.

Otherwise, it is worth noting that women, particularly unnamed women, are prominent in the Book of Judges, where an assortment of women play public roles in this portrayal of prenational Israelite life. The women who appear sporadically in the narratives of the monarchies in Israel and Judah, however, achieve their place by virtue of their social class — most are relatives (mothers, wives, sisters, daughters) of the biblical kings.

The relative paucity of female figures in the poetic books of the Hebrew Bible — most of the Major and Minor Prophets as well as Psalms and Lamentations — should not necessarily be seen as sexist. The type of literature in those books is much less focused on specific persons, male or female; and specific individuals and even generic types of either gender are mentioned far less often than in the historical books. Because we do not have counts of the number of times that unnamed men or male images appear, it is uncertain how unbalanced those books are with respect to gender. In the prophetic books, the frequent use of military language — of destruction or impending doom — and the focus on national leadership would lead us to believe that male figures substantially outnumber female ones. Yet, with respect to named individuals, the poetic portions of those books are nearly as devoid of men as they are of women. Apart from

the superscriptions identifying the prophets, for example, the names of neither men nor women are found in the books of Habakkuk and Zephaniah.

The stories about certain women were apparently known to the authors of more than one book of the Hebrew Bible. At least thirty-five named women appear in two different biblical books. Many of them are royal women mentioned in a narrative of 2 Kings that is repeated in a parallel account in 2 Chronicles. Eight women appear in three biblical books: Abigail 1 (wife of Naboth and then of David), Achsah (daughter of Joshua's associate Caleb), Ahinoam 2 (another of David's wives), Haggith (another of David's wives), Michal (yet another of David's wives), Serah (daughter of Asher, son of Jacob), Tamar 1 (daughter-in-law of Judah), and Zeruiah (sister of David). Even more prominent across biblical books is the matriarch Rachel, who is mentioned in Ruth, 1 Samuel, and Jeremiah in addition to the Genesis narratives. Bathsheba (wife of Solomon and mother of David) also appears in four books: 2 Samuel, 1 Kings, 1 Chronicles, and Psalms (superscription to Psalm 51). And perhaps it is fitting that the woman who appears in the most books of the Hebrew Bible (Exodus, Numbers, Deuteronomy, 1 Chronicles, and Micah) is Miriam, a woman whose leadership and prophetic status stand on their own, without a link to a male relative. Despite the androcentric interests of the canonical books, Miriam's contribution to the Israelite story was exemplary and perhaps represents that of many other female figures who are not mentioned at all but who participated in significant ways in the family life, if not the public life, of the ancient Israelites.

The Apocryphal/ Deuterocanonical Books

⟶

Toni Craven

THE Apocryphal/Deuterocanonical Books are ancient Jewish religious writings that are not included in the Hebrew Bible but form part of various Christian Old Testaments. All these works originate in the Greek version of the Hebrew Bible, the Septuagint, with the exception of 2 Esdras (which is found in Old Latin translations). Since Christian Bibles were based on the Septuagint, most Bibles included these books until the sixteenth-century Protestant Reformation. Even though they were eventually excluded from the canon of sacred Scripture in the Hebrew Bible, copies of some of the books have been discovered in the Dead Sea Scrolls, suggesting that in the last few centuries B.C.E. and the first century C.E. at least some of these works (the Letter of Jeremiah, Tobit, and Sirach, together with other religious writings) were being used by the Qumran community (a settlement near the northwest shore of the Dead Sea associated with producing the Dead Sea Scrolls).

The eighteen books in the NRSV Apocryphal/ Deuterocanonical Books (various parts of which complete Roman Catholic, Greek Orthodox, and Slavonic Orthodox Old Testaments) include literary forms similar to those found in the Hebrew Bible. Some works revise and complete earlier books of the Hebrew Bible (Esther, Baruch, the Letter of Jeremiah, Daniel), some are historical writings (1 Maccabees, 2 Maccabees in a more limited sense, and 1 Esdras), some are edifying short stories that are ostensibly historical but actually imaginative fictions (Tobit, Judith, Susanna, and Bel and the Dragon), one is apocalyptic (2 Esdras), others are wisdom treatises (Sirach, which is sometimes called Ecclesiasticus, the Wisdom of Solomon, and 4 Maccabees), and some are psalms and prayers (the Prayer of Manasseh, Psalm 151, and the Prayer of

Azariah and the Song of the Three Jews). Establishing a chronology for these books is difficult, but most agree that they were taking shape from 200 B.C.E. to 100 C.E. (or 200 C.E.).

The stories of how Jews and Protestants came to regard the Apocrypha as noncanonical and how Catholics and Orthodox Christians viewed them as deuterocanonical ("second canon") parts of the Bible illustrate how ideas about canon and what constitutes "the Bible" depend upon multiple factors, including religious and political ones. Canonical status and terminology for these books present special problems, particularly in ecumenical and interfaith exchanges. Even when there is sensitivity to difference in canons of Scripture, what to call these books is problematic. The designation Intertestamental simplistically suggests the existence of two "testaments" between which these works developed, although in reality the process of the formation of the various canons was much more complex. Apocrypha (Greek for "hidden") is an inaccurate identifier because none of these writings were "hidden" or "concealed." The title Apocrypha may be linked to the legend in 2 Esdras 14 that ninety-four books were dictated by Ezra to five scribes in forty days, with the instruction from the Most High that twenty-four (the traditional number of books in the Hebrew Bible) were for public use and the remaining seventy were to be kept only for the wise.

Deuterocanonical Books for Roman Catholics include Tobit, Judith, Greek Additions to the Book of Esther, the Book of Wisdom, Sirach (Ecclesiasticus), Baruch, the Letter of Jeremiah, Greek Additions to the Book of Daniel (the Prayer of Azariah and the Song of the Three Jews, Susanna, Bel and the Dragon), and 1 and 2 Maccabees. The Greek

Orthodox Bible adds the Prayer of Manasseh, Psalm 151, 1 Esdras, and 3 Maccabees (with 4 Maccabees in an appendix). The Slavonic Orthodox Bible, in addition to all the preceding, contains 3 Esdras (called 2 Esdras in the NRSV). These eighteen books or parts of books constitute the NRSV Apocryphal/ Deuterocanonical Books.

The 1987 "Guidelines for Interconfessional Co-operation in Translating the Bible," published by the Secretariat for Promoting Christian Unity and the United Bible Societies, responded to the need for editions of the Bible that contain the Apocryphal/Deuterocanonical Books and respect for confessions that exclude the books from canon by offering the reconciling position that they be published in a separate section. This, in fact, was the practice followed by the 1989 New Revised Standard Version (NRSV), which places the books after The Hebrew Scriptures Commonly Called the Old Testament, with the heading The Apocryphal/Deuterocanonical Books of the Old Testament. Bibles containing additional writings need somehow to differentiate them, yet using the term Old Testament perpetuates what many regard as the anti-Judaism — latent or active — in Christian division of the "old" from the "new" (and better) Christian covenant. First Testament and Second Testament, more neutral designations employed by some, have not gained widespread usage.

The Late Writings of the Old Testament (a designation widespread in Europe) can misleadingly suggest that these works are later in origin than the Hebrew Bible (which is not always the case) or worse, that the Judaism of this period is late Judaism — that is, Judaism nearing its end — from which early Christianity emerges. One covenant did not, of course, eradicate the other. Calling these writings postbiblical or noncanonical is considered inaccurate according to Catholic and Orthodox perspectives. And most awkwardly, until recently the books referred to as Apocrypha by Catholics were labeled by Protestants as Pseudepigrapha (other noncanonical Jewish religious writings designated as "writings with false superscriptions" because, in some cases, the character with whom they are identified is not the author). Apocryphal/Deu-

terocanonical Books, the NRSV term that uses a slash to create a hybrid word, is an inclusive practice with a good deal to commend it.

After generations of using Bibles without the Apocryphal/Deuterocanonical Books, many Protestants lost sight of the fact that these books were once part of their Bible. The earliest copies of English Bibles that exclude the Apocrypha are certain 1599 Geneva Bibles, in which the omission was presumably due to a binder's mistake, because the books are listed in the table of contents. Some speculate that Protestant Bibles without the Apocrypha became popular because they were less expensive and less bulky. In 1615, George Abbot, archbishop of Canterbury, one of the translators of the 1611 King James Version, specifically directed that no Bibles without the Apocrypha were to be produced or sold on pain of one year's imprisonment. Nonetheless, the 1616, 1618, 1620, 1622, 1626, 1627, 1629, 1630, and 1633 King James Versions appeared without the disputed books.

Martin Luther's 1534 German Bible broke with the tradition of interspersing the additional books among the uncontested (protocanonical) Old Testament books by recognizing only those thirty-nine books original to the Hebrew Bible as canonical. Luther separated Judith, Wisdom, Tobit, Sirach, Baruch (including the Letter of Jeremiah), Maccabees, parts of Esther, and parts of Daniel, in that order, to a section with the special heading "Apocrypha, that is, books which are not held as equal to holy Scripture, yet which are useful and good to read." Later, he added the Prayer of Manasseh, for which he had high regard, as the last book in this collection. Luther acted boldly in separating the Apocrypha, changing the order in which the books appeared in the Vulgate ("common text," Jerome's fourth-century Latin translation, prepared at the instruction of Pope Damasus I), and deleting some of the writings. Though Luther never got rid of the Apocrypha, he opened the door to serious questioning of the value of these books. His decisions regarding their choice, ordering, and placement were carefully followed for the hundred years of Wittenberg Bible printing, when no complete Bible was printed without the Apocrypha.

The preface attributed to Zwingli in the 1529 Zurich Bible, which also included the Apocrypha in an appendix, refers to them as "Church Books" in contrast to the "Canonical Books" and contains the admonition that the books should be read (not preached!) for they are holy books. The other well-known Swiss Bibles followed the decision of the Wittenberg and Zurich Bibles to print the Apocrypha after the canonical books of the Old Testament. The 1546 Geneva Bible contains an introduction attributed to Calvin in which he maintains that the Apocrypha are "profane books" distinguished from "Holy Scripture." Thus, the Apocrypha, though included in the Bible, came to be regarded as "profane writings" for "private" use that had no legal validity or value in the formation of doctrine. Other Reform traditions went so far as to exclude the Apocrypha from the Bible. The Westminster Confession of Faith (1647) unequivocally stated, "The books commonly called Apocrypha, not being of divine inspiration, are not part of the canon of Scripture; and therefore of no authority to the Church of God, not to be otherwise approved, or made use of, than any other human writings."

Reacting to the Reformers' challenges, the Council of Trent (1546) declared the wider Old Testament canon, including the Apocrypha, as sacred and canonical. By Trent's decision, all Catholic Old Testaments contain thirty-nine protocanonical books and seven deuterocanonical books, plus additions to Esther and Daniel. Trent condemned "anyone who does not accept these books in their entirety, with all their parts, according to the text usually read in the Catholic Church and as they are in ancient Latin Vulgate." Although Trent was an ecumenical council, the Vulgate was used only in Western churches. Eastern churches had, and have to this day, different practices regarding an even wider canon. Trent did not accept 1–2 Esdras and the Prayer of Manasseh, even though these books were widely used and even appear in some versions of the Vulgate.

The early church used a variety of Jewish sacred books during the formative Christian period because there was no fixed canon in Judaism in the first and early second century. As a result, the church fathers held varying positions on what, in addition to the New Testament, constituted the canon of Scripture. Leaders of the Eastern Church like Justin (c. 100–c. 165 C.E.) recognized only books in the Hebrew Bible. Melito of Sardis (died c. 190 C.E.) listed only books that were part of the Jewish canon, though he excluded Esther. Others, most significant of whom is Athanasius (c. 296–373 C.E.) — who had Jewish teachers — insisted on only twenty-two books but used the Deuterocanonical Books in practice.

Western fathers more rigorously advocated the narrower Jewish canon, as can be seen in Hilary of Poitiers (c. 315–367); Rufinus (c. 345–c. 410), until he moved to Rome in 397, when he accepted a wider canon; and most notably Jerome (c. 342–420). In the Latin Vulgate, Jerome, who was the first to call the additional books the Apocrypha, insisted that the canon be limited to books found in the Hebrew Bible ("Hebrew truth") and urged that the Apocrypha not be used for establishing doctrine (a practice that the Reformers later adopted).

The great majority of the Greek and Latin fathers, on the other hand, incorporated the Deuterocanonical Books into the canon. Most influential of all these was Augustine (354–430), who argued for inclusion of the extra Greek books on the basis of apostolic usage. Augustine's defense of a wider canon endorsed what had become the general consensus in the West and in large parts of the East. Through a series of ecclesiastical decisions, a broader canon was gradually authorized. Editions of the Latin Vulgate, officially approved by the Roman Catholic Church, incorporated the Deuterocanonical Books within the sequence of the Old Testament and placed the Prayer of Manasseh and 1 and 2 Esdras in an appendix after the New Testament.

Authorship for the Apocryphal/Deuterocanonical Books is likely male, though assumptions that women were not literate and could not have produced documents or translations are no longer unchallenged. Such matters related to gender roles will perhaps be unlocked by the very kind of work that *Women in Scripture* has produced and will encourage. The few cases where an author or translator's name is given are patronymic (derived from the name of a paternal ancestor). Only Sirach specifies the proper name of its author (Sir 50:27). The original Hebrew title, according to the subscription of Cairo ms. B (one of the four extant Hebrew manuscripts), was "Yeshua ben Eleazar ben Sira" (Jesus son of Eleazar son of Sirach). Sirach is actually the name of the grandfather of the author, Yeshua (Jesus).

Judith, Esther, and Susanna are titled by the name of a female character, but that character is not identified as the author. Other books have a pseudepigraphic author who sometimes assumes the voice of the character for whom the book is titled, such as Tobit, the Wisdom of Solomon, Baruch, the Letter of Jeremiah, the Prayer of Azariah, and the Prayer of Manasseh. Such is also the case with Ezra, who is associated with 1 Esdras (called 3 Ezra in the Latin Bible) and 2 Esdras (also called 4 Ezra, which sometimes is used only for chaps. 3–14, with chaps. 1–2 then designated 5 Ezra and chaps. 15–16 designated 6 Ezra). Two translators, both of whom are male, receive notice: an unnamed grandson, who explains his difficulty in translating his grandfather's Hebrew original into Greek (Prologue to Sirach); and Lysimachus of Jerusalem, who allegedly translated Esther into Greek (11:1). An unnamed epitomist (one who is summarizing) explains in a preface that 2 Maccabees is the digest of a five-volume Greek work by Jason of Cyrene (2 Macc 2:19–32). Could this epitomist have been a woman? One can only say that, when discussing "anonymous," anything is possible.

On the whole, the Apocryphal/Deuterocanonical Books are more important as sources for postexilic Jewish piety than as historical documents. Many are fictionally placed in settings associated with the political and religious traumas of the sixth and fifth centuries B.C.E., such as the fall of Jerusalem in 586 B.C.E. and the resulting exile in Babylonia; the dispersion of large numbers of Judeans to Egypt, Babylonia, and Assyria; the return from the exile in 538 B.C.E.; and the ensuing restoration of the Jewish community. These events, which function as archetypes for survival and faithful practice of religion in times of trial, offered inspiration and comfort dur-

ing the religious persecution inflicted by the Seleucid ruler Antiochus IV Epiphanes (168 B.C.E.) and the Roman destruction of Jerusalem (70 C.E.). The Maccabean Revolt against Seleucid domination (166–160 B.C.E.), also called the Hasmonean Revolt, and the years afterward to 142 B.C.E., when Judea became independent, up to the time of the Romans and the First and Second Jewish Revolts (66–73 C.E. and 132–135 C.E., respectively) also figure in some of this literature.

The religious ideas in the Apocryphal/Deuterocanonical Books were influenced by belief in communal survival, hope for political restoration, the expectation of a Davidic heir, and adherence to the idea of the covenant people. Concern for Jerusalem and the temple is regularly expressed. Differing conceptions of life in obedience to the Torah are reflected in this literature. Monotheism that acknowledged the existence of no God other than YHWH, the God of the ancestors, became a belief for which the faithful were willing to be tortured and killed. Lives defined by the Torah and its interpretation, circumcision, observance of the Sabbath, fidelity to dietary laws, and repudiation of idolatry assumed great significance in the Jewish pluralism that emerged from these times.

The social structures depicted in this literature are patrilinear (descent was reckoned through the male line) and patrilocal (women joined the households of their husbands). Inheritance was generally patrimonial (through the father or husband, with the notable exception of Jdt 16:23–24). It was the duty of all to have and care for children, who were taught obedience to Torah and respect for parents (though see Jdt 16:22). In the idealized world of these works, the solidarity of the Jewish family, with its concerns for the maintenance of economy, reproduction, nurturance, and education, served as the cornerstone for a religion that endured and survived the radical cultural changes, warfare, and poverty of the Hellenistic and Roman eras. Because so much of this literature is didactic fiction constructed in support of various ideals of postexilic Jewish piety, it is unclear how these works square with the social realities of the period.

Like other parts of the Bible, the Apocryphal/

Deuterocanonical Books contain both negative and positive portrayals of women, though this literature contains examples of excesses in both directions. For instance, no biblical assessment of women is more negative than that in Sirach: "Better is the wickedness of a man than a woman who does good; it is woman who brings shame and disgrace" (Sir 42:14). And no portrayal of another biblical woman equals Judith in its positive depiction of and praise for a woman as an autonomous agent through whom God's purposes are accomplished.

In all but three of the eighteen books or parts of books found in the NRSV (the Prayer of Azariah, the Prayer of Manasseh, and Psalm 151), women figure as named or unnamed characters or in female representations. Notably, in prayer and relationship with God, women such as Sarah (in Tobit), Judith, Esther, Susanna, and the unnamed martyred mother in 2 and 4 Maccabees achieve a measure of independence from androcentric societal norms. God hears and values these women's voices, even when sociopolitical structures silence them. Three books are titled by the names of women who are models of courageous faithfulness to covenant in times of crisis: Judith, Esther, and Susanna (compared to the Hebrew Bible's two eponymous books — Ruth and Esther — and the New Testament, in which no book is titled by the name of a woman).

The seventeen named women in the Apocryphal/Deuterocanonical Books appear in only nine books. The main characters among these women are faithful Jewish wives, mothers, daughters, or widows. Passing references cite women from the Hebrew Bible and other non-Jewish women, most of whom have royal associations. Judith and Susanna are the only named women in their books. Tobit includes four Jewish female characters — Deborah, Anna, Sarah, and Edna — and it refers in a prayer to Eve of the Book of Genesis (Tob 8:6). The Book of Judith alludes to the Genesis story of the rape of Dinah (compare Jtd 9:2; Gen 34:2). Baruch makes reference to another woman of Genesis, Hagar (Bar 3:23). Greek Additions to the Book of Esther names Esther and three other women: Vashti, Zosara (she is the same woman as Zeresh in Esther 5), and

Cleopatra (mentioned in the postscript). 1 Maccabees names and makes references to another Cleopatra (Cleopatra Thea). 2 Maccabees mentions one woman, Antiochis, the king's concubine. 3 Maccabees tells of Arsinoë, Philopator's courageous sister, and 1 Esdras names two women: Agia, whose sons returned from the exile to claim the priesthood, and Apame, who exercises powerful control over the king as his concubine.

Unnamed women, who for the most part reflect androcentric stereotypes, appear throughout (except in the Prayer of Azariah, the Prayer of Manasseh, and Psalm 151) as community members, brides, widows, wives, mothers, daughters, nurses, servants, prostitutes, and worshippers. More attention is given to Jewish unnamed women than to foreigners. Most notable and most thoroughly developed of the unnamed Jewish women is the mother martyred with her seven sons, mentioned in 2 and 4 Maccabees. Typical of the ideology of most of the Apocryphal/Deuterocanonical Books is the sentiment that "because of their birthpangs" mothers "have a deeper sympathy toward their offspring than do the fathers. Considering that mothers are the weaker sex and give birth to many, they are more devoted to their children" (4 Macc 15:4–5). Praise is intended by the conclusion that "If, then, a woman advanced in years and mother of seven sons, endured seeing her children tortured to death, it must be admitted that devout reason is sovereign over the emotions" (4 Macc 16:1).

Female deities and personifications appear in five of the eighteen books. Two goddesses are cited, both in 2 Maccabees: in the temple of Nanea, the Seleucid ruler Antiochus IV (Epiphanes) is stoned and decapitated (2 Macc 1:13–17); in the temple of Atargatis, Judas Maccabeus, the leader of the second-century B.C.E. Jewish revolt, put to death twenty-five thousand Gentiles (12:26). God, and in some instances the church, is personified as a mother, nurse, and hen in 2 Esdras. In the same book, Earth, Zion, Babylon and Asia, righteousness, and iniquity are personified as females. Wisdom is depicted as a woman in the Wisdom of Solomon, Sirach, Baruch, and 2 Esdras.

The New Testament

Ross S. Kraemer

CONTEMPORARY New Testament scholarship has much in common with the study of the Hebrew Bible and the Apocryphal/Deuterocanonical Books, but it also has distinctive aspects. This section introduces readers to some significant issues in the study of the New Testament and early Christianity, particularly as they pertain to women.

The twenty-seven books of the New Testament were originally composed in Greek, probably in scroll form. As is true for the Hebrew Bible and the Apocryphal/Deuterocanonical Books, no original manuscripts of any book of the New Testament survive. The earliest copy of any New Testament book appears to be a small fragment of the Gospel of John dating to the second quarter of the second century C.E. The earliest copies of Paul's letters date to about 200 C.E., as do the earliest full manuscripts of the Gospels. Not until the fourth century C.E. do we begin to have complete manuscripts of all books of the New Testament, made possible by the development of the large-scale codex, in which individual leaves or sheets of writing material were inscribed on both sides and then bound together along one edge.

Whereas Jewish copyists of the Hebrew Bible (at least from the Greco-Roman period and onward) seem to have taken considerable care to ensure the accurate copying of biblical manuscripts, the situation with New Testament manuscripts is more complex. More than five thousand handwritten copies of part or all of the New Testament have survived from the period between the second century C.E. and the sixteenth century; the printing press, invented in the fifteenth century, made handwritten copies virtually obsolete. Except for some very tiny fragments, none of these manuscripts agrees entirely in its wording with any other manuscript.

Some scholars (called text critics) specialize in analyzing these similarities and differences and attempt to recover the earliest available readings, which may or may not be the same as what the authors first wrote. They concur that although many of the differences between manuscripts result from scribal errors, others are the product of intentional revision. Some of these changes do nothing more than smooth out awkward Greek constructions, but others are far more significant for biblical interpretation. Ancient copyists altered the texts of the Synoptic Gospels to bring them into harmony with one another and changed theologically problematic passages to more acceptable readings.

As a result, all modern editions of the Greek New Testament are really only careful approximations of the ancient books, and these editions usually contain at least some critical apparatus noting major differences in the existing manuscripts. Obviously then, all translations into English (or any other language) reflect textual decisions made by the translators. Many newer editions of the Bible in English, such as the HarperCollins Study Bible or the Oxford Study Bible, provide the reader with notes that indicate significant alternative readings.

Text-critical questions sometimes become quite significant for the study of women. Reading the name of the person "prominent among the apostles" in Rom 16:7 as the feminine Junia, rather than the masculine Junias (the preferred reading until quite recently), restores a female apostle to early Christian history and has significant ramifications for contemporary debates about women's roles and titles in early Christian communities. A famous fourth-century Christian preacher, John Chrysostom of Antioch, seems to have known a version of Acts 18:26 that reads, "When Priscilla heard [Apollos, an Alexandrian preacher] she took him aside and explained the Way of God to him more accurately," whereas all the ancient manuscripts now known to us have both Priscilla and Aquila (called her husband in Acts) take Apollos aside and correct his teachings. The reading apparently known to Chrysostom gives us an unambiguous example of a woman teaching a man authoritatively, something expressly prohibited in 1 Tim 2:12. This may be an example of intentional suppression of a tradition about a woman because of its theological and political implications. Concerns about women and gender have influenced both ancient copyists and modern text critics and the readings they have transmitted.

Text-critical issues also greatly affect discussions about the identity of the young dancer who asks for the head of John the Baptist in Matthew 14 and Mark 6. Some ancient manuscripts of Mark 6:22 identify the dancer as "the daughter of Herodias, herself." Others call her "his [Herod's] daughter, Herodias" (this could even be translated as "his [Herod's] daughter by Herodias," although it is not usually construed this way). One manuscript of Matt 14:6 calls the dancer "Herodias, his daughter," but other manuscripts generally identify her as "the daughter of Herodias." Although Christian tradition has long identified the dancer as Salome, daughter of Herodias, these several textual variants complicate any attempt to sort out early Christian traditions about the woman implicated in the death of John.

The twenty-seven books of the New Testament reflect the work of multiple authors. All but six of these books identify themselves as the works of male writers, but these six include major works: the four Gospels, the Acts of the Apostles, and Hebrews. Contemporary biblical scholarship questions many of these attributions, as well as the early Christian traditions that assign names and identities to the authors of the originally anonymous Gospels. Although most biblical scholars continue to call the authors of the Gospels by their traditional names, we cannot be certain of the actual names or identities of these writers, and most scholars consider later Christian traditions about these evangelists to

have little historical value. Recently, some scholars have even suggested that women could have authored one or more of the Gospels, including perhaps those attributed to Mark and to John. Precisely because we know so little about the authors, this remains only a tantalizing possibility.

Of the thirteen letters in the name of Paul, only seven are generally accepted as the work of this early and prominent apostle to the Gentiles (Romans, 1 and 2 Corinthians, Galatians, Philippians, 1 Thessalonians, and Philemon). Scholars continue to be divided about whether this same person wrote Colossians; a few maintain Pauline authorship for Ephesians; the vast majority of critical scholars are persuaded that Paul did not write the Pastoral Epistles (1 and 2 Timothy and Titus). Likewise, biblical scholars consider the Epistles of James, Jude, and 1 and 2 Peter to be "pseudonymous" — that is, written under the name of another person.

For some modern readers, the idea that early Christian authors might have intentionally written works in someone else's name suggests a disturbing deceitfulness. In fact, in antiquity, people did sometimes write in the name of another person or alter another person's works with the intention of deceiving readers. Numerous ancient authors complain that writings have been forged in their names or that their genuine works have been spuriously altered. Such a claim even appears in the New Testament itself, in 2 Thessalonians 2, where the author, writing in the name of Paul, urges the letter's recipients not to be persuaded by letters purporting to come from him.

It is particularly important to recognize, however, that writing in the name of another person was not always considered fraudulent and devious. Young men learned to compose in the style of venerated authors as part of a classical education. Writing in one's own name was sometimes considered immodest. Many Jewish and Christian writings from the Greco-Roman period, apart from the New Testament, claim to be the writings or revelations of religious luminaries ranging from Abraham to Moses to Mary. It is difficult to know how many of these might be deliberate deceptions and how many the works of pious persons who considered themselves only the conduits for divine words. They might truly have understood the source of their writings to be Abraham or Moses, Peter or Paul, Mary Magdalene or the Blessed Virgin Mary, mediated through visions and other forms of revelation.

A significant number of pseudepigraphic works in the New Testament are central to Christian debates about gender and women's roles. Writers claiming the authority of Paul set forth stringent regulations for the behavior of women in New Testament books including Ephesians, Colossians, and the Pastoral Epistles; 1 Peter does so in the name of Peter. Invoking someone else's authority thus seems to be an effective device for many early Christian writers seeking to contain the power and prestige of early women prophets and teachers. Yet, ironically, proponents of women's autonomy also invoked the authority of Paul pseudepigraphically in works such as the second-century C.E. *Acts of (Paul and) Thecla,* in which Paul commissions a celibate aristocratic woman to "go and teach the word of God." Further, the practice of pseudepigraphy might even have allowed women to write under a "cloak of respectability" — masking their identity with a male name.

Just as scholars have demonstrated the composite nature of many books of the Hebrew Bible, so too have New Testament scholars recognized the complex composition of many New Testament writings. The letter known as 2 Corinthians, for example, almost certainly contains at least two different letters from Paul to believers at Corinth, arranged differently from their original order of composition. Romans 16, which contains greetings from Paul to a long list of women and men in the early movement, may not have originated as part of this letter. Many scholars believe that some of Paul's letters contain interpolations by later writers, including one of the most famous passages pertaining to women, 1 Cor 14:33b–36 (which advocates women's silence in the communal assembly).

Some of the most significant debates about the integrity of New Testament books concern the four Gospels. Modern scholarship has demonstrated that Matthew, Mark, Luke, and John draw extensively on earlier materials, both oral and written. Both Mark and John are thought to have undergone significant revision and perhaps to have circulated in antiquity in several different versions. This is especially visible in the Gospel of John, including John 8:1–11, the story of the woman caught in the act of adultery, and chap. 21, which is almost certainly a later addition.

Scholars have been particularly intrigued by the relationship between the Gospels of Mark, Matthew, and Luke. These three are known as the Synoptic Gospels, because when "seen together" (the meaning of *synoptic*), it is clear that they have some strong literary relationship. Most contemporary New Testament scholars subscribe to some form of what is often called the two-source hypothesis. According to this model, the Gospel of Mark was composed first (probably around the year 70 C.E.) and known (although perhaps in somewhat different forms) to the authors of both Matthew and Luke, neither of whom read the other. In addition, both Matthew and Luke are thought to have drawn from a collection of sayings about Jesus designated as "Q" (for the German word *Quelle,* meaning "source"). The existence of Q has been hypothesized in order to account for the significant body of sayings material found both in Matthew and Luke but neither in Mark nor John. Matthew and Luke each also contain material found nowhere else, suggesting that each evangelist had access to additional collections of traditions about Jesus not known to the other. Both Gospels are usually dated to the late first century C.E., although some scholars think Luke and Acts may have been written in the early decades of the second century C.E.

By carefully comparing the Synoptic Gospels, with painstaking attention to those places where Matthew and Luke diverge from the Markan text, scholars have been able to discern the specific interests and perspectives of the writers. Close textual analysis has demonstrated that the Gospel writers sometimes intentionally revise traditions about Jesus and has strongly suggested that, at times, they also create at least some of the material unique to each Gospel. The author of Luke, for instance, regularly includes parables about women not found in either Mark or Matthew, and these passages are parallel to parables about men (the raising of the widow's son in Luke 7:11–17 paired with the raising of the centurion's daughter; the woman sweeping for the lost coin in Luke 15:8–10 paired with the man searching for the lost sheep).

Comparative analysis of the Gospels also reveals divergent early Christian traditions about whether the first person(s) to see the risen Jesus were female (Matt 28:9; John 20:14–18) or male (Luke 23:34; compare Luke 24:13–27). The primary contenders are Mary Magdalene and Peter, but other persons figure in various Gospel narratives as well. These competing traditions have had significant repercussions regarding the authority of women in Christian communities.

None of the books of the New Testament specifies the date of its composition. Individual writings must be dated on the basis of evidence such as their earliest known quotation in other works, mention of them in later writings whose own date is secure, and other indirect references. Since none can predate the ministry of Jesus, and all are attested by about the late second century C.E., it is safe to say that the books of the New Testament were written over a period of no more than about one hundred years, from the late 40s or early 50s C.E. to about 150 C.E. Many scholars would argue for a span of only seventy-five years or so. The earliest books are the seven undisputed letters of Paul, written from perhaps 48–51 C.E. (1 Thessalonians) to about 58 C.E. (Romans). Identifying the latest book of the New Testament is more difficult: candidates include the Acts of the Apostles (which may have been written as late as c. 135 C.E.), Jude, 2 Peter, and the so-called Pastoral Epistles to Timothy and Titus. Written in the name of Paul, these last two letters may have been written as late as the mid–second century C.E.

Perhaps the most important consequence of modern critical New Testament scholarship is the recognition that the writings of the New Testament cannot be used uncritically for historical reconstruction of the life and teachings of Jesus or of the subsequent experiences of his followers and the development of early Christian communities. On the contrary, biblical scholars recognize that all of the writings of the New Testament are fundamentally theological in nature. They are much less interested in what we might think of as the niceties and fine points of "objective history," and much more concerned with the meaning and interpretation of events and experiences, particularly those understood to illuminate the relationship between humans and the divine.

Scholars also understand that the New Testament by no means comprises the totality of early Christian traditions about the life and teachings of Jesus, nor are its books necessarily the earliest such traditions, or the most historically reliable. Relying on the full range of literary and archaeological evidence related to the first and second centuries C.E., contemporary scholarship has demonstrated the rich diversity of early Christian communities, beliefs, and practices. Other early Christian gospels that are not part of the canon, including those attributed to Thomas and to Peter, are now thought to contain important early traditions of comparable value to historians (although not necessarily to contemporary believers, who tend to privilege the canonical texts). These include the various works gathered in the so-called *Apostolic Fathers* (such as the letters of Ignatius of Antioch, *1 and 2 Clement,* the *Shepherd of Hermas,* and the *Didache*), all composed in the late first or early mid–second century C.E., contemporaneous with some writings in the New Testament. In the first few centuries, Christianity produced an extensive literature attesting to Christians' multiple understandings of who Jesus was and what it meant to be his follower. This literature included numerous ancient Christian gospels, such as the *Gospel of Peter,* the *Gospel of Thomas,* the *Gospel of the Hebrews,* and even one known as the *Gospel of Truth.* Several, including the *Gospel According to Mary* and the *Dialogue of the Savior,* feature women as prominent disciples and as recipients of major divine revelation.

Yet although Christianity was not initially (and

perhaps has never been) a homogeneous, unified tradition, by the fourth century C.E. certain Christian beliefs, practices, and writings had attained a privileged status. This process is intricately intertwined with the Christianization of the Roman Empire, a phenomenon usually associated with the Roman emperor Constantine (d. 337 C.E.), the first emperor to endorse and legalize Christianity. The books of the New Testament may all have been written by the mid–second century C.E., but it is not until the late fourth century that a definitive list of authoritative Christian Scripture can be documented that contains precisely the twenty-seven books that we think of as the New Testament. This list is found in the Festal Letter of Athanasius, bishop of Alexandria, in 367 C.E. Earlier such "canon" lists contain many of the books in the New Testament, but they frequently lack some books (such as 1 and 2 John, 2 Peter, and Revelation) and contain books now excluded from the New Testament, such as the *Shepherd of Hermas* and the *Apocalypse of Peter*. The same is true for some actual codices.

Canonization has particularly significant implications for women and understandings of gender. Favoring canonical writings obscures and marginalizes early Christian traditions about women's leadership and authority, as well as early Christian use of feminine imagery for the divine. Such imagery is far more prevalent in extracanonical texts, from the *Shepherd of Hermas* to the Gnostic *Thunder, Perfect Mind*. When we consider that 1 and 2 Timothy (which prohibit women teachers and encourage marriage and childbearing) are ultimately included in the canon, whereas the *Acts of (Paul and) Thecla* was relegated to the category of Christian "apocrypha" and the *Gospel of Mary* to the category of "heresy," we might well conclude that at least one implicit criterion for the canon was precisely conformity to fourth-century and earlier orthodox views on the leadership of women and on appropriate gender differentiation.

∽

As was true for the Hebrew Bible entries and those for the Apocryphal/Deuterocanonical Books, com-

piling the New Testament entries for *Women in Scripture* produced some unexpected findings. One of the most startling was our realization of precisely how much evidence for the presence of women in the New Testament comes from Luke-Acts and Romans 16. Without these, the majority of material for women would disappear. Luke and Paul (in the undisputed Epistles) account for three quarters of the entries in Part I (excluding New Testament references to women of the Hebrew Bible). Luke contains most of the references to individual widows and various other female characters. By comparison, it is almost as startling to see that Matthew, Mark, and John each name only four women. Since in John the mother of Jesus is never called Mary by name, the only woman named in each of the four canonical Gospels is Mary Magdalene.

Counting the number of named women in the New Testament itself proved surprisingly difficult. In Part I, the alphabetical listing of names, fifty-one entries are taken from New Testament passages. Ten of these refer to women of the Hebrew Bible who are mentioned in the New Testament. Yet the remaining forty-one entries — women depicted as members or contemporaries of the Jesus movement and early Christian communities — may represent as few as thirty-five actual women. Tabitha and Dorcas are two names for the same person; as are Prisca and Priscilla, reducing the list to no more than thirty-nine. "Jezebel" (Rev 2:20) is a likely pseudonym for a woman prophet whose real name is unknown, and Candace is an Ethiopian title for a female ruler (the Kandake), reducing the list to thirty-seven actual named women. Further, despite enduring tradition, the dancing daughter of Herodias who demands the head of John the Baptist is never named Salome in the New Testament, reducing the list of named women to thirty-six. Two of the seven women named Mary might be the same person, reducing the list to thirty-five. Finally, some manuscripts name the dancing daughter Herodias, expanding the list to thirty-six again.

Other surprising statistics emerged as we identified the entries for the dictionary. Of the twenty-seven books of the New Testament, slightly more than one third (ten books) mention both named and unnamed women: all four Gospels, Acts, Romans, 1 Corinthians, Philippians, Colossians, and 2 Timothy. Four books — 2 Thessalonians, 1 and 3 John, and Jude — are devoid of references to women, named or unnamed. The only mentions of women in 2 Corinthians are a reference to Eve (11:3) and an apparent quotation of 2 Sam 7:14 (6:18). Nine books, all in the form of letters, contain no named women, even from the Hebrew Bible: Ephesians, 1 and 2 Thessalonians, Titus, 2 Peter, 1–3 John, and Jude. Another six books name only women from the Hebrew Bible, but no women from the author's own milieu: 2 Corinthians, Galatians, 1 Timothy, Hebrews, James, and 1 Peter.

Drawing up these lists was complicated by the reference in Rev 2:20 to a woman prophet called Jezebel. Almost certainly, this is a polemical pseudonym taken from the idolatrous queen Jezebel of 1 and 2 Kings and is not the true name of an otherwise historical woman. Revelation does contain female figures such as the Whore of Babylon, the Woman Clothed with the Sun, and the Bride of the Lamb (all discussed in Part III), but names no other contemporaneous women nor any other figures from the Hebrew Bible. Should Revelation be listed among the books that name women? that name women from the Hebrew Bible? that name contemporaneous women? Including or excluding Revelation from each of these categories does not significantly alter the general picture, but it does demonstrate the difficulty of making a precise count.

Compiling the list of entries for unnamed women was complicated by the fact that several recent English translations of the Bible have sought to use gender-inclusive language whenever possible, at least for passages referring to human beings. In particular, the translators of the NRSV have rendered the Greek masculine plural *adelphoi* (literally "brothers") with the inclusive phrase "brothers and sisters" in the majority of cases, reserving the exclusively male translation "brothers" for those few passages where the translators thought the Greek was gender-specific. Similarly, in many cases where the Greek has *adelphos* ("brother"), the NRSV reads "brother or sister."

In some cases, such as the use of *adelphoi* for the addressees of Paul's letters, or the use of *adelphos* to designate an individual member of the community in ethical material, the decision of the NRSV translators seems highly appropriate. Given the actual content of Paul's letters, particularly Romans, it is inconceivable that Paul envisioned his audience as wholly male or his instructions for appropriate behavior as limited to men. Here the translation of "brothers and sisters" or "brother and sister" illuminates the presence of women where the more literal "brothers" might obscure it.

Elsewhere, however, the matter is more complicated. In 1 Cor 15:6, Paul presents a list of persons who have seen the resurrected Jesus. The list includes various male disciples (concluding with Paul himself) and five hundred *adelphoi*. The NRSV renders this as "five hundred brothers and sisters," thereby presenting a list of resurrection appearances that unambiguously includes women. As noted in the entry for this passage, Paul's list is already curious in that it contains no mention of either Mary Magdalene or the other women who are said to have seen the resurrected Jesus in Matthew and John. If Paul was either unaware of a tradition of Jesus' appearance to women or chose here not to repeat it, are we warranted in translating *adelphoi* here as "brothers and sisters"?

The NRSV translators helpfully flag their decisions in accompanying footnotes. Readers alert to these notes will soon see, though, that the translators were far from consistent in their translation of *adelphos* and *adelphoi*. In a considerable number of cases, they sought to produce inclusive translations through the use of apparently gender-neutral or inclusive terms such as "beloved" (used for both singular and plural), "friend(s)," "believer(s)," "comrades," and "relatives." Readers who ignore the small footnotes might be misled about the presence of explicit references to women in the New Testament. Interestingly, only a few instances of this problem crop up in the translation of the Hebrew Bible and the Apocryphal/Deuterocanonical Books.

For us, these translation decisions had practical consequences. The use of such translations affects any attempt to calculate the presence of women in individual books. In the NRSV (and in translations such as the New Revised English Bible), Epistles such as Galatians and 2 Corinthians appear to include multiple references to women. Yet apart from these inclusive translations of *adelphoi,* these books contain no references to particular contemporaneous women, although Galatians makes extensive use of the story of Sarah and Hagar and contains the famous baptismal formula "there is no longer male and female . . . in Christ Jesus" (3:28), itself an allusion to Gen 1:27.

Most significant, in close to one hundred places the NRSV renders either *adelphos* or *adelphoi* inclusively. Although we have tried to be as comprehensive as possible in this book, writing entries for each of these instances seemed excessive and redundant. Instead, we have chosen to provide entries only for those instances where the Greek is explicitly inclusive (for example, Jas 2:15) or where the translators' choice raises interesting questions (for example, Rom 16:23; 1 Cor 15:6; Jas 3:1).

For Further Reading

The following reference works are recommended to readers who wish to know more about some of the technical issues or other aspects of biblical study alluded to in the Introduction or elsewhere in this book. Articles about individual biblical books are especially recommended for those interested in the context of the passages discussed by our contributors.

Anchor Bible Dictionary, 6 vols. New York: Doubleday, 1992.

Cambridge Companion to the Bible. Cambridge: Cambridge University Press, 1997.

Harper's Bible Commentary. San Francisco: Harper & Row, 1988.

HarperCollins Bible Dictionary. San Francisco: HarperSanFrancisco, 1996.

New Interpreter's Bible. Nashville: Abingdon Press, 1994.

New Jerome Bible Commentary. Englewood Cliffs, N.J.: Prentice-Hall, 1990.

Oxford Companion to the Bible. New York: Oxford University Press, 1993.

Oxford History of the Biblical World. New York: Oxford University Press, 1998.

Feminist Biblical Scholarship

—◦◦◦—

Alice Ogden Bellis

ALTHOUGH women have been reading the Bible with sensitivity to issues of sex (biologically determined) and gender (culturally constructed) for centuries, they have not always done so with the critical awareness that characterizes contemporary feminism. The roots of feminist biblical interpretation lie ultimately in the European Enlightenment and, in the United States, in the nineteenth-century women's suffrage movement, which overlapped in some instances with the struggle to emancipate slaves. The Grimké sisters, for example, were abolitionists who were drawn into the women's rights movement as a result of male opposition to their outspoken views. They were criticized for stepping outside of their proper place by speaking in public, especially to mixed groups (groups composed of both women and men).

Opponents of women's suffrage used the Bible as ammunition. They understood the Garden of Eden story to say that Eve was created from Adam's rib, and they took this as a sign that women were secondary to men. For them, Eve's leading role in eating the forbidden fruit and offering it to Adam signified women's evil nature. In the early nineteenth century some women, mainly white Protestants, responded with their own counterreadings. Judith Sargent Murray used metaphorical interpretations of the Eve and Adam story in her arguments for women's suffrage. Lucy Stone was determined to learn the biblical languages because she believed that the Scriptures, if properly translated, would support women's rights. In 1843 she went to Oberlin, the first American college to admit women along with men, to study Hebrew and Greek.

Black women, such as Sojourner Truth, Anna Julia Cooper — who entered the struggle for women's rights after the emancipation of slaves — and Jarena Lee, a member of the African Methodist Episcopal Church in the 1830s and 1840s, were also reading the Bible in new ways and using biblical interpretations to buttress their pro-women arguments.

Not all early feminists believed that the Bible, if rightly interpreted, could support their struggle. For example, Matilda Joslyn Gage became convinced that Christianity had degraded women in a variety of ways, including through its Scriptures, most especially the Eve and Adam story, its (Roman Catholic) canon law, and its advocacy of celibacy. In 1893, she published *The Original Exposé of Male Collaboration Against the Female Sex.*

At about the same time, Elizabeth Cady Stanton, one of the most prominent suffragists, led the effort to compile *The Woman's Bible* in order to interpret the Bible in a way that affirmed women's full humanity and thus to combat the interpretations used by men to hold women back. Like Gage, she believed that the story of Eve and Adam was the most problematic biblical text and that feminist interpretation could not solve all the problems. The contributors to *The Woman's Bible* (including Stanton herself) were not trained biblical scholars and were unable to use the then new methods of higher criticism. *The Women's Bible* also contains numerous anti-Jewish comments, reflecting views prevalent in nineteenth-century Christianity. Nevertheless, it was a serious effort and in some ways foreshadowed approaches that have emerged nearly a century later.

The Society of Biblical Literature (SBL), the "establishment" of biblical scholarship, did not vote admission to a woman until almost fifteen years after the society was founded (in 1880). Anna Ely Rhoads, educated at Bryn Mawr College and the University of Leipzig, became a member in 1894, and four more women had joined the society by the turn of the century. Yet the earliest female members neither delivered papers at the society's meetings nor published them in its journal. The barrier to such full participation in the SBL was not broken until the second decade of the twentieth century, when women began to make contributions to the academic study of the Bible. Like their male colleagues, they did not address gender issues. Many of them were active in women's causes, but as biblical scholars they dealt with more "acceptable" topics.

Treatments of women's roles in the Bible in the early twentieth century came from women who were not credentialed biblical scholars. In 1900, Dr. Katherine Bushnell, a medical missionary to China and a Women's Christian Temperance Union leader, published *God's Word to Women: One Hundred Bible Studies on Women's Place in the Divine Economy* (London: Women's Correspondence Bible Class). The Reverend Lee Anna Starr, a Methodist minister, wrote *The Bible Status of Women* (New York: Fleming H. Revell, 1926). Both believed that the Bible, when correctly translated and interpreted, supported women's full humanity.

One of the most noteworthy books on women in the Bible, also by a writer who is not a biblical scholar, appeared in 1955. Edith Deen, a Texas newspaper columnist, published *All the Women of the Bible* (New York: Harper and Row). Pious anthologies of biblical women had been appearing since early in the nineteenth century. But Deen's book was different. A monumental undertaking, it gave detailed treatment to major women as well as an alphabetical listing of named women and a chronological listing of unnamed women. It was the first attempt to be comprehensive and include all women in the Bible. Deen's work is not the work of a specialist, it does not actually include *all* biblical females, it often takes a pious tone, and it sometimes supplies details not provided by the biblical text. Yet, the author of a subsequent such volume

(*All the Women of the Bible,* Grand Rapids, Michigan: Zondervan, 1971), the clergyman Herbert Lockyer, rightly acknowledged Deen's work as a classic. Although his own work often exhibits sexist bias, his acknowledgment of Deen's superb classificatory and expositional skills is valid. In some measure, this present volume is taking up the same interest as Deen's, for in fact, to this day, despite titles to the contrary, no comprehensive listing and analysis of all the women of the Bible has been produced.

A second wave of feminist biblical scholarship emerged in the mid–twentieth century. Just as nineteenth-century feminist biblical scholarship had its origins in the suffrage movement, which in turn was rooted in the abolitionist movement, so also twentieth-century feminist biblical scholarship had its roots in the women's movement, which was an outgrowth of the civil rights movement. In 1963 Betty Friedan published *The Feminine Mystique* (New York: Norton), a book that marked the beginning of the second wave of feminism in the United States. Margaret Crook, professor of religion and biblical literature at Smith College and thirty-nine-year member of the Society of Biblical Literature, published *Women and Religion* (Boston: Beacon) in 1964 and called for the full and equal participation of women with men in a crucial rethinking of ideas about God and religion. A few years later, Elsie Culver, a lay church professional, wrote *Women in the World of Religion* (Garden City, New York: Doubleday, 1967), in which she took biblical scholars to task for their failure to research women's status and roles in the Bible. She suggested how important this research would be for contemporary women. By the 1970s biblical scholars were taking up the challenge. An influential anthology, *Religion and Sexism* (New York: Simon and Schuster), appeared in 1974. Edited by Roman Catholic theologian Rosemary Radford Ruether, it contains programmatic essays, including several on women in Jewish and Christian Scripture. These essays showed that the Bible contained both positive and negative material with respect to women.

At this time, the assumption of many feminists was that, once the Bible was stripped of its androcentric and even misogynist interpretations, its real meaning would support women's claims to equality. Protestant theologian Letty Russell's *The Liberating Word: A Guide to Nonsexist Interpretation of the Bible* (Philadelphia: Westminster, 1985) was typical in its optimistic premises. Before long, however, it was recognized that the problems often went deeper than sexist interpretations. The Bible itself was often androcentric. Much of it was written by men from a male perspective and intended for a male audience.

From biblical law to biblical narrative, the marginalization of women was frequently evident. This recognition prompted questions about the Bible's authority. How could a book that contained so much material apparently oppressive of women be considered authoritative by feminists? Protestant Hebrew Bible scholar Phyllis Trible put it this way:

I face a terrible dilemma: Choose ye this day whom you will serve: the God of the fathers or the God of sisterhood. If the God of the fathers, then the Bible supplies models for your slavery. If the God of sisterhood, then you must reject patriarchal religion and go forth without models to claim your freedom. ("Depatriarchalizing in Biblical Interpretation," *Journal of the American Academy of Religion* 41 [1973]: 31)

On one end of the spectrum were the revolutionaries, those who found the Bible so androcentric, patriarchal (literally, "ruled by the father"), and misogynist (woman hating) that they rejected the Bible and sought other sources of religious inspiration. Theologian and former Roman Catholic Mary Daly is a good example. Already in the late 1960s, she moved from a reformist position — the conviction that the Bible and religious communities could be purged of their bias against women — to a revolutionary stance. In her famous book *The Church and the Second Sex* (New York: Harper and Row, 1968), she rejects biblical authority outright.

On the other end of the spectrum were the reformists, those who believed that the Bible was God's inspired word and there had to be a way of resolving the tension between their feminist convictions and their acceptance of the Bible's authority. Some of these Christian feminists read specific statements in light of general, timeless ones. For example, they understood Gal 3:28 ("There is no longer Jew or Greek, there is no longer slave or free, there is no longer male and female; for all of you are one in Christ Jesus") to state a truth for all time, that in Christ distinctions of servitude, ethnicity, and sex and gender are irrelevant. Thus 1 Cor 11:2–16a, which seems to deal with head coverings and hairstyles for women, had its origin in a particular historical setting, but must now be read in light of Gal 3:28.

The reformists also claim that much of the narrative in the Bible is descriptive rather than prescriptive. For them, just because the Bible says something does not mean that things are supposed to be that way for all time. For example, Col 3:22 says, "Slaves, obey your earthly masters," but Gal 3:28 and other texts suggest that slavery is not God's intention for humanity.

Finally, reformists look for positive notes. Although God is usually described with male images in the Bible, sometimes female images are used. Male imagery may predominate, but it only takes one female image to indicate that God is neither male nor female. Similarly, the reformists point to women such as Miriam, Deborah, Ruth, Esther, Judith, Mary (the sister of Martha), and Priscilla (Prisca) as major biblical figures. Furthermore, their presence may indicate that there were many other significant women who were simply ignored by male authors.

Between the two extremes of the revolutionary feminists who totally reject the Bible's authority and the reformists who have a high view of its authority are those who adopt other strategies for dealing with the issue of biblical authority. One popular strategy is to define a canon within the canon. The term *canon* refers to the writings that are accepted as sacred by a religious community. Those who use the canon-within-a-canon strategy sometimes look for a principle, text, or theme within Scripture as the key for unlocking the interpretive door. In other words, they seek a touchstone by which the variety of texts in Scripture can be evaluated. For example, African American and Latin American liberation theologians often view the exodus experience as the central event of the Hebrew Bible/Old Testament.

Related to the various canon-within-a-canon approaches is the method of correlation. Theologian Rosemary Ruether correlates the secular principle of women's full humanity with the biblical prophets' critique of injustice. Although she views the principle of women's full humanity as nonbiblical, the Bible is not silent on the liberation of women, though it does not use that terminology. For example, the Book of Ruth may have been written, at least in part, as protest literature against those in the Jerusalem establishment at the time of Ezra and Nehemiah (fifth century B.C.E.) who blamed much of the community's problems on foreign women. Similarly, the stories of Judith and Susanna in the Apocryphal/Deuterocanonical Books can be understood as positive pictures of their female heroes that may imply protest against misogynist views. In the New Testament, Jesus' interactions with women and the statement in Gal 3:28 are also taken to suggest women's full humanity.

Elisabeth Schüssler Fiorenza, a Roman Catholic New Testament scholar, shifts authority from the biblical text to the interpretive community who experience God's presence in their struggle for liberation. The focus is on the *process* of biblical interpretation, which includes four "moments" or tasks: a hermeneutics of suspicion, a hermeneutics of historical interpretation and reconstruction, a hermeneutics of ethical and theological evaluation, and a hermeneutics of creative imagination and ritualization.

The term *hermeneutics* comes from the Greek *hermeneuein,* meaning the practice and principles of interpretation. Not merely a synonym for the term *interpretation,* it includes a thoughtful awareness of the principles employed in the process of interpretation. The hermeneutics of suspicion involves approaching texts with an awareness of the possibility of their androcentrism. In the past women have often unconsciously accommodated

themselves to texts that really assumed their absence. For example, the commandment not to covet one's neighbor's wife (Exod 20:17; Deut 5:21) is directed at males. Women sometimes unconsciously edit the commandment to include themselves.

The hermeneutics of historical interpretation and reconstruction seeks to figure out what happened, to the extent that this can be known, including what happened to women, whether or not they are explicitly included in the text. The hermeneutics of ethical and theological evaluation goes beyond historical reconstruction to evaluate the implications of our understanding of what happened or may have happened. The hermeneutics of creative imagination and ritualization involves filling in gaps and rewriting ancient stories to transform them for contemporary use.

None of the approaches to the authority of Scripture outlined here has won universal acceptance among feminists. Each reads in a historical and social context that shapes understanding of the texts and their authority. Although there is much in the Bible that is uncongenial to contemporary women, there is also much that nourishes feminists and helps keep alive their struggle to have women's full humanity affirmed.

Not all feminists who read and study the Bible do so from a religious perspective. Thus, the issue of the Bible's religious authority is not an issue for all feminist biblical interpreters. Some read the Bible as a historical or literary document that sheds light on the past. The interest is not simply antiquarian. The Bible in all of its various canons and translations has probably been the most influential body of literature in the West and certainly has been the most significant with respect to women's rights and roles. To understand it and the history of its interpretation empowers the interpreter to shape the present and the future.

Most feminists recognize that no one comes to the task of interpretation detached or neutral. We all bring our beliefs as well as our personal history. This does not make feminists — female or male — different from other interpreters, as if feminist interpretation were ideological and androcentric interpretation universal and objective. Rather, everyone comes to the text with convictions, assumptions, and perspectives. They influence the questions we ask, the way we ask them, the approaches we use to find the answers, and the answers themselves.

In addition, the texts themselves are often multivalent; they are open to a number of different interpretations. For example, in Esth 1:11, when King Ahasuerus demands that Vashti appear at his party "wearing the royal crown, in order to show the peoples and the officials her beauty," does she refuse because she understands that he has requested her to appear with nothing on but her crown or, alternatively, does she refuse not because he requests her nude appearance but because she does not wish to appear even clothed before the drunken, rowdy party? The text can be read either way.

This multivalence of many texts does not mean, however, that interpreters are free to rewrite the texts. Although we may struggle to identify the criteria with which to judge, some interpretations are generally conceded to be better than others. Mary Ann Tolbert suggests that critical discourse involves "clarity of thought, logical argument, and analysis" ("Defining the Problem: The Bible and Feminist Hermeneutics," *Semeia* 28 [1983]: 115).

Reading modern values back into the text can be problematic, but contemporary values and perspectives can sometimes be helpful in opening up the text. Until recently, virtually all biblical scholars and interpreters were white males, and rarely did any of them think to ask questions about women's roles and status. When they did, the results now often sound ridiculous. For example, in his book *All the Women of the Bible,* Lockyer states that "Human nature remains very much the same, as millenniums come and go. As long as history continues, women remain women, in spite of their present effort to become more masculine." It took the combination of women's experience of marginalization and acquisition of the tools of academic biblical interpretation to open up this rich area of research.

Similarly, as long as the vast majority of commentators were white, few people even considered the question of the ethnicity of biblical characters. Now that a variety of ethnic and national groups have entered the world of professional biblical interpretation in significant numbers, many new questions are being considered. Among these are matters relating to the intersection of gender and ethnic heritage.

Black feminists, who often call themselves womanists — a term coined by poet and novelist Alice Walker from black folk idioms — have raised this issue with particular urgency. Womanists feel a stronger bond with black men than white women often experience with white men because of their common experience of slavery. Thus a tension exists between loyalty to gender and loyalty to ethnicity. Jewish feminists sometimes experience a similar conflict. Scholars of Hispanic heritage (who call themselves *feministas* or *mujeristas,* Spanish for "feminists" and "womanists") also read the Bible in the context of their ethnic heritages as well as their gender. For instance, Mexican Hebrew Bible scholar Elsa Tamez believes that Latin American women need to distance themselves from the macho culture that implicitly views women as inferior to men. They also need to be sensitive to the poverty, malnutrition, repression, torture, Indian genocide, and war that mark the lives of many women and men in Latin America. Similarly, Asian feminists such as Chung Hyun Kyung, a Korean Christian feminist, do biblical interpretation in the context of the history of Western colonization in which the Bible was sometimes used oppressively.

Regardless of these diverse perspectives, feminist biblical interpreters approach the texts with an eye on the way women are presented, hidden, understood, and treated in the Bible. They look at stories about women or that at least include female characters, whether named or unnamed. They look at the stories of women who are strong and virtuous and those who are weak, victimized, or portrayed in negative ways. Stories that do not include women, but in which their absence screams loudly, are scrutinized. Feminist scholars attend to female images of God. They also consider the biblical laws affecting women and wonder if the biblical texts are accurate representations of reality, or biased distortions produced by elite male leaders and authors, or even idealizations.

Yet many feminists are concerned with more than issues of gender. Being sensitized to problems of oppression in one area of one's life tends to open one's eyes to other kinds of oppression. African American Hebrew Bible scholar Renita Weems believes African American women should read the Bible to uncover the voice of the oppressed. Elisabeth Schüssler Fiorenza emphasizes the importance of going beyond gender to address the whole range of categories of oppression.

One area of particular concern is the anti-Judaism of some Christian feminists. Sometimes, in an attempt to present Jesus in positive terms, they depict the Jews and Judaism of Jesus' day in extremely negative ways. Jewish restrictions on women's roles, known only from later sources, are read back into the first century C.E. so that a feminist Jesus is contrasted with a misogynist Judaism. As Katharina von Kellenbach shows in *Anti-Judaism in Feminist Religious Writings* (Atlanta: Scholars Press, 1994), the reality was far more complex.

Feminist biblical interpreters approach the biblical texts from a wide variety of angles. Some of these can be placed on a continuum. On one end of the continuum — we'll call it the right-hand end — the text is viewed as the product of authors and editors. The goal is to determine the intention of the authors and editors at various stages in the process that resulted in the final form of the text. In the center of the continuum is the text as finished product. The goal is to determine what the text says, regardless of what its producers intended. Although what the author or editor intended and what the text says might seem to be synonymous, it is often true that authors say more than they themselves realized at the time of writing. On the left end of the continuum is the reader's understanding of the text. The goal is neither the author's or editor's intention or the text's meaning, but what the reader understands the text to mean. Again, it might seem that what the text says and what the interpreter understands it to mean should be the same. In real-

ity, because of the multivalence of the text and the various perspectives interpreters bring to the text, the reader's understandings are not necessarily synonymous with the bare text.

Interpreters on the right-hand side of the continuum ask mostly historical questions and utilize many different approaches including archaeology, comparative anthropology, and analysis of other ancient documents. They ask, for example, what women's life was like at various times in biblical history or how women's lives in ancient Israel or early Christianity compare with the lives of women in other ancient cultures. Those on the left-hand side engage in what is called reader-response criticism, a type of criticism that focuses on the reader's understanding of the text. Those in the middle ask mostly literary questions and use a variety of forms of literary criticism.

The most famous example of the literary approach to texts about women is Phyllis Trible's handling of the Eve and Adam story in *God and the Rhetoric of Sexuality* (Philadelphia: Fortress, 1978), in which she understands the first person created to have been a sexually undifferentiated creature, that is, a human without biological sex. She looks at what the text says in Genesis 2–3, rather than what its producers may have intended. She has been criticized because some interpreters do not believe the author(s) and editor(s) could possibly have meant what she interprets the texts to say. Her reading is consistent with the words of the text, but words can be intended in various ways.

In reality, the rigid distinctions between the ends of the interpretive continuum cannot and should not be maintained. Whether our focus is on what the authors or editors intended or on what we understand the text to mean, we are dealing with historical texts in ancient languages that cannot be understood at all without a knowledge of how the ancients used language. Thus, all interpretation of biblical texts must be somewhat historically oriented. On the other hand, all readers view the ancient texts through the lens of their own experience. Thus, all interpretation is, to some degree, reader-response oriented. Nevertheless, some interpreters are more interested in historical matters, others in literary questions, and others still in the psychological, sociological, and other factors that influence readers' understanding of biblical texts.

Because they believe that ancient authors were rarely, if ever, interested in the kinds of questions modern historians pose, most biblical scholars are extremely cautious about the use of biblical materials to consider historical questions. Feminist biblical scholars often avoid historical reconstruction because of its difficulties, but some of the most exciting feminist biblical criticism is in this area. Carol Meyers's sociohistorical reconstruction of the life of a typical woman before the monarchy in *Discovering Eve: Ancient Israelite Women in Context* (New York: Oxford, 1988), Ross Kraemer's work on women in the Greco-Roman world in *Her Share of the Blessings: Women's Religions Among Pagans, Jews, and Christians in the Greco-Roman World* (New York: Oxford, 1992), and Luise Schottroff's New Testament historical work *Lydia's Impatient Sisters: A Feminist Social History of Early Christianity* (Louisville: Westminster/John Knox, 1995) are prime examples.

In the area of literary criticism, scholars such as Trible and Toni Craven (*Artistry and Faith in the Book of Judith;* Chico, California: Scholars Press, 1983) use a method called rhetorical criticism or compositional analysis. It is a kind of literary criticism involving close reading of the text with an eye on rhetorical strategies. Other forms of literary criticism have emerged, including structuralism, deconstructionism, and narrative criticism. Structuralist critics look at the binary oppositions such as good and evil, woman and man, body and spirit, that at a deep level provide structure for literary works. Deconstructionists consider the ways in which structural conflicts can tear down a message: for example, a movie whose message is that reading is preferable to video presentations. Narrative critics look at the text and the interrelationship of its various elements and how the reader relates to the text. Some of these methodologies have grown out of secular literary criticism and have provided fresh new approaches, as in Mieke Bal's *Lethal Love:*

Feminist Literary Readings of Biblical Love Stories (Bloomington: Indiana University Press, 1987).

Although many feminists have often assumed that most biblical texts were authored and edited by men, the majority of biblical authors are anonymous or pseudonymous, and the process by which the texts came into final form was a complex one. Thus some feminists such as Athalya Brenner and Fokkelien van Dijk-Hemmes (*On Gendering Texts: Female and Male Voices in the Hebrew Bible;* Leiden: E. J. Brill, 1993) try to hear women's voices in the biblical texts.

Because women's presence and perspectives are often hidden or absent in the biblical texts, feminists sometimes imaginatively re-create biblical stories, inserting constructed roles for women characters. For example, when Jephthah sacrifices his daughter in fulfillment of a vow to God (Judges 11), where was her mother? Where was Sarah when Abraham went out to sacrifice Isaac (Genesis 22)? Where were Jesus' female disciples during the Last Supper (Matthew 26; Mark 14; Luke 22)? Feminists sometimes tell the biblical stories from the perspective of female characters rather than from the point of view of a male character. How would David's adultery with Bathsheba (2 Samuel 11) look if the story was told from her perspective rather than his? How would the story of Hosea and his allegedly promiscuous wife Gomer (Hosea 1–3) sound if Gomer was the narrator? How would the story of Susanna, falsely accused of adultery, sound if Susanna had spoken at her own trial? How would the story of the sisters Mary and Martha (Luke 10:38–42) read if Martha was telling it?

An area of growing interest is the history of interpretation. Because feminists initially believed that the problem was only in androcentric interpretation rather than in the texts themselves, the history of this interpretation was of little interest. Now that feminists have come to the conclusion that some parts of the Bible contain much difficult material, but that difficulties have been intensified through androcentric interpretation, interest has grown in the way texts have been interpreted by various communities down through the centuries and the way this history has influenced contemporary interpretation.

For example, many people are more familiar with Milton's version of the Eve and Adam story in *Paradise Lost* than with the original story in Genesis. The servant songs in Isaiah are often first encountered in Handel's *Messiah*. Some feminists are taking a new look at Jewish elaborations of biblical stories known as Midrash. Others trace the way stories have been used in Christian traditions. Still others observe how some biblical material made its way into Muslim traditions. It is amazing to see what happens to the queen of Sheba, for example, in Midrashic, Ethiopic-Christian, and Muslim renditions of the story. Jacob Lassner's *The Demonization of the Queen of Sheba* (Chicago: University of Chicago Press, 1993) recounts the Midrashic elaborations and Muslim retellings, in which the queen of Sheba is depicted very negatively with hairy legs or a misshapen foot and is sometimes virtually turned into a demon. In the Ethiopic version, known as the *Kebra Nagast*, or "Glory of Kings," she is tricked into sex with King Solomon of Israel, and from the union is born King Menelik I of Ethiopia. In addition to literary retellings, artistic and musical interpretations, both serious and popular, are being studied.

Another important area for feminists is translation. Because the biblical languages use masculine pronouns as gender-inclusive pronouns, it is not always clear from the pronoun alone who the referents are. Similarly, masculine nouns may sometimes be intended as gender-specific and sometimes as gender-inclusive. Sometimes "sons" refers to sons, and sometimes it refers to children. So the phrase "sons of Israel" is variously translated as "sons of Israel," "children of Israel," and "Israelites." Although Israelite men were always included in the phrase "sons of Israel," for some purposes the women and children were considered part of the Israelites as well. Feminists often argue for more inclusive and less ambiguous translations, at least where the original language allows for it. Many feminists, when referring to God, avoid the use of pronouns altogether, since God is personal and

therefore not an it, but neither male nor female. As a result of feminists' concerns in this area, new, more inclusive translations of the Bible are becoming available.

Finally, many feminist biblical interpreters have a keen interest in the theological and ethical implications of the texts. They preach sermons, teach in seminaries, and write in a devotional vein. This religious interest is not inherently separate from the historical, literary, and sociological approaches.

Biblical scholars of both genders have often been more comfortable describing the theological understandings found in various biblical texts than in constructing contemporary biblically based theology. Theologians are sometimes not immersed in biblical texts in the way that biblical scholars are. Thus, there is a dearth of constructive theology grounded in modern biblical scholarship, especially from a feminist perspective. This will no doubt be remedied as feminist biblical theologians and scholars begin to grapple with the implications of recent biblical scholarship.

Although the Bible has been used as a tool to prevent women from exercising their full humanity, it nevertheless has also been a rich resource for women struggling to attain liberation. The struggle continues. Progress has been made in the past thirty years, and feminist biblical interpretation has been instrumental in achieving some of these gains. Much work remains to be done, and feminist biblical interpretation no doubt will continue to develop as we seek to meet the challenges of the twenty-first century.

For Further Reading

Anderson, Janice Capel. "Mapping Feminist Biblical Criticism: The American Scene, 1983–1990." In *Critical Review of Books in Religion: 1991*, ed. Eldon Jay Epp, 21–44. Atlanta: Scholars Press, 1991.

Bass, Dorothy C. "Women's Studies and Biblical Studies: An Historical Perspective." *Journal for the Study of the Old Testament* 22 (1982): 6–12.

Bellis, Alice Ogden. *Helpmates, Harlots, and Heroes:*

Women's Stories in the Hebrew Bible. Louisville: Westminster/John Knox, 1994.

Brenner, Athalya, and Carole Fontaine, eds. *A Feminist Companion to Reading the Bible: Approaches, Methods, and Strategies*. Sheffield: Sheffield Academic Press, 1997.

Cannon, Katie Geneva, and Elisabeth Schüssler Fiorenza, eds. *Interpretation for Liberation. Semeia* 47 (1989).

Castelli, Elizabeth. "Heteroglossia, Hermeneutics and History: A Review Essay of Recent Feminist Studies of Early Christianity." *Journal of Feminist Studies in Religion* 10 (1994): 73–95.

———. *Reimagining Christian Origins: A Colloquium Honoring Burton L. Mack*. Valley Forge, Penn.: Trinity Press International, 1996.

Collins, Adela Yarbro, ed. *Feminist Perspectives on Biblical Scholarship*. Chico, Calif.: Scholars Press, 1985.

Hackett, JoAnn. "Women's Studies and the Hebrew Bible." In *The Future of Biblical Studies: The Hebrew Scriptures*, ed. Richard E. Friedman and Hugh G. M. Williamson, 141–64. Atlanta: Scholars Press, 1987.

Milne, Pamela. "Feminist Interpretations of the Bible: Then and Now." *Bible Review* 8 (1992): 38–43, 52–54.

Newsom, Carol A., and Sharon H. Ringe, eds. *The Women's Bible Commentary*. Louisville: Westminster/John Knox, 1992.

Newsom, Carol A., and Sharon H. Ringe, eds. *Women's Bible Commentary: Expanded Edition with Apocrypha*. Louisville: Westminster John Knox Press, 1998.

Russell, Letty, ed. *Feminist Interpretation of the Bible*. Philadelphia: Westminster Press, 1985.

Sakenfeld, Katherine Doob. "Old Testament Perspectives: Methodological Issues." *Journal for the Study of the Old Testament* 22 (1982): 13–20.

Schüssler Fiorenza, Elisabeth, ed. *Searching the Scriptures*, 2 vols. New York: Crossroad, 1993–94.

———. "The Ethics of Interpretation: De-centering Biblical Scholarship." *Journal of Biblical Literature* 107 (1988): 3–17.

Selvidge, Marla. *Notorious Voices: Feminist Biblical Interpretation, 1550–1920*. New York: Paragon, 1995.

Tolbert, Mary Ann, ed. *The Bible and Feminist Hermeneutics. Semeia* 28 (1983).

Names and Naming in the Biblical World

Karla G. Bohmbach

What's in a name? Shakespeare's answer to this question was "a rose by any other name would smell as sweet" *(Romeo and Juliet,* Act II). This suggests that a name has no intrinsic connection to that which is named. Any convenient collocation of sounds would function as well as any other to identify a person, place, or thing.

Such a viewpoint has no place in the Bible. Rather, in ancient Near Eastern literature generally, names often carry enormous significance, being inextricably connected to the very nature of that which is named. Hence, to know the name is to know something of the fundamental traits, nature, or destiny of the name's bearer. Names can provide insights into a person's character, social location, or future, or the way in which others perceive the person. In the Bible, the name often represents the very essence of a person.

Names provide significant information about the women of the Bible, both individually and as a whole. Indeed, given the Bible's overall androcentrism (male-centeredness), attention to the seemingly small detail of a woman's name may provide key information about her characterization. What, then, is known about the names of the women in the Bible — especially the frequency of their occurrence and their meanings? And what, too, can be said about other name-related issues — such as women who themselves name others and women who have no names? These issues will be taken up in the following pages.

Calculating the frequency with which women's names appear in the Bible presents several challenges. Some biblical names are ambiguous; they could be used to name either women or men (for

example, Abihail, Nahash). When contextual clues indicating otherwise are absent or unclear, translators have tended to assume that such a name refers to a male, not a female (see, notably, the Junia/Junias dispute occasioned by Rom 16:7). A second challenge is the existence of alternate name forms for the same person (for example, Sarah/Sarai, Bathsheba/Bath-shua). A third challenge emerges when names appear different because of the different languages involved, even though the name may well have the same meaning or refer to the same person (for example, Hannah/Anna; Zeresh/Zosara). Finally, the Hebrew occasionally makes use of a hypocoristic name form, that is, a shortened form of an originally longer name; both forms may or may not appear in the text to refer to the same, or a different, person (for example, Abi may derive from Abijah). All three of these latter name-related challenges may well necessitate decisions about whether to count each various name form separately, or, instead, to treat the variations as one name, especially if the specific name variations under consideration all refer to the same person. And the outcome of those decisions will, of course, affect the final tally.

Depending, then, on who is doing the counting and how it proceeds, different totals of biblical women's names are possible. One recent calculation put the number of named individuals in the Hebrew Bible and the New Testament at approximately 3,000–3,100, of which 2,900 are men and 170 are women. But because many names designate more than one individual, another calculation identified only about 1,700 distinct personal names in the Bible, with about 1,563 of these being men's names and 137 being those of women. In yet another enumeration, one that looked only at the Hebrew Bible and also Hebrew inscriptions, the total came to 1,426 names, with 1,315 belonging to men and 111 to women. Despite the disparities among these different calculations, in all of them, women or women's names represent between 5.5 and 8 percent of the total, a stunning reflection of the androcentric character of the Bible.

This dictionary contains 205 separate entries about named women. Because some of these names are shared by more than one woman, or because the same woman is referred to in the different main sections of the Bible and so counted separately, the number of distinct women's names comes to 162. Moreover, the vast majority (approximately 70 percent) of both the names and the named women derives from the Hebrew Bible. Thus, in considering more precisely qualitative aspects of women's names, we shall turn first to the Hebrew Bible, with subsequent consideration of women's naming patterns in the Apocryphal/Deuterocanonical Books and the New Testament.

Discerning the meanings of names in the Bible, like counting them, is difficult. The meanings of names are sometimes doubtful or contested. Occasionally the Bible itself provides more than one meaning for a name. Or, more often, no meaning at all is provided, forcing us to depend on our knowledge of biblical languages (Hebrew, Aramaic, and Greek), as well as their cognates, for derivation of a name's meaning. Also, a certain name may have originally had a specific allusion attached to it that is now lost, or it may have had none at all. Given these difficulties, we must proceed cautiously. Although we cannot always provide precise details, we can identify general patterns and trends with some confidence.

In the Hebrew Bible the connection between a woman's name and her identity or nature appears in a number of different ways. Frequently, a woman is named for an abstract quality. Presumably those doing the naming have either already identified such a quality in her or are hoping for such a quality to be made manifest as she matures. Another

possibility is that the author of a biblical text has deliberately chosen or created a name to suit the aims of the narrative. Whatever the case, the qualities delineated tend to be positive (such as Naamah, "lovely one"; Hannah, "grace"; Shua, "independent"). However, a few do have negative connotations (such as Shemamah, "desolate"; Mara, "bitter"). Rather less often, the quality identified is not abstract, but instead represents some physical feature probably found in the one named (for example, Zilpah, "short-nosed"; Zeruah, "having a skin disease").

Expressing a woman's nature through her name may also be achieved by taking a name from the world of animals, plants, or material objects. The animal world, for example, is the source for twelve women's names (such as Deborah, "bee"; Huldah, "weasel"; Eglah, "heifer"; Jael, "mountain goat"). The floral world is also a source, though much less frequently (Hadassah, "myrtle"; Tamar, "date-palm"). And, finally, a very common practice (eleven instances) is to utilize certain material objects — many connected with ornamentation (jewelry or cosmetics) — to name women (for example, Keturah, "incense"; Adah, "ornament"; Kerenhappuch, "cosmetics case").

Another naming pattern for women is to identify them according to their social location, perhaps either as currently realized, as a hoped-for future attainment, or as part of a strategy effected by a storyteller. Within this pattern two separate categories can be identified: names designating social roles and those denoting kin relationships. In the former we find names such as Milcah ("queen") and Naarah ("girl"). In the latter are names such as Ahinoam ("my brother is pleasantness"), Abital ("my father is dew"), and Abihail ("my father is strength").

It has been suggested that at least some of the "father" names just mentioned actually allude to the deity. These names would then be more properly assigned to another important category of women's names in the Hebrew Bible — theophoric ones (names containing an element that derives from a divine name). In such names some statement about a deity is made. As such, they belong to a name type known as the compound name, in which two or more elements are combined to form either a descriptive phrase or a complete sentence. Approximately eighteen separate examples of women's names in the Hebrew Bible are theophoric. In the majority (about ten) the compound consists of the element Yah- or Yahu- (a shortened form of the divine name YHWH [Yahweh]) together with some commentary on that divine name (for example, Abijah means "my father is Yah"; Athaliah means "Yah is exalted"; Micaiah means "who is like Yah?"). Far fewer women's theophoric names (about five) are compounded with El, a generic Hebrew term for "god" and also the designation for the chief god of the Canaanite pantheon (for example, Elisheba means "my God is an oath"; Michal means "who is like God?"). Associations with non-Israelite deities are also, arguably, made with other names (Asenath may mean "she belongs to Neith [an Egyptian goddess]"; Jezebel may mean "where is Zebul [that is, Baal]?").

The categories mentioned above are the ones most readily adduced from the women's names appearing in the Hebrew Bible. Although not every woman's name is captured under these categories, neither do any other significant categories suggest themselves. That aside, when we compare the categories that can be discerned for women's names with those evident in men's names in the Hebrew Bible, we find remarkable similarities. Men's names, too, derive from abstract qualities, physical features, the natural world, material objects, social roles, and kin relationships — and all in about the same proportions as women's names.

The one exception occurs in theophoric names. Although such names represent only about 15 percent of all women's names, men's theophoric names in the Hebrew Bible form a much higher percentage of total men's names (upwards of 30 percent). But rather than attribute this difference to the notion that women played a much smaller part in Israelite religion, one may point to the case of Genesis, which contains a high concentration of women's names — about thirty named women — probably because the book focuses on domestic life, where women tend to be prominent. Significantly fewer theophoric names exist for both women and men in Genesis. Indeed, most of the theophoric names, whether for women or men, come from the literature situated in or referring to the monarchic period; women in that literature are much less prominent because of the focus on public official life, in which men were the major figures. Finally, note that women who are said to name their children give them names with YHWH elements far more often than male name-givers do.

Another feature of theophoric names in the Hebrew Bible is that they collectively favor both Yahwism and that which is masculine. For both women's and men's theophoric names, the highest percentages, by far, are those linked to the name YHWH, even though the ancient Israelites worshipped deities other than YHWH. And among the non-YHWH names, most are connected to the god Baal, even though, again, other deities were worshipped. Especially notable is that no theophoric element of such names can be clearly connected to a female deity. In fact, among the whole corpora of both women's and men's names, the name of a goddess virtually never serves as the source for a person's name, even though female deities such as Asherah and Astarte were surely worshipped by the Israelites. Besides the name Asenath, with its possible reference to the Egyptian goddess Neith, the only other instance is probably the father of Shamgar. His name is Anath, a Semitic goddess of war of that name.

It was earlier suggested that names can represent the nature or identity of a person. If a person changes in a significant way, a name change would follow. When YHWH initiates a covenant with Abram, it results in name changes for both him and his wife, Sarai. The former becomes Abraham, and the latter becomes Sarah. Another example is Naomi, who, in response to her altered personal circumstances renames herself, changing Naomi ("pleasant") to Mara ("bitter"). Variations of this practice occur when kings get throne names (for example, Mattaniah becomes Zedekiah in 2 Kgs

24:17), when people have double names (for example, Jedidiah/Solomon in 2 Sam 12:24–25), or when a person has names in two languages (Esther/Hadassah).

Other situations seem to represent exceptions to the notion that a name expresses a person's nature. For instance, some names may have been eponyms, identifying a real or created person for whom a place, clan, or tribal group is named (for example, Benjamin is the name of the man considered the father of the tribe of Benjamin; the names of the five daughters of Zelophehad may also have been the names of Manassite clans). Other names, notably in the prophetic texts, functioned as symbols of the whole people toward whom a prophet was directing his message. An example would be Hosea's daughter Lo-ruhamah ("not pitied"). Finally, over time a certain name likely came to have value in a family or community in remembrance of a person or persons who had borne that name. In such instances, the name might be reused not for its inherent meaning, but rather for being identified with the person linked to it and the presumably positive connotations arising from that linkage. Thus, some of the many different women named Mary in the New Testament might well have received their names because it was deemed desirable to be associated with and to honor the heroism and leadership of the Miriam of the Hebrew Bible (Mary being the anglicized form of the Greek word for the Hebrew Miriam).

Taken as a whole, the variety of meanings evident in women's names in the Hebrew Bible may reflect deeply held social and cultural values of the ancient Israelites. For example, the names testify to the Israelites' strong awareness of and connection to the natural world (plants, animals, stars). They reveal the value placed on a woman's physical appearance. They also generally demonstrate the Israelite sense of family relationships. The significance of male linkages is apparent too; compound names involving males (such as "father," "brother") far outnumber those mentioning female kinship roles. They also signify not only the importance of YHWH in the community, but also the communal recognition of women's legitimate connections to the deity. And finally, that women's names derive from approximately the same categories and in the same proportions as men's names might suggest a certain complementarity between the women and men of ancient Israel.

Two features of women's names in the Apocryphal/Deuterocanonical Books and the New Testament are particularly apparent. First, far fewer names of women are present (seventeen in the Apocryphal/Deuterocanonical Books, forty-one in the New Testament). Second, many of the women's names in both of these collections somehow depend on women mentioned in the Hebrew Bible. For instance, of the seventeen women named in the Apocryphal/Deuterocanonical Books, five are characters from the Hebrew Bible (Eve, Hagar, Vashti, Esther, and Zeresh). Three other women have names that also designate women of the Hebrew Bible — though the women named in the Apocryphal/Deuterocanonical Books are different persons from those named in the Hebrew Bible (Deborah, Judith, Sarah). Other types of links to the Hebrew Bible can be identified in the following three women's names: Anna, a Grecized form of the Hebrew name Hannah; Zosara, the wife of Haman, whose name appears as Zeresh in the Hebrew Bible; and Agia, the unnamed daughter of Barzillai in both Ezra and Nehemiah. This naming of Agia in 1 Esdras exemplifies a practice that becomes prominent in the pseudepigraphical literature: assigning names to otherwise unnamed persons in biblical texts. Meanwhile, in the New Testament, forty-one different names are used to name a total of forty-nine women. Of the women named, ten are present in either, or both, the Hebrew Bible and Apocryphal/Deuterocanonical Books (for example, Tamar, Sarah, Ruth, Rahab, Eve). And as many as twelve additional women have names that are Hellenized forms of Hebrew ones (for example, Anna is Hannah; Joanna is Yehohannah; Elizabeth is Elisheba; Mary is Miriam, in six or seven instances). This dependence on names found in the Hebrew Bible means that the same naming patterns tend also to be found in these two collections; that is, here, too, women are named for plants, animals, social roles, physical features, and abstract qualities with pleasing connotations. Approximately the same proportions pertain, at least for the New Testament (the Apocryphal/Deuterocanonical Books have too few examples to provide meaningful statistics).

But the repertoire of women's names in the Apocryphal/Deuterocanonical Books and the New Testament also differs from that of the Hebrew Bible in a number of ways. For one thing, fewer theophoric names are present. The Apocryphal/Deuterocanonical Books have no theophoric names at all, whereas the New Testament has only two (Elizabeth, meaning "God is an oath/good fortune"; Joanna, meaning "God has been gracious"). Also, both collections reflect the wider sociocultural contexts in which they were written and disseminated. They both, for instance, incorporate names from an ever wider variety of languages (Hebrew, Aramaic, Persian, Greek, Latin). In addition, they both reflect naming practices not found in the Hebrew Bible, such as naming children after ancestors (for example, Berenice, Herodias, and Judith), which was done for both daughters and sons and is probably a sign of Hellenistic influence, although the practice may have begun in the Persian period.

Finally, to summarize, the two most often used woman's names in all the Bible are Mary (which appears as Miriam in the Hebrew Bible and is used for at least six and possibly seven women in the New Testament) and Maacah (found for seven women in the Hebrew Bible). And the names of only two women appear in all three collections: Eve and Hagar.

With considerable weight placed on people's names, those who actually give the names should be regarded as significant. In the act of name giving, they may reflect society's recognition of their acumen in discerning correctly the character of the person whom they are naming — and so name the person aright. Or, perhaps in some cases, the name-giver, by virtue of the name given, may actually be *determining* the named person's eventual character or future destiny. Either way, the act of naming, whether a literary construction or a social reality,

may have expressed the name-giver's authority over the named.

In the Hebrew Bible, women outnumber men as name-givers. Of the approximately forty-seven instances in which a name-giver is specified, twenty-nine involve women. In all except one, a mother names a child. The same mother sometimes appears in multiple naming accounts, as when Leah names individually all of the nine children she claims as her own (Gen 29:32–35; 30:11, 13, 18, 20–21), when Rachel names the four sons she considers to be hers (Gen 30:6, 8, 24; 35:18), when Shua (Judah's wife) names Onan and Shelah (Gen 38:4–5), and when Eve names, separately, both Cain and Seth (Gen 4:1, 25). The other name-giving mothers in the Hebrew Bible — each of whom names just a single child, but some of whom are themselves without names — are Hagar (Gen 16:11), the two unnamed daughters of Lot (Gen 19:37–38), Sarah (Gen 21:6–7), Zipporah (in some manuscripts of Exod 2:22; the NRSV has the father as name-giver), the unnamed wife of Manoah (Judg 13:24), Hannah (1 Sam 1:20), the unnamed wife of Phinehas (1 Sam 4:21), Bathsheba (in the Hebrew of 2 Sam 12:24; the NRSV has the father as name-giver), the unnamed mother of Jabez (1 Chr 4:9), and Maacah (1 Chr 7:16). The one account in which women other than the mother bestow a name on a child is found in the Book of Ruth: the women friends of Naomi name Ruth's child Obed (Ruth 4:17).

In comparing the accounts of women naming children with those in which men give names, several similarities emerge. As with the women, the focus for men is on the parent-child relationship: eighteen fathers name their own children (Gen 4:26; 5:3, 29; 16:15; 21:3; 35:18; 41:51–52; Exod 18:3–4; Judg 8:31; 1 Chr 7:23; Job 42:14; Hos 1:4–9). And, as with the women, some men name more than one child: Job names all three of his daughters, and Hosea names all of his children (two sons and one daughter).

This latter example, however, is complicated insofar as God instructs Hosea to give his children certain names. This situation parallels the namings of both Ishmael and Isaac: God or God's agent informs the parent (Hagar for Ishmael, Abraham for Isaac) what the child's name shall be, and then presumably the parent actually gives the name to the child. Another peculiarity of the naming accounts concerns the few instances in which, though both parents name the same child, they do not work together in doing so. (Indeed, the act of naming, whether done by a woman or a man, is a very individualistic enterprise in the Hebrew Bible.) For instance, Seth is named by both Eve and Adam (Gen 4:25; 5:3), Isaac by both Sarah and Abraham (Gen 21:3, 6–7), Gershom by both Zipporah and Moses (Exod 2:22; 18:3), and Ben-oni/Benjamin by both Rachel and Jacob (Gen 35:18). Because in many of these instances the mother is the first to name the child, the accounts of fathers-as-namers may stem from a male narrative perspective, giving a man the function of namer when in actuality the namer was a woman.

That the majority — 62 percent — of name-givers in the Hebrew Bible are women is perhaps attributable at least partly to the intimacy of the mother-child relationship in the child's early years. It may also be a consequence of the high preponderance of such accounts in Genesis, a book that focuses on family life, the expected sphere of a woman's parental authority in ancient Israel.

But though women may dominate in the giving of names, the focus of such actions is largely male. In the forty-seven total naming accounts, only five females are named by a parent. One involves the symbolic naming of Hosea's daughter Lo-ruhamah (Hos 1:6). The three daughters of Job, a non-Israelite, are named Jemimah, Keziah, and Keren-happuch (Job 42:14); their father names them in the only instance in the Hebrew Bible of a father naming female children. And Dinah is named by her mother, Leah, the only instance in which a mother names a daughter (Gen 30:21).

Unlike the Hebrew Bible, both the Apocryphal/Deuterocanonical Books and the New Testament have far fewer naming accounts, which makes it far less possible to draw any significant conclusions about naming practices. For the Apocryphal/Deuterocanonical Books, Tob 1:9 refers briefly to the naming of Tobias by his father, Tobit. And in 1 Macc 2:2–5, mention is made of the names of the five sons of Mattathias; besides their given names, each is also provided with a surname, which seems to function rather like a nickname. The New Testament, meanwhile, reports the birth and thus the naming of only two children: John the Baptist and Jesus. For the latter, an angel is actually the source of the name (Matt 1:21; Luke 1:31). For the former, both the mother and father, individually, name the child, with the mother doing so first, a practice already noted for the Hebrew Bible. Perhaps the only significant new custom mentioned in the New Testament is that of waiting eight days to name the child, so that naming occurs concurrently with circumcision (Luke 1:59; 2:21). Of course, such a practice would be relevant only for male children; what might have been done for the naming of daughters remains entirely conjectural.

Given all that has been said about the significance of names, name giving, and name taking, what is to be concluded about those women (and men) who are without names in the Bible? The issue of anonymity is best evaluated on a case-by-case basis, taking into account the other features of the anonymous figure's portrayal, other characters with whom the anonymous figure interacts, and the socioliterary contexts of the writing in which the figure appears. It has been suggested, for instance, that anonymity can function positively to throw into sharper relief the role(s) — familial or professional — of nameless characters (such as the daughter of Jephthah (Judges 11), the daughter of Herodias (Mark 6:22), the wise woman of Tekoa (2 Samuel 14), and the martyred mother of seven sons (2 Maccabees 7). Anonymous characters may also shift attention to the named characters with whom they interact or foster the overall development of the narrative plot. Biblical characters without names may invite the reader to identify with them more easily, a function with arguably either positive or negative aspects. Indeed, it has also been argued that names may have been withheld from certain characters in order to prevent overidentification with them or even glorification of them.

Names are a wonderfully rich source of information about the biblical world. Their meanings, as well as the patterns of their occurrences, can help inform our understandings of women's and men's roles in biblical times, ancient society's respective valuation of women and men, and the constructions of gender (sex roles as understood in a particular cultural context) found in the Bible. But much work remains to be done, especially in comparing the biblical repertoire of names with those of the cultural milieus in which the people of the Bible lived. Such works will surely deepen and enhance our knowledge of the workings of gender in the Bible and the biblical world.

For Further Reading

Abba, Raymond. "Name." In *The Interpreter's Dictionary of the Bible*, ed. George A. Buttrick, 3:500–508. Nashville: Abingdon Press, 1965.

Beck, David R. "The Narrative Function of Anonymity in Fourth Gospel Characterization." *Semeia* 63 (1993): 143–58.

de Vaux, Roland. "The Name." In *Ancient Israel: Its Life and Institutions*, 43–46. Trans. John McHugh. New York: McGraw-Hill, 1965.

Fowler, Jeaneane D. *Theophoric Personal Names in Ancient Hebrew: A Comparative Study.* Sheffield, Eng.: JSOT Press, 1988.

Freund, Richard A. "Naming Names: Some Observations on 'Nameless Women' Traditions in the MT, LXX, and Hellenistic Literature." *Scandinavian Journal of the Old Testament* 6 (1992): 213–32.

Gray, G. Buchanan. *Studies in Hebrew Proper Names.* London: Adam and Charles Black, 1896.

Hess, Richard S. "Getting Personal: What Names in the Bible Teach Us." *Bible Review* 6 (1997): 30–37.

Horsley, G. H. R. "Names, Double." In *The Anchor Bible Dictionary*, ed. David Noel Freedman, 4:1011–17. New York: Doubleday, 1992.

Hudson, Don Michael. "Living in a Land of Epithets: Anonymity in Judges 19–21." *Journal for the Study of the Old Testament* 62 (1994): 49–66.

Ilan, Tal. *Jewish Women in Greco-Roman Palestine: An Inquiry into Image and Status.* Tubingen: J. C. B. Mohr, 1995.

Ljung, Inger. "Women and Personal Names." In *Silence or Suppression: Attitudes Towards Women in the Old Testament*, 15–33. Stockholm: Almqvist & Wiskell International, 1989.

Noth, Martin. *Die israelitischen Personennamen im Rahmen der gemeinsemitischen Namengebung.* Hildesheim/New York: Georg Olms Verlag, 1928.

Odelain, O., and R. Séguineau. *Dictionary of Proper Names and Places in the Bible*, preface by R. Tournay, trans. Matthew J. O'Connell. Garden City, N.Y.: Doubleday, 1981.

Pardes, Ilana. "Beyond Genesis 3: The Politics of Maternal Naming." In *Countertraditions in the Bible: A Feminist Approach*, 39–59, 162–65. Cambridge, Mass.: Harvard University Press, 1992.

Pike, Dana M. "Names, Hypocoristic." In *The Anchor Bible Dictionary*, ed. David Noel Freedman, 4:1017–18. New York: Doubleday, 1992.

———. "Names, Theophoric." In *The Anchor Bible Dictionary*, ed. David Noel Freedman, 4:1018–19. New York: Doubleday, 1992.

Reinhartz, Adele. "Anonymity and Character in the Books of Samuel." *Semeia* 63 (1993): 117–41.

———. "Samson's Mother: An Unnamed Protagonist." *Journal for the Study of the Old Testament* 55 (1992): 25–37.

——— *"Why Ask My Name?": Anonymity and Identity in Biblical Narrative.* New York: Oxford University Press, 1998.

Tigay, Jeffrey H. *You Shall Have No Other Gods: Israelite Religion in the Light of Hebrew Inscriptions.* Atlanta: Scholars Press, 1986.

———. "Israelite Religion: The Onomastic and Epigraphic Evidence." In *Ancient Israelite Religion: Essays in Honor of Frank Moore Cross*, ed. Patrick D. Miller, Jr., Paul D. Hanson, and S. Dean McBride, 157–94. Philadelphia: Fortress, 1987.

Watty, William W. "The Significance of Anonymity in the Fourth Gospel." *The Expository Times* 90 (1979): 209–13.

Zadok, Ran. *The Pre-Hellenistic Israelite Anthroponymy and Prosopography.* Leuven, Belgium: Uitgeverij Peeters, 1988.

PART I

Named Women

Abi

"my father," from Hebrew *'āb*, "father," a shortened form of Abijah

See Abijah 2 (Part I).

Abigail 1

meaning uncertain; perhaps "my father rejoices" or "my father is joy," from Hebrew *'ābî*, "my father," and either the verb *gyl*, "to rejoice," or the noun *gîl*, "rejoicing, joy"

(1 Sam 25; 27:3; 30: 3, 5, 18; 2 Sam 2:2; 3:3; 1 Chr 3:1)

Abigail is the wife of Nabal the Calebite from Carmel and later becomes the second wife of David. According to 1 Samuel 25, Abigail is married to Nabal, a wealthy rancher, and she is described as beautiful and intelligent. Her husband is just the opposite: mean and churlish. Despite Nabal's shortcomings, Abigail is an ideal wife, always protecting her husband's interests, taking the initiative when he is unable or unwilling to act, and apologizing for his rude behavior.

In her encounter with David, who is fleeing from Saul and trying to build up a following, Abigail is polite far beyond what is required. She is a woman of high socioeconomic status, by virtue of Nabal, whereas David, not yet king, is an outlaw on the run. Yet she acts toward David and addresses him as though he is the lord and she the servant. Abigail's good manners and diplomatic strategy succeed in protecting Nabal from David's wrath when Nabal fails to respond to David's request for gifts in payment for treating Nabal's shepherds well. When Nabal learns of Abigail's actions, after sobering up from a drunken state, "his heart died within him" (1 Sam 25:37). Shortly afterward he dies, and David loses no time in marrying Abigail. Whether it is because this bright and articulate woman catches his fancy, or, more likely, because the marriage is an astute political move calculated to win support in Judah, we cannot know for sure.

Abigail is mentioned along with Ahinoam the Jezreelite (David's third wife) when they accompany David in seeking refuge in Philistine territory and when they are captured by Amalekites and rescued by David (1 Sam 30:3, 5, 18). Abigail again appears with Ahinoam when these two wives go with David to Hebron, where they settle and where David is anointed king (2 Sam 2:2). Abigail is the mother of David's second son, Chileab (2 Sam 3:3; Daniel, according to 1 Chr 3:1), born in Hebron.

As a character, Abigail is not very well developed and does not figure to any great extent in the stories of David outside of 1 Samuel 25. Yet she serves the important function of glorifying and validating David's kingship. First, her prescient words, representing the narrator's pro-David point of view, foreshadow the future kingship of David and validate the legitimacy of his rule: "the Lord will certainly make my lord a sure house, because my lord is fighting the battles of the Lord. . . . When the Lord has done to my lord according to all the good that he has spoken concerning you, and has appointed you prince over Israel . . ." (1 Sam 25:28–30).

Moreover, 1 Samuel 25 is situated between two episodes in which David has the opportunity to kill Saul, but resists. In this article's episode, too, David maintains extraordinary self-control and leaves it to God to dispatch his opponent. The Abigail story, like the Saul stories, is a strong endorsement of David's destiny to reign as the chosen favorite of God.

1 Samuel 25 stands in stark contrast to, and serves as a mirror image of, the Bathsheba story in 1 Samuel 11–12. Both Abigail and Bathsheba are originally married to other men, and both become the wives

of David, yet by very different courses of events. In the Abigail story, the woman is married to an evil husband, yet David is prevented by the woman from murdering her husband, as he clearly acknowledges (1 Sam 25:33–34). In the case of Bathsheba, whose husband is portrayed as a good man, David is led to order the murder of the husband because of his desire for the woman. The Abigail story contains no illicit sex, though the opportunity was present; the Bathsheba story revolves around an illicit relationship. In the Abigail story, David, the potential king, is seen as increasingly strong and virtuous, whereas in the Bathsheba story, the reigning monarch shows his flaws ever more overtly and begins to lose control of his family.

ADELE BERLIN

SEE ALSO Part I: Ahinoam 2; Bathsheba; Bath-shua 2; Eglah; Haggith; Maacah 2; Michal; Part II: Wives of David (2 Sam 12:11, etc.); Concubines of David (2 Sam 15:16, etc.).

FOR FURTHER READING: Berlin, Adele. *Poetics and Interpretation of Biblical Narrative.*

Levenson, Jon D. "1 Samuel 25 as Literature and History."

———. and B. Halpern. "The Political Import of David's Marriages."

Abigail 2

(2 Sam 17:25; 1 Chr 2:16–17)

Abigail and Zeruiah are sisters of King David (reigned c. 1005–965 B.C.E.) and mothers of the rivals Amasa and Joab, respectively. Chronicles lists Abigail among the children of Jesse, David's father. However, Samuel's reference to Abigail as "daughter of Nahash" (king of Ammon), usually dismissed as a scribal error, may indicate that David and his sisters have different fathers.

Biblical sources conflict over the ethnicity of Abigail's husband, who is identified as Ithra the "Israelite" (2 Sam 17:25) and Jether the "Ishmaelite" (1 Chr 2:17). Nabal, a wealthy herdsman from Maon, also had a wife named Abigail who saved their household by countermanding her husband's refusal to feed David's men (1 Samuel 25). Nabal, meaning

"fool," probably was not his actual name. If Ithra/Jether is the real name of Nabal, as Levenson and Halpern suggest, then David marries his (half?) sister.

Later tradition would suppress the memory of this incestuous union. This match might have been politically desirable if Abigail was the daughter of Nahash, king of Ammon (2 Sam 17:27). The Ammonites were enemies, and the simplest way to avoid conflict with one's foes was to make a marriage alliance.

RHONDA BURNETTE-BLETSCH

SEE ALSO Part I: Abigail 1; Zeruiah.

FOR FURTHER READING: Levenson, Jon D., and Baruch Halpern. "The Political Import of David's Marriages."

Abihail 1

meaning uncertain; perhaps "father is," from Hebrew *'āb*, "father," and *hyh*, "to be"; or "my father is strength," from Hebrew *'ābî*, "my father," and *ḥāyil*, "strength," with the first letter miswritten (1 Chr 2:29)

Abihail is named as the mother of Ahban and Molid and the wife of Abishur, a fifth-generation descendant of Hezron, who also is David's ancestor. The genealogies in 1 Chronicles are designed to emphasize the primary role of the tribe of Judah within the national unit known as Israel, and also within Judah, the importance of the house of David.

DIANA VIKANDER EDELMAN

Abihail 2

(2 Chr 11:18)

This sexual partner, presumably a wife, of King David (reigned c. 1005–965 B.C.E.), is named only once in the Hebrew Bible, in connection with David's grandson King Rehoboam. Rehoboam's wife, Mahalath, is the granddaughter of Abihail and King David. The text identifies Abihail's father as Eliab, who, like David, is a son of Jesse. This seems to make Abihail not only David's wife, but also his niece. This double connection to David brings together Jesse's oldest son, Eliab, and his youngest son, David, perhaps reconciling them. Eliab becomes head of the tribe of Judah (1 Chr 27:18), and David becomes king.

ALICE L. LAFFEY

SEE ALSO Part I: Mahalath 2; Part II: Women of Rehoboam (Eighteen Wives, Sixty Concubines, and Sixty Daughters) (2 Chr 11:21).

Abijah 1

"my father is Yah," from Hebrew *'ābî*, "my father," and *yāh*, a shortened form of YHWH

(1 Chr 2:24)

Abijah is the wife of Hezron, ancestor of an important clan in the tribe of Judah. She is mentioned at the end of the complicated genealogy of Hezron's family in 1 Chronicles 2, and it is not clear if she is the mother of Hezron's first three sons (1 Chr 2:19), the daughter of Machir, whom he married when he was sixty years old (2:21), or a third wife. Furthermore, perhaps because Abijah is more often a man's name than a woman's, the difficulties in this passage are sometimes resolved by eliminating Abijah from the translation (as in the RSV, NAB, and REB) and by assuming that 2:24 is referring to Ephrathah as the wife of Hezron.

JULIA MYERS O'BRIEN

SEE ALSO Part I: Ephrath/Ephrathah.

FOR FURTHER READING: Williamson, H. G. M. "Source and Redaction in the Chronicler's Genealogy of Judah."

Abijah 2/Abi

Abi: "my father," from Hebrew *'āb*, "father"; a shortened form of Abijah

(2 Kgs 18:2; 2 Chr 29:1)

Abijah was the chief wife of Ahaz, king of Judah from 743 to 727 B.C.E., and the daughter of Zechariah, a Judean aristocrat possibly associated with the prophet Isaiah (Isa 8:2). At the coronation of her son, Hezekiah, Abijah/Abi became queen mother, perhaps the highest position for a female in the Judean royal court. She is often identified as the "young woman," mother of the symbolic child Immanuel (meaning "God is with us"), in Isa 7:14.

RHONDA BURNETTE-BLETSCH

SEE ALSO Part I: Maacah 4; Hamutal/Hamital; Nehushta; Part II: Young Woman (Isa 7:14).

FOR FURTHER READING: Ackerman, Susan. "The Queen Mother and the Cult in Ancient Israel."

Abishag

"my father goes astray," from Hebrew *'ābî*, "my father," and the verb *šgg*, "to go astray"

(1 Kgs 1:1–4, 15; 2:13–25)

When King David (reigned c. 1005–965 B.C.E.) ages and his health fails, a beautiful young woman is sought throughout Israel to lie in his bosom and keep him warm. The king does not have sexual relations with Abishag (1 Kgs 1:4). This physical impotence mirrors his political impotence; the next verse reports the premature claim of his son Adonijah (son of his fourth wife, Haggith) to his throne. Bathsheba, David's major wife at this point in his life story, responds to Adonijah's preemption by convincing David to name her son Solomon as his successor, in a conversation at which Abishag is also present (1:15). After the death of David, the temporary reconciliation of Adonijah and Solomon ends when Adonijah uses Bathsheba as an intermediary to request from the new king Abishag's hand in marriage. Solomon responds violently, ordering Adonijah's assassination (2:13–25).

The unspeaking Abishag is more a tool to move the plot along than a developed character: she marks first the inability of David to continue his rule and, later, the inability of Adonijah to assume that power. The latter incident has perplexed commentators: why would Solomon react so strongly against Adonijah's marriage proposal? Many assume Adonijah makes a move on David's harem and, thus, a symbolic claim to his father's throne, although this seems to be an unlikely maneuver for a politically weakened man. This and other texts in which a king's sexual partner(s) are seized by other men (2 Sam 3:6–11; 16:20–22) may reflect broader cultural norms regarding male honor and "the traffic in women" — the roles women play as mediators between men — rather than specific political claims. Solomon thus asserts his claim on his mother's loyalty, and his right to determine the sexual fate of the female members of what is now *his* household, against Adonijah's insinuations of status.

CLAUDIA V. CAMP

SEE ALSO Part I: Abigail 1; Bathsheba; Rizpah; Part II: Concubines of David (2 Sam 15:16, etc.)

FOR FURTHER READING: Fewell, Danna Nolan, and David M. Gunn. *Gender, Power, and Promise.*

Stone, Ken. "Sexual Power and Political Prestige: The Case of the Disputed Concubines."

Abital

"my father is dew," from Hebrew *'ābî*, "my father," and *ṭal*, "dew"

(2 Sam 3:4; 1 Chr 3:3)

Abital is the wife of King David (reigned c. 1005–965 B.C.E.) and the mother of Shephatiah. She is fifth on a list of six mother-son references concerning David's sons born in Hebron (2 Sam 3:2–5; 1 Chr 3:1–4). David's wives were apparently carefully chosen to form alliances with various factions in the emerging monarchy, thus securing loyalty of important segments of the tribal groups.

LINDA S. SCHEARING

SEE ALSO Part I: Abigail 1; Ahinoam 2; Bathsheba; Eglah; Haggith; Maacah 2; Part II: Wives and Concubines of David, Taken in Jerusalem (2 Sam 5:13); Wives of David (2 Sam 12:11, etc.).

Achsah

"anklet, bangle," from Hebrew *'ekes*, "anklet, bangle"

(Josh 15:16–17; Judg 1:12; 1 Chr 2:49)

Achsah is the daughter of Caleb, according to the genealogy of the tribe of Judah. She is given to Othniel, son of Kenaz, brother of Caleb, in exchange for his taking of Kiriath-sepher (identified as Debir in Judges). Achsah encourages her new husband to ask Caleb for a field. Her father also asks

what she wants; at her request he gives her the upper and lower springs in the Negev (named Gulloth-mayim in Judges). Like the daughters of Zelophehad, Achsah succeeds in gaining some of her family's land and water resources, which were normally not available to women in ancient Israel's patrilineal system; in both cases, however, the women remain vulnerable within the patriarchal system.

JULIA MYERS O'BRIEN

SEE ALSO Part I: Sheerah; Part II: Daughters of Zelophehad (Num 26:33, etc.).

FOR FURTHER READING: Fewell, Danna Nolan. "Deconstructive Criticism: Achsah and the (E)razed City of Writing."

Adah 1

"ornament, adornment," from the Hebrew *'dh*, "to adorn, ornament oneself"

(Gen 4:19–20, 23)

According to the genealogy of Gen 4:17–19, Adah is one of the two wives of Lamech and the mother of two sons. Those sons, along with the son and daughter of her co-wife, Zillah, are in the seventh generation of naturally born human beings. They are the founders of the civilized arts, which are thus presented as a fully human product and not as a gift of the gods, as in many mythological beginnings stories of other cultures. Adah and Zillah are both addressed in Lamech's poetic account of a violent deed he has committed. Perhaps he anticipated that they will respond with a song celebrating his deed, in keeping with the tradition in ancient Israel for women to compose victory songs.

The name Adah, in signifying aesthetic qualities, is common in the ancient Semitic world and may point to the fact that female beauty was deemed important. It should be noted, however, that several men's names in the Hebrew Bible are based on the same root (*'dh*, "to adorn, ornament oneself").

CAROL MEYERS

SEE ALSO Part I: Naamah 1; Zillah; Part II: Daughters (and Sons) of Adam, Seth, Enosh, Kenan, Mahalalel, Jared, Enoch, and Methuselah (Gen 5:4, etc.); Women with Hand-Drums, Dancing (Exod 15:20, etc.).

Adah 2

(Gen 36:2, 4, 10, 12, 16)

Adah, the daughter of Elon the Hittite, marries Esau, one of the two sons of Jacob and Rebekah, to whom she bears Eliphaz. Esau's marriage to a woman outside his family's descent line results in his exclusion from the endogamous patrilineage of Abraham's father, Terah. However, the inclusion of Adah's and other women's names in the Genesis 36 genealogy indicates the importance of women and marriage for understanding the formation of kinship and descent groups in the world described in the Book of Genesis.

There is a contradiction between Gen 36:2, which identifies Adah as the daughter of the Hittite Elon, and Gen 26:34, which names Basemath as Elon's offspring; Gen 36:3 lists Basemath as the daughter of Ishmael.

NAOMI STEINBERG

SEE ALSO Part I: Basemath 1/Bashemath; Judith 1; Mahalath 1; Oholibamah.

Agia

Greek *Augia*, corruption of Hebrew *hgl'd*, "the Gileadite"

(1 Esdr 5:38)

Agia is named as the wife of Jaddus and daughter of Barzillai in an inventory of people returning to Jerusalem from exile in Babylon, which appears in 1 Esdras, a work focusing on the temple and its leadership. 1 Esdras probably dates to the late second century B.C.E. The list of returnees (1 Esdr 5:7–46) has been copied from Ezra 2:1–70 and shows close similarities to Neh 7:6–73; indeed, none of the other Apocryphal/Deuterocanonical Books so closely repeats the Hebrew Bible as does this one (compare 2 Chr 35–36; the whole of Ezra; and Neh 7:38–8:12). The list of returnees in 1 Esdras, as in Ezra and Nehemiah, includes three groups of priests who could not prove their ancestry and thus are barred from service in the Jerusalem temple. Agia does not appear by name in either of the parallel lists, which mention only a marriage to "one of the daughters

of Barzillai the Gileadite" (Ezra 2:61; Neh 7:63). Most unusual in each of the three lists is that the descendants of Jaddus take their name from his wife's father, tracing themselves as descendants of Barzillai (a Gileadite who supported David in 2 Sam 17:27–29; 19:31–40). This is the only case in the Hebrew Bible where a man derives his name and the name of his progeny from his wife's father. Ezra-Nehemiah makes reference to two men named Barzillai: one who befriended David, and the other who married his daughter.

1 Esdras gives names to the daughter and to the man who married her, explaining that the unregistered priests returning to Jerusalem include "the descendants of Jaddus who had married Agia, one of the daughters of Barzillai, and was called by his name" (5:38). These names are both doubtful. "Jaddus" can be understood as the corrupted Greek transliteration of the Hebrew *zlly*, from which a first syllable, *br*, was lost, and the Greek *Augia* is a corrupt transliteration of the Hebrew *hgl'd*, "the Gileadite." If Agia and Jaddus's sons had a legitimate claim to the privileges and duties of priests in postexilic Jerusalem, then Jaddus or Barzillai (if that was his original name) compromised his status as a priest by appropriating the name of his father-in-law, the non-priestly Barzillai the Gileadite, with the effect that his and his son's names were deleted or excluded from priestly registers.

TONI CRAVEN

SEE ALSO Part I: Apame; Part II: Daughter of Barzillai the Gileadite (Ezra 2:61, etc.); Women as Strongest (1 Esdr 3:12, etc.).

FOR FURTHER READING: Myers, Jacob. *I & II Esdras.* Petter, Gerald J. "Barzillai."

Ahinoam 1

"my brother is pleasantness," from Hebrew *'āḥî*, "my brother," and *nōʿam*, "pleasantness"

(1 Sam 14:50)

Ahinoam is the daughter of Ahimaaz and wife of Saul ben Kish, king of Israel, who reigned during the early decades of the tenth century B.C.E. She is the implied mother of Merab, Jonathan, Ishvi, Malchishua and Michal (1 Sam 14:49–50) and probably also the mother of Abinadab, who appears in 1 Sam 31:2 and in 1 Chr 8:33 and 9:39. Her name is given in the summary of Saul's reign in 14:48–50. It seems unlikely that Saul's Ahinoam is indeed Ahinoam the Jezreelite, who would become David's wife. The two are clearly distinguished in the text by the different means used to identify each woman's background.

Unlike the normal summary of a royal reign that refers the reader to a source for further information about the king's accomplishments during his reign (as in 2 Kgs 10:34; 12:8), 1 Sam 14:49–50 includes a list of Saul's children and a note about his relative Abner, who is in a position of power. This unusual genealogical information seems to serve two functions. Placed at the end of the summary of Saul's reign, it signals, on a literary level, the effective end of Saul and his family as leaders of Israel on the eve of his rejection by God (1 Samuel 15) and David's anointing to take his place (1 Samuel 16). At the same time, with the exception of Abinadab, it introduces a roster of Saulide characters who will appear in the subsequent narrative. Abinadab's name may have been added to 1 Sam 31:2 later by a scribe who found it in the family lists in 1 Chronicles 8 and 9.

As is customary, Ahinoam is identified first by her relationship to her father and then by her relationship to her husband. Women were under the legal custody of their fathers until they were married, at which point custody was transferred to the husband and his male relatives (Exod 20:17; Deut 5:21). In ancient Israel, the function of marriage was to guarantee legitimate offspring for a lineage and to consolidate or maintain the wider social structure in which the family functioned.

DIANA VIKANDER EDELMAN

SEE ALSO Part I: Ahinoam 2; Merab; Michal.

FOR FURTHER READING: Edelman, Diana Vikander. *King Saul in the Historiography of Judah.*

Hiebert, Paula S. "'Whence Shall Help Come to Me?': The Biblical Widow."

Levenson, Jon D. "1 Samuel 25 as Literature and History."

Ahinoam 2

(1 Sam 25:43; 27:3; 30:5; 2 Sam 2:2; 3:2; 1 Chr 3:1)

Ahinoam, said to come from Jezreel, is King David's wife and the mother of his eldest son, Amnon. All references to her occur with, or in close literary proximity to, Abigail (another wife of David, king of Israel, c. 1005–965 B.C.E.).

Following Abigail's marriage to David (1 Sam 25:42), David "also" marries Ahinoam from Jezreel (v. 43). Ahinoam and Abigail are with David during his stay with King Achish of Gath (1 Sam 27:3); are taken captive when Amalekites raid Ziklag, David's Philistine base (1 Sam 30:5); and are among those who go with David to Hebron when he becomes king over Judah (2 Sam 2:2). The last reference to Ahinoam occurs in the list of David's sons born at Hebron (2 Sam 3:2–5; 1 Chr 3:1–4), where she is noted in the first (Abigail is in the second) of six mother-son references. Of the five contexts in which Ahinoam appears, only in her marriage notice (1 Sam 25:43) does she come after Abigail.

Since Ahinoam's name usually precedes that of Abigail, it has been suggested that David married Ahinoam before he married Abigail (contrary to 1 Sam 25:42–43; see Levenson and Halpern). However, if Ahinoam's son Amnon was David's firstborn son (as both lists of sons affirm), then the order of their names might indicate Ahinoam's status as the crown prince's mother.

Only one other character named Ahinoam appears in the Hebrew Bible (Saul's wife; see 1 Sam 14:50). Because she is roughly a contemporary of David's wife, it is possible that "Ahinoam of Jezreel" is Saul's wife Ahinoam. Citing YHWH's words (via the prophet Nathan) to David, "I gave you . . . your master's wives" (2 Sam 12:8), Levenson and Halpern argue that David's marriage to Ahinoam constituted a claim to Saul's throne (see Absalom's actions in 2 Sam 16:22). Perhaps David, like other kings who appropriated the harems of their predecessors or rivals, strengthened his claim to the throne in this way.

LINDA S. SCHEARING

SEE ALSO Part I: Ahinoam 1; Part II: Wives of Saul (2 Sam 12:8); Wives of David (2 Sam 12:11, etc.).

FOR FURTHER READING: Levenson, Jon D., and Baruch Halpern. "The Political Import of David's Marriages."

Ahlai

meaning uncertain; perhaps an onomatopoeic interjection "ah!" from Hebrew *'āḥ*
1 Chr 2:31, 34–35; 11:41)

A figure in the genealogy of the tribe of Judah, Ahlai appears as a male, the "son of Sheshan" (1 Chr 2:31), in virtually all translations. However, because the text states that Sheshan had "no sons, only daughters" (2:35) and that he gave his daughter in marriage to his Egyptian servant Jarha (Gen 2:34–38), it is likely that Ahlai denotes a female. The Hebrew text of 2:31 actually has the plural "sons of" in a term often used generically to indicate "descendants of" and thus to represent both female and male offspring. Ahlai, because her father had no sons, becomes founder of an important branch of one of the clans of the tribe of Judah.

One of her male descendants, Zabad, appears in the list of the mighty men of David's armies in 1 Chr 11:41. It appears in the translation that Zabad's parent is male; but the Ahlai of 1 Chr 11:41 is probably the same as the Ahlai of 1 Chr 2:31–36, where she is said to be an ancestor (grandmother) of Zabad.

CAROL MEYERS

Anah

from Hebrew root *'nh*; meaning unknown
(Gen 36:2, 14, 18, 25)

Anah, the daughter of Zibeon the Hivite (a pre-Israelite people living in the Transjordan), is the mother of Oholibamah, one of Esau's wives. Anah can be either a feminine or a masculine name. The NRSV follows the Septuagint (Greek translation of the Hebrew Bible) rather than the Hebrew, in identifying Anah as a male. Whether female or male,

Anah's origins reflect Esau's alliances outside the Hebrew lineage.

NAOMI STEINBERG

SEE ALSO Part I: Oholibamah.

Anath   SEE Anath (Part III).

Anna 1

"grace," Grecized from Hebrew *ḥēn*, "favor, grace"
(Tob 1:9, 20; 2:1, 11–14; 4:3–4; 5:18–6:1; 10:4–7; 11:5–6, 9; 14:12)

Tobit's wife, Anna, appears in various short references that illustrate some of the central concerns of the Book of Tobit: endogamy (marriage within one's own group; Tob 1:9), proper burial practices (Tob 4:4; 14:12), and respect for one's parents (Tob 4:3–4). The book also features Anna in several longer scenes that focus on the relationships between husband and wife, and mother and son.

Anna is important not merely as the wife of righteous Tobit, but in her own right. A patriarchal world often confines women within narrow boundaries, and Anna crosses a line. After her husband's zeal to do good deeds leads to his being blinded, Anna earns the family's living by doing "women's work," weaving. But taking on a man's role as wage earner, even when forced by circumstances beyond her control, raises suspicion. When Anna brings home a young goat that her employers gave her as a bonus, Tobit accuses her of stealing it and does not believe her explanation. She, like her namesake Hannah in 1 Samuel 1, refuses to crumple before an unjust accusation from a righteous man and defends herself against it. She upbraids him for his self-righteousness and mistrust, asking, "Where are your righteous deeds now?" (Tob 2:11–14).

The next scene between Anna and Tobit shows a different side of the couple's relationship. After their previous argument, Tobit prays for death as relief from his misery and the "undeserved" insults he has suffered. Expecting to die, Tobit remembers some money he once left in trust in a distant city and, wishing to ensure his son's financial security, sends him to get it. As their only child sets out on the long and potentially dangerous journey, Anna and Tobit have another emotional exchange. Tearfully asking "Why?", she suggests that the continued presence of their child in their daily life is more important than money could ever be, and in any case they should be satisfied with the life God has given them (compare Hannah's words in 1 Sam 2:7). This time Tobit does not argue, but comforts and reassures his wife, and she stops weeping (Tob 5:18–6:1).

Anna's next appearance in the text shows the couple once again at odds. When the time of Tobias's expected return passes with no word of him, Anna fears he has died. Daily she watches the road; at night she can get no sleep. Now her husband's attempts at comfort wear thin. When he says, "Be quiet; he's all right," she snaps, "Be quiet yourself!" (Tob 10:7). Probably aware that Tobit is also worried (Tob 10:3), Anna accuses him, "Stop lying! My child has perished" (Tob 10:4–7).

In Anna's final extended appearance, before the notice of her death in Tob 14:12, she is again on good terms with her spouse. One day as she continues her vigil at the road, she spots her son returning. Instead of rushing toward the child she feared she had lost forever, Anna's first impulse is to go and share the wonderful news with her husband, who cannot see it for himself. Only then does she run to Tobias, expressing her joy at his return (Tob 11:5–6, 9).

Three of Anna's scenes illustrate the depth of a mother's love. Although the emotion is realistic, there may be an economic reality behind Anna's desperate concern for her son's return. Her husband has been blind for four years and now expects to die. Even for a woman like Anna, who has been earning wages, to lose both husband and son would have been a serious threat to her financial security. How long could a childless widow survive and avoid destitution? It is no wonder that Tobias's departure and continued absence are a cause of contention between Anna and Tobit.

The scenes involving Anna and Tobit depict a complex and realistic relationship between spouses.

Tobit can be, alternately, solicitous and patronizing. He loves his wife, but he does not trust her to live up to his standards of righteousness. Anna also cares for her husband, but she does not believe everything he says. Nor is she a docile, subservient, silent wife, afraid to speak her mind. In the couple's first argument, the reader knows which of the two *really* received the undeserved insult; in the second, the reader empathizes with Anna's grief and forgives her sharp retort to Tobit, even while knowing that this time he is right.

The presentation of Anna in the Book of Tobit upholds a patriarchal worldview in that Anna's world revolves around her family, in the private sphere. She has none of the religious or community obligations her husband and son have. At the same time, the figure of Anna challenges patriarchy. She is not defined solely by her relationship with the men in her family. Unexpectedly, she has a life outside the home, however limited and unasked for. The author deliberately paints a sympathetic picture of Anna that presents her as both independent from and in conformity with the conventional roles of wife and mother.

BEVERLY BOW

SEE ALSO Part I: Edna; Hannah.

FOR FURTHER READING: Bow, Beverly, and George W. E. Nickelsburg, "Patriarchy with a Twist: Men and Women in Tobit."

Anna 2

(Luke 2:36–38)

Anna is a female prophet, one of six mentioned in the New Testament (see also Philip's four daughters, Acts 21:9; Jezebel, Rev 2:20). Within Luke's corpus, prophets hold a prominent position because they possess a spiritual gift bestowed on only a select few, of either gender. Prophecy understood as a "gift" could in part explain the name Anna, which means "grace." Women are accorded the gift of prophecy specifically as "a privilege of virginity, either as virgins or widows" (Seim, p. 756).

This pericope about Anna concludes the story of the wondrous births of John the Baptist and Jesus and also ends the infancy narrative of Jesus. Each miraculous birth involves a female/male pair: Elizabeth and Zechariah, Mary and Joseph. In Luke's literary pairing, Anna corresponds to the prophet Simeon.

After Jesus is born, Mary and Joseph fulfill a pair of ritual requirements: circumcision and purification. When Mary, Joseph, and Jesus enter the temple, the blind prophet Simeon "sees" Jesus, praising the child in song. Anna recognizes Jesus as the one who will redeem Jerusalem, and she proclaims this to everyone.

Luke describes at some length Anna's circumstances as a pious widow, reminiscent of the virtuous widow Judith, who saves her people in the Apocryphal/Deuterocanonical book that bears her name. This is consistent with Luke's frequent favorable portrayal of widows, who are not to be pitied but emulated as examples of faith and piety (see Seim). Anna had lived as a wife for only seven years before her husband died. Although Luke calls her "Anna, the daughter of Phanuel, of the tribe of Asher" (v. 36), his social description of Anna focuses on her own biography and virtues, not those of her father, husband, or possible children. When she sees Jesus, she is eighty-four years old.

Curiously, Luke tells us that Anna never left the temple. There she prayed and fasted. That a pious woman could have lived in the women's court of the temple (described by the Jewish historian Josephus in *The Jewish War*) is possible, but no other known examples attest to this. Judging from Luke-Acts as a whole, Luke's poor knowledge of Palestinian geography, Jerusalem, and the temple cult would lend support to the idea that Anna is a literary construction. Her character focuses Luke's concerns about ascetic widowhood in the service of God. This has been understood by Kraemer, Seim, and Schaberg as a possible reference to the order of widows in the early church.

VASILIKI LIMBERIS

FOR FURTHER READING: Kraemer, Ross Shepard. *Her Share of the Blessings.*

Schaberg, Jane. "Luke."

Seim, Turid Karlsen. "The Gospel of Luke."

Antiochis

"opposer," Greek feminine form of Antiochus
(2 Macc 4:30)

Nothing is known of this concubine of Antiochus IV (Epiphanes) apart from this reference in 2 Maccabees. Here the Seleucid king hands over the Cilician towns of Tarsus and Mallus as a present to Antiochis, and the people revolt (4:30). Antiochus IV goes to settle the trouble, leaving Andronicus in charge of affairs in Antioch (4:31).

While the king is thus occupied, Menelaus, the high priest of the Jerusalem temple, plunders its golden vessels and presents some to Andronicus, either as a bribe to have Onias III, the rightful Jerusalem high priest, murdered (4:32–34) or as payment of the overdue tribute.

The purpose of the passage in 2 Maccabees is to portray the villany and evil character of both Menelaus and Andronicus. The upheaval in the Cilician towns of Tarsus and Mallus, known only from 2 Macc 4:30, is an invented narrative strategy to legitimate the absence of the king from Antioch.

Coins of Tarsus indicate that Antiochus IV conferred upon it the privileges of an Antiochene city, and an inscription from 166 B.C.E. shows that the privileges were still in force at that time. Since Seleucid kings ruled by right of conquest and had the power to dispose of subject communities by gift or sale, it would have been legitimate for Antiochus to give Tarsus and Mallus to Antiochis. That she was female and his concubine may have been an affront to the towns, since she would have had the king's authority to intervene in their affairs and the right to receive their revenues. It is an interesting quirk that her very name is the feminine form of his.

The narrative in 2 Macc 4:30 must have been a believable invention. That Antiochus honored Antiochis with the extravagant gift of Tarsus and Mallus suggests the ancient audience thought it possible that a woman could have great influence with a king.

TONI CRAVEN

SEE ALSO Part I: Apame.

FOR FURTHER READING: Carroll, Scott T. "Antiochis."

Doran, Robert. "2 Maccabees."

Goldstein, Jonathan A. *II Maccabees: A New Translation with Introduction and Commentary.*

Apame

meaning uncertain; perhaps "the latest" or "the most recent born," derived from Avestan (eastern dialect of Old Persian) *apama*

(I Esdr 4:29–31)

Apame is one of the two women mentioned by name (Agia, the other, appears in 5:38) in 1 Esdras, a rather free Greek version of biblical history from the time of Josiah's Passover to Ezra's reforms. The present version of 1 Esdras, which repeats all of Ezra as well as parts of 2 Chronicles and Nehemiah, dates to the second half of the second century B.C.E.

Apame is identified as daughter of the illustrious Bartacus (Greek: Thaumastos Bartacus) and concubine of the Persian king Darius 1 (522–486 B.C.E.) in the story of the three young bodyguards who try to best each other with answers to the riddle "What one thing is strongest?" (3:1–5:6; material unique to 1 Esdras, that is, not taken from the Hebrew Bible). The first two propose that wine and the king, respectively, are strongest and argue persuasively for the superior strength of each. The third contestant, who is established in an obvious textual insertion as Zerubbabel (4:13), the Jewish leader of the second return from exile and builder of the Second Jerusalem Temple, wins by wittily defending the position "Women are strongest, but above all things truth is victor" (3:12). To illustrate his argument, Zerubbabel cites an incident when Apame, King Darius's concubine, dominated the king.

Sitting at the right hand of Darius, Apame teased and mocked him, even putting his crown on her head and slapping him. The king responded by simply opening his mouth and gaping at her, laughing when she smiled at him and humoring her when she was exasperated with him (1 Esdr 4:29–31). While indeed an extraordinary display of fe-male power, such behavior may have been inconsistent with gender roles and expectations in royal settings where even queens survived at the mercy of the king (see Esth 4:16; Add Esth 15: 10).

Scholars are divided on whether Apame is a fictional character or a historical one. Association with the Persian king Darius gives her story a credible royal setting, though Darius could be one of several kings with this same name. Apame's father, Bartacus, is otherwise unknown. Apame is a Persian name, which appears in royal contexts during the Achaemenid and Hellenistic periods in association with four different powerful women. Further evidence of the importance of the historical women named Apame is the fact that in Hellenistic times at least six sites in Seleucia were named Apamea.

WILLIAM R. GOODMAN, JR.

SEE ALSO Part I: Agia; Esther; Part II: Women as Strongest (1 Esdr 3:12, etc.).

FOR FURTHER READING: Brosius, Maria. *Women in Ancient Persia: 559–331 B.C.*

Myers, Jacob. *I & II Esdras.*

Apphia

origin and meaning uncertain; attested as a personal name in ancient Phrygia (Turkey); in Greek, a term of endearment, particularly between siblings

(Phlm v. 2)

Paul's briefest letter is addressed to three individuals: Philemon (by whose name the letter is known), called "beloved" (NRSV, "dear friend") and "coworker"; Apphia, called "the sister"; and a second man named Archippus, called "our fellow soldier." It is also addressed to "the church in your [singular] house," which is often assumed to be that of Philemon, although it might also be that of Archippus.

From the address, we cannot be certain what sort of relationships existed between these three. Apphia is often assumed to have been the wife (or even the daughter) of Philemon. The term "sister" does sometimes have marital connotations in antiquity, but it is regularly used as a term for members of early Christian churches (Paul refers to the cowriter of this letter, Timothy, as "our brother").

D'Angelo has suggested that "sister" may sometimes designate the female partner of a female-male missionary team. Read from this perspective, Apphia might have been part of such a team, perhaps with Philemon, affiliated with the church in Archippus's house. That Paul explicitly names Apphia suggests that he seeks her consent to his request concerning Philemon's runaway slave, Onesimus, and therefore acknowledges her influential role in this church (often thought to have been in Phrygia, a region in ancient Asia Minor, now modern Turkey).

Ross S. Kraemer

For further reading: D'Angelo, Mary Rose. "Women Partners in the New Testament."

Gilman, Florence Morgan. "Apphia."

Petersen, Norman. *Rediscovering Paul: Philemon and the Sociology of Paul's Narrative World.*

Arsinoë

> meaning unknown
>
> (3 Macc 1:1, 4)

3 Maccabees opens with a brief romantic story about Queen Arsinoë's rallying of the troops of her consort-brother in the Battle of Raphia (217 B.C.E.). Ptolemy IV Philopator, king of Egypt (221–204 B.C.E.) moves out with his infantry and cavalry to do battle with the Seleucid ruler Antiochus III of Syria on the frontier between Palestine and Egypt. Ptolemy takes his sister Arsinoë along with him. When the first tide of battle runs against Ptolemy, her dramatic intervention saves the day and ensures victory for the Egyptian forces.

As a warrior queen/princess, Arsinoë goes to the troops "with wailing and tears, her locks all disheveled, and exhorted them to defend themselves and their children and wives bravely, promising to give them each two minas of gold if they won the battle"

A third-century B.C.E. *limestone statue depicting Arsinoë. An inscription on the base reads, in part, "Mistress of the Two Lands, Arsinoë, the divine, beloved of the king who lives forever." See* Arsinoë.

(3 Macc 1:4). Two minas of gold would be equal to about 698 grams or the equivalent of 200 drachmas. This seems an extravagant sum, but Egyptian queens did own extensive private property.

Arsinoë of 3 Maccabees is also so named by the Greek historian Polybius (c. 200–118 B.C.E.), who affirms that she appeared before the troops, but she is later called Cleopatra by the Roman historian Livy (59 B.C.E.–17 C.E.) and Eurydice by Justin (c. 100–165 C.E., a Greek theologian who founded a school of Christian philosophy at Rome). Polybius's story of the encounter differs only in detail and probably has a basis in actual fact.

Arsinoë was the daughter of Ptolemy III and the sister of Ptolemy IV Philopator. In accordance with Egyptian custom, she later became his wife, queen, and the mother of Ptolemy V. As wealthy and influential a woman as Arsinoë was, she exerted power only as consort of her brother. She displayed courage, generosity, and intelligence in support of his rule. Like Cleopatra Thea, another resourceful Egyptian queen, Arsinoë's prominence was occasioned by her royal marriage.

HUGH ANDERSON

SEE ALSO Part I: Cleopatra 2; Cleopatra 3.
FOR FURTHER READING: Anderson, Hugh. "Third Maccabees."
———. "3 Maccabees (First Century B.C.): A New Translation and Introduction."
Emmet, C. W. "The Third Book of Maccabees."
Lefkowitz, Mary R. "Influential Women."
Young, Robin Darling. "3 Maccabees."

Artemis   SEE   Artemis (Part III).

Asenath

"she belongs to Neith," from Egyptian *sw,* "she belongs," and *Nt,* "Neith," the name of an Egyptian goddess
(Gen 41:45, 50; 46:20)

When the Hebrew shepherd Joseph becomes prime minister, he receives an Egyptian name and an Egyptian wife, named Asenath, who is the daughter of Potiphera (different from Potiphar), a priest of On. In bearing a theophoric name relating her to the ancient Egyptian goddess Neith, Asenath brings to her marriage with Joseph strong overtones of royalty and world creation, for the goddess appears both as mother of the king and as primordial creator. Thus the marriage represents a full joining, both literally and figuratively, of Egypt and Israel on multiple levels. It also indicates that marriage to foreigners (exogamy) can produce politically valuable alliances.

A later story of Asenath's marriage to Joseph appears in a tale composed in Greek, usually known as *Joseph and Aseneth.*

SUSAN TOWER HOLLIS

FOR FURTHER READING: Bohak, Gideon. *"Joseph and Aseneth" and the Jewish Temple in Heliopolis.*
Kraemer, Ross Shepard. "The Book of Aseneth."
———. *When Aseneth Met Joseph.*
Yee, Gale A. "Asenath."

Asherah   SEE   Asherah/Asherim (Part III).

Ashima/Ashimah   SEE   Ashima/Ashimah (Part III).

Astarte   SEE   Astarte (Part III).

Atarah

"crown," from Hebrew *'tr,* "to surround"
(1 Chr 2:26)

Atarah is the second of at least two wives of Jerahmeel, the great-grandson of Judah in the genealogy of Chronicles. Atarah's ancestors are not identified, but her husband's father is listed as Hezron, a son of Perez, one of two sons of the union between Judah and Tamar. Atarah became the mother of Onam and grandmother of Shammai and Jada.

ALICE L. LAFFEY

SEE ALSO Part I: Tamar 1.

Atargatis   SEE   Atargatis (Part III).

Athaliah

meaning uncertain; perhaps "YHWH is great" or
"YHWH is exalted," apparently from a Semitic root,
'*tl*, meaning "to be great, exalted," and *yāh*, a shortened form of YHWH

(2 Kgs 8:18, 26; 11; 2 Chr. 21:6; 22–24)

Queen Athaliah is the only woman in the Hebrew
Bible reported as having reigned as a monarch
within Israel/Judah. She is the daughter of either
Omri, king of Israel (2 Kgs 8:26; 2 Chr 22:2), or,
more probably, of his son King Ahab (2 Kgs 8:18; 2
Chr 21:6; the Jewish historian Josephus cites this in
Antiquities), who ruled from 873 to 852 B.C.E. There
is no evidence that she was the daughter of Ahab's
chief wife, Jezebel. Athaliah married Jehoram
(reigned 851–843 B.C.E.) of Judah (2 Kgs 8:18; 2 Chr
21:6). After Jehoram's death, their son Ahaziah
reigned for one year, and "his mother was his counselor in doing wickedly" (2 Chr 22:3).

After Ahaziah is killed in a dynastic struggle (2
Kings 9), Athaliah sets out to kill the rest of the
royal dynasty and seizes the throne of Judah in
Jerusalem (2 Kings 11; 2 Chr 22:10–23:21). She man-
ages to remain sole monarch for six years (842–836
B.C.E.). In the seventh year a revolution led by Jehoiada the priest puts on the throne the seven-year-
old Joash, Ahaziah's child who was rescued by his
paternal aunt (and Jehoiada's wife) Jehosheba from
the royal bloodbath six years earlier. The overthrow
takes place in the Jerusalem temple. Athaliah is
killed in what she terms "treason" (2 Kgs 11:14; 1 Chr
23:13) against her reign.

The biblical evaluation of her rule is negative.
Both 2 Kings 11 and 1 Chronicles (especially chap.
24) connect Athaliah with Baal worship, even
though her name contains the theophoric element
-*yāh[û]* (YHWH), like the names of other figures
in the story. The priestly objection to her could also
be motivated by hatred for a non-Davidic ruler and,
particularly, a woman ruler. However, that she
managed to sustain her reign for six years can be
attributed to her successful use of various sources
of power: her royal origins and connections, involvement in her husband's and son's reigns, economic independence, personal ability, and political
knowledge — all of which are not mentioned, apart
from notes on her wicked influence on her husband
and son.

ATHALYA BRENNER

SEE ALSO Part I: Azubah 1; Jehosheba/Jehoshabeath;
Jezebel 1.

FOR FURTHER READING: Brenner, Athalya. "Athaliah."
Katzenstein, Hanna J. "Who Were the Parents of
Athaliah?"

Azubah 1

"forsaken," from Hebrew '*zb*, "to leave, forsake"

(1 Kgs 22:42; 2 Chr 20:31)

Azubah is the daughter of Shilhi (whose place of
origin is unknown), wife of Asa, third king of Judah
(reigned 908–867 B.C.E.) and mother of his successor, King Jehoshaphat. Her name occurs in the introduction to her son's reign (1 Kgs 22:41–44; 2 Chr
20:31–33).

Although kings' mothers like Azubah are often
mentioned in their sons' introductions, very little
information survives concerning their activities.
Only the accounts of Bathsheba, Maacah, Hamutal,
Jezebel, Athaliah, and Nehushta contain details beyond the mother's place of origin and the names
of her father, husband, and son. Did these royal
women occupy an institutional position ("queen
mother") in Judah and Israel? If so, what was its
origin? Was it imported from a nation with such an
institution (such as the Hittites), or is it evidence of
a prior matriarchal period in Israel? What did the
queen mother do? Were her duties cultic, political,
or personal? According to Ben-Barak, women such
as Bathsheba, Maacah, Hamutal, and Nehushta secured the throne for their sons who, being very
young, did not yet have the right to succession.
They derived their power and influence from personal charisma and were exceptions to, not examples of, typical kings' mothers. Ackerman, however,
argues that duties of queen mothers were both political (king's adviser) and cultic (Asherah's representative in the Judean royal court). Unlike Ben-
Barak, Ackerman suggests that queen mothers in
Judah were second only to the king in power and
influence.

LINDA S. SCHEARING

SEE ALSO Part I: Athaliah; Bathsheba; Hamutal/Hamital; Jezebel 2; Maacah 3/Micaiah; Nehushta.
FOR FURTHER READING: Ackerman, Susan. "The Queen Mother and the Cult in Ancient Israel."
Ben-Barak, Zafrira. "The Status and Right of the *gᵉbîrâ*."

Azubah 2

(1 Chr 2:18–19)

Azubah is one of Caleb's wives, although the somewhat confusing genealogy of the tribe of Judah in which she is found makes it difficult to determine whether she, or her co-wife, Jerioth, is the mother of the three sons of Caleb mentioned in v. 18. When Azubah dies, Caleb takes another wife.

JULIA MYERS O'BRIEN

SEE ALSO Part I: Ephrath/Ephrathah; Jerioth.

Azubah 3   SEE Azubah/Forsaken, Jerusalem (Part III).

Baara

meaning uncertain; perhaps "possessor of strength," from Hebrew *ba'al*, "ruler, possessor" and *rĕ'ēm*, "wild ox"; or "brutish," from Hebrew *ba'ar*, "brutishness"

(1 Chr 8:8)

Baara was one of at least three wives of Shaharaim; two of them, including Baara, were discarded, and one, Hodesh, was retained. Shaharaim was a descendant of Benjamin. Because the text lists no offspring for Baara, in contrast to Shaharaim's other wives, it is possible that Baara was barren. Another possibility is that she was discarded because she was a foreigner and a worshipper of Baal, as her name suggests. The text mentions that Shaharaim had children in Moab after he sent away his wives. The discarded wives were perhaps Moabites, and the Bible records a long history of hostility between them and the Israelites (for example, Deut 23:4).

ALICE L. LAFFEY

SEE ALSO Part I: Hodesh; Hushim.

Basemath 1/Bashemath

"fragrance," from Hebrew *bośem*, "spice, balsam, perfume"

(Gen 26:34; 36:3–4, 10, 13, 17)

Cross-cultural studies of family life reveal that the contemporary emphasis on romantic love as the basis for marriage appears to be the foundation for family life beginning in the nineteenth century. Prior to that century, marriages were formed on the basis of one's social group, rather than on the basis of the affective nature of relationships. Marriage reflected in the Hebrew Bible was normally an economic or social arrangement, intended to serve one of two purposes: either to keep property within the kinship group or to initiate an alliance between kinship groups through the exchange of marriage partners.

Marriage to a spouse within one's own kinship group is known as endogamy, whereas marriage to a spouse from outside the group is labeled exogamy. Moreover, the biblical texts reveal a correlation between marriage and patrilineal descent. From the internal perspective of the kinship group of Abraham (the founding family, according to the biblical narrative) a man must be the son of both a woman and a man within this patrilineage, as well as marry a woman descended from this patrilineage, in order to be considered a primary heir to this important patrilineage. A primary heir is a man who is entitled to both the name and the property of the patrilineage descended through Terah and Abraham. Thus, the biblical texts reveal a preference for patrilineage endogamy. However, a marriage of alliance — that is, exchange — between two unrelated groups occurs when Basemath, the daughter of Ishmael (who is excluded from the patrilineage traced through Abraham and Isaac because his mother, Hagar, is an Egyptian) and sister of Nebaioth, becomes one of Esau's wives.

In Gen 26:34, Basemath is identified as the daughter of Elon the Hittite, whereas Gen 36:2 names the latter as father of Adah. Regardless of whether Basemath is the daughter of either Ishmael or Elon, neither descent line is acceptable from an Israelite perspective. Consequently, the Israelite preference for patrilineal endogamous marriage results in Esau's exclusion from the Terahite descent line, due to his exogamous marriage.

NAOMI STEINBERG

SEE ALSO Part I: Adah 2; Anah; Judith 1; Mahalath 1; Oholibamah.

FOR FURTHER READING: Steinberg, Naomi. *Kinship and Marriage in Genesis: A Household Economics Perspective.*

Wilson, Robert R. *Genealogy and History in the Biblical World.*

Basemath 2

(1 Kgs 4:15)

Among the organizational acts of King Solomon (reigned c. 968–928 B.C.E.), according to 1 Kgs 4:7–19, is the division of the kingdom into twelve fiscal districts, each with a governor and each to provide provisions for the royal household for one month a year. The governor of the eighth district, Naphtali in eastern Galilee, is Ahimaaz; he is married to Basemath, one of Solomon's daughters. The text does not indicate her mother's name, so her status within the royal household cannot be ascertained. Nonetheless, her marriage to a high official indicates political patronage.

Perhaps because the eighth district was the northernmost one, far from Jerusalem, the marital connection with the royal house was calculated to maintain the distant governor's loyalty to the crown.

CAROL MEYERS

SEE ALSO Part I: Taphath.

Bathsheba

meaning uncertain; perhaps "daughter of Sheba" or "daughter of abundance," from Hebrew *bat*, "daughter," and *šebaʿ*, "Sheba" or "abundance" (2 Samuel 11–12; 1 Kings 1–2; 1 Chr 3:5; Ps 51:superscription)

Bathsheba, the wife of David (reigned c. 1005–965 B.C.E.) and the mother of Solomon (reigned c. 968–

Terra-cotta figurine (3 inches high) of a woman in a bathtub, dating to the Iron II period (ninth–early sixth century B.C.E.). It was discovered at Achzib on the Mediterranean coast of Israel. See Bathsheba.

928 B.C.E.), is featured in each of these roles in one major narrative sequence in the David stories, and she is characterized quite differently in each.

The account in 2 Samuel 11–12 of how Bathsheba came to be David's wife makes clear that the circumstances are morally problematic. Yet because her character is suppressed, she emerges untainted by the adultery and murder for which David receives full blame. Bathsheba, daughter of Eliam and wife of Uriah the Hittite, becomes the object of David's lustful gaze. The story implies that David should have been at the battlefield, leading his troops, but instead he is at home in Jerusalem. From his rooftop he sees a woman bathing; David has her brought to his royal residence and lies with her. Afterward she returns to her home. The adultery results in a pregnancy; this sets in motion David's plan to pass the child off as Uriah's and, when this fails, to legitimize the child as his own by ensuring that Uriah will be killed in battle so that David can marry the widowed Bathsheba.

Bathsheba seems to know nothing of David's plan, and, indeed, it unfolds outside her purview. Bathsheba is "on stage" in this story very infrequently and is silent except for the announcement of her pregnancy, which she does not deliver in person. No hint is given of her inner life or of her complicity with or resistance to David's actions. We see her next after her husband, Uriah, has died, and she reacts as a proper wife would. 2 Sam 11:26 emphasizes her status as Uriah's wife: "When the wife of Uriah heard that her husband was dead, she made lamentation for him." Immediately after the mourning period, David marries her and she bears him a son.

The child born to David and Bathsheba becomes ill and soon dies. David is portrayed as a distraught father, praying and fasting that the child might live. Of the mother we hear nothing, except that after the child has died, "Then David consoled his wife Bathsheba, and went to her, and lay with her; and she bore a son, and he [or she] named him Solomon" (12:24).

One should not conclude that Bathsheba was a callous woman, but rather that the narrator has intentionally shaped the portrayal of her character for a purpose. Bathsheba's role is intentionally minimized to focus the story on David. David bears the responsibility and the condemnation, and from this point on he is beset by problems within his family that have political implications for his reign. This David is quite different from the man depicted in the Abigail story.

If Bathsheba is portrayed as passive in her early relationship with David, she becomes strongly active toward the end of David's life in her successful attempt to ensure that her son Solomon will inherit the throne. 1 Kings 1 shows her plotting, along with the prophet Nathan and other supporters of Solomon, to convince David that he has promised the kingship to Solomon. David is by now a pathetic figure who had lost control over his sons long ago. The first three of David's sons have already died, and the succession will be decided between the fourth son, Adonijah, and the destined heir, Solomon. The operative familial relationship is the mother-son relationship, and it is emphasized in the way the narrator refers to the characters: "Adonijah, son of Haggith" (1 Kgs 1:5), and "Bathsheba, Solomon's mother" (1 Kgs 1:11).

Bathsheba succeeds in having her son designated as David's successor, but her importance in the narrative does not stop when he has become king, as we see in 1 Kings 2. When David dies, the unsuccessful Adonijah, who has been assured by Solomon that no harm will come to him if he proves worthy, asks Bathsheba to convey a request to Solomon, for she is considered influential. Adonijah requests that one of David's concubines, Abishag, be given to Adonijah as his wife. It sounds innocent enough — a small consolation prize from the king to his brother who has lost the throne. Bathsheba conveys the request, with a small change in the wording, to Solomon, whereupon Solomon reacts violently, interpreting the request as an attack on his position as king. The request costs Adonijah his life.

Why did Bathsheba agree to convey this request? There are several possible explanations. Perhaps Bathsheba understood the impropriety of the request (it has been interpreted as tantamount to claiming the throne) and knew how Solomon would react. She might have been happy to see Adonijah killed so that he could not remain a rival to her son.

Or perhaps Bathsheba would have been only too happy to have Abishag removed from Solomon's household and transferred to Adonijah's. Abishag had been in David's bed when Bathsheba came to convince the feeble old king to designate Solomon as his successor. And, although David did not have sexual relations with Abishag, she was, in a sense, a younger rival to Bathsheba herself for David's favors and perhaps for future influence over Solomon. Whatever the explanation, Bathsheba plays an important role in the succession of Solomon to the throne.

ADELE BERLIN

SEE ALSO Part I: Abihail 1; Abishag; Azubah 1; Bath-shua 2; Part II: Wife of Uriah (Matt 1:6).

FOR FURTHER READING: Bailey, Randall C. *David in Love and War: The Pursuit of Power in 2 Samuel 10–12.*

Berlin, Adele. *Poetics and Interpretation of Biblical Narrative.*

Gunn, David M. *The Story of King David: Genre and Interpretation.*

Levenson, Jon D., and Baruch Halpern. "The Political Import of David's Marriages."

Sternberg, Meir. *The Poetics of Biblical Narrative.*

Bath-shua 1

"daughter of Shua," from Hebrew *bat,* "daughter,"
and *šûʿa,* "Shua"

(Gen 38:2–5, 12; 1 Chr 2:3)

In the story of Judah and Tamar in Genesis 38,
Judah marries a Canaanite woman identified as the
daughter of Shua (v. 2). She becomes the mother of
Er (who marries Tamar), Onan, and Shelah (vv.
3–5). When her death is recorded in v. 12, she is
called "Bath-shua, wife of Judah." The NRSV maintains her namelessness by translating this verse
"wife of Judah, daughter of Shua" (but in the genealogy of the tribe of Judah in 1 Chr 2:3, it presents
her as "the Canaanite woman Bath-shua"). When
Judah has completed his time of mourning for his
wife, his widowed daughter-in-law Tamar realizes
that she will not be given to her living brother-in-
law Shelah, and she seeks to secure her husband's
lineage and her own future.

TIKVA FRYMER-KENSKY

SEE ALSO Part I: Tamar 1.

Bath-shua 2

(1 Chr 3:5)

Bath-shua is here identified as the daughter of Ammiel and as one of David's wives. She is the mother
of four of his sons, Shimea, Shobab, Nathan, and
Solomon, who are born in Jerusalem. These four
sons are also listed in 2 Sam 5:14–16 and 1 Chr
14:4–7, but without the name of their mother. Bath-
shua is probably an alternate form of Bathsheba.
According to 2 Sam 11:3, Bathsheba's father was
Eliam, not Ammiel (a change explained by the in-
terchange of the two elements in the name). Solomon is the only son of Bathsheba mentioned in
Samuel and Kings. The Chronicles passage, whose
purpose was to provide as complete a genealogical
record as possible, seems to have drawn on the
sources in Samuel and Kings and combined the
information in them.

ADELE BERLIN

SEE ALSO Part I: Bathsheba.

Ber(e)nice

from Greek *pherenikē,* "bearing victory"

(Acts 25:13–26:32)

Two women members of the Herodian family, the
Jewish sisters Drusilla (Acts 24:24) and Bernice,
make brief appearances in Acts. In what seems a
straightforward narrative, King Agrippa, Bernice,
and a substantial retinue hear Paul's defense and
collectively pronounce him blameless (Acts 25:13–
26:32). Bernice is explicitly named three times in
this passage: when she and Agrippa arrive at Caesarea to welcome Festus (25:13), when they arrive
with much "pomp" the next day to hear Paul's case
(25:23–24), and at the conclusion (26:30–31). Acts
identifies Agrippa as king, but never reveals
Bernice's identity. Continuously present in this
scene, she is nevertheless largely obscured. Festus
addresses "King Agrippa and all here present with
us" (25:24) and then says, "I have brought [Paul]
before all of you, and especially before you, King
Agrippa" (25:26). Each time, Festus presumably in-

A first-century C.E. *Latin inscription from Beirut,
commemorating the restoration of a building by Berenice, here called "Queen," and her brother, King
Agrippa II. Berenice's name precedes Agrippa's and
identifies her as the daughter of their father, Agrippa
I. See* Ber(e)nice.

cludes Bernice, but does not acknowledge her directly. Agrippa, but not Bernice, speaks to Paul (26:1), and Paul addresses only Agrippa explicitly (26:2, 19, 27). Only at the end (26:30–31) is Bernice explicitly named among those who proclaim Paul's apparent blamelessness to one another.

Because history has bequeathed us considerable additional evidence for Bernice and her family, we are able to see how Bernice may be deliberately masked and reshaped in Acts for the author's own purposes.

Bernice figures prominently in the pages of her Jewish contemporary the historian Josephus, who spells her name Berenice and who says nothing of the events in Acts 26. Later Roman historians chronicle her intense love affair with the Roman general Titus, better known in Jewish history for his major role in the destruction of the second temple.

Born in about 28 C.E., Bernice was a great-granddaughter of Herod the Great (ruled 37 B.C.E.–4 B.C.E.). She and her siblings Drusilla and Agrippa were among the five children of Agrippa I (37 C.E.–44 C.E.) and Cypros, his first cousin. At about age fifteen, she was married to a man from an exceedingly prominent Alexandrian Jewish family. Marcus Julius Alexander was a nephew of the great philosopher Philo and the son of Alexander, alabarch (a Roman official) of Egypt. Bernice's brother-in-law, Tiberius Julius Alexander, became procurator of Judea, prefect of Egypt, and a staff general for Titus during the siege of Jerusalem; Josephus claims that he had abandoned the ancestral practices of his people. When Marcus died, Agrippa married Bernice to his own brother, Herod of Chalcis. In 50 C.E., at age twenty-two, she was again a widow, with two small sons.

Bernice, unmarried, then ruled as queen with Agrippa II. An inscription from this period on a statue in Athens honors her as "great" queen. A Latin inscription from Beirut also calls her "Queen."

Josephus reports the otherwise unattested rumor that Bernice's relationship with Agrippa was incestuous, and that, to deflect criticism, Bernice arranged to marry a non-Jew, Polemo, king of Cilicia

(who agreed to be circumcised). Josephus claims that Bernice deserted (or perhaps divorced) Polemo, motivated by *akolasia* (inappropriate sexual desire).

Though we do not know precisely when Bernice and Titus met, Agrippa and Bernice went to Rome with Titus after the First Jewish Revolt (66–30 C.E.). The Roman historian Dio Cassius says that Bernice acted in all respects as though she were Titus's wife, creating enough tension between Titus and the Roman aristocracy that she was forced to leave Rome. Another Roman historian, Suetonius, notes that when Titus was proclaimed emperor, Bernice returned to Rome, apparently hoping, finally, to become his legitimate wife, but sufficient pressure was brought to bear on Titus that he dismissed her for good.

Bernice receives mixed but largely negative reviews from ancient male historians. Roman writers seem offended by a foreign, Jewish, aristocratic woman who aspired to a position beyond her grasp; licit wife of the emperor of Rome. Josephus, who knew many of the first-century cast of characters far better, frequently vilifies Bernice, accusing her of jealousy toward her beautiful sister, Drusilla, and of various sexual improprieties. Elsewhere, though, he offers a sympathetic portrait of a barefoot, penitent Bernice, at considerable peril to her own life, imploring the Roman procurator Gessius Florus to desist from his slaughter of Jews in Jerusalem.

Bernice's support for Josephus's political opponent, Justus of Tiberias, may have affected his judgment. But Josephus may also have found offensive the ability of Bernice (and other elite Herodian Jewish women) to circumvent the strictures of gender to live relatively autonomously and to play significant roles in first-century affairs. Such an interpretation accords well with his more favorable treatment of women like Bernice and Drusilla's mother, who conformed more closely to ancient expectations for elite women.

Of her ancient male chroniclers, Luke alone appears uncritical. All that appears to interest the author of Acts about Bernice is that she is yet another example of a Jewish aristocrat who is aligned with Rome and who vindicates Paul. We cannot say how much Luke (writing no earlier than the late first century C.E., and in my view, more likely in the first third of the second century C.E.) actually knew of Bernice and her subsequent role in Roman and Jewish history. But Luke omits key data about Bernice, including her well-attested title of queen and her identity as Agrippa's (and Drusilla's) sister and as Titus's future lover. He reduces her role in this scene to one of a passive observer whose assessment of Paul's innocence is commingled with that of the entire elite retinue.

Luke's distinctive portrait may reveal his intent to exploit Bernice's prestige while muting the more embarrassing details of her life that might weaken her credibility as a witness to Paul's innocence and to Luke's larger theme: that Rome never found fault with the Christians. Luke's representation of Bernice is also consistent with a pattern identified by recent feminist scholarship: the author repeatedly presents aristocratic, non-Christian women as sympathetic to early Christians. Further, Luke seems greatly concerned to cast both those women and Christian women themselves as conforming to ancient Roman conventions of gender, which may also explain why he depicts Bernice as largely ornamental and mute. Finally, recent commentators have observed that, although Acts tends to emphasize the conversion of elite women to Christianity, nothing is said here about Bernice's response to Paul's preaching. Partly this is because Bernice was not ever a supporter of Christians (nothing else we know about her suggests that), but partly it may be that she functions all the more effectively as an elite Roman-allied vindicator of Paul if her judgment is clearly impartial.

We may catch a glimpse of Bernice's legacy in several second-century C.E. papyri, which mention a woman named Julia Crispina, an elite landowner and legal guardian of several children. Crispina's father was named Berenicianus, an unusual name known to have been that of Bernice's son by Herod of Chalcis. Possibly, Julia Crispina was Bernice's granddaughter. But of Bernice's ultimate fate we know nothing, and we last see her for certain on the

stage of history as she is cast out of Titus's palace. Had Titus and Bernice succeeded in their desire to marry legally, Jewish and Roman history might have been altogether different.

Bernice is one of the few women in the Bible well attested in ancient nonbiblical sources. Roman writers' references to her may be found in Stern, *Greek and Latin Authors on Jews and Judaism.* Inscriptions may be found in the collections *Inscriptiones Graecae* (III. 556) and *L'Année Épigraphique* (1928:82).

Ross S. Kraemer

See also Part I: Drusilla.

For further reading: Ilan, Tal. *Jewish Women in Greco-Roman Palestine: An Inquiry into Image and Status.*

Macurdy, Grace H. "Julia Berenice."

————. "Royal Women in Judea."

Beulah   See Beulah/Married, Jerusalem (Part III).

Bilhah

meaning unknown

(Gen 29:29; 30:3–7; 32:22–23; 33:1–3; 35:22; 37:2; 46:25; 49:4; 1 Chr 7:13)

When Rachel marries Jacob, her father Laban gives her a maid, Bilhah (Gen 29:29; 46:25), whom she gives to Jacob as a wife (Hebrew *'iššâ*) when she finds herself barren (Gen 30:3–7). Rachel did not have to do this for Jacob's sake, for Jacob already had children to be his heirs by his other wife, Leah; rather, she is said to do this so that Jacob could fulfill her demand to give her children. Rachel plans to "have children through her" (as Sarah did with Hagar) by having Bilhah give birth "upon my [Rachel's] knees," probably a phrase that comes from adoption ritual. The story is silent about Bilhah's reaction. The plan succeeds, so that when Bilhah's son is born, Rachel names him, an act expressing her maternal authority. The child's name, Dan, means "he judged" and indicates Rachel's relationship to the boy: she claims that "God has judged me [Hebrew *dānannî*] and has also heard my voice and given me a son" (Gen 30:6). Bilhah bears another son to Jacob under this arrangement, with Rachel again naming the child. She calls him Naphtali, which means "I have prevailed," because she has "prevailed" (Hebrew *niptaltî*) over her sister in a divine contest (Hebrew *naptûlê 'ĕlōhîm*; NRSV, "mighty wrestlings").

Despite this relationship to Rachel, Dan and Naphtali continue to be considered Bilhah's sons, and that influences their standing in the family. When faced with what he thinks might be a tense confrontation with his brother, Esau, Jacob places the "two maids and their children" at the front of his household, Leah and her children next, and Rachel and Joseph bringing up the (protected) rear (Gen 33:1–3; compare 32:22–23).

Bilhah's own status in the household is somewhat ambiguous. She is given to Jacob as his "wife" (Hebrew *'iššâ*), although in one instance she is called his "secondary wife" (*pilegeš*; NRSV, "concubine"). Yet in the potentially dangerous situation with Esau, she reverts to being called a "maid" (Hebrew *šipḥâ*). Furthermore, in the listing of Jacob's twelve sons in chap. 35, Dan and Naphtali are presented as the "sons of Bilhah, Rachel's maid" (v. 25). And the maids apparently must share a tent, whereas the wives have their own (Gen 31:33). Nevertheless, when the danger from Esau has passed, Bilhah again is called Jacob's wife; and her sons are not disadvantaged, for Rachel's biological son Joseph becomes a shepherd, "a helper to the sons of Bilhah and Zilpah, his father's wives" (Gen 37:2).

Bilhah must have been very young when she bore her children, because Jacob's eldest son Reuben (by Leah) has sex with her (Gen 35:22). Sleeping with one's father's wife was considered a great offense in biblical law (Lev 18:8; 20:11); perhaps that is why Bilhah is called his secondary wife (*pilegeš*) in this one text — to diminish the gravity of the act. Jacob hears about what Reuben did and does nothing at the time. But apparently he considered it a major offense, for in his deathbed speech, he removes

Reuben from his extra inheritance as firstborn and alludes to Reuben's dreadful deed (Gen 49:4).

Nothing is said about Bilhah's fate, but she continued to be remembered as the ancestress of major clans in Israel (1 Chr 7:13).

TIKVA FRYMER-KENSKY

SEE ALSO Part II: Female (and Male) Slaves (Gen 12:16, etc.).

Bithiah

"daughter of God," from Hebrew *bat*, "daughter," and *yāh*, a shortened form of YHWH
(1 Chr 4:17)

A daughter of an unnamed pharaoh, Bithiah is one of two wives of Mered, a man in the lineage of Caleb, probably part of the tribe of Judah. Her name, meaning "daughter of God," may indicate that in spite of being Pharaoh's daughter, she has adopted the culture of the group into which she has married. According to the genealogy in 1 Chronicles, she bears two sons and a daughter, Miriam.

SUSAN TOWER HOLLIS

SEE ALSO Part I: Miriam 2; Part II: Daughter of Pharaoh (Exod 2:5–10).

FOR FURTHER READING: Lo, Hing Choi. "Bithiah."

Candace

In older translations, the Ethiopian queen mentioned in Acts 8:27 was thought to be named Candace. Newer translations recognize that Kandake is an Ethiopian title, not a proper name.

ROSS S. KRAEMER

SEE ALSO Part II: The Candace, Queen of the Ethiopians (Acts 8:27).

Chloe

"verdant, blooming," from Greek *chloē*
(1 Cor 1:11)

In 1 Cor 1:11, Paul explains that conflicts among believers in Corinth have been reported to him by "Chloe's people" (literally, "[those] of Chloe"). The term refers to members of Chloe's household, which would typically have included relatives, slaves, and former slaves (freedpersons). Women heads of household are well attested in the Roman Empire and were often prosperous in business (Lydia of Thyatira in Acts 16:14–15 is another example from the New Testament). Whether Chloe was herself a believer cannot be determined with certainty.

ROSS S. KRAEMER

FOR FURTHER READING: Gilman, Florence Morgan. "Chloe."

Claudia

> "limping, lame," from Latin *claudo* or *claudeo*, "to limp or be lame"; also, the name of two prestigious Roman *gentes* (clans), hence a female member of the *gens* Claudia
>
> (2 Tim 4:21)

Among the relatively large number of individuals named in 2 Timothy is a group of three persons, a woman, Claudia, and two men, Pudens and Linus. All three are apparently with the author of the letter and send their greetings to the recipient.

Some of the persons named in 2 Timothy are known also from the undisputed letters of Paul (such as Prisca and Aquila, from Romans and 1 Corinthians; and Timothy himself, from 2 Corinthians, Philippians, 1 Thessalonians, and Philemon) but most are attested only here. Since 2 Timothy is widely held to have been written in Paul's name by someone else, it is not clear whether we should take the persons named only in this letter as otherwise unattested members of Paul's circle, as persons known to the author (but not to the historical Paul), as creations of the author designed to lend authenticity to a letter in the name of Paul, or perhaps even as some combination of all three.

A woman with this name would have been in some way associated with the Roman *gens* Claudia, either as a member of the family by birth, or as a slave or freedperson of a family member. 2 Timothy clearly associates Claudia with the "Pauline" mission, although it does not indicate whether she should be understood as a missionary herself, or as a person in whose home traveling missionaries stayed and who provided significant support for them, or even as the head of a household church, analogous to women such as Prisca (who is actually greeted by the author in 4:19) or Phoebe (Rom 16:1–2). 2 Timothy appears to link Claudia with Pudens and Linus, yet despite extensive speculation on the part of interpreters, it does not indicate how, if at all, the three constitute a group.

Collectively the Pastoral Epistles (1 and 2 Timothy and Titus) envision women as particularly prone to error and deceit (for example, 1 Tim 4:7; 2 Tim 3:6), and are concerned to circumscribe the roles of women in Christian communities (1 Tim 2:8–15; 5:3–16; Titus 2:3–5). Yet Claudia is represented here in a manner consistent with the evidence for women in mid-first-century C.E. Pauline communities. Although Claudia may not have been a historical person, her inclusion in the final greetings of 2 Timothy may reflect the author's awareness that the real Paul routinely did associate with women as colleagues. The absence of any specific description of Claudia's roles may reflect the author's desire to avoid explicit representation of women as the leaders and patrons known from the authentic Pauline Epistles.

ROSS S. KRAEMER

SEE ALSO Part I: Phoebe; Prisca/Priscilla; Part II: Wives (and Husbands) Exhorted (Eph 5:22–33); (Col 3:18–19); (1 Pet 3:1–7).

Cleopatra 1

> "[born] of a famous father," from Greek *kleō*, "to be famous," and *patēr*, "father"
>
> SEE Dan 11:17 Wife of the King of the South (Part II)

Cleopatra 2

> (Add Esth 11:1)

The name Cleopatra, which goes back to the Macedonian dynasty in Greece, in the fifth century B.C.E., became popular in the Hellenistic period among the Ptolemaic rulers in Egypt and the Seleucid rulers in Syria. These two dynastic successors to Alexander in the East struggled to control Palestine in the last centuries B.C.E.

The Greek version of Esther, a Hellenistic Jewish novel based on the Hebrew Bible's Book of Esther, concludes with a colophon (a notation providing facts about its production) reporting that the story was brought to the Egyptian Jewish community in the fourth year of the "reign of Ptolemy and Cleopatra" (11:1). Because at least five Ptolemaic rulers had wives or co-regents named Cleopatra, it is difficult to be certain which Cleopatra is referred to in this verse.

Some scholars suggest that it must be Cleopatra II, wife and sister of Ptolemy VI Philometor, who was well disposed toward the Jewish community in Egypt. During his reign (180–145 B.C.E.), the exiled high priest Onias IV was allowed to build a Jewish temple at Leontopolis in Egypt. After Philometor's death, the Jewish community in Egypt supported his widow (and sister) Cleopatra II in her struggle for power against her younger brother, and sometime husband, Ptolemy VIII Euergetes.

Other scholars opt for either Ptolemy IX (reigned 116–107 and 88–81 B.C.E.) or Ptolemy XII (reigned 80–58 and 55–47 B.C.E.). The former was co-regent with his mother, Cleopatra III; he was also married to a Cleopatra IV, whom he divorced, and then he married yet another Cleopatra, Cleopatra Selene, both of whom are candidates for the Cleopatra of the Additions to Esther. Ptolemy XII Auletes was married to his sister Cleopatra V Tryphaenes, in accordance with Pharaonic and Ptolemaic custom; she too could be the woman of Add Esth 11:1. Whoever the Cleopatra of the colophon may be, the dates of the most likely ones would place the composition of the Additions to Esther in the late second or early first century B.C.E.

Whereas the Hebrew Bible gives regnal dates according to the name of the king alone, as does also the beginning of Greek Additions to Esther (11:2), the use of Cleopatra's name along with Ptolemy may indicate the power of the queen in Ptolemaic Egypt.

JOHN J. COLLINS

SEE ALSO Part I: Cleopatra 3; Part II: Wife of the King of the South (Dan 11:17).

FOR FURTHER READING: Bickerman, Elias J. "The Colophon of the Greek Book of Esther."
Moore, Carey A. *Daniel, Esther, and Jeremiah: The Additions.*
Whitehorne, John. "Cleopatra."

Cleopatra 3
(1 Macc 10:54, 57–58; 11:9–12)

A number of rulers in the Ptolemaic (based in Egypt) and Seleucid (based in Syria) dynasties, which ruled parts of the eastern Hellenistic empire after the death of Alexander in 323 B.C.E., were married to women named Cleopatra. This name was popular in the late centuries B.C.E. probably because of its prominence among the Macedonian Greek rulers of the fifth century B.C.E. The Apocryphal/Deuterocanonical Book of 1 Maccabees, which tells the story of the Jewish revolt against the Syrian king Antiochus IV Epiphanes, refers to one of these women, Cleopatra Thea.

Cleopatra Thea was the eldest daughter of Ptolemy VI Philometor ("who loves his mother"), the son of Cleopatra I, and husband of Cleopatra II. 1 Macc 10:57–58 reports that Philometor gave Cleopatra Thea in marriage to the Syrian king Alexander Balas. The marriage was arranged in response to Alexander's request that he marry her in order to "establish friendship" with Philometor (1 Macc 10:54). Such acts might be called diplomacy through marriage, whereby an alliance is sealed by the member of one royal house taking in marriage a woman from another, often rival dynasty. The wedding of Cleopatra Thea and Alexander Balas, which took place in 150 B.C.E., proved unsatisfactory. Four years later, Philometor took back his daughter, alleging that Alexander had plotted to kill him, and gave her in marriage to Alexander's rival, Demetrius II Nicator (1 Macc 11:9–12).

Although Cleopatra Thea seems to have been a mere pawn of international diplomacy, she subsequently proved to be a resourceful and formidable woman. When Demetrius was captured while invading Parthia in 139–138 B.C.E., Cleopatra Thea continued as queen by marrying his brother Antiochus VIII Sidetes. When Sidetes died in 129 B.C.E., she ruled in her own right for a short period and then as regent for her son Antiochus VIII Grypus (125–121 B.C.E.), whom she tried to have poisoned. Her plot was discovered, and she was forced to commit suicide by drinking the poison intended for her son.

JOHN J. COLLINS

SEE ALSO Part I: Arsinoë; Cleopatra 2; Part II: Wife of the King of the South (Dan 11:17).

FOR FURTHER READING: Goldstein, Jonathan A. *I Maccabees.*

Whitehorne, John. "Cleopatra."

Cozbi

"attractive"; related to Akkadian *kuzbu,* "voluptuous, sexually vigorous"; Israelites may have associated it with Hebrew *kzb,* "to lie, to be deceitful"

(Num 25:15, 18)

Although Cozbi's name is given only near the end of Numbers 25, her story is told in vv. 6–9. A certain Israelite man brings a Midianite woman (Cozbi) into the Israelite camp and to his family tent to have sexual relations with her. This happens even as Moses and the people are mourning over the apostasy resulting from similar relations with Moabite women. The Israelite man and Cozbi are pierced through together with a single spear thrust by the grandson of the priest Aaron. It seems that the story is told to legitimate the perpetual priesthood of the Aaronic line (v. 13). For that purpose Cozbi's name is not of interest, but only that she is Midianite; the priest's action is central.

Cozbi's name and the name of the man (Zimri) are introduced late in the story with an emphasis on their lineage as important personages among their respective peoples. Cozbi is daughter of a clan head; Zimri is himself a clan head. Perhaps this rank lends a level of symbolic fulfillment to Moses' command in v. 4 that all the chiefs should be put to death, a command not otherwise carried out in this story.

The story concludes (vv. 16–18) with a command to defeat the Midianites on account of the affair of Cozbi, thus preparing the reader for the battle recorded in Numbers 31. Only in this conclusion is any blame attached to Cozbi and the other foreign women of this story. In the preceding sections there is no indication that the women enticed the Israelite men sexually, and there is no punishment announced for the foreign women.

KATHARINE DOOB SAKENFELD

SEE ALSO Part II: Moabite Women (Num 25:1); Midianite Women (Num 31:9, etc.).

Damaris

meaning uncertain; apparently a variant of Greek *damalis,* "heifer"

(Acts 17:34)

Acts reports that Paul gained some converts in Athens, two of whom are named: Dionysius, a member of the prestigious Areopagus (the high council of Athens, which met on a hill of the same name), and Damaris. The identity of the latter has long been an object of speculation: was she the wife of Dionysius, the wife or mother of one of the philosophers present, or a reformed prostitute? The last of these possibilities draws on the stereotype that "respectable" women did not appear in public. Some ancient manuscripts ascribe to her the epithet "of high standing" (compare Acts 13:50; 17:12); others delete the reference to her, perhaps to suppress recognition of independent women. Damaris (and Dionysius) may be legendary (compare 1 Cor 16:5).

RICHARD I. PERVO

FOR FURTHER READING: Pervo, Richard I. "Social and Religious Aspects of the Western Text."

Deborah 1

"bee," from Hebrew *dĕbôrâ,* "bee"

(Gen 24:59; 35:8)

Deborah, Rebekah's wet nurse, is mentioned twice in the Genesis narratives. First, though her name does not appear, she is said to have accompanied own children. The exceptions may have been elite or royal women. That Rebekah is said to have had a nurse may be a literary embellishment pointing to her prominence among the matriarchs.

CAROL MEYERS

SEE ALSO Part I: Jochebed; Part II: Nurse (Num 11:12); Nurse of Joash (2 Kgs 11:2, etc.); Nursing Mothers (Isa 49:15, etc.).

FOR FURTHER READING: Gruber, Mayer I. "Breast-feeding Practices in Biblical Israel and in Old Babylonian Mesopotamia."

Terra-cotta statuette (2 inches high) of a woman with a child at her breast, from Uruk in Mesopotamia, early first millennium B.C.E. See Deborah 1; Nurse of Joash (2 Kgs 11:2–3, etc.).

Rebekah on the journey from her natal household in Mesopotamia to that of her fiancé, Isaac, in the land of Canaan (Gen 24:59). Then, when Deborah dies, her burial place under an oak — the "oak of weeping" — near Bethel is noted (Gen 35:8).

Because the mention of wet nurses is so rare in the Hebrew Bible (the only other specific instances are for Moses, where his biological mother is "hired" to be his nurse, and for Joash, a Judean king whose mother was apparently murdered), it may be assumed that most Israelite women nursed their

Deborah 2

(Judges 4–5)

Deborah is one of the major judges (meaning charismatic leaders, rather than juridical figures) in the story of how Israel takes the land of Canaan.

The only female judge, and also the only judge to be called a prophet, Deborah is a decisive figure in the defeat of the Canaanites, a victory told in two accounts, a prose narrative in Judges 4 and an ancient song known as the Song of Deborah, probably composed not long after the original events, possibly by Deborah herself, and preserved in Judges 5. In Judg 4:4, Deborah is identified as 'ēšet lappîdôt, which may mean "woman of [the town] Lappidoth," "wife of [the man] Lappidoth," or "woman of torches" (that is, "fiery woman").

As the story opens in Judges 4, Deborah is already a judge, settling disputes brought to her while she sits under the "palm of Deborah" in the hill country of Ephraim (4:5). Most of the major figures in the Book of Judges are acknowledged as leaders after military victory; Deborah is a judge before the battle, but the narrative does not include the story of how she became judge, why she is called a "prophetess," or the way in which God commanded her to begin the battle against Jabin, the Canaanite king of Hazor, and his general, Sisera.

Deborah summons Barak to be her general, relaying God's command to take ten thousand men to Mount Tabor to begin the battle. When he responds that he would go only if she will, she agrees to go, but informs him that Barak will get no glory from the victory, for "the LORD will deliver [NRSV, sell] Sisera into the hand of a woman" (4:9). The reader naturally assumes that the woman will be Deborah. Sisera deploys his army against Deborah, and Barak and the troops near Mount Tabor in Galilee. Deborah announces to Barak that the day of victory has come, and "the LORD is indeed going out before you." Barak and his warriors destroy all the Canaanites except Sisera, who flees from the battle and seeks refuge with a Kenite woman, Jael, who kills him; Jael is in fact the woman who seals Sisera's fate.

The Song of Deborah, preserved in Judges 5, tells more about this final battle. It describes the chaotic conditions that exist until "you arose, Deborah, / arose as a mother in Israel" (5:7). The poem hints that the battle against Canaan was instigated by the people, who call, "Awake, awake, Deborah! / Awake, awake, utter a song! / Arise, Barak, lead away your captives, / O son of Abinoam" (5:12). Deborah's job would not be to fight. As the prophetic leader, her job would be to sing encouraging war chants and a victory song (such as Judges 5); the actual fighting would be Barak's job.

YHWH takes part in the actual battle, causing a sudden flood storm: "The stars fought from heaven, / from their courses they fought against Sisera. / The torrent Kishon swept them away" (5:21). This disabled the Canaanite chariots, enabling Israel's infantry to win.

The Song of Deborah concludes with a heroic depiction of Jael as a woman warrior and with a taunt of Sisera's mother, waiting anxiously and in vain for Sisera to return after the battle. Deborah does not show sympathy toward another woman, Sisera's mother. Quite the contrary — she portrays her as the quintessential enemy woman, already anticipating the riches that the fighters will bring as spoil when they return. These riches would include both material wealth and captive women — "a girl or two [Hebrew, a womb-girl, two womb-girls] for every man" (5:30). The battle is between Israelites and Canaanites, and the women align solidly with their own group.

There is no other heroine like Deborah in the Hebrew Bible, but other women did have some of her many roles. She is called a "mother in Israel" (Judg 5:7) perhaps because she was a biological mother. This would be important, showing that mothers might attain political prominence. More likely, the phrase may indicate that her arbitration powers as judge were parental, even maternal. "Mother," like "father," can be an honorific title for an authority figure or protector in the community (compare 1 Sam 24:1 and Isa 22:21). Another possibility is that she was a strong administrator of God's plan, like the matriarchs in Genesis. As a respected politico-judicial authority, she has a counterpart in the wise woman of Abel, who spoke for and rescued the city of Abel where, she said, the people of Israel brought their disputes to be settled (2 Sam 20:15–22). As a singer of victory songs, she echoes Miriam and foreshadows latter women who celebrate David's military success (1 Sam 18:6–7). And as a prophetess, like Miriam, she anticipates later female prophetic figures, such as Huldah, who prophesied the end of Israel's time in Canaan, and Noadiah, who appeared during the restoration from exile. But there are differences in these roles. Women singers and prophets continue throughout Israel's history, but with the consolidation of the Israelite monarchy, politico-judicial authority of the type enjoyed by Deborah and the wise woman of Abel was handed over to the royal bureaucracies. And except perhaps for some queen mothers, they apparently did not include women.

TIKVA FRYMER-KENSKY

SEE ALSO Part I: Jael; Part II: Mother of Sisera (Judg 5:28–30); Wisest Ladies (Judg 5:29–30); Girls as Booty (Judg 5:30).

FOR FURTHER READING: Ackerman, Susan. *Warrior, Dancer, Seductress, Queen: Women in Judges and Biblical Israel.*

Exum, J. Cheryl. "Mother in Israel: A Familiar Story Reconsidered."

Fewell, Dana Nolan. "Judges."

Frymer-Kensky, Tikva. *Victors, Victims, Virgins, and Voice: Rereading the Women of the Bible.*

Stager, Lawrence. "Archaeology, Ecology, and Social History: Background Themes to the Song of Deborah."

Deborah 3

(Tob 1:8)

The Deborah of the Book of Tobit, like her biblical namesake in Judges 4–5, is notable in that she performs a role traditionally considered a male prerogative. According to Tobit's first-person account of his background, he learned the law from his grandmother Deborah because his father had died and left him an orphan. The full impact of this astonishing casual remark takes a moment to be felt.

Rabbinic literature compiled many centuries after the Book of Tobit suggests that it was uncommon for Jewish women to study the law, much less to teach it to a male. Some rabbinic authorities in the Talmud were adamant that women not be allowed to study Torah (Jerusalem Talmud Soṭah 3:4; Babylonian Talmud Yoma 66b) or even claimed that teaching a daughter Torah was equivalent to teaching her obscenity (Babylonian Talmud Soṭah 20a). The Talmud mentions only one woman, Beruriah, said to have been the wife of the famous Rabbi Meir, who was learned in the law (Babylonian Talmud Pesahim 62b; Babylonian Talmud Eruvin 53b).

The fact that Tobit had no father to teach him may have sanctioned Deborah's unusual performance of a man's duty. However, in some rabbinic literature, if a father failed to teach his son the law, the son was supposed to teach himself (Mekilta, Pisha 18). Deborah, like Beruriah, may be an exception; there is no indication that the other three named female characters in Tobit (Anna, Edna, Sarah) know the law. Yet the author does not indicate that there is anything odd about the way in which Tobit receives his education. Tobit, who is presented as scrupulously observant of the law, seems proud of his knowledge and unashamed of how he got it. Perhaps what Deborah did was not, after all, as uncommon as later traditions have led us to believe.

BEVERLY BOW

SEE ALSO Part I: Anna 1; Deborah 1; Sarah 2.

FOR FURTHER READING: Bronner, Leila L. *From Eve to Esther: Rabbinic Reconstructions of Biblical Women.*

Kraemer, Ross S. *Her Share of the Blessings: Women's Religions among Pagans, Jews, and Christians in the Greco-Roman World.*

Delilah

meaning uncertain; perhaps "flirtatious," related to Arabic *dallatum*, "flirt"; or "languid," possibly from Hebrew *dll*, "to languish"

(Judges 16)

Delilah is the only woman in the Samson story whose name is given. Whatever its etymology, her name is a wordplay on Hebrew *laylâ*, "night," for as the night overcomes the mighty sun (the name Samson, *šimšôn*, is related to "sun," *šemeš*), so Delilah overcomes the apparently invincible strong man, Samson.

The biblical story, in which Samson falls in love with her and then the Philistines use her to learn the secret of his strength, leaves us with more questions than answers about Delilah. She is not, as biblical women typically are, identified in terms of a man (husband, father, or brother). All we know is her name, which is a Hebrew name, and the place where she lives, the valley of Sorek, which lay between Israelite and Philistine territory. She and Samson are apparently lovers but are not married. What is her status in society? Is she a wealthy widow, like Judith? A sexually autonomous woman, like the woman in the Song of Solomon? A harlot, as is commonly supposed?

Delilah is not called a harlot. Samson is the profligate, and it is perhaps because he visits a harlot in Judg 16:1–3 that some readers conclude that Delilah is also a harlot (the phrase "and after that he fell in love with a woman . . ." [Judg 16:4] also links the two women). Delilah is not even called a Philistine, though it is usually assumed that she is because (1) Samson is attracted to Philistine women, (2) she has dealings with the Philistine rulers and it is unlikely that the Philistines would seek to enlist the aid of an Israelite woman, and (3) she betrays the Israelite hero to his enemies, and it is unlikely that a biblical author would portray one of his countrywomen doing such a scandalous thing without further comment. All are good reasons, but none is conclusive. Actually, only one of the three women with whom Samson is involved — his wife — is specifically identified as a Philistine.

Delilah accepts a bribe to reveal the source of Samson's strength to the Philistines. The bribe would make sense if the woman was Israelite — she would probably need enticement to betray a leader of her people. Each of the Philistine rulers (probably five of them, representing the five important Philistine city-states) pays her eleven hundred pieces of silver. On the other hand, if Delilah is Philistine, perhaps the bribe simply underscores what a treacherous woman she is.

The text reports that Samson loves Delilah (16:4), but not that she loves him — a hint, perhaps, that she does not love him and will have no qualms about betraying him.

Three times Delilah tries unsuccessfully to learn the secret of Samson's strength. The Philistines instruct her to "entice" (NRSV, "coax") Samson, which suggests something sexual, but the text reports only her persistent questioning and nagging. She makes no secret of her intention. By the fourth time, it is apparent that she will carry out whatever procedure Samson describes, but Samson tells her anyway, and she cuts his hair, enabling the Philistines to capture him. The Hebrew text has Delilah cut Samson's hair, just as she did the binding (twice) and weaving of his hair. The text is rather difficult, however, and some of the versions introduce a "man" or a "barber" and have him cut Samson's hair.

J. Cheryl Exum

See also Part II: Wife of Samson (Judg 14:1–15:6); Prostitute of Gaza (Judg 16:1–3); Philistine Women (Judg 16:27)

For further reading: Bal, Mieke. *Lethal Love: Feminist Literary Readings of Biblical Love Stories.*

Exum, J. Cheryl. *Fragmented Women: Feminist (Sub)versions of Biblical Narratives.*

———. *Plotted, Shot, and Painted: Cultural Representations of Biblical Women.*

Sasson, Jack M. "Who Cut Samson's Hair? (And Other Trifling Issues Raised by Judges 16)."

Dinah

"judgment, cause," from Hebrew *dyn,* "to execute judgment, plead the cause"
(Gen 30:21; 34; 46:15)

Dinah is the daughter of Jacob, the father of twelve sons (and thus the twelve tribes) in the ancestor narratives of Genesis. She is born to Leah after Leah has given birth to six sons. Leah names her (Gen 34:21), as biblical women often did as part of the maternal role. Of Jacob's daughters (others are noted in Gen 46:15), only Dinah is mentioned by name.

The story of Dinah deals with the Israelites' attempt to establish social boundaries for marriage. It seems to advocate an inclusive perspective (represented by Dinah and Jacob) in which, when mutual respect and honor characterize the relationship, cooperation and bonding ("give and take") with outsiders (represented by Shechem, Hamor, and the Shechemites) can take place.

The story is set during the ancestral period in the city of Shechem, the geographical center of a movement in which people of diverse backgrounds, customs, and religious beliefs merged to become the community of Israel. Dinah goes out "to visit the women of the region" (the indigenous people, 34:1). The phrase implies an openness to and acceptance of outsiders. Dinah's subsequent sexual intercourse with Shechem, the Hivite prince of the region, is the ultimate symbol of acceptance. And Hamor speaks to Jacob about "giving" his daughter in marriage to Shechem, in the same way that the Jacobites and Shechemites will "give and take" wives, live and trade in the same region, and hold property together peacefully.

But separatist tendencies within Jacob's community (represented by Simeon, Levi, and the other sons of Jacob) are threatened by this possibility and by Shechem's intercourse with Dinah. They want to resist intermarriage. Their idea of "give and take" is "taking" the sword, killing all the Shechemite males, plundering the city, and taking their wives and children. The story passes "judgment" (the meaning of Dinah's name) on their friendly attitude.

The story invites two opposing interpretations.

The traditional understanding is that Dinah has been raped by Shechem. Her brothers Simeon and Levi retaliate by violently slaying and plundering Shechem, Hamor, and the Shechemite community. But the retaliation puts Jacob's group in jeopardy by making subsequent social intercourse and peaceful coexistence impossible. Jacob thus reprimands his sons for their behavior. But concerning the question of whether Dinah has been raped, the final clue comes in the last sentence of the story. Simeon and Levi say, "Should our sister be treated like a whore?" (34:31). Prostitutes engage in sexual intercourse for financial gain, and their sexual actions involve mutual consent. Rape therefore does *not* characterize either prostitution or what has happened to Dinah. Furthermore, one of the purposes of sexual intercourse in the ancient world was to create permanent bonding and obligation; but in prostitution, there is no bonding or obligation. By saying that Dinah has become like a prostitute, Simeon and Levi might be suggesting that, from their perspective, Dinah and Shechem's intercourse could never lead to bonding and obligation. They are not suggesting that she was raped.

Upon hearing the news about his daughter, Jacob is at first silent; then he negotiates Dinah's marriage to Shechem. If Dinah has been raped, Jacob ignores his obligation to protect the women of his household and ignores Dinah's suffering. This seems peculiar — does it suggest that Dinah was not raped? In the Hebrew Scriptures, rape is generally indicated by a cry for help from the woman (showing lack of consent) and violence on the part of the man (indicating a forcible, hostile act).

But the intercourse of Shechem does not fit this pattern. Genesis 34:2 reports that he sees Dinah, takes her (the Hebrew word for "take" is often used for taking a wife), lies with her (a euphemism for sexual intercourse), and shames her (the NRSV combines the last two verbs, rendering "lay with her by force," a reading that should be contested). Then the text (v. 3) provides three expressions of affection: first it says he bonds with her (the NRSV uses "was drawn" to her, but the word *bonds* more appropriately represents a word used for marital bonding), then that he loves her, and finally that

he speaks tenderly to her. From this description Shechem appears to be a man in love, not a man committing an exploitative act of rape. Rapists feel hostility and hatred toward their victims, not closeness and tenderness.

So why does the text include the verb *to shame* (or *to humble, put down*), and why does it record that Jacob's daughter has been "defiled" (34:5; compare 34:13, 27)? Shame, or intense humility, usually relates to failure to live up to societal goals and ideals. Because sexual intercourse should be part of marital bonding, it is shameful for an unmarried woman like Dinah to have sex. The declaration of love and desire for marriage comes after she and Shechem have intercourse. Furthermore, Dinah's intercourse with Shechem makes her "defiled," a term (Hebrew *ṭm'*) indicating here an unacceptable sexual act. The unacceptability of premarital sex in this case is intertwined with the response of Dinah's brothers, who insist that Shechem's requested marriage with her would be an unacceptable union.

Ironically, if there is a rape in this story, it is Simeon and Levi who "rape" the people of Shechem's city. It is their behavior that is violent, hostile, and exploitative. Shechem's desire for marital bonding stands in tension with Simeon and Levi's determination that no such liaison take place. The tension between marriage within a group (endogamy) and marriage with outsiders (exogamy) is dramatized in this story of love and violence. The premarital sexual act is the narrative's representation of the violation of group boundaries. Also, the fact that Shechem figures prominently first as a friend and then as a victim of Jacob's group may prefigure what another biblical narrative reports — that Shechem is peacefully incorporated into Israel but then is violently destroyed (see Judges 9).

LYN M. BECHTEL

SEE ALSO Part II: Daughters/Women of the Region; Daughters of the Jacob Group (Gen 34:1, etc.); Virgin (Exod 22:16–17, etc.); Daughters of the Inhabitants of the Land as Marriage Partners (Exod 34:16, etc.); Prostitute (Lev 19:29, etc.).

FOR FURTHER READING: Bechtel, Lyn. "What If Dinah Is Not Raped? (Genesis 34)."

Brueggemann, Walter. *Genesis.*

Sheres, Ita. *Dinah's Rebellion: A Biblical Parable for Our Times.*

Dinah in the Apocryphal/Deutero-canonical Books SEE JDT 9:2 Virgin Defiled (Part II).

Dorcas

Greek *dorkas,* "gazelle"

(Acts 9:36–42)

Dorcas was the Greek name of Tabitha, the disciple at Joppa who dies and is raised back to life by the apostle Peter.

LUCINDA A. BROWN

SEE ALSO Part I: Tabitha.

Drusilla

feminine diminutive form of Drusus, one of the elite Roman families of the *gens,* or clan, Livius; Latin

(Acts 24:24)

One of three members of the royal Herodian family who appear in the pages of Acts, and about whom we have external testimony, Drusilla was a child of Agrippa I (37–44 C.E.) and his first cousin, Cypros, along with her brother, Agrippa II (44–75? C.E.), and her sister, Bernice. The Herodians had complex ties with the imperial family in Rome, and Drusilla was apparently named after the sister of Caligula, emperor of Rome (37–40 C.E.).

According to the first-century C.E. Jewish historian Josephus, Drusilla's great beauty had a significant impact on her life. Her father, who died when she was about six, had arranged for her to marry Epiphanes, son of Antiochus IV of Commagene (on the Euphrates River), but he reneged, refusing to undergo circumcision and adopt Judaism. Subsequently, her brother, Agrippa II, arranged a marriage between Drusilla and Azizus, king of Emesa (also in Syria), who was willing to be circumcised, but the marriage was short-lived. Drusilla's appearance dazzled the Roman procurator of Judea, Felix, who sent an intermediary to persuade Drusilla to leave Azizus and marry him. Josephus claims that Drusilla had suffered so much from Bernice's jealousy of her beauty that she "was persuaded to transgress the ancestral law and to marry Felix" (*Antiquities,* book 20, section 143). Josephus appears to be suggesting that Drusilla married Felix while her first marriage was still legally valid, either because she instigated divorce proceedings against Azizus (something that Josephus elsewhere characterizes as against Jewish law) or perhaps because she simply left Azizus without any legal proceedings. Noting that Josephus accuses three of Agrippa's daughters of illicitly leaving their husbands, Ilan suggests that these stories may reflect anti-Agrippan polemic, while Macurdy remarks that Josephus's narratives about both Drusilla and her sister may reflect his own anger at Agrippa II and Bernice for their support of one of Josephus's major opponents.

None of this is apparent from Drusilla's brief appearance in Acts 24:24. In Acts 24, Felix holds several hearings on charges against Paul. In v. 24, Drusilla, described only as Felix's Jewish wife, is present when Felix sends for Paul and hears him preach Christ. Distressed by Paul's talk of future judgment, Felix terminates that meeting, but according to Acts 24:26, Paul and Felix have frequent subsequent conversations. Like other Roman officials in Acts, Felix is presented as sympathetic to Paul: that he leaves Paul in prison when his term as procurator ends is explained as a favor to the Jews.

What, if any, role Drusilla is represented as playing in all this is unclear. Throughout Acts, aristocratic, non-Christian women are repeatedly presented as sympathetic to early Christians, and its author seems concerned to cast both those women and Christian women themselves as conforming to ancient Roman conventions of gender. This may explain why both Drusilla and Bernice are depicted as largely ornamental and mute. Interestingly, in contrast to Acts 25:13–26:32, where Bernice is among those who find him blameless, Acts gives no hint of Drusilla's response to Paul. Conceivably, Drusilla's presence in Acts 24:24 is intended to explain why Felix wishes to do a favor for the Jews, but if so, the connection is not explicit.

ROSS S. KRAEMER

SEE ALSO Part I: Ber(e)nice.

FOR FURTHER READING: Ilan, Tal. *Jewish Women in Greco-Roman Palestine: An Inquiry into Image and Status.*

Macurdy, Grace. "Royal Women in Judea."

Edna

    "delight," from Hebrew *'ednâ,* "delight," and related to the name Eden

    (Tob 7:2–8, 13, 15–16; 8:11–12, 19, 21; 10:12–13; 14:13)

In the Book of Tobit, Edna is Raguel's wife, Sarah's mother, and the mother-in-law of Tobias, Tobit's son. Edna has no biblical namesake; unlike the other women named in Tobit (Anna, Deborah, Eve, Sarah), her name does not evoke images from the Hebrew Bible. Perhaps the author of Tobit means to recall Eden's idyllic existence, or, more likely, to convey by the name something about the type of woman, wife, and mother Edna is.

What makes Edna a "delight" may be her deportment within her family. One cannot help comparing Edna with Anna, the other matriarch in Tobit. Both women are devoted mothers and good wives, but unlike Anna, Edna never appears outside the home or argues with her husband. She does what her husband asks (Tob 7:13, 15; 8:12, 19) and seems to be always in accord with him. Raguel, in turn, treats her as his partner, not his servant (Tob 8:21). On her daughter's wedding night, Edna encourages Sarah (Tob 7:16), who has reason to be apprehensive (Tob 3:8). She welcomes Tobias, whom she has just met, into her family as a son (Tob 10:12). The author may want readers to see Edna as the ideal wife and mother and chooses her name as a hint to that effect.

Edna operates only within the home and almost exclusively in conjunction with her husband. Although the text mentions Raguel twice (Tob 3:7; 6:11) before Tobias and his companion arrive in Ecbatana, the reader first encounters Edna only when the guests come to her house (Tob 7:2). Whenever Edna appears in the story, she is usually either in the company of Raguel (Tob 7:8; 8:21; 14:13) or Sarah (Tob 7:16), or doing something Raguel has told her to do (Tob 7:13, 15; 8:12, 19).

However, there are unexpected, if small, challenges to the patriarchal view that Edna's subordination to her husband upholds. Edna, not Raguel, interviews their guests, even though Raguel is present (Tob 7:2–8). According to one manuscript tradition, she may also have actively participated in the signing of her daughter's marriage contract; the Greek says, *"they* set their seals to it" (Tob 7:13; emphasis added). This would give Edna a larger part in the proceedings than does the other manuscript tradition, in which she merely fetches the scroll for her husband. Finally, she blesses Tobias at the newlyweds' departure, performing a function rarely associated with biblical women (Tob 10:12).

If the meaning of Edna's name indeed reflects her character, then her charm stems from both the way she fits her patriarchally defined role and the way she gently nudges its limitations. Matriarch of a harmonious household, she is an agreeable but not silent partner for her husband, a loving and supportive mother, a warm mother-in-law, and a gracious host — all delightful aspects.

BEVERLY BOW

SEE ALSO Part I: Anna 1; Deborah 1; Sarah 2.

FOR FURTHER READING: Bow, Beverly, and George W. E. Nickelsburg, "Patriarchy with a Twist: Men and Women in Tobit."

Eglah

    "heifer," from Hebrew *'eglâ,* "heifer"

    (2 Sam 3:5; 1 Chr 3:3)

Eglah is King David's wife and the mother of Ithream. She is sixth on a list of six mother-son references concerning David's sons born at Hebron, the first capital of David's kingdom (2 Sam 3:2–5; 1 Chr 3:1–4). Of the six women, only Eglah is designated "wife of David." These six wives may have represented political alliances as the new king sought to solidify his power base among various tribal groups.

LINDA S. SCHEARING

SEE ALSO Part I: Abigail 1; Abital; Ahinoam 2; Bathsheba; Haggith; Maacah 2; Michal; Part II: Wives and Concubines of David, Taken in Jerusalem (2 Sam 5:13); Wives of David (2 Sam 12:11, etc.).

Elisheba

"God is an oath," from Hebrew *'ēl*, "God," and
šeba', "oath"
(Exod 6:23)

Daughter of Amminadab, sister of Nahson, Elisheba is the wife of the high priest Aaron and the mother of four sons, Nadab, Abihu, Eleazar, and Ithamar. She never appears in any story, and the mention of her name in this brief genealogy must be related to the purpose of this family listing. Such listings don't ordinarily include female ancestors. This genealogy foregrounds Moses and Aaron, and the addition of named women to their family tree — Moses' mother Jochebed as well as Elisheba — perhaps contributes to the prominence of their lineage. Moreover, the inclusion of a mother's name indicates how significant these women were to the destiny of their children.

TIKVA FRYMER-KENSKY

SEE ALSO Part I: Jochebed.

Elizabeth

Grecized form of the Hebrew name Elisheba
(Luke 1:5–80)

Luke chooses to begin his Gospel with the story of Elizabeth and Zechariah, an aged, married couple who become the parents of John the Baptist. Adept at infusing his literary creations with rich allusions to familiar themes from the Hebrew Bible, Luke relies heavily on the Abraham and Sarah traditions of Genesis 17–21 as the hermeneutic for understanding Elizabeth and Zechariah, whose story is unique to this Gospel.

Elizabeth is of priestly descent from the lineage of Aaron. Her lineage, although not required, would have made her marriage to the priest Zechariah all the more ideal. By their heredity and character, they are exemplary Jews: "both of them were righteous before God, living blamelessly according to all the commandments and regulations of the Lord" (Luke 1:6). But like Abraham and Sarah, Zechariah and Elizabeth are old and childless, specifically because Elizabeth carries the opprobrium of barrenness (Luke 1:25). Despite her upright life, her childlessness is a sign of God's punishment for sin or his "forgetting" of the woman (1 Sam 1:11). Socially, failure to bear children had grave consequences for women: disfavor with the husband and his family, possible occasion for divorce, embarrassment to the woman's father, contempt, shame, humiliation, and, on the barren woman's part, envy.

One day when Zechariah is in the temple, the angel Gabriel terrifies him by appearing to him. Gabriel announces that Elizabeth will conceive a son in her old age, as God's response to Zechariah's prayer. Awestruck, Zechariah responds with doubt. Impatient, Gabriel censures the old priest, declaring that he will be mute until the child's birth.

Zechariah's shameful display of doubt only highlights Elizabeth's strong faith. Although, according to Seim, the narrative begins as an annunciation with a "patriarchal slant," it later focuses clearly on Elizabeth as Zechariah's role recedes. Since Gabriel does not pay her a visit, occasion for her to express any initial disbelief is avoided. Luke simply relates that when Elizabeth conceives, she secludes herself for five months. Given her responses to God, Elizabeth's name would most likely be translated "God is good fortune" in the Gospel.

The Sarah story acts as a hermeneutic, Luke's way of theologically "correcting" the Genesis account. In Gen 18:9–12, Sarah overhears the LORD, in the guise of three male visitors, discussing the promise of her conception. Sarah, who may well have not recognized the men's identity, laughs in response. Later, fearful of God, she denies having done so. The Genesis text (18:15) is genuinely ambiguous as to whether God speaks to Sarah directly. Nevertheless, God's promise comes true in the birth of Isaac. In contrast, Elizabeth immediately responds positively in Luke 1:25: "This is what the Lord has done for me when he looked favorably on me and took away the disgrace I have endured among my people." In a series of events that theologically supersede one another, showing the unfolding of God's blessing over the course of biblical history from Abraham onward, Luke gives Elizabeth, and then Mary, stronger and more central roles in the divine plan of salvation.

Elizabeth's joy at her pregnancy sets the stage for the next section: Gabriel's annunciation to another woman, a betrothed virgin, Mary, who lives in Nazareth. At first these two stories seem unrelated, but at the end of the angel's visit, Luke masterfully weaves them together. Gabriel proclaims to Mary the miracle of Elizabeth's pregnancy as a proof of God's great works now at hand. The angel's promise of Mary's own conception by the Holy Spirit is simply an even greater miracle than Sarah's and Elizabeth's. Finally, in a brilliant literary coup, Luke has Gabriel refer to Elizabeth as Mary's "relative." This statement, about a woman Mary knows, would help her trust the angel's news. Thus Luke intertwines the fates of Elizabeth and Mary and their sons, allowing the two women to share friendship and mutual support. The reader has a rare glimpse of two Jewish women in the first century C.E., both miraculously pregnant, related to each other, living together for three months. It also sets up the theological subordination of Isaac and John to Jesus in Luke's work as a whole. Finally, it implies that Mary and Jesus may be of priestly descent.

Mary does pay a visit to Elizabeth. Filled with the Holy Spirit, Elizabeth greets Mary with a loud blessing, exclaiming that she is the mother of Elizabeth's Lord. Thus the first Christological confession of the Gospel is in a woman's voice. All this serves to confirm Mary's decision to submit to God's plan. Significantly, unborn John leaps at Mary's presence. Only in the unborn state do John and Jesus meet in this Gospel.

VASILIKI LIMBERIS

SEE ALSO Part I: Mary 1; Sarah 1/Sarai.
FOR FURTHER READING: Schaberg, Jane. "Luke."

Seim, Turid Karlsen. *The Double Message: Patterns of Gender in Luke-Acts.*
————. "The Gospel of Luke."

Ephah

meaning uncertain; perhaps "darkness," from the Hebrew root *'wp,* "to be dark"; or possibly the name of a tree, as Arabic *ġâfah*
(1 Chr 2:46)

One of the two concubines of Caleb (who was himself a descendant of Judah), Ephah bears Haran, Moza, and Gazez. The text lists a son of Haran named Gazez, but it is not clear who his mother was. The genealogy in Chronicles follows the Calebite family through several wives and two concubines, an indication of the family's prominence within the tribe of Judah in the Hebron district.

ALICE L. LAFFEY

SEE ALSO Part I: Azubah 2; Ephrath/Ephrathah; Jerioth; Maacah 5.

Ephrath/Ephrathah

meaning uncertain; perhaps "fruitful," from Hebrew *prh,* "to bear fruit"
(1 Chr 2:19, 50; 4:4)

According to the tribal genealogies in 1 Chronicles, Ephrath (variant name, Ephrathah) marries Caleb after the death of his wife Azubah. Ephrath's firstborn son, Hur, is the ancestor of an important group of Judeans living in the vicinity of Bethlehem. Some texts (for example, Ruth 1:2) call that group Ephrathites, thereby making Ephrath the matriarch of a lineage that includes King David.

ALICE L. LAFFEY

SEE ALSO Part I: Azubah 2; Ephah; Jerioth; Maacah 5.

Esther

"star," from Persian *stâra,* "star"; sometimes connected with the Babylonian goddess Ishtar; alternative name: Hadassah

Cylindrical ivory perfume bottle with a long narrow neck ending in a female head, on top of which is a spoon; from a thirteenth-century B.C.E. Canaanite temple at Lachish, in southern Israel. Tilting the bottle allowed a few drops of perfume to drip into the spoon, ready for use. Perfumes were a precious commodity, and expensive containers were fashioned for them. See Esther; Daughters as Perfumers, Cooks, and Bakers (1 Sam 8:13).

ESTHER IN THE HEBREW BIBLE
(Book of Esther)

The heroine of the book named for her, Esther is a young Jewish woman living in exile in the Persian diaspora, who through her youth and beauty becomes queen of the Persian Empire, and then by her wits and courage saves the Jewish people from destruction. The message of the Book of Esther, a work of historical fiction written in the diaspora in the late Persian–early Hellenistic period (fourth century B.C.E.), gives encouragement to the exiled Jews that they, although powerless in the Persian Empire, can, by their resourcefulness and talents, not only survive but prosper, as does Esther.

Esther first appears in the story as one of the young virgins collected into the king's harem as possible replacements for Vashti, the banished wife of King Ahasuerus (Xerxes I, reigned 485–465 B.C.E.). She is identified as the daughter of Abihail (Esth 2:15) and the cousin and adopted daughter of Mordecai, from the tribe of Benjamin (Esth 2:5–7). Not much is revealed about her character, but she is described as beautiful (2:7) and obedient (2:10), and she appears to be pliant and cooperative. She quickly wins the favor of the chief eunuch, Hegai, and, when her turn comes to spend the night with the king, Ahasuerus falls in love with her and makes her his queen. All this takes place while Esther keeps her Jewish identity secret (Esth 2:10, 20).

After Esther becomes queen, her cousin Mordecai becomes involved in a power struggle with the grand vizier Haman the Agagite, a descendant of an Amalekite king who was an enemy of Israel during the time of King Saul (1 Sam 15:32). Mordecai refuses to bow before Haman, and this so infuriates Haman that he resolves not only to put Mordecai to death, but also to slaughter his entire people. He secures the king's permission to do this, and a date is set, Adar 13 (this episode determines the date of the festival of Purim, a popular Jewish festival). When Mordecai learns of Haman's plot, he rushes to the palace to inform Esther, weeping and clothed in sackcloth (Esth 4:1–3).

At this point in the story, Esther's character comes to the fore. When she first learns of Haman's plot and the threat to the Jews, her reaction is one of helplessness. She cannot approach the king without being summoned, on pain of death, and the king has not summoned her in thirty days, implying that she has fallen out of favor (Esth 4:11). However, following Mordecai's insistent prodding, she resolves to do what she can to save her people, ending with the ringing declaration "After that I will go to the king, though it is against the law; and if I perish, I perish" (Esth 4:16). The pliant and obedient Esther has become a woman of action.

She appears unsummoned before King Ahasuerus, who not only does not kill her, but promises to grant her request (the text here, as throughout, does not mention God, but God's providence is clearly in the background). In a superb moment of understatement, Esther asks the king to a dinner party (Esth 5:4)! The king, accompanied by Haman, attends Esther's banquet and again seeks to discover her request, which she once more deflects with an invitation to another dinner party. Only at the second dinner party, when the king is sufficiently beguiled by her charms, does she reveal her true purpose: the unmasking of Haman and his plot. She reveals, for the first time, her identity as a Jew and accuses Haman of the plot to destroy her and her people. The volatile king springs to the defense of the woman to whom he was indifferent three days earlier, Haman is executed, and the Jews receive permission to defend themselves from their enemies, which they do with great success (Esther 7–9). The book ends with Mordecai elevated to the office of grand vizier and power now concentrated in the hands of Esther.

Esther and her book have suffered much at the hands of interpreters through the centuries. Although very popular among the Jewish people, it was one of the last books to be accepted into the canon, and was accepted only because of its connection with the festival of Purim. The book has been taken to task for irreligiosity: God is not mentioned, and the only Jewish religious practice referred to is fasting (Esth 4:16). The rabbis were troubled by Esther's failure to live as a Jew: she has sexual intercourse with and marries a Gentile, lives in the Persian court, and does not follow Jewish dietary laws (the Septuagint, the Greek translation of the Hebrew Bible, tries to remedy this by adding prayers and repeatedly invoking God, as well as having Esther declare that she loathes her present lifestyle). In addition, Esther has been taken to task by both female and male commentators for her apparent willingness to participate in Persian harem customs, and by Christian commentators for

her evident bloodthirstiness in destroying Gentiles (Esth 9:1–15). All these criticisms, however, fail to grasp the true purpose of the book.

The purpose of the Book of Esther is to demonstrate to Jews living in exile that it is possible to achieve success in the country of one's exile without giving up one's identity as a Jew. In this, the Book of Esther is similar to books such as Daniel or Tobit, or, in fact, to the historical character Nehemiah. However, the Book of Esther is unique in two important respects. First, the protagonist of the book, and the one with whom the audience should identify, is a woman, Esther (Mordecai is, of course, the other leading character and finishes the story at a very high rank, but this is basically because of his relationship to, and through the efforts of, Esther). This choice of a female hero serves an important function in the story. Women were, in the world of the Persian diaspora, as in many other cultures, essentially powerless and marginalized members of society. Even if they belonged to the dominant culture, they could not simply reach out and grasp power, as a man could; whatever power they could obtain was earned through the manipulation of the public holders of power, men. In this sense the exiled Jew could identify with the woman: he or she too was essentially powerless and marginalized, and power could be obtained only through one's wits and talents. But, as the actions of Esther demonstrate, this can be done. By astutely using her beauty, charm, and political intelligence, and by taking one well-placed risk, Esther saves her people, brings about the downfall of their enemy, and elevates her kinsman to the highest position in the kingdom. Esther becomes the model for the Jew living in exile.

The second unique aspect of the Hebrew Book of Esther is the absence of any overt religious element. (God is not mentioned in the book. There are no religious practices observed, with the minor exception of fasting.) Many commentators have argued that religious beliefs, such as a belief in God's protection of the chosen people, are present (Esth 4:14). This argument may be valid; however, it remains true that the presence of God is conspicuously absent. Jewish identity seems to be primarily ethnic, not religious. It is who Esther is that makes her Jewish, rather than what she practices or believes. This indicates that the audience for the book was primarily in the diaspora, where certain religious practices, such as worship in the temple, were simply not possible, and Jewish ethnic identity was in danger of disappearing in the great melting pot of the ancient Near East. The Book of Esther shows that this does not have to happen; in fact, Jews can thrive as Jews (although the danger they may live in is also clearly acknowledged).

The character of Esther serves as a positive role model for Jewish women and men living in diaspora, both in the time the book was written and down through the centuries to the present day. The contemporaneity of the message helps to account for the enduring popularity of the book, and Esther herself, in the Jewish community.

SIDNIE WHITE CRAWFORD

SEE ALSO Part I: Hadassah; Vashti; Part II: Young Virgins/Women (Esth 2:2–3, etc.); Mother of Esther (Esth 2:7); Maids of Esther (Esth 2:9, etc.).

FOR FURTHER READING: Levenson, Jon D. *Esther.*
Moore, Carey A. *Esther.*
White, Sidnie A. "Esther."
———. "Esther: A Feminine Model for Jewish Diaspora."

ESTHER IN THE APOCRYPHAL/
DEUTEROCANONICAL BOOKS

(Greek Additions to Esther)

The Greek version of the Hebrew Bible Book of Esther is designated Additions to Esther and preserves many details of the Hebrew account. Its portrayal of Esther herself, however, is appreciably different, primarily because of Additions C and D (Add Esth 13:8–14:19; 15:1–16). The Additions to Esther consist of six extended passages (107 verses) that have no counterpart in the Hebrew version. They are numbered as chaps 11–16, designated A–F, and added to the Hebrew text at various places. Another important "addition" to Greek Esther is the mention of God's name over fifty times. This has the effect of making the story explicitly relig-

ious, in sharp contrast to the Hebrew text, which does not mention God at all. The Additions, which probably were not composed at the same time by the same person, can be dated to the second or first centuries B.C.E. because of their literary style, theology, and anti-gentile spirit.

After the death of her parents, Esther, daughter of Aminadab (Add Esth 2:7, 15; 9:29; not Abihail, as in the Hebrew Esth 2:15), is raised by her cousin, Mordecai, son of Aminadab's brother. Like many beautiful virgins throughout the Persian Empire (Add Esth 2:7), Esther is compelled, by the officials conducting the search for a new queen, to go to Susa to compete for the queenship (Add Esth 2:8).

With the other virginal contestants, Esther undergoes an elaborate year-long beauty treatment (Add Esth 2:12), designed to make a candidate for the queenship as desirable as possible. Even though Esther is given preferential treatment by the eunuch in charge, including the promptest service, special cuisine, the finest perfumes, seven choice maids, not to mention his good advice (Add Esth 2:9), she is wretchedly unhappy from the time of her arrival through the next five years of her marriage (Add Esth 2:16; 3:7). Her wretchedness, described in detail in Addition C (Add Esth 14:15–18), is not even hinted at in the Hebrew account.

Addition C corrects all the "flaws" in the Hebrew version of Esther, which was rejected as authoritative by some Jews even as late as the third century C.E. and was one of the last books to enter the Jewish canon, presumably because of its "inexcusable" omissions. In Addition C, Esther prays to "the Lord God of Israel" (Add Esth 14:3), mentions Israel's "everlasting inheritance" (Add Esth 14:5) and God's holy altar and house in Jerusalem (Add Esth 14:9), and strictly observes dietary laws (Add Esth 14:17). Moreover, Esther confesses her hatred for every alien, the pomp and ceremony of her office, and her abhorrence at being married to a Gentile (Add Esth 14:15–16). Despite her regal environment, Esther does not partake of nonkoshered food or wine dedicated to idols (Add Esth 14:17). Later Jewish commentators credit her with eating only kosher food and faithfully observing the Sabbath

(*Megillah* 13a). The rabbis, however, go even further than the Greek version, claiming that Esther is one of the four most beautiful women in the world (*Megillah* 15a) and one of only seven female prophets of the Bible (*Megillah* 14b).

When Esther is finished praying and fasting, she dresses in her finest and, with two maids, approaches the king's throne unsummoned. What is described by three verses in the Hebrew (Esth 5:1–3) requires sixteen verses in Addition D (Add Esth 15:1–16). Unlike the Hebrew account, here Esther is "frozen with fear" (Add Esth 15:5) and finds the king so terrifying that she falters, turns pales, and collapses on her maid (Add Esth 15:7). Comforted by the king, who sweeps her up in his arms, Esther says to him, "I saw you, my lord, like an angel of God, and my heart was shaken with fear at your glory" (Add Esth 15:13). And then she faints again (Add Esth 15:15).

This high drama in the Greek finds no parallel in the Hebrew, where Esther simply appears and is immediately and favorably received. But the truly great difference in the Greek is that "Then God changed the spirit of the king [from "fierce anger" in 15:7] to gentleness, and in alarm he sprang from his throne and took her in his arms until she came to herself. He comforted her with soothing words" (Add Esth 15:8). *This* is the high point in the Greek version, in contrast to Hebrew Esther 9, where the establishment of the festival of Purim represents the book's climax. In the Greek version, God, not Queen Esther, is the "hero"! In other words, just as Queen Vashti was demoted by the king, so Queen Esther is, in effect, demoted by Addition D. In the Greek Additions, Esther is a negative stereotype of female weakness and helplessness, although her fainting spells, like her feminine allure, serve to change the king's mind and lead to the defeat of the enemy.

CAREY A. MOORE

SEE ALSO Part II: Maids of Esther (Add Esth 2:9, etc.).

FOR FURTHER READING: Crawford, Sidnie A. White. "Esther."

Moore, Carey A. "Esther, Additions to."

———. "Esther, Book of."

Reinhartz, Adele. "The Greek Book of Esther."

Eunice

Greek *eunikē*, "good [or happy] victory"
(2 Tim 1:15)

A co-missionary of Paul's called Timothy is well known from the undisputed letters of Paul, which provide no biographical information about him. According to Acts 16:1–3, however, Timothy was the uncircumcised son of a Jewish mother, who was herself a "believer" (*pistēs*), and a gentile father. The author of the second letter to Timothy, writing in the name of Paul perhaps as late as the mid–second century C.E., identifies Timothy's mother as a woman named Eunice and his grandmother as one Lois, both of whom are now said to have been believers in Christ. That this information appears only in the relatively late and pseudonymous 2 Timothy suggests that its historical value is questionable. The addition of a pious grandmother to Timothy's lineage and the assignment of names to these women probably point to a tendency to provide additional material about venerated figures, including proper names for persons previously anonymous. The first-century C.E. pseudonymous work, the *Biblical Antiquities* of Pseudo-Philo, provides numerous examples of this phenomenon, including the provision of names for Jephthah's unnamed daughter (Judg 11:29–40) and the judge Samson's unnamed mother in Judges 13.

The oblique allusion in 3:15 to "how from childhood you have known the sacred writings that are able to instruct you for salvation through faith in Christ Jesus" is often understood to mean that the two women were responsible for Timothy's childhood education, thus presenting us with an image of Jewish women knowledgeable in sacred Scriptures. If 2 Timothy is the work of a Christian author in the second century C.E., however, this allusion may say more about the education of Christian women than of contemporaneous Jewish women, if it says anything reliable about actual social practices.

Although the author presents Eunice and Lois in a most favorable light, the author's approval of these women may be closely related to his representation of them as devout mothers who, perhaps, diligently educate their children within the confines of the home. They may be implicitly contrasted with the "little women" (NRSV, "silly women") of 2 Tim 3:6 who are easily deceived by false teachers, and the depiction of Eunice and Lois should be understood within the broader context of the same author's instructions about appropriate and inappropriate behavior for women: 1 Tim 2:9–14 (the author forbids women to teach or have authority over men — presumably the instruction of children is not intended by this prohibition), 3:11 (on women deacons), and 5:2–6 (on widows).

ROSS S. KRAEMER

SEE ALSO Part I: Lois; Part II: Mother of Timothy (Acts 16:1); Women Who Profess Reverence for God (1 Tim 2:9–15); Women Deacons (1 Tim 3:11); Older and Younger Women (1 Tim 5:2).

FOR FURTHER READING: Freund, Richard A. "Naming Names: Some Observations on 'Nameless Women': Traditions in the MT, LXX and Hellenistic Literature."

Metzger, Bruce M. "Names for the Nameless in the New Testament: A Study in the Growth of Christian Tradition."

Euodia

"success, prosperity," from Greek *euodoō*, "help," or, in the passive, "succeed"

(Phil 4:2–3)

Euodia was a coworker of both Paul and another woman named Syntyche; they are described in 4:3 as "having struggled beside me . . . with Clement and the rest of my coworkers." The athletic image ("struggled" or "co-contested") portrays their earlier missionary endeavors with Paul in a heroic vein. Because of their importance in founding the church at Philippi, one or the other was sometimes identified with Lydia (reinterpreted as "the Lydian"; Acts 16:11–15). Other interpreters have treated them as symbols of Jewish and Gentile communities rather than real women leaders.

In Phil 4:2, Paul formally appeals to the two women "to be of the same mind in the Lord"; the usual interpretation depicts the two women in conflict with each other, and, because of their status as leaders in the community, causing dissension in the

community in Philippi. But when Paul asks the Corinthians to be of the same mind, he means the same mind with him (1:10; compare 4:14–21). The estrangement may thus have been between the two women and Paul; his complaints about preachers who proclaim Christ out of rivalry (1:15) and his elaborate appeal for agreement (2:1–11) and obedience (2:12) may have been directed to or against them.

Euodia and Syntyche may have functioned as a missionary couple; Romans 16 includes a pair of missionary women, Tryphaena and Tryphosa (16:12), as well as female-male pairs (16:3–5, 7, 16), whose partnerships may reflect commitments to each other as well as to the mission. Perhaps Euodia and Syntyche belong on a "lesbian continuum," a prehistory of women's same-sex commitments.

MARY ROSE D'ANGELO

SEE ALSO Part I: Martha; Mary 2; Syntyche; Tryphaena; Tryphosa.

FOR FURTHER READING: D'Angelo, Mary Rose. "Women Partners in the New Testament."

Gillman, Florence Morgan. "Euodia."

Eve

"living, life giver," from the Hebrew root *ḥyh*, "to live"; or from another Semitic root, *ḥwy*, also meaning "to live"

EVE IN THE HEBREW BIBLE

(Gen 2–3; 4:1–2)

The first woman, according to the biblical creation story in Genesis 2–3, Eve is perhaps the best-known female figure in the Hebrew Bible. Her prominence comes not only from her role in the Garden of Eden story itself, but also from her frequent appearance in Western art, theology, and literature. Indeed, the image of Eve, who never appears in the Hebrew Bible after the opening chapters of Genesis, may be more strongly colored by postbiblical culture than by the biblical narrative itself. For many, Eve represents sin, seduction, and the secondary nature of woman. Because such aspects of her character are not actually part of the Hebrew narrative of Genesis, but have become associated with her through Jewish and Christian interpretive traditions, a discussion of Eve means first pointing out some of those views that are not intrinsic to the ancient Hebrew tale.

Although Eve is linked with the beginnings of sin in the earliest mentions of her outside the Hebrew Bible — in the Jewish noncanonical Book of Sirach, as well as in the New Testament and in other early Jewish and Christian works — she is not called a sinner in the Genesis 2–3 account. To be sure, she and Adam disobey God; but the word *sin* does not appear in the Hebrew Bible until the Cain-Abel narrative, where it explicitly refers to the ultimate social crime, fratricide. Another misconception is that Eve tempts or seduces Adam. In reality she merely takes a piece of fruit — not an apple — and hands it to him; they both had been told not to eat of it, yet they both do. Also, the story is often thought to involve God's cursing of Eve (and Adam), yet the text speaks only of cursing the serpent and the ground. And the Eden tale is frequently referred to as the "Fall" or "Fall of Man," although there is no fall in the narrative; that designation is a later Christian application of Plato's idea (in the *Phaedrus*) of the fall of heavenly beings to earth in order to express the idea of departure from divine favor or grace.

Such views are entrenched in Western notions of Eden, making it difficult to see features of Eve and her role that form part of the Hebrew tale. These features have been largely unnoticed or ignored by the interpretive tradition. This situation, and also the way in which the Genesis 2–3 story appears to sanction patriarchal notions of male dominance, has made a reconsideration of the Eden tale an important project of feminist biblical study ever since the first wave of feminist interest in biblical exegesis, which was part of the nineteenth-century suffrage movement in the United States. Contemporary feminist biblical study for the most part, but not entirely, has tended to remove negative theological overlay, to recapture positive aspects of Eve's role, and generally to understand how this famous beginnings account might have functioned in Isra-

elite culture. The literature dealing with Eve and her story is voluminous, and only a sample of the new perspectives can be discussed here.

The well-known Eden tale begins with the scene of a well-watered garden — so unlike the frequently drought-stricken highlands of the land of Canaan in which the Israelites lived. God has placed there an 'ādām, a person formed from the "dust of the ground ['ădāmâ]" (2:7). This wordplay evokes the notion of human beings as earth creatures. The traditional translation of 'ādām as "man" (NRSV and most English versions) at the beginning of the Eden story can be contested. The Hebrew word 'ādām can indeed mean a male and even be the proper name Adam; but it can also be a generic term for a mortal, or a human being. Such may be the case here, according to some current feminist readings of biblical inclusive language as well as some medieval Jewish commentaries, thus implying that the original human was androgynous and that God had to divide it into two gendered beings in order for procreation and continued human life to begin.

God tells this first being that anything in the garden may be eaten except for the fruit of a certain tree. God then decides that this person should not be alone and tries animals as companions. Creating animals serves to populate the world with living creatures but doesn't quite meet God's intentions. God then performs cosmic surgery on the first person, removing one "side" (NRSV, "rib"; 2:21) to form a second person. The essential unity of these first two humans is expressed in the well-known words (Gen 2:23) "bone of my bones / and flesh of my flesh," which the "Man" (Hebrew 'îš) says to the "Woman" (Hebrew 'iššâ). This unity is reenacted in copulation, indicating the strength of the marital bond over the natal one: "therefore a man leaves his father and his mother and clings to his wife, and they become one flesh" (2:24). The relationship between this first pair of humans is also expressed by the term 'ēzer kĕnegdô, translated "helper as his partner" by the NRSV and "helpmeet" or "helpmate" in older English versions (2:18). This unusual phrase probably indicates mutuality. The noun *helper* can mean either "an assistant" (subordinate) or "an expert" (superior); but the modifying prepositional phrase, used only here in the Bible, apparently means "equal to." The phrase, which might be translated literally as "an equal helper," indicates that no hierarchical relationship exists between the primordial pair.

The serpent now enters the scene. An intelligent being, it begins a dialogue with the woman, who is thus the first human to engage in conversation (a reflection perhaps of female skill with words?). The woman is the one who appreciates the aesthetic and nutritional qualities of the forbidden tree and its fruit, as well as its potential "to make one wise" (3:6). The woman and the man both eat and ultimately are expelled from Eden for their misdeed, lest they eat of the tree of life and gain immortality along with their wisdom. Eating of the forbidden fruit has made them like God, able to know, perceive, and understand "good and bad" (3:22) — meaning everything. But they must never eat of the life tree and gain immortality too.

The riveting and controversial story of human origins can best be understood as portraying archetypal human qualities, whereby the first humans represent all humans. The woman's name is Eve, which apparently is derived from a root meaning "to live." The introduction of her name is followed by a folk etymology; she is "mother of all living" (3:20). Her name is rich in symbolism, characterizing her archetypal role — as the first woman, Eve represents the essential life-giving maternal function of all women. Eve is also the one who provides the first morsel of food, in a narrative in which the words for "food" and "eat" (from the same Hebrew root, *'cl*) appear repeatedly. The repetition of such words in the story of human origins reflects the Israelite concern with sustenance in the difficult environment of the Canaanite highlands. Eve's action in handing the man some fruit may thus derive from the reality of women's roles in food preparation rather than from a depiction of temptation or seduction.

The Eden story also serves etiological purposes. It helped ancient Israelites deal with the harsh reali-

ties of daily existence, especially in contrast with life in the more fertile and better watered areas of the ancient Near East, by providing an "explanation" for their difficult life conditions. The punitive statements addressed to the first couple prior to the expulsion from the garden depict the realities they will face. Men (Gen 3:17–19) will experience unending toil (*'iṣṣābôn*) in order to grow crops from ground that is "cursed." And women?

This brings us to perhaps the most difficult verse in the Hebrew Bible for people concerned with human equality. Gen 3:16 seems to give men the right to dominate women. Feminists have grappled with this text in a variety of ways. One possibility is to recognize that the traditional translations have distorted its meaning and that it is best read against its social background of agrarian life. Instead of the familiar "I will greatly increase your pangs in childbearing," the verse should begin "I will greatly increase your work and your pregnancies." The word for "work," *'iṣṣābôn,* is the same word used in God's statement to the man; the usual translation ("pangs" or "pain") is far less accurate. In addition, the woman will experience more pregnancies; the Hebrew word is *pregnancy,* not *childbearing,* as the NRSV and other versions have it. Women, in other words, must have large families and also work hard, which is what the next clause also proclaims. The verse is a mandate for intense productive and reproductive roles for women; it sanctions what life meant for Israelite women.

In light of this, the notion of general male dominance in the second half of the verse is a distortion. More likely, the idea of male "rule" is related to the multiple pregnancies mentioned in the first half of the verse. Women might resist repeated pregnancies because of the dangers of death in childbirth, but because of their sexual passion ("desire," 3:16) they accede to their husbands' sexuality. Male rule in this verse is narrowly drawn, relating only to sexuality; male interpretive traditions have extended that idea by claiming that it means general male dominance.

Eve does not disappear from the biblical story at the expulsion from the garden. In a little-noticed introduction (4:1–2a) to the ensuing Cain and Abel narrative, Eve is said to have "created a man together with the LORD." The NRSV translation — "produced a man with the help of the LORD" — obscures highly unusual language. The word for "create" is the same as the word used in the Bible for the creative power of God (Gen 14:19, 22) and in extrabiblical texts for the creativity of Semitic mother goddesses. Women in the Bible are said to "bear children," not "create a man"; and creating a man "with" God puts female creative power alongside that of God. This view of the woman as the source of life, together with the more conventional notice of the birth of her second son, Abel (Gen 4:2a), is the last direct reference to Eve in the Hebrew Bible (although she is mentioned indirectly in Gen 4:25, where she gives birth to Seth). It follows the scene in which Adam names her, presumably signifying his power over her. Is that a male narrator's attempt to compensate for the awesomeness of female creativity, akin to God's?

CAROL MEYERS

SEE ALSO Part II: Woman (and Man) in the First Creation Story (Gen 1:26–28, etc.); Part III: Lilith.

FOR FURTHER READING: Bal, Mieke. "Sexuality, Sin, and Sorrow: The Emergence of the Female Character."

Bellis, Alice Ogden. "The Story of Eve."

Clines, David J. A. "What Does Eve Do to Help? And Other Irredeemably Androcentric Orientations in Genesis 1–3."

Layton, Scott C. "Remarks on the Canaanite Origin of Eve."

Meyers, Carol. *Discovering Eve: Ancient Israelite Women in Context.*

Morris, Paul, and Deborah Sawyer, eds. *A Walk in the Garden: Biblical, Iconographical, and Literary Images of Eden.*

Pardes, Ilana. "Creation According to Eve."

———. "Beyond Genesis 3: The Politics of Maternal Naming."

Trible, Phyllis. "A Love Story Gone Awry."

EVE IN THE APOCRYPHAL/DEUTEROCANONICAL BOOKS

(Tob 8:6; Sir 25:24, 40:1, 42:13; 4 Macc 18:7)

Eve, the first woman according to the Eden story (Genesis 2–3), is mentioned very rarely in the Apocryphal/Deuterocanonical Books. One text mentions her by name (Tob 8:6), and four others allude to her (Sir 25:24; 40:1; 42:13; 4 Macc 18:7). Only Sirach (also known as Ecclesiasticus or Ben Sira) presents the negative theological judgment that women are the source of sin.

The Book of Tobit tells the story of two families who have experienced various misfortunes. Through the marriage of Tobias, son of a father who has been blinded, and Sarah, whose first seven husbands have died on the wedding night, the two families come together and are blessed. Before Tobias and Sarah consummate their marriage, they pray (in Tob 8:5a, both pray; in Tob 8:5b, only Tobias speaks). This prayer contains one of only two named references to both Eve and Adam outside Genesis in the Hebrew Bible (the other mention of both occurs in 1 Tim 2:13). Echoing and quoting Gen 2:18, Tobias says, "You made Adam, and for him you made his wife Eve / as a helper and support. / From the two of them the human race has sprung. / You said, 'It is not good that the man should be alone; / let us make a helper for him like himself.' I now am taking this kinswoman of mine, / not because of lust, but with sincerity. / Grant that she and I may find mercy / and that we may grow old together" (Tob 8:6–7). When the prayer is finished, they both say, "Amen, Amen" (Tob 8:8). As in Genesis, the word *helper* likely signals mutuality. Tobias's addition of the word *support* further indicates his understanding of gender relations, as does his statement that *he* takes this woman. Man (not a generic human being) was created first in this interpretation, and the family is unquestionably patriarchal.

The other possible references to Eve in the Apocryphal/Deuterocanonical Books do not refer to her by name. The most well known is in the Book of Sirach, which reads: "From a woman sin had its beginning, / and because of her we all die" (Sir 25:24). The context of this verse is a longer passage about good and evil wives (Sir 25:13–26:18). It reviles a wicked wife and reveals a very negative view of women. If Sir 25:24 is understood as a reference to Eve, it is related to the material that precedes and follows as a generalized association of evil with women and the legitimation of harsh treatment of a disobedient wife.

Although Sirach does not name Eve, interpreters have often held that the author is referring to the Garden of Eden story (Genesis 2–3). If this view is correct, then Sir 25:24 is the earliest attribution of the origin of sin to Eve. Later developments of this idea can be found in several pseudepigraphical works (noncanonical Jewish documents that were influential in popular religious circles, especially Christian ones): the Books of Adam and Eve (chaps. 3, 5, 16, 18), the Apocalypse of Moses (24:1–3), 2 Enoch (30:16–18; 31:6), and Targum Pseudo-Jonathan.

Attribution of the origin of sin to Eve was not typical of Jewish interpretation at the time Sirach was written (second century B.C.E.). The common view was that sin had its beginning in the cohabitation of evil angels with human women described in Gen 6:1–4 (see the pseudepigraphical books of 1 Enoch 6:1–6; 7:1–6; 15:2–16; Jubilees 5:1–6; 10:1, 5–9, 11; the Cairo Damascus Document 11:16–18). Later, the rabbis usually traced the origin of sin and death to Adam rather than to Eve. If Ben Sira is referring to Eve in Sir 25:24, then he held an uncommon view for his time.

It is possible that Sir 25:24 does not refer to Eve, but to the evil wife who is the subject of the passage. She (and collectively all bad wives) causes her husband to sin and thus brings death to her unfortunate husband, who may have been understood as all (or almost all) men. This view is more consistent with Ben Sira's remarks on this subject found elsewhere in Sirach, with the immediate context in Sirach 25, and with the common view of the time. It is also possible that Ben Sira intended the reader to understand the primary reference as evil wives, but nevertheless was making a veiled allusion to the Genesis story of the garden.

Sir 40:1 includes another phrase that sounds like a reference to Eve: "Hard work was created for everyone, / and a heavy yoke is laid on the children of Adam, / from the day they come forth from their mother's womb / until the day they return to the mother of all the living." In Gen 3:20, Eve is called the "mother of all living" because the Hebrew word ḥawwâ is related to the Hebrew word for "life." In Sirach, however, it is clear that the womb from which new life emerges and to which all return is Mother Earth. As in Job 1:21, earth is both womb and tomb. The phrase "the living" in Sir 40:1 may be an addition, since it appears in the Hebrew but not the Greek. If these words are removed, then this is likely not an allusion to Eve.

A clear, though indirect, allusion to Eve is found in 4 Macc 18:7. In this verse a righteous woman says, "I was a pure virgin and did not go outside my father's house; but I guarded the rib from which woman was made." The reference is to Gen 2:22. The following verse offers further clarification when the woman declares "no seducer corrupted me on a desert plain, nor did the destroyer, the deceitful serpent, defile the purity of my virginity" (4 Macc 18:8). Her words embody the ancient Jewish belief that women were in danger of seduction by evil spirits (Genesis 6; Jubilees 4, 5; Enoch 6; Testament of Reuben 5:6) who were thought to inhabit deserts. The descendants of the first union of human women and spirits (Genesis 6), the giants known as Nephilim, became demons who corrupt humanity (Jubilees 7:27) and seduce women (Enoch 15). The reference to "the destroyer, the deceitful serpent" suggests the serpent of the Garden of Eden, whose allure is here understood to have been sexual.

ALICE OGDEN BELLIS

SEE ALSO Part II: Wife (Sir 7:19, etc.); Woman as Evil (Sir 9:2, etc.).

FOR FURTHER READING: Collins, John J. *Jewish Wisdom in the Hellenistic Age.*

Freedman, R. David. "Woman, a Power Equal to Man: Translation of Woman as a 'Fit Helpmate' for Man Is Questioned."

Kvam, Kristen E., Linda S. Schearing, and Valarie H. Ziegler, eds. *Eve and Adam: Jewish, Christian, and Muslim Readings on Genesis and Gender.*

Levison, Jack. "Is Eve to Blame? A Contextual Analysis of Sirach 25:24."

Phillips, John A. *Eve: The History of an Idea.*

Trenchard, Warren C. *Ben Sira's View of Women: A Literary Analysis.*

EVE IN THE NEW TESTAMENT
      (2 Cor 11:3; 1 Tim 2:13–14)

In his appeal to the Corinthians to remain faithful to his message, Paul expresses his fear that "as the serpent deceived Eve by its cunning, your thoughts will be led astray from a sincere and pure devotion to Christ" (11:3). So he not only identifies his (Jewish-Christian) opponents with Satan (for which the serpent is here a symbol), but he also compares his addressees, whom he accuses of submitting readily enough to false preachers (2 Cor 11:4), to Eve, who was easy prey to the devil. It would seem that the author does not (or not yet) regard Eve as the prototype of all women, but that notion will very soon be developed; it is significant that here he personifies his opponents as a woman.

The (non-Pauline) author of 1 Timothy perhaps knew this passage from 2 Corinthians, since he too emphasizes, but much more strongly than Paul did, that it was Eve who was deceived by Satan (the same Greek verb, which could also imply sexual seduction, is used again). He even states that Eve, not Adam, became a transgressor (1 Tim 2:14)! Moreover, the author stresses the fact that "Adam was formed first, [only] then Eve" (2:13) to make it abundantly clear that, in his view, Eve is inferior to Adam (according to the generally accepted principle in the ancient world that older or earlier is better). This argument is then used to justify severe strictures: women have to submit themselves to men, or wives to their husbands, and they have to keep silent in the church (2:12), that is, they are forbidden to be teachers or leaders; their only permissible role is that of wife and mother. This passage, inspired by a specific form of contemporaneous Jewish exegesis of the story of "the fall" in Genesis 3, has exerted a baneful influence in the history of the Christian church, and it still does so in certain traditional circles.

PIETER W. VAN DER HORST

Gomer

"perfection," from Hebrew *gmr,* "to accomplish, complete"; perhaps a shortened form or nickname of the theophoric name Gemariah (Jer 29:3), "YHWH has accomplished it (the child's birth)" (Hosea 1–3)

The eighth-century B.C.E. prophet Hosea's famous metaphor of God as faithful husband to Israel, his adulterous wife (Hosea 2), is juxtaposed with the story of Hosea's own disastrous marriage to Gomer, Diblaim's daughter (Hosea 1; 3). It is difficult, however, to separate historical facts about the couple's domestic problems from the theological message expressed through them.

Scholars have advanced a number of theories to reckon with historical questions about the portrayal of Gomer in Hosea 1–3. Some commentators regard Hosea and Gomer's marriage as an allegory, not meant to be taken literally. Such an interpretation would perhaps preserve Gomer's moral goodness by erasing her existence as a real woman and having her serve God's purposes. Others think that Gomer actually was a licentious woman, maybe even a prostitute, whom Hosea felt obliged to marry and whose illegitimate children Hosea adopted. A mediating position interprets the command to marry the immoral Gomer proleptically (after the fact): Gomer was chaste at the time of marriage, but subsequently became unfaithful to Hosea as an adulteress, a common harlot, or a temple prostitute. Some try to vindicate Gomer's reputation by insisting that she should not be equated with the woman in Hosea 3, another wife, whom Hosea was commanded to marry and whose promiscuity is unfairly laid upon Gomer. A variant of this position regards the blameless Gomer of Hosea 1 becoming wrongly identified with the prostitute whom Hosea hires (rather than marries) in Hosea 3. In order to preserve the sanctity of marriage, still other interpreters argue that Hosea did not actually marry Gomer. The verb *take* in 1:2 could mean "marry a wife" or "take a woman sexually." Following the latter sense, Hosea was commanded to have sex with two unchaste women: Gomer and the unnamed woman of Hosea 3. His symbolic actions are not meant to parallel the marriage between God and Israel (Hosea 2).

Most commentators today understand the unnamed woman in Hosea 3 to be Gomer of Hosea 1. The standard opinion that Gomer was a prostitute is based on misleading translations of 'ēšet zĕnûnîm in 1:2, which have Hosea marrying "a wife of whoredom" (NRSV, JPS), "a wife of harlotry" (RSV), "a harlot wife" (NAB), or simply "a whore" (NJB). However, Gomer is never labeled as a zônā, the technical term for a prostitute. Nor is Gomer called a qĕdēšâ (literally, "holy one"), wrongly translated as "temple prostitute" or "cult prostitute" to describe the daughters of Israel in 4:14. Qĕdēšâ refers to a woman serving in the cult. The nature of her activity (whether sexual or not) is, however, difficult to reconstruct from the extant evidence. In the prophet's mind, her rituals involved sexuality, but it would be a mistake to accept his polemical condemnations at face value.

For Hosea, Gomer is a "wife of whoredom," not because she is a prostitute, but because, according to the mores of Israel, she is blatantly licentious and wanton. In her sexual activity, Gomer is condemned as being "like a whore," although she is not a prostitute by profession. As a promiscuous wife, Gomer is much more threatening to the social order than a prostitute — a woman marginalized but still tolerated in Israel. An adulterous woman could never be permitted in a patrilineal society based on the principle of male descent and inheritance through legitimate sons. Through prostitution, men were allowed socially condoned sexual access to "other" women who were not their wives. Women, on the contrary, were permitted no other men besides their husbands. Because of this unequal sexual access to other partners, which itself is based on other gendered asymmetries, ancient Israelite marriage becomes a powerful metaphor, delineating the exclusive boundaries of God's covenant with Israel and Israel's infidelity to that covenant by worshipping other gods.

During the course of their marriage, Gomer bears Hosea three children with symbolic names: a son, Jezreel, meaning, "God sows" (1:4–5); a daughter, Lo-ruhamah, meaning "not pitied" (1:6–7); and another son, Lo-ammi, meaning "not my people" (1:8–9). Each child symbolically represents the deteriorating state of the nation.

The story of God's marriage to Israel interrupts that of Hosea's marriage to Gomer and becomes a paradigm for Hosea's treatment of Gomer in Hosea 3. Highlighted in Hosea 2 is the forgiving love of God, who renews covenantal vows with his wayward but repentant Israel. However, the metaphorical vehicles, describing God's punishment of "his wife" to make her repent, become dangerously similar to acts of domestic violence. God the husband will "strip her naked," "make her like a wilderness," "kill her with thirst" (2:3), isolate her (2:6), refuse to provide for her well-being (2:9), humiliate her before her lovers (2:10), and so forth.

Like God the husband, Hosea is commanded to "love" the adulterous wife (Hos 3:1), whom he was bidden to marry (Hos 1:2–3). As God does for Israel, Hosea restores provisions for Gomer's livelihood that he had withdrawn: silver for clothes, barley for food, and wine for drink (3:2; compare 2:14). Just as God isolates Israel from her lovers (2:6–7), so does Hosea segregate Gomer from her paramours and even refrains from sexual intercourse with her himself.

Whereas Hosea 2 clearly describes the physical and emotional violence God inflicts upon his wife to punish her, Hosea 3 is selective in portraying the prophet's chastisement of Gomer: no descriptions of Hosea stripping and humiliating her, no reports of his withholding her food and clothing, and no accounts of his physical mistreatment of her. Yet if Hosea models God to the fullest extent, these acts of "love" are certainly implied in Hosea 3. But what a man views as love, a woman experiences as abuse. The text's silence about these acts of "love" coincides with the reality that most cases of wife battering are private, not public, matters.

It is tragic that Gomer is silent in Hosea 1 and 3. She is basically remembered as Hosea's unfaithful wife. Yet one wonders about her account of domestic life with her famous prophetic spouse, who had immortalized their marriage as a significant, but problematic, metaphor of covenantal love. Gomer's muteness only emphasizes the extent to which women have been left out of discussions that visualize the deity as male and the sinful as female.

These discussions, by both feminists and traditional interpreters, are rooted in paradigmatic Western dichotomies that link God with the male, and matter and nature with the female and with sexuality. Because the prophet Hosea's life precedes the development of this dualistic structure, it is also possible to read his metaphor as a commentary on eighth-century B.C.E. sociopolitical conflicts. His true metaphor may be a family metaphor rather than a marriage one. He may be using the centrality of family life to critique the larger social body. Like the family, the community of Israel is disintegrating. This reading calls into question the authority of traditional interpretations, which are embedded in the sexism and misogyny of Western culture, and calls for new ways of thinking about the body, woman, and the sacred.

GALE A. YEE

SEE ALSO Part I: Lo-ruhamah; Part II: Prostitute (Lev 19:29, etc.); Adulteress (Lev 20:10, etc.); Temple Prostitute (Deut 23:17–18, etc.).

FOR FURTHER READING: Bird, Phyllis. "'To Play the Harlot': An Inquiry into an Old Testament Metaphor."

Keefe, Alice. "The Female Body, the Body Politic, and the Land: A Sociopolitical Reading of Hosea 1–2."

Weems, Renita J. *Battered Love: Marriage, Sex, and Violence in the Hebrew Prophets.*

Yee, Gale A. "Hosea."

Hadassah

"myrtle," from Hebrew *hădas,* "myrtle"
(Esth 2:7)

Hadassah is the Hebrew name of the heroine Esther, the Jewish queen of the Persian Empire. Characters in postexilic (fifth century B.C.E. and later) literature often had two names, a Hebrew name and a name of the country of their exile (for example, Dan 1:7).

SIDNIE WHITE CRAWFORD

SEE ALSO Part I: Esther.

Hagar

meaning uncertain; perhaps "wanderer," from Arabic *hajara,* "to migrate"; or "town," from Sabean and Ethiopic *hagar,* originally meaning "splendid"

HAGAR IN THE HEBREW BIBLE
(Gen 16; 21:9–21; 25:12–16)

Hagar is Sarai's Egyptian slave girl, whom Sarai (later Sarah) gives to Abram (later Abraham) as a wife who would bear a child that would be considered Sarai's (Gen 16:3). Although it bears a resemblance to modern technological surrogate motherhood, this custom may seem bizarre. However, cuneiform texts of the second and first millennia B.C.E. attest to this custom in ancient Mesopotamia. The first such text, from the Old Assyrian colony in Anatolia, dates from around 1900 B.C.E. A marriage contract, it stipulates that if the wife does not give birth in two years, she will purchase a slave woman for the husband. The most famous text, in the Code of Hammurabi (no. 146), concerns the marriage of a *nadītu,* a woman, attached to a temple, who is not allowed to bear children. Her husband has the right to take a second wife, but if she wishes to forestall this, she can give her husband a slave. In the world of the ancient Near East, a slave woman could be seen as an incubator, a kind of womb-with-legs.

Sarai and Abram see Hagar in this role and never call her by name. She, however, sees herself as a person and, once pregnant, does not see Sarai as superior; "she looked with contempt on her mistress" (Gen 16:4). With Abram's permission, Sarai regains authority over Hagar. She "degrades her" (NRSV, "dealt harshly with her"), possibly by treating her as an ordinary slave (Gen 16:6). The Hammurabi laws acknowledge the possibility that the pregnant slave woman might claim equality with her mistress, and they allow the mistress to treat her as an ordinary slave (law 146). This seems to be what Sarai is doing. However, Hagar is not passive. Rather than submit, she runs away to the wilderness of Shur, where she meets God's messenger, who tells her to return to submit to Sarai's abuse for then she will bear a son who will be a "wild ass of a man" (Gen 16:12). Just as the wild ass was never domesticated, so too Hagar's son would never be subject to anyone, and would live "with his hand against everyone" and "in everyone's face" (Gen 16:12).

The angel's annunciation to Hagar is similar to announcements to Hannah, to the mother of Samson, and to Mary the mother of Jesus: all would have children with special destinies, and all are addressed personally, not through their husbands. God's request that Hagar become a slave again and return to be degraded by Sarai seems strange: why should God respect property rights over the freedom of persons? This is particularly odd, considering the legal code of Israel, which, alone among ancient law systems, specified that runaway slaves should not be returned to their masters (Deut 23:16). But the angel's speech here parallels God's speech to Abram in Gen 15:13, which states that his children would be enslaved and degraded before their redemption. Both passages use the key terms that Israel uses to describe the Egypt experience. Hagar, the slave from Egypt, foreshadows Israel, the future slaves in Egypt. Her very name, Hagar, could be heard as *haggēr,* meaning "the alien"; Hagar is an alien in Abram's household as Israel will be aliens, *gērîm,* in a foreign land. Hagar is to be degraded as Abram's descendants will be degraded, and YHWH has "given heed to affliction" as God will hear the affliction of Abram's descendants.

Hagar is Abram's counterpart. God speaks directly to her, forging a relationship independent of God's relationship with Abram, and she responds in that way. She names God ("You are El-roi," meaning "the one who sees me"; Gen 16:13) and the place (Beer-lahai-roi, "the well of the Loving One who sees"; Gen 16:14) and then goes back to Abram's household and bears a son, whom Abram (not Sarai) names Ishmael.

Hagar and Ishmael are freed at Sarai's instigation (Gen 21:9–14). Here too their destiny is parallel to later Israel's, for the newly freed slaves head to the desert and struggle with thirst. God then saves the dying Ishmael, not because of Hagar's cries or God's promises to Abram, but because God heard Ishmael's voice (Gen 21:15–21). God's relationship with Hagar is resealed with her son, as God's relationship with Abram is resealed with Isaac and his son Jacob.

Like Jacob, Ishmael has twelve sons. Hagar is the ancestor of these twelve tribes of Ishmael (Gen 25:12–15). She may also be the ancestor of the Hagrites, tent dwellers mentioned along with Ishmaelites in Ps 83:7 (see also 1 Chr 5:10; 27:30).

The Qur'an, like some Jewish Midrash, remembers Hagar as a princess. In more modern times, Hagar is often admired as the symbol of downtrodden women who persevere.

TIKVA FRYMER-KENSKY

SEE ALSO Part I: Bilhah; Sarah 1/Sarai; Zilpah.

FOR FURTHER READING: Frymer-Kensky, Tikva. "Patriarchal Family Relationships and Near Eastern Law."
———. "Sarah and Hagar."
———. *Victors, Victims, Virgins, and Voice: Rereading the Women of the Bible.*
Gossai, Hemchand. *Power and Marginality in the Abraham Narrative.*
Trible, Phyllis. "Hagar: The Desolation of Rejection."

HAGAR IN THE APOCRYPHAL/
DEUTEROCANONICAL BOOKS
    (Bar 3:23)

Reference to Hagar appears in a wisdom poem (Bar 3:9–4:4) that is itself part of an apocryphal letter written sometime between 200 to 60 B.C.E. to the priests and people of Jerusalem from Baruch, the scribe and close friend of Jeremiah (Jeremiah 36).

The climax of the wisdom poem is that Wisdom is "the book of the commandments of God, / the law that endures forever" (Bar 4:1). Humans cannot find wisdom except by seeking it directly from God. Like Job 28, the wisdom poems asks, "Who has found her place?" (Bar 3:15). This rhetorical question is answered through a listing of those who have not found her — mighty rulers and later generations of seekers (Bar 3:16–21), giants of old (Bar 3:26–28), those with gold or silver (Bar 3:17–19).

Bar 3:22 indicates that wisdom has not been heard of in places traditionally associated with it: Canaan, renowned for its wealth and wisdom (see Ezek 28:3–5), and Teman, reputed for its wisdom (Jer 49:7). Bar 3:23 continues in a similar vein, enumerating others who have not found wisdom, and among them "the descendants of Hagar," the Ishmaelites (Gen 16:11–12), who stand for the Ishmaelite territory in northwest Arabia (see Gen 25:18).

The inclusion of "the descendants of Hagar" in the group whom the poet claims have not found wisdom suggests, to the contrary, that the Ishmaelites were thought to be wise. The story of the Ishmaelites (or Midianites) to whom Joseph is sold (Gen 37:25–28) could be the background for the inclusion of the "descendants of Hagar" in Bar 3:23. Traders and traveling merchants sometimes transported culture as well as goods (travel and wisdom are associated in Ezek 28:5 and Sir 39:4). It is also possible that Hagar's descendants could be associated with wisdom because of her Egyptian background (Gen 16:1) and their Egyptian heritage.

ALICE OGDEN BELLIS

SEE ALSO Part III: Woman Wisdom.

HAGAR IN THE NEW TESTAMENT
(Gal 4:24–25)

Hagar appears in an allegory in Gal 4:21–31. Paul uses the figure of Hagar to represent the Sinai covenant and its granting of the Jewish law. It contrasts her with the figure of Sarah (here unnamed) who represents the new covenant brought through Christ. The force of the allegory depends on the stark contrast between slaves and free persons, and it draws its metaphors from the institution of slavery and the sexual use of women slaves.

Both Hagar and Sarah bear Abraham a son, but only Sarah's son is to be recognized as the legitimate heir of Abraham. Hagar receives a promise from God that her descendants too will be a multitudinous people (Gen 16:10; compare 21:13). Hagar is driven out with Ishmael from Abraham's household as a result of Sarah's jealousy and fear that Ishmael will rival her son, Isaac, for Abraham's inheritance. Without resources, Hagar and her son would have perished, but God intervenes and preserves their lives (Gen 21:17–19).

Paul's description of Hagar and her fate is significantly more negative than the original Genesis account. He says nothing of the divine promise to Hagar and her descendants nor of the divine rescue of her and her son. Sarah's fears and jealousy are presented by Paul as divinely warranted opposition between free and slave. Hagar's child is portrayed as persecuting the legitimate heir, and their expulsion is justified in order to preserve the inheritance of Sarah's son (Gal 4:29–30). This divergence from the Genesis account is motivated by Paul's overall aim in Galatians to deny the authority of the Jewish law for believers in Christ. Hagar and her descendants are the type of the Jewish law and those who observe it. They are, in Paul's opinion, enslaved with no rightful title to be considered the spiritual heirs of Abraham. Paul identifies Christians with the children of the free woman, Sarah, and therefore as Abraham's true descendants.

An interesting counterpoint to Paul's interpretation of the Hagar story can be found in contemporary African American womanist theology. Here Hagar the slave woman and her son become representative of African American slave women and their descendants, and the divine promises to and rescue of Hagar become symbols of God's concern for the survival of African American women and their children.

SHEILA BRIGGS

SEE ALSO Part I: Sarah 1/Sarai; Part II: The Free Woman, Mother of a Son of Abraham (Gal 4:22).

FOR FURTHER READING: Briggs, Sheila. "Galatians."

Castelli, Elizabeth A. "Allegories of Hagar: Reading Galatians 4:21–31 with Postmodern Feminist Eyes."

Haggith

"festal," from the Hebrew verb *ḥgg*, "to make pilgrimage, keep a pilgrim-feast"

(2 Sam 3:4; 1 Kgs 1:5, 11; 2:13; 1 Chr 3:2)

Haggith is wife of King David (reigned c. 1005–965 B.C.E.) and the mother of his son Adonijah. She is fourth on a list of six mother-son references concerning David's sons born at Hebron (2 Sam 3:2–5; 1 Chr 3:1–4), where he established his first capital and also his power base by making carefully chosen marriage alliances.

Haggith is mentioned three times in epithets

concerning Adonijah (her son and rival of Solomon, the son of another wife, Bathsheba). Adonijah, "son of Haggith," declares himself king (1 Kgs 1:5), while later, the prophet Nathan remarks, "Have you not heard that Adonijah son of Haggith has become king. . . ?" (v. 11). After Solomon's accession (c. 968 B.C.E.), Adonijah asks Bathsheba for her help with Solomon. Once again the narrator points out that "Adonijah son of Haggith came to Bathsheba, Solomon's mother" (2:13). Thus, on the level of epithets, rivalry exists between royal half-brothers and their mothers. The many offspring of David represented, in part, rival factions desiring to inherit the throne. The rise to power of Solomon, apparently not the first of David's sons, no doubt caused a power struggle in the royal court.

LINDA S. SCHEARING

SEE ALSO Part I: Abigail 1; Abital; Ahinoam 2; Maacah 5; Michal; Part II: Wives and Concubines of David; Taken in Jerusalem (2 Sam 5:13); Wives of David (2 Sam 12:11, etc.).

Hamital SEE Hamutal/Hamital (Part I).

Hammolecheth

"she who reigns," from Hebrew *mlk,* "to reign"
(1 Chr 7:18)

Hammolecheth is one of several women in the tribe of Manasseh mentioned in the Chronicler's genealogy. She is unusual in that her husband is not named, although her three sons (Ishhod, Abiezer, and Mahlah) are listed.

She is identified as "his sister," but the antecedent of "his" is unclear because five male names appear in the preceding verse. The third one, Gilead, is most like Hammolecheth's brother; her father then would have been Machir and her grandfather, Manasseh.

JULIA MYERS O'BRIEN

Hamutal/Hamital

meaning uncertain; perhaps "his/my husband's father is the dew," from Hebrew *ḥām,* "husband's father," and *ṭal,* "dew"; or "his/my husband's father is protection," from Hebrew *ḥām,* and *ṭll,* "to protect"
(2 Kgs 23:31; 24:18; Jer 13:18; 52:1; Ezekiel 19)

Hamutal was the daughter of Jeremiah of Libnah, the consort of Josiah, king of Judah from 639 to 609 B.C.E., and the mother of two Judean kings, Jehoahaz and Zedekiah. Since most Judean regnal formulas include the name of the king's mother and several of these women appear to wield considerable influence in political and cultic matters, the queen mother may have served as an official functionary of the royal court. Alternatively, Ben-Barak suggests that the activities of the more prominent queen mothers do not represent official roles. Rather, their prominence may be the result of personal influence earned by individual women who successfully garnered the support necessary to advance a younger son ahead of an older sibling in the royal succession.

Hamutal's son Jehoahaz, for example, becomes king with the support of the people of the land, although he has an elder half brother (2 Kgs 23:30–36). This group of landed aristocracy is involved in succession only when the rising queen mother originates from the outlying provinces of Judah. Presumably, the loyalties of Hamutal of Libnah and of her son would rest outside Jerusalem.

Hamutal apparently does not accompany Jehoahaz when he is exiled by Necho of Egypt, because she later serves as queen mother under another son, Zedekiah (2 Kgs 24:18; Jer 52:1). Ezekiel's lamentation on the mother (Ezekiel 19) may be interpreted as a reference to Hamutal's involvement in her sons' reigns. Likewise, Jeremiah's joint criticism of the king and the queen mother (Jer 13:18) may refer to Zedekiah and Hamutal and indicate their shared authority.

RHONDA BURNETTE-BLETSCH

SEE ALSO Part I: Azubah 1; Bathsheba; Maacah 4; Part II: Mother of Princes (Ezekiel 19).

FOR FURTHER READING: Ackerman, Susan. "The Queen Mother and the Cult in Ancient Israel."
Berlyn, P. J. "The Great Ladies."
Ben-Barak, Zafrira. "The Status and Right of the *gᵉbîrâ*."

Hannah

"grace, favor, supplication, prayer for favor," from Hebrew *ḥnn*, "to be gracious, merciful, compassionate"

(1 Sam 1:1–2:21)

The narrative in 1 Samuel 1–2, in which Hannah is protagonist, is set in the late premonarchic period (eleventh century B.C.E.). It opens obliquely with the introduction of her husband, Elkanah, who is identified by name, location, and extensive genealogy. Elkanah's two wives conclude the exposition, and they are presented without genealogy. The significance of the women lies in their relationship to Elkanah and in their childbearing capacity: "The name of one was Hannah, and the name of the other Peninnah. Peninnah had children, but Hannah had no children" (1:2). The use of chiasmus (the inversion of elements in two parallel phrases) underscores the standing of the women: Hannah is the primary wife, yet Peninnah has succeeded in bearing children. It also foreshadows the tension in the relationship between the women.

Hannah's status as primary wife and her barrenness recall Sarah and Rebekah, and an implicit comparison with these earlier women underlies the entire narrative. The matriarchs sought the recognition of motherhood through surrogate females, a solution that brought more grief than honor. Against this background, the reader of the Hannah narrative may suppose that Elkanah took Peninnah as second wife because of Hannah's barrenness; but Hannah, unlike Sarah and Rebekah, never doubts her capacity for motherhood. Although vexed by Peninnah, Hannah does not enter into the rivalry that characterizes the matriarchal narratives. With a loving (but tactless) husband and a jealous rival wife, Hannah keeps her counsel and her suffering to herself.

At the annual sacrifice at the major shrine of Shiloh, Hannah's predicament is intensified by her husband's allocation of sacrificial portions, one to each of his wives and children: the value of the women is demonstrably enhanced by their childbearing capacities. Though he gives a generous portion to Hannah, this gesture still emphasizes the fact that she has borne no children and thus does not comfort her. When she weeps and does not eat, Elkanah tries to assuage her misery with a series of "Why" questions, concluding with "Am I not more to you than ten sons?" (1:8). This "consoling" might be understood as a touching gesture by a sensitive husband. Or his words might convey the image of an insensitive man who does not realize how greatly his wife wants to bear children. Elkanah's chain of rhetorical questions does not allow Hannah an opportunity to answer, and she wisely remains silent to his last question. Not granted the dignity of her suffering, Hannah suffers even more under Elkanah's "comforting."

At Shiloh, the scene of her acute isolation and Peninnah's tormenting, Hannah turns to YHWH in the temple. She prays fervently, vowing that if YHWH will grant her a male child, she will give that child back to YHWH after weaning him. The desperation of Hannah's vow indicates that merely bearing a male child would establish her in the community; she would forgo the joys of raising him. Her vow does assume that within the social structure of early Israel, when women made vows, their husbands had to uphold them.

Hannah's prayer is observed by Eli the priest, who presumes her moving lips indicate that she is drunk; thus Hannah is wrongly accosted (and this time wrongly judged) by a second male character in the story. At a time when prayer was said aloud, Hannah's personal and private prayer was an innovation and regarded skeptically by the priest. Her muted voice may represent the "muted" position of women: she retreats from the control of religious and social authorities — husband and priest — into herself, to offer a prayer that they can neither hear nor understand. She assumes that God can hear and respond to a woman's prayer. Hannah answers Eli humbly and poignantly. In response, the priest offers no apology — merely trite phrases.

Hannah's prayers are answered by YHWH, who

"remembers" her (1:19), much as he remembered Rachel, suggesting that women's wombs are controlled by the deity, who acts upon them by closing or opening. Upon birth, it is Hannah who chooses a name for her son, for women's authority over children was often expressed by their naming of their offspring. She calls him Samuel, because she asked God (El) for him. Elkanah is not mentioned in this action. At the time of the next pilgrimage to Shiloh, strengthened by the self-assurance of motherhood, Hannah chooses to remain at home until the boy is weaned. Hannah's exchange with her husband on this occasion takes on an entirely different tone. She initiates the dialogue and establishes the conditions under which she will resume travel (when the boy has been weaned), and Elkanah offers a mere confirmation of her words.

When Hannah finally does relinquish her son to YHWH, she brings him to Eli, with significant sacrifices to YHWH; and she reminds the priest of her earlier prayer. The earliest translation and transmission traditions (Septuagint and 4QSam^a) show "patriarchalizing" of the text in removing Hannah's agency in performing the sacrifice, depriving her of a cultic role that legitimately belongs to her. In the Hebrew text, Hannah presents the child and also the sacrifices.

A poem of thanksgiving, the Song of Hannah (2:1–10), (and a brief digression concerned with Eli's sons) interrupts the narrative. The attribution of this poetic utterance to Hannah distinguishes her among biblical personages. Her song is essentially a hymn of praise to YHWH for good fortune, and the theme of reversal includes reference to a previously barren woman. The song also includes many themes of Israel's national culture: defeat of enemies and creation, battle and YHWH's relationship to Israel's leaders, wisdom and storm-god images. Fertility and childbirth are thus included as equal in importance to other motifs and worthy of Israel's singers.

Hannah's narrative concludes with a comment on her annual visit with her husband to offer the yearly sacrifice. At that time, her motherhood is emphasized: it is not "Hannah" but "his [Samuel's] mother" who makes a "little robe" and brings it to him at Shiloh (2:20). Elkanah and Hannah receive the blessings of Eli the priest, who prophesies that she will have other children because of her vow to YHWH. Indeed, Hannah's story concludes with fulfillment of YHWH's blessing in the form of three additional sons and two daughters.

Hannah's image is secure indeed: she is recognized as mother of Samuel — who becomes a prophet, judge, and king-maker — and as a good woman. She proves herself independent and resourceful, never abandoning her goals or demeaning others as a means to achieve them; she demonstrates women's activity in family ritual practices; she discloses social responsibility by making a vow that is upheld by her husband; and she links the realms of private and public religious life by vowing dedication of her son and by bringing her own sacrifice to YHWH in fulfillment of that vow.

LILLIAN R. KLEIN

SEE ALSO Part I: Peninnah; Rebekah; Sarah 1/Sarai; Part II: Person (Female or Male) Presenting an Offering (Lev 2:1, etc.); Woman Making a Vow (Num 30:3–15); Mother of Micah (Judg 17:1–4); Daughters (and Sons) of Hannah (1 Sam 2:21).

FOR FURTHER READING: Bird, Phyllis A. "Images of Women in the Old Testament."

Brenner, Athalya, and Fokkelien van Dijk-Hemmes. *On Gendering Texts: Female and Male Voices in the Hebrew Bible.*

Hackett, Jo Ann. "1 and 2 Samuel."

Klein, Lillian R. "Hannah: Victim and Redeemer."

Meyers, Carol. "Hannah and Her Sacrifice: Reclaiming Female Agency."

———. "The Hannah Narrative in Feminist Perspective."

Hassophereth/Sophereth

"the scribe" (feminine) or "scribe" (feminine), from Hebrew *spr*, "to count, relate, account," related to *sēper*, "document, book"
(Ezra 2:55; Neh 7:57)

Meaning literally "the female scribe" or "female scribe" (respectively), Hassophereth or Sophereth is the head of a family or guild whose descendants returned to Jerusalem from Babylonia during the

Persian period (c. 538–400 B.C.E.), after the Babylonian exile. There is no reason to suppose that the reference is to a male guild; indeed, a relevant grammatical, and perhaps vocational, parallel is the female herald (*měbaśśeret*) in Isa 40:9. Thus we can presume a guild whose ancestor was a female scribe, especially since the presence of female scribes in Babylonia (whence this group came) is well attested. Scribes were skilled professionals whose duties may have included record keeping and related administrative tasks.

TAMARA COHN ESKENAZI

SEE ALSO Part II: Those Who Bear Tidings/Herald (Ps 68:11, etc.).

FOR FURTHER READING: Eskenazi, Tamara Cohn. "Out from the Shadows: Biblical Women in the Postexilic Era."

Hazzelelponi

"he gives my face shade," from Hebrew *ṣll*, "to give shade," and *pānîm*, "face"

(1 Chr 4:3)

Hazzelelponi is the sister of Jezreel, Ishma, and Idbash, according to the Chronicler's genealogy of the tribe of Judah. Etam, named early in the verse but nowhere else in the Bible, may be the father of these siblings. Like Ashhur and Mered, other descendants of Judah who appear — with female members of their families — only in Chronicles, the presence of Etam and his children helps emphasize their tribe, Judah, which is probably the most important tribe in the Chronicler's estimation.

JULIA MYERS O'BRIEN

SEE ALSO Part I: Helah; Miriam 2; Naarah.

Helah

meaning unknown

(1 Chr 4:5, 7)

Helah is one of the two or more wives of Ashhur, great-grandson of Judah. Helah bore Ashhur four sons: Zereth, Izhar, Ethnan, and Koz. Her co-wife, Naarah, bore four. The text lists another son (Tekoa) by an unnamed wife.

The inclusion of names of wives of various members of the tribe of Judah, which is not done for other tribes in the genealogy of Chronicles, attests to the author's disproportionate interest in Judah, the source of the Southern Kingdom and the Davidic dynasty.

ALICE L. LAFFEY

SEE ALSO Part I: Hazzelelponi; Naarah.

Hephzibah 1

"my delight is in her," from Hebrew *ḥepṣî*, "my delight," and *bâ*, "in her"

(2 Kgs 21:1; 62:4)

Hephzibah is the chief wife of Hezekiah of Judah and the queen mother during the reign (698–642 B.C.E.) of their son, Manasseh, although her name is omitted from his regnal formula by the Chronicler (2 Chr 33:1). She is the only Judean queen mother for whom neither patronym nor place of origin is recorded, perhaps because of the extremely negative evaluation of her son, who undid his father's reforms and instigated extensive idolatry and evil behavior. Yet her name, ironically, appears as a designation for Zion restored, in Isa 62:4 — "you shall be called My Delight Is in Her."

RHONDA BURNETTE-BLETSCH

SEE ALSO Part III: Hephzibah/My Delight Is in Her, Jerusalem.

FOR FURTHER READING: Ben-Barak, Zafrira. "The Status and Right of the *gᵉbîrâ*."

Hephzibah 2 SEE Hephzibah/My Delight Is in Her, Jerusalem (Part III).

Herodias 1

feminine form of Herod, from the Greek *heros*, "hero, heroic"; the term can also designate the revered, deified dead

(Mark 6:17–28; Matt 14:1–11; Luke 3:19–20)

A granddaughter of Herod the Great (king of Judea, 37 B.C.E.–4 B.C.E.), Herodias is vilified in the Gospels of Mark and Matthew as the instigator of the gruesome execution of John the Baptist (an event not narrated in the Gospel of Luke). Herodias's antipathy toward the Baptist is ascribed to her problematic marital history. The first-century C.E.

Jewish historian Josephus tells us that Herodias's first husband was her uncle, Herod (a son of Herod the Great). After the birth of their daughter, Salome, she appears to have deserted (or perhaps actually divorced) Herod in order to marry her first husband's half brother (and also her uncle), confusingly also named Herod, called Antipas, the tetrarch of Galilee (*Antiquities* 18.136). Josephus characterizes Herodias's behavior as an intentional transgression of ancestral traditions. Most interpreters consider the marriage a violation of Lev 18:16 and 20:21, but Josephus's objection is unspecified and may (also) have to do with the irregular dissolution of the first marriage.

According to all three Synoptic Gospels, John the Baptist criticizes Herod for marrying his brother's wife: Herod, in response, imprisons John. Both Mark and Matthew relate that, at a celebratory banquet (possibly his birthday), Herod is so delighted at the dancing of the daughter of Herodias that he offers the daughter anything she wishes. Both Gospels concur that Herodias has engineered the daughter's request for the head of John the Baptist on a platter.

Yet the two accounts differ significantly. In Mark, it is Herodias who wants to have John killed but cannot, since Herod fears this righteous and holy man. Here, Herodias is consistently the instigator and the actor, although always indirectly, through the immediate agency and power of her husband. In Matthew, it is Herod who from the start desires to execute John but who fears the crowd, which regards the Baptist as a prophet (14:5). Matthew minimizes the role of Herodias, limiting her action to "prompting" her daughter and receiving the severed head.

Herodias's actual complicity in the death of John the Baptist is historically suspect. Josephus, whose version of these events postdates Mark and probably Matthew, contradicts the Gospels on key issues. Josephus blames both Herodias (*Antiquities* 18.136) and Herod (*Antiquities* 8.110) for their irregular marriage and places the blame for John's death squarely on Herod, with no mention of Herodias's participation. Whereas Josephus understands Herod to have been motivated by fear that

John's popularity might incite an uprising (*Antiquities* 18.116–19), the Gospels portray Herod's actions as grounded in lust and lack of self-control. Although Josephus criticizes the marriage of Herodias and Herod, he nowhere suggests that John the Baptist did so. Josephus is often a suspect source: a general during the Jewish revolt against Rome, Josephus was either captured by or surrendered to the Romans at the siege of Jotapata in Galilee (he provides conflicting narratives in the *Antiquities* and in his subsequent account of the war), and all his writings were composed with the financial support of the Roman imperial family, whose client he became after the war. It seems difficult to understand why he would have omitted Herodias's role in John's death, had he known of it.

Some scholars have questioned the entire story. Corley and Crossan both suggest that Mark has created the narrative, borrowing from a story about Lucius Quinctius Flaminius, who was expelled from the Roman senate in 184 B.C.E., allegedly for beheading a condemned man at a dinner party at the request of a courtesan whom he loved and who had expressed a desire to see such an act performed.

If we assume that Josephus's narrative is accurate in two details at least — the agency of Herod and his political motivation — assigning the blame to Herodias in the Gospels cannot be explained as a mere derivative of an older Roman narrative. On the contrary, if such a narrative does underlie the Gospels, it may be because the story of Flaminius lent itself to assigning blame to Herodias, rather than to Herod. Such a revision would be consistent with early Christian tendencies to deflect blame for the persecution of key Christian figures away from the Romans and their allies (which the Herodians clearly were) and onto more vulnerable and safer targets. Matthew's awkward recasting, attributing to Herod the desire to kill John but the actual instigation of the act to Herodias, may reflect both knowledge of Herod's actual responsibility and a desire to correct the Gospel of Mark without altogether refuting it.

If Herodias may have been innocent of the Gospels' charges against her, she nevertheless emerges from Josephus's narratives as a complex woman desirous of power and prestige (not unusual for members of the Herodian family). Although Christian sources have portrayed (and some continue to portray) Herodias as evil personified, Herodias appears in Josephus as a stereotypical schemer but also a loyal if misguided wife to Herod Antipas. After the emperor Gaius (37 C.E.–41 C.E.) made her brother Agrippa a king (37 C.E.–44 C.E.), Herodias persuaded Herod to seek the same honors for himself. Herod was ultimately accused, by Agrippa, of conspiring against Gaius, who then confiscated Herod's tetrarchy and banished him. Learning that Herod's wife was Agrippa's sister, Gaius offered to spare Herodias from exile and to allow her to keep her property. But Herodias demurred, insisting that having shared in her husband's former prosperity, she would be wrong to abandon him in his present misfortune. Gaius apparently then banished Herodias with her husband, confiscating her resources and giving them over to her brother (*Antiquities*. 18.240–55; see also *The Jewish War* 2.181–83).

Josephus sees these events as divine retribution, punishing Herod for listening to the "light speech" of a woman and punishing Herodias for resenting that her manipulative, spendthrift brother had become a king while her own husband, a member of the royal family, remained only a tetrarch, a lesser prince. A feminist perspective prompts other understandings. From Herodias's point of view, Agrippa's success at her husband's expense might seem unjust indeed, and her subsequent appeal to the emperor Gaius on her husband's behalf highly understandable. Perhaps what particularly offended ancient writers (including Josephus, Mark, and Matthew) about Herodias, was precisely her autonomy and her attempts to exercise control over her life, something women were not generally expected to do. If her complicity in the death of the Baptist is, in fact, manufactured, it is all the more interesting to consider that such blame functions as a telling critique of autonomous women.

Ross S. Kraemer

See also Part I: Herodias 2; Salome 2.

For further reading: Corley, Kathleen S. *Private Women, Public Meals: Social Conflict in the Synoptic Tradition.*

Crossan, John Dominic. *Jesus: A Revolutionary Biography.*
Macurdy, Grace H. "Royal Women in Judea."

Herodias 2
(Mark 6:22–28; Matt 14:6–11)

According to Mark 6:14–29, manipulative females brought about the death of John the Baptist. John had criticized Herod (the tetrarch of Galilee and Perea, 4 B.C.E.–37 C.E.) for marrying Herodias, who had previously been married to Herod's brother. Herodias wished to kill John but was prevented by Herod's fear of John's righteousness and holiness.

At his birthday banquet, however, Herod is so entranced by the dancing of a young girl that he promises her anything she wishes. At her mother's behest, the girl asks for the head of John the Baptist on a platter. A dismayed Herod complies to preserve his honor before his guests. At the end of the scene, John's head is brought to the daughter, who gives it to her mother.

Ancient manuscripts of the Gospel of Mark are divided in their identification of the dancer. According to a famous fourth-century C.E. manuscript, Codex Alexandrinus, and other witnesses, the dancer is called "the daughter of Herodias herself." But other equally famous and major witnesses, including Codices Sinaiticus, Vaticanus, and Bezae, name the dancer Herodias and identify her as the daughter of Herod.

Influenced by the report of the first-century C.E. Jewish historian Josephus that Herod's wife, Herodias, had a daughter named Salome by her first husband (*Antiquities* 18.136), and by the long history of Christian identification of the dancer as Salome, many editions of the Greek New Testament have preferred the manuscripts that call the dancer "the daughter of Herodias." However, some recent editions of the Greek New Testament now prefer the reading "his [Herod's] daughter, Herodias," and the NRSV of Mark 6:22 follows them. This decision is based on a text-critical principle that copyists are more likely to change a "difficult" reading to something easier than they are to make an "easy" reading harder. In this case, scholars reason that ancient scribes would more likely have changed the "difficult" reading, "his daughter, Herodias," to the less problematic "the daughter of Herodias" than vice versa; hence, this "difficult" reading is preferable.

If the reading "his [Herod's] daughter, Herodias" is earlier, identifying this daughter with Salome becomes implausible. In the notes to the HarperCollins Study Bible of the NRSV for Mark 6:22, C. Clifton Black points out that it seems strange for Mark to call the dancer Herodias, when according to Josephus her name was Salome. The real problem here is not so much the dancer's name but rather her paternity. According to Josephus, Salome was not the daughter of the Herod (Herod Antipas) for whom the dancer performs in the Gospels, but the daughter of his half brother by the same name (who is called Philip in both Mark and Matthew, although Josephus reports no additional name for that Herod). Herod Antipas is not known to have had a daughter, either by his first wife or by Herodias. But if he did, she might well have been named Herodias after her father. At least one scholar has argued that the dancer is to be identified with an actual daughter of Herod and his first wife, a princess of Nabatea (an ancient kingdom whose capital was Petra, in present-day Jordan) whose name is not preserved.

Although the verses that describe the interaction between mother and daughter never explicitly name the mother, the Gospels clearly assume that the dancer's mother is Herodias. Thus, Herodias the daughter could only also be Salome if she went by both names, a practice occasionally attested among Judean royalty in antiquity (for example, Queen Alexandra Salome). Since the historical Salome's father was also named Herod, she could conceivably have also been called Herodias. But if the parents of the dancer were Herod Antipas and Herodias, she cannot have been the historical Salome.

The textual situation for Matt 14:6 is much simpler. Codex Bezae calls the dancer "Herodias, his daughter," as it does also for Mark 6:22, but other manuscripts generally identify her as the daughter of Herodias. In the mid–second century C.E., Justin

Martyr (a convert to Christianity from Samaria), retelling this story, names neither the mother nor the daughter, but does identify the dancer as the niece (*exadelphē*) of Herod (*Dialogue with Trypho* 49:4–5). By this, Justin may mean that he understands her to be the daughter of Herod's brother, which in turn suggests that Justin knows a version of the story in which the dancer is the daughter of Herod's wife and her first husband.

If, as seems likely, the entire narrative is a fabrication, reconstructing the original reading of Mark will only help us identify the dancer intended within the Markan narrative. Nevertheless, if we accept the reading prevalent in Matthew ("the daughter of Herodias herself") as also reflecting the older Markan reading, the identification of the dancer with Salome might initially seem plausible, since Josephus records no other children of Herodias, daughters or sons, from either marriage. The authors or knowledgeable early readers of Mark and Matthew, or both, might well have drawn such an inference. Yet what we know of the historical Salome may make it less likely that she could ever have been the dancer.

Ross S. Kraemer

SEE ALSO Part I: Herodias 1; Salome 2; Part II: Young Dancer Who Asks for the Head of John the Baptist (Matt 14:6–11).

Hodesh

"new, new moon, month," from Hebrew *ḥōdeš,* "month"

(1 Chr 8:9)

Hodesh is one of at least three wives of Shaharaim, within the genealogy of the tribe of Benjamin. 1 Chr 8:9–10 suggests that her children — Jobab, Zibia, Mesha, Malcam, Jeuz, Sachia, and Mirmah — were born in Moab after her husband sent away two other wives (Baara and Hushim). The reasons for this connection between Benjaminites and Moabites are unclear.

Julia Myers O'Brien

SEE ALSO Part I: Baara; Hushim.

Hodiah

"My splendor is Y H W H," from Hebrew *hôd,* "splendor," and *yāh,* a shortened form of Y H W H
S E E Jehudijah (Part I).

Hoglah

"partridge," from semitic root *ḥgl,* "to hop," hence "partridge"

(Num 26:33; 27:1; 36:11; Josh 17:3)

Hoglah is one of the five daughters of Zelophehad who approach Moses to ask for an inheritance of land alongside their male relatives.

K A T H A R I N E D O O B S A K E N F E L D

S E E A L S O Part I: Mahlah 1; Milcah 2; Noah; Tirzah; Part II: Daughters of Zelophehad (Num 26:33, etc.).

Huldah

meaning uncertain; perhaps from Hebrew *ḥeled,* "duration" or from *ḥōled,* "weasel"

(2 Kgs 22:14–20; 2 Chr 34:11–28)

Huldah is depicted as a temple prophet who validates a scroll, called "the book of the law [or covenant]," purportedly found in the temple during repairs ordered by King Josiah, the last of Judah's "good" kings (reigned 640–609 B.C.E.). The narrative of this book is tied to the nationalistic political and economic policies known as Josiah's cultic reform. Whether Josiah's new policies began before or after the discovery of the book is a point of contention between the versions of events in Kings and in Chronicles. The exact content of the book is not specified: Josiah's destruction of non-Yahwistic cultic sites is in line with positions expressed in the Book of Deuteronomy, as is Huldah's reference to "all the curses that are written in the book" (2 Chr 34:24). In Chronicles, the allusion to "the book of the law of the LORD given through Moses" (2 Chr 34:14) may suggest that later author's (historically unlikely) assumption that it was the whole Pentateuch. Some historians question whether an ancient document was really found and suggest it had

been produced to serve Josiah's purposes. Others tie it to documents that may have survived from an earlier reform — that of Josiah's great-grandfather Hezekiah (727–698 B.C.E.), whose efforts were negated by the subsequent misdeeds of his son Manasseh (698–642 B.C.E.).

Modern readers, unaccustomed to thinking of ancient women in positions of authority, may find Huldah's story remarkable. The biblical evidence, however, makes clear that prophecy was a role open to women on an equal basis with men (other examples include Miriam, Deborah, and, in the New Testament, Anna), and the narrators of Kings and Chronicles take no notice of Huldah's gender. Though she is identified by her husband's ancestry, such a formal convention does not detract from her own royally recognized authority to speak in the name of Y H W H. Mesopotamian parallels suggest this story fits a type of account in which a king ostensibly receives a divine directive for cult reform and then validates it through temple personnel. Such parallels confirm Huldah's role as typical.

Although it is certainly possible to envision a woman like Huldah as a temple prophet in the time of Josiah, some scholars suggest that this narrative segment is the literary creation of a postexilic writer seeking to explain the exile, rather than a report (or justification) of events during the monarchy. Indeed, Huldah's rather generic prophetic oracle deals with the inevitability of divine punishment of Judah, not the hope promised by Josiah's cultic reform. If so, the idea of a female prophet was presumably taken for granted in the later period as well (compare Noadiah in Neh 6:14).

Whatever the case, Huldah's story is notable in the biblical tradition in that her prophetic words of judgment are centered on a written document: she authorizes what will become the core of Scripture for Judaism and Christianity. Her validation of a text thus stands as the first recognizable act in the long process of canon formation. Huldah authenticates a document as being God's word, thereby affording it the sanctity required for establishing a text as authoritative, or canonical.

C L A U D I A V. C A M P

SEE ALSO Part I: Noadiah.
FOR FURTHER READING: Camp, Claudia V. "Female
Voice, Written Word: Women and Authority in He-
brew Scripture."
Swidler, Arlene. "In Search of Huldah."

Hushim

meaning uncertain; perhaps "enjoyment," from
Hebrew ḥwš, "to feel, enjoy"; or "hurried," from
Hebrew ḥwš, "to hasten, make haste"

(1 Chr 8:8, 11)

Hushim is one of at least three wives of Shaharaim,
a descendant of Benjamin. Two of his wives, including Hushim, were discarded; the third, Hodesh, was
retained. Hushim bears Shaharaim two sons, Abi-
tub and Elpaal; the names of five of Elpaal's children are listed as well, indicating the importance of
this family in Aijalon, an area west of Jerusalem.

According to the genealogy, Shaharaim had sons
in the country of Moab after he sent away his wives.
Perhaps this means that the discarded wives were
Moabites. The text may reflect the long-held hostil-
ity between Israelites and Moabites (for example,
Deut 23:4).

ALICE L. LAFFEY

SEE ALSO Part I: Baara; Hodesh.

Iscah

"perfume," from Hebrew nsk, "to pour," as perfume; or "favored," from Hebrew skh, "to see," a
sign of divine favor

(Gen 11:29)

The genealogy of Genesis 11 lists Iscah as a daughter
of Haran and thus the sister of Lot and of Milcah
(the wife of Nahor, Abraham's brother). This elaboration on Nahor's marital ties, and not on Abraham's, may be a function of the important role the
Nahor group will have in providing a kinswoman as
a spouse for the next generation of ancestors: Isaac
will marry Rebekah, granddaughter of Milcah and
grand-niece of Iscah.

CAROL MEYERS

SEE ALSO Part I: Milcah 1; Rebekah.

FOR FURTHER READING: Steinberg, Naomi. *Kinship
and Marriage in Genesis: A Household Economics Perspective.*

Jael

"ibex," from Hebrew yāʿēl, "ibex"

(Judg 4:17–22; 5:6, 24–27)

The wife of Heber the Kenite, Jael plays an important role in the story of Israel's wars with the Canaanites, described in the Book of Judges. In the
narrative about the military heroine Deborah, Jael
kills Sisera, the Canaanite general of King Jabin,
after he escapes from the battle with Deborah's general, Barak. Jael's deeds are recounted in Judges 4
and in the poetic Song of Deborah in Judges 5. The
song is old, most probably dating to the late twelfth
century B.C.E., and may be the earliest poem in the
Hebrew Bible.

In the prose account, Deborah first sends Barak
to fight the Canaanites and then she agrees to accompany him. She prophesies that the victory
would not be a glory for him, for Sisera would fall
"by the hand of a woman" (Judg 5:9); that woman
will be Jael. Sisera flees the battle and goes to Jael's
tent, for there was "peace" between King Jabin and
the Kenites (14:17). This peace might mean that,
since the Kenites may have been metal smiths, Heber was nearby in order to repair Canaanite weapons.

When Sisera approaches her tent, Jael greets him,
invites him in, covers him with a blanket (NRSV,
"rug"), and, at his request for a little water, gives
him milk. He then tells her to stand at the entrance
to her tent and respond negatively to whoever asks
whether anyone is inside (4:18–20). As he lies asleep,
exhausted from the battle, Jael takes a tent peg and
drives it through his forehead into the ground and
then shows his dead body to Barak, who has come
in pursuit of the enemy general (4:21–22).

Jael thus fulfills Deborah's prophecy, but she con-
founds other expectations. The reader or the listener to the tale, seeing a general at war come into a
woman's tent, fears for the woman, not for the man.
Yet when the outside world of national battles

comes into her domestic space, Jael takes up a domestic "weapon of opportunity" and becomes a heroine. Her actions are not explained. Does she act, like Rahab, out of loyalty to God and Israel, or does she react to the general's imperious behavior? When Jael's hospitality induces him to feel secure, he issues commands to her. Did this make Jael wonder what would happen to her when he awoke? Whatever her motives, the story considers her action the will of God. At the same time, it conveys the notion that being killed by a woman shames both the dead general and the live Israelite general, who had not slain him himself.

The poetic account in Judges 5 shows none of this unease about women warriors. Near the opening of the poem, Jael is linked with Shamgar, son of Anath, another fighter hero of early Israel (4:7; compare 3:31). And in the account of her slaying, of Sisera, the poet calls for her to be blessed by women in tents (NRSV, "most blessed of women"; 5:24). Her deed is clearly heroic: she is a ferocious woman warrior, offering milk in a princely bowl, taking a tent pin and hammer in her hands, and crushing Sisera's head (5:25–27). Nothing is said about blankets or sleep. This Sisera is standing when he is fatally struck by Jael; he then sinks to the ground "between [NRSV, to]" her feet, a fallen warrior.

The stealthy heroine of the prose account and the fierce warrior of the poem are both dramatic inversions of motherhood. One offers maternal nurturing before she strikes, and the other stands with the slain foe between her legs in a grim parody of birth. When the greater world of national battles intrudes into her domestic space, this Kenite women becomes one of the "mothers" of Israel.

TIKVA FRYMER-KENSKY

SEE ALSO Part I: Deborah 2; Part II: Tent-Dwelling Women (Judg 5:24).

FOR FURTHER READING: Ackerman, Susan. *Warrior, Dancer, Seductress, Queen: Women in Judges and Biblical Israel.*

Bal, Mieke. *Murder and Difference: Genre, Gender, and Scholarship on Sisera's Death.*

Niditch, Susan. "Eroticism and Death in the Tale of Jael."

van Wolde, Ellen. "Ya'el in Judges 4."

Yee, Gale A. "By the Hand of a Woman: The Metaphor of the Woman Warrior in Judges 4."

Jecoliah

"YHWH is able" or "YHWH prevails," from Hebrew
ykl, "to be able, prevail," and *yāh*, a shortened
form of YHWH
(2 Kgs 15:2; 2 Chr 26:3)

This Jerusalemite of unknown parentage becomes the consort of King Amaziah, ninth king of Judah (reigned 798–769 B.C.E.), and queen mother of his successor, Azariah/Uzziah. She may have wielded considerable influence as queen mother during the early years of her son's reign (he was sixteen when he became king) and during her son's illness (he suffered from a skin disease for much of his long reign).

RHONDA BURNETTE-BLETSCH

SEE ALSO Part I: Athaliah.

FOR FURTHER READING: Ackerman, Susan. "The Queen Mother and the Cult in Ancient Israel."

Jedidah

"beloved," from Hebrew *yādîd*, "beloved"
(2 Kgs 22:1)

Jedidah is the daughter of Adaiah of Bozkath (a city southwest of Jerusalem), the consort of King Amon of Judah, and the mother of Josiah, Amon's successor, who ruled from 639 to 609 B.C.E. She is mentioned only in Josiah's regnal formula. Because these formulas typically name the mother of Judean kings and the biblical record portrays more than one of these women in active cultic and political roles, the queen mother may have served as an official functionary in the southern royal court. Alternatively, Ben-Barak argues that few queen mothers are portrayed prominently in the Bible and explains that those who receive such treatment must have been exceptional individuals. However, the scarcity of biblical data on the role of the queen mother is not surprising, since the Bible is dominated by an androcentric perspective that often precludes any mention of women's activities.

As is always the case when the people of the land are involved in matters of succession, Josiah's mother originates from the outlying provinces of Judah rather than from Jerusalem. Thus, Jedidah's rural connections are likely instrumental in the choice of Josiah as successor to the murdered Amon.

RHONDA BURNETTE-BLETSCH

SEE ALSO Part I: Azubah 1.

FOR FURTHER READING: Ackerman, Susan. "The Queen Mother and the Cult in Ancient Israel."

Andreasen, Niels-Erik. "The Role of the Queen Mother in Israelite Society."

Ben-Barak, Zafrira. "The Status and Right of the *gᵉbîrâ*."

Jehoaddin/Jehoaddan

"YHWH gives delight," from Hebrew *'ēden*, "luxury, delight," and *yāh*, a shortened form of YHWH

(2 Kgs 14:2; 2 Chr 24:3; 25:1)

This Jerusalemite woman of unknown parentage becomes one of two wives of Joash/Jehoash, eighth king of Judah (reigned 836–798 B.C.E.), in a marriage arranged by the influential priest Jehoiada. She is also queen mother of his successor, Amaziah (reigned 798–769 B.C.E.).

The role of queen mother probably bore political or cultic significance. She certainly exerted personal influence over the reigning monarch and may also have held institutionalized status as a political adviser or the sponsor of the goddess Asherah's cult.

RHONDA BURNETTE-BLETSCH

SEE ALSO Part I: Athaliah.

FOR FURTHER READING: Ackerman, Susan. "The Queen Mother and the Cult in Ancient Israel."

Jehosheba/Jehoshabeath

"YHWH's oath," from Hebrew *yĕhô*, prefix form of YHWH, and *šbʿ*, "to swear"

(2 Kgs 11:2–3; 2 Chr 22:11)

Identified as the daughter of King Jehoram (reigned 851–843 B.C.E.) and the sister of his successor King Ahaziah (reigned 843–842 B.C.E.). Jehosheba is credited with saving the royal line in the person of Ahaziah's son, her nephew Joash. After the violent death of Ahaziah, Queen Athaliah kills all of the king's other descendants — potential heirs — and would likewise have killed Joash, had Jehosheba not hidden him and his nurse for the six years of Athaliah's reign.

In the Chronicler's account (in which she is named Jehoshabeath), she is further identified as the wife of the priest Jehoiada. Because of his priestly interests, the Chronicler perhaps wished to lay claim to her and her heroism. At the same time, Chronicles often contains reliable information not present in the parallel Kings materials. In this case, Jehoshabeath's marriage to Jehoiada prefigures his influence on Joash.

ALICE L. LAFFEY

SEE ALSO Part I: Athaliah; Part II: Nurse of Joash (2 Kgs 11:2, etc.).

Jehudijah/Hodiah

"the Judahite [feminine]," from Hebrew *yĕhûdâ*, the name of the tribe of Judah

(1 Chr 4:18–19)

In the Chronicles genealogy of the tribe of Judah, Jehudijah appears as the proper name of one of the wives of a man named Mered. Alternatively, the name may be translated "his Judean wife," in light of the mention later in the verse that Mered also married an Egyptian woman, Bithiah. To confuse the matter further, 4:19 mentions "the wife of Hodiah, the sister of Naham," but it is not clear if Hodiah is the same person as Jehudijah. To clarify this kinship enigma, the verse is often emended to equate the two women mentioned.

JULIA MYERS O'BRIEN

SEE ALSO Part I: Bithiah.

Jemimah

meaning uncertain; perhaps "bright day," from Hebrew root *yôm*, "day"; or "dove," related to Arabic *yamāmah*, "dove"

(Job 42:14)

Jemimah is one of the three daughters, along with seven sons, born to Job in later life, after God restored his fortunes. The sons are not named, but all of the daughters are, and all their names signify beauty. If Jemimah means "dove," then her name may also be related to an epithet of the Canaanite goddess Anath.

ILANA PARDES

SEE ALSO Part I: Keren-happuch; Keziah; Part II: Daughters of Job (Job 1:2–19, etc.); Part III: Anath.

Jerioth

> meaning uncertain; perhaps "fearful one," from Hebrew *yr'*, "to tremble, be afraid"
> (1 Chr 2:18)

Listed within a textually problematic verse within the genealogy of Judah, this woman may be either a wife of Caleb, according to the Hebrew text (so NRSV), or a child of Caleb and another wife, Azubah, following the Syriac and the Vulgate.

JULIA MYERS O'BRIEN

SEE ALSO Part I: Azubah 2; Ephah; Ephrath/Ephrathah; Maacah 5.

Jerusha/Jerushah

> "possession, inherited one," from Hebrew *yěruššâ*, "possession, inheritance"
> (2 Kgs 15:33; 2 Chr 27:1)

Jerusha, daughter of Zadok, was the chief wife of Azariah/Uzziah, king of Judah from 785 to 733 B.C.E. and the mother of his successor, King Jotham. Some scholars have suggested that the queen mother served in an official capacity in the Judean court, based upon the regular occurrence of her name in the regnal formulas of southern kings and other hints in the biblical narrative of the cultic and political power she wielded. Others emphasize the scarcity of biblical evidence for the existence of such an official role. However, this silence is not surprising, since the Bible is dominated by an androcentric perspective that often precludes any mention of women's activities. If the queen mother was an official functionary of the court, Jerusha, who may have come from a prominent priestly family, would have risen to power early because of

the co-regency of Azariah and Jotham, necessitated by the former's illness (2 Kgs 15:5).

RHONDA BURNETTE-BLETSCH

SEE ALSO Part I: Athaliah; Jezebel 1.

FOR FURTHER READING: Ackerman, Susan. "The Queen Mother and the Cult in Ancient Israel."

Andreasen, Niels-Erik. "The Role of the Queen Mother in Israelite Society."

Ben-Barak, Zafrira. "The Status and Right of the *gᵉbîrâ*."

Jezebel 1

> "heap of dung"; pronunciation dictated by the pointing in the Hebrew *'izebel;* originally, probably "Zebul [another name for the god Baal] exists," "Zebul is," or "where is Zebul"; perhaps later understood as a parody: "no [Hebrew *'i*] Zebul," meaning "Baal is not," or "Baal does not exist"
> (1 Kgs 16:31; 18; 19; 21; 2 Kings 9)

Jezebel was the daughter of Ethbaal, king of the Phoenician city-state of Tyre, and wife of Ahab, king of Israel (1 Kgs 16:31), in the mid–ninth century B.C.E. She was undoubtedly the chief wife of Ahab and co-ruler with him. It is implied that she was the mother of Ahab's son and successor Ahaziah (1 Kgs 22:53) and alternately implied and stated that she was mother of the next king, Jehoram (2 Kgs 3:2, 13; 9:22). Ahab had other unnamed wives as well and many unnamed sons (1 Kgs 20:3, 5, 7; 2 Kings 10). Hence, whether Jezebel had other children or, specifically, was Athaliah's mother is unclear.

The extent of Jezebel's power is evidenced by the necessity for Jehu, the founder of the next royal dynasty in Israel, to murder her before his rule can be established (2 Kgs 9:30–37) — even though her royal husband and sons are by now dead. The biblical text insists that she is evil through and through.

Jezebel is the enemy of YHWH's prophets: she "killed the prophets of the LORD" (1 Kgs 18:13). On the other hand, there are "the four hundred fifty prophets of Baal and the four hundred prophets of Asherah, who eat at Jezebel's table" (v. 19). Elijah kills Jezebel's prophets on Mount Carmel (chap. 18). As a result, she swears that she will kill him (19:3). He takes her threat seriously and flees to the south, beyond the Israelite territory. His fleeing indicates Jezebel's power in the realm.

Another indication of her power is the story of Naboth (1 Kings 21). Ahab wishes to buy Naboth's vineyard, which is adjacent to the royal complex in Jezreel. Naboth refuses to give or sell it, claiming its status as nontransferable ancestral land. Ahab is depressed by this but cannot do anything. Jezebel, who sees the matter as a test case of monarchic power (v. 7), finds a way: she writes to the elders and dignitaries of Jezreel, asking them to bring two false witnesses to claim that Naboth has cursed the king and God. Such behavior signifies treason; Naboth is stoned to death, and his property reverts to the king. Although the letter is ostensibly signed with the king's seal (v. 8), the report comes back to Jezebel (v. 14). She tells Ahab that he can inherit Naboth's land, and he does so. Elijah protests to Ahab, "Thus says the LORD: Have you killed, and also taken possession?" (v. 19); he prophesies that Ahab's male descendants will die prematurely, his dynasty will perish, and that the "dogs shall eat Jezebel within the bounds of Jezreel" (v. 23). Ahab dies a brave soldier's death in Samaria (1 Kings 22); his son and Jezebel's, Ahaziah, succeeds to the throne for two years and then dies. His brother Jehoram succeeds him and is killed by Jehu, the new contender for the throne (2 Kings 9). Jezebel is killed by Jehu as well (2 Kgs 9:31–37): as she regally awaits Jehu and her doom in the Jezreel palace, some palace officials drop her through the lattice window. By the time Jehu has finished eating and orders that she be buried "for she is a king's daughter" (2 Kgs 9:34), the dogs have already eaten most of her carcass — in keeping with Elijah's prophecy.

Jezebel is characterized as totally evil in the biblical text and beyond it: in the New Testament her name is a generic catchword for a whoring, nonbelieving female adversary (Rev 2:20); in Judeo-Christian traditions, she is evil incarnate (see Pippin). The Bible is careful not to refer to her as queen. And yet, this is precisely what she seems to have been. Some early Jewish, albeit postbiblical, sources deconstruct the general picture: "Four women exercised government in the world: Jezebel and Athaliah from Israel, Semiramis and Vashti

from the [gentile] nations" (in a Jewish Midrash for the Book of Esther, *Esther Rabbah*). Clearly, Jezebel acted as queen even though the Bible itself refuses her the title and its attendant respect, not to mention approval. In the biblical text, as Trible notes, Jezebel is contrasted with and juxtaposed to the prophet Elijah, to the extent that they both form the two panels of a mirrored dyptich. She is a Baal supporter, he is a YHWH supporter; she is a woman, he is a man; she is a foreigner, he is a native; she has monarchic power, he has prophetic power; she threatens, he flees; finally he wins, she is liquidated. The real conflict is not between Ahab (the king) and Elijah, but between Jezebel (the queen in actuality, if not in title) and Elijah. Ultimately the forces of YHWH win; Jezebel loses. It remains to be understood why she gets such bad press.

It seems reasonable that Jezebel, a foreign royal princess by birth, was highly educated and efficient. Also, although her son's theophoric names have the element -*yāh* or -*yāhû* (referring to YHWH) in them, she seems to have been a patron and devotee of the Baal cult. It is not incomprehensible that, whereas Ahab devoted himself to military and foreign affairs, Jezebel acted as his deputy for internal affairs: the Naboth report comes back to her, as if the king's seal was hers (see Avigad's identification of a seal, "*lyzbl*," as possibly Jezebel's); she has her own "table," that is her own economic establishment and budget; she has her own "prophets," probably a religious establishment that she controls. All these point toward an official or semiofficial position that Jezebel held by virtue of her character, her royal origin and connections, her husband's and later her children's esteem, and her religious affiliation to the Baal (possibly also Asherah) cult. Perhaps she had the status of *gĕbîrâ*, "queen mother" (Ben-Barak), or of "co-regent" (Brenner). At any rate, there is no doubt that the biblical and later accounts distort her portrait for several reasons, among which we can list her monarchic power, deemed unfit in a woman; her reported devotion to the Baal and Asherah cult and her objection to Elijah and other prophets of YHWH; her education and legal know-how (shown in the Naboth affair); and her foreign origin. Ultimately, the same passages that disclaim

Jezebel as evil, "whoring," and immoral are witness to her power and the need to curb it.

ATHALYA BRENNER

SEE ALSO Part I: Athaliah; Azubah 1; Jezebel 2; Part II: Wives of Ahab (1 Kgs 20:3, etc.); Part III: Asherah/ Asherim.

FOR FURTHER READING: Avigad, Nahman. "The Seal of Jezebel."

Ben-Barak, Zafrira. "The Status and Right of the gᵉbîrâ."

Brenner, Athalya. *The Israelite Woman: Social Role and Literary Type in Biblical Narrative.*

Pippin, Tina. "Jezebel Re-Vamped."

Trible, Phyllis. "The Odd Couple: Elijah and Jezebel."

Jezebel 2

(Rev 2:20–23)

The name Jezebel appears once in the New Testament in the Revelation to John in the letter to the church in Thyatira (Rev 2:20). After praising the church for its service, the "one like the Son of Man" (Rev 1:13) speaks critically of "that woman Jezebel, who calls herself a prophet" (2:20). He accuses her of false prophecy, deceiving the church's people "to practice fornication and to eat food sacrificed to idols" (2:20). It is not clear whether or not the woman's actual name was Jezebel. What is important is that Revelation links her with the Jezebel of the Hebrew Bible. The name designates a deceptive woman who leads believers into sin. Though described as illicit sex, the sin could stand for broader behavior deemed sinful by the author. This reference takes the fornication metaphor further by calling Jezebel's followers adulterers (Rev 2:22). In the Hebrew Bible, adultery is frequently used as a metaphor for idolatry. Jezebel's punishment, and the punishment of her followers, is severe. She will be thrown into "great distress" and "her children" — that is, her followers — will be struck dead (2:22–23). This apocalyptic vision reflects the fate of the idolatrous Queen Jezebel in 1 and 2 Kings. Jezebel and her prophets are destroyed (in 2 Kings 9 and 1 Kings 18, respectively).

Revelation reveals only one opinion of this prophet Jezebel. The reader does not hear her perspective. She may have been a teacher or preacher in the congregation with views different from those of the author of this text; though we cannot prove her historical existence we can explore the cultural implications of giving a powerful woman with differing opinions the name Jezebel. It is a way of dismissing and shaming her. Powerful women are often humiliated and disempowered in the biblical text through accusations of sexual promiscuity. Beginning with Eve, women have been blamed as temptresses and seducers of men. As a foreign woman, Jezebel is doubly "other," bringing with her both dangerous religion and sexuality.

In Revelation Jezebel serves as an apocalyptic bad woman whose actions lead to the end of the world. God destroys both her and the evil whore of Babylon. Jezebel is not linked with a political power as the whore is, but her connection with a different religious teaching is clear. Traditional commentaries have sided with Revelation in presenting Jezebel as an evil presence. Feminist readings propose alternative readings of the women of Revelation, focusing on the ambiguities of the figure of Jezebel.

TINA PIPPIN

SEE ALSO Part I: Jezebel 1; Part III: Great Whore.

FOR FURTHER READING: Pippin, Tina. "'And I Will Strike Her Children Dead': Death and the Deconstruction of Social Location."

Joanna

"God is/has been gracious," a Grecized version of many Semitic proper names; from Hebrew *yāh* (an alternative form of YHWH) and *ḥnn*, "to grace or favor"

(Luke 8:3; 24:10)

Luke 8:3 singles out three women from a group characterized by having been healed from demons or illness, by possessing presumably independent means, and by having decided to join the itinerant Jesus movement and serve as its benefactors. The name of Joanna stands second both in Luke 8:3 and on the list of witnesses to the empty tomb (Luke 24:10). Whereas Mary of Magdala is characterized by her place of origin (a common ancient designation) and the severity of her previous misfortune (seven demons), Joanna is identified by reference to her husband, Chuza, an officer of Herod, presumably the ruler of Galilee. His title, *epitropos*, might well refer to the management of an estate farmed by slaves, tenants, or day laborers (compare Matt 20:8). Such managers were often themselves slaves or former slaves. Since there is no reason to think that Chuza joined her on this journey, one must imagine that either a very tolerant husband is in view or that, more likely, Joanna has left him — purse, dowry, or inheritance in hand — to follow Jesus. Wives of this sort populate the non-canonical *Acts of the Apostles,* where their rebellion and embracing of celibacy make considerable contributions to the plots of these second- and third-century works. Joanna's unknown story requires reevaluation of the view that no such wives can be found in the New Testament.

Luke 23:55–24:11 changes the Markan source in significant ways; all affect the portrayal of the women. Their visit to the tomb is an attempt to complete burial activities interrupted by the Sabbath. Preparation of corpses was "women's work." As wealthy women they could purchase expensive fragrant oils. The evangelist thus portrays them as continuing their benefactions to Jesus even after the men had faded from the scene. Unlike Mark 16:1–8, where the women are given a commission that they fail to execute, Joanna and the other women in Luke 24 are reminded of the teaching that Jesus had directed to *them* (24:6) and, on their own initiative, report their experience to the men. That they are disbelieved (24:11, 22–24) is not to their discredit. They shall, of course, have the last laugh. Their discipleship and witness are strongly underlined but found ineffective. Luke knows that opponents of the church ridiculed resurrection stories as reports of "mere" women, often considered to be unreliable witnesses. The fourth evangelist celebrates this witness (John 20:11–18). Luke neither celebrates nor suppresses it, but does ground the subsequent community in appearances of Jesus to the men (24:36–49).

RICHARD I. PERVO

SEE ALSO Part I: Mary 3; Susanna 2; Part II: Unnamed Women Who Provide for the Jesus Movement (Luke 8:2–3); Unnamed Women at the Cross (Luke 23:49).

FOR FURTHER READING: Seim, Turid Karlsen. *The Double Message: Patterns of Gender in Luke-Acts.*
———. "The Gospel of Luke."

Jochebed

meaning uncertain; perhaps "YHWH is glory,"
from *yāh,* a shortened form of YHWH, and *kābôd,*
"glory"
(Exod 2:1–9; 6:20; Num 26:59)

Jochebed, wife of Amram and mother of Moses, Aaron, and Miriam, is mentioned by name only in Exod 6:20 and Num 26:59, both genealogical listings. The narrative in Exodus 2 about Moses' birth introduces her, without providing her name, as a member of the priestly tribe Levi; she marries a Levitical man, also unnamed here. The mother, in defiance of the Pharaoh's order that every male Hebrew child be killed, hides her newborn son for three months and then places him in a basket in the Nile. Pharaoh's daughter (also unnamed) finds the child and accepts the offer of Moses' sister Miriam, who witnesses the rescue of her brother, to find a Hebrew woman as a wet nurse for the infant. The narrative cleverly places Jochebed as the caregiver for her own son.

The story in Exodus 2 clearly focuses on Moses, whose rescue from the river resembles other birth tales presenting culture heroes. The omission of the names of the child's family members contributes to the heightened interest in Moses. The genealogical information about his mother, as not only the daughter of Levi but also as the wife (and aunt!) of a Levite, serves to highlight the priestly pedigree of both Moses and Aaron. In addition, Jochebed, whose name (Hebrew *yôkebed*) apparently means "YHWH is glory," is notable as the first person in the Bible to have a name with the divine element *yāh,* a shortened form of YHWH. The tradition that Moses announces to the Israelites that YHWH is the name of their God (Exod 6:1–8) is thus embedded in his maternal lineage: if his mother bears YHWH's name, Moses learned it from her.

CAROL MEYERS

SEE ALSO Part I: Miriam 1; Part II: Daughter of Pharaoh (Exod 2:5–10).

Judith 1

"Judean, Jewess," from Hebrew *yĕhûdâ*, the name
of the tribe Judah
(Gen 26:34)

When Judith, a Hittite woman, becomes the wife of
Esau, the latter is excluded as a direct heir of the
Terahite lineage because of the Hebrew preference
that a man take a spouse from within the patrilineage.

The narrative's claim that Judith and Basemath,
and their husband, Esau, caused problems for Isaac
and Rebekah may reflect rivalry between the lineages of Esau and Jacob. Judith's name is not included in the genealogical listing of Esau's wives
found in Gen 36:1–5, which may mean that the
Genesis 26 reference is an addition to highlight the
Jacob-Esau conflict.

The use of a woman's name reflecting the people (Jews) of the late postexilic community (fourth
century B.C.E.) for a woman of non-Jewish origins
living a millennium or more before this time period
suggests that the genealogy of Esau was compiled
well after the time of the ancestral era.

NAOMI STEINBERG

SEE ALSO Part I: Adah 2; Anah; Basemath 1/Bashemath;
Mahalath 1; Oholibamah.

Judith 2

"Jew" or "Judean woman"; Greek *ioudith* represents the Hebrew *yĕhûdît*
(Jdt 8:1–16:25)

The Book of Judith (second or early first century
B.C.E.) is an imaginative, highly fictionalized, romance that entertains as it edifies. From a literary
perspective, the book is an artistic masterpiece,
constructed in two parts (1:1–7:32, 8:1–16:25), with
each internally ordered by a threefold chiastic pattern. Numerous correspondences between the two
halves of the story provide elegant compositional
symmetries. The Book of Judith is a story of balance and counter-balance that makes the point that
God's people have all they need to survive if they
rely wholeheartedly on the convenant.

Judith, the character from whom the book takes
its name, is not mentioned in the story's first half
(1:1–7:32). In the opening chapters, God's divine
sovereignty over Israel comes into direct conflict
with Nebuchadnezzar's political sovereignty over
all the nations of the western world. Holofernes,
commander-in-chief of the Assyrian armies of
Nebuchadnezzar (which, of course, is impossible
historically since Nebuchadnezzar is a Babylonian!), leads a massive force in a punitive campaign
against the western vassal nations — including Israel — who refused to send auxiliary forces against
the Medes. The people of Israel block his retaliatory
advancement against all the nations of the west at
their little town of Bethulia (related to Hebrew for
"virgin"), which strategically guards his route of
access to Jerusalem. Despite the warning of Achior
the Ammonite that the Jews cannot be conquered
unless they sin against their God, Holofernes lays
siege to Bethulia, cutting off its water supply. After
thirty-four days, the exhausted Bethulians are ready
to surrender, even though it will mean worship of
Nebuchadnezzar (3:8). Uzziah, their town magis-
trate, urges a compromise to give God five additional days to deliver them, temporarily postponing
what seems inevitable apostasy, slavery, and destruction of the Jerusalem sanctuary.

In Part 2 (8:1–16:25), Judith, a pious widow in
Bethulia, comes forward to challenge the five-day
compromise that has imposed conditions on God's
sovereignty. Once she takes the stage, she surrenders it to no other character, figuring in every scene
until the book's end. She sends her maid to summon the town magistrates, Uzziah, Chabris, and
Charmis to her house. Upbraiding them for putting
themselves in the place of God (8:12), she argues
that God is simply testing them, and has the power
to help them at any time (8:15). She urges, "Do not
try to bind the purposes of the Lord our God; for
God is not like a human being, to be threatened, or
like a mere mortal, to be won over by pleading"
(8:16). Judith proposes that they wait for deliverance and together call upon God who will listen, if
so disposed (8:17). She insists that God will not
disdain Israel because they know no other god and

that capture by the Assyrians will mean the desolation of the temple as well as their way of life. Judith counsels, "let us set an example for our kindred" (8:24).

Uzziah responds that all she has said is true and that this is not the first time her wisdom has been shown (8:28–29). But, the people were thirsty; the magistrates made an oath; and she can best help by praying for rain. On her account, the Lord will fill the cisterns and the people will no longer faint from thirst (8:31). Thus he saves himself from losing face by rescinding his foolish vow to hand over the town to the Assyrians in five days if God does not act (7:30–31), blaming the people who forced him to this oath, victimizing the victims as Jephthah did his daughter (Judg 11:35).

Giving up the idea that she and the town officials can set an example together, Judith decides to act independently. Explaining that she will do something all the generations will remember, she tells them to meet her at the town gate that evening when she and her maid will go out. Before the five days of their compromise are gone, she pledges "the Lord will deliver Israel by my hand" (Jdt 8:33). She refuses to tell them exactly what she is about to do (8:33–34).

Once the magistrates leave, Judith prostrates herself and cries out to God, begging the strength to be like Simeon, who took vengeance against the Shechemites who violated his virgin sister, Dinah. She implores God to hear her widow's prayer (9:4), crediting God with full knowledge of past, present, and future (9:5–6). Judith asks God to see the pride of the enemy, to send fury on their heads, to give her — a widow — a strong hand, to strike down the enemy "by the deceit" of her lips (9:10), and to "crush their arrogance by the hand of a woman" (9:10). In an androcentric setting, there is no greater dishonor for a male than to die at the hand of a female (see Judg 9:53–54; 2 Sam 11:21).

Judith is the only biblical woman who asks God to make her a good liar. In Jdt 9:10 and again in 9:13, she petitions God for "deceitful words" that will wound those who have planned cruelties against the Jerusalem Temple and their homeland. Judith is part of a larger company of women in the Bible who practice deceits that have positive national and personal consequences, including Rebekah who tricks her husband, Isaac, for the sake of their son Jacob (Genesis 27); Tamar who steals the next generation by tricking her father-in-law Judah into impregnating her (Genesis 38); the midwives, Shiphrah and Puah, who lie to the king of Egypt about why they have not killed the Hebrew males at birth (Exod 1:19); Moses' sister who offers to call a nurse for the daughter of Pharaoh, but calls the baby's own mother, (Exod 2:7–8); the daughter of the Pharaoh who adopts and names the child Moses, in direct violation of her father's instruction (Exod 2:10); Rahab, who preserves the lives of Joshua's spies by lying to the king of Jericho (Joshua 2); and Jael, a Kenite, who smashes the skull of the enemy general seeking the hospitality of her tent (Judges 4–5).

When her prayer is finished (Jdt 9:14), Judith dresses beautifully, "to entice the eyes of all the men who might see her" (10:4). Taking ritually pure foods to eat (10:5), she and her maid go out that night to the camp of the enemy. She meets the Assyrian patrol and tells her first lie when she says, "I am a daughter of the Hebrews, but I am fleeing from them, for they are about to be handed over to you to be devoured. I am on my way to see Holofernes the commander of your army, to give him a true report" (10:12–13). Her words and beauty greatly excite the soldiers who choose one hundred men from their ranks to assist her to the tent of Holofernes (10:14–17).

She prostrates herself before Holofernes, who tells her his first lie, saying he has never hurt anyone who chose to serve Nebuchadnezzar (11:2; conveniently forgetting how he destroyed the shrines and sacred places of seacoast peoples after they had surrendered in 3:1–8). Equal to the encounter, and playful with her use of the address "lord," which Holofernes hears as deference to him, but Judith means as reference to God, Judith promises to tell him nothing false (11:5). She explains she will go out into the valley and pray to God each night and God will tell her when the Bethulians have sinned by eating sacrifices, so that Holofernes can safely attack Bethulia (11:16–19). Well-pleased, Holofernes praises her beauty and wise speech, pledging, "If you do as you have said, your God shall be my God, and you shall live in the palace of King Nebuchadnezzar" (11:23; compare Ruth 1:16).

Four uneventful days pass in the enemy camp before Holofernes sends his personal attendant Bagoas to invite Judith to a banquet in his tent (Jdt 12:10–12). Judith accepts the invitation and dresses in her best finery (12:14–15). Seeing her, Holofernes is ravished, "for he had been waiting for an opportunity to seduce her from the day he first saw her" (12:16). She drinks and eats what her maid prepares (12:18–19). He drinks "much more than he had ever drunk in any one day since he was born" (12:20).

Evening comes and all withdraw from the tent, save Judith and Holofernes who is stretched out on his bed, dead drunk (13:2). Judith's maid waits outside, as instructed. Judith prays twice for God's help (13:4–5, 7), then taking Holofernes' own sword, she strikes his neck twice and cuts off his head (13:8). She gives his head to her maid, who puts it in the food bag, and the two women go out of the camp, as was their nightly habit to pray, except this night they return to Bethulia (13:10).

The people run to welcome Judith and her maid, and Judith displays the head of Holofernes, telling how God protected her so that no sin was committed to defile or shame her (13:15–16). The people bless God (13:17), and Uzziah hails her as "blessed by the Most High God above all other women on earth" (13:18). Judith then instructs the people to wait until daybreak and then attack the Assyrians (14:1–4). When Achior the Ammonite is brought to verify that the head belongs to Holofernes, he faints (see Add Esth 15:7), blesses Judith, believes firmly in God, and is circumcised (14:6–10).

The Israelites successfully rout the Assyrians and plunder their camp. Joakim, the high priest of Jerusalem arrives to celebrate the victory. A triumphant procession of the women and the men, with Judith in the lead singing a hymn of praise like that of Miriam and Moses in Exodus 15, makes its way to Jerusalem where all worship God for three months (16:1–20).

In the end, Judith goes back to her estate in Bethulia. "Many desired to marry her, but she gave herself to no man all the days of her life after her husband Manasseh" (16:22). At one hundred five years of age, she frees her faithful maid and distributes her property to all those who were next of kin to her husband (compare Num 27:1–11; 36:1–11; Tob 6:11–13). This dispersal of her estate supports the unexpressed fact that Judith is a childless widow.

Judith is conventional in upholding inheritance and purity rights, in prayer and fasting, in her ideas about God's providence. She is unconventional in upbraiding the male leaders of her town for what they have said about God, though she does this within the privacy of her own home. No other woman in the Bible has another woman in charge of her estate; no other childless woman refuses to marry. On her account, "No one ever again spread terror among the Israelites during the lifetime of Judith, or for a long time after her death" (16:25).

TONI CRAVEN

SEE ALSO Part II: Widows (Exod 22:22, etc.); Daughters of Zelophehad (Num 26:33, etc.); Woman of Thebez (Judg 9:53–54, etc.); Kinship Wife (Tob 1:9, etc.); Maid of Judith (Jdt 8:10, etc.); Virgin Defiled (Jdt 9:2).

FOR FURTHER READING: Craven, Toni. *Artistry and Faith in the Book of Judith.*

———. "Women Who Lied for the Faith."

Hopkins, Denise Dombkowski. "Judith."

Moore, Carey A. *Judith: A New Translation with Introduction and Commentary.*

Julia

"a woman of the *gens,* or clan, Julius"; Latin
(Rom 16:15)

Julia is one of nine women whom Paul greets at the conclusion of his letter to the Romans. The name was common in the Roman Empire, even among slaves. Julia is paired with Philologus (unlike most English translations, the NJB correctly and directly pairs these two), who is perhaps her husband or brother. These two, together with the others mentioned in v. 15, probably constituted the nucleus of one of several small congregations in Rome, which perhaps met in their house.

JOUETTE M. BASSLER

FOR FURTHER READING: MacDonald, Margaret. "Reading Real Women through the Undisputed Letters of Paul."

Junia

"a woman of the *gens,* or clan, Junius"; Latin
(Rom 16:7)

In Rom 16:7, Paul greets Andronicus and Junia as "prominent among the apostles." Paul describes them as relatives and states that they were in prison with him and had come to belief in Christ before he did. "Relatives" could mean fellow Jews or could denote actual blood relation, but according to either interpretation, Junia and Andronicus were Jews. We do not know their relationship to each other.

Since Junia fulfilled the Pauline criteria for apostleship (see 1 Cor 9:1), she must have claimed to have seen the risen Christ and have been engaged in missionary work. As a Jewish Christ-believer before Paul was converted, Junia may have lived in an eastern province of the Roman Empire and been among those who brought the message of Christ to the Roman Jewish community. Perhaps the Romans imprisoned Junia and Andronicus because of conflicts about this missionary work.

Junia's leadership role as an apostle corresponds with female leadership roles within ancient Judaism (such as head of the synagogue or elder) and within other Greco-Roman religions. Junia was one of several female church leaders associated with Paul. Others include Prisca (Rom 16:3–4; 1 Cor 16:19; 2 Tim 4:19), whom Acts describes as a teacher (Acts 18:26); Phoebe, described by Paul as a patron (Rom 16:1–2); and Euodia and Syntyche, whose conflict with each other caused problems for the church in Philippi (Phil 4:2–3). (See also the extracanonical *Acts of (Paul and) Thecla,* which describes the missionary Thecla as an associate of Paul.) Thus, Junia may have already carried out leadership functions within the Jewish community before becoming an apostle of Christ, and she carried out her apostolic work in communities led by women and men.

Christians have frequently overlooked the apostle Junia because many interpreters have argued that one should translate the name as Junias, a male name. Early church writers either explicitly interpreted Junia as a female name (the fourth-century prelate John Chrysostom praises her as a female apostle) or did not comment on the gender of the name. In later centuries, however, interpreters assumed that a woman could not have been an apostle and therefore that the name (in the Greek accusative case, Iounian) must be a masculine name, Junias. This hypothetical name Junias is, however, as yet unattested in ancient inscriptions, but the female Latin name Junia occurs over 250 times among inscriptions from ancient Rome alone. Further, the ancient translations and the earliest manuscripts with accents support reading Iounian as Junia. Finally, Junias would be an irregular form. Therefore, critical scholars today increasingly interpret the name as the feminine Junia. This Latin family name *(nomen gentile)* indicates that Junia was possibly a freedwoman or a descendant of a slave freed by a member of the Junian clan.

BERNADETTE J. BROOTEN

SEE ALSO Part I: Euodia; Phoebe; Prisca/Priscilla; Syntyche.

FOR FURTHER READING: Brooten, Bernadette. "'Junia . . . Outstanding Among the Apostles' (Romans 16:7)."

Cervin, Richard. "A Note Regarding the Name 'Junia(s)' in Romans 16.7."

Thorley, John. "Junia, a Woman Apostle."

Keren-happuch

"horn of antimony/kohl," that is, "cosmetics case"; from Hebrew *keren,* "horn, flask," and *pûk,* "antimony, kohl"
(Job 42:14)

Keren-happuch is one of three daughters (and seven sons) born to Job late in his life, after God restored his fortunes. Her name signifies a container of antimony or kohl, black powder used to beautify the eyes. It is compatible with the renowned beauty of Job's daughters.

ILANA PARDES

See also Part I: Jemimah; Keziah; Part II: Daughters of Job (Job 1:2–19, etc.).

Keturah

"incense," or possibly, "the perfumed one," from Hebrew *qĕṭōret*, "incense"

(Gen 25:1, 4; 1 Chr 1:32–33)

The marriage of Abraham (the first major male figure in the ancestor narratives of Genesis) to Keturah represents a secondary union, one that separates the procreation of offspring from the inheritance of immovable property (land), which in this case goes only to Abraham's primary heir, Isaac — not to Keturah's six children. From the story, it is impossible to tell whether Keturah's marriage to Abraham took place while Sarah was still alive; the secondary nature of this marriage would not have required Sarah's death.

The names Keturah and those of her children probably reflect the region of Arabia, the land from which incense derives.

NAOMI STEINBERG

See also Part I: Hagar; Sarah 1/Sarai.

Keziah

"cassia," from Hebrew *qĕṣî'â*, "cassia"

(Job 42:14)

Keziah is one of three daughters (and seven sons) born to Job at the end of his life, after God restored his fortunes. Her name stands for a perfume made from cassia, a variety of cinnamon used as an ingredient in scents and anointing oils. It evokes an aura of feminine fragrance that is compatible with the renowned beauty of Job's daughters, whose names all signify natural or augmented female attractiveness.

ILANA PARDES

See also Part I: Jemimah; Keren-happuch; Part II: Daughters of Job (Job 1:2–19, etc.).

Leah

Hebrew *lē'â*, "cow," possibly meaning "strength," as Akkadian *littu*, "cow," is related to *lē'ûtu*, "strength, power"

(Gen 29:16–34:1; 35:23, 26; 46:5, 14, 18; 49:31; Ruth 4:11; compare Hos 12:13)

Leah is the elder daughter of Laban and the wife of Jacob, father of twelve sons who will become the twelve tribes of Israel. Leah and her sister Rachel, whose names mean "cow" and "ewe," give Jacob many sons; and their father gives him actual livestock. Leah is described as having "soft (lovely) eyes" (Gen 29:7). Some translations (such as NJPS, RSV, NEB, and REB), perhaps influenced by Jacob's preference for Rachel, render this as "dull-eyed" or "weak eyes," but the more appropriate translation is "soft eyes" (as in NRSV and NAB) — what we might call "cow eyes." She has six sons, who become six of the Israelite tribes (Gen 35:23; 46:5, 14).

Jacob sets out to Mesopotamia to marry from his parents' collateral line. His father Isaac had married a first cousin, once removed; Jacob will marry his matrilineal first cousins and his paternal second cousins, once removed. In so doing, he too will marry into the family of Terah, the father of Abraham and Nahor, the grandfather of Rebekah, and the great-grandfather of Rachel and Leah. Jacob meets Rachel at a well (compare the stories of Zipporah and Rebekah) and falls in love. Penniless, he contracts to work seven years as his bride wealth. After the wedding feast, in the dark of evening, Jacob goes in to consummate the marriage, but Leah has been substituted for her sister; in the morning, Jacob claims that "it was Leah!" (Gen 29:25). This is a multiple reversal: the trickster has been tricked, and the man who supplanted his elder brother marries the elder sister. Laban makes the message clear as he declares that the younger must not be married first. Jacob then arranges to receive Rachel at the end of the wedding week and thereafter to work another seven years to pay off her bride price.

The two sisters are co-wives in competition for status in the household. Jacob clearly prefers Rachel (Gen 29:30). In compensation, God "opened her

[Leah's] womb" (Gen 29:32), whereas Rachel proves to be barren. Perhaps the significance of Leah's name comes into play here. Cows are a great symbol of fertility in Mesopotamia, partially because of the similarity between the words *littu,* "cow," and *alittu,* "birthgiver." Leah's fertility quickly results in four sons. Nevertheless, because of Jacob's obvious preference for Rachel, Leah remains insecure and in the naming of her sons shows how she hopes to gain favor through bearing them. She names her first son Reuben ("see, a son") her next one Simeon ("God heard that I am unloved"), the third one Levi ("now my husband will be with me"), and the fourth one Judah ("thanks! [NRSV, praise]"). At this point Rachel is jealous and has her maid Bilhah give birth to two sons; Leah, no longer fertile, responds by having her own maid Zilpah bear two sons (Gen 30:9–13; 35:26; 46:18).

The climax in the rivalry between the sisters/co-wives comes when Reuben finds mandrakes. Both sisters want them for their fertility-inducing powers and perhaps also for their aphrodisiac qualities. They strike a bargain: Leah will give Rachel the mandrakes in return for a night with Jacob. Leah crudely announces to Jacob that she has "hired" him with the mandrakes, and Jacob spends the night with her (Gen 30:14–17). When co-wives unite in purpose, husbands must comply. The new accord between the sisters helps Leah become pregnant (or the mandrakes work), for she gives birth to two more sons — Issachar ("God has given me my hire") and Zebulon ("now my husband will honor me") — and a daughter, Dinah (Gen 30:17–21).

The sisters are also in accord when Jacob asks them to come back with him to Canaan, but they are unhappy that their father gave them nothing of the bride wealth that Jacob provided in his fourteen years of service (Gen 31:3–15). Yet, like Rebekah, they affirm their choice to leave their parental home. They depart together, but despite all her children, Leah is still second best. When Jacob believes that danger threatens in his meeting with Esau, he arranges his family so that the maids and their children are placed first, then Leah and her children, and last and most protected, Rachel and Joseph

(Gen 33:1–2; compare 32:22). Even after Rachel's death, Jacob will continue to favor her son, Joseph.

Leah does not play the kind of role in determining the fate of her sons that Rebekah and Sarah did, perhaps because she never feels as secure as they did, and possibly because in a polygamous situation, co-wives have less influence except when they are united. The absence of a clear matriarchal hand shows itself in the uncontrolled friction between the children, but all the children of Jacob are to inherit the blessing. Nothing more is heard of Leah other than Jacob's statement that he buried her in the Cave of Machpelah with Abraham and Sarah, Isaac and Rebekah (Gen 49:31).

In Israelite tradition, the maid-mothers were forgotten, but Rachel and Leah were remembered. The prophet Hosea relates how Jacob went to Aram to search for a wife (Hos 12:13), and the wedding blessing for Ruth remembers Rachel and Leah as the ancestresses "who built up the house of Israel" (Ruth 4:11).

TIKVA FRYMER-KENSKY

SEE ALSO Part I: Bilhah; Rachel; Zilpah.

FOR FURTHER READING: Brenner, Athalya. "Female Social Behaviour: Two Descriptive Patterns Within the 'Birth of the Hero' Paradigm."

Cohen, Norman J. "Two That Are One: Sibling Rivalry in Genesis."

Jagendorf, Zvi. "'In the Morning, Behold, It Was Leah': Genesis and the Reversal of Sexual Knowledge."

Ross-Burstall, Joan. "Leah and Rachel: A Tale of Two Sisters [Gen 29:31–30:24]."

Lilith SEE Lilith (Part III).

Lois

Greek *lois,* probably meaning "more pleasant, more desirable"
(2 Tim 1:5)

According to Acts 16:1–3, a coworker of Paul's named Timothy was the uncircumcised son of a Jewish mother, who was herself a "believer" (*pistēs*), and a Gentile father. Timothy is well known from the undisputed letters of Paul, which say nothing about his family. However, the author of the letter known as 2 Timothy (who writes in the name of Paul, perhaps as late as the mid–second century C.E.) identifies Timothy's grandmother as a woman named Lois, and her daughter, his mother, as one Eunice, both of whom are now said to have been believers in Christ.

The historical value of this information is dubious. The addition of a pious grandmother to Timothy's lineage and the assignment of names to these women probably points to a well-known tendency in both ancient Jewish and Christian literature to provide additional material about venerated figures, including proper names for persons previously anonymous.

The oblique allusion in 3:15 to "how from childhood you have known the sacred writings that are able to instruct you for salvation through faith in Christ Jesus" is often understood to mean that the two women were responsible for Timothy's childhood education, thus presenting us with an image of Jewish women knowledgeable in sacred Scriptures. If 2 Timothy is the work of a Christian author in the second century C.E., however, this allusion may say more about the education of Christian women than of contemporaneous Jewish women, if it says anything reliable about actual social practices. It is worth noting, though, that in the Apocryphal/Deuterocanonical Book that bears his name, Tobit's paternal grandmother, Deborah, is said to have been knowledgeable in the observance of law (Tob 1:8).

The author's positive presentation of Eunice and Lois should be contrasted with the denigration of those "little women" (NRSV, "silly women") of 2 Tim 3:6 who are easily deceived by false teachers, and should be understood within the broader context of the same author's instructions about appropriate and inappropriate behavior for women in 1 Tim 2:9–14 (where the author forbids women to teach or have authority over men — presumably the instruction of children is not intended by this prohibition), 3:11 (on women deacons), and 5:2–6 (on widows).

ROSS S. KRAEMER

SEE ALSO Part I: Eunice; Part II: Mother of Timothy (Acts 16:1); Women Who Profess Reverence for God (1 Tim 2:9–15); Women Deacons (1 Tim 3:11); Older and Younger Women (1 Tim 5:2).

FOR FURTHER READING: Metzger, Bruce M. "Names for the Nameless in the New Testament: A Study in the Growth of Christian Tradition."

Lo-ruhamah

"not pitied, loved," from Hebrew lō', "no," and rḥm, "to have pity, have compassion, love"
(Hos 1:6, 8; 2:1, 23)

Lo-ruhamah is the second of three children born to the prophet Hosea (eighth century B.C.E.) and his wife, Gomer; she is sister to brothers Jezreel ("God sows") and Lo-ammi ("not my people"). All three offspring symbolically represent the corruption of Israel. Associated with the noun reḥem ("womb"), ruḥāmâ refers to one receiving God's maternal compassion, which issues forth from the divine womb. However, Lo-ruhamah's birth signifies that God will no longer have such compassion upon the kingdom of Israel (1:6). When Israel is reconciled with God, the meaning of Lo-ruhamah's name will be reversed, along with her brothers'. Instead of being unpitied, God will now have pity on her (2:1, 23); and she will be called Ruhamah ("pitied, loved").

GALE A. YEE

SEE ALSO Part I: Gomer.

Lydia

meaning uncertain; probably a woman from Lydia, a region in western Asia Minor
(Acts 16:11–15)

The Lydia story appears only in Acts 16 and may be fictitious. Acts is not historical in the traditional Western sense of the word, but rather was written to tell a story, entertain, present a theological argument, and convert. In particular, Acts told the story of the conversion of the Gentiles to Christianity.

Luke (the author of Acts and the Gospel of Luke)

describes Lydia as a seller of purple (goods) from Thyatira who worships the God of Israel. Thyatira, a Macedonian colony in Asia Minor, was known in antiquity for its excellent dye industry. The Greek term for "dealer in purple goods," *porphyropōlis,* indicates that Lydia dealt in a very precious commodity: purple dye was used primarily for the clothing of royalty and the wealthy. Inscriptions have been found honoring the city's guild of dyers, and Luke's readers may have associated Lydia with such a guild. If she is a fictitious figure, her name may have been adopted by Luke to refer to the region of Lydia in Asia Minor, in which Thyatira was located.

In the passage, Lydia is baptized "with her household" (v. 15) and then offers her home as a center for Paul and his fellow evangelists. This indicates that she, like many other women in antiquity, owned a home and employed a number of servants or owned slaves. (It does not necessarily mean that she was wealthy or high-born, since she may have been a freedwoman; but she was at least comfortable and self-supporting.) Since no husband is mentioned in the passage, she was probably widowed; demographically, this was more likely than being divorced or never married.

The Lydia story, and probably Acts in general, would have been circulating in the Christian community in the late first century and thereafter. At that time, women leaders in the early Christian communities were viewed by some (mostly male leaders) as threatening and by others as normal and positive, on a par with male leaders. Such female leadership reflected a broad trend in religious worship at the time. At Philippi, the archaeological evidence shows that polytheism, especially goddess worship, was thriving in the middle of the century after Acts was produced. Women often held positions of authority in such cults. The Diana/Artemis cult, in which women figured prominently, became highly popular by the end of the second century — long after Paul's time, but it may have existed during his time as well. Devotion to the goddess Isis was widespread in the Roman period, attracting many women; a cult to the divinized Livia, wife of Augustus, was refounded in the second century;

women were also involved in a cult to the gods Liber, Libera, and Hercules, which was unusual because women in the Greco-Roman environment did not generally participate in cults to Hercules; and early Byzantine evidence points to the veneration of Mary and to women's leadership roles in the early church. Literary evidence, including the letter of Polycarp, bishop of Smyrna, to the Philippians (c. 110 C.E.), also intimates the existence of strong women, and Paul himself mentions the women leaders Euodia and Syntyche (Philippians 4).

Luke's placing of Lydia (Eastern businesswoman turned Christian heroine) at Philippi (a city where many were converted by Paul, yet where polytheism and female participation in religions were thriving) was theologically driven. O'Day points out that Luke's treatment of Lydia is self-serving. His ideal women throughout Acts merely provide housing and some economic resources; they do not lead the growing Christian community on a par with men. For Luke, then, Lydia presents an example to "wayward" women of Philippi: even businesswomen who own homes and have servants should convert to Luke's understanding of Christianity, offer their wealth and resources to (male) Christian missionaries, and allow men to preserve or assume leadership roles in the community.

Luke's judgment does not have to be the final word, however. Today, instead of viewing Lydia and other women like her as pawns in male leaders' games, women can recognize them as strong, well-off, and independent people who, upon embracing the new Christ cult, became leaders in it.

VALERIE ABRAHAMSEN

SEE ALSO Part II: Women at the Place of Prayer at Philippi (Acts 16:13).

FOR FURTHER READING: Abrahamsen, Valerie. "Women at Philippi: The Pagan and Christian Evidence."

O'Day, Gail R. "Acts of the Apostles."

Olson, Mark J. "Lydia."

Maacah 1

meaning uncertain; perhaps from Hebrew *m'k,*
"to press, squeeze"
(Gen 22:24)

Reumah, the secondary wife (concubine) of Nahor, bears Maacah as one of four offspring to her husband, Abraham's brother. The feminine grammatical formation of the name suggests that Maacah is a daughter of Nahor. The NRSV understands Maacah to be a man. Here and in several other passages, ancient as well as modern translators obscure the presence of women.

The meaning of the name is uncertain, but it may refer to a geographical region in the northern Transjordan.

NAOMI STEINBERG

SEE ALSO Part I: Matred; Reumah.

Maacah 2

(2 Sam 3:3; 1 Chr 3:2)

Maacah is King Talmai of Geshur's daughter, King David's wife, and the mother of David's son Absalom. She is third on a list of six mother-son references concerning David's sons born at Hebron (2 Sam 3:2–5; 1 Chr 3:1–4). Her royal origins may indicate that her marriage had diplomatic implications for Geshur, an Aramean kingdom, and Judah.

LINDA S. SCHEARING

SEE ALSO Part I: Abigail 1; Abital; Ahinoam 2; Bathsheba; Bath-shua 2; Haggith; Michal; Part II: Wives and Concubines of David, Taken in Jerusalem (2 Sam 5:13); Wives of David (2 Sam 12:11, etc.).

Maacah 3/Micaiah

(1 Kgs 15:2; 2 Chr 11:20–22; 13:2)

The best-loved wife of King Rehoboam (reigned 928–911 B.C.E.; the first king of the southern kingdom of Judah) and the mother of King Abijam/Abijah (reigned 911–908 B.C.E.), Maacah is also the mother of Attai, Ziza, and Shelomith. According to 1 Kgs 15:2, she is the daughter of a man named Abishalom, whereas 2 Chr 11:20–22 calls her the daughter of Absalom. Another discrepancy appears in 2 Chr 13:2, where the wife of King Rehoboam and the mother of King Abijah is named Micaiah, the daughter of Uriel of Gibeah.

ALICE L. LAFFEY

SEE ALSO Part I: Azubah 1; Shelomith 3; Part II: Women of Rehoboam (Eighteen Wives, Sixty Concubines, and Sixty Daughters) (2 Chr 11:21).

Maacah 4

(1 Kgs 15:10, 11, 13; 2 Chr 11:20–23; 15:16)

The regnal formula of Asa, king of Judah from 908 to 867 B.C.E., claims that his mother is Maacah the daughter of Abishalom (1 Kgs 15:10). This is problematic because the same woman is alleged to be the mother of Asa's father, Abijah/Abijam (1 Kgs 15:2). An alternative tradition, calling Abijah's mother Micaiah the daughter of Uriel of Gibeah, is most likely an attempted harmonization of this difficulty (2 Chr 13:2). Either Abijah and Asa are brothers, not father and son, or Maacah was Asa's grandmother, not his mother. Thus, Maacah is the wife of Rehoboam (2 Chr 11:20–23), whose favored status with her husband ensured Abijah's succession. This tradition also offers the variant spelling "Absalom" for Maacah's father. If this refers to the half-Geshurite son of David, Maacah and Rehoboam's marriage would be politically advantageous. After serving as queen mother during Abijah's short reign, Maacah continues in that position under her son or grandson, Asa. If Asa is her grandson, this atypical retention of Maacah's title adds support to the contention that the queen mother was an official functionary in the Judean court and not simply the female parent of the king. Maacah's role appears most clearly to be an office when Asa removes her from her position as *gĕbîrâ* ("great lady") after she makes a cult object associated with the goddess Asherah. Ackerman suggests that the primary and generally accepted responsibility of the queen mother's office was to devote herself to the cultic worship of Asherah. Thus, the lack of biblical evidence for this office might be partly explained by the Bible's reluctance to admit Asherah worship was ever part of the official royal court.

RHONDA BURNETTE-BLETSCH

SEE ALSO Part I: Abijah 2/Abi; Azubah 1; Hamutal/ Hamital; Maacah 3/Micaiah; Nehushta; Part III: Asherah/Asherim.

FOR FURTHER READING: Ackerman, Susan. "The Queen Mother and the Cult in Ancient Israel."

Andreasen, Niels-Erik. "The Role of the Queen Mother in Israelite Society."

Ben-Barak, Zafrira. "The Status and Right of the gᵉbîrâ."

Spanier, Kitziah. "The Queen Mother in the Judean Royal Court: Maacah — A Case Study."

Maacah 5

(1 Chr 2:48)

Maacah is identified in a genealogy as one of Caleb's two concubines. Caleb, who also had several wives, was a descendant of Judah. Maacah bore four sons and probably one daughter, Achsah, who figures prominently in the story of Othniel (Josh 15:15–19; Judg 1:12–15).

The elaboration of wives and concubines, unusual in the Chronicles genealogy, conveys the importance of Caleb and his descendants.

ALICE L. LAFFEY

SEE ALSO Part I: Achsah; Azubah 2; Ephah; Ephrath/ Ephrathah; Jerioth.

Maacah 6

(1 Chr 7:15–16)

The wife of Machir, the firstborn son of Manasseh by Manasseh's union with an Aramean concubine, Maacah bore a son, Gilead. The Hebrew text seems to indicate that Maacah was also Machir's sister. Her double relation to Machir may point to his strong position as the source of military officers (Judg 5:14). Her Aramean background suits the role of her son as the eponymous ancestor of Gilead, in Transjordan; it was usually under the influence of the Arameans.

ALICE L. LAFFEY

Maacah 7

(1 Chr 8:29; 9:35)

The wife of Jeiel in the tribe of Benjamin, Maacah seems to have been the mother of Gibeon as well as of several other sons, including Abdon, Zur, Kish,

Baal, Nadab, Gedor, Ahio, Zeker, Mikloth, and also, according to 1 Chr 9:35, Ner. Ner was the grandfather of Israel's first king, Saul (reigned c. 1025–1005 B.C.E.).

ALICE L. LAFFEY

Mahalath 1

"mild, sweet, gracious," from Hebrew ḥlh, "to appease, make agreeable"; or "adornment," from unattested Hebrew root, also ḥlh

(Gen 28:9)

The daughter of Ishmael, granddaughter of Abraham (the first major male ancestor in the Genesis narrative) and Hagar, an Egyptian woman outside the Hebrew descent line, Mahalath marries Esau. Because of the Israelite preference for marriage to a woman within the kinship group, the marriage between Mahalath and Esau results in Esau's displacement from the direct Israelite patrilineage. Mahalath's name is not included in the genealogical listing of Esau's wives found in Gen 36:1–5, and her appearance in 28:9 may be part of the emphasis on the Esau-Jacob rivalry.

NAOMI STEINBERG

SEE ALSO Part I: Anah; Basemath 1/Bashemath; Oholibamah.

Mahalath 2

(2 Chr 11:18–19)

Wife of King Rehoboam of Judah (reigned 928–911 B.C.E.), Mahalath also seems to be related to Rehoboam as a second cousin, since both of their fathers were sons of King David. Mahalath was the daughter of Jerimoth, who was the son of David and Abihail; she was the mother of three sons (Jehush, Shemariah, Zaham) who are not mentioned elsewhere in the Bible.

ALICE L. LAFFEY

SEE ALSO Part I: Abihail 2; Part II: Women of Rehoboam (Eighteen Wives, Sixty Concubines, and Sixty Daughters) (2 Chr 11:21)

Mahlah 1

meaning uncertain; perhaps "wounded," from Hebrew *ḥll*, "pierce"; or "pleasing, ornament," from
Hebrew *ḥlh*, "to mollify, appease"

(Num 26:33; 27:1; 36:11; Josh 17:3)

Mahlah is one of the five daughters of Zelophehad
who approaches Moses to ask for an inheritance of
land alongside their male relatives.

KATHARINE DOOB SAKENFELD

SEE ALSO Part I: Hoglah; Milcah 2; Noah; Tirzah; Part II:
Daughters of Zelophehad (Num 26:33, etc.).

Mahlah 2

(1 Chr 7:18)

According to the genealogical lists of 1 Chronicles,
Mahlah is one of the children of Hammolecheth,
the sister of Machir who is the son of Manasseh
and the ancestor of a major clan in the tribe of
Manasseh. The mention of women, including sisters and daughters, in kinship lists that are largely
patrilineal served to reinforce the importance of the
group.

ALICE L. LAFFEY

SEE ALSO Part I: Hammolecheth.

Mara

"bitter," from Hebrew *mar*, "bitter, bitterness"

(Ruth 1:20)

When Naomi returns to Bethlehem with Ruth, she
is met by the women of the city, who ask, "Is this
Naomi?" (1:19). She replies by asking them to "call
me Mara," a name meaning "bitter," rather than
Naomi, which means "pleasant." Her new name
alludes to her difficulties — the death of her husband and sons, and her sojourn in a foreign land. It
also provides a wordplay with her claim that "the
Almighty has dealt bitterly [Hebrew *hēmar*] with
me" (1:20).

CAROL MEYERS

SEE ALSO Part I: Naomi.

Martha

Aramaic *mārtâ or mārtā'*, "lady" or "mistress"

(Luke 10:38–42; John 11:1–6, 17–44; 12:2)

Martha, identified as the sister of Mary, tends to be
remembered primarily as she is depicted in Luke's
very short exemplary story. This story appears to pit
Martha and Mary against each other. It shows Jesus
affirming the silent Mary who "sits at his feet"
(learns from him as a disciple), against a complaining, bustling Martha who is busy with what is seen
as the women's work of serving. The story is often
read as permitting women to step out of the gender
roles assigned to them (as Mary supposedly does),
but at the cost of denigrating the "Marthas" who
engage in the work of sustaining life.

The stories in John 11:1–12:19 present a quite different picture; they show the two women acting in
concert on behalf of their brother Lazarus (11:17–
44) and in gratitude for his restoration to them
(12:1–8). In John's version of the story, Martha in
particular is an example of faith (11:20–27). But the
roles Martha plays in both stories require a second
look.

Luke's story begins by mentioning Martha, saying that she "received" Jesus; in the context of Luke,
this means that she offered him the hospitality of
her home. Therefore she seems to have been the
head of the household. The text goes on to say she
had a sister called Mary; the standard translations
say, "who sat at the Lord's feet and listened to what
he was saying" (10:39). Thus Mary takes on the role
of the student of a rabbi, in contrast to Martha,
who is "distracted by her many tasks" (10:40). But
many ancient manuscripts include the word *also* in
10:39; it would be better translated: "She had a sister
named Mary who also sat at the Lord's feet and
listened to what he was saying." This version introduces Martha as a disciple and hearer of Jesus and
introduces Mary as her sister and her companion in
discipleship.

Reading the verse this way helps to bring out the
real meaning of the next verse, "But Martha was
distracted by her many tasks" (10:40) The word
translated as "tasks" is *diakonia;* the related verb
diakonein in her question is translated "to do

work." Although these words can mean "serving, waiting on table" in many contexts, throughout the New Testament they convey a double reference to table service and Christian ministries (Mark 10:41–45; Acts 6–7; 2 Cor 3:4–11; 4:1). The later Christian terms *deacon* and *dean* derive from these words. This context celebrates Martha as a minister (*diakonos;* compare Rom 16:1). But the approval Jesus gives to the silent Mary seems to discourage women from the ministry of preaching and charity. Unfortunately, this reading accords well with Luke's interest in including women in the narrative while carefully restricting their roles.

Martha is even more prominent in John's narrative. John 11:1–12:19 forms a unit bound together by references to the persons of Martha, Mary, and Lazarus. The section opens with the introduction of Lazarus as being from "Bethany, the village of Mary and her sister Martha" (11:1). The author goes on to identify Mary as "the one who anointed the Lord" (11:2), apparently expecting the reader to know both the anointing story and the names Mary and Martha. The progress of the story is explained through the relationships between Jesus and the three, but the emphasis is placed on Martha: "Jesus loved Martha and her sister and their brother Lazarus" (11:5).

When Jesus arrives in Bethany, Martha takes the initiative in going out to meet him, presenting him with an oblique request for his help (11:20–22). The dialogue between Martha and Jesus is used by the author to convey the special Johannine understanding of resurrection (vv. 24–26). Martha responds with a full confession of faith in Jesus (v. 27). With no prompting from Jesus, she returns and sends Mary back to meet Jesus, claiming that he has asked for her. Thus it seems that Martha has expectations from Jesus and is guiding the events that will ensue. This impression is undercut by Martha's objection to opening the tomb (11:39); but this objection gives Jesus the opportunity to recall for the reader their dialogue about resurrection (11:41). Martha's reaction to the miracle is not described, but the dinner in 12:1–8 appears to be a celebration of Lazarus's restoration; in 12:2, Martha is said to "serve." This

elaborate and dramatic narrative, usually referred to as the resurrection of Lazarus, actually focuses more on the two sisters, and particularly on Martha. It appears to have been developed from an earlier and simpler story about a woman whose brother Jesus raised; another version appears in the *Secret Gospel of Mark,* a version of Mark attested in a letter of Clement of Alexandria (late second to early third century). The author, or community of John, identified the woman with the famous disciple or minister *(diakonos)* Martha and introduced her sister into the story.

What then lies behind the two different Marthas? Should one be accepted over the other? The two stories appear to reflect the theological interests and gender assumptions of Luke and John, having only a few common features. In both, Martha is said to serve or minister *(diakonein;* Luke 10:39–40; John 12:1), whereas Mary is designated as "sister." In both, Martha welcomes Jesus (Luke 10:38; John 11:20); this may imply that she is the head of the house. This slender information appears to reflect the memory of the roles these two women played in the post-resurrection early Christian mission. Martha was known and remembered as Martha the *diakonos* ("minister"; compare Rom 16:1, Phoebe the *diakonos* of the church of Cenchreae).

Perhaps, like Prisca and Aquila, Philemon, and Nympha, Martha the *diakonos* was also the host to a house church along with "Mary the sister." Like Paul, who signed letters with his missionary companion (for example, Paul the apostle and Sosthenes the brother in 1 Cor 1:1), Martha may have worked with Mary in a missionary pair. Similar partnerships appear in Matt 10:1–4 and Romans 16. The latter includes female-and-male pairs who may have been marital partners (Prisca and Aquila, Junia and Andronicus, Nereas and his "sister"), and a pair consisting of two women, Tryphaena and Tryphosa. The title "sister," which applies to Martha as well as Mary, may indicate kin, erotic partners, and Christians in general, as well as specific roles in the mission. Here sisterhood may represent not blood relationship, but a shared commitment to the mission and perhaps to each other, hinting at a prehistory of women's same-sex commitments.

MARY ROSE D'ANGELO

SEE ALSO Part I: Euodia; Mary 2; Syntyche; Tryphaena; Tryphosa.

FOR FURTHER READING: D'Angelo, Mary Rose. "Women Partners in the New Testament."

———. "Women in Luke-Acts: A Redactional View."

Reinhartz, Adele. "From Narrative to History: The Resurrection of Mary and Martha."

Schüssler Fiorenza, Elisabeth. "A Feminist Critical Interpretation for Liberation: Martha and Mary, Luke 10:38–42."

Mary 1

anglicized form of Maria, which is a Greek form of Hebrew Miriam or Mariamme, meaning unknown

(Matt 1–2; 12:46–50; 13:53–58; Mark 3:31–35; 6:3–4; Luke 1–2; 3:23; 4:16–30; 8:19–21; 11:28–29; John 2:1–12; 6:42; 19:25–27; Acts 1:14; Rom 1:3; Gal 4:4)

This article deals mainly with New Testament references to Mary the mother of Jesus and to Jesus' mother, rather than texts on how Jesus was born or his genealogy. It omits consideration of John 1:1–5, 10–18; Phil 2:6–12; and Revelation 12.

Traditions about Mary the mother of Jesus ultimately become so central in Christianity that many readers may be surprised to see how few of these are found in the New Testament itself. Rather, stories of Mary's own birth, life, death, and bodily ascension to heaven first appear in Christian narratives dating no earlier than the second century C.E. and usually significantly later, the best known of which is the *Protevangelium (Infancy Gospel) of James.*

The first two chapters of Luke are known as the infancy narrative. They give a beautiful, poetic account of the miraculous events resulting in the birth of Jesus, the Christ for Luke. Thought by many scholars to be a Jew from a Greek-speaking Roman province, Luke infuses these chapters with allusions to scriptural events while casting the story as a contemporary Greco-Roman birth narrative of

a "divine man." This ploy in some ways resembles how the Roman poet Vergil heralded of the birth of Augustus as the dawn of the new age and how the Roman historian Suetonius posited Apollo as the father of Augustus.

Luke introduces Mary in the middle of his story about Elizabeth and Zechariah. Thanks to God's help, Elizabeth has miraculously conceived a son, John the Baptist, in her old age. Next Luke surprises his audience, inverting the familiar scriptural topos of God granting sons to childless married women. Shockingly, a betrothed virgin is reported as God's choice as a mother for his son. The angel Gabriel visits a young virgin, Mary, living in Nazareth. She is betrothed to Joseph, a descendent of the Davidic line. Unlike the earlier miracle, in which Zechariah received the angel's message, Gabriel announces his news to the prospective mother and tells her that the son must be named Jesus. Despite her fear of the supernatural being, Mary musters the courage to ask how she could conceive a child, since she did not "know a man" (1:34; "since I am a virgin," in NRSV). She, too, appears to understand God's miracles as working through the natural order. Gabriel answers that the miracle God will perform for her will surpass that of Elizabeth and Zechariah and, by implication, that of Sarah and Abraham (Gen 18:1–15; 21:1–2). God's Holy Spirit will father Mary's son, and as a result, Jesus will be called "Son of God" (1:35).

At 1:36 Luke intertwines these two miracle narratives. Gabriel tells Mary that her own relative, the aged Elizabeth, is six months pregnant. One can only imagine Mary's surprise that another female member of her family has been visited by God in a similar manner. This information seems to allay Mary's fears — she will not be alone in her pregnancy and will have a confidante in Elizabeth, who will understand the divine event. Mary submits to God and agrees to the divine impregnation. She calls herself the "servant [literally "slave," in the Greek] of the Lord" and accedes to the angel's message: "let it be to me according to your word" (1:38).

When Mary arrives to stay with Elizabeth for three months, Elizabeth exclaims, "Blessed are you among women, and blessed is the fruit of your womb" (1:42). Unborn John leaps in the womb at this greeting to the unborn Jesus. The elder Elizabeth humbles herself before the younger Mary, calling her the "mother of my Lord" (1:43). Mary responds with an extended song, traditionally called the Magnificat (1:46–55), which recalls Hannah's prayer in 1 Sam 2:10.

This joyous response is all the more remarkable because of Mary's vulnerability due to her young age and her liminal marital status. Her pregnancy places her in a precarious position socially. She is promised to Joseph, but is not quite his wife (meaning his property). Yet the betrothal implies a commitment pledging Mary to Joseph and to no other man. God, however, usurps Joseph's place, suspending his legitimate rights. Joseph has no say in this matter. (In fact, Luke does not even introduce him in the descriptions of events preceding the miraculous birth.) God does not violate Mary, since the conception can happen only with her agreement. And in the Magnificat we see that Mary utterly submits to the will of God.

Schaberg has proposed that Luke knew of a tradition holding that Jesus was illegitimate. In her view, rather than erase the tradition that Mary was an unmarried mother, Luke purposely includes her social humiliation of being pregnant and unmarried — a condition far more ignominious than Elizabeth's embarrassment due to her childlessness. Then he transforms this shameful situation into a story of exaltation. Schaberg argues that Mary finds protection and empowerment from God, expressed in the Magnificat, as she accepts the bitterness of her situation: the stigma of being an unwed mother. But Schaberg also notes that the story is not presented in a way that will empower other women. Luke has merely exchanged Mary's patriarchal master — a mortal husband, Joseph — for the all-powerful God, to whom she dutifully submits.

Three later episodes in chap. 2 allow us a glimpse of Mary as fiancée, wife, and mother. Joseph takes Mary to Bethlehem for the imperial census. There she gives birth to Jesus. When they receive accolades from the shepherds who come to see the baby, Luke says that Mary treasures their praises, pondering them in her heart (2:19). Mary and Joseph act as Torah-observant parents, having their son circumcised and then going to the temple for ritual purification. There Simeon, the blind prophet, "sees" in Jesus the salvation of Israel. He takes Mary aside, warning her about Jesus' future. Finally the young family returns to Nazareth, where the boy grows up.

When Jesus is twelve and the family is in Jerusalem for Passover, Jesus wanders off to the temple without telling his parents. After a three-day search, they find him, and Mary scolds him. Jesus retorts with a cryptic answer about already being in his father's house. Luke tells us that Mary "treasured all these things in her heart" (2:51). Much later in the Luke-Acts corpus (Acts 1:14), there is one reference to Mary as part of the small group who returned to Jerusalem after Jesus' ascension — a further hint of her understanding and support of her son's special identity and mission.

In these passages Mary takes no initiative to act outside her role as model "slave," patient listener, dutiful mother. Luke has succeeded in legitimating her as a woman of appropriate behavior and demeanor according to society's standards, a worthy choice to play such an important role in God's plan. Mary's childbearing is presented as the culmination of God's salvation history with Israel.

That God takes a virgin, Mary, to be the mother of his son reveals Luke's Greco-Roman hermeneutic. Although the idea that a mortal woman could conceive and bear the son of God is foreign to all Jewish writings, it is a familiar Greco-Roman theme in explaining the origin of many "divine men": Heracles, Alexander the Great, Octavian, the Augustus, Pythagoras, and Plato. In fact, such a genealogy would be a minimum requirement in legitimating a new god in the Greco-Roman world. What is unique to Luke's story is Mary's virginity, which will be dealt with shortly.

In presenting Mary the mother of Jesus, Matthew's contrast with Luke is noteworthy. Matthew's Mary is nearly absent from the narrative, much like Luke's Joseph. She is not the confidante of God through Gabriel; Joseph is. The scandalous quality of the pregnancy out of wedlock is underscored in this Gospel. As a "righteous man," Joseph struggles with the shock and shame of his beloved's betrayal and finally decides to divorce Mary "quietly" (1:19). When Gabriel reveals that the pregnancy has been conceived through the Holy Spirit, Joseph responds obediently and "acts" as Mary's husband until the birth of the baby, legitimating them both.

The audience can barely imagine what Mary is like, based on Matthew's Gospel. Unlike Luke, Matthew gives no clue as to Mary's response to God's will, leaving open the possibility that Mary was tricked into a divine conception. Schaberg points out that Matthew, more than Luke, leaves open the possibility that Mary's pregnancy may have resulted from adultery or from brutality or abuse, such as rape.

Mary's virginity at the time of the divine conception is important to both Luke and Matthew, but for different reasons. Luke's story holds that miracles progress in greatness over the course of biblical history. God has given many childless women sons, culminating with Elizabeth's experience; but God's choice of a young virgin to bear his son is completely new, and in magnitude it supersedes the earlier wonders. First, it is miraculous that a young virgin could become pregnant while never having "known a man" (Luke 1:34). Second, that God would choose to father a child in the manner of a pagan god is dealt with in the narrative by stating that the conception took place through the Holy Spirit. Luke avoids the typical pagan scenario in which a deity descends in the guise of a mortal being in order to have sexual intercourse with a mortal. Thus Mary's body, impregnated by incorporeal means, remains virginal. Also, Luke's narrative preserves God's essential incorporeality and even morality — qualities that pagan gods could never claim when they engendered offspring through mortals. No other mortal mother of a "divine man" had remained a virgin. Luke has carefully crafted a narrative to spread the word about a new god who is superior to others yet, as a variation on the "divine man," surprisingly familiar to his pagan contemporaries. Finally, Luke shows that what may have appeared to some as a degrading situation — an untimely pregnancy — was legitimated by Mary's virginity and by God.

Matthew uses the concept of Mary's virginity in much less creative ways. First, consistent with Matthew's interest in Jesus as fulfilling specific scriptural prophecies, it is a proof that the prediction of Isa 7:14 has been fulfilled. Second, Matthew casts God in the role of "rescuer," addressing the shameful situation caused by a pregnant virgin. He directs Joseph, who responds dutifully. An earthly patriarchy is replaced by a higher one.

The next mention of Jesus' mother is in Matt 12:46–50, parallel to Luke 8:19–21. They are identical teaching sayings, giving us no particular information about Jesus' mother. Matt 13:55–56 contains more elaboration than Luke 4:22 in describing the rejection of Jesus in his own village. Luke simply has the people ask if Jesus is not Joseph's son (Luke 3:23 states explicitly that Joseph was the supposed father of Jesus), whereas Matthew offers a series of rhetorical questions identifying Jesus as a carpenter's son, giving his mother's name (Mary) and his brothers' names, and pointing to the presence of his sisters. Although Matthew gives a profile of Jesus' family, he does not tell whether Mary was mother or stepmother to Jesus' siblings.

The Gospels of Mark and John provide no useful information about Mary. Kelber, among other scholars, have noted Mark's apparent hostility toward Mary and the family of Jesus. Neither Gospel has a birth narrative; out of the combined six references to Jesus' mother, only Mark 6:3 gives her name (Mark 3:31–35; 6:3; John 2:1–11; 2:12; 6:42; 19:25–27). Mary remains unnamed in John. In this Gospel, Jesus addresses his mother twice as "woman," (2:4; 19:26). Mark 6:3 is parallel to Matt 13:53–58, Luke 4:16–30, and John 6:42, passages in which Jesus states that a prophet is rejected in his own home, implying that Mary is not his most ardent supporter. Mark 3:31–35 is the parallel to Matthew's and Luke's pericope on the eschatological definition of Jesus' family, in which his followers take pride of place over his own close relatives.

John's miracle at Cana (2:1–11) is often cited for the prominent role Mary plays in it. Close reading, however, reveals that she is an unnamed catalyst for the enactment of Jesus' first sign. Jesus' testy reply to his mother suggests tension between them. There is certainly none of Luke's contemplative Mary here. Near the end of John 19:25–27, John tells us that "his mother" is at the foot of the cross. Jesus entrusts his mother to the "disciple whom he loved" (v. 26) in a quasi adoption scene: she gets a new son, and the disciple gets a new mother.

Interestingly, the earliest writings in the New Testament, the seven undisputed letters of Paul, contain no explicit mention of Jesus' mother, although Rom 1:3 and Gal 4:4 are sometimes taken as oblique references to her. Rom 1:3 tells us that Jesus was a descendant of David "according to the flesh." In first-century genealogies, this heritage would ordinarily be traced through the father; how Paul understands it is not clear here. Gal 4:4 says that "God sent his Son, born of a woman, born under the law." We are not told how this took place, only that it did. Paul must have received this information from another believer, since he did not know Jesus.

VASILIKI LIMBERIS

SEE ALSO Part I: Elizabeth; Part II: Born of a Woman (Gal 4:4).

FOR FURTHER READING: Brown, Raymond, Karl P. Donfried, Joseph A. Fitzmyer, and John Reumann, eds. *Mary in the New Testament.*

Gaventa, Beverly Roberts. *Mary: Glimpses of the Mother of Jesus.*

Graef, Hilda. *Mary: A History of Doctrine and Devotion.*

Kelber, Werner. *The Oral and the Written Gospel.*

Limberis, Vasiliki. *Divine Heiress: The Virgin Mary and the Creation of Christian Constantinople.*

Schaberg, Jane. *The Illegitimacy of Jesus.*

———. "Luke."

Mary 2

(Luke 10:38–42; John 11:1–5, 17–20, 28–33; 12:1–8)

Mary, identified as the sister of Martha, is frequently remembered as she is depicted in Luke's very short exemplary story, or confused with either the anonymous woman penitent who washes and anoints Jesus' feet in Luke 7:36–50 or the famous disciple and witness to the resurrection, Mary of Magdala.

Luke's story appears to pit Martha and Mary against each other. It shows Jesus affirming the si-

lent Mary who "sat at the Lord's feet and listened to what he was saying" (10:39) against a complaining, bustling Martha who is busy with what is seen as the women's work of serving a meal. A long tradition of interpretation made Mary represent the contemplative life, and Martha the "lesser" active life. Much ink has been spilled identifying the "better part" that Mary has chosen (10:42) and discussing whether the original text proclaimed "one" or "few" things necessary (10:42). Recently, the phrase "at his feet" has been reinterpreted as a term for learning from a teacher as a disciple (compare Acts 22:3, where Paul claims to have been educated "at the feet of" the famous teacher Gamaliel). Jesus' rebuke to Martha is then read as permitting women to transcend the gender roles assigned to them, since Jesus appears to affirm Mary's choice to sit at his feet and listen. But this reading denigrates the "Marthas" who engage in the work of sustaining life. Even if the words translated "tasks" and "to do work" *(diakonia, diakonein)* refer to Christian ministry, Martha's role as minister is disparaged in favor of Mary's discipleship.

The more complex stories of John 11:1–12:19 are bound together by references to the persons of Mary, Martha, and Lazarus. The section opens with the introduction of Lazarus as being from "Bethany, the village of Mary and her sister Martha" (11:1). The author identifies Mary as "the one who anointed the Lord" (11:2), apparently expecting the reader to know both the anointing story and the names Mary and Martha. The narrative stresses Jesus' friendship with the three, but particularly with Martha: "Now Jesus loved Martha and her sister and their brother Lazarus" (11:5). Mary's only speech repeats Martha's reproachful greeting word for word (11:31; compare v. 21); she disappears from the story after speaking.

In 12:1–8, Mary takes center stage; Martha is introduced to the scene as one having "served" *(diēkonei)* and Lazarus as one of the guests. The scene that follows bears a complex relationship to two other stories. Mark 14:1–11 (parallel to Matt 26:1–16) narrates an anointing in Bethany, associated with the Passover and the death of Jesus; in it an anonymous woman prophet anoints Jesus on the head, designating Jesus as messiah ("anointed, king"; Mark 14:3), in the same way that Samuel anointed Saul and David as king. In Luke 7:36–50, a woman sinner washes Jesus' feet with her tears, dries them with her hair, kisses them, and anoints them with ointment (Luke 7:37–38); Jesus interprets her gesture as signifying love and repentance (v. 47). Features of both of these stories appear in John 12:1–8; John's version could revise both Mark and Luke, or all three might derive from a single older story. The best explanation seems to be that John combines two different traditions that lie behind Mark's and Luke's versions. As in Mark, the story is set in Bethany, close to Passover and Jesus' death (12:1); a contrast is made with the betrayer (v. 6; compare Mark 14:10–11); Mary is said to use pure nard worth three hundred denarii (vv. 3, 5; compare Mark 14:3–4); Jesus defends her with a prediction of his own death (vv. 7–8; compare Mark 14:8–9). Like Luke's anonymous woman, Mary anoints Jesus' feet and wipes them with her hair (12:3). No penitence is implied here. Rather, her gesture looks forward to Jesus' washing and wiping of his disciples' feet (13:1). As a task allotted to a wife or a special disciple (*diakonos;* see Davies), it conveys intimacy and service. An atmospheric note follows her gesture: "The house was filled with the fragrance of the perfume" (12:3). Coupled with the picture of Jesus reclining for the meal, this observation evokes the voice of the woman lover in Song of Solomon: "While the king was on his couch, my nard gave forth its fragrance" (1:12). The reference adds the messianic overtones of kingly anointing, while retaining and intensifying the erotic charge. Thus Mary's gesture identifies her as disciple, perhaps *diakonos,* and as friend of Jesus, but possibly also as a prophetic figure designating the messianic king.

What then lies behind the two different versions of Mary in Luke and in John? Should one be accepted over the other? The two stories have only few common features. In both, Mary is designated as "sister," whereas Martha is said to serve or minister (*diakonein;* Luke 10:39–40; John 12:1). Further, Mary is located "at the feet of" Jesus (she "sat at the Lord's feet and listened to what he was saying" in Luke 10:39; "knelt at [Jesus'] feet" in John 11:32; "anointed Jesus' feet" in John 12:3). These details suggest two aspects of her career. First, this sister may have been famous among later believers as a disciple instructed directly by Jesus himself — "at his feet" and not through other missionaries and disciples. Second, the title "sister," which applies to Martha as well as Mary, may indicate kin, erotic partners, Christians in general, or a specific role in the mission. Like the missionary companions with whom Paul signed his letters (for example, Paul the apostle and Sosthenes the brother in 1 Cor 1:1), Mary worked with Martha in a missionary pair. Similar partnerships appear in Matt 10:1–4 and Romans 16. The latter includes female/male pairs (Prisca and Aquila, Junia and Andronicus, Nereas and his "sister"; Rom 16:3–5, 7, 16) who may have been spouses or lovers, and a pair of women, Tryphaena and Tryphosa (16:12). Thus sisterhood may represent a blood relationship, a shared commitment to the mission, or a commitment to each other.

MARY ROSE D'ANGELO

SEE ALSO Part I: Euodia; Martha; Mary 3; Syntyche; Tryphaena; Tryphosa; Part II: Woman Who Anoints Jesus (Mark 14:3–9); (Luke 7:36–50).

FOR FURTHER READING: D'Angelo, Mary R. "Women Partners in the New Testament."

———. "Women in Luke-Acts: A Redactional View."

Reinhartz, Adele. "From Narrative to History: The Resurrection of Mary and Martha."

Schüssler Fiorenza, Elisabeth. *But She Said: Feminist Practices of Biblical Interpretation.*

Mary 3

(Matt 27:55–56, 61; 28:1; Mark 15:40–41, 47; 16:1, 9; Luke 8:2; 24:10; John 19:25; 20:1, 11, 16, 18)

This elusive figure is the most famous of Jesus' women disciples and the one who has been most misinterpreted in Christian history. It has been suggested that the epithet *Magdalene* meaning "tower of strength," was given her as a descriptor but it much more likely refers to her provenance, the town of Magdala (Aramaic) or Migdal (Hebrew), known in Greek as Taricheae ("salted fish") because of its major industry. The town lies on the northwest side of the "Sea" of Galilee (actually a lake), about three miles north of Tiberias. It thrived in the first century and through the Byzantine period. It was partially excavated in 1971–74.

Luke 8:2–3 describes a number of women who accompanied Jesus with the twelve in his travels, all having been healed of evil spirits and illnesses: Mary Magdalene, exorcised of seven demons; Joanna, wife of Herod's agent Chuza; Susanna; and many others. From the resources they had, whether economic or other, they functioned as patrons, performing the *diakonia*, or ministry of supplying provisions in the group. That Mary was exorcised of seven demons appears also in the second ending of Mark (16:9). Demons were widely believed to be the cause of various illnesses, both physical and mental; such exorcism is thus another way to speak of healing, perhaps of illness with a mental component.

The Gospels do not explain how Mary or some of her companions came to be traveling independently. Whenever she is mentioned in the company of other women, her name appears first, with the sole exception of John 19:25, where female members of Jesus' family are listed before her. This would suggest a prominent place for her both historically and in the early tradition.

Outside this Lukan passage, Mary appears in the Gospels only in the passion and resurrection narratives. The tradition unanimously places her among the women at the cross. Mark and Matthew also relate that she and the "other Mary" (Matt 27:61), the mother of Joses (Mark 15:47), were present at the burial.

Early on the first day of the week, Mary Magdalene leads the women who come to the tomb (John whittles down the group to Mary alone). The portrayal of Mary in John 20 as an impetuous and loving disciple has been decisive in the creation of later images of her. Seeing that the stone has been rolled away from the tomb and not understanding what has happened, she immediately assumes that

"they" have stolen the body of Jesus. Her recognition of Jesus, when he speaks her name, echoes John 10:3, in which Jesus' sheep know the sound of his voice. The ensuing conversation between Jesus and Mary in the garden (John 20:11–18) has been thought to evoke the woman's pursuit of her lover in Song 3:1–5. Her testimony to the other disciples, "I have seen the Lord" (v. 18), followed by a report of the things he said to her, gave rise to a rich tradition celebrating her as the first to receive the inside story from the risen Jesus. In keeping with the figure of the beloved disciple in John's Gospel, he becomes the first to believe Mary's news that Jesus is risen.

The later traditions about Mary Magdalene developed in two directions. The earlier tradition, which has prevailed more strongly in the East, concerns her stature as discloser of special revelations from Jesus, as shown in a number of noncanonical Gnostic works. The *Gospel of Philip* interprets the presence of the three Marys in John's crucifixion scene as an expression of their faithful and exemplary discipleship: the three Marys (Jesus' mother, aunt, and Mary Magdalene, his companion) "always walked with the Lord." The *Gospel of Peter* repeats the synoptic scene. Mary — who is here specifically called a disciple (*mathētria*) of Jesus — again leads a group of women, of which she is the only one named. *The Dialogue of the Savior* features three partners in conversation with Jesus: Matthew, Mary, and Judas (not the betrayer, but the other member of the twelve by that name). Which Mary is never specified, but in light of the many Gnostic dialogues in which Mary Magdalene plays a key role, it is surely she. Here she is called "a woman who had understood completely." In the *Pistis Sophia*, Mary Magdalene is again a major speaker, and she and John "the virgin" are said by Jesus to be the greatest of the disciples.

Mary Magdalene's prominent role among the women disciples in the canonical Gospels and as a communicator of revelation in noncanonical tradition leads to the assumption that she was a leader and spokeswoman who held a position of spiritual authority among many Christians. As the figure of

Peter increasingly took on a similar stature, it was inevitable that the two should clash. In the concluding saying of the *Gospel of Thomas*, Peter suggests to Jesus that he get rid of Mary "because women are not worthy of life." Jesus answers according to Neoplatonic and Gnostic gender typology, in which the female is considered inferior to the male because it is associated with earth and matter, whereas the superior male is associated with heaven and spirit: Jesus says that he will make Mary male because every female made male will enter the kingdom of heaven. Though the symbolism sounds strange and offensive to the modern reader, Mary here exemplifies the transformation, according to Gnostic belief, that is necessary for all human believers, whether women or men. She is the prototype of humanity.

The Gnostic *Gospel of Mary* brings the tension between the authority of Mary and that of Peter to its peak. Here Mary is recognized as a privileged recipient of special revelation from the risen Jesus. At a moment of discouragement about their mission, Mary rallies the disciples. Then Peter asks her, as the woman Jesus loved more than any other woman, to tell them some of what she received. When she does, however, Peter and his brother Andrew attack her credibility, questioning whether Jesus would really have spoken with a woman and preferred her to them. Levi rebukes them, warning that the savior both knows and loves her more than them.

By the early third century, Hippolytus (a schismatic leader of the Roman church) would call Mary Magdalene an apostle, and an early medieval tradition referred to her as the "apostle of the apostles," since it was she who brought to the men the news of the empty tomb and her encounter with Jesus. For the most part, however, Western tradition developed a very different perspective on Mary of Magdala. Onto her was projected the male fascination with the repristinated sex object. In spite of a total lack of evidence in the canonical Scriptures or early church tradition, Mary became identified with the woman who "was a sinner" in Luke 7:36–50, who washed the feet of Jesus with her tears and dried them with her hair (perhaps this is because the story occurs immediately before Luke 8:2–3, where she is first named). In the male imagination, only one sin could require such dramatic repentance: she had to be a reformed prostitute. She then became conflated with Mary of Bethany, sister of Martha and Lazarus. In the Middle Ages, legend had them emigrate to Marseilles where Mary continued to exercise her spiritual authority by preaching.

In the West, the figure of Mary Magdalene has connoted suppressed eroticism. In circles wherein such can be contemplated of Jesus, a sexual liaison between him and her is suggested. She is represented as young and alluring, yet at the same time she is said to have spent her reformed life in penance and monastic asceticism. In the modern period, paintings of Mary Magdalene usually reflect male fantasies and are intended to titillate. In spite of the ascetic context, such depictions usually include sensually flowing hair and enough clothing carelessly out of place to be provocative. Her name has become synonymous with barely repentant sensuality.

How can Mary Magdalene be restored to her original image as prominent disciple and spokeswoman of the gospel? She is thought of as young and beautiful, though to have had the economic means and social freedom to spend her income and time the way she chose, she is likely to have been widowed or divorced at the time of her encounter with Jesus. To have acquired her reputation for closeness to Jesus, there must have been a certain intimacy in their relationship, which may just as well have been motherly or patronal as anything else. Her unquestioned presence at both the cross and at the tomb on Easter morning, thus involving her in two seminal events of the Christian faith, points up her preeminence as disciple. At the darkest and most uncertain moments, when others had withdrawn — even Jesus' mother, according to the Synoptic Gospels — Mary Magdalene faithfully remained in Jesus' presence. This was a strong woman.

CAROLYN OSIEK

SEE ALSO Part II: Unnamed Women at the Cross (Luke 23:49); Unnamed Companion of Cleopas (Luke 24:13–35).

FOR FURTHER READING: Haskins, Susan. *Mary Magdalene: Myth and Metaphor.*

Moltmann-Wendel, Elisabeth. "Mary Magdalene."

Ricci, Carla. *Mary Magdalene and Many Others: Women Who Followed Jesus.*

Schaberg, Jane. "How Mary Magdalene Became a Whore."

Thompson, Mary R. *Mary of Magdala: Apostle and Leader.*

Mary 4

(Matt 27:56; Mark 15:40, 47; 16:1; Luke 24:10)

Variously called the mother of James and Joses (or Joseph, a manuscript variant in these references — Matt 27:56), mother of little James and Joses (Mark 15:40), of Joses (Mark 15:47), or of James (Mark 16:1; Luke 24:10), this otherwise unknown woman is no doubt the same as "the other Mary" (Matt 27:61; 28:1), since she is called by that name only after she has been introduced by her maternal connections, and in passages parallel with Marcan passages that name her as mother (Mark 15:47; 16:1). She is one of the companions of Mary Magdalene present at the cross of Jesus and the empty tomb on Easter morning. Her name does not appear in the group of women disciples mentioned by Luke during the Galilean ministry (Luke 8:2–3). Her sons James and Joses appear elsewhere in parallel passages (Matt 13:55; Mark 6:3) among the brothers of Jesus, which would make this Mary also a relative of Jesus. If James and Joses are meant to be true siblings of Jesus rather than cousins, there is a possible conflation in the tradition of this Mary with the mother of Jesus. Some think that this was how the Synoptic Gospels put the mother of Jesus in the death and resurrection narratives, but it is highly unlikely that Luke, who portrays the mother of Jesus as a disciple, would continue this confusion. However, she may be the same as Mary, the wife of Clopas, at the cross in John 19:25.

CAROLYN OSIEK

SEE ALSO Part I: Mary 5; Part II: Unnamed Women Who Provide for the Jesus Movement (Luke 8:3, etc.); Unnamed Women at the Cross (Luke 23:49).

Mary 5

(John 19:25)

According to John, there were three or four women standing by the cross of Jesus: his mother and her sister, Mary (probably wife) of Clopas, and Mary Magdalene. The grammar in Greek is as ambiguous as it is in English: the third named may be the sister of Jesus' mother (who is never named in John's Gospel) or a third woman. She may also be the same as Mary the mother of James and Joses (Matt 27:56, 61) and the mother of James (Luke 24:10). If Clopas is identical to Cleopas, which is possible but by no means necessary, this Mary may also be identified with the unnamed disciple who accompanies Cleopas to Emmaus (Luke 24:13, 18), called variously by her marital or maternal relationship.

CAROLYN OSIEK

SEE ALSO Part II: Unnamed Companion of Cleopas (Luke 24:13–35); Sister of Jesus' Mother (John 19:25).

FOR FURTHER READING: Daniels, Jon B. "Clopas."

Mary 6

(Acts 12:12)

This Mary, mother of John Mark, was hostess of a house church in Jerusalem where Peter went when he was miraculously released from prison during the night (Acts 12:12–17). The story confirms the early Christian practice of gathering in homes for prayer — especially homes of prominent women believers — as well as the function of women as heads of households even in Palestine and the function of women's homes as centers of hospitality and refuge in time of persecution.

CAROLYN OSIEK

FOR FURTHER READING: Martin, Clarice J. "The Acts of the Apostles."

Mary 7

from either the Hebrew/Aramaic name Miriam/
Mariamme, or "a woman of the clan of Marius";
Latin

(Rom 16:6)

Mary is the first of four women who are identified
in the closing greetings of Paul's letter to the Romans as having "worked hard" in the young church
in Rome (see also v. 12). The nature of the work is
not indicated, but Paul uses the same Greek word to
refer to his own missionary work (1 Cor 15:10) and
the work of leaders within local congregations (1
Cor 16:16). Her name appears early in the list of
greetings, among those who are obviously known
personally to Paul. She certainly exercised a leadership role in the Roman church.

Most interpreters have taken her name to be Semitic and consider her to be of Jewish birth. However, since her name is given as Maria, not Mariam,
and she is associated with Christians in the city of
Rome, her name may derive from the Roman clan
of Marius.

JOUETTE M. BASSLER

SEE ALSO Part I: Euodia; Persis; Syntyche.

Matred

meaning uncertain; perhaps "spear," related to the
Aramaic and Arabic root ṭrd, "to drive"; or "flowing speech," from Hebrew ṭrd, "to flow continuously"

(Gen 36:39; 1 Chr 1:50)

Matred, daughter of Mezahab, is the mother of Mehetabel, who is the wife of Hadar, an Edomite king.
The Septuagint (Greek translation of the Hebrew
Bible) lists Matred as a man. This is one of several
instances in which translators, both ancient and
modern, have obscured the presence of women.

NAOMI STEINBERG

SEE ALSO Part I: Maacah 1; Mehetabel.

Mehetabel

"God does good," from Hebrew yṭb, "to do well or
good," and 'ēl, "God"

(Gen 36:39; 1 Chr 1:50)

Mehetabel, daughter of Matred and granddaughter
of Me-zahab (who may be a woman), marries the
Edomite king Hadar. The listing of these three
women in the Edomite genealogy indicates that
they married into this patrilineage from kinship
groups outside the Edomite descent line.

NAOMI STEINBERG

SEE ALSO Part I: Matred.

Merab

"increase," from Hebrew rbb, "to increase"

(1 Sam 14:49; 18:17–19)

Merab is the older of two daughters of King Saul
(reigned c. 1025–1005 B.C.E.) according to the genealogical summary presented in 1 Sam 14:49, and
one of six children by his primary wife, Ahinoam
the daughter of Ahimaaz (compare 1 Sam 31:2; 1 Chr
8:33; 9:39; these note the fourth son, Abinadab, who
is not mentioned in 1 Sam 14:49). The genealogical
summary serves two functions in the larger narrative of Saul. First, it helps signal the effective end
of his reign as king on the eve of his rejection by
God as part of a general summary of his accomplishments to that point in his career; second, it
introduces the names of family members (with the
exception of Abinadab) who will appear in the remaining portion of the narrative.

In the Masoretic version (the standard Hebrew
version) of 1 Sam 18:17–19, Saul is depicted to have
offered Merab in marriage to David in order to
make him a soldier for life and thus get him killed
by the Philistines. His plan to kill David helps further develop the story line. It shows Saul trying to
thwart the divine plan, which calls for David to
succeed him on the throne instead of his eldest son,
Jonathan. Saul's plan does not work, however; at
the appointed time of the marriage to David, Merab
is wed to Adriel of Meholah instead. Although no
explicit reason for the failed marriage is given, it is

implied in the ensuing narrative that David was unable to raise the money for the bride price. His initial statement in 18:18 of being from a different socioeconomic class when offered Merab as bride is made more explicit when he is offered Saul's second daughter, Michal: "I am a poor man and of no repute" (18:23). With the second marriage offer, David is allowed to present one hundred Philistine foreskins for the normal marriage gift, substituting military prowess for social standing. In ancient Israelite society, daughters were under the legal custody of their fathers, and marriages were used regularly as a way of strengthening a father's social or economic position or, as in this case, as a way for royalty or the elite to pursue political interests.

Another ancient version of 1 Samuel, Codex Vaticanus of the Greek version, which is earlier in date than the Masoretic version and which reflects a different form of the book, does not include the story of 1 Sam 18:17–19. A later scribe may have composed the story in order to show that the eldest daughter was married first, according to custom. He would have derived the name of Merab's husband from the Greek version of 2 Sam 21:8, which reports how David tried to strengthen his claim to the throne of Israel by killing off Saulide heirs who could challenge him by virtue of their royal blood.

DIANA VIKANDER EDELMAN

SEE ALSO Part I: Ahinoam 1; Michal.

FOR FURTHER READING: Edelman, Diana V. *King Saul in the Historiography of Judah.*

Steinberg, Naomi. "Kinship and Gender in Genesis."

Meshullemeth

"rewarded," from Hebrew *šlm,* "to recompense, reward"

(2 Kgs 21:19)

Meshullemeth is the daughter of Haruz of Jotbah, the wife of Manasseh of Judah (reigned 698–642 B.C.E.), and the mother of King Amon (reigned 641–640 B.C.E.). Her name occurs in the introduction to her son's reign in 2 Kgs 21:19–22 but is missing from the corresponding introduction in 2 Chr 33:1–2. The writer may have wished to downplay the significance of the "evil" king Manasseh by not mentioning the queen mother.

The significance of Meshullemeth's marriage to Manasseh depends, in part, on the location of her city of origin, which is uncertain. If Jotbah is the Galilean site of Yodefat, then Manasseh's marriage to Meshullemeth may represent an attempt to strengthen Judah's ties to the north. If Jotbah is located in the south (at el-Taba), it is possible that Meshullemeth was of Arab or Edomite origin. If either site identification is correct, Manasseh's marriage to Meshullemeth may represent an attempted alliance with a non-Judean people.

A Hebrew seal bearing the name *mšwlmt,* Meshullemeth, has been discovered in Israel. But any connection between the woman mentioned on the seal (used as a signature in business transactions) and the wife of Manasseh remains speculative.

LINDA S. SCHEARING

SEE ALSO Part I: Azubah 1.

Micaiah

meaning uncertain; perhaps "who is like YHWH?" from Hebrew *mî,* "who," *kĕ,* "like," and *yāh,* a shortened form of YHWH

SEE Maacah 3/Micaiah (Part I).

Michal

probably a shortened form of Michael, meaning "who is like God?" from Hebrew *mî,* "who," *kî,* "like," and *'ēl,* "God"

(1 Sam 14:49; 18:20–29; 19:11–17; 25:44; 2 Sam 3:13–16; 6:16, 20–23; 21:8–9; 1 Chr 15:29)

Michal's appearances in 1–2 Samuel reflect her confinement as a woman caught in the fierce struggle over the kingship between her father, Saul, and her husband, David. After her introduction in 1 Sam 14:49 as Saul's younger daughter, she appears next in 18:20, where we read, "Michal loved David." Saul uses her, as he did her older sister Merab, as a "trap," in the hope that David will be killed while trying to meet the bride price of one hundred Philistine foreskins. David pays double the bride price, and Michal becomes his wife.

Michal's love for David helps explain both the risk she takes to save David's life in 1 Samuel 19 and, later, her angry outburst at him in 2 Samuel 6, when her love has turned to hate. These two scenes, the only ones in which Michal plays an active role, are framed by scenes in which Michal is acted upon: 1 Samuel 19, where she actively takes David's part against her father Saul, is framed by scenes in which she is acted upon by her father (1 Sam 18:20–29 and 25:44); 2 Samuel 6, where she takes the part of her father's house against her husband, David, is framed by scenes in which she is acted upon by her husband (2 Sam 3:13–16 and 21:8–9).

Michal saves David's life by orchestrating his escape through the window when Saul's envoys come for him (1 Samuel 19). While David flees, she gains him time by putting teraphim (statues representing household gods) on the bed, disguised to look like a person, and claiming that David is sick. Some commentators take the presence of teraphim as a sign that Michal holds to false religious beliefs, but it should be noted that the teraphim are in David's house. There are parallels between this scene, in which Michal deceives her father, and Rachel's theft of the family teraphim and deception of her father, Laban (Genesis 31), in which the teraphim are ridiculed. But ridicule is not evident in 1 Samuel 19. Michal lies to her father to conceal her involvement; that she took a great risk is indicated by the parallel to her brother Jonathan, whom Saul tries to kill for abetting David (1 Sam 20:30–33).

The fact that the Bible reports that "Michal loved David" (the only place in the Hebrew Bible where it is stated that a woman loves a man), but not that he loves her, suggests he does not. After he flees Saul's court, David has two secret meetings with Jonathan, but none with Michal. He does not attempt to provide for her or take her with him, though he arranges for his parents' safety in Moab and has other wives with him in the wilderness and in the land of the Philistines.

Saul gives Michal to another man (1 Sam 25:44) in an apparent move to block David from claiming the kingship through her. After Saul's death, when it is politically expedient, David demands the return of his wife in his negotiations over the kingship (2 Samuel 3). Michal's husband Paltiel is grief-stricken, but of Michal's feelings we hear nothing until 2 Samuel 6, where she watches David dancing before the ark and "despise[s] him in her heart" (v. 16). Her rebuke, accusing him of sexual vulgarity, gives vent to her anger over his treatment of her (it also isolates her from David and from the servant women she speaks of as witnessing his cavorting). Their quarrel raises another important issue by repeatedly referring to the kingship: the rejection of the house of Saul in favor of the house of David. Michal is identified as "Saul's daughter," for she speaks as the representative of her father's house, and, by doing so, forfeits her role in the house of King David. David's rude reply is his only speech addressed to her in the narrative. Michal's childlessness is not accounted for (did David confine her, as he shut away other wives [2 Sam 20:3]?) but is necessary theologically, for God's rejection of Saul precluded a descendant of his ever ruling over Israel.

The statement that Michal had no children (2 Sam 6:23) does not square with the Hebrew text of 2 Sam 21:8–9, where David hands over "the five sons of Michal, Saul's daughter" to the Gibeonites for execution. Some manuscripts therefore read "Merab" in place of "Michal," for Merab was the wife of Adriel.

J. CHERYL EXUM

SEE ALSO Part I: Merab; Part II: Maids of David's Servants (2 Sam 6:20, etc.).

FOR FURTHER READING: Clines, David J. A., and Tamara C. Eskenazi, eds. *Telling Queen Michal's Story: An Experiment in Comparative Interpretation.*

Edelman, Diana Vikander. *King Saul in the Historiography of Judah.*

Exum, J. Cheryl. *Fragmented Women: Feminist (Sub)versions of Biblical Narratives.*

———. *Tragedy and Biblical Narrative: Arrows of the Almighty.*

Milcah 1

meaning uncertain; a feminine form of Hebrew
verb *mlk,* "to rule," perhaps meaning "queen"
(Gen 11:29; 22:20, 23; 24:15, 24, 47)

A daughter of Abraham's brother Haran, Milcah
marries Nahor, another brother of Abraham, according to the ancestral narratives of Genesis. Milcah bears eight sons to her husband, Nahor. One of
these sons, Bethuel, fathers Rebekah. Thus Milcah is
the grandmother of Rebekah, who later will marry
Isaac.

According to the marriage customs in biblical
Israel, a man from the patrilineage of Terah, father
of Abraham, was required to marry a woman who
was descended from this same lineage in order for
their offspring to be reckoned as heir to the family
name and inheritance. This marriage pattern,
known as patrilineal endogamy, establishes the circles of kinship narrowly — the Israelite lineage is
traced through the descendants of the sons of
Terah. It helps focus the sequence of Genesis narratives on the one family considered to be the ancestors of all Israel.

NAOMI STEINBERG

SEE ALSO Part I: Rebekah.

Milcah 2

(Num 26:33; 27:1; 36:11; Josh 17:3)

Milcah is one of the five daughters of Zelophehad
who approach Moses to ask for an inheritance of
land alongside their male relatives.

KATHARINE DOOB SAKENFELD

SEE ALSO Part I: Hoglah; Mahlah 1; Noah; Tirzah; Part
II: Daughters of Zelophehad (Num 26:33, etc.).

Miriam 1

meaning unknown
(Exodus 15; Numbers 12, 20, 26; Deut 24:9; 1 Chr
6:3; Mic 6:4)

Exod 2:1–10 features an unnamed sister of Moses
who helps deliver him at the Nile River. Many com-

*Terra-cotta figurine (6 inches high) of a woman play-
ing a hand drum, from the Iron II period (ninth–early
sixth century B.C.E.). The place of origin is uncertain,
but it is probably from the northern coast of Israel.
Women rather than men are typically represented as
percussionists in the repertoire of terra-cotta musicians from the ancient Near East. See Miriam 1;
Women with Hand-Drums, Dancing (Exod 15:20,
etc.).*

mentators identify her as Miriam. Two genealogies
listing Moses, Aaron, and Miriam as the sole children of Amram support the identification (Num
26:59; 1 Chr 6:3). She first appears by name, however, in the crossing of the Red Sea (Exod 15:20–21).
Called "the prophet Miriam, Aaron's sister," she
leads Hebrew women in singing, dancing, and playing drums.

Though the meaning of the term *prophet* is here
indeterminate, Miriam is the first woman ever to
bear it. She becomes thereby the archetype of the
female prophetic tradition, even as Moses heads the
male (compare Deut 34:10). Contrary to the im-

pression that her one stanza sung at the sea (Exod 15:21) is but an abridgement of the lengthy song attributed to Moses (Exod 15:1–18), historical and literary studies show that the latter version is itself the Song of Miriam. It belongs to a corpus of women's traditions that include the long Songs of Deborah (Judg 5:1–31) and Hannah (1 Sam 2:1–10).

After the episode at the sea, Miriam surfaces in the wilderness narratives. Accompanied by her brother Aaron, she speaks out against Moses (Num 12:1–16), faulting him for marrying a Cushite woman. But the text fails to explain the issue. The woman is not named. She may be Zipporah, the known wife of Moses (Exod 2:21, 18:2), or another woman. The meaning of "Cushite" is uncertain. It may refer to the African country of Cush (see Gen 10:6; 1 Chr 1:8) or to Midian, the region east of the Gulf of Aqabah from which Zipporah came (see Exod 3:1; 18:1 Hab 3:7). Most probably, the attack implicates Miriam in a struggle over the priestly leadership of Moses.

Miriam with Aaron also challenges the prophetic authority of Moses. She asks, "Has the LORD spoken only through Moses? Has he not spoken through us also?" (Num 12:2). She understands leadership to embrace diverse voices, female and male. But the price of speaking out is severe. Though God rebukes both Miriam and Aaron, the deity punishes only her. Metaphorically, the divine nostril burns in anger to leave her stricken with scales like snow. Aaron pleads with Moses on her behalf, and Moses appeals to God. God responds by confining her outside the camp for seven days. This period of time verifies her cleanliness but does not restore her to wholeness. Whatever her particular disease, Miriam remains a condemned woman, a warning for generations to come (see Deut 24:8–9). After her punishment, she never speaks, nor is she spoken to. Indeed, she disappears altogether from the narrative until the announcement of her death and burial at Kadesh (Num 20:1).

Negative as well as positive traditions about Miriam testify to her prominence, power, and prestige in early Israel. She participates with Moses and Aaron to lead the Israelite community during the

exodus and the wanderings. Her role in saving her baby brother and in celebrating the crossing of the sea highlights her concern for her people. Later they reciprocate. Despite the instructions of God and Moses, the people refuse to continue the march in the wilderness until the diseased Miriam is restored (Num 12:15). Three references to them at her death further underscore their loyalty to her.

Nature also honors Miriam. At her triumphal entry, the living waters of the Red Sea surround her (Exod 15:19–20); at her demise the wells in the desert dry up (Num 20:2). Centuries later, prophecy remembers her as the equal of Moses and Aaron in representing God before the people (Mic 6:8). Moreover, prophecy includes her, though not by name, within its eschatological vision. Jeremiah says that in days to come, Israel will have a new exodus. It will go forth again with drums, dances, and merrymakers (Jer 31:4). As the inaugurator of a performance and composition tradition of song, drums, and dances in Israel, Miriam continues to resonate throughout its musical life (see Pss 68:25; 81:2; 150:4).

Unlike most women in the Bible, Miriam is never called wife or mother. She has neither husband nor children. Jewish traditions, however, cannot tolerate her status as single. The historian Josephus deems Hur the husband of Miriam (Antiquities 3.54; see Exod 17:10–12). Rabbinic sources give her Caleb for a husband and Hur for a son (but compare 1 Chr 2:19).

In the New Testament Miriam's afterlife continues through her name and her deeds. The Greek name Mary is the equivalent of the Hebrew Miriam. In singing a song of deliverance (Luke 1:46–55), in embodying a demonic or diseased condition (Luke 8:2), and in challenging male authorities (Matt 28:10; Luke 24:10; John 20:11–18), the various Marys of the Gospels reflect their namesake.

PHYLLIS TRIBLE

SEE ALSO Part I: Deborah 2; Hannah; Huldah; Zipporah; Part II: Women with Hand-Drums, Dancing (Exod 15:20, etc.).

FOR FURTHER READING: Brenner, Athalya. The Israelite Woman.

Bronner, Leila Leah. *From Eve to Esther: Rabbinic Reconstructions of Biblical Women.*

Burns, Rita J. *Has the Lord Indeed Spoken Only Through Moses?: A Study of the Biblical Portrait of Miriam.*

Trible, Phyllis. "Bringing Miriam out of the Shadows."

Miriam 2

(1 Chr 4:17)

Miriam is a daughter of Mered, a descendant of Judah. Most modern translators transfer the mention of Mered's Egyptian wife Bithiah in 4:18 to this verse, granting Miriam and her brothers mixed heritage.

JULIA MYERS O'BRIEN

SEE ALSO Part I: Bithiah; Hazzelelponi; Helah; Naarah.

Naamah 1

"loved, lovely one" or "singer," from Hebrew *n'm,*
"to be pleasant, lovely," or "to sing"

(Gen 4:22)

Naamah is one of only three females included in the genealogies of the early chapters of Genesis. Those lists of names serve the literary purpose of expanding the world's population from the primal pair (Eve and Adam) to the populated territories of the known world that form the backdrop to the emergence of the Israelite ancestors (Sarah and Abraham) at the end of Genesis 11. The three females are the two wives and one daughter of Lamech, whose offspring constitute the seventh generation after creation. The symbolism of the number seven in the Bible points to the seventh generation as significant: humanity is now fully launched. Lamech's children thus are the human founders of vocations, in contrast to divine creators of cultural roles that characterize many mythological beginnings tales.

As the daughter of Zillah, Naamah is the sister and half sister of three brothers, all founders of an aspect of human culture. Their names are linked to their archetypal occupation (for example, the name Jubal, ancestor of instrumental musicians, may be related to the Hebrew word for "horn" or "trumpet"). No vocational role is ascribed to Naamah; however, her name may signify one. It comes from the Hebrew root *n'm,* which means "to be pleasant" or "lovely" (compare Naomi); but the same stem can mean "to sing," which would make her the ancestral singer. The intimate connection between women and song, going back to the maternal tuneful, rhythmic soothing of infants and found widely across cultures, would support the idea that Naamah is the archetypal founder of vocal music.

CAROL MEYERS

SEE ALSO Part I: Adah 1; Zillah.

FOR FURTHER READING: Meyers, Carol. "An Archaeomusicological Study of Women's Performance in Ancient Israel."

Naamah 2

(1 Kgs 14:21, 31; 2 Chr 12:13)

Naamah is one of the wives of Solomon, king of all Israel (reigned c. 968–928 B.C.E.), and the mother of Rehoboam, first king of the southern kingdom of Judah. The text refers to her as "the Ammonite" rather than in the usual way — as the daughter of someone. Three explanations are possible. She could have been a commoner of foreign origin. The narrator could have used this connection with the Ammonites, traditional enemies of Israel, to express displeasure with the reign of her son. Finally, she could have been from a prominent Ammonite family, named as part of a diplomatic agreement sealed through a marriage alliance, but then remembered by tradition simply as the foreign Ammonite wife.

DIANA VIKANDER EDELMAN

SEE ALSO Part II: Women of Solomon (1 Kgs 3:1, etc.).

Naarah

"girl, damsel," from Hebrew *na'ărâ,* "girl, damsel"

(1 Chr 4:5–6)

Naarah is one of the two wives of Ashhur, great-grandson of Judah according to the genealogy in

Chronicles. In an unusual repetition of the wife's procreative role, the text announces Naarah as the mother of four sons (Ahuzzam, Hepher, Temeni, and Haahashtari) and then concludes with the statement that they were her sons. That her sons Temeni and Haahashtari may be eponymous ancestors of peoples may explain the emphasis.

ALICE L. LAFFEY

SEE ALSO Part I: Helah.

Nahash

"serpent," from Hebrew *nāḥāš*, "serpent"
(2 Sam 17:25)

According to 2 Sam 17:25, King David's rebellious son Absalom appoints a man named Amasa to be chief military officer in place of the general Joab. Amasa is the son of a man whose wife is Abigail, "daughter of Nahash, sister of Zeruiah." Most commentators take Nahash to be a man's name. However, it is not clear from the Hebrew text whether "sister of Zeruiah" refers to Abigail or Nahash. If it is the former, and since Abigail and Zeruiah are sisters and Jesse is their father, Nahash would then be their mother, whose name is otherwise not mentioned. Amasa as general would thus have a lineage parallel to that of Joab, whose mother was Abigail.

CAROL MEYERS

SEE ALSO Part I: Abigail 2; Zeruiah.

Nanea   SEE Nanea (Part III).

Naomi

"my pleasant or delightful one," from Hebrew *n'm*,
"to be pleasant or delightful"
(Book of Ruth)

The Book of Ruth is one of two in the Hebrew Bible that bears a woman's name (the other is Esther). Ruth depicts the struggles of Naomi and Ruth for survival in a patriarchal environment. Though the story takes its name from the younger woman, the older is the dominant character. Naomi's plight shapes the narrative, and her plan brings it to resolution.

Scene one (1:1–22) opens with a famine that sends a Judean family across the Jordan to Moab, a foreign land. In introducing the family, the storyteller subordinates Naomi to the man Elimelech. She is "*his* wife," and their children are "*his* sons" (1:1–2) (emphasis added). But his death changes the situation. He becomes "the husband of Naomi," and she is "left with *her* two sons" (1:3) (emphasis added). They marry Moabite wives, Orpah and Ruth, but die without progeny. So Naomi shrinks again. From wife to widow, from mother to no-mother, this woman is stripped of all identity.

Upon hearing that the LORD has restored food to Judah, Naomi begins the journey home. She tells each of her daughters-in-law to return to her "mother's house" and implores the *ḥesed* ("faithfulness" or "loyalty") of YHWH upon them (1:8–9). Strikingly, the basis on which Naomi invokes divine *ḥesed* is the loyalty that Orpah and Ruth have already shown her family. She lifts up these female foreigners as models for what God ought to do. Then she spells out the content of *ḥesed* for women who live in a man's world: to find a home, "each of you in the house of your husband" (1:9). Naomi shapes a theology that paradoxically subverts and serves patriarchy.

When the daughters-in-law insist upon returning with her, she seeks to dissuade them (1:10–13). Using rhetorical questions, she resorts to sound reasoning. She has no sons now in her womb to provide them husbands and no husband to impregnate her. Moreover, she is too old to bear sons, and even if she did, why would these women wait for them to grow up? Describing her situation, Naomi concludes that the LORD has turned against her. The deity whom she hopes will show *ḥesed* to her daughters-in-law has shown hostility to her.

Naomi convinces only Orpah; Ruth accompanies her to Bethlehem. When the women of the town focus attention upon Naomi (1:19), she instructs them not to call her "Naomi" (meaning "pleasant") but instead "Mara" (meaning "bitter"). In a wordplay, she explains the name change by faulting the "Almighty" who has "dealt bitterly with me" (1:20–21). Yet no one ever follows her instruction.

Naomi dominates scene one. Nine times her name appears, most often as the active subject of verbs. Numerous pronouns also attest to her centrality in a time of famine, dislocation, and death — and of return home at the beginning of the barley harvest.

Naomi's prominence continues in scene two (2:1–23). Her name is the first word. It links her to a wealthy kinsman named Boaz. Meanwhile, Naomi grants Ruth permission to glean wherever she is received (2:2). When Ruth finds favor in the field of Boaz, a servant identifies her to him by invoking the name of Naomi (2:6). Boaz also alludes to Naomi as Ruth's mother-in-law (2:11). In the evening Ruth returns to Naomi, who initiates (2:19) and concludes (2:22) their conversation. Passing judgment on Ruth's day, Naomi utters words of blessing for the first time (2:19–20). They pertain to the man, as yet unidentified for her, who helped Ruth (2:19). Upon learning that the man is Boaz, Naomi adds the name of the LORD to her blessing (2:20) and so invokes the God whom she has earlier faulted as the giver of bitterness (1:13, 21). Naomi is changing (2:20–22).

As the last to speak in scene two (2:22) and the first to speak in scene three (3:1–18), Naomi continues to direct the plot of the narrative. Not waiting for matters to take their course or for God to intervene, she plans to secure Boaz as husband for Ruth. In seeking security through marriage, her plan fits the strictures of patriarchy, but it departs from them in proposing a dangerous scheme. Naomi tells her "daughter" to dress in fine clothes and visit Boaz in secret at the threshing floor. There she will ask him to make good on his prayer for her blessing (3:3–5). The plan succeeds. The scene ends with the two women discussing the events of the night. Naomi again initiates (3:16) and concludes (3:18) their exchange. From being the receiver of calamity, she has become the agent of change and challenge.

Naomi never speaks again; her work is finished. Nevertheless, she figures prominently in the last scene (4:1–21), her name appearing six times. Boaz depicts Naomi as the owner of property (4:3, 5, 9). The women of Bethlehem invoke YHWH's blessing upon Naomi through Ruth and the grandchild Ruth bears her (4:14–15). The narrator reports that Naomi embraces the child and becomes his nurse. And at the end, the women even declare that the child has been born to Naomi (4:17).

Feminist assessments of Naomi diverge widely, depending often upon the cultural, social, ideological, and experiential biases of readers. A sampling includes the following: Naomi is a cipher for male values that find fulfillment for women in marriage and children. In contrast to the loss of status for childless widows in patriarchy, Naomi achieves importance as a mother-in-law and an independent character. Naomi is an overbearing, interfering, and domineering mother-in-law. Naomi is a caring, gracious, and altruistic mother-in-law. Naomi the Judean rejects Ruth (and Orpah) because she is a Moabite. Naomi embraces Ruth the Moabite within the family of Judah. Naomi and Ruth are rivals, with Naomi eventually achieving the greater prestige. Naomi and Ruth are friends, indeed sisterlike, each seeking the good of the other in a world over which they have little control. Naomi schemes, connives, and manipulates. Naomi plans, reflects, and executes. Naomi is an embittered old woman who denounces God for her troubles but fails to thank the deity when she recovers. Naomi is a profound figure of faith who experiences God as enemy but then wrestles blessing from adversity. All such disparate judgments attest to Naomi's commanding, if ambiguous, presence in one of the few biblical stories focused on women.

PHYLLIS TRIBLE

SEE ALSO Part I: Mara; Orpah; Ruth; Part II: Women of Bethlehem (Ruth 1:19, etc.); Women of the Neighborhood (Ruth 4:17).

FOR FURTHER READING: Kates, Judith A., and Gail Twersky Reimer, eds. *Reading Ruth.*

Levine, Amy-Jill. "Ruth."

Trible, Phyllis. "A Human Comedy."

Nehushta

meaning uncertain; perhaps "serpent," from Hebrew *nāḥāš*, "serpent"; or "bronze," from Hebrew *nĕḥōšet*, "bronze"

(2 Kgs 24:8, 12, 15; Jer 13:18; 22:26–27; 29:2)

Nehushta was the daughter of Elnathan of Jerusalem, the consort of Jehoiakim, king of Judah from 608 to 598 B.C.E., and the mother of his successor, Jehoiachin. According to the regnal formula in 2 Kgs 24:8, Jehoiachin was eighteen years old when he succeeded his father. However, in the Chronicler's account (2 Chr 36:9), which does not mention Nehushta, he was only eight years old. If the king was indeed a minor, the queen mother might have wielded considerable influence during her son's short reign. This contention is supported by three deportation lists (2 Kgs 24:12, 15; Jer 29:2) that mention the queen mother as a captive immediately after the king. The explicit mention of Nehushta in these lists seems to indicate her importance in the Judean court and as a potential threat to the Babylonians. Both references in Jeremiah give Nehushta the title *gĕbîrâ*, or "great lady," perhaps indicating that the queen mother was recognized as an official functionary in the Judean court. Jer 13:18 indicates that both she and her son wore crowns, possibly as a symbol of their shared authority. Nehushta's fate in exile is unknown, but she may have shared her son's privileges (2 Kgs 25:27–30).

RHONDA BURNETTE-BLETSCH

SEE ALSO Part I: Abijah 2/Abi; Hamutal/Hamital; Maacah 4; Part II: Mother of Princes (Ezekiel 19).

FOR FURTHER READING: Andreasen, Niels-Erik. "The Role of the Queen Mother in Israelite Society." Ben-Barak, Zafrira. "The Status and Right of the *gᵉbîrâ*."

Noadiah

"YHWH has met" or "YHWH has become manifest," from Hebrew *y'd*, "to meet, appear," and *yāh*, a shortened form of YHWH

(Neh 6:14)

Noadiah is one of only four named women prophets in the Hebrew Bible (the others are Deborah, Huldah, and Miriam). She appears once in Nehemiah's reference to high-placed opponents who sought to intimidate Nehemiah, the governor of the postexilic province of Yehud (c. 444 B.C.E.). Context implies that she too had high status. Like the other prominent opponents in this verse (Tobiah and Sanballat), she could have opposed his building of the walls of Jerusalem.

Noadiah was probably Judahite; otherwise, Nehemiah would have called her foreign. We know nothing further about her, but her presence establishes the fact that in the postexilic era, as before, a woman could be a prophet and thus serve in a role of inspired leadership as a recognized spokesperson for the divine.

TAMARA COHN ESKENAZI

SEE ALSO Part I: Deborah 2; Huldah; Miriam 1.

FOR FURTHER READING: Eskenazi, Tamara Cohn. "Out from the Shadows: Biblical Women in the Postexilic Era."

Noah

meaning uncertain; perhaps a place name used as a woman's name

(Num 26:33; 27:1; 36:11; Josh 17:3)

Noah is one of the five daughters of Zelophehad who approaches Moses to ask for an inheritance of land alongside their male relatives.

KATHARINE DOOB SAKENFELD

SEE ALSO Part I: Hoglah; Mahlah 1; Milcah 2; Tirzah; Part II: Daughters of Zelophehad (Num 26:33, etc.).

Nympha

"bride," from Greek, *nymphē*, "bride"; or "young wife," "young woman eligible for marriage"; also "sister-in-law"

(Col 4:15)

At the conclusion of the letter to the church at Colossae (in western Asia Minor, now modern Turkey), the author sends greetings to believers in the nearby city of Laodicea, and to a person whose name is probably Nympha and the church in that person's house.

Many ancient biblical manuscripts understand this person to have been a man named Nymphas, as evidenced by their use of the masculine pronoun in the phrase "the church in his house," whereas others read, "the church in her house." This confusion occurs because, when used as a direct object, both the masculine Nymphas and the feminine Nympha are written as Nymphan.

Older translations of the Bible, such as the KJV, preferred to see the head of this house church as a man, just as they also saw the apostle Junia in Rom 16:7 as the male Junias. No listing occurs for Nympha (or Junia) in works such as Edith Deen's *All the Women of the Bible* (1955) or Herbert Lockyer's collection of the same title (1967). More recently, however, scholars have preferred the female Nympha, operating on the principle that ancient scribes, troubled by a woman church leader, were more likely to have corrected the feminine pronoun to the masculine than vice versa. This judgment is now reflected in newer translations such as the NRSV, the REB, the NJB, the NAB, and others. Since the masculine Nymphas is not found among Roman inscriptions from this period, whereas the feminine Nympha is attested more than sixty times (mostly for slaves and freedwomen), it seems reasonably safe to assume that this newer reading is correct.

Nympha's historicity is problematic as well. Colossians is one of several New Testament Epistles, written in the name of Paul, whose authenticity is questioned by many scholars. The probable pseudonymous character of the letter raises the possibility that Nympha and other persons named here but not known from the undisputed letters of Paul may be creations of the author intended to give Colossians the appearance of a genuine Pauline work.

Although we cannot know whether there was an actual Nympha, she is presented here as a woman in whose house a local church meets (other house churches mentioned in the New Testament include that of Prisca and Aquila, Rom 16:5, and another in Phlm v. 2). This implies that she owned a house big enough to accommodate a gathering of believers, although this number need not have been particularly large. No male relative, whether husband, father, or son, is associated with Nympha, suggesting that she was either independent of male authority or sufficiently wealthy or powerful to allow the church to meet in her home. Given what we know of early house churches and of Greco-Roman associations that met in private houses, Nympha would most likely have been both the financial patron of the church and a significant leader in its affairs and practices.

Ross S. Kraemer

SEE ALSO Part I: Prisca/Priscilla.

Oholah SEE Oholah, Woman Samaria (Part III).

Oholibah SEE Oholibah, Woman/Whore Jerusalem (Part III).

Oholibamah

meaning uncertain; perhaps "my tent [protection] is in them," from Hebrew *'ohŏlî*, "my tent," plus preposition for "in," plus third-person-plural suffix

(Gen 36:2)

Oholibamah, daughter of Anah, who was of a Hivite (non-Israelite) family, becomes one of Esau's wives through an exogamous marriage (one based on an alliance between two unrelated kinship groups). Esau's exogamous marriages separate him from the major lineage, that of his brother, Jacob. Oholibamah bears Esau three children. The name may be related to Oholiab from the tribe of Dan (Exod 31:6) and Oholibah and Oholah (Ezekiel 23).

Naomi Steinberg

SEE ALSO Part I: Anah; Basemath 1/Bashemath; Judith 1; Mahalath 1.

Orpah

"nape of the neck," from Hebrew *'orep*, "neck, back of neck"

(Ruth 1:4, 14)

Named twice in the Book of Ruth, Orpah is the Moabite wife and widow of the Judean Chilion, son of Naomi and Elimelech (1:4–5; see 4:9–10), and the daughter-in-law who chooses not to return with Naomi from the foreign land of Moab to Bethlehem (1:14). Orpah speaks only once, and then in concert with Ruth (1:10). She weeps twice (1:9, 14), and she kisses her mother-in-law in farewell (1:14). The etymology of her name may evoke this posture of turning back. Naomi herself commends Orpah for loyalty (1:8), wishes for her the security of a second husband (1:9), and cites her choice as a model for Ruth to emulate (1:15). Yet her behavior contrasts with that of Ruth, who leaves her Moabite kin behind and becomes an ancestor of the Davidic dynasty.

One feminist judgment deems Orpah's return sound. It fits societal strictures and offers her a future. A counter judgment deems the return dangerous. As the widow of a foreigner, Orpah would experience rejection by her own people and so have no future. But on such possibilities the story is silent.

PHYLLIS TRIBLE

Peninnah

"pearl; red coral," from Hebrew *pĕnînîm,* "corals"
(1 Sam 1:2, 4)

The second wife to Elkanah in the Hannah narrative (1 Samuel 1–2, set in the tribal period — eleventh century B.C.E.) Peninnah is unloved — hence hated — but fertile. She is also jealous of Hannah, Elkanah's first wife, who is loved but barren. Peninnah's prestige as mother of Elkanah's children is emphasized at the annual pilgrimage to Shiloh, when Elkanah gives each wife and each child a sacrificial portion. Peninnah taunts Hannah on this occasion. Because the reader's sympathies are directed toward the motherless Hannah, Peninnah comes across as a malicious woman. In fact, she is probably a literary convention, a foil for the independence and goodness of Hannah, and should be regarded as such. The text does not suggest Peninnah has an independent personality in any way.

Peninnah represents a woman who accepts social paradigms without examining them, thus acting out the type of jealousy between co-wives known from the matriarchal texts of Genesis. Unlike the fecund second wives in Genesis, Peninnah has no voice in the text and is mentioned only in three capacities: as second wife to Elkanah, as mother of an unspecified number of daughters and sons, and as tormentor of Hannah. She disappears from the narrative when Hannah conceives.

LILLIAN R. KLEIN

SEE ALSO Part I: Hannah; Part II: Daughters (and Sons) of Peninnah (1 Sam 1:4).

Persis

from Greek *Persis,* "Persian woman"
(Romans 16:12)

Persis, one of nine women greeted by Paul in his letter to the Romans, is singled out for special praise. Paul often indicates his affection for particular Christians, especially coworkers, by referring to them as "my beloved [Name]" (Rom 16:5, 8–9), but here he says "*the* beloved Persis" (italics added), which probably indicates the esteem that Roman Christians have for her. Paul describes her further as having "worked hard in the Lord," using a word he employs elsewhere for his own apostolic labors (for example, Phil 2:16) and for the work of leaders within local congregations (for example, 1 Thess 5:12). Though her name suggests slave or freedwoman status, she was clearly a pillar, if not one of the founders, of the Roman church.

JOUETTE M. BASSLER

SEE ALSO Part I: Euodia; Mary 7; Syntyche.

Phoebe

"bright, radiant," from Greek *Phoibē,* in the masculine form, an epithet of the Greek god Apollo
(Rom 16:1–2)

Paul commends this woman to the Christians in Rome at the conclusion of his letter to them and provides, in two brief verses, just enough information to indicate her significant role in the early church. She was probably a gentile Christian (her name derives from Greek mythology), but because of Paul's brevity, the precise nature of her role or position in the church has been a matter of some dispute.

It has been argued that Romans 16, with its long list of greetings, was not originally part of Paul's letter to Rome, a city the apostle had never visited. In fact, a few early manuscripts of the letter lack this chapter, so some think it was once a separate letter intended, perhaps, for Ephesus. It has never been suggested, though, that Paul did not write the chapter, and many scholars are now convinced that it was part of the original letter to Rome. Indeed, Phoebe was probably the one who carried the letter from Paul to the church in Rome, just as Epaphroditus probably carried Paul's letter to the Philippians (Phil 2:25-30) and Tychicus probably carried the letter to the Colossians (Col 4:7-9).

Paul does not explicitly state why Phoebe is traveling to Rome; he only encourages the Roman Christians to "help her in whatever she may require from you" (v. 2). Some have speculated that she was traveling for business reasons or because of some litigation and that she had agreed to carry the letter as a favor to Paul. Others, however, understand the travel and the recommendation to be associated with her role as a church leader.

Paul, for example, notes that Christian missionaries and church leaders regularly carried letters of recommendation (see 2 Cor 3:1; also Acts 18:27), or a letter that included recommendations (1 Cor 4:17), and he introduces Phoebe first to the Romans as "our sister" (v. 1), suggesting that she, like Timothy (introduced in 1 Thess 3:2 as "our brother"), was a coworker. Jewett has suggested that she had been sent ahead by Paul to begin the complex arrangements for his mission to Spain, though Paul's comments are far too terse to confirm this hypothesis.

If the purpose of Phoebe's trip to Rome is not specifically stated, her status in her home church is somewhat clearer. She is identified as *diakonos* of the church of Cenchreae, the eastern port of Corinth. Though this title is sometimes translated as "servant" (NIV) or "deaconess" (RSV, NJB), and sometimes defined in terms of informal service or limited ministry to women or to the sick, it is the same title (with no gender distinctions) that Paul applies to himself and to others engaged in a ministry of preaching and teaching (1 Cor 3:5; 2 Cor 6:4; Phil 1:1). The word clearly points to a leadership role over the whole church, not just part of it; and the way the title is introduced suggests a recognized office, though doubtless not as well defined as it later became in the church (1 Tim 3:8-13). Phoebe is thus a church official, a minister of the church in Cenchreae.

She is also described as *prostatis,* the feminine form of a noun that can denote a position as leader, president, presiding officer, guardian, or patron (see 1 Thess 5:12; 1 Tim 3:4-5; 5:17, where the related verb occurs). Because she is presented as *prostatis* "of many and of myself as well" (v. 2), and not specifically as *prostatis* of the church, the emphasis is probably on her role as patron or benefactor, though the title also reinforces the concept of authority conveyed by her position as deacon. As a patron she would, of course, have provided funds for the church and probably publicly represented it when necessary. She would also have used her influence — derived from her wealth and social standing — to resolve any difficulties that might arise for the congregation. Paul himself is personally indebted to her in some way (that is, he is her "client"), and he asks the Roman church to help him repay that debt by providing her with a generous welcome and whatever support she requires.

Paul thus recommends Phoebe as his coworker ("sister"), as leader of an established church ("deacon"), and as a generous benefactor of many Christians. She is obviously an independent woman (she is not defined in terms of husband, father, or family) of considerable means. She may well have been traveling to or through Rome as a missionary or church worker. Paul's acknowledgment of her in this letter is brief, but it offers a tantalizing glimpse of the leadership of women in early Christianity.

JOUETTE M. BASSLER

SEE ALSO Part I: Prisca/Priscilla.

FOR FURTHER READING: Castelli, Elizabeth A. "Romans."

Jewett, Robert. "Paul, Phoebe, and the Spanish Mission."

MacDonald, Margaret. "Reading Real Women through the Undisputed Letters of Paul."

Schüssler Fiorenza, Elisabeth. "The 'Quilting' of Women's History: Phoebe of Cenchreae."

Prisca/Priscilla

"venerable," from Latin *priscus,* "belonging to former times," hence venerable; Prisca is the feminine form of the common Roman surname Priscus (masculine); Priscilla is a diminutive

(Acts 18:2–3, 18–19, 24–26; Rom 16:3–5; 1 Cor 16:19; 2 Tim 4:19)

Prisca (called "Priscilla," a diminutive of Prisca, in Acts) is mentioned six times in the New Testament: twice in Paul's letters, several times in Acts 18, and once in 2 Timothy. Paul's letters provide the most reliable information about her; the story in Acts, written somewhat later and amplified by novelistic concerns, nevertheless contains some useful details; the brief reference to her in 2 Timothy, probably written several decades after Paul's death, provides nothing more than evidence of an enduring memory of Prisca's connections with Paul's ministry.

Prisca is always mentioned with Aquila, her husband. She was obviously a very important, well-traveled missionary and church leader whose work on occasion intersected with that of Paul. Though Acts describes her husband as a Jew from the region of Pontus (on the southern coast of the Black Sea), we know nothing of Prisca's origins. (Both names are Latin and provide no clues of ethnic or geographic origin; Acts 18 contributes information only about Aquila.) Acts reports that the two were forced to leave Rome because of an edict of the emperor Claudius, expelling all Jews from the city (Acts 18:2). As described by the Roman historian Suetonius, this expulsion (in 49 C.E.) was in response to "disturbances at the instigation of Chrestus," which is widely (and probably correctly) interpreted as a reference to quarrels between believing and nonbelieving Jews generated by believers' proclamation about Christ (in Greek, *Christos*). Both groups in Rome were affected by the edict, and it seems likely that Prisca and Aquila were already believers, since Acts, which picks up their story after the expulsion, nowhere describes their conversion. Thus it appears that they were already active as missionaries for Christ in Rome before their encounter with Paul.

According to Acts, Paul met them in Corinth soon after their arrival from Rome. The author of Acts focuses on Paul's missionary work, so we do not learn of Prisca's (or Aquila's) church work in Corinth, though it was probably fairly extensive. (We are told, however, of their secular trade: like Paul's, it was tent making.) Certainly the two were well known to the Corinthian community, for when Paul wrote to Corinth some time later, he included warm greetings from "Aquila and Prisca, together with the church in their house" (1 Cor 16:19).

Paul's letter to the Corinthians was written from Ephesus (1 Cor 16:8), and obviously Prisca and her husband were with him in that city, having moved there from Corinth with Paul (see also Acts 18:18–19). Paul's apostolic work caused him to leave Ephesus, but Prisca and Aquila stayed behind, overseeing the church that met in their house. House churches were a common feature of the early Christian movement (Rom 16:5; 1 Cor 16:19; Col 4:15; Phlm 2), and in each city there were probably a number of these base units, which included not only members of the immediate family, but also slaves, freedmen, freedwomen, workers associated with the family, and other converts as well. The head of the house naturally assumed leadership of the group, and the fact that in four of six instances the New Testament sources mention Prisca before her husband (inverting the usual custom) probably points to her more active role in the life of the church.

After the edict banning Jews (including Jewish believers in Christ) was lifted in 54 C.E., Prisca and Aquila must have returned to Rome, for when Paul wrote to the community in that city (in 56 or 57 C.E.) he sent greetings first of all to them (Rom 16:3–5). They again used their home to establish a house church, which Paul greeted as well. The evidence presented thus far suggests that Prisca and her husband were obviously people of relatively comfortable means: they were independent artisans, able to move frequently, and owned houses large enough to accommodate modest congregations.

Paul's comments in his letter to Rome reveal more about Prisca's work for the church. Prisca is mentioned before her husband, though both are described as his coworkers, a term Paul uses for associates actively engaged with him in missionary work (Rom 16:9, 21 — Urbanus and Timothy; 1 Cor 3:9 — Apollos; 2 Cor 8:23 — Titus; Phil 2:25 — Epaphroditus; 4:2–3 — Euodia, Syntyche, and Clement; 1 Thess 3:2 — Timothy; Phlm v. 1 — Philemon, v. 24 — Mark, Aristarchus, Demas, and Luke). He also asserts that they both "risked their necks for my life" (Rom 16:4), an indication that they acted as patrons or benefactors of Paul at some point (perhaps in Ephesus; see 1 Cor 15:32), using their wealth and status — at some personal risk — to gain protection for the apostle when his life was endangered. He gives thanks to them for their work and affirms that "all the churches of the Gentiles" (Rom 16:4) join him in this. Though perhaps an exaggeration, these words indicate how widespread Prisca's influence was — whether through her missionary preaching, her generous patronage, or other forms of support.

Acts reports that Apollos, an early missionary remembered for his powerful and eloquent speech (Acts 18:24–28) and for his work in Corinth (1 Corinthians 3–4), received much of his instruction about Christ from Prisca and Aquila — and again Prisca is given prominence by being listed first. This account is not entirely reliable, but it does reflect an enduring memory in the early church that Prisca was an authoritative teacher who not only performed missionary work herself, but also helped train others.

Missionary couples were apparently relatively common in early churches (1 Cor 9:5), and our sources suggest that Prisca and Aquila were prominent among them. Moreover, they suggest that Prisca was the leader of the pair. Her work would have involved preaching, teaching, presiding over the church in her house, and serving as patron to

other believers. According to one legend, the fourth-century church, Saint Priscae, on the Aventine Hill in Rome was built on the site of her house church. It has also been suggested that Prisca was the author of the anonymous letter to the Hebrews. These legends cannot be confirmed, but they attest to the power of her memory in the early church.

JOUETTE M. BASSLER

SEE ALSO Part I: Phoebe.

FOR FURTHER READING: D'Angelo, Mary Rose. "Hebrews."

Lampe, Peter. "Prisca."

Richter Reimer, Ivoni. *Women in the Acts of the Apostles: A Feminist Liberation Perspective.*

Schüssler Fiorenza, Elisabeth. "Missionaries, Apostles, Coworkers: Romans 16 and the Reconstruction of Women's Early Christian History."

Puah

"girl" or "shining one," from Hebrew *yp'*, "to shine"; or "speaker," from Hebrew *p'h*, "to cry out"
(Exod 1:15–21)

The first chapter of Exodus relates that, as the Israelites in Egypt begin to proliferate following the death of Joseph, the Egyptian king seeks to curb the Israelite population lest its numbers threaten the security of Egypt in time of war. When enslavement of the Israelites fails to achieve Pharaoh's goal, he commands the Hebrew midwives, of whom only two are known by name — Shiphrah and Puah — to kill at birth all the male Hebrews, but to permit the females to live. Since, however, the midwives stand in awe of God, they violate Pharaoh's command and permit the boys to live.

Called to account for failing to carry out Pharaoh's order, they report that the Hebrew women are more "vigorous" than Egyptian women and tend to deliver their babies before the arrival of the midwife. Convinced by the midwives' explanation, Pharaoh does not punish them. Their explanation is probably accepted because of a universal human tendency to dehumanize victims — especially women — as a prelude to depriving them of basic civil rights, their reproductive freedom, their progeny, and ultimately their very lives.

The identity of the midwives is somewhat ambiguous. The Hebrew text of Exod 1:15 supports either the view that Puah and Shiphrah were "Hebrew midwives" or the view that they were "midwives to the Hebrews." The former is more likely because both names are Semitic, not Egyptian. Ancient Jewish commentators vary widely in their understanding of who these women were; some even propose that Puah was Moses' sister Miriam, and others suggest they were proselytes.

Whatever their identity, the fact that they are rewarded with progeny indicates that they may have been barren and especially that they were young enough to begin a family. The latter piece of information contests the supposition by some that midwives were typically older, perhaps postmenopausal, women. Such was indeed the case in ancient Greece — Athenian law specified that a midwife had to have herself given birth and be past childbearing age — but not everywhere in the ancient world.

Modern commentators have wondered how two midwives could have served a whole community, even if the figure of 600,000 people (given in Num 1:46) is not taken literally. The obvious answer is that the text does not claim that Shiphrah and Puah were the only midwives to serve the Hebrews, but rather were two among many. Why then were they singled out? The tale implies that they are mentioned because of their virtue in fearing God more than they feared Pharaoh. In the Hebrew Bible, the phrase "fear God" can mean "obey God's ethical imperatives" (see Lev 19:14; Job 28:28). It is noteworthy that Exod 1:1–2, in its highly schematic survey of Hebrew history from the descent of Jacob into Egypt until the birth of Moses, mentions by name only the midwives Shiphrah and Puah. The crucial role of the midwives in subverting Pharaoh's decree is, perhaps, reflected in the Talmudic attribution of the redemption from Egypt to the merit of the virtuous women of that generation.

It is not clear whether Shiphrah and Puah worked together or alone. Ancient Egyptian pictorial art depicts midwives working in teams. Yet the other explicit biblical references to members of this profession (Gen 35:17; 38:28) each mention a single midwife.

The Hebrew term for "birth stool" in Exod 1:16, 'obnayim, means literally "two stones." It refers to the primitive form of the birth stool, which was simply two bricks (or stones) placed under each of the buttocks of the woman in labor. Such birth stools are depicted in the later forms of the hieroglyphic symbol for "birth" and are referred to in ancient Egyptian folk sayings, such as "He left me like a woman on the bricks." Ancient Egyptian pictorial art shows that the two bricks were replaced by a chair with an opening in the middle (like a toilet seat) through which, with the help of gravity, the mother could push out her baby into the deft hands of the midwives.

Mayer I. Gruber

See also Part I: Shiphrah; Part II: Midwife (Gen 35:17, etc.); Hebrew Women in Egypt (Exod 1:19, etc.).

For further reading: Exum, J. Cheryl. "Second Thoughts about Secondary Characters: Women in Exodus 1.8–2.10."

———. "'You Shall Let Every Daughter Live': A Study of Exodus 1:8–2:10."

Ghaliounghi, Paul. *The House of Life.*

Paul, Shalom M. "Exodus 1:21: 'To Found a Family,' a Biblical and Akkadian Idiom."

Rachel

"ewe," from Hebrew *rāḥēl*, "ewe"

RACHEL IN THE HEBREW BIBLE

(Gen 29–31; 33; 35:16–21, 24–25; 46:19, 22, 25; 48:7; Ruth 4:11; 1 Sam 10:2; Jer 31: 11–21)

The younger daughter of Laban and wife of Jacob, Rachel is the mother of Joseph and Benjamin, who become two of the twelve tribes of Israel (Gen 35:24; 46:15–18). Her maid Bilhah is ancestor of two more (Gen 35:25; 46:23–24).

When Jacob goes to Mesopotamia to find a wife from his mother's family (the line of Terah), he meets the shepherd Rachel at a well. He waters her flock, kisses her, and announces their kinship, for Jacob is both Laban's nephew (through his mother Rebekah) and his second cousin (through his father). Rachel runs home to tell of his presence, and Laban invites Jacob to the house (Gen 29:9–14). Jacob loves Rachel and arranges to marry her and to work seven years as her bride wealth. At the wedding, however, Laban substitutes Leah, his older daughter, for Rachel. Explaining that it was not the custom to give the younger in marriage first, he promises Rachel to Jacob at the end of the week of the wedding feast, on the proviso that Jacob work another seven years to pay off a second bride price (Gen 29:15–30).

Like Sarah and Rebekah before her, Rachel experiences a long period of barrenness. The infertility of the matriarchs has two effects: it heightens the drama of the birth of the eventual son, marking Isaac, Jacob, and Joseph as special; and it emphasizes that pregnancy is an act of God. For when God "saw that Leah was unloved, he opened her womb" (Gen 29:31), giving Leah four sons (Gen 29:32–35). Rachel, envious of her sister, forcefully demands children from Jacob: "Give me children or I shall die!" (Gen 30:1). Jacob is incensed, declaring that he can do nothing because it is God who has denied Rachel children (Gen 30:2). As a consequence of her demand, Jacob agrees to her plan, to give Bilhah, whom her father had given her (Gen 29:29), to Jacob as a wife. Jacob already has children, but Rachel herself wishes to acquire children through her surrogate (as does Bilhah). The plan works, and Rachel names the child Dan, explaining "God judged [that is, vindicated] me" (Gen 30:5–6). Still competing with her sister, Rachel has Bilhah bear another son, whom she names Naphtali (meaning "I have prevailed"), in reference to the "contest" with her sister that she has been waging and winning (Gen 30:7–8).

The competition between the sisters/co-wives continues as Leah gives her maid Zilpah in turn. Despite the birth of children to these surrogates, Rachel and Leah still want to conceive their own. A turning point comes when Leah's son Rueben finds mandrakes. A mandrake root, which looks like a newborn baby, was often considered a fertility charm and an aphrodisiac. Rachel wants the mandrakes, and she has something that Leah wants even more than mandrakes. She has occupancy of Jacob's bed and trades a night with Jacob for the mandrakes. When they reach an agreement, Leah announces to Jacob that she has "hired" him (Gen 30:14–16). Co-wives are normally rivals, which is perhaps why biblical law forbids a man from marrying sisters (Lev 18:18). But when the co-wives cooperate, Jacob, like other husbands, complies with their wishes.

This agreement proves fruitful for both wives. Leah bears three more children; and finally, after eleven children have been born to Jacob, Rachel bears a son and names him Joseph ("he adds"). Her two explanations for the name reveal her state of mind: "God has taken away my reproach" and "may the LORD add to me another son!" (Gen 30:22–24). In the very moment of relief and joy, she is not satisfied: she wants more. Rachel, like Jacob, is simply not content with what is given her. Her lack of satisfaction becomes clear when the family leaves Laban and sets out for the land of Canaan. Like Rebekah before them, both sisters actively agree to leave for Canaan. At the same time, they both express their anger at Laban, who never gave them any of the bride wealth earned by Jacob's fourteen years of service for them (Gen 31:14–16).

But Rachel alone takes action: she steals her father's teraphim, his household gods (Gen 31:19). Her behavior often bears a shadowy resemblance to Jacob's. Jacob supplanted his elder brother, but Rachel didn't succeed in supplanting hers at marriage. Jacob had received Esau's birthright; Rachel takes the teraphim, which may have had something to do with property rights, perhaps to secure some inheritance. Or they may have been primarily religious images, intended to invoke the protection of the ancestors. In either case, possession of the teraphim was the prerogative of the head of household. Laban would never have given them to her, and he comes looking for them. Unaware of what Rachel has done, Jacob takes an oath that "anyone with whom you find your gods will not live" (Gen 31:32). The reader knows what Jacob does not — that Rachel has taken the gods and is now in danger, not only from her father, but also from the oath. Laban must not find the gods; Rachel, a trickster like her father, her aunt (Rebekah), and her husband, thinks of a stratagem. She places the gods under her seat and declines to rise because she is menstruating (Gen 31:33–35). Her womanhood perhaps disqualifies her from receiving the teraphim legitimately; so she uses her womanhood to prevent Laban from taking them away once she has taken them illegitimately.

In the end, Rachel's stratagem comes to naught. She could not keep the teraphim, for Jacob commands his household to bury (NRSV, "put away") all their foreign gods, which almost certainly would include these teraphim (Gen 35:2). More tragically, in a sad irony, the very womanhood that has helped her trick Laban thwarts her daring and her ambition in a way that has plagued women through the ages. Finally fertile, she dies bearing her second child, Benjamin. Jacob buries her where she died, in her own tomb (Gen 35:20; 48:17) and not in the ancestral tomb at Machpelah.

There is one more twist to the story. Rachel, who died young, becomes an image of tragic womanhood. Her tomb remained as a landmark (see 1 Sam 10:2) and a testimony to her. She and Leah were remembered as the two "who together built up the house of Israel" (Ruth 4:11). Rachel was the ancestress of the Northern Kingdom, which was called Ephraim after Joseph's son. After Ephraim and Benjamin were exiled by the Assyrians, Rachel was remembered as the classic mother who mourns and intercedes for her children. More than a hundred years after the exile of the North, Jeremiah had a vision of Rachel still mourning, still grieving for her lost children. Moreover, he realized that her mourning served as an effective intercession, for God promised to reward her efforts and return her children (Jer 31:15–21). After the biblical period, "Mother Rachel" continued to be celebrated as a powerful intercessor for the people of Israel.

TIKVA FRYMER-KENSKY

SEE ALSO Part I: Bilhah; Leah; Rebekah.

FOR FURTHER READING: Greenberg, Moshe. "Another Look at Rachel's Theft of the Teraphim."

Niditch, Susan. *Underdogs and Tricksters: A Prelude to Biblical Folklore.*

Pardes, Ilana. *Countertraditions in the Bible: A Feminist Approach.*

Spanier, Ktziah. "Rachel's Theft of the Teraphim: Her Struggle for Family Primacy [Gen 31]."

van der Toorn, Karel. "The Nature of the Biblical Teraphim in the Light of the Cuneiform Evidence."

RACHEL IN THE NEW TESTAMENT
(Matt 2:18)

Characteristic of the Gospel of Matthew is the repeated claim that various events in the life of Jesus fulfill particular prophecies found in Jewish Scripture. In Matthew's version of the birth and infancy of Jesus (a narrative with striking resemblances to the birth and infancy of Moses in Exodus), Herod the Great (ruled 37 B.C.E.–48 C.E.) learns that a child has been born who will be king of the Jews. Terrified at the prospect, Herod authorizes the slaughter of all children (probably meaning all boys) of two years of age and younger, in Bethlehem and its vicinity, thus recalling Pharaoh's response to news of the birth of Moses (Exod 1:15–22). According to Matthew 2:18, this wholesale infanticide fulfills a prophecy in the Book of Jeremiah, in which the matriarch Rachel weeps inconsolably for her children. In its own context, Gen 31:15 depicts Rachel, second wife of the patriarch Jacob, grieving over the exile of northern Israelite tribes by the conquering Assyrians in the eighth century B.C.E.

ROSS S. KRAEMER

Rahab

Hebrew *rāḥāb*, from the root *rḥb*, "to be wide, enlarge"; possibly a shortened form of a theophoric name meaning "God has enlarged"

RAHAB IN THE HEBREW BIBLE
(Josh 2; 6:16–25)

A Canaanite woman living in Jericho, Rahab is a prostitute who is also a biblical heroine. According to the narrative in Joshua 2, before the conquest of Canaan, Joshua sends two men as spies to see the land. They come to Rahab's house for lodging, information, and/or sex. The king, hearing about the two men, demands that Rahab give them up. Like the midwives in Egypt, Rahab is faced with a "moment of truth." Like them, Rahab defies the ruler and rescues the Israelites. She tells the king's men that the two men have left and that the king's men should chase them. Meanwhile, she has hidden the men under the flax drying on her roof (2:4); the writer uses the unusual word *tiṣpĕnô*, "she hid him" (even though there are two men), perhaps as an allusion to Exod 2:2, where Moses' mother hides her newborn *(tiṣpĕnēhû)*. Rahab is midwife and mother to Israel in its beginnings in Canaan.

Rahab lets the two men out through her window, which is in the town wall. She requests a return for her act of *ḥesed* ("special benevolence": NRSV, "I have dealt kindly"). She asks that she and her family be spared once the Israelites attack Jericho. The spies give her a crimson thread to hang from her window, with the injunction that she is to gather her family and wait inside her house; as long as they stay indoors, they will be spared. When the Israelites destroy Jericho, as described in Joshua, Rahab and her whole extended family indeed escape doom by waiting inside a house marked with a red thread, just as the Israelites who stayed in houses marked with the blood of the paschal lamb were spared the fate of the Egyptians. They are exempted from the *ḥerem*, Israel's obligation to destroy all Canaanites (see 6:17), and are brought out of the city to live "in Israel ever since" (6:25). Rahab and her family are a new Israel.

Rahab has a special function in the biblical narratives of Israel's existence in the land. When uncovering the men, she explains that she knows that God will give Israel the land (2:8). She has heard about the events of the Red Sea and the defeat of the Amorite kings Og and Sihon, and she declares (quoting from the Song of Miriam in Exodus 15; see v. 11) that "dread" has fallen on the inhabitants and that they all "fear" Israel (2:9). This is the message that the men bring back to Joshua. Rahab is thus

the oracle of Israel's occupation of the land. Another woman, the prophet Deborah, announced a major victory in the taking of Canaan; and the end of Israel's occupation of the land is pronounced by yet another woman, the prophet Huldah. Rahab, who begins as triply marginalized — Canaanite, woman, and prostitute — moves to the center as bearer of a divine message and herald of Israel in its new land. Even though later generations of readers have been squeamish about her occupation, preferring to think of her as an "innkeeper," she is remembered in Jewish tradition as the great proselyte, as ancestress of kings and prophets, and, in the New Testament, as ancestress of Jesus.

TIKVA FRYMER-KENSKY

SEE ALSO Part II: Mother (and Father) and Sisters (and Brothers) of Rahab (Josh 2:13, etc.); Women (and Men) of Jericho and Ai (Josh 6:21, etc.).

FOR FURTHER READING: Bird, Phyllis. "The Harlot as a Heroine: Narrative Art and Social Presuppositions in Three Old Testament Texts."

Frymer-Kensky, Tikva. "Reading Rahab."

RAHAB IN THE NEW TESTAMENT
  (Matt 1:5)
The prostitute from Jericho (Joshua 2, 6), Rahab is the second woman named in Jesus' genealogy. According to Matt 1:5, "Salmon [was] the father of Boaz by Rahab," and thus Rahab is Ruth's mother-in-law. There is no hint of this relationship in the Hebrew Scriptures; to the contrary, Salmon lived two centuries after Rahab (Ruth 4:20, at the end of the period of the judges; no wife is here listed for Salmon). According to the Talmud (*b. Megillah* 14b–15a), Rahab is the wife of Joshua. Her anomalous presence, along with that of Tamar, Ruth, the wife of Uriah (Bathsheba), and Mary, has been explained by several theories.

The early Christian male writers traditionally known as the church fathers argued that the women represent sinners redeemed by Jesus. However, according to contemporaneous Jewish and Christian literature, the women were regarded not as sinners but as manifesting righteousness. Although all five women lack direct contact from heaven — the deity does not appear to Tamar, Rahab, Ruth, or Bathsheba, and according to Matthew, the heavenly messages come not to Mary but to Joseph — to view them as sinners associates women with sin in a way that is absent from the Gospel.

The women's various unexpected sexual activities — Rahab is a prostitute (although she is never depicted engaging in any sort of sexual act); Tamar poses as a prostitute and seduces her father-in-law; Ruth, of Moabite origins and therefore associated with incest (see Gen 19:30–38), has a possibly indiscreet meeting with Boaz on the threshing floor; and Bathsheba, while married to Uriah, conceives a child with David — may be seen to anticipate Joseph's concern with Mary's pregnancy and, perhaps, to serve as responses to claims of Jesus' illegitimacy.

Although their inclusion in the conventional pattern of the genealogy implies that they lived in traditional domestic arrangements, not one of the women is identified as married at the time of her child's conception; thus a trace of independence, if not subversive status, remains. In this perspective, the women can represent members of the community associated with the author of the Gospel of Matthew: independent of biological families and seen as potentially disruptive by those on the outside. Moreover, they are also to some extent independent of their natal communities: Tamar is inappropriately housed in her father's house, since she is legally a member of Judah's family; Rahab survives the destruction of Jericho; Ruth leaves Moab; and Bathsheba is identified as the wife of Uriah, the Hittite who fights for the Israelite king. So too will Mary be forced to leave her home in Bethlehem and relocate first to Egypt and then to Nazareth in Galilee.

In their willingness to act and to move, the women may also indicate the higher righteousness that Matthew frequently endorses: Rahab acts righteously in order to save the spies sent by Joshua, just as Tamar forces Judah to act; Ruth motivates Boaz, and Bathsheba, here identified as "she of Uriah," recollects the Hittite's fidelity while David

stayed home at the time when kings go off to war. Joseph, the major actor in the infancy account, also subverts expectation: "being a righteous man" (Matt 1:19), he had resolved to divorce Mary quietly. Yet he is convinced by an angelic dream to marry.

Rahab is, finally, the first Gentile clearly mentioned in the genealogy. Ruth, too, is a Gentile, and the ethnic origins of Tamar and Bathsheba were debated by Jews and Christians in the early centuries. Rahab thus may foreshadow the entry of Gentiles into the Matthean church. However, in Jewish literature of the period, Rahab, along with Ruth, was regarded as a righteous proselyte to Judaism.

AMY-JILL LEVINE

SEE ALSO Part I: Bathsheba; Ruth; Tamar.

RAHAB IN THE NEW TESTAMENT
(Heb 11:31; Jas 2:25)
Rahab, the prostitute who hid Joshua's spies from the authorities in Jericho, became an example of conversion in early Christianity and Judaism because she and her family escaped the ban on Jericho and continued to live in Israel "to this day" (Joshua 2; 6:17, 23–25). She appears in the historical example lists of Hebrews, James, and the late-first-century letter called *1 Clement,* to the Corinthians. In Heb 11:31, Rahab is presented as an example of faith; having "received the spies in peace," she escapes the fate of the unbelievers. The Epistle of James, which emphasizes the relationship between faith and works, offers her deed as an example of the works that show faith. In *1 Clement,* she exemplifies faith and hospitality. This common emphasis on faith probably derives from the deduction that she became a proselyte, a view that also appears in a number of early Jewish commentaries.

MARY ROSE D'ANGELO

Rebecca
Greek transliteration of the Hebrew name Rebekah; the different spelling reflects the use of the double kappa for the Hebrew koph (q) as well as the English letter c for the Greek kappa.

SEE ALSO Part I: Rebekah: Rebecca in the New Testament.

Rebekah

perhaps "cow," Hebrew *bāqār*, a metathesis of *ribqâ;* or "knot," from the unattested Hebrew root *rbq,* "to tie fast"

REBEKAH IN THE HEBREW BIBLE

(Gen 24–27; 28:5; 29:12; 35:8; 49:31)

The second (after Sarah) of the matriarchal figures in the ancestral stories of Genesis, Rebekah is one of the most prominent women — in terms of her active role and her control of events — in the Hebrew Bible. The beautifully constructed narratives in Genesis 24–27 describe how she becomes Isaac's wife, gives birth to twin sons after initial barrenness, and finally obtains the primary place in the lineage for her younger son, Jacob, who is destined to become ancestor of all Israel.

The story of the wooing of Rebekah unfolds in Genesis 24, the longest chapter in the Book of Genesis. A spouse for Isaac is to be obtained from his uncle Nahor's family; the ensuing cousin marriage, with Rebekah and Isaac both members of the same kinship group, serves to emphasize the importance of their lineage. Abraham dispatches a trusted but unnamed servant to Mesopotamia, the land of his birth and where some of his family still resides, to find a wife for his son. Rebekah secures her role as wife-elect for Isaac by befriending the servant and his ten camels in the famous well scene, which has been called a type-scene — a narrative episode with certain expected motifs that appears at the critical juncture in the life of a hero. Indeed, the account of Rebekah at the well is the premier biblical example of such a scene. It ostensibly draws attention to Isaac, but, in his absence, reveals the beauty and especially the virtues of his wife-to-be.

After the well incident, Rebekah brings the servant home, enters into the marriage arrangement, and sets off to meet her future husband. She seems to have some input into the marriage negotiations, or at least into the decision about her departure from her homeland and birth family. Once she arrives in the promised land, she enters Isaac's home (called "his mother Sarah's tent," 24:67). There she is "loved" (24:67) by her husband, the first woman in the Hebrew Bible for whom marital love is proclaimed.

After twenty years of marriage, when Rebekah fails to become pregnant, Isaac prays to God, who grants the prayer that she may conceive. Another type-scene, that of the barren wife, thus enters the Rebekah story, calling attention to the special role of the children ultimately born to her. A divine oracle is addressed to her when she is pregnant, making her the only matriarch to receive a direct message from God (although Abraham's slave wife Hagar also receives an oracle). YHWH proclaims that "two nations" are in her womb and will contend with each other (25:23). This oracle foreshadows the tensions that will characterize the relationship between her sons, Jacob and Esau, as figures in the Genesis narrative and as eponymous ancestors of Israel and Edom.

In the next episode in the Rebekah story, Isaac passes her off as his sister. This narrative, similar in many ways to two such accounts about Sarah, at first seems to contribute little to the role or character of Rebekah. However, it does differentiate her in a significant way from Sarah; in one of the two wife-sister episodes in which she figures, Sarah seems to have had sexual relations with Pharaoh (Gen 12:13–14, 19) to ensure the safety of her husband and their household. Rebekah's marital fidelity, in contrast, is never compromised (Gen 26:7–11). Her relationship with her husband is consistently monogamous, unlike that of Sarah, who not only has extramarital sex, but also provides her husband with the slave wife Hagar, and of Rachel and Leah, who are co-wives and also provide slave wives to Jacob.

The final scene in which Rebekah appears is another well-known biblical episode: Isaac blesses Jacob rather than Esau, the first to emerge from the womb and thus the expected recipient of the paternal blessing. This designation of Jacob as heir to the ancestral lineage, which will mean his becoming progenitor of all Israel, is orchestrated by Rebekah. Through clever manipulation, whereby Isaac is deceived, she achieves her purpose and controls the family destiny.

Evaluating Rebekah's role in the biblical story of pre-Israelite ancestral beginnings has evoked varying perspectives. Two millennia of Jewish and Christian biblical interpretation have focused largely on the male ancestors — the patriarchs Abraham, Isaac, and Jacob. Furthermore, virtually all scholarly studies and Bible textbooks, until very recently, designated the pre-Mosaic era as the patriarchal period, thereby providing an inherent male bias to any consideration of the family stories of Genesis. That bias rightly reflects the biblical concern with patrilineage — tracing families through the male line. Yet it obscures the fact that those family stories include strong female characters.

This is especially true in the case of Rebekah, whose position in the second generation of ancestors is actually more prominent than that of her spouse. For one thing, Rebekah is far more dynamic and proactive than Isaac, for whom no independent episode is reported. The very fact that the verb *to go* is used of Rebekah *seven* times (a number used in the Bible for emphasis) in the courtship narrative of chap. 24 highlights her active character. In addition, Rebekah's behavior in Genesis 24 is depicted by a series of action verbs — she runs, draws water, fills jars, and rides a camel — that contribute to a sense of her individuality and vitality, in contrast to Isaac's passivity. Also noteworthy is the way the language used in reference to Rebekah's journey from Mesopotamia to Canaan, and in anticipation of her role as progenitor of countless offspring, echoes that found in the Abraham narratives (compare Gen 24:4, 38, 60 with Gen 12:1 and 22:17). Furthermore, Rebekah is said to have had a nurse (Gen 35:8), a highly unusual circumstance in the Hebrew Bible and one that thus signifies her unusual stature.

Finally, the long courtship account of Genesis 24, which is considered by many to be a self-contained novella, can perhaps be called a woman's story. Rebekah's dynamic presence in that episode may indicate its origin in women's storytelling, as do certain other features. The term "mother's household," for example, appears in 24:28. That phrase is found only four times in the Hebrew Bible, all in texts that reveal women's lives and agency. It signifies the important role of the senior woman in a family household, at least when considered from a female perspective, as does the use of the phrase "his mother Sarah's tent" for Isaac's home.

Because of the centrality of Rebekah, in contrast to Isaac, the ancestral sequence might more accurately be called Abraham, Rebekah, and Jacob. Indeed, when Rebekah's favored son, Jacob, is sent to Mesopotamia to secure a spouse, he identifies himself to his future bride (and cousin) Rachel not as the son of Isaac, but rather as "Rebekah's son" (Gen 29:12); his paternal ancestry is eclipsed by Rebekah's lineage. This incident may signify a reality of maternal dominance, at least in the case of Rebekah, that is too powerful for the androcentric interests of biblical narrative to obscure.

CAROL MEYERS

SEE ALSO Part I: Deborah 1; Sarah 1/Sarai; Part II: Mothers of Ruth and Orpah (Ruth 1:8, etc.).

FOR FURTHER READING: Allen, Christine Garside. "Who Was Rebekah? 'On Me Be the Curse, My Son.'"

Alter, Robert. *The Art of Biblical Narrative.*

Meyers, Carol. "Parashat Ḥayyei Sarah (Genesis 23:1–25:18)."

Stansell, Gary. "Mothers and Sons in Ancient Israel."

Steinberg, Naomi. *Kinship and Marriage in Genesis: A Household Economics Perspective.*

Teugels, Lieve. "'A Strong Woman Who Can Find?' A Study of the Characterization in Genesis 24 with Some Perspectives on the General Presentation of Isaac and Rebekah in the Genesis Narrative."

REBEKAH (REBECCA) IN THE NEW TESTAMENT
(Rom 9:10–12)

Paul argues here that Abraham's only true descendants are those born to him by virtue of a promise (Gen 18:10) and that therefore, from the moment of the births of his offspring, distinctions were drawn between his descendants. He exemplifies this principle further by arguing that it is not only valid in the case of *two* different mothers (Sarah and Hagar), but also in the case of *one,* referring to the fact that "something similar happened to Rebecca when she had conceived children by one husband, our ancestor Isaac," for even before the twins Esau and Jacob were born, she was told by God: "the elder shall serve the younger" (Gen 25:23). So only Jacob is heir to the promise.

PIETER W. VAN DER HORST

Reumah

meaning uncertain; perhaps "darling," related to Akkadian *râmu,* "to love"

(Gen 22:24)

The secondary wife (concubine) of Nahor (brother of Abraham, the first major male figure in the ancestral narratives of Genesis), Reumah bears Nahor four children, in addition to the children borne to him by his primary wife, Milcah. The names of these children are the names of Aramean tribes, which are indirectly related to the Israelites through this genealogy and whose history intersects with that of Israel in the period of the monarchy.

NAOMI STEINBERG

SEE ALSO Part I: Maacah 1; Milcah 1; Part II: Aramean Concubine of Manasseh (1 Chr 7:14).

Rhoda

"rose," from Greek *rhodon,* "rose"

(Acts 12:13–15)

A slave (Greek *paidiskē,* diminutive of *pais,* "girl") in the household of Mary, the mother of John Mark, Rhoda is not presented as a believer but as one free to watch the door while others pray. In this capacity she responds to the knock of the recently rescued Peter, but does not open the gate immediately; instead she runs to announce his arrival.

As a social figure Rhoda embodies the anonymous slaves of Christian owners addressed or discussed in several later New Testament texts. As a literary figure she evokes two important cross-references. Like the women of Luke 24:10–11, her report is disbelieved. She turns the tables on Peter — now he must pay a penalty for denying Jesus to another (anonymous) slave girl (NRSV, "servant-girl"; Luke 22:56–57). This lowly slave is a perfect, if imaginary, flower of poetic justice.

RICHARD I. PERVO

SEE ALSO Part II: Two Servant-Girls Who Accuse Peter (Matt 26:69–72); Servant-Girl, of the High Priest, Who Accuses Peter (Mark 14:66–69); Servant-Girl Who Accuses Peter (Luke 22:56–57); Slave Girl Healed of a Spirit (Acts 16:16–18).

Rizpah

"baking stone" or "hot coal," from Hebrew *riṣpâ,* "coal"

(2 Sam 3:7; 21:8, 10, 11)

The daughter of Aiah, Rizpah is the concubine of Saul, the first king of Israel (reigned c. 1025–1005 B.C.E.). Since Saul's wife Ahinoam has borne him four sons and two daughters, the reason for his taking of a concubine is not to produce an heir. Rizpah bears Saul two sons, Armoni and Mephibosheth. They become potential claimants to the Saulide throne after Saul because Saul's three eldest sons die in battle at Mount Gilboa (1 Sam 14:49; 31:2), and the youngest son, Eshbaal, who had not been old enough to fight, is crowned Saul's successor (1 Sam 14:49; 2 Sam 2:8; 1 Chr 8:33; 9:39) and then is assassinated (2 Samuel 4). In order to usurp the throne, David uses a three-year famine as a pretext to turn over the remaining seven eligible Saulide male heirs to the Gibeonites for ritual execution to atone for the bloodguilt Saul was supposed to have incurred against this group. Rizpah's two sons and the five sons of Saul's fertile daughter are killed. Rizpah prevents the executed bodies from being defiled by animals until David agrees to give them proper burial.

At some point after Eshbaal's installation as king, his great-uncle Abner, the seasoned commander of the Israelite army, makes a bid to wrest the throne from the inexperienced youth by sleeping with

Rizpah. It may have been the practice in ancient Near Eastern kingdoms to lay claim to the throne by having sexual relations with the former king's wives or concubines (see also 2 Sam 15:13–17; 16:17–22).

DIANA VIKANDER EDELMAN

SEE ALSO Part I: Abishag; Ahinoam 1; Part II: Wives of Saul (2 Sam 12:8); Concubines of David (2 Sam 15:16, etc.).

FOR FURTHER READING: de Vaux, Roland. *Ancient Israel: Its Life and Institutions.*

Matthews, Victor H., and Don C. Benjamin. *Social World of Ancient Israel, 1250–587* B.C.E.

Patai, Raphael. *Sex and Family in the Bible and the Middle East.*

Ruhamah

"pitied, loved," from Hebrew *rḥm,* "to pity, have compassion, love"

SEE Lo-ruhamah (Part I).

Ruth

"satiation, refreshment," from Hebrew *rwh,* "to be saturated, to drink one's fill"

RUTH IN THE HEBREW BIBLE

(Book of Ruth)

Ruth's name provides the title for the Book of Ruth, probably a piece of historical fiction set in the time of the judges. Ruth is a Moabite woman who marries a Judean immigrant named Mahlon (1:1–4; 4:10). Upon his death she becomes a childless widow who chooses to accompany her mother-in-law, Naomi, to Judah. Naomi protests the decision (1:11–13), but Ruth perseveres. She pledges total loyalty, even unto death, to Naomi, her people, and her god YHWH (1:16–17). When the women of Bethlehem greet them both, Naomi fails to acknowledge that Ruth is with her. Instead, the storyteller reports her presence as Moabite immigrant (a foreigner) and daughter-in-law (1:19–22).

In scene one (1:1–22) Ruth emerges in tension with her culture. She marries outside her own people, disavows the solidarity of her family, abandons her national identity, and renounces her religious affiliation. In the entire biblical epic of Israel, only Abraham approaches this radicalness, but then he had a call from God (Gen 12:1–3) and also a wife. Ruth stands alone, without support human or divine. Moreover, she reverses sexual allegiance. A young woman commits herself to an old woman in a world where life depends upon men.

Scene two (2:1–23) portrays Ruth taking the initiative to find food. By chance (a code for the divine) she comes to the field of a prosperous man named Boaz, a relative of Naomi (2:1–3). He asks, "To whom does this young woman belong?" — truly a patriarchal question. Though the question fits his culture, it does not fit Ruth, who remains in tension with the culture. The servant's answer fails to give her name but identifies her as "the Moabite who came back with Naomi from the country of Moab" (2:6). It derives her identity from her strangeness and from another woman.

Boaz allows Ruth to glean in his field and arranges for her safety. She responds with appropriate deference, noting his favor and her foreignness (2:8–9). Yet ironic subtlety marks her speech. The favor Boaz gives her is the favor that she has sought. Therefore, she (and chance), not he, is shaping her destiny. Boaz recognizes her distinctiveness. He describes her as one who has left her mother and father and her native land to live among a people she did not know (2:11). His language echoes the call of Abraham (Gen 12:1) and so locates Ruth within the saga of Israel. Further, Boaz invokes blessing upon her from YHWH under whose protective "wings" *(kĕnāpayim)* she has taken refuge (2:12). At evening, when Ruth reports to Naomi, the daughter learns that Boaz is a redeemer within their larger family. Her own concerns, however, remain loyalty to Naomi and the availability of food (2:17–23).

If scene two portrays Ruth's struggle to survive physically, scene three represents her struggle to survive culturally (3:1–18). It involves a bold act, potentially dangerous and compromising. At the insistence of Naomi, Ruth agrees without question to pursue marriage with Boaz. The plan calls for her to visit him on the threshing floor after he has celebrated the harvest and gone to sleep. She is to uncover his "feet," a euphemism for genitals, and then he will tell her what to do.

Ruth's actions elicit from Boaz a second question (see 2:5). Unlike his first, it addresses her directly and asks for her personal identity: "Who are you?" (3:9). In answering, Ruth gives her name. Then, contrary to Naomi's assurance, she tells Boaz what to do: "Spread your wing [*kānāp*, translated "cloak" in the NRSV] over your servant, for you are next-of-kin." By a wordplay on *wing* Ruth challenges Boaz to heed his earlier prayer for her blessing (2:12). This foreign woman calls an Israelite man to responsibility.

Even though Boaz informs Ruth that another man has first rights to her, Boaz himself responds graciously to her proposal. He calls Ruth a "worthy woman" (*'ēšet ḥayil*), the same phrase that Proverbs uses to depict the "capable wife" (Prov 31:10). He protects Ruth from discovery and provides her with food (3:14–15). In the morning she reports to her mother-in-law all that Boaz has done, yet omitting any report of her own bold words and deeds. Characteristically, Ruth's last words focus on her mother-in-law and the availability of food (3:17).

In scene four (4:1–22) Ruth, like Naomi, does not talk but is talked about. Before the male elders at the city gate, the place where issues are settled by the community, Boaz presents the case of the women to the unnamed man who has first rights. When this man learns that his obligation to purchase land from Naomi entails the marrying of Ruth, he refuses (4:1–6). The way is then open for Boaz to do the redeemer's part. The elders who witness the transaction address him with words about Ruth, though they never use her name. She is "the woman" and "this young woman" whom they compare to the ancestral mothers Rachel, Leah, and Tamar. These men see her as fulfilling the traditional values of fertility and the continuation of a male lineage (4:7–12). Accordingly, Boaz takes her as his wife, and she bears a son (4:13). A man's concerns have subsumed the woman Ruth.

Her story ends, however, not with the male elders but with the women of Bethlehem (see 1:19). In transferring Ruth's child to Naomi, they remind her that "your daughter-in-law who loves you, who is more to you than seven sons, has borne him" (4:14–15). Ruth leaves the story exalted above the ideal number of male children and identified through the woman to whom she swore allegiance even beyond death.

Feminist readings of Ruth diverge sharply. One perspective faults her for perfection, for being compliant, self-effacing, and a mere pawn of Naomi. Another praises her for faithfulness, for making radical moves, for risking dangerous acts, and for being a devoted partner of Naomi. Still another sees her used to espouse the patriarchal values of marriage and progeny, and then discarded. The counter view sees her challenging patriarchy even while trapped within it. Her foreign identity also receives opposing interpretations. One view holds that the story affirms this Moabite woman, embracing her fully within Judah as the great-grandmother of David (see 4:17–21). Another view holds that the story rejects this Moabite woman, erasing her at the end by giving her child to Naomi and so according David a pure genealogy.

Outside the story, the Gospel of Matthew claims Ruth as the mother of her child. Moreover, it places her alongside Tamar, "the wife of Uriah," and Mary as the only women in the genealogy of Jesus (Matt 1:3, 5, 6, 16).

PHYLLIS TRIBLE

SEE ALSO Part I: Naomi; Orpah; Part II: Mothers of Ruth and Orpah (Ruth 1:8, etc.); Women of Bethlehem (Ruth 1:19, etc.).

FOR FURTHER READING: Brenner, Athalya, ed. *A Feminist Companion to Ruth.*

Kates, Judith A., and Gail Twersky Reimer, eds. *Reading Ruth.*

La Cocque, André. "Ruth."

Levine, Amy-Jill. "Ruth."

Trible, Phyllis. "A Human Comedy."

RUTH IN THE NEW TESTAMENT
      (Matt 1:5)

David's great-grandmother (Ruth 4:18–22), the Moabite Ruth, is the third woman named in Matthew's genealogy of Jesus. Like Rahab, Tamar, and Bathsheba, Ruth takes righteous if unexpected action, anticipates Mary's sexually problematic situation (see Gen 19:30–38 on the incestuous origins of the Moabites; Ruth 3:6–15), may have served to counter claims concerning Jesus' illegitimacy, and foreshadows gentile participation in Matthew's church.

AMY-JILL LEVINE

SEE ALSO Part I: Rahab.

Salome 1

a Hellenized (and abbreviated) form of the Hebrew name Shelamzion, "peace of/to Zion," from Hebrew *šālôm*, "peace," and *ṣiyyon*, "Zion."

(Mark 15:40; 16:1)

Salome is one of three women named in Mark as present both at Jesus' crucifixion (15:40) and his tomb (16:1). She is not identified by her town (as is Mary of Magdala) or by her children (as is Mary the mother of James and Joses); surprisingly, none of the three is identified by her husband, as might have been expected. Even though the three named women are said to be looking on "from a distance" (compare 14:54, of Peter), what is surprising is their presence — in the absence of all of Jesus' male disciples. More startling is the flashback at 15:41, re-

A coin from 54 C.E. depicting Salome, queen of Chalcis, on one side, and her husband, King Aristobulus, on the other. See Salome 2.

vealing that these and "many other women" had been followers of Jesus in Galilee, and had ministered to (NRSV, "provided for") him there. The audience must now rethink the first part of the Gospel to include faithful women followers and assistants! Faithful and serving to the end, Salome and the two Marys come to the tomb to complete the burial rituals and are the first to hear the incredible resurrection message. Because Matt 27:56 does not mention Salome but does include — along with two Marys — the unnamed mother of the sons of Zebedee, some later readers have harmonized the texts and identified Salome as Zebedee's wife.

ELIZABETH STRUTHERS MALBON

SEE ALSO Part II: Mother of the Sons of Zebedee (Matt 20:20, etc.); Unnamed Women at the Cross (Mark 15:40–41).

Salome 2

(Mark 6:17–28; Matt 14:1–11; Luke 3:19–20)

According to the first-century C.E. Jewish historian Josephus, Salome was the daughter of Herodias and her first husband, Herod (a son of Herod the Great). She is never explicitly named in the New Testament, but she has long been identified as the daughter who, prompted by her mother, asks for the head of John the Baptist after her dancing has enchanted her stepfather, Herod Antipas (tetrarch of Galilee and Perea, 4 B.C.E.–39 C.E.), at a celebratory banquet.

The historicity of this entire event is suspect for various reasons, including its major discrepancies with Josephus's account of the death of John. The narrative bears a troubling resemblance to an earlier Roman story about Lucius Quinctius Flaminius, who was expelled from the senate in 184 B.C.E., allegedly for beheading a condemned man at a dinner party at the request of a courtesan whom he loved and who had expressed a desire to see such an act performed.

What we know of the historical Salome raises additional doubts about her identification as the dancer. One major issue is whether Salome's age is consistent with the probable date of John's death (anywhere from 27–28 to 33 C.E.) and the Gospels' description of the dancer as a young girl (*korasion;* Justin Martyr, a second-century C.E. Christian writer, calls her a child [*pais*]). Presumably, though, the dancer would have been no older than her early teens. Some scholars have suggested that she could have been as old as nineteen, but such arguments have been formulated to resolve tensions between the Gospels and the few fixed chronological points in the historical Salome's life. Presumably, also, to have provoked Herod's implicitly erotic response, the dancer would most likely have been postpubescent, and so at least twelve, although these estimates are based on imperfect knowledge of the ages at which girls matured in antiquity.

Since we do not know the date of Salome's birth, the date of John's death, nor the date of Herodias's marriages, it is difficult to determine whether Salome was in fact of the right age to be the dancer. We do know that Salome's first husband, Philip, died in 33–34 C.E., and that, according to Josephus, she subsequently married her cousin Aristobulus, who became king of Armenia Minor in 54 C.E. Neither marriage, though, resolves the issue definitively; in fact, the two together pose a somewhat different dilemma. The earlier a date of birth we propose for Salome, the more probable that she would have been the right age to have danced before Herod and yet made her first marriage to Philip before his death in 33–34.

Yet, since Aristobulus is usually thought to have been much younger — perhaps turning twenty-one in 54 C.E. — the earlier we date the birth of Salome, the more difficult it becomes to accommodate the second marriage and the three children it produced (*Antiquities* 18.137). If she was born between 10 and 18 C.E., she would have been fifteen to twenty-three years older than her husband. Such a marriage, although not impossible, contravenes much of what we know about marriages in this period, royal and otherwise. These difficulties have caused at least one scholar to suggest that two different Salomes are meant. Conversely, the later we date Salome's birth (while still allowing for the marriage to Philip, for she could have been as

young as twelve as late as 33 C.E.), the more likely it is that Salome was young enough to marry Aristobulus and bear him three children. Then, however, she would almost certainly have been too young to have danced before Herod Antipas.

In any case, Salome, wife of Aristobulus, was queen of Chalcis and is commemorated on a coin dating to 54 C.E., which is interesting in part for the light it may shed on head coverings and hairstyles of the era. The obverse of the coin depicts the king; the reverse depicts Salome's head, and she wears a crown of some sort, with her hair hanging down loose. Since a coin from 61 C.E. depicts only Aristobulus, Queen Salome may have died by then.

Ross S. Kraemer

See also Part I: Herodias 1; Herodias 2; Part II: Young Dancer Who Asks for the Head of John the Baptist (Matt 14:6–11).

For further reading: Kokkinos, Nikos. *The Herodian Dynasty: Origins, Role in Society and Eclipse.*
———. "Which Salome Did Aristobulus Marry?"

Sapphira

"beautiful, good," from Aramaic *šappîrāʾ*, "beautiful, good"; Hebrew similar, as is the name of a gem in Hebrew and Greek
(Acts 5:1–11)

Punitive miracles, which are characteristic of Acts and the non-canonical *Acts of the Apostles,* troubled early Christian theologians. Sapphira (a name mainly restricted to wealthy Jerusalem women) appears to have been added to an earlier legend about Ananias in order to provide emphasis and to leave no uncertainty regarding the supernatural cause of their deaths. This may also be an example of a proclivity exhibited by Luke and others (for example, the parables of Luke 15:1–10) for pairing female and male characters. The verbs in Acts 5:1–2 are singular and refer to Ananias. Two additional phrases make his wife a co-conspirator. The narrative evidently presumes that spouses could act as joint owners, making mutual decisions. Mutuality does not benefit Sapphira. Following the death of Ananias, the assembly remains in unexplained session for three hours, at which time Sapphira, who has not been informed of her husband's death, arrives. Narrative variation gives her the more dramatic, spoken role of the two partners. The providential return of Ananias's burial party at the moment of her false assertion further enhances the drama of this well-structured piece.

The story, part of a unit extending from Acts 4:32 to 5:16, puts into narrative form the kind of scene envisioned in 1 Cor 5:3–5. One source is Josh 7:16–26 (concerning Achan). In this instance, however, the Greco-Roman notion of personal agency applies. The couple are not destroyed by a bolt from heaven together with their family and possessions. Each dies after an individual affirmation. Both are also comparable to the figure of Judas, likewise motivated by financial considerations. Ironically, Sapphira, portrayed as a responsible moral actor, may be the most fully "equal" woman in the New Testatment.

RICHARD I. PERVO

FOR FURTHER READING: Martin, Clarice J. "The Acts of the Apostles."

Pervo, Richard I. *Luke's Story of Paul.*

Sarah 1/Sarai

"princess," from Hebrew *śārâ,* "princess"; Sarai is an older form of the name

SARAH IN THE HEBREW BIBLE

(Gen 11:29–13:1; 16:1–18:15; 20:2–21:12; 23:1–2, 19; 24:36; 25:10, 12; 49:31; Isa 51:2)

Sarah is the wife of Abraham, the mother of Isaac, and thus the ancestress of all Israel. The Bible explains that Sarai was her earlier name and that she was renamed at the annunciation of the birth of Isaac (Gen 17:15).

Sarah's ancestry is not clear. Genesis 11 relates that Abram and his brother Nahor married Sarai and Milcah, respectively (v. 29). It does not name Sarah's father, even though it relates that Milcah was the daughter of Haran, Terah's other son, and then names Haran's other daughter, Iscah. When Gen 11:31 tells that "Terah took his son Abram and

his grandson Lot son of Haran, and his daughter-in-law Sarai, his son Abram's wife" from Ur to Haran, it does not call Sarai Terah's granddaughter. However, in Genesis 20, when Abraham explains his wife-sister ruse to Abimelech of Gerar, he claims that Sarah is his non-uterine sister (v. 12). This contradiction has led some readers to identify Sarah with the otherwise unknown Iscah. But this would make Sarai Abram's niece, not his half sister; it would not explain why she is identified as daughter-in-law to Terah, not as his daughter.

Sarah and Abraham come to Israel as part of God's promise of numerous progeny and the land (Gen 12:1–5). Because Sarah's importance to this promise is not at first obvious, the promise is immediately endangered. Forced by famine to leave the land, Abraham is fearful that Egyptians will kill him in order to take the beautiful Sarah. His concerns make sense in the biblical milieu, for in the Bible, beauty sets up the beautiful to be desired and taken. Indeed, Esther and Judith, at the close of the biblical period, are the first to use their beauty to their people's advantage. Furthermore, in the ancient world adultery was considered a very grievous offense, possibly even worse than murder. Thus Abraham's solution seems bizarre; he asks Sarah to say that she is his sister. They would still take her, but they would not kill Abraham, who would thus "share a wife and save a life." The ruse might have some advantage for Sarah, for a brother was somewhat of a protector, whereas a widow had no protection of any kind. It certainly enriched Abraham, who was given bride wealth for a sister, something that he would never have received as a husband.

Genesis 12 relates this strange wife-sister episode in a matter-of-fact fashion. Genesis 20, the parallel account in which Abraham tries this ruse in Gerar, adds new details that perhaps show concern about Abraham's actions that developed after the original telling of the story. The Gerar story emphasizes that Abimelech never touched Sarah because God immediately intervened with dreams. Moreover, the narrator is not at ease with the wife-sister ruse and may no longer understand it. So Abraham not only relates that Sarah is his half sister, but also makes it clear that the ruse is done by the grace and benevolence of Sarah.

Although the wife-sister stories are difficult to understand, the fact that Sarah becomes a slave in Pharaoh's house serves to foreshadow Israel's later bondage in Egypt. She herself is not in danger of her life — but the reader knows that nascent Israel is in danger of losing its ancestress. And so God acts to protect Sarah by afflicting "Pharaoh and his house with great plagues" (Gen 12:17) until he realizes the problem and sends Sarah away. Protection and plague foreshadow Israel's later redemption at the exodus.

Sarah's barrenness also endangers the promise and prompts her to give her handmaiden Hagar to Abraham as a surrogate womb (Gen 16:1–2), a custom known also from Mesopotamia. The plan goes awry when the pregnant Hagar no longer acknowledges Sarah's superiority. Sarah feels displaced and turns her anger on Abraham, declaring, "May the wrong done to me be on you!" and "May the LORD judge between you and me!" (Gen 16:5). Her own experience of servitude in Egypt perhaps has made her feel threatened by the Egyptian Hagar rather than sympathetic to her. Her status as first wife is not invulnerable: she has been given away before, in the wife-sister ruse, and she may now be vulnerable to Hagar, who conceives and will bear Abraham's heir. Abraham then restores the authority over Hagar to Sarah. However, Hagar's child Ishmael is never considered part of Sarah's domain; Abraham has all the authority in the family, and he, rather than Sarah, names Ishmael (compare the stories of Rachel and Leah, who do name the offspring of their surrogates Bilhah and Zilpah).

Abraham seems content to keep Sarah out of the loop and to consider Ishmael the child of the promise. The miracles that God performed for Sarah in Egypt have not taught him her importance. God informs him that, although Ishmael will have his own destiny, the promise — as formalized in God's covenant — will come through Sarah. God therefore renames her and blesses her when announcing the birth of Isaac (Gen 17:15–21).

Abraham falls on his face, laughing (Gen 17:17) because of their age (he is one hundred years old, and she is ninety) just as Sarah laughs when she hears the second announcement of the birth (Gen 18:11–15). God ignores Abraham's laughter, but reacts to Sarah's. After all, Sarah should understand how important she is, for God has already worked miracles for her. Sarah's importance in God's scheme means that God will have zero tolerance for skepticism from her.

Sarah's importance is certainly clear after she sees Ishmael "sporting" (NRSV, "playing"; Hebrew *mĕṣaḥēq*) at Isaac's weaning. The Septuagint reads "playing with him" (with Isaac), which has led some readers to suspect abuse. But however innocent this act may have been, it was Isaac named as "the one who plays" who was supposed to be doing it. Sarah therefore intervenes, urging Abraham to send Hagar and Ishmael away. Abraham, who considers Ishmael his son, is reluctant; but God once again emphasizes Sarah's importance and tells Abraham to do what she says. As a result, Abraham emancipates Hagar and Ishmael and sends them away as freed slaves.

Having secured Isaac's position in the family, Sarah disappears from Genesis. She plays no role in the near sacrifice of Isaac. She dies at the age of 127 in Hebron (Gen 23:1–2). Abraham buys his first real property in the land of Israel, the Cave of Machpelah, in order to bury her (Gen 23:19). She is mentioned three more times in the Book of Genesis (24:36; 25:10–12). She is remembered in the prophecies of Isaiah 51 (v. 2) as the ancestress of her people.

TIKVA FRYMER-KENSKY

SEE ALSO Part I: Hagar; Iscah; Leah; Rachel; Rebekah.

FOR FURTHER READING: Biddle, Mark E. "The 'Endangered Ancestress' and Blessing for the Nations."

Bledstein, Adrien J. "The Trials of Sarah."

Eichler, Barry. "On Reading Genesis 12:10–20."

Exum, J. Cheryl. "Who's Afraid of 'the Endangered Ancestress'?"

Trible, Phyllis. "Genesis 22: The Sacrifice of Sarah."

SARAH IN THE NEW TESTAMENT

(Rom 4:19, 9:9; Heb 11:11; 1 Pet 3:6)

For early Christians, Sarah was a model of faith. Sarah is mentioned in Paul's letters in the context of commending Abraham's faith and declaring believers in Christ to be his true descendants. So in Rom 4:19 Abraham's faith in God's promise (that he would become "the father of many nations") did not weaken when he considered that Sarah was infertile. In Rom 9:9 Paul identifies Sarah as the mother of the "children of promise." Here and in the Hagar-Sarah allegory of Gal 4:21–31, the motherhood of Sarah (there referred to not by name, but as "free woman") becomes the symbol of authentic descent from Abraham. In Gal 4:21–31 the two women correspond to two covenants, Hagar representing that of the Mosaic law and Sarah, that of God's covenant with Abraham fulfilled in Christ. In Romans 9 the focus has shifted more to the descendants, to Sarah's son Isaac and especially Isaac's two sons, Jacob and Esau. Isaac's two sons replace Abraham's two wives as the figures of true and merely physical descent from Abraham.

Hebrews 11 extols both women and men in ancient Israel whose faith makes them models for believers in Christ. Sarah is mentioned in Heb 11:11 in a text that has several variants in the Greek manuscripts and in a grammatical construction, yielding no certain meaning. This difficulty is reflected in modern translations. For example, the RSV reads, "By faith Sarah herself received power to conceive, even when she was past the age, since she considered him faithful who had promised." However, the NRSV translates the same passage, "By faith he [Abraham] received power of procreation, even though he was too old — and Sarah herself was barren — because he considered him faithful who had promised." What is at stake here is whether Sarah herself is the model of faith or whether she constitutes a parenthetical comment on Abraham's faith.

In 1 Pet 3:6, Sarah as a model of faith whose true descendants are Christians has changed into Sarah as a model for Christian wives. Sarah is seen in this text as Abraham's obedient wife. Christian women, as her daughters, should likewise submit to their husbands.

SHEILA BRIGGS

SEE ALSO Part I: Hagar; Part II: The Free Woman, Mother of a Son of Abraham (Gal 4:21).

FOR FURTHER READING: Balch, David L. *Let Wives Be Submissive: The Domestic Code in 1 Peter.*

D'Angelo, Mary Rose. "Hebrews."

Kitteredge, Cynthia Briggs. "Hebrews."

Sarai   SEE Sarah 1/Sarai (Part I).

Sarah 2

(Tob 3:7–17; 6:11–18; 7:8–13, 16; 8:4–8, 20; 10:10–12; 11:3, 15–17; 12:12, 14)

In the Book of Tobit the primary function of Sarah is to become the wife of the protagonist, Tobias. Once they have wed, Sarah adds very little to the story. From the reader's standpoint, Sarah is a more interesting character before her marriage takes place.

Sarah's name recalls her namesake in the Hebrew Bible, and her introduction into the story reinforces the connection. When the reader first encounters Sarah, her maids are reproaching her and "cursing" her with perpetual childlessness (Tob 3:7–9). This scene recalls elements of the story of Abraham's barren wife Sarah, whose maid, Hagar, reviled her after Hagar conceived a child by Abraham (Gen 16:1–4). In the Book of Tobit, Sarah mirrors her biblical namesake in her eagerness to bear a child (Tob 3:15) and because God intervenes to rectify her situation (Tob 3:16–17).

The precise circumstances of Sarah's predicament in Tobit differ from the situation of her counterpart in Genesis, however. In Tobit, Sarah is not only childless, but also husbandless, because a demon who plagues her has killed seven husbands before their marriages to Sarah could be consummated (Tob 3:8). The text is ambiguous about whether Sarah or anyone in her family knows the cause of the deaths, but Tobias has heard a rumor about the demon before ever meeting his intended bride or visiting the distant city where she lives (Tob 6:14–15).

Initially Sarah is paralleled with Tobit, although she eventually fades from the story in a way that he does not. Together their plights form twin problems that the plot will resolve. Both require healing: Sarah from the demon, Tobit from blindness — and both from despair. Both cry out for help to God, who heals them via the archangel Raphael and the entrails of a dead fish (Tob 3:17; 6:8–9).

The parallel prayers of Sarah and Tobit provide a comparison that highlights positive aspects of both characters (Tob 3:2–6, 11–15). Both turn to God after being reproached by someone who should have respected them, and both ask for death as a release from their unbearable situations. The prayers are structured similarly and use some of the same vocabulary.

But there are significant thematic differences. Tobit's prayer is larger in scope than Sarah's. Sarah is concerned with how her marital situation affects her own father and prays about her particular dilemma, whereas Tobit speaks of his ancestors and presents himself as paradigmatic for all (the men of) Israel. Their prayers suggest that a man's religious interests and obligations are more far-reaching than a woman's, whose primary interests are home and family.

In tone, however, Sarah's prayer is more commendable. The scene that immediately precedes and thus seems to prompt her prayer appears much more serious than the scene preceding Tobit's. She has seven dead husbands, no heir, and maids who wish her to die childless. He has a fight with his wife. True, he is blind, but he has been living with that problem for four years (Tob 2:10); it does not seem to be the immediate stimulus for his prayer. Further, although parts of Tobit's prayer imply a concern for all Israel, Sarah's repeated references to solicitude for her father's reputation reveal her prayer to be actually less self-centered than Tobit's whining about Anna's "insults." Finally, Tobit sees death as the only answer to his problems, but Sarah, who also asks to die, allows that God may have other ideas. The narrative has already established Tobit's righteousness, but under the surface of the parallel prayers the text presents a subtle contrast between an unselfish, besieged woman who defers to God and a self-centered, somewhat petty man

who arrogantly assumes that what he desires is equivalent to the divine will.

After her prayer Sarah appears as a passive figure in several places in the story. She is the topic of a long conversation between Raphael and Tobias in which the angel easily overcomes Tobias's objections and persuades him that he deserves Sarah (and her inheritance) and that in fact she was predestined to be his wife (Tob 6:11–18). She is again the topic of the negotiations between Tobias and Raguel about the marriage; Sarah is not even consulted (Tob 7:9–13). Her mother leads her to the bridal chamber (Tob 7:16), and Tobias leads her in prayer (Tob 8:4–8). Here she speaks her only word outside of her introductory scene in Tobit 3, saying with Tobias, "Amen" (8:8). Finally, Sarah is welcomed and blessed by her new father-in-law, but again, she says nothing in response (Tob 11:15–17).

At first glance the union between Sarah and Tobias seems a greater asset to the groom. Tobias fulfills his father's wish that he marry a kinswoman (Tob 4:12), and he profits financially through Sarah's dowry and inheritance (Tob 6:12; 8:21). In contrast, Sarah "loses" her home by moving to that of her husband. However, the marriage does benefit Sarah as well: she loses the demon plaguing her (Tob 8:2–3), and she gains both a husband who survives the wedding night (Tob 8:12–14) and children (Tob 14:3, 12).

Sarah occupies a curious place in the story: she is a central character who has very little action. Her plight is necessary for the plot, but her mere presence is more important in most scenes than what she says or does. Her function is to become Tobias's wife; what she does, says, thinks, or feels is irrelevant compared to fulfilling that function. Sarah is not an active participant in the story after her first scene, but her character remains important for the resolution of the plot.

BEVERLY BOW

SEE ALSO Part I: Sarah 1/Sarai.

FOR FURTHER READING: Bow, Beverly, and George W. E. Nickelsburg. "Patriarchy with a Twist: Men and Women in Tobit."

Serah

meaning uncertain

(Gen 46:17; Num 26:46; 1 Chr 7:30)

Serah is the daughter of Asher, one of the two sons of the patriarch Jacob borne to him by Zilpah, the concubine of Leah. She is the only female offspring of Jacob's sons mentioned in the Genesis and Numbers genealogies, and it is not clear why she is included.

Although the precise meaning of the name is uncertain, it may be related to the Akkadian word *surḫu*, in which case it would be an abbreviation of the phrase "may God grant success."

NAOMI STEINBERG

SEE ALSO Part I: Zilpah.

Sheerah

"flesh, kin," from Hebrew *šě'ēr*, "flesh"

(1 Chr 7:24)

Listed within the genealogy of the tribe of Ephraim in Chronicles, Sheerah is the daughter of Beriah. Sheerah is said to have built Lower Beth-horon and Upper Beth-horon, two sites on the southern (Benjaminite) border of Ephraim, northwest of Gibeon. She is also said to have built Uzzen-sheerah, an otherwise unknown settlement. The attribution of territory to a woman is unusual, but not unique; Caleb's daughter Achsah was awarded an allotment by her father.

JULIA MYERS O'BRIEN

SEE ALSO Part I: Achsah. Part II: Daughter of Zelophehad (Num 26:33, etc.).

Shelomith 1

"tranquil [one]," from Hebrew root *šlm*, "to be complete" or "to be sound"; related to the noun *šālôm*, "peace, tranquility"

(Lev 24:10–16)

Daughter of Dibri of the tribe of Dan and wife of an Egyptian, Shelomith is the only woman mentioned by name in the Book of Leviticus. She appears in the narrative about her son, a man who pronounces the name of God in blasphemy during a fight with another Israelite man. Her unnamed son is brought to Moses and placed in custody to await the decision of God. God then commands Moses to take him outside the camp and have the whole community stone him. At this point, a general policy is set forth, proclaiming that all who blaspheme God's name, "aliens as well as citizens," will be punished by being stoned to death (Lev 24:16). Stoning in ancient Israel was the penalty for very serious offenses — ones considered to endanger the universe.

This story may have served a pedagogical purpose by showing that blasphemy was a direct trespass on the holy and that stoning was sanctioned by God through special instruction to Moses. Other stories, such as the tale of the man who gathered wood on the Sabbath day (Num 15:32–36), carry the same message. Such stories also indicate the way a precedent might have developed into a general law.

The fact that the story, whether true or invented, presents a precedent for an important law may explain why it provides details of the man's parentage: his father's identity as an Egyptian and his mother's name and lineage. The fact that the father is Egyptian helps justify the law's application to non-Israelites ("aliens") as well as Israelites. His mother's name, along with her father's name and tribe, is important in establishing him as an Israelite, perhaps because one's lineage was usually reckoned through the father's family. Shelomith's name may have been preserved because she does not serve as an example of women in general.

TIKVA FRYMER-KENSKY

FOR FURTHER READING: Westbrook, Raymond. "Cuneiform Law Codes and the Origins of Legislation."

Shelomith 2

(1 Chr 3:19)

Shelomith was the daughter of Zerubbabel, a governor (c. 520–510 B.C.E.) of the postexilic province of Yehud. She is the only woman mentioned among the descendants of David in 1 Chronicles 1–24. As a woman's name, Shelomith is otherwise mentioned only in Leviticus (24:11). It is a fairly common man's name (1 Chr 23:9, 18; 26:28; 2 Chr 11:20; 26:25; Ezra 8:10), although in Ezra and 2 Chronicles 11, the names could just as well designate women. In 1 Chr 3:19, Shelomith is listed as the sister of Meshullam and Hananiah rather than as the daughter of Zerubbabel, their father. This awkward designation led some older commentators to suggest that she was either the head or founder of an important family or had a "marked personality."

The discovery of a late-sixth-century B.C.E. Judean seal (an inscribed stone used as an official "signature") with the name Shelomith inscribed alongside that of Elnathan the governor has opened new possibilities for understanding Shelomith's role in Judean society. The seal reads: "Belonging to Shelomith, maidservant of Elnathan the governor." The word for "maidservant" is 'āmâ, which can connote a high status or honorific title, as well as marital status, when it is associated with an important official such as Elnathan the governor. Shelomith could well have been the co-regent as well as spouse of Elnathan, who is mentioned as governor in another seal.

The importance of Shelomith's marriage to the governor who succeeded her father, Zerubbabel, a scion of the royal Davidic family, cannot be overstated. In the Judean restoration, Zerubbabel's acceptance of limited civil power alongside Joshua the high priest was symbolic of the commitment of the new Jewish leadership to cooperate with Persian imperial policy. Scholars have regularly asserted that the transition to limited autonomy under Zerubbabel and Joshua was traumatic. The inclusion of a female Davidic descendant as 'āmâ with Elnathan was certainly one way of solidifying local support for the Persian-appointed administration. In any case, Shelomith's involvement in the public arena may testify to the changing status of women in the Persian period.

ERIC M. MEYERS

SEE ALSO Part I: Basemath 2; Shelomith 1, 4; Taphath; Part II: Daughters of Shallum (Neh 3:12); Women, Part of the Assembly of People (Neh 8:2, etc.).

FOR FURTHER READING: Avigad, Nahman. *Bullae and Seals from a Post-exilic Judean Archive.*

Meyers, Carol L., and Eric M. Meyers. *Haggai, Zechariah 1–8.*

Meyers, Eric M. "The Shelomith Seal and the Judean Restoration: Some Additional Considerations."

Shelomith 3
(2 Chr 11:20)

Shelomith was one of four children, possibly a daughter, born to King Rehoboam (reigned 928–911 B.C.E.) by his wife Maacah. The name Shelomith occurs elsewhere designating males, but in 1 Chr 3:19 Shelomith is identified as the daughter of Zerubabbel. The name can thus refer to a female.

ALICE L. LAFFEY

SEE ALSO Part I: Maacah 3/Micaiah; Shelomith 2.

Shelomith 4
(Ezra 8:10)

Shelomith, an ancestor of Josiphiah, is listed among the heads of households going to Jerusalem from Babylonia with Ezra (458 B.C.E.), according to the Hebrew text. The name Shelomith can be masculine. However, the reference to a daughter of Zerubbabel named Shelomith (1 Chr 3:19) and to a Danite woman named Shelomith (Lev 24:11) and the discovery of a seal of a woman named Shelomith indicate a feminine use for the name, especially in the postexilic era, and suggests that here also it refers to a woman. Most English translations, including the NRSV, supply a man's name (Bani) present in 1 Esdr 8:36, so that the Ezra verse reads "of the descendants of Bani" rather than rendering the Hebrew as "of the descendants of Shelomith."

This unusual mention of a female ancestor may account for the fact that the text of this verse differs in form from others in the same list. This Shelomith, whose descendants now return to Jerusalem, is conceivably the sister of Zerubbabel.

TAMARA COHN ESKENAZI

SEE ALSO Part I: Shelomith 2.

FOR FURTHER READING: Eskenazi, Tamara Cohn. "Out from the Shadows: Biblical Women in the Postexilic Era."

Shemamah SEE Shemamah/Desolate, Jerusalem (Part III).

Shimeath/Shomer/Shimrith

meaning of Shimeath uncertain, perhaps from Hebrew *šmʿ*, "to hear"

(2 Kgs 12:21; 2 Chr 24:26)

The two assassins (Jozacar and Jehozabad) of the Judean king Joash (c. 800 B.C.E.) are identified in the narratives of Kings and Chronicles by parental names as well as by their own. In 2 Kings, the male parent seems to be named. The parent of Jozacar (Zabad in 2 Chronicles) is called Shimeath, which is grammatically feminine, although such a construction in a man's name is not unknown (compare Goliath). Shomer, the designation of Jehozabad's parent in 2 Kings, is a masculine form. In 2 Chronicles, however, Shomer is changed to (the feminine) Shimrith. Also in Chronicles, nationalities are assigned to the two women in feminine constructions: Shimeath is an Ammonitess and Shimrith is a Moabitess. The possible fathers have become certain mothers, and foreign ones at that! But why?

Strange women usually signify danger, especially of apostasy, and Ezra 9:1, a likely source for the author of Chronicles, identifies Ammonites and Moabites among the foreign wives who must be divorced by the men of Ezra's community. This could, then, be a polemic against relationships with foreigners, especially women: only men of mixed ancestry would murder a king! On the other hand, 2 Chr 24:25 states that King Joash was killed because he ordered the murder of the son of the good priest Jehoiada (and this after beginning idol worship himself). Moral evaluation is thus ambiguous at best, an ambiguity mirrored by the status of Ammonites and Moabites vis-à-vis Israel: excluded from "the assembly of the LORD" (Deut 23:3; but note the murderers' loyalty to the priestly family in 2 Chr 24:25), they are also recognized as kin of Israel through the dubious ancestry of Lot's intercourse with his daughters (Lot is Abraham's nephew) (Gen 19:30–38). This symbolically intermediary position

of Shimeath and Shimrith may, then, reflect Chronicles' mixed review of Joash's reign.

CLAUDIA V. CAMP

SEE ALSO Part II: Daughters of Lot (Gen 19:8, etc.); Daughters of Judah and Foreign Daughters/Wives (Ezra 9:2, etc.).

Shimrith

"guardian, steward," from Hebrew *šmr*, "to guard, keep"

SEE Shimeath/Shomer/Shimrith (Part I).

Shiphrah

"beauty," from common Semitic root *špr*, "to be fair"

(Exod 1:15)

Shiphrah is one of the two named midwives who serve the Hebrew women in Egypt and who contravene Pharaoh's order to kill at birth all Hebrew males. The feminine proper name Shiphrah is also attested as the name of an Asiatic slave woman in an eighteenth-century B.C.E. papyrus from Egypt.

MAYER I. GRUBER

SEE ALSO Part I: Puah; Part II: Midwife (Gen 35:17, etc.).

FOR FURTHER READING: Albright, W. F. "Northwest-Semitic Names in a List of Egyptian Slaves from the 18th Century B.C."

Shomer

"guardian, steward," from Hebrew *šmr*, "to guard, keep"; masculine form of Shimrith

SEE Shimeath/Shomer/Shimrith (Part I).

Shua

"independent, noble," from Hebrew *šôʿa*, "free"

(1 Chr 7:32)

Shua is the daughter of Heber, who was a grandson of Asher, according to the genealogy in Chronicles. Heber fathered sons, Shua's brothers: Japhlet, Shomer, and Hotham. The biblical text records the descendants of the three sons but omits information about Shua's children. Perhaps she was child-less, but it is more likely that the patrilineal interests of the author did not usually extend to a daughter's lineage.

ALICE L. LAFFEY

Sophereth   SEE   Hassophereth/Sophereth
(Part I).

Susanna 1

"lily," Greek *Sousanna,* derived from Hebrew *šôšannâ*

(Sus vv. 2–3, 7–8, 10–12, 15–24, 26–46, 48–49, 54, 57–58, 63)

The brief, self-contained story of Susanna appears in Greek but not Hebrew manuscripts of the Book of Daniel. Most modern editions of the Bible include it among the Apocryphal/Deuterocanonical Books as Daniel 13. Although readers will respond to and remember most vividly Susanna and her predicament, the story's conclusion emphasizes Daniel's emergence as a young figure of wisdom. On account of this, some ancient Greek versions place the Book of Susanna before Daniel 1.

The text first introduces Joakim, a wealthy man living in the Babylonian diaspora (Greek for "scattered abroad," Jews who lived outside Palestine after the Babylonian exile of 587 B.C.E.). Joakim, however, plays a minimal role in the unfolding of the story. Susanna's introduction defines her in terms of her relationships to two men, as wife of Joakim and daughter of Hilkiah, and tells that she is beautiful and righteous and was trained "according to the law of Moses" by her parents (vv. 2–3).

Joakim's house functions as a courthouse for the Jewish community. Two elders who serve there as judges separately develop lustful feelings toward Susanna, whom they spy walking in the garden when the house empties at midday for the community to go to their own homes for lunch (vv. 8–12). One day the two elders catch each other lingering behind in order to watch Susanna, and they conspire together to entrap her (vv. 13–14).

On a hot day Susanna decides to bathe in the garden (v. 15). She believes herself to be alone with her maids because the elders have concealed themselves (v. 16). When Susanna sends her maids away to bring ointments for her bath (vv. 17–18), the elders reveal themselves and try to coerce her into sexual relations. They say that, unless she lies with them, they will testify that she sent her maids away in order to be with a young lover (vv. 19–21). Susanna's dilemma is this: to submit to the elders is to disobey the law of Moses, which she has been raised to follow, but to resist the elders is to invite the death penalty for adultery (Lev 20:10; Deut 22:22). She articulates her decision, "I choose not to do it; I will fall into your hands, rather than sin in the sight of the Lord" (v. 23). Susanna cries aloud, and so do the elders (v. 24). Their shouting attracts members of the household (v. 26), specifically identified as "servants," who, when they hear the elders' story, are "very much ashamed, for nothing like this had ever been said about Susanna" (v. 27).

Susanna's trial occurs on the following day at her home, described as "the house of her husband Joakim" (v. 28). Susanna comes before the two elders and the people, accompanied by her parents, her children, and other unspecified relatives — her husband is not mentioned (vv. 29–30). The lascivious elders ask that she be unveiled so that they may continue to look at her (v. 32). Those who weep with her weep at this disgrace (v. 33), which in Theodotion's version amounts to an unveiling of Susanna's face. (The NRSV follows Theodotion, an alternate Greek translation of the Hebrew Bible.) In the Septuagint version, Susanna is stripped naked, in accordance with ritual Jewish law (Ezek 16:37–39; Hos 2:3–10). The elders proceed with their accusations (v. 34). They claim that they saw Susanna in the garden, embracing a young lover whose strength enabled him to elude them as they attempted to detain him; they further claim that Susanna has refused to cooperate in naming the lover (vv. 36–41a). Because of the credibility of the elders in the community, the assembly believes them and condemns Susanna to death (v. 41b).

No one offers testimony on Susanna's behalf.

She, however, turns to heaven for help, crying aloud to God that she is innocent (vv. 42–43). The text records, "The Lord heard her cry" (v. 44). Just as Susanna is being taken to her death, God stirs "the holy spirit of a young lad named Daniel" (v. 45). Announcing that he cannot be part of Susanna's execution (v. 46), he asks the assembly for the right to cross-examine the elders (vv. 47–49). Before the reassembled court, Daniel separates the two elders and questions each about the location of the lovers' intimacies. The first elder identifies a mastic tree (v. 54) as the site of the illicit coupling, and the second elder identifies an evergreen oak (v. 58). Daniel thus reveals their deceit and the innocence of Susanna, "a daughter of Judah," a descendant of southern Judah (v. 57). The two elders are then sentenced to the fate they intended for their victim: death (v. 62).

At the close of the tale, Susanna's parents and husband rejoice, not because Susanna will live, but because she was "found innocent of a shameful deed" (v. 63). Susanna's own reaction is not described. Instead, the text notes that "from that day onward Daniel had a great reputation among the people" (v. 64).

Although the story has a Babylonian setting, it was written during the Hellenistic period (after the death of Alexander the Great in 323 B.C.E.) and reflects the concerns of that time. One of Israel's major concerns was how to maintain its integrity living in diaspora among alien peoples. Susanna's community does not seem economically or politically vulnerable to external pressures; rather, it seems wealthy and secure. The wickedness of the elders in the garden suggests the potential for a community accustomed to luxury to self-destruct through laxity and inattentiveness to proper boundaries. As in other Hellenistic narratives, the principal female character represents the community under attack. In the Book of Judith, for example, Judith represents the community under siege, protecting its cultic boundaries from foreign penetration. In the Book of Susanna, Susanna represents the community besieged by internal problems.

Critics have persistently labeled Susanna a tale of seduction, although feminist critics have insisted that it is really a tale of attempted rape. To call the story a tale of seduction is to visualize the events through the eyes of the elders. In fact, the story is written in a way that emphasizes this point of view; the reader is invited to consider Susanna and her beauty, to see what the elders see. The reader is not invited to look at the elders — to see what Susanna sees. Susanna remains the object of the elders' and the reader's vision, rather than emerging as a subject whose vision defines her own story. Such a representation of Susanna may be difficult for women readers, who can align themselves with neither the gaze of the elders nor with Susanna's unrepresented gaze. Susanna presents a further challenge to contemporary readers. On the one hand, Susanna's resistance to rape and adherence to the Mosaic law is laudable. On the other hand, Susanna's understanding of her dilemma unfortunately supports the problematic notion that victims are somehow themselves guilty. For these reasons Susanna is an ambiguous heroic figure for some contemporary feminists.

JENNIFER A. GLANCY

SEE ALSO Part I: Judith 2; Part II: Adulteress (and Adulterer) (Lev 20:10, etc.); Daughter(s) of Israel/Daughter of Judah (Sus v. 57).

FOR FURTHER READING: Glancy, Jennifer A. "The Accused: Susanna and Her Readers."

Levine, Amy-Jill. "'Hemmed in on Every Side': Jews and Women in the Book of Susanna."

Susanna 2

(Luke 8:3)

Susanna, who shares the name of the heroine of the Apocryphal/Deuterocanonical Book of Susanna, is the third and last of those named in Luke 8:3, one of a group of women of evidently independent means who had been healed by Jesus and had joined his entourage, of which they were benefactors. Her position on the list, together with the absence of concrete description and the failure to mention her in Luke 24:10, suggests that she was less notable than Mary Magdalene and Joanna, but sufficiently prominent to be singled out. For a revealing comparison, see the biblical references to James and

John, the sons of Zebedee, often grouped with Peter as members of a "big three."

The view that Luke alone mentions Joanna and Susanna because they served as sources for that Gospel is a sentimental rationalization that does not comport with ancient practice and scarcely conforms to the Lukan depiction of their ministries.

RICHARD I. PERVO

SEE ALSO Part II: Unnamed Women Who Provide for the Jesus Movement (Luke 8:2–3).

Syntyche

"fortunate"; from the Greek *syn–* "with" and *tychē* "fortune, chance, luck"; Tychē was personified as a goddess in the Greco-Roman period

(Phil 4:2–3)

Syntyche was a coworker of both Paul and another woman, Euodia. The Christian theologian Theodore, bishop of Mopsuestia from 392 to 428 C.E., revised her name to Syntyches (masculine), claiming that she was Euodia's husband and Paul's onetime jailer (Acts 16:27-34). Thus Syntyche suffered the same gender transformation that Junia (Rom 16:7) and Nympha (Col 4:15) did. (For full discussion, see the article on Euodia.)

MARY ROSE D'ANGELO

SEE ALSO Part I: Euodia; Junia; Nympha.

FOR FURTHER READING: Brooten, Bernadette. "'Junia . . . Outstanding Among the Apostles' (Romans 16:7)." Gillman, Florence Morgan. "Syntyche."

Tabitha

probably from Aramaic *ṭabyā᾽*, "gazelle" (Tabitha's Greek name is Dorcas, from Greek *dorkas*, "gazelle") but perhaps from *ṭabtā᾽*, "good" or "precious"

(Acts 9:36–42)

The story of the raising of Tabitha is one of a number of miracle stories in the Acts of the Apostles. Following the account of Paul's conversion, the story of Tabitha is included in an extended narrative about Peter, inserted between the story of Aeneas's healing in Lydda and Peter's encounter with the Roman centurion, Cornelius, in Caesarea. The story is one of many in Acts relating how God's mighty acts, worked through the lives of Jesus' followers, were made known throughout the Mediterranean world and facilitated the growth of the early church.

Acts 9:36–42 tells how Tabitha, a disciple in Joppa who is well known for her piety and good works, falls ill, dies, and is subsequently raised to life again. The story concludes by noting that news of Tabitha has spread throughout Joppa and that many thus believe in the Lord.

The story has literary parallels in both the Hebrew Scriptures and the New Testament Gospels, most notably in the accounts of the prophet Elijah's raising of the widow of Zarephath's son (1 Kgs 17:17–24), the prophet Elisha's raising of the Shunammite woman's son (2 Kgs 4:18–37), and Jesus' raising of the widow of Nain's son (Luke 7:11–17). New Testament parallels also include the raising of Jairus's daughter (Luke 8:41–42, 49–56), Lazarus (John 11:1–44), and Eutychus (Acts 20:9–12).

A port city in Judea's coastal plain, Joppa had been a predominantly Jewish city since its conquest in 143 B.C.E. by Simon Maccabeus (see 1 Macc 12:33; 13:11). It was a center of the Jewish Revolt in 66 C.E. and was subsequently destroyed by the Romans under Cestius Gallus. According to the Jewish historian Josephus, Joppa became a refuge for Jews who had escaped from neighboring cities and who were later crushed by Vespasian. The story of Tabitha, although probably written after the Jewish-Roman Wars and the destruction of Joppa, is set in the years between 30 and 40 C.E. within the context of a predominantly Jewish Christian community.

Tabitha is introduced into the narrative as a disciple, this being the only New Testament occurrence of the feminine form of the Greek word for "disciple" (*mathētria*). She is, however, introduced by means of the indefinite article, suggesting at least the possibility that there may have been other female disciples at Joppa.

Further, Tabitha is introduced not only by her

Aramaic name, but also by its Greek translation (Dorcas), meaning "gazelle." It may have been that she was known among both Aramaic- and Greek-speaking members of her community. It is even more likely that the story was addressed to, and circulated among, Greek-speaking as well as Aramaic-speaking Christians, thus necessitating the Greek translation of her name.

The name itself appears to have originated as a nickname, rather than as a proper name. Its use is attested in rabbinic traditions thought to date to the late first century C.E., where it appears to have been common among the slave population; it is possible that Tabitha herself was either a slave or a freedwoman of slave origins.

Tabitha's association with the widows of Joppa has been the subject of considerable speculation. In the ancient world, the term widow was fairly inclusive, designating any woman who lacked male protection or support. A widow might be a once-married woman whose husband had died, a divorced woman, or simply an unmarried woman who was no longer under her father's protection. Throughout Jewish history, widows had been the object of charity. Care of the widow, the fatherless, and the stranger — those who were unprotected by standard means of support — had long been one of the ways by which God's righteousness and justice were demonstrated.

By the first century C.E., widows had also come to be associated with the act of mourning — perhaps even as professional mourners — so that the presence of widows at the time of Tabitha's death would not be entirely unexpected. The story seems to indicate, however, that Tabitha had a personal association with the widows of Joppa.

Some commentators have suggested that Tabitha was a philanthropist who supported local widows out of her own (rather than the church's) resources and upon whom the widows of Joppa depended for their economic survival. The story itself, however, does not necessarily suggest that Tabitha was a woman of independent means. On the contrary, the apparently humble origins of her name, along with the fact that she worked with textiles, would

seem to suggest that Tabitha was a woman responsible for her own economic support.

It is possible that Tabitha herself was a widow. Devotion to good works and acts of charity were commended as virtues in the ancient Mediterranean world. Elsewhere in the New Testament, widows are admonished to be known by their hospitality and good works (see 1 Tim 5:10).

Or Tabitha may have belonged to a community of widows that was active within the church at Joppa and was perhaps even a prototype for the order of widows that was to emerge later within the early church. As disciples, Tabitha and the other widows of Joppa would have studied and followed Jesus' teachings and confessed Jesus as Lord in both word and deed. Tabitha's death would have been a tragic loss to the church at Joppa — not because of her contributions to the economic well-being of its members, but because of her role as a devout and faithful member, perhaps even leader, of the early Christian community.

Although the historical existence of Tabitha has typically been assumed, traditional interpretations have focused on Peter as a miracle worker. As a miracle story, the text thus assumed some literary embellishment layered upon the basic historical facts. Luke's focus on Peter as the key player in the story, as well as his characterization of Tabitha in terms of the traditional virtue of charity, diverts attention from the possibility that Tabitha may have been an economically self-sufficient leader in the Joppa community. Indeed, a close reading of the story supports the idea that women took an active leadership role within the early church. ·

LUCINDA A. BROWN

SEE ALSO Part II: Widows (Exod 22:22, etc.); (Tob 1:8); Widows of Hellenists and Hebrews (Acts 6:1); Widows (1 Tim 5:3–16).

FOR FURTHER READING: O'Day, Gail R. "Acts."

Richter Reimer, Ivoni. *Women in the Acts of the Apostles: A Feminist Liberation Perspective.*

Witherington, Ben, III. *Women and the Genesis of Christianity.*

Tahpenes

"the wife of the king," from Egyptian *ta*, "the"
hmt, "wife," *pa*, "of the," and *nsw*, "king"

(1 Kgs 11:19–20)

Tahpenes is an Egyptian queen during the time of
King Solomon (tenth century B.C.E.). She is mentioned in the Solomon narrative because her sister
is given in marriage to Hadad, an Edomite ruler
and adversary of Solomon. Tahpenes provides a
court upbringing for her sister's son, Genubath, in
line with a long-established Egyptian tradition of
caring for foreign royal sons, usually a diplomatic
move evidencing good faith and alliance. The boy is
the son of the refugee crown prince Hadad, probably giving the Egyptians no more than a minor
card to play against Israel at a suitable time.

Because the name Tahpenes is an epithet, it gives
no clue as to the woman's identity. Particularly notable is the biblical author's use of the Hebrew term
gĕbîrâ ("queen") with Tahpenes, a title normally
reserved for the Judean queen mother, the most
important female in the royal family who usually
exercised considerable authority in the affairs of the
court.

SUSAN TOWER HOLLIS

FOR FURTHER READING: Schearing, Linda S. "Queen."
Troy, Lana. *Patterns of Queenship in Ancient Egyptian
Myth and History.*

Tamar 1

"palm-tree," from Hebrew *tāmār*, "palm-tree"

TAMAR 1 IN THE HEBREW BIBLE

(Genesis 38; Ruth 4:12; 1 Chr 2:4)

Tamar, whose story is embedded in the ancestor
narratives of Genesis, is the ancestress of much of
the tribe of Judah and, in particular, of the house of
David. She is the daughter-in-law of Judah, who
acquires her for his firstborn son, Er. When Er dies,
Judah gives Tamar to his second son, Onan, who is
to act as levir, a surrogate for his dead brother who
would beget a son to continue Er's lineage. In this
way, Tamar too would be assured a place in the
family. Onan, however, would make a considerable

economic sacrifice. According to inheritance customs, the estate of Judah, who had three sons,
would be divided into four equal parts, with the
eldest son acquiring one half and the others one
fourth each. A child engendered for Er would inherit at least one fourth and possibly one half (as
the son of the firstborn). If Er remained childless,
then Judah's estate would be divided into three,
with the eldest, most probably Onan, inheriting two
thirds. Onan opts to preserve his financial advantage and interrupts coitus with Tamar, spilling his
semen on the ground. For this, God punishes Onan
with death, as God had previously punished Er for
doing something wicked.

Although the readers know that God has killed
two of Judah's sons, Judah does not. He suspects
that Tamar is a "lethal woman," a woman whose
sexual partners are all doomed to die. So Judah is
afraid to give Tamar to his youngest son, Shelah. As
a result, Judah wrongs Tamar. According to Near
Eastern custom, known from Middle Assyrian laws,
if a man has no son over ten years old, he could
perform the levirate obligation himself; if he does
not, the woman is declared a "widow," free to
marry again. Judah, who is perhaps afraid of
Tamar's lethal character, could have set her free. But
he does not — he sends her to live as "a widow" in
her father's house. Unlike other widows, she cannot
remarry and must stay chaste on pain of death. She
is in limbo.

Ostensibly, Tamar is only waiting for Shelah to
grow up and mate with her. But after time passes,
she realizes that Judah is not going to effect that
union. She therefore devises a plan to secure her
own future by tricking her father-in-law into having sex with her. She is not planning incest. A father-in-law may not sleep with his daughter-in-law
(Lev 18:15), just as a brother-in-law may not sleep
with his sister-in-law (Lev 18:16), but in-law incest
rules are suspended for the purpose of the levirate.
The levir is, after all, only a surrogate for the dead
husband.

Tamar's plan is simple: she covers herself with a
veil so that Judah won't recognize her, and then she
sits in the roadway at the "entrance to Enaim" (He-

brew *petaḥ 'ênayim;* literally, "eye-opener"). She has chosen her spot well. Judah will pass as he comes back happy and horny (and maybe tipsy) from a sheep-shearing festival. The veil is not the mark of a prostitute; rather, it simply will prevent Judah from seeing Tamar's face. And women sitting by the roadway are apparently fair game. So Judah propositions her, offering to give her a kid for her services and giving her his seal and staff (the ancient equivalent of a credit card) in pledge.

Judah, a man of honor, tries to pay. His friend Hirah goes looking for her, asking around for the *qĕdēšâ* in the road (Gen 38:21). The NRSV translates this as "temple prostitute," but a *qĕdēšâ* was not a sacred prostitute; she was a public woman, who might be found along the roadway (as virgins and married women should not be). She could engage in sex, but might also be sought out for lactation, midwifery, and other female concerns. By looking for a *qĕdēšâ*, Hirah can look for a public woman without revealing Judah's private life. The woman, of course, is nowhere to be found. Judah, mindful of his public image, calls off the search rather than become a laughingstock.

But there is a greater threat to his honor. Rumor relates that Tamar is pregnant and has obviously been faithless to her obligation to Judah to remain chaste. Judah, as the head of the family, acts swiftly to restore his honor, commanding that she be burnt to death. But Tamar has anticipated this danger. She sends his identifying pledge to him, urging him to recognize that its owner is the father. Realizing what has happened, Judah publicly announces Tamar's innocence. His cryptic phrase, *ṣādqâ mimmenî,* is often translated "she is more in the right than I" (Gen 38:26), a recognition not only of her innocence, but also of his wrongdoing in not freeing her or performing the levirate. Another possible translation is "she is innocent — it [the child] is from me." Judah has now performed the levirate (despite himself) and never cohabits with Tamar again. Once she is pregnant, future sex with a late son's wife would be incestuous.

Tamar's place in the family and Judah's posterity are secured. She gives birth to twins, Perez and Zerah (Gen 38:29–30; 1 Chr 2:4), thus restoring two sons to Judah, who has lost two. Their birth is reminiscent of the birth of Rebekah's twin sons, at which Jacob came out holding Esau's heel (Gen 25:24–26). Perez does him one better. The midwife marks Zerah's hand with a scarlet cord when it emerges from the womb first, but Perez (whose name means "barrier-breach") edges his way through. From his line would come David.

Tamar was assertive of her rights and subversive of convention. She was also deeply loyal to Judah's family. These qualities also show up in Ruth, who appears later in the lineage of Perez and preserves Boaz's part of that line. The blessing at Ruth's wedding underscores the similarity in its hope that Boaz's house "be like the house of Perez, whom Tamar bore to Judah" (Ruth 4:12). Tamar's (and Ruth's) traits of assertiveness in action, willingness to be unconventional, and deep loyalty to family are the very qualities that distinguish their descendant, King David.

TIKVA FRYMER-KENSKY

SEE ALSO Part I: Bath-shua 1; Ruth; Part II: Midwife (Gen 35:17, etc.); Prostitute (Lev 19:29, etc.).

FOR FURTHER READING: Bos, Johanna. "Out of the Shadows: Genesis 38; Judges 4:17–22; Ruth 3."

Friedman, Mordechai. "Tamar, a Symbol of Life: The 'Killer Wife' Superstition in the Bible and Jewish Tradition."

Frymer-Kensky, Tikva. *Victors, Victims, Virgins, and Voice: Rereading the Women of the Bible.*

Niditch, Susan. "The Wronged Woman Righted: An Analysis of Genesis 38."

Westenholz, Joan Goodnick. "Tamar, *Qedesa, Qadistu,* and Sacred Prostitution in Mesopotamia."

TAMAR 1 IN THE NEW TESTAMENT
(Matt 1:2)

The first woman named in Jesus' genealogy, Tamar, who posed as a prostitute and seduced her father-in-law, Judah, is proclaimed righteous (Gen 38:26); she thus anticipates both Mary's unexpected pregnancy and Joseph's righteous behavior. Early Jewish tradition regards her as either Hebrew or a proselyte; in this latter role, she foreshadows (as do Rahab, Ruth, and Bathsheba through Uriah) the Gentiles of Matthew's church.

AMY-JILL LEVINE

SEE ALSO Part I: Rahab.

Tamar 2

(2 Samuel 13; 1 Chr 3:9)

Tamar, daughter of King David (c. 1005–965 B.C.E.), is listed after David's secondary wives' children in 1 Chr 3:9 without maternal lineage. However, in 2 Sam 13:1 she is introduced as apparently a full sister of Absalom (third son of David — 2 Sam 3:3; 1 Chr 3:2) and paternal half sister of Amnon (David's eldest son — 2 Sam 3:2; 1 Chr 3:1). She is good-looking and a virgin. Amnon desires or loves her (or both), so much that he becomes ill, but finds it impossible to "do anything to her" because "she was a virgin" (2 Sam 13:2).

Jonadab, Amnon's companion and cousin, advises him to ask David to send Tamar to Amnon's apartments, ostensibly to cook for him and make him well. Amnon does that, and Tamar is ordered by David to go to her brother's apartments. After she prepares food for him, Amnon dismisses all the servants. He asks Tamar to come to his sickroom with the food, where he takes hold of her and asks her directly to have sexual relations with him (v. 11). She refuses (vv. 12–13), citing shame and scandal as reasons. Also, she says, they can get married — David would allow it (which suggests the possibility of accepted royal sibling incest and unions in ancient Israel). Amnon does not listen to her; instead, he overpowers and rapes her. After the event, his "love" immediately turns into "hate." He dismisses her with two words, "Get out!" (v. 15). In spite of Tamar's protests, Amnon orders his servant to throw her out.

Apparently, Tamar feels at this point that she has to protect her reputation and that publicizing her state (the loss of her virginity) is better than concealment. She wears a "long robe with sleeves" or simply "a long outer garment" (Hebrew *kĕtōnet passîm*, like Joseph's unique garment in Genesis 37) as signifier of her royal and virginal state (v. 18).

This tiny brown jasper seal from the seventh century B.C.E. is inscribed with the words "Belonging to Ma'adana, Daughter of the King." It depicts a lyre, which she may have played. Because seals with inscribed names were used to "sign" documents, a seal bearing a woman's name suggests that she could transact business, such as buying or selling property. See Tamar 2; Royal Daughters and Their Garments (2 Sam 13:18).

She tears her garment and displays other signs of mourning: placing ashes and her hand on her head and wailing. This is the last time we will hear Tamar's voice or even of her voice. When she comes to her brother Absalom's house, he immediately understands what has happened. He advises her to keep quiet and forget: she stands no chance against Amnon, "her brother" — implying that Amnon's status as firstborn and heir apparent to David would make legal redress impossible (v. 20). Tamar remains, desolate and mourning — for her virginity, for her life? — in Absalom's compound.

At this point, Tamar virtually disappears from the story. But this is not the end of the incident. Absalom is angry and hates Amnon "because he had raped his sister Tamar" (v. 22), although he does not take up the matter with Amnon. He bides his time. Two years later he murders Amnon and escapes David's wrath by running away to Geshur, to his maternal royal grandfather (2 Sam 13:23–38). Absalom eventually returns to Jerusalem (chap. 14). The chain of events started with Tamar's outrageous treatment by Amnon continues with Absalom's eventual revolt against David and his death, and the elimination of previously born heirs from the inheritance line in favor of Solomon (2 Samuel 15–20; 1 Kings 1–2).

Tamar is indirectly (through her actions and, especially, speech) characterized as a strong, generous, sexually moral, and shrewd woman. She is presented as intelligent and possessing considerable rhetorical skills. She is good-looking and an obedient daughter and devoted sister to full and half brothers alike. But her many virtues do not save her from her fate: to be raped without redress, to remain with her shame without being able to complain (until she disappears from the story), and to lose all prospects of marriage and bearing progeny (although it is implied, according to at least one source [2 Sam 14:27], that Absalom had a daughter and called her Tamar — after his sister?).

In fact, all the male kin who should support Tamar and look after her well-being (her father, David, and Amnon, Absalom, and Jonadab) betray her in one way or another: David by uncritically ordering Tamar to go to Amnon's chambers and by not translating his anger about the rape into action against Amnon (v. 21); Amnon by raping, then discarding, her; Absalom by plotting revenge that may seem conventionally acceptable but, ultimately, would benefit his own ambition for the throne without affecting Tamar's desolate state; Jonadab by engineering the encounter. Tamar is *not* protected by her male relatives or other male figures in the story, such as the servants. She is a pawn in the power politics between her brothers and between them and their king-father. Indeed, this is how she is introduced: "David's son Absalom had a beautiful sister whose name was Tamar; and David's son Amnon fell in love with her" (13:1 — she is situated between the political ambitions of her two brothers). Her rape is narrated as an indirect, albeit decisive, argument against Amnon's suitability for the throne, in the unfolding story of King David's domestic affairs and political rivalries. The silence concerning Tamar and her fate, together with the story's development leading to her brothers' doom, indicates her less-than-central role in her own story. It is, ultimately, more about Amnon and Absalom and their competition vis-à-vis their king-father than about a raped royal daughter. This is well within a framework that attributes motifs of sexual impropriety to David (exemplified by his relations with Bathsheba) and his lineage.

In some ways the story is reminiscent of another rape story, that of Jacob's sons and their sister Dinah (Genesis 34). There too brothers avenge their sister's rape (although, here, by an outsider). Ostensibly the same principle of sister's honor and family honor is at stake. But in fact, the revenge advances the brothers' political, military, and territorial ambitions. In this story, too, the raped woman is silent — even more so than in Tamar's case — and her eventual fate is not resolved in the text. Another character named Tamar in David's lineage, foremother of his ancestor Perez, also involves a narrative of illicit sex (Genesis 38).

ATHALYA BRENNER

SEE ALSO Part I: Dinah; Tamar 1; Tamar 3.
FOR FURTHER READING: Bar-Efrat, Shimon. "Narrative Art in the Bible."
Bledstein, Adrien. "Was *Habbiryâ* a Healing Ritual Performed by a Woman in King David's House?"
Stone, Ken. *Sex, Honor, and Power in the Deuteronomic History.*
van Dijk-Hemmes, Fokkelien. "Tamar and the Limits of Patriarchy: Between Rape and Seduction."

Tamar 3

(2 Sam 14:27)

According to the narrative in the Book of 2 Samuel, King David's third son, Absalom, had four children while living in Jerusalem. One of these is a daughter, who is named Tamar, perhaps after Absalom's sister. Tamar's prominence among Absalom's offspring is suggested by the information that "she was a beautiful woman," much as her father was said to have been praised for his beauty, from head to toe, throughout the land (2 Sam 14:25). Variant traditions in some ancient translations have the name Maacah instead of Tamar in 2 Sam 14:27. If those traditions are accurate, Absalom's only daughter becomes the wife of her uncle Rehoboam, Solomon's successor, thereby partially realizing her father's dynastic hopes.

CAROL MEYERS

SEE ALSO Part I: Maacah 3/Micaiah; Tamar 2.

Taphath

"a drop," from Hebrew *nṭp*, "to drip, drop"

(1 Kgs 4:11)

Taphath, a daughter of Solomon, third king of Israel from c. 968 to 928 B.C.E., is married to the son of Abinadab, the supervisor in charge of the administrative district called Naphath Dor. Her mother's name is not preserved, so it is not possible to learn how much status she would have enjoyed within the royal family. Had she been the offspring of a concubine, she would probably have been deemed less important than the daughter of a full wife.

Her marriage illustrates well how the kingdom of ancient Israel functioned on the principles of a patronage society. The king used the marriages of his daughters as a way to create alliances and to ensure loyalty to his rule. In the case of the son of Abinadab, he gained a son-in-law who was personally bound to serve Solomon faithfully by virtue of the marriage.

DIANA VIKANDER EDELMAN

SEE ALSO Part I: Basemath 2.

FOR FURTHER READING: de Vaux, Roland. *Ancient Israel: Its Life and Institutions.*

Patai, Raphael. *Sex and Family in the Bible and the Middle East.*

Timna 1

meaning uncertain; related to the Hebrew root *mn'*, "to withhold, hold back"

(Gen 36:12)

The secondary wife (concubine) of Eliphaz, son of Esau, Timna bore Amalek, eponymous ancestor of

a southern people who often were enemies to Israel. Some commentators argue that this Timna is the same woman as Timna in Gen 36:22 and 1 Chr 1:39, which would mean that the marriage between Eliphaz and Timna was an alliance marriage between the Edomites and the Horites.

This name appears in the Bible as both a masculine and a feminine proper name.

NAOMI STEINBERG

SEE ALSO Part I: Timna 2.

Timna 2

(Gen 36:22; 1 Chr 1:39)

After listing the seven sons of Seir the Horite, the Edomite genealogy of Esau indicates that one of these seven sons, Lotan, had a sister whose name was Timna. The presence of Timna's name in this genealogy indicates her importance in tracing the descent line of Esau.

NAOMI STEINBERG

SEE ALSO Part I: Timna 1.

Tirzah

meaning uncertain; perhaps "pleasure" or "beauty" from Hebrew *rṣh*, "to be pleased with"

(Num 26:33; 27:1; 36:11; Josh 17:3)

Tirzah is one of the five daughters of Zelophehad who approaches Moses to ask for an inheritance of land alongside their male relatives.

KATHARINE DOOB SAKENFELD

SEE ALSO Part I: Hoglah; Mahlah 1; Milcah 3; Noah; Part II: Daughters of Zelophehad (Num 26:33, etc.).

Tryphaena

"delicate, luxurious, voluptuous," from Greek *tryphaō*, "to live delicately, luxuriously"

(Rom 16:12)

Tryphaena, with Tryphosa, is greeted by Paul in Rom 16:12 as "workers in the Lord" — that is, engaged in missionary work. The women's related names may mean that they are sisters; their meaning makes it more likely that they are slaves or freedwomen of the same patron. The verb from which their names derive has sexual overtones when applied to women; thus these women may have once been sex-workers, perhaps in the same brothel. That they are greeted with a single verb and adjective suggests that they function as missionary partners. Romans 16 includes similar partnerships of women and men, perhaps spouses or lovers (Prisca and Aquila, 16:3–5; Junia and Andronicus, 16:7; Nereas and his "sister" 16:15). These partnerships may reflect commitments to each other as well as to the mission; Tryphaena and Tryphosa may be such a couple.

MARY ROSE D'ANGELO

SEE ALSO Part I: Euodia; Martha; Mary 2; Syntyche; Tryphosa.

FOR FURTHER READING: D'Angelo, Mary Rose. "Women Partners in the New Testament."

Lampe, Peter. "Tryphaena and Tryphosa."

Tryphosa

"living delicately, luxuriously," from Greek *tryphaō*, "to live delicately, luxuriously"

(Rom 16:12)

Tryphosa, with Tryphaena, is greeted by Paul in Rom 16:12 as "workers in the Lord," meaning that

(Below) *Detail of an eighth-century B.C.E. bronze belt from Urartu (present-day Armenia). The elaborate banquet scenes depict women preparing and being served food and drink, dancing, and playing musical instruments; because no men appear in these scenes, they probably represent a women's feast or celebration. See Vashti; Women at Vashti's Banquet (Esth 1:9); Wives and Concubines of Belshazzar (Dan 5:2-3, etc.).*

they are engaged in missionary work. (For full discussion, see the entry on Tryphaena.)

MARY ROSE D'ANGELO

SEE ALSO Part I: Euodia; Martha; Mary 2; Syntyche; Tryphaena.

Vashti

from Persian *vahista*, "best"

VASHTI IN THE HEBREW BIBLE

(Esth 1:9–19; 2:1, 4, 17)

The first wife of Ahasuerus (Xerxes I, reigned 485–465 B.C.E.), the king of Persia, Vashti is the featured character in the first episode (thought by some scholars to come from a "Vashti" source) of the Book of Esther, a work of historical fiction of the late Persian–early Hellenistic period (fourth century B.C.E.). King Ahasuerus, in the midst of a drinking banquet with his noblemen, summons Vashti to appear before the company with her royal crown upon her head, so that he can show off her beauty. She refuses (her reasons are not given, although the rabbis speculated that she was summoned to appear naked), and the king, enraged, puts her away permanently, thus setting in motion the chain of events that will make the Jewish girl Esther the queen of Persia.

Vashti stands out in the Book of Esther as the only woman who directly disobeys an order from a man. This makes her admirable to some modern readers, although the results of her disobedience are not particularly desirable. Not only is Vashti banished, but also a decree requires all women to honor (and obey?) their husbands. However, the author's customary irony may be at work here: Vashti does

not wish to appear before the king, and her "punishment" grants her wish.

SIDNIE WHITE CRAWFORD

SEE ALSO Part I: Esther; Part II: Women at Vashti's Banquet (Esth 1:9); Noble Ladies of Persia and Media (Esth 1:18–20).

FOR FURTHER READING: White, Sidnie A. "Esther."

VASHTI IN THE APOCRYPHAL/
DEUTEROCANONICAL BOOKS
    (Add Esth 1:9, 12–13, 15–16; 2:1, 4)
Greek Esther, like its Hebrew counterpart, is set in the royal court of Susa where Queen Vashti gives a party for the royal women in the house of the king (1:9), while King Artaxerxes (Ahasuerus) hosts a week-long banquet for his officials and courtiers. On the seventh day, the king orders seven eunuchs "to escort the queen to him in order to proclaim her as queen and to place the diadem on her head, and to have her display her beauty to all the governors and the people of various nations, for she was indeed a beautiful woman" (1:11). Vashti is summoned not only to display her beauty, as in the Hebrew version, but also to be proclaimed queen. This detail is the only real difference between the Hebrew and Greek depictions of Vashti.

Queen Vashti's refusal (1:12) is interpreted as an insult to the king and a potential disruption to marital harmony and male authority. The king's male friends advise him to issue a royal decree barring the queen from the king's presence, giving the queen's royal rank to "a woman better than she" (1:19), and proclaiming "all women will give honor to their husbands, rich and poor alike" (1:20).

While Vashti's demotion is necessary to the plot in which Esther is promoted to queen, her dethronement is a delicious irony: the king deposes one defiant queen only to enthrone another who is ultimately even more so.

Ancient Jewish commentators were especially critical of Vashti, maintaining that she, a granddaughter of wicked Nebuchadnezzar, was a woman of poor character. Some rabbis thought she had been asked to appear with *only* the crown, that is, nude (1:11). Martin Luther advised husbands whose wives were disobedient, "If she still refuses, get rid of her; take an Esther and let Vashti go, as King Ahasuerus did."

Others applaud Vashti's boldness, viewing her as heroic, the first woman in the Bible, albeit a "pagan," to refuse to be treated as either chattel or a sex object. She was a queen who, in the face of the ideology of male dominance, sets for women a fine example of female independence, assertiveness, and a high concept of self-worth.

CAREY A. MOORE

FOR FURTHER READING: Darr, Katheryn Pfisterer. *Far More Precious Than Jewels.*

Zebidah

    "gift," from Hebrew *zbd,* "to bestow upon, give"
    (2 Kgs 23:36)
Zebidah is the daughter of Pedaiah of Rumah, wife of Josiah (sixteenth king of Judah; reigned 639–609 B.C.E.), and mother of King Jehoiakim (reigned 609 B.C.E.). Her name occurs in the introduction to her son's reign in 2 Kgs 23:36–37, but not in its parallel in 2 Chr 36:11–12.

LINDA S. SCHEARING

Zeresh

meaning uncertain; a name of Persian origin
(Esth 5:10, 14; 6:13)

Zeresh is the wife of Haman, grand vizier of Persia and enemy of Mordecai, the cousin of Queen Esther. It is Zeresh, equally with Haman's advisers, who recognizes that Haman will be unable to defeat the Jewish Mordecai.

SIDNIE WHITE CRAWFORD
SEE ALSO Part I: Esther; Zosara.

Zeruah

"having a skin disease," from the Hebrew verb ṣrʻ, "to have a skin disease"
(1 Kgs 11:26)

Zeruah is the widow of Nebat, an Ephraimite servant of Solomon, and the mother of Jeroboam, who would become the first king (reigned 928–907 B.C.E.) of the northern kingdom of Israel.

Although the names of Judean queen mothers usually appear in the regnal formulas of their sons, mothers of northern kings are rarely identified — possibly because of that kingdom's lack of dynastic stability. Alternatively, the anonymity of northern queen mothers might indicate that these women did not serve in an official capacity in the court. According to another tradition, preserved only in the Septuagint (1 Kgs 12:24), Jeroboam's mother is named Sarira ("lepers") and is called a harlot. This epithet, as well as her name in both Hebrew and Greek, may be intended as pro-Judean polemics against Jeroboam.

RHONDA BURNETTE-BLETSCH

Zeruiah

"YHWH has let flow, from Hebrew ṣrh, "to bleed, let flow," and yāh, a shortened form of YHWH
(1 Sam 26:6; 2 Sam 2:13, 18; 3:39; 8:16; 14:1; 16:9, 10; 17:25; 18:2; 19:21–22; 21:17–18; 23:37; 1 Kgs 1:7; 2:5, 22; 1 Chr 2:16; 11:6, 39; 18:12, 15; 26:28; 27:24)

The sister of Abigail and King David (2 Sam 17:25; 1 Chr 2:15), Zeruiah is the mother of three sons, all prominent in the royal bureaucracy: Joab (2 Sam 2:13, 18; 8:16; 14:1; 17:25; 23:27; 1 Kgs 1:7; 2:5, 22; 1 Chr 2:16; 11:6, 39; 18:15; 26:28; 27:24), Abishai (1 Sam 26:6; 2 Sam 2:18; 16:9; 18:2; 19:22; 21:17; 19:23; 23:18; 1 Chr 2:16; 18:12), and Asahel (2 Sam 2:18; 1 Chr 2:16). Due to her status as sister of the king, the most famous king of Israel (reigned c. 1005–965 B.C.E.), each of her sons is known by her name, "the son of Zeruiah," rather than by the name of their father or their place of origin, which were the standard practices. Their father's name is not preserved in tradition. All three men gain positions of power and importance in David's kingdom because of their blood ties to him; monarchic Israel operated as a patronage society.

Zeruiah's status as sister of the king would have allowed her to enjoy some privileges and honor, and she would also have received even more prestige because of her status as the mother of three sons, all of whom had important court appointments. Marriage and motherhood were the expected norm for women in ancient Israel and Judah. A large family was seen as a blessing, and sterility a trial or chastisement from God. Sons were valued more highly than daughters because they perpetuated the family lineage, so Zeruiah's three sons would have led her to be esteemed for her own sake within the community, in spite of her ties to the king.

DIANA VIKANDER EDELMAN
SEE ALSO Part I: Abigail 2.
FOR FURTHER READING: de Vaux, Roland. *Ancient Israel: Its Life and Institutions.*
Patai, Raphael. *Sex and Family in the Bible and the Middle East.*

Zibiah

"gazelle," from Hebrew ṣĕbiyyâ, "gazelle"
(2 Kgs 12:1; 2 Chr 24:1)

Zibiah is the wife of Ahaziah, sixth king of Judah (reigned 843–842 B.C.E.), and the mother of King Jehoash (Joash). Her place of origin is Beersheba, but her lineage is unknown. Ahaziah's marriage to Zibiah may imply an attempted alliance with the Negev tribes close to the Edomite border. Her name occurs in the introduction to her son's reign (2 Kgs

12:1–3; 2 Chr 24:1–2). The writer of Chronicles does not always mention the names of queen mothers. Perhaps it is included here as a mark of status for Joash, who is considered a good ruler.

LINDA S. SCHEARING

SEE ALSO Part I: Azubah 1.

Zillah

meaning uncertain; perhaps "shadow, protection," from Hebrew *ṣēl*, "shade"; or "shrill cry, melody," from Hebrew *ṣll*, "to shrill, tinkle" and related to the word for "cymbals," *ṣelṣēlîm*
(Gen 4:19, 22–23)

The genealogies in the early chapters of Genesis are critical in advancing the story of the world from the original population of two (Eve and Adam) to the full global population that becomes the backdrop for the story of the Israelite ancestors. All of these lists of begetters and those begotten (Gen 4:17–26; 5:1–32; 10:1–32) are comprised of male names with one exception, the family of Lamech, an ancestor appearing in the sixth generation after Cain. Lamech has two wives, and the names of both are given, the second being Zillah. In addition, the daughter (Naamah) of Zillah is named along with one of her sons and the two sons of the other wife (Adah).

The unusual appearance of Zillah and two associated females in the male genealogies of Genesis 1–10 may be linked to the special role of the children of Zillah and of her co-wife. In the genealogical sequence, those children are the seventh generation of naturally born humans. In the biblical idiom in which seven represents totality, the seventh generation indicates the beginning of "fully launched" humanity. It is precisely at that point that the civilized arts are said to have begun, represented by the four children of Zillah and Adah: pastoralists (Jabal), instrumentalists (Jubal), metallurgists (Tubal-Cain), and vocalists (Naamah). Civilization is thus portrayed as the product of human creativity and not, as in most mythological beginnings stories, the gift of various gods to certain individuals. The *mothers* of the persons representing the beginning of civilized arts appear in the text, thus acknowledging that human creativity is inextricably linked to female parentage.

The names of Zillah, her co-wife, and her daughter are all interesting in relation to the Lamech story (Gen 4:19–26) as a foundational tale of the beginnings of civilization. If Zillah in fact does have a musical meaning (instead of, or in addition to, its possible meaning of "protector"), it combines with the meaning of Adah (something to do with adornment or decoration) and Naamah ("lovely one" or perhaps "singer") to link the female with aspects of aesthetic expression.

Zillah and her co-wife are addressed in Gen 4:23 in their husband's brief war taunt. This appeal to women in an archaic poem concerning military exploits is probably related to the fact that, in Israelite tradition, the prominent role of women as musicians includes the custom of women composing and performing victory psalms or songs (as by Miriam and Deborah) following an outstanding military victory. The names of the wives and daughter of Lamech, as well as their implied relation to his enigmatic slaying of an enemy, reflect the inherent connection of music and women in this biblical conception of humanity.

CAROL MEYERS

SEE ALSO Part I: Adah 1; Naamah 1; Part II: Women with Hand-Drums, Dancing (Exod 15:20, etc.); Singing Women (and Men) (2 Sam 19:35, etc.).

FOR FURTHER READING: Cassuto, Umberto. *A Commentary on the Book of Genesis.*

Meyers, Carol. "Mother to Muse: An Archaeomusicological Study of Women's Performance in Ancient Israel."

Niditch, Susan. "Genesis."

Zilpah

meaning uncertain; perhaps "short-nosed," related to Arabic
(Gen 29:24; 30:9–10; 35:26; 37:2; 46:18)

Marriage customs in the Hebrew Bible are depicted from the male point of view and allow for a man to have more than one wife, though a woman could not have more than one husband. Social scientists categorize a marriage between one man and two or more women of equal social status as polygyny, whereas the term *polycoity* refers to a marriage pattern in which a man takes an additional wife, beyond his primary wife, who is of lower social status than the primary wife. In the latter case, this secondary wife is usually a concubine or a handmaid, whose role within the family unit is either to bear children in order to build up the husband's lineage or to provide sexual enjoyment for the husband. The distinction between a primary and a secondary wife is based on economic considerations: marriage to a primary wife is established on the basis of a conjugal fund property to which both spouses contribute and which becomes the foundation of the economic and legal rights of the primary wife. A secondary wife is a woman without economic standing in her husband's household.

Zilpah was given as a wedding gift to Leah by her father Laban on the occasion of Leah's marriage to Jacob. The economic basis of the marriage between Leah and Jacob meant that Leah was Jacob's primary wife. However, after Leah's marriage to Jacob, Leah's sister Rachel also became a primary wife to Jacob — a marriage arrangement known as sororal polygyny. Despite the equal socioeconomic status of Leah and Rachel as primary co-wives of Jacob, the two sisters competed against each other for a place of honor within their husband's family through their ability to bear children. Their competition went so far as to have Jacob father children through their handmaids (Rachel's handmaid was Bilhah) in each woman's attempt to establish herself as the victor in a competition of baby-making. Perhaps the competition between sisters who are wives is related to the Levitical stipulation prohibiting a man from marrying his sister-in-law (Lev 18:18).

Through the initiative of Leah, Zilpah became a secondary wife to Jacob and bore him two sons, Gad and Asher. Though Gad ("fortune") and Asher ("happy") were borne to Jacob by Zilpah, they were considered to be children of Leah, who gave them names symbolic of her perspective on their births and their ability to gain favor for her with Jacob.

Thus, Zilpah's role would be comparable to what contemporary society refers to as surrogate motherhood. In this family system, a woman's biology is part of her destiny, or even tragedy, in the case of a barren woman. A woman establishes her worth as a wife through her ability to increase her husband's lineage; her prestige is determined by her reproductive capabilities. Additional progeny also augment the family workforce and thus its economic potential.

The equal status of Rachel and Leah as primary wives of Jacob resulted in a shift in the generation of Jacob's offspring from a vertical genealogy to a horizontal one; instead of choosing only one primary heir in the descending generation, multiple heirship occurred as all the offspring of Jacob, presented as ancestors of the twelve tribes of Israel, were reckoned as his heirs. The secondary status of Zilpah as a wife to Jacob did not result in secondary status for her sons within the patrilineage of Jacob. The status of the mother in this case was separate from the status of her children. Asher and Gad were considered direct heirs to the patrilineage of Terah, their great-great-grandfather, and are listed among the twelve sons/tribes of Jacob/Israel. However, Asher and Gad represent the most peripheral of the tribal territories, probably the first two to cease to be included in the nation of Israel. Their marginal status may be foreshadowed by their having been the children of the secondary wife associated with the unpreferred primary wife, Leah.

NAOMI STEINBERG

SEE ALSO Part I: Bilhah; Leah; Sarah 1/Sarai; Part II: Women in Incest Regulations (Lev 18:7–18, etc.).

FOR FURTHER READING: Steinberg, Naomi. *Kinship and Marriage in Genesis: A Household Economics Perspective.*

Zipporah

"bird," from Hebrew *ṣippôr,* "bird"

(Exod 2:21–22; 4:20, 24–26; 18:2–6; Num 12:1)

Zipporah is a Midianite woman who becomes the wife of Moses. After Moses kills an Egyptian, he flees from the pharaoh and settles among the Midianites, an Arab people who occupied desert areas in southern Transjordan, northern Arabia, and the Sinai. He meets the seven daughters of Reuel, priest of Midian, at a well; rescues them from shepherds who are harassing them; and fills their jugs with water. In gratitude, Reuel (called Jethro or Hobab in other biblical passages) offers Moses hospitality, then gives him his daughter Zipporah in marriage (Exod 2:21–22). She and Moses have two sons, Gershom and Eliezer (Exod 18:3–4).

Zipporah is the heroine of a bizarre incident that takes place as Moses heads back to Egypt with his wife and sons (Exod 4:20). On their way, at a night encampment, "The LORD met him [Moses] and tried to kill him" (Exod 4:24). No reason is given, just as no reason is given for the angel's attack on Jacob as he came back from Mesopotamia (Gen 32:24). Jacob was alone and wrestled with the angel all night; Moses is with his wife, who comes to his rescue. She takes a flint and cuts off her son's foreskin. She then flings the foreskin at "his" feet, declaring that he is ḥătan dāmîm to her (Exod 4:26). Zipporah's enigmatic statement has two possible explanations: she flings the foreskin at *Moses'* feet, saying, "You are a bridegroom of blood to me" (NRSV), or she flings it at *God's* feet, saying, "You are a blood father-in-law to me." (*Dāmîm* means "blood," and ḥātan can mean either "bridegroom" or "father-in-law.") Either way, her deed and words stop the attack. The story is already difficult for the narrator, who adds a comment that ḥātan dāmîm refers to circumcision. The situation remains unclear to us. Zipporah, however, understood it and acted decisively to rescue Moses. Zipporah's name, meaning "bird," combined with her protection of Moses, is reminiscent of the fierce loyalty to her husband Osiris of the Egyptian goddess Isis, who is often portrayed as a bird of prey.

Zipporah is not well rewarded. At some point before the exodus from Egypt, Moses sends her and the children away (Exod 18:2). After the exodus, her father, the priest of Midian (here called Jethro), comes to visit Moses, bringing Zipporah and her two sons. Moses is told that his father-in-law Jethro is "coming to see you, with your wife and her two sons" (Exod 18:6). Moses goes out to greet Jethro and takes him into his tent, but nothing is said about his greeting Zipporah.

Moses' neglect of Zipporah is obvious, as he (not God) tells the men at Sinai not to approach any women in preparation for God's approach in three days (Exod 19:2). Since he himself is apparently always in preparation for meeting with God, we can infer that he never sleeps with Zipporah. In Num 12:1, Miriam and Aaron speak against Moses because of the "Cushite woman" whom he married, but they do not mention her name. Midrashic tradition assumed they were discussing Moses' neglect of Zipporah. Other interpreters see the Cushite woman as a second wife, with Miriam and Aaron opposed to the marriage. But no children are ever recorded for a second wife of Moses.

TIKVA FRYMER-KENSKY

SEE ALSO Part II: Woman (Women) Not to Be Approached at Sinai (Exod 19:15).

FOR FURTHER READING: Ashby, Godfrey. "The Bloody Bridegroom: The Interpretation of Exodus 4:24–26."

Pardes, Ilana. *Countertraditions in the Bible: A Feminist Approach.*

Propp, William. "That Bloody Bridegroom (Exodus iv 24–6)."

Robinson, Bernard P. "Zipporah to the Rescue: A Contextual Study of Exodus 4:24–6."

Zosara

an Elamite or Persian name of uncertain etymology; the Greek transliteration of Hebrew *zereš*
(Add Esth 5:10, 14; 6:13)

Zosara, identical to Zeresh in the Hebrew Book of Esther, is the wife and principal confidant of Haman, the villainous prime minister of King Artaxerxes (Add Esth 3:1; 5:11) who tries to destroy all the Jews in the Persian Empire (Add Esth 3:6–11). In the Hebrew version, Haman is "son of Hammedatha the Agagite," an Amalekite enemy of the Jews (Esth 3:1). In the Greek, Haman is "a

Bougean" (3:1; 9:10; 12:6), a designation of uncertain origin and meaning that carries a sense of scorn. Later Greek editions replace it with "Macedonian," a term meaningful to Greek-reading Jews. Thus Zosara and Haman are hated Greeks, not Amalekites, in Greek Esther.

As befitting the spouse of a conniving official, Zosara is a strong, ruthless woman, quite at home with court intrigues. Like Jezebel (1 Kings 21), she is solicitous for her husband's happiness to the point of utter ruthlessness. When Haman's delight at being included in Esther's dinners with the king is destroyed because Mordecai neither stands or trembles as he passes him in the courtyard, Zosara and Haman's friends advise, "Let a gallows be made, fifty cubits high, and in the morning tell the king to have Mordecai hanged on it. Then, go merrily with the king to the dinner" (Add Esth 5:14). The exaggerated height of a 75-foot-high gallows accents Zosara's vengeance.

When the king decides to honor Mordecai, Haman seeks his friends and Zosara, who now play the prophet, saying, "If Mordecai is of the Jewish people, and you have begun to be humiliated before him, you will surely fall. You will not be able to defend yourself, because the living God is with him" (Add Esth 6:13).

Zosara, who shared in her husband's rise to power, shares in his precipitous defeat. She presumably pays dearly for her viciousness toward Mordecai, for she ends up losing her husband on the infamous gallows (Add Esth 7:10), all his estate (Add Esth 8:1), and their ten sons, each of whom is mentioned by name as being among the five hundred people killed by the Jews (Add Esth 9:7–10).

CAREY A. MOORE

SEE ALSO Part I: Esther; Zeresh.

FOR FURTHER READING: Moore, Carey A. *Daniel, Esther and Jeremiah: The Additions.*

PART II

Unnamed Women

Gen 1:26–28; 5:1–2
Woman (and Man) in the First Creation Story

According to the creation story in Genesis 1, the first woman was created on the sixth day of creation as part of a single female-male pair (vv. 26–27). This pair is 'ādām, which can be a gender-inclusive word meaning "earthling" or "human" (see NRSV, "humankind"). Some translations (such as the NAB, NEB, NJPS, and RSV) obscure the inclusiveness of the Hebrew term by rendering it "man." Because the 'ādām clearly consists of "male and female" (v. 27), many interpreters have acclaimed this as the simultaneous creation of female and male, as evidence of a Hebraic conception of gender equality. A pair is necessary for biological reasons, for the first pair is blessed by God and instructed to "be fruitful and multiply and fill the earth" (v. 28). Nevertheless, it is noteworthy that the two biological partners are mentioned equally, rather than as "a man and his mate."

The wording in the text is strange: God is said to create "them" and to bless "them"; but when it states that God created 'ādām in the image of God, it says, "in the image of God he created 'it' [singular 'ōtô, also 'him']," a preposition repeated in 5:1, "He created it." (The NRSV changes "it" to "them.") Several interpretations are possible: only the male is created in the image of God (an interpretation frequent in Christian tradition); humanity is made in the image of God precisely when female and male are together; or female and male represent two parts of a whole, a human. Another strange aspect of this text is that it reports God as saying, "Let us make humankind in our [plural] image." The plural pronoun is open to various interpretations, for example, that God's being includes both female and male.

Readers have also long been concerned with the relationship between the creation of the first woman and man in Genesis 1 and the story of the creation of humanity in Genesis 2. There, after God creates 'ādām, God looks for a suitable companion for this creature. After creating the animals, who are unsuitable as companions, God "splits the 'ādām," creating woman and man. The man is now called Adam, the woman Eve. Some readers have harmonized the two stories, understanding Genesis 2 to be a more detailed account of the creation of the first woman. Other readers, recognizing the differences between the two stories, developed a legend of "the first Eve" (Lilith). Finally, many see the two accounts as separate, each relating distinct views about the nature of female and male.

TIKVA FRYMER-KENSKY

SEE ALSO Part I: Eve; Part III: Lilith.

FOR FURTHER READING: Bird, Phyllis. "Male and Female He Created Them: Genesis 1:27b in the Context of the Priestly Account of Creation."

Frymer-Kensky, Tikva. *Motherprayer.*

Gen 4:17
Wife of Cain

After Cain is punished for killing his brother, Abel, by being made a fugitive, he is said to have had sexual relations with his wife. She conceives and bears a son, Enoch, whose name becomes the name of the first city. If Cain is of the first generation after Eve and Adam, his wife would have to be his sister, a possibility based on the information in Gen 5:4 that the primal couple had other sons and daughters after Abel's death. Such a marriage, which would have been considered incestuous, is problematic. Other similar difficulties — such as the notion of a city being built without enough people in the world

— suggest that the Cain narrative was taken from some other context and placed after the Eden story, making it less likely that it implies or condones sister-brother sexuality, which is forbidden in Levitical laws.

CAROL MEYERS

SEE ALSO Part II: Women in Incest Regulations (Lev 18:7–18, etc.).

GEN 5:1–2
First Woman Created by God

SEE GEN 1:26–28, etc. Woman (and Man) in the First Creation Story (Part II).

GEN 5:4, 7, 10, 13, 16, 19, 22, 26
Daughters (and Sons) of Adam, Seth, Enosh, Kenan, Mahalalel, Jared, Enoch, and Methuselah

The daughters of Adam (and of Seth, Enosh, Kenan, Mahalalel, Jared, Enoch, and Methuselah) are part of a genealogy in Genesis 5 that spans the time period between creation and the flood. The family tree is a vertical genealogy, that is, a family lineage that tracks the offspring of only one person — in this case, a son — in each generation. The Genesis 5 listing differs in number and detail from the preceding genealogy in Genesis 4, which is meant to introduce the tale of Lamech and his children, the founders of cultural vocations in the seventh generation. In the Genesis 5 list, Lamech and Noah, with their daughters and sons, come after Methuselah, providing ten generations of humanity to populate the world before the flood. The formulaic presentation of each generation is similar to that of the postflood genealogies in Genesis 11, where ten more generations separate the flood from Abraham. The lists in Genesis 5 and 10 provide a symmetry between the world after the creation and the world after the flood.

Unlike many other biblical genealogies, such as

those of Gen 4:17–18 and the table of nations in Genesis 10, the preflood and postflood lists mention daughters as well as sons. Those lists provide population suitable to the narrative's purposes: the presence of daughters conveys the requisite notion of demographic increase, which depends on the reproductive role of women. The inclusion of daughters thus is more important in some lists, such as these, than in those governed by patrilineal principles, which omit females.

CAROL MEYERS

SEE ALSO Part II: Daughters (and Sons) of Lamech (Gen 5:30); Daughters (and Sons) of Shem, Arpachshad, Shelah, Eber, Peleg, Reu, Serug, and Nahor (Gen 11:10–11, etc.).

GEN 5:30
Daughters (and Sons) of Lamech

The daughters (and sons, including Noah) of Lamech constitute the tenth generation before the flood according to the genealogical listing in Genesis 5, which balances the sequence of ten generations of daughters and sons after the flood, from Noah to Abraham, in Genesis 11. Lamech's offspring appear in a different genealogical tradition in Genesis 4, where his three sons and one daughter are founders of the civilized arts.

CAROL MEYERS

SEE ALSO Part I: Naamah 1; Part II: Daughters (and Sons) of Adam, Seth, Enosh, Kenan, Mahalalel, Jared, Enoch, and Methuselah (Gen 5:4, etc.); Daughters (and Sons) of Shem, Arpachshad, Shelah, Eber, Peleg, Reu, Serug, and Nahor (Gen 11:10–11, etc.).

GEN 6:1–4
Daughters of Men, Wives of the Sons of God

The small mythical notice in Gen 6:1–4 relates that human women attracted divine beings and became the mothers of the renowned "heroes" and the

Nephilim. This story should be read together with Gen 1:26–28, 3:22–24, and 11:1–9 as a progressive discovery of the nature of humanity in relationship to the heavenly court of divine beings, and humanity's gradual attainment of their current attributes and destiny. Humanity was created in the likeness and image of God, placed on earth as God's representative to administer the cosmos and work the world. As humans began to acquire cultural knowledge, they became more godlike. As a result, they were sent out from the Garden of Eden. The expulsion has two consequences: it prevents them from becoming immortal and thus just like the gods, and it sets them one step closer to fulfilling their destiny, as they begin to work the ground.

Now, when humans begin to multiply, their very similarity to divine beings means that the human women look beautiful to the divine beings of the heavenly court (v. 2). The beauty of these women, like the beauty of Sarah, Rebekah, and Bathsheba, sets them up to be taken by powerful males, in this case the "sons of God," the heavenly beings of the divine court. The women taken by these males give birth to the famous Nephilim and (or who are) the heroes. The idea of divine males mating with human females is reminiscent of Greek mythology; for Mesopotamian tradition, goddesses choose powerful men, particularly kings, as lovers. In the context of Genesis, this mating sets up a crisis, for the lines between humanity and divinity are thereby blurred and the role of humanity is thus endangered. In order to keep human and divine separated, God decrees a maximum human life span of 120 years (Gen 6:3), a life span traditional in Mesopotamian mythology. Here the purpose of the limitation is to create a separation between the gods and humanity; presumably human women, decaying so quickly, would no longer be attractive to the gods.

TIKVA FRYMER-KENSKY

FOR FURTHER READING: Clines, David J. A. "The Significance of the 'Sons of God' Episode (Genesis 6:1–4) in the Context of the 'Primeval History.'"

Eslinger, Lyle. "A Contextual Identification of the *bene ha'elohim* and *benoth ha'adam* in Genesis 6:1–4."

Hendel, Ronald. "Of Demigods and the Deluge: Toward an Interpretation of Genesis 6:1–4."

Klein, Jacob. "The Bane of Humanity: A Lifespan of One Hundred and Twenty Years."

Gen 6:18; 7:7, 13; 8:16, 18
Wife of Noah

As commanded by God at the time of the great flood, Noah's wife accompanies her husband, her sons, and her son's wives into and out of the ark. Having already had children, her fertility was not the reason for her survival of the flood; she comes as part of the family unit, and her inclusion shows the importance of companionship in the biblical concept of marriage. Noah's wife is not mentioned after the flood.

In Mesopotamian mythology, which has a similar flood story, the flood hero also brings his wife on the boat, and they become immortal together.

TIKVA FRYMER-KENSKY

Gen 6:18; 7:7, 13; 8:16, 18
Wives of Noah's Sons

As commanded by God at the time of the great flood, the wives of Noah's three sons accompany their husbands and their in-laws into the ark and come out with them. Because the whole world is destroyed by the flood, the presence of wives for Noah's sons is essential so that they can carry out God's post-diluvian mandate to "be fruitful and multiply" (8:17). They have also become the family of Noah and are thus saved along with him.

TIKVA FRYMER-KENSKY

Gen 11:10–11, 13, 15, 17, 19, 21, 23, 25
Daughters (and Sons) of Shem, Arpachshad, Shelah, Eber, Peleg, Reu, Serug, and Nahor

The story of Noah (Genesis 6–9), the table of nations (Genesis 10), and the story of the tower of Babel (Gen 11:1–9) together explain how the earth had become fully populated by the time the prehistory of Israel begins. Gen 11:10–27 provides a long genealogical sequence that connects the Israelite ancestors (Abraham and Sarah and their successors) with human beginnings (Noah and his wife and their family, sole survivors of the flood). The Israelites saw themselves as Shemites (Semites), and so they traced themselves back to Shem, Noah's first son. For every generation after Shem and before Terah (the father of Abraham), the genealogical pattern (called a vertical genealogy because it tracks only one member of each generation) follows a formula: first the major son of the ancestor is named, along with the number of years the ancestor lived before and after the birth of that son; then the fact that the ancestor had "other sons and daughters" is provided.

The listing in Genesis 11 of both daughters and sons of Shem and his descendants differs from the genealogy of Shem in the table of nations in Genesis 10. Four generations of that genealogy coincide with the Genesis 11 list, but mention only sons. That is, in the conceptualization of the origins of the general world population, female offspring are omitted until the Hebrew ancestors are mentioned. The appearance of the word *daughters* along with *sons* in Genesis 11 thus may represent an acknowledgment of the role of females in Hebrew lineage. Though reckoned patrilineally (that is, through the male line), these biblical lists contain daughters as well as sons, thereby indicating the critical role of women in Israelite family structure and continuity.

CAROL MEYERS

SEE ALSO Part I: Naamah 1; Part II: Daughters (and Sons) of Adam, Seth, Enosh, Kenan, Mahalalel, Jared, Enoch, and Methuselah (Gen 5:4, etc.); Daughters (and Sons) of Lamech (Gen 5:30).

Gen 12:16; 20:14; 24:35; 30:43; 32:5; Exod 11:5; 1 Sam 25:41; 2 Kgs 5:26; Esth 7:4
Female (and Male) Slaves

The Hebrew term *šipḥâ*, "maid, maidservant," is often translated "female slave" in the NRSV and other English versions, which tend to reserve the translation "maidservant" for another word indicating a female subordinate, *'āmâ*. The two words may sometimes be synonymous, especially because they are each used in combination with *'ebed*, the word for "male servant, slave" (as in Exodus 20 and 21 and Jeremiah 34). However, the word *šipḥâ*, in the texts mentioned here, usually denotes a level of menial labor or servitude that seems to be more servile than does *'āmâ*.

In Exod 11:5, in order to indicate that all firstborn Egyptians will die, the narrator uses a merismus — a figure of speech in which two extremes represent everything in between. In this text, someone at the top of the social, economic, and political realms is represented by "Pharaoh who sits on his throne," that is, a seated male ruler. At the other extreme is the "female slave who is behind the handmill," that is, a woman servant hard at work. The firstborn of those two people, and thus the firstborn of everyone in between, will perish.

More often, "female slave" does not appear alone but rather is paired with "male slave." Together they can represent an array of possessions, such as those representing Abraham's wealth (Gen 12:12; 24:35); those presented, along with sheep and oxen, in apology, to Abraham by King Abimelech of Gerar when returning Sarah to her husband (Gen 20:14); and those, along with animals, apparently available as conciliatory gifts to Esau from Jacob (Gen 30:43; 32:5). Similarly, when the prophet Elisha's servant, Gehazi, is given a reward for healing the Aramean general Naaman, Elisha taunts Gehazi for having accepted money and also "clothing, olive orchards and vineyards, sheep and oxen, male and female slaves" (2 Kgs 5:26). And Esth 7:4 mentions "slaves, men and women," as occupying a status better only than death.

Because of the lowly status of such servants, the term for "female slave" is also sometimes used as an expression of the humility of a speaker. In 1 Sam 25:41, Abigail expresses her willingness to become David's wife by telling his emissaries that she is their "servant," willing to wash their feet (compare the wise woman of Tekoa, in 2 Samuel 14, who repeatedly refers to herself as "your servant" in addressing the king). However, this word (*šiphâ,*) for female servant, unlike "maidservant" (*'āmâ*), is never used to express humility before God.

CAROL MEYERS

SEE ALSO Part II: Female (and Male) Hebrew Slaves (Exod 21:7–11, etc.); Serving Girls (and Male Servants) of Job (Job 19:15, etc.); Female (and Male) Slaves (Isa 14:2); Female (and Male) Slaves (Joel 2:29).

GEN 19:8, 12, 14–17, 30–38
Daughters of Lot

When the men of Sodom demand sexual relations with two messengers from God, Lot, who has given the messengers hospitality, offers his two daughters to the men of Sodom instead. The daughters are living with their parents and have not had sexual relations with any man (19:8), although they are apparently betrothed (19:14). Lot's offer indicates that, at least from the perspective of the men who produced the text, a father might find it less shameful to allow his own daughters to become objects of forced sexual relations than to allow male visitors to become such objects (compare Judg 19:24). Lot's daughters are spared this fate, however, and escape with their father before Sodom is destroyed.

Lot's daughters live with their father in a cave after the destruction of Sodom, Gomorrah, and the other cities in the area. Fearing that no men are available to father their children, they make Lot drink wine on two consecutive nights and, while he is drunk, have sexual relations with him. In this manner the daughters bear sons, one of which becomes the ancestor of the Moabites and the other of which becomes the ancestor of the Ammonites; both people become enemies of the Israelites.

The story may be in part an attempt to slander Israel's enemies by associating their origins with dubious sexual unions. At the same time, the desperate measures taken by the daughters probably indicate that, for many women as well as men in the ancient world, having children was the route by which one's future welfare could be secured. Thus, the daughters' apparently radical actions might also be read as an initiative to ensure their survival (compare Genesis 38).

KEN STONE

SEE ALSO Part II: Wife of Lot (Gen 19:15–16, etc.); Concubine (Secondary Wife) of a Levite (Judges 19–20).

GEN 19:15–16, 26
Wife of Lot

When the large cities of the plain of Jordan are destroyed because of their people's lack of discernment of good and bad, Lot's wife looks back and turns into a pillar of salt. Salt preserves her in a fixed state. Is this symbolic of her still being tied to the security that city culture is assumed to offer?

LYN M. BECHTEL

SEE ALSO Part II: Daughters of Lot (Gen 19:8, etc.).

GEN 20:14
Female Slaves of Abimelech
SEE GEN 12:16, etc.   Female (and Male) Slaves (Part II).

GEN 20:17
Wife and Female Slaves of Abimelech

In the second of two "wife-sister" tales involving Sarah and Abraham, King Abimelech of Gerar, takes Sarah into his household, presumably intending to have sex with her. He desists when God warns him in a dream that she is a married woman. Not only is Abimelech mortified that he might inadvertently have sinned, but also he apparently suffers from some physical problem as the result of his near-indiscretion.

What was that problem? The answer can be inferred from the account of what happens when Abimelech restores Sarah to her husband and also provides generous gifts. God then restores Abimelech to his normal physical condition. Furthermore, God also does so for "his wife and female slaves" (20:17) with the result that they bear children. The episode ends on an explanatory note, indicating that God "had closed all the wombs of the house of Abimelech" (20:18) because of the Sarah incident. The implication is that Abimelech and his women experienced infertility, which is viewed as a punishment for Abimelech's having acquired Sarah. The subsequent fertility of his family signals the return to rightful behavior.

The word rendered "female slave" in this passage is 'āmâ, which would be better translated "maidservant." This Hebrew word usually connotes a woman occupying a somewhat higher status than does "(female) slave," for which there is another term. That other term appears earlier in the narrative of this episode to denote the female slaves Abimelech gives to Abraham, along with male slaves, animals, and silver, when Sarah is restored.

CAROL MEYERS

SEE ALSO Part I: Sarah 1/Sarai; Part II: Female (and Male) Slaves (Gen 12:16, etc.); Serving Girls (and Male Servants) of Job (Job 19:15, etc.); Female (and Male) Slaves (Isa 14:2).

GEN 24:3
Daughters of the Canaanites

> SEE EXOD 34:16, etc.   Daughters of the Inhabitants of the Land as Marriage Partners (Part II).

GEN 24:11, 13
Women Drawing Water

When Abraham's servant travels to Mesopotamia to find a wife for Isaac, he stops outside the city where Abraham's brother Nahor lives. He waters his camels there at a "well of water" in the evening, which is described as "the time when women go out to draw water" (Gen 24:11). This phrase indicates that, in the division of labor by gender characteristic of traditional societies, the task of fetching water in ancient Israel was usually assigned to women. Indeed, the servant soon notices that the "daughters of the townspeople are coming out to draw water" (Gen 24:13). Similar well scenes figure in the narratives about Rachel (Gen 29:2–10) and Zipporah (Exod 2:15–16), both of whom meet their husbands (Jacob and Moses, respectively) at a well.

These well scenes are sometimes called type scenes — narrative episodes with certain expected motifs. In the Hebrew Bible, they signal the appearance of a hero (Isaac, Jacob, and Moses). In the case of Rebekah, however, Isaac is not actually present; she thus commands the scene herself, as befits the most dynamic of the matriarchs.

CAROL MEYERS

SEE ALSO Part I: Rachel; Rebekah; Zipporah; Part II: Maidens Going Out to Draw Water (1 Sam 9:11).

GEN 24:35   Female Slaves of Abraham

> SEE GEN 12:16, etc.   Female (and Male) Slaves (Part II).

GEN 24:53–60
Mother of Rebekah

Although Rebekah's father (Bethuel) and grandmother (Milcah, wife of Abraham's brother Nahor) are named in the narrative about her marriage to Isaac, her mother remains nameless. The mother appears directly only in Gen 24:53, when Abraham's servant presents her and her son with bride wealth — "costly ornaments" — and in Gen 24:54–60, when she and her son ask if Rebekah is willing to journey to Canaan to marry Isaac, arrange for the trip, and give Rebekah their blessing. She appears indirectly in 24:28, when Rebekah, after meeting Abraham's emissary, runs to "her mother's household."

CAROL MEYERS

SEE ALSO Part I: Deborah 1; Rebekah; Part II: Maids of Rebekah (Gen 24:61).

GEN 24:59   Rebekah's Nurse
SEE Deborah 1 (Part I).

GEN 24:61
Maids of Rebekah

When Rebekah journeys with Abraham's servant to the land of Canaan to marry Isaac, she takes "her maids" (Gen 24:61) with her. Because her two daughters-in-law, Rachel and Leah, are given maids when they marry (Gen 29:24, 29), it is possible that Rebekah's maids have been similarly bestowed upon her. Rebekah's attendants are called *nĕʿārôt.* That word can mean "young women" as well as "female servants"; it thus may indicate a somewhat higher status for Rebekah's maids than the *šĕpāḥôt,* or maidservants, presented to Rachel and Leah.

Unlike both her mother-in-law (Sarah) and daughters-in-law, whose maidservants alleviate their infertility by providing sons for their husbands, Rebekah solves her problem with barrenness directly, by prayer to YHWH. That she does not use maids as surrogate mothers helps emphasize her uniquely prominent role as a matriarch.

CAROL MEYERS

SEE ALSO Part I: Deborah 1; Rebekah; Part II: Mother of Rebekah (Gen 24:53–60).

GEN 25:6
Concubines of Abraham

The status of these unnamed women as secondary wives of Abraham results in their sons' being ex-

cluded from the primary lineage of their father; they also do not receive a share of the land inheritance given to Isaac.

Secondary wives were of a lower social and economic status than primary wives.

NAOMI STEINBERG

SEE ALSO Part I: Hagar; Sarah 1/Sarai.

GEN 27:46   Hittite Women
SEE EXOD 34:16, etc.   Daughters of the Inhabitants of the Land as Marriage Partners (Part II).

GEN 28:1   Canaanite Women
SEE EXOD 34:16, etc.   Daughters of the Inhabitants of the Land as Marriage Partners (Part II).

GEN 28:2   Daughters of Laban
SEE LEAH; RACHEL IN THE HEBREW BIBLE (Part I).

GEN 28:6, 8   Canaanite Women
SEE EXOD 34:16, etc.   Daughters of the Inhabitants of the Land as Marriage Partners (Part II).

GEN 30:43   Female Slaves of Jacob
SEE GEN 12:16, etc.   Female (and Male) Slaves (Part II).

GEN 31:50
Daughters of Laban to Be Jacob's Only Wives

Jacob finally leaves the home of his father-in-law Laban after having worked for him for fourteen years and having amassed considerable property. The struggle for control of the property culminates in a covenant between Jacob and Laban in which Laban arranges to maintain his connection to his daughters Leah and Rachel, who are Jacob's co-wives, and their children. The covenant seems to ensure that Jacob will not mistreat his wives nor "take wives in addition" to Laban's daughters. The lineage of Jacob, uniquely involving his maternal ancestry (in that Rachel and Leah are from his mother's family) as well as that of his father, is thus secured.

CAROL MEYERS

SEE ALSO Part I: Leah; Rachel.

GEN 32:5 Female Slaves of Jacob
SEE GEN 12:16, etc. Female (and Male) Slaves (Part II).

GEN 34:1, 9, 16, 21, 29
Daughters/Women of the Region; Daughters of the Jacob Group

The tensions between the Jacob group (Israelites) and the people of Shechem, which are dramatized in the narrative about Dinah in Genesis 34, probably reflect the difficult status of Shechemites as a group of Canaanites who eventually become Israelite. That transformation of political (and ethnic) identity is fraught with in-group–out-group issues that play out in the complex dynamics of in-group (endogamous) and out-group (exogamous) marriage.

In this tale, Jacob's daughter Dinah is with her family in the area of Shechem and, quite naturally, socializes with her female cohort, other local women: "daughters of the region" (Gen 34:1; NRSV, "women of the region"). The phrase "daughters of the region" probably refers to other "daughters" like Dinah, that is, unmarried females living in their parents' household (compare Judg 11:40). While Dinah is visiting with her peers in the Shechem area, the son of Hamor, a Shechemite leader, sees her, has sex with her, falls in love with her, and wants to marry her. Would this be considered desired endogamy or problematic exogamy? Hamor opts for the former: he repeatedly speaks of the "daughters" of his group (vv. 9, 21) as being legitimate spouses for "daughters" of the Jacob group. Such marriages

would do what in-group marriages should do — enhance kin prosperity and secure property (vv. 10, 21, 23). Dinah's brothers, negotiators for their father, apparently agree to consider the union endogamous; but they insist on the circumcision of all Shechemites, a physical sign of common identity (vv. 13–17).

The brothers, however, are duplicitous in their negotiations. Apparently they cannot accept the Shechemites as kin. They attack the Shechemites (who are recovering from painful adult circumcision), killing all the males and taking their wealth, their women (v. 29; NRSV, "wives"), and their children as booty. This slaughter, explained as being precipitated by improper sexual advances toward Dinah, is an example of the ideological culture of warfare, in which destruction is justified as a carrying out of God's punishment. Usually, in the biblical treatment of such annihilation of conquered cities, the sparing of women, children, and property is depicted only for towns not within Israel's allotted territory. That the women (and property and children) are spared here perhaps is related to the fact that Shechem ultimately does become Israelite. Some Shechemites can remain alive to constitute the core of what eventually will be an Israelite city.

CAROL MEYERS

SEE ALSO Part I: Dinah; Part II: Daughters of the Inhabitants of the Land as Marriage Partners (Exod 34:16, etc.); Women in Distant Towns as Booty (Deut 20:14, etc.); Companions of Jephthah's Daughter (Judg 11:37–38).
FOR FURTHER READING: Bechtel, Lyn M. "What If Dinah Is Not Raped? (Genesis 34)."

GEN 35:17; 38:28
Midwife

When the matriarch Rachel is giving birth to her second son (Benjamin), she is attended by a midwife (Gen 35:17). The presence of such a health care professional, called *měyalledet* ("one who causes, helps birth"), was probably routine in Israelite and pre-Israelite society, and the explicit reference to her in this case is not necessarily related to the difficulty of Rachel's labor.

Similarly, the presence of a midwife at the birth of Tamar's twin sons seems routine (Gen 38:28). But the role of the midwife in this narrative is hardly routine. She witnesses and verifies the strange reversal of the birth sequence whereby Perez precedes Zerah, although the latter's hand had appeared first and had been marked with a crimson thread. Further, the midwife apparently suggests appropriate names for the newborns, usurping a role usually played by one of the parents, often the mother. The remarkable reversal gives priority and recognition to Perez ("breach"), who becomes an ancestor of King David.

Midwifery is among the earliest and most ubiquitous specialized functions in human society. It virtually always is a woman's profession: it involves women assisting other women in a natural biological process. As a profession, it involves the instincts and emotions of the practitioners as well as technical knowledge and clinical skill. The care of a midwife tends to be holistic, providing emotional as well as physical support and assistance, as the case of Rachel indicates. In her duress, Rachel evidently exhibits fear, and the midwife consoles her.

The existence of texts with rules and procedures for obstetrics in second-millennium B.C.E. Egypt, where midwives (and birth deities) were female, indicates that bodies of knowledge about obstetrical practice were collected and transmitted, whether in written or oral form. Very little direct knowledge about Israel's health care system is available, but biblical clues and comparative research indicate the existence of a developed system with several consultative options. The midwife was the only one of those options outside priestly or prophetic circles. The professional aspects of midwifery meant that midwives had to train their successors. Informal associations of midwives helped maintain and add to the knowledge of delivery techniques, medications given to women in labor, and also prayers to be uttered at childbirth (Isa 46:16–18). Midwives in ancient Israel thus represent one of several female professions — others were wise women, musicians, and mourners — that afforded women the oppor-

tunity to meet with one another, instruct novices, and garner respect for their skills from the community. The status of midwives — and their power to transform childbirth from what might be a negative experience to a positive one — did not erode until the advent of modern, male-dominated medicine.

CAROL MEYERS

SEE ALSO Part I: Puah; Shiphrah; Part II: Woman in Labor (Isa 13:8, etc.); Women of the Neighborhood (Ruth 4:17)

FOR FURTHER READING: Meyers, Carol. "Guilds and Gatherings: Women's Groups in Ancient Israel."

Towler, Jean, and Joan Bramall. *Midwives in History and Society.*

GEN 36:6
Daughters (and Sons) of Esau

Most of the second half of the Book of Genesis presents the story of Jacob and his sons as the ancestors of all Israel. Yet the right of Jacob and his descendants to possess the land was apparently contested by closely related groups of people represented by Jacob's brother Esau, the ancestor of the Edomites. Genesis 36 focuses entirely on Esau and his descendants. In so doing, it mentions his daughters as well as his sons, wives, and other household members (v. 6). The sons and wives have names elsewhere in the chapter, but not so the daughters. Perhaps they are included in the description of Esau's household to parallel the presence of daughters in Jacob's family.

CAROL MEYERS

SEE ALSO Part I: Adah 2; Basemath 1/Bashemath; Oholibamah; Part II: Daughters (and Sons) of Jacob (Gen 37:35).

GEN 37:35
Daughters (and Sons) of Jacob

Although the Genesis narratives provide the name of only one daughter, Dinah, Gen 37:35 indicates that the ancestor Jacob had more daughters in addition to his twelve or more sons (see Gen 46:15). All these children attempt to console him when he receives news suggesting that his preferred son, Joseph, is dead. The inclusion of daughters as well as sons in this glimpse of family sorrow preserves the notion of mourning as an occasion affecting all family members. At the same time, it may reflect the special role of women in funeral customs.

CAROL MEYERS

SEE ALSO Part II: Weeping Daughters (2 Sam 1:24); Mourning Women (Jer 9:17–22, etc.).

GEN 38:2–5   Wife of Judah
SEE Bath-shua 1 (Part I).

GEN 38:11   Tamar as a Widow
SEE EXOD 22:22, etc.   Widows (Part II).

GEN 38:12   Wife of Judah
SEE Bath-shua 1 (Part I).

GEN 38:15   Prostitute
SEE LEV 19:29, etc.   Prostitute (Part II).

GEN 38:21   Temple Prostitute
SEE DEUT 23:17–18, etc.   Temple Prostitute (Part II).

GEN 38:22   Prostitute
SEE LEV 19:29, etc.   Prostitute (Part II).

GEN 38:28   Midwife
SEE GEN 35:17, etc.   Midwife (Part II).

GENESIS 39
Wife of Potiphar

The attempted seduction by Potiphar's wife of her husband's Hebrew slave Joseph presents a theme common in narratives from the ancient eastern Mediterranean world: a powerful woman attempts to seduce a virile young male. Joseph's response highlights his ethical behavior and devotion to his deity. An Egyptian parallel appears in the first part of the XIX dynasty "Tale of Two Brothers," and other ancient Near Eastern parallels may be found in the Canaanite tale of Aqhat and in Ishtar's attempt to marry Gilgamesh. Although the narrative threads of these tales are similar, once placed in context, each carries its own set of meanings (the Egyptian is patently multivalent).

Discussions of the Potiphar's wife episode generally revolve around the foreign woman and her evil actions, but in fact, she is pivotal — as the story is transmitted — to the survival of the Hebrews in a time of famine. As a result of her (mis)actions, Joseph demonstrates his loyalty to his god and the moral precepts of behavior inherent within those beliefs. Her behavior ultimately brings him to the notice of Pharaoh and a position of high authority through which he organizes food supplies in Egypt, the bread basket of the ancient world (compare Gen 12:10). Despite her attempt at seduction, this woman fills a positive narrative role; she initiates the story line that will bring the Hebrews to Egypt, thus setting the stage for the exodus — perhaps the most important event related in the Hebrew Bible.

SUSAN TOWER HOLLIS

FOR FURTHER READING: Hollis, Susan Tower. *The Ancient Egyptian "Tale of Two Brothers": The Oldest Fairy Tale in the World.*

———. "The Woman in Ancient Examples of the Potiphar's Wife Motif, K2111."

GEN 46:7, 15
Daughters and Granddaughters of Jacob

When Jacob leaves the land of Canaan to be reunited with his son Joseph, he takes his entire family with him, including his unnamed daughters and his unnamed granddaughters.

The mention of his female descendants anticipates the growth of the Israelites in Egypt (Exod 1:7) as well as the role of daughters in the continuation of the prenational Israelite story at the beginning of Exodus.

NAOMI STEINBERG

SEE ALSO Part II: Hebrew Female Babies in Egypt (Exod 1:16, etc.); Hebrew Women in Egypt (Exod 1:19, etc.).

GEN 46:10
Canaanite Mother of Shaul

The list of individuals who traveled to Egypt with Jacob is arranged according to the wives of Jacob. In the portion of the list of Leah's sons, there is mention of a Canaanite woman who bore a son named Shaul to Simeon. The same information is repeated in Exod 6:15. The lowly status of the tribe of Simeon, later to be absorbed into Judah, may reflect the fact that Simeon married a woman from outside the patrilineage descended from Terah.

NAOMI STEINBERG

GEN 46:15   Daughters of Jacob
SEE GEN 46:7, etc. Daughters and Grand-daughters of Jacob (Part II).

EXOD 1:16, 22
Hebrew Female Babies in Egypt

Apparently concerned with the burgeoning population of Hebrews in Egypt, Pharaoh issues an edict calling on the Hebrew midwives to kill male newborns but to let female infants live. This directive hardly makes sense historically: why would a king intent on using Hebrew laborers want to cut off his supply? On a literary level, however, it serves several purposes. It echoes the theme of males representing death and females representing life that is presented in the tale of Abraham and Sarah in Egypt (Gen 12:12 has Abraham say that the Egyptians will kill him but let Sarah live), thus providing continuity between the ancestral narratives of Genesis and the

deliverance tale in Exodus. The death of Hebrew male children also foreshadows the death of all Egyptian firstborns (Exod 11:5).

In addition, this directive positions the midwives as heroic figures who defy the king's edict; those who assist in bringing living beings into the world intensify that role by allowing the condemned male infants to live (Exod 2:17–18). Furthermore, God rewards the brave midwives with "houses" (probably large families), a word that in Hebrew is a pun on the word for "girl" (Hebrew "daughter") in Exod 1:16 and 22. The midwives are the first two in a series of twelve women who figure prominently in Exodus 1–2, allowing the twelve sons (that is, the twelve tribes) to survive.

CAROL MEYERS

SEE ALSO Part I: Puah; Shiphrah; Part II: Seven Daughters of the Priest of Midian (Exod 2:16–20).

FOR FURTHER READING: Siebert-Hommes, Jopie. "But If She Be a Daughter . . . She May Live! 'Daughters' and 'Sons' in Exodus 1–2."

EXOD 1:19; 2:7
Hebrew Women in Egypt

Two references to women at the beginning of the story of the exodus focus on aspects of childbirth and lactation. Women are prominent in this narrative — as givers of life. They perhaps prefigure the "birth" of Israel in the story that follows.

In his attempt to curb the growth of the Hebrew population, Pharaoh commands the midwives to kill at birth every boy, but to let the girls live. When the midwives are called to account for their failure to carry out the royal edict, they explain that the Hebrew women are "vigorous" (from the word ḥāyôt; Exod 1:19). This term is related to the word for "animal" and may suggest that Hebrew women gave birth with ease.

Regardless of the precise meaning of the adjective or noun in question, virtually all interpreters agree that the midwives' claim that Hebrew women typically give birth before the arrival of the midwife is a means to avoid infanticide out of obedience to God and also to avoid incurring Pharoah's wrath by putting the blame on the Hebrew women. In both cases, the women outsmart the authorities and contribute to the survival of their people.

The biological functions of the Hebrew women come to the fore again in the next sequence. Exod 2:4–8 reports that when Pharaoh's daughter discovers the infant Moses in a basket along the riverbank and identifies him as a Hebrew child, the baby's older sister offers to find a wet nurse from among the Hebrew women. The wet nurse provided by the cunning sister is none other than Moses' natural mother, who succeeds by this ruse not only in saving the life of the eventual liberator of the Hebrews, but also in getting the foolish Egyptian princess to pay Moses' mother, Jochebed, a wet nurse's wages. Again, women, representing all Hebrews held in servitude in Egypt, take part in a scheme to subvert authority and outwit the Pharaonic establishment, thus ensuring the survival and health of their future leader.

It is taken for granted by all the characters in the narrative of Exod 2:6–9 that, even when enslaved, the Hebrew women in Egypt continued to employ wet nurses. This rare use of wet nurses is a possible explanation for the unusual growth of the Israelite population, the supposed threat to Egyptian security that prompted Pharaoh to enslave the Hebrews (Exod 1:7–11). Natural nursing on demand, without supplemental food or liquid and without the use of a pacifier, leads to suspension of ovulation for as long as ten or even fifteen months. This lactational ovulation can be more effective than all other forms of birth control in reducing population growth. On the other hand, women who hand over their infants to wet nurses may become pregnant as early as six weeks after delivery, thus giving birth to up to five times the number of children they would bear if they were nursing their offspring themselves.

MAYER I. GRUBER

SEE ALSO Part I: Deborah 1; Jochebed; Miriam 1; Puah; Shiphrah; Part II: Midwife (Gen 35:17, etc.); Hebrew Female Babies in Egypt (Exod 1:16, etc.).

FOR FURTHER READING: Exum, J. Cheryl. "Second Thoughts about Secondary Characters: Women in Exodus 1:8–2:10."

———. "'You Shall Let Every Daughter Live': A Study of Exodus 1.8–2.10."

Gruber, Mayer I. "Breast-Feeding Practices in Biblical Israel and in Old Babylonian Mesopotamia."

EXOD 1:22
Hebrew Female Babies in Egypt

SEE EXOD 1:16, etc. Hebrew Female Babies in Egypt (Part II).

EXOD 2:5
Attendants of the Daughter of Pharaoh

When the daughter of Pharaoh bathes in the Nile and finds a basket containing the infant Moses, she is accompanied by female "attendants," who walk along the river. The Hebrew word for these attendants is nĕ'ārôt, which can mean "young women" in general as well as "maidservants" or "attendants," especially those of royalty (as the maids of King David's wife Abigail and of Queen Esther). The women with Pharaoh's daughter are surely her servants; one of them — her "maid" (Hebrew 'āmâ) — is sent to fetch the basket in which Moses has been hidden.

CAROL MEYERS

SEE ALSO Part II: Maids of Rebekah (Gen 24:61); Maids of Abigail (1 Sam 25:42); Maids of Esther (Esth 2:9, etc.).

EXOD 2:5–10
Daughter of Pharaoh

Moved by compassion, Pharaoh's daughter takes an infant, whom she recognizes as a Hebrew baby, out of the Nile, defying her father's command to throw male babies into the river. She readily embraces the idea of engaging a Hebrew nurse and keeping the child as her own. Sometime after the weaning (usually about three years after birth), "she took him as her son" (v. 10), perhaps a reference to some form of adoption. The unnamed princess gives her son an Egyptian name that she explains in relation to a Hebrew word, *māšâ*, meaning "to draw out." The name Moses thus both recalls the princess's deed and anticipates Moses' future as the one who draws Israel out of bondage.

J. CHERYL EXUM

SEE ALSO Part II: Daughter of Pharaoh (1 Kgs 3:1, etc.).

FOR FURTHER READING: Ackerman, James S. "The Literary Context of the Moses Birth Story (Exodus 1–2)."

Exum, J. Cheryl. *Plotted, Shot, and Painted: Cultural Representations of Biblical Women.*

EXOD 2:7 Hebrew Women in Egypt
SEE EXOD 1:19, etc. Hebrew Women in Egypt (Part II).

EXOD 2:16–20
Seven Daughters of the Priest of Midian

After killing an Egyptian official, Moses flees to the land of Midian, the desert territory, inhabited by nomads, that lay south and east of the land of Canaan. Resting there at a well, he meets seven daughters of a Midianite priest and helps them by warding off some shepherds who were interfering with their task of watering their father's flocks. The daughters are instructed to bring Moses home for a meal, and one of them — Zipporah — marries Moses.

The motif of women at a well, known also from the story of Rebekah (Gen 24:11, 13) and from an incident in one of the narratives about Saul (1 Sam 9:11), is probably drawn from the fact that, in the division of labor by gender in ancient Semitic societies, unmarried daughters were responsible for

fetching water. Here the well scene introduces seven women; together with the two midwives of Exodus 1, Pharaoh's daughter of Exodus 2, Jochebed (Moses' mother), and Miriam (Moses' sister), they constitute twelve women who figure prominently in the opening chapters of Exodus. Moses is the major figure of the Exodus story, but he would not have been able to carry out his role without those twelve women. As a group, they save Moses, who in turn saves the twelve tribes. Furthermore, as members of a priestly family, the Midianite daughters contribute to Moses' pedigree of sanctity (his mother Jochebed is from the priestly tribe of Levi) when he marries one of them.

CAROL MEYERS

SEE ALSO Part I: Jochebed; Zipporah; Part II: Maidens Going Out to Draw Water (1 Sam 9:11).

FOR FURTHER READING: Siebert-Hommes, Jopie. "But If She Be a Daughter . . . She May Live! 'Daughters' and 'Sons' in Exodus 1–2."

EXOD 3:22
Daughters (and Sons) of Israelites in Egypt

The Israelite women and men in Egypt are told to procure jewelry and clothing from their Egyptian neighbors in anticipation of the exodus, their departure from servitude. The valuables are not to be transported in packages or bundles, but rather to be worn by the daughters and sons of the Israelites (Exod 3:22) in keeping with the custom of transient people to carry valuables on their persons. Just as both women and men collect the items that will ultimately provide the materials for building the wilderness tabernacle (so Exod 11:2), both female and male children participate in preserving those items until the journey out of Egypt is complete and the time for constructing a cultic center has arrived.

CAROL MEYERS

SEE ALSO Part II: Women (and Men) with Jewelry and
    Clothing (Exod 3:22, etc.); Skilled Women (and Men)
    (Exod 35:25–26, etc.).

EXOD 3:22; 11:2; 32:2–3; 35:22–24, 29;
36:2–7

Women (and Men) with Jewelry and Clothing

Before the Israelites depart from Egypt, they are
said to have become well regarded by the Egyptians
(Exod 3:21). The Egyptians then respond favorably
to the request of Israelite women (3:22) for silver
and gold jewelry and also clothing. A reiteration of
this incident (11:3) includes men in the act of asking
for precious items: men approach Egyptian men,
and women go to Egyptian women.

*Gold pendant in the shape of a flying hawk, part of a
large collection of jewelry discovered at Tell el-Ajjul,
near Gaza on the Mediterranean coast. Dating to the
Late Bronze Age (1550–1200 B.C.E.), this hoard of lo-
cally produced items shows the influence of Egyptian
art in both workmanship and motifs. See Women
(and Men) with Jewelry and Clothing (Exod 3:22,
etc.).*

The Israelites thus leave Egypt with great wealth,
thereby fulfilling the divine promise of Gen 15:13–14
that Abraham's descendants would be oppressed
in a foreign land for a long time but would ultimately leave their bondage "with great possessions
(v. 14)." At the same time, this incident anticipates
the Deuteronomic law stipulating that emancipated
servants not go out empty-handed (Deut 15:13).
Aside from the way it connects both with the ancestor narratives that precede the Exodus account and
with the Pentateuchal law that follows, the incident indicates something about gender bonding.
Women and men apparently have gender-specific
informal networks with their "neighbors" that allow them to request valuable items.

The ultimate use of these items is specified in the
texts that describe the tabernacle to be constructed
in the wilderness. After Moses tells the people of
God's intentions for an elaborate portable sanctuary, he enlists skilled artisans to do the work. Yet he
does not need to solicit building funds or materials.
Both women and men donate jewelry, precious
metals, fabrics, and skins as a "freewill offering" to
YHWH (Exod 35:22–24, 29; 36:2–7) in great quanti-
ties, more than enough to construct the tabernacle
with all its appurtenances. The establishment of
Israel's first national cultic center is thus attributed
equally to the generosity of women and men.

CAROL MEYERS

SEE ALSO Part II: Daughters (and Sons) of Israelites in
    Egypt (Exod 3:22); Egyptian Women (Exod 3:22, etc.);
    Skilled Women (and Men) (Exod 35:25–26, etc.).
FOR FURTHER READING: Meyers, Carol. "'Women of
    the Neighborhood' (Ruth 4.17) — Informal Female
    Networks in Ancient Israel."

EXOD 3:22; 11:2

Egyptian Women

Before the Israelites depart from Egypt, God informs them that the Egyptians will hold them in
high regard and thus will respond favorably to their
request for valuables when they are about to leave.

That request is to be made by women, who are to ask for items of precious metal and of clothing from their female Egyptian neighbors as well as from any other women living in the neighbors' households (Exod 3:22). God's instructions for this solicitation of valuables appear again, with the addition of men requesting objects from their male Egyptian neighbors (Exod 11:2).

The description of obtaining possessions, so as not to leave Egypt empty-handed (see Deut 15:13), provides information about women's roles. First, it implies gender-specific interactions between the Israelites and their neighbors; women approach Egyptian women, and men go to Egyptian men. Second, the feminine noun for the neighboring women, used only here and in Ruth (4:17), indicates a close relationship, perhaps a neighborhood network, of women living near one another. Third, the concept of women approaching neighboring women and also any other women in their households implies that the households have a senior female. All of these features are perhaps projections of women's roles in Israelite households rather than depictions of Egyptian peasant life.

CAROL MEYERS

SEE ALSO Part II: Daughters (and Sons) of Israelites in Egypt (Exod 3:22); Women (and Men) with Jewelry and Clothing (Exod 3:22, etc.); Women of the Neighborhood (Ruth 4:17).

EXOD 6:15
Canaanite Mother of Shaul

> SEE GEN 46:10, etc. Canaanite Mother of Shaul (Part II).

EXOD 6:25
Daughter of Putiel

Within a complex genealogical series lies the information that one of the daughters of Putiel, a man with a composite Egyptian-Hebrew name ("the one given," from Egyptian *pa di*, and "of God," from Hebrew *'ēl*) marries into the Aaronide family. This

liaison may represent a common occurrence: the marriage between two members of geographically proximate peoples. No apparent stigma appears attached to this act, since her son's name is Phinehas, an Egyptian name meaning "the Nubian." Whether Putiel's daughter participates in a diplomatic alliance is unclear, but it is unlikely, given that there is no evidence that she is a daughter of the pharaoh.

The appearance of this woman, perhaps unnamed because she was a foreigner, along with several named women (Elisheba, Jochebed) is unusual in this tribe-by-tribe genealogy (6:14–25). Female ancestors are noted only for the tribe of Levi. This genealogy focuses on Levi, and including women may have added to the aristocratic claims for the priestly line, just as queen mothers are frequently noted for Judean kings (see 1 Kgs 15:2; 22:42).

SUSAN TOWER HOLLIS

FOR FURTHER READING: Hostetter, Edwin C. "Puti-el."

EXOD 11:2
Women with Jewelry and Clothing

> SEE EXOD 3:22, etc. Women (and Men) with Jewelry and Clothing (Part II).

EXOD 11:2   Egyptian Women

> SEE EXOD 3:22, etc. Egyptian Women (Part II).

EXOD 11:5   Female Slaves in Egypt

> SEE GEN 12:16, etc. Female (and Male) Slaves (Part II).

EXOD 15:20; 1 SAM 18:6–7; 2 SAM 1:20; PS 68:25; JER 31:4, 13
Women with Hand-Drums, Dancing

After the Israelites escape from Egypt and from the Pharaoh's army at the Sea of Reeds (NRSV, "Red Sea"), the prophet Miriam leads a celebration. Accompanied by "all the women," who are dancing and playing hand-drums (Exod 15:20–21), she sings of YHWH's victory. Most English translations, including the NRSV, use the word *tambourines* in this passage. That word, however, is anachronistic, for there is no evidence that tambourines were invented until the Roman period at the earliest, and perhaps not for several centuries later. The Hebrew word *tōf* represents a hand-held frame-drum, a hoop-shaped drum with a diameter wider than its depth and well known as a popular membranophone (percussion instrument) from artistic representations preserved from the ancient Near East.

The scene of Miriam with her chorus of women drummers and dancers is echoed in several other instances in which song, dance, and drums appear in connection with women musicians. After a victory over the Philistines, David is welcomed by women singing, dancing, and playing frame-drums (1 Sam 18:6–7). Two other passages probably present, elliptically, a similar situation: Deborah sings out after YHWH brings victory for the Israelites over the Canaanites in Galilee (Judg 5:1), and Jephthah's daughter welcomes her father with dancing and drumming after his God-granted defeat of the Ammonites (Judg 11:34). The elements of drum, dance, and song constitute a women's performance genre: the musical celebration of military victory. Another elliptical passage, 2 Sam 1:20, claims that Philistine women would perform a victory song if they heard the news that Saul and Jonathan had died. The celebratory nature of the genre is extended, in prophetic eschatology, to the rejoicing that accompanies God's restoration of Israel (Jer 31:4, 13).

The 2 Sam 1:20 passage, which refers to Philistines, suggests that this performance genre was part of the general culture of the eastern Mediterranean in biblical times. Archaeological evidence supports that possibility. Egyptian wall paintings, scenes on metal and ivory vessels from Cyprus and Phoenicia as well as Mesopotamia, and most notably small terra-cotta figurines from many Near Eastern sites all depict musicians playing a significant repertoire of musical instruments. Musicologists have assigned them to various categories: wind instruments, stringed instruments, instruments that are self-striking (such as cymbals), and percussion instruments. In virtually every instance, the frame-drum players are female. This evidence, along with cross-cultural materials as well as a reference to the Canaanite goddess Anath with a hand-drum, suggests that the playing of these percussion instruments was a specifically female role in the ancient Mediterranean world.

The identification of the frame-drum as a woman's instrument has implications for the understanding of several biblical texts mentioning musical performance. The Bible mentions dozens of musical instruments of the various types; but only one percussion instrument is named — the *tof*, or hand-drum — even though other kinds of drum were known elsewhere in the biblical world. Whenever this word is found, it is quite likely that the presence of female instrumentalists is implied. This is particularly true in a series of psalms that depict cultic processions and celebrations in praise of YHWH. In Ps 68:25, a procession into the temple involves singers, female hand-drummers, and other musicians. The word for drum players is unambiguously feminine. The words for the singers and musicians are masculine, but they may include females and males, given the nature of Hebrew as a gendered language with masculine nouns often used for both genders. The references to musical ensembles in several other psalms (Pss 81:2; 149:3; 150:4) can be interpreted, because they include the hand-drum, as including female instrumentalists in cultic musical performance.

Clearly the frequent claim that women did not take part in public religious occasions in ancient Israel needs to be contested in light of readings that take extrabiblical artifactual evidence into account. In addition, recognizing the existence of women's performance traditions allows us to acknowledge that women had the benefit of participating together in professional associations. Gathering to rehearse, compose, and perform provided women with the opportunity to experience leadership and camaraderie, as well as the esteem of their colleagues and also of their audiences. Such experience is empowering.

CAROL MEYERS

SEE ALSO Part I: Miriam 1; Naamah 1; Part II: Daughter of Jephthah (Judg 11:34–40); Singing Women (and Men) (2 Sam 19:35, etc.); Singing Women (and Men) Who Lament (2 Chr 35:25); Female (and Male) Singers Returning to Judah (Ezra 2:65, etc.); Mourning Women (Jer 9: 17–20, etc.).

FOR FURTHER READING: Goitein, S. D. "Women as Creators of Biblical Genres."

Meyers, Carol. "Of Drums and Damsels: Women's Performance in Ancient Israel."

Redmond, Layne. *When the Drummers Were Women.*

EXOD 19:15
Woman (Women) Not to Be Approached at Sinai

The Decalogue (Ten Commandments, Exod 20:1–17) and the covenant "code" (Exod 20:22–23:33) are framed by several narratives that depict how the Israelites received the covenant at Sinai. Most of these accounts are silent or ambiguous concerning the role of women at that event. Exod 19:15, however, reads, "And he [Moses] said to the people [*hā'ām*], 'Prepare for the third day; do not go near a woman.'" (The prohibition of "going near," namely having intercourse, with a woman, reflects a biblical notion that sexual intercourse causes ritual impurity [compare, for example, Lev 15:18; 1 Sam 21:5–6] and is thus incompatible with God's theophany.) This verse thus suggests quite clearly that, at least according to one biblical author, women were not considered part of the people *(hā'ām)* who were present at Sinai.

MARC ZVI BRETTLER

SEE ALSO Part II: Women in the Decalogue (Exod 20:8, etc.); Women and Bodily Emissions (Lev 15:18–33, etc.); Women Kept Away from David's Men (1 Sam 21:4–5).

EXOD 20:8, 10, 12, 17; DEUT 5:14, 16, 18; LEV 19:3
Women in the Decalogue

Although the origin of the Decalogue (the Ten Commandments), its original form, and development continue to be debated within biblical scholarship, the texts of Exodus and Deuteronomy present the Decalogue as the only section of biblical law recited by YHWH directly to the people (*hā'ām*), rather than mediated by Moses. This gives it a unique, prestigious status within the Hebrew Bible. The citation of parts of the Decalogue in other places in the Hebrew Bible (for example, Jer 7:9) suggests that already in the biblical period it had attained a special role. These factors make the question of the inclusion or exclusion of women in the Decalogue even more pressing than their presence or absence in other sections of biblical law.

The positive and negative commandments of the Decalogue are all addressed in the masculine singular. However, Hebrew has no neuter, and the masculine singular *may* be used when a man or woman is the intended addressee, so little may be learned from the form of the verbs. Other evidence is ambiguous. The commandment to honor one's parents (v. 12; Deut 5:16) explicitly includes both parents: "Honor your father and your mother." The father is listed first, as is typical of cases in which both parents are listed; it is unclear if this is simply a stylistic feature of Hebrew or if it reflects upon the relative status of the parents. In any case, Lev 19:3, which seems to be a quotation of the Decalogue, reads: "You shall each revere your mother and father." *Mother* appears before *father;* this might reflect a balancing of the Decalogue's order or perhaps ancient Hebrew stylistics, whereby a quotation frequently cites its source in chiastic (ABBA) order. It is significant, however, that here too both parents are included. Perhaps, because Hebrew lacks a generic term for "parent," *mother* and *father* must always appear together to indicate what in English is conveyed by *parent.*

The final commandment is not inclusive (v. 17; Deut 5:21): "You shall not covet your neighbor's house; you shall not covet your neighbor's wife . . ."

No parallel law prohibiting a woman from coveting her neighbor's husband is found in the Decalogue. Perhaps this commandment suggests that the Decalogue was addressed primarily to men. Alternatively, the focus of the commandment might be the possessions of the head of the household, almost always a male. In this case, it is important to recall that in certain aspects the husband was the *ba'al,* or "lord" of his wife, having exclusive right to her sexuality. This would explain the one-sided nature of the commandment.

The Sabbath commandment is even more complicated. The list of those prohibited from working consists of "you, your son or your daughter, your male or female slave, your livestock, or the alien resident in your towns" (v. 10; Deut 5:14). Given the pairing of son and daughter, the lack of "you and your wife" is especially noteworthy. It is possible that women are not being explicitly addressed here, as in the final commandment, though it is equally possible that "you" (*'attâ;* masculine singular) could also be used as a neuter, thereby including the adult woman.

MARC ZVI BRETTLER

SEE ALSO Part II: Woman (Women) Not to Be Approached at Sinai (Exod 19:15); Adulteress (and Adulterer) (Lev 20:10, etc.).

Exod 21:3–5
Wife of a Hebrew Slave

In describing what belongs to the slave and what belongs to his master, the slave law in the covenant "code" (Exod 20:22–23:33) distinguishes between a wife who entered servitude with the male slave, who belongs to the slave (Exod 21:3b), and a wife who is given by the master and who bears children — this wife, with her children, belongs to the master (v. 4). In both cases, in matters of sexuality and the offspring that result, the wife is viewed as property. Significantly, the parallel law in Deut 15:12–18 omits the particular laws concerning the male slave's wife; this may reflect a more liberalized attitude toward women.

MARC ZVI BRETTLER

SEE ALSO Part II: Daughters (and Sons) of a Hebrew Slave (Exod 21:4–5); Female (and Male) Hebrew Slaves (Exod 21:7–11, etc.).

Exod 21:4–5
Daughters (and Sons) of a Hebrew Slave

The laws in Exodus 21 dealing with the manumission of temporary, or debt, slaves in ancient Israel mandate the release of an indentured Hebrew male after six years of servitude. If he is single or married at the time he begins his service, he is to be released with the same marital status. However, if his master gives him a wife, that woman is to remain with the master when her husband is freed. Likewise, any daughters and sons produced by the marriage during bondage are to remain with the master when their father is released (v. 4). The only way for such a family to remain intact would be for the husband to relinquish his right to freeman status; he can choose freedom, but the offspring and spouse acquired during bondage cannot (v. 5).

It is difficult to know the reason for the permanent servitude of the children of a male debt slave. As a single man or a man with a spouse but no children, he probably was not himself a household head at the time his servitude began, but rather became a debt slave as the dependent of his father. He therefore may have lacked the possibility for financial solvency as a free man, and his offspring would thus be better cared for in the master's household. It also may be that the master, as possessor of their mother, possessed the daughters and sons too. The law does not mention what would happen to children of a wife who entered servitude with her husband. Presumably, because she would be released with him, so would their daughters and sons.

CAROL MEYERS

SEE ALSO Part II: Wife of a Hebrew Slave (Exod 21:3–5); Female (and Male) Hebrew Slaves (Exod 21:7–11, etc.) .

FOR FURTHER READING: Chirichigno, Gregory C. *Debt-Slavery in Israel and the Ancient Near East.*

Exod 21:7–11, 20, 26–27; Lev 19:20;
25:6, 44; Deut 5:14; 15:12–18; 1 Sam
8:16; Jer 34:8–16

Female (and Male) Hebrew Slaves

For the most part, biblical laws treat female and male slaves with parity. Bondswomen and bondsmen are to enjoy Sabbath rest (Exod 20:10; Deut 5:14) and must be included in religious feasts (Deut 12:12; 16:11, 14). Masters who injure or kill female or male debt-slaves (that is, those who could gain freedom after paying off debt through labor) are dealt with evenhandedly (Exod 21:20–21, 26–27).

The case of the enslaved daughter (Exod 21:7–11) is a notable exception to such evenhandedness. The preceding law, Exod 21:2–6, requires anyone who acquires a Hebrew bondsman to release him at the end of six years. Exod 21:7–11 explicitly excludes from the law of release a girl whose father is forced to sell her into slavery.

Some commentators argue that Exod 21:7 excludes all female slaves from release, but it is more likely that the drafters of the law intended to except only enslaved *daughters*. The provisions of the previous law make it clear that a *wife* followed her husband into servitude and was released with him. The *widow* or *abandoned wife*, not mentioned in the laws, is most likely implicitly included in the release mandated in v. 2.

Most recent commentators rightly explain the exclusion of the daughter in terms of the purpose for which she was acquired. The primary economic value of a daughter would have been her sexual and reproductive capacity. The subcases indicate that the master could have purchased her as a slave wife for himself or his son. Most likely, he could also acquire her for one of his slaves or in order to obtain her bride price. In a culture in which a free wife could not sever her husband's authority over her, it is not surprising that a slave wife could not choose to leave her master.

The law is not altogether indifferent to the enslaved daughter's welfare. If the master purchases the girl for himself, when she is old enough he must either take her as his concubine or allow her kinfolk to buy her back. He may not sell her to "outsiders" (that is, non-Israelites, or more probably, anyone outside the master's family). A master who acquires a slave girl for his son must accord her the "customary rights of daughters," probably the rights not to be physically abused or prostituted. Once the master uses the girl as his concubine, he is to continue to maintain her even if he takes another wife or concubine. (The Hebrew term that the NRSV translates as "another wife" in v. 10 simply means "another.") The master must provide three things for the girl: food, clothing, and a third item whose meaning is uncertain. It has been traditionally translated as "marital rights," but recent studies suggest it may mean "oil." In any case, he must provide for her needs (as also indicated by Lev 25:6) or let her go free.

The law, then, views a daughter sold into concubinage as more than mere chattel. She has some rights. Her status is not that of a free wife, however. She is "bought," not "taken in marriage"; she is "set free" or "redeemed," not divorced. Her purchaser is called master (*'adōn*), not husband (*ba'al*), and unlike the bondsman, who may choose whether to go free or opt for the security of remaining, the slave wife is given no choice.

A later version of the law of the Hebrew slave, Deut 15:12–18, pointedly includes the Hebrew bondswoman in the seventh-year release and altogether omits the law excluding daughters from release. These differences have to do with the treatment of enslaved daughters and should not be overgeneralized.

Wives would continue to be expected to follow their husbands in and out of bondage (compare Lev 25:39–44, a later slave law). Widows and other women not under male authority who become enslaved are likely implicitly included in the release of Exod 21:2, as they are explicitly included in the Deuteronomic text. It is possible that the Deuteronomic version of the law does not allow for the sale of daughters as slave wives, either to protect them or because the drafters resisted the very notion that a woman could be at the same time a man's wife and his slave. It is also possible that the Deuteronomic law simply presupposes that enslaved daughters are excluded from release.

The relationship of the slave laws to actual legal practice is debated. Certainly fathers (and mothers) could and did find it economically necessary to sell their sons or daughters into servitude (2 Kgs 4:1; Neh 5:5; see also 1 Sam 8:16). A master (or mistress) could give a slave girl to a son, a slave, or some other man as a concubine (see Lev 19:20). Whether the release mandated by Exod 21:2 was regularly practiced is uncertain. Jer 34:8–16, which reports a proclamation of liberty, setting free female and male slaves, suggests that the release of slaves was observed sporadically, if at all. It is also unknown whether the subcases protecting the slave wife were enforced. In practice, the welfare of a slave wife or any slave was probably dependent upon the master's goodwill.

CAROLYN PRESSLER

SEE ALSO Part II: Wife of a Hebrew Slave (Exod 21:3–5); Female (and Male) Servants Returning to Judah (Ezra 2:64–65, etc.); Daughters (and Sons) and Wives in Rebuilt Jerusalem (Neh 4:14, etc.); Mistress (Ps 123:2).

FOR FURTHER READING: Bird, Phyllis A. "Translating Sexist Language as a Theological and Cultural Problem."

Chirichigno, Gregory C. *Debt-Slavery in Israel and the Ancient Near East.*

Pressler, Carolyn. "Wives and Daughters, Bond and Free: Women in the Slave Laws of Ex 21:2–11."

Turnbam, Timothy John. "Male and Female Slaves in the Sabbath Year Laws of Exodus 21:2–11."

EXOD 21:15, 17; LEV 20:9
Mother (or Father) Cursed or Struck by Offspring

Anyone today reading the family laws of Exod 21:15, 17 and the similar stipulations of Lev 20:9 and Deut 27:16 is likely to be appalled at the severity of the regulations. The texts in Exodus and Leviticus invoke the death penalty for what seems to be the abuse of parents: striking or cursing one's mother or father. The Deuteronomy text curses those who do not honor their parents. These laws, however, are not based on the same family frame of reference that influences our contemporary response to these extremely grave punishments. The families in the agrarian communities of biblical Israel were likely to have been multigenerational, or extended, families, rather than the nuclear families (conjugal pair plus offspring) of today's industrial world.

The children referred to in these biblical laws are undoubtedly young or even middle-aged adults. Daughters remained in the parental household until they married, and sons remained there after marriage. The laws stipulate punishment for adult offspring who challenge parental authority. Despite romantic notions regarding the support and care that extended families provide for their members, multigenerational families are characteristically difficult to manage. As children become adults and take on increasingly more of the economic and other functions of family life, they understandably might question or challenge parental authority. The harshness of the punishment must be seen as an attempt to maintain the fundamental order and stability of the Israelite family, since disorder could jeopardize its functioning and hence the very survival of the household unit in the precarious environment of ancient Israel.

The stipulations regarding punishment for threats to parental authority are the negative counterparts of the Fifth Commandment, which calls for the honoring of one's parents. Indeed, the word for "curse" in Exod 21:17 and Lev 20:9 is the semantic opposite of the word for "honor" in the Decalogue (Exod 20:12; Deut 5:16). Furthermore, the consequence of obeying that commandment (survival) is the opposite of the consequence (death) of not obeying it according to the motive clause ("that your days may be long in the land that the LORD your God is giving you") attached to the Fifth Commandment (Exod 20:12; compare Deut 5:15).

Family authority, in its positive presentation in the Decalogue and also in its negative formulation in the legal materials, involves both parents. In other Near Eastern laws, the father alone appears in similar stipulations; Hammurabi no. 195, for example, penalizes a son for striking a father. (Hammurabi, d. 1750 B.C.E., was a Babylonian king.) The authority of the senior female in Israelite families, at least with respect to internal governance and jurisdiction, seems to be the same as that of the senior male, a situation that is optimal for family dynamics and management in the farming households in which most Israelites lived.

CAROL MEYERS

SEE ALSO Part II: Women in the Decalogue (Exod 20:8, etc.); Mother (and Father) Dealing with a Rebellious Son (Deut 21:18–21); Women in Covenant Curses (Deut 27:16, etc.).

FOR FURTHER READING: Perdue, Leo G., Joseph Blenkinsopp, John J. Collins, and Carol Meyers, *Families in Ancient Israel*.

ribution is mandated, including the death penalty, should she die (Exod 21:23–25).

The Hebrew phrase used here for miscarriage is, literally, "her children emerge," which is peculiar in being a plural form. It gives the impression, however, of a pregnancy in its later stages. Perhaps the proviso giving the judges leeway to determine the amount of restitution implies taking into account the age of the fetus, as Hittite laws do. Aside from the issue of what constitutes a human life, this case and especially the related one in Deut 25:11 provide examples of women using physical violence to protect their interests, whatever risk to themselves that might entail.

CAROL MEYERS

SEE ALSO Part II: Woman Who Mutilates a Man's Genitals (Deut 25:11–12).

EXOD 21:22–23
Woman Caused to Miscarry

Directly preceding the famous *lex talionis* (the law of retaliation — an eye for an eye, and so on) of the covenant code of Exodus is the strange case of a pregnant woman who happens to be injured in a physical fight between two men (21:22). The NRSV refers to "people" who are fighting, but the term for "fighting," or "striking," is used in the Hebrew Bible exclusively for men involved in fistfights (for example, Lev 24:10; 2 Sam 14:6; compare Isa 58:4). That sometimes women tried to intervene in such fights (as Deut 25:11), especially if their husbands were involved, would explain how the pregnant woman in this case suffered bodily injury leading to miscarriage.

The penalty imposed upon the woman's assailant is monetary restitution for the loss of the fetus, as in several other ancient Near Eastern law codes dealing with similar cases. The fact that capital punishment is not stipulated in the Bible suggests that the fetus lost in the incident was not considered a vital human, whose death would have required the death penalty according to the concept of "a life for a life." Indeed, if other harm befalls the woman, exact ret-

EXOD 22:16–17; DEUT 22:13–21, 23–29; 28:30
Virgin

"Virgin" is a misleading translation of the Hebrew word *bĕtûlâ*, which means a pubescent "young woman," often a woman of marriageable age. It can denote an engaged woman, as in Deut 22:23, but it can also be used for a married (Isa 62:5) or even widowed (Joel 1:8) woman. The word is the female counterpart to *bāḥûr*, "young man," with which it is often paired (as in Amos 8:13). Biological virginity is usually specified by the addition of phrases such as "who has not known a man" or "whom a man has not known"; Jephthah's daughter, for example, "had never known [NRSV, slept with] a man" (Judg 11:39).

The marriage laws in Exodus and Deuteronomy indicate the desirability of virgins as brides in ancient Israel. The reasons for such desirability are difficult to determine, but several possibilities can be considered. Most importantly, virgins may have been considered blank slates whose future identities would be determined by their sexual partner. Their "deflowering" stamped them as their husband's flesh. "Deflowering" may also have been prized because of the expected vaginal tightness of virgins. A commonly offered explanation for the prizing of virginity in brides is that husbands wanted to be assured of the paternity of their offspring. This may have played some part, but paternity could be assured by considering all children born in the first nine months of marriage to be members of the wife's family. The control of daughters that the desire for virgin brides demands may also have been part of the reason virginity was desired.

The stipulation in Exod 22:16–17 that a man who seduces a virgin will have to pay the "bride-price for virgins" as a fine if her father will not let her be married to her seducer indicates that the bride wealth for virgins was higher than that for nonvirgins. It also indicates that nonvirgins did in fact marry — at a reduced bride price. In fact, only a priest was *required* to marry a virgin (Lev 21:14). Nevertheless, girls were expected to remain chaste until marriage. And one of the horrors in the covenant curses at the end of the Book of Deuteronomy is that a man's fiancée would sleep with another man (28:30). The law in Exodus 22 probably helped make sure young women remained chaste, and it gave the father the right to decide whether he wanted to marry a seduced daughter to her lover. Such a normalized procedure helps rule out any violent solution to the seduction of virgins. It also indicates that a father's rights over his daughter's sexuality were apparently absolute.

Deuteronomic regulations dealing with virgins and premarital sex are more elaborate; and the father has less control. Betrothed girls were bound by adultery rules and were considered in their husband's domain even before marriage.

Chastity was still expected of daughters, and a bridegroom's accusation that his bride was not a virgin was taken seriously (Deut 22:13–21). The father could not himself punish the daughter, but he could determine if she was to be punished. The mother and the father (and not the accusing bridegroom) bring the marital sheets of an accused bride before the town elders. Presumably, if the father knew she was not a virgin, or if he sympathized with her plight, he might bloody the sheets. She

would then be acquitted, her husband would have to pay a fine to her father, and she could never be divorced. If he presented unbloodied sheets, she would be convicted and stoned at her father's doorway "because she committed a disgraceful act in Israel by being faithless to her father's household" (Deut 22:21).

The Deuteronomic regulations in Deut 22:23–28 deal with the case of a man having sex with a young woman (NRSV, "virgin") engaged to someone else. Even though she is not yet married, the woman is considered his wife, and the case is treated as if it were adultery. In such a case, the legislation distinguishes between consensual and nonconsensual sex. If the act of intercourse takes place in a town, where a woman could presumably have called for help if she did not want to have sex, she is assumed to be in complicity. Both she and her lover are stoned to death at the city gate (vv. 23–24). If the illicit intercourse takes place in the countryside, where presumably no help would be available to her, she is acquitted, but the offending man is put to death (vv. 25–27).

Finally, Deut 22:28–29 requires a father to marry a girl to her lover who is not her fiancé (and who even may have raped her). The man must also pay a fine of fifty shekels of silver to her father. Furthermore, a man who acquires a wife in this way could never divorce her, a stipulation that may have helped minimize frivolous seduction. Overall, this law meant that if a single, unbetrothed girl was taken sexually, she was stuck and had to marry the lover. On the other hand, it allowed for a girl to "elope" — she could have sex with someone that her parents may not have chosen for her, and the father had to marry her to that person.

TIKVA FRYMER-KENSKY

SEE ALSO Part II: Women Whom a Priest Can and Cannot Marry (Lev 21:7–8, etc.); Royal Daughters and Their Garments (2 Sam 13:8); Virgins/Young Women (Esth 2:2–3, etc.); Virgin (Job 31:1).

FOR FURTHER READING: Frymer-Kensky, Tikva. "Virginity in the Bible."

Exod 22:18; Isa 57:3
Female Sorcerer

Sorcery is one of nine kinds of magic and divination condemned in Deut 18:9–14 as abominable foreign practices, tantamount to idolatry. The alien origins of sorcery are indicated by its frequent association with non-Israelites: Egyptian sorcerers perform tricks to demonstrate their power (Exod 7:11); in Daniel (2:1–3) sorcery is associated with Babylonian dream interpretation; and in 2 Kings (9:22) the Phoenician princess Jezebel, married to Israel's king Ahab, introduces sorcerers to Israel. The catalogue of forbidden cultic professionals in Deuteronomy 18 uses the masculine form of the terms for those practitioners, as is the case elsewhere in the Hebrew Bible, although those terms may include females. (All Hebrew nouns are gendered, but some nouns are used inclusively.)

Only for one practitioner, the sorcerer, are female practioners specifically and separately mentioned. (But compare Lev 20:27, where men and women mediums and wizards are together mentioned, and also 1 Sam 28:7–25, which describes an individual woman who is a medium.) Apart from any consideration of other illegal cultic practices, Exod 22:18 states that female sorcerers must be given the death penalty. Why the female sorcerer is singled out by the Exodus text is difficult to determine except by considering the nature of sorcery itself.

In terms of the various "occult" arts of Near Eastern antiquity, sorcerers were probably magicians rather than diviners. Indirect comparative evidence suggests that sorcerers used their magic to function as "health care consultants," or folk healers, who could use various potions and herbal substances along with incantations to treat illness and exorcize evil spirits. The traditional role of women in food preparation may have made them more likely than men to acquire the expertise to become sorcerers. If most sorcerers were women, they undoubtedly had lively practices, for one of the most ubiquitous features of human life is the concern for maintaining or recovering health. Sorcerers were threats to the role of YHWH, the sole source of and cure for illness, according to the biblical perspective.

The repeated condemnation of various forms of magic and divination (for example, 1 Sam 28:3; 2 Kgs 21:6; 2 Chr 33:6; Jer 27:9), including sorcery, makes it clear that they were an established part of Israelite society and competed with the "true prophets" of YHWH, whom the Bible considers the only legitimate avenues of assisted communication with God. Isaiah 57:3 concerns female sorcerers along with adulterers because both represent infidelity.

CAROL MEYERS

SEE ALSO Part II: Medium/Wizard (Lev 20:27); Medium of Endor (1 Sam 28:7–25).

FOR FURTHER READING: Avalos, Hector. *Illness and Health Care in the Ancient Near East: The Role of the Temple in Greece, Mesopotamia, and Israel.*

Exod 22:22, 24; etc.
Widows

In biblical studies, widows have been under-studied. Even in the comprehensive six-volume *Anchor Bible Dictionary* (1992), there is no separate entry on widows, but only a few scattered references. Most studies of the widow in the Hebrew Bible consist mainly of commenting on texts in which the word for "widow" (*'almānâ*) occurs. There has been little attempt to create an overall picture of the widow in the Bible or in her social context in ancient Israel.

The Hebrew word *'almānâ* has cognates in other Semitic languages, but its derivation is uncertain. The Akkadian equivalent is *almattu*, which is found in early texts, but is clearly defined only in the Middle Assyrian laws:

[If] a woman is still dwelling in her father's house, (and) her husband is dead and [she] has none, [she shall dwell in a] house [belonging to them where she chooses. If] she has no [son, her father-in-law shall give her] to whichever [of his sons] he likes . . . or, if he pleases, he shall give her as a spouse to her father-in-law. If her husband and her father-in-law are [indeed] dead and she has no son, she becomes [in law] a widow [al-mattu]; she shall go wherever she pleases.

According to the final lines of this law, to be considered an *almattu*, both a woman's husband and father-in-law must be deceased, and she must have no son. She is thus a woman with no males obligated to support her.

Certain aspects of a widow's situation are highlighted in the Bible. She is pictured as a vulnerable person due special consideration in Israelite society (2 Sam 14:5; 1 Kgs 17:9–20; Job 24:21; 31:16). Over half of all biblical references to the widow group her with the orphan (Exod 22:22, 24; Job 31:16; Isa 1:17, 10:2), and with orphans and sojourners (Deut 10:18; 14:29; 24:19–21; 26:12–13; 27:19; Pss 94:6; 146:9; Jer 7:6; 22:3; Ezek 22:7; Mal 3:5). In Zech 7:10 this grouping of disadvantaged or marginalized persons expands to include the poor. The fact that the widow is frequently linked with the orphan and the sojourner implies that these three groups shared something in common. The *gēr*, commonly translated "sojourner, stranger, resident alien," but better understood as "client," was one living apart from his or her own kin group. He or she was, therefore, in need of protection or sustenance not available from his or her family because of geographical dislocation. The *gēr*, or client, required connection to a patron for protection and economic assistance. Like the *gēr*, the widow existed on the margins of society. She was not considered a proper marriage partner for a priest (Lev 21:14; Ezek 44:22). Her life could be lonely (Lam 1:1) and even humiliating (Isa 54:4).

The Bible illuminates two particular aspects of widowhood in ancient Israel: levirate marriage and inheritance rights.

Levirate Marriage

Levirate marriage was an important Jewish institution, one of the foci of the tractate *Yebamot* in the Babylonian Talmud. Rabbis valued the institution because it protected the widow and helped com-

pensate the family for loss. In this the rabbis apparently continued the biblical view of levirate marriage as a socially beneficial institution. The social world of the Bible ordinarily permitted a young woman only two proper family roles. She could be either an unmarried virgin in her father's household, or a child-producing wife in her husband's household. Levirate marriage allowed society to avoid social misfits — namely, young childless widows. Levirate marriage continued the lineage of the deceased and the transfer of his property to the next generation; it also reaffirmed the young widow's place in the home of her husband's family.

The Hebrew Bible deals with levirate marriage in Genesis 38, Deut 25:5–10, and Ruth 4. Deut 25:5–10 provides for marriage between a woman whose husband died childless and the brother of the deceased. If a brother-in-law would not marry his brother's widow (Deut 25:7–10), a ceremony followed in which the widow removed the brother-in-law's sandal (Ruth 4:9) and spat in his face. This is the *only* law in the Bible to include an act of humiliation as penalty against the offender. The removal of the shoe by the woman is not part of the insult. Rather, in this act, witnessed by the town's elders, the woman appropriates the right to her freedom and full control of her affairs.

Two narratives portray levirate marriage in operation: Genesis 38 and Ruth 4. Genesis 38 tells the story of Judah and his daughter-in-law Tamar. When Judah's son, Onan, dies after refusing to father a son for his deceased brother, Er, Judah says to Tamar: "Remain a widow in your father's house . . ." (Gen 38:11), suggesting that a childless widow should return to the home of her birth.

When these stories are compared with the law in Deuteronomy, significant differences appear. In Deuteronomy and Genesis the levirate is compulsory; in Ruth it is not. Deut 25:5–10 limits the levirate to brothers who "reside together." In Genesis 38 it is extended to the father-in-law and, in the case of Ruth, to a more distant relative. Genesis 38 appears to be akin to Middle Assyrian Law no. 33, in which the brother is the normal partner but allows his father to assume this role. Another discrepancy appears when Deut 25:7 stipulates that the levir's responsibility is "to perpetuate his brother's name." In the genealogy that concludes Ruth, however, Judah and Boaz, the biological fathers, are mentioned in the genealogies of Perez and Obed, not Er and Mahlon whose places they took.

Levirate marriage in the Hebrew Bible is thus not concerned solely with the protection of patrimony by producing male offspring, nor with bringing forth an heir. It is equally concerned with the support and protection of the widow.

Widows' Inheritance Rights

Whereas other ancient Near Eastern societies describe widows' inheritance rights, the inheritance rights of widows in ancient Israel are less explicit. The Book of Ruth is cited as evidence that widows inherited property. In Ruth 4:3 it seems that a childless widow, taking precedence over her husband's male relatives, inherits her husband's estate. Others insist that widows had no such rights. They observe that the Bible (in contrast to other ancient Near Eastern texts) has no provisions guaranteeing a widow's inheritance rights. Num 27:8–11 says that if the widow had children, her husband's estate would pass to them; if she had none, then her husband's nearest kinsman was the heir. This would obviously compound the plight of the childless widow in Israel, since she would have no claim to her husband's property.

An entirely different situation is portrayed in the Book of Judith in the Apocrypha. Judith is a young, childless widow, wealthy and well respected, the very antithesis of the common biblical picture of a poor, marginalized widow. Judith did not return to her natal home, but remained in her own. She inherited "gold and silver, men and women slaves, livestock and fields" from her husband, and she managed the estate (Jdt 8:4, 7). Here is a Jewish widow who was *not* "inherited" by a husband's kinsman, *not* pitied as an object of charity, and who did *not*, out of desperation or duty, return to her father's house. She was not reabsorbed into society through remarriage to one of her deceased husband's lineage and was *not* forced to do so by levi-

rate or another form of remarriage. Judith is a widow who lived alone and had independent control of her estate.

FRANK S. FRICK

SEE ALSO Part I: Judith 2; Ruth; Tamar 1; Part II: Daughters of Zelophehad (Num 26:33, etc.); Wife in Levirate Marriage (Deut 25:5–10); Widow of Zarephath (1 Kgs 17:8–24); Widow Whose Oil Is Multiplied (2 Kgs 4:1–7).

FOR FURTHER READING: Beattie, D. R. G. "The Book of Ruth as Evidence for Israelite Legal Practice."

Davies, E. W. "Inheritance Rights and the Hebrew Levirate Marriage."

Frick, Frank S. "Widows in the Hebrew Bible: A Transactional Approach."

Hamilton, Victor P. "Marriage: Old Testament and Ancient Near East."

Hiebert, Paula S. "'Whence Shall Help Come to Me?' The Biblical Widow."

EXOD 23:26; JOB 24:21; PS 113:9; ISA 54:1

Barren Woman

Ancient Israel's agrarian economy depended upon large families, yet the constant threat of endemic and epidemic disease made infant and child mortality high. Clearly, the continued life of the community as well as the survival of individual families depended upon female fertility. Many biblical narratives not only encourage and emphasize childbearing (as do the stories of the matriarchs) but also decry its opposite, barrenness.

In Exod 23:26, God promises the absence of barrenness and miscarriage, that is, the presence of human fecundity, when the Israelites, faithful to their god, enter the promised land. Barrenness is also mentioned in poetic passages. Divine power is expressed by the notion that God can end barrenness and thereby make women joyful (Ps 113:9). The future restoration of Israel, after the exile during the sixth century B.C.E., will be a time when a barren woman will celebrate new fertility (Isa 54:1). Childless women, like widows, are considered marginal (Job 24:21) — neither contribute new human life to their families and to society — whereas pregnant women represent survival

CAROL MEYERS

SEE ALSO Part II: Sterile Female (and Male) (Deut 7:14); Pregnant Women Killed in War (2 Kgs 8:12, etc.); Mothers Killed in War (Hos 10:14, etc.); Pregnant Women of Gilead (Amos 1:13).

Exod 32:2–3
Women with Jewelry and Clothing

SEE EXOD 3:22, etc. Women (and Men) with Jewelry and Clothing (Part II).

Exod 34:16; Gen 24:3; 27:46; 28:1, 6, 8; Deut 7:3; Josh 23:12–13; Judg 3:5–6
Daughters of the Inhabitants of the Land as Marriage Partners

Marital patterns reflected in biblical narratives vary in their stance on in-group (endogamous) and out-group (exogamous) marriages. On the one hand, many notable Israelite men are said to have married foreigners: Abraham's slave wife is the Egyptian Hagar; Samson marries a Philistine woman; David marries the Geshurite princess Maacah; Solomon's wife Bathsheba was formerly married to a Hittite man; and Ruth, wife of Boaz and ancestor of David, is from Moab. These marriages with foreigners are apparently condoned, although other important figures, such as Solomon and Ahab, are criticized for such marital practices.

In addition to the negative evaluation given to several kings who take wives from other peoples, many biblical passages contain explicit stipulations against marrying the daughters of neighboring groups. Prominent among these are Pentateuchal passages warning about marriage with the inhabi-

tants of the land in which the Israelites settle (Exod 34:11–16; Deut 7:1–4). In the ancestral narratives, Isaac, the very first patriarch born in the promised land, is told not to take a Canaanite wife, but rather to procure a spouse from his clan group, which remained in Mesopotamia (Gen 24:3). Similarly, Jacob is sent to fetch a wife from his Mesopotamian family lest he wed a Hittite or Canaanite woman (Gen 27:46; 28:1, 6, 8). The narratives of Israelite settlement likewise warn against intermarrying with any members of the local population (Josh 23:12–13) and then report that the Israelites failed to heed that interdiction (Judg 3:5–6). It is important to note, however, that the Hebrew Bible has no absolute interdiction of marriage with all outsiders; only marriage with local Canaanite groups is forbidden.

The critiques of those who marry foreigners provide the justification for avoiding such a practice: mixing with other people, the texts warn, will inevitably mean worship of the gods of those foreigners and concomitant disloyalty to YHWH. This "religious" motivation for prohibiting marriage with outsiders should be understood in more general cultural terms. Because religion was not a discrete aspect of Israelite society, but rather an integral part of its political, economic, social, as well as cultic identity, the anxiety about intermarriage and the worship of foreign deities actually expresses a broader concern about cultural boundaries.

Condemnation of intermarriage also appears in late biblical texts (as in Ezra 9:2, 12; 10:2); it reflects a mechanism used to maintain cultural or ethnic identity among people who have lost their territory or their political autonomy. One must ask whether this aspect of the exilic experience colors the negative attitudes toward marriage to foreigners presented in the ancestral and settlement narratives, which may have reached their final form during the exile of Judeans from their land. Or is some other cultural dynamic at work? Again, Ezra is concerned with marriage to local people, not all people.

The study of marriage patterns in other communities, particularly those that, like ancient Israel, inhabited natural environments that made group survival precarious, offers data relevant to that question. Families in such situations thrive best when new spouses moving into the groom's family are familiar with the social, technical, and historical heritage that governs daily life. The highlands occupied by Israelite groups consisted of unusually diverse microenvironments, making it most advantageous for families to find mates for their offspring from related families — those most familiar with their particular strategies for survival. The theological language about avoiding foreign spouses encodes the awareness that members of a foreign culture would threaten the optimal use of Israelite habitats. Also, if daughters are sent out to other peoples, they are lost as potential brides for Israelite men, an intolerable situation demographically, given the fact that premodern societies typically have shortages of women of childbearing age (because of significant incidence of death in childbirth). And if men procure wives from outside their group, they find themselves with women who are deficient in the cultural expertise necessary for household life. Furthermore, marriage with related family groups ensures mutual aid in times of economic or military difficulty and diminishes the possibility of disputes with such groups. Clearly there were important functional reasons for endogamy in preexilic as well as later periods, and the notion of Israelite cultural exclusivity or ethnic purity as reasons for endogamy should be questioned.

The prohibition of *all* intermarriage became an important characteristic of postbiblical Judaism — Jews may not marry non-Jews. The process leading to such a policy probably began in the postexilic period and can be discerned in the Book of Ezra, but it was not a feature of Israelite life as expressed in the Hebrew Bible.

CAROL MEYERS

SEE ALSO Part I: Maacah 2; Part II: Canaanite Mother of Shaul (Gen 46:10); Women (Daughter, Wife) (and Men: Brother, Son) Who Lead a Person to Idolatry (Deut 13:6); Daughters of Judah and Foreign Daughters/Wives (Ezra 9:2, etc.); Daughter of a Foreign God (Mal 2:11); Part III: Woman Wickedness.

FOR FURTHER READING: Cohen, Shaye J. D. "From the Bible to the Talmud: The Prohibition of Intermarriage."

Hamilton, Victor P. "Marriage: Old Testament and Ancient Near East."

Meyers, Carol. "The Family in Early Israel."

EXOD 35:22–24
Women with Jewelry and Clothing

SEE EXOD 3:22, etc. Women (and Men) with Jewelry and Clothing (Part II).

EXOD 35:25–26; 36:6
Skilled Women (and Men)

After Moses provides God's instructions for the tabernacle to be built in the wilderness, many people, both women and men, make contributions of precious metals and fabrics that they have brought with them from Egypt and also of acacia wood that they possess (Exod 35:21–24, 27–29). Inserted in this account of donations to the building fund is the in-

Wall painting on an early-second-millennium B.C.E. *Egyptian tomb, showing two women spinning thread and two women operating a loom. Textile production was largely women's work in the ancient Near East. See* Skilled Women (and Men) *(Exod 35:25–26, etc.);* Weaving Women *(2 Kgs 23:7).*

formation (35:25–26) that fabrics of colored yarns and linen and also goat's hair were prepared by women. These women are called "skilled," from a Hebrew root (ḥkm) that usually indicates "wisdom," but that also, as here, can denote the learned technical abilities of artisans.

The association of women with textile production appears frequently in many cultures. In most traditional societies, women are typically the producers of fabric in village settings. When textiles are needed for ritual purposes, as is the case in the tabernacle texts, women's skill in preparing fabrics and converting them to specific forms situates them in positions of social or religious prominence; it gives them a public role that has been little noticed.

The account of material gifts to the tabernacle and of women's textile craftwork is followed by Moses' recruitment of several talented artisans to teach others all the skills required to do the myriad tasks involved in building a shrine. They instruct volunteers, both women and men, who enthusiastically produce more than enough material, so that Moses must call a halt to their labors and gifts (Exod 36:6). Because women are included in this general injunction and also because women textile workers are specified, any references to "artisan or skilled designer" (Exod 35:35), words that are grammatically masculine in Hebrew, may be meant inclusively to signify women as well as men who are trained in craft specialties. Clearly both women and men participate in, as well as contribute to, the construction of the national wilderness shrine.

CAROL MEYERS

SEE ALSO Part II: Women (and Men) with Jewelry and Clothing (Exod 3:22, etc.); Weaving Women (2 Kgs 23:7).

FOR FURTHER READING: Schneider, Jane, and Annette B. Weiner. "Cloth and the Organization of Human Experience."

EXOD 35:29; 36:3–7
Women with Jewelry and Clothing
SEE EXOD 3:22, etc.   Women (and Men) with Jewelry and Clothing (Part II).

EXOD 36:6   Skilled Women
SEE EXOD 35:25–26, etc.   Skilled Women (and Men) (Part II).

EXOD 38:8; 1 SAM 2:22
Women at the Entrance to the Tent of Meeting

The priestly texts in the Bible seem to indicate that only males, from the tribe of Levi, were cultic functionaries. Yet two texts, one in Exodus (38:8) and one in 1 Samuel (2:22), preserve information about women in service of the central Israelite shrine. Those passages both refer to "women who served at the entrance to the tent of meeting." The Hebrew term for "serve" is related to the word describing the Levitical men who performed menial labor (for example, Num 4:23). The women who served likely performed maintenance tasks as well. (Temple service in the ancient Near East involved a range of activities, from exalted sacred acts to routine manual labor.)

The fact that these serving women are said to be at the entrance to the "tent of meeting" rather than the tabernacle (or temple) may reflect a separate and old sacred tradition, in which the tent was not a ritual space but rather the site of oracular contact between God and a prophetic figure. The incident of the daughters of Zelophehad takes place at the same location, showing that women had access to that sacred space and that people came there to approach the deity with a petition needing divine response. It is thus possible that the old tradition of the tent of meeting was more gender-inclusive than the tabernacle-temple tradition into which it was absorbed, and in which authority and service were restricted to men of the priestly class.

CAROL MEYERS

SEE ALSO Part II: Daughters of Zelophehad (Num 26:33, etc.); Daughters (and Sons) of Heman (1 Chr 25:5–6).

FOR FURTHER READING: Haran, Menahem. "The Non-Priestly Image of the Tent of MŌʿĒD."

Lev 2:1; also Lev 4:2, 27; 5:1–2, 4, 15, 17, 21, 25, 27; 23:29–30b; Num 5:6; 15:27, 30; 19:22; 31:19, 28; 35:11, 15, 30b

Person (Female or Male) Presenting an Offering

The priestly texts of Leviticus and Numbers present in great detail the kinds of sacrificial offerings that were part of the Israelite cultic system. Those texts are generally interpreted as mandating the participation of males far more than females in sacrificial acts. The language used for the persons who bring sacrifices, however, is likely to be gender-inclusive, despite traditional translations that obscure the fact that both women and men are given instructions about offerings to YHWH.

A case in point is the use of the word *person* (NRSV, "anyone") in Lev 2:1 and twenty-six other times in Leviticus and Numbers (Lev 4:2, 27; 5:1–2, 4, 15, 17, 21, 25, 27; 23:29–30b; Num 5:6; 15:27, 30; 19:22; 31:19, 28; 35:11, 15, 30b), as well as elsewhere in the Bible. The Hebrew term *nepeš* means "person, anyone." That it includes females as well as males is clear from Num 5:6, which refers to "a man or a woman [who] wrongs another" as a "person" *(nepeš)*. Such a person is instructed to make restitution, either as payment to the wronged person's family or as a donation to the sanctuary, and also to make an atonement offering. In that case, *nepeš* explicitly denotes both genders. Other uses of the word *person* in the ritual legislation of the Bible should likewise be understood as gender-inclusive. Women are thus participants along with men in extradomestic cultic practice as offerers of sacrifice, an activity preserved in biblical narrative in the story of Hannah and in the specific stipulations for sacrifices to be brought by new mothers.

CAROL MEYERS

SEE ALSO Part I: Hannah; Part II: Women after Childbirth (Lev 12:1–8); Daughters (and Sons) and Female (and Male) Slaves, Rejoicing (Deut 12:12, etc.); Women, Part of the Assembly of People (Neh 8:2–3, etc.).

FOR FURTHER READING: Gruber, Mayer I. "Women in the Cult According to the Priestly Code."

Lev 10:14–15; 22:12–13; Num 18:11, 19

Daughters (and Sons) of a Priest

Unlike the rest of the Holiness Code, a section of Leviticus (chaps. 17–26) dominated by the theme of holiness, chaps. 21–22 are addressed primarily to the priests rather than to the people as a whole. Chap. 22 deals with the "sacred donations" brought by the Israelites to YHWH. Because the priests owned no land and had no vocation apart from their cultic office, they and their families, including daughters and sons, were dependent upon receiving as their livelihood a share of the sacrificial offerings brought to the sanctuary (Num 18:19–20; compare Lev 10:14, 15). Those products, set aside as the "perpetual due" of the priests and their daughters and sons, include the choicest of crops and livestock (Num 18:11–15).

A priest's son inherited his father's office and retained the right to partake of the offerings. A priest's daughter, however, was entitled to partake of such foodstuffs only as long as she resided in her parents' household. If she should marry a non-priest (NRSV, "layman"), who presumably owned land and animals, she would lose her right to sacral provisions. However, if she returned to her natal home because of divorce or widowhood, she regained access to sacrificial victuals. But that would not be the case if she had children. Presumably they could continue to work their family land and thus provide for their mother, whereas a childless woman left alone by death or divorce would have to rejoin her original household. If her father was no longer alive, her brothers would probably have taken her in.

CAROL MEYERS

SEE ALSO Part II: Prostitute (Lev 19:29, etc.); Wives and Daughters (and Sons) of Priests (2 Chr 31:18).

Lev 12:1–8
Women after Childbirth

The discharge of lochia — blood and tissue from the vagina — after childbirth is a normal bodily function. Like other normal discharges, from men (seminal emissions) as well as from women (menstrual blood), it rendered a person temporarily "impure" or "unclean," that is, disqualified from entering the sacred realm. The NRSV translation "unclean" should not be understood as meaning "dirty" or "soiled." Furthermore, the lochial fluids, not childbirth itself, produced this unfitness for ritual or cultic activity; and the mother, but not the child, was considered impure. This discharge of fluid rendered people impure in many ancient cultures, but the reasons are usually difficult to understand. In ancient Israel, perhaps the loss of fluid from the body was thought to make a person temporarily less whole or perfect and thus unfit to enter God's perfect realm without special purification procedures.

Two stages of impurity after childbirth are distinguished in Lev 12:1–8. In the first stage, for seven days following the birth of a son or fourteen days following the birth of a daughter, a woman's status was analogous to that of a menstruant. She was barred from entering the sanctuary and from engaging in sexual intercourse, and her body and objects beneath it could transfer her impurity to others (Lev 15:18–24).

The second stage of impurity lasted thirty-three days after the birth of a son or sixty-six days after the birth of a daughter. During this time the impurity was no longer considered contagious and intercourse could resume, although the new mother still could not enter the sanctuary. At the end of the second stage, two sacrifices marked her readmission into the cult as an active participant. The animals required for the sacrifices varied according to the parturient's economic status, but were equivalent for either a female or male child. Of all genital discharges, childbirth occasioned the longest fixed period of impurity. The length of each of the two stages (seven and fourteen; thirty-three and sixty-

six) and their totals according to the sex of the child (forty or eighty) are multiples of the common biblical numbers seven and forty; they suggest totality — a completed period of ritual impurity.

The difference in the duration of the mother's impurity following the birth of a daughter or a son is often interpreted as a sign that greater social value was placed on male children. However, if this was the case, one would expect a greater sacrifice following the birth of a son. The gender distinction could stem from a female's greater potential role in reproduction. Another possible explanation is that the discrepancy resulted from male circumcision on the eighth day of life. Originally, the duration of the mother's impurity may have been identical for daughters and sons. However, the institution of the practice of circumcising male infants may have necessitated that the mother's impurity be shortened so that she could comfort her son during this ritual procedure.

The relatively small space devoted to a discussion of childbirth in the biblical text suggests that this was predominantly a female sphere of activity, attended to by midwives and other women.

RHONDA BURNETTE-BLETSCH

SEE ALSO Part II: Midwife (Gen 35:17, etc.); Woman (Women) Not to Be Approached at Sinai (Exod 19:15); Person (Female or Male) Presenting an Offering (Lev 2:1, etc.); Women and Bodily Emissions (Lev 15:18–33, etc.); Women of the Neighborhood (Ruth 4:17).

FOR FURTHER READING: Wright, David P., and Richard N. Jones. "Discharge."

Lev 13:29, 38; Num 5:2–4
Blemished Women (and Men)

The intersection of medical problems, cultic practice, and ritual purity in ancient Israel is reflected in several priestly texts dealing with disease and bodily discharge. Although all illnesses were considered punishment from God, these texts seem to focus on skin ailments, perhaps because they were most visible and tended to be contagious but not fatal. In any case, persons with skin diseases or with bodily emissions and also those who had touched corpses (which might contaminate) were considered unfavored by God. They were thus not ritually fit to come near YHWH's sanctuary, which epitomized purity, wholeness, and moral perfection. Both women and men were subject to regulations banning such people from the sacred precincts (Num 5:2–4).

A diseased person, however, was not irrevocably excluded from the realm of sanctity. As guardians of that realm, priests functioned as health care practitioners, quarantining people with suspicious symptoms, examining lesions to see if they represented minor or major disease, and authorizing the attainment of a state of health tantamount to ritual purity. Women along with men are specified in some of the passages dealing with specific dermatological symptoms (Lev 13:29, 38). The pronouncement that some of these afflicted persons may eventually be deemed "clean" (that is, ritually fit) is tantamount to making them eligible to participate in cultic activities such as the offering of sacrifices.

CAROL MEYERS

SEE ALSO Part II: Person (Male or Female) Presenting an Offering (Lev 2:1, etc.); Women and Bodily Emissions (Lev 15:18–33, etc.).

FOR FURTHER READING: Avalos, Hector. *Illness and Health Care in the Ancient Near East: The Role of the Temple in Greece, Mesopotamia, and Israel.*

Meyers, Carol. "Illness and Health in the Hebrew Bible."

LEV 15:18–33; 18:19; 20:18
Women and Bodily Emissions

Bodily discharges related to the reproductive physiology of both women and men in ancient Israel rendered persons temporarily "impure" with the consequence that they were banned from activities in the sacred realm. This taboo applied to both normal discharges, such as menstrual blood and seminal emissions, and pathological discharges, such as irregular genital secretions of blood or pus.

For Israelite women, the most common normal discharge was menstruation (Lev 15:19–23), resulting in a seven-day period of impurity during which she could not enter the sanctuary; it was viewed as possessing a mild contagion. Both a menstruant herself and objects beneath her could transfer her impurity to others. Anyone who touched a menstruant or these objects would contract a one-day impurity and had to wash themselves and their clothes. However, a man who had intercourse with her was either impure for seven days (Lev 15:24) or cut off from his people, along with the woman (Lev 20:18). Thus, in addition to a menstruant's ban from cultic activity, her movements and activities within the profane realm were also somewhat restricted by her menstrual status. Unlike many societies, however, ancient Israel did not socially isolate menstruating women. Neither was a sacrifice required to end her impurity. Rectification appears to rest solely upon the passage of time. Postmenstrual ablutions are not mentioned but may have been practiced as they were for similar states of impurity (as for seminal emissions, Lev 15:16–18).

Pathological female discharges (Lev 15:25–33) would include bleeding outside of or beyond the normal duration of the menorrheal period. This situation was handled exactly as the analogous case for males. The affected woman persisted in her impurity for the duration of her discharge and for seven days following its cessation. During this time her condition barred her from the sanctuary, and she, as well as objects beneath her, were considered a source of contagion. Her readmission into the sacred realm required an offering.

The severity of the impurity occasioned by a genital discharge depended upon its normalcy, frequency, and duration. The impurity contracted for normal seminal discharges or sexual intercourse lasted only one day because of the frequency and short duration of these acts. Because normal menstruation occurred less frequently and lasted longer, it carried a seven-day impurity. Compared to contemporary Western women, Israelite women would likely have experienced relatively few unproductive cycles because of the early age of marriage, the large optimal family size, and the time spent pregnant or breastfeeding. Malnutrition might have also affected the regularity of menstrual cycles and shortened the childbearing years. Pathological discharges were more severe because they were much less frequent and could potentially last longer. The impurity associated with such conditions lasted for seven days beyond the condition itself and had to be followed by a sacrifice.

Many cultures have similar customs related to bodily discharges. Anthropologists have suggested several different explanations for them, such as these five: (1) Some anthropologists hold that purity regulations may be an expression of male dominance and a means of distinguishing between female and male spheres within a given society. This seems unlikely in ancient Israel, where most of the population throughout its history lived in rural, agricultural contexts lacking separate domestic and public spheres of activity. (2) Douglas relates purity to social ideas of normalcy and wholeness. The passage of fluids from the body makes people incomplete and abnormal; it thus disqualifies them temporarily from approaching the realm of a perfect deity. She also suggests that rules pertaining to the margins of the body reflect concerns about the boundaries of society. However, several scholars have objected, noting that "normal" genital discharges, such as menstruation and all heterosexual intercourse, are also associated with impurity. (3) A modified form of Douglas's schema relates impurity to death rather than normalcy. The loss of "life liquids" gives persons an aura of death and disqualifies them from approaching a perfect deity. However, no evidence suggests that loss of semen was viewed as sapping a man's vitality. (4) Purity laws are linked to liminal states, or moments of transition from one status to another. Procreation and menstruation move a person from childhood to adulthood. Pathological discharges might move a person from life to death. Rituals of purification would serve to reincorporate individuals from dangerous liminal states back into society. However,

Israelite regulations appear more concerned with isolating impure people from the sacred realm than from other people. (5) Finally, purity regulations concerning a menstruating woman might serve as a form of population management that encourages procreation by banning intercourse during less fertile periods of a woman's cycle. None of these explanations by itself accounts for all of Israel's purity regulations.

RHONDA BURNETTE-BLETSCH

SEE ALSO Part II: Woman (Women) Not to Be Approached at Sinai (Exod 19:15); Women after Childbirth (Lev 12:1–8); Women Kept Away from David's Men (1 Sam 21:4–5); Menstruating Women (Ezek 18:6, etc.).

FOR FURTHER READING: Douglas, Mary. "Couvade and Menstruation: The Relevance of Tribal Studies."

Wenham, Gordon J. "Why Does Sexual Intercourse Defile (Lev 15:18)?"

LEV 18:7–18, 20; 20:11–14, 17, 19–21; DEUT 22:30; 27:20; 22, 23
Women in Incest Regulations

Though modern definitions vary, incest is traditionally defined as sexual relations between closely related persons. Incest regulations or taboos are prohibitions that identify family members with whom sexual relations are forbidden. Almost every culture has such a list; however, the family members included on that list vary from culture to culture. According to some investigators, variations are indicative of the sociological setting of the culture.

Recent anthropological studies claim that the number of relatives included in incest taboos or laws are often predictors of family organization, system of governance, and degree of social stratification and technological and economic sophistication. These studies are important to Leviticus 18 and 20 because they demonstrate that incest taboos vary across cultures, and across time periods within cultures.

The term *incest* does not have a single-word Hebrew equivalent in the Hebrew Bible. "Incestuous" relations are clearly prohibited in Leviticus 18, where incest is described euphemistically as "uncovering the nakedness" of a near kinswoman. Leviticus 18 presents twelve categories of relationships that are prohibited. Leviticus 20 presents a somewhat shorter version — seven forbidden liaisons — with punishments prescribed. Sexual relations are forbidden not only between biological relatives, but also between persons related by marriage.

Curiously, one person is missing from the Leviticus regulations — the daughter. Given the regularity of father-daughter prohibitions in incest taboos, it is likely that its absence here is unintentional. A scribal error may account for the missing father-daughter prohibition.

Yet the missing father-daughter prohibition is complicated by the treatment of incest in stories like that of Lot and his daughters, in which their sexual behavior is not condemned. Perhaps more important issues were at stake (see Brenner). When initiated by men fighting for power or women striving to protect male lineages, incest is treated as a minor infraction (Gen 19:30–38). Considering its literary structure, the story of Lot's daughters was not written to address incest; rather, it explains the Israelites' hostility toward Moabites and Ammonites (see Bailey). Part of the difficulty in understanding apparent ethnical ambiguities is that narratives and law are entirely different literary genres, or types of writing. A story about power struggles or maintaining family lineages may not tell us what is generally sanctioned or prohibited in a society.

At the same time, the particular relatives included in incest taboos reveal certain periods in the social and economic development of a culture. In studies of simple societies, anthropologists have found a way to correlate the number of relatives included in incest taboos and the severity of punishment with certain socioeconomic settings. One of the most likely socioeconomic settings suggested by Leviticus 18 and 20 is the early Iron Age (1200–1000 B.C.E.), a date that is much earlier than the generally accepted fifth-century B.C.E. designation

of Levitical laws. If the incest regulations date to the tenth century B.C.E., what are we to make of a narrative that does not condemn incestuous relations? Was the recorder of Rachel's story unaware of the incest regulations or indifferent to them? Was the priestly writer overlooking the incest to make another point? Is the narrative older than the laws, or vice versa? Variations in attitudes toward incest (in narratives and laws) may reflect changing incest taboos and perhaps changing family structures.

Incest regulations are almost universal. Anthropological theory deals with them in a variety of ways. Rather than reflecting an innate avoidance of close relatives or a sociobiological awareness of the deleterious effects of inbreeding, incest prohibitions should be viewed as attempts to create order in social relations. Forbidding marriage within the immediate family necessitated exogamy (marriage outside the family) thus creating alliances that helped maintain peace among neighboring families or groups of families. Marriage ties also increased the likelihood that those families would assist each other in times of trouble (such as crop failures, illness, and enemy threats). In short, incest taboos encouraged mutual aid between groups that might otherwise resist such interactions. Some simple societies stated marriage rules positively, specifying the makeup of desirable unions. Israelite prohibitions, with their negative or exclusionary statements, are evidence of a more complex system.

Although the functional origins of Israelite regulations lie in the need to organize social relations between groups, their presentation in Leviticus 18 states that incestuous relations are prohibited because — "they are your flesh" and "it is depravity" (v. 17). A certain community ethic underlies these motive clauses (clauses that explain the reason for something). The rationale that certain women were off limits may be illuminated by the analysis of anthropologist Mary Douglas. Douglas provides a paradigm for understanding the ethical imperative of many regulations in Leviticus. She sees "uncleanness" as "matter out of place" and is "something that must not be included if order is to be maintained." Having sexual relations with a close relative may have represented a kind of disorder, an "intimacy out of place" an uncleanness or "depravity." The severe punishments (Lev 20:11–12, 14, 17, 19–21), usually death, banishment, or childlessness, are a means of establishing sanctions for acts that interfere with the welfare of the group.

These Levitical prohibitions, like many biblical laws, are addressed to *men*. It is enigmatic that women are held equally liable in the punishments of Leviticus 20. The only mitigating consideration is that the Hebrew terminology for sexual relations in this chapter neither explicitly nor implicitly describes a sexual relationship involving force or coercion, in which case the liability of both the man and the woman may be explainable. We cannot uncritically assume, however, that all incestuous liaisons were consensual. Numerous studies on incest have shown that where power differentials exist, coercion or force is rarely needed to ensure the compliance of a reluctant person. Consequently, the incest regulations also served to protect females from sexual predators and problematic dynamics within the extended family, in which most rural Israelites probably lived.

The incest regulations in Deuteronomy (22:30; 27:20, 22–23) are much less extensive, perhaps because the urban orientation of the book reflects a different social setting, in which political bureaucracies, rather than kinship ties, provide security and assistance to families.

MADELINE GAY MCCLENNEY-SADLER

SEE ALSO Part II: Daughters of Lot (Gen 19:8, etc.).

FOR FURTHER READING: Bailey, Randall C. "They're Nothing but Incestuous Bastards: The Polemical Use of Sex and Sexuality in Hebrew Canon Narratives."

Brenner, Athalya. "On Incest."

Douglas, Mary. *Purity and Danger: An Analysis of the Concepts of Polution and Taboo.*

Wegner, Judith Romney. "Leviticus."

Zonabend, Françoise. "An Anthropological Perspective on Kinship and the Family."

LEV 18:19   Menstruating Women

SEE LEV 15:18–33, etc.   Women and Bodily Emissions (Part II).

LEV 18:20   Wife of a Kinsman

SEE LEV 18:7–18, etc.   Women in Incest Regulations (Part II).

LEV 18:22, 23; 20:16
Women as Legitimate Sexual Partners for Men; Women (and Men) Prohibited from Practicing Bestiality

Lev 18:23 forbids women and men from having sexual relations with any animal; and Lev 20:15 and 16 decree the death penalty for the persons and also the beasts who commit such an act. The extreme penalty indicates the gravity of the sin of bestiality. Yet one must keep in mind that the death penalty appears more frequently than might be expected because ancient Israel had no incarceration system for lesser crimes. Nonetheless, the reason for forbidding bestiality is not stated, nor is the reason for forbidding male homosexuality (men are enjoined not to "lie with a male as with a woman," Lev 18:22).

One anthropological reading of these prohibitions and many others in the Levitical codes understands them to be part of a structural mapping of the world that lays out distinct categories of objects and living things. Confusing the boundaries between categories is considered abominable and hence strongly interdicted.

A more functionalist or ecosystem approach would take into account the demographic situation in early Israel, in which large families were essential for providing agrarian labor and for maintaining territorial claims. Bestiality and male homosexuality involve wasted semen and hence lost opportunities for reproduction. The death of Onan in the Judah and Tamar narrative for having "spilled his semen on the ground" expresses such a perspective (Gen 38:9). That women are not explicitly forbidden from homosexual acts may reflect the awareness that no "seeds" are wasted in female homosexuality. Prohibitions against intercourse with animals or with (for men) members of the same sex may thus be considered the negative expression of the procreation-affirming positive command given to both female and male at creation (Gen 1:28) and to Noah and his sons at the second, postflood creation (Gen 9:7): to "be fruitful and multiply."

CAROL MEYERS

SEE ALSO Part II: Woman (and Man) in the First Creation Story (Gen 1:26–28, etc.).

FOR FURTHER READING: Douglas, Mary. *Purity and Danger: An Analysis of the Concepts of Pollution and Taboo.*

LEV 19:3   Mother to Be Revered

SEE EXOD 20:8, etc.   Women in the Decalogue (Part II).

LEV 19:20   Female Slave

SEE EXOD 21:7–11, etc.   Female (and Male) Hebrew Slaves (Part II).

LEV 19:29; 21:7–9, 14; GEN 38:15–22; DEUT 23:18; MIC 1:7
Prostitute

Lev 19:29 is the second of two laws in Leviticus 19 that attempt to regulate female sexual behavior. The first concerns the betrothed slave girl who is presumably seduced (vv. 20–22). Whereas v. 29 speaks of the dangers of premarital sex, the law of vv. 20–22 suggests the serious implications of illicit sexual behavior after betrothal.

The key term in Lev 19:29 is the verb *zānâ*, which generally refers to premarital sex and prostitution. Here the Israelite father is warned not to "profane" (*ḥillēl*) his daughter by allowing her to engage in premarital sex, or alternatively, by exploiting her through prostitution. In the Hebrew Bible, the objects of the verb *profane* are generally those things regarded as holy, such as God's name (Lev 20:3), God's sanctuary (Ezek 23:39), the Sabbath (Neh

13:18), or the priestly family (Lev 21:9, 15). The idea that an Israelite woman can be "profaned" through premarital intercourse is unique to this verse, although a nearly synonymous term, "defile" (*ṭimmē'*), is often used to describe the consequences of illicit sex (Gen 34:5; Num 5:13–29). It is also possible that the term *profane* is used here because a prostitute was also called a *qĕdēšâ*, from the root *qdš*, "holy" (Gen 38:21–22; Deut 23:17; Hos 4:14). Thus, the verse is emphasizing that prostitution is not the sanctification of a daughter, but rather the opposite, her profanation.

The second half of the verse reads literally "that the land doesn't commit prostitution and the land is [not] filled with depravity." Most commentators think that "the land" in the first case refers to "the people of the land," so that the verse suggests that the prostitution of a daughter, or immorality on a small scale, could eventually lead to widespread promiscuity. The suggestion of the medieval Jewish commentator Rashi may be more compelling: "the land" in the first case refers to the actual land, and its "prostitution" refers to the degeneration of its fertility as the consequence of sexual immorality. This linking of fidelity to the covenant and agricultural productivity is found elsewhere in the Pentateuch (Lev 26:3–5; Deut 7:12–13; 11:13–14). The term *zimmâ*, "depravity," is used often in the Bible to describe illicit sex, whether adultery (Job 31:11), incest (Lev 20:14), or the gang rape of a secondary wife (Judg 20:6).

As repugnant as these texts make prostitution seem, it is never expressly forbidden. The presence of prostitutes as apparently uncensured heroines (such as Tamar in Genesis, and Rahab) in several biblical narratives would support this point, as does indirectly the text in Deuteronomy about a prostitute's wages. Deut 23:18 declares money gained from prostitution inadmissible for the payment of vows. This is not surprising, as in the Bible, especially among the prophets, the source of a temple donation is critical to its acceptability (Isa 1:10–18; Amos 5:21–24). Although the prohibition certainly includes the hire of a professional harlot, also alluded to is temporary prostitution by Israelite women specifically for the payment of a vow. In ancient Israel, women were no less likely than men to vow goods and money to the temple (Numbers 30; 1 Sam 1:11; Prov 31:2). However, since women were financially dependent upon the men in their households, whether husbands or fathers, the actual fulfillment of the vow could have been difficult. Thus, prostitution, though temporary, was one means by which an Israelite woman might fulfill her vow. Prov 7:10–14 may supply a graphic illustration of this practice, and Mic 1:7 states that the divine images in Samaria were funded by the "wages of a prostitute."

According to Lev 21:7, 14, the prostitute is rejected as an appropriate bride for a member of the priesthood because the indiscriminate sexuality of a prostitute is inconsistent with the priesthood's requirement of holiness. The verse implies the possibility, however, that the nonpriestly Israelite might find a prostitute to be a fitting bride. In both v. 7 and v. 14, *prostitute* is paired with *ḥălālâ*, "a woman who has been defiled." The two terms may be understood as a hendiadys, the use of two nouns to express a single concept — in this case "a woman defiled through prostitution." Or they may be two of a set of four categories of sexually experienced women unsuitable for priestly marriage, the other two being widows and divorced women.

According to Lev 21:9, the daughter of a priest who "profanes herself" through "prostitution," whether premarital relations or real prostitution, is executed by burning, an unusually harsh punishment in the biblical context. Elsewhere this penalty is found regarding the marriage of a man to a mother and her daughter (Lev 20:14). In Genesis 38, Judah condemns Tamar to death by burning for having sexual relations while awaiting levirate marriage to his son Shelah. Because the capital punishment prescribed here is inconsistent with more lenient biblical laws regarding premarital sexual activity (Exod 22:16–17; Deut 22:28–29), the priest's daughter in Lev 21:9 may be either married or betrothed. The harsh penalty imposed in Lev 21:9, however, can be explained by the unique status of the actor, the daughter of a priest. Through her

illicit relations, she "profanes her father," who is holy by virtue of his lineage and office.

The holiness, or separateness, of biblical priests (like that of other temple servitors in the ancient Near East) was linked to their purity and fitness to maintain the rituals of their deity. Marriage to virgins protected the priestly lineage by making certain that a priest's offspring were indeed his own.

ELAINE ADLER GOODFRIEND

SEE ALSO Part I: Rahab; Tamar 1; Part II: Female (and Male) Hebrew Slaves (Exod 21:7–11, etc.); Women a Priest Can and Cannot Marry (Lev 21:7–8, etc.); Temple Prostitute (Deut 23:17–18, etc.); Prostitute, Mother of Jephthah (Judg 11:1–2); Prostitute (Prov 6:26, etc.).

FOR FURTHER READING: Goodfriend, Elaine Adler. "Prostitution."

Levine, Baruch A. *The JPS Torah Commentary: Leviticus.*

LEV 20:9
Mother Cursed by Offspring

SEE EXOD 21:15, etc.   Mother (or Father) Cursed or Struck by Offspring (Part II)

LEV 20:10; DEUT 22:22
Adulteress (and Adulterer)

In the passage about adultery in Lev 20:10, the verb used is *nā'ap*, "to commit adultery." In the Hebrew Bible, this legal term indicates sexual intercourse between a married or betrothed woman and any man other than her husband. Some suggest that the redundancy of the Hebrew of Lev 20:10 ("If a man commits adultery with a married woman, commits adultery with the wife of his neighbor . . .") is the result of scribal error (compare NRSV). More likely, the repetition in the verse is intended to heighten the treachery of the act described; adultery is an evil perpetrated not only against a "man," but more so, against one's "neighbor" or friend.

Because only the marital status of the female partner determines whether a sexual act is adulterous, the circumstances of her paramour are irrelevant. Married men are admonished for infidelity

(Prov 5:15–20; Mal 2:14–1), yet a legal penalty is lacking. Both Lev 20:10 and Deut 22:22 prescribe the death penalty for both parties in an act of adultery. The reasons for the gravity of this crime are never explicitly stated in the legal sections of the Pentateuch. The patrilineal nature of Israelite society, however, makes it certain that mistaken paternity was viewed with dread, as the family inheritance would then be bequeathed to an illegitimate heir. Indeed, in such a circumstance, the unknowing husband may leave his fortune to the product of his wife's disloyalty. Thus, adultery is disruptive in multiple ways: social, economic, and religious.

The need to maintain social stability by preventing adultery is apparent in the strong biblical sanctions against it. Consorting with a married woman is viewed as an act of treachery (Ps 50:16–21; Jer 9:2; Mal 3:5) and is called in the Hebrew Bible a "great sin" (ḥăṭā'â gĕdōlâ), a label it shares with apostasy (Gen 20:9; Exod 32:21, 30–31; 2 Kgs 17:21). Adultery is prohibited in the Decalogue, the Israelite God's only direct and unmediated address to Israel (Exod 20:14, 19; Deut 4:12; 5:18, 22), and is an assault upon the sanctity of the nuclear family, which is favored by God (Gen 2:18, 24, Prov 18:22). According to the later Jewish texts, including the Septuagint (Greek translation of the Hebrew Bible), the issue from an adulterous union, as from incest, is the mamzēr or "bastard" of Deut 23:2, who is excluded from membership in the assembly of the LORD. It is not clear, however, that such status obtained in biblical times.

Both Lev 20:10 and Deut 22:22 emphasize that both parties to the adulterous act must be put to death. The equal punishment of both parties is typical of most Mesopotamian law (see Code of Hammurabi no. 129, Middle Assyrian Law no. 13, and Hittite Law nos. 197–98 in *Ancient Near Eastern Texts*). This precludes the possibility that two of the involved parties have conspired against the third.

The means of execution for the guilty pair are not stated specifically in either Lev 20:10 or Deut 22:22. Deut 22:21, 24 specifies execution by stoning for the unchastity of the betrothed maiden, and Jesus, according to John 8:5, believed that the penalty for adultery was stoning.

Despite the uncompromising demand of Lev 20:10 and Deut 22:22 that adulterers be executed, some scholars think that the legal reality was otherwise, or at least that it varied throughout the many centuries of Israelite history. The prosecution of adultery in Israel may have resembled the legal custom of Mesopotamia, where the husband had the right to pardon his wife and her lover. On the other hand, it is possible that this ability to pardon was extrajudicial and facilitated by bribery (Prov 6:34–35).

ELAINE ADLER GOODFRIEND

SEE ALSO Part II: Women in the Decalogue (Exod 20:8, etc.); Woman Accused of Unfaithfulness (Num 5:11–31); Adulterous Woman (John 8:3–11); Part III: Woman Stranger (Loose Woman/Adulteress) (Prov 2:16–19, etc.).

FOR FURTHER READING: Goodfriend, Elaine Adler. "Adultery."

Greenberg, Moshe. "Some Postulates of Biblical Criminal Law."

Milgrom, Jacob. "Adultery in the Bible and the Ancient Near East."

Pritchard, James B., ed. *Ancient Near Eastern Texts Relating to the Old Testament*.

LEV 20:11–14, 17, 19–21
Women in Incest Regulations

> SEE LEV 18:7–18, etc. Women in Incest Regulations (Part II).

LEV 20:16
Woman Practicing Bestiality

> SEE LEV 18:22, etc. Women as Legitimate Sexual Partners for Men; Women (and Men) Prohibited from Practicing Bestiality (Part II).

LEV 20:18   Menstruating Women

> SEE LEV 15:18–33, etc. Women and Bodily Emissions (Part II).

LEV 20:27
Medium/Wizard

These two types of divination, virtually always mentioned together (Lev 19:31; 20:6, 27; 1 Sam 28:3–9; Isa 8:19), are explicitly stated to have been practiced by both women and men. The Hebrew terms (literally meaning "a man or woman who has a ghost or familiar spirit") refer to people thought to have access to the spirits of the dead and by extension to diviners who consult them (for example, 1 Sam 28:8; Isa 19:3). The Hebrew Bible frequently condemns such forbidden cultic practitioners (for example, Deut 18:9–14), which indicates that such professionals were well established among the Israelites. Indeed, King Saul consults the medium of Endor (1 Sam 28:7–25). However, only the medium, wizard, and sorcerer are specifically condemned to death (Exod 22:18; Lev 20:27). Apparently their services directly conflicted with the notion that the prophets of YHWH were the only legitimate channel of communication between YHWH and Israel. Perhaps gender was also an issue, for these are the three divinatory or magical professions for which female practitioners are explicitly mentioned.

THOMAS W. OVERHOLT

SEE ALSO Part II: Female Sorcerer (Exod 22:18, etc.); Medium of Endor (1 Sam 28:7–25); Daughters Who Prophesy (Ezek 13:17–23).

LEV 21:1–3, 11; EZEK 44:25
Women Whom a Priest Can and Cannot Bury

Contact with corpses was considered defiling in ancient Israel, and it disqualified individuals from approaching the divine realm. Hence, in order to perform their sacred duties, priests had to limit this type of contact as much as possible. Levitical law allowed ordinary priests to attend to the funerary needs of only co-residential, consanguine relatives (21:1–3). Because married couples typically resided with the husband's family, the women included in both of these categories were a priest's mother, daughters, and unmarried sisters. In addition, because the term *bat*, "daughter," can refer to kinship positions extending several generations, all direct lineal female descendants, such as granddaughters, constituted exemptions from the corpse prohibition for priests. The high priest, however, could have no contact with a dead body (Lev 21:11). Ezekiel reiterates the rule for ordinary priests and further forbids them even to enter a house containing a corpse (44:25). These stringent funerary restrictions may have been intended to distance Israelite religious leadership from the cult of the dead, which was widely practiced elsewhere in the biblical world.

An especially interesting aspect of the texts limiting priestly contact with corpses are the categories of women within an ordinary priest's family that he was not allowed to bury. Legal tradition explicitly prohibited him from defiling himself on behalf of affinal kin (relatives by marriage). This category would include his wife, any of her consanguine kin other than their children, his sisters-in-law, and their consanguine relatives. Neither could he bury his own consanguine kinswomen who had either transferred into or always belonged to another residential unit. This category would include married sisters, married paternal aunts, or any maternal relatives other than his mother herself. Finally, he could not participate directly in the funerary rituals of co-residential, consanguine kinswomen who were neither in his direct line of descent (daughters) or ascent (mother), nor in his lateral generation (sisters). This category would include nieces.

Assuming that special rules for priests functioned to set them apart from the rest of Israelite society, other Israelites were typically obliged to bury many, or even all, of these relatives. This suggests that, for most Israelites, both affinal and consanguine kinship created networks of alliance entailing mutual responsibilities.

RHONDA BURNETTE-BLETSCH

SEE ALSO Part II: Women Whom a Priest Can and Cannot Marry (Lev 21:7–8, etc.).

Lev 21:7–8, 13–14; Ezek 44:22
Women Whom a Priest Can and Cannot Marry

Several priestly texts limit the potential marriage partners for a priest in ancient Israel. The legal tradition (Lev 21:7–8, 13–14) insists that ordinary priests must not marry harlots or divorcees. For the high priest, it adds a prohibition against widows and also stipulates that an appropriate bride should be sought among his kin. Among the forbidden categories of females, the common limiting characteristic is sexual experience. A virginal bride and an endogamous marriage would help to ensure the purity of priestly lineages. A prophetic text (Ezek 44:22), discussing the marriage of ordinary priests, explicitly excludes as prospective mates only divorced women and widows whose late husbands were not also priests. Marriage to the widow of another priest would still preserve the purity of the priestly line, if not necessarily that of a given priest's own household.

Because these regulations clearly intend to set priests apart from the rest of Israelite society, this requirement must represent a higher level of conjugal discrimination than commonly exercised in nonpriestly circles. This suggests that many Israelite men would marry divorcees, widows, former harlots, or women in other categories of sexual experience. Although the image of a virginal bride may have been a social ideal in ancient Israel, it apparently was not always a social reality.

These texts also demonstrate that the word *bĕtûlâ* does not have the technical meaning "virgin" that is frequently ascribed to it; it is better translated "girl of marriageable age." If the term did indicate sexual experience, then it would suffice to describe the appropriate conjugal partner for a priest without the need to specify particular categories of women with sexual experience.

RHONDA BURNETTE-BLETSCH

SEE ALSO Part II: Virgin (Exod 22:16–17, etc.); Widows (Exod 22:22, etc.); Prostitute (Lev 19:29, etc.); Woman Being Divorced (Deut 24:1–4).

Lev 21:7–9,14   Prostitute
SEE LEV 19:29, etc.   Prostitute (Part II).

Lev 21:11   Corpse of a Mother
SEE LEV 21:1–3, etc.   Women a Priest Can and Cannot Bury (Part II).

Lev 21:13–14
Women Whom a Priest Can and Cannot Marry
SEE LEV 21:7–8, etc.   Women Whom a Priest Can and Cannot Marry (Part II).

Lev 22:12–13   Daughter of a Priest
SEE LEV 10:14–15, etc.   Daughters (and Sons) of a Priest (Part II).

Lev 25:6,44   Female Slaves
SEE EXOD 21:7–11, etc.   Female (and Male) Hebrew Slaves (Part II).

Lev 26:26
Women as Bread Bakers

The covenant curses at the end of the Book of Leviticus set forth the terrible consequences of disobeying God. Among the disasters is the great reduction in the availability of the "staff of bread," a Hebrew idiom, denoting bread as supportive of life and the basis for the English aphorism describing bread as the "staff of life." The paucity of bread is expressed in the scenario of ten women baking bread in a single household oven (Lev 26:26). That is, there is so little flour to make dough that the bread of ten households can fit in the space usually used to bake loaves for one.

The providers of bread in this text are women, which accords well with the general pattern across cultures. In premodern societies household and productive tasks are allotted to subsets of the family

Clay model (3 inches high) dating to the Iron II period (ninth–early sixth century B.C.E.) of a female figure bending over a trough and kneading dough, from Achziv on the northern coast of Israel. Preparing flour and baking bread were typically women's tasks in ancient Israel. See Women as Bread Bakers (Lev 26:26); Women as Perfumers, Cooks, and Bakers (1 Sam 8:13); Women Who Grind (Eccl 12:3); Women Making a Fire (Isa 27:11); Women Worshipping the Queen of Heaven (Jer 7:18, etc.).

group. Some tasks are performed by men and others by women; and some may be shared. This division of labor by gender differs from culture to culture, but a number of tasks are associated with one gender rather than the other in virtually all societies. Food preparation, epitomized by the many steps necessary to convert grain into flour and then bread, is nearly always women's work in domestic settings.

The women of the Leviticus text not only produce the bread, but also dole it out by weight, that is, in limited portions. This situation stands in contrast to the abundance of bread available when God bestows blessings (Lev 26:5), so that in Lev 26:26 no one is sated (compare Ezek 4:16). This description of near starvation provides a glimpse of women in

control of food portions. That they are the ones to allocate vital domestic resources indicates their power in household life.

CAROL MEYERS

SEE ALSO Part II: Daughters as Perfumers, Cooks, and Bakers (1 Sam 8:13); Women Who Grind (Eccl 12:3); Women Making a Fire (Isa 27:11); Women Worshipping the Queen of Heaven (Jer 7:18, etc.).

FOR FURTHER READING: Meyers, Carol L. "Everyday Life: Women in the Period of the Hebrew Bible."

LEV 26:29; DEUT 28:53–57; JER 19:9; LAM 2:20; 4:10

Mother (and Father) Cannibalizing Their Daughters (and Sons)

Perhaps the greatest horror associated with the deprivations of war or other disaster is the way some people will eat human flesh in order to survive. That horror is particularly powerful if it involves parents cannibalizing their children. It is no wonder, then, that such an act appears in the curses that constitute the concluding section of ancient Near Eastern treaties. The closing chapters of both Leviticus and Deuteronomy conform to Near Eastern treaty types in significant ways, among which is the depiction of eating one's children as part of the severe punishment that will result if the terms of the treaty or covenant are not obeyed.

In both Leviticus (26:29) and Deuteronomy (28:53–57), which list the cannibalizing of children among the consequences of disobeying God, as well as in Jer 19:9, which anticipates such a tragedy, both daughters and sons will be the victims of this horrific act. In Lamentations one verse records the eating of "offspring" and "children" (2:20) and another the eating of "children" (4:10). Although three different Hebrew words are used in these texts, they are either collective or masculine plural nouns that almost certainly, in light of the other texts mentioning cannibalism, are gender-inclusive.

But what about the gender of those who consume their offspring? The Lamentations passages mention only women. The Deuteronomy text is quite explicit that both women and men, even "the most refined and gentle" among them (vv. 54, 56), will eat their children. Women will even consume the placenta; and both women and men will refuse to share the flesh with any of their closest kin (vv. 55, 57). The other two references to cannibalism, in Leviticus and Jeremiah, use masculine plural language. In light of the Lamentations reference to the mother alone, and because of the very full and gender-inclusive description in the Deuteronomy curses, the Leviticus and Jeremiah passages can be interpreted as referring to both parents committing this horrendous deed. Though not always recognized or acknowledged, it is often the case in the gendered language system of ancient Hebrew that the use of masculine gender words is meant to be gender-inclusive. Surely the warning contained in the covenant curses is meant for all the people (Lev 26:12). What could be a more fitting threat to society than the specter of a woman, the creator of life, taking back into her body as food the very ones to whom she has given birth!

CAROL MEYERS

SEE ALSO Part II: Two Mothers Who Agreed to Eat Their Sons (2 Kgs 6:26–33); Mothers and Widows (Lam 2:12, etc.).

LEV 27:2–8
Female (and Male) Valuations in Votary Pledges

The concluding chapter of the priestly Book of Leviticus concerns the economic support base for the national sanctuary — for maintaining the physical plant and supporting its large staff. Tithes of livestock and farm products and donations of property are all possible contributions, especially if their value in silver is provided rather than the materials themselves. This is especially true in the first set of donation pledges (vv. 2–8) set forth in Leviticus 27: the votive offering of humans, which probably represents their labor potential.

The contribution of humans to the sanctuary is presented in terms of their silver "equivalent" (Hebrew 'erek), a technical term in biblical and other ancient Near Eastern cultic texts for the assessed value of goods in a votive offering system. The human values here are organized by gender and age, with assessments provided separately for females and males in four age groups — one month to four years old (v. 6), five to twenty years old (v. 5), twenty to sixty years old (v. 3–4), and over sixty years old (v. 7).

The first group listed, for people between ages twenty and sixty, involves the highest values; and the lowest values are for the infant-toddler group. That is, in this passage concerned with economic transactions, those whose labor potential is greatest are "worth" the most. As might be expected, the monetary equivalents — in silver shekels according to the "sanctuary weight" (compare Lev 27:25) — are greater for males than for females. Consequently, this passage is often thought to express the notion that males are valued more than females.

That idea, however, can be contested if the labor potential behind the equivalences is properly understood. Adding together the value of the two genders in each age category provides an absolute number representing the value of a female-male pair in each set. Except for the group at five to twenty years, in which childbearing (beginning at puberty) would reduce female labor potential, the female percentage of that combined male-female value hovers at or near 40 percent.

The near 40 percent figure is striking in light of the findings of social scientists who study the relative contributions of women and men to the productive tasks needed for family survival in premodern societies. Women and men, across cultures, provide varying amounts to the family labor pool. Within the wide range of possibilities, a 2:3 ratio (women 40 percent, men 60 percent) of female-male contributions has been found to be optimal for gender relations in general and to indicate maximum prestige accorded to females. The Leviticus text, viewed in such socioeconomic terms, thus presents a favorable view of female worth and indicates a relatively high status for women in Israelite society.

CAROL MEYERS

FOR FURTHER READING: Meyers, Carol. "Procreation, Production, and Protection: Male-Female Balance in Early Israel."

Sanday, Peggy R. "Female Status in the Public Domain."

NUM 5:2–4   Blemished Women

> SEE LEV 13:29, etc.   Blemished Women (and Men) (Part II).

NUM 5:6
Woman (or Man) Who Wrongs Another

Num 5:5–10 concerns an individual who has confessed after defrauding another and having sworn falsely. The culprit is called "a man or a woman" (v. 6); this is unusual, and it is unclear why women should be specifically included in this law. Their inclusion, however, suggests that women could own (and steal) property in ancient Israel.

The archaeological recovery of sealing stones (or their impressions) from Iron Age Palestine that are inscribed with women's names supports the idea that women could own movable goods. These seals were used as "signatures" in business transactions.

MARC ZVI BRETTLER

See also Part I: Achsah; Part II: Daughters of Zelophehad (Num 26:33, etc.).

NUM 5:6
Woman Who Wrongs Another

> SEE LEV 2:1, etc.   Person (Female or Male) Presenting an Offering (Part II).

Num 5:11–31
Woman Accused of Unfaithfulness

One of the longest and most detailed legal cases in the Hebrew Bible concerns the problem of a married woman whose husband suspects infidelity but lacks evidence. It involves a unique biblical example of trial by ordeal that combines legal, cultic, and magical procedures. Because there are no witnesses to the alleged adulterous behavior, the case must be brought directly to God. It is resolved through the performance of a ritual intended to expunge both guilt and suspicion.

The woman accused of infidelity undergoes a quasi trial before a priest in which divine judgment is invoked before she drinks a potion of ink and dust dissolved in water. An innocent woman is expected to suffer no ill effects and is promised fertility. No penalty faces the husband whose suspicions prove false. A guilty woman, however, is supposed to suffer some sort of sexual dysfunction ("her womb shall discharge, her uterus shall drop," v. 27), although the precise meaning of the curse is debated. Suggested interpretations include miscarriage (assuming the accused woman is pregnant), sterility, a prolapsed uterus, or false pregnancy. The law allows no punishment of the presumably guilty woman other than the effects of the potion itself. This contrasts strongly with the death penalty demanded for witnessed adultery (Lev 10:20; Deut 22:22) and may suggest a greater social tolerance for sexual promiscuity and illegitimacy than biblical law otherwise admits.

Because of its excessive repetition and awkward structure, the text is often viewed as a compilation of two or more separate adultery laws. The priest employs a sacrifice, an oath, and a potion to test the suspected woman. The first two verses (5:12–13) explicitly state that she has been unfaithful, but the next phrase attributes the husband's charges to an unsubstantiated fit of jealousy. Twice the woman is set before the altar. Twice the priest gives her an oath that she never expressly utters. Three times he makes her drink the potion.

Despite these difficulties, several recent analyses suggest that the text is a unified composition. Through an analogy with similar legislation in the Code of Hammurabi, some argue for the presence of two mutually exclusive, but related, cases of unwitnessed adultery, the first involving an oath and the second an ordeal. They are to be distinguished by the origin of the allegation and the nature of the evidence supporting it. The first case may arise from public gossip and the second from the husband's jealousy. However, such a distinction is not made clear in the biblical law, which relates the allegations only to the husband.

Other scholars attribute the complex nature of the text to literary technique or authorial intention. Repetition could be used to unify a complex passage by allowing the reader to resume a thought following a short digression. However, the excessive use of repetition in this passage could also indicate an intentional effort to create an air of pomp and ceremony. Because the potion imbibed by the suspected woman is fairly innocuous, the most likely outcome of the trial is her exoneration. The text refers to the lack of evidence supporting the husband's allegations in four separate phrases in v. 13 ("hidden," "undetected," "no witness," and "not caught in the act"), and it scrupulously avoids the technical term for an adulteress. Thus, while lending a tongue-in-cheek dignity to male paranoia, the law ultimately provides an almost transparent charade to pacify the distraught husband. The terms of the ordeal virtually ensure that the fertility, health, and reputation of a suspected woman will be preserved intact. Even though the husband is given a forum for voicing his suspicions, the law reveals a willingness to accept a woman's word in matters of adultery in the absence of contrary evidence.

RHONDA BURNETTE-BLETSCH

SEE ALSO Part II: Adulteress (and Adulterer) (Lev 20:10, etc.); Part III: Woman Stranger (Loose Woman/Adulteress).

FOR FURTHER READING: Fishbane, Michael. "Accusations of Adultery: A Study of Law and Scribal Practice in Numbers 5:11–31."

Frymer-Kensky, Tikva. "The Strange Case of the Suspected Sota (Numbers V 11–31)."

Milgrom, Jacob. "The Case of the Suspected Adulteress, Numbers 5:11–31: Redaction and Meaning."

NUM 6:2–21
Nazirite Woman

Nazirites were persons who made special vows to God, usually asking for some particular benison and promising to observe a period of ardent devotion in return. Outward practices marking the Nazirite varied over time, but in most periods they consisted of three ritual observances: refraining from cutting the hair, from drinking wine or strong drink, and from coming into contact with the dead. The earliest Nazirites (in roughly the tenth through eighth centuries B.C.E.) lived as permanent devotees, but the priestly regulations of the postexilic period assumed that Nazirite vows were to be made for limited intervals, concluded by rituals of sacrifice, purification, and shaving of the head.

Num 6:2–21 clearly identifies both women and men as potential Nazirites, regarding Naziriteship as a particularly demanding type of vow (v. 2). The chapter details Nazirite distinctives (vv. 3–8), prescribes a purification procedure for accidental defilement (vv. 9–12), and recounts the extensive sacrifices required for "desacralization" upon completion of the period (vv. 13–21).

Samson's unnamed mother observed some Nazirite practices before her son was born. The divine messenger who predicted her conception instructed her to avoid wine, strong drink, and unclean foods (Judg 13:4–5). In this narrative, Samson's only proscription is that his hair not be cut: it is Samson's mother who abstains from alcohol, at least during pregnancy.

Hannah became the mother of Samuel after she had prayed for a son, promising to devote her child to God's service. The text does not call Hannah a Nazirite, but suggests that she raised Samuel as a Nazirite (1 Sam 1:11, 22; clearer in the fuller texts preserved by the Septuagint and the main Qumran manuscript of 1 Samuel).

Nazirite vows by women and men apparently

continued into the period of the New Testament and early Judaism. The New Testament speaks of Nazirite vows (Acts 21:23–26), but mentions no Nazirite women. During the first century C.E., however, the Jewish historian Josephus mentioned a Nazirite vow made by Bernice, the wife of King Agrippa. Josephus used the occasion to describe current Nazirite practices: a thirty-day period of abstention from wine before shaving the hair and offering sacrifices (*The Jewish War*, 2.15.1).

The Mishnah (a collection of Jewish legal interpretations of the Torah, dating from the second century C.E.) also mentions female Nazirites. It relates the case of a proselyte, Queen Helene of Adiabene, who promised to become a Nazirite for seven years if her son should return safely from battle. Upon his return, she began fulfilling her vow, but unfortunate technicalities required her to serve twenty-one years before satisfying the rabbis (*Nazir* 3.6).

No vow in Israel was considered more sacred than the Nazirite vow: even the high priest was not so restricted in drinking wine or touching the dead as was the Nazirite. In a culture that thought of a woman's hair as her "glory" (1 Cor 11:15), the willingness to surrender it suggests a true depth of devotion. The Scriptures' testimony that women participated fully in making Nazirite vows reveals one avenue through which biblical women demonstrated their personal piety on equal footing with men.

TONY W. CARTLEDGE

SEE ALSO Part I: Hannah; Part II: Mother or Sister of a Nazirite (Num 6:7); Woman Making a Vow (Num 30:3–15); Mother of Samson (Judg 13:2–25, etc.).

FOR FURTHER READING: Cartledge, Tony W. *Vows in the Hebrew Bible and the Ancient Near East.*
———. "Were Nazirite Vows Unconditional?"

NUM 6:7
Mother or Sister of a Nazirite

Nazirites were required to avoid all contact with the dead, even if the corpse belonged to a close relative such as mother or sister (Num 6:7; compare Lev 21:1–3). Two biblical examples are Samson's unnamed mother (Judg 13:4–5) and Samuel's mother Hannah (1 Sam 1:11, 22), both parents of sons who seem to have lived as Nazirites.

TONY W. CARTLEDGE

SEE ALSO Part II: Women Whom a Priest Can and Cannot Bury (Lev 21:1–3, etc.); Nazirite Woman (Num 6:2–21).

NUM 11:12
Nurse

In a passage in Numbers about the dissatisfaction of the Israelites as they traverse the wilderness from Egypt to the promised land, Moses chafes at his responsibilities. Drawing upon maternal images for God, he poses a series of rhetorical questions to YHWH. Because God has conceived the people, shouldn't God, not Moses, be the one to "carry them in your bosom, as a nurse carries a sucking child?" (11:12). The word translated as "nurse" is actually not the term for a wet nurse. Rather, it designates a "deliverer of child care," and it is grammatically masculine here because it refers to God. In this context, in which Moses demands that YHWH take responsibility for the Israelites, "nurse" indicates general caregiving rather than simple provision of nourishment. In so doing it reveals the assumption that mothers, who conceive children and carry them in their bosoms, were responsible for the well-being of their offspring.

CAROL MEYERS

SEE ALSO Part I: Deborah 1; Part II: Nursing Mothers (Isa 49:15, etc.); Part III: Female Images of God in the Hebrew Bible.

NUM 11:12
Image of God as Conceiving, Bearing, and Nursing the Israelites

SEE Female Images of God in the Hebrew Bible (Part III).

Num 12:1
Cushite Woman, Wife of Moses

Cush is the Hebrew term for ancient (not modern) Ethiopia, the area of the Nile Valley between the first and second cataracts south of Aswan, in modern Sudan. In Num 12:1, Moses is said to have married a Cushite woman. Was she the same as Moses' wife Zipporah, who elsewhere is referred to as Midianite (Exod 2:15–21; 3:1; Num 10:29) and Kenite (Judg 1:16; 4:11)? If the Kenites, a subgroup of the Midianites, had migrated from Cush, then it is plausible that Moses' Cushite wife could be Zipporah. Another possibility is that Cush refers to a place in Midianite territory.

In Num 12:1, Miriam and Aaron speak against Moses because of his Cushite wife. The motivation suggested in 12:2, their questioning whether "the LORD [has] spoken only through Moses," would seem to have little to do with Moses' having a Cushite wife. However, if the wife is Zipporah, a plausible explanation lies in the suggestion that Zipporah's father Jethro may have been instrumental in introducing Moses to the worship of YHWH. Miriam and Aaron could have feared that Moses was acquiring additional authority by marriage to Jethro's daughter, who was a religious functionary herself (Exod 4:24–26). If the Cushite wife is not Zipporah, then the objection may have been to Moses' marriage to a foreign woman; this would reflect the Israelite tendency to favor endogamy (marriage within one's group).

ALICE OGDEN BELLIS

SEE ALSO Part I: Zipporah; Part II: Daughters of the Inhabitants of the Land as Marriage Partners (Exod 34:16, etc.).

FOR FURTHER READING: Bellis, Alice Ogden. *Helpmates, Harlots, and Heroes: Women's Stories in the Hebrew Bible.*

Rice, Gene. "The Africans and the Origin of the Worship of Yahweh."

Num 14:3
Wives (and Children) as Booty

The complaining of the people about the perils and deprivation of the wilderness is a recurrent and jarring theme of the accounts, in Exodus and Numbers, of the post-exodus period of wandering in the Sinai Peninsula en route to the promised land. Incredibly, the people even long to return to Egypt, the place where they had lived in bondage. A new dimension to this longing appears in Num 14:2–3, where people fear the process of entering the land promised to their ancestors, lest the men be killed and the women and children become spoils of war.

This statement differentially favors women (and their offspring), who will live, whereas men will die in the expected military encounters with the inhabitants of the land. The advantage women have in this context is their reproductive capacity. In-

Wall relief from the seventh century B.C.E. palace of Ashurbanipal at Nineveh (in Assyria), showing four women in a cart being transported by their conquerors. Female captives often became slaves or slavewives in the households of the victors. See Wives (and Children) as Booty (Num 14:3); Girls as Booty (Judg 5:30); Women (Wives and Daughters [and Sons]) of Ziklag (1 Sam 30:2, etc.).

deed, it is not uncommon in many premodern cultures, in which there are relatively fewer women of childbearing age than men because of the death of women in childbirth, for the ethics of military victory to allow for claiming wives among the female survivors. The Israelites themselves do this when they defeat the Midianites (Num 31:9–20).

CAROL MEYERS

SEE ALSO Part II: Midianite Women (Num 31:9, etc.); Women in Distant Towns as Booty (Deut 20:14, etc.); Girls as Booty (Judg 5:30); Women (Wives and Daughters [and Sons]) of Ziklag (1 Sam 30:2–3, etc.).

NUM 15:27, 30
Person (Female or Male) Who Sins and Atones

SEE LEV 2:1, etc.   Person (Female or Male) Presenting an Offering (Part II).

NUM 16:27–33
Wives of Dathan and Abiram

These women, along with their children, are judged on account of their husbands' rebellion against Moses, although there is no indication that the women participated in the rebellion. The women and children apparently die (see Deut 11:6), together with their husbands, as punishment. Probably involved in a power struggle among early Israelite leaders, this group is thus irrevocably silenced.

KATHARINE DOOB SAKENFELD

NUM 18:11, 19   Daughters of Aaron

SEE LEV 10:14–15, etc.   Daughters (and Sons) of a Priest (Part II).

NUM 19:22
Person Becoming Purified

SEE LEV 2:1, etc.   Person (Female or Male) Presenting an Offering (Part II).

NUM 21:25   Villages as Daughters

SEE Mother/Daughter (NRSV, Village) as Territory (Part III).

NUM 21:29
Daughters of Moab

"Daughters," in this poetic verse attributed to the "ballad singers," refers to all the women of the land of Moab. They are described as war captives of King Sihon of the neighboring Amorites. Removal of progeny and women is a vivid way to express the defeat of a people.

KATHARINE DOOB SAKENFELD

SEE ALSO Part II: Moabite Women (Num 25:1).

NUM 25:1
Moabite Women

Near the end of the forty years of wandering in the wilderness, Israelite men join these foreign women in sexual relations and in worship of their gods. The results are disastrous for the Israelites.

This is one of many narratives that depict tensions with the Moabites, who are sometimes enemies and sometimes in close relationship to the Israelites. These narratives show struggles in setting political and social boundaries, which are sometimes crossed through intergroup sexual relations.

KATHARINE DOOB SAKENFELD

SEE ALSO Part I: Cozbi; Part II: Daughters of Moab (Num 21:29).

NUM 26:33; 27:1–11; 36:1–12; JOSH 17:3–6; 1 CHR 7:15
Daughters of Zelophehad

The story of the five daughters of Zelophehad provides legitimation of a limited right of Israelite women to inherit land. It also places specific marriage restrictions upon any women who inherit under this right. The story celebrates women's boldness and at the same time offers comfort for men who have the misfortune (from the Bible's androcentric point of view) to have no sons.

Zelophehad has five daughters, Mahlah, Noah, Hoglah, Milcah, and Tirzah; he has no sons. Zelophehad is part of the generation of Israelites who departed from Egypt under Moses' leadership and died during the forty years in the wilderness. His five daughters belong to the new generation that would enter and possess the promised land. (Their mother is never mentioned.)

According to God's decree, the promised land is to be apportioned according to the "number of names" of members of the second generation counted in the census recorded in Numbers 26 (see 26:52–56). Since only men were counted in the census, however, Zelophehad's daughters would be left without an inheritance.

Mahlah, Noah, Hoglah, Milcah, and Tirzah come forward to appeal this regulation, stating their case in front of the sacred tent of meeting in the presence of Moses, Eleazar the priest, the leaders, and indeed the whole community (Num 27:2). They argue that their father's name (lineage) should not be cut off from his clan just because he had no son and that they should be permitted to inherit his land portion (v. 4) in order to avoid this potential injustice to their father's name (and property). The story presumes a culture that recognizes a connection between landholding and preservation of a male name in a family lineage.

Moses consults God, and God announces the decision to Moses: the proposal of the daughters of Zelophehad is to be implemented (vv. 5–7). The text then moves beyond the particular case to report God's further generalized regulation for order of inheritance: when there are no sons, daughters shall have first inheritance rights, followed by other male relatives in a set sequence (vv. 8–11).

Later on, the male relatives of the Manassite clan to which Zelophehad belonged recognize what to them appears to be a large loophole in this ruling. Their appeal to Moses is recorded in Numbers 36.

The male relatives point out that when the daughters of Zelophehad get married, the land that they have inherited will go with them to the clans of their husbands. (The possibility that a man might change clans in such a case was presumably beyond Israel's imagining.) The relatives are concerned that the marriage of any of the daughters outside their own tribe will lead to diminution of the Manassite landholdings. Moses announces that God does not intend any moving of land from tribe to tribe. As insurance against such movement, the daughters of Zelophehad (and any other daughters who inherit land) must marry within the clan of their father's tribe.

The daughters do marry within their clan (Num 36:10–12) and eventually receive their inheritance (Josh 17:3–6).

KATHARINE DOOB SAKENFELD

SEE ALSO Part I: Achsah; Hoglah; Mahlah 1; Milcah 2; Noah; Tirzah.

FOR FURTHER READING: Graham, M. Patrick. "Mahlah."

Sakenfeld, Katharine Doob. "Feminist Biblical Interpretation."

NUM 30:3–15
Woman Making a Vow

In the Bible, the making of vows was a popular means of expressing personal piety and of seeking divine favor. Many examples of vows made by women have survived in texts and inscriptions from the ancient Near East. The Hebrews, like their neighbors, made conditional vows: one asked a special request of God and promised some gift or service in return. These could include extra sacrificial offerings, gifts to the temple, or special acts of worship.

For example, childless Hannah requested a son and promised to return him to YHWH (1 Sam 1:11). Priestly legislation governing the vows of Nazirites speaks to women as well as to men (Num 6:2–21), and material from the later Jewish sources (the

Mishnah, tractates *Nedarim* and *Nazir*) also addresses both genders.

In Num 30:3–15, however, the power of certain women to make vows was restricted. Independent women (widows and divorcees), presumably because they controlled property and their own labor, were free to make vows as they wished (v. 10), but the vows of other women were subject to validation by their father or husband. Even so, the authoritative male could annul the vow only by declaring his displeasure upon first hearing of it. Otherwise, it became binding.

TONY W. CARTLEDGE

SEE ALSO Part II: Nazirite Woman (Num 6:2–21).

FOR FURTHER READING: Cartledge, Tony W. *Vows in the Hebrew Bible and the Ancient Near East.*

NUM 31:9, 15–18, 35
Midianite Women

After a confrontation with the Midianites, during the period of wandering in the wilderness after the exodus, the victorious Israelites take all the women captive. Moses asserts that Midianite women were the cause of Israelite apostasy (see Numbers 25) and requires that all women who have had sexual relations be put to death. Virgin girls may be kept as war captives and are apportioned in the same way as animal booty. The total of sixteen thousand virgin captives (v. 35) is unrealistic historically, as is the equally fantastic claim of over 800,000 animals taken in booty.

The taking of virgins may have been allowed for demographic reasons. Because of death in childbirth, marriageable women were often scarce in supply in premodern societies. In addition, virgins would not have been pregnant with a child of the enemy.

Deut 21:10–14 offers protections for women taken captive in warfare, but such protection may have been available only to captives selected for marriage.

KATHARINE DOOB SAKENFELD

SEE ALSO Part I: Cozbi; Part II: Daughters of the Inhabitants of the Land as Marriage Partners (Exod 34:16, etc.); Wives (and Children) as Booty (Num 14:3).

NUM 31:19, 28; 35:11, 15, 30b
Person (Female and Male)

SEE LEV 2:1, etc. Person (Female or Male) Presenting an Offering (Part II).

NUM 36:1–12
Daughters of Zelophehad

SEE NUM 26:33, etc. Daughters of Zelophehad (Part II).

DEUT 2:34; 3:6
Women (and Men and Children) in Towns of the Amorite Kings Sihon and Og

In Deuteronomy 2 and 3, Moses summarizes the most recent events in Israel's history, their trek out of the Sinai Peninsula to the area on the east side of the Jordan River and the battles fought there against two Amorite kings, Sihon of Heshbon and Og of Bashan. In every town of each king, the Israelites are said to have killed every man, woman, and child, leaving no survivors, although livestock and material goods were kept as booty (2:34–35; 3:6–7). This same chilling pattern of killing all human beings appears in stories of capture of land west of the Jordan (for example, Josh 6:21; 8:25–26; 10:40; 11:20). The practice of killing all human beings is called "devotion to destruction" (Hebrew *ḥērem*; Josh 6:21). Historically, the practice was probably never fully carried out. The Hebrew Bible itself has different ideologies of war and provides differing justifications for this horrific aspect of military encounters. Some traditions claim that God required it because of the wickedness of those being destroyed. The intent also is represented as expediency: prevention of apostasy by eliminating all sources of temptation.

Israelite treatment of enemies in battle varies in

different narratives and laws, although the modern idea of distinction between combatants and civilians does not appear. In Numbers 31, for example, virgin Midianite women are kept as war captives, whereas those women who had had sexual relations are killed. A law in Deut 20:14–16 requires death of all persons in nearby towns (as in the case of the lands of Sihon and Og) but allows women and children of more distant towns to be taken captive. Often, women in war are treated differently than men because of their reproductive potential. Not so the Amorite women. The Amorites (sometimes called Canaanites) occupied land designated for Israel, and they had to be annihilated for Israel to realize its territorial claims.

KATHARINE DOOB SAKENFELD

SEE ALSO Part II: Wives (and Children) as Booty (Num 14:3); Daughters of Moab (Num 21:29); Midianite Women (Num 31:9, etc.); Women in Distant Towns as Booty (Deut 20:14, etc.).

FOR FURTHER READING: Fewell, Danna Nolan. "Joshua."

Niditch, Susan. *War in the Hebrew Bible: A Study in the Ethics of Violence.*

DEUT 3:19
Israelite Wives

A retrospective survey of the Israelite occupation of the promised land, which includes territory on both sides of the Jordan River, is presented in the opening three chapters of Deuteronomy. The decidedly military tone of the narrative appears in the directive to the members of tribes that take hold of the Transjordanian allotment: the men of these tribes — the fighting men — shall serve as a vanguard for the tribes meant to occupy the territory west of the Jordan. Those men, who will already have settled their families, will serve as shock troops. They must, therefore, leave behind their households, which consist of women (NRSV, "wives"), dependents (NRSV, "children"), and animals (NRSV, "livestock").

The technical Hebrew term *ṭap* ("dependent") is used here, rather than the more common *bēn* ("child"), because it signifies a range of household members — servants and the elderly, as well as children. Women are usually part of that collective term (as in Gen 47:12) and thus are often invisible in translations that render the term "little ones" or "children" rather than "dependents" or "household" (as Exod 10:10, 24; Judg 18:21). In the military context of Deut 3:19, because women are considered inherently ineligible for combat, they are listed separately, apart from those household members unfit for military service for reasons other than gender.

CAROL MEYERS

FOR FURTHER READING: Locher, C. "*ṭap.*"

DEUT 4:16   Female Idol
SEE Female (and Male) Idol (Part III).

DEUT 5:14, 16, 18
Women in the Decalogue
SEE EXOD 20:8, etc.   Women in the Decalogue (Part II).

DEUT 5:14   Female Slave
SEE EXOD 21:7–11, etc.   Female (and Male) Hebrew Slaves (Part II).

DEUT 7:3
Daughters of the Nations in the Land
SEE EXOD 34:16, etc.   Daughters of the Inhabitants of the Land as Marriage Partners (Part II).

DEUT 7:14
Sterile Female (and Male)

The introductory materials for the Book of Deuteronomy include many motivational statements, providing encouragement for the people to obey God's word. One such statement proclaims that fidelity to God will bring about the blessings of survival, that is, good health and bountiful sustenance. The latter is specified in Deut 7:13 as the promise of fertility of family ("fruit of your womb"), crops ("fruit of your ground, your grain and your wine and your oil"), and livestock ("increase of your cattle and . . . flocks").

In the next verse (7:14), the message of fecundity is reiterated in the statement that there will be no "sterile male or sterile female among you or your livestock." The NRSV, by translating this passage "neither sterility nor barrenness among you or your livestock," obscures the way in which the Hebrew text uses the masculine and feminine forms of a root (*'qr*) signifying infertility. That usage apparently indicates an awareness that failure to produce offspring can result from male impotence or sterility as well as female barrenness.

CAROL MEYERS

SEE ALSO Part II: Barren Woman (Exod 23:26, etc.).

DEUT 10:18   Widow

SEE EXOD 22:22, etc.   Widows (Part II).

DEUT 12:12; 16:11, 14
Daughters (and Sons) and Female (and Male) Slaves, Rejoicing

The general Deuteronomic stipulations for bringing offerings to the central sanctuary appear in chap. 12. The command to bring all sacrifices and donations is addressed to the collective "you" (masculine plural), which here is gender-inclusive because in v. 12 the text specifies that the rejoicing of those who bring offerings will include, in addition to the addressed "you" and also Levites in the community, all members of the household: daughters and sons, and female and male slaves. Wives are not designated apart from the masculine "you," which thus is being used in a neuter sense to designate the senior female-and-male conjugal pair of a family group, just as the language of the Decalogue

does (except in the last commandment). Deut 12:12, which expands the language of 12:7 (addressed to "you [masculine plural] and your households together"), thus includes all members of the households among the participants in the responsibilities and joys of the sacrificial system enjoined upon the people as a whole. A similar injunction in Deuteronomy 16 (vv. 11, 14) lists all who are to keep the festivals. In that list, again the addressed "you" includes the senior female as well as the senior male in the household, the female and male children and servants, and the Levites in the community. The list expands the specified celebrants to include the "strangers, the orphans, and the widows resident in your towns" (16:14).

CAROL MEYERS

SEE ALSO Part II: Women in the Decalogue (Exod 20:8, etc.); Israelite Women in the Covenant Community (Deut 29:11; etc.); Women (and Men) of the Ark Ceremony (2 Sam 6:19); Women, Part of Assembly of People (Neh 8:2–3, etc.).

DEUT 12:31; 18:10; 2 KGS 17:17; 23:10; PS 106:37–38; JER 7:31; 32:35; EZEK 16:20
Daughter (or Son or Child) Passed Through Fire, Burned, or Sacrificed

The phrase "to cause one's son/daughter/child to pass [Hebrew *'br*] through fire," followed by the name of a god, is a fixed expression referring to child sacrifice (Lev 18:21; Deut 18:10; 2 Kgs 16:3; 17:17; 21:6; 23:10; 2 Chr 28:3; 33:6; Jer 32:35; Ezek 16:21; 20:26, 31; 23:37). Similar passages referring to child sacrifice use other verbs, such as *to burn* (Deut 12:31; 2 Kgs 17:31; Jer 7:31; 19:5), *to sacrifice* (Ps 106:37–38; Ezek 16:20), or *to give* (Lev 20:2–4). Some of these verses delete the name of the god or the word *fire*. Some mention sons *and* daughters (Deut 12:31; 18:10; 2 Kgs 17:17; 23:10; Ps 106:37–38; Jer 32:35; 7:31; Ezek 16:20), others only sons (2 Kgs 16:3; 21:6; 2 Chr

28:3; 33:6), others the firstborn in particular but without reference to gender (Ezek 20:26), and others only children in general (Lev 18:21; 20:2–4; 2 Kgs 17:31; Jer 19:5; Ezek 16:21; 20:31; 23:37).

The Israelite attitude toward child sacrifice can be seen in Exod 13:11–15, which states that all firstborn males were to be "set apart [*'br*] to the LORD." Exod 13:15 reveals that *to set apart* actually means "to sacrifice"; thus, all firstborn male animals and children conceptually belonged to God and were subject to sacrifice. The passage makes an exception, however, for firstborn male donkeys and firstborn sons. These could be "redeemed," meaning that another animal could be substituted for them. This law, as well as the story of the binding of Isaac in Genesis 22, illustrates the special status of the firstborn child.

Despite its many condemnations of child sacrifice, the biblical text contains several accounts of it. The Judean kings Ahaz and Manasseh sacrificed their sons (2 Kgs 16:3; 21:6; 2 Chr 28:3; 33:6), as did Hiel of Bethel (1 Kgs 16:34) and Mesha of Moab (2 Kgs 3:27). Unlike Abraham, who was prevented from sacrificing Isaac, Jephthah sacrificed his daughter (Judg 11:31) in exchange for extraordinary divine intervention. It should be noted, however, that all of these incidents refer to extraordinary situations. Often the sacrifices were meant to offset military defeat and do not represent regularly occurring rituals.

Other references, perhaps involving regular rituals, appear to mention a deity named Molech, who received child sacrifice (Lev 18:21; 20:2–5; 2 Kgs 23:10; Jer 32:35); however, certain scholars believe that the word *molech* is not the name of a deity, but rather the name of a particular type of child sacrifice ritual. Another technical term related to child sacrifice is *tophet* (2 Kgs 23:10; Jer 7:31–32; 19:6, 11–14), a cultic installation where child sacrifice occurred and where the victims were buried.

Child sacrifice may be rooted in the notion that God gives children and therefore God has the right to demand their return through sacrifice. Inscriptional material from child sacrifice burial grounds, however, such as the one excavated at Punic Carthage (containing more than twenty thousand

burials dating from the eighth through second centuries B.C.E.), indicates that animal surrogates were often used in child sacrifice rituals. In the earliest strata, as many as one in three burials represents animal surrogates. Other Punic inscriptions, such as the Ngaous III stele from Algeria, also record the use of surrogates. The sacrifice of one's actual child, as described in inscriptions such as those found in Idalion in Cyprus, was believed to carry a great deal of power. This power, however, seems only to have been invoked in periods of extreme distress.

ELIZABETH C. LaROCCA-PITTS

SEE ALSO Part II: Daughter of Jephthah (Judg 11:34–40).

FOR FURTHER READING: Cross, Frank Moore. "A Phoenician Inscription from Idalion: Some Old and New Texts Relating to Child Sacrifice."

Green, Alberto R. W. *The Role of Human Sacrifice in the Ancient Near East.*

Heider, George C. "Molech."

Stager, Lawrence E., and Samuel R. Wolff. "Child Sacrifice at Carthage — Religious Rite or Population Control?"

DEUT 13:6
Women (Daughter, Wife) (and Men: Brother, Son) Who Lead a Person to Idolatry

The Deuteronomic abhorrence of disloyalty to YHWH is so powerful that the text mandates death by stoning for those who follow other deities (Deut 17:2–5). The intensity of the prohibition appears in the stipulation that this death penalty be enforced even by someone whose closest kin or companion worships other gods. That is, a person with a family member or friend who thus violates the covenant shall be the first to take part in the execution of the transgressor. The list of such transgressors who are kin delineates the core of a patrilineal group — wife, brothers (including half brothers: "father's son" or "mother's son"), children (both female and male).

The specification of "wife" is augmented by the information that she is the one whom "you embrace" (literally, "of your bosom"), which implies sexual relations. This language focuses on the intimacy of the relationship and thus indicates how extreme is the demand to put her to death should she try to introduce idolatry into the household. A similar though nonsexual intimacy is implied for the person's friend (literally, "the friend who is as your own being"). A wife and a close friend thus represent a man's two most intimate relationships in this grim scenario.

CAROL MEYERS

SEE ALSO Part II: Women (and Men) Who Break the Covenant (Deut 17: 2–5, etc.).

DEUT 14:29   Widows

SEE EXOD 22:22, etc.   Widows (Part II).

DEUT 15:12–18   Female Hebrew Slaves

SEE EXOD 21:7–11, etc.   Female (and Male) Hebrew Slaves (Part II).

DEUT 16:11, 14   Widows

SEE EXOD 22:22, etc.   Widows (Part II).

DEUT 16:11, 14
Women Keeping the Festivals

SEE DEUT 12:12, etc.   Daughters (and Sons) and Female (and Male) Slaves, Rejoicing (Part II).

DEUT 17:2–5; 29:18
Women (and Men) Who Break the Covenant

The covenant community includes women as well as men. Women are enjoined to bring offerings and to keep the festivals, all as part of a system connecting the people to one god, YHWH. Conversely, therefore, women are culpable, as are men, for breaking the covenant by worshipping other gods (Deut 17:2–7). The death penalty is mandated for that transgression. Furthermore, everyone is required to help identify such an abhorrent act. If two or three witnesses testify at the city gate — the site of judicial proceedings — against a suspected idolater, that person, female or male, shall be stoned to death, with the witnesses throwing the first stone.

This principle — that idolatry is a capital and unforgivable offense — is reiterated at the end of Deuteronomy in chap. 29, where the naming of women (and men) who break the covenant is expanded to the corporate level — "family or tribe" (29:18).

CAROL MEYERS

SEE ALSO Part II: Daughters (and Sons) and Female (and Male) Slaves, Rejoicing (Deut 12:12, etc.); Women (Daughter, Wife) (and Men: Brother, Son) Who Lead a Person to Idolatry (Deut 13:16); Women in Covenant Curses (Deut 27:16, etc.).

DEUT 17:14–20
Wives of the King

Deut 17:14–20, in its final form a late utopian text critical of the concentration of political power in monarchic rule, reluctantly permits Israel to have a king. It then seeks to prohibit the typical perquisites of kingship. The king is not to amass wealth, build up his cavalry, or "acquire many wives" (v. 17). Marriage in ancient Israel represented an alliance between two families, or, in the case of the king and a non-Israelite wife, two peoples. The prohibition against acquiring many wives seeks to limit such alliances, perhaps partly because they represent trust in political stratagems rather than in YHWH, but primarily out of fear that foreign wives might lead the king to worship foreign gods (compare Deut 7:3; 1 Kgs 11:1–8; 16:30–31).

CAROLYN PRESSLER

SEE ALSO Part II: Wives and Concubines of David, Taken in Jerusalem (2 Sam 5:13); Wives of Saul (2 Sam 12:8); Wives of David (2 Sam 12:11, etc.); Women of Solomon (1 Kgs 3:1, etc.).

DEUT 18:10
Daughter Passed Through Fire

SEE DEUT 12:31, etc. Daughter (or Son or Child) Passed Through Fire, Burned, or Sacrificed (Part II).

DEUT 20:7; 24:5
Fiancée/Wife of a Soldier

Deut 20:5–7 enumerates three cases in which men are exempt from army service: the man who has built a new house, but has not initiated it; the man who has planted a vineyard, but has not yet eaten from it; and the man who has become engaged to a woman, most likely by transferring money to the bride's household, but has not yet married her. Jer 29:5–6 suggests that these three activities — building houses, planting vineyards, and marrying (and having children) — represent normal life. All three activities have two separable stages, but these stages naturally belong together, and the jurist is concerned that the man who began the larger activity be allowed to complete it.

A law complementary to Deut 20:7, in Deut 24:5, prohibits a man from serving in the army during his first year of marriage to a "new wife" so he may "give pleasure" to her (author's translation).

MARC ZVI BRETTLER

DEUT 20:14; 21:11–14
Women in Distant Towns as Booty

The narrative and legal portions of Deuteronomy are replete with assumptions about the Israelites as a military presence in the promised land, on both sides of the Jordan River. Laws dealing with troops and an army include stipulations for dealing with conquered settlements. The enemy population that is found within the boundaries of the land allotted to the Israelites is to be totally destroyed, under the application of the so-called ban *(ḥērem)*; see Deut 20:16–18. The origins of this horrific practice are obscure; but, couched in the language of sacred warfare and found in other ancient cultures, it may have functioned to help establish and preserve political communities by removing populations that could erode or threaten their physical or cultural boundaries. References to the ban in the Bible, however, present the objects of annihilation as sacrifices to God; and they often justify this extreme level of violence by claiming that the enemies were so sinful that they deserved destruction as divine punishment.

For conquered towns located outside Israel's territory, the requisite slaughter is not total: only the warriors — the men — need be slain (Deut 20:13). Women and children and also livestock are spared, although the reasons for this differential treatment are difficult to discern. Perhaps because of the demographic crises precipitated by warfare, drought, and famine and also because women of childbearing age were in short supply as the result

Detail of a wall relief from the ninth-century B.C.E. palace at Nimrud (in Assyria), showing three female captives, two of whom have a child. One lifts her hands in a mourning gesture. Such captives became slaves to the conquerors and were unlikely ever to return to their own families. See Women in Distant Towns as Booty *(Deut 20:14, etc.);* Daughters of Moab *(Num 21:29);* Midianite Women *(Num 31:9, etc.);* Girls as Booty *(Judg 5:30).*

of death in childbirth, the captured women and children constituted needed population (and potential population) and labor. And livestock provided capital and a drought-resistant food supply. At the same time, in the male culture of warfare, women and children, along with material goods, are considered war trophies, chattels that denote the valor and success of the male warriors.

Whatever the origin of the stipulation that foreign women could be spared and then be taken as wives, their status as such evoked special consideration. The captive women taken as wives are treated in a prescribed way that allows them to make the transition from their culture of birth to that of their new households (Deut 21:11–13). The period of one month allotted to a captive wife to mourn the loss of her natal family also allows the new husband to be sure she is not pregnant before initiating marital relations with her. Thus he can be certain of the paternity of children she may bear. Should such a woman's new husband change his mind about her desirability, he cannot treat her as he would a slave. Rather, he must free her because he has "dishonored" her (Deut 21:14). The word for dishonor (from Hebrew ʿnh) indicates (sexual?) humiliation, perhaps because the usual contractual procedures for marriage were not followed. That is, the woman was forced to become his wife, whereas women otherwise often consented to the marital liaisons arranged by their parents.

CAROL MEYERS

SEE ALSO Part II: Wives (and Children) as Booty (Num 14:3); Daughters of Moab (Num 21:29); Midianite Women (Num 31:9, etc.); Women (and Men) of Jericho and Ai (Josh 6:21, etc.); Girls as Booty (Judg 5:30); Women (Wives and Daughters [and Sons]) of Ziklag (1 Sam 30:2–3, etc.).

FOR FURTHER READING: Niditch, Susan. *War in the Hebrew Bible: A Study in the Ethics of Violence.*

Pressler, Carolyn. *The View of Women Found in the Deuteronomic Family Laws.*

Washington, Harold C. "'Lest He Die in the Battle and Another Man Take Her': Violence and the Construction of Gender in the Laws of Deuteronomy."

Deut 21:13
Mother (and Father) of Captive Women

Although Israelite men typically took wives from their own people and usually from their own or nearby villages, occasionally they acquired foreign wives who were brought into their households as prisoners of war. That is, a female captive who became a man's slave could become his wife. Deuteronomic law shows respect for such a wife and imposes moral obligations upon her husband. Included in those features is the stipulation that the husband give a captured woman a month of mourning for her mother and her father before he establishes conjugal relations (21:13).

Because the thirty days represent a typical period of mourning for the dead (see Num 20:29; Deut 34:8), a captured woman, who will never again see her parents, is evidently to regard them as if they were dead. This procedure for a foreign wife implies that the opposite would be true for indigenous wives. That is, a woman would move in with her husband's family, according to the Israelite custom of patrilocal marriage (marriage in which the wife resides with her husband's kin), but she would continue to have some contact with her natal family.

CAROL MEYERS

SEE ALSO Part II: Female (and Male) Hebrew Slaves (Exod 21:7–11, etc.); Daughters of the Inhabitants of the Land as Marriage Partners (Exod 34:16, etc.); Concubine of Gideon Jerubbaal (Judg 8:31, etc.).

Deut 21:15–17
Two Wives and Their Offspring

Deuteronomy provides that a man who has two wives, one of whom he clearly favors, cannot name the first male child born of the beloved wife his firstborn in place of the firstborn child of the disliked wife. The "firstborn," Hebrew *bĕkôr*, inherited a double portion of the father's estate and may also have inherited a ceremonial position in relationship to the ancestors. Near Eastern documents, particularly those from Nuzi, show that naming the firstborn was originally at the discretion of the father. Moreover, a full wife's children would be expected to take precedence over a concubine's, and a beloved wife's son over that of a less favored one. The story of Isaac's blessing (Genesis 27) shows that the father had the ability to choose in ancestral Israel. So too in Jacob's family, in which Reuben was the firstborn of Leah and Joseph the firstborn of the beloved Rachel. Joseph's dreams (Gen 37:5–11) show that he believed that his father might make him the firstborn; the brothers' reaction to the dreams show that they thought so too.

Deuteronomic laws often eliminate the power of the head of household, providing set procedures where the men had previously had the ability to choose. As part of this trend, Deuteronomy eliminates the role of choice in the designation of the firstborn. In Deuteronomy, the first male born becomes the firstborn, and only the date of birth determines this designation.

TIKVA FRYMER-KENSKY

FOR FURTHER READING: Frymer-Kensky, Tikva. "Patriarchal Family Relationships and Near Eastern Law." Frymer-Kensky, Tikva. "Deuteronomy."

DEUT 21:18–21
Mother (and Father) Dealing with a Rebellious Son

The family household in the Israelite village communities, in which most people lived in biblical times, was the major locus of daily life in all its aspects. It served primary economic, social, educational, religious, and even juridical functions. Because farming households were usually formed by compound (or extended) families, maintaining the authority of the senior female-male pair over their offspring, especially once the offspring became adults but remained in their parents' house-

hold, was critical for family stability. Grown children faced capital punishment for disobeying or abusing their parents (see Exod 21:15, 17).

Household justice could apparently be initiated by parental action. Deuteronomic law provides procedures for both mother and father to bring a "rebellious son" to an extrafamilial panel of elders, who will implement the death penalty. A rebellious daughter is not included in this text because adult female offspring were no longer present in their natal homes; they would have moved to their husbands' households when they married.

CAROL MEYERS

SEE ALSO Part II: Mother (or Father) Cursed or Struck by Offspring (Exod 21:15, etc.); Mother (and Father) of a Slandered Bride (Deut 22:15).

FOR FURTHER READING: Pressler, Carolyn. *The View of Women Found in the Deuteronomic Family Laws.*

DEUT 22:5
Women's (and Men's) Clothing

In all societies, clothing protects people and keeps them warm (see Exod 22:26–27); it can also signify sexual attractiveness, as does a bride's attire (Jer 2:32). The garments people wear can supply information about the wearer. In ancient Israel, for example, women in mourning apparently wore certain garb, as did prostitutes (see Gen 38:14); high priests had distinctive raiment (Exod 28:2–5), as perhaps did some prophetic figures (2 Kgs 2:8–14; Zech 13:4). Whatever specific status, role, or ethnicity garments may indicate, gender is virtually always signified by some differences in dress; and the law in Deut 22:5, instructing women not to don male "apparel" (Hebrew kĕlî, which can also denote "weapon") and men not to wear a woman's "garment," assumes that certain items of clothing can be identified with one or the other gender.

The reasons that this text forbids women and men to wear each other's gender-specific items of dress are not clear. Some commentators suggest that it is a direct prohibition of transvestism or an indirect measure for preventing homosexuality. Others have noted that it is linked to the claim that cross-dressing is "abhorrent to YHWH your God" and may thus indicate an underlying polemic against foreign cultic practices; the phrase "abhorrent to YHWH" in Deuteronomy seems to refer to matters of proper cultic behavior (as Deut 7:25) and, in reference to gendered clothing, may be prohibiting certain practices of other ancient peoples. One other possibility is that the text simply expresses a propensity for order, whereby distinct categories are not mixed (as in the prohibition in Deut 22:11 about making fabrics with a wool and cotton blend): female and male, with associated items of apparel, have separate gendered identities.

CAROL MEYERS

DEUT 22:13–21
Young Woman Accused of Not Being a Virgin

SEE EXOD 22:16–17, etc.   Virgin (Part II).

DEUT 22:15
Mother (and Father) of a Slandered Bride

A legal case presented in Deut 22:13–21 concerns the slander of a new bride. It consists of an original case involving the slander of a wife by her new husband (vv. 13–19) and a later addition, which considers the possibility that the slander might prove correct (vv. 20–21). The mother of the slandered woman explicitly appears only in the original case, whereas the secondary verses emphasize her father's house. Because the later (Deuteronomic) redactor of this law assumes a more masculine perspective, the mother's role in the trial is obscured. This might explain why only the father is explicitly named as the recipient of monetary damages.

Although a married daughter is no longer part of their residential household, both mother and father bring their slanderous son-in-law to trial in order to restore their daughter's honor and their own.

The involvement of both parents in these proceedings indicates shared responsibility for their children and shared authority within kinship matters (compare Deut 21:18–21). It also indicates that married women retained contact with and the support of their parents, who could continue to intercede on their behalf in conflicts with affinal relatives.

The nature of the parents' involvement depends upon the slander circulated about their daughter. The husband may have accused her of premarital unchastity, which he discovered from the absence of bleeding associated with the breaking of the hymen during initial intercourse. Because her parents disprove this rumor by producing a blood-stained cloth, this presupposes a ritual of examination on the wedding night. Although such rituals are common in cultures concerned with female virginity, typically the husband or his family takes possession of the stained bedclothes. If the charge does involve premarital unchastity, then the bride's parents had a more active role in this custom in ancient Israel, possibly because they had been responsible for safeguarding their daughter's virginity.

However, the word *bĕtûlâ,* often translated "virgin" in the NRSV, typically denotes any adolescent female, regardless of her sexual experience. Hence, the stained cloth could show menstrual blood. If so, the husband has wrongly charged his new wife with being pregnant by another man prior to their wedding night. By refuting the slander, her parents are contending that they did not attempt to pass off another man's child on the prospective husband when they arranged the marriage. Thus, parents would be motivated to preserve the virginity of their daughters, not because virginity was considered valuable in itself, but for reasons of paternity.

RHONDA BURNETTE-BLETSCH

SEE ALSO Part II: Virgin (Exod 22:16–17, etc.); Mother (and Father) Dealing with a Rebellious Son (Deut 21:18–21).

FOR FURTHER READING: Frymer-Kensky, Tikva. "Virginity in the Bible."

DEUT 22:22   Adulteress

SEE LEV 20:10, etc.   Adulteress (and Adulterer) (Part II).

DEUT 22:23–29
Unmarried Young Women Who Have Sex

SEE EXOD 22:16–17, etc.   Virgin (Part II).

DEUT 22:30
Father's Wife in Incest Regulations

SEE LEV 18:7–18, etc.   Women in Incest Regulations (Part II).

DEUT 23:17; GEN 38:21; HOS 4:14
Temple Prostitute

Deut 23:17 can be translated literally, "There shall be no female temple prostitute from the women of Israel, and there shall be no male temple prostitute from the men of Israel." The two halves of the verse thus correspond word for word. The key terms are *qĕdēšâ* for the female temple prostitute and *qādēš* for the male. The Hebrew root *qdš* refers generally to "holiness." Thus, this verse has long been interpreted as a blanket prohibition, for both females and males, of temple prostitution in Israel.

Temple prostitution in this case would be defined as the performance of sexual acts for payment on the part of a specific class of temple personnel, but the term could include an act of prostitution by a member of the laity for the benefit of a temple. A priestess who participated in a "sacred marriage" could also be included under this heading, along with the laywoman who participated in sexual activities as part of a ritual. Often scholars project a magical dimension onto this sexual act, especially "sacred marriage," and suggest that it promoted the fertility of the land and its inhabitants. Although Greek and Latin authors, along with modern scholars, detect all these forms of temple prostitution in their descriptions of ancient Israelite and Mesopotamian religious life, primary texts from these cultures offer little unambiguous testimony to confirm them.

Recent research regarding the terms used in Deut 23:17, *qĕdēšâ* and *qādēš*, place in doubt the widespread assumption that both refer to temple prostitutes. In Mesopotamian documents, we encounter a kind of female religious professional with the title *qadištu*, also from the Semitic root *qdš*, "holy." Her supposed role as a temple prostitute has been thought to provide proof that her Israelite counterpart, the *qĕdēšâ*, likewise had a sexual function in the cult. The reevaluation of the texts that mention the *qadištu* suggests that she assumed various cultic roles, yet none of these are explicitly sexual. In the Ugaritic texts, which reflect Canaanite culture in the Late Bronze Age (1550–1200 B.C.E.), *qdšm* signifies a class of cult personnel, who are generally mentioned after the priests. Any insinuation of sexual activity is lacking. Nor does the Septuagint provide proof for the translation "temple prostitute."

In the Hebrew Bible, the assumption of a sexual/cultic role for the *qĕdēšâ* and *qādēš* may result from the confusion of their distinct functions. On the basis of Ugaritic texts and various biblical passages that refer to the *qādēš* (1 Kgs 14:24; 15:12; 22:46; 2 Kgs 23:7), it can be concluded that the term *qādēš* refers to a priestly class rejected as illegitimate by the editor of Kings. The nature of their activities is not specified in these texts. In contrast, the feminine *qĕdēšâ* always appears as a synonym of *zōnâ*, the Hebrew word for the common prostitute (Gen 38:21–22; Deut 23:17–18; Hos 4:14). This could suggest that these two closely related words, *qādēš* and *qĕdēšâ*, masculine and feminine, refer to two different professions. The bipartite structure of Deut 23:17, with each half referring to a different gender, could suggest that the feminine and masculine nouns should be distinguished and refer to two distinct classes of people, common harlots and pagan priests. The author of Deuteronomy treated both of these classes in the same verse because both were detested by the pious writer and obviously, because of the homonymy of the two words, *qādēš* and *qĕdēšâ*. This proposed distinction contrasts with the traditional view of commentators that both terms refer to females and males who engage in a single profession, temple prostitution.

The *qĕdēšâ* is mentioned in two other biblical passages. In Genesis 38, Judah encounters Tamar at a crossroads, not a temple, and assumes that she's a *zōnâ*, a common harlot (v. 15). Judah's Canaanite friend, Hirah, introduces the word *qĕdēšâ* in his query to the people of Timnah, who reply with the same term (vv. 21–22). The variation might be a function of their different ethnic backgrounds, as Hirah inquires of the harlot's whereabouts with a term that suggests her identity as he and the locals knew it, a term different than that used by the Israelite Judah. Hos 4:13–14 offers a cultic setting for the activities of the *qĕdēšâ*, with the mention of mountaintops, shade trees, burning incense, and sacrifice. What is not certain is the relationship of her professional activities to the religious context. The presence of prostitutes at a religious festival could simply indicate an atmosphere of merrymaking, and we needn't assume that her sexual activity was a feature of the ritual.

If the *qĕdēšâ* was not a temple prostitute, the association with holiness suggested by her name is then problematic. A medieval Jewish commentator, Nahmanides, explains it as the result of the phenomenon in Hebrew that one word can have a certain meaning along with its opposite; thus, she who *separates* herself from holiness could be labeled with the root *qdš* (commentary on Deut 23:18). Further, the root *qdš* also has the sense "to separate," "set apart" (Josh 20:7; Jer 12:3), and the prostitute, by virtue of her promiscuity and ill repute, is alienated from the community and so "set apart," like the "foreign woman" of Proverbs, who may not really be foreign, only promiscuous (Prov 2:16; 5:3; 7:5).

ELAINE ADLER GOODFRIEND

SEE ALSO Part I: Tamar 1; Part II: Prostitute (Lev 19:29, etc.); (Prov 6:26, etc.).

FOR FURTHER READING: Goodfriend, Elaine Adler. "Prostitution."

van der Toorn, Karel. "Prostitution (Cultic)."

Westenholz, Joan Goodnick. "Tamar, *Qedesa*, *Qadistu*, and Sacred Prostitution in Mesopotamia."

DEUT 23:18 Prostitute

SEE Lev 19:29, etc.   Prostitute (Part II).

DEUT 24:1–4; ISA 50:1
Woman Being Divorced

These two passages in the Hebrew Bible refer to a bill of divorce, which would presumably formalize the dissolution of a marriage. There is no way of concluding, however, whether such a document was always required to end a conjugal union. As with many customs associated with family life, there is little direct information on this subject in the biblical text. Neither passage describes a straightforward case of divorce. Isaiah uses the bill as a metaphor for the broken covenant between the deity/husband and the nation/wife, whereas Deuteronomic law deals with one very specific situation that might arise among divorcees. The law forbids a man to reconcile with his wife after she has remarried another man and subsequently found herself either widowed or divorced again. Motive clauses, rather than a specific penalty, reinforce the prohibition: infraction of the law is not only abhorrent to the deity, but it also defiles the woman and brings sin upon the land.

Most attempts to understand the rationale behind the Deuteronomic law fail to explain the complexity of the case and the nature of its consequences. The law is sometimes seen as an attempt to impede an accelerating divorce rate by encouraging individuals to deliberate before ending a marriage. If so, this goal is pursued in a remarkably circuitous manner. It seems unlikely that an irate husband would consider the remote possibility that he might someday wish to remarry his wife after she had been widowed or divorced in a later marriage. The protasis of this case is far too complicated for such a simple purpose.

It has also been suggested that the law aims to protect second marriages by eliminating any cause for jealousy stemming from the wife's prior relationship. However, this does not explain why remarriage would be prohibited even after the death of the second husband, nor does it explain why this action would pollute the land.

Others explain its association with pollution by viewing the case as a variation of incest. According to this understanding, marriage creates a kinship bond between spouses that persists even after divorce. Thus, to remarry an ex-wife would be as incestuous as wedding another close relative. However, because this should be the case whether or not a second marriage occurs, such a rationale does not account for the complexity of the law.

It has also been argued that the law deals with two different types of divorce and divorce settlements. The first marriage ends because the husband has found something displeasing about his wife. Other ancient Near Eastern laws suggest that, in this type of divorce, a husband was neither required to return his wife's dowry nor to make other financial provisions for her. The second divorce results from the husband's hatred of his wife. Assuming that this indicates the absence of an objective reason, then the wife would receive financial compensation. Likewise, some ancient Near Eastern laws require that widows receive monetary provisions. If such laws were operative in ancient Israel, and if this text indeed envisions two different types of divorce, then it would protect a wealthy widow or divorcee from the avarice of her ex-husband. Although this explanation might account for the complexity of the law, it does not explain its motive clauses. It also rests on the problematic assumption that particular ancient Near Eastern laws were mirrored in biblical Israel.

Other interpreters view the remarriage of the original spouses in this case as a legalized form of committing adultery. These interpreters define adultery as sexual intercourse between a woman and man A, man B, and then man A again. Although divorce and remarriage are permitted, once the divorced woman has remarried, any reunion with her first husband would produce a case of "adultery after the fact." However, biblical laws typically mandate capital punishment for adultery rather than threatening the couple and the land with sexual defilement. Nor does this view explain why legally dissolved and contracted relationships should cause pollution.

Because none of the proposed rationales adequately explain the prohibition and its conse-

quences, it probably rests on several rationales working together. The law could be motivated by a concern for the well-being of the second marriage, preventing a mild form of adultery, and other more practical concerns as well. Especially in an agrarian society, the uncontrolled movement of women from one patrilocal, extended family to another could damage the cohesion and productivity of a kinship group. Once a household has been disrupted by an unhappy marriage and a divorce, this law attempts to preserve it from future instability. The close tie between kinship groups and land in agrarian societies would account for the otherwise bizarre third motive clause.

Because this text does not regulate the dissolution of marriage, it cannot be used to justify common presuppositions about divorce in ancient Israel. For example, this law is often used to illustrate that only husbands could initiate divorce proceedings. The story of the Levite's concubine suggests that wives could, in fact, leave their husbands and seek refuge in their natal home. Likewise, evidence that women in the seventh-century B.C.E. Judean colony at Elephantine could initiate divorce might suggest a similar practice in biblical Israel. Neither does the Deuteronomic law define acceptable grounds for divorcing a wife.

RHONDA BURNETTE-BLETSCH

SEE ALSO Part II: Women Whom a Priest Can and Cannot Marry (Lev 21:7–8, etc.); Concubine (Secondary Wife) of a Levite (Judges 19–20).

FOR FURTHER READING: Pressler, Carolyn. *The View of Women Found in the Deuteronomic Family Laws.*

Wenham, Gordon J. "Divorce."

Westbrook, Raymond. "The Prohibition of the Restoration of Marriage in Deuteronomy 24:1–4."

DEUT 24:5   New Wife of a Soldier
SEE DEUT 20:7, etc.   Fiancée/Wife of a Soldier (Part II).

DEUT 24:17, 20–21; 25:5–10   Widow
SEE EXOD 22:22, etc.   Widows (Part II).

Deut 25:5–10
Wife in Levirate Marriage

According to the custom of levirate marriage, when a man died without sons, his nearest kinsman was to marry his widow. The first son of the levirate union was counted as the dead man's son. The law of levirate marriage (Deut 25:5–10) imposes the obligation of levirate marriage on a surviving brother if he and the deceased had not divided their inheritance. The last section of the law (vv. 7–10), concerns the case in which the brother refuses to marry the widow. She is to bring a complaint to the elders, who establish her brother-in-law's unwillingness to take her. She then performs three actions designed to humiliate the brother-in-law for his refusal. Presumably this frees the widow and the dead man's brother from levirate obligation.

One purpose of this law may be to protect the widow by providing her with the social status and economic security of marriage and a child. Its primary concern, however, is for the deceased himself. The law emphatically states that the purpose of levirate marriage is to bear a son to succeed to the dead man's "name" (that is, to perpetuate his memory). This, in turn, was believed vital to the continued existence, or afterlife, of the deceased.

The law assumes that the widow is an agent, not merely an object. She can bring a complaint to court and can perform legally binding ritual acts. Nonetheless, the family structure presupposed by the text is clearly male-centered. Both lineage and inheritance are traced from father to son. Moreover, the law assumes that a man's claims over his wife may extend even beyond his death.

CAROLYN PRESSLER

SEE ALSO Part I: Ruth; Tamar 1; Part II: Widows (Exod 22:22, etc.).

FOR FURTHER READING: Frymer-Kensky, Tikva. "Deuteronomy."

Pressler, Carolyn. *The View of Women Found in the Deuteronomic Family Laws.*

Westbrook, Raymond. *Property and the Family in Biblical Law.*

Deut 25:11–12
Woman Who Mutilates a Man's Genitals

The case of a married woman intervening in a brawl between her husband and another man is presented in Deut 25:11–12. The woman who defends her husband by grabbing his opponent's genitals is punished by having her hand severed from her body. The text bears many similarities to Exod 21:22–25, which discusses a pregnant woman injured in a brawl. Both cases begin with the same phrase describing a fight between two men; it ends when the wife of one party becomes somehow involved, and an injury results. In each case, the injury is associated with reproductive physiology. These texts are also the only two biblical laws that prescribe mutilation as a penalty. Both laws define how the *lex talionis* (law of retaliation, or exact retribution) is to be extended when it cannot be applied literally. The Deuteronomic passage, however, assumes that the injury is intentional, whereas the harm caused in the other text is accidental.

By modern standards, the penalty seems very severe, especially given the extenuating circumstances of the case. This may be because the woman has enacted a serious breach of modesty by contacting the genitals of a man other than her husband. More compelling is the possibility that the severity of the penalty is because the injury to the man would impede his ability to perform sexually or to sire children. Similar ancient Near Eastern laws mandate the amputation of a woman's finger if one testicle is damaged and a more radical mutilation for damage to both testicles. Assuming this law derives from an actual case, it indicates that an Israelite woman was willing to use physical force and risk bodily harm in order to help her spouse.

RHONDA BURNETTE-BLETSCH

SEE ALSO Part II: Woman Caused to Miscarry (Exod 21:22–23).

DEUT 26:12–13   Widows

SEE EXOD 22:22, etc.   Widows (Part II).

Deut 27:16, 19–20, 22–23; 28:30, 32, 41, 53–54, 68

Women in Covenant Curses

Deuteronomy 27 narrates a ritual of imprecation, or formal, solemn curses: v. 16 mentions cursing one's mother as well as one's father; v. 19, reflecting a main concern of Deuteronomy, includes perverting the widow's trial; and vv. 22–23 prohibit having intercourse with one's sister or mother-in-law. Brother and father-in-law are lacking; this suggests that the real audience of this ritual is the male community.

In parts of chap. 28, the great rebuke (a series of escalating grave punishments to befall Israelites if they abrogate the covenant), the perspective is largely male; thus fiancées and wives are mentioned, without any male counterparts (vv. 30, 54). However, consistent with the pattern of Assyrian treaty curses, both sons and daughters are sometimes mentioned (vv. 32, 41, 53). The final verse of the rebuke (v. 68) suggests that those who had violated the commandments will be sold as female and male servants, incorporating women into the chapter.

MARC ZVI BRETTLER

SEE ALSO Part II: Female (and Male) Hebrew Slaves (Exod 21:7–11, etc.); Widows (Exod 22:22, etc.); Women (and Men) Who Break the Covenant (Deut 17:2–5, etc.).

Deut 27:19   Widows

SEE Exod 22:22, etc. Widows (Part II).

Deut 27:20, 22–23
Mother, Sister, and Mother-in-law in Incest Regulations

SEE Lev 18:7–18, etc. Women in Incest Regulations (Part II).

Deut 28:30   Engaged Woman

SEE Exod 22:16–17, etc. Virgin (Part II).

Deut 28:30, 32, 41, 53–54
Women in Covenant Curses

SEE Deut 27:16, etc. Women in Covenant Curses (Part II).

Deut 28:54–57
Mother Cannibalizing Her Daughters (and Sons)

SEE Lev 26:29, etc. Mother (and Father) Cannibalizing Their Daughters (and Sons) (Part II).

Deut 28:68   Female Slaves

SEE Deut 27:16, etc. Women in Covenant Curses (Part II).

Deut 29:11; 31:12; Josh 8:35

Israelite Women in the Covenant Community

The covenant is an agreement, well known from other ancient Near Eastern cultures, that creates an oath-bound relationship between two parties. One or both parties make promises to carry out certain stipulations. The Sinai covenant tradition thus expresses a binding relationship between the people of Israel and their god, YHWH. According to the Deuteronomic account of the covenant, women are part of the population that constitutes "all Israel" (31:11), that is, the covenant community. Women are included in 29:10–11 in the list of those who enter into the covenant: leaders, elders, officials, men, children, women, and aliens living in the community.

Though the nouns denoting the first three groups in the Deuteronomy 29 list are masculine plural, the possibility that women are included in those positions must be raised. Ordinary people are designated in the categories of women, men, and children. But because one of the groups with a different status, the "aliens" (Hebrew gērîm), certainly included women, the other groups also could have had female members (see Ruth 1:1 and also 2 Kgs 8:1, where the related verb designates women dwelling in another community).

The responsibility to keep the covenant is incumbent upon the entire community, to which the document is read aloud every seventh year during the feast of booths (Tabernacles, or Succoth). All the people are to assemble to listen. According to Deut 31:12, that assembly is to consist of women along with men, children, and aliens. The same groups are mentioned in Josh 8:35, which recounts the reading of the covenant by Joshua to "all the assembly of Israel" in the promised land.

CAROL MEYERS

SEE ALSO Part II: Daughters (and Sons) and Female (and Male) Slaves, Rejoicing (Deut 12:12, etc.); Women (and Men) of the Ark Ceremony (2 Sam 6:19); Women, Part of the Assembly of People (Neh 8:2–3, etc.).

FOR FURTHER READING: Eckart, Otto. "False Weights in the Scale of Biblical Justice? Different Views of Women from Patriarchal Hierarchy to Religious Equality in the Book of Deuteronomy."

Weinfeld, Moshe. *Deuteronomy and the Deuteronomic School.*

DEUT 29:18
Woman Who Breaks the Covenant
SEE DEUT 17:2–5, etc.   Women (and Men) Who Break the Covenant (Part II).

DEUT 31:12
Israelite Women in the Covenant Community
SEE DEUT 29:11, etc.   Israelite Women in the Covenant Community (Part II).

DEUT 32:19, 25
Daughters (and Sons) Spurned by God; Young Women (and Men) Punished by God

The poem of Deuteronomy 32 describes the relationship between YHWH and Israel, focusing on Israel's sin and punishment. Both daughters and sons sin (v. 19), and young women and men are punished (v. 25). The poem thus explicitly includes women within its intended audience; this fits the

gender-inclusive tendency present elsewhere in Deuteronomy (for example, 31:12).

MARC ZVI BRETTLER

SEE ALSO Part II: Women in Covenant Curses (Deut 27:16, etc.); Israelite Women in the Covenant Community (Deut 29:11, etc.).

DEUT 33:9
Mother (and Father) of Levi

Deuteronomy 33 is an archaic poem, introduced as Moses' deathbed charge to the Israelite tribes. The reference in this poem to Levi, the eponymous ancestor of the priestly tribe, alludes to the incidents of Massah and Meribah in the wilderness, in which Moses and Aaron somehow displease God in their response to the complaints of the Israelites (Exod 17:7; Num 20:12–13). The strife in this episode is represented by the image of a person (Levi, ancestor of Aaron and Moses?) ignoring close kinfolk: parents — "father and mother" — and children (Deut 33:9).

CAROL MEYERS

JOSH 1:14
Wives (and Children) of Two and a Half Tribes

When the Israelites are about to cross the Jordan River to begin the process of acquiring the land designated for the nine and a half tribes west of the river, their leader Joshua instructs the men from the two and half tribes east of the Jordan to cross along too. A military campaign is anticipated, and the "warriors" of Reuben, Gad, and the half-tribe of Manasseh will be needed. However, the rest of the population of those tribes — "your wives, your little ones" (Josh 1:14) — are to remain east of the Jordan. Warfare is viewed as a male endeavor; and by excluding women and children from battle, the future of those tribes is assured.

CAROL MEYERS

SEE ALSO Part II: Wives (and Children) as Booty (Num 14:3).

JOSH 2:13, 18; 6:17, 22–25
Mother (and Father) and Sisters (and Brothers) of Rahab

Rahab's parents and siblings, who live with her in Jericho, are saved with her when the Israelites destroy Jericho. As reward for saving the spies, Rahab had requested that she and her family be spared. She had specified that she would save her mother and father, her sisters and her brothers, and all that belong to them (Josh 2:13). The explicit mention of "sisters" emphasizes the extent of the family she will save; the stipulation "and all who belong to them" implies that the group to be saved extends collaterally into her sisters' households.

When the spies and Joshua rescue Rahab and her family, the narrative mentions only her mother, her father, and her brothers; presumably the sisters are included with the brothers. Rescued from the destruction of Jericho in a manner reminiscent of Israel's rescue from the plague of the firstborn in Egypt, all of them are spared and dwell "in Israel ever since" (Josh 6:25; Hebrew "to this very day").

TIKVA FRYMER-KENSKY

SEE ALSO Part I: Rahab.

JOSH 6:21; 8:25
Women (and Men) of Jericho and Ai

The military aspect of the Israelite occupation of the promised land involved what seems to us a component of unnecessary violence: all inhabitants of conquered settlements, such as Jericho (Josh 6:21) and Ai (Josh 8:25), including women and children along with men and livestock, were to be put to death under the "ban" (Hebrew ḥērem).

This feature of sacred warfare — in which the destroyed lives are "devoted" to God — is known from other ancient Near Eastern cultures. Perhaps it represents the way a people at risk of losing their identity or integrity protected their spatial and cul-

tural boundaries. Another possibility is that this practice reflects a mechanism for coping with the epidemic disease prevalent in the east Mediterranean basin at the time when the Israelites are thought to have emerged in Palestine. The total destruction of cities, theologized in biblical language, may have been a kind of plague control imposed in desperation upon crowded urban settlements.

Whatever its origin, the ideological recasting of the annihilation of Israel's enemies as a sacral act serves the dubious purpose of making war and killing acceptable, reducing the guilt of survivors, and increasing the group solidarity of the victors.

CAROL MEYERS

SEE ALSO Part II: Women (and Men and Children) in Towns of the Amorite Kings Sihon and Og (Deut 2:34, etc.); Women in Distant Towns as Booty (Deut 20:14, etc.); Daughters (and Sons) of Achan (Josh 7:24); Girls as Booty (Judg 5:30); Women (Wives and Daughters [and Sons]) of Ziklag (1 Sam 30:2–3, etc.).

FOR FURTHER READING: Niditch, Susan. *War in the Hebrew Bible: A Study in the Ethics of Violence.*

JOSH 6:22–25   Mother of Rahab

SEE JOSH 2:13, etc. Mother (and Father) and Sisters (and Brothers) of Rahab (Part II).

JOSH 7:24
Daughters (and Sons) of Achan

Joshua contains a narrative accounting for a major setback in the story of Israel's military exploits in occupying the promised land. The requisite annihilation and "devotion" (Hebrew ḥērem) to YHWH of enemy populations and their possessions — known as the "ban" — was violated by a man named Achan. God's fury at this act of disobedience becomes manifest in the defeat of three companies of fighting men (NRSV, "three thousand" people) at Ai. Ultimately, Achan is punished along with his children ("sons and daughters," 7:24), and Ai is subsequently destroyed.

The inclusion of family and also animals in the punishment of Achan is not so much an expression of corporate responsibility, but rather may stem from the fear that the objects taken from Ai as booty may have been a source of contagion and contamination. This possibility is related to the notion that the ban is a theologized sanction for a public health measure — utterly destroying conquered cities — in a period of widespread epidemic disease at urban sites.

At the same time, Achan and his family serve as scapegoats; their suffering releases the rest of the people to carry out their mission. Also, they are burned, like sacrifices; and a heap of stones, like an altar, marks the place of the conflagration. Thus the concept of the ban as God's sacrificial due dominates this incident, while the idea of Achan and his family justly being destroyed for their sins is also present. The scapegoat motif may in fact mediate the tension between the idea of the ban as sacrifice and the idea that it is divine justice. In either case, the inclusion of Achan's innocent daughters and sons signals the gravity of the situation.

CAROL MEYERS

SEE ALSO Part II: Women in Towns of the Amorite Kings Sihon and Og (Deut 2:34, etc.); Women in Distant Towns as Booty (Deut 20:14, etc.); Women (and Men) of Jericho and Ai (Josh 6:21, etc.).

FOR FURTHER READING: Boling, Robert G., and G. Ernest Wright. *Joshua.*

Niditch, Susan. *War in the Hebrew Bible: A Study in the Ethics of Violence.*

JOSH 8:25   Women of Ai (Part II)
SEE JOSH 6:21, etc.   Women (and Men) of Jericho and Ai (Part II).

JOSH 8:35
Israelite Women in the Assembly of All Israel
SEE DEUT 29:11, etc.   Israelite Women in the Covenant Community (Part II).

JOSH 17:3–6
Daughters of Zelophehad
SEE NUM 26:33, etc.   Daughters of Zelophehad (Part II).

JOSH 23:12–13   Women of the Nations
SEE EXOD 34:16, etc.   Daughters of the Inhabitants of the Land as Marriage Partners (Part II).

JUDG 3:5–6
Daughters of Other Nations
SEE EXOD 34:16, etc.   Daughters of the Inhabitants of the Land as Marriage Partners (Part II).

JUDG 5:24
Tent-Dwelling Women

In the Song of Deborah, an ancient poem (c. 1100 B.C.E.) celebrating a major Israelite victory over the Canaanites, Deborah says, *tĕborak minnāšim yā'ēl . . . minnāšim bā'ōhel tĕbōrāk* (Judg 5:24). The NRSV translates this line as "Most blessed of women is Jael . . . of tent-dwelling women most blessed." It identifies Jael as belonging to a nomadic group, the Kenites; and it states that she is exemplary among them. The line can also be translated, "Let Jael be blessed by women . . . by women in their tents may she be blessed." This would have Jael praised by her peers, not as different from other tent-dwelling women, but as a model who shows that they can rise to heroic heights when war invades their homes.

TIKVA FRYMER-KENSKY

SEE ALSO Part I: Deborah 2; Jael.

JUDG 5:28–30
Mother of Sisera

In the Song of Deborah (Judges 5), an ancient poem (c. 1100 B.C.E.) celebrating a major Israelite victory over the Canaanites, Deborah taunts the mother of the Canaanite general Sisera. Sisera's mother is sitting and peering through the lattice of her window, wondering what delays her son's return from battle (v. 28). Potentially poignant, this is not a sympathetic woman-to-woman vision, for Deborah sees Sisera's mother and her attendants ("wisest ladies") imagining that the delay is due to Sisera's victory and thus an abundance of booty, both in material goods (textiles) and in captive women. Deborah and Sisera's mother, on opposite

Ivory carving in open relief in Syrian style, from eighth-century B.C.E. Nimrud (in Assyria), showing a women looking through a window. See Mother of Sisera *(Judg 5:28–30);* Women Looking Through Windows *(Eccl 12:3).*

sides, are in sympathy with their men rather than with each other.

TIKVA FRYMER-KENSKY

SEE ALSO Part I: Deborah 2; Jael; Part II: Wisest Ladies (Judg 5:29–30); Girls as Booty (Judg 5:30).

JUDG 5:29–30
Wisest Ladies

The female companions of the mother of Sisera appear near the end of the Song of Deborah, an ancient poem preserved in Judges 5, about Israel's victory over the Canaanites. The word in Hebrew for these women is *śārôt,* a term meaning "princesses, noble women, or female courtiers." Coupled with "wisest," it may refer to the role of such women as advisers to the mother of Sisera, a prominent general and perhaps even one of the coalition of kings fighting against the Israelites (Judg 5:19–20). The NRSV's "her wisest ladies" thus denotes the wise advisers among her female courtiers.

Deborah has no sympathy for these women. They are enemies, yet they don't fight in war (as Deborah and Jael do for the Israelites). They may be wise, but they act foolishly. They gloatingly wait at home for the booty, including nubile women, that they expect their men to bring back; but they wait in vain.

TIKVA FRYMER-KENSKY

SEE ALSO Part I: Deborah 2; Jael; Part II: Mother of Sisera (Judg 5:28–30); Girls as Booty (Judg 5:30).

JUDG 5:30
Girls as Booty

The biblical account of the Israelite occupation of the promised land is presented as military conquest, and many of its features reflect general patterns and practices of warfare in the ancient Near East. Various biblical war texts, for example, deal with the issue of booty, often forbidding the taking of both human and material spoils of war. The poetic account in Judges 5 of the victory over the

Canaanites under Deborah and Barak concludes with a poignant scene. The enemy general's mother anxiously awaits the returning troops, expecting that the delay is because the Canaanites have tarried to collect and divide the spoil, which is epitomized by costly fabrics and by girls of childbearing age (5:30). The expectation that the Canaanite soldiers and their general (Sisera) will take girls as booty provides an ironic twist to the story: it is at the hands of a woman (Jael) that Sisera is killed, with the result that the battle is lost and the soldiers will not return home, let alone take girls captive.

The word for "girls" in this text is the dual of *raḥam* ("womb"), an unusual usage of that term to denote not simply wombs, but rather the female bodies that contain them. This poetic *pars pro toto* term emphasizes that the female captives are nubile women. The acquisition of such women as booty, like the taking of costly goods, enhanced the prestige and power of the victors. Also, in ancient societies in which there was a shortage of women because of death in childbirth, it provided valuable reproductive as well as labor potential. Women, like children and livestock, are treated as chattel, as trophies of war. Israelite policy in many of the narratives of settlement was quite different: the conquered were "devoted" as sacrifice to God, meaning all humans were killed and all property destroyed, except that women in enemy lands outside Israelite territory were spared.

CAROL MEYERS

SEE ALSO Part I: Deborah 2; Jael; Part II: Wives (and Children) as Booty (Num 14:3); Midianite Women (Num 31:9, etc.); Women in Distant Towns as Booty (Deut 20:14, etc.); Women (and Men) of Jericho and Ai (Josh 6:21, etc.); Edomite Women (NRSV, Pity) Cast Off (Amos 1:11).

FOR FURTHER READING: Niditch, Susan. *War in the Hebrew Bible: A Study in the Ethics of Violence.*

JUDG 8:19
Mother of Gideon

When the Israelite judge Gideon captures the two enemy Midianite kings (Zebah and Zalmunna), he accuses them of having slain his "brothers," that is, his "mother's sons" (Judg 8:19), at an otherwise unmentioned battle at Tabor. This could mean, literally, Gideon's blood brothers, which might explain the personal revenge he seems to be taking by killing them. At the same time, "brothers" can mean "kinsmen" and, by extension, compatriots. Usually, this notion of kindred folk is presented by calling them descendants of a common male ancestor. Perhaps in this case, invoking common female ancestry conjures up the special intimacy among those who have shared the same mother's womb, which likewise would signify the appropriateness of Gideon's slaughter of the kings.

CAROL MEYERS

SEE ALSO Part II: Wives of Gideon (Judg 8:30).

JUDG 8:30
Wives of Gideon

The judge Gideon is said to have had many wives, who together bore seventy sons. The symbolic value of the number seventy, indicating a plenitude of male offspring (compare Judg 12:14), probably is meant to signify Gideon's importance and political power. Similarly, the "many wives" (8:30) who bore those sons point to his prominence.

CAROL MEYERS

SEE ALSO Part II: Concubine of Gideon (Jerubbaal) (Judg 8:31, etc.); Daughters (and Sons) and Daughters-in-Law (and Sons-in-Law) of Ibzan (Judg 12:9); Women of Rehoboam (Eighteen Wives, Sixty Concubines, and Sixty Daughters) (2 Chr 11:21).

JUDG 8:31; 9:1, 3, 18
Concubine of Gideon (Jerubbaal)

In addition to his many wives, the judge Gideon — probably to be identified with Jerubbaal (see Judg 6:32 and 8:35) — is said to have had at least one secondary wife. She is called a "concubine" in 8:31 and a "maidservant" (NRSV, "slave woman") in

9:18. This unnamed woman is from Shechem, a strategic site in northern Israel. The story of this concubine's son and also the Dinah episode of Genesis 34 indicate that the history of Shechem apparently involved a troubled transition from being a Canaanite stronghold to becoming an Israelite city; in both tales, the narrator is highly critical of Shechem.

The concubine gives birth to Abimelech, who has himself declared king with the support of the Shechemites — "his mother's kinfolk . . . the whole clan of his mother's family" (9:1; see also 9:3) — and in defiance of traditions resistant to the notion of monarchy (8:22–23). Abimelech's kingship ends in disaster after only three years. The wicked city (9:57) of Shechem is destroyed, and Abimelech himself is killed by a woman (9:53–55). The narrator's hostile attitude toward both Shechem and also the renegade king Abimelech is expressed by linking the two in the person of Abimelech's mother. Her Shechemite origin and her secondary marital status together prefigure the ruin of a rebellious city and the end of an ill-conceived experiment in royal rule. At the same time, the fact that Abimelech seeks help from his mother's family suggests that married women maintained contact with their natal households.

CAROL MEYERS

SEE ALSO Part I: Dinah; Part II: Wives of Gideon (Judg 8:30); Woman of Thebez (Judg 9:53–54, etc.).

JUDG 9:49
Women (and Men) in the Tower of Shechem

A rebellious tribal leader, Abimelech, tries to establish a monarchy during the premonarchic tribal period of Israel, according to the narrative of Judges 9. With his followers, he burns an Israelite stronghold at Shechem, in the central hill country, where "a thousand men and women" — both genders representing the population threatened by Abimelech's coercive political activities — had taken refuge (Judg 9:49). This use of deadly military aggression

against Israelites is intolerable; and Abimelech himself is soon killed, ironically by a woman, an act that biblical ideology approves.

CAROL MEYERS

SEE ALSO Part II: Women (and Men) of Jericho and Ai (Josh 6:21, etc.); Concubine of Gideon (Jerubbaal) (Judg 8:31, etc.); Women (and Men) in the Tower of Thebez (Judg 9:51); Woman of Thebez (Judg 9:53–54, etc.).

JUDG 9:51
Women (and Men) in the Tower of Thebez

The rebellious activities of Abimelech, the son of the judge Gideon, are set in Israel's premonarchic period. His attempt to make himself king culminates in his burning the stronghold of Shechem and all the people (both women and men) who had taken refuge there. This intolerable act is followed by a scene in which all the people (again, both women and men, Judg 9:51) find refuge in the stronghold of nearby Thebez. From its tower a woman casts a millstone at Abimelech, resulting ultimately in his death. The women and men of the Thebez tower, who thereby live, become part of a tale of divine justice, with Abimelech's death serving as recompense for all the wrongs he had committed, including the burning of the women and men of the Shechem tower.

CAROL MEYERS

SEE ALSO Part II: Concubine of Gideon (Jerubbaal) (Judg 8:31, etc.); Women (and Men) in the Tower of Shechem (Judg 9:49); Woman of Thebez (Judg 9:53–54, etc.).

JUDG 9:53–54; 2 SAM 11:21
Woman of Thebez

The story of Abimelech, a man who tries to establish a monarchy in Israel long before the period of the first Israelite kings, is set in the days of the judges. The character of Abimelech is presented in an extremely negative light, from beginning to end, perhaps in part because of his origins in Shechem, a city with a troubled and volatile political and ethnic relationship to the Israelites (compare the story of Dinah). The narrator's critique finds expression in the details, involving women, of Abimelech's origin and demise.

Abimelech is introduced as the son of the heroic figure Gideon, a man with many wives; Abimelech's mother, however, is his only "concubine," or secondary wife, a fact that may signify a problematic son from the start. In the dramatic conclusion to the Abimelech episode, a heroic woman causes his death. When he attacks the city of Thebez, a woman, who was one of those who sought refuge in the city's tower, seizes an upper millstone and throws it down at him, thereby crushing his head. She saves her city, but the dying Abimelech finds it unbearable that a woman has delivered this mortal blow. He orders his armor bearer to thrust a sword through him, so that people who see his body will think he has been slain in battle and thus won't say "a woman killed him" (9:54). Abimelech tries to avoid the ignominious fate of being done in by a woman. His ruse fails, for generations later King David refers to this incident (2 Sam 11:21), and the woman's heroism is vindicated because she is linked to valiant warriors, albeit ones who kill some of David's men. What is demeaning to a renegade king is simultaneously an incident of military valor.

CAROL MEYERS

SEE ALSO Part I: Dinah; Part II: Wives of Gideon (Judg 8:30); Concubine of Gideon (Jerubbaal) (Judg 8:31, etc.); Women (and Men) in the Tower of Thebez (Judg 9:51).

JUDG 11:1–2
Prostitute, Mother of Jephthah

Jephthah, who delivered Israel from the oppression of the Ammonites during the period of the judges (c. 1200–1000 B.C.E.), was born to an unnamed prostitute (Judg 11:1). Although the pater-

nity of a prostitute's children may often be uncertain, the biblical author identifies Gilead as Jephthah's father. (Gilead in this context may be an eponym — an individual, at times fictitious, who is assumed to be the forefather of a tribe or ethnic group.) Gilead also had sons with an unnamed legal wife. Jephthah's half brothers (perhaps after the death of Gilead) banish him from the tribal patrimony on the grounds that he is "the son of another woman" (Judg 11:2). They use this terminology, rather than "prostitute," perhaps out of reverence for their father, or because they are fearful that Jephthah, who is described as a "mighty warrior," might resent his half siblings' calling his mother a zônâ, "prostitute," often a term of disdain in Israel.

As a landless son of a prostitute, Jephthah might have occupied a marginal social position in ancient Israel. The same seems to have been true for the other major judges (for example, Abimelech was a son of a concubine [Judg 8:31]) and that these figures became judges indicates that, before the monarchy, lineage and status were not required in order to be called by YHWH to leadership positions. Having a mother who was a prostitute was not a liability.

ELAINE ADLER GOODFRIEND

SEE ALSO Part I: Rahab; Tamar 1; Part II: Prostitute (Lev 19:29, etc.); Concubine of Gideon (Jerubbaal) (Judg 8:31, etc.); Wife of Gilead (Judg 11:2).

JUDG 11:2
Wife of Gilead

In the narrative of Jephthah, who delivers Israel from the Ammonites during the period of the judges (c. 1200–1000 B.C.E.), a man named Gilead has a legitimate, unnamed wife with multiple sons. She is contrasted with a prostitute who bears him only one son, Jephthah. The disparity in the status of these women leads to a perceived inequality among their children: the legitimate sons drive their illegitimate half brother away and deny him any inheritance.

RHONDA BURNETTE-BLETSCH

SEE ALSO Part II: Prostitute, Mother of Jephthah (Judg 11:1–2).

JUDG 11:34–40
Daughter of Jephthah

The story of this unnamed woman appears near the end of her father's story (see Judg 11:1–12:7). Its position, as well as the events that it narrates, suggests that it functions primarily, though not necessarily solely, as a further explication of the character of her father. It is, further, one of the most enigmatic stories in the Hebrew Bible.

The woman's father, Jephthah, has a rather unconventional background. His mother is a prostitute; his father is identified as Gilead. But since Gilead also names the region in Transjordan from which Jephthah comes, the text may be implying that any of the men of Gilead could be Jephthah's father. This questionable parentage leads to Jephthah's being driven away from his home by his kinsmen. He becomes an outlaw and presumably builds up a reputation as a fighter. When his people are threatened militarily by the Ammonites, they appeal to Jephthah to be their commander. Jephthah agrees, being enticed by the promise that he will become their overall leader if he is victorious. But before going into battle, he seeks a guarantee of success by vowing to YHWH that if victory is granted to him, he will sacrifice to YHWH "whoever [whatever] comes out" of his house first on his return from the fight (11:31). (The Hebrew allows either the personal or impersonal pronoun.)

The ensuing conflict proves victorious for Jephthah and his forces. The rejoicing is short-lived, however, for on the return to his house it is his daughter that he sees coming out to meet him. But while Jephthah bemoans the fate to which his vow has brought him, his daughter merely affirms that he must do what he has vowed to do. She asks only that she be allowed a two-month reprieve so as to spend time with her women friends on the mountains, mourning her virginity. This request is granted. When she comes back to her father, he does with her "according to the vow he had made" (Judg 11:39).

The episode involving Jephthah's daughter, partly because of its very brevity, generates numerous questions. Readers want to know why Jephthah makes such a vow. The text does not offer any hints, such as doubts about his chances for military success. Does the spirit of YHWH actually move him to the pronouncement of the vow? And in making the vow, does he not know that it was customary in Israel for women to come out and greet with song and dance victorious male warriors upon their return from battle (compare Exod 15:19–21; 1 Sam 18:6–7) and that it is quite likely that his daughter will also follow this custom? Or does he think that an animal will be first out of his house? (Animals were often stabled in a small room inside, and quite near the entrance of, the typical Israelite house. And animals were a common object of sacrifice in ancient Israel.)

Another question concerns whether Jephthah's daughter has prior knowledge of her father's vow before she steps out of the house. The text suggests that Jephthah's vow was made in their hometown of Mizpah; if pronounced publicly, presumably she would have heard it. Perhaps that was Jephthah's intention — that she hear it and so take warning not to come out of the house first. But even if the vow was spoken in private, it is still conceivable that word could have gotten back to the daughter. And yet if the daughter did know, one wonders why she went out to greet him.

Just as troubling as the daughter's apparent complicity is that of others. We wonder why no one — not even YHWH — intervenes. In the narrative of Abraham's near-sacrifice of his son, Isaac, YHWH sends an angel to prevent the killing. That sacrifice, however, was YHWH's idea in the first place (Gen 22:1–14). And why do the people of the community not countermand the vow's fulfillment? Why do the women friends of the daughter not convince her to run away and so escape her doom? And where is the daughter's mother? Why is she not even mentioned in this story, much less presented as an advocate for her daughter?

Another ambiguity of the narrative concerns

the daughter's actual fate. The text does not explicitly state that Jephthah actually kills her. Perhaps he merely offers her up to the service of YHWH; presumably she would have then gone to work for a lifetime in a sanctuary dedicated to YHWH. In that case, the lamenting done by both father and daughter would have concerned the loss for the daughter of the normative Israelite roles of wife and mother (a tragedy for Jephthah, too, since she is his only child and, without her children, his patrimony will most likely be lost forever.)

Finally, what is the function of this story in the biblical text? Some suggest that it is meant to point up the rash and foolish behavior of Jephthah. But his unconscionable behavior would also have been a sign of Israel's depravity and thus an argument for instituting monarchical rule, presumably a more stable and upright form of government than what is currently in place. This message is here mediated primarily through the victimization of a woman. Women's lives and reproductive potential were essential for community and family survival. The loss of the daughter perhaps represents, in dramatic form, the dangers (amid apparent success) of the leadership of the judges. As a potential mother, the daughter represents the future for family and community. Her father's shortsightedness signifies the chaos of premonarchic life.

Despite the possibilities of comprehending the narrative as part of the propaganda of the Book of Judges, the story of Jephthah's daughter remains enigmatic and disturbing to today's readers. Indeed, this tale of a nameless young woman, with scarcely a voice of her own and with her violent fate precipitated and carried out by her own father, is surely one of the most horrifying tales in the whole Bible.

KARLA G. BOHMBACH

SEE ALSO Part II: Women with Hand-Drums, Dancing (Exod 15:20, etc.); Daughter (or Son or Child) Passed Through Fire, Burned, or Sacrificed (Deut 12:31, etc.); Companions of Jephthah's Daughter (Judg 11:37–38); Daughters of Israel Lamenting Jephthah's Daughter (Judg 11:40).

FOR FURTHER READING: Day, Peggy L. "From the Child Is Born the Woman: The Story of Jephthah's Daughter."

Exum, J. Cheryl. "Murder They Wrote."

Fewell, Danna Nolan. "Judges."

Trible, Phyllis. "The Daughter of Jephthah: An Inhuman Sacrifice."

JUDG 11:37–38
Companions of Jephthah's Daughter

These women accompany Jephthah's daughter during her two months of mourning — presumably to support her and even to participate in the grieving over her imminent death. It has been suggested that their mourning rite subsequently became regularized in Israelite society; that is, it came to be a custom for young women to go out annually together (see Judg 11:40). Some have further suggested that this custom functioned as a rite of passage: a formal recognition, by means of ritual, of the crossover from childhood to adulthood; for women, such a rite would have signaled their readiness for marriage. However, other evidence for the existence of such a rite in ancient Israel is lacking. Still, the passage does seem to indicate the presence of women-only associations — informal and formal networks that contributed to female social power — in the biblical world.

KARLA G. BOHMBACH

SEE ALSO Part II: Daughter of Jephthah (Judg 11:34–40); Daughters of Israel Lamenting Jephthah's Daughter (Judg 11:40); Women of the Neighborhood (Ruth 4:17); Mourning Women (Jer 9:17–22, etc.).

JUDG 11:40
Daughters of Israel Lamenting Jephthah's Daughter

Certain ritual practices in ancient Israel, as in many cultures, are relegated to men; so too are some the prerogative of women. The androcentric interests of the Hebrew Bible rarely are concerned with women's practices, whether they are part of household religion or wider community observance. One exception is a custom tied to the tragic death of Jephthah's daughter in fulfillment of a vow made by her father. According to Judg 11:40, the "daughters of Israel" would annually commemorate the death of Jephthah's daughter with four days of lamenting. This reference to Israelite daughters perhaps designates Israelite women in general; but more likely it has in mind females like Jephthah's daughter — unmarried females still residing in their parental homes.

The details of the commemorative practice are not given, but the fact that these young women "go out" to carry out this custom indicates that it was not done in a domestic setting. Perhaps they went out into the hills near Mizpah (where the death had occurred), just as the companions of Jephthah's daughter had done at the time of her death (Judg 11:38).

Several features of the annual event are noteworthy. As a practice carried out only by women, it is one example of the social and religious practices that were part of the lives of Israelite women but are not generally visible in the androcentric biblical record. Like the wailing after her death, the commemorative mourning is particularly suitable for an annual female custom, given the fact that women, rather than men, tended to be specialists in funerary practices in ancient Israel. This custom also provides an example of female bonding; the dynamics of a single-gender gathering that lasted for four days inevitably would have fostered extensive interaction, shared experience, and a sense of connection. Finally, it is unusual, among biblical rituals, in marking a human character rather than a divine deed or a seasonal event.

CAROL MEYERS

SEE ALSO Part II: Daughter of Jephthah (Judg 11:34–40); Companions of Jephthah's Daughter (Judg 11:37–38); Mourning Women (Jer 9:17–22, etc.).

FOR FURTHER READING: Ackerman, Susan. *Warrior, Dancer, Seductress, Queen: Women in Judges and Biblical Israel.*

Bird, Phyllis. "The Place of Women in the Israelite Cultus."

JUDG 12:9
Daughters (and Sons) and Daughters-in-Law (and Sons-in-Law) of Ibzan

One of the minor judges (a leader without an attached narrative) in the Book of Judges is a Bethlehemite named Ibzan. He is said to have had sixty children, thirty of each gender. That number seems to be significant, perhaps as an indication of power; note that another minor judge, Jair, is said to have had thirty sons riding on thirty donkeys in thirty towns (Judg 10:3–4; see also 14:13, 19). Ibzan may have been a regional chieftain who controlled a large number of settlements (thirty), each represented by a son placed in a local leadership role. He would then have doubled his domain (from thirty to sixty) by using the patronage system, that is, by marrying his daughters to families in settlements outside his domain.

The NRSV translation "outside his clan" is misleading, because no word for "clan" appears in the Hebrew text. In any case, the marriages of Ibzan's offspring epitomize the pattern of sons maintaining the father's lineage or position by marrying women from outside the immediate family group and of daughters being sent out to marry. The idea of "outside" here does not mean that spouses were obtained from non-Israelites, but rather from Israelite groups somewhat more distant than usual.

CAROL MEYERS

SEE ALSO Part II: Daughters of the Inhabitants of the Land as Marriage Partners (Exod 34:16, etc.).

JUDG 13:2–25; 14:2–9, 16; 16:17
Mother of Samson

The birth announcement of a son to a sterile woman is a typical biblical scene. Here no background is offered — whether like Sarah the woman was old, or like Rachel she complained to her husband about childlessness, or like Sarah and Rachel she tried other means of obtaining a child. She does not pray for a child, as does Hannah, nor does her husband pray for her, as Isaac prays for Rebekah. Even her name is not reported, though her role in the story is as important as that of her husband, Manoah.

She is alone when the divine messenger appears to her to announce Samson's birth. The Nazirite injunctions against drinking alcohol and eating unclean food are placed upon her, since the child is to be a Nazirite "from birth" (13:5). She immediately shares the news with her husband, but apparently this is not enough for him and he prays to God to send the man again "to us" to "teach us" (v. 8). God grants the prayer, but the messenger appears again to the woman only (to underscore this point, the text adds in v. 9, "and Manoah her husband was not with her"). She must bring Manoah to the man. When Manoah questions the messenger, he never receives as much information about the child as his wife does (he never hears the prohibition against cutting the boy's hair or that Samson will begin to deliver Israel from the Philistines).

The woman is more perceptive than her husband. Although they both call the emissary a "man of God" (a term for a prophet) until he reveals his divine identity (v. 20), she senses at once something otherworldly about him (v. 6) and does not, as Manoah later does, ask about his ineffable name.

The woman and her husband together witness the messenger's ascension. Upon realizing that they have seen a divine being, Manoah fears they will die — a common response to such a revelation — but the woman recognizes a divine purpose behind the revelation, and thus assures Manoah that they will not die. Usually, in such circumstances, this assurance is given by God.

The woman, as is frequently the case in the Bible, names the child. She is included in the events leading up to Samson's marriage, but her role in arranging it is not clear (parents typically arranged their children's marriages). Samson tells both his father and his mother about seeing the woman he wants

to marry, and both parents object to his choice of a Philistine (neither knows that this is all part of a divine plan). Both parents accompany Samson to Timnah in Judg 14:5, but his mother is not included in v. 10. Samson does not tell either parent about killing the lion or finding honey in its carcass (he gives both some honey to eat). These two events give rise to his famous riddle. Samson's question "I have not told my father or my mother. Why should I tell you?" (14:16) indicates that the man's primary allegiance is to his parents, not to his wife.

J. CHERYL EXUM

SEE ALSO Part I: Delilah; Part II: Nazirite Woman (Num 6:2–21); Wife of Samson (Judg 14:1–15:6).

FOR FURTHER READING: Exum, J. Cheryl. *Fragmented Women: Feminist (Sub)versions of Biblical Narratives.*

Fuchs, Esther. "The Literary Characterization of Mothers and Sexual Politics in the Hebrew Bible."

Reinhartz, Adele. "Samson's Mother: An Unnamed Protagonist."

JUDG 14:1–15:6
Wife of Samson

Of the three women involved with Samson, the unnamed woman who becomes Samson's wife in Judges 14 is the only one clearly identified as a Philistine. She lives in a Philistine town, Timnah, located in the valley of Sorek in south central Palestine. Samson's (mis)adventures begin when, upon visiting Timnah, he sees this woman and decides he wants her for his wife (14:1–4). The reason he gives, "she is the right one in my eyes" (v. 3; author's translation), is not the usual way to indicate beauty; it alludes to Judg 17:6 and 21:25. Following Israelite custom, the parents are expected to arrange the marriage (vv. 2, 10). The animosity that the Israelites felt toward the Philistines, their archenemy in the struggle for the land, is reflected in the incredulous response of Samson's parents, who do not understand why he does not choose a wife from his own people (14:3). Unknown to them, his decision, which results in havoc, is part of the divine plan. The word *this* in v. 4 ("this was from the LORD") refers either to Samson's decision, or, since the Hebrew word can mean "she," to the woman herself.

At the wedding feast, the thirty Philistine (male) guests threaten Samson's wife with death by fire in order to force her to discover for them the answer to Samson's riddle. She obtains the answer by means of tears, by accusing Samson of not loving her, and by nagging him. It is not clear how long it takes her to break down Samson's resistance; 14:17 says she wept the seven days that the feast lasted, but in v. 15 the Hebrew text has the Philistines threatening the woman on the seventh day (the NRSV, following the Septuagint, reads "on the fourth day," but this still does not square with her seven days of weeping).

Samson's union is sometimes described as a type of marriage in which the woman remains in her father's house and her husband visits her there. The story does not support this view, however. When Samson abandons his bride and returns to his father's house in anger, his father-in-law apparently takes this gesture as an act of divorce (this is what his explanation in 15:2 implies) and marries off his daughter to Samson's best man. Samson apparently still believes he is married to the woman, but when he returns some time later to visit her, her father explains the situation and offers Samson his "prettier" younger daughter in her place (15:2).

Ironically, the fate the woman sought to avoid by disclosing the answer to Samson's riddle befalls her anyway. When Samson burns the Philistine grain fields in retaliation for losing his wife (15:3–5), the Philistines retaliate in turn and burn the woman and her father (15:6; in 14:15 they threatened to "burn you and your father's house with fire"; either the word *house* has dropped out of the text in 15:6 or the rest of the household, including the woman's younger sister, is spared). Samson avenges their deaths by slaughtering Philistines.

J. CHERYL EXUM

SEE ALSO Part I: Delilah; Part II: Mother of Samson (Judg 13:2–25, etc.); Younger Sister of Samson's Wife (Judg 15:2); Prostitute of Gaza (Judg 16:1–3).

FOR FURTHER READING: Bal, Mieke. *Death and Dissymmetry: The Politics of Coherence in the Book of Judges.*

Exum, J. Cheryl. *Fragmented Women: Feminist (Sub)versions of Biblical Narratives.*

Greenstein, Edward L. "The Riddle of Samson."

JUDG 14:2–9, 16   Mother of Samson
SEE JUDG 13:2–25, etc.   Mother of Samson (Part II).

JUDG 15:2
Younger Sister of Samson's Wife

Samson's Philistine father-in-law offers Samson his younger daughter as a wife in place of the bride Samson had walked out on at his wedding feast. He tries to persuade Samson by suggesting she is a "better" choice (NRSV, "prettier") than her older sister, but Samson will accept no substitute and vows to take vengeance.

J. CHERYL EXUM

SEE ALSO Part II: Mother of Samson (Judg 13:2–25, etc.); Wife of Samson (Judg 14:1–15:6); Philistine Women (Judg 16:27).

JUDG 16:1–3
Prostitute of Gaza

It is usually assumed that the prostitute whom Samson visits in Gaza is Philistine, but she could be an Israelite woman who happens to live in a Philistine city-state, a "foreign woman" in Gaza, like the dangerous "foreign woman" that the Book of Proverbs warns about. Samson leaves her in the middle of the night (when a lesser man would be exhausted from lovemaking), thereby escaping the Philistine ambush set for the morning. Twice, with the help of a woman, the Philistines get the better of Samson. In this case they fail, suggesting that only when a woman helps them can they overcome him.

J. CHERYL EXUM

SEE ALSO Part I: Delilah; Part II: Wife of Samson (Judg 14:1–15:6).

For further reading: Bird, Phyllis. "'To Play the Harlot': An Inquiry into an Old Testament Metaphor."
Exum, J. Cheryl. *Fragmented Women: Feminist (Sub)versions of Biblical Narratives.*

JUDG 16:17 Mother of Samson

See Judg 13:2–25, etc. Mother of Samson (Part II).

JUDG 16:27
Philistine Women

Philistine women are specifically mentioned, along with men, as being among the spectators in the temple of Dagon and on the roof when Samson pulls down the temple, killing them all.

J. Cheryl Exum

See also Part I: Delilah; Part II: Wife of Samson (Judg 14:1–15:6).

JUDG 17:1–4
Mother of Micah

A woman living in the hill country of Ephraim in the period of the judges discovers that eleven hundred pieces of silver have been stolen from her. She then utters a curse (Hebrew *'ālâ*) in the hearing of her son Micah, who is the thief. The wording of the curse is not preserved, although that of a subsequent blessing appears in v. 3. The curse, which must have had a formulaic quality similar to that of the blessing, would have proclaimed her hope that God would punish the thief. Micah immediately confesses his theft and returns the sum — a goodly amount, indicating a prosperous household — thereby escaping God's punishment.

Apparently if a curse was spoken audibly (compare Lev 5:1, "audible curse"; NRSV, "public adjuration"), it constituted a conditional rather than an absolute imprecation: it allowed the guilty party to come forth and make restitution (in the case of theft). The use of both blessing and cursing formulas were part of ancient Near Eastern legal tradition, used either to protect property or to attempt to establish guilt. The mother of Micah clearly is presented as having the right to utter a legally valid imprecation; indeed this text is the only biblical narrative that presents a property-protection use of a curse.

The story does not end with the return of the stolen property. The woman decides that the silver, or at least a portion of it (two hundred pieces), should be consecrated to YHWH. She goes to a silversmith and commissions an "idol of cast metal" (v. 4). The idol is subsequently installed in the household shrine, which includes two other cult objects (an ephod and teraphim) and, eventually, a resident priestly officiant (Judg 17:7–13). This incident provides a rare glimpse into household, or private, religion. Most of the Hebrew Bible's cultic texts concern official public practices at the tabernacle or temple. Yet ancient Israelite religion in its totality included domestic as well as the more visible official practices. The narrative of Micah's mother, along with several other texts, indicates that women were major participants in household religious activities in ancient Israel, as is typically the case in traditional societies. It also suggests that women had some control over household assets.

Carol Meyers

See also Part II: The Shunammite (2 Kgs 4:8–37, etc.); Women Worshipping the Queen of Heaven (Jer 7:18, etc.); Women Who Went to Egypt (Jer 43:6, etc.); Part III: Queen of Heaven.

For further reading: Bird, Phyllis. "The Place of Women in the Israelite Cultus."

JUDGES 19–20
Concubine (Secondary Wife) of a Levite

The story of the unnamed woman in Judges 19–20 is one of the most disturbing texts in the Hebrew Bible. The woman, who is from Bethlehem but lives with a Levite in the hill country of Ephraim, north of Jerusalem, is referred to in Hebrew as the *pilegeš* of the Levite. The precise nature of the relationship between a man and his *pilegeš* is not always clear from the biblical texts, however, and scholars have sometimes disagreed about the term's meaning. It is usually translated into English as "concubine" and understood to refer to a wife or sexual partner of secondary status. Although certain men in the Hebrew Bible have both wives and concubines, no wives or additional concubines are referred to in Judges 19. The Levite is referred to as the "husband" of the woman (19:3; 20:4) and the "son-in-law" of the woman's father (19:5), who in turn is referred to as the Levite's "father-in-law" (19:4, 7, 9). The uncertain nature of the differences between a wife and a concubine reveals the complexities involved in understanding notions of kinship and marriage presupposed by biblical narratives.

The Hebrew text states that the woman "prostituted herself against" the Levite (19:2). Thus, it has often been assumed that she was sexually unfaithful to him. Certain Greek translations, however, state that she "became angry" with him. The latter interpretation is accepted by a number of commentators and modern English translations, including the NRSV, since the woman goes to her father's house rather than the house of a male lover. It is also possible that the woman's "prostitution" does not refer to literal sexual infidelity but is a sort of metaphor for the fact that she leaves her husband. The act of leaving one's husband is quite unusual in the Hebrew Bible, and the harsh language used to describe it could result from the fact that it was viewed in a very negative light.

Four months after the woman returns to Bethlehem, the Levite goes after her. Although the Hebrew text states that he wishes to "speak to her heart" (19:3; NRSV, "speak tenderly to her"), no discussion between the Levite and the woman is recounted. Indeed, the text never records any of the woman's words. The woman's father acts as if he is glad to see the Levite, but for several days he delays the return of the Levite and the woman to Ephraim. Because of this delay the travelers finally set out at a late hour and, due to the unwillingness of the Levite to spend the night in a city of "foreigners" (19:12), arrive at the Benjaminite city of Gibeah after the sun has gone down.

Although hospitality to strangers was an important custom in the ancient world, the travelers initially have a difficult time finding a place to spend the night. They are finally offered hospitality by an old man who, like the Levite, is from Ephraim. While the travelers are eating, the house is surrounded by men of the city who, according to the Hebrew text, wish "to know" the Levite (19:22). "To know" is probably a euphemism for sexual intercourse here, as it is in other biblical texts and as the NRSV translates it. The Ephraimite host attempts to dissuade the men of the city from raping his male guest, offering to them his own daughter and the Levite's concubine in place of the Levite.

Several elements in this part of the story, including the offer of two women as objects of rape in the place of a male object, are very similar to elements of the story of Lot and his daughters (Gen 19:1–8). Apparently the sexual violation of women was considered less shameful than that of men, at least in the eyes of other men. Such an attitude reflects both the social subordination of women and the fact that homosexual rape was viewed as a particularly severe attack on male honor.

When the men of Gibeah refuse to accept the two women, one of the men inside the house throws the concubine outside. Interpreters generally agree that it is the Levite who throws her to the crowd, though the text only states ambiguously that "the man seized his concubine, and put her out to them" (Judg 19:25) without noting specifically which man is meant. The woman is then raped by the men of Gibeah throughout the night. They do not kill her, however, for in the morning she returns to the house from which she was thrown and collapses at the door. The Levite finds her there when he rises to leave and orders her to get up. When she does not respond, for she apparently is near death, he places her on the back of his donkey and returns to Ephraim.

The text does not tell us exactly when or how the woman dies. The Levite, upon his arrival in

Ephraim, cuts the woman's body into twelve pieces and sends these pieces throughout the land. As a result of this action, the Israelites gather at Mizpah, a traditional site of tribal assembly, to listen to the Levite's story and plan a response to the Benjaminites. A cycle of violence ensues, resulting in the slaughter of many Benjaminite men, women, and children (20:35–48), the slaughter of most of the inhabitants of the city of Jabesh-gilead (21:8–12), and the kidnapping of young women at Shiloh (21:15–24).

It unlikely that any of the characters in this troubling tale are meant to be understood in an entirely positive light. The story is placed in a section of Judges (chaps. 17–21) illustrating the social and religious chaos that preceded the institution of Israelite kingship. The horror of the tale represents extreme disorder, to be rectified only by the establishment of monarchic rule. The fate of the concubine is particularly gruesome, however, and the story has appropriately been called a "text of terror" by one feminist commentator (Trible).

KEN STONE

SEE ALSO Part II: Daughters of Lot (Gen 19:8–17, etc.); Virgin Daughter of the Old Man of Gibeah (Judg 19:24); Young Women of Shiloh (Judg 21:21–23).

FOR FURTHER READING: Exum, J. Cheryl. *Fragmented Women: Feminist (Sub)versions of Biblical Narratives.*

Stone, Ken. "Gender and Homosexuality in Judges 19: Subject-Honor, Object-Shame?"

Trible, Phyllis. *Texts of Terror: Literary-Feminist Readings of Biblical Narratives.*

Yee, Gale A. "Ideological Criticism: Judges 17–21 and the Dismembered Body."

JUDG 19:24
Virgin Daughter of the Old Man of Gibeah

When Gibeonite men seek to rape his male guest, the Levite's host offers them his virgin daughter and the Levite's wife (concubine) instead. Perhaps two women are offered because two women are offered

in the parallel story of Lot (Genesis 19). The host's daughter is not thrown to the mob. Literarily speaking, perhaps she is not sexually abused because, unlike the Levite's wife, who flaunted her husband's authority by leaving him, she has done nothing to deserve punishment in the narrative.

J. CHERYL EXUM

SEE ALSO Part II: Daughters of Lot (Gen 19:8, etc.); Concubine (Secondary Wife) of a Levite (Judges 19–20).

FOR FURTHER READING: Exum, J. Cheryl. *Fragmented Women: Feminist (Sub)versions of Biblical Narratives.*

JUDG 21:7, 16–18
Daughters of Israel as Potential Wives for Benjaminites

Civil war between Benjamin and the other Israelite tribes begins and ends with sexual violence against women (Judges 19; 21). Whereas unwarranted Benjaminite lust provokes the military conflict and the slaughter of numerous Benjaminites, the necessity for sexual relations with women to maintain a tribal group's patrimony legitimizes rape in another context.

The surviving Benjaminites need wives to continue their line, but a vow prevents traditional marriage alliances with other tribes. They had "sworn by the LORD" not to give their daughters to Benjaminite men: "Cursed be anyone who gives a wife to Benjamin" (Judg 21:7, 18). Israelite men solve this dilemma by allowing the Benjaminites to capture the virgins of Jabesh-gilead (Judg 21:8–12) and permitting them to kidnap the daughters of Shiloh (presumably also virgins).

This story demonstrates concern for perpetuating tribal properties by providing heirs, and it indicates the existence of appropriate marriage alliances. The tension in the story lies between the need to punish the Benjaminites and the need to preserve their territorial integrity.

RHONDA BURNETTE-BLETSCH

See also Part II: Concubine (Secondary Wife) of a
Levite (Judges 19–20); Women of Jabesh-gilead (Judg
21:10–14); Young Women of Shiloh (Judg 21:21–23).

Judg 21:10–14
Women of Jabesh-gilead

The people of Jabesh-gilead are punished because
they did not participate in a vow, taken by all Israelites at Mizpah, to root out the anarchic evil prevalent before the monarchy and represented by the
incident of the Levite's concubine (Judges 19). Because of their recalcitrance, the inhabitants of
Jabesh-gilead are subjected to the policies of military annihilation that elsewhere in the biblical narratives of conquest have been applied to Israel's
enemies. A large Israelite force is dispatched to kill
all the Jabesh-gileadites, including "women and the
little ones" (Judg 21:10). This wholesale slaughter is
conceptualized as a "ban," a destruction devoted to
God because it carries out divine justice. In this
instance, however, not every woman is killed: sexually experienced women — whoever "has lain with
a male" (v. 11) — are slain, but "young virgins who
had never slept with a man" (v. 12) are allowed
to live.

That these young women escape the mass killing
is a function of their marriageability and reproductive potential, for they are subsequently given as
wives to the Benjaminites, a tribal group to whom
wives were being denied (Judg 21:7, 16–18) because a
group of Benjaminite men had perpetrated the evil
against the Levite's concubine. The virgins of
Jabesh-gilead become military booty, captured as
the result of a horrible inter-Israelite struggle.

The mass killing of Israelite enemies usually
meant the slaughter of the whole population. But if
the enemy was located outside Israelite territory,
females would be brought home as spoil and as
potential wives for the victors. The case of Jabesh-
gilead reflects that custom, except that only virgins
were spared. Perhaps because the Jabesh-gilead
women were Israelites, it was important to ensure

that none of them were pregnant when they married Benjaminites; otherwise inner-Israelite inheritance patterns would be jeopardized. In any case,
the portrayal of social divisiveness in the era before
the monarchy entails an unusual application of the
principle of military destruction and the differential sparing, according to sexual status, of some
people — female virgins — from a doomed city.

CAROL MEYERS

See also Part II: Women in Distant Towns as Booty
(Deut 20:14, etc.); Girls as Booty (Judg 5:30); Concu-
bine (Secondary Wife) of a Levite (Judges 19–20);
Daughters of Israel as Potential Wives for Benjaminites
(Judg 21:7, etc.).

For further reading: Niditch, Susan. *War in the
Hebrew Bible: A Study in the Ethics of Violence.*

Judg 21:21–23
Young Women of Shiloh

According to the concluding narrative of the Book
of Judges, the young women of Shiloh are kidnapped by Benjaminite warriors who have survived
the war waged in the premonarchic period against
their tribe by an alliance of other Israelite tribes.
The members of the alliance had taken an oath that
none among them would give his daughter to a
Benjaminite (21:1). Thus, wives for these warriors
had to be acquired from other sources, lest Israel be
reduced by one tribe. Women are provided for the
six hundred remaining Benjaminites first from
Jabesh-gilead, a city marked for slaughter because
its leaders neglected to send troops for the Israelite
campaign.

Another strategy is undertaken when the league's
leaders realize that an annual festival will be celebrated the following day at Shiloh, a city about
twenty miles north of Jerusalem. The Benjaminites
are advised to wait in the vineyards until the young
women (literally, "daughters") of the town come
out to dance, and each man is to abduct one to be
his wife. This they do and return home to their
tribal territory. In both cases, the intended brides
are not given freely by their fathers, and the oath
mentioned earlier therefore is not violated.

The biblical narrator implicitly condemns this event in several ways. First, the verb used in v. 23, *gāzal* ("steal," but translated in the NRSV as "abduct"), censures the deed as a trespassing of the Torah's laws (Lev 19:13). Further, the leaders of Israel's tribal league are made to look ludicrous: they direct the slaughter of one of their own tribes, and then they anguish over the possible obliteration of a tribe from Israel (21:2–3). The editor's summary in v. 25, "In those days there was no king in Israel; all the people did what was right in their own eyes," suggests that deeds such as this, the kidnapping of young women and their forcible marriage, are indicative of the violent anarchy that preceded the rise of the monarchy. The seizure of the maidens of Shiloh is the last in a series of outrageous acts by Israelites that are recorded in Judges 18–21.

Shiloh was an important religious center before the rise of the monarchy (Josh 18:1; 22:9, 12; 1 Samuel 1–2). The religious festival mentioned in Judges 21 was perhaps associated with the vintage, like the one at Shechem (Judg 9:27).

This narrative reflects concern about the availability of spouses at a time when the life spans of women were significantly shorter than those of men. Women of childbearing age were in demand. Depriving Benjaminites of brides was tantamount to negating their territorial claims. The story also preserves a tradition about women's religious activities. The annual dance at Shiloh is an example of a public ritual performed by women, apparently as part of a harvest festival. Women's religious practices in ancient Israel were largely domestic and are invisible in the text of the Hebrew Bible. But this public occasion, mentioned because of its place in a complex narrative, attests to women's roles in communal as well as private cultic life.

ELAINE ADLER GOODFRIEND

SEE ALSO Part II: Concubine (Secondary Wife) of a Levite (Judges 19–20); Women of Jabesh-gilead (Judg 21:10–14); Daughters of Israel as Potential Wives for Benjaminites (Judg 21:17, etc.).

FOR FURTHER READING: Bird, Phyllis. "The Place of Women in the Israelite Cultus"

RUTH 1:8; 2:11
Mothers of Ruth and Orpah

A woman from Bethlehem, Naomi, takes refuge with her husband and sons in Moab because of famine in her land. Her sons, who marry Moabite women, die, as does her husband. When she decides to return to Bethlehem, she urges her Moabite daughters-in-law, Ruth and Orpah, to remain in their land by insisting that each one go back to her "mother's house" (Ruth 1:8). Orpah agrees, but Ruth instead accompanies Naomi on her journey home.

The phrase "mother's house" is rare in the Hebrew Bible, occurring elsewhere only in Genesis (once, 24:28) and in the Song of Solomon (twice, 3:4; 8:2), whereas the term "father's house" is quite common. Both apparently designate the same social unit: the family household. The prevalence of "father's house" would be expected in the Bible, where an androcentric perspective governs language choice. However, the Ruth passage and the other texts using "mother's house" are all women's texts — either they speak in the female voice or they tell a woman's story. For that reason, "mother's house" can be regarded as the term used for the household when women are referring to their family and its abode. Furthermore, because women in the agrarian households of ancient Israel controlled many of the domestic activities, the term may be accurate in designating internal household dynamics; the term "father's house" may be more appropriate in referring to the household in its relation to supra-household interactions.

Once Ruth arrives in Bethlehem, she meets and marries Boaz, a kinsman of Naomi's deceased husband. Boaz praises her good deeds in accompanying Naomi, thereby leaving her parents — "father and mother" (2:11) — and her homeland to join an unfamiliar people. That language echoes God's command to Abraham in Gen 12:1. Ruth is thus cast in the mold of Abraham, as a righteous pioneer coming to the promised land and choosing YHWH as her god.

CAROL MEYERS

SEE ALSO Part I: Naomi; Orpah; Rebekah; Ruth; Part II: Wise Woman Building Her House (Prov 14:1); Mother of Woman/Lover/ Shulammite (Song 1:6, etc.).

FOR FURTHER READING: Meyers, Carol. "Returning Home: Ruth 1.8 and the Gendering of the Book of Ruth."

Trible, Phyllis. "Two Women in a Man's World: A Reading of the Book of Ruth."

RUTH 1:19; 4:14–15
Women of Bethlehem

The women of Bethlehem, the Judahite town from which Naomi migrates to Moab, appear at the beginning and the end of the account of her experience when she returns to her native land with her daughter-in-law Ruth, according to the narrative in the Book of Ruth. The whole town is excited about her return, but it is the women who greet their kinswoman Naomi — "Is this Naomi?" (1:19) — and evoke her poetic response. At the end of this historical fiction set in the period of Israel's judges, when Ruth bears the son who will be ancestor of King David, the women reappear to remind Naomi of her good fortune in having such a faithful and devoted daughter-in-law. The women mentioned in 4:14–15 in the context of Obed's birth are not, however, called women of Bethlehem. Perhaps these verses refer indirectly to the women attendant at the birth event, women from nearby households, the "women of the neighborhood" of 4:17.

The presence of female townspeople at the beginning and ending of the part of the story set in Bethlehem represents female solidarity and augments the female bonding between the major characters, Naomi and Ruth.

CAROL MEYERS

SEE ALSO Part I: Naomi; Ruth; Part II: Women of the Neighborhood (Ruth 4:17).

RUTH 2:8, 22; 3:2
Young Women of Boaz

After Ruth, Naomi's Moabite daughter-in-law, accompanies her mother-in-law back to the latter's home in Bethlehem, she goes out to glean in the fields to help obtain sustenance for herself and Naomi. The fields belong to Boaz, a wealthy relative of Naomi's late husband; and the grain is being reaped by teams of "young women" (2:8, 22; 3:2) and young men. Ruth is urged to stay close to the young women as she gleans, presumably to avoid what would have been sexual harassment in the workplace.

The term for "young women," a feminine form of the word *na'ar*, or "youth," probably refers to girls near marriageable age. Agricultural field work, at least at harvest time, was apparently a female as well as a male role for young people. Because Ruth eats with the reapers, according to 2:14, and because the reapers include young women, the masculine noun *reapers*, at least in this case, refers to both females and males. This is one of many examples of grammatically masculine nouns in the Hebrew Bible that, though often unnoticed, are gender-inclusive.

CAROL MEYERS

SEE ALSO Part I: Ruth.

FOR FURTHER READING: Carasik, Michael. "Isolating a Contemporary Issue in the Bible."

RUTH 2:11   Mother of Ruth
SEE RUTH 1:8, etc.   Mothers of Ruth and Orpah (Part II).

RUTH 2:22; 3:2
Young Women of Boaz
SEE RUTH 2:8, etc.   Young Women of Boaz (Part II).

RUTH 4:14–15   Women of Bethlehem
SEE RUTH 1:19, etc.   Women of Bethlehem (Part II).

RUTH 4:17
Women of the Neighborhood

At the end of the biblical book that bears her name, Ruth gives birth to a son who will be an ancestor of King David. The infant is named Obed by "women of the neighborhood" (4:17), a subset of the "women of Bethlehem" who welcomed Ruth and her mother-in-law Naomi when they returned from a sojourn in Moab. These neighboring women were probably the ones closest to Ruth and Naomi, both spatially and socially. Their presence at the birth of the child was one of many ways in which women who lived in adjacent households provided mutual aid and support and also joined together to celebrate family events. Such associations of women would have served as an informal yet highly significant network, providing important economic and social functions across households. The term for "neighbor," as a feminine noun, occurs only here and in Exod 3:22. The existence of such women's networks is thus barely visible in the Hebrew Bible, though other terms (such as "companions" in Judg 11:37–38) may signify a related instance of extrafamilial female bonding.

That a group of women name the child is unusual, as is also the implication that both Ruth and Naomi are mothers of the infant. Usually mothers, but sometimes fathers, bestow names on newborns. Having two mothers and a whole group of female name-givers perhaps signifies Obed's role as progenitor of the future dynastic founder, who will belong to a whole nation.

CAROL MEYERS

SEE ALSO Part I: Naomi; Ruth; Part II: Women (and Men) with Jewelry and Clothing (Exod 3:22, etc.); Companions of Jephthah's Daughter (Judg 11:37–38); Women of Bethlehem (Ruth 1:19, etc.).

FOR FURTHER READING: Meyers, Carol. "'Women of the Neighborhood' (Ruth 4.17) — Informal Female Networks in Ancient Israel."

1 Sam 1:4
Daughters (and Sons) of Peninnah

Peninnah is the mother of an unspecified number of daughters. They receive sacrificial portions equally with their brothers in the family's annual pilgrimage to the shrine at Shiloh. The participation of all members of the family in this ritual attests to the inclusiveness of private or family religious activity.

LILLIAN R. KLEIN

SEE ALSO Part I: Peninnah; Part II: Women Worshipping the Queen of Heaven (Jer 7:18, etc.).

1 SAM 2:21
Daughters (and Sons) of Hannah

At the end of the long narrative in 1 Samuel 1–2 about Hannah and her quest for offspring, the text notes that she has three more sons and two daughters after bearing the son Samuel, whom she dedicates to God. She had asked for only one son, but the priest Eli petitioned God to give her more children because of her admirable vow.

LILLIAN R. KLEIN

SEE ALSO Part I: Hannah; Part II: Daughters (and Sons) of Peninnah (1 Sam 1:4).

1 SAM 2:22
Women at the Entrance to the Tent of Meeting

SEE EXOD 38:8, etc.   Women at the Entrance to the Tent of Meeting (Part II).

1 Sam 4:19–22
Mother of Ichabod, Wife of Phinehas

In this narrative, set in the period of the judges (c. 1200–1000 B.C.E.), the Israelites are losing the Battle of Ebenezer to the Philistines and have brought into their battle camp the ark of the covenant, the symbol of the invisible presence of YHWH (1 Sam 4:1–4). The Philistines understand that the ark signals YHWH's presence (4:7–9), and their fear of the god(s) who plagued the Egyptians spurs them on to defeat the Israelites and to capture the ark. Hophni and Phinehas, the priest Eli's two wicked sons, die, as had been predicted (2:34).

On the same day, when Eli is told about the ark and the defeat, he falls over dead. When his pregnant daughter-in-law, Phinehas's wife, hears about the capture of the ark and the deaths of her father-in-law and husband, the shock sends her into labor. She assumes the crouching or squatting position ("she bowed" [4:19, NRSV]) in which Israelite women gave birth. Just before she dies, she gives birth to a son and names him Ichabod — literally, "Where is the glory?" — referring to the loss of the ark and therefore YHWH, Israel's glory. This episode exhibits the piety of an Israelite woman, whose last act is to name her son to commemorate a tragic event in her people's religious history.

Women often name their children in the Hebrew Bible (Eve in Gen 4:1, 25, and the wives of Jacob in Genesis 29–35, for example).

JO ANN HACKETT

SEE ALSO Part II: Women Attending the Wife of Phinehas (1 Sam 4:20)

1 Sam 4:20
Women Attending the Wife of Phinehas

The word *midwife* is not used, but these women who "stand by" (NRSV, "attend") Phinehas's wife surely help in the delivery of the dying woman's child, since it is they who tell her not to be afraid, for she has borne a son. Their assistance is typical of midwives; they provide both emotional and physical support to the birth process.

JO ANN HACKETT

SEE ALSO Part I: Puah; Shiphrah; Part II: Midwife (Gen 35:17, etc.); Woman in Labor (Isa 13:8, etc.).

1 SAM 8:13
Daughters as Perfumers, Cooks, and Bakers

When the people of early Israel clamor for a king to govern them, the prophet Samuel tries to dissuade them by warning them about the realities of monarchic rule. A king may provide stability and justice, but the cost will be paid in heavy taxation and in the conscription of young women and men to be servitors in the military and palace bureaucracy. The tasks Samuel describes for females and males reflect common patterns in the division of labor by gender. Young men will serve as soldiers, makers of armaments, and laborers in the king's fields. Young women will serve as "perfumers and cooks and bakers" (1 Sam 8:13).

These female tasks are found widely in domestic contexts in traditional societies. Usually, however, when such jobs in the ancient Near East became specialty occupations connected with courts or temples, they were performed by men, who took over the processes, recipes, and formulas that women had developed. According to the Samuel text, women in ancient Israel retained these specializations as they became linked to the upper levels of the political hierarchy.

CAROL MEYERS

SEE ALSO Part II: Women as Bread Bakers (Lev 26:26); Women Who Grind (Eccl 12:3); Women Making a Fire (Isa 27:11).

FOR FURTHER READING: Goody, Jack. *Cooking, Cuisine, and Class: A Study in Comparative Sociology.*

1 Sam 8:16   Female Slaves

See Exod 21:7–11, etc.   Female (and Male) Hebrew Slaves (Part II).

1 Sam 9:11

Maidens Going Out to Draw Water

Several passages, such as 1 Sam 9:11, make clear that drawing water was often women's work, especially for the unmarried daughters of a family. The well is thus a place where many biblical men find their wives: Abraham's servant (for Isaac) and Rebekah (Gen 24:13), Jacob and Rachel (Gen 29:9), and Moses and Zipporah (Exod 2:16). Drawing water is not always women's work, however: in Ruth 2:9, Boaz's young men draw water that Ruth is to drink; in Deut 29:11, strangers ("aliens") draw water. Joshua 9, especially v. 23, illustrates the inferior or marginal status of water-drawers, whether female or male.

Jo Ann Hackett

See also Part I: Rebekah; Part II: Women Drawing Water (Gen 24:11, etc.).

1 Sam 15:33

Mother of Agag

The mother of King Agag (an Amalekite king in the days of the judges) and the mothers of those his troops killed are identified as victims of war, along with the soldiers who died. The loss of offspring in war is well known in the Hebrew Bible (for example, Deut 32:25; Lam 2:12), and mothers' reactions to the threat or reality of such a loss are also reported: the naive disbelief of Sisera's mother (Judg 5:28–30), Jezebel's outrage (2 Kgs 9:30–31), and Athaliah's cold-blooded securing of power (2 Kgs 11:1). In this case, the prophet and judge Samuel asserts that Agag's sword has cut off the future of many Israelites by killing their children, and so, in fitting retribution, Agag must die: his "mother shall

be childless." The king of one of Israel's traditional enemies (Num 14:43–45) is then violently slain.

Jo Ann Hackett

See also Part II: Mother of Sisera (Judg 5:28–30).

1 Sam 15:33

Childless Women

The Amalekites were enemies of the Israelites during the period of the judges, according to the narrative of 1 Samuel. King Saul defeats them and destroys them but allows their king, Agag, to live, against the biblical concept of the *ḥērem* ("ban"), which required the total destruction of the enemy. This displeases the prophet Samuel, who had anointed Saul king. Samuel himself thus brutally slays Agag, justifying the killing as an act of retribution. That is, because Agag's sword had made women childless (1 Sam 15:33), Agag must be slain. The horror of war is epitomized by the implied grief of a woman losing offspring in time of war.

Carol Meyers

See also Part II: Women (and Men) of Jericho and Ai (Josh 6:21, etc.); Mother of Agag (1 Sam 15:33); Pregnant Women of Gilead (Amos 1:13).

1 Sam 18:6–7
Women Coming to Meet King Saul

See Exod 15:20, etc.   Women with Hand-Drums, Dancing (Part II).

1 Sam 21:4–5

Women Kept Away from David's Men

When David is outlawed from Saul's court, he flees to Nob, a "city of priests" (1 Sam 22:19) just north of Jerusalem. There he seeks assistance — food for his "young men" and a weapon for himself — from the priest Ahimelech. The priest provides both, but he is concerned about giving bread to David's men. Ahimelech has "only holy bread" (v. 4), that is, bread that has been sanctified for an official offering to YHWH (v. 7). Such bread should not be consumed by people who are ritually unfit, and Ahimelech was well aware of what would make a group of young men unfit to eat sanctified food.

The ancient Israelites believed that bodily discharges, including both normal ones such as menstrual blood and seminal emissions as well as those produced by disease, rendered persons temporarily "impure," that is, unfit to participate in activities in the sacred realm. Many cultures have similar views about bodily discharges, and anthropologists have suggested many different reasons for them. For the Israelites, perhaps the loss of fluid from the body was understood to make a person incomplete and thus not perfect — such a person would be disqualified from approaching the deity's perfect realm. In any case, David's young men could very well have had sex recently and thus experienced a discharge of seminal fluid; they would not then have been given the holy bread. Ahimelech doesn't say this directly; rather, he agrees to make the bread available only if the "young men have kept themselves from women" (v. 4).

David assures the priest that his men have abstained from sex: "women have been kept from us as always when I go on an expedition" (v. 5). The policy of always abstaining from sex during military forays is not because sex was thought to diminish a man's prowess, but rather because war could be considered a holy enterprise (see Josh 3:5); indeed, Deuteronomic regulations require a man who has had a seminal emission to temporarily absent himself from the military camp (Deut 23:9–11).

This incident raises the question about just who were the women that David's young men were avoiding. The text doesn't provide any information, and one can only speculate. The term for "young man" in this narrative is Hebrew *na'ar*. Although this word can sometimes denote servants or retainers, it is usually used to designate males from infancy up to marriageable age (see Gen 34:19; Exod 2:6; 1 Sam 20:35). It is thus unlikely that the men

with David were being intimate with wives. Perhaps camp followers were available to such young men on a military expedition, as is the case in many societies. Whoever these women may have been, David is adamant that his men had nothing to do with them.

CAROL MEYERS

SEE ALSO Part II: Woman (Women) Not to Be Approached at Sinai (Exod 19:15); Women and Bodily Emissions (Lev 15:18–33, etc.).

FOR FURTHER READING: Wright, David P., and Richard N. Jones. "Discharge."

1 SAM 22:3–4
Mother (and Father) of David

The first Israelite king, Saul (reigned c. 1025–1005 B.C.E.), feels threatened by the success of the young warrior David and ultimately seeks to kill him. David becomes a fugitive, according to a lengthy narrative sequence in 1 Samuel. Not only does he flee with his closest supporters, but also he sends his mother and father to the protective custody of the king of the Moabites at a place in Moab called Mizpeh (1 Sam 22:3–4).

The elaborate account of David's flight from Saul includes the mention of many geographical sites, all in Judah. The reference to a foreign site, presumably a Moabite royal city, is unusual. Furthermore, because Saul and David were both at war with the Moabites, it is difficult to understand why Moab becomes the refuge for David's parents, especially since the rest of his family goes into hiding with him in the "cave of Adullam" (1 Sam 22:1–3). The Moabite refuge for his parents is probably an allusion to David's Moabite ancestry as a descendant of the Moabite woman Ruth. The emphasis on David's partial non-Israelite origins may be intended to foreshadow the inclusivity of David's eschatological rule.

CAROL MEYERS

SEE ALSO Part I: Nahash; Ruth.

1 SAM 22:19
Women (and Men) of Nob

Because the priest Ahimelech, who has helped David in his struggle against King Saul, is from Nob, Saul strikes out against that city. He imposes the *ḥērem* ("devotion" or "ban"), killing all Nob's inhabitants: "men and women, children and infants, oxen, donkeys, and sheep" (1 Sam 22:19). This total annihilation, a feature of "sacred warfare" in biblical Israel and other ancient Near Eastern cultures, is usually depicted as imposed on Israel's enemies. Its application to an Israelite city, in the case of Nob, may reflect the pro-David and anti-Saul stance of this narrative; it shows Saul using the ban illegitimately, destroying an important priestly lineage for political reasons. When used against external enemies, the ban justified the use of violence as God's will, perhaps reducing the guilt of participating in warfare and increasing the solidarity of the victors. Using it to exterminate political opponents within the community, as Saul does at Nob, could expose the danger of an ideology condoning the destruction of human life.

CAROL MEYERS

SEE ALSO Part II: Women in Towns of the Amorite Kings Sihon and Og (Deut 2:34, etc.); Women (and Men) of Jericho and Ai (Josh 6:21, etc.); Daughters (and Sons) of Achan (Josh 7:24).

FOR FURTHER READING: Niditch, Susan. *War in the Hebrew Bible: A Study in the Ethics of Violence.*

1 SAM 25:42
Maids of Abigail

When the ill-natured and surly Nabal dies, David immediately marries Nabal's beautiful and intelligent widow, Abigail. Abigail comes to David with "five maids" in attendance (1 Sam 25:42). The word for these female companions, *nĕʿārôt*, can mean "young women" as well as maidservants and often designates the attendants of royalty (as of Pharaoh's daughter in Exod 2:5 and of Esther in Esth 2:9 and

4:9, 16). The presence of these attendants, as Abigail approaches the king in order to marry him, signals her impending royal status.

CAROL MEYERS

SEE ALSO Part I: Abigail 1; Part II: Maids of Rebekah (Gen 24:61); Attendants of the Daughter of Pharaoh (Exod 2:5); Maids of Esther (Esth 2:9, etc.).

1 SAM 27:9, 11
Women (and Men) Killed in David's Raids

When exiled by King Saul, David (along with his six hundred troops and their households) seeks refuge in the Philistine city of Gath (1 Sam 27:1–4). From there, David attacks enemies of Israel, while telling Achish, the king of Gath, that he is attacking Israel and its allies. David kills everyone he attacks, "leaving neither man nor woman alive" (27:9, 11).

Usually Israel's annihilation of enemies is "presented" as a sacrifice to God or as a "ban" securing God's justice (see Deut 20:16; Josh 6:21; 1 Sam 15:3). No such justification appears here. David kills everyone so that survivors cannot tell Achish, David's patron, that David has lied. David's motivation for mass killing is purely pragmatic and is not embedded in the language of religious duty.

ELIZABETH C. LAROCCA-PITTS

SEE ALSO Part II: Women in Distant Towns as Booty (Deut 20:14, etc.); Women (and Men) of Jericho and Ai (Josh 6:21, etc.).

FOR FURTHER READING: Niditch, Susan. *War in the Hebrew Bible: A Study in the Ethics of Violence.*

1 SAM 28:7–25
Medium of Endor

The story of Saul's visit to the medium at Endor gives a clear picture of the purpose and dynamics of this type of divination. Eager to consult YHWH on matters of both personal and national importance (an impending military encounter with the Philistines), Saul asks his servants to seek out "a woman who is a mistress of a ghost" (v. 7; author's translation). He visits this medium at night and requests that she "divine for [him] by means of a ghost," specifically, the ghost of the dead judge Samuel, who had anointed Saul as king. Though we are not told exactly how she accomplishes the feat, the woman brings up Samuel's ghost, which she refers to as a "god" (v. 13). Saul then communicates with this spirit and is profoundly disturbed by what he learns of YHWH's intentions for him.

According to the narrative, Saul first had tried consulting YHWH by standard (accepted) methods of divination (dreams, Urim, and prophets; v. 6), but "the LORD did not answer him." He then sought out this woman diviner, though the narrative says he had earlier "cut off the mediums and wizards from the land" (v. 9). Apparently, Saul had enough confidence in the ability of mediums to employ one when more acceptable forms of consulting the deity proved inconclusive. Deuteronomic polemics against divination notwithstanding (for example, Deut 18:9–14), this story suggests that various types of divination were well established in Israel, though only a few enjoyed official status within the Yahwistic establishment.

The narrative does not present it as remarkable that a woman is the medium recommended to Saul. Of all the various diviners forbidden in the Bible, mediums, wizards, and sorcerers are the only ones explicitly said to have been both female and male. Being a medium, which today is certainly a position outside mainstream culture, was an opportunity for women to have a professional role in ancient Israel.

THOMAS W. OVERHOLT

SEE ALSO Part II: Female Sorcerer (Exod 22:18, etc.); Medium/Wizard (Lev 20:27).

FOR FURTHER READING: Cryer, Frederick H. *Divination in Ancient Israel and Its Near Eastern Environment: A Socio-Historical Investigation.*

Overholt, Thomas W. *Cultural Anthropology and the Old Testament.*

1 SAM 30:2–3, 6, 19, 22
Women (Wives and Daughters [and Sons]) of Ziklag

The city of Ziklag, nearly forty miles southwest of Jerusalem, served for a short time as the base of David's military operations before he became king. During that period, while David is away with his warriors, the city is captured by Amalekite raiders, who burn it and take its women captive (1 Sam 30:2). All women, including two of David's wives (Abigail and Ahinoam), are carried off: "both young and old [NRSV, both small and great]." The next verse (30:3), as well as subsequent references to the captives (30:6, 19, 22), indicate that the "sons" of David and his men, as well as their daughters and wives, are also taken captive.

Unlike the way in which victorious Israelites treat enemy cities within Israelite territory, calling for total annihilation of the population, the Amalekites spare women and children. The Israelites likewise spare women and children when they destroy towns outside their territory (Deut 20:14). Perhaps such a policy was typical of the taking of spoils in warfare in the Levant in the Iron Age, at least in the bardic tradition in the Bible that celebrates heroes and chivalrous conduct. Women and children in such contexts serve as trophies of war as well as slave labor and sources of population increase.

In any case, the women and children of Ziklag do not remain with their captors, for David and his men overtake and kill the Amalekites and take their herds and flocks as spoil. The wives and children are restored to their menfolk (30:19, 22), along with equitable shares of the spoil.

CAROL MEYERS

SEE ALSO Part II: Wives (and Children) as Booty (Num 14:3); Midianite Women (Num 31:9, etc.); Women in Distant Towns as Booty (Deut 20:14. etc.); Women (and Men) of Jericho and Ai (Josh 6:21, etc.).

FOR FURTHER READING: Niditch, Susan. *War in the Hebrew Bible: A Study in the Ethics of Violence.*

2 SAM 1:20
Daughters of the Philistines

SEE EXOD 15:20, etc. Women with Hand-Drums, Dancing (Part II).

2 SAM 1:24
Weeping Daughters

King David's eulogy over the slain Saul (David's predecessor as king) and Saul's son Jonathan contains several female images, including the contrasting ones of women celebrating military victory (2 Sam 1:20) and of women mourning the death of those fallen in battle. Both draw upon cultural roles played by women in ancient Israel and other Near Eastern societies. With respect to the latter image, the "daughters of Israel" are called upon to "weep over Saul" (1 Sam 1:24). This reflects the predominance of women as experts in funerary practices and in the recitation or chanting of laments.

The word *daughters* is used poetically here to refer to Israelite women in general, or at least to those, perhaps members of the royal court, who have prospered materially under Saul's leadership.

CAROL MEYERS

SEE ALSO Part II: Women with Hand-Drums, Dancing (Exod 15:20, etc.); Mourning Women (Jer 9:17–20, etc.).

2 SAM 1:26
Women's Love, Compared with That of Jonathan and David

At the conclusion of his lyrical lament over the fallen heroes — King Saul and his son Jonathan — David expresses his intense sorrow over the latter's death. He refers to the great love he and Jonathan had for each other; he proclaims that Jonathan's love for him was greater than the "love of women" (2 Sam 1:26).

Although this phrase, along with the general theme of love throughout the narrative of the close personal relationship between David and Jonathan has led to suggestions of a homosexual relationship between them, the use of the word for "love" to describe their intimate bond can also refer to the covenant (1 Sam 18:1–4; 23:17–18) they make with each other. Despite the literary character of the narratives depicting the succession of David rather than Jonathan to the throne, political overtones color virtually every episode. Thus Near Eastern covenant terminology, which includes the word for "love," would have a legitimate place in David's lament. The image of a woman's love does have undeniable erotic qualities, yet the love of Jonathan for David is not compared to such love, but is said to surpass it.

CAROL MEYERS

SEE ALSO Part II: Weeping Daughters (2 Sam 1:24).

2 SAM 4:4
Nurse of Mephibosheth

The nurse (Hebrew 'ōmenet) of Mephibosheth, son of Jonathan and grandson of Saul, Israel's first king (reigned c. 1025–1005 B.C.E.), is not necessarily a wet nurse (Hebrew mēneqet), but rather simply someone who takes care of him. The same root is used for female and male caretakers elsewhere in the Hebrew Bible.

In this case, the caregiver is made responsible for the lameness of her five-year-old charge. The child falls as the nurse whisks him away from danger. His physical incapacity foreshadows his inability to become his grandfather's heir to the throne.

JO ANN HACKETT

SEE ALSO Part II: Nurse (Num 11:12); Nursing Mothers (Isa 49:15, etc.).

2 Sam 5:13
Wives and Concubines of David, Taken in Jerusalem

Whatever personal attraction may have existed between David and his wives and secondary wives, or concubines, all of his marriages, except perhaps with Bathsheba, were probably made to secure political advantage. Seven of his named wives — Abital, Abigail, Ahinoam, Eglah, Haggith, Maacah, Michal — become part of David's household before he is anointed king at Hebron, his first capital city; these marriages probably helped solidify his early base of support. When the capital is moved to Jerusalem, David not only builds a royal residence there and plans a national temple, but also takes additional wives and secondary wives, or concubines (2 Sam 5:13). All these actions are politically motivated; the buildings secure and legitimate his regnal powers, and the marriages provide additional loyal connections in his enlarged domain.

CAROL MEYERS

SEE ALSO Part II: Wives of the King (Deut 17:14–20); Daughters of David (2 Sam 5:13, etc.); Wives of David (2 Sam 15:16, etc.); Concubines of David (2 Sam 12:11, etc.).

2 SAM 5:13; 19:5; 1 CHR 14:3
Daughters of David

Female royal offspring were often used in ancient Israel and surrounding lands to establish alliances through diplomatic marriages and to ensure the loyalty of the nobility through marriage into the royal house. This was surely the case for David, the second king of Israel (reigned c. 1005–965 B.C.E.). David's many wives bore him numerous daughters and sons (2 Sam 5:13; 1 Chr 14:3). The daughters were raised within the palace precincts and wore special robes. It was the father's duty to protect and provide for all his family members and to put family loyalty ahead of individual loyalty (2 Sam 19:5).

DIANA VIKANDER EDELMAN

SEE ALSO Part I: Tamar 2; Part II: Royal Daughters and Their Garments (2 Sam 17:18).

FOR FURTHER READING: Matthews, Victor H., and Don C. Benjamin. *Social World of Ancient Israel, 1250–587 B.C.E.*

2 SAM 6:19
Women (and Men) of the Ark Ceremony

When the ark of YHWH, a symbol of the divine presence among the people, is returned to the Israelites after having been captured by the Philistines, King David decides to bring it to Jerusalem. The transfer of this central icon to the new capital at Jerusalem, which is described in 2 Samuel 6, is a highly significant event; it marks God's favor for David's regime and thereby justifies David's political control of Jerusalem and the kingdom. With the pomp and ceremony known to characterize other ancient Near Eastern cultures when the people escorted a deity to its city and temple, the ark is brought to Jerusalem with music, dancing, and offerings. Once it is safely ensconced in a special tent shrine, David offers more sacrifices, blesses the people, and gives all of them, "both men and women" (2 Sam 6:19), shares of the ceremonial food. The community participation in these important political and religious festivities is clearly gender-inclusive.

CAROL MEYERS

SEE ALSO Part II: Daughters (and Sons) and Female (and Male) Slaves, Rejoicing (Deut 12:12, etc.); Israelite Women in the Covenant Community (Deut 29:11, etc.); Women, Part of the Assembly of People (Neh 8:2, etc.).

2 SAM 6:20, 22
Maids of David's Servants

David's "servants" could be anyone in his retinue and need not be people of inferior status. The passage implies that their maids, however, are maidservants. They are being used as a foil to Michal, who is a king's daughter. Her jealousy for her father's dynasty blinds her to the piety in David's ecstatic dance before the ark, and she uses the presence of lowly maidservants looking on to shame David. David believes that women without the burdens of high birth and lost status will recognize his zeal for YHWH and praise him for it.

JO ANN HACKETT

SEE ALSO Part I: Michal.

2 SAM 11:21   Woman of Thebez
SEE JUDG 9:53–54, etc.   Woman of Thebez (Part II).

2 SAM 12:8
Wives of Saul

In a speech delivered by the prophet Nathan on behalf of God to David, condemning the king for committing adultery with Bathsheba, reference is made to God's granting of the kingship to David, giving him his "master's house" and "his master's [Saul's] wives." This transfer of wives may refer to the standard practice in which a new king took control of the former king's harem to assert a right to the throne.

DIANA VIKANDER EDELMAN
SEE ALSO Part I: Abishag; Ahinoam 1; Rizpah.

2 SAM 12:11; 19:5
Wives of David

As one of many punishments for committing adultery with Bathsheba, David (the second king of Is-rael, reigned c. 1005–965 B.C.E) is told that God plans to turn his wives over to a "neighbor" within his own house, who will sleep with them in broad daylight (2 Sam 12:11). This prediction is fulfilled in 2 Sam 16:21–22, when his son Absalom is proclaimed king after David's flight from Jerusalem. In order to demonstrate his claim to the throne, Absalom sleeps with the ten concubines of the royal harem who were left behind to keep the house (2 Sam 15:17). The reference to David's wives in 2 Sam 19:5 is made within the context of David's misplaced loyalty to one son, which overrides his concern for all others bound to him by loyalty oath or blood ties.

DIANA VIKANDER EDELMAN
SEE ALSO Part I: Ahinoam 2; Bathsheba; Eglah; Haggith; Maacah 2; Michal; Part II: Wives and Concubines of David, Taken in Jerusalem (2 Sam 5:13); Concubines of David (2 Sam 15:16, etc.).
FOR FURTHER READING: Berlin, Adele. "Characterization in Biblical Narrative: David's Wives."
Bird, Phyllis. "Images of Women in the Old Testament."

2 SAM 13:18
Royal Daughters and Their Garments

The narrative in 2 Samuel 13 about King David's daughter Tamar mentions a special garment worn by the unmarried daughters of the king. The NRSV calls these women "virgins," but the Hebrew term in fact designates young pubescent women, not necessarily biological virgins. The garment that these princesses wear is called *kĕtōnet passîm* (v. 18), variously translated "long robe with sleeves" (NRSV) or "ornamented tunic" (NJPS). This is the same phrase as that designating the garment that Jacob gives to Joseph (Gen 37:31). It is a sign of special privilege and thus not, in the case of the king's daughters, a mark of their unmarried status.

The garment offers no protection for Tamar, the most prominent of David's daughters, who is raped by her half-brother Amnon and then cast out by his servant. After this horrendous experience, Tamar puts ashes on her head, rips the garment, puts her hand on her head, and cries aloud (v. 19). These actions are the typical responses to death in ancient Israel; they call attention to the gravity of the incestuous rape and perhaps also to the family and national violence that ensues.

TIKVA FRYMER-KENSKY

SEE ALSO Part I: Tamar 2; Part II: Daughters of David (2 Sam 5:13, etc.).

FOR FURTHER READING: Frymer-Kensky, Tikva. *Victors, Victims, Virgins, and Voice: Rereading the Women of the Bible.*

2 SAM 14:1–20
Wise Woman of Tekoa

Tekoa — a Judean hill country village ten miles south of Jerusalem — was home to one of two women designated as "wise," both appearing in 2 Samuel. One defining attribute of "wisdom," in the biblical tradition, is skill in rhetoric (Prov 1:5–6 and *passim*), and the speeches of both this woman and her counterpart from the town of Abel (20:14–22) are highlighted in their respective stories. More obvious in the latter story is the wise woman's role as village leader, likely akin to the male role of elder. In the present narrative, subterfuge hides overt indications of such status, while at the same time offering under-the-surface allusions to its social and symbolic grounding. This narrative, however, to some degree clouds a clear judgment about the quality of the woman's wisdom.

2 Samuel 13 tells of the rape of King David's daughter Tamar by her half brother and David's heir, Amnon; Amnon's murder by her full brother, Absalom (now the heir!); Absalom's subsequent flight; and David's grief. It is now three years later, and Joab, David's general, devises a ruse to reconcile David and his son. He instructs (forces? — her willingness is never stated) the wise woman of Tekoa to act the role of a widowed mother of two sons, one of whom has murdered the other. She ostensibly seeks mercy for the fratricide in the face of the family's will to execute him, thus preserving her dead husband's name and also the mainstay of her own familial status and survival.

The woman thus acts out a parable, not unlike the ewe-lamb story told by the prophet Nathan after David's adultery with Bathsheba and murder of her husband. Both prophet and wise woman force David to clear thinking and action on his own situation by indirect means, though there are also differences in the two performances. Whereas the speech of Nathan, the divinely appointed prophet, is clear in both syntax and judgment, that of the humanly appointed female outsider is grammatically broken and employs the servile flattery of a social inferior. The wisdom of having Absalom return to Jerusalem is also questionable: four years later, he revolts against his father.

Despite these narrative ambiguities, the outline of an ancient Israelite woman's leadership role shows through. Her story is not as dramatically effective as is Nathan's, yet she persists through the dangerous and unpredictable turns in her conversation with David: she clearly understands that "with patience a ruler may be persuaded, and a soft tongue can break bones" (Prov 25:15). Her effective use of a proverbial simile (2 Sam 14:14), the sage's stock-in-trade, further indicates her experience in such dealings. Finally, although her story may have originated with Joab (14:3, 19), the wise woman is represented as one able to appropriate the fundamental cultural values of ancient Israel: the preservation of patriarchal lineage (14:7) and the people of God (14:13), and the king's obligation to protect the right of widow and orphan to enjoy God's heritage (14:16). Although her self-presentation as a mother is in one sense artifice, it also indicates an acknowledged source of women's authority and wisdom in ancient Israel, as attested by the phrase "mother in Israel" applied to the judge Deborah (Judg 5:7) and used by the wise woman of Abel (2 Sam 20:19).

CLAUDIA V. CAMP

SEE ALSO Part II: Wise Woman of Abel of Beth-maacah (2 Sam 20:14–22); Part III: Woman Wisdom .

FOR FURTHER READING: Brenner, Athalya. *The Israel-ite Woman: Social Role and Literary Type in Biblical Narrative.*

Camp, Claudia V. "The Wise Women of 2 Samuel: A Role Model for Women in Early Israel."

Willey, Patricia K. "The Importunate Woman of Tekoa and How She Got Her Way."

2 SAM 15:16; 16:21–22; 19:5; 20:3, 1 CHR 3:9

Concubines of David

When Absalom, son of King David (reigned c. 1005–965 B.C.E.), attempts to become king of Israel in place of his father, David and his household flee the city of Jerusalem. David leaves behind ten "concubines," however, "to look after the house" (2 Sam 15:16). The practice of having numerous wives and concubines (who were perhaps secondary wives or sexual partners) seems to have been accepted in Israel, at least for Israel's patriarchs and kings. The book of 1 Chronicles, which portrays David in a positive light and seldom mentions his negative characteristics, notes that David had sons by his concubines (1 Chr 3:9).

After Absalom and his supporters enter Jerusalem, David's former adviser Ahithophel encourages Absalom to have sexual intercourse with the ten concubines. Ahithophel states that this action will make Absalom "odious" to his father and encourage Absalom's supporters. Following Ahithophel's advice, Absalom has a tent set upon the roof of the house and has sexual relations with his father's concubines "in the sight of all Israel" (2 Sam 16:22). This act seems to have been an attempt to shame David and increase Absalom's prestige. In addition, it fulfills an oracle given to David by the prophet Nathan, in which it is acknowledged that God previously gave the wives of Saul to David (2 Sam 12:8). Nathan's oracle states that, because of David's actions with Bathsheba and Uriah, God will cause another man to lie with David's wives "before all Israel" (2 Sam 12:12). This sordid episode perhaps reflects the political practice of a king's taking over his predecessor's or rival's harem as a way of asserting dynastic control or shaming his predecessor or rival.

When David regains control of Israel, he places the concubines in a house where they live as widows (2 Sam 20:3); he apparently cannot reestablish marital relations with them once Absalom has had sexual relations with them. David's concubines are also referred to by his general Joab, who complains that David has shamed his own supporters and members of his own household, including his wives and concubines, by grieving over his son Absalom (2 Sam 19:5).

KEN STONE

SEE ALSO Part II: Wives of Saul (2 Sam 12:8); Wives and Concubines of David, Taken in Jerusalem (2 Sam 5:13); Wives of David (2 Sam 12:11, etc.).

FOR FURTHER READING: Levenson, Jon D., and Baruch Halpern. "The Political Import of David's Marriages."

2 SAM 17:17

Servant Girl of En-rogel

When Absalom's revolt forces David to flee Jerusalem, this servant girl carries military intelligence obtained by David's spy, Hushai, from the loyal high priests (Zadok and Abiathar) to their sons (Jonathan and Ahimaaz) who were hiding in En-rogel, near Jerusalem. Since she does not attract attention leaving and entering Jerusalem, females of her status must have enjoyed freedom of movement.

Although the text does not say for whom she worked, it is likely that she worked in the temple complex or for a wealthy loyalist, since most small landholders probably could not afford servants. The fact that the text mentions her role in an incidental way suggests the historical veracity of this story.

RHONDA BURNETTE-BLETSCH

2 SAM 17:18–20
Woman at Bahurim

When servants of Absalom pursue David's messengers (Jonathan and Ahimaaz), who are carrying vital military intelligence, a woman at Bahurim hides them in a well and conceals its opening with a covering strewn with grain. Although the house, well, and courtyard are identified as her husband's property, it is the woman who chooses to use these resources on David's behalf. Likewise, Absalom's servants address her, not her husband. Though the phrasing may indicate male ownership of the household, in many cases the senior women controlled its daily activities. The narrator even gives her the only voice in the story by phrasing her response in direct address. Like many biblical heroines (and heroes), she accomplishes her goals through deception when she misdirects her questioners. Her actions contrast with the condemned behavior of Shimei of Bahurim, who cursed and threw stones at the fugitive King David (2 Sam 16:5–14). Possibly they represent a division between pro- and anti-Davidic groups in this Benjaminite village.

RHONDA BURNETTE-BLETSCH

2 SAM 19:5   Daughters of David

SEE 2 SAM 5:13, etc.   Daughters of David (Part II).

2 SAM 19:5   Wives of David

SEE 2 SAM 12:11, etc.   Wives of David (Part II).

2 SAM 19:5   Concubines of David

SEE 2 SAM 15:16, etc.   Concubines of David (Part II).

2 SAM 19:35; ECCL 2:8; 12:4
Singing Women (and Men)

Women's musical traditions in ancient Israel, as in many cultures, can be broadly classified as either secular or religious, although the boundaries between the two are often blurred. Several biblical passages seem to refer unambiguously to women (and men) whose musical performances can be considered secular. Two of these texts are in the Book of Ecclesiastes, the work of a teacher who at first questions the meaning of pleasurable pursuits. Among the sensory delights he mentions is the performance of "singers, both men and women" (Eccl 2:8). A similar reference to performers of both genders appears in an earlier biblical book, where the delights of palace life in Jerusalem are said to include visual beauty, fine food and drink, and "the voice of singing men and singing women" (2 Sam 19:35).

These texts indicate that professional singers of both genders were available to provide entertainment for individuals or groups. Such professionals were likely to have been participants in loosely organized guilds, a term that denotes an association of people pursuing common interests. Knowledge of songs and of performance techniques depended upon opportunities for learning and practice, which guilds would provide.

It is difficult to assess whether these pairs of references to female and male singers mean that the groups were mixed. The fact that they are mentioned individually by gender, rather than simply by a collective word for "singers," may indicate that separate performance groups were involved. That possibility finds some support in the reference in Eccl 12:4 to "daughters of song," where the word *daughters* (like *sons* in expressions such as "sons of the prophets") is used to indicate membership in a professional group, in this case a women's association.

Because recent ethnomusicological study of performance dynamics provides information about the experience of people who perform singly and in groups, the meaning of membership in organized women's performance groups in ancient Israel can be ascertained. Women who belong to such groups have the opportunity to act autonomously, to experience female solidarity, and, for some, to act as leaders or mentors. Furthermore, professional women singers, like professional mourning women and members of women's drumming and dancing ensembles, were part of performance traditions for women that contributed significantly to Israelite culture in a variety of public settings.

CAROL MEYERS

SEE ALSO Part II: Women with Hand-Drums, Dancing (Exod 15:20, etc.); Singing Women (and Men) Who Lament (2 Chr 35:25); Mourning Women (Jer 9:17–20, etc.).

FOR FURTHER READING: Meyers, Carol. "Mother to Muse: An Archaeomusicological Study of Women's Performance in Ancient Israel."

2 SAM 19:37
Mother (and Father) of Barzillai

Barzillai is a Gileadite who provides support for King David (reigned c. 1005–965 B.C.E.) when he has problems with his subversive son Absalom. In gratitude, David invites him to come to Jerusalem and partake of the pleasures of the royal court. Barzillai declines. At the age of eighty, he wants only to return home, to be near his family tomb, presumably feeling that his days on earth are coming to an end.

The phrase Barzillai uses for the family tomb is "the grave [NRSV, graves] of my father and my mother." The word translated as "grave" is the Hebrew *qeber,* which probably refers to a rock-hewn tomb rather than a pit grave, especially because the word is singular in the Hebrew and because it is accompanied by the words for both "mother" and "father," indicating multiple burial. Burial practices in ancient Israel typically involved an ancestral tomb located on the family's land, so that the tomb served as a physical marker of the family rights to the land. Although the land itself was transmitted through the male lineage, the concept of family associated with the burial site included both female and male ancestors, as Barzillai's comment indicates. (Compare the references to the cave of Machpelah, as a burial place of both female and male family members, in Gen 49:29–33.)

CAROL MEYERS

SEE ALSO Part II: Daughter of Barzillai the Gileadite (Ezra 2:61, etc.).

FOR FURTHER READING: Bloch-Smith, Elizabeth. *Judahite Burial Practices and Beliefs about the Dead.*

2 SAM 20:3   Concubines of David
SEE 2 SAM 15:16, etc.   Concubines of David (Part II).

2 SAM 20:19
Mother as Designation for the City of Abel
SEE Mother/Daughter (NRSV, Village) as Territory (Part III).

2 SAM 20:14–22
Wise Woman of Abel of Beth-maacah

The second of two "wise women" portrayed in 2 Samuel lived in a fortified city in northern Israel. More straightforwardly than the story of the wise woman of Tekoa (2 Samuel 14), this narrative depicts what must have been typical leadership activities of a woman in this accepted position against the larger political tensions of David's reign.

Hostility between the "people of Judah" (David's tribe of origin in the south) and the "people of Israel" (the ten northern tribes) surfaces following David's suppression of his son Absalom's revolt (2 Sam 19:41–43). A Benjaminite, Sheba son of Bichri, capitalizes on the sentiment with a call for the northerners to forsake their "share in David" (20:1) — that is, to rebel or secede. The scene is thus set for Sheba's flight to the north and refuge in Abel, where David's general Joab chases him down.

As Joab's forces batter the city wall, the wise woman calls out to him for negotiations. His immediate response suggests his familiarity with her position and his acknowledgment of its claim to authority. Her next speech (20:18–19) is a masterpiece of manipulation. Using a proverb unfortunately not fully recoverable from a corrupt text, she rhetorically links her city's reputation for wise counsel with her own claim to be one of the "peaceable and faithful in Israel" (20:19). She then accuses Joab of seeking to destroy "a city that is a mother in Israel" and demands why he would "swallow up the heritage of the LORD" (20:19). Reference to a city as "mother" indicates its preeminent position among a cluster of smaller towns. Here, however, the woman's rhetoric suggests as well a wider metaphorical connotation to "mother in Israel": used by a woman who was no doubt a mother as well as being wise, it ties back to her self-reference as a "peaceable and faithful" citizen of a city known for wise counsel (compare the attribution of the title to Deborah, Judg 5:7); at the same time it anticipates by means of parallelism the theologically freighted "heritage of the LORD" (compare the Tekoite wise woman's allusion to the "heritage of God," 2 Sam 14:16). Joab can only defensively backpedal: "Far be it from me, far be it, that I should swallow up or destroy!" (20:20). Joab then asks only for the head of Sheba, perhaps unwilling to risk demanding "all the Bichrites" who would remain in safety behind Abel's walls. The wise woman accedes to this request, with apparent confidence in her people's subsequent agreement.

Like that of her counterpart in Tekoa, this story of a wise woman attests to what must have been a regularized public role for women, at least through the early period of the Israelite monarchy: we have no further record of such female leadership after the time of David (reigned c. 1005–965). Although the increasing political encroachment of the monarchy may have undercut the wider power of the village wise women, it is unlikely, however, to have eliminated their authority among their own people. Rather, the interests of the male court historians became focused more on urban life and male leaders than on life in rural communities.

CLAUDIA V. CAMP

SEE ALSO Part II: Wise Woman of Tekoa (2 Sam 14:1–20); Part III: Woman Wisdom.

FOR FURTHER READING: Camp, Claudia V. "The Wise Women of 2 Samuel: A Role Model for Women in Early Israel."

1 KGS 3:1; 7:8; 10:8; 11:1–8; NEH 13:26
Women of Solomon

Solomon, third king of Israel (reigned c. 968–928 B.C.E.), is said to have had a harem that included seven hundred wives and three hundred concubines (1 Kgs 11:3). His wives were to have included the daughter of Pharaoh, as well as women of Moabite, Edomite, Sidonian, and Hittite origins (1 Kgs 7:8; 11:1). The latter group is usually understood to represent wives who were added to the harem as a means of sealing treaty agreements with these five foreign powers. Throughout human history, marriage alliance has been the most common way for rulers to attempt to secure peaceful relationships with potential enemies.

The tradition in 1 Kgs 11:1–8 about Solomon's marriage to foreign wives, whether based on historical records or not, employs the motif of the dangerous foreign woman to condemn Solomon for idolatry in his later years (see Neh 13:26). It seems to illustrate the prohibition in Deut 7:3 against marrying foreign women and also to echo the exclusion of Moab and Edom from the congregation of the LORD in Deut 23:4–9. Foreign women were considered a potential source of trouble because they might not always adopt the culture and values of their husbands and their new place of residence. If they chose to continue to practice their native customs and cults, they would pass these on to their children and might also influence their husbands to adopt some non-Israelite practices as well. Loyalty to and identity with Israelite tradition would be threatened. In biblical literature, foreign women, seduction, prostitution, sexual disloyalty, and fertility cults were often linked together, yet not all foreign women were viewed as evil. Tamar (Genesis 38), Ruth (Book of Ruth), Rahab (Joshua 2), and Jael (Judges 4–5) provide positive images of foreign women; each demonstrates through her behavior her adoption of Israelite or Judahite society and religion and gains acceptance in her new community. Solomon's foreign wives, by contrast, depict the negative side of foreign women. Like Potiphar's wife (Genesis 39), Samson's wife (Judges 14–16), and the foreign woman of Proverbs 1–9, they remain loyal to their own personal or political interests and, as a result, disrupt law and order in their adoptive Israelite community.

DIANA VIKANDER EDELMAN

SEE ALSO Part I: Naamah 2; Part II: Concubines of David (2 Sam 15:16, etc.); Daughter of Pharaoh (1 Kgs 3:1, etc.); Queen of Sheba (1 Kgs 10:1–13, etc.); Women of Rehoboam (Fourteen Wives and Sixteen Daughters) (2 Chr 11:21); Wives and Daughters of Abijah (Eighteen Wives, Sixty Concubines, and Sixty Daughters) (2 Chr 13:21).

FOR FURTHER READING: Reinhartz, Adele. "Anonymous Women and the Collapse of the Monarchy: A Study in Narrative Technique."

Brenner, Athalya. *The Israelite Woman: Social Role and Literary Type in Biblical Narrative.*

Miller, J. Maxwell, and John H. Hayes. *A History of Ancient Israel and Judah.*

1 KGS 3:1; 7:8; 9:16, 24; 11:1; 2 CHR 8:11
Daughter of Pharaoh

These references to Pharaoh's daughter foreground the concept of diplomatic marriages, a common method of alliance in the eastern Mediterranean region during the second and first millennia B.C.E. Attested in Egypt no later than the reign of Thutmose III (1504–1450 B.C.E.), Egyptian diplomatic marriages of the XVIII and XIX dynasties involved the marriage of a foreign king's daughter to Pharaoh, thus denoting an Egyptian position of strength; reciprocal marriages — a daughter of Pharaoh to a foreign ruler — did not occur, as attested by the tablets known as the Amarna letters (with the exception of Ankhesenamen's attempt to marry a Hittite prince following Tutankhamen's death). Thus the marriage of Solomon to a daughter of Pharaoh at the end of the XXI dynasty may evidence a shift in power relations between the two

states, one in which Egypt found it advantageous to make a marriage alliance with Israel. (Israel's political power may have exceeded that of Egypt during the reign of Solomon in the tenth century B.C.E.)

Use of Pharaoh's daughter as a pawn to cement relationships between nations appears to be — and is — contrary to the common understanding of the Egyptian woman as independent, a concept amply attested in Egyptian sources. As in the case of multiple wives for an Egyptian pharaoh, which was most uncommon among nonroyalty, one may say that royal women also could be used for the perceived good of the state, although such was not the case among nonroyal persons. Furthermore, with each change of ruler, this type of alliance needed to be renewed.

The pharaoh's daughter of diplomatic marriages presents a strikingly different picture from the one in the Moses narrative.

SUSAN TOWER HOLLIS

SEE ALSO Part II: Daughter of Pharaoh (Exod 2:5–10); Women of Solomon (1 Kgs 3:1, etc.).

FOR FURTHER READING: Brenner, Athalya. *The Israelite Woman: Social Role and Literary Type in Biblical Narrative.*

Camp, Claudia V. "1 and 2 Kings."

Robins, Gay. *Women in Ancient Egypt.*

Schulman, Alan R. "Diplomatic Marriage in the Egyptian New Kingdom."

Setel, Drorah O'Donnel. "Exodus."

1 KGS 3:16–28
Two Prostitutes as Mothers

Immediately after he requests that God grant him "an understanding mind to govern your people" (1 Kgs 3:9), King Solomon (reigned c. 968–928 B.C.E.) is confronted by two prostitutes and their enigmatic case. One function of the story, therefore, is to illustrate God's fulfillment of Solomon's plea. The story further demonstrates that Solomon provides access to justice even to the most marginalized of Israel's subjects, in this case women bereft of male benefactors, whether husband or father. The narrator informs the reader at the outset that these women are prostitutes, so that the lack of a corroborating witness in their home is understood; in ancient Israel, one would expect to find a husband in the home of a woman after childbirth. Further, the tale expresses the intensity of maternal affection, which exceeds jealous possessiveness. (Moses' mother, in Exodus 2, behaves similarly in renouncing her claim to her child in order to save his life.) The fact that these women are prostitutes only strengthens the depiction of authentic love (or envy), as the live son is not desired as an object to win the affections of a husband, but rather for his own sake.

The narrator presents us with two women, referred to vaguely as "the one woman" and "the other woman." We know nothing of their appearance and can distinguish between them only by their words. The "one woman" offers a full version of the events, that she and "the other woman" gave birth to sons only three days apart. The rest of her account, however, provides only logical speculation as she herself admits that she was asleep (v. 20) during the episode. She claims that the other woman unintentionally killed her baby by lying on it and then exchanged the dead baby for her live son. Since no other people were at home, the reader (and the king) have only her version, a reconstruction of events that happened as she slept so soundly that she did not perceive the switch. She assumes that her companion's negligence caused her baby's demise, because he had showed no symptoms of illness previously; if he did, perhaps witnesses could have been called to verify his condition.

The other woman does not dispute this account, but states briefly, "No, the living son is mine, and the dead son is yours" (v. 22). It is difficult for the reader to sympathize with her because of the terseness of her words. Rather than summon character witnesses, cross-examine the women, pursue physical evidence, or even take time to ponder the dilemma, the king calls for a sword and gives directions to one of his courtiers to divide the live baby in two and give each woman half.

At this point the narrator identifies for us the mother of the living child — the woman who offers her son to her counterpart in order to save him.

The reader, however, does not know whether the mother of the live child is the first or the second woman, the complainant or the respondent. The conventional and most probable understanding of the story is that the first woman, who gave the speculative yet full account of what transpired, is the mother of the living child. Her spontaneous outburst is motivated by the "compassion for her son [that] burned within her" (v. 26). The Hebrew word translated as "compassion," *rǎḥamîm*, is related to *reḥem*, "womb," and is especially suitable for evoking maternal pathos. The narrator assumes that strong, spontaneous emotion offers a reliable reflection of a person's true nature.

What motivates the other woman to demand the splitting of the child even after her rival, at least verbally, surrenders him? Perhaps fierce envy prompts her to demand that her housemate's child suffer the same tragic fate as did her own child. Because she is not his real mother, her desire for vengeance transcends her love for the child. Further, she may fear that her claim to the child will never be secure, or she may be seeking to flatter the king by affirming his judgment. By exposing the falseness of her claim, Solomon's ruse amazes his subjects and demonstrates his God-given wisdom in executing justice.

ELAINE ADLER GOODFRIEND

SEE ALSO Part I: Rahab; Part II: Prostitute (Lev 19:29, etc.); Two Mothers Who Agree to Eat Their Sons (2 Kgs 6:26–33).

FOR FURTHER READING: Lasine, Stuart. "The Riddle of Solomon's Judgment and the Riddle of Human Nature in the Hebrew Bible."

———. "Solomon, Daniel, and the Detective Story: The Social Functions of a Literary Genre."

van Wolde, Ellen. "Who Guides Whom? Embeddedness and Perspective in Biblical Hebrew and in 1 Kings 3:16–28."

1 KGS 7:8　Daughter of Pharaoh

SEE 1 KGS 3:1, etc.　Daughter of Pharaoh (Part II).

1 Kgs 7:13–14; 2 Chr 2:14
Mother of Hiram

The skilled artisan hired by King Solomon to fashion all the metal vessels and appurtenances for the Jerusalem temple was a man named Hiram (1 Kgs 7:13) or Huram-abi (according to 2 Chr 2:14). In providing information about Hiram's parentage, the Kings and Chronicles accounts both indicate that his father was Tyrian. Their statements about his mother diverge: Kings claims that his mother was a "widow of the tribe of Naphtali" (v. 14), and Chronicles states that she was a Danite woman.

The divergence in maternal lineage, the somewhat different names, and also the statement in Chronicles that Hiram produces the fabrics for the temple as well as the metalwork can probably be explained by the Chronicler's special priestly interests. Chronicles changes the earlier tradition in a way that makes Hiram's work on the temple equivalent to the artistic component of the construction of the first sacred structure, the tabernacle. One of the two artisans whom Moses appointed to construct the tabernacle was Oholiab, whose name has the same "ab" component as does Huram-abi. Oholiab is also a member of the tribe of Dan (Exod 31:6), and he works on both the fabrics and the metalwork for the tabernacle.

The tradition that Hiram's craft expertise comes from his father, a foreigner, is offset by having his mother be explicitly identified as an Israelite. His maternal lineage is critical: the central shrine must be built by someone who is at least half Israelite. That his mother was a widow may further stress his Israelite identity by suggesting that he was raised by his mother alone.

CAROL MEYERS

FOR FURTHER READING: Dillard, Raymond B. 2 Chronicles.

1 Kgs 9:16, 24   Daughter of Pharaoh
SEE 1 Kgs 3:1, etc.   Daughter of Pharaoh (Part II).

1 Kgs 10:1–13; 2 Chr 9:1–12
Queen of Sheba

An independent woman ruling a fabulously wealthy Arabian or African kingdom to the south of Judah, this unnamed queen appears in one of the many stories emphasizing the grandeur of Solomon's court and his international reputation for extraordinary wisdom. In the brief notice of her visit, the 1 Kings and 2 Chronicles narratives highlight her wealth and intelligence, as well as Solomon's. Despite the legendary nature of her story, extrabiblical records from Egypt and Mesopotamia, which amply attest to the presence of strong women rulers of international reputation in Egypt and Arabia both before and after the general time period in which the Hebrew Bible places Sheba (c. tenth century B.C.E.), lend credibility to the biblical account. Although some have attempted to identify Sheba's visit with the Egyptian queen Hatshepsut's famed expedition to Punt, the land of incense in the Horn of Africa (catalogued on the walls of the queen's temple at Deir el-Bahri in Egypt), this connection is far too early to fit within biblical chronology. Nevertheless, connections between the Horn of Africa and the kingdoms of southwest Arabia have been well established by archaeology, so the possibility of Sheba's African origin is not out of the question. Some later traditions connect Sheba with the "dark and lovely" companion of Solomon in the Song of Solomon.

While her presence in the Hebrew Bible is due to a desire to show Solomon's magnificence and knowledge, certain terms in the story have given rise to a rich folkloric tradition about her in Jewish, Islamic, and Christian postbiblical legends. Both the phrases "she came" (1 Kgs 10:1) and "Solomon gave to the queen of Sheba all that she desired" (v. 13a), for example, have led to the suggestion of a sexual relationship between the two, which issued in a son, variously called Menelik (Ethiopian Christian), Rehoboam (Islamic), or Nebuchadnezzar (Jewish). For Christians, she is identified with the queen of the South (Matt 12:42; Luke 11:31) or Candace (Acts 8:27) of Ethiopia, and she typifies the "outsider" female who has more good sense than "insider" men.

The queen of Sheba appears in the *Antiquities* of Josephus (8.5.5) with the name Nicaulis, a noble philosopher and ruler from Egypt or the Horn of Africa. She also appears in the Qur'an (Sura XXVII) as a queen who submits to Solomon, the prophet of Allah, and converts to Islam. In Jewish legend, she is identified with Lilith, queen of demons. Although her riddles ("hard questions") do not appear in the Bible, they are given in subsequent sources and show her vast knowledge of the world, including the history of the ruling families of Judah.

Sheba, despite the mystery of her origins, presents us with a valid memory of women who managed to carve out high-ranking positions for themselves in worlds dominated by men. Her "chutzpah" in "testing" — that is, challenging — God's chosen king with riddles is in no way out of character for such a monarch. It may be that the Bible's anxiety over the existence of such women is the reason for the suppression of her riddling tradition. Extrabiblical legends also show her to be a facile user of riddles and other wisdom forms, by which she displays her cunning and statecraft. Whether viewed as a dangerous demonic partner or a noble ancestress, traditional sources portray her as an able ruler, and hence, a powerful human incarnation of the virtues and abilities residing in Woman Wisdom of Proverbs 1–9.

CAROLE R. FONTAINE

SEE ALSO Part I: Candace; Part II: Queen of the South (Matt 12:42); (Luke 11:31); Part III: Lilith; Woman Wisdom.

FOR FURTHER READING: Abbott, Nabia. "Pre-Islamic Arab Queens."

Fontaine, Carole R. "More Queenly Proverb Performance: The Queen of Sheba in the Targum Esther Sheni."

Lassner, Jacob. *Demonizing the Queen of Sheba: Boundaries of Gender and Culture in Postbiblical Judaism and Medieval Islam.*

Pritchard, James B., ed. *Solomon and Sheba.*

1 KGS 10:8; 11:1–8   Wives of Solomon

SEE 1 KGS 3:1, etc.   Women of Solomon (Part II).

1 KGS 11:19–20
Queen Tahpenes' Sister, Hadad's Wife

The fruitful marriage of Egyptian queen Tahpenes' sister to the refugee Edomite crown prince Hadad represents an example of the diplomatic marriages of this era (tenth century B.C.E.)

SUSAN TOWER HOLLIS

SEE ALSO Part I: Tahpenes; Part II: Daughter of Pharaoh (1 Kgs 3:1, etc.).

1 KINGS 14
Wife of Jeroboam

This episode features the unnamed wife of Jeroboam I (reigned 928–907 B.C.E.), the first king of the northern kingdom of Israel. On instructions from her husband, she disguises herself and goes to inquire of the prophet Ahijah about the fate of her sick son, Abijah. The prophet, his eyes dimmed with age, has been forewarned by God of her arrival, and he recognizes the sound of her footsteps despite the disguise.

The prophet's message to the woman is a harsh one, foretelling the end of the newly installed house of Jeroboam because of the idolatry of the king. The sick son, she is told, will die when she returns to her city and will be the only member of the family to receive a proper burial. These words are to be delivered to King Jeroboam.

Jeroboam's wife does not utter a word in this episode. She passively follows her husband's orders, does not greet the prophet or respond to his dire message, but returns home, knowing that when she does so, the son will die. There is no record of her repeating the prophetic message to Jeroboam.

Her role in the story is best understood as a literary vehicle through which the sharp reversal in Jeroboam's fortune is conveyed to the reader. By serving as a silent intermediary between Jeroboam and the prophet Ahijah (the same prophet who earlier announced directly to Jeroboam that he would be given the kingdom of Israel), she becomes the means through which the message is given to the reader.

At the same time, the need for an intermediary and the accompanying deception and generous gifts suggest that Jeroboam knows that he has already lost the favor of God and Ahijah. Indeed, this chapter confirms the message of chap. 13 — that because of the altar that Jeroboam established at Bethel, perceived as illegitimate by the biblical author, Jeroboam has lost God's favor.

Accordingly, we should not view the wife's characterization as an attempt to minimize a historical wife of a king, but rather as the effective use of an anonymous character to fill an important literary function. She is intentionally not portrayed as a real individual in her own right. Her individual personhood is thrice removed from the narrative — by the absence of her name, by her disguise, and by her role as an agent rather than as a full-fledged character. She is an extension of Jeroboam and a vehicle through which the text portrays his present state and his future doom.

ADELE BERLIN

SEE ALSO Part II: Widow of Zarephath (1 Kgs 17:8–24).

FOR FURTHER READING: Reinhartz, Adele. "Anonymity and Character in the Books of Samuel."

1 KGS 17:8–24
Widow of Zarephath

Narratives about the ninth-century B.C.E. prophet Elijah are found in 1 Kings 17–19 and 21 and in 2 Kings 1–2. Like his successor, Elisha, he is depicted as having many of the attributes of Israel's later prophetic figures. One of these characteristics —

concern for the oppressed and socially marginalized — is revealed in the story of the widow of Zarephath. The narrative of 1 Kings 17 contains three episodes that serve to introduce the figure of Elijah.

After an introductory section (1 Kgs 17:1–7) in which YHWH announces a drought and commands ravens to feed the prophet, an episode unfolds concerning a widow living in a non-Israelite village near Sidon during the drought (1 Kgs 17:8–16). The prophet requests food, but the woman is unable to acquiesce. She plans to prepare a meager meal for her son and herself with her few remaining supplies and then die. Autonomous widows, unless their spouses and fathers were wealthy, were socially and economically marginalized, barely able to survive in times of plenty and clearly at risk during droughts. In this case, the prophet as miracle worker saves the widow and her son. Invoking God's authority, Elijah causes her jar of grain and jug of oil to be miraculously replenished until the drought ends.

In a third episode (1 Kgs 17:17–24), which may originally have been a separate narrative because the woman does not seem as poor as the one in vv. 8–16, the widow's son dies. She seems to blame the prophet for her son's death, or perhaps for suggesting that his death was the result of a transgression of her own. Elijah invokes divine help and stretches himself out on the corpse. The child is brought to life, and the foreign widow becomes a follower of Elijah's God.

These stories of miracle working, which make Elijah a favorite prophetic figure in the New Testament, are artfully situated in their Kings setting. They connect narratively to an earlier event in which Jeroboam's wife tries to save her sick son (1 Kgs 14:2–18). And they effect a transition to Elijah's larger national mission. A foreign widow — socially marginal and religiously outside the true community of God — is fed, her son is brought to life, and she acknowledges YHWH. The individual incident prefigures the national message. God will provide for the Israelites and give them life; they must commit themselves to God.

FRANK S. FRICK

SEE ALSO Part II: Widows (Exod 22:22, etc.); Widow Whose Oil Is Multiplied (2 Kgs 4:1–7).

FOR FURTHER READING: Camp, Claudia. "1 and 2 Kings."

1 KGS 19:20

Mother (and Father) of Elisha

Elisha, a northern prophet of the ninth century B.C.E., is successor to Elijah, one of the most famous prophetic figures in the narratives of 1 and 2 Kings. In the highly symbolic account of Elijah's designation of Elisha to succeed him, Elisha agrees to follow Elijah. He says, however, that he must first kiss his parents — "my father and my mother" (1 Kgs 19:20) — goodbye. He understands well that his prophetic mission will take him away from his agricultural work (he was plowing when Elijah beckoned him) and his family, represented by both parents.

CAROL MEYERS

1 KGS 20:3, 5, 7

Wives of Ahab

In the context of a preexisting vassalship between the king of Syria and Ahab, king of the northern kingdom of Israel (reigned c. 873–852 B.C.E.) (1 Kgs 20:32–33), the Syrian monarch claims ownership of Ahab's harem, children, silver, and gold in a confrontation that presumes that the Israelite king had rebelled against his Syrian master. As the overlord in the treaty, the Syrian king is said to comment on owning Ahab's wives, which would have been a symbolic means of asserting his claim to political superiority and thus to his demand for the Israelite king's reaffirmation of his status. Possession of the royal harem, along with the children of the king's wives, was the prerogative of the ruling monarch. The Syrian king would not have hesitated to demonstrate his claim by publicly sleeping with members of the harem in order to drive home the point more graphically, had Ahab failed to cooperate or had he lost the ensuing two battles (1 Kgs 20:12–21:30). Ahab is said to have renegotiated his status, becoming the ally of his former overlord in the wake of his military victories (2 Kgs 20:31–34). His wives and children were spared being handed over to the foreign ruler.

DIANA VIKANDER EDELMAN

SEE ALSO Part I: Jezebel 1.

FOR FURTHER READING: de Vaux, Roland. *Ancient Israel: Its Life and Institutions.*

Gray, John. *I & II Kings: A Commentary.*

Matthews, Victor H., and Don C. Benjamin. *Social World of Ancient Israel, 1250–587 B.C.E.*

1 KGS 22:38

Prostitutes Washing in Ahab's Blood

According to the episode reported in 1 Kings 22, King Ahab of Israel (reigned 873–852 B.C.E.) was mortally wounded when, alongside his Judean counterpart Jehoshaphat, he fought the Arameans. 1 Kgs 22:35 records that his blood flowed into the chariot, which was then flushed out with water by the pool of Samaria. Elijah, in 1 Kgs 21:19, had told Ahab that dogs would lick his blood "in the place" that dogs licked the blood of Naboth, whom Ahab and Jezebel had executed on spurious charges in order to obtain his property. In fulfillment of Elijah's prediction, dogs lap up Ahab's blood and the prostitutes wash in it.

Dogs are mentioned here because of their status as perhaps the only carnivorous scavengers encountered in ancient Israel on a daily basis. The consumption of human flesh by canines is mentioned in several biblical passages (1 Kgs 14:11; 16:4; 21:24; 2 Kgs 9:10; Jer 15:3). Canines were thus generally viewed with contempt, despite their occasional role in shepherding. Prostitutes supplement canines as an additional affront to Ahab's dignity. They are depicted as bathing in public, perhaps because they are viewed by the biblical author as immodest by nature. Thus, canines and prostitutes, as objects of loathing, symbolize Ahab's final disgrace; both are again linked in Deut 23:18. The Septuagint (Greek translation of the Hebrew Bible) version of 1 Kgs 22:38 adds swine to dogs to further degrade Ahab.

ELAINE ADLER GOODFRIEND

SEE ALSO Part I: Rahab; Tamar; Part II: Prostitute (Lev 19:29, etc.); Two Prostitutes as Mothers (1 Kgs 3:16–28).

1 KGS 22:52   Mother of Ahaziah
SEE   Jezebel 1 (Part I).

2 KGS 3:2, 13   Mother of Jehoram
SEE   Jezebel 1 (Part I).

2 KGS 4:1–7
Widow Whose Oil Is Multiplied

Several stories, such as this one about the ninth-century B.C.E. prophet Elisha, parallel narratives about his mentor, Elijah. 2 Kgs 4:1–8 tells of Elisha's ministry to the needs of a widow, a member of a socially marginalized group in ancient Israel. In some ways this account parallels 1 Kgs 17:8–24, in which Elijah responds to the needs of a destitute widow in Zarephath by increasing her supply of meal and oil, and later reviving her dead son. In the Elisha story, the widow is in debt but not impoverished, and her children are in danger of servitude, not death. The prophet miraculously multiplies the widow's oil supply so that she can pay off her deceased husband's debts and thus prevent her two children from being sold into debt servitude. She has enough left over for her and her children to live on (presumably for an indefinite period).

This narrative does not develop the prophet's relationship with the woman to the extent of the story about Elijah and the widow. It is more concerned with prophetic power and the working of

miracles. Yet it also addresses social concerns in its portrayal of a woman whose livelihood is threatened by her husband's death. Her family unit was probably a simple nuclear one, not an extended farm family, which would more likely have provided for her. Her husband was a "salaried professional" — a member of a prophetic guild.

FRANK S. FRICK

SEE ALSO Part II: Widows (Exod 22:22, etc.); Widow of Zarephath (1 Kgs 17:8–24).

2 KGS 4:8–37; 8:1–6
The Shunammite

The "great woman of Shunem" appears twice in the narratives about the ninth-century B.C.E. prophet Elisha. Her title suggests wealth, but also, as the story unfolds, independence of mind and faith. She recognizes Elisha as a man of God, offering him meals and building and furnishing a roof-chamber for his convenience (a decision announced to her husband, not submitted for his approval!). In response, the prophet offers her a boon, proposing to use his influence with the king or army commander. Although this offer foreshadows later events, here she proudly refuses such help, expressing confidence in her own people. Following up on his servant Gehazi's observation of the woman's childlessness, Elisha then announces she will bear a son. Again (and surprisingly, given the conventions of such announcement stories) she resists: "No, my lord, O man of God; do not deceive your servant" (2 Kgs 4:16). The child is born and grows into a youth. One day, while helping his father in the fields, he falls sick. He is sent to his mother, the parent charged with health care and, in this case, with deciding what to do when the child dies. Brushing off her husband's questions about her actions, the woman orders him to fetch her a servant and a donkey so that she might ride to Elisha at Mount Carmel. Notably unaware of what troubles her, Elisha sends Gehazi to question her. The woman, however, refuses to deal with an intermediary: she neither responds to Gehazi's queries nor accepts Elisha's wish to send his servant in his place. He accedes to her demand, returns with her, and restores the child to life.

The Shunammite woman appears again in 2 Kgs 8:1–6. Having accepted Elisha's suggestion that she move her household away from Israel during a seven-year famine, she returns to appeal to the king for return of her house and her land. It so happens that she and her son appear at court just at the moment that Gehazi is regaling the king with the story of Elisha's resurrection of the boy. Apparently impressed with this sight of a miracle in the flesh, the king restores the woman's possessions.

Prophet legends such as these (compare 1 Kgs 17:8–24; 2 Kgs 4:1–7) usually serve to impress the reader or listener with the prophet's power. The characterization of the great woman of Shunem both supports and subverts this purpose. In some respects she is stereotypically subordinated to Elisha: he is named, whereas she is not; he rarely speaks directly to her, even when she is present; he decides that she should have a child, when she has expressed no such desire; she speechlessly bows in the face of his resurrecting power. On the other hand, she is presented as the decision-making head of her household and as the initiating and unintimidated actor in her relationship with the prophet — indeed, one who reveals the limits of Elisha's own communication with God.

CLAUDIA V. CAMP

SEE ALSO Part II: Widow of Zarephath (1 Kgs 17:8–24); Widow Whose Oil Is Multiplied (2 Kgs 4:1–7).

FOR FURTHER READING: Camp, Claudia V. "1 and 2 Kings."

Long, Burke. "The Shunammite Woman: In the Shadow of the Prophet?"

Shields, Mary E. "Subverting a Man of God, Elevating a Woman: Role and Power Reversals in 2 Kings 4."

van Dijk-Hemmes, Fokkelien. "The Great Woman of Shunem and the Man of God: A Dual Interpretation of 2 Kings 4:8–37."

2 Kgs 5:2–4
Wife and Servant Girl of Naaman

The wife of Naaman (the commander in chief of the Aram-Damascus army in the ninth century B.C.E.) probably enjoyed a higher social status than most females in her culture because of her husband's position. An Israelite captive of war, who becomes her servant girl, represents the other end of the socioeconomic spectrum for women. However, as a servant in a wealthy house, she may have had more advantages than most other captives. She suggests that Naaman, who suffers from a skin disease, could be cured by a prophet, Elisha, from her native land. He takes her suggestion seriously, is eventually cured, and as a result becomes a worshipper of YHWH.

Although primarily intended to glorify Elisha, this story also belongs to the genre of traditions that portrays women (such as Esther and Judith) exerting considerable influence over foreign leaders despite their lack of authority.

RHONDA BURNETTE-BLETSCH

2 KGS 5:26   Female Slaves
SEE GEN 12:16, etc.   Female (and Male) Slaves (Part II).

2 KGS 6:26–33
Two Mothers Who Agree to Eat Their Sons

During a siege of Samaria by Aram, the hereun-named king of Israel walks about the city walls, surveying his starving populace, when a woman begs him for help in achieving justice in a bargain she had made with another woman. Both had agreed to kill and share their sons as food, one on one day and the other on the next. The speaker's child was duly consumed, but the other mother has now reconsidered and hidden her son.

The story is similar to the riddle posed to Solomon (reigned c. 968–928 B.C.E.) by two prostitutes, each laying claim to a living child after the death of another (1 Kgs 3:16–28). Both are folktales that use readers' or listeners' expectations about female characters, mothers in particular, to comment on social order or disorder and to evaluate male leaders. Solomon counts on predictable "maternal instinct" to determine the true mother and thereby to publicly display his God-given wisdom. Social disorder in Samaria, however, seems so great that the king cannot depend on such verities. He tears his clothes in distress, unable to render justice. This is probably a folktale, however, not history, and one marked by the grotesque irony of the "world turned upside down" motif. Not only the cannibalism (not unknown in conditions of siege; compare Lev 26:29; Jer 19:9), but especially the woman's self-righteous plea for the "justice" of a second child's death, point to deeper issues of social disruption, distrust, and greed. As such, it is theologically noteworthy that the beleaguered king assigns blame for the situation to YHWH and the prophet Elisha (2 Kgs 6:27, 31, 33).

Claudia V. Camp

SEE ALSO Part II: Mother (and Father) Cannibalizing Their Daughters (and Sons) (Lev 26:29, etc.); Two Prostitutes as Mothers (1 Kgs 3:16–28).

FOR FURTHER READING: Camp, Claudia V. "1 and 2 Kings."

Lasine, Stuart. "Jehoram and the Cannibal Mothers (2 Kings 6.24–33). Solomon's Judgment in an Inverted World."

2 KGS 8:1–6   The Shunammite

SEE 2 KGS 4:8–37, etc.   The Shunammite (Part II).

2 KGS 8:12; 15:16
Pregnant Women Killed in War

During one of a series of royal coups in the northern kingdom of Israel, the usurper Menahem (reigned 747–737 B.C.E.) is said to have "ripped

open all the pregnant women" in Tiphsah (15:16), a town whose location is uncertain. This heinous act is one usually ascribed only to Israel's foreign enemies, as in Amos 1:13 and Hos 13:16. In 2 Kgs 8:12 the prophet Elisha weeps when he foresees a similar action perpetrated by Hazael, the future king of Aram, against the people of Israel. Here, however, YHWH's precognizance of Hazael's rise to power leaves open the question of the deity's ultimate responsibility for the women's fate. The ripping open of Israel's pregnant women and the dashing of their little ones to pieces (compare 2 Kgs 8:12) is attributed to YHWH's will to punish the people.

Whether perpetrated by Israel's foreign enemies, or, indeed, by YHWH, the slaughter of women and children — and both, in the case of pregnant women — creates a powerful image. It signals the denial of a future. The continuity of human life is disrupted, as is the political life of the nation or city whose pregnant women's wombs are slashed.

Claudia V. Camp

Small terra-cotta figurines of pregnant women from a late Iron Age (seventh–sixth century B.C.E.) house in Achziv, on the northern coast of Israel. The right arm of each woman reaches over her belly, perhaps in a protective gesture. See Pregnant Women Killed in War *(2 Kgs 8:12, etc.);* Mothers Killed in War *(Hos 10:14, etc.);* Pregnant Women of Gilead *(Amos 1:13).*

SEE ALSO Part II: Mothers Killed in War (Hos 10:14, etc.); Pregnant Women of Gilead (Amos 1:13).

2 KGS 8:18
Wife of Jehoram (Daughter of Ahab)
SEE Athaliah (Part I).

2 KGS 10:13   Queen Mother
SEE Jezebel 1 (Part I).

2 KGS 11:2–3; 2 CHR 22:11–12
Nurse of Joash

In 842 B.C.E., the queen mother, Athaliah, attempts to hold royal power after the assassination of her son, King Ahaziah (reigned 843–842 B.C.E.), by annihilating all heirs to the Davidic royal house. Ahaziah's sister Jehosheba rescues Joash, Ahaziah's one-year-old son, successfully hides him, together with a woman designated as his nurse, in the temple of Jerusalem. Joash eventually becomes king.

The use of the term *nurse,* because it is from the Hebrew root *ynk* ("to suck"), implies that Joash's caregiver was responsible for suckling him — she was in fact his wet nurse. Her presence in this narrative raises the issue of who used wet nurses as paid employees in ancient Israel and why such women were hired.

In ancient Israel, as in most ancient Near Eastern societies, the employment of wet nurses was generally confined to the upper socioeconomic classes. In royal Egypt, the wet nurse of the king and queen was an important person in the court. Mesopotamian laws are replete with regulations for the proper payment and responsibilities of women hired to breast-feed the infants of wealthy urban citizens. Granted, the elite texts that provide such information are not likely to reveal the wet nurse practices of the lower classes. Yet biblical information suggests that, for most Israelites, it was the norm for women to nurse their own children (see the examples of Sarah, Gen 21:7–8, and Hannah, 1 Sam 1:22). It is unlikely that they hired wet nurses, not even as a solution to the two problems that could confront any family: maternal death or insufficient milk supply. For most non-elite people, the deceased mother's network of friends and family probably provided assistance in feeding a motherless infant. The same would be the case for lactational insufficiency, which was probably rare except in instances of maternal illness or severe malnutrition.

If using wet nurses was an upper-class phenomenon, not typically related to natural death or lack of milk, one must ask whether it served any purpose other than to provide leisure for a wealthy woman. Because extended lactation is a natural, if imperfect, form of birth control, the limiting of lactation increases the likelihood of more pregnancies. If large families were desirable for all, they were much more likely to occur among the affluent, where multiple wives were possible, as was the use of wet nurses to maximize female fertility. In contrast, most Israelite peasant families, with only one wife, were probably relatively small. The biblical references to the use of wet nurses, such as Joash's nurse, usually reflect the lives of privileged families.

MAYER I. GRUBER

SEE ALSO Part I: Athaliah; Deborah 1; Jehosheba/Jehoshabeath; Part II: Nursing Mothers (Isa 49:15, etc.).

FOR FURTHER READING: Gruber, Mayer I. "Breast-Feeding Practices in Biblical Israel and in Old Babylonian Mesopotamia."

2 KGS 15:16
Pregnant Women Killed in War
SEE 2 KGS 8:12, etc.   Pregnant Women Killed in War (Part II).

2 KGS 17:17
Daughter Passed Through Fire
SEE DEUT 12:31, etc.   Daughter (or Son or Child) Passed Through Fire, Burned, or Sacrificed (Part II).

2 KGS 19:21   Daughter Zion/ Jerusalem
SEE Daughter (Part III).

2 Kgs 23:7
Weaving Women

These women, during the reign of King Josiah of Judah (reigned 639–609 B.C.E.), worked within the temple compound, weaving garments that clothed the cult statue of the goddess Asherah. Josiah, as part of his great religious reformation, which included removing all traces of Asherah worship from Israel, destroyed the houses in which these women worked. Yet the fact that these women served a cult statue of Asherah that stood in the temple, as well as the text's implication that their work was supported by the temple economy, indicates that at least some in ancient Israel saw the worship of Asherah as appropriately paired with the worship of YHWH. Moreover, the biblical association of women with textiles in a cultic context, here and in Exod 35:25–26, probably reflects the fact that women in ancient Israel, as in many other cultures, were the producers of cloth and clothing. The reference in Exod 35:25 to these weaving women as "skillful" may further indicate that the preparation of cultic fabric was an organized, even "professional," group activity for women.

SUSAN ACKERMAN

SEE ALSO Part II: Skilled Women (and Men) (Exod 35:25–26, etc.); Part III: Asherah/Asherim.

2 Kgs 23:10
Daughter Passed Through Fire
SEE DEUT 12:31, etc. Daughter (or Son or Child) Passed Through Fire, Burned, or Sacrificed (Part II).

2 Kgs 24:15
Mother of Jehoiachin
SEE Nehushta (Part I).

2 Kgs 24:15
Wives of Jehoiachin

2 Kgs 24:15 is part of a list of groups who were taken hostage after Nebuchadnezzar's siege of Jerusalem (2 Kgs 24:10–17) in 597 B.C.E. The order of the hostages — Jehoiachin, the king's mother (Nehushta), the king's wives, his officials, the elite of Jerusalem, and finally military men and artisans — indicates the importance of these women for whom we no longer have names.

LINDA S. SCHEARING

SEE ALSO Part I: Nehushta.

1 Chr 2:21
Daughter of Machir, Wife of Hezron

This unnamed woman, a wife taken by Hezron (a grandson of Judah) when he was sixty years old, became the mother of Segub. She figures in the genealogy because of the prominence of her descendants in Gilead, but perhaps her name is omitted because Gileadites were of little interest to the Chronicler. Whether she is the same woman who is named (Abijah) in 1 Chr 2:24 as being the mother of Ashhur is doubtful but uncertain.

ALICE L. LAFFEY

SEE ALSO Part I: Abijah 1; Part II: Aramean Concubine of Manasseh (1 Chr 7:14).

1 Chr 2:34–35
Daughter of Sheshan

Sheshan, of the tribe of Judah, is the son of Ishi. Since Sheshan has no sons, but only daughters (we do not know how many) he gives one of them to an Egyptian slave, Jarha. This unnamed daughter gives birth to Attai, and twelve more generations are listed as the descendants of Attai. The patrilineal principle, by which descent is traced through the line of legitimate males, is successfully violated in this case.

ALICE L. LAFFEY

1 Chr 3:9   Concubines of David
SEE 2 SAM 15:16, etc. Concubines of David (Part II).

1 CHR 4:9
Mother of Jabez

This woman bore a son who was among the descendants of Judah. Although her name is not mentioned, she does what many Israelite women did — she gives her son a name. She names him Jabez (related to a Hebrew word meaning "distress") because, according to her testimony, she bore him "in pain." He is said to be more honored than his brothers. Jabez is reported to have called on the God of Israel with these words: "Oh that you would bless me and enlarge my border, and that your hand might be with me, and that you would keep me from hurt and harm!" (4:10). Perhaps his favored status had caused his brothers to attempt to harm him. The text records that God granted Jabez's petition; the potentially detrimental effect of his name was overcome.

ALICE L. LAFFEY

1 CHR 4:18
Judean Wife of Mered

The unnamed Judean wife of Mered, a member of the tribe of Judah, bore three sons (Jered, Heber, and Jekuthiel); one son is in turn listed for each of them. Mered's other wife, the Egyptian Bithiah, was a daughter of a pharaoh. Fewer descendants are listed for the foreign wife, perhaps indicating the Chronicler's preference for endogamous marriages.

ALICE L. LAFFEY

SEE ALSO Part I: Bithiah.

1 CHR 4:19
Wife of Hodiah, Sister of Naham

Referred to indirectly in a genealogy of the descendants of Judah, this woman is cited as having sons and grandsons. The biblical text does not list her sons, but it does name two grandsons, Keilah the Garmite and Eshtemoa the Maacathite. She appears in the Chronicles genealogy of the tribe of Judah, along with a number of other women. This contrasts with the paucity of women given in the lineages of other tribes. Clearly the presence of women in Judah's family line in some way reinforces the prominence of that tribe.

ALICE L. LAFFEY

1 CHR 4:27
Daughters of Shimei

Shimei, a member of the tribe of Simeon, is listed as having six daughters as well as sixteen sons. Shimei's brothers, in contrast, did not have many children — far fewer than many Judeans. These assertions suggest that the descendants of Simeon were not as numerous as those of Judah, which is the most important tribe in the Chronicler's estimation. Yet Shimei's fertility, expressed by mention of daughters as well as sons, played a key role in maintaining the Simeon lineage.

ALICE L. LAFFEY

1 CHR 7:4
Wives of Descendants of Issachar

The genealogy in which reference is made to these women identifies them as wives of descendants of the five sons of Uzzi, all of whom were chiefs. The biblical text, intent on asserting the significance and strength of the descendants of Issachar, includes the mention of wives as progenitors of a large fighting force.

ALICE L. LAFFEY

1 Chr 7:14
Aramean Concubine of Manasseh

This unnamed concubine, an Aramean, is the only sexual partner connected to Manasseh, son of Joseph, in the Bible. Her son Machir fathers Gilead. Manasseh, Machir, and Gilead are named as the ancestors of Zelophehad's daughters in Num 27:1 (compare especially Num 36:1 and Josh 17:2–3, as well as Num 32:39–40 and Josh 13:31). That there is only one partner listed for Manasseh, and a foreign concubine at that, is a way of downplaying, even discrediting, the tribe.

ALICE L. LAFFEY

SEE ALSO Part II: Daughters of Zelophehad (Num 26:33, etc.); Daughter of Machir, Wife of Hezron (1 Chr 2:21).

1 CHR 7:15
Wives of Huppim and Shuppim

Nothing is known of the identities of these two women except for the fact that Machir took them as wives for Huppim and Shuppim, who may have been from the tribe of Benjamin. But the fact that Machir, a Manassite, arranges their marriage suggests that they were members of the tribe of Manasseh, because marriages were usually arranged by parents.

ALICE L. LAFFEY

SEE ALSO Part II: Aramean Concubine of Manasseh (1 Chr 7:14).

1 CHR 7:15   Daughters of Zelophehad
SEE NUM 26:33, etc.   Daughters of Zelophehad (Part II).

1 CHR 7:23
Wife of Ephraim

When the first three sons of Ephraim (eponymous ancestor of the tribe of Ephraim) raided the cattle of the people of Gath, they were killed by the victims of their theft. In sorrow, Ephraim and his wife have another son, Beriah, so named because of the disaster (bĕrā'â) that had befallen his brothers. Beriah's offspring, with a daughter (Sheerah) named first, become the most prominent Ephraimites. Perhaps for this reason, his mother is included in the Chronicles genealogy — women typically appear to reinforce the importance of a group.

ALICE L. LAFFEY

SEE ALSO Part I: Sheerah.

1 CHR 14:3   Daughters of David
SEE 2 SAM 5:13, etc.   Daughters of David (Part II).

1 CHR 15:20   Alamoth
SEE PSALM 46: SUPERSCRIPTION Alamoth (Young Women) (Part II).

1 CHR 23:22
Daughters of Eleazar

According to Chronicles, in King David's organization of the Levites (a priestly group), the third son (Merari) of one of Levi's three sons, had five grandchildren, one of whom (Eleazar) had daughters only. These women marry their cousins (sons of Kish), presumably in keeping with the provisions of Num 36:6–9. Marriage within the clan helped maintain the status of this priestly group.

ALICE L. LAFFEY

SEE ALSO Part II: Daughters of Zelophehad (Num 26:33, etc.).

1 Chr 25:5–6
Daughters (and Sons) of Heman

The writer of Chronicles is interested in connecting King David with the temple and its service, even though the structure was built by Solomon. This interest is manifest in having David appoint the Levitical singers who perform in the temple service. Another possibility is that the Chronicler wants to give the singers, as cult personnel, status equal to that of the other priestly officials and therefore lists them as Davidic appointees.

Included in the 1 Chronicles 25 list of musicians that David appoints is the family of Heman, to whom "God had given . . . fourteen sons and three daughters" (v. 5). Heman directs all of them (v. 6) in song and instrumental play in the temple, which implies that his daughters are among the musicians. Only the sons, however, are named in the subsequent list of the order of service. It may not be possible to resolve this ambiguity about whether Heman's daughters participate in the musical service. It is worth noting, however, the presence of temple singers of both genders in many Mesopotamian texts dealing with cultic officials. Perhaps women could be included in the musical service because, in ancient Israel and elsewhere in the ancient Near East, it was of a lower status than other priestly tasks. Also, two other biblical texts (Exod 38:8 and 1 Sam 2:22) apparently refer to low-status female cultic functionaries.

CAROL MEYERS

SEE ALSO Part II: Women at the Entrance to the Tent of Meeting (Exod 38:8; etc.); Singing Women (and Men) (2 Sam 19:35, etc.).

FOR FURTHER READING: Gruber, Mayer I. "Women in the Cult According to the Priestly Code."

Henshaw, Richard A. *Female and Male: The Cultic Personnel: The Bible and the Rest of the Ancient Near East.*

2 CHR 2:14   Danite Woman
SEE 1 KGS 7:13–14, etc.   Mother of Hiram (Part II).

2 CHR 8:11   Daughter of Pharaoh
SEE 1 KGS 3:1, etc.   Daughter of Pharaoh (Part II).

2 CHR 9:1–12   Queen of Sheba
SEE 1 KGS 10:1–13, etc.   Queen of Sheba (Part II).

2 CHR 11:21
Women of Rehoboam (Eighteen Wives, Sixty Concubines, and Sixty Daughters)

Only two wives of Rehoboam (first king of the southern kingdom of Judah; reigned 928–911 B.C.E.) are named: Mahalath, daughter of Jerimoth, son of David; and his favorite wife, Maacah, daughter of Absalom and mother of Rehoboam's heir, Abijah. His other sixteen wives, his sixty concubines, and his sixty daughters remain unnamed and undifferentiated, though the text does state that his daughters far outnumbered his twenty-eight sons. The great numbers of wives, concubines, and children, especially sons but also daughters, assert Rehoboam's power and prestige. The wives and concubines may represent liaisons with various political factions, made to strengthen his dynastic legitimacy in the power struggle that caused the division of the monarchy of his father, Solomon. Such marriages often cemented alliances meant to secure relations among rival groups. Solomon's numerous marriages are the prime example of this principle in the Hebrew Bible.

ALICE L. LAFFEY

SEE ALSO Part I: Maacah 3/Micaiah; Mahalath 2; Part II: Women of Solomon (1 Kgs 3:1, etc.).

2 CHR 13:21
Wives and Daughters of Abijah (Fourteen Wives and Sixteen Daughters)

The biblical reference to the several wives and daughters of Abijah, second king of Judah (reigned 911–908 B.C.E.), is a way of asserting that his reign was a strong one. None of his wives or his daughters are named, except perhaps, in 2 Chr 15:16, where reference is made to Maacah, the queen mother during the reign of Abijah's son Asa. The presence of many wives and children, especially sons but also daughters, was a mark of power and prestige. Also, Abijah's many marriages may have been politically motivated. His war with the northern kingdom of Israel necessitated drawing upon local loyalties in his kingdom, which were often achieved through marital alliances.

ALICE L. LAFFEY

SEE ALSO Part II: Women of Solomon (1 Kgs 3:1, etc.); Women of Rehoboam (2 Chr 11:21).

2 CHR 15:13
Women (and Men) Who Do Not Seek the LORD

Whereas 1 Kgs 15:8–14 briefly describes the reforms of King Asa of Judah (reigned 908–867 B.C.E.), the Chronicler's version of the story transforms Asa into a religious reformer much like David and Josiah. In this account, Asa, encouraged by the prophecy of Azariah, leads all of Judah into a covenant with God; anyone who will not seek YHWH is put to death. The explicit mention that women as well as men (and children as well as adults) were held accountable to the covenant underscores the pervasiveness, with respect to gender and age, of Asa's reform and the understanding that all Judah entered into the covenant.

JULIA MYERS O'BRIEN

SEE ALSO Part II: Wives of All Judah (2 Chr 20:13).

2 CHR 18:1
Israelite Wife of Jehoshaphat

Unnamed, this woman is identified as a "marriage alliance," which is a marriage made between two parties who are from two different countries; both parties recognize a political advantage to the union. In this case the fourth Judean king Jehoshaphat (reigned 870–846 B.C.E.) marries a princess, daughter of King Ahab (reigned 873–852 B.C.E.) from the northern kingdom of Israel. Jehoshaphat hopes that this marriage will be beneficial, both economically and politically, to him and his kingdom. Peace between Judah and Israel, which were often involved in a sort of civil war with each other, was essential at this point because of the Aramean threat to both countries (1 Kings 22; 2 Chronicles 18).

ALICE L. LAFFEY

2 CHR 20:13
Wives of All Judah

This passage implies that Judean males represent the whole community: in the days of Jehoshaphat (reigned 870–846 B.C.E.) an assembly of "all Judah" is said to be accompanied by wives and children (2 Chr 20:13). In contrast, in 2 Chr 15:13, "all Judah" consists of women and men, children and adults.

JULIA MYERS O'BRIEN

SEE ALSO Part II: Women (and Men) Who Do Not Seek the LORD (2 Chr 15:13).

2 CHR 21:6   Daughter of Ahab
SEE Athaliah (Part I).

2 CHR 21:14, 17
Wives of Jehoram

In 2 Chr 21:14, the prophet Elijah is writing a letter to the evil king Jehoram (reigned 851–843 B.C.E.), announcing that a plague will come upon Jehoram's people, meaning his children, his unnamed wives, and his possessions. The royal family, consisting of wives and children, is seen as distinct from the general populace. As it happened, his wives and children ("sons," in NRSV) were carried into exile by the Philistines and Arabs (2 Chr 14:17).

JULIA MYERS O'BRIEN

SEE ALSO Part I: Athaliah.

2 CHR 22:11–12   Nurse of Joash

SEE 2 KGS 11:2–3, etc.   Nurse of Joash (Part II).

2 CHR 24:3
Wives and Daughters of Joash

According to the biblical text, Joash, eighth ruler of Judah (reigned 836–798 B.C.E.), had at least two wives, both of whom were acquired for him by the priest Jehoiada. Joash's wives bore him an unspecified number of daughters and sons. Joash's fertility, together with the priestly involvement in arranging his marriages, contributes to the high regard the narrator has for him.

ALICE L. LAFFEY

2 CHR 28:8, 10–15; 29:9
Judean Women and Daughters (and Sons) Captured by Israelites

For the writer of the Book of Chronicles, the division of the monarchy into a northern kingdom (Israel) and a southern one (Judah) was a tragic event, as were the various episodes of enmity between the two kingdoms. A case in point is the account in which the Israelite king Pekah (reigned 735–732 B.C.E.) slaughters Judean warriors and takes captive a large number of their families — "wives [NRSV, women], sons, and daughters" (2 Chr 28:8; compare 29:9). He brings them along with the spoils of war to the capital in Samaria.

The narrative explains this military devastation as an act of divine justice: death and captivity are punishments for Judean apostasy. Yet the Israelites are equally criticized, through the outcry of a prophet (Oded), not for slaying warriors, but rather for taking captives — "male and female" (2 Chr 28:10–15) — to be their servants. Because those captives are their kinfolk, they should not be subjugated, lest YHWH punish the Israelites in turn. In response to Oded's warning, the captives are ultimately released and given clothes and provisions from the booty.

This incident illustrates the differential treatment, according to gender and also age, of an enemy population in biblical times: under most circumstances women were allowed to live, as were offspring of both genders. It also provides several examples of how masculine words can be used inclusively. The word for "kin" or "kindred" (2 Chr 28:8, 11) literally means "brothers," but clearly refers to compatriots of both genders; and the "people" (literally "sons" or "children," v. 10) being enslaved includes females and males. Similarly, the masculine plural word for "captives" (vv. 11–15) refers to both women and men.

CAROL MEYERS

SEE ALSO Part II: Wives (and Children) as Booty (Num 14:3); Girls as Booty (Judg 5:30).

2 CHR 31:18
Wives and Daughters (and Sons) of Priests

The wives and daughters of priests are referred to within the context of the apportionment of part of the sacrifices to the priests. Hierarchical order assigns the portions according to priests' ancestry and takes into consideration their families — wives, daughters, and sons. In contrast, the Levites receive their portions according to their function and by their divisions, with no indication that consideration is given to family size. In both cases, the provision of part of the sacrificial commodities to the priests and Levites is not only an indication of their status, but also an economic necessity. Priestly groups had no land of their own and thus depended on others' agricultural productivity.

ALICE L. LAFFEY

2 CHR 35:25
Singing Women (and Men) Who Lament

Virtually all of the biblical references to professional mourners indicate that those practitioners were women. One passage in 2 Chronicles (35:25) seems to be an exception; it states that "all the singing men and singing women" (that is, professional singers) utter laments for King Josiah (reigned 639–609 B.C.E.), who was killed in a battle with the Egyptians. Because the tradition of women as experts in funerary customs and laments in ancient Israel and in many other cultures is so strong, it is possible that the mourning for Josiah, one of the few kings considered a righteous ruler, called for an extraordinary outpouring of mourning, which would have involved professional singers of both genders.

The narrative goes on to report that these singers continue to sing the laments for Josiah long after his death and that those dirges are recorded in "the Laments," which may be a reference to the biblical Book of Lamentations. If so, then that book, usually attributed to Jeremiah or to other male authorship, actually contains some women's compositions. The richness of female imagery in Lamentations accords with that possibility.

CAROL MEYERS

SEE ALSO Part II: Weeping Daughters (2 Sam 1:24); Mourning Women (Jer 9:17–22, etc.); Grieving Girls (Lam 1:4, etc.); Part III: Daughter; Princess Jerusalem.

FOR FURTHER READING: Brenner, Athalya, and Fok-kelein van Dijk-Hemmes. *On Gendering Texts: Female and Male Voices in the Hebrew Bible.*

2 CHR 36:17
Young Women (and Men) Slaughtered

In the Babylonian conquest of Jerusalem in 587–586 B.C.E., the nation's leaders were exiled, the poorest people were allowed to stay in the land, and many others were killed. The priestly officials were among those put to death after being carried away to the Babylonian king's headquarters (2 Kgs 25:18–21). Other Judeans — young women and young men, as well as the elderly — were slaughtered in their temple. These may have been lesser temple servitors, which included women as well as men. A similar allusion is found in Ezek 24:21.

CAROL MEYERS

SEE ALSO Part II: Daughters (and Sons) of Heman (1 Chr 25:5–6).

EZRA 2:61; NEH 7:63
Daughter of Barzillai the Gileadite

This ancestor of a priestly group is reported in relation to those returning from the Babylonian exile to Jerusalem after 538 B.C.E. According to the text, the name of the clan goes back to a male head who had married a daughter of Barzillai the Gileadite (Barzillai had been greatly favored by David; see 2 Sam 19:32–40; 1 Kgs 2:7) and assumed her family name.

This reference is a rare biblical example of a familiar phenomenon in antiquity by which a son-in-law appropriated the name and property of a prominent man by marrying the daughter. Typically this happened when a man had no sons.

TAMARA COHN ESKENAZI

SEE ALSO Part I: Agia; Part II: Mother (and Father) of Barzillai (2 Sam 19:37).

SEE ALSO Part II: Singing Women (and Men) (2 Sam 19:35, etc.); Daughters (and Sons) of Heman (1 Chr 25:5–6).

EZRA 2:64–65; NEH 7:67
Female (and Male) Servants Returning to Judah

Ezra and Nehemiah specify that 7,337 female and male servants return to Judah with 42,360 people ("the whole assembly") from the Babylonian exile after 538 B.C.E. Nothing further is said about the servants; the ratio of women to men is unknown. Their ethnic background is not noted; it is possible that they were foreigners, Judeans, or both.

TAMARA COHN ESKENAZI

SEE ALSO Part I: Female (and Male) Hebrew Slaves (Exod 21:7–11, etc.); Female (and Male) Singers Returning to Judah (Ezra 2:65, etc.).

EZRA 2:65; NEH 7:67
Female (and Male) Singers Returning to Judah

Female and male singers (200 according to Ezra 2:65; 245 in Neh 7:67) reportedly come to Jerusalem some time after 538 B.C.E. with the more than forty-two thousand Judeans who return to their homeland after the Babylonian exile. Although cultic singers, usually associated with Levites and other temple officials, are frequently mentioned in Ezra and Nehemiah (see, for example, Ezra 2:70; 7:7, 24; Neh 10:28), the 200/245 singers who include women are most likely entertainers. Such secular singers are undoubtedly of lower status than temple singers, for the list places them between servants and horses.

TAMARA COHN ESKENAZI

EZRA 9:2, 12; 10; NEH 10:30; 13:25–27
Daughters of Judah and Foreign Daughters/Wives

The concern with setting boundaries for the sake of religious, political, and economic survival figures prominently in the sixth and fifth centuries B.C.E., when the inhabitants of the postexilic province of Yehud were a minority among peoples with significantly different religious and cultural positions. Because the household was the primary unit in society, marriage played a crucial role in maintaining and transmitting cultural heritage.

The struggle of the people of Yehud to retain identity and land is reflected in the way the books of Ezra and Nehemiah (fifth century B.C.E.) perceive endogamy (marriage within the group) as vital for Israel's continuity. Echoing Deut 7:3, the text opposes marriage to foreign women and men.

Although marriages of the daughters of the people of Yehud to foreign men are proscribed in Ezra 9–10, marriages, especially those of religious leaders, with women from "the peoples of the land" (Ezra 9:1; compare Neh 10:30) apparently constitute the central crisis. According to Ezra (an important postexilic leader, a priest, and a scribe), such marriages reenact the religious corruption that originally led to exile. Under his influence, the community determines to separate from the peoples of the land and remove foreign wives (10:2–15). Four intermarried priests agree to send their wives away (10:19); 106 other intermarried men are identified (10:20–44), but it is not clear what, if anything, they do.

Neither the Hebrew text nor the Septuagint mentions, in the concluding verse (v. 44), that these wives were sent away. Unfortunately, most English translations (such as the NRSV) and commentators obscure the silence of the text by supplying a misleading closure, adding (on the basis of the later Hellenistic book 1 Esdras) that the men dismissed their wives and children. The silence in Ezra 10 may reflect the writer's sensitivity to the tragic situation. Perhaps it is an accurate reflection that no further steps were taken because the marriages of those who were not priests were not as problematic and did not require further recording. Another possibility is that the silence reflects a lack of interest in certain details once the main goal — a communal consensus banning marriage with certain people — had been achieved.

Nehemiah also singles out marriages with women from certain neighboring peoples as being dangerous (Neh 13:23). He opposes marrying daughters to foreign men as well as bringing in foreign daughters as wives for the men of Yehud (13:25). He blames the religious influence of foreign women for King Solomon's sin (13:26–27). Ezra and Nehemiah both assert that marriages with foreigners involve Israelite men in the prohibited religious practices of other local people. In doing so, they echo other biblical texts that make claims about the dangers of intermarriage (for example, Deut 7:36; Josh 23:12–13). But the use of an unusual verb to refer to these marriages, a term translated "taken [in marriage]" by the NRSV but which really means "settled" (Ezra 10:14), suggests socioeconomic and political concerns, which were probably part of the prohibitions of exogamy (marriage outside the group). Who is settled on the land — and thus who owns it — underlies the controversy over these marriages. Foreign wives pose a threat because, through them, land can transfer out of the newly reestablished province of Yehud. Such transfer can occur when women inherit land (as they can, according to some sources).

Ezra and Nehemiah both follow Deut 7:3 in prohibiting exogamy (marriage outside the group) for both the women and men of Yehud. It appears, however, that exogamy involving the women of Yehud was rare since Ezra and Nehemiah, with one possible exception (Neh 6:18), do not record any such incident.

TAMARA COHN ESKENAZI

SEE ALSO Part II: Daughters of the Inhabitants of the Land as Marriage Partners (Exod 34:16); Daughter-in-Law of Tobiah, Daughter of Meshullam, Wife of Jehohanan (Neh 6:18); Women of Ashdod, Ammon, and Moab (Neh 13:23–24); Part III: Woman Wickedness.
FOR FURTHER READING: Eskenazi, Tamara Cohn. "Ezra-Nehemiah."
———. "Out of the Shadows: Biblical Women in the Postexilic Era."
Perdue, Leo G., Joseph Blenkinsopp, John J. Collins, and Carol Meyers. *Families in Ancient Israel.*
Williamson, H. G. M. *Ezra, Nehemiah.*

EZRA 10:1
Women (and Men and Children) in Assembly

Ezra, the leader of the postexilic community in the mid–fifth century B.C.E., confesses in a prayer to God that the people have sinned by marrying the daughters and sons of foreigners. In response, the people — "a very great assembly of men, women, and children" (10:1) — approach Ezra. Like him, they "weep bitterly" and, through a spokesman, echo his confession. The specific inclusion of women in this group, gathered before God at the temple, indicates their membership in the assembly (*qāhāl*).

CAROL MEYERS

SEE ALSO Part II: Daughters of Judah and Foreign Daughters/Wives (Ezra 9:2, etc.); Women, Part of the Assembly of People (Neh 8:2–3, etc.).

NEH 2:6
Queen, Wife of Artaxerxes

Nehemiah was an exiled Judean living in Persia in the fifth century B.C.E. He apparently ranked high in the royal court in Persia before he became a governor of the postexilic province of Yehud. He mentions an unnamed royal spouse sitting next to King Artaxerxes (reigned 464–424 B.C.E.) at the time when Nehemiah requests permission to rebuild Jerusalem's walls. Her presence may account for the king's positive response to Nehemiah. The royal wife mentioned in Neh 2:6 may have been Queen Damaspia (died 424 B.C.E.) or perhaps a lesser royal consort. Greek sources emphasize women's influence on Achaemenid (Persian) royal courts (as do the books of Daniel and Esther), but Persian sources do not mention or portray royal women.

TAMARA COHN ESKENAZI

FOR FURTHER READING: Brosius, Maria. *Women in Ancient Persia: 559–331 B.C.*

NEH 3:12
Daughters of Shallum

Neh 3:12 mentions these unnamed daughters of Shallum, who was an official in charge of a district in Jerusalem among those who rebuilt Jerusalem's walls in 444 B.C.E., under the leadership of Nehemiah. The walls signified the resurgence of national, religious, and social life for the Judahites (Yehudites)in the province of Yehud after the exile. Some commentators earlier in this century considered the participation of women in building activities so incredible that they reinterpreted or emended the verse to eliminate the presence of women, reading instead "sons"(!) or claiming that "daughters" here refers to outlying towns. The Hebrew text and context, however, are clear. The mention of these daughters shows that women played a role in every important event during the reconstruction of Judahite life in the century after the return from exile.

TAMARA COHN ESKENAZI

SEE ALSO Part I: Hassophereth/Sofereth; Part II: Women, Part of the Assembly of People (Neh 8:2, etc.).

FOR FURTHER READING: Eskenazi, Tamara Cohn. "Out from the Shadows: Biblical Women in the Postexilic Era."

Neh 4:14; 5:1–2, 5
Daughters (and Sons) and Wives in Rebuilt Jerusalem

The people living in Jerusalem during the period of rebuilding after the exile faced numerous political and economic problems. In the fifth century B.C.E., when the Persian-appointed governor Nehemiah is overseeing the reconstruction of Jerusalem's walls, the Samaritans and other groups become angered at that enterprise. Nehemiah urges the male leaders and the men working on the walls not to be afraid, but rather to fight if necessary for their kin and households, including daughters (and sons) and wives (4:14).

No sooner does Nehemiah refocus the people on their rebuilding project than internal dissension erupts. Some people and their wives are concerned that they don't have enough food to feed themselves or their daughters and their sons (5:1–2). Furthermore, their economic plight is so severe that they have to indenture "sons and daughters" to wealthier Jerusalemites to pay off debts or to secure loans. Indeed, some of their daughters have already been indentured (5:5; compare Deut 15:12). The NRSV uses the word "ravished," which probably misrepresents the shortened form of an idiom meaning "subdued as servants, forced into servitude."

Although only the male leaders and workers on the wall voice their concerns about the external threat, which endangers everyone, both women and men protest economic inequity — the food scarcity that could lead to the indenturing of female and male offspring. Women may not be political leaders or construction workers, but they share with men the concern and responsibility for the welfare of their families as well as membership in the restored community and religious assembly (see Neh 8:28; 12:43).

CAROL MEYERS

SEE ALSO Part II: Female (and Male) Hebrew Slaves (Exod 21:7–11, etc.); Women, Part of the Assembly of People (Neh 8:2, etc.).

NEH 6:18
Daughter-in-Law of Tobiah, Daughter of Meshullam, Wife of Jehohanan

Tobiah was a major opponent of the rebuilding of Jerusalem's walls under Nehemiah in 444 B.C.E., whereas Meshullam is a prominent Judahite (Yehudite) supporter of Nehemiah (Neh 3:4, 30). Since Nehemiah portrays Tobiah as a foreigner ("the Ammonite slave," Neh 2:19), the marriage of Meshullam's daughter to Tobiah's son suggests either that women (not only men) intermarried among the upper-class returnees or, more likely, that Tobiah was regarded by some as a member of the community of Israel and a Yahwist (as his name, which means "Yah(weh) is good," implies).

TAMARA COHN ESKENAZI

SEE ALSO Part II: Daughters of Judah and Foreign Daughters/Wives (Ezra 9:2, etc.).

NEH 7:63   Daughter of Barzillai
SEE EZRA 2:61, etc.   Daughter of Barzillai the Gileadite (Part II).

NEH 7:67
Female Slaves Returning to Judah
SEE EZRA 2:64–65 Female (and Male) Servants Returning to Judah (Part II).

NEH 7:67
Female Singers Returning to Judah
SEE EZRA 2:65, etc.   Female (and Male) Singers Returning to Judah (Part II).

NEH 8:2; 10:28; 12:43
Women, Part of the Assembly of People

Nehemiah 8–10 depicts the climax of return and reconstruction of life in Judah (Yehud) in the fifth century B.C.E., after the destruction of Jerusalem and exile to Babylonia in 586 B.C.E. Here the reconstituted community celebrates its renewal by gathering to hear the priest Ezra read the book of Torah and by formally affirming its commitment to God and to the teachings of the Torah. The returnees (Ezra 2; Nehemiah 7) had already rebuilt the temple (Ezra 1–6), redefined communal ethnic and religious boundaries (Ezra 9–10), and rebuilt the wall of Jerusalem (Nehemiah 1–6). Now comes the covenantal reaffirmation. In these chapters, in a ritual that echoes Israel's covenant with God at Sinai (Exodus 19–24), the assembly of rededicated people hears and accepts the Torah.

Women are specifically included in this religiously reconstituted assembly (qāhāl) and people ('am). They hear (Neh 8:2–3) and carry out its teachings; their commitment is affirmed by an oath (10:2–30), and they rejoice in the subsequent festivities (Neh 12:43). Since Ezra and Nehemiah (and later Judaism) present the Torah ritual in Nehemiah 8–10 as a second Sinai, with Ezra as a Moses-like figure, the specific inclusion of women in this event of Torah teaching and affirmation represents a counterpoint to the ambiguity at Sinai (see Exod 19:15). The postexilic community, to which these women belong, promises to avoid the transgressions of the past. The very specificity of women as members of the community itself functions as an overcoming of earlier neglect; it presents women as full participants in the covenantal life of the reconstituted community.

TAMARA COHN ESKENAZI

SEE ALSO Part II: Woman (Women) Not to Be Approached at Sinai (Exod 19:15); Women (and Men) of the Ark Ceremony (2 Sam 6:19); Daughters (and Sons) and Wives in Rebuilt Jerusalem (Neh 4:14, etc.); Women (and Men and Children) in Assembly (Ezra 10:1).

FOR FURTHER READING: Eskenazi, Tamara Cohn. *In an Age of Prose: A Literary Approach to Ezra-Nehemiah.*

———. "Out from the Shadows: Biblical Women in the Postexilic Era."

NEH 10:28
Women, Part of the Covenant Community

SEE NEH 8:2, etc. Women, Part of the Assembly of People (Part II).

NEH 10:30
Daughters of Judah and Foreign Daughters

SEE EZRA 9:2, etc. Daughters of Judah and Foreign Daughters/Wives (Part II).

NEH 12:43
Women at the Dedication of Jerusalem's Wall

SEE NEH 8:2, etc. Women, Part of the Assembly of People (Part II).

NEH 13:23–24
Women of Ashdod, Ammon, and Moab

Foreign women, according to the books of Ezra and Nehemiah, pose a special threat to the religious and national identity of the newly restored community in the province of Yehud after the Babylonian exile. Nehemiah, the governor (444–432 B.C.E.) of Yehud, attacks such marriages between the men of Yehud and the women of Ashdod, Ammon, and Moab (Ammonites feature frequently as opponents of Nehemiah). It is noteworthy that the Hebrew text specifically labels the women Ashdodite, Ammonite, and Moabite (not simply daughters or women of Ashdod, and so on). These designations seem to acknowledge these women as citizens, not just related to the male citizens, of those cities. Nehemiah decries the linguistic influence of these women, whose children no longer speak yĕhûdît (the language of Yehud/Judah, presumably what we now call Hebrew); he charges that such marriages repeat the sin of Solomon, who swerved from God

because of the influence of foreign women. Even though he considers such influence pernicious, Nehemiah's objections indicate his view that women have strong power over their husbands' behavior. His focus on the failure of the children to speak "the language of Judah" represents a more general indictment of the cultural estrangement of the children of foreign women. He thereby, tacitly, also acknowledges that women have a central role in the transmission of language and all that is implicit in such primary orientation.

TAMARA COHN ESKENAZI

SEE ALSO Part II: Women of Solomon (1 Kgs 3:1, etc.); Daughters of Judah and Foreign Daughters/Wives (Ezra 9:2, etc.).

NEH 13:25–27
Daughters of Judah and Foreign Daughters

SEE EZRA 9:2, etc. Daughters of Judah and Foreign Daughters/Wives (Part II).

NEH 13:26 Women of Solomon

SEE 1 KGS 3:1, etc. Women of Solomon (Part II).

ESTH 1:9
Women at Vashti's Banquet

Feasts figure prominently in the Book of Esther, which dates to the late Persian or early Hellenistic period (c. fourth century B.C.E.). At the beginning of the narrative, three elaborate banquets are reported: one for the king's "officials and ministers" as well as military personnel, nobles, and governors (1:2–3); another for "all the people" present in the citadel of Susa (1:5); and a third given by the queen (Vashti), concurrent with the end of the second one, for "the women in the palace of King Ahasuerus" (1:9). These women are not otherwise identified; they might be the women of the harem

(2:3, 8, 12) or the women associated with those banqueting with the king.

Although the depiction of a woman's banquet is found in the art of Urartu in northern Mesopotamia, in the eighth century B.C.E., there is no evidence that women and men banqueted separately in ancient Persia. Indeed, the Greek historian Herodotus reports that both concubines and wives sat next to men at such occasions. Whether or not single-sex feasts are historical, the women's banquet in Esther may be understood as an element that serves the plot, enhances the banquet theme, and is suggestive of female cohorts that balance the male cohorts in this historical novel.

CAROL MEYERS

SEE ALSO Part I: Vashti; Part II: Women of the Harem (Esth 2:3, etc.); Wives and Concubines of Belshazzar (Dan 5:2–3, etc.).

FOR FURTHER READING: Berg, Sandra Beth. *The Book of Esther: Motifs, Themes and Structure.*

ESTH 1:18–20
Noble Ladies of Persia and Media

These women are the wives of the nobles and officials of the Persian king in the Book of Esther, a work of historical fiction of the late Persian–early Hellenistic period (fourth century B.C.E.) After Queen Vashti refuses a direct order from the king (Esth 1:12), his counselors turn what is essentially a marital conflict into a national crisis by declaring that these noble ladies will follow Vashti's example and refuse to obey their husbands, thus bringing chaos into the kingdom. The king is persuaded to put Vashti away, thus setting in motion the chain of events that leads to Esther's becoming queen. He is also persuaded to issue a decree requiring all women to honor their husbands. The pattern of irony that the author of Esther uses throughout the book begins here, in which supposedly powerless women actually control the actions of the "all-powerful" males.

SIDNIE WHITE CRAWFORD

SEE ALSO Part I: Esther; Vashti; Part II: Women at Vashti's Banquet (Esth 1:9).

ESTH 2:2–3, 8, 12–14, 17, 19
Young Virgins/Women

These young women have been gathered from all parts of the Persian Empire to the harem of the royal palace of Susa, in order that King Ahasuerus might find a replacement for Queen Vashti, whom he has put away. Esther, who eventually becomes the queen, is among this group of women (Esth 2:8).

This episode is distasteful to many modern commentators, female or male, Jewish or Christian, because the women are apparently used strictly for the pleasure of the king. They are taken from their homes, put into the harem, given a year of special beauty treatments, and then taken to spend one night with the king. If they manage to titillate his jaded sexual appetite, they may be called back; if not, they are locked away in a second harem, never to be seen again, for they are the property of the king. Even Esther, with whom the king falls in love and makes his queen, cannot approach him on her own initiative, but must wait to be summoned on pain of death (Esth 4:11). The text gives no thought to the question of the women's desires or wishes; they simply do as they are told.

However, in defense of the Book of Esther, it should be noted that the author of this piece of historical fiction uses the reality of the powerlessness of women in Persian society to deliver a message of hope to his also powerless Jewish audience: by the conclusion of the book, the powerless young virgin Esther has completely triumphed over all of the males in the book, including the king, and taken the reins of power into her own hands (Esth 8:1–2, 9:29).

SIDNIE WHITE CRAWFORD

SEE ALSO Part I: Esther; Vashti; Part II: Women of the Harem (Esth 2:3, etc.).

FOR FURTHER READING: White, Sidnie A. "Esther: A Feminine Model for Jewish Diaspora."

Esth 2:3, 8, 12
Women of the Harem

These women dwell in the harem (cloistered quarters for women belonging to the king) of the royal citadel in the Persian capital of Susa. Esther becomes one of them.

SIDNIE WHITE CRAWFORD

SEE ALSO Part I: Esther; Part II: Young Virgins/Women (Esth 2:2–3, etc.).

Esth 2:7
Mother of Esther

This otherwise unidentified character died while Esther, later the queen of Persia, was still a minor. Esther's unnamed father also died, leaving Esther orphaned and thus the ward of her cousin Mordecai.

SIDNIE WHITE CRAWFORD

SEE ALSO Part I: Esther.

Esth 2:9; 4:4, 16
Maids of Esther

Seven women are specially chosen by the eunuch Hegai from the king's palace to serve Esther in the harem (Esth 2:9). They are an indication of her favored status. Esther's maids are also mentioned in 4:4, after she becomes queen; they are to join her in fasting (4:16). It is unclear whether these are all the same women.

SIDNIE WHITE CRAWFORD

SEE ALSO Part I: Esther; Part II: Maids of Rebekah (Gen 24:61).

Esth 2:12–14, 17, 19
Young Virgins/Women in the Harem
SEE Esth 2:2–3, etc. Young Virgins/Women (Part II).

Esth 3:13
Women in the King's Decree

According to the Book of Esther, a historical novel probably dating to the fourth century B.C.E., a high official named Haman in the court of King Ahasuerus is incensed that the Jew Mordecai will not bow down to him. He avenges this slight by plotting to destroy not only Mordecai, but also Mordecai's entire people. A decree issued in the king's name proclaims that, on a certain date, all Jews are to be annihilated, including "young and old, women and children" (3:13).

The specific mention of these four categories may mean that all these groups were not ordinarily slaughtered; a military campaign, for example, would usually spare those groups. But this political purge would be genocidal, with women as well as children and the aged to be killed. Such anticipated total destruction makes Esther's deeds in saving her people all the more heroic. In addition, the inclusion of women along with youth and the elderly in the decree for destruction implies that the injunction for all Jews, when they are ultimately spared, to celebrate their survival was incumbent upon Jews of all ages and both genders.

CAROL MEYERS

SEE ALSO Part I: Esther; Part II: Women, Part of the Assembly of People (Neh 8:2, etc.).

Esth 4:4, 16   Maids of Esther
SEE Esth 2:9, etc. Maids of Esther (Part II).

Esth 4:11
Woman (or Man) Going Unbidden to the King

In the dramatic novella about the survival of Jews living in Persia, the heroine Esther is urged by her uncle Mordecai to go to the king to appeal the edict condemning her people to death. She resists, claiming that anyone, female or male, who approaches the king without being summoned would be put to death (4:11).

It is not certain whether this was a Persian policy to protect the privacy or safety of the king, but it is an effective literary ploy. The specter of death to an unbidden supplicant heightens the sense of danger to Esther and thus intensifies the bravery she exhibits when she finally presents herself to the king (5:1–2).

CAROL MEYERS

SEE ALSO Part I: Esther.

ESTH 7:4   Female Slaves
SEE GEN 12:16, etc.   Female (and Male) Slaves (Part II).

JOB 1:2–19; 41:5; 42:13–15
Daughters of Job

Job's daughters are first mentioned in the opening of the book. They serve as a token of Job's prosperity. Job supposedly has the best of all worlds: seven sons, three daughters, many slaves, and much cattle. As a result of Satan's intervention, however, the three daughters, much like the rest of Job's household, die suddenly in a succession of tragic events. Curiously enough, they seem to spring back to life again in the happy ending, for here, just as in the beginning, Job has seven sons and three daughters.

The second set of daughters looms large with the enigmatic power of figures in a dream. Job endows them with captivating names that match their renowned beauty: Bright Day (or possibly Dove), Cassia (a type of perfume), and Horn of Antimony (a black powder used to beautify the eyes). This is the only place in the Bible where a father names his daughters. To record the act of naming means to accentuate the importance of a given birth, which is why such attention is primarily given to male characters. Job undermines patriarchal conventions not only as a name-giver but also in his distribution of property. Job, we are told, gave his daughters "inheritance along with their brothers" (42:15). According to biblical law (see Numbers 36), only in

the absence of male heirs were daughters permitted to receive their father's estate. Here, therefore, is a clear deviation from the law, for Job's daughters inherit alongside their brothers.

ILANA PARDES

SEE ALSO Part I: Jemimah; Keren-happuch; Keziah; Part II: Daughters of Zelophehad (Num 26:33, etc.).

JOB 1:21; 3:3, 10–11; 14:1; 15:14; 17:14; 31:18
Mother of Job

Job's mother does not appear as a character in the text, but her body, her womb in particular, is evoked time and again. The mother's womb is first mentioned in Job's well-known acceptance of the tragedies that befall him: "Naked I came from my mother's womb, and naked shall I return there" (1:21). This parallelism likens the womb to the earth as it portrays the life cycle from birth to death. Death is construed as a return to the mother's womb. The mother's body is thus associated not only with life, but also with the darker realm of death. Job's fear, or even disgust, vis-à-vis the maternal body is more conspicuous in his initial series of curses: "Let the day perish in which I was born . . . Let the stars of its dawn be dark . . . because it did not shut the doors of my mother's womb, / and hide sorrow from my eyes. / Why did I not die at birth? . . . Why were there knees to receive me, / or breasts for me to suck?" (3:2–12). The mother who supposedly has the power to turn her womb into a tomb is accused of giving life — of giving birth and then suckling with her breasts. Life, for Job, is a punishment meted out by merciless mothers who are the agents of a merciless God. The lowliness of the human condition is inextricably related to the fact that humans are "born of woman" (14:1; 15:14) and as such are destined to a life full of trouble and agony, and ultimately to death. Both female and male imagery, however, represent Sheol, the shadowy place of the dead, in 17:13–14. Female and male imagery, for birth ("mother's womb") and youth, also appear in 31:18.

ILANA PARDES

JOB 2:9–10; 19:17; 31:10
Wife of Job

In the well-known biblical story dealing with the problem of undeserved suffering, Job loses his children, his possessions, and his health. Job's nameless wife turns up after the final blow, after Job has been struck with boils. Seeing her husband sitting in the dust, scraping his sores silently, she bursts out, "Do you still persist in your integrity? Curse God, and die" (2:9). She cannot bear her husband's blind acceptance of the tragedies that befall them. Indeed, the attention to Job's suffering usually ignores the fact that she too, after all, is a victim of these divine tests in addition to being pained by exposure to his afflictions (19:17). To cling to a model of perfect devotion to a supposedly perfect God when reality is so far from perfection seems to Job's wife to be not exemplary strength, but an act of cowardice. Such "integrity," she seems to be saying, lacks a deeper value. What Job must do is to challenge the God who has afflicted him so, even if the consequence is death.

Much has been written about the unusual challenge the Book of Job offers in its audacious questioning of the ways of God, but one never hears of the contribution of Job's wife to the anti-dogmatic bent of the text. Job's wife prefigures or perhaps even generates the impatience of the dialogues. She opens the possibility of suspending belief, of speaking against God. Job's initial response to his wife's provocative suggestion is harsh: "You speak as any foolish woman would speak. Shall we receive the good at the hand of God, and not receive the bad?" (2:10). When the dialogues begin, however, Job comes close to doing what his wife had suggested. He does not curse God directly, but by cursing his birth he implicitly curses the creator who

gave him life. Much like Eve, Job's wife spurs her husband to doubt God's use of divine powers. In doing so she does him much good, for this turns out to be the royal road to deepening one's knowledge, to opening one's eyes.

Job's wife disappears after her bold statement. She is mentioned in passing only once more in the course of Job's debate with his friends. In protesting his innocence of various wrongdoings, Job insists that if his "heart was enticed by [the wife of his neighbor]/ . . . then let my wife grind for another,/ and let other men kneel over her" (31:9–10). He regards his wife's fate as a mere extension of his own lot.

Job's wife is conspicuously absent from the happy ending in which Job's world is restored. Job's dead children spring back to life, as it were, because he ends up having, as in the beginning, seven sons and three daughters. Yet his wife, who actually escaped death, is excluded from this scene of familial bliss. The challenge of the outsider — and woman is something of an outsider in divine-human matters — seems far more threatening than a critique voiced from within.

ILANA PARDES

JOB 3:3, 10–11; 14:1   Mother of Job
SEE JOB 1:21, etc.   Mother of Job (Part II).

JOB 14:1; 25:4
Born of Woman

Among the various terms for human beings, or mortals, in the Hebrew Bible, the phrase "son of man" is frequently found as a designation for a human being, often with human mortality being emphasized, in contrast to divine immortality. That mortality is typically expressed in masculine terms

— "son of [child of]" a man (or human) — is not surprising, given the androcentric nature of much of Scripture. Two texts in Job, however, express human mortality in feminine language. Job laments the brevity and difficulty of human life: of "a mortal, born to a woman" (14:1). And Bildad, one of the friends who try to help Job in his suffering, refers to a "human" (NRSV, "mortal") in parallel to "born of woman" in 25:4; and in 25:6, he refers to a "human" (NRSV, "mortal") in parallel to "son of man/human" (NRSV, "human being"). Similarly, the common humanity of all is expressed by female imagery in 31:15, which stresses that all people of all classes are formed by God in the womb.

CAROL MEYERS

SEE ALSO Part II: Mother's Womb (Eccl 5:15, etc.).

JOB 15:14; 17:14   Woman/Mother
SEE JOB 1:21, etc.   Mother of Job (Part II).

JOB 17:14
Sister and Mother (and Father) of Job

In one of his responses to Eliphaz, the first of three friends who try to comfort him in his misery, Job apparently accepts, even welcomes, the inevitability of death as an escape from his suffering. The anticipated intimacy with death is conveyed by calling the Pit (that is, the grave, or the underworld) "my father" and by addressing the worm (that will enter his decomposing flesh) as "my mother" or "my sister" (17:14). Although his wife and children appear as minor characters elsewhere in the book, the idea of life's end brings Job back to his birth family — parents and sister — rather than his marital one.

CAROL MEYERS

SEE ALSO Part II: Daughters of Job (Job 1:2–19, etc.); Mother of Job (Job 1:21, etc.); Wife of Job (Job 2:9–10, etc.); Sisters (and Brothers) of Job (Job 42:11).

JOB 19:15 (AND 16); 31:13
Serving Girls (and Male Servants) of Job

In one of his responses to Bildad, a friend who tries to comfort him in his misery, Job bemoans the way God has distanced him from those who were once closest to him. These include family, friends, relatives, and others who dwell in his house. In the last category are the household servants, both female ("serving girls," 19:15) and male ("servants," 19:16). This list of people who reject him consists of those who know him best. One might expect him to be less concerned with the alienation of servants, and their inclusion here indicates that the intimacy of a shared household may be stronger than class differences.

Similarly in the series of self-imprecations that constitute his final apology in chap. 31, Job expresses concern (in v. 13) that he may have failed to attend to the well-being of his female and male servants (NRSV, "slaves"). Like the other items in this catalogue, the mention of the need to treat servants well expresses high ethical ideals. It may even reflect an egalitarian attitude toward humanity, given the lofty statement (in v. 15) that all people are children of God: "Did not one [that is, God] fashion us [servants and masters alike] in the womb?"

CAROL MEYERS

SEE ALSO Part II: Born of Woman (Job 14:1, etc.); Mistress (Ps 123:2); Maid, Mistress (Prov 30:23).

JOB 19:17   Wife of Job
SEE JOB 2:9, etc.   Wife of Job (Part II).

JOB 24:3, 21   Widow
SEE EXOD 22:22, etc.   Widows (Part II).

JOB 24:21   Childless Woman
SEE EXOD 23:26, etc.   Barren Woman (Part II).

JOB 25:4   Born of Woman
> SEE JOB 14:1, etc.   Born of Woman (Part
> II).

JOB 29:13   Widow
> SEE EXOD 22:22, etc.   Widows (Part II).

JOB 31:1
Virgin

Toward the end of the Book of Job, after he has heard and answered all the discourses of the friends who have tried to help him accept that his sins have caused his suffering, Job utters a series of apologies. He begins with a statement that is difficult to understand: "I have made a covenant with my eyes; / how then could I look upon a young woman [NRSV, virgin]?" (31:1). The word for "young woman" is *bĕtûlâ* and usually indicates a pubescent woman, not necessarily one who is biologically a virgin. But the term does connote sexual readiness, and its use in Job seems to say that Job has contracted with himself to avoid looking at young women and thereby risk the temptation of illicit sexuality. Similar ideas appear in 31:9–12.

CAROL MEYERS

SEE ALSO Part II: Wife of Job (Job 2:9–10, etc.); Women in Illicit Sex (Job 31:9–10).

JOB 31:9–10
Women in Illicit Sex

Job states that if he "has been enticed by a woman" (v. 9), his wife should "grind for another" (v. 10), a euphemism for intercourse. V. 9 suggests that women's sexuality is dangerous to men, whereas v. 10 invokes a common pattern of measure for measure — if Job has had an illicit sexual relationship, he should be punished by seeing his wife (his sexual property) doing the same.

Although the context suggests that the woman who might have enticed Job is married (v. 9b, "and I have lain in wait at my neighbor's door"), Job's offense is not viewed as a capital one, in contrast to Torah legislation (compare Lev 20:10). As a work of wisdom literature with a non-Israelite protagonist, the Book of Job is not expected to agree with this Torah notion; like other biblical wisdom literature, it shares the ancient Near Eastern idea that adultery is an offense against the husband (compare Prov 6:26–35), rather than a religious, capital offense.

MARC ZVI BRETTLER

SEE ALSO Part II: Adulteress (and Adulterer) (Lev 20:10, etc.); Wife of Job (Job 2:9, etc.); Virgin (Job 31:1); Part III: Woman Stranger (Loose Woman/Adulteress).

JOB 31:10   Wife of Job
> SEE JOB 2:9, etc.   Wife of Job (Part II).

JOB 31:13   Female Slaves
> SEE JOB 19:15, etc.   Serving Girls (and Male Servants) of Job (Part II).

JOB 31:6, 18   Widow
> SEE EXOD 22:22, etc.   Widows (Part II).

JOB 31:18   Mother of Job
> SEE JOB 1:21, etc.   Mother of Job (Part II).

JOB 38:8, 29
Image of God as Womb/Mother
> SEE Female Images of God in the Hebrew Bible (Part III).

JOB 41:5   Girls of Job
> SEE JOB 1:2–19, etc.   Daughters of Job (Part II).

Job 42:11
Sisters (and Brothers) of Job

At the very end of the Book of Job, God restores doubly to Job all that had been taken from him at the beginning of the tale. Job is then visited by family and friends: "all his brothers and sisters and all who had known him before" (v. 11). These visitors share a meal in his home and comfort him because of all the miseries he has endured; and "each of them" gives him some money (Hebrew *qĕśîṭâ*, which probably was a sizable amount) and a gold ring. The term translated "each" is Hebrew *'îš*, which is the usual term for "man" (male) but can sometimes, as here, refer to a generic person, meaning "each, one." In this text, therefore, Job's sisters as well as his brothers and friends have resources that they can use to make generous gifts.

The reference to both sisters and brothers in this passage makes it possible to identify the use of inclusive language in another verse in Job. The readiness of friends and relatives to visit, once Job's fortunes are restored, contrasts with their behavior in 19:14, in which Job bemoans the fact that his "relatives" and his "close friends" have deserted him. The term translated "my close friends" is literally "those who know me," the same as in 42:11. The word translated "relatives" is the equivalent of "brothers and sisters" of 42:11. The inclusive NRSV translation "relatives" in 19:14 is appropriate.

CAROL MEYERS

SEE ALSO Part II: Sister and Mother (and Father) of Job (Job 17:14); Sisters (and Brothers) of the Psalmist (Ps 22:22).

Job 42:13–15   Daughters of Job
SEE Job 1:2–19, etc.   Daughters of Job (Part II).

Ps 9:14   Daughter Zion
SEE Daughter (Part III).

Pss 22:9–10; 27:10; 35:14; 50:20; 51:5; 71:6; 86:16; 109:14; 116:16; 131:2; 139:13
Mother of Psalmist (God's Serving Girl)

The mother of the psalmist is mentioned in eleven psalms of various genres. These references should be divided into three categories: psalms in which the mother is mentioned in the second part of a verse, parallel to a male in the first part (27:10; 35:14; 50:20; 86:16; 109:14; 116:16); psalms that contain images of birth or sustenance in the womb (22:9–10; 51:5; 71:6; 139:13); and Ps 131:2, which contains a more extended image of a baby nursing from its mother.

The six cases in which *mother* or *maidservant* appears parallel to a male term are of little significance for understanding a mother's role in the psalms or the cult. Biblical poetry has relatively set pairs of poetic terms that are distributed between both parts of the verse; a term in the first part often naturally calls for a particular term in the second. Thus, in Ps 35:14, "brother" evokes "mother"; in Ps 50:20, "kin" evokes "mother's child"; in Pss 86:16 and 116:16, "servant" (male) evokes "serving girl"; and in Pss 27:10 and 109:14, "mother" is paired with "father" as parents of the psalmist or his enemy.

Of the references to birth, Pss 22:9–10, 71:6, and 139:13 all connect YHWH to human birth and sustenance. Of these verses, 139:13 is the clearest and least ambiguous: "For it was you who formed my inward parts; you knit me together in my mother's womb." YHWH is without question given a central role in the formation of the child in utero; the expression "you knit me together" is particularly picturesque in this regard. This thought is especially appropriate in a psalm that emphasizes YHWH's power. Pss 22:10–11 and 71:6 both refer to YHWH's power (*mibbeṭen* "from the womb"; it is unclear if the preposition, "from," should be understood in the sense of Ps 139:13, of the child being already dependent upon YHWH in utero, or if it should be understood as "from the [time I exited the] uterus." In either case, these verses certainly are suitable for women and men, and there is nothing in them or their context to suggest particular sensitivity to women's perspectives. This role of YHWH is also reflected in many Hebrew personal names, which express thanksgiving to YHWH for the successful completion of the birthing process.

One instance, Ps 51:5, is somewhat anomalous; it reads, "I was born guilty, a sinner when my mother conceived me." In his effort to be cleansed of his transgression, the psalmist acknowledges a lifetime of iniquity. He feels as if he has been sinful since birth, or even since his "mother conceived" him.

Ps 131:2, a difficult verse, reads, "But I have calmed and quieted my soul, like a weaned child with its mother; my soul is like the weaned child that is with me." Because the previous verse (131:1) emphasizes the psalmist's extreme submission, some have suggested that this psalm was recited by women. Though this is plausible, weaning was a central event for both genders in ancient Israel, since it represented the independence of the child, and thus it would have been valued by women and men alike.

The presence of female imagery in these psalms raises some fundamental issues concerning women composing and reciting psalms in ancient Israel. Although the psalter covers many situations, no psalm is specifically appropriate for women's life-cycle events, even central events such as the birth of a child. Additionally, although several historical characters are mentioned in Psalms, the matriarchs are never mentioned. These factors make it quite likely that none of the canonical psalms were composed specifically for or by women.

This does not mean, however, that women never could have recited these psalms, that women did not have access to cultic prayer in ancient Israel, or that women did not compose songs or prayers. In 1 Samuel 2, a royal prayer is put in Hannah's mouth — it is seen as appropriate especially because of its reference to the barren mother giving birth (v. 5). Furthermore, in 1 Sam 1:11, Hannah recites a prose prayer that is fully appropriate to her situation. This evidence suggests that when women prayed in ancient Israel, they could either compose their own (prose) prayers or could use ready-made poetic prayers that were only somewhat appropriate to

their situations. It must also be remembered that the Book of Psalms is one particular collection of prayers, collected by a male (priestly?) elite; it is thus not surprising that types of prayers such as birth incantations, which most likely existed in ancient Israel, would not be included there.

MARC ZVI BRETTLER

SEE ALSO Part I: Hannah; Part II: Alamoth (Young Women) (Psalm 46: superscription, etc.); Woman in Labor (Isa 13:8, etc.).

FOR FURTHER READING: Brettler, Marc Zvi. "Women and Psalms: Toward an Understanding of the Role of Women's Prayer in the Israelite Cult."

Miller, Patrick D. *They Cried to the Lord: The Form and Theology of Biblical Prayer.*

Ps 22:22
Sisters (and Brothers) of the Psalmist

In this psalm of lament, the poet agonizes over his misfortunes. But, convinced that God will help him, he vows to praise YHWH to all, including his "brothers and sisters" (22:22). The Hebrew here is the word for "brothers," which usually denotes biological kinfolk or, even more broadly, people of the same political or ethnic group. Many such broad usages should not necessarily be construed as gender-inclusive; but instances such as this verse, which expresses the psalmist's apparent desire for everyone to hear his praise, seem to justify the translation "brothers and sisters." Also, the term is used parallel to "congregation," which probably refers to a broad community of both genders, further supporting the inclusive translation.

CAROL MEYERS

SEE ALSO Part II: Sisters (and Brothers) of Job (Job 42:11).

Pss 27:10; 35:14   Mother of Psalmist
SEE Pss 22:9–10, etc.   Mother of Psalmist (God's Serving Girl) (Part II).

Ps 45:9–14
Women in the Royal Household

Psalm 45 was written for the marriage of an Israelite king. No ruler is named, however, and the psalm may have been used by various kings. The psalm describes the bridegroom (vv. 2–9) before moving on to address the bride (vv. 10–12a), to describe her (vv. 12b–14a), and to depict her companions (vv. 14b–15).

In v. 9 the psalmist mentions "daughters of kings," referred to in Hebrew as the bridegroom's "precious ones." The reference to daughters of kings among these women was probably meant to illustrate the bridegroom's power and prestige. The phrase "precious ones" is sometimes translated "ladies of honor" but may refer to a royal harem, for Israelite kings often had numerous wives and secondary wives (concubines).

It is possible that the bride for whom the psalm was originally written was not an Israelite, since she is told in v. 10 to "forget your people and your father's house." A reference to Tyre in v. 12 may imply that she was Phoenician. According to the psalmist, the queen's loyalty, like that of all women who marry outside their natal group, should be to her husband, the king, who is referred to as her "lord" and to whom she is instructed to bow down (v. 11). The bridegroom desires her beauty, which is enhanced by her colorful clothing. She is followed by young female companions.

The psalm indicates that the queen was accorded a great deal of respect in Israel, noting that wealthy people pay homage to her (v. 12). Her functions included giving birth to the king's sons, promised to the king in v. 16.

KEN STONE

SEE ALSO Part II: Daughters of David (2 Sam 5:13, etc.);
   Royal Daughters and Their Garments (2 Sam 13:18).

Ps 45:12   Daughter of Tyre
SEE Daughter (Part III).

PSALM 46: SUPERSCRIPTION; 1 CHR 15:20
Alamoth (Young Women)

The fifth word of the superscription to Psalm 46 is *'ălāmôt*, which may be understood as a plural of *'almâ*, the usual biblical word for a woman of marriageable age. It has therefore been suggested by some that this psalm was sung by young women, therefore showing that women played a significant role in the ancient biblical cult. Although not apparent in the NRSV, this superscription may also be reflected in the superscription to Psalm 9 and in Ps 48:14; see also 1 Chr 15:20.

The technical terms used in the superscriptions, however, are extremely difficult to understand; even the translators of the Septuagint often did not understand them. Those introduced by the Hebrew preposition *'al*, "on," may refer to a melody (for example, Psalm 22, *'al 'ayyelet haššahar*, "according to The Deer of the Dawn") or to a musical instrument (for example, Psalms 6 and 12, *'al haššĕmînît*, best rendered "on an eight-stringed instrument"). It is likely that *'al 'ălāmôt* should similarly be understood in one of these two ways, most likely as a musical instrument (note the parallelism in 1 Chr 15:20, *'al 'ălāmôt*, to v. 21, *'al haššĕmînît*, "on an eight-stringed instrument"). Nothing in the contexts of the psalms in which *'al 'ălāmôt* appears would make them particularly appropriate for women. Thus, the superscription of Psalm 46 does not provide information on the important questions of women in the cult and of women reciting psalms in ancient Israel.

MARC ZVI BRETTLER

SEE ALSO Part II: Mother of Psalmist (God's Serving
   Girl) (Pss 22:9–10, etc.).

Ps 48:7
Woman in Labor

As a celebration of Jerusalem's impregnability, and thus of the supremacy of YHWH, whose earthly dwelling, the temple, is situated there, the psalmist depicts the effect that the holy city has on all people, both God's people and others. The former celebrate Jerusalem and what it represents. The latter, represented by enemy kings who might attack the city, recognize God's power and flee in panic.

The visceral response of those kings is conveyed by the term *ḥîl*, which is translated "pains" (that is, labor pains) by the NRSV (v. 7), but is really a more inclusive term. When it accompanies the word for a woman in labor, as it virtually always does in the Hebrew Bible, it signifies the entire labor process. Because the recurring contractions of labor are not subject to conscious control, *ḥîl* is used figuratively to depict similar situations of helplessness in the face of an inevitable outcome. The enemy kings are overcome and tremble, as do women in labor, at the inevitable universality of YHWH's realm.

CAROL MEYERS

SEE ALSO Part II: Woman in Labor (Isa 13:8, etc.); Woman in Labor (Jer 4:31, etc.).

FOR FURTHER READING: Bauman, A. "*ḥyl; chîl; chîlah; chalchālāh.*"

Pss 50:20; 51:5 Mother of Psalmist
SEE Pss 22:9–10, etc. Mother of Psalmist (God's Serving Girl) (Part II).

Ps 68:5 Widows
SEE Exod 22:22, etc. Widows (Part II).

Ps 68:11; Isa 40:9
Those Who Bear Tidings; Herald

The Hebrew verb *bśr* means "to bring a good message," and several times the feminine participle (*mĕbaśśeret*) is used to denote the "herald" who delivers glad tidings. Although male heralds are mentioned as bearers of both secular and religious good news, in two instances the heralds of joyful announcements about God's saving deeds are specifically female (although this is not apparent in the NRSV and most English translations). In Ps 68:11, great numbers of female messengers proclaim di-

vine victory over enemy forces; and in Isa 40:9 a "[female] herald" is twice addressed as one who brings good tidings of God's presence to Zion and to Jerusalem. The role of female heralds in announcing divine victory is perhaps related to the professional role of women as victory singers (Exod 15:20).

CAROL MEYERS

SEE ALSO Part II: Women with Hand-Drums, Dancing (Exod 15:20, etc.).

FOR FURTHER READING: Schilling, O. "*bśr.*"

Ps 68:12
Women Dividing the Spoil

The Hebrew text for Ps 68:12 does not have a word designating "women." Rather, it has a plural feminine form of a verb meaning "to dwell, abide." Together with the word for "house," it indicates females waiting at home while warriors fight on the battlefield. The structure and syntax of this archaic poem make it one of the most difficult psalms to understand. It seems clear, however, that this particular verse uses irony to convey its message. It contrasts the defeat of enemy rulers with the false sense of victory contained in the image of the women already dividing up the expected booty that will never come. A further ironic twist is implied: those women will themselves become booty, because the defeat of their menfolk will render them vulnerable to the practice of carrying off women as spoils of war.

CAROL MEYERS

SEE ALSO Part II: Wives (and Children) as Booty (Num 14:3); Mother of Sisera (Judg 5:28–30); Girls as Booty (Judg 5:30).

Ps 68:25 Girls Playing Hand-Drums
SEE Exod 15:20, etc. Women with Hand-Drums, Dancing (Part II).

Ps 71:6 Mother of Psalmist
SEE Pss 22:9–10, ETC. Mother of Psalmist (God's Serving Girl) (Part II).

Pss 78:63; 148:12
Young Women (and Young Men)

The pair "young woman" (Hebrew *bĕtûlâ;* NRSV, "girls") and "young man" (Hebrew *bāḥûr*) appears frequently in the Hebrew Bible, as do other gender pairs (for example, old women and old men, daughters and sons), to represent the totality of people in a particular age or relational cohort. The male half of the set virtually always precedes the female, an indication of the androcentric perspective of the biblical writers.

Ps 78:63 is a good example of how the young woman/young man pair is used to indicate the destruction of Israel's posterity (compare Deut 32:25). Because both words refer to young people in the prime of early adulthood, with the promise of fertility and virility, the psalm's description of the youthful males being devoured by fire (of war? of divine wrath?) and of their female counterparts having no wedding to celebrate with song means that God is truly destroying the rebellious people. Those people are probably the inhabitants of the northern kingdom of Israel, which was conquered by the Assyrians in 721 B.C.E.

An opposite image appears in Ps 148:12, where young women and men, together with the elderly and children, praise YHWH, creator of the natural world and its plenitude. In that verse, the procreative potential of the pair of young people is muted; instead, they represent people in all the age groups between childhood and old age. The latter two terms are inclusive masculine plural forms (as also in Deut 32:25 and in contrast to Zech 8:4–5, which mentions old women and men, and girls and boys, separately), indicating both genders; but for those in between, the productive and procreative members of society, separate words are retained. Taken together, these gender and age terms express the totality of the people.

CAROL MEYERS

SEE ALSO Part II: Daughters (and Sons) Spurned by
   God; Young Women (and Men) Punished by God

(Deut 32:19, etc.); Old Women (and Men) and Girls (and Boys) (Zech 8:4–5); Young Women (and Men) (Zech 9:17).

Ps 86:16   Serving Girl
SEE Pss 22:9–10, etc.   Mother of Psalmist (God's Serving Girl) (Part II).

Ps 106:37–38
Daughters Sacrificed to Idols
SEE Deut 12:31, etc.   Daughter (or Son or Child) Passed Through Fire, Burned, or Sacrificed (Part II).

Ps 109:9   Widow
SEE Exod 22:22, etc.   Widows (Part II).

Ps 109:14   Mother of Psalmist
SEE Ps 22:9–10, etc.   Mother of Psalmist (God's Serving Girl) (Part II).

Ps 113:9   Barren Woman
SEE Exod 23:26, etc.   Barren Woman (Part II).

Ps 116:16   Serving Girl
SEE Pss 22:9–10, etc.   Mother of Psalmist (God's Serving Girl) (Part II).

Ps 123:2
Mistress

The highest-ranking female of a given household was in charge of household management (see Prov 31:10–3), including the supervision of female servants. The Hebrew word used here (*gĕbîrâ*) is used for Sarah in her relationship to Hagar in Genesis 16 and is derived from the same root (*gbr*) as "mighty man/champion" and indicates the prominence of senior women in their managerial role. Here, the "hand" of the mistress gives orders (by gesture) and administers blessings and punishments. Often appearing with "maid," over whom the mistress has authority, it (like "master" in this passage) is a metaphor for divine authority in Psalm 123.

CAROLE R. FONTAINE

SEE ALSO Part I: Sarah 1/Sarai; Part II: Maid (Ps 123:2); Maid, Mistress (Prov 30:23); (Isa 24:2).

FOR FURTHER READING: Brettler, Marc Zvi. "Women and Psalms: Toward an Understanding of the Role of Women's Prayers in the Israelite Cult."

PS 123:2
Maid

Such a servant (Hebrew *šipḥâ*, meaning "female servant" or "maidservant") of unspecified age, status, nationality, and marital status, was sometimes obtained as a wedding present or other type of gift (Gen 12:16; 29:24, 29). Normally, this kind of maid was under the control of the senior female ("mistress," in NRSV) of the household, but she might be assigned by her mistress to provide sexual services, as were Hagar (Genesis 16) and Bilhah (Genesis 30).

The "uppity" behavior of female slaves toward their mistresses is a standard motif in ancient Near Eastern texts. However, in this text the female (and male) servants obey the authority of the mistress (and master) of the household, thereby providing a metaphor for human acknowledgment of divine authority.

CAROLE R. FONTAINE

SEE ALSO Part I: Bilhah; Hagar; Zilpah; Part II: Female (and Male) Slaves (Gen 12:16, etc.); Mistress (Ps 123:2); Maid, Mistress (Prov 30:23); (Isa 24:2).

FOR FURTHER READING: Driver, Godfrey R., and John C. Miles. *The Babylonian Laws.*

PS 128:3
Fruitful Wife

The production of children is the means to individual and group survival. The fertile woman produces many children and "builds" not only the household, but the nation. In an agricultural nation, children help produce food to sustain the household and the national economy. They also are providers and caregivers for aged parents. In Psalm 128, the fruitful wife is not celebrated in her own right, but rather, from the psalm's androcentric perspective, as a sign that her husband is blessed.

LYN M. BECHTEL

SEE ALSO Part II: Barren Woman (Exod 23:26, etc.).

PS 131:2   Mother of Psalmist
SEE PSS 22:9–10, etc.   Mother of Psalmist (God's Serving Girl) (Part II).

PS 137:8   Daughter Babylon
SEE Daughter (Part III).

PS 139:13   Mother of Psalmist
SEE PSS 22:9–10, etc.   Mother of Psalmist (God's Serving Girl) (Part II).

PS 144:12
Daughters Compared to Pillars

The second part of Psalm 144 — vv. 12–15 — is a leader's prayer that the people of the land will experience prosperity and peace. The hope for plenitude opens with paired male and female images: of sons being like flourishing trees or vines (literally, "planted ones") and with daughters being like the pillars that support the family dwelling. These two carefully chosen images reflect the division of labor in ancient Israelite agrarian households. Men had primary responsibility for the outdoor work of planting and sowing (although women certainly contributed to agricultural tasks). Women were responsible for the technologies of food production and other transformative tasks performed in or close to their domiciles, and they also managed the activities of young children and servants. The metaphoric link between women and the support structure of a house is reminiscent of the image of Woman Wisdom hewing pillars for her house (Prov 9:1; compare Prov 14:1).

CAROL MEYERS

SEE ALSO Part II: Wise Woman Building Her House (Prov 14:1); Part III: Woman Wisdom.

Ps 146:9   Widow

SEE EXOD 22:22, etc.   Widows (Part II).

Ps 148:12
Young and Old Women (and Men)

Psalm 148, which praises YHWH, first exhorts the elements of the cosmos, from the highest heavens to the netherworld, to give praise. The psalmist then invokes the praise of the earth and its creatures, including those with political power and all those over whom they rule, that is, the rest of the world's population. The former are specified as the kings, princes, and rulers of the entire earth (v. 11). The latter are designated by two sets of categories: "young men and women alike" and "old and young together" (v. 12). The first set uses the feminine and masculine terms for young people of marriageable age (bĕtûlôt [feminine] and baḥûrîm [masculine]). The second set uses two masculine plural nouns for the aged and the young; those terms are probably gender-inclusive here, given the universal scope of this psalm. By using age and gender categories, the psalmist underscores the totality of humanity meant to acknowledge and exalt YHWH.

CAROL MEYERS

Ps 148:12   Young Women

SEE Ps 78:63, etc.   Young Women (and Young Men) (Part II).

PROV 1:8; 4:3; 6:20; 10:1; 15:20; 19:26; 20:20; 23:22, 25; 28:24; 30:11, 17, PAIRED WITH FATHER; PROV 29:15; 31:28, MOTHER ALONE
Mother

"Mother" appears as the second half of the traditional antithetical word pair (father/mother), a teaching device much favored by wisdom literature, especially in the discussion of parental care, authority, and duties in the Book of Proverbs. Here the mother is a figure of power and influence precisely because she *is* a mother and also, at some point in her life, probably mistress (manager) of her own domestic unit. As such, she is a strong figure in the home, representing order, right practice, and the child's first contact with religious and ethical teaching (hence, emphasis on the "mother's torah" in 1:8; 6:20). In fact, one of the reasons that Woman Wisdom (compare Prov 1:20–33; 3:13–20; 4:5–9; 8; 9:1–6) is imaged as female may be the all-encompassing roles played by the mother or senior female in the typical family household.

Because of her role as first teacher of her children, the mother takes a special interest in the proper behavior and success of her offspring (Prov 10:1; 15:20; 23:25; 29:15), since they reflect upon her performance (as well as that of the father). Due to her leadership in the home, she is entitled to expect obedience, respect, and honor from her household, including her grown male children (Prov 30:17; 31:28). In fact, the majority of references to father/mother in Proverbs concern the care owed to parents in their later years of increasing dependency, because of *their* labor-intensive contributions to the well-being of the dependent child (Prov 19:26; 20:20; 23:22; 28:24; 30:11, 17), a theme also found in Egyptian wisdom literature. These strongly motivational proverbs are in harmony with the religious and social duties of covenant obligations (Exod 20:12; 21:15, 17; Deut 5:16; 21:18–21; 27:16; Sir 3:1–16), forming a sort of "social welfare" system for the care of the aged.

The impressive preponderance of proverbs and admonitions warning against abuse of the mother and father suggest that all might not have been peaceful in the ancestral home, however. The large (extended) families of biblical Israel involved complicated family dynamics and issues of control, especially when adult children continued to live in their parents' household. Parents used threat and physical discipline to socialize their children (Prov 19:18; 22:15; 29:15, 17; compare Deut 21:18–21). Could it be that "elder abuse" was a mechanism favored by grown children striving to achieve authority in the household, thus necessitating proverbial commands to honor parents?

Prov 31:10–31 presents the best all-around portrait of the idealized mother of wisdom literature. Seen in the context of a family, she is portrayed as fulfilling many managerial tasks in the household economy. But she also fulfills reproductive (childbearing and nurturing) functions, for which she merits her family's highest praise (Prov 31:28).

CAROLE R. FONTAINE

SEE ALSO Part II: Wife (Prov 5:18–19, etc.); Mother of King Lemuel (Prov 31:1–9); Part III: Woman Wisdom.

FOR FURTHER READING: Camp, Claudia V. "The Female Sage in Ancient Israel and in the Biblical Wisdom Literature."

———. *Wisdom and the Feminine in the Book of Proverbs.*

Fontaine, Carole R. "The Sage in Family and Tribe."

———. "The Social Roles of Women in the World of Wisdom."

Meyers, Carol. *Discovering Eve: Ancient Israelite Women in Context.*

Pilch, John. "'Beat His Ribs While He Is Young' (Sirach 30:12): A Window on the Mediterranean World."

PROV 1:20–33   Woman Wisdom
SEE Woman Wisdom in the Hebrew Bible (Part III).

PROV 2:16–19
Loose Woman/Adulteress
SEE Woman Stranger (Loose Woman/Adulteress) (Part III).

Prov 3:13–18; 4:5–9   Woman Wisdom
SEE Woman Wisdom in the Hebrew Bible (Part III).

PROV 5:3–8, 20
Loose Woman/Adulteress
SEE Woman Stranger (Loose Woman/Adulteress) (Part III).

PROV 5:18–19; 12:4; 18:22; 19:13–14; 21:9, 19; 25:24; 27:15–16; 30:23; 31:10–31
Wife

Along with that of mother, the role of wife is the one most approved by the sages, and indeed motherhood may be considered a subset of the wife's role. For all of wisdom literature's characterization of women as dangerous and as potential troublemakers, an able, active, fruitful wife is viewed as an absolute necessity for male participation in the larger community (compare 12:4; 31:10–31), a theme also found in Egyptian wisdom instructions. In fact, the presence of a prudent, hardworking woman as manager of the household and as contributor to the domestic economy is so important that a man who finds her is said to have obtained a divine blessing (18:22; 19:14). Her many duties are amply catalogued, albeit in idealized form, in the image of the good or "capable" (NRSV) wife of Prov 31:10–31, which is a veritable job description of the senior female in a large household. The term for this woman in Hebrew (*'ēšet ḥayil*) indicates a woman of power and valor or a woman who produces prosperity. In the Bible, the term *wife* encodes a set of productive and managerial tasks that, along with a woman's reproductive role, were essential to the existence of the Israelite household. There is no equivalent understanding of "wife" as a social category in the modern West, where women's household work does not usually contribute to the family economy and tends to be ignored, trivialized, minimized, or otherwise degraded. The often insulting idea of "just a wife and mother" would have had no meaning in the biblical world.

The list of a capable wife's chores in Prov 31:10–31 includes providing food for her household (vv. 14–16) and working in textile production (vv. 13, 19,

21–22, 24, 25?), both being common female roles in Near Eastern family and commercial traditions. She also has a strong social consciousness (v. 20) and good business sense (vv. 16, 18, 24); and her attention to household management frees her husband to fulfill extradomestic tasks (v. 23). Significantly, this wife and mother is linked with wisdom and instruction (v. 26), a connection that may have contributed to the depiction of Woman Wisdom as female.

At the opposite end of the continuum, an angry, verbally abusive, fretful woman is portrayed as a curse that rots the entire fabric of a man's existence (12:4; 19:13; 21:9, 19; 25:24; 27:15–16). An unloved (unlovable?) woman would not even have a husband (20:23). A "contentious" wife's nagging is seen as a kind of water-torture for her spouse ("a continual dripping of rain," 19:13). The adulterous wives of other men are a pitfall of smooth invitations and illicit pleasures that must be avoided at all costs (5:3; 6:29–35; 7:19–23; 12:4). Far better is fidelity and appreciation of the "wife of one's youth," who provides all a man and his household could ever need (5:18; 31:10–31).

For a woman, becoming a wife and mother are the most important events of her life. Virtually all women in Israelite society left their natal families and formed households with their husbands. For both men and women, life outside of marriage was considered precarious, if not impossible.

CAROLE R. FONTAINE

SEE ALSO Part II: Mother (Prov 1:8, etc.); Part III: Woman Wisdom; Woman Stranger (Loose Woman/ Adulteress).

FOR FURTHER READING: Camp, Claudia V. *Wisdom and the Feminine in the Book of Proverbs.*

Fontaine, Carole R. "The Social Roles of Women in the World of Wisdom."

Perdue, Leo G., Joseph Blenkinsopp, John J. Collins, and Carol Meyers. *Families in Ancient Israel.*

PROV 6:20 Mother
SEE PROV 1:8, etc. Mother (Part II).

PROV 6:24–26, 29, 32
Adulteress/Neighbor's Wife
SEE Woman Stranger (Loose Woman/Adulteress) (Part III).

PROV 6:26; 7:10; 23:27; 29:3
Prostitute

One of the more dangerous kinds of women against which the sages warn their male pupils, the prostitute (RSV, "harlot") has much in common with her wicked sisters: the loose woman, the foolish woman, the strange/foreign woman, and the adulteress. Although it may seem that it costs little ("a loaf of bread") to obtain her services, such behavior can actually cost a man his life as well as his livelihood (6:26; 7:22–23, 27; 23:27; 29:3). Mythic imagery of goddesses of love and war who bear their lovers down to the underworld underlies the description of the harlot as a "deep pit" (23:27), whose house is "the way to Sheol" (the underworld from which none but deities return) (7:10–27). Her dress is distinctive (with or without a veil, depending on the time period; compare Gen 38:14 with Song 5:7), a feature preserved in other ancient Near Eastern societies (where a veil is usually the symbol of married or noble status). Her behavior is also another telltale marker, for she is brazen and aggressive, openly frequenting public places where she searches for her prey (7:11–12). Since there is little compelling evidence for cultic prostitution in the Hebrew Bible, the prostitutes represented in Proverbs are probably "secular" ones, whose activity is generated by pragmatic need (Lev 19:29) or incorrigible (from the sages' point of view) temperament. Prostitutes appear as dangerous figures in the wisdom instructions and proverbs of surrounding nations: such women are thought to be intrinsically "disloyal" because of their many partners and financial independence; and as such, they make poor wives (7:19–20).

CAROLE R. FONTAINE

SEE ALSO Part II: Prostitute (Lev 19:29, etc.); Part III: Woman Folly (Foolish Woman); Woman Stranger (Loose Woman/Adulteress).

FOR FURTHER READING: Bird, Phyllis A. "To Play the Harlot: An Inquiry into an Old Testament Metaphor."

————. "The Harlot as Heroine: Narrative Art and Social Presupposition in Three Old Testament Texts."

Fontaine, Carole R. "The Social Roles of Women in the World of Wisdom."

PROV 7:1–5   Woman Wisdom

SEE Woman Wisdom in the Hebrew Bible (Part III).

PROV 7:5–27
Loose Woman/Adulteress

SEE Woman Stranger (Loose Woman/Adulteress) (Part III).

PROV 7:10   Prostitute

SEE PROV 6:26, etc.   Prostitute (Part II).

PROV 8:1–9:6   Woman Wisdom

SEE Woman Wisdom in the Hebrew Bible (Part III).

PROV 9:3
Wisdom's Servant Girls

Female servants are part of the retinue of female personified Wisdom, who sends them out to extend her invitation of life and insight to those in the highways and byways (compare the invitation to the messianic banquet in Matt 22:3–4). Some scholars have speculated that the text invents an imaginary cult of a "goddess" Wisdom as a form of polemic against the worship of Ishtar/Astarte. Wisdom and her servants could as easily, however, reflect denizens of a wealthy household setting a table for guests (compare Prov 31:15, 20). Just as the household is depicted as that of a woman (9:1), the preparations for the banquet (9:2) and the invitation of guests are carried out by women.

CLAUDIA V. CAMP

SEE ALSO Part II: Attendants of the Daughter of Pharaoh (Exod 2:5); Wife (Prov 5:18–19, etc.); Part III: Woman Wisdom.

PROV 9:13–18   Foolish Woman

SEE Woman Folly (Foolish Woman) (Part III).

PROV 10:1   Mother

SEE PROV 1:8, etc.   Mother (Part II).

PROV 11:16
Gracious Woman

The NRSV uses Greek, Syriac, Aramaic, and Latin versions, very different from the Hebrew, to augment this verse with the concept of shameful behavior in women. The original Hebrew reads "A gracious woman acquires honor, but ruthless [men] acquire wealth," with the word for "ruthless" being a masculine plural form. The word translated here as "gracious" is ḥēn, which can be used to refer to both females and males and to animate or inanimate objects (stones, words); it carries the notion of making oneself agreeable (as well as beautiful) in the eyes of another. It can also refer to showing kindness to those less fortunate. "Honor" here refers to good reputation brought by embodying these standard virtues; in Ps 84:11, honor is again paired with "grace" as gifts bestowed by God on those who are faithful and trusting. Proverbs consistently teaches that honor and humility are to be preferred to ill-gotten gains or haughty dispositions (15:16; 18:12; 21:21; 22:4). Honor is thought to be a gift that Woman Wisdom bestows upon her followers (compare 3:34–35; 4:8).

CAROLE R. FONTAINE

SEE ALSO Part II: Wife (Prov 5:18–19, etc.); Part III: Woman Wisdom.

Prov 11:22
Beautiful Woman

Compared to a bejeweled pig or boar, led about by an incongruous golden nose-ring, physical beauty in women is found to be no substitute for discerning or discreet behavior, according to the sages (Prov 11:22). The metaphor uses these fertile but unclean and repulsive animals forbidden in the Hebrew diet to show that a woman's outward form ("golden ring") must be accompanied by virtuous disposition and actions (she should not act like a pig). Since the sages habitually speak of women's beauty as dangerous to men, this shows once more their emphasis on inner nature over outward appearance (compare 6:25; 31:30). Virtuous fulfillment of female roles (wife, mother, household manager, and so on) is to be valued more than external beauty.

CAROLE R. FONTAINE

SEE ALSO Part II: Mother (Prov 1:8, etc.); Wife (Prov 5:18–19, etc.); Prostitute (Prov 6:26, etc.).

PROV 12:4　Wife
SEE PROV 5:18–19, etc.　Wife (Part II).

Prov 14:1
Wise Woman Building Her House

The Hebrew text for the first verse of Proverbs 14 reads that the "wisdom of women builds her house," but translations often adjust the language somewhat. The NRSV reads, "the wise woman builds her house"; the NJPS has "the wisest of women builds her house." Despite the difficult syntax in the Hebrew, the association between "woman" and "house" as well as "wisdom" is clear. This verse can thus be added to the four explicit uses of "mother's house" (Gen 24:28; Ruth 1:8; Song 3:4; 8:2), a term for the family household (otherwise commonly referred to as "father's house") that reflects a woman's perspective and also expresses female agency in managing an agrarian household in ancient Israel. The link here with wisdom adds the dimension of female technological expertise and sagacity to the managerial aspects of senior women in family life.

CAROL MEYERS

SEE ALSO Part II: Mothers of Ruth and Orpah (Ruth 1:8, etc.); Daughters Compared to Pillars (Ps 144:12); Mother of Woman/Lover/Shulammite (Song 1:6, etc.); Part III: Woman Wisdom.

FOR FURTHER READING: Meyers, Carol. "'To Her Mother's House': Considering a Counterpart to the Israelite Bêt 'āb."

PROV 14:1　Wise Woman
SEE Woman Wisdom in the Hebrew Bible (Part III).

PROV 14:1　Foolish Woman
SEE Woman Folly (Foolish Woman) (Part III).

PROV 15:20　Mothers
SEE PROV 1:8, etc.　Mother (Part II).

PROV 15:25　Widow
SEE EXOD 22:22, etc.　Widows (Part II).

PROV 18:22; 19:13–14　Wife
SEE PROV 5:18–19, etc.　Wife (Part II).

PROV 19:26; 20:20　Mother
SEE PROV 1:8, etc.　Mother (Part II).

PROV 21:9, 19　Wife
SEE Prov 5:18–19, etc.　Wife (Part II).

PROV 22:14　Loose Woman
SEE Woman Stranger (Loose Woman/Adulteress) (Part III).

PROV 23:22, 25　Mother
SEE PROV 1:8, etc.　Mother (Part II).

PROV 23:27   Prostitute
SEE PROV 6:26, etc.   Prostitute (Part II).

PROV 23:27–28   Adulteress
SEE Woman Stranger (Loose Woman/Adulteress) (Part III).

PROV 25:24; 27:15–16   Wife
SEE PROV 5:18–19, etc.   Wife (Part II).

PROV 27:27; 31:15

Daughters (NRSV, Servant Girls)

The extensive attention to family life in Proverbs is striking in its omission of daughters, especially in light of the many verses dealing with female offspring in the similar, although later, collection of wise sayings in Ecclesiasticus (Sirach). However, two verses in Proverbs contain a term, traditionally translated "serving girls" (Prov 27:27; 31:15), that might be better rendered as "daughters." The Hebrew word is *něʿārôt* and can designate "young women, daughters," especially girls of marriageable age. Less often it denotes "maids," that is, the attendants of royalty (as for Pharaoh's daughter, Esther, and even Woman Wisdom in Prov 9:3).

The household depicted in Proverbs 31 might be that of an upper-class family, which could indeed have female servants. Yet such maids would more likely be designated by the term *šiphâ* (as in Prov 30:23). Thus the "servant girls" of 31:15 might in fact be the unmarried daughters of the household. They are provided with food; then they are assigned their allotted duties by their mother — that was how the girls of a household typically learned their gender-specific tasks. Similarly, Prov 27:27 refers first to the food needed by a household and then to its "daughters." Perhaps the concern in this verse for the "nourishment" of daughters was related to their marriageability; well-fed young women would seem desirable as wives and mothers.

CAROL MEYERS

SEE ALSO Part II: Attendants of the Daughter of Pharaoh (Exod 2:5); Wife (Prov 5:18–19, etc.); Wisdom's Servant Girls (Prov 9:3); Maid, Mistress (Prov 30:23).

PROV 28:24   Mother
SEE PROV 1:8, etc.   Mother (Part II).

PROV 29:3   Prostitute
SEE PROV 6:26, etc.   Prostitute (Part II).

PROV 29:15; 30:11, 17   Mother
SEE PROV 1:8, etc.   Mother (Part II).

PROV 30:19

Girl

The Hebrew word for young woman or girl is *ʿalmâ*, a term for a nubile young woman (compare Song 1:3). The "way of a man with a girl" probably refers to intercourse or, more broadly, to courtship and seduction. In this verse, three seemingly inexplicable or mysterious features of the natural world are followed, in a kind of climax, with an example from human behavior.

CAROLE R. FONTAINE

SEE ALSO Part II: Maidens (Song 1:3, etc.); Young Woman (Isa 7:14).

PROV 30:20   Adulteress
SEE Woman Stranger (Loose Woman/Adulteress) (Part III).

PROV 30:23

Maid, Mistress

The two ends of the female status continuum are yoked together in this "numerical" wisdom saying about the reversal of the natural orders of patriarchy, a frequent wisdom theme. In this case, a woman in authority (a "mistress") is replaced by her subordinate (a "maid," or female servant).

When roles are inverted, expected behaviors shift, causing the earth — that is, society — to tremble at its foundations.

CAROLE R. FONTAINE

SEE ALSO Part II: Mistress (Ps 123:2); Maid (Ps 123:2); Maid, Mistress (Isa 24:2).

PROV 30:23   Unloved Woman

SEE PROV 5:18–19, etc.   Wife (Part II).

PROV 31:1–9
Mother of King Lemuel

This queen presents a royal "wisdom instruction" ("oracle" in NRSV) given by a mother to her son (normally the father speaks; compare Prov 1:1–19; 2:1–22; 3:1–12, and so on). Some scholars interpret the word *oracle* as the proper name Massa (compare Prov 30:1), hence referring to a place or a tribe in northern Arabia; numerous extrabiblical texts make mention of powerful queen-priestesses ruling in this region (for example, the queen of Sheba of 1 Kings 10 may be a memory of such women). The queen's advice about leadership and other typical wisdom themes (drunkenness, sexual indiscretion, and so on) provides a concrete example of "the mother's teaching" mentioned elsewhere (Prov 1:8b; 6:20).

CAROLE R. FONTAINE

SEE ALSO Part II: Queen of Sheba (1 Kgs 10:1–13, etc.); Mother (Prov 1:8, etc.).

FOR FURTHER READING: Abbott, Nabia. "Pre-Islamic Arab Queens."

Fontaine, Carole R. "The Social Roles of Women in the World of Wisdom."

PROV 31:3   Loose Women

SEE Woman Stranger (Loose Woman/Adulteress) (Part III).

PROV 31:10–31   Wife

SEE PROV 5:18–19, etc.   Wife (Part II).

PROV 31:15   Servant Girls

SEE PROV 27:27, etc.   Daughters (NRSV, Servant Girls) (Part II).

ECCL 2:7   Female Slaves

SEE EXOD 21:7–11, etc.   Female (and Male) Hebrew Slaves (Part II).

ECCL 2:8
Concubines(?)

A list of pleasures pursued by the Teacher, the first-person narrator of the Book of Ecclesiastes, includes a two-word Hebrew phrase that appears nowhere else in the Bible. Although its meaning is uncertain, the similarity of the phrase to the Hebrew word for "breast" leads some interpreters to argue that it refers to women. Thus, it is sometimes translated "concubines," as it is in the NRSV.

KEN STONE

ECCL 2:8   Women Singers

SEE 2 SAM 19:35, etc.   Singing Women (and Men) (Part II).

ECCL 5:15; 11:5
Mother's Womb

Ecclesiastes' (or the Teacher's) use of the term "mother's womb" relates to his overall view of life as vain and unprofitable, due to the leveling effects of death. In 5:15, the term denotes the ultimate point of origin, from which a person emerges naked and possessionless. This parallels one's condition at death (compare Job 1:21; Psalm 139; Sir 40:1) and represents a paramount example of "vanity" or emptiness. In 11:5, the mother's womb is a source of supreme mystery, since no one knows how or when the "breath" of life (compare Gen 2:7) enters the bones of a fetus. Rather than consider this a sign of God's miraculous work in the world, Ecclesiastes sees this as just another worrisome example of how much is hidden from a humanity toiling and suffering without purpose.

CAROLE R. FONTAINE

SEE ALSO Part II: Born of Woman (Job 14:1, etc.).

ECCL 7:26–28
Woman Who Is a Trap

In its account of the search for wisdom, the Book of Ecclesiastes contains negative statements about women that are similar to warnings against the adulterous woman made in Proverbs (2:16–19; 5:1–4; 7:22–23; 9:13–18). The Teacher (the first-person narrator of Ecclesiastes) describes in 7:26–28 how women are the downfall of all but the righteous and how difficult it is to find a good woman. Women as traps are "more bitter than death" (v. 26), but *bitter* might also be translated "stronger," perhaps echoing the sentiment made in Song 8:6 ("love is strong as death"). But the translation "bitter" seems more likely here, because similar terms characterize women negatively elsewhere, as in Prov 5:4 ("bitter as wormwood"), and because the idea of trapping is also negative, as in 6:25. Some interpreters have suggested that "thousand" in v. 28 represents a military unit (reasonable, perhaps, if one reads "snare" as "fortification"; compare 9:14), a male domain — hence, Ecclesiastes has found not one woman there. If the adulteress represents a kind of death trap in v. 26, at least she has nothing to do with formal war. "They have devised many schemes" in v. 29 refers, then, not to women in particular but to all humankind.

Although such interpretations exempt Ecclesiastes from the worst possible reading of this passage, it still reflects a misogyny typical of male-oriented wisdom traditions. The Middle Kingdom Egyptian "Instruction of Ptahhotep" makes strikingly similar points in warning young bureaucrats:

. . . beware of approaching the women, for no good comes to a place where this is done, nor is it

clever to reveal them; a thousand men are turned aside from what is good for them. A little moment, the semblance of a dream, and death reaches you because of knowing them. (9, 10)

Whether a man escapes such dangers is a matter determined by God.

CAROLE R. FONTAINE

SEE ALSO Part III: Woman Folly (Foolish Woman); Woman Stranger (Loose Woman/Adulteress).

FOR FURTHER READING: Faulkner, Raymond O. "The Maxims of Ptahhotep."

Fontaine, Carole R. "Ecclesiastes."

ECCL 9:9
Wife

Although generally cynical about family life (compare Eccl 2:18–19; 6:3; 7:28), Ecclesiastes pauses to consider what pursuits might have value, given the brevity and "vanity" of life. He recommends enjoyment of life because in death no one knows, much less enjoys, anything (7:7–10). This is reminiscent of Prov 5:18–19, though there the tone is considerably more optimistic. Ecclesiastes' guarded advocacy of enjoying life is related to his notion of the "portion" God has given to humanity. Men ought to enjoy what they can, including a family — "enjoy life with the wife whom you love" — as compensation for the toil and misfortune of the human condition. Similar advice is given by the barmaid Siduri to the despondent hero Gilgamesh in the important Mesopotamian *Epic of Gilgamesh* (Tablet X:iii), composed during the late third millennium B.C.E. and known to biblical authors.

CAROLE R. FONTAINE

SEE ALSO Part II: Wife (Prov 5:18–19, etc.).

FOR FURTHER READING: Murphy, Roland E. *Ecclesiastes.*

ECCL 11:5   Mother's Womb
SEE ECCL 5:15, etc.   Mother's Womb (Part II).

ECCL 12:3
Women Who Grind

The writer of Ecclesiastes extols the joys of youth, which will one day give way to the struggles of old age. In 12:3, he presents two gender-paired images depicting the diminution of powers as people age. One of these depicts strong men, able to carry out the physically demanding tasks of an agrarian household, becoming "bent" and unable to work, and then mentions that "women who grind" will cease working. The Hebrew text does not use a word for "woman," but rather a feminine plural participle of the verb "to grind" *(ṭāḥan)*.

Just as the essence of a man's contribution to the household economy is represented by male physical power, so is a woman's role epitomized by grinding grain, a *pars pro toto* designation for the lengthy and technologically complex process of converting wheat to bread. In the division of labor by gender in ancient Israel, as in most societies, the preparation of the basic carbohydrate food was the responsibility of women. The many operations required to convert cereal crops into an edible form could take as much as two hours a day. This intensive labor was not without its rewards. Social scientists suggest that the integrated sequence of activities required to produce bread (and other foodstuffs, as well as textiles — all largely women's work) and the fact that essential and usable products result from it immediately can produce more satisfaction and a more direct sense of gratification than do the results of male labor. Men produce quantitatively measurable goods, but ones that usually cannot be used at once, whereas women literally put bread on the table.

CAROL MEYERS

SEE ALSO Part II: Women as Bread Bakers (Lev 26:26); Daughters as Perfumers, Cooks, and Bakers (1 Sam 8:13); Women Looking Through Windows (Eccl 12:3); Women Making a Fire (Isa 27:11); Women Worshipping the Queen of Heaven (Jer 7:18, etc.).

FOR FURTHER READING: Meyers, Carol. "The Family in Early Israel."

Eccl 12:3
Women Looking Through Windows

The image of women peering from windows but seeing little is part of a gender pair, one of two such pairs, used by the writer of Ecclesiastes in 12:3 to bemoan the transition from vigorous youth to difficult old age. The first and last lines of the verse reflect aspects of protection from one's enemies. In the first lines the male role is that of guardian or defender. As they age, such men "tremble" and thereby lose their effectiveness. The last line concerns what women do when men go out against their foes: they traditionally gaze from their windows, expecting to greet returning victors (compare Judg 5:28; 2 Sam 6:16).

In this verse, such women have failing eyesight. Although the word *woman* does not appear in the Hebrew, the participial form of the verb, meaning "to see, look," is feminine plural, indicating that those peering out the window in vain are indeed women.

CAROL MEYERS

SEE ALSO Part II: Mother of Sisera (Judg 5:28–30); Women Who Grind (Eccl 12:3).

ECCL 12:4   Daughters of Song
SEE 2 SAM 19:35, etc.   Singing Women (and Men) (Part II).

BOOK OF SONG OF SOLOMON
Woman/Lover/Shulammite

The Shulammite (from Hebrew *šûlammît,* "woman of Jerusalem") is the central figure in the Song of Solomon (also called Song of Songs or Canticles) and one of the most positive representations of young womanhood in the Hebrew Bible. As the embodiment of erotic pleasure, innocent and savored for its own sake, she is to be contrasted, on the one hand, with the wily seductress of Proverbs

7, whose sexuality is insidious and destructive, and on the other with figures such as Tamar and Ruth, whose sexual boldness is in the service of perpetuating the family line. In the Shulammite, indeed, we find one of the most unqualified celebrations of female eroticism in all of Western literature.

Like her lover, she is not given a proper name. The epithet "the Shulammite," which occurs (twice) in only one verse of the Song (6:13) and nowhere else in the Bible, is of uncertain meaning. Medieval Jewish exegetes such as Ibn Ezra understood the word as "the Jerusalemite," a feminine epithet derived from Salem (Hebrew *šālēm*), an ancient poetic name for Jerusalem (Ps 76:2). The epithet *Shulammite*, with its root *š-l-m*, may have been chosen also because of its allusions to Solomon (*šĕlōmōh*), who figures in the poem, and to the young woman's role of bringing "peace" *(shalom)* to her lover (8:10). Other less likely interpretations involve the village of Shunem or Shulem (the home of King David's attendant, Abishag, 1 Kgs 1:1–4), or the Mesopotamian war goddess Shulmanitu, perhaps Ishtar.

Although she is not as fully articulated as the characters in biblical prose fiction, the Shulammite has a distinct consistency of characterization throughout the Song. That she is probably just past the age of puberty is implied by the dialogue with her brothers in 8:8–10. They consider her a child ("We have a little sister, / and she has no breasts"); her spirited response ("my breasts are like towers") indicates that she has already reached sexual maturity (see Ezek 16:7–8). There is no mention of a father in the poem; thus the Shulammite's brothers take responsibility for her conduct, about which they have rebuked her (1:6), as well as for marriage negotiations with potential suitors (8:8–9).

Her relationship with her mother appears to be close and tender. The Shulammite is called her mother's favorite (6:9). She speaks of bringing her lover to her mother's house (3:4; 8:2), perhaps to signify a more binding relationship or perhaps in reference to the fact that, from a female perspective, the family household was the mother's domain. In one possible reading of 8:2, her mother can be seen

as instructing her in the arts of love. The Shulammite addresses her feelings about love and her lover to a group of young women, the daughters of Jerusalem, who serve as a kind of chorus in the poem.

The Shulammite's beauty is celebrated in three formal praise songs, often called by the Arabic term *wasfs* (4:1–7; 6:4–10; 7:1–7; compare the praise of the man's beauty in 5:10–16). The homage to the nude body is unique in the Bible and may perhaps indicate the influence of Hellenistic art. The poet's metaphors and similes are not literally descriptive; they convey the delight of the lover in contemplating the beloved, finding in the body a reflected image of the world in its freshness and splendor.

Like her lover, the Shulammite is portrayed in images that suggest tenderness (lilies, doves, gazelles), as well as strength and stateliness (pillars, towers). The poet's metaphors move back and forth between the actual landscape, suffused with erotic associations, and the landscape of the body: the Shulammite waits for her lover in a garden, but she herself is a garden. The lovers go out to the vineyards to make love, but she herself is a vineyard, her breasts like clusters of grapes, and their kisses an intoxicating wine. When the lovers are compared to animals, it is in tribute to their beauty and undomesticated freedom. Like her lover, the Shulammite has dovelike eyes and is associated with deer and gazelles. Perhaps strange to the contemporary reader is the comparison of the Shulammite in 1:9 to a mare (a familiar trope in Greek poetry), suggesting her elegant gracefulness.

The Shulammite calls herself "black and beautiful" (1:5–6). This is apparently a reference to her sunburned skin — according to her poetic phrase "the sun has gazed on me" (1:6). Working outdoors (she is "keeper of the vineyards" in 1:6) is perhaps associated with a lower social status; those who could afford not to work outdoors would have a fair complexion. The Shulammite's need to account for her dark skin may sound apologetic; on the other hand, it is likely that she is boasting, not apologizing.

Apart from her youth and beauty, the Shulammite's most striking characteristic is her assertiveness. She is described by her lover as 'ăyummâ (6:10); the word *daunting* conveys the spirit of the Hebrew better than the commonly rendered *terrible*. Only she makes dramatic statements about herself (1:5; 8:10), and only she commands the elements (4:16). She goes out into the streets of Jerusalem at night to search for her lover — bold and unusual behavior for an unmarried woman (3:1–4; 5:6–7). Her invitations to love (4:16; 7:11–13; 8:2) are more outspoken than his, and she is the one who apparently takes the initiative in their lovemaking: "I awakened you" (8:5).

The Shulammite speaks the first words in the poem — "kiss me" (1:2) — and the last (8:14); she delivers most of the lines, including the rousing speeches about the power of love (2:7; 8:6–7). Her voice and thoughts come directly to the reader, unmediated by a narrator. Her repeated adjurations to the daughters of Jerusalem (2:7; 3:5; 8:4), filled with awe at love's power, convey the seriousness with which she regards this relationship. When she asks her lover to be true to her forever (8:6), she is expressing a hope for a permanent bond in language that is characteristically emphatic.

The lover's affectionate phrase "my sister, my bride" (4:9–10, 12; 5:1–2) is not to be taken literally; both epithets express closeness and intimacy. (In Egyptian love poetry, the lovers refer to each other as "sister" and "brother" as a sign of closeness.) In 8:1, the Shulammite says she wishes her lover was "like a brother"; then she could kiss him in the streets and no one would scorn her. The word *bride* reflects the young man's desire for a permanent relationship; the Shulammite expresses a similar wish in 8:6. There is no indication in the poem that the lovers are married; that they meet secretly in the countryside at night and part at daybreak implies the contrary.

The most complex portrait of the Shulammite is also the most dramatic scene in the poem (5:2–8), conveying passion, coquetry, self-reproach, and yearning in quick succession. Her lover knocks at her door at night, ardent and impatient, but the Shulammite coyly pretends reluctance; as soon as he leaves, she is filled with regret and longing. Run-

ning through the streets of Jerusalem to search for him, she is apprehended and beaten by the city watchmen — one of the few dark moments in a poem filled with delight and celebration.

CHANA BLOCH

SEE ALSO Part II: Daughters of Jerusalem, Zion (Song 1:5–6, etc.); Mother of Woman/Lover/Shulammite (Song 1:6, etc); Part III: Woman Stranger (Loose Woman/Adulteress).

FOR FURTHER READING: Bloch, Ariel, and Chana Bloch. *The Song of Songs: A New Translation with an Introduction and Commentary.*

Fox, Michael V. *The Song of Songs and the Ancient Egyptian Love Songs.*

Pope, Marvin H. *Song of Songs: A New Translation with Introduction and Commentary.*

Weems, Renita. "Song of Songs."

SONG 1:3; 6:8–9
Maidens

The female lover in the Song of Solomon opens her initial song by declaring that her beloved, whom she beckons to kiss her, is attractive to all "maidens." The Hebrew word for "maiden" ('almâ), which indicates nubile young women (sexually mature but not necessarily virgins), contributes to the erotic mood of her words. The term *maiden* appears again in 6:8–9, joined by "queens and concubines." In the male lover's view, his beloved is praised by the very women who also may be drawn to him.

CAROL MEYERS

SEE ALSO Part II: Girl (Prov 30:19); Queens and Concubines (Song 6:8–10); Young Woman (Isa 7:14).

SONG 1:5–6; 2:7; 3:5, 10–11; 5:8–9, 16; 8:4
Daughters of Jerusalem, Zion

Women play a prominent role in the Song of Solomon. Aside from the Shulammite, three mothers are mentioned — the Shulammite's (3:4; 6:9; 8:2), her lover's (8:5), and King Solomon's (3:11) — as well as a group of young women, the daughters of Jerusalem, who act as a foil to the Shulammite and an audience for her. She addresses her feelings about love to them and turns to them for help. Like the young women who accompany Jephthah's daughter in her mourning (Judg 11:37–38) or the women of Bethlehem who come out to greet Naomi (Ruth 1:19), the daughters of Jerusalem represent the social milieu in which she moves, answering the Shulammite's need for public testimony and public validation. The young man's companions, mentioned briefly in 1:7 (and perhaps in 5:1 and 8:13), may serve a similar purpose, though unlike the daughters of Jerusalem they are given no voice in the poem.

The presence of the daughters of Jerusalem in the Song heightens the dramatic quality of this lyrical cycle of poems. Apart from a set piece about the splendors of King Solomon's court (3:7–11), where they are also called the "daughters of Zion," they always appear in dialogue with the Shulammite. In 1:5–6 the Shulammite boasts to them of her dark beauty. Her emphatic self-defense suggests that they are critical of her sunburned skin, which is typically associated with outdoor work and hence perhaps with a low social status. In the repeated refrain of 2:7, 3:5, and 8:4, the Shulammite urges them to swear that they will not awaken love until the moment is ripe. Since she instructs them as one who has the wisdom of experience, they are presumably less experienced than she is in matters of love. Finally, in 5:8–16, the Shulammite encounters them while searching for her lover at night in the streets of Jerusalem. Their question to her in 5:9 about the qualities that distinguish her lover need not be taken as hostile, but rather as a rhetorical device to elicit her formal praise of his beauty in 5:10–16.

CHANA BLOCH

SEE ALSO Part II: Woman/Lover/Shulammite (Book of Song of Solomon); Maidens (Song 1:3, etc.); Queens and Concubines (Song 6:8–10).

FOR FURTHER READING: Bloch, Ariel, and Chana

Bloch. *The Song of Songs: A New Translation with an Introduction and Commentary.*

Fox, Michael V. *The Song of Songs and the Ancient Egyptian Love Songs.*

SONG 1:6; 3:4; 6:9; 8:1–2

Mother of Woman/Lover/Shulammite

The mother of the female lover in the Song of Solomon is mentioned five times; and the word *mother* also appears in designating Solomon's female parent in 3:11 and that of the male lover in 8:5. This total of seven occurrences of the word *mother* provides a literary emphasis on the female parent, in that seven is a symbolic biblical number designating totality or completeness. The prominence of *mother*, especially in the absence of the word *father*, has led some commentators to suggest that the father was deceased or that the Song reflects a primitive matriarchy.

Such suggestions fail to take into account the possibility that this biblical book represents a woman's voice. Because women in many cultures are the creators of love poetry, and because of various literary features of the Song of Solomon that seem to indicate a specifically female perspective, a strong case can be made that it is a product of women's culture. The multiple uses of the term *mother* certainly form one of those features.

Four of the references to the woman's mother portray the intimacy of the mother-daughter relationship and the bonds that connect the two, going back to the daughter's birth (3:4; 6:9; 8:1–2). The emphasis on this primal closeness serves as a metaphor for the intimacy between the woman and her beloved. The fifth mention (1:6) uses the unusual phrase "mother's sons" to designate the woman's brothers. One might expect such a phrase, in poetic usage, to stand as a parallel to the word *brothers;* but such is not the case. Thus the use of "mother's sons" may simply be part of the female orientation of the Song.

Two occurrences of the word *mother* form part of the phrase "my mother's house" = "house of my mother" (3:4; 8:2). This unusual phrase is found elsewhere only twice in the Hebrew Bible (in Gen 24:28, in reference to Rebekah, and in Ruth 1:8); and it is also used indirectly several times in Proverbs (for example, 14:1). It is probably the female equivalent of "father's house," a common biblical expression denoting the family household, the fundamental unit of Israelite society. The household provided basic subsistence needs for all its members; and it was also the setting for many religious, educational, and judicial functions that in the modern world take place outside the home. The fact that "mother's house" appears in biblical passages that deal with women's lives indicates that those texts provide a woman's perspective. Furthermore, the identification of the household with the mother may reflect the important managerial role of women, seen from within, in maintaining the complex set of operations that constituted daily life for agrarian families in biblical times.

CAROL MEYERS

SEE ALSO Part I: Rebekah; Part II: Mothers of Ruth and Orpah (Ruth 1:8, etc.); Wise Woman Building Her House (Prov 14:1); Part III: Woman Wisdom.

FOR FURTHER READING: Brenner, Athalya, and Fokkelein van Dijk-Hemmes. *On Gendering Texts: Female and Male Voices in the Hebrew Bible.*

Meyers, Carol. "'To Her Mother's House': Considering a Counterpart to the Israelite *Bêt 'āb.*"

SONG 2:7 Daughters of Jerusalem
SEE SONG 1:5–6, etc. Daughters of Jerusalem, Zion (Part II).

SONG 3:4
Mother of Woman/Lover/Shulammite
SEE SONG 1:6, etc. Mother of Woman/Lover/Shulammite (Part II).

SONG 3:5, 10–11
Daughters of Jerusalem, Zion
SEE SONG 1:5–6, etc. Daughters of Jerusalem, Zion (Part II).

SONG 3:11
Mother of Solomon

Although tradition ascribes the Song of Solomon to the Israelite King Solomon, modern scholarship generally agrees that neither the author nor the date of this biblical book can be established. The references to Solomon in this series of love poems were perhaps motivated by his reputation for having had countless marital liaisons. In 3:11, Solomon's mother appears at his marriage — she supplies the crown, which is probably a wedding garland rather than his royal crown of office. She seems to sanction the marriage with this gesture, which may reflect either a queen mother's royal power or any mother's role in seeing her son wed.

The role of the mother in the wedding and also the presence of the "daughters of Jerusalem" and "daughters of Zion" give a decidedly female cast to the event and contribute to the overall sense that the Song of Solomon is, at least in part, a woman's composition. In addition, the use of the word *mother* here, and in six other passages, means that the word appears *seven* times in this book. Given the symbolic meaning of seven, as indicating totality or completeness, the sevenfold use of the term is another indication of the female orientation of the Song of Solomon.

CAROL MEYERS

SEE ALSO Part II: Daughters of Jerusalem, Zion (Song 1:5–6, etc.); Mother of Woman/Lover/Shulammite (Song 1:6, etc.); Mother of Male Lover (Song 8:5).

SONG 5:8–9, 16
Daughters of Jerusalem
SEE SONG 1:5–6, etc. Daughters of Jerusalem, Zion (Part II).

SONG 6:8–9 Maidens
SEE SONG 1:3, etc. Maidens (Part II).

Song 6:8–10
Queens and Concubines

According to an interpretation popular in the Victorian era, the Song of Solomon tells the story of a love triangle in which King Solomon (King of Israel, c. 968–928 B.C.E.) attempts (unsuccessfully) to win the Shulammite maiden away from her humble shepherd-lover to a life at court. There are, indeed, many allusions to the golden age of Solomon in the Song. These include references to the cedars of Lebanon, horses and chariots, gold, silver, ivory, and spices, as well as to queens and concubines — all signs of Solomon's wealth and power. But the king is best seen as a central figure in the lovers' fantasies, not a character in the poem. His reign is invoked as a symbol of legendary royal splendor that enhances and ennobles the two young lovers.

According to 1 Kings, Solomon had a harem of seven hundred wives and three hundred concubines (1 Kings 11) — women of Moabite, Ammonite, Edomite, Sidonian, and Hittite origin who, in the view of the biblical historian, enticed him to worship foreign gods. In Song 6:6–8, the king's women make a cameo appearance, freed from the negative judgment of the historian. Here the lover's enumeration of sixty queens, eighty concubines, and "maidens without number" sets off the uniqueness of the Shulammite, and the extravagant praise attributed to the royal harem adds luster to his gallant compliment.

CHANA BLOCH

SEE ALSO Part II: Women of Solomon (1 Kgs 3:1, etc.); Woman/Lover/Shulammite (Book of Song of Solomon).

FOR FURTHER READING: Bloch, Ariel, and Chana Bloch. *The Song of Songs: A New Translation with an Introduction and Commentary.*

Fox, Michael V. T*he Song of Songs and the Ancient Egyptian Love Songs.*

Song 6:9
Mother of Woman/Lover/Shulammite

SEE SONG 1:6, etc. Mother of Woman/Lover/Shulammite (Part II).

Song 8:1–2
Mother of Woman/Lover/Shulammite

SEE SONG 1:6, etc. Mother of Woman/Lover/Shulammite (Part II).

Song 8:4   Daughters of Jerusalem

SEE SONG 1:5–6, etc. Daughters of Jerusalem, Zion (Part II).

Song 8:5
Mother of Male Lover

Near the end of the lyrical songs that comprise the Song of Solomon, the female lover imagines a scene in which she awakens her beloved under an apple tree, the very place where his mother gave birth to him. The word translated "awakened" by the NRSV is better rendered "aroused"; the Hebrew word indicates stirring someone to intense action for a pursuit such as love or war. The erotic implications of that term, and also of the apple tree, lead well to the subsequent image of a mother in labor, a condition that originated in her own arousal nine months earlier.

The word *mother* is found six additional times in the Song of Solomon — five references to the Shulammite's female parent and one to that of Solomon. The frequent appearance of mother and other female characters, and the dearth of male ones (no father is mentioned, for example), contributes to the sense that women's voices dominate this book.

CAROL MEYERS

SEE ALSO Part II: Daughters of Jerusalem, Zion (Song 1:5–6, etc.); Mother of Woman/Lover/Shulammite (Song 1:6, etc.); Mother of Solomon (Song 3:11).

Isa 1:17, 23   Widow

SEE EXOD 22:22, etc. Widows (Part II).

Isa 1:21–23   Woman Jerusalem/Zion

SEE Woman Jerusalem/Zion in Isaiah (Part III).

ISA 3:12
Women as Rulers

Many commentators emend this verse, which includes the statement "women rule over them," to read "money-lenders [extended to any kind of oppressors] rule over them." Others assume that the prophet Isaiah is referring to the women of the court: some queen or the queen mother is exerting undue influence in the court of Ahaz (reigned 743–727 B.C.E.). Because the context includes a series of unnatural reversals (see vv. 4–5), the sentence is probably meant as a simple insult to Judah's rulers, since rule by women was not acceptable during the time of the monarchy, even though certain women (Athaliah and Jezebel) exerted royal power.

JO ANN HACKETT

SEE ALSO Part I: Athaliah; Jezebel 1; Part II: Troops as Women (Nah 3:13).

ISA 3:16–26; 32:9–11
Daughters of Zion

In Isa 3:16–26 the daughters of Zion are castigated as "haughty," concerned solely with perfumes, jewels, and similar items of luxury. The eighth-century B.C.E. prophet Isaiah warns that such ostentatiousness will not be tolerated, describing how YHWH will turn the perfumes of these women to stench, their fine girdles to rope, their elaborate hairstyles to baldness, and their rich robes to sackcloth. The prophet concludes by depicting Jerusalem/Zion, personified as a woman, as ravaged and sitting on the ground.

A similar condemnation of daughters who are "complacent" and "at ease" is found in Isa 32:9–11, and, as in Isa 3:16–26, these women are told that, as part of God's punishment, they will have to strip off their finery and clothe themselves in sackcloth. Yet despite the misogynistic tenor of both these passages, in which the prophet Isaiah singles out Jerusalem's women as the object of his special scorn, there are hints in these texts of an important place

for women in ancient Israelite religion: to play the role of mourners. The sackcloth donned in Isa 3:24 and 32:11 was typical mourning garb in ancient Israel; the baldness that replaces the women's elaborate hairstyles in Isa 3:24 also seems to have been required in Israelite mourning rituals; sitting on the ground, as does the ravaged Zion in Isa 3:26, was similarly a typical rite of Israelite lamentation. This more positive female imagery gives rise to texts like Isa 49:22, in which the daughters of Zion are carried triumphantly on the nations' shoulders as God celebrates a redeemed relationship with Jerusalem's people.

SUSAN ACKERMAN

SEE ALSO Part II: Daughters (and Sons) (Isa 49:22, etc.); Mourning Women (Jer 9:17–22, etc.); Part III: Woman Jerusalem/Zion in Isaiah.

FOR FURTHER READING: Ackerman, Susan. "Isaiah."

ISA 3:25–26   Woman Jerusalem/Zion
SEE Woman Jerusalem/Zion in Isaiah (Part III).

ISA 4:1
Seven Women

Isa 4:1 is part of a longer oracle (Isa 3:16–4:1) in which the eighth-century B.C.E. prophet Isaiah describes the doom that is to come upon the city of Jerusalem because of its arrogance. Jerusalem's population shall be decimated; Isa 3:25 indicates that, in particular, Jerusalem's men will die in battle. This shortage of men, according to Isa 4:1, will lead to such desperation that seven women (a traditional biblical number of wholeness and completeness, as in the seven days of creation) will seek marriage with every remaining man. The women's desperation is further indicated by their volunteering to provide their own food and clothing once wed, although this responsibility is normally assumed by a woman's husband.

SUSAN ACKERMAN

ISA 7:14
Young Woman

Isa 7:14 describes a "young woman" (Hebrew *'almâ*) who is pregnant with and soon to bear the child Immanuel. This boy's name, which means "God is with us," signifies to King Ahaz of Judah (reigned 743–727 B.C.E.) that YHWH will protect him and his people from the attacks of King Pekah of Israel and King Rezin of Damascus.

The identity of the young woman is debated. At two other points in Isaiah 7–8, children with symbolic names are presented to Ahaz as signs that God will deliver him from the threats of Pekah and Rezin, and in both of these cases the child is identified as Isaiah's son. These children's mother is therefore presumed to be Isaiah's wife. Some scholars propose that the "young woman" of Isa 7:14 is likewise Isaiah's wife. The fact that Isa 7:16, where it is said that salvation will come to Ahaz by the time that Immanuel is weaned, is remarkably parallel to Isa 8:4, where salvation is similarly promised within the first year of the life of the third child, Maher-shalal-hash-baz, whose name means "swift the spoil, prompt the plundering" (author's translation), further suggests this identification; that is, as Maher-shalal-hash-baz's mother is Isaiah's wife, so too should the wife be the mother of this boy's counterpart, Immanuel. Others, however, point out that in the mythological "Epic of Kirta" from the Late Bronze Age city-state of Ugarit in Syria, the cognate of the Hebrew *'almâ*, "young woman," refers to the wife of a king. They thus suggest that the young woman of Isa 7:14 is Abi (Abijah), the wife of King Ahaz, and the child is Ahaz's heir, Hezekiah, or some other royal prince.

When the Hebrew Bible was translated into Greek, beginning the third century B.C.E., Hebrew *'almâ* was rendered as *parthenos*, "virgin," and it is this tradition that is quoted in Matt 1:23, where the "virgin" is taken as Jesus' mother Mary and the child Immanuel as Jesus himself. Matthew engages here in his well-known practice of using fulfillment quotations, whereby he cites a Hebrew Bible passage and sees it as applying to the life of Jesus. To find in Isa 7:14, however, references to a virginal conception and to Jesus' divinity goes well beyond the intentions of the original text.

SUSAN ACKERMAN

SEE ALSO Part I: Abijah 2/Abi; Part II: Prophetess (Wife of Isaiah) (Isa 8:3–4).
FOR FURTHER READING: Gottwald, Norman K. "Immanuel as the Prophet's Son."
Roberts, Jimmy J. M. "Isaiah and His Children."

ISA 8:3–4
Prophetess (Wife of Isaiah)

With this woman, the prophet Isaiah of Jerusalem engenders a son, Maher-shalal-hash-baz. This boy's name, which means "swift the spoil, prompt the plundering" (author's translation), signifies to King Ahaz of Judah (reigned 743–727 B.C.E.) that his enemies, King Pekah of Israel and King Rezin of Damascus, will swiftly and promptly be spoiled and plundered, threatening Ahaz no more. The prophetess is probably also the mother of Shear-jashub ("a remnant shall return"), mentioned in Isa 7:3, whose name is again meant to serve as a sign to Ahaz, telling him that only a remnant of his enemies in the northern kingdom of Israel will survive. Some commentators, moreover, believe that the prophetess is the "young woman" mentioned in Isa 7:14 who bears the child Immanuel, whose name, meaning "God is with us," is yet another sign to Ahaz that YHWH will protect him from enemy attacks. Others identify the "young woman" of Isa 7:14 as King Ahaz's wife, Abi (Abijah).

Several prophetesses in the biblical tradition seem to exercise significant political or religious power: Miriam (Exod 15:20–21), Deborah (Judg 4:4), Huldah (2 Kgs 22:14–20), and Noadiah (Neh 6:14). But the prophetess of Isaiah 7–8 takes no action other than bearing Isaiah's children. This suggests that her title "prophetess" is merely an honorific bestowed upon her because of her husband's role as prophet, in much the same way that the wife of a king is assigned the title of queen.

SUSAN ACKERMAN

SEE ALSO Part I: Abijah 2/Abi; Part II: Young Woman (Isa 7:14).
FOR FURTHER READING: Ackerman, Susan. "Isaiah."
Gottwald, Norman K. "Immanuel as the Prophet's Son."
Roberts, Jimmy J. M. "Isaiah and His Children."

ISA 9:17; 10:2   Widows

SEE EXOD 22:22, etc.   Widows (Part II).

ISA 10:30   Daughter Gallim

SEE Daughter (Part III).

ISA 13:8; 21:3; 26:17–18; 42:14; 45:10; 66:7–9; MIC 4:9–10

Woman in Labor

The familiarity of most people with the sounds, if not the sights, of women in labor and childbirth meant that the process of giving birth could provide powerful imagery in Hebrew poetry. Several prophetic passages employ such imagery — some emphasizing the ordeal of the birth process, and others celebrating the creative aspect of new life.

In Isa 13:8 and 21:3, trembling as an expression of fear or anxiety is compared to the uterine contractions experienced by women in labor. Isa 13:8, for example, refers to the reaction of the people of Babylon when that nation, which had terrorized the civilized world, will in its turn be humbled by more powerful nations not yet imagined.

Likewise, in Isa 26:17–18 and Mic 4:9–10, persons' and nations' fear or anxiety, expressed by both trembling and screaming, is compared to the combination of uterine contractions and screaming observed in many women in labor. Isa 26:16–18 mentions that a prayer was addressed to the LORD during an earlier time when the people of Judah writhed and experienced anxiety like a woman in labor. This mention of a prayer is perhaps an indication that women recited certain prayers at the time of their delivery. This passage, along with the knowledge that women in neighboring Semitic cultures offered prayers during childbirth, allows us to suggest that women turned toward God at this mo-

mentous event in the creation of new life. Additional biblical evidence concerning prayer and sacrifice by women in connection with the desire to give birth, a difficult pregnancy, and the joy of giving birth is found in Gen 4:1; 25:22–23; 29:35; 1 Sam 1:9–13, 24–28; 2:1–10, 19.

A different aspect of labor appears in Isa 42:14; 45:9–10; and 66:7–9. In these passages, images of giving birth are used to depict God as parent or midwife. God's distress at having destroyed Israel (by acting as a soldier) is expressed by comparing God to a woman gasping and panting in labor (42:14). In Isa 45:9–10, the prophet rebukes xenophobic elements among the Judeans who call into question God's choice of the non-Israelite Cyrus as the instrument of salvation. In doing so, he compares God to both a father (who begets) and a mother (who is in labor). Israel is thus the offspring of God's procreative activity.

In Isa 66:7–9, in another gynomorphic image, God is pictured as the midwife who delivers Zion (the personified Jerusalem or land of Israel), the mother whose newborn children are the people Israel. Their return from exile is compared to the birth of children. The vivid image of childbirth — the creation of new life — expresses the new life that God is creating for the Israelites by restoring them to Zion.

MAYER I. GRUBER

SEE ALSO Part II: Woman in Labor (Ps 48:7); Part III: Female Images of God in the Hebrew Bible.
FOR FURTHER READING: Gruber, Mayer I. "The Motherhood of God in Second Isaiah."
Trible, Phyllis. "God, Nature of, in the Old Testament."

ISA 13:16

Ravished Wives of Babylonians

In an oracle against Babylon, the prophet Isaiah describes how Babylon's punishment will include the ravishing of its wives, an atrocity frequently endured by a conquered people during war. Men may be killed in battle, but surviving women suffer horrors of their own.

SUSAN ACKERMAN

SEE ALSO Part II: Wives (and Children) as Booty (Num 14:3); Raped Women and Virgins (Lam 5:11); Raped Women (Zech 14:2).

SEE ALSO Part II: Female (and Male) Slaves (Gen 12:16, etc.); Female (and Male) Hebrew Slaves (Exod 21:7–11, etc.); Female (and Male) Slaves (Joel 2:29).

ISA 16:1 Daughter Jerusalem/Zion
SEE Daughter (Part III).

ISA 14:2
Female (and Male) Slaves

Most of the first thirty-nine chapters of Isaiah date to the eighth century B.C.E and are concerned with the emergence of Assyrian imperialism, which threatens to destroy Israel. However, several of those chapters, including Isaiah 14, see Babylon as the threat and thus date to the sixth century, the time of the Babylonian conquest and captivity. The beginning of chap. 14 deals with that captivity: Israel will be released from bondage among the "nations" (plural). This restoration will not be simply a matter of renewed residence of YHWH's people in their homeland. Rather, the entire balance of political power will be reversed. According to 14:2, those who once ruled over the "house of Jacob" will themselves become captive: they will become "servants [masculine] and maidservants [NRSV, male and female slaves]."

The two Hebrew words for "servitude" in this verse — 'ebed for the male servants and šiphâ for the female — are often used together, especially in nonlegal contexts, to indicate menial servitude rather than a state of political subordination. Their use in Isaiah 14 makes the passage vindicatory. Israel's oppressors will not simply release their captives and themselves be subjected to the rule of YHWH's people. Rather, all of them — women and men — will become laborers in YHWH's land. This harsh view of the fate of the enemy emerges from the "pain and turmoil and the hard service" (14:3) that the Israelites themselves had experienced, in which both women and men had been subjected to enforced labor by their Babylonian captors.

CAROL MEYERS

ISA 16:2
Daughters of Moab

In an oracle concerning Moab (Isa 15:1–16:14), the people of Judah are told that after the destruction of that nation by unknown agents, Moabite refugees, identified in Isa 16:2 as the daughters of Moab, will seek asylum in their land. The most obvious interpretation identifies these daughters as female Moabites. But the word *daughters* in the Bible can also refer to the small villages that surround a larger town (Num 21:25, 32; Josh 15:45; Judg 11:26), and given that the oracle contains several references to Moabite cities (Ar, Kir, Dibon, and many more), it is possible that *daughters* in Isa 16:2 is to be understood as a geographical term.

Another interpretive problem concerns the words spoken by the "daughters of Moab" subsequent to Isa 16:2. Commentators generally agree that v. 3 and the first half of v. 4, which contain a plea for refuge, form an address by the Moabite daughters to Judah and Jerusalem. But the second half of v. 4 and v. 5, which contain a promise that when the catastrophe is past, a righteous king shall rule "in the tent of David," are less easily understood. Some suggest that the daughters here proclaim that some future king of Moab will maintain a proper (that is, righteous) vassal relationship to the Davidic house in Jerusalem. The passage, however, seems more to identify the righteous king as Judah's own. Yet if this is the case, it is difficult to understand why foreigners would be delivering this eschatological promise.

Perhaps this passage reflects both the traditional enmity between Israel and Moab (for example, Deut 23:3–4) and also their intimate connection, whereby a Moabite woman (Ruth) is the ancestor of King David and Moab's father, Lot, is Abraham's nephew (Gen 19:30–38).

SUSAN ACKERMAN

SEE ALSO Part III: Daughter; Mother/Daughter as Territory.

FOR FURTHER READING: Kaiser, Otto. *Isaiah 13–39: A Commentary.*

Miller, J. Maxwell. "Moab."

ISA 19:16
Trembling Women

The idea of trembling as a manifestation of fear, particularly as part of female behavior, is used in Isaiah's oracle against the Egyptians (Isaiah 19). The prophet proclaims (v. 16) that when YHWH turns against the Egyptians, they will "be like women, and tremble with fear before . . . the LORD."

SUSAN ACKERMAN

SEE ALSO Part II: Women in Labor (Isa 13:8, etc.).

ISA 21:3   Woman in Labor
SEE ISA 13:8, etc.   Woman in Labor (Part II).

ISA 23:4
Young Women (and Men) of Sidon

In the oracle in Isaiah 23 against Tyre and Sidon, Phoenician cities on the coast north of ancient Israel, Sidon is negatively personified as a barren mother, having neither reared young men nor brought up young women. This is an allusion to the city's depopulation in time of war.

SUSAN ACKERMAN

SEE ALSO Part III: Daughter; Woman Jerusalem/Zion in Isaiah; Women Sidon and Tyre.

ISA 23:4   Woman Sidon
SEE Women Sidon and Tyre (Part III).

ISA 23:10
Daughter (NRSV, Ships of) Tarshish
SEE Daughter (Part III).

ISA 23:12   Daughter Sidon
SEE Daughter (Part III).

ISA 23:15–18   Woman Tyre
SEE Women Sidon and Tyre (Part III).

ISA 24:2
Maid, Mistress

Amid threats of apocalyptic destruction, Isa 24:2 describes how all classes in society will be brought low. The passage lists various people and professions in pairs of opposites, including the maid along with her mistress, the servant along with his master, the buyer along with the seller, and so on. The passage implies, however, that in times other than those of apocalyptic chaos, such social distinctions are perfectly acceptable.

SUSAN ACKERMAN

SEE ALSO Part II: Mistress (Ps 123:2); Maid, Mistress (Prov 30:23).

ISA 26:17–18   Woman in Labor
SEE ISA 13:8, etc.   Woman in Labor (Part II).

ISA 27:11
Women Making a Fire

The cosmic eschatological judgment depicted in Isaiah 24–27 concludes with the image of fortified cities reverting to their pre-urban rural state. Vegetation will grow (where buildings once stood), and animals will graze there. In the final scenario, before the prophet concludes this section on the divine judgment of wayward Israelites, women gather wood and build a fire.

Isaiah's reference to this activity, performed by women, probably reflects one of the subsistence tasks generally carried out by females, perhaps aided by children, rather than by males in the division of labor by gender in ancient Israel. Because building a fire in the courtyard oven was an integral part of the series of processes involved in converting grain to bread, as well as the preparation of other foods, it was natural for the prophet to use women to depict this aspect of the demise of normal life.

CAROL MEYERS

SEE ALSO Part II: Women as Bread Bakers (Lev 26:26); Daughters as Perfumers, Cooks, and Bakers (1 Sam 8:13); Women Who Grind (Eccl 12:3).

ISA 32:9–11
Complacent Women/Daughters
SEE ISA 3:16–26, etc.   Daughters of Zion (Part II).

ISA 37:22   Daughter Jerusalem/Zion
SEE Daughter (Part III).

ISA 40:9   Herald
SEE Ps 68:11, etc.   Those Who Bear Tidings; Herald (Part II).

ISA 42:14   God as a Woman in Labor
SEE Female Images of God in the Hebrew Bible (Part III).

ISA 45:10   Woman in Labor
SEE ISA 13:8, etc.   Woman in Labor (Part II).

ISA 45:10–11; 46:3–4   God as a Mother
SEE Female Images of God in the Hebrew Bible (Part III).

ISA 47:1, 5
Daughter Babylon/Chaldea
SEE Daughter (Part III).

ISA 47:5–7   Mistress Babylon
SEE Mistress Babylon (Part III).

ISA 47:8   Widow
SEE EXOD 22:22, etc.   Widows (Part II).

ISA 49:1, 5
Mother of the Servant

In the second servant song of Isaiah, the "servant," who is the poem's subject, speaks of being called to God's service while still in the womb. The identity of the servant is debated. Sometimes, it seems that the term refers to the prophet, in which case this verse should be compared to Jeremiah's commission *in utero* described in Jer 1:5. Yet at other points, the servant seems to be understood as the entire nation of Israel. If this is the case here, perhaps the "mother" should be identified as Jerusalem, who is also described as the Israelite people's mother in Isa 51:17–18, 54:1–10, and 66:7–13.

Yet whomever the mother represents, it is clear from Isa 49:1 that YHWH names the child. Since often in the Hebrew Bible, it is a child's mother who names him or her, YHWH's role as namer here suggests the presence of female imagery in this poem's conception of God. Because there are several examples, though, of a father naming his child, no definitive analysis can be secured.

SUSAN ACKERMAN

SEE ALSO Part II: Mother of Jeremiah (Jer 1:5, etc.); Part III: Female Images of God in the Hebrew Bible; Woman Jerusalem/Zion in Isaiah.

ISA 49:15, 23
Nursing Mothers

In Isaiah 49, the sixth-century B.C.E. prophet uses the image of nursing mothers in two different ways. In v. 15, he uses it to depict god as exhibiting maternal characteristics; in v. 23, it portrays the reversal of Israel's political fortunes.

In Isa 49:15 the prophet asks rhetorically whether

a woman could possibly abandon either a child she had carried in her womb or a child she had breast-fed. The assumption behind the question is the fact that carrying a child in the womb or breast-feeding often leads to a very close attachment, called "bonding," between mother and child. This bonding makes it unlikely that she will abandon the child. Speaking in the name of God, the prophet declares that God, in the role of Mother of Israel, will not forget Israel.

In Isa 49:22–23 the prophet promises Israel, personified as a mother, that God will restore to her her rightful inhabitants, the Israelites, who had been exiled in 586 B.C.E. by the Babylonians. Thus the political order will be subverted: the conquerors of Israel will become the servants of Israel. This reversal is depicted in God's announcement that kings will become male child-care providers and queens will become wet nurses. This classic example of gender-matched parallelism suggests that, as in modern egalitarian families, child care is a responsibility shared by males and females; women perform the biological function of lactation, and men take on nonbiologically determined tasks such as diaper changing (said to have been performed by God the adoptive father in Ezek 16:6–8). Throughout the Hebrew Bible a distinction is maintained between *mêneqet*, "wet nurse" and *'ōmenet*, "female deliverer of child care (in general)." The latter is the feminine counterpart of the noun *'omēn*, "male deliverer of child care," attested in Isa 49:23.

MAYER I. GRUBER

SEE ALSO Part II: Hebrew Women in Egypt (Exod 1:19, etc.); Nurse (Num 11:12); Nurse of Mephibosheth (2 Sam 4:4); Part III: Female Images of God in the Hebrew Bible.

FOR FURTHER READING: Forster, Brenda. "The Biblical *'Omēn* and Evidence for the Nurturance of Children by Hebrew Males."

Gruber, Mayer I. "Breast-Feeding Practices in Biblical Israel and in Old Babylonian Mesopotamia."

ISA 49:15   God as Mother

SEE Female Images of God in the Hebrew Bible (Part III).

ISA 49:18   Jerusalem/Zion as a Bride

SEE Woman Jerusalem/Zion in Isaiah (Part III).

ISA 49:22; 56:5
Daughters (and Sons)

In Isa 49:22–23, which dates to the sixth century B.C.E., the prophet envisions the homecoming the Israelites will enjoy when the Babylonian exile, under which they currently suffer, comes to an end. The oracle is addressed to Jerusalem, who is personified here as the mother of her people, and it promises the city that YHWH will cause her daughters and sons to be brought back by the inhabitants of the nations in which the exiled Israelites dwell, borne in these foreigners' bosoms and carried upon their shoulders. Although the nations are pictured in the role of benevolent foster parents to the Israelites in this text, they are nevertheless viewed as inferiors of the people's real mother, Jerusalem, to whom it is said they will bow down and lick the dust off her feet. Isa 56:1–8, however, embraces foreigners and also eunuchs as full equals within the Israel of the future, so welcome that they will be given a monument and a name "better than sons and daughters" (56:5), who are otherwise envisioned here as the most precious things humans could want.

SUSAN ACKERMAN

SEE ALSO Part II: Daughters of Zion (Isa 3:16–26, etc.); Daughters (and Sons) (Jer 3:24, etc.); Part III: Woman Jerusalem/Zion in Isaiah.

ISA 49:23
Queens

The sixth-century B.C.E. prophet Second Isaiah (chaps. 40–55) envisions all peoples coming to Jerusalem (Zion) and acknowledging YHWH as their God. So integrated with Israel will those foreigners become that their royalty — "kings . . . and their queens" — will become like parents to Israel's children; the kings will be child-care providers (not "foster fathers," as the NRSV has it) and the queens, wet nurses. At the same time, this vision indicates social leveling, with the highest-status foreigners (royalty) taking on everyday marital parenting tasks and thereby becoming subservient to Zion.

CAROL MEYERS

SEE ALSO Part II: Nursing Mothers (Isa 49:15, etc.).

ISA 49:23   Nursing Mothers
SEE ISA 49:15, etc. Nursing Mothers (Part II).

ISA 50:1   Divorced Mother
SEE DEUT 24:1–4, etc. Woman Being Divorced (Part II).

ISA 51:17–52:2
Woman Jerusalem/Zion
SEE Woman Jerusalem/Zion in Isaiah (Part III).

ISA 52:2   Daughter Jerusalem/Zion
SEE Daughter (Part III).

ISA 54:1   Barren Woman
SEE EXOD 23:26, etc. Barren Woman (Part II).

ISA 54:1–10   Woman Jerusalem/Zion
SEE Woman Jerusalem/Zion in Isaiah (Part III).

ISA 54:4   Widowhood
SEE EXOD 22:22, etc. Widows (Part II).

ISA 56:5   Daughters
SEE ISA 49:22, etc. Daughters (and Sons) (Part II).

ISA 57:3   Sorceress
SEE EXOD 22:18, etc. Female Sorcerer (Part II).

ISA 57:3–13
Jerusalem/Zion as Prostitute
SEE Woman Jerusalem/Zion in Isaiah (Part III).

ISA 61:10
Bride (and Bridegroom)

Marital imagery in the Book of Isaiah typically presents Jerusalem (or Zion) as the bride or spouse of YHWH. In one passage, however, the prophet compares himself to both bride and bridegroom. In 61:10, the beautiful adornments of a newlywed couple represent the clothing — garments of righteousness and salvation — worn by the prophet as he gives himself over to exultation in God.

SUSAN ACKERMAN

SEE ALSO Part II: Bride (and Bridegroom) (Jer 2:2, etc.); Part III: Woman Jerusalem/Zion in Isaiah.

ISA 62:4–5   Woman Jerusalem/Zion
SEE Woman Jerusalem/Zion in Isaiah (Part III).

ISA 62:11   Daughter Zion
SEE Daughter (Part III).

ISA 66:7–9   Woman in Labor
SEE ISA 13:8, etc. Woman in Labor (Part II).

ISA 66:7–9, 12–13
God as Midwife and Mother
SEE Female Images of God in the Hebrew Bible (Part III).

ISA 66:7–13
Woman Jerusalem/Zion
SEE Woman Jerusalem/Zion in Isaiah (Part III).

JER 1:5; 15:10; 20:14, 17, 18
Mother of Jeremiah

Jeremiah's role as a prophet is one of great personal agony for him in two respects: he feels called by God to condemn his own family and compatriots for their disobedience to YHWH and the covenant, and these very people to whom he brings God's message in turn call him a traitor and seek his life. It is no wonder that Jeremiah wishes that he were not alive to carry out such a painful mission. He gives voice to his predicament by reversing traditional birth imagery; his mother's womb represents sorrow, not joy.

Jeremiah's designation as a spokesperson for God comes before he was born (formed in the womb; 1:5), and his anguish at being alive (coming forth from the womb; 20:18) is expressed in the desire never to have been born at all (15:10). Thus his day of birth is considered one of curses, not of blessings (20:14), and the person who announced his birth should have killed him at that moment so that his mother's womb would have been his grave — his place of death rather than life (20:17).

CAROL MEYERS
SEE ALSO Mother of the Servant (Isa 49:1, etc.).

JER 2:2, 20, 23–28, 32–37
Women in Imagery for Jerusalem
SEE Women in Imagery for Jerusalem, Judah, and Israel in Jeremiah (Part III).

JER 2:2, 32; 7:34; 16:9; 25:10; 33:11
Bride (and Bridegroom)

The sixth-century B.C.E. prophet Jeremiah, who foresees and then witnesses the destruction of Jerusalem and Judah, provides many accounts of the horrible devastation of the land. In addition to the awful prospect of corpses strewn about and cities in ruin is the sense of what will be missing. The poignant image of the absence of joy in the voices of a bride and bridegroom epitomizes the grave tragedy of the end of the Southern Kingdom. Jeremiah

uses the bride-bridegroom pair four times: three times to bemoan the absence of marital joy (7:34; 16:9; 25:10) and once to herald its expected return (33:11). The word *bridegroom* precedes *bride* in all these instances (although the NRSV inexplicably puts *bride* first in 7:34). In addition, he twice uses the image of the bride alone: once to convey Jerusalem's love for YHWH (2:2), and once in reference to her essential wedding garments (2:32).

The words for "bride" *(kallâ)* and "bridegroom" *(ḥātān)* regularly appear together in the Hebrew Bible, but never in reference to specific persons. Rather, the terms are a stereotyped pair that together indicate great human joy; in Jeremiah they always are found together with the words *mirth* and *gladness*. Marriage in ancient Israel, as elsewhere in the ancient Near East, was probably a contractual arrangement, with parents selecting spouses for their offspring. Yet the element of joyful celebration was clearly present too. The idea of a newlywed couple also connotes the hopefulness of marital fecundity, making bride and bridegroom apt metaphors, in Jeremiah, for communal life and death.

CAROL MEYERS
SEE ALSO Part II: Bride (and Bridegroom) (Isa 61:10); (Joel 2:16); Wife of One's Youth (Mal 2: 14–16).

JER 3:1, 20; 6:11–12; 14:16; 15:8; 16:2; 18:21; 29:6, 23; 35:8; 44:9
Wife/Wives

During a time of crisis, invasion, war, and impending exile, as depicted in the Book of Jeremiah, women play significant roles in the community and in their families. In the latter context, women as wives are prominent. They are depicted negatively, as part of the community of Judeans that is sinful and that God will punish. They are also treated sympathetically, as those who suffer from destruction and exile at the hand of the Babylonians in 586 B.C.E. Finally, they appear positively as the prophet envisions survival and restoration.

Jerusalem's apostasy, in 3:20, is compared to that of a "faithless wife." In an indictment of two false prophets (Zedekiah and Ahab) in 29:23, Jeremiah places adultery with others' wives among the outrages for which they are condemned. The crimes of the wives of the kings and of all Judean wives are condemned, along with those of their husbands, in the stinging rhetorical question of 44:9. Perhaps the most disturbing image is that of the divorced wife in 3:1. The woman who has been divorced (literally, "sent out") remarries; in so doing she represents God's people, who have wed themselves to other gods. But should she want to go back to her first husband, he wouldn't take her — she would be "polluted." Even such awful pollution, represented by the notion of a woman having lain with another man, would not, however, prevent God from ultimately taking Israel back (4:1–2).

The devastation that must occur before God reclaims Israel involves death for many. In 14:16 wives (along with men and children) die by the sword or from starvation. Many become widowed (15:8 and 18:21); and many others are taken captive with their husbands or are given to other men (6:11–12). The death, deportation, and disruption awaiting virtually all wives is poignantly signified by God's command to Jeremiah not to take a wife at all (16:2). Defying custom, whereby it was unthinkable not to marry, Jeremiah's single (and childless) status will be a symbolic action, representing the way in which the people will soon be punished with the disruption of their normal lives and perhaps even their survival.

Ultimately, however, the prophet envisions restoration. Because eventually they will be returned to the land, he encourages all those exiled to Babylon by Nebuchadnezzer to live normal lives there. To do so, they should all take wives for themselves and their sons (29:6). The model for future righteous behavior of God's people should be the Rechabites, a tent-dwelling ascetic group; the resolute obedience of all Rechabites, wives and children included (35:8), exemplifies the way all the people should obey God.

ANGELA BAUER

SEE ALSO Part II: Daughters (and Sons) (Jer 3:24, etc.);
    Women Worshipping the Queen of Heaven (Jer 7:18, etc.); Mothers (and Fathers) (Jer 15:8–9, etc.).

FOR FURTHER READING: Bauer, Angela. *Gender in the Book of Jeremiah: A Feminist Literary Reading.*

JER 3:1–3, 6–10, 30–31
Women in Imagery for Jerusalem, Judah, and Israel
SEE Women in Imagery for Jerusalem, Judah, and Israel in Jeremiah (Part III).

JER 3:7–10   Sister Judah
SEE Sister Judah (Part III).

JER 3:20   Wife
SEE JER 3:1, etc.   Wife/Wives (Part II).

JER 3:24; 5:17; 11:22; 14:16; 16:2–3; 29:6; 35:8; 48:46
Daughters (and Sons)

The sixth-century B.C.E. prophet Jeremiah depicts the people of Judah and Jerusalem before, during, and after they are conquered by the Babylonians in 586 B.C.E. In so doing he refers to various components of the population: women, men, and children. Although women and men are prominent among those indicted for sins as well as those who suffer at the hands of the Babylonians and are later to be restored, children — daughters and sons — appear not as sinners but only as victims of war and then as part of the future hope.

The death of daughters and sons is twice paired with the devastation of fields and herds (3:24; 5:17), indicating the loss of the biological progeny as well as the agricultural sustenance that together represent the future. In other passages, several unrighteous groups are singled out as ones that will suffer the loss of daughters and sons: the people of Anathoth, who have persecuted Jeremiah (11:22); Jerusalemites who have been duped by false prophets (14:16); and even a foreign people, the Moabites (48:46).

This tragic picture of the loss of children and thus of a future has its opposite in Jeremiah, mainly in the image of bride and bridegroom and the fecundity they represent. Indeed, children themselves are mentioned as part of the future. In 29:6, the people who have been exiled to Babylon are encouraged to marry and to have their daughters and sons marry so that all will have daughters and sons. The exiles will thereby "multiply" and ultimately be restored to their land. Children also are part of the model of righteous behavior provided by the Rehabites, an ascetic, tent-dwelling group (35:8); the daughters and sons, as well as the wives, of the Rehabites keep their vows and exemplify how all people should obey God.

ANGELA BAUER

SEE ALSO Part II: Mothers (and Fathers) Cannibalizing Their Daughters (and Sons) (Lev 26:29, etc.); Bride (and Bridegroom) (Jer 2:2, etc.); Mothers (and Fathers) (Jer 15:8–9, etc.).

JER 4:31; 6:24; 13:21; 22:23; 30:6; 31:8; 48:41; 49:22, 24; 50:43

Woman in Labor

The sixth-century B.C.E. prophet Jeremiah, in agony because he foresees and then witnesses the destruction of his country and because he feels compelled to announce its doom, rues the day of his own birth (Jer 20:17–18). It is no wonder that the image of a woman in labor figures prominently in his prophecies. In several places the impending suffering of the people about to be destroyed (Jer 6:24) and their rulers (Jer 13:21) is compared to the experience of a woman in labor.

Perhaps because in biblical Hebrew the words for "city" and "country" are feminine, cities and states tend to be personified as women. Personified Jerusalem (Jer 4:31), about to be destroyed, is depicted as crying out in anguish, like a woman in labor with her first child. Jerusalem's reliance on deities other than its own God is likened to a woman committing adultery, and the pain in the guts of personified Israel (or Jerusalem) at the ill fate of her metaphoric lovers is compared to the uterine contractions of a woman in labor (Jer 22:20–23). Similarly, in Jer 48:41, the defeat of Moab will mean that her military leaders will experience abdominal pains comparable to uterine contractions, as also will the Edomite warriors (Jer 49:22). The reaction of the personified Aramean city-state of Damascus to impending devastation is like that of a woman in labor (Jer 49:24). In Jeremiah 50, the prophet consoles the exiled Judeans by announcing that the Babylonians, instrument of God's punishment of Judah, will themselves be punished. Their king will be in anguish: he will experience abdominal pains like those of a woman in labor (50:43).

In all of these passages, the less familiar, less frequent, and not universal experience of abdominal pain resulting from anxiety and stress is compared to the uterine contractions during labor of a significant portion of all adult females. The inevitability, as well as the anguish, becomes attached to the fate of Israel/Jerusalem and then of her enemies.

A somewhat different use of the image of a woman in labor appears in Jer 31:8. There, a pregnant woman and a woman in labor appear, along with the blind and the lame, among those exiled Israelites to be returned to their homeland. This prophecy of consolation points out that even those with some physical limitation, whether temporary or chronic, will be able to make the trek safely because god will lead them.

MAYER I. GRUBER

SEE ALSO Part II: Woman in Labor (Isa 13:8, etc.); Part III: Woman Jerusalem/Zion in Isaiah.

FOR FURTHER READING: Bauer, Angela. *Gender in the Book of Jeremiah: A Feminist Leterary Reading.*

JER 4:31   Daughter Zion
SEE Daughter (Part III).

JER 5:7   Prostitutes
SEE Lev 19:29, etc.   Prostitute (Part II).

JER 5:7–9
Women in Imagery for Jerusalem
SEE Women in Imagery for Jerusalem, Judah, and Israel in Jeremiah (Part III).

JER 5:17   Daughters
See Jer 3:24, etc.   Daughters (and Sons) (Part II).

JER 6:2, 23   Daughter Zion
See Daughter (Part III).

JER 6:11–12   Wife/Wives
See Jer 3:1, etc.   Wife/Wives (Part II).

JER 6:24   Woman in Labor
See Jer 4:31, etc.   Woman in Labor (Part III).

JER 7:6   Widow
See Exod 22:22, etc.   Widows (Part II).

JER 7:18; 44:15–19, 25
Women Worshipping the Queen of Heaven

Judean women are condemned by the seventh- and sixth-century B.C.E. prophet Jeremiah in Jer 7:18 for making offering cakes for a goddess called the queen of heaven. Elsewhere (Jer 44:19), Jeremiah condemns a second group of Judean women for making cakes for the queen. Although Jeremiah indicates that the queen of heaven was also worshipped by men, children, and even the "kings" and "officials" in Jerusalem (Jer 44:17), the special stress on women as the makers of the queen's cakes, as well as their role in pouring out libations and offering incense to the goddess (Jer 44:15, 19, 25), probably indicates that the queen's cult was particularly appealing to females. Given, moreover, that women were generally excluded from official or public religion, we should probably see the cult of the queen of heaven as an example of domestic or household-centered religion and note in this regard the important, if not leading, role women could play in this more private form of worship.

SUSAN ACKERMAN

See also Part II: Women as Bread Bakers (Lev 26:26); Daughters as Perfumers, Cooks, and Bakers (1 Sam 8:13); Women Who Went to Egypt (Jer 43:6, etc.); Women Weeping for Tammuz (Ezek 8:14); Part III: Queen of Heaven.
For further reading: Ackerman, Susan. "'And the Women Knead Dough': The Worship of the Queen of Heaven in Sixth-Century Judah."
Bird, Phyllis. "The Place of Women in the Israelite Cultus."

JER 7:18   Queen of Heaven
See Queen of Heaven (Part III).

JER 7:31
Daughters Passed Through Fire
See Deut 12:31, etc.   Daughter (or Son or Child) Passed Through Fire, Burned, or Sacrificed (Part II).

JER 7:34   Bride
See Jer 2:2, etc.   Bride (and Bridegroom) (Part II).

JER 9:17–20; EZEK 32:16
Mourning Women

A major theme of the prophet Jeremiah is that God's people will be destroyed because of their apostasy. Images of destruction and the demise of their nation-state abound. One extended passage (Jer 9:17–20) portrays the sequel to death and destruction, namely, lamenting the dead nation. Specifically, the prophet solicits the services of professional mourners, women who are "skilled" (v. 17). The use of this term, which can denote a specialized craft or profession, indicates that women who knew or could compose appropriate laments and dirges were considered trained experts. In fact, such women were probably organized in loose association or guilds in order to maintain their specialty.

A glimpse of the function of guilds of women mourners appears in Jeremiah's exhortation to

A limestone coffin used for Ahiram, a king of Byblos (on the coast of Lebanon) in the early tenth century B.C.E. The relief on the end panel depicts four women making typical mourning gestures: two beating their breasts, two tearing their hair. Professional mourners in the biblical world were usually women. See Weeping Daughters (2 Sam 1:24); Singing Women (and Men) Who Lament (2 Chr 35:25); Mourning Women (Jer 9:17–22, etc.); Grieving Girls (Lam 1:4, etc.).

them to compose, with divine inspiration, songs of grief: "teach to your daughters a dirge, and each to her neighbor a lament" (v. 20). The words *daughter* and *neighbor* are probably not meant literally, but probably refer to members of groups of women that gathered to develop and transmit Israelite mourning culture. The words *daughters*, (as in "daughters of song," Eccl 12:4) and *sons* (as in "sons of prophets"; in NRSV, "company of prophets," 2 Kgs 2:3, 5, 7, 15) sometimes designate members of a professional guild — the experts and their disciples. The term *neighbors* similarly represents colleagues in a group that serves a specific social function.

In considering biblical references to mourning behaviors, the distinction between outpouring of grief and organized funeral practices should be kept in mind. Virtually all people experience the need to express the loss of loved ones, and the Bible frequently refers to the cries of despair of both women

and men, young and old. But the chanting of laments, although apparently practiced by some men, was largely a woman's profession. Cross-cultural studies show that in many societies women are the traditional experts in mourning rituals and in the recitation of dirges selected from an established and extensive repertoire. It is not surprising, therefore, that a passage in Ezekiel indicates an awareness of mourning expertise as a female role among non-Israelite peoples: the prophet calls upon the "daughters [NRSV, women] of the nations" to lament over fallen Egypt (32:16).

Associations of mourning women were one of several such groups organized for professional purposes in ancient Israel. Like the women in song-drum-dance ensembles and the female singers, the mourning women were performers. Their role in society as well as their interaction with one another in practice sessions and in performance events offered them the opportunity to experience leadership, female solidarity, and the status that comes from carrying out an activity involving specialized expertise. Furthermore, some of their laments may be preserved in the Book of Lamentations, in the two verses in Jeremiah (9:21–22) that follow the prophet's summoning of mourning women, and also in other laments usually attributed to men.

CAROL MEYERS

SEE ALSO Part II: Women with Hand-Drums, Dancing (Exod 15:20, etc.); Weeping Daughters (2 Sam 1:24); Singing Women (and Men) (2 Sam 19:35, etc.); Singing Women (and Men) Who Lament (2 Chr 35:25); Grieving Girls (Lam 1:4, etc.).

FOR FURTHER READING: Goitein, S.D. "Women as Creators of Biblical Genres."

Meyers, Carol. "Guilds and Gatherings: Women's Groups in Ancient Israel."

JER 11:15
Women in Imagery for Jerusalem and Judah

SEE Women in Imagery for Jerusalem, Judah, and Israel in Jeremiah (Part III).

JER 11:22   Daughters
> SEE JER 3:24, etc.   Daughters (and Sons) (Part II).

JER 12:7; 13:20–27
Women in Imagery for Jerusalem, Judah, and Israel
> SEE Women in Imagery for Jerusalem, Judah, and Israel in Jeremiah (Part III).

JER 13:21   Woman in Labor
> SEE Jer 4:31, etc.   Woman in Labor (Part II).

JER 14:16   Wife/Wives
> SEE JER 3:1, etc.   Wife/Wives (Part II).

JER 14:16   Daughters
> SEE JER 3:24, etc.   Daughters (and Sons) (Part II).

JER 14:17   Daughter
> SEE Daughter (Part III).

JER 15:8   Widows
> SEE EXOD 22:22, etc.   Widows; Jer 3:1, etc. Wife/Wives (Part II).

JER 15:10   Mother of Jeremiah
> SEE JER 1:5, etc.   Mother of Jeremiah (Part II).

JER 15:8–9; 16:3–4, 7
Mothers (and Fathers)

The image of mothers experiencing the ravages of war is part of the indictment of the people for their sins and the anticipation of destruction found in the oracles of the sixth-century B.C.E. prophet Jeremiah. In a passage depicting the terror and shame experienced by a mother who loses her children (15:8–9), the phrase "she who bore seven" is used to denote a suffering mother, with the number seven, symbolizing totality or completeness, perhaps indicating a "perfect mother" who will nonetheless succumb to the impending tragedy. (This image may be the basis for the figure of the martyred mother of seven sons in 2 and 4 Maccabees.)

When Jeremiah is commanded by God to remain single, the explanation for this highly unusual and symbolic act is that if he married, he would have children; he would then experience the anguish of all the mothers and fathers who will witness their children die by disease, war, and starvation (16:3–4). To intensify this calamity, the dead children would not be buried, nor would there be anyone to help the bereft mothers and fathers mourn their losses (16:7).

ANGELA BAUER

SEE ALSO Part II: Mothers (and Fathers) Cannibalizing Their Daughters (and Sons) (Lev 26:29, etc.); Mother of Jeremiah (Jer 1:5, etc.); Wife/Wives (Jer 3:1, etc.); Daughters (and Sons) (Jer 3:24, etc.).

JER 16:2   Wife
> SEE JER 3:1, etc.   Wife/Wives (Part II).

JER 16:2–3   Daughters
> SEE JER 3:24, etc.   Daughters (and Sons) (Part II).

JER 16:3–4, 7   Mothers
> SEE JER 15:8–9, etc.   Mothers (and Fathers) (Part II).

JER 16:9   Bride
> SEE JER 2:2–32, etc.   Bride (and Bridegroom) (Part II).

JER 18:13
Israel as a Maiden (NRSV, Virgin)
> SEE Daughter (Part III).

JER 18:21   Wife/Wives
> SEE JER 3:1, etc.   Wife/Wives (Part II).

JER 20:14, 17–18   Mother of Jeremiah
> SEE JER 1:5, etc.   Mother of Jeremiah (Part II).

Jer 22:18
Sister

Among the prophet Jeremiah's indictments of several kings of Judah is a particularly seething oracle against Jehoiakim (reigned 608–598 B.C.E.). The ultimate ignominious fate awaits him: denial of a proper burial and its attendant mourning ritual. The latter is represented by quotations of actual funeral laments, examples of what will *not* be said at the king's demise. These laments include the apostrophes "Alas, my brother!" and "Alas, sister!" (22:18). The use of "brother" alone might be taken to mean a cry of pain to a deceased man by a mourner (as 1 Kgs 13:30). The presence of both "sister" and "brother," however, probably indicates that the two words together were used in a broader sense to signify the company of mourners, both female and male.

CAROL MEYERS

SEE ALSO Part II: Singing Women (and Men) Who Lament (2 Chr 35:25); Mourning Women (Jer 9:17–20, etc.).

JER 22:23   Woman in Labor
SEE JER 4:31, etc.   Woman in Labor (Part II).

JER 22:26–28, 29:2   Mother of Coniah/Jeconiah (Jehoiacin)
SEE Nehushta (Part I).

JER 25:10   Bride
SEE JER 2:2, etc.   Bride (and Bridegroom) (Part II).

JER 29:6   Daughters
SEE JER 3:24, etc.   Daughters (and Sons) (Part II).

JER 29:6, 23   Wives
SEE JER 3:1, etc.   Wife/Wives (Part II).

JER 30:6   Woman in Labor
SEE JER 4:31, etc.   Woman in Labor (Part II).

JER 31:4, 13
Young Women/Israel with Hand-Drums, Dancing
SEE EXOD 15:20, etc.   Women with Hand-Drums, Dancing (Part II).

JER 31:4, 21–22   Virgin/Maiden Israel
SEE Daughter (Part III).

JER 31:8   Women in Labor
SEE JER 4:31, etc.   Woman in Labor (Part II).

JER 31:22
Woman Encompassing a Man

Located in the eschatological chapters of Jeremiah (30–33), Jer 31:22 is part of the enigmatic climax of a salvation oracle proclaiming a new creation, in which "a woman encompasses a man" (31:22b). Three Hebrew words (*nĕqēbâ*, "female"; *tĕsôbēb*, "surrounding"; and *geber*, "warrior male") connote the parameters of this divinely created "new thing" (31:22a). As the crowning expression of newness after destruction and exile, Jeremiah proclaims a turning upside down of gender relations.

The verse's meaning is considered problematic and has elicited many explanations. Traditional interpretations fall into three main categories: (1) notions of protection, whereby woman protects man, and thus the whole community, from enemies in a peaceful time (Septuagint, RSV, NIV); (2) notions of procreation with somehow transformed involvement of women (NIV, NRSV); and (3) versions of mutation in which woman becomes man (NEB).

Some feminist biblical scholars suggest that the passage indicates new roles for women in a peaceful society, with active involvement in procreation or possible role reversals. Others suggest innerbiblical meanings of the passage's womblike structure.

ANGELA BAUER

SEE ALSO Part II: Woman (and Man) in the First Creation Story (Gen 1:26–28, etc.); Women (and Girls) in Babylon (Jer 50:37, etc.).

FOR FURTHER READING: Bozak, Barbara A. *Life 'Anew': A Literary-Theological Study of Jer. 30–31.*

O'Connor, Kathleen M. "Jeremiah."

Trible, Phyllis. "Journey of a Metaphor."

JER 32:35
Daughters Sacrificed to Moloch

SEE DEUT 12:31, etc. Daughter (or Son or Child) Passed Through Fire, Burned, or Sacrificed (Part II).

JER 33:11   Bride

SEE JER 2:2, etc. Bride (and Bridegroom) (Part II).

JER 34:8–16   Female Hebrew Slaves

SEE EXOD 21:7–11, etc. Female (and Male) Hebrew Slaves (Part II).

JER 35:8   Wife/Wives

SEE JER 3:1, etc. Wife/Wives (Part II).

JER 35:8   Daughters

SEE JER 3:24, etc. Daughters (and Sons) (Part II).

JER 38:22–23; 41:10, 16; 43:6–7
Women (Wives and Daughters) in Zedekiah's Court

In a vision report to Zedekiah, last king of Judah (reigned 596–586 B.C.E.), Jeremiah warns that "all the women" in his house (Jer 38:22–23) will be taken hostage if Zedekiah does not surrender to the Babylonians. After Jerusalem's fall (587–586 B.C.E.), the "king's daughters" are held briefly at Mizpah (Jer 41:10), just north of Jerusalem, after which they

are taken to Tahpanhes in Egypt (41:16; 43:6–7). In contrast, his sons apparently are slaughtered (2 Kgs 25:7). Although Jer 43:7 is the last unambiguous reference to these royal women, Jeremiah 44–45 contains references to Judeans in Egypt, including at Tahpanhes, and to wives (see especially the description of women's worship practices in Jer 44:15–19). Other narratives of Jerusalem's fall (2 Kgs 24:18–25:30; 2 Chr 36:15–21; Jeremiah 52) are silent concerning the fate of these royal women.

LINDA S. SCHEARING

SEE ALSO Part II: Young Women (and Men) Slaughtered (2 Chr 36:17); Women Worshipping the Queen of Heaven (Jer 7:18, etc.); Women Who Went to Egypt (Jer 43:6, etc.); Part III: Queen of Heaven.

JER 40:7
Women (and Men) Remaining in the Land

The books of Jeremiah and of 2 Kings both report that, when the Babylonians conquered Judah and Jerusalem in 586 B.C.E., they carried the leaders and most of the people into exile in Babylon. However, in order to maintain a minimal level of agricultural productivity, the poorest people of the land were allowed to remain (2 Kgs 25:12; Jer 39:10; 40:7). Of these three verses mentioning that poor people remained in the land, only Jer 40:7 specifies who they were: "men, women, and children." Because the poor people are expected to keep the vineyards and till the soil, the role of women as well as children in the agrarian economy is indicated.

CAROL MEYERS

SEE ALSO Part I: Eve.

FOR FURTHER READING: Meyers, Carol. "Everyday Life: Women in the Period of the Hebrew Bible."

JER 41:10, 16
Women (Wives and Daughters) in Zedekiah's Court

SEE JER 38:22–23, etc. Women (Wives and Daughters) in Zedekiah's Court (Part II).

JER 43:6; 44:7, 15, 24–25
Women Who Went to Egypt

Women are specified (Jer 43:6) among the people of Judah who sought refuge in Egypt in the aftermath of the destruction of Jerusalem and its temple in 586 B.C.E. (see Jeremiah 41–43). The prophet Jeremiah, in Egypt, accuses the refugees of idolatrous practices. He holds that such practices by their ancestors (including leaders) were responsible for the destruction and claims that they will again destroy those who fled to Egypt. Far from repenting, the people, especially women, challenge Jeremiah's theology with a countertheology and a different interpretation of history. Their response exposes a crucial biblical conflict between the exclusive worship of YHWH and the tolerance or advocacy of other gods as well.

Women are spokespersons and actors in this challenge to exclusive Yahwism. Their rationale is grounded in a historical observation: the nation prospered as long as the queen of heaven was worshipped. Evil days arrived in Judah only when such worship was neglected (possibly as a result of the Deuteronomic reforms of 622 B.C.E.). This historical and religious challenge is not easy to refute and Jeremiah offers nothing more than a repetition of earlier threats.

The challenge comes from "all the men who were aware that their wives had been making offering to other gods," and "all the women standing in the [NRSV, who stood by, a] great assembly" (44:15); note that the NRSV makes the women bystanders when in fact they constituted a great assembly. It also came from the women who insist that their men were knowing partners in these practices (44:19). Women's prominence in both the practice of such worship and its defense is emphasized by the quoting of women's statements and also by the use of verbs conjugated in the third-person *feminine* plural for "declared in words" and "in deeds" in Jeremiah's response (44:24–25; NRSV).

This last recorded event in the life of Jeremiah, following the destruction of Jerusalem and its temple, offers a rare representation of *both* sides of a pivotal religious conflict over the interpretation of Israel's crucial events and highlights women's important role in it. The views that the women articulate here lost out to the official position of the final form of the Hebrew Bible, which considers the exclusive YHWH worship as normative. Nevertheless, later Jewish writings from Egypt, such as the Elephantine documents from the fifth century B.C.E., attest to the continuity of some such "inclusive" practices as well as to the continued importance and participation of women in religious and sociopolitical life.

TAMARA COHN ESKENAZI

SEE ALSO Part II: Women Worshipping the Queen of Heaven (Jer 7:18, etc.); Part III: Queen of Heaven.

FOR FURTHER READING: Ackerman, Susan. "'And the Women Knead Dough': The Worship of the Queen of Heaven in Sixth-Century Judah."

Eskenazi, Tamara Cohn. "Ezra-Nehemiah."

JER 43:6–7
Women in Zedekiah's Court
SEE JER 38:22–23, etc.   Women (Wives and Daughters) in Zedekiah's Court (Part II).

JER 44:7, 15, 24–25
Women Who Went to Egypt
SEE JER 43:6, etc.   Women Who Went to Egypt (Part II).

JER 44:9   Wife/Wives
SEE JER 3:1, etc.   Wife/Wives (Part II).

JER 44:15–19, 25
Women Worshipping the Queen of Heaven
SEE JER 7:18, etc.   Women Worshipping the Queen of Heaven (Part II).

JER 44:17–19, 25   Queen of Heaven
SEE   Queen of Heaven (Part III).

JER 46:11, 19, 24   Daughter Egypt
SEE   Daughter (Part III).

JER 48:18   Daughter Dibon
> SEE Daughter (Part III).

JER 48:19
Woman (and Man) of Aroer

The woman of Aroer appears in God's judgment of Moab, part of Jeremiah's oracles against the nation. She represents women trying to escape destruction, fleeing alongside the male inhabitants of Aroer — an Arnon River fortress (modern Khirbet Ara 'ir).

ANGELA BAUER

SEE ALSO Part II: Daughters of Moab (Isa 16:2); Part III: Daughter.

JER 48:41   Woman in Labor
> SEE JER 4:31, etc.   Woman in Labor (Part II).

JER 48:46   Daughters
> SEE JER 3:24, etc.   Daughters (and Sons) (Part II).

JER 49:4   Rabbah as Daughter
> SEE Daughter (Part III).

JER 49:11   Widows
> SEE EXOD 22:22, etc.   Widows (Part II).

JER 49:22, 24   Woman in Labor
> SEE JER 4:31, etc.   Woman in Labor (Part II).

JER 50:37; 51:22, 30
Women and Girls in Babylon

The judgment on Babylon in Jeremiah 50–51, part of the prophet's oracles against the nation during the sixth century B.C.E., includes a threat that Babylon's mercenary troops will become feminized ("become women") as part of Babylon's doom (50:37; 51:30). Also, the description of Babylon's de-

struction depicts the brutal death (by "smashing"; 51:22) of all its inhabitants — women and girls, as well as men and boys.

ANGELA BAUER

SEE ALSO Part II: Woman in Labor (Jer 4:31, etc.).

JER 50:42   Daughter Babylon
> SEE Daughter (Part III).

JER 50:43   Woman in Labor
> SEE JER 4:31, etc.   Woman in Labor (Part II).

JER 51:22, 30
Women and Girls in Babylon
> SEE JER 50:37, etc.   Women and Girls in Babylon (Part II).

JER 51:33   Daughter Babylon
> SEE Daughter (Part III).

LAM 1:1   Widow
> SEE EXOD 22:22, etc.   Widows (Part II).

LAM 1:1   Princess Jerusalem
> SEE Princess Jerusalem (Part III).

LAM 1:4; 2:10
Grieving Girls

Among the many female images in the Book of Lamentations, a series of laments over the loss of Jerusalem and its temple in 586 B.C.E., is that of young women grieving over the devastation wrought by the Babylonians. In one text (1:4), their grief is paired with that of the priests of Jerusalem. In another passage (2:10), they perform traditional mourning rites together with the city's elders; they don sackcloth, put dust on their heads, and bow to the ground (compare Job 2:12–13; Jer 4:8; 6:26; Jonah 3:6). This pairing of young women — the word for these women is *bětûlôt*, which usually denotes female adolescents of marriageable age — with senior male leaders perhaps functions as a merismus (two extremes representing everything in between), indicating the totality of the grief among the survivors.

ANGELA BAUER

SEE ALSO Part II: Mourning Women (Jer 9:17–20, etc.).

LAM 1:6   Daughter Zion
SEE Daughter (Part III).

LAM 1:15   Daughter Judah
SEE Daughter (Part III).

LAM 1:18; 2:21; 3:51
Fallen and Captive Young Women (and Men)

The atrocities of war inflicted upon Jerusalem and its population by the Babylonians in 586 B.C.E. included death for some people and exile for others. These people are poetically represented in several passages in the Book of Lamentations by a gendered pair: young women and young men. In a troublesome passage that presents God as abuser, Zion (Jerusalem), portrayed as a female, concedes to divine punishment, resulting in young women together with young men going into captivity (1:18). Similarly, God's anger results in the death of young women and young men by the sword (in 2:21). In both passages, the young women are mentioned before the young men; and when Zion, surveying the devastation, mourns her losses in a tender scene, the fate of the young women alone is mentioned (3:51).

ANGELA BAUER

SEE ALSO Part II: Raped Women and Virgins (Lam 5:11); Beautiful Young Women (and Young Men) (Amos 8:13); Part III: Daughter.

LAM 2:1, 2, 4–5, 8, 10, 13, 15, 18
Daughter Jerusalem/Zion and Daughter
SEE Daughter (Part III).

LAM 2:10   Young Girls in Mourning
SEE Lam 1:4, etc.   Grieving Girls.

LAM 2:12; 5:3
Mothers and Widows

The family images in the Book of Lamentations include that of mother. The utter hopelessness of the people in the destroyed city of Jerusalem is indicated by the fact that mothers, who are providers of nourishment, can no longer feed their children; and even worse, that their children die from starvation at their dried-up breasts (2:12). Mothers are also bereft of their husbands, for they are compared to widows in the concluding communal lament (5:13), which echoes the opening verse of Lamentations depicting Jerusalem as a widow (1:1).

ANGELA BAUER

SEE ALSO Part II: Mother (and Father) Cannibalizing their Daughters (and Sons) (Lev 26:29, etc.); Grieving Girls (Lam 1:4, etc.).

LAM 2:20
Women Eating Their Children
SEE Lev 26:29, etc.   Mother (and Father) Cannibalizing Their Daughters (and Sons) (Part II).

LAM 2:21; 3:51   Fallen Young Women
SEE Lam 1:18, etc.   Fallen and Captive Young Women (and Men) (Part II).

LAM 4:10
Women Boiling Their Children for Food
SEE Lev 26:29, etc.   Mother (and Father) Cannibalizing Their Daughters (and Sons) (Part II).

LAM 4:21–22   Daughter Edom
SEE Daughter (Part III).

LAM 4:22   Daughter Zion
SEE Daughter (Part III).

LAM 5:3   Widows

SEE EXOD 22:22, etc. Widows (Part II).

LAM 5:3   Mothers and Widows

SEE LAM 2:12, etc. Mothers and Widows (Part II).

LAM 5:11
Raped Women and Virgins

Lam 5:11 is part of a community lament that describes the atrocities committed in Jerusalem and Judah during and following the Babylonian conquest of 587–586 B.C.E. In typical Hebrew poetic form, the second half of the verse extends and strengthens the image portrayed in the first. The parallel verse structure works to say that women, including virgins, are raped throughout the land, emphasizing the widespread nature of this horror. Claiming women as booty was a legal right awarded to victors in the ancient Near East, where this practice may also have served to procure women, whose longevity was markedly less than that of men in biblical antiquity and who were therefore needed as wives. Such conduct was not typically seen as rape. Explicit references to the rape of women in war are thus rare in the Hebrew Bible.

SANDRA L. GRAVETT

SEE ALSO Part II: Ravished Wives of Babylonians (Isa 13:16); Raped Women (Zech 14:2); Part III: Oholah, Woman Samaria.

EZEK 5:5–6, 16
Female Imagery for Jerusalem

SEE Oholibah, Woman/Whore Jerusalem (Part III).

EZEK 8:14
Women Weeping for Tammuz

In chaps. 8–11, the sixth-century B.C.E. prophet Ezekiel recounts a vision in which he is transported to Jerusalem, where he sees four abominations taking place in or near YHWH's temple (8:1–18). Third among these abominations (8:14–15) is the presence of women "weeping for Tammuz" (v. 14). For Ezekiel, this practice, like the other abominable activities, is idolatrous, since the cult's participants venerate a deity other than YHWH.

The Mesopotamian shepherd god Tammuz (Sumerian Dumuzi), husband of the goddess Inanna (Babylonian Ishtar), was originally a Sumerian deity, but also is found in the pantheons of Babylon and Assyria. Tammuz was manifest in nature's fecundity: rising tree sap, the fruits of the date-palm, grains for making bread and beer, the quickening of the fetus in its mother's womb, and breast milk. Most of the materials preserved about him depict his relationship with Inanna/Ishtar; they describe the courtship and marriage of the two deities and then the death of Tammuz. In one version, Inanna proclaims annual lamenting for her beloved deceased husband. Such weeping may be reflected in this passage in Ezekiel.

The cult of Tammuz was especially popular among women who, perhaps at different stages of their lives, cherished Tammuz as a sister loves a brother, a bride her bridegroom, a mother her adored son. Their laments for him took place in the fourth month of the year (June/July) called Tammuz in his honor, when nature waned beneath the summer sun. Ezekiel's vision of the weeping women occurs in September, however. The apparent popularity of the cult of Tammuz in Jerusalem should be seen in the context of rites practiced for millennia throughout the ancient Near East as part of women's religious observances related to childbirth and fertility.

Jacobsen has criticized Tammuz for lacking "proper manly virtues" and his devotees for the nature of their love for him — ostensibly neither unselfish nor mature, but a form of self-love motivated by need. His critique should be challenged both for its sexist polarization of "manly virtues" versus women's "emotional" nature, and for its marginalization of physiological experiences — pregnancy, birth, lactation — linking women to the Tammuz cult.

KATHERYN PFISTERER DARR

SEE ALSO Part II: Women Worshipping the Queen of Heaven (Jer 7:18, etc.); Part III: Astarte; Queen of Heaven.

FOR FURTHER READING: Jacobsen, Thorkild. *Toward the Image of Tammuz and Other Essays on Mesopotamian Culture.*

EZEK 9:6
Women and Young Women (and Young Men)

The sixth-century B.C.E. prophet Ezekiel is transported to Jerusalem in a vision (chaps. 8–11). There he hears YHWH command executioners to kill all of the city's inhabitants who bear no protective mark on their foreheads. Noncombatants, who might otherwise be spared in battle but who would suffer greatly and even die from the ravages of war, are themselves to be directly annihilated, so enormous will be the devastation. Included in that comprehensive list of victims (9:6) are "young men and young women," the latter indicated by a term, *bĕtûlâ*, that usually denotes an adolescent girl of marriageable age. Another such pair of people usually not part of a battle scene are "little children and women." Everyone will be vulnerable when the divine wrath is poured out upon Jerusalem (9:8).

KATHERYN PFISTERER DARR

SEE ALSO Part II: Wives (and Children) as Booty (Num 14:3); Fallen and Captive Young Women (and Men) (Lam 1:18, etc.).

EZEK 13:17–23
Daughters Who Prophesy

In 13:17–23, the sixth-century B.C.E. prophet Ezekiel excoriates his people's prophetesses, who, like their male counterparts (13:1–16), ostensibly are guilty of prophesying "out of their own imagination" (vv. 2, 17). Their false prophecy is an outrage to Ezekiel, whose account of his call emphasizes the divine

origin of his oracles (Ezekiel 2–3). The activities of these women remain obscure, although the passage does allude to séance-like practices, perhaps intended to summon the dead. Ezekiel pejoratively casts their actions in the mold of divination, magic, and necromancy. He accuses them of disheartening the righteous while encouraging the wicked to persist in their evil ways (v. 22), but he believes that YHWH will release their victims and put an end to their false visions and practices (v. 23).

Ezekiel's complaint against female soothsayers, like the account of the medium of Endor in 1 Samuel 28, may indicate that the raising of spirits was practiced mainly by women.

KATHERYN PFISTERER DARR

SEE ALSO Part II: Medium/Wizard (Lev 20:27); Medium of Endor (1 Sam 28:7–25).

FOR FURTHER READING: Bowen, Nancy. "The Daughters of Your People: Female Prophets in Ezekiel 13:13–17."

EZEK 14:16–23; 23:4, 10, 25, 47; 24:21, 25
Daughters (and Sons)

The gender pair "sons and daughters," representing children, appears in several contexts in the prophecies of the sixth-century B.C.E. prophet Ezekiel. In one passage, Ezekiel proclaims that the depravity of the land is so great, virtually no one will survive God's punitive wrath. Only three examples of rectitude — Noah, Daniel, and Job — would be saved by their own righteousness (14:14). Yet, so completely sinful is the land that not even the presumably innocent daughters and sons of those men would be saved (14:16, 18, 20).

In a somewhat different vein, people who are exiled in Babylon will suffer grief over "sons and daughters" left behind to die. But just as the prophet can't properly lament the loss of his wife, so too will bereft parents be denied the rites of mourning (24:21, 23; compare 24:25).

One other appearance of the daughters-and-sons pair is in the scathing treatment of Samaria (Oholah) and her sister Jerusalem (Oholibah), personified as women in Ezekiel 23. The slaughter of the inhabitants of those cities, the "sons and daughters" of the whoring sisters, is justified because of their mothers' unabashed and unabating lewdness.

KATHERYN PFISTERER DARR

SEE ALSO Part II: Wife of Ezekiel (Ezek 24:18); Part III: Oholah, Woman Samaria; Oholibah, Woman/Whore Jerusalem.

EZEKIEL 16
Female Images for Nations

SEE Female Images for Nations in Ezekiel (Part III).

EZEK 16:20   Daughters Sacrificed

SEE DEUT 12:31, etc.   Daughter (or Son or Child) Passed Through Fire, Burned, or Sacrificed (Part II).

EZEK 16:41; 23:48
Women

In the context of the scathing depictions of Samaria and Jerusalem (called Oholah and Oholibah respectively) as whores, the sixth-century B.C.E. prophet Ezekiel refers several times to women in general. He claims that the negative example of those apostate women/cities should make other women refrain from such behavior (16:41). Furthermore, he warns "all women" that if they don't take heed, they too will suffer the consequences, namely, annihilation of them and their families. The lewd behavior of women is to be an object lesson, especially for women.

KATHERYN PFISTERER DARR

SEE ALSO Part III: Female Images for Nations in Ezekiel; Oholah, Woman Samaria; Oholibah, Woman/Whore Jerusalem.   .

EZEK 16:46–61
Sister Sodom and Her Daughters

SEE Sister Sodom and Her Daughters (Part III).

EZEK 18:6, 11, 15; 22:11; 33:26
Neighbor's Wife, Daughter-in-Law, and Sister as Illicit Sexual Partners

These several passages in the prophetic Book of Ezekiel (sixth century B.C.E.) list adultery with a neighbor's wife as one way in which male Israelites have forgotten their God and broken divine law. In all of these passages, a series of behaviors defines those men who are unrighteous and deserving of punishment. Because the lists include acts such as intercourse with a menstruating woman and incest with a female relative, as well as adultery with a neighbor's wife, they are addressed exclusively to a male audience. These behaviors are juxtaposed with murder, charging interest on loans, retaining a pledge, robbery, failure to provide for needy members of society, extortion, idolatry, filial disobedience, profanation of the Sabbath, slander, incest, and perversion of justice. This array of unrighteous behavior includes an interesting mix of principles contained in the Decalogue and ordinances or principles drawn from cases found in other biblical laws. In short, the unrighteous man has behaved inappropriately in cultic, economic, and sexual matters.

Although legal codes typically mandate capital punishment for one or both parties involved in adultery, only one of these passages appears to presuppose the death penalty. Ezekiel 18 declares that men are no longer held accountable for the sins of their fathers or sons. Each man is to be punished or rewarded according to his own deeds (18:13, 18). The assumption in this text is that those men who have sexual intercourse with their neighbor's wife will be executed, as is specified in Lev 20:10. Because these oracles are addressed to men, it is unclear whether the author intends to include women in this declaration of individual responsibility, or if they would still be held accountable for the sins of their relatives. Nor is it clear whether men would be held accountable for the sins of their female kin. In any case, these passages regarding individual (male) responsibility and punishment differ from the corporate responsibility and punishment expressed elsewhere in Ezekiel.

RHONDA BURNETTE-BLETSCH

SEE ALSO Part II: Women in the Decalogue (Exod 20:8, etc.); Adulteress (and Adulterer) (Lev 20:10, etc.); Woman Accused of Unfaithfulness (Num 5:11–31); Menstruating Women (Ezek 18:6, etc.); Daughter-in-Law and Sister (and Mother) Taken in Incest (Ezek 27:10–11).

EZEK 18:6; 22:10; 36:17
Menstruating Women

Three separate oracles in Ezekiel specifically mention menstruating women. The first of these texts (18:6) is part of an oracle depicting the behavior of three generations of males. It begins with a list of the righteous behavior of the first generation (18:5–9). Second only to refraining from idolatry is this man's avoidance of illicit sex of two kinds: adultery and intercourse with a menstruating woman. Other actively positive deeds such as justice and charity follow. Yet such a man's son might be iniquitous, acting in just the opposite way in all these deeds (18:10–13). Finally, that man's son might revert to righteousness in all these deeds (18:14–18). The three catalogues of deeds are virtually the same. With respect to sexual misconduct, however, intercourse with a menstruant appears only for the first generation. It is difficult to know why it is omitted for the next two generations. Perhaps it is subsumed under adultery. More likely, because it causes no harm and because the resulting impurity lasts only seven days (Lev 15:24), it was dropped from the second two lists.

The second text (22:10) dealing with menstruants appears in an oracle against Jerusalem that cites abominations committed by the city's inhabitants against the deity and against one another. The men of Jerusalem are accused, among other things, of several illicit sexual acts, including raping women during their menstrual periods. This compounds the crime of rape with the condition of ritual impurity, which is not itself sinful. Such connecting of a violent act with the ritual unfitness of menstruation may be one of the ways in which the negative evaluation of women's emissions emerges.

The third text (36:17) related to menstruants uses this ritually impure state as a symbol for the sinfulness of the house of Israel in its apostasy. A menstruating woman is disqualified from approaching the sacred realm and may potentially spread her unfit ritual status to others. Similarly, an idolatrous nation cannot approach the deity, and it defiles the land through its worship of idols. Thus, Ezekiel applies the concept of ritual impurity to places as well as persons.

Whereas legal texts are more descriptive in their discussion of menstruation and describe ritual impurity but not sin, the prophet implies a negative value judgment on the female body and its natural conditions by listing it among sinful acts and transforming it into a metaphor of shame and humiliation. If the legal materials are dated prior to prophetic texts, with Ezekiel dating to the first half of the sixth century B.C.E., differences in the treatment of menstruation in these literary genres may result from historical developments. They could also result from the prevalence of the marriage/covenant metaphor in prophetic texts and the resulting devaluation of the feminine Israel in relation to masculine images of the deity.

RHONDA BURNETTE-BLETSCH

SEE ALSO Part II: Women and Bodily Emissions (Lev 15:18–33, etc.); Neighbor's Wife, Daughter-in-Law, and Sister as Illicit Sexual Partners (Ezek 18:6, etc.); Daughter-in-Law and Sister (and Mother) Taken in Incest (Ezek 27:10–11); Part III: Oholah, Woman Samaria; Oholibah, Woman/Whore Jerusalem.

EZEKIEL 19
Mother of Princes

The sixth-century B.C.E. prophet Ezekiel "laments" certain princes of Israel (19:1), using two metaphors to depict their mother: a lioness who raises and then witnesses the demise of her cubs (19:2–9) and a well-watered vine that suddenly is uprooted and burned (19:10–14). The catchphrase "your mother" links the two parts of the lament (19:2, 10).

A noble lioness ("a lioness . . . among lions!"; 19:2) raises and trains her cubs. When the first devours humans, he is captured and deported to Egypt. This may refer to Judah's king Jehoahaz (reigned 609 B.C.E.), who was taken by Pharaoh Necho to Egypt, where he died (2 Kgs 23:31, 35). His mother was Hamutal, daughter of Jeremiah of Libnah (not the prophet Jeremiah). The lioness then pins her hopes on a second cub, but it also kills people and is deported to Babylon (v. 9). The identity of this cub is disputed, but it is likely Zedekiah, another of Hamutal's sons.

In vv. 10–14, the mother is the "vine"; and her destruction is linked to that of her towering (prideful) offshoot. In this case, critics have argued that "she" is either Hamutal, mother of Jehoahaz and Zedekiah, or Nehushta, mother of the Judean king Jehoiachin (reigned 597 B.C.E.) who was exiled to Babylon with her son (see 2 Kgs 24:8, 12, 14).

Both of these images — a powerful lion and a fruitful vine — fit the roles of Hamutal and Nehushta, queen mothers who were considerably involved in the reigns of their sons. Because poetry can have more than one meaning, both the lioness and the vine may also represent Judah, the Davidic dynasty, or Jerusalem (which elsewhere in Ezekiel is personified as YHWH's wife and the murderous mother of their children; 16:20–21).

KATHERYN PFISTERER DARR

SEE ALSO Part I: Hamutal/Hamital; Nehushta; Part III: Oholibah, Woman/Whore Jerusalem.

EZEK 22:7
Mother

Many of the oracles uttered by the sixth-century B.C.E. prophet Ezekiel condemn the bloody city of Jerusalem for its violence, idolatry, and immorality. The rulers of the city are denounced, in 22:7–12, for a long series of misdeeds, some of which are related to the stipulations of the Decalogue. First on the list is the accusation that they have done what is tanta-

mount to violating the Fifth Commandment: "father and mother are treated with contempt" (22:7). This precedes the castigation for profaning the Sabbath (the Fourth Commandment), perhaps because respecting parental authority was considered so basic.

KATHERYN PFISTERER DARR

SEE ALSO Part II: Women in the Decalogue (Exod 20:8, etc.); Women and Young Women (and Young Men) (Ezek 9:6); Mother of Princes (Ezekiel 19); Daughters-in-Law and Sister (and Mother) Taken in Incest (Ezek 27:10–11).

EZEK 22:7   Widow
SEE   Exod 22:22, etc.   Widows (Part II).

EZEK 22:10   Menstruating Women
SEE   EZEK 18:6, etc.   Menstruating Women (Part II).

EZEK 22:10–11
Daughter-in-Law and Sister (and Mother) Taken in Incest

In a list of abominable behaviors that characterize unrighteous men deserving divine punishment, the sixth-century B.C.E. prophet Ezekiel includes a series of sexual offenses. In addition to adultery and sex with a menstruant, he deplores incest with three female relatives — a mother, a daughter-in-law, and a paternal sister ("father's daughter") — in 22:10–11. The mother is not explicitly mentioned in v. 10, which condemns men who "uncover their father's nakedness"; but the incest prohibitions of Leviticus 18 explain that such an act is the same as uncovering "the nakedness of your father's wife," that is, a man's mother or possibly his stepmother.

It is not clear why these three forms of illicit family sex, among the many liaisons forbidden in Leviticus 18 and 20, are specified in this passage. Perhaps they were the most common violations and stand, *pars pro toto,* for all. At least with respect to sister-brother incest, the fact that it is mentioned twice in Leviticus 18 (vv. 8 and 9) suggests that it was especially troublesome. In any case, these sexual offenses by males, along with the horrendous depictions of women as whores, make sexual misconduct of all kinds a prominent metaphor in Ezekiel for Israel's depravity.

KATHERYN PFISTERER DARR

SEE ALSO Part II: Women in Incest Regulations (Lev 18:7–18, etc.); Women (Ezek 16:41, etc.); Neighbor's Wife, Daughter-in-Law, and Sister as Illicit Sexual Partners (Ezek 18:6, etc.); Menstruating Women (Ezek 18:6; etc.); Part III: Oholah, Women Samaria; Oholibah, Woman/Whore Jerusalem.

EZEK 22:11
Neighbor's Wife, Daughter-in-Law, and Sister as Illicit Sexual Partners

SEE EZEK 18:6, etc. Neighbor's Wife, Daughter-in-Law, and Sister as Illicit Sexual Partners (Part II).

EZEKIEL 23   Woman Samaria

SEE Oholah, Woman Samaria (Part III).

EZEK 23:4, 10, 25, 47   Daughters

SEE EZEK 14:16–23, etc. Daughters (and Sons) (Part II).

EZEK 23:48   Women

SEE EZEK 16:41, etc. Women (Part II).

EZEK 24:18
Wife of Ezekiel

YHWH informs Ezekiel that when his unnamed wife, "the delight of your eyes," dies, he must not engage in the expected mourning rituals (24:16–18). This symbolic prophetic action — or rather, lack of action — represents the fact that the people will not be allowed the comfort of mourning when their temple is profaned and their daughters and sons, left behind as the parents go into exile, are slain. The pain of a man unable to grieve for his beloved wife represents the agony of Judeans unable to lament their loss of temple and posterity.

KATHERYN PFISTERER DARR

SEE ALSO Part II: Daughters (and Sons) (Ezek 14:16–23, etc.).

EZEK 24:21, 25   Daughters

SEE EZEK 14:16–23, etc. Daughters (and Sons) (Part II).

EZEK 26:6, 8   Daughter-towns

SEE Mother/Daughter (NRSV, Village) as Territory (Part III).

EZEK 32:16
Women Chanting a Lamentation

SEE JER 9:17–20, etc. Mourning Women (Part II).

EZEK 33:26
Neighbor's Wife as Illicit Sexual Partner

SEE EZEK 18:6, etc. Neighbor's Wife, Daughter-in-Law, and Sister as Illicit Sexual Partners (Part II).

EZEK 36:17   Menstruating Woman

SEE EZEK 18:6, etc. Menstruating Women (Part II).

EZEK 44:22
Women a Priest Can and Cannot Marry

SEE LEV 21:7–8, etc. Women Whom a Priest Can and Cannot Marry (Part II).

EZEK 44:25
Women a Priest Can and Cannot Bury

SEE LEV 21:1–3, etc. Women Whom a Priest Can and Cannot Bury (Part II).

DAN 5:2–3, 23
Wives and Concubines of Belshazzar

Fictionally set during the time of Judean captivity in Babylon (sixth century B.C.E.), the Book of

Daniel contains numerous tales of the wise visionary Judean exile, Daniel, in the Babylonian court.
Daniel 5 relates the famous story of the mysterious
writing that appears on the palace wall of King
Belshazzar. The tale begins with Belshazzar, son of
Nebuchadnezzar, holding a great feast. Drunk, he
orders the gold and silver vessels that his father had
taken from the temple in Jerusalem to be brought
in, so that his lords, his wives, and his concubines
might all drink from them (5:2–3). Once they have
committed this act of desecration and praised their
gods, the fingers are seen writing on the wall.

When none of the king's enchanters, diviners,
and wise men can decipher and interpret the writing, Daniel is called. He tells the king that the hand
has come from God, in response to the impious acts
of Belshazzar, his lords, his wives, and his concubines, when they drank from the sacred vessels of
the temple, and praised false gods (5:23). The words
on the wall are MENE, MENE, TEKEL, PARSIN, and
they predict the death of the king (which transpires
that very night) and the subsequent division of his
land among the Medes and the Persians.

Although the Babylonians' use of the vessels
from the Jerusalem temple may strike modern
readers as contrived, banquet halls in the ancient
world, and drinking, are often closely associated
with religious devotion and even cults of the dead.
Further, rulers and gods were intimately linked, and
military conquest and political domination were
regularly understood in theological terms: the
power of rulers was a function of the power of the
gods they worshipped. This tale thus shows that,
despite the destruction of the temple, the true God,
the God of Daniel, continues to control history and
to reward piety and punish the impious, not only of
Israel, but of all nations.

It is not entirely clear what function the participation of the women of the court plays in the story.
The presence of his wives and concubines may intensify the culpability of Belshazzar, thus making it
seem particularly appropriate that not only he, but
also his family and heirs, should suffer from the
dissolution of his kingdom.

How, if at all, the presence of the wives and concubines corresponds to actual ancient social prac-

tices is also unclear, particularly since the story is set
in the sixth century B.C.E., but was given its present
form in the second century B.C.E. The Book of
Esther (which may have also been composed in the
later Hellenistic period, despite its fictional setting
in an earlier Persian period) offers conflicting evidence. At the outset, King Ahasuerus holds an all-
male banquet, while his queen, Vashti, holds a separate one for women; yet later the new queen, Esther,
holds a banquet for her husband and his scheming
adviser, Haman. Vashti's absence from her husband's banquet, though, is required by the narrative, and what we know of Persian banqueting practices indicates that women did sometimes dine with
men. In ancient Greece, respectable women did not
generally dine with men, and women who attended
banquets were usually assumed to be sexually available. In the Hellenistic and Roman periods, however, it became increasingly common for respectable women to dine publicly with men, although
the practice was more acceptable in Roman circles,
and women who dined with men were still often
presumed to be prostitutes.

ROSS S. KRAEMER

SEE ALSO Part II: Women at Vashti's Banquet (Esth 1:9);
   Queen (of Babylon) (Dan 5:10–12).
FOR FURTHER READING: Corley, Kathleen. *Private
   Women, Public Meals.*
Craven, Toni. "The Greek Book of Daniel."

DAN 5:10–12
Queen (of Babylon)

Daniel 5 contains the famous story of the hand that
mysteriously writes on the palace walls of Belshazzar, king of Babylon, after he, his wives and concubines, and his courtiers have sacrilegiously drunk
from vessels looted from the destroyed temple in
Jerusalem. When none of the kings' specialists can
decipher the words and interpret their meaning, the
queen enters the banquet hall and informs him, in a
lengthy speech, that there is a man in the kingdom
who has the power to read and interpret the writing, namely, Daniel (vv. 10–12).

Although the kings' wives and concubines are already present in the banquet hall, the queen enters the hall only in v. 10, having overheard the anxious discussion of the king and his lords concerning the writing. Because she is thus distinguished from the wives and concubines, and because she informs the king that his father, Nebuchadnezzar, had made Daniel chief of all his diviners, scholars have tended to see her as the queen mother, rather than as Belshazzar's wife. Although the story may indeed understand her in this way, her absence from the banquet, and thus her implicit abstinence from the impious activity, align her with Daniel and remove any taint from her recommendation. What scholars have thus taken as evidence for her identity may have more to do with her role in the introduction of Daniel.

ROSS S. KRAEMER

SEE ALSO Part II: Wives and Concubines of Belshazzar (Dan 5:2–3, etc.).

DAN 5:23
Wives and Concubines of Belshazzar

SEE DAN 5:2–3, etc. Wives and Concubines of Belshazzar (Part II).

DAN 6:24
Wives of Daniel's Accusers

Daniel 6 relates one of the most famous biblical tales, that of Daniel in the lions' den. The tale opens with Darius, king of the Medes, making Daniel one of three "presidents" of the former kingdom of the Babylonians, which he had received at the end of the previous tale in Daniel 5. Daniel soon so excels in his performance that the king plans to make him sole ruler. The other two presidents and the 120 satraps conspire against Daniel, prevailing on the king to issue an ordinance forbidding the worship of anyone other than the king himself, whether human or divine, for a period of thirty days. When Daniel is found praying to God, he is thrown into the den of lions, where, miraculously, he remains

unharmed, protected by an angel of God. In a classic scene of reversal, the greatly relieved king orders that those who had accused Daniel be thrown into the den, where the lions destroy them.

Although they appear to have played no part in the plot against Daniel, the wives and children of the presidents and satraps are also thrown to the lions (6:24). The destruction not only of the culpable men, but also of their innocent families, deprives the men (and the women) of descendants to perform rituals of veneration for the dead and probably guarantees that their estates will be given to others. The Bible offers several other instances of women and children put to death for the transgressions of men (for example, Num 16:25–33; Josh 7:24); such actions are characteristic of patriarchal cultures that consider women and children of both genders as the rightful property of their husbands and fathers.

ROSS S. KRAEMER

SEE ALSO Part II: Wives of Dathan and Abiram (Num 16:27–33); Daughters (and Sons) of Achan (Josh 7:24).

DAN 11:6–7
Daughter of the King of the South

Although the Book of Daniel is set in Babylon after the destruction of the first Jerusalem temple by Nebuchadnezzar in the sixth century B.C.E., Daniel 11 retrospectively "predicts" the conquest of Persia by Alexander the Great and the subsequent history of Alexander's successors through the early second century B.C.E., indicating that Daniel was actually composed shortly before 164 B.C.E. Dan 11:5–7 offers a highly condensed summary of historical events in the mid–third century B.C.E. Ptolemy II of Egypt (here called the king of the south) arranges a marriage between his daughter, Berenice, and Antiochus II of Syria (here called the king of the north) in 251 B.C.E. According to Daniel, the daughter "shall not retain her power," nor will her offspring with the king survive, but she, her child, her attendants, and "the one who supported her" will die. Subsequently, however, "a branch from her roots" will prevail against the king of the north (vv. 6–7).

From a variety of ancient extrabiblical sources, we know these events were worthy of a contemporary soap opera. Antiochus II already had a wife, Laodice, and children, to whom he was apparently devoted, but he assented to the marriage nevertheless, perhaps because Berenice's dowry was so enormous that she was called by the epithet "Phernophorus" (dowry-bringer). Although he lived with Berenice for a short time in the Syrian city of Antioch and fathered a son with her, he soon returned to Laodice in Ephesus. Fearing, however, that Antiochus would succumb to pressure from Ptolemy and return to Berenice, Laodice is said to have poisoned her husband. When Berenice responded by having her infant son, Seleucus, proclaimed king in Ephesus, Laodice had the baby kidnapped and killed; ultimately, Berenice, too, was murdered. Her brother, Ptolemy III, invaded much of the Seleucid Empire, bringing back to Egypt vast spoils in revenge.

ROSS S. KRAEMER

SEE ALSO Part II: Wife of the King of the South (Dan 11:17).

FOR FURTHER READING: Craven, Toni. "The Greek Book of Daniel."

Macurdy, Grace Harriet. *Hellenistic Queens: A Study of Woman-Power in Macedonia, Seleucid Syria, and Ptolemaic Egypt.*

Pomeroy, Sarah B. *Women in Hellenistic Egypt from Alexander to Cleopatra.*

DAN 11:17
Wife of the King of the South

The apocalyptic revelations of the Book of Daniel contain allusions to several figures of the second century B.C.E., when the Ptolemaic rulers of Egypt and the Seleucid dynasties of Syria were struggling for control of Palestine. The angel who provides the visionary review of Hellenistic history at the end of the book refers to the Ptolemaic ruler (204–180 B.C.E.) Ptolemy V, as the "king of the south" (11:2, 6). He is opposed by a Seleucid ruler — the "king of the north" (11:7, 15) — who is identified as Antiochus III the Great (reigned 223–187 B.C.E.). As part of his plot to overthrow Ptolemy, Antiochus gives him his daughter in marriage, presumably hoping that she can influence or subvert the regime from within. This daughter is Cleopatra I (c. 215–176 B.C.E.), the first of several Seleucid and Egyptian queens who bore this name, which was probably popular because of its Macedonian associations. The first Cleopatra of historical importance was the wife of Perdiccas II of Macedonia in the fifth century B.C.E.

The passage in Daniel alluding to Cleopatra I has several textual difficulties. The NRSV reads, "In order to destroy the kingdom, he [Antiochus III] shall give him [Ptolemy V] a woman [Cleopatra I] in marriage" (Dan 11:17). The Hebrew text actually reads "daughter of woman," but a fragment of Daniel found among the Dead Sea Scrolls (4QDan) reads "daughter of men." In either case, the title, omitted from the NRSV translation, is probably honorific and reflects the author's admiration for the queen because of her loyalty to the Ptolemaic house. The Hebrew text also reads "to destroy her"; but the Qumran fragment, which the NRSV follows in its translation "destroy his kingdom," reads "destroy him."

The marriage of Cleopatra I to Ptolemy V took place at Raphia in southern Palestine in 193 B.C.E. Her dowry was supposed to have included Coele-Syria, Samaria, Judea, and Phoenicia, according to the Jewish historian Josephus (*Antiquities* 12.154). Cleopatra's father hoped to gain influence in Ptolemaic Syria through this marriage, but his plan failed. Daniel alludes to Antiochus III's failed strategy in declaring that the marriage, intended to "destroy" the Ptolemies, "shall not succeed nor be to his advantage." Cleopatra was more loyal to her husband than to her father; and, when Ptolemy V died (180 B.C.E.), she ruled as regent for her son Ptolemy VI (known as Philometor — he "who loves his mother") until her death. Similarly, a half-century later, her daughter (Cleopatra II) and then her granddaughter (Cleopatra III) also served as co-regents.

JOHN J. COLLINS

SEE ALSO Part I: Cleopatra 2; Cleopatra 3; Part II: Daughter of the King of the South (Dan 11:6–7).

FOR FURTHER READING: Collins, John J. *Daniel.*

DAN 11:37
Women Worshippers of an Unnamed Deity

Set in Babylon after the destruction of the first Jerusalem temple by Nebuchadnezzar in the sixth century B.C.E., the Book of Daniel was nevertheless actually composed shortly before 164 B.C.E., when the forces of a rebel leader named Judah the Maccabee (Judas Maccabeus) brought to an end the persecution of pious Jews and the desecration of the temple in Jerusalem wrought by the Seleucid king Antiochus IV Epiphanes. Two Apocryphal/Deuterocanonical Books, 1 and 2 Maccabees, explicitly relate these events at great length, while Daniel 11 retrospectively "predicts" them in a cryptic manner that is nevertheless sufficiently transparent.

In the course of recounting Antiochus's many atrocities and impieties, Dan 11:36–37 claims that Antiochus considered himself above all the gods and failed to pay honor to the gods of his own ancestors or to "the one beloved by women." Most scholars take this to refer to women's worship either of Tammuz or of Adonis. Tammuz was an ancient Mesopotamian deity, whose devotion by women weeping over his death (in anticipation of his subsequent resurrection) is mentioned in Ezek 8:14. Adonis was originally a Phoenician deity whose worship was popular in ancient Athens; women mourned him (Aphrodite's beloved consort) at a summer festival known as the Adonia. In the Hellenistic period, women's ritual mourning of the adored young Adonis was widespread. The third-century B.C.E. poet Theocritus provides an exten-

sive account of women's celebration of the Adonia in Alexandria, Egypt, in rites that offered them a rare day of freedom from household chores, and whose symbols and myths temporarily reversed the powerlessness and boredom of many women's daily lives. Because the object of the women's affections is ambiguous in Hebrew and could conceivably be feminine, some scholars have also suggested that the goddess Astarte is intended.

Why the author of Daniel singles out Antiochus's failure to worship a deity "beloved by women" is unclear, but it may be connected with the fact that Adonis was the consort of the great Syrian goddess known simply as Dea Syria, and Antiochus was the Syrian king.

ROSS S. KRAEMER

SEE ALSO Part II: Women Weeping for Tammuz (Ezek 8:14); Part III: Astarte.

FOR FURTHER READING: Griffith, Frederick. "Home Before Lunch: The Emancipated Woman in Theocritus."

Kraemer, Ross S. "Women's Devotion to Adonis."

HOS 4:5
Mother of Priest

Included among the indictments of the eighth-century B.C.E. prophet Hosea against the wayward Israelites are strong charges of idolatry and promiscuity against the priestly leaders. This condemnation takes the form, in chap. 4, of a diatribe against the chief priest and his family. God will punish them, in essence, by the dissolution of the priestly line: not only will the priest's offspring (Hebrew "sons") be forgotten (v. 6), but also his mother will be destroyed (v. 5), thereby precluding family continuity.

Some critics wonder why it is the priest's mother that is mentioned, and not his father or both parents. Because the chief priest holds his office by having inherited it from his father, his father probably is dead. The notion of discontinuity of the priestly line, however, is served better by focusing on the destruction of the mother as childbearer.

CAROL MEYERS

SEE ALSO Part II: Daughters and Daughters-in-Law of Priest (Hos 4:13–14).

Hos 3:1   Adulteress
SEE Gomer (Part I).

Hos 4:13–14
Daughters and Daughters-in-Law of Priest

The eighth-century B.C.E. prophet Hosea, in chap. 4, condemns the apostate actions of, among others, the chief priest and his family. Punishment will apparently involve destroying the priestly line — forgetting (that is, expelling) the chief priest's sons (Hebrew; in NRSV, "children," v. 6) and ruining or destroying his mother (v. 5). Later in the chapter, he mentions the sins of the priest (vv. 10b–12) and of his sons (v. 13a), daughters, and daughters-in-law (vv. 13b–14). Hos 4:14, however, indicates that God "will not punish" these two groups of women.

Commentators have suggested deleting the word *not* from this phrase or have found other ways to try to include the daughters and the sons' wives in the punishment. However, if one understands the whole chapter to be an indictment of the priest and his powerful negative impact on the people, beginning with his family and with the result that the priestly line is in jeopardy, then only the priests' mother and sons need be destroyed. Priestly lineage is through the male line. Thus the chief priest's mother must not bear more children, nor must his sons survive. And his father must already be dead or he would not be chief priest. But his female descendants, by blood or by his sons' marriages, are apparently spared; they are not implicated in the concept of destroying the lineage.

CAROL MEYERS

SEE ALSO Part II: Mother of Priest (Hos 4:5).

Hos 4:14   Temple Prostitute
SEE DEUT 23:17-18.   Temple Prostitute (Part II).

Hos 10:14; 13:16
Mothers Killed in War

Hosea's prophecies (eighth century B.C.E.) regarding the destruction of the northern kingdom of Israel are laced with brutal depictions of the fate of mothers, the nation's life-givers, and children, the nation's future. The prophesied annihilation of Israel's military strongholds is compared to a past devastation still vivid in the people's collective memory (10:14). Although the identities of the conqueror and conquered (Shalman and Beth-arbel) elude us now, the battle evidently was one of unparalleled cruelty and sadism, in which "mothers were dashed in pieces with their children (10:14)." Likewise Israel's capital, Samaria, will become the site of atrocities, targeting the most vulnerable — children and pregnant women (13:16). Moreover, Hosea personifies Samaria as a guilty and rebellious pregnant woman who will suffer a brutal fate. Her swollen belly will be ripped open and the fruit of her promiscuity, her bastard child Ephraim (compare 13:12–13), torn from her.

GALE A. YEE

SEE ALSO Part II: Pregnant Women Killed in War (2 Kgs 8:12, etc.); Pregnant Women of Gilead (Amos 1:13).

Hos 11:3–4   God as Mother
SEE Female Images of God in the Hebrew Bible (Part III).

Hos 12:12   Wives of Jacob
SEE Leah; Rachel (Part I).

Hos 13:16
Pregnant Women Killed in War
SEE Hos 10:14, etc.   Mothers Killed in War (Part II).

JOEL 1:8
Young Woman in Mourning

The postexilic prophet Joel calls to Jerusalem (or Judah), traditionally personified as a woman, to mourn because of God's punitive judgment. In so doing, he uses the feminine of the imperative form of the verb *lament* (1:8). His poetic simile portrays the mourner as a young woman, rather than a virgin, as the NRSV translates it. She is grieving over a dead husband, which would preclude the use of the latter term; and the Hebrew word usually means "young woman" — a chronological designation rather than one dealing with the status of her genitals. The image of a woman bemoaning the loss of the "husband of her youth" implies his death early in marriage, a particularly poignant loss.

Although women in ancient Israel had a significant role as professional mourners, this verse draws upon the general expression of grief that any person would experience when a loved one dies.

CAROL MEYERS

SEE ALSO Part II: Daughters of Zion (Isa 3:16–26, etc.); Young Woman (Isa 7:14); Mourning Women (Jer 9:17–20, etc).

JOEL 2:16
Bride (and Bridegroom)

The prophet Joel, after portraying God's judgment against Judah, calls on the people to return to YHWH. The inclusive notion of the people in 2:16 is conveyed by two paired groups: a pair involving opposite ages (the elderly and the suckling infants) to represent all ages in between, and a gender pair — a bride and bridegroom — to represent all women and men. The choice of newlyweds as the second pair balances the use of the elderly and infants in the first. It emphasizes people in the prime of life, in contrast to those just beginning and ending life. It also connotes reproductive potential and thus Judah's posterity, in contrast to the doom of the past, in which the merry sounds of bride and

Lovers on a terra-cotta bed, seen from above, dating to the second millennium B.C.E. See Bride (and Bridegroom) (Jer 2:2, etc.); (Joel 2:16).

bridegroom had ceased (as in Jer 7:34; 16:9; 25:10; 33:11).

CAROL MEYERS

SEE ALSO Part II: Bride (and Bridegroom) (Jer 2:2, etc.).

JOEL 2:28
Daughters (and Sons) Who Prophesy

In the latter part of the Book of Joel, the prophet focuses on the day of the LORD, a momentous future event marked by terrible strife and a divine judgment, as well as the eventual establishment of a new world order. One aspect of this new world order, according to Joel 2:28–29, is the breakdown of many hitherto accepted social distinctions, resulting from, and signaled by, a general outpouring of God's spirit. Hence, differential treatment based on gender will disappear insofar as daughters, as well as sons, will prophesy. Differences based on age will also be inconsequential, since both young and old men will have visionary experiences. And, finally, distinctions based on class will also be of little account, since even slaves (both female and male) will be endowed with the divine spirit.

KARLA G. BOHMBACH

SEE ALSO Part I: Noadiah; Part II: Daughters Who Prophesy (Ezek 13:17–23); Female (and Male) Slaves (Joel 2:29); Prophesying Daughters and Female Slaves (Acts 2:17–18).

JOEL 2:29
Female (and Male) Slaves

The end of Joel 2 presents YHWH's promise for restoration, which involves revolutionary concepts: certain distinctions based on age, gender, and social status will be removed. For example, in v. 29, both female and male slaves will have access to God's spirit, apparently meaning that even they, people at the bottom of the social hierarchy, will have the

status of YHWH's prophets, divinely chosen to receive visions.

CAROL MEYERS

SEE ALSO Part II: Female (and Male) Hebrew Slaves (Exod 21:7–11, etc.); Daughters (and Sons) Who Prophesy (Joel 2:28).

JOEL 3:3 Prostitutes
SEE LEV 19:29, etc. Prostitute (Part II).

JOEL 3:3
Girls Sold for Wine (and Boys Traded for Prostitutes)

The prophet Joel expresses great contempt for the nations that have destroyed and plundered Judah and Jerusalem. The image he uses to show how little regard Israel's enemies had for human life is that of trafficking in children — selling girls for wine and boys for prostitutes (3:3). In this scenario, children of both genders are valued as representatives of all God's people.

CAROL MEYERS

SEE ALSO Part II: Daughters (and Sons) to Be Sold by Judeans (Joel 3:8).

JOEL 3:8
Daughters (and Sons) to Be Sold by Judeans

Joel's oracles about divine judgment of the nations that have destroyed God's people involve an unusual instance of exact retribution. The people who enslaved Judean children will see their own daughters and sons (3:8) sold by the Judeans. Rather than depict God as punishing the wrongdoers, the prophet proclaims that Judean victims, or at least the parents of the enslaved Judean children, will become the agents of the enslavement of the enemy's offspring. This rare situation of direct revenge perhaps is meant to convey the great horror of trafficking in children.

CAROL MEYERS

SEE ALSO Part II: Girls Sold for Wine (and Boys Traded for Prostitutes) (Joel 3:3).

Amos 1:11
Edomite Women (NRSV, Pity) Cast Off

The opening section of the Book of Amos comprises oracles against the nations, particularly ones that have threatened or damaged Israel's territory or population. Edom, Israel's neighbor to the southeast, is third in the sequence of doomed peoples. The Edomites, considered distant kin of the Israelites because Jacob's twin brother, Esau, is the eponymous ancestor of the Edomites, are accused of pursuing their kin "with the sword." This probably reflects the militant stance Esau takes against his brother in Gen 27:41–42; 32:6–8. In the next clause of this poetic passage, Edom is said to have "cast off all pity," a strained translation (by the NRSV) of the Hebrew, which others have read as "stifling their natural affection" (REB). Neither rendering does justice to the Hebrew text.

Because this clause uses the root *rhm*, which can mean "womb" as well as "compassion, pity," it might equally be translated as "destroyed his womenfolk." The word for "womb" would thus indicate childbearing women, just as it does, *pars pro toto*, in another poetic war text, Judg 5:30. Furthermore, an allusion to wombs appears in the next oracle, where the Ammonites are accused of ripping open pregnant women (Amos 1:13). The first two lines describing Edom's sins are thus complementary: killing men and destroying women. Standard translations have failed to notice a poetic gender pair and have thus obscured the presence of literary imagery representing women.

CAROL MEYERS

SEE ALSO Part II: Girls as Booty (Judg 5:30); Pregnant Women of Gilead (Amos 1:13).

FOR FURTHER READING: Paul, Shalom M. *Amos: A Commentary on the Book of Amos.*

Amos 1:13
Pregnant Women of Gilead

Amos 1:3–2:3 indicts six neighbors of Israel — Aram, Philistia, Tyre, Edom, Ammon, and Moab — for war crimes. The Ammonites to the east were a traditional enemy of Israel (Judges 10–11; 1 Sam 10:27–11:15), and Gilead, a fertile land east of the Jordan, was a disputed territory claimed by Israel but repeatedly invaded by various groups (see, for example, 1:3). "Ripping up pregnant women" appears in prophetic writings as a stereotypical representation of the horrors of war. It was predicted of Aram's and Assyria's invasions of Israel (2 Kgs 8:12; Hos 13:16) and attributed to one Israelite king, Menachem (2 Kgs 15:16). Outside the Bible, the practice was attributed to the Assyrian king Tiglath-pileser I and urged in Homer's *Iliad*.

For these three reasons, it is uncertain whether this verse refers to a specific campaign, and if so, one remembered from the past or one from Amos's time (eighth century B.C.E.). Another possibility is that all six specific accusations in this series constitute one evocation of atrocities frequently associated with warfare: gratuitous brutality ("threshing"), deportations, treaty violations, relentless cruelty, slaughter of the most vulnerable noncombatants (pregnant women and unborn babies), and desecration. In that case, the Ammonites would not have resorted to the battle strategy of slaying pregnant women more than the other nations would have, nor would the Israelites in Gilead have been victimized by this practice more than others; rather, the prophet Amos would be accusing all six nations of a variety of war crimes.

In general, the practice constituted one of several methods of total warfare and terror in a border war. The specific practice can be explained either as a means of ensuring that all potential soldiers of the next generation are wiped out or as a symbolic

Terra-cotta figure of a pregnant woman with a protective arm across her belly, dating to the late Iron Age (seventh–sixth century B.C.E.) from Achziv, on the northern coast of Israel. See Pregnant Women Killed in War (2 Kgs 8:12, etc.); Mothers Killed in War (Hos 10:14, etc.); Pregnant Women of Gilead (Amos 1:13).

emasculation of the fathers. Both motives seem appropriate precisely because they focus attention away from women to males, whether sons or husbands. Another possibility is that slaughtering pregnant women and their unborn children signifies that there will be no future whatsoever for the victimized people.

JUDITH E. SANDERSON

SEE ALSO Part II: Pregnant Women Killed in War (2 Kgs 8:12, etc.); Mothers Killed in War (Hos 10:14, etc.); Edomite Woman (NSRV, Pity) Cast Off (Amos 1:11).

FOR FURTHER READING: Hayes, John H. *Amos, the Eighth-Century Prophet: His Times and His Preaching.*

AMOS 2:7
Girl

In this eighth-century B.C.E. prophetic book, in the midst of several indictments of Israelites for acts of injustice to the poor (2:6–8) appears a very difficult line, literally "a man and his father go/walk to the girl." If they are going for sex, this would be the only use of this verb with that meaning; and if so, is this the *same* girl, and is she a prostitute or their slave or the son's intended wife? Why did Amos use this general term for "young female (of marriageable age)"? Whereas nothing in the Bible suggests profanation by father and son visiting the same prostitute, Exod 21:7–11 and Lev 19:20–22 call for a slave to be used sexually by one man only, and Lev 18:15 and 20:12 prohibit sex with one's (intended?) daughter-in-law. These latter two interpretations would fit with the context of socioeconomic injustices in Amos 2:6–8. A very different interpretation, attempting to account for the difficult Hebrew, envisions generations of men walking to worship in the shrine of "the" female deity (perhaps the perpetual adolescent Anath?).

JUDITH E. SANDERSON

SEE ALSO Part II: Female (and Male) Hebrew Slaves (Exod 21:7–11, etc.); Women in Incest Regulations (Lev 18:7–18, etc.).

FOR FURTHER READING: Sanderson, Judith E. "Amos."

AMOS 4:1
Women ("Cows") of Bashan

The eighth-century B.C.E. prophet Amos, in calling for social justice, calls an elite group of women "cows of Bashan." Although clearly denouncing the wives of wealthy and powerful men in the capital city Samaria for their affluent ease while oppressing the poor, Amos is not necessarily ridiculing their appearance or their relationships with their husbands. Animal metaphors were frequently used for humans, and often quite positively, as when the lover likened his beloved to "a mare among Pharaoh's chariots" or her breasts to "two fawns, twins of a gazelle" (Song 1:9; 7:3), and leading men were called "bulls" or "rams" (for example, Ps 68:30). Bashan, east of the Jordan River, was renowned for its fertility, and Micah eagerly anticipated the future grazing of all Israelites, imaged as a flock of sheep, in Bashan "as in the days of old" (7:14). Further, it is not clear that suggesting that one's husband "Bring something to drink!" would have been considered unwifely behavior in ancient Israel. In the Bible prosperity, including the enjoyment of wine, was considered a blessing from YHWH (Deut 7:13; Ps 104:14–15); it was prosperity gained by exploitation of others — as here — that was condemned (see Amos 5:11).

Although it could be argued that Amos has misunderstood the reality of these women's lives, attributing to them power and wealth that they enjoy only as borrowings from their husbands, it is noteworthy that he predicts punishment as the result of what he understands as their own sin. This emphasis on the personal responsibility of women contrasts with the multitude of biblical exhortations and laws addressed exclusively to the adult males of Israel (for example, Exod 20:17) and the many cases in which wives and children suffer for the sins of husbands and fathers (for example, Amos 7:17).

JUDITH E. SANDERSON

FOR FURTHER READING: Sanderson, Judith E. "Amos."

AMOS 5:2 Maiden Israel
SEE Daughter (Part III).

AMOS 7:17
Wife and Daughters (and Sons) of Amaziah

Amaziah, priest in the royal shrine of the Northern Kingdom in Bethel in the mid–eighth century B.C.E., tries to stop the prophet Amos from preaching there. Amos responds with a defense of his role as prophet of YHWH and a threat of disaster for

Amaziah's unnamed wife and children, his property, himself, and the nation of Israel. In a premodern society with a communal understanding of guilt and punishment, it would be natural to see Amaziah's wife and children as directly deserving of punishment for Amaziah's sin and to see their fate as direct punishment of Amaziah (see, for example, Exod 20:5 and 2 Sam 12:9–14; this approach would be questioned later, in Ezekiel 18). Whether the wife and children are guilty of their own sin is not an issue for Amos.

Whereas his daughters and sons are threatened with death at the hands of invading armies, Amaziah is to die in exile in the conquerors' land. His wife, left without family and home, is to become a prostitute, a common fate of unattached women in time of conquest and occupation. Will she be forced into this activity physically by the conquering armies or economically by her destitution? Such matters probably do not concern Amos, who presumably is more interested in irony: Lev 21:7 prohibits priests from marrying prostitutes or even divorced women. As Amaziah tries to stop the prophet Amos from prophesying in Israel, so Amos predicts that the priest Amaziah will no longer be worthy of priesthood. Israelites would recognize this threat as poetic justice.

JUDITH E. SANDERSON

SEE ALSO Part II: Women Whom a Priest Can and Cannot Marry (Lev 21:7–8, etc.).

AMOS 8:13
Beautiful Young Women (and Young Men)

Among the diatribes of the eighth-century B.C.E. prophet Amos against the sinful people is an eschatological passage delineating the punishment to be meted out to those who worship the goddess Ashimah. Both women and men will be affected by drought, suggesting general desolation. This pronouncement ("The beautiful young women and the young men / shall faint for thirst") is made in several unusual ways. The text mentions "young women" before "young men" (8:13), reversing the more typical order. Also, the only verb in this verse, *faint*, is feminine; and both nouns thus go with the feminine verb. Finally, only the word for "young women" is modified by an adjectival form: "beautiful." Clearly the female is the dominant one in this gender pair of apostates, perhaps reflecting that the worship of Ashimah in Samaria was dominated by women.

CAROL MEYERS

SEE ALSO Part II: Women Who Went to Egypt (Jer 43:6, etc.); Part III: Ashima/Ashimah; Queen of Heaven.

BOOK OF OBADIAH
No Women Mentioned

The shortest book in the Hebrew Bible, Obadiah consists of twenty-one verses dealing with the painful tension between two national groups, Judah and Edom. The rivalry between the two peoples is portrayed in terms of the struggle between their eponymous ancestors, the brothers Jacob and Esau. Although the date of Obadiah is open to some question, the depiction of the destruction of Judah and the opportunistic response of Edom seems to fit the situation following the Babylonian conquest of Judah and Jerusalem in 586 B.C.E. The prophet castigates the Edomites, in language similar to the oracle against Edom in the Book of Jeremiah, and anticipates the day of divine judgment. When YHWH restores the Israelites to their land, Edom will not simply be dispossessed, but rather will be annihilated.

The international politics of Obadiah is played out in vivid imagery that focuses on male sibling rivalry. The absence of females from this biblical book is thus not surprising. Yet, although masked by the gendered nature of Hebrew language, females do appear in several places. The term "grape-gatherers" in v. 5, for example, probably refers to both women and men; picking grapes was likely an activity that involved female as well as male la-

bor in the initial harvesting and certainly in the gleaning (Deut 24:21). Similarly, the "fugitives" and "survivors" of v. 14 are certainly denoted by gender-inclusive terms. And the "eagle" (probably a griffin-vulture and not an eagle) of v. 4 is linked with nest building and thus provides female imagery, in this case for the arrogance of the Edomites.

CAROL MEYERS

FOR FURTHER READING: Glazier-McDonald, Beth. "Obadiah."

BOOK OF JONAH
No Women Mentioned

The Book of Jonah is part of the canonical grouping of twelve short ("minor") prophetic works, but it differs from the others in literary form and characterization. The book is more a short story or novella, replete with folkloristic motifs, than a series of prophetic utterances or oracles. Although called by God to cry out against wickedness, as are many biblical prophets, Jonah is a kind of anti-hero whose behavior is often perplexing and even outrageous, rather than a man of God.

The story of Jonah is set in the days of Assyrian domination of the Near East, during the reign of Jeroboam II (788–747 B.C.E.), who has a court prophet named Jonah son of Amittai. The author of Jonah has used this reference to contextualize the tale; but the actual date of the book, although difficult to pinpoint, is undoubtedly several centuries later. The theme of God's favorable response to human repentance seems to fit the circumstances of Judah's sixth-century B.C.E. destruction and exile, when the efficacy of repentance would have been an important component of the hope for restoration.

As a dramatic tale involving the memorable image of Jonah swallowed by a large fish, Jonah has captured the attention of audiences for millennia and has become part of Jewish and Christian liturgical tradition. The world of seafaring and sailors that provides the book's setting is a male domain, and the universalistic message of divine forgiveness transcends gender. Yet an illusion to a female role may be present in the attributes of God mentioned in 4:2. This verse is excerpted from a longer creedal formula about God (Exod 34:6–7) that is quoted many other times in the Hebrew Bible. It includes a designation — "merciful" — that is used in the Bible only for God. Because this abstract adjective is related to the noun *reḥem* ("womb"), the use of the word *merciful* to describe God can be deemed a female image of a deity exhibiting maternal compassion for humanity.

CAROL MEYERS

SEE ALSO Part III: Female Images of God in the Hebrew Bible.

FOR FURTHER READING: Trible, Phyllis. "Journey of a Metaphor."
White, Marsha C. "Jonah."

MIC 1:7   Prostitute
SEE LEV 19:29, etc.   Prostitute (Part II).

MIC 1:13; 4:8, 10, 13   Daughter Zion
SEE Daughter (Part III).

MIC 4:9–10   Woman in Labor
SEE ISA 13:8, etc.   Woman in Labor (Part II).

MIC 5:3
Woman in Labor

If metaphorical, the woman in this prophetic text is Zion. She suffers the labor pains of exile in Babylon, to whom YHWH has surrendered Judah (see 4:9–10), and the limited duration of the agony is emphasized. Otherwise, the emphasis is on the birth of the son whose kingship will bring relief to Judah.

JUDITH E. SANDERSON

SEE ALSO Part II: Woman in Labor (Isa 13:8, etc.); (Jer 4:31, etc.).

MIC 7:5
Embraced Woman

Using hyperbole to lament his sense of utter isolation, the prophet finds absolutely no one trustworthy: neither public figures (vv. 3–4) nor household members (v. 6). Thus he warns his male listener to confide neither in his closest male friend (compare Jer 9:4–6) nor even in the woman he embraces. The family setting of v. 6 may suggest that this is most naturally his wife, though it would not rule out a prostitute.

JUDITH E. SANDERSON

MIC 7:6
Daughter (and Son) and Daughter-in-Law; Mother (and Father) and Mother-in-Law

The late-eighth-century B.C.E. prophet Micah presents a grim scene of how unstable society has become because of the idolatry of the people. Although elsewhere he portrays political doom and physical devastation, in 7:5–6 he depicts the disruption of the most intimate of relationships: the bonds between friends and loved ones, especially those between family members (v. 6). The pairs of connections that go sour — father and son, mother and daughter, mother-in-law and daughter-in-law — curiously omit father-in-law and son-in-law.

This omission can be understood as a reflection of family structure and marital patterns in ancient Israel. Sons brought wives into their family households, making daughters-in-law live in close proximity to their husbands' mothers. Daughters, however, married out, with the result that sons-in-law were not part of the household of their wives' fathers. The troubled family dynamics of this verse, therefore, exclude the relationship of fathers to their daughters' spouses.

CAROL MEYERS

SEE ALSO Part II: Daughters of the Inhabitants of the Land as Marriage Partners (Exod 34:16, etc.); Embraced Woman (Mic 7:5).

NAH 2:7
Slave Women of Nineveh

In announcing the destruction of the Assyrian capital Nineveh, the seventh-century B.C.E. prophet Nahum says its slave women will be carried away. Whether literal slaves, or attendants of the queen, or women devoted to the patron goddess Ishtar, these women of Nineveh will be carried off lamenting into exile, their disgrace symbolizing the fall of the capital of Assyria.

JUDITH E. SANDERSON

SEE ALSO Part III: Woman Nineveh.

NAH 3:4–7
Female Imagery for Nineveh
SEE Woman Nineveh (Part III).

NAH 3:8–10
Female Imagery for Thebes
SEE Woman Thebes (Part III).

NAH 3:13
Troops as Women

The soldiers of Nineveh, the capital of Assyria, which had been the mightiest empire in Israel's world, are in this description of Nineveh's defeat called women, one of the most insulting threats or curses that could be made, from an androcentric point of view (compare Isa 3:12). As their fortresses fall like first-ripe figs (v. 12), their soldiers will be fearful (compare Isa 19:16), weak (compare Jer 51:30), and easily defeated (compare Jer 50:37). Typically representing power, these soldiers instead, like women, completely lack military clout.

JUDITH E. SANDERSON

SEE ALSO Part II: Women as Rulers (Isa 3:12); Trembling Women (Isa 19:16); Women and Girls in Babylon (Jer 50:37, etc.).

BOOK OF HABAKKUK
No Women Mentioned

One of the twelve Minor Prophets of the Hebrew Bible, the Book of Habakkuk is a poetic work attributed to the prophet Habakkuk. The prophet is mentioned twice (1:1; 3:1); but unlike most of the Minor Prophets, no biographical information is provided for him. The dearth of identifying data about the prophet or about the time in which he lived makes it difficult to establish the context for the oracles that comprise the book. The references to Babylonian (Chaldean) militance, however, make it likely that Habakkuk's oracles were uttered in the late seventh century B.C.E., when the neo-Babylonian Empire was expanding.

The Book of Habakkuk consists of several literary forms, all dealing with human and divine violence. First, in an extended address to God, the prophet bemoans the horrible destruction perpetrated by the evil Babylonians; God then instructs him to write down a somewhat enigmatic vision that the enemy will ultimately be vanquished. A series of oracles of woe follows; each specifies the heinous deeds of the oppressor. Finally, the third chapter of the book is called a prayer and expresses the prophet's hope that God will use divine might to wipe out the enemy.

The theme of violence is prominent in all three parts of Habakkuk. It is no wonder that the book's images of human and divine power, drawn from the arena of warfare, include no females. Although women may be considered part of the populations devastated by the enemies and then ultimately by God's retributive onslaught, they are absent from the specific depictions of violence and domination. Those depictions include features of male military operations as well as troubling metaphors for God's power.

CAROL MEYERS

FOR FURTHER READING: Sanderson, Judith E. "Habakkuk."

BOOK OF ZEPHANIAH
No Women Mentioned

Zephaniah, whose book is included in the canonical grouping of twelve Minor Prophets, uttered his prophetic oracles in Judah during the reign of King Josiah (639–609 B.C.E.). A contemporary of Jeremiah, Zephaniah likewise focuses his message on his people's sins and the divine judgment that will necessitate sweeping destruction. God's punitive actions will also be visited upon Judah's neighbors on all sides. Ultimately, however, those nations will turn to YHWH. Similarly, the remnant of Jerusalem and Israel will be returned to their homeland and restored in their role as God's people.

The national and international interests of Zephaniah are devoid of reference to specific individuals of either gender, except for several categories of male leaders in Jerusalem (3:3–4). However, his indictment of "those who bow down on the roofs / to the host of the heavens" (1:5) probably is directed at worshippers in household shrines, which included women and may even have been the responsibility of women; and the deities worshipped on the rooftops probably included goddesses such as the queen of heaven. In addition, all people, female and male, are included in his general mention of those who have sinned and those who will be saved. Also, in one instance he refers to Jerusalem as "daughter Zion" (3:14), a term related to the fact that cities are often personified as women.

CAROL MEYERS

SEE ALSO Part III: Daughter; Mother/Daughter as Territory; Queen of Heaven.

FOR FURTHER READING: Sanderson, Judith A. "Zephaniah."

ZEPH 3:14   Daughter Zion
SEE Daughter (Part III).

BOOK OF HAGGAI
No Women Mentioned

The prophet Haggai, to whom one of the twelve minor prophetic books is attributed, is linked with his contemporary Zechariah, the prophet responsible for Zechariah 1–8 (First Zechariah). Both men utter their oracles during the reign of Darius I (521–486 B.C.E.), the Persian emperor whose kingdom had dominion over the tiny province of Yehud in the postexilic period. The Book of Haggai contains five date formulas, which indicate that the prophet's words were spoken over a brief period of several months, from August 29 to December 18 in 520 B.C.E. Haggai is concerned with practical matters of the community restored to semi-autonomy under Persian rule, especially with the project of refurbishing the temple in Jerusalem. God's dwelling place on earth must be rebuilt to serve as the religious center of Yehud and also, now that there is no longer a royal ruler, to function as the site of broader national and political leadership.

Some of Haggai's oracles are directed to all the people, presumably women as well as men, who are suffering from the difficult economic conditions of the late sixth century. He offers them hope that their contributions to the restoration of the temple will lead to God's blessing, and thus to prosperity; and ultimately, he claims, all nations will contribute to the glory of Jerusalem. In addition, Haggai addresses some of his prophecies to specific leaders — the high priest Joshua and the Persian-appointed governor Zerubbabel. These public officers are both men; the priesthood, of course, is limited to men, but Zerubbabel may be part of a series of gubernatorial appointments that involves at least one woman, Zerubbabel's daughter Shelomith.

CAROL MEYERS

SEE ALSO Part I: Shelomith 2.

FOR FURTHER READING: Meyers, Carol, and Eric M. Meyers. "Haggai, Book of."

ZECH 2:7   Daughter Babylon
SEE Daughter (Part III).

ZECH 2:10   Daughter Zion
SEE Daughter (Part III).

ZECH 5:6–11   Woman in the Basket
SEE Woman Wickedness (Part III).

ZECH 5:9   Two Winged Women
SEE Two Winged Women Carrying a Basket (Part III).

ZECH 7:10   Widow
SEE EXOD 22:22, etc.   Widows (Part II).

ZECH 8:4–5
Old Women (and Men) and Girls (and Boys)

The eschatological visions that conclude the prophecies of First Zechariah, a sixth-century B.C.E. prophet whose oracles and visions appear in Zechariah 1–8, include the concept of Zion and Judah gloriously restored. One image that conveys the peace and prosperity of the future age is that of the young (8:5) and the elderly (8:4) enjoying their place in the life span. Old people are free of the onerous tasks of daily life and can sit in public places ("open places of Jerusalem"; NRSV, "streets of Jerusalem"), enjoying companionship and watching the pulse of city life. Similarly, children — both girls and boys — will be playing in the same public places, with similar freedom from household tasks and delight in one another's company.

These two pairs of gender terms marking the two ends of the life span not only represent equality between each part of the pair, but may also function as a merismus. That is, the two age extremes represent all ages in between, meaning that in the future age all people will find release from the trials and tribulations of daily life. God will restore Israel, reversing the horrible devastation that befell both young and old (see Lam 2:21).

CAROL MEYERS

SEE ALSO Part II: Grieving Girls (Lam 1:4, etc.); Fallen and Captive Young Women (and Men) (Lam 1:18, etc.).

ZECH 9:9   Daughter Zion/Jerusalem
SEE Daughter (Part III).

ZECH 9:17
Young Women (and Men)

The poetic opening of the oracles of the fifth-century B.C.E. prophet Second Zechariah (Zechariah 9–14) presents a future vision of God's people restored through divine intervention. The final image is that of a plenitude of "new wine" and of "grain," which will cause "young women" and "young men" to flourish (9:17). Wine in this passage is associated with the young women, probably because, in the division of labor by gender in ancient Israel, women often worked in the vineyards and in wine making (see Judg 21:21). Similarly, this verse connects men with grain production, reflecting male responsibility for field crops.

It is to be noted, however, that the verse has only one verb; the flourishing includes both genders. This suggests that the boundaries between female and male tasks were not rigid — women worked in the fields, especially at harvest time (see Ruth 2:3, 17), and men had responsibilities in wine production. The emphasis in this complementary gender pairing of *young* women and men is part of the future orientation of Zechariah's oracles and the promise of human, as well as agricultural, fertility. It reverses the biblical image of doom, such as that of Lam 2:21, represented by the death of young women and men.

CAROL MEYERS

SEE ALSO Part II: Fallen and Captive Young Women (and Men) (Lam 1:18, etc.).

Zech 12:12–14

Women of the Houses of David, Nathan, and Levi, and of the Shimeites, and of All the Families

The fifth-century B.C.E. prophetic book Second Zechariah (Zechariah 9–14) depicts a glorious future for Zion, Israel, and all the nations. It also reviews the destruction of God's people and others. In one such section, at the end of chap. 12, there is a catalogue (vv. 12–14) of people mourning the devastation. "All the families" are to grieve, namely the houses of David, Nathan, Levi, and of the Shimeites, and of all the rest. These five groups include two royal lineages, two priestly ones, plus all the remaining people. For each of them the text indicates that "their women [NRSV, wives] by themselves" are to mourn.

It is difficult to determine why the mourning activities of the women are mentioned separately. Perhaps it may indicate that women and men had separate rituals of grieving. It may mean that women cared for the corpses of women and men for the corpses of men, as is the case in contemporary Judaism and as was done already in early postbiblical Judaism. At the same time, it may reflect the special role of women as professional mourners. All the people experienced and expressed the loss of loved ones; the experts who keened traditional laments were often women.

CAROL MEYERS

SEE ALSO Part II: Weeping Daughters (2 Sam 1:24); Singing Women (and Men) Who Lament (2 Chr 35:25); Daughters of Zion (Isa 3:16–26, etc.); Mourning Women (Jer 9:17–20, etc.).

Zech 13:2–3

Mothers (and Fathers) of False Prophets

The oracles on the end of false prophecy in Second Zechariah (Zechariah 9–14), a postexilic prophetic book, contain an unusual example of household judicial action. The prophet begins with YHWH acting to remove false prophets from the land (13:1). But he then cites a case in which the mothers and fathers of those who "speak lies in the name of the LORD" take responsibility for dealing with that sinful behavior (Zech 13:2–3). Once the problem of false prophecy is recognized, the parents deliver a verdict (guilty) and then carry out the penalty (death). In several pentateuchal texts (Deut 21:18–21; 22:15), parents have authority in domestic juridical-legal matters — ones affecting family stability — but other people carry out the penalty. In Zechariah 13, the scope of the problem has shifted to one affecting the well-being of the entire postexilic community; and the parents themselves, as representatives of that community, impose the death sentence. Second Zechariah portrays both parents as responsible for punishing their errant offspring and thus as agents of national justice.

CAROL MEYERS

SEE ALSO Part II: Mother (or Father) Cursed or Struck by Offspring (Exod 21:15, etc.); Mother (and Father) Dealing with a Rebellious Son (Deut 21:18–21); Mother (and Father) of a Slandered Bride (Deut 22:15).

FOR FURTHER READING: Meyers, Carol L., and Eric M. Meyers. *Zechariah 9–14.*

ZECH 14:2

Raped Women

In describing the future day of the LORD (an eschatological term in the Hebrew Bible), the writer of Zechariah 14 draws images from the destruction of Jerusalem in 587–586 B.C.E. These images include the rape of women who remain in the city and virtually mirrors the wording of Isa 13:16, in which Babylonian women are the subject. Rape in wartime was both a reality for women in the ancient Near East as well as a literary figure used to describe the subjugation of peoples by their enemies. Here, use of perhaps the harshest language for sexual abuse available in Hebrew underscores the violence and offensiveness of this act.

SANDRA L. GRAVETT

SEE ALSO Part II: Ravished Wives of Babylonians (Isa 13:16); Raped Women and Virgins (Lam 5:11)

MAL 2:11
Daughter of a Foreign God

Most scholars identify this figure as a foreign woman involved in — and enticing Judean men to — idolatry. Combined with standard treatments of "wife of one's youth" (2:14–16), this rendering is usually seen as evidence that Malachi decries the mixed marriages later outlawed by the reforms of Ezra and Nehemiah and that the book dates to the years immediately before Nehemiah's mission (which began in 445 B.C.E.).

A minority of interpreters argues that the offense described is not intermarriage, but worship of a female deity. Vocabulary is consistent with biblical passages describing idolatry, and "daughter of a god" logically may be a goddess.

JULIA MYERS O'BRIEN

SEE ALSO Part II: Daughters of the Inhabitants of the Land as Marriage Partners (Exod 34:16, etc.); Wife of One's Youth (Mal 2:14–16); Part III: Woman Wickedness.

MAL 2:14–16
Wife of One's Youth

Most interpreters understand this passage as addressing a concrete problem in the postexilic community: Judean men who had returned to the land

after the Babylonian exile were divorcing their original (Judean) wives in order to marry more affluent foreign women — the "people of the land" whose ancestors had not been exiled and who owned property. According to this view, the prophet Malachi (fifth century B.C.E.) describes the mixed marriages that were later outlawed by the reforms of Ezra and Nehemiah.

Several objections to such an interpretation, however, have been offered. First, if Mal 2:16 is accurately understood to claim that God hates divorce (literally, the Hebrew reads "sending"), then it conflicts with the action of Ezra and Nehemiah, which *mandates* divorce of non-Judean women.

Second, the language "wife of one's youth" is not unique to Malachi. It appears frequently in other prophetic books in the context of the "marriage metaphor," in which the relationship between YHWH and Israel is compared to that between a husband and a wife, and idolatry is compared to adultery. In passages such as Hos 2:17 and Ezek 16:60, YHWH is said to have "married" the land; infidelity is called "treachery"; and "youth" is considered the time of happiness and fidelity.

If Malachi indeed is using this common prophetic vocabulary, then the author has done so with an interesting gender twist: if Judah is accused of being unfaithful to the wife of *his* youth, then within the metaphorical system the wife must be the deity. Several interpreters have made such a suggestion: Petersen identifies YHWH as the female spouse, and O'Brien explores the grammatical shifts in Mal 2:10–16 that leave Judah's gender unstable.

JULIA MYERS O'BRIEN

SEE ALSO Part II: Daughter of a Foreign God (Mal 2:11).

FOR FURTHER READING: O'Brien, Julia M. "Judah as Wife and Husband: Deconstructing Gender in Malachi."

Petersen, David. *Zechariah 9–14 and Malachi.*

MAL 3:5 Widow
SEE EXOD 22:22, etc. Widows (Part II).

The Apocryphal/
Deuterocanonical Books

TOB 1:8
Widows

The Book of Tobit is an extended fourteen-chapter narrative, sometimes called a romance of diaspora Judaism (communities outside Palestine where Jews "scattered" to live after the Babylonian exile) because it is an entertaining and edifying story that encourages righteousness, prayer, and almsgiving. The story is about two related Jewish families who, through no fault of their own, experience great misfortune: the family of Tobit, Anna, and their son, Tobias; and the family of Raguel, Edna, and their daughter, Sarah. The story, set in the eighth century B.C.E., is often dated to the second century B.C.E. but compositionally could be earlier. It gives special attention to marriage, family, extended family, and care for aging parents and other vulnerable groups, including widows.

In 1:8 Tobit's acts of piety include the charitable almsgiving of "a third tenth" to the orphans and widows. It is unclear whether this is a tri-annual tithe (as in 2 Macc 3:10; 8:28, 30) or an annual gift of one of three tithes (based upon the laws on tithing in Lev 27:30–33; Num 18:21–32; Deut 14:28–29). The practice of sharing resources with those in need, most particularly those who reside together yet have no allotment of land (resident aliens, orphans, and widows) is part of the social fabric of ancient Israel. Concern for widows (and orphans) spans the entire Bible. Good acts, like care for widows, usually bring God's blessing, though such is not the case for Tobit, who has been blinded by bird droppings despite his pious practices.

TONI CRAVEN

SEE ALSO Part II: Widows (Exod 22:22, etc.); (2 Macc 3:10, etc.); Widow (Wis 2:10); (Sir 35:17–18); (Ep Jer v. 38); (2 Esdr 2:2–4, etc.).

FOR FURTHER READING: Moore, Carey A. "Tobit, Book of."

TOB 1:9; 4:12–13; 6:11–13, 16; 7:10; 8:21
Kinship Wife

The ideal in the Book of Tobit is that a wife should be specifically from the father's tribe (1:9; 4:12; 6:11–13, 16; 7:10). Such endogamy ensures that inheritance rights are preserved. Since Sarah is an only child, Tobias, as the nearest kin, can legally take her and all her father's possessions (6:11–13; 7:10; 8:21). This model follows the case of the five daughters of the sonless Zelophehad (Num 27:1–11; 36:1–11), who were granted legal right to their father's inheritance, but were required to marry within their father's own tribe to avoid transfer of property from one tribe to another.

In 4:12, Tobit instructs his son, Tobias, to follow the way of the great ancestral figures Noah, Abraham, Isaac, and Jacob who "took wives from among their kindred." In Diaspora Judaism, endogamy (marriage within one's own group) was important for preserving national and religious identity. Endogamous marriage is the norm in the ancestral stories; Isaac, for example, marries his cousin Rebekah (Gen 24:15). But exogamous marriages are also found in these narratives, demonstrating that endogamy was not inviolable: Joseph, for example, marries an Egyptian (Gen 41:45), and Moses a Midianite/Cushite (Num 12:1). Thus, Tobit overstates the case to his son in saying, "Our ancestors of old, *all* took wives from among their kindred" (Tob 4:12).

Tobit's closing words that his son "love your kindred" (4:13) express the romantic tenderness found elsewhere in the book (6:17–18; 8:5–8).

TONI CRAVEN

SEE ALSO Part II: Daughters of the Inhabitants of the Land as Marriage Partners (Exod 34:16, etc.); Daughters of Zelophehad (Num 26:33, etc.); Daughters of Judah and Foreign Daughters/Wives (Ezra 9:2, etc.)

FOR FURTHER READING: Hamilton, Victor P. "Marriage (OT and ANE)."

Tob 3:7–9; 8:12–14; 10:10
Female (and Male) Servants

Servants are assumed in the household structure of Raguel, Edna, and their daughter, Sarah. One of her father's maids reproaches Sarah, saying of the deaths of her seven husbands, "You are the one who kills your husbands! See, you have already been married to seven husbands and have not borne the name of a single one of them. Why do you beat us? Because your husbands are dead? Go with them! May we never see a son or daughter of yours!" (3:8–9). Sarah, falsely accused of acts of the demon Asmodeus, is reduced to praying for death (3:10–15). She is likely not innocent of the charge of physical abuse, even if she does not deserve the servant's wish that she will be barren. Only the female servant censures Sarah's beating of her slaves; Sarah does not confess remorse in her prayer for such actions, nor does anyone else in the narrative confront this issue. Abusive domestic violence is thus given no attention in this narrative, except by one female servant.

Early on the day after Sarah's marriage to Tobias, Raguel calls his male servants and instructs them to dig a grave, thinking to divert additional ridicule if Tobias meets the same fate as the previous seven husbands (8:9–10). He tells his wife to send one of her maids to see if Tobias is still alive (8:12). The maid finds the couple sound asleep and returns to inform Edna and Raguel that nothing is wrong (8:13–14). Thus male and female servants are portrayed as obedient to the commands of those they serve. Men do heavy digging work; female servants are household assistants.

When Sarah and Tobias plan their return to his parents' home in Nineveh, Raguel gives Tobias Sarah as his wife, "as well as half of all his property: male and female slaves, oxen and sheep, donkeys and camels, clothing, money, and household goods" (10:10). In this hierarchy of ownership women belong to men, as do human slaves, animals, and material goods.

TONI CRAVEN

SEE ALSO Part I: Sarah 2; Part II: Maid of Judith (Jdt 8:10, etc.); Maids (Sus v. 15, etc.).

FOR FURTHER READING: Glancy, Jennifer A. "The Mistress-Slave Dialectic: Paradoxes of Slavery in Three LXX Narratives."

Tob 3:8
Wives

In the Book of Tobit, the fulfillment of marriage through the first act of sexual intercourse "customary for wives" (Tob 3:8) is denied Sarah, who remains a virgin. Her misfortune is caused by Asmodeus, an evil demon, who kills each of her seven briedgrooms before the consummation of her marriage. On this account, Sarah is unable to fulfill the biblical instruction that "a man leaves his father and his mother and clings to his wife, and they become one flesh" (Gen 2:24).

Sarah's enemy, the demon Asmodeus (which probably means "the destroyer"; see the destroying angel of 2 Sam 24:16; Wis 18:25; Rev 9:11), also appears in *Testament of Solomon* (a first- to third-century C.E. folktale about the building of the temple) where the whole of chap. five is given over to Solomon's interrogation of this being. Solomon learns that he is the son of a human mother and an angel, the Great Bear (or Offspring of a Dragon) constellation. He tells Solomon, "I am the renowned Asmodeus; I cause the wickedness of men to spread throughout the world. I am always hatching plots against newlyweds; I mar the beauty of virgins and cause their hearts to grow cold" (TSol 5:7). "I spread madness about women through the stars and I have often committed a rash of murders" (TSol 5:8). Solomon learns that Asmodeus is thwarted by the angel Raphael and by the smoking liver and gall of the sheatfish (a large catfish) found in the rivers of Assyria. Asmodeus begs Solomon not to condemn him to the water. In the end, Solomon subdues Asmodeus, requiring him to wear irons, mold clay for the vessels of the temple, and sit surrounded by ten water jars. Then Solomon takes the liver and the gall of the fish and lights a fire under Asmodeus.

With the help of the angel Raphael and the incense of fish liver and heart, Tobias safely enters the bridal chamber, and the demon flees and is never again seen near Sarah (Tob 6:16–18; 8:2–3).

TONI CRAVEN

SEE ALSO Part I: Sarah 2; Part II: Virgin (Exod 22:16-17, etc.).

FOR FURTHER READING: Duling, D. C. "Testament of Solomon."

TOB 3:9
Daughter (and Son)

One of the female servants in the household of Raguel and Edna outspokenly charges Sarah with wrongdoing, both in murdering her seven husbands on their wedding nights and in physically abusing the servants.

The hateful imprecation of the female servant, "May we never see a son or daughter of yours!" (3:9), is intended to make Sarah the object of reproach. Since both barrenness and fertility were traced to God (Gen 20:17–18; 30:2; 33:5; 1 Sam 1:6), it is appropriate that Sarah addresses her distress over this exchange, not to the servant, but to God in her prayer (3:11–15). Contention between a servant and another mistress named Sarah appears in Genesis, when Hagar, having become pregnant by Abraham, "looked with contempt on her mistress" (Gen 16:4–6).

TONI CRAVEN

SEE ALSO Part I: Hagar; Part II: Female (and Male) Servants (Tob 3:7–9, etc.).

TOB 4:12
Foreign Wife

Tobit's instruction to his son, Tobias, to marry within his own tribe is immediately followed by the negative restatement of this same command: "Do not marry a foreign woman, who is not of your father's tribe" (Tob 4:12). This repeats the preference for endogamy over exogamy, making even more specific the command that the woman is to be

from Tobit's tribe, that is, the tribe of Naphtali in the northern regions of Israel around the eastern parts of Galilee (Tob 1:1). Thus a "foreign woman" here is conceivably a woman from another tribe of Israel as well as a woman from another people.

TONI CRAVEN

SEE ALSO Part II: Kinship Wife (Tob 1:9, etc.).
FOR FURTHER READING: Nowell, Irene. "Tobit."

TOB 4:12–13; 6:11–13, 16; 7:10
Kinship Wife
SEE TOB 1:9, etc.   Kinship Wife (Part II).

TOB 8:12–14   Maids
SEE TOB 3:7–9, etc.   Female (and Male) Servants (Part II).

TOB 8:21   Kinship Wife
SEE TOB 1:9, etc.   Kinship Wife (Part II).

TOB 10:10   Female Slaves
SEE TOB 3:7–9, etc.   Female (and Male) Servants (Part II).

TOB 13:9   Jerusalem as Mother
SEE Jerusalem/Zion as Widow and Mother (Part III).

JDT 4:10–12; 13:18; 15:12–13
Women/Wives of Israel

In the Book of Judith, a highly fictionalized sixteen-chapter narrative dating to the end of the second or beginning of the first century B.C.E., at least five centuries of historical and geographical information are intermingled with imaginary details.

Women in this book play stock communal female roles that are for the most part associated with the maintenance of the androcentric family in times of warfare and deliverance. With the exceptions of Judith, eventually hailed as "blessed by the Most High God above all other women on earth" (13:18), and her maid, the women appear in silent chorus. When the singular word "woman" is used, it refers only to Judith (see 8:31; 9:10; 11:1, 21; 12:11, 12; 13:15; 14:18; 16:5).

Women (and children) are not only family members, but also property men do not want to lose in war. Their fate as prisoners of war is usually slavery, but to lose women (and children) is to lose the battle. As the Assyrians approach, the Judeans fortify their mountain passes and pray fervently that God will not allow the Gentiles to take their wives and infants as booty (4:12). Protection of women and children symbolizes preservation of the family household and continuance of a way of life that carries with it important political, religious, economic, and cultural consequences.

Women of Israel as a group are supplicants in communal worship, though only cultic actions, not words, are attributed to them in the Book of Judith. In 4:9, "every man of Israel cried out to God with great fervor," with women as "their wives and their children and their cattle and every resident alien and hired laborer and purchased slave" (4:10), putting on sackcloth and ashes and humbling themselves before the Jerusalem temple (4:11).

Only in 15:12–13 do women of Israel take initiative, gathering to see Judith upon her triumphant return from the enemy camp. While they act in ways typical of women's celebration of a military victory (see Judg 11:34; 1 Sam 18:6), their action is distinctive in that it is another woman whose victory they celebrate. They bless her, and some perform a dance in her honor. She, in turn, gives them ivy-wreaths, which they put on their heads (a Greek custom associated with the cult of Dionysus in 2 Macc 6:7; 10:7). Then Judith leads the women — with the men following — in a joyous procession to Jerusalem. Like those who danced in victory with Miriam at the Red Sea (Exod 15:20), the women of Israel dance their deliverance and Judith's great victory.

TONI CRAVEN

SEE ALSO Part II: Women with Hand-Drums, Dancing (Exod 15:20, etc.); Women/Wives of Bethulia (Jdt 6:16, etc.); Women/Wives Defended by Judas and Simon (1 Macc 3:20, etc.).

FOR FURTHER READING: Craven, Toni. *Artistry and Faith in the Book of Judith.*
Hopkins, Denise Dombkowski. "Judith."
Moore, Carey A. *Judith: A New Translation with Introduction and Commentary.*

JDT 6:16; 7:22–23, 32
Women/Wives of Bethulia

In the story of Judith, unnamed Jewish women play communal roles as part of the people of the imaginary little town guarding the pass to Jerusalem. They appear in the public assembly when Uzziah, an official in Bethulia, questions Achior the Ammonite, who has just arrived from the Assyrian camp (6:16). After thirty-four days without water, faint and collapsing and without "any strength" (7:22), women are part of the crowd that gathers before Uzziah and the other rulers of Bethulia (Chabris and Charmis) to demand the surrender of their town to the Assyrians (7:23). After Uzziah proposes his compromise plan to postpone surrender for five more days, he dismisses the townspeople, including the women and children, whom he sends home (7:32). Typical of the gender roles in the androcentric family, the men take up military posts to defend Bethulia; the women return to family households with their children. For all the women in Bethulia, a town whose very name suggests "virgin," patriarchy is the norm.

TONI CRAVEN

SEE ALSO Part II: Women/Wives of Israel (Jdt 4:10–12, etc.); Sisters (and Brothers) (Jdt 7:30).

JDT 7:30
Sisters (and Brothers)

In the NRSV translation, Uzziah urges his brothers and "sisters" in the little town of Bethulia to have courage and hold out for five days more before surrendering to the Assyrian forces camped at the foot of the hill below who have cut off their water supply for thirty-four days (7:30). The Greek lacks the word for "sisters." In this instance, the women of Bethulia are in the crowd that gathers around Uzziah (7:23) and are specifically dismissed by him (7:32). Here and in two other Apochryphal/Deuterocanonical Books (Sir 25:1 and 2 Macc 15:18), the NRSV translation includes reference to "sisters" for inclusiveness and the sense of the text.

TONI CRAVEN

SEE ALSO Part II: Women/Wives of Bethulia (Jdt 6:16, etc.); Sisters (and Brothers) (Sir 25:1); Wives and Sisters (and Brothers) of Judas' Men (2 Macc 15:18).

JDT 7:32   Women of Bethulia

SEE JDT 6:16, etc.   Women/Wives of Bethulia (Part II).

JDT 8:7
Women (and Men) Slaves

In Jdt 8:7, widowed Judith inherits the estate of her husband, Manasseh, including women (and men) slaves. A regular part of wealthy households in the Diaspora, like those of Raguel in the Book of Tobit and Joakim in the Book of Susanna, slaves figure in the economy of estate management. They are listed as property with no indication of national or religious identity. Whether they are Jewish or Gentile is unclear. According to Deut 15:12, if they are Jewish, the law protects them with promise of freedom following seven years of service. If Gentile, they are bound to life service.

TONI CRAVEN

SEE ALSO Part II: Female (and Male) Hebrew Slaves (Exod 21:7–11, etc.); Female (and Male) Servants (Tob 3:7–9, etc.); Maid of Judith (Jdt 8:10, etc.); Maids (Sus v. 15, etc.).

JDT 8:10, 33; 10:2, 5, 10, 17; 12:15, 19; 13:3, 9; 16:23
Maid of Judith

A woman (variously designated *abran*, literally "graceful one" or "favorite slave," 8:10, 33; 10:2, 5, 17;

13:9; 16:23; "maid," *paidiskē*, 10:10; or "servant," *doule*, 12:15, 19; 13:3) is in charge of Judith's household and serves as her body slave, helping with personal matters (compare Sus vv. 15, 17, 19, 21, 36). Like Abraham's servant (Gen 15:2; 24:2), this woman has administrative charge of the affairs of Judith's estate ("gold and silver, men and women slaves, livestock, and fields" [Jdt 8:7] of Judith's dead husband, Manasseh). In Jdt 8:10, Judith's first act in the story is to send this unnamed woman to summon the town officials (Uzziah, Chabris, Charmis) to come to her house to review the compromise they have just struck with the people of Bethulia, which gives God five days to deliver their town before its surrender to the Assyrians. Later, this unnamed woman accompanies Judith to the enemy camp (8:33; 10:10) after helping Judith prepare (10:2) and carrying the food her mistress will eat in the enemy camp (10:5).

Upon their arrival in the enemy camp, the soldiers choose one hundred men to escort Judith and her maid to the tent of Holofernes (10:17). On the night of the climactic party in the Assyrian camp, the maid goes ahead of Judith into the tent of the enemy general Holofernes to spread out lambskins for her use in reclining (12:15). While with Holofernes, Judith eats and drinks only the foods her maid prepares (12:19). As instructed, the maid waits outside Holofernes' bedchamber for Judith, "for she said she would be going out for her prayers" (13:3). When Judith comes out with the head of the enemy, she gives the decapitated head to her maid (13:9), who puts it in the food bag. The two women return to Bethulia (13:10) and are welcomed by the excited townspeople (13:13). Upon their arrival, only Judith speaks and receives acclaim.

The maid does not reappear until the very end of the story, where Judith's last action before her own death is to free this faithful servant (Jdt 16:23). As Judith risked her life for her people, so did this maid. Manumission comes for this woman with no name, no family connection of her own, no unambiguous national identity — save that she regularly prays with her mistress — in her old age. The only hint that this female servant is Jewish is that "the two of them went out together, as *they* were accustomed to do for prayer" (13:10). Their habit of prayer, in this last instance, is the ruse that gets them out of the enemy camp after Judith has beheaded Holofernes. With Judith to the end, this unnamed servant is constant and faithful. No jealousy or tensions arise between them, like those that plague Hagar and Sarah in Genesis or the female servant and Sarah in Tobit. No seventh-year release (see Deut 15:12) figures in the life of this silent woman. Only the note that Judith, now 105 years old, "set her maid free" tells her fate (Jdt 16:23). This unnamed servant and her mistress Judith are the only female characters in the Book of Judith who play individual female roles. Only Judith's death separates them (16:23).

TONI CRAVEN

SEE ALSO Part I: Hagar; Judith 2; Part II: Female (and Male) Servants (Tob 3:7–9, etc.); Women/Wives of Israel (Jdt 4:10–12, etc.); Women/Wives of Bethulia (Jdt 6:16, etc.); Maids (Sus v. 15, etc.).
FOR FURTHER READING: Craven, Toni. "Judith."
Glancy, Jennifer A. "The Mistress-Slave Dialectic: Paradoxes of Slavery in Three LXX Narratives."

JDT 9:2
Virgin Defiled

In Judith's personal prayer of lament, the longest prayer in the Book of Judith (9:1–14), she asks God to crush the Gentiles who threaten the safety of the Jerusalem temple (9:8, 13). Recalling how God empowered Simeon to annihilate those who defiled his sister, Dinah, by means of a sword given into his hand by God (9:2–4), Judith begs God to hear her (9:4, 12). Identifying with Simeon, Judith prays to carry out heaven-sent vengeance against Israel's enemies (9:5–6).

The reference to "strangers who had torn off a virgin's clothing to defile her" (9:2) is to Shechem, the Hivite prince of the city that bears his name, who violated Dinah, Jacob and Leah's daughter (Gen 34:2). Judith's prayer appeals to this scriptural precedent in Genesis, even as it anticipates her use

of the sword given into her hand — Holofernes' very own — to cut off his head and annihilate those who sought to defile the temple (Jdt 13:6–8).

TONI CRAVEN

SEE ALSO Part I: Dinah; Judith 2.
FOR FURTHER READING: Chesnutt, Randall D., and Judith Newman. "Prayers in the Apocrypha and Pseudepigrapha."
Craven, Toni. "Judith Prays for Help (Judith 9:1–14)."

JDT 9:4
Wives/Daughters of Shechem

Judith's personal prayer of lament (9:2–14) mentions that Simeon's annihilation of the Shechemites who defiled his sister, Dinah, included the capture of their wives (and children) as booty (9:4). In Gen 34:25–31, Simeon and Levi do attack and kill the newly circumcised Shechemite males, plundering the wealth of Shechem and taking their wives and children, as is customary in warfare.

TONI CRAVEN

SEE ALSO Part II: Daughters/Women of the Region; Daughters of the Jacob Group (Gen 34:1, etc.).

JDT 10:2, 5, 10, 17, 12:15, 19; 13:3, 9–10; 16:23   Maid of Judith
SEE JDT 8:10, etc.   Maid of Judith (Part II).

JDT 12:13
Assyrian Women

On Judith's fourth day in the enemy camp — with one day remaining before her townspeople surrender to the Assyrians — Bagoas, Holofernes's eunuch in charge of his personal affairs, invites Judith to a banquet in his master's tent. His master had earlier expressed desire to have "intercourse with her. If we do not seduce her, she will laugh at us" (Jdt 12:12). Bagoas translates this to Judith in language intended to flatter her: "Let this pretty girl not hesitate to come to my lord to be honored in his presence, and to enjoy drinking wine with us, and to become today like one of the Assyrian women who serve in the palace of Nebuchadnezzar" (12:13). The reference to Assyrian women serving in the palace of the Babylonian Nebuchadnezzar is, of course, historically impossible and reflects the fantasy of the scene. Royal women and drinking parties evoke Vashti's plight in the Book of Esther and in Greek Esther with Additions. Judith will obey the command to appear at the party, but on her own terms.

TONI CRAVEN

SEE ALSO Part I: Vashti; Part II: Women at Vashti's Banquet (Esth 1:9); Women at Vashti's Party (Add Esth 1:9).

JDT 13:18; 15:12–13   Women of Israel
SEE JDT 4:10–12, etc.   Women/Wives of Israel (Part II).

JDT 16:23   Maid of Judith
SEE JDT 8:10, etc.   Maid of Judith (Part II).

JDT 16:4
Virgins as Spoil

Judith's triumphant hymn of praise (16:1–17) is a liturgical celebration of God's deliverance and great victory. The poem narrates in epic fashion how the Assyrians boasted they would burn the territory of Israel, kill the young men with the sword, dash the infants to the ground, seize the children as booty, and take the virgins as spoil (Jdt 16:4). These practices reflect the ban, in which enemy males are annihilated and women, children, livestock, and other things of value are taken as spoil (Deut 20:10–15). This is a stock listing of the atrocities of warfare designed to destroy a people and its future. Capture of virgins represents destruction of potential fecundity for a community. The language is reminiscent of horrors associated with the persecutions of the Seleucid ruler Antiochus IV (Epiphanes) as recounted in the Maccabean literature. It also evokes language from Judith's great opening prayer in

which she begs God to allow her to carry out vengeance like that taken by Simeon on behalf of his sister, Dinah, defiled by "strangers who had torn off a virgin's clothing" (Jdt 9:2).

TONI CRAVEN

SEE ALSO Part II: Women in Distant Towns as Booty (Deut 20:14, etc.); Virgin Defiled (Jdt 9:2); Women/Mothers with Circumcised Sons (1 Macc 1:60–61); Women/Wives as Victims of War (2 Macc 5:13, etc.); Martyred Mother with Seven Sons (4 Macc 1:8, etc.).

JDT 16:12
Slave Girls

In her final epic prayer (Jdt 16:1–17), Judith celebrates how "sons of slave girls" attacked the enemy "and wounded them like the children of fugitives" (16:12), so that they perished. Sons of young slave mothers would be mere children themselves, indicating the undoing of this enemy by those not counted powerful by age or social status. These poetic figures offer illustration of the poem's earlier claim that this mighty enemy did not fall at the hand of the Titans, or tall giants (16:6). The powerful are reduced to special vulnerability like that of the unprotected children of fugitives. The identity of these slaves is not specified. If they are Gentiles, this is attack from within their own ranks and is doubly insulting. The slaves could be the Israelites, since in 14:13, the Assyrians try to awaken Holofernes, whom they do not yet know is dead, with the words, "the slaves have been so bold as to come down against us" in battle.

TONI CRAVEN

FOR FURTHER READING: Moore, Carey A. *Judith: A New Translation with Introduction and Commentary.*

ADD ESTH 1:9
Women at Vashti's Party

The Greek version of the Book of Esther (NRSV Additions to Esther) translates the Hebrew Book of

Esther verse for verse, but there is scarcely a verse without some alteration. The reference to women at Vashti's party differs from the Hebrew version in that, in the Greek version, both Vashti's "drinking party" for women (Add Esth 1:9) and the King's "drinking party" for men (Add Esth 1:5) follow a "marriage festival" (Add Esth 1:5, 11). Presumably the women were drinking the same "sweet wine" as King Artaxerxes (the Greek name for Hebrew Ahasuerus) and his guests (Add Esth 1:7).

TONI CRAVEN

SEE ALSO Part I: Vashti; Part II: Women at Vashti's Banquet (Esth 1:9).

FOR FURTHER READING: Moore, Carey A. "Esther, Additions to" and "Esther, Book of."

Reinhartz, Adele. "The Greek Book of Esther."

ADD ESTH 1:18–20
Wives of Persian and Median Governors

With minor alterations in wording, the Greek version repeats the parallel Hebrew text. After Vashti defies the king's order to appear before his male guests (Add Esth 1:12), Muchaeus (equivalent to Memucan, Esth 1:16), spokesman for the king's seven chief counselors, expresses concern that "the other ladies who are wives of the Persian and Median governors, on hearing what she [Vashti] said to the king, will likewise dare to insult their husbands" (Add Esth 1:18). He advises that the king depose Queen Vashti, seek a new queen, and issue a royal decree "that all women will give honor to their husbands, rich and poor alike" (Add Esth 1:20), lest Vashti's example of disobedience spread to every household in the realm, resulting in great social upheaval when wives no longer obey their husbands. As in Hebrew Esther, Vashti's refusal is perceived as a threat to male authority and marital harmony throughout the kingdom.

TONI CRAVEN

SEE ALSO Part I: Vashti; Part II: Noble Ladies of Persia and Media (Esth 1:18–20).

ADD ESTH 2:2–3, 8, 12–14, 17
Young Virgins/Girls

Hebrew Esther's description that "beautiful young virgins" (Esth 2:2) are to be sought out for the king is restated in the Greek: "Let beautiful and virtuous girls be sought out for the king" (Add Esth 2:2). The process of selection by "officers in all the provinces" is much the same as in the Hebrew. The "beautiful young virgins" (Add Esth 2:3) are brought to Susa, where they are placed in the custody of Gai (Haggai in Hebrew Esther) for a twelve-month beautification program, "six months while they are anointing themselves with oil of myrrh, and six months with spices and ointments for women" (Add Esth 2:12). By turn, each goes to the king in the evening and departs in the morning to the second harem, not to go in to the king again "unless she is summoned by name" (Add Esth 2:14). As in the Hebrew version, Esther finds "favor above all the other virgins, so he put on her the queen's diadem" (Add Esth 2:17).

The selection process reflects the patriarchal standard regarding sexual behavior that is characteristic of the ancient Near East. Powerful males are free to exploit female beauty or to act on erotic attraction. The king is allowed multiple sexual partners, but the young girls must not have experienced sexual intercourse outside their encounter with him.

TONI CRAVEN

SEE ALSO Part II: Young Virgins/Women (Esth 2:2–3, etc.).

FOR FURTHER READING: Frymer-Kensky, Tikva. "Sex and Sexuality."

ADD ESTH 2:3, 8, 13–14
Girls/Women of the Harem

References to the harem in Greek Additions to Esther illustrate male entitlement in sexual matters. The king is free to possess and control young females who are selected for their beauty and virginity and are rewarded for giving him pleasure. These young women are virtual slaves who belong to the cloistered harem of the king.

Those in the harem (Add Esth 2:3) are subordinate to the king's eunuch, Gai. After twelve months of training (Add Esth 2:12), one of these girls will achieve status as queen-wife. Following intercourse with the king, life in the "second harem" is the fate of the rest (Add Esth 2:14).

TONI CRAVEN

SEE ALSO Part II: Women of the Harem (Esth 2:3, etc.); Young Virgins/Girls (Add Esth 2:2–3, etc.).

FOR FURTHER READING: Frymer-Kensky, Tikva. "Sex and Sexuality."

ADD ESTH 2:7
Mother of Esther

Because Esther's mother and father are dead, Esther has been adopted and raised by a paternal relative. Mordecai is her cousin, and Esther is the daughter of his uncle, Aminadab (Add Esth 2:7). No name or familial lineage is accorded Esther's dead mother.

TONI CRAVEN

SEE ALSO Part I: Esther; Part II: Mother of Esther (Esth 2:7).

ADD ESTH 2:8
Young Virgins/Girls

SEE ADD ESTH 2:2–3, etc.   Young Virgins/Girls (Part II).

ADD ESTH 2:8   Girls/Women of the Harem

SEE ADD ESTH 2:3, etc.   Girls/Women of the Harem (Part II).

ADD ESTH 2:9; 4:4; 15:2–4, 7
Maids of Esther

Because Esther finds favor with the eunuch Gai early in her period of training, she is given special treatment, including "seven maids chosen from the palace" who also benefit from the special treatment given to their mistress (Add Esth 2:9). "Maids and eunuchs" communicate Mordecai's concerns to Queen Esther (Add Esth 4:4). And "two maids" accompany Esther when she goes before the king: "on one she leaned gently for support, while the other followed, carrying her train" (Add Esth 15:2–4). When the king reacts angrily to Esther's approach, she falters and collapses "on the head of the maid who went in front of her" (Add Esth 15:7).

Esther's maids were personal or body slaves whose domestic role was to serve their mistress. They appear to have been involved primarily with Esther's personal concerns. That Esther approached the king with one maid in front of her and one maid behind suggests that these servants functioned to guard their mistress, buffering her from potential hostility. There is no hint that Esther was physically abusive to her female servants, as Sarah was (Tob 3:9). Like their mistress, the maids held subordinate roles, though in their case subordination was to another woman.

TONI CRAVEN

SEE ALSO Part I: Esther; Sarah 2; Part II: Maids of Esther (Esth 2:9, etc.).

FOR FURTHER READING: Glancy, Jennifer A. "The Mistress-Slave Dialectic: Paradoxes of Slavery in Three LXX Narratives."

ADD ESTH 2:12–14, 17   Young Virgins/Girls

SEE ADD ESTH 2:2–3, etc.   Young Virgins/Girls (Part II).

ADD ESTH 2:13–14
Girls in the Harem

SEE ADD ESTH 2:3, etc.   Girls/Women of the Harem (Part II).

ADD ESTH 4:4   Maids of Esther

SEE ADD ESTH 2:9, etc.   Maids of Esther (Part II).

ADD ESTH 13:6
Wives

Between Hebrew Esth 3:13 and 3:14, the Greek inserts Addition B, the text of the king's decree against the Jews (Add Esth 13:1–7). In the edict, Haman is charged to massacre all the Jews, "wives and children included" (Add Esth 13:6) on the fourteenth day of the twelfth month of the twelfth year of King Artaxerxes (the fifth year of Esther's queenship) so that the Persian Empire will be rid of this hostile people. The letter is a clever piece of propaganda written in the name of Artaxerxes, who has authorized Haman to dictate its contents (Add Esth 3:10–12). In other words, Haman charges himself to utterly destroy all the Jews! Haman's inclusion of "wives and children" ensures that all the Jews will die in the massacre.

TONI CRAVEN

SEE ALSO Part II: Women in the King's Decree (Esth 3:13).

FOR FURTHER READING: Moore, Carey A. *Daniel, Esther, and Jeremiah: The Additions.*

ADD ESTH 4:11
Woman (or Man) Who Goes Unbidden to the King

Both the Hebrew and Greek texts include the admonition that no one may go to the king inside the inner court without being called. Both texts invoke this custom as a Persian law, but such a law is otherwise unknown. Its significance is to heighten narrative tension by making it a deadly serious action for Esther to go unbidden before the king.

TONI CRAVEN

SEE ALSO Part II: Woman (or Man) Going Unbidden to the King (Esth 4:11).

ADD ESTH 7:4
Female (and Male) Slaves

In both Hebrew and Greek Esther, at Esther's second banquet, she explains to the king that she and her people are "to be destroyed, plundered, and made slaves — we and our children — male and female slaves" (Add Esth 7:4). Esther petitions for her own life and the life of her people.

This reading suggests, as does its Hebrew counterpart, that if the Jews had only been sold into slavery, she would have kept quiet. Slavery would have been acceptable to Esther, but destruction was not. As slaves, the Jews would have constituted movable property, just like livestock, but their lives would have been preserved. Since Addition B, the text of the king's decree against the Jews (Add Esth 13:1–7), entitles Haman to massacre all the Jews, "wives and children included" (Add Esth 13:6), Esther's request to the king averts this impending disaster.

TONI CRAVEN

SEE ALSO Part II: Female Slaves (Esth 7:4); Wives (Add Esth 13:6).

ADD ESTH 15:2–4, 7   Maids of Esther
SEE ADD ESTH 2:9, etc.   Maids of Esther (Part II).

WIS 2:10
Widow

The Wisdom of Solomon is a pseudonymous work by a Hellenized Jew, almost certainly part of the thriving Jewish community in Alexandria, Egypt. It was probably written between 30 B.C.E. and 40 C.E. The author is clearly familiar with Greek philosophy as well as Hebrew Scripture and draws on both to present Judaism in intellectually respectable terms to a sophisticated Jewish audience. His vigorous attacks on "the ungodly," however, suggest a political climate of conflict between Jews and others or, perhaps, within the Jewish community. Reflected here may be new laws passed in Alexandria in the late first century B.C.E., demoting Jews to the status of aliens and foreigners. Ensuing tensions led to anti-Jewish riots in 38 C.E. Such an environment may provide the setting for sections of this work, such as 2:1–20, where the author invents a speech by the ungodly, who argue that life's brevity calls for full enjoyment of earthly pleasures while they last. What could have passed as superficial Epicureanism is, however, grossly distorted as the imagined reprobates go on to assert that might makes right, urging, in parody of the Hebrew Bible prophets' defense of the disenfranchised, "let us oppress the righteous poor man; / let us not spare the widow" (2:10).

In this male-authored and male-oriented text, little attention is given to real women, as this and the other entries on this text indicate. In contrast, the author of the Wisdom of Solomon exalts the idealized figure Woman Wisdom in a manner previously unsurpassed, personifying her with such personal and mythic qualities that there is barely distinction between her and God.

CLAUDIA V. CAMP

SEE ALSO Part III: Woman Wisdom.

FOR FURTHER READING: Pomeroy, Sarah B. *Women in Hellenistic Egypt.*

Tanzer, Sarah J. "The Wisdom of Solomon."

WIS 3:12
Foolish Wives

Among the punishments for the ungodly envisioned by the pseudonymous author of the Wisdom of Solomon are foolish wives and accursed offspring. "Folly" is a topos in the biblical wisdom tradition of which this book is a part. Whereas it can mean mere silliness, it also carries more sinister connotations: Woman Folly in Prov 9:13–18 is a personification of deadly evil. At the very least, a foolish wife can tear down a house with her own hands (Prov 14:1). Marriage to such a woman destroys family and society.

CLAUDIA V. CAMP

SEE ALSO Part III: Woman Folly (Foolish Woman).

FOR FURTHER READING: Camp, Claudia. "The Strange Woman of Proverbs: A Study of the Feminization and Divinization of Evil in Biblical Thought."

———. *Wisdom and the Feminine in the Book of Proverbs.*

WIS 3:13
Blessed Barren Woman

In marked contrast to the Hebrew Bible's typical promise of pregnancy to the barren woman, the pseudonymous author of the Wisdom of Solomon interprets and remedies her condition in spiritualized terms. He blesses her for remaining "undefiled" by any "sinful union" and promises that "she will have fruit when God examines souls" (Wis 3:13). Spiritual fertility is related to Wisdom's doctrine of the preexistent soul and Wisdom's theory of immortality, new emphases in Jewish tradition, although parts of a continuous development in Hellenistic Jewish thought (Wis 1:1–6:21). Childlessness and death of the human body are superseded by the immortal destiny of the righteous, and fruitfulness is spiritualized to life after death.

CLAUDIA V. CAMP

FOR FURTHER READING: Tanzer, Sarah J. "The Wisdom of Solomon."

Winston, David. *The Wisdom of Solomon.*

WIS 6:12–11:1   Woman Wisdom
SEE Woman Wisdom in the Apocryphal/Deuterocanonical Books (Part III).

WIS 7:1
Mother's Womb

The pseudonymous author of the Wisdom of Solomon, writing under the guise of King Solomon, stresses his mortal status by reference to his own conception and birth, including a brief but graphic depiction of his ten months "in the womb of a mother," where he "was molded into flesh, . . . compacted with blood" (Wis 7:1). This is the first biblical attestation that pregnancy lasted ten months, a view common in the ancient world. The rabbis generally considered the ordinary duration of pregnancy to consist of nine solar months. The point, however, is that human mortality did not prevent Solomon's intimate relationship with divine Wisdom.

CLAUDIA V. CAMP

FOR FURTHER READING: Winston, David. *The Wisdom of Solomon.*

WIS 9:5
Serving Girl

In the author's own expanded version of Solomon's prayer (compare 1 Kgs 3:6–9; 2 Chr 1:8–10), "Solomon" prays to God for wisdom, stressing his human shortcomings by reference to a lowly birth as "the son of your serving girl" (Wis 9:5). This conventional language of humility stands in ironic relationship to the Hebrew Bible narratives of Solomon's royal conception and birth to King David and Bathsheba daughter of Eliam (2 Sam 11:3) or alternatively to King David and Bath-shua daughter of Ammiel (1 Chr 3:5). Here, as in the Hebrew Bible parallels, though, Solomon's request to God for wisdom is an important feature of his prayer.

CLAUDIA V. CAMP

SEE ALSO Part I: Bathsheba; Bath-shua 2.

WIS 9:7
Daughters (and Sons)

Solomon's prayer (Wis 9:1–18) continues with a commemoration of God's choice of him to be "king of your people / and to be judge over your sons and daughters" (Wis 9:7). The poetic parallelism makes explicit that women as well as men constitute God's

"people." This set of gender-inclusive terms is not found in the parallel texts to this prayer in the Hebrew Bible (1 Kgs 3:6–9; 2 Chr 1:8–10), but it does appear in prophetic speeches like Isa 43:6 and Joel 2:28.

CLAUDIA V. CAMP

WIS 10:7
Wife of Lot

Wis 10:1–11:1 rehearses key events in the biblical narrative from creation to the exodus, but puts female personified Wisdom, rather than YHWH, in the role of divine protector of several unnamed figures who can, nonetheless, be easily identified as Adam, Abraham, Lot, Jacob, the enslaved Israelites, and Moses. Vv. 6–9 contrast "a righteous man" (Lot) with the ungodly who perished in "the fire that descended on the Five Cities" (v. 6). The author suggests that evidence of their wickedness can still be seen in the "continually smoking wasteland" and in "a pillar of salt standing as a monument to an unbelieving soul" (Wis 10:7). The allusion to Lot's wife (who even in Genesis is unnamed) is fleeting but powerful. With it, the author places her firmly in the category of the violent men of Sodom (Genesis 19).

CLAUDIA V. CAMP

SEE ALSO Part II: Wife of Lot (Gen 19:15–16, etc.).

SIR 1:1–20   Woman Wisdom
SEE Woman Wisdom in the Apocryphal/Deuterocanonical Books (Part III).

SIR 1:14; 10:18; 40:1; 49:7; 50:22
Mother's Womb

The Book of Sirach was written by a Jerusalem sage named Jesus ben Eleazar ben Sira in about 180 B.C.E. and was translated into Greek by his grandson in Egypt sometime after 132 B.C.E. Much of the book consists of instructional poems, addressed to young men and dealing with matters typical of biblical wisdom literature like Proverbs: attainment of wisdom, both pious and worldly, through fear of the Lord and adherence to the teachings of one's elders. Crucial to life's learning is acceptance of one's place in the patriarchal family structure, whether as controlling father/husband, submissive but industrious wife/loving mother, or obedient child. Ben Sira also deploys the female personification of Wisdom found in Proverbs, both as reinforcement for the father's teaching and as a cosmic being identified with God's Torah.

The image of the mother's womb (or being born of woman, as in Sir 10:18) is used to foreground different aspects of human destiny. Wisdom herself is said to be "created with the faithful in the womb" (1:14), whereas pride and violent anger are not (10:18). A prophet, Jeremiah, is consecrated in his mother's womb (compare Jer 1:5), but it is also from the womb (so Greek and Hebrew; compare the NRSV's "from birth," Sir 50:22) that God nurtures us all.

The complex allusion to Genesis 3 in Sir 40:1 multiplies mother/womb imagery to make the case that hard work is the lot of the "children of Adam, from the day they come forth from their mother's womb / until the day they return to the mother of all the living." The phrase "mother of all the living" is a double-entendre. It refers, on the one hand, to Eve (compare the parallelism with "children of Adam"), whose name is so interpreted in Gen 3:20, as well as to the earth to which mortals return (Gen 3:19). The latter sense is reinforced by the tendency in the wisdom tradition, of which Ben Sira is a part, to equate woman's womb/vagina/mouth with the "pit" or the house of death (Prov 2:16–18; 5:3–5; 7:21–27; 9:13–18; 18:21; 22:14; 23:27). The "mother of all the living" is thus also, paradoxically, the signifier of death.

CLAUDIA V. CAMP

SEE ALSO Part I: Eve; Part II: Mother of Jeremiah (Jer 1:5, etc.); Part III: Woman Stranger (Loose Woman/Adulteress).

FOR FURTHER READING: Skehan, Patrick W., and Alexander A. Di Lella. *The Wisdom of Ben Sira.*

SIR 3:2–11, 16; 4:10; 7:27–28; 15:2; 23:14; 41:17
Mother(s)

In the Jewish wisdom book Sirach (second century B.C.E.), the mother is typically named as deserving of respect and honor in parallel with the father (although the father is sometimes mentioned without his female counterpart, the reverse is not true). Both respect and lack thereof for one's mother are tied to one's relationship to the Lord: "those who honor their mother obey the Lord" (Sir 3:6), a mother's curse uproots her children's foundations (Sir 3:9), and "whoever angers a mother is cursed by the Lord" (Sir 3:16). A son's sense of obligation to his parents derives, in the first instance, from the fact that they gave him life: even his mother's birth pangs should be part of his consciousness (Sir 7:27–28), and memory of his parents should keep him from acting like a fool in the presence of the great and thus regretting his very birth (Sir 23:14). Fear of shame before his mother and father should also prevent a young man from engaging in sexual immorality (Sir 41:17).

A mother's love is used rhetorically to define the relationship between a man and the deity. He should be "like a husband" to the mother of orphans in order to become "like a son of the Most High," who will then love him more than does his mother (Sir 4:10). Likewise, one who fears the Lord will be met by Woman Wisdom "like a mother" (and a bride; Sir 15:2).

CLAUDIA V. CAMP

SEE ALSO Part III: Woman Wisdom.

FOR FURTHER READING: Camp, Claudia V. "Understanding a Patriarchy: Women in Second Century Jerusalem Through the Eyes of Ben Sira."

McKinlay, Judith E. *Gendering Wisdom the Host: Biblical Invitations to Eat and Drink.*

SIR 4:11–19; 6:18–37   Woman Wisdom
SEE Woman Wisdom in the Apocryphal/Deuterocanonical Books (Part III).

Sir 7:19, 26; 9:1; 25:1, 8, 13–26; 26:1–4,
6–9, 13–18, 19–27; 28:15; 33:20; 36:26–31;
37:11; 40:19, 23; 42:6, 12

Wife

Wives fall into one of two categories for Ben Sira —
either good or evil. As if this dichotomy were not
extreme enough, however, at some points in the
text it seems as if achieving "goodness" may be
outside any real woman's reach. "Do you have a
wife who pleases you? Do not divorce her / but do
not trust yourself to one whom you detest" (Sir
7:26; compare 7:19). How, then, might a wife please
her husband and avoid his hatred?

The good wife is wise (Sir 7:19), sensible (Sir 25:8;
40:23), loyal (Sir 26:2), fertile (Sir 26:20), pious (Sir
26:23), kind and humble (Sir 36:28), and blameless
(Sir 40:19). Beauty is desirable in a wife, as long as it
is accompanied by silence, self-discipline, modesty,
chastity, and industry (Sir 26:13–18). She is the manager of her husband's household: "her skill puts
flesh on his bones" (Sir 26:13). And yet she is also a
piece of this household: "he who acquires a wife
gets his best possession / a helper fit for him and a
pillar of support" (Sir 36:29). As "pillar," the wife
becomes "part of the house" in a rather literal
sense! The same figure occurs in Ben Sira's highest
praise of the good wife, which begins by picturing
her in her house and then envisions her as part of
the holiest of houses: "Like the sun rising in the
heights of the Lord, / so is the beauty of a good wife
in her well-ordered home. / Like the shining light
on the holy lampstand, / so is a beautiful face on a
stately figure. / Like golden pillars on silver bases, /
so are shapely legs and steadfast feet" (Sir 26:16–18).

Although the status of honored and honorable
wife was the highest a woman could achieve in the
ancient world, the position could be tenuous. The
sage twice admonishes his readers not to divorce a
good wife (why would they?! — 7:19, 26) and notes
with chagrin that "slander has driven virtuous
women from their homes" (28:15). His admonition
not to "consult with a woman about her rival" (Sir
37:11; compare 26:6) suggests, moreover, that a wife
could belong to a polygamous household, with all

its potential for jealousy and hierarchy among
women. Thus, a situation that the man creates
might justify the dismissal that the problem wife in
Ben Sira's view deserves (Sir 25:26).

A good wife is "among the blessings of the man
who fears the Lord"; she will make him happy and
double the number of his days (Sir 26:1–4; 26:26).
Thus, Ben Sira commends harmony between wife
and husband (25:1), but this possibility can be easily
disrupted by the many forms of female wickedness:
"Dejected mind, gloomy face, / and wounded heart
come from an evil wife. / Drooping hands and
weak knees / come from the wife who does not
make her husband happy" (Sir 25:23). A wife's anger
(Sir 25:15), garrulousness (Sir 25:20; 26:27), jealousy
of a rival (Sir 26:6; 37:11), or drunkenness (Sir 26:8)
can all earn her the epithets "chafing yoke" and
"scorpion" (Sir 26:7).

Even deeper fears are evident in this sage's
thought about a man's relationship to his wife, and
they center on her capacity to bring him shame and
the power this gives her over him. The wife's dangerous power derives, ironically, from two of her
most valued traits, her control of the household
economy and her sexuality (Sir 25:21–22). Thus the
female dilemma: she should be beautiful, but he
must resist the attraction of mere beauty; she
should support him (Sir 36:29), but not support
him (Sir 25:22)! She may be responsible for putting
fat on his bones, but she should never be given the
power of ownership of his property (Sir 33:20). He
may, moreover, lose trust in her (how?), in which
case he should resort to seals and locks (Sir 42:6).

But which sort of treasure box would need such a
seal? Ben Sira's rhetoric slips back and forth between sexual and economic codes. Sir 42:6 appears
in the midst of an instruction about handling one's
money, which, however, moves shortly thereafter to
strong advice about controlling a daughter's sexuality. Crucial in this regard is that she not spend time
with married women (including her mother?) lest
she learn "woman's wickedness" from them (Sir
42:12–13).

Here, as elsewhere in Ben Sira, all women seem
to fall under the shadow of the possible shame their

sexuality may bring (compare Sir 26:24). At one point, he seems to place some responsibility on the husband not to teach his wife jealousy by harboring jealousy of his own (Sir 9:1). In the larger context of this instruction, however, which goes on to condemn contact with loose women of various sorts (Sir 9:1–9), one wonders if the real problem is not that the husband might teach his wife jealousy, but rather teach her infidelity! He is clearly worried about the possibility of her unfaithfulness (Sir 23:22–27; 26:9), an anxiety whose most profound expression comes just after his acclamation of the wife as a man's "best possession, a helper fit for him and a pillar of support," in Sir 36:30–31: "Where there is no fence, the property will be plundered; / and where there is no wife, a man will become a fugitive and a wanderer. / For who will trust a nimble robber / that skips from city to city? So who will trust a man that has no nest, / but lodges wherever night might overtake him?" In Ben Sira's construction, the wife stands at the border of his property, both his strongest defense against his own shameful tendencies and also the weakest link in his armor against others.

CLAUDIA V. CAMP

FOR FURTHER READING: Camp, Claudia. "The Strange Woman of Proverbs: A Study of the Feminization and Divinization of Evil in Biblical Thought."

McKinlay, Judith E. *Gendering Wisdom the Host: Biblical Invitations to Eat and Drink.*

SIR 7:24–25; 22:3–5; 26:10–12, 24; 42:9–12

Daughter

"The birth of a daughter is a loss" (Sir 22:3). Daughters are the bane of a man's existence, a lifelong threat to a father's ability to control the threat of shame that female sexuality can bring on a man's household (Sir 22:4–5; 42:11). While living in the father's household, a daughter must not be indulged (Sir 7:24), but rather thrashed and disciplined (Sir 22:6), lest her chastity be impugned. The

windows of her room must not overlook the street; she must be kept from the gaze of men and the company of married (that is, sexualized) women (Sir 44:11–12). Sir 42:9–10 details the many forms of paternal anxiety, a man robbed of sleep "when she is young, for fear she may not marry, / or if married, for fear she may be disliked; / while a virgin, for fear she may be seduced / and become pregnant in her father's house; / or having a husband, for fear she may go astray, / or, though married, for fear she may be barren."

Odious as a modern reader finds such thoughts, we may yet have some sympathy for the burden that maintaining male honor put upon a man in the ancient world: on one level Ben Sira was himself also a victim of patriarchy. Sympathy is much harder to maintain, however, when his deeper misogyny surfaces, a misogyny closely tied to his view of female sexuality: "As a thirsty traveler opens his mouth / and drinks from any water near him / so she will sit in front of every tent peg / and open her quiver to the arrow" (Sir 26:12). In the Greek text (we have no extant Hebrew for 26:12), this calumny is targeted at the daughter, though the passage occurs in a longer unit on wives. One might imagine that there is little difference, in Ben Sira's view.

CLAUDIA V. CAMP

FOR FURTHER READING: Berquist, Jon L. "Controlling Daughters' Bodies in Sirach."

SIR 7:27–28   Mother

SEE SIR 3:2–11, etc.   Mother(s) (Part II).

SIR 9:1   Wife

SEE SIR 7:19, etc.   Wife (Part II).

SIR 9:2; 25:13–15; 24; 42:12–14; 47:19

Woman as Evil

Although Ben Sira tends to write about women in terms of their social roles (wife, mother, daughter, prostitute), he occasionally remarks on women in general, always in strongly misogynistic terms. Because in both Hebrew and Greek the word for "woman" is also used for "wife," it is sometimes hard to maintain the distinction between evil wives and the generalized evil he associates with women. Thus, a passage whose main concern is a wicked wife (Sir 25:13–26) begins with three verses that could be understood to revile women more generally. Likewise, Sir 9:1–9 deals with dangers posed to men by a variety of women, from the wife to the harlot. The passage includes, however, the more generalized warning against "giv[ing] yourself to a woman" lest she "trample down your strength" (v. 2; compare the teaching of Lemuel's mother in Prov 31:3).

Here, as is typical for Ben Sira, female sexuality constitutes the heart of the problem. Thus, Solomon's downfall is brought about by the "women" who lay at his side (Sir 47:19). Male fear of female sexuality is virulently expressed in 42:12–14, where the sage advises against allowing a virgin daughter to spend time with married women, for "from a woman comes women's wickedness / better is the wickedness of a man than a woman who does good / it is woman who brings shame and disgrace." Ben Sira also provides the earliest extant "blame the woman" interpretation of Genesis 3, justifying harsh measures against a disobedient wife with the assertion that "from a woman sin had its beginning, / and because of her we all die" (Sir 25:24).

CLAUDIA V. CAMP

SEE ALSO Part II: Mother of King Lemuel (Prov 31:1–9).

FOR FURTHER READING: Camp, Claudia V. "Honor and Shame in Ben Sira: Anthropological and Theological Reflections."

Trenchard, Warren C. *Ben Sira's View of Women: A Literary Analysis.*

SIR 9:3, 6–7; 19:2–3; 26:22; 41:20
Prostitute(s)

As in all urban societies, prostitutes were a fact of life in Ben Sira's world, though he seems less tolerant of male indulgence in this regard than most

of his biblical predecessors. Whereas Prov 6:26 distinguishes clearly between the cost of a prostitute ("only a loaf of bread") and the price of adultery ("a man's very life"), Ben Sira warns that a man who gives himself to prostitutes may lose his inheritance (Sir 9:6), "decay and worms" taking possession of him (19:3). These formulations may be related to the fact that, in 9:3, Ben Sira picks up Proverbs' reference to the "strange woman" (so Hebrew; NRSV, "loose woman"), who also causes loss of inheritance and death (Prov 2:16–19; 5:10–20), by catching a man in her "snares" (Prov 7:23). In Proverbs, however, the figure of the strange woman poetically embodies a larger sense of evil, while the later sage seems to use the term for a prostitute of a more mundane sort (compare the Greek "female companion, courtesan").

CLAUDIA V. CAMP

SEE ALSO Part III: Woman Stranger (Loose Woman/ Adulteress).

FOR FURTHER READING: Camp, Claudia V. "The Strange Woman of Proverbs: A Study of the Feminization and Divinization of Evil in Biblical Thought."

———. *Wisdom and the Feminine in the Book of Proverbs.*

SIR 9:4
Singing Girl

Sir 9:2–9 comprises a list of women whose sexual attractions might lead a man astray. Among these is the singing girl who entertains at the banquets held by the rich and powerful men whom Ben Sira's students would serve as scribes (compare Sir 29:22–27).

CLAUDIA V. CAMP

SIR 9:5; 42:10
Virgin

The high value placed on female virginity before marriage causes Ben Sira anxiety in more ways than one. He fears, on the one hand, his own temptation to do more than "look intently" at such a young woman, thus incurring penalties for her (9:5; compare Exod 22:16–17; Deut 22:28–29). On the other hand, he worries lest his own daughter "become pregnant in her father's house" (Sir 42:10). Biblical law prescribes that a bride be stoned in her father's doorway if he cannot produce "the tokens of her virginity" to a suspicious husband (Exod 22:13–21). We do not know if such executions were typically practiced in Ben Sira's day, but this author's high concern for avoiding public shame was sufficient to induce a bit of hand-wringing as well as significant restrictions on his daughters.

CLAUDIA V. CAMP

See also Part II: Virgin (Exod 22:16–17; etc.).

SIR 9:8–9; 23:22–27; 26:9; 41:21
Wife of Another Man/Woman as Adulterer

The topic of adultery again provides occasion for Ben Sira's fearful and fearsome misogyny to manifest itself. Desperately concerned for self-control, yet seemingly incapable of it, he warns that merely looking at another man's attractive wife can lead to the path of destruction (Sir 9:8–9; compare 41:21). He also fears encroachment on his own female property: two extended instructions warn against both female and male adulterers (Sir 23:16–21, 22–27; compare 26:9). The latter unit identifies three separate sins committed by the faithless wife: disobeying God's law, wronging her husband, and bearing another man's child (Sir 23:23).

The distinction between the second and third suggests that adultery as such is defined in rather precise terms: it is not merely the sexual act, but rather the bearing of another man's children, that is at issue. The problem concerns inheritance. The husband needs certainty that his wife has not presented him "with an heir by another man" (Sir 23:22). The punishment for an adulterous wife seems severe yet is somewhat unclear: "She herself

will be brought before the assembly, / and her punishment will extend to her children. / Her children will not take root, / and her branches will not bear fruit. / She will leave behind an accursed memory / and her disgrace will never be blotted out" (Sir 23:24–25).

Does this mean that both she and her children will be executed or, more likely, that they will suffer some sort of public shaming and disinheritance from the husband's family? And which children are included — only those presumed to be the fruit of her adultery or those she bore to her husband as well? Perhaps, regarding the children, the sage simply remarks on the reality that, in his culture, the shame produced by a woman in one generation could affect a family for many to come. However, a sense of impotence also colors Ben Sira's articulation of this woman's fate: whether or not her disgrace is eternal and her children rootless is to some degree in the hands of God, as is, perhaps, her apprehension in the first place.

CLAUDIA V. CAMP

SEE ALSO Part III: Woman Stranger (Loose Woman/ Adulteress).

FOR FURTHER READING: Camp, Claudia V. "Honor and Shame in Ben Sira: Anthropological and Theological Reflections."

Trenchard, Warren C. Ben Sira's View of Women: A Literary Analysis.

SIR 9:8; 25:21; 26:16–18; 36:27; 42:12
Women and Beauty

Ben Sira's ambivalence toward women, especially as sexual beings, is evident in his comments on female beauty. Beauty in itself seduces; thus a man must turn his gaze from a "shapely woman" lest his passion be kindled, for she may be the wife of another (Sir 9:8). Nor should a woman's beauty (or her wealth!) ensnare him into marriage with an evil wife (Sir 25:21; compare 36:27). A daughter's beauty should not be paraded before any man, presumably for the mutual protection of both the daughter and the man (Sir 42:12)! On the other hand, the "beauty of a good wife in her well-ordered home" is "like the sun rising in the heights of the Lord"; her face, figure, legs, and feet are compared to holy objects in the temple (Sir 26:16–18).

CLAUDIA V. CAMP

FOR FURTHER READING: Di Lella, Alexander A. "Women in the Wisdom of Ben Sira and the Book of Judith: A Study in Contrasts and Reversals."

SIR 10:18 Woman

SEE SIR 1:14, etc. Mother's Womb (Part II).

SIR 14:20–15:10 Woman Wisdom

SEE Woman Wisdom in the Apocryphal/Deuterocanonical Books (Part III).

SIR 15:2
Bride

Ben Sira uses the simile of a man's encounter with his young bride to articulate his relationship with Woman Wisdom. Interestingly, this simile occurs in parallel with another comparison that likens Wisdom to his mother, hinting at a rather desexualized ideal of the wife-husband relationship.

CLAUDIA V. CAMP

SEE ALSO Part III: Woman Wisdom.

SIR 15:2 Mother

SEE SIR 3:2–11, etc. Mother(s) (Part II).

SIR 19:2–3 Prostitute

SEE SIR 9:3, etc. Prostitute(s) (Part II).

SIR 19:11; 34:5; 48:19
Woman/Women in Labor

The image of women's childbearing labor is used metaphorically in two quite different ways in the wisdom writings of Sirach. Sir 48:19 presents a typi-cal biblical metaphor. The verse is part of a review of Israel's history, here commenting on the time that the Assyrian ruler Sennacherib invaded Judah during the reign of Hezekiah (727–698 B.C.E.), caus-ing anguish among the inhabitants of Zion like that of "women in labor." Many such metaphors occur in the Hebrew Bible (see, for example, Isa 13:8; Jer 6:24).

In a different vein, Sir 19:7–12 uses the image of a woman in labor as Ben Sira counsels discretion in repeating confidential information. The passage ac-knowledges in vivid terms how difficult it can be not to "burst" with such knowledge. Especially a fool and a gossip, "having heard something," will suffer "birth pangs like a woman in labor" (v. 11). This sense of the urgency of childbirth also informs Sir 34:5, where the fantasies of the mind are com-pared to those of a woman in labor. One may not be able to prevent these imaginings, but one should certainly pay no attention to them unless, of course, they come from God.

CLAUDIA V. CAMP

SEE ALSO Part II: Woman in Labor (Jer 4:31, etc.).

SIR 22:3–5 Daughter

SEE SIR 7:24–25, etc. Daughter (Part II).

SIR 23:14 Mother

SEE SIR 3:2–11, etc. Mother(s) (Part II).

SIR 23:22–27 Woman as Adulterer

SEE SIR 9:8–9, etc. Wife of Another Man/Woman as Adulterer (Part II).

SIR 24:1–34 Woman Wisdom

SEE Woman Wisdom in the Apocryphal/Deuterocanonical Books (Part III).

SIR 25:1
Sisters (and Brothers)

Although the NRSV translation reads, "I take plea-sure in three things, and they are beautiful in the sight of God and of mortals: agreement among brothers and sisters, friendship among neighbors, and a wife and a husband who live in harmony," the word "sisters" does not appear in the original. The NRSV follows the Syriac and Latin; in the Greek, Wisdom says of herself, "In three things I was beautiful and I stood in beauty before the Lord and mortals." Here, and in two other Apocryphal/ Deuterocanonical Books (Jdt 7:30; 2 Macc 15:18), the NRSV translators made the decision to include references to "sisters" for inclusiveness and their sense of the text.

TONI CRAVEN

SEE ALSO Part II: Sisters (and Brothers) (Jdt 7:30); Wives and Sisters (and Brothers) of Judas' Men (2 Macc 15:18).

SIR 25:1, 8, 13–26   Wife
SEE SIR 7:19, etc.   Wife (Part II).

SIR 25:13–15, 24   Woman as Evil
SEE SIR 9:2, etc.   Woman as Evil (Part II).

SIR 25:21   Woman's Beauty
SEE SIR 9:8, etc.   Women and Beauty (Part II).

SIR 25:24
Woman and Sin's Beginning
SEE Eve in the Apocryphal/Deuterocanonical Books (Part I).

SIR 26:1–4, 6–9   Wife
SEE SIR 7:19, etc.   Wife (Part II).

Sir 26:9   Adulterous Wife
SEE SIR 9:8–9, etc.   Wife of Another Man/Woman as Adulterer (Part II).

SIR 26:10–12   Daughter
SEE SIR 7:24–25, etc.   Daughter (Part II).

SIR 26:13–18   Wife
SEE SIR 7:19, etc.   Wife (Part II).

SIR 26:16–18   Women and Beauty
SEE SIR 9:8, etc.   Women and Beauty (Part II).

SIR 26:19–27   Wife
SEE SIR 7:19, etc.   Wife (Part II).

SIR 26:22   Prostitute
SEE SIR 9:3, etc.   Prostitute(s) (Part II).

SIR 26:24   Daughter
SEE SIR 7:24–25, etc.   Daughter (Part II).

SIR 28:15; 33:20   Virtuous Woman/ Wife
SEE SIR 7:19, etc.   Wife (Part II).

SIR 34:5   Woman in Labor
SEE SIR 19:11, etc.   Woman/Women in Labor (Part II).

SIR 35:17–18
Widow

Like a typical biblical prophet, Ben Sira admonishes his reader to care for weaker members of society, denoted in the stereotypical image of the widow and the orphan (Sir 35:17–18).

CLAUDIA V. CAMP

SEE ALSO Part II: Mothers and Widows (Lam 2:12, etc.); Mother(s) (Sir 3:2–11, etc.).

SIR 36:26–31   Wife
SEE SIR 7:19, etc.   Wife (Part II).

SIR 36:27   Women and Beauty
SEE SIR 9:8, etc.   Women and Beauty (Part II).

SIR 37:11   Rival Woman
SEE SIR 7:19, etc.   Wife (Part II).

SIR 36:29
Wife as Fit Helper

As part of his portrayal of the wife, Ben Sira alludes to the Genesis account of Eve's creation as a "fit helper" (see Gen 2:18, 20), here literally "a help like himself" (Sir 36:29b). There is, however, no gender complementarity in Sirach. The first half of the verse contextualizes this reference to indicate the wife has the status of property, and thus belongs to the man as he belongs to himself: "He who acquires a wife gets his best possession, a helper fit for him and a pillar of support."

TONI CRAVEN

SEE ALSO Part I: Eve; Part II: Wife (Sir 7:19, etc.).

SIR 40:1   Mother's Womb
SEE SIR 1:14, etc.   Mother's Womb (Part II).

SIR 40:19, 23   Wife
SEE SIR 7:19, etc.   Wife (Part II).

SIR 41:17   Mother
SEE SIR 3:2–11, etc.   Mother(s) (Part II).

SIR 41:20   Prostitute
SEE SIR 9:3, etc.   Prostitute(s) (Part II).

SIR 41:21   Wife of Another Man
SEE SIR 9:8–9, etc.   Wife of Another Man/Woman as Adulterer (Part II).

SIR 41:22
Servant Girl

In the Book of Sirach, the serving girl appears — along with the prostitute and another man's wife — in a series of women whom a man should "be ashamed" to look at and whom he should avoid "meddling with" (41:20–22). In the midst of this list is a different sort of admonition, against "taking away someone's portion or gift" (v. 21). The verse

intimates that all these women are the possessions of other men, thus to be avoided.

CLAUDIA V. CAMP

SEE ALSO Part II: Wife (Sir 7:19, etc.); Prostitute(s) (Sir 9:3, etc.).

SIR 42:6   Wife
SEE SIR 7:19, etc.   Wife (Part II).

SIR 42:9–12   Daughter
SEE SIR 7:24–25, etc.   Daughter (Part II).

SIR 42:10   Virgin
SEE SIR 9:5, etc.   Virgin (Part II).

SIR 42:12   Women and Beauty
SEE SIR 9:8, etc.   Women and Beauty (Part II).

SIR 42:12   Married Women
SEE SIR 7:19, etc.   Wife (Part II).

SIR 42:13–14   Woman as Evil
SEE SIR 9:2, etc.   Woman as Evil (Part II).

SIR 42:13
Woman and Sin's Beginning
SEE Eve in the Apocryphal/Deuterocanonical Books (Part I).

SIR 47:19
Women of Solomon

Ben Sira rehearses the wisdom and fame of Solomon, but also recounts his downfall because of the women he "brought in" to lie at his side. There is no explicit mention here that the wives were foreign or that they led Solomon to worship foreign gods, the issue dominant in 1 Kings 11. Typical of this sage, this verse concerns the staining of Solomon's honor (Sir 47:20) through contact with female sexuality.

CLAUDIA V. CAMP

See also Part II: Women of Solomon (1 Kgs 3:1, etc.).

For further reading: Skehan, Patrick W., and Alexander A. Di Lella. *The Wisdom of Ben Sira.*

SIR 47:19
Women Cause of Subjection

See Sir 9:2, etc. Woman as Evil (Part II).

SIR 48:19 Women in Labor

See Sir 19:11, etc. Woman/Women in Labor (Part II).

SIR 49:7; 50:22 Womb/Birth

See Sir 1:14, etc. Mother's Womb (Part II).

SIR 51:13–30 Woman Wisdom

See Woman Wisdom in the Apocryphal/Deuterocanonical Books (Part III).

BAR 2:3
Cannibalized Daughters (and Sons)

According to the legendary tradition reflected in the Book of Baruch and other Jewish sources (*Seder Olam Rabbah* 26; *Midrash Rabbah Song* 5:5; *Megillah* 16b), Baruch, the scribe and close friend of Jeremiah, went to Babylon (not Egypt as in Jer 43:1–7). From here, he is credited with writing an edifying letter (which is considered deuterocanonical in Roman Catholic and all Orthodox Bibles) to the priests and people of Jerusalem. The Book of Baruch actually consists of three loosely connected sections: a prose prayer (Bar 1:15–3:8), a wisdom poem (3:9–4:4), and a poem of consolation (4:5–5:9), which were originally independent sections whose individual dates of composition are difficult to determine. Most scholars favor a date between 200 and 60 B.C.E. for the compilation of the book as a whole, thus dating this book to long after the sixth-century Babylonian exile and time of the prophet Jeremiah and his faithful scribe, Baruch.

Two references to unnamed women appear in the prose prayer of Baruch (1:15–3:8), which is considered one of the great prayers in the Apocryphal/Deuterocanonical Books. Both are found in gender-matched pairs: daughters and sons (2:3); brides and bridegrooms (2:23, see the following entry) in illustrations of the great desolation of the exiles. An introduction (1:1–14) explains that the letter and prayer are being sent in 597 B.C.E. (or 586) from the exiles in Babylon, together with money and silver temple vessels, to the high priest and people in Jerusalem together with requests for prayer and the public reading of the letter. A contrite confession of the sins of the exiles and an appeal for God's mercy (1:15–2:10) accompany a petition for deliverance (2:11–3:8). Throughout is the view that the law is God's great gift (see Deuteronomy 28); that obedience brings prosperity; disobedience brings disaster and exile; and repentance and renewed obedience are the conditions of restoration (see Dan 9:4–19). God is depicted as just (Bar 2:9), kind and compassionate (2:27), ready to reward obedience (2:31), willing to increase the people (2:34), to make an everlasting covenant with them (2:35a), and never again exile them from Israel (2:35b).

The exiles confess that their great diminishment of numbers and separation from the homeland resulted from their hideous depravity during the siege of Jerusalem when "some of us ate the flesh of their sons and others the flesh of their daughters" (2:3). Cannibalism of one's own children in time of war is mentioned as perhaps the greatest horror in other texts, including Lev 26:29; Deut 28:53–57; 2 Kgs 6:24–31; Jer 19:9; Lam 2:20; 4:10. According to Baruch, God drove both women and men to eat their young (contrast 2 Kgs 6:24–31 and Lam 2:20; 4:10 where the sin is attributed to mothers) as a most severe punishment. The community recognizes its present struggle as rooted in the bleak sins of a previous time.

TONI CRAVEN

See also Part II: Mother (and Father) Cannibalizing Their Daughters (and Sons) (Lev 26:29, etc.); Bride (and Bridegroom) (Bar 2:23).

For further reading: Tull, Patricia, K. "Baruch."

BAR 2:23
Bride (and Bridegroom)

In the prose prayer of Baruch (1:15–3:8), which is considered one of the great prayers in the Apocryphal/Deuterocanonical Books, the Jewish exiles in Babylon pray for deliverance (2:11–3:8), confessing their disregard of God's instruction to submit to the king of Babylon. They disobeyed, despite God's threat to "make to cease from the towns of Judah and from the region around Jerusalem the voice of mirth and the voice of gladness, the voice of the bridegroom and the voice of the bride" (2:23). They ask now that God show them mercy, acknowledging, "You are enthroned forever, and we are perishing forever" (3:3).

The threats to society contained in God's destruction of the gladness and mirth associated with the gender-matched pairs of brides and bridegrooms (compare daughters and sons in Bar 2:3) strike at the roots of the community's continuance. Destruction of females near or at the childbearing stage of their lives represents destruction of potential or actual fecundity. It is difficult to imagine greater signs of desolation than those graphically contained in this prayer.

TONI CRAVEN

SEE ALSO Part II: Bride (and Bridegroom) (Jer 2:2–32, etc.); Cannibalized Daughters (and Sons) (Bar 2:3).
FOR FURTHER READING: Mendels, Doron. "Baruch."

BAR 3:9–4:4   Woman Wisdom
SEE Woman Wisdom in the Apocryphal/Deuterocanonical Books (Part III).

BAR 4:5–5:9
Jerusalem/Zion as Widow and Mother
SEE Jerusalem/Zion as Widow and Mother (Part III).

BAR 4:10, 14, 16
Daughters (and Sons) of Zion

In the poem of consolation that closes the Book of Baruch (4:5–5:9), Widow Zion mourns for her captive children, whom the Everlasting has exiled (4:10) on account of their sins (4:12). She calls to her neighbors to come and remember the capture of her daughters and her sons (4:14), who were led away by a distant nation: "They led away the widow's beloved sons, and bereaved the lonely woman of her daughters" (4:16). Bereft Zion encourages her children to go (4:19), promising to intercede for them with the Everlasting all the days of her life (4:20). Zion instructs her children to take courage and to cry to God, who will deliver them from the power and hand of the enemy (4:21). Widow Zion is sure in her hope that she and her neighbors will soon see her children's "salvation by God" (4:24).

Israel is here poignantly depicted as the very flesh and blood of Zion, who, personified as the female figure of mother and widow, intercedes for and encourages her children. A vision of hope that soon the exiles will be returned safely by God in glory, to take up residence within Jerusalem, closes the book (5:1–9). That Zion is a devastated mother is understandable; that she is a widow raises a troubling question: who and where is her husband? Are not the daughters and sons of Zion God's very own? God is named Everlasting (4:10, 14, 20, 22, 24, 35; 5:2) and Holy One (4:22, 37; 5:5), but never father to Israel or husband to Zion in the Book of Baruch.

TONI CRAVEN

SEE ALSO Part III: Enemy Cities as Female; Jerusalem/Zion as Widow and Mother.
FOR FURTHER READING: Tull, Patricia K. "Baruch."

BAR 4:32–35   Enemy Cities as Female
SEE Enemy Cities as Female (Part III).

EP JER v. 9
Girl Who Loves Ornaments

The Letter of Jeremiah (which is chap. 6 of the Book of Baruch in the Latin Vulgate and the King James Bible) is not a letter, nor was it written by its reputed author, the sixth-century B.C.E. prophet Jeremiah. Rather, this book of seventy-three verses is actually a sarcastic homily, or tirade, against Babylonian idols and, by implication, idolatry everywhere. It is usually dated to between the late fourth and late first century B.C.E. and was likely composed in Palestine. The author took the name of Jeremiah to lend credibility to this new work and to align it with Jeremiah's idol satire (Jer 10:2–16) and instruction to the exiles in Babylon (Jeremiah 29).

The Letter's attack on Babylonian women, which by implication represents an attack upon all women, including Jewish women, is devastating. The author's demeaning and chauvinistic attitude toward women in general is quite evident: "People take gold and make crowns for the heads of their gods, as they might for a girl who loves ornaments" (Ep Jer v. 9). Although in every time and place women have loved jewelry, such love is certainly not unique to females; kings, priests, and the wealthy males in the Bible have also valued gold and jewelry. Gold represents wealth and power, and Solomon, more than any other in the Bible, received spectacular amounts of gold, some 666 talents (1 talent = 75 pounds) per year, according to 1 Kgs 10:14–15, that he used for decorative armaments, his throne, vessels, and sacred equipment for the Jerusalem temple. Yet the author of the Letter of Jeremiah makes no such mention of male fascination with jewelry and gold.

CAREY A. MOORE

FOR FURTHER READING: Moore, Carey A. *Daniel, Esther, and Jeremiah: The Additions.*

Platt, Elizabeth E. "Jewelry, Ancient Israelite."

EP JER V. 11
Prostitutes

The Letter of Jeremiah voices Israel's negative attitude toward secular prostitution, which, though outlawed by legislation (Lev 19:29), was nonetheless ambivalently tolerated as an institution (Genesis 38; Joshua 2, 6; Judg 16:1). Israelite priests came under even stricter standards, with specific prohibitions

forbidding their marriage to prostitutes and legislating death by burning for their daughters who practiced prostitution (Lev 21:7, 9, 14). It is doubly insulting, then, when Babylonian priests come under attack in the Letter of Jeremiah: "Sometimes the priests secretly take gold and silver from their gods and spend it on themselves, or even give some of it to the prostitutes on the terrace" (vv. 10–11). This allusion evidently refers to secular prostitution (in contrast to vv. 42–43). While decrying the immorality of the Babylonian priests, the ancient writer expresses no concern for the degradation and misery of the prostitutes themselves. Association with prostitutes is used here as a metaphor for the depravity of the Babylonian religious system, which suits the Letter's attack on idolatry.

CAREY A. MOORE

SEE ALSO Part I: Rahab; Tamar 1; Part II: Prostitute (Lev 19:29, etc.); Temple Prostitute (Deut 23:17, etc.); Prostitute of Gaza (Judg 16:1–3).

FOR FURTHER READING: Goodfriend, Elaine Adler. "Prostitution (OT)."

EP JER VV. 28, 33
Wives of Priests

For the author of the Letter of Jeremiah, the depravity of Babylonian priests in selling sacrifices and keeping the money for themselves (v. 28) is paralleled by their wives' actions: "Likewise their wives preserve some of the meat with salt, but give none to the poor or helpless" (v. 29). In their role as cooks, wives of Babylonian priests are damned either way: they don't share their meat with the needy; but then, they themselves should not be preserving such meat in the first place!

To make matters worse, "The priests take some of the clothing of their gods to clothe their wives and children" (v. 33), thereby destroying their loved ones' cultic purity, the latter being (at least from a Jewish point of view) an indispensable precondition for performing any religious or cultic acts.

These attacks on the wives of priests illustrate the

author's attack on the religious system of Babylonia. Priests and their wives are here caricatured as immoral and dishonest.

CAREY A. MOORE

FOR FURTHER READING: Tull, Patricia K. "The Letter of Jeremiah."

EP JER V. 29
Women and Bodily Emissions

Worst of all the illustrations in the Letter of Jeremiah of the depravity of Babylonian religious practices is that "sacrifices to them [idols] may even be touched by women in their periods or at childbirth" (v. 29). The author shares the deep-seated fear expressed in Leviticus 15, where all genital discharges — and especially blood — render female and male alike cultically unclean. Such an individual is to be totally excluded from religious or cultic practices until purified. Moreover, that cultic impurity contaminates all persons and objects touched by the unclean person. A vaginal flow of blood from any cause, menstrual or postpartum, renders a woman ritually polluted, unfavored by God, and banned from the sacred precincts (Num 5:2–4). For the author of the Letter of Jeremiah, that ritually unclean Babylonian women are allowed to touch sacrifices provides the crowning evidence that these idols are not gods. Such women — which in effect includes all women, Babylonian and Jewish — are to be totally banned from true worship.

CAREY A. MOORE

SEE ALSO Part II: Blemished Women (and Men) (Lev 13:29, etc.); Women and Bodily Emissions (Lev 15:18–33, etc.).

FOR FURTHER READING: Schuller, Eileen M. "Introduction to the Apocrypha."

Wegner, Judith Romney. *Chattel or Person? The Status of Women in the Mishnah.*

EP JER V. 30
Women Who Serve Idols

Babylonian women's priestly service to the gods and their giving of food to statues is ridiculed as complete foolishness by the author of the Letter of Jeremiah. "For how can they [the idols] be called gods?" when "women serve meals for gods of silver and gold and wood" (v. 30). From this author's perspective, only males born to priestly families could perform priestly functions. Priestly instructions in Exodus, Leviticus, and Numbers do specify the offering of sacrifices, "the food of God" (Lev 21:6), as chief among the duties of priests. But it is unthinkable to this author that women could perform such service.

CAREY A. MOORE

FOR FURTHER READING: Schiffman, Lawrence H. "Priests."

EP JER V. 33   Wives of Priests
SEE EP JER V. 28, etc.   Wives of Priests (Part II).

EP JER V. 38
Widow

Unlike Israel's God (see Ps 146:9), the Babylonian idols "cannot take pity on a widow or do good to an orphan" (v. 38). For the author of the Letter of Jeremiah, idols are worthless to women whose husbands have died. Care for the widow and the fatherless is noted as one of God's special concerns in much of the Hebrew Bible. The author's concern, however, is not to promote the well-being of Babylonian widows, but to illustrate in one more way the meaninglessness of the Babylonian religious system.

CAREY A. MOORE

SEE ALSO Part II: Widows (Exod 22:22, etc.).

EP JER VV. 42–43
Women with Cords

In a passage about how the Chaldeans (the word is used here in its restricted sense of a priestly magician, astrologer, or diviner) themselves dishonor their idols (vv. 40b–44), the author of the Letter of Jeremiah addresses the worst form of prostitution: sacred, or cultic, prostitution (contrast vv. 10–11). He states, "And the women, with cords around them, sit along the passageways, burning bran for incense. When one of them is led off by one of the passers-by and is taken to bed by him, she derides the woman next to her, because she was not as attractive as herself and her cord was not broken" (vv. 42–43). The passage alludes to a Babylonian practice long ago noted by the Greek Herodotus (*History*, c. 450 B.C.E.) and repeated by Strabo (born c. 63 B.C.E.) in *Geography*.

Although prohibited by Deut 23:17–18, women becoming sexual mercenaries, as sacred or secular prostitutes, plagued Israel throughout the days of the Israelite monarchy and beyond. Here, prostitution is used as a metaphor for defection from God, in order to debunk Babylonian worship.

CAREY A. MOORE

SEE ALSO Part II: Temple Prostitute (Deut 23:17, etc.); Prostitutes (Ep Jer v. 11).

FOR FURTHER READING: Moore, Carey A. *Daniel, Esther, and Jeremiah: The Additions.*

THE PRAYER OF AZARIAH AND THE SONG OF THE THREE JEWS
No Women Mentioned

One of the Greek additions to the Book of Daniel, the Apocryphal/Deuterocanonical Prayer of Azariah and the Song of the Three Jews is inserted between 3:23 and 3:24 of the Hebrew version of Daniel. Date, author, and place of composition for the insertion are unknown. In Daniel 3, Daniel's three friends face martyrdom on account of their refusal to worship a huge golden statue (87.5 feet tall and 8.75 feet wide) that Nebuchadnezzar set up in the plain of Dura (an unknown Babylonian location). In the Septuagint and Latin versions of Daniel, vv. 24–90b (the same as Pr Azar vv. 1–68) detail what happens while the three, using their Hebrew names only (see Dan 1:7) — Hananiah (Shadrach), Mishael (Meshach), and Azariah (Abednego) — are in the fiery furnace. They fell, bound, into a furnace of blazing fire (Dan 3:23), and "they walked around in the midst of the flames, singing hymns to God and blessing the Lord" (Pr Azar v. 1).

The insertion includes two prayers and a brief connective narrative. In the first prayer (vv. 3–22), a national lament that makes no mention of the fiery furnace, Azariah praises God's wisdom and justice, confesses the sinfulness of his own nation, and petitions God's deliverance, for the sake of the divine name (v. 11; compare Ezek 20:9–39; 36:21; 39:25). While Azariah prays, the king's men continue to stoke the furnace, and its scorching hot flames devour those nearby (Pr Azar vv. 23–25). An angel of God drives the flames from the furnace, so that a moist wind whistles through the furnace, and the fire does not touch the three young Jews (vv. 26–27).

In response to their miraculous deliverance, the three young men sing a song of praise and thanksgiving to the Lord for saving them from the raging fire (vv. 28–68; compare Psalm 148). Hebrew Dan 3:24 resumes with the king's astonishment that he sees "four men unbound, walking in the middle of the fire, and they are not hurt; and the fourth has the appearance of a god" (Dan 3:25). Nebuchadnezzar calls the three "servants of the Most High God" to come out of the fire (Dan 3:26) and blesses their God who has sent an angel of deliverance (3:28). The king then decrees that anyone who blasphemes this God will be cut to pieces and their houses destroyed, for "there is no other god who is able to deliver in this way" (3:29). The story ends with the promotion of the three young Jews in the province of Babylon (3:30).

There are no references to women in the Prayer of Azariah and the Song of the Three Jews. Even though vv. 35–68 elicit all God's creation to "bless the Lord," women are not explicitly so summoned.

Vv. 60–68 list various worshippers of God — people, priests, servants of the Lord, spirits and souls of the righteous, holy and humble in heart, Hananiah, Azariah, and Mishael. But this descending hierarchy, from corporate worshippers to individual males, makes no specific mention of women.

TONI CRAVEN

FOR FURTHER READING: Craven, Toni. "The Greek Book of Daniel."

Moore, Carey A. *Daniel, Esther, and Jeremiah: The Additions.*

SUS VV. 3, 30, 33, 63
Mother of Susanna/Wife of Hilkiah

The mother of Susanna plays a minor role in the story of Susanna, which is chap. 13 of the Greek version of Daniel but is found as a separate book in the NRSV. She is included in the reference to Susanna's righteous parents "who trained their daughter according to the law of Moses" (v. 3), a hint that women in the Hellenistic diaspora may have been students and even teachers of Torah within domestic confines. Together with Susanna's children and relatives (both of which may include some females), Susanna's mother is again included in a reference to her "parents," who appear with her at her trial (v. 30) and are among those who weep at her unveiling (v. 33). At Susanna's acquittal, her "parents," husband, and relatives rejoice "because she was found innocent of a shameful deed" (v. 63). This final reference lists Susanna's mother as "Hilkiah's wife," an affirmation of the restored integrity of the patriarchal household: "Hilkiah and his wife praised God for their daughter Susanna" (v. 63). In keeping with the androcentric nature of this story, Susanna's father, but not her mother, is named. In fact, no woman, save Susanna, is named in the entire Book of Daniel.

JENNIFER A. GLANCY

SEE ALSO Part I: Susanna 1.

SUS VV. 15, 17, 19, 21, 36
Maids

Susanna's maids (typically enslaved women) play a peculiar role in the narrative: their absence, and how to interpret it, is central to the story whereas their appearance is only incidental. Two maids accompany Susanna to the garden (v. 15) and bring her ointments so she can bathe (v. 17). Their departure from the garden (v. 19) affords the elders a chance to threaten Susanna with the accusation that she sent the maids away in order to meet her lover (v. 21). The maids are presumably among the people of the house who run through the side door when they hear the cries of Susanna and the elders (v. 26), though they are not specifically mentioned again until v. 36 in the two elders' testimony.

JENNIFER A. GLANCY

SEE ALSO Part II: Female (and Male) Servants (Tob 3:7–9, etc.); Maid of Judith (Jdt 8:10, etc.).

FOR FURTHER READING: Glancy, Jennifer A. "The Mistress-Slave Dialectic: Paradoxes of Slavery in Three LXX Narratives."

SUS VV. 30, 33 Mother of Susanna
SEE SUS v. 3, etc. Mother of Susanna/Wife of Hilkiah (Part II).

SUS V. 36 Maids
SEE SUS v. 15, etc. Maids (Part II).

SUS VV. 48, 57
Daughter(s) of Israel/Daughter of Judah

In his cross-examination of the two wicked elders (vv. 47–64), Daniel makes an obscure reference to "daughters of Israel" whom the elders coerced into sexual relations; he contrasts these women with Susanna, a "daughter of Judah" who resisted the elders' advances (v. 57). It is difficult to square the distinction in v. 57 that Susanna is a "daughter of Judah" with Daniel's earlier words, "Are you such fools, O Israelites, as to condemn a daughter of

Israel [meaning Susanna] without examination and without learning the facts?" (v. 48). The differentiation between Judah and Israel may reflect the bias of Babylonian Jews who were primarily Judean exiles, but it may also represent a postexilic prejudice of Palestinian Jews toward their northern Israelite neighbors, the Samaritans.

JENNIFER A. GLANCY

SEE ALSO Part I: Susanna 1.

FOR FURTHER READING: Moore, Carey A. *Daniel, Esther and Jeremiah: The Additions.*

SUS V. 63 Mother of Susanna

SEE SUS V. 3, etc. Mother of Susanna/Wife of Hilkiah (Part II).

BEL VV. 10, 15, 20, 21
Wives/Women of Priests

Chap. 14 of the Greek version of Daniel, the Apocryphal/Deuterocanonical Bel and the Dragon, is composed of two very brief, entertaining detective stories (or confrontation narratives) about the folly of revering idols. These idol parodies show that one god, Bel, cannot eat (Bel, vv. 1–22); the other, the Dragon — actually a large snake — dies when it eats a concoction of pitch, hair, and fat (vv. 23–30). Likely composed sometime between the third and first centuries B.C.E., these tales are tests of loyalty to the living God, similar to Daniel 3 (Shadrach, Meshach, and Abednego in the fiery furnace) and Daniel 6 (Daniel in the lions' den).

The only references to women appear in the story of Bel (vv. 1–22). The seventy priests of Bel, with their wives and children (v. 10), stage a deceptive demonstration of how Bel consumes food and wine by having the king shut and seal the door to the temple of Bel. Each night, however, the priests and their wives and children (v. 15) come into the temple through a hidden entrance and consume the offerings themselves. Daniel persuades Cyrus that the Babylonian god Bel (meaning Marduk, the patron deity of Babylon) does not consume the

daily sacrifices. Daniel puts ashes on the sanctuary floor, so that the next morning, the king sees the footprints of men, women, and children (v. 20). Enraged, Cyrus arrests the priests and their wives and children (v. 21) and executes them. As the property of men, wives and children could be punished along with them.

TONI CRAVEN

SEE ALSO Part II: Wives of Dathan and Abiram (Num 16:27–33); Daughters (and Sons) of Achan (Josh 7:24); Wives of Daniel's Accusers (Dan 6:24).

FOR FURTHER READING: Craven, Toni. "The Greek Book of Daniel."

Moore, Carey A. *Daniel, Esther, and Jeremiah: The Additions.*

1 MACC 1:26–27
Young Women (and Young Men); Brides (and Bridegrooms)

1 Maccabees, likely composed around 100 B.C.E., is a chronological record of apostasy and persecution and the Hasmonean revolt begun by the Jewish priest Mattathias and carried on by his five sons and grandson against the Greco-Macedonian Seleucid kings. Written in the manner of other biblical historical works like Judges, Samuel, and Kings, 1 Maccabees is a chronicle of events in Palestine from the death of Alexander the Great (323 B.C.E.) through the reign of the Seleucid king Antiochus IV (175–164 B.C.E.), who took the name Epiphanes ("god manifest").

Women are conspicuously absent in 1 Maccabees, except as unnamed members of Jewish patriarchal family households, as Judahite mourners for the temple and victims of oppression, as non-Jewish women of the indigenous people of the Judean area, or as wives and women of the Greco-Roman invaders. There are no named women in this story of the struggle for national liberation.

The first references to women appear in chap. 1, in a poetic lament describing Judah's distress:

"Young women and young men became faint, the beauty of the women faded. Every bridegroom took up the lament; she who sat in the bridal chamber was mourning" (1:26–27). Using traditional lamentation imagery like that in Jeremiah and Baruch, the poem poignantly describes the destruction of the strength and beauty, gladness and mirth associated with young women and young men, brides and bridegrooms. Such weakening of persons, near or at the childbearing stages of their lives, represents destruction of potential or actual fecundity for the community. These are graphic signs of the desolation effected by the pillaging of the Jerusalem temple by Antiochus IV.

RONALD S. KLINE

SEE ALSO Part II: Bride (and Bridegroom) (Bar 2:23).

FOR FURTHER READING: Doran, Robert. "1 Maccabees."

Young, Robin Darling. "1 Maccabees."

1 MACC 1:32; 2:30, 38; 5:13
Women/Wives Persecuted by Antiochus IV

In 1 Maccabees, a story of Jewish struggle for national liberation, Jewish women are portrayed as victims of the persecutions of the Seleucid king Antiochus IV Epiphanes. Their demise represents a blow to the very fabric of society. Women, children, and livestock (listed in that order) are seized in the initial capture of Jerusalem (1:32). At the same time that the priest Mattathias, his five sons, and his followers flee to the hills, leaving everything behind them (2:28), others go out into the Judean wilderness, taking rudiments of family households with them, "their sons, their wives, and their livestock" (2:30). One thousand of these seekers of righteousness — men, wives, children, with their livestock — choose to die rather than fight the Gentiles on the Sabbath day (2:38). Another thousand who live in Tob (possibly Hippos, twelve miles southeast of the Sea of Galilee) are captured and, possibly with some of "their wives and children and goods," are de-

stroyed (5:13). In each of these instances, religious-political oppression of women (together with children and livestock) represents the economic and cultural consequences embodied in the ideological conflict of the Hasmonean revolt against Hellenism.

RONALD S. KLINE

SEE ALSO Part II: Martyred Mother with Seven Sons (2 Macc 7:1–42); (4 Macc 1:8, etc.).

FOR FURTHER READING: Doran, Robert. "1 Maccabees."

Young, Robin Darling. "1 Maccabees."

1 Macc 1:38–40
Jerusalem as Widow and Mother
SEE Jerusalem/Zion as Widow and Mother (Part III).

1 MACC 1:60–61
Women/Mothers with Circumcised Sons

Antiochus IV Epiphanes' subjugation of Jerusalem included prohibitions against temple worship, observance of Sabbaths and holy days, circumcision, and the keeping of Torah. Immediately following his desecration of the temple, on the twenty-fifth day of Chislev (1:59; that is around mid-December in 167 B.C.E.; compare 2 Macc 10:5), the author illustrates the cruelty of the attempt to destroy the traditions of the Jews. In one of the most hideous acts of persecution, women who have their sons circumcised are killed, and their infants are hung from their necks (1:60–61). The deaths of mothers (and their sons) represent the actual destruction of the community and its future. 2 Maccabees 6 as well as 4 Maccabees 4 contain similar stories of martyrdoms of mothers who circumcised their sons.

RONALD S. KLINE

SEE ALSO Part II: Women/Mothers with Circumcised Sons (2 Macc 6:10); (4 Macc 4:25).

FOR FURTHER READING: Doran, Robert. "1 Maccabees."

Young, Robin Darling. "1 Maccabees."

1 MACC 2:8–11
Jerusalem as Widow and Mother
SEE Jerusalem/Zion as Widow and Mother
(Part III).

1 MACC 2:30, 38
Wives Persecuted by Antiochus IV
SEE 1 MACC 1:32, etc.   Women/Wives Persecuted by Antiochus IV (Part II).

1 MACC 3:20; 5:23, 45; 13:6, 45
Women/Wives Defended by Judas and Simon

Early in his victories against the Seleucids, a Hellenistic dynasty in Syria, Judas Maccabeus goes to
battle with Seron of Syria. Judas's own small Jewish
army are fearful when they see the size of the approaching enemy force. Judas encourages them to
believe that victory in battle does not depend on the
size of the army, but on strength that comes from
heaven. Even though the usual fate of wives and
children taken as prisoners of war was slavery, not
death, Judas claims, "They come to destroy us and
our wives and our children, and to despoil us; but
we fight for our lives and our laws" (3:20–21).

After Judas Maccabeus defeats the Seleucid
forces and, following a lengthy delay, the temple is
cleansed (164 B.C.E.; 2 Macc 4:36–61), he sends Simon to evacuate the remote Galilean Jews. Women
return to Jerusalem with Simon and his army and
with others who will rebuild the community. The
return in 5:23 is like a triumphant liturgical procession of men, women, and children, similar to that
in Psalm 126, Isa 35:10, and 51:11.

Later, when Simon believes his four brothers —
Eleazar, Judas, John, and Jonathan — have perished, though actually Jonathan is held prisoner by
Trypho the usurper of the Syrian throne, he vows
to avenge the "nation and the sanctuary and your
wives and children" (1 Macc 13:6). His commitment
points to the close connection between preservation of the temple and preservation of the family

household as foundational to the nation's identity.
Protection of women and children symbolizes
maintenance of a distinctive way of life based on
the observance of Torah and temple worship. Such
protection carries with it important political, religious, economic, and cultural consequences.

In 13:45, Simon and his armies are portrayed as
sparing enemies in Garara (Gezer, an important site
on the road from Jerusalem to Joppa), including
men, their wives, and children (see also 11:65–66).
Simon cleanses the city, expelling the gentile population, and repopulates it with observant Jews. Simon's practice of ethnic cleansing is in sharp contrast to that of his brother Judas, who practiced the
ban (see 5:28, 35, 51), the annihilation of the enemy
males and the taking of their women, children, livestock, and other things of value as spoil (Deut
20:10–15). Simon did not take the gentile women
and children, but rather turned them, with their
husbands, out of their houses as war refugees (1
Macc 13:47). The fate of these gentile women, so
spared, is not detailed.

RONALD S. KLINE

SEE ALSO Part II: Women in Distant Towns as Booty
(Deut 20:14, etc.).
FOR FURTHER READING: Doran, Robert. "1 Macca-
bees."
Goldstein, Jonathan. I Maccabees: A New Translation with
Introduction and Commentary.

1 MACC 3:45
Jerusalem as Widow and Mother
SEE Jerusalem/Zion as Widow and Mother
(Part III).

1 MACC 5:13
Wives Persecuted by Antiochus IV
SEE 1 MACC 1:32, etc.   Women/Wives Persecuted by Antiochus IV (Part II).

1 MACC 5:23, 45
Wives Defended by Simon and Judas
SEE 1 MACC 3:20, etc.   Women/Wives Defended by Judas and Simon (Part II).

1 Macc 8:10; 9:37–42
Greek Brides and Wives

Because the Romans were successful in defeating the Seleucids, a Hellenistic dynasty that ruled Syria, 1 Maccabees idealizes friendly relations between Rome and the Jews. 1 Macc 8:10 approvingly records the Roman capture of Greek wives (and children) and defeat of the confederation of Greek cities known as the Achaean League, which had rebelled against Rome (these events, which occurred in 147 B.C.E., are anachronistic here, since they do not happen until fifteen years after the Jewish embassy to Rome described in 8:17–32). Just as the Seleucids had repeatedly victimized Jewish women and children (1:32, 2:30, 38; 5:13), now the Romans victimize Seleucid women and children. At stake is partisan interest in the defeat of the enemy and any possibility of its future.

1 Macc 9:37–42 offers another such illustration. In 1 Macc 9:35–36, Jonathan sends his brother John, "the multitude" (which likely would have included women, children, and the elderly), and all their baggage to their friends, the Nabateans (an Arab kingdom south of the Dead Sea). But the Jambrites, a clan of uncertain descent from Medeba (in Moab, twelve miles southeast of the north end of the Dead Sea), kill John (see 9:38) and seize all with him. To avenge their brother John's death, Jonathan and Simon attack a wedding procession of a certain Jambri (likely an Arab), slaying the wedding party of a Jambrite who was marrying a Canaanite woman. The Jews take all the goods of the wedding party whose mirth is turned into mourning and "the voice of their musicians into a funeral dirge" (9:41).

RONALD S. KLINE

SEE ALSO Part II: Singing Women (and Men) Who Lament (2 Chr 35:25); Women/Wives Persecuted by Antiochus IV (1 Macc 1:32, etc.).

FOR FURTHER READING: Doran, Robert. "1 Maccabees."

Goldstein, Jonathan. *I Maccabees: A New Translation with Introduction and Commentary.*

1 Macc 13:6
Wives Defended by Simon and Judas

SEE 1 Macc 3:20, etc. Women/Wives Defended by Judas and Simon (Part II).

1 Macc 13:28
Mother (and Father) of Simon

Simon, the second son of Mattathias, was the last of the Maccabean brothers to ascend to a position of leadership, taking over from Jonathan, whom Trypho (the usurper of the Seleucid throne) murdered in 142 B.C.E. (see 13:4–8). Amid national lamentation, Simon buries his brother in their home village of Modein and builds a huge monument of polished stone over the burial places of his father (the priest Mattathias) and his four brothers — Eleazar, Judas, John, and Jonathan (13:27). In addition, he sets up seven pyramids for his father, four brothers, his unnamed mother, and perhaps himself (13:28). Pyramids, more usually associated with Egypt, here are symbols of wealth and power to honor a family of great national importance.

Simon, the founder of the Hasmonean dynasty, honors his deceased family, who gave their lives for what he brought to fruition — military, religious, and political power and national independence from the deteriorating Seleucid Empire. His mother, for whom he constructed a pyramid, is otherwise unknown.

RONALD S. KLINE

SEE ALSO Part II: Women/Wives Defended by Judas and Simon (1 Macc 3:20, etc.).

FOR FURTHER READING: Doran, Robert. "1 Maccabees."

Goldstein, Jonathan. *I Maccabees: A New Translation with Introduction and Commentary.*

1 Macc 13:45
Wives Defended by Simon and Judas

SEE 1 Macc 3:20, etc. Women/Wives Defended by Judas and Simon (Part II).

2 MACC 3:10; 8:28, 30
Widows

2 Maccabees, composed probably before 63 B.C.E., tells the story of the family of Judas Maccabeus and the mid-second-century B.C.E. revolt of the province of Judea against the Seleucid Empire. The book is organized around three attacks on the Jerusalem temple and the defeat of these by supernatural agents or by Judas.

References to widows appear in the stories of the first two attacks on Jerusalem. Heliodorus, an official from the court of Seleucus IV Philopater, arrives in Jerusalem to strip the temple treasuries because Simon had said that "the treasury in Jerusalem was full of untold sums of money" (3:6). The high priest Onias, who kindly welcomed Heliodorus, explains that Simon misrepresented the facts. In addition to some money belonging to a prominent man, Hyrcanus, there are only "deposits belonging to widows and orphans" (3:10). These funds may be the triannual tithe for orphans and widows described in Tob 1:8 (see also Deut 14:29). Throughout Scripture, care for those without husband (or father) is put forth as an ideal. To be without a male is to be without protection and inheritance in the patrilineal world of the Bible. Neglect or oppression of the defenseless provoked divine wrath (Deut 27:19; Isa 1:23; Ezek 22:7). Thus, violation of the funds belonging to the widow (and orphan) would be a most hideous act, as Onias tries unsuccessfully to convince Heliodorus.

In 2 Macc 8:28 and 30, Judas is an exemplary warrior who gives some of the spoils of his successful battles to widows (and orphans), as well as to those who had been tortured or those who were aged. In line with Deut 26:12–13 and other similar texts, Judas shows concern for observance of God's command to care for the unfortunate.

The practice of sharing resources with those in need, most particularly those who reside together — resident aliens, orphans, and widows — is part of the social fabric of ancient Israel. The custom of concern for widows (and orphans) spans the entire Bible. Good acts, like care for the widow, brings God's blessing (as in the case of Judas, who will successfully rout the Seleucids). Conversely, failure to do good acts brings catastrophe (as in the case of Heliodorus, who will eventually fail in his attempt to strip the temple treasury).

TONI CRAVEN

SEE ALSO Part II: Widows (Exod 22:22, etc.); (Tob 1:8); Widow (Wis 2:10); (Sir 35:17–18); (Ep Jer v. 38); (2 Esdr 2:2–4, etc.).
FOR FURTHER READING: Doran, Robert. "2 Maccabees."
Goldstein, Jonathan A. *II Maccabees: A New Translation with Introduction and Commentary.*
Price, James L. "Widow."

2 MACC 3:19–20
Women Suppliants

In 2 Maccabees 3, Heliodorus, a Seleucid official, under order from Seleucus IV to plunder the Jerusalem temple treasury, sets a day to confiscate the money kept for widows, orphans, and a wealthy man, Hyrcanus, ignoring the pleas of the high priest, Onias. In great distress, the whole city laments and makes supplication to God because Heliodorus purposes to dishonor the sanctity of temple. "Women, girded with sackcloth under their breasts, thronged the streets. Some of the young women who were kept indoors ran together to the gates, and some to the walls, while others peered out of the windows. And holding up their hands to heaven, they all made supplication" (3:19–20).

The public actions of these unnamed women on behalf of the Jerusalem temple are graphic signs of distress. While some only look out their windows (compare Sir 42:9–12), other unmarried young women race outside. Crisis emboldens these women to go out in public — some wearing sackcloth (the classic symbol of mourning, see Neh 9:1; Jonah 3:6; Esth 4:1; Jdt 4:10–14; 9:1) — and join in the community's prayer. This disruption of stereotyped behavioral patterns is like that of the women of Jerusalem in 3 Macc 1:18–20, where the details are even more elaborate.

The prayers of the Jerusalem community are effective. As Heliodorus goes into the treasury, miraculously, a great horse and rider rush at him, and two angelic figures flog him continuously, rendering him unconscious. Only the prayer of Onias saves him from death. Following his experience, Heliodorus converts to Judaism. When the king asks what kind of man would be suitable for another mission to Jerusalem, Heliodorus replies, one whom the king would like to see thoroughly flogged, if he survives at all (3:37–38).

TONI CRAVEN

SEE ALSO Part II: Daughter (Sir 7:24–25, etc.); Widows (2 Macc 3:10, etc.); Women Supplicants (3 Macc 1:18–20).

2 MACC 5:13, 24; 12:3–4, 21
Women/Wives as Victims of War

In 2 Maccabees, atrocities against women are perpetrated explicitly only by the enemy. Jewish attacks and counterattacks, which surely resulted in the death of women, never single out women as victims. Women massacred as casualties of war represent a death blow to individuals as well as to the community and its future. Slavery, not death, is the more usual fate of women (and children) taken in war. In a society like that of Jerusalem, organized around preservation of the temple and of the family household, attack on women carries with it political, religious, economic, and cultural devastation.

During Antiochus IV's brutal three-day attack of Jerusalem, Jewish women are both massacred and enslaved. Eighty thousand people die, which is surely an inflated number (2 Macc 5:12–14). Of those still left following this attack, grown men are slated to be killed and women and boys sold as slaves (5:24).

In 12:3–4 unsuspecting Jewish inhabitants of Joppa (an important harbor city) are cruelly tricked by their gentile neighbors to set out on boats; when at sea, two hundred of them are drowned. Here as elsewhere in 2 Maccabees, the Jews are portrayed as peaceful, desirous only of following their own customs undisturbed.

When Judas Maccabeus and his Jewish freedom fighters come against Timothy, a military officer of the Ammonites who joined forces with the Syrians, he sends off all the gentile women and the children to Carnaim, the site of a temple to the Syrian goddess Atargatis (2 Macc 12:26). As many as thirty thousand Gentiles are put to death in Judas's attack (12:23), but Timothy is spared by arguing that he "held the parents of most of them, and the brothers of some, to whom no consideration would be shown" (12:24). No mention of women is made in Timothy's pleading. This text, which is either misplaced or about another Timothy, follows 10:24–38, where "Timothy" was earlier killed by Judas and his army in a stronghold called Gazara, while hiding in a cistern (a large plastered pit used for collecting water during the rainy season).

TONI CRAVEN

SEE ALSO Part II: Women in Distant Towns as Booty (Deut 20:14, etc.); Women/Wives Persecuted by Antiochus IV (1 Macc 1:32, etc.); Part III: Atagartis.

FOR FURTHER READING: Doran, Robert. "2 Maccabees."

Goldstein, Jonathan A. *II Maccabees: A New Translation with Introduction and Commentary.*

2 MACC 6:4
Prostitutes/Women in Sacred Precincts

In 2 Maccabees, the condensation of an otherwise unknown Jason of Cyrene's five-volume history of the mid-second-century B.C.E. revolt of the province of Judea against the Seleucid Empire, the sole information regarding the desecration of the Jerusalem temple under Antiochus IV appears in 6:4–5. The author caricatures the licentiousness of gentile men and female temple prostitutes (see Ezek 23:36–49; Ep Jer vv. 11, 42–43) to illustrate their barbarity in profaning the Jerusalem temple: "For the temple was filled with debauchery and reveling by the Gentiles, who dallied with prostitutes and had intercourse with women within the sacred precincts, and besides brought in things for sacrifice that were unfit" (2 Macc 6:4).

It is highly probable that the source for this report of temple prostitution is Dan 11:31, where the Hebrew *zr'ym* is usually read as *zĕrō'îm*, with the translation "forces sent by him shall occupy and profane the temple." But Theodotion, a mid-second-century C.E. Jewish translator, read *zĕrā'îm*, with the translation "seeds . . ." 2 Maccabees seems to favor this sexual reading of Antiochus's desecration of the temple, which results in forbidden temple prostitution (Deut 23:17).

Both Daniel and 1 Maccabees are concerned with Antiochus IV's introduction of foreign worship into the Jerusalem temple, "the abomination that makes desolate" (Dan 11:31), or its equivalent, "the defiled stones" (1 Macc 4:43), which may have been another altar on top of the altar of burnt offering, or, less likely, a statue of Zeus, or even a stone structure of three meteorite cult-stones representing the God of the Jews, the Queen of Heaven (God's consort), and God's divine son. Perhaps the reference in 2 Macc 6:4 to the Gentiles bringing in "things for sacrifice that were unfit" is an allusion to one of these forms. 2 Maccabees does not use the full term, "abomination that makes desolate," nor does it make reference to cessation of burnt offerings, as do Dan 11:31 and 1 Macc 1:45.

TONI CRAVEN

SEE ALSO Part II: Temple Prostitute (Deut 23:17, etc.); Prostitutes (Ep Jer v. 11); Women with Cords (Ep Jer vv. 42–43).

FOR FURTHER READING: Goldstein, Jonathan A. *II Maccabees: A New Translation with Introduction and Commentary.*

Wenham, David. "Abomination of Desolation."

2 MACC 6:10
Women/Mothers with Circumcised Sons

The Seleucid ruler Antiochus IV's savage subjugation of Jerusalem in 2 Maccabees outlaws temple worship, observance of Sabbaths and holy days, circumcision, and the keeping of Torah. In 2 Macc 6:9, he rules that the Jews who will not adopt Greek customs are to die. While 2 Macc 6:10 repeats the hideous illustration of women with their circumcised sons hung around their necks, also found in 1 Macc 1:60–61 and 4 Macc 4:25, its purpose is distinct. The writer urged "those who read this book not to be depressed by such calamities, but to recognize that these punishments were designed not to destroy but to discipline our people" (6:12).

2 Macc 6:7–7:42 lists examples of cruel tortures and martyrdoms meant to encourage the faithful when so disciplined. The first martyrs are two women with their circumcised sons hanging at their breasts, who are first paraded around the city and then hurled from the city wall. The last martyr is the widowed mother of seven sons who dies after encouraging each to endure in his faith. In 2 Maccabees, these are not examples of Antiochus's destruction of the community and its future; rather they are signs of his inability to destroy this community or its future.

TONI CRAVEN

SEE ALSO Part II: Women/Mothers with Circumcised Sons (1 Macc 1:60–61); (4 Macc 4:25); Martyred Mother with Seven Sons (2 Macc 7:1–42); (4 Macc 1:8, etc.).

2 MACC 7:1–42
Martyred Mother with Seven Sons

According to 2 Maccabees, in the second century B.C.E. the Seleucid king Antiochus IV outlaws temple worship, observance of Sabbaths and holy days, circumcision, and the keeping of Torah, and rules that the Jews who will not adopt Greek customs are to die (2 Macc 6:9). The martyrology in 2 Macc 6:7–7:42 (the first of its kind in the Bible) lists stories of those who choose death over apostasy. The last martyr is the unnamed mother who dies after witnessing each of her seven sons cruelly tortured. Her family story appears here in 7:1–42 and in a considerably expanded version in 4 Maccabees (see that entry). Exactly where the martyrdoms in 2 Maccabees take place is debated. No scene other than Jerusalem and Judea is ever established in the narrative, yet Antioch is a possible setting for chap. 7 since the king seems so thoroughly on his own turf.

The 2 Maccabees 7 version of the martyr family story opens with the arrest of the seven brothers and their mother, who are beaten in an effort to force them to eat swine's flesh (prohibited by Lev 11:7–8). The first six sons each defy the king and are cruelly tortured. The six brothers' exchanges with Antiochus IV, the king (7:2–19), build a coherent argument, which is arranged chiastically (three elements and their reverse): (A) Jewish refusal of the king's command results in suffering and death; (B) Jewish hope in eternal life is born of serving *the King;* (C) Jewish belief in bodily resurrection makes mortal life meaningless; (C′) for the gentile king there will be no resurrection to life; (B′) for this mortal king and his descendants there is no hope; (A′) the king's "fight against God" (7:19) will not go unpunished. God, not the gentile king, is in charge of the happenings.

Attention then turns to the mother (7:20–23), "especially admirable and worthy of honorable memory" (7:20). Because her hope was in the Lord, she had encouraged each of her sons, in Aramaic or Hebrew, to persevere. "Filled with a noble spirit, she reinforced her woman's reasoning with a man's courage" (7:21). Addressing these sons — not Antiochus — she claims not to comprehend how life came to them in her womb, even as she expresses confidence in the Creator, who "will in his mercy give life and breath back to you again, since you now forget yourselves for the sake of his laws" (7:23). What mother, beholding the brutal deaths of six sons, could speak such words?

Antiochus interprets her words, which he cannot understand since they are not in his language, as reproach, and so appeals to her seventh and youngest son that he will make him rich and will befriend him if he will but turn away from the ways of his ancestors (7:24). When the youngest will not listen, Antiochus calls the mother and urges her to persuade her son (7:25). The mother leans close to her remaining child and, speaking only to him, urges him to take pity on her and accept death (7:27–29). Three matters in her words merit notice: (1) the mother speaks only to her family members, never the king; (2) the mother remarks in passing that she had nursed her son for three years; (3) God creates out of nothing, which may reflect the philosophical argument *creatio ex nihilo,* or more likely, with 7:11, 22–23, belief that life comes from the Creator of the world.

While his mother was still speaking, her youngest says to the king, "What are you waiting for? I will not obey the king's command, but I obey the command of the law that was given to our ancestors through Moses" (7:30). Repeating much of what his brothers said as they faced their deaths, the seventh brother claims that the king will not go unpunished, that suffering is discipline for human sinfulness, and that reconciliation with God is at hand (7:31–36). Antiochus falls into a rage and treats the youngest brother worse than the others (7:39). "So he died in his integrity, putting his whole trust in the Lord" (7:40).

"Last of all, the mother died, after her sons" (7:41). With only this brief statement the mother's death is recorded.

Antiochus's brutal efforts are completely ineffective. Death has lost its power in the face of obedience to the laws of the ancestors and belief in God's mercy and resurrection of the dead. Resurrection cancels fears of earthly death for faithful Jews. Which sins merit martyrdom is a question left unanswered. Vengeance and vindication belong to God alone — not the earthly king, Antiochus.

2 Maccabees, like 4 Maccabees, shows that *eusebēs logismos,* "reason adhering to the law" triumphs over human emotions (see 4 Macc 1:16–19). Those who might be expected to be weak show themselves strong in holding fast to the teachings of the Torah. Ironically, the king is the only one in the story who loses control. The author's claim that the mother bore the deaths of her sons with good courage because of her hope in the Lord and the reinforcement of "her woman's reasoning with a man's courage" (7:20–21) reflects the Greek cultural norm, mediated through Hellenism, that courage and

control are distinctively masculine virtues. Thus praise comes for being like a man. This mother, unlike her counterpart in Jer 15:5–9, did not swoon, nor is she disgraced by her children or her own actions. She is mother of a martyr family that was unified in facing death, with no husband or father offering protection. The unexplained absence of her husband makes her a virtual widow. Courage such as hers and that of her sons won God's mercy and made possible the victories of Judas Maccabeus (7:37–38; 8:3–5).

The martyrology, set in Judea and Jerusalem, that stretches from 2 Macc 6:10 to 7:42, beginning with the deaths of the circumcising mothers and climaxing with the martyrdom of the mother and her seven sons, now comes to an end. Antiochus and his ideology do not win the day. Two Jewish women, Sabbath observers assembled in caves, an old man (Eleazar), seven brothers, and a single mother have shown conclusively that God disciplines the faithful, but never withdraws mercy (see 6:12–17).

TONI CRAVEN

SEE ALSO Part II: Mothers (and Fathers) (Jer 15:8–9, etc.); Women/Mothers with Circumcised Sons (2 Macc 6:10); (4 Macc 4:25); Mother/Woman's Womb (2 Esdr 4:40–43, etc.); Martyred Mother with Seven Sons (2 Macc 7:1–42); (4 Macc 1:8, etc.).

FOR FURTHER READING: Doran, Robert. "2 Maccabees."

Goldstein, Jonathan A. *II Maccabees: A New Translation with Introduction and Commentary.*

Young, Robin Darling. "2 Maccabees."

———. "The 'Woman with the Soul of Abraham': Traditions about the Mother of the Maccabean Martyrs."

2 MACC 8:28, 30   Widows

SEE 2 MACC 3:10, etc.   Widows (Part II).

2 MACC 12:3–4, 21   Wives of Joppa

SEE 2 MACC 5:13, etc.   Women/Wives as Victims of War (Part II).

2 Macc 15:18
Wives and Sisters (and Brothers) of Judas' Men

Nicanor, a Syrian general assigned by the Seleucid king Antiochus IV (Epiphanes) to suppress the Maccabean uprising in Judea, furious that the Jewish freedon fighter Judas has gone into hiding, threatens to level the Jerusalem temple if the priests do not hand Judas over to him as a prisoner (14:33). Hearing that Judas and his troops are in the region of Samaria, Nicanor prepares to attack on the Sabbath, assuming they will not defend themselves (15:1). Judas arms his men "not so much with confidence in shields and spears as with the inspiration of brave words" (15:11), telling them his dream of Onias, the noble high priest, bringing word that Jeremiah prays for the city of Jerusalem and sent Judas a golden sword, as a gift from God, to strike down his adversaries (15:16). This holy sword was a sign that God approved the Jews' self-defense on the Sabbath. Judas's words inspire his troops to attack bravely to protect the holy city and the temple.

Here, just before the last great battle in 2 Maccabees in which Nicanor will be defeated, "Their concern for wives and children, and also for brothers and sisters and relatives, lay upon them less heavily; their greatest and first fear was for the consecrated sanctuary" (15:18). More usual in this book that highly values preservation of the family is great concern for the safety of women and children (see 2 Macc 5:13, 24; 12:3–4).

Another unusual feature of 15:18 is the inclusion of "sisters." This word is not explicit in the Greek text, but appears in the NRSV translation. Here, and in two other Apochraphal/Deuterocanonical Books (Jdt 7:30; Sir 25:1), the NRSV translators made the decision to include references to "sisters" for inclusiveness and the sense of the text.

TONI CRAVEN

SEE ALSO Part II: Sisters (and Brothers) (Jdt 7:30); (Sir 25:1); Women/Wives as Victims of War (2 Macc 5:13, etc.).

1 ESDR 1:32
Mourning Women (and Men)

1 Esdras, a canonical book for only the Eastern Orthodox Church, is a rather free Greek version of important historical events in Judah from the time of Josiah's Passover (621 B.C.E.) to Ezra's reforms (444 B.C.E.). Probably written after 165 B.C.E., it opens with Josiah's reinstatement of the Passover (1:1–22) and the story of his untimely death when he opposed Pharaoh Neco of Egypt at Carchemish (1:23–33), accounts parallel to 2 Chronicles 35.

In 1 Esdr 1:32 women of Israel, together with principal men, the prophet Jeremiah, and all Judea, lament the untimely death of the upright King Josiah (1:32). Whereas 2 Chr 35:25 says "singing men and singing women" mourn Josiah's death, 1 Esdras reads "principal men, with the women [or wives]." This subordination of women as wives rather than professional mourners seems to reflect a misreading of the Hebrew, mistaking *haššārîm wĕhaššārōt* ("the singing men and the singing women") for *haśārîm wĕhaśārôt* ("princes and princesses") to result in the Greek translation "principal men, with the women."

WILLIAM R. GOODMAN, JR.

SEE ALSO Part II: Singing Women (and Men) Who Lament (2 Chr 35:25).

FOR FURTHER READING: Goodman, William R. "Esdras, First Book of."

Klein, Ralph W. "1 Esdras."

Myers, Jacob. *I & II Esdras.*

Schuller, Eileen M. "1 Esdras."

1 ESDR 1:53
Young Woman (and Young Man) as War Victims

In the Jewish book 1 Esdras (late second century B.C.E.), except for some minor variants in the text, the compiler simply let the Chronicler's work (1–2 Chronicles; Ezra; Nehemiah), with its point of view, prevail. Such is the case with the description of the last kings of Judah and the fall of Jerusalem in 1 Esdr 1:34–58, which closely follows 2 Chronicles 36.

1 Esdr 1:53 rewords 2 Chr 36:17 in describing how God gave over all in Jerusalem to the Chaldeans (the people who ruled Mesopotamia during the Neo-Babylonian period) in its attack on Jerusalem. "These killed their young men with the sword around their holy temple, and did not spare young man or young woman, old man or child, for he gave them all into their hands" (1 Esdr 1:53). "Young woman" here is the Greek word "virgin." The devastation of the passage is poignant. 1 Esdras follows the Chronicler's reasoning that Jerusalem fell because its inhabitants mocked God's prophets and incurred God's wrath, as executed by the Chaldeans, against themselves and the temple.

WILLIAM R. GOODMAN, JR.

SEE ALSO Part II: Young Women (and Men) Slaughtered (2 Chr 36:17).

FOR FURTHER READING: Myers, Jacob. *I & II Esdras.*

1 ESDR 3:12; 4:13–32, 34
Women as Strongest

The story of the three bodyguards and the riddle contest held at the Persian court of Darius in 1 Esdr 3:1–5:6 is the only distinctive passage in a book that is otherwise a rather free Greek version of materials that closely — though not exactly — parallel 2 Chronicles and Ezra-Nehemiah. In this important composite tale, each young man tries to best the other's statement of "What one thing is strongest" (3:5). They put their answers under the pillow of the king, who, they believe, will reward the wisest with gifts and honors. Upon waking, the king summons an audience and requests each youth to give a public defense of his answer to the riddle. The first two argue that wine and the king, respectively, are strongest. But the third wins with his witty defense of women and truth (3:12; 4:13–32, 34). The king grants the winner's request that the exiled Jews be permitted to return to Jerusalem, that the city and the temple be rebuilt, and that the temple vessels be

returned. This third youth is identified in an obvious gloss as Zerubbabel (4:13), the illustrious leader
of the second return from exile and the builder of
the second temple, making this an edifying legend
about an important leader of the Jews during the
Babylonian exile.

The view here, from a male perspective, is that
women have the most power in the world sexually,
economically, and socially, and therefore are the
strongest. Simply put, "men cannot exist without
women" (4:17). While the king and all people who
rule over the sea and land are powerful, it is women
who are most powerful since they give birth to
these leaders (4:15). Women raise the men who
plant the vineyards that produce wine, also a powerful — but not most powerful — force (4:16).
Women make clothes for men and bring them re-
nown (4:17). Female form exercises direct power
over men: "If men gather gold and silver or any
other beautiful thing, and then see a woman lovely
in appearance and beauty, they let all those things
go, and gape at her, and with open mouths stare at
her" (4:18–19).

Restating Gen 2:24, the third youth claims that a
man will leave his father and country and live out
his days with his wife, and then adds the negative
assessment that relationship with a woman causes a
man to forget both parents and country (1 Esdr
4:20–21). The young man tells the king and his nobles that all this proves "women rule over you"
(4:22a), a reversal of Gen 3:16 in which a man rules
over the woman. He argues that men will do anything for women — give them all the fruits of their
labor, rob and steal for them, face lions, walk in
darkness, love them more than their own parents,
lose their minds because of them, and even become
slaves on their account (4:22b–26). The third youth
concludes, "Many have perished, or stumbled, or
sinned because of women" (4:27).

To clinch his argument, the third youth cites an
incident (4:29–32) that occurred at another (unnamed) king's banquet when Apame, the king's
concubine, sitting in a place of honor at the king's
right hand, took the crown from the king's head,
slapping him with her left hand. That the king allowed her these liberties and was willing to do anything to make her happy proves, according to the
third youth's logic, that women are strongest. His
listeners — all males — appreciate these ideas
about gender and male-female relationships.

Apparently favoring the third youth's argument
for women as strongest, over the arguments for
wine and king, the king and nobles look knowingly
at each other (4:33). Just then the riddle contest
takes an unexpected turn: the third young man
begins to speak again, now defending truth as
strongest (4:33–41). No doubt an addition to the
original folk tale, this enigmatic addition displaces
women as the winning answer. Ironically, the third
youth wins by cheating; he introduces a second
entry, while the other youths got only one. "Gentle-
men, are not women strong?" he begins (4:34).
Then, adding an ethical dimension to the original
secular story, he argues, "Wine is unrighteous, the
king is unrighteous, women are unrighteous, all
human beings are unrighteous, all their works are
unrighteous, and all such things. There is no truth
in them and in their unrighteousness they will perish. But truth endures and is strong forever" (4:37–
38). When Zerubbabel prays, "Blessed be the God
of truth!" (4:40), all the people acclaim, "Great is
truth, and strongest of all!" (4:41).

Truth (*alētheia*) is a feminine noun, and the description of truth in the youth's defense bears great
similarity to the power of the Egyptian *Ma'at*, the
Greek *Sophia* (Wisdom), the Hebrew *ḥokmâ*,
and the Persian *Arta*, all feminine in gender and all
subjects of hymns of praise extolling their cosmic
and earthly powers.

In the end, women are not considered the
strongest; they are labeled as unrighteous (4:37);
they cause men to stumble and sin (4:27); they
make men forget their fathers and country (4:21).
The third youth voices negative views regarding
women that were likely reflections of popular culture in the Persian or early Hellenistic period. This
story makes Zerubbabel an important person in
the postexilic era. It objectifies and ultimately denigrates women of the same period.

WILLIAM R. GOODMAN, JR.

SEE ALSO Part I: Apame.

FOR FURTHER READING: Goodman, William R. "Esdras, First Book of."

Klein, Ralph W. "1 Esdras."

Myers, Jacob. *I & II Esdras.*

Schuller, Eileen M. "1 Esdras."

1 ESDR 5:1, 41–42
Women as Returning Exiles

In 1 Esdras, the Persian king Darius rewards the third bodyguard, Zerubbabel, the winner of a riddle contest, with generous royal support and approval for the exiles to return to Jerusalem and rebuild the temple (4:42–57). In preparation for the return, Jewish male leaders are chosen, according to their tribes, to go up (perhaps from Susa) with their households. Wives, daughters, and female slaves (5:1) are listed among the exiles allowed to return to Jerusalem, with a cavalry escort of one thousand provided by Darius. The female and male servants listed as returning from the exile number 7,337, of a total of 42,360 over twelve years of age (5:41–42).

Lists of exiles returning to Judea (the province of Yehud in Hebrew) also appear in Ezra 2:1–70 and Neh 7:6–73a, though neither records that exiles returned in the time of Darius or mentions selection of those exiles as the list described in 1 Esdras. All the lists include parallel references to returning female (and male) slaves (1 Esdr 5:1, 41–42; compare Ezra 2:65; Neh 7:67), but only 1 Esdras specifically mentions wives and daughters (1 Esdr 5:1). In each instance, though, family groups, which would have included wives and daughters, are mentioned as returning from exile. The Hebrew Bible lists thirty-three family groups in Ezra 2 and thirty-one in Nehemiah 7. The Greek Bible (Septuagint) lists thirty-three in Ezra 2, thirty-four in Nehemiah 7, and thirty-five in 1 Esdras 5. Thus the women mentioned as returning exiles were likely involved with the maintenance of the household and its tasks in a variety of roles.

Although women are listed as part of the return-ing entourage, they are not mentioned in the instruction to the young men to fast for the safety of the returning exiles (8:50). However, some scholars have suggested that the translation "for the young men" may be a misreading of the word for "river." If this is the case, then there is no omission of women at all in this passage as they would be included in the petition for "ourselves and for our children and the livestock that were with us" (8:50).

WILLIAM R. GOODMAN, JR.

SEE ALSO Part II: Female (and Male) Servants Returning to Judah (Ezra 2:64–65, etc.); Female (and Male) Singers Returning to Judah (Ezra 2:65, etc.).

FOR FURTHER READING: Myers, Jacob. *I & II Esdras.*

1 ESDR 8:70, 84, 92–93; 9:7, 9, 12, 17–36
Foreign Daughters/Wives; Daughters of Judah

In 1 Esdr 8:1–9:55, as in Ezra 7:1–10:44 and Neh 7:73–8:12, Ezra's reforms (444 B.C.E.) confront the problem of intermarriage. In his prayer-address on mixed marriages (1 Esdr 8:74–90), Ezra regards marriage with "alien peoples of the land" as pollution of the "holy race" (8:70) and states that there are to be no mixed marriages with alien women and that Judahite daughters are not to be given to the foreigners (8:84). Ezra confesses that, by the intermarriage of their sons and daughters with foreigners, the people have violated God's commandment given through the prophets. However, this claim that the prophets make such a statement (8:82–85) is not borne out in any extant biblical prophecy. Some have suggested that the author was thinking of Leviticus 18.

Ezra's ruling outlaws exogamy (marriage outside the clan) in favor of endogamy (marriage within the clan). At stake here is preservation of the ethnic and religious identity of the Judahite community, as well as its land rights. Given the greatly reduced area that comprised the province of Yehud (with boundaries roughly twenty miles in any direction around Jerusalem) under the rule of the Persian

Empire, preservation of the actual land belonging to the Judahite community was important. Outlawing marriage outside the community ensured that no partner or child of such a marriage would be able to seize legal control over property once a Jewish spouse had died.

In response to Ezra's prayer-address, one of the men of Israel, a certain Shecaniah (as in Ezra 10:2) says to Ezra, "We have sinned against the Lord, and have married foreign women from the peoples of the land; but even now there is hope for Israel. Let us take an oath to the Lord about this, that we will put away all our foreign wives, with their children" (1 Edsr 8:92–93). The law sanctioned divorce in the case of a man finding "something objectionable" about his wife (Deut 24:1–4), and here, that something is seemingly her foreign birth. No provisions are made and no concerns are expressed for the foreign women and children thus expelled from the Judahite community. In fact, the ethnic identity of these women and children is unclear. They may have been outsiders to the Judahite community (Ammonites, Moabites, or others), or they may have been Judahite families who had not gone into exile, since for Ezra-Nehemiah the returning exiles constituted the only authentic Judahites.

In 1 Esdras 9, the people respond to Ezra's summons (9:7–9) and agree to separate themselves from their foreign wives (9:12). On account of severe winter weather, they ask for three months so that local committees, composed of elders and judges, can decide upon each case (9:17). The lists of those required to put away foreign wives include priests (9:18), Levites (9:23), and laity (9:26–36). Thus the people purged themselves of guilt by dissociating themselves from the people of the land.

WILLIAM R. GOODMAN, JR.

SEE ALSO Part II: Woman Being Divorced (Deut 24:1–4); Daughters of Judah and Foreign Daughters/Wives (Ezra 9:2, etc.).

FOR FURTHER READING: Goodman, William R. "Esdras, First Book of."

Myers, Jacob. *I & II Esdras.*

1 Esdr 8:91; 9:40–41
Women (and Men) in Assembly

1 Esdr 8:1–9:55 is a rather free Greek version of Ezra's reforms (444 B.C.E.) that parallels Ezra 7:1–10:44 and Neh 7:73–8:12. Women from Jerusalem are among those who gather around Ezra (8:91) following his prayer-address on the problem of mixed marriages (8:74–90) and form part of the great crowd who hear Ezra read the law to the "men and women" (9:40–41). These passages closely parallel Ezra 10:1 and Neh 8:2, respectively.

WILLIAM R. GOODMAN, JR.

SEE ALSO Part II: Women (and Men and Children) in Assembly (Ezra 10:1); Women, Part of the Assembly of People (Neh 8:2, etc.).

THE PRAYER OF MANASSEH
No Women Mentioned

No women are mentioned in the Prayer of Manasseh. When the prayer invokes the "God of our ancestors" (vv. 1, 8), it is Abraham, Isaac, and Jacob who are named.

The Apocryphal/Deuterocanonical Prayer of Manasseh, which is included in Greek Orthodox and Slavonic Bibles, is a penitential prayer composed by a Palestinian Jew, sometime before the destruction of the Jerusalem temple in 70 C.E. It supplies a prayer attributed to Manasseh — son of Hezekiah, the arch-villain of the Davidic kings of Judah (reigned 687–642 B.C.E.). According to 2 Chr 33:10–17, Manasseh is briefly exiled to Babylon, where he repents and prays, and the Lord hears his prayer and restores him again to Jerusalem (contrast 2 Kings 21, where his apostasy necessitates the nation's exile).

Only fifteen verses long, Manasseh's individual lament of his personal sin and petition for forgiveness is a poetic jewel. The convictions that contrition and repentance are effective and that God's justice comes with mercy run throughout the prayer. The theme that God restores those who repent (v. 13) was important in postexilic Judaism, which constantly lived under repressive regimes. Forgiveness is available for those, like Manasseh, who "bend the knee of my heart" (v. 11) and implore God's mercy.

TONI CRAVEN

FOR FURTHER READING: Charlesworth, James H. "Manasseh, Prayer of."

Tull, Patricia K. "The Prayer of Manasseh."

PSALM 151
No Women Mentioned

Only seven verses long, Psalm 151, one of the Apocryphal/Deuterocanonical additions, is known in four ancient text forms (Hebrew, Greek, Latin, and Syriac) and is included in Greek Orthodox and Slavonic Bibles. Like the Prayer of Manasseh, Psalm 151 relates an episode from the life of a notable male character from the Hebrew Bible. Likely composed during the Hellenistic period, Psalm 151 is ascribed to David as his own composition.

No women are mentioned in Psalm 151. Only males — David and his seven brothers — are considered when the prophet Samuel searches for God's chosen ruler (compare 1 Samuel 16–17).

TONI CRAVEN

SEE ALSO Part II: The Prayer of Manasseh.

FOR FURTHER READING: Charlesworth, James H., with James A. Sanders. "Psalm 151."

Newsom, Carol A. "Psalm 151."

3 MACC 1:4
Wives (and Children) of Troops

3 Maccabees, a historical romance describing three episodes in the reign of Ptolemy IV Philopater, king of Egypt (221–204 B.C.E.), opens with a brief ro-

mantic story about how the Egyptian queen Arsinoë saved the day for her consort-brother, Ptolemy IV, during the Battle of Raphia (217 B.C.E.). When the tide of battle turned to favor the forces of the Seleucid ruler Antiochus III of Syria, Arsinoë went into the Egyptian forces "with wailing and tears, her locks all disheveled, and exhorted them to defend themselves and their children and wives bravely, promising to give them each two minas of gold if they won the battle" (3 Macc 1:4).

Raphia, the site of the battle, is a strategic location on the main road between Egypt and Palestine, called the "Way of Horus" by the Egyptians, the "Way of the Land of the Philistines" in the Hebrew Bible (Exod 13:17), and the "Way of the Sea" by the Romans. Arsinoë encourages the Egyptian troops to defend the very entry road to their homeland, appealing to the warriors' honor in bravely defending their women and children. She invokes protection of the defenseless in this society for the preservation of the state, with motives more political than ethical. Her promise to pay each soldier the equivalent of 200 drachmas for success testifies to her own wealth and ability to buy what she wants, specifically military success.

TONI CRAVEN

SEE ALSO Part I: Arsinoë.

FOR FURTHER READING: Keck, Brian E. "Raphia."

3 MACC 1:18–20
Women Supplicants

Women are prominent in a group of supplicants featured in 3 Maccabees, a book that deals with the struggles of Egyptian Jews who suffered under Ptolemy IV Philopater, the Hellenistic king of Egypt (reigned 221–204 B.C.E.). Although it reads as history, the story of Ptolemy's efforts to destroy the Jews is probably a highly dramatized fictionalized account. It is best regarded as an edifying and apologetic tract, perhaps composed in the first century B.C.E. in Alexandria (Egypt), designed to keep the lamp of orthodox Jewish faith burning and to exhibit the loyalty of Jews as subject people in the territories of their sojourn.

On arrival in Jerusalem direct from his victory over Antiochus III at Raphia on the frontier between Palestine and Egypt (217 B.C.E.), Ptolemy insists on his right to enter the temple's Holy of Holies (3 Macc 1:9–16). The populace, aghast at what might happen, crowds into the streets. At this critical moment, the women of the city are given pride of place in the narrative. Women of different stages of life, in relation to childbearing, move out in throngs toward the temple (1:18–20). Young women rush out from their rooms, and into the streets with their mothers, sprinkling dust on their hair as a token of mourning and loudly lamenting the dire fate about to overtake their beloved holy place (1:18). Brides leave their bridal chambers and, betraying the modesty normally expected of them, run around the city in disorder (1:19). Mothers and wet nurses, both charged with the care of the youngest children, in their extreme haste to reach the temple, are ready to abandon the children in houses or in the streets en route (1:10).

The public actions of these unnamed women on behalf of the Jerusalem temple and their burning desire to preserve their Jewish faith could scarcely be more graphically portrayed. Three categories of women are depicted: nubile girls, new brides, and the mothers and nurses of newborns. This set, comprised of women near or at the childbearing stage of their lives, represents potential or actual fecundity. Their appearance in public view is unusual. Crisis emboldens them to rush out and join in prayer and protest of Ptolemy's attempt to enter the Jerusalem temple. They join a crowd of outraged Jewish citizenry — an extended family of faith — who offer supplications because of what Ptolemy IV planned (1:17–29).

3 Maccabees shares two important theological themes with 1, 2, and 4 Maccabees: the absolute loyalty of the Jews to law and temple, and ineradicable belief in God as the protector of the covenant people. One salient motif stands out in particularly bold relief in all four: the invincible devotion of Jewish women to the ancestral faith.

HUGH ANDERSON

SEE ALSO Part II: Young Women (and Young Men); Brides (and Bridegrooms) (1 Macc 1:26–27); Women Supplicants (2 Macc 3:19); Women Faithful in Persecution (3 Macc 3:25; etc.).

3 MACC 3:25; 4:6–7; 5:49–51; 7:10–23
Women Faithful in Persecution

In 3 Maccabees, a highly fictionalized drama likely composed in the first century B.C.E., Ptolemy IV Philopator (reigned 221–204 B.C.E.) is portrayed as persecuting Egyptian Jews. Ptolemy is convinced that punishment of *all* Jews, including women and children (3:25) in Alexandria and beyond, would ensure the permanence of his government. All the Jews are rounded up, bound fast in iron chains, and herded with ferocious cruelty onto ships for the voyage to Alexandria. Even young brides "exchanged joy for wailing, their myrrh-perfumed hair sprinkled with ashes, and were carried away unveiled, all together raising a lament instead of a wedding song" (4:6). These young women are probably singled out for special mention because of their symbolic role of representing survival.

The next scene shifts to Alexandria, where Ptolemy orders Hermon, the commander of his elephant brigade, to annihilate the Jews (5:1–2). The whole multitude of deported Jews is to be mustered in the hippodrome (an open-air stadium with an oval course for horse and chariot races) on the city's outskirts and trampled to death by five hundred elephants drugged with frankincense and wine. However, the plot is foiled three times by divine intervention.

The third time that God intervenes to save the Jews, women play a decisive part. The drugged elephants, followed by armed forces, are at last set on the move. The Jews crowded in the hippodrome believe their fate is finally sealed. Parents and children, daughters and nursing mothers bewail their impending destruction. The nursing mothers put aside the infants at their breasts, prostrate themselves as supplicants (the author of 3 Maccabees is always anxious about the correct posture for prayer), and implore the God of all power for mercy (5:45–51). The aged priest Eleazar also appeals to God to save them, and two angels, visible to all except the Jews, strike terror into the king and his troops and turn the elephants back upon the king's forces (6:1–21). Seeing all this, Ptolemy has a change of heart; he begs the forgiveness of the "living God of heaven" (6:28) and orders not only that the Jews be released, but that they celebrate a festival for seven days at his expense (6:22–29).

In the conclusion of 3 Maccabees, the women featured in the account of the rescue of the Jews are not explicitly mentioned; but surely they are included among the company of Jews who return to their homelands in festive celebration (7:17–23). These persecuted women, with their public laments and prayers, have helped to save their people, as do other women in the Apocryphal/Deuterocanonical Books. Not mentioned by name or role, but surely part of the restored community, women would have returned to the customary seclusion of private nuclear households as times of persecution were replaced by times of peace. In the Apocryphal/Deuterocanonical Books, the courageous public actions and laments of Jewish women in 3 Maccabees parallel those of Judith (Jdt 8–16) and other unnamed brides (1 Macc 1:27).

HUGH ANDERSON

SEE ALSO Part I: Arsinoë; Judith 2; Part II: Mourning Women (Jer 9:17–20, etc.); Young Women (and Young Men); Brides (and Bridegrooms) (1 Macc 1:26–27); Women Supplicants (3 Macc 1:18–20).

FOR FURTHER READING: Anderson, Hugh. "Third Maccabees."

———. "3 Maccabees (First Century B.C.)."

Archer, Léonie J. "The Role of Jewish Women in the Religion, Ritual, and Cult of Graeco-Roman Palestine."

Emmet, C. W. "The Third Book of Maccabees."

Kasher, Aryeh. *The Jews in Hellenistic and Roman Egypt: The Struggle for Equal Rights.*

Rostovtzeff, M. "Ptolemaic Egypt."

Young, Robin Darling. "3 Maccabees."

2 ESDR 1:15–30; 2:2–4   God as Mother
SEE Female Images of God in the Apocryphal/Deuterocanonical Books (Part III).

2 ESDR 2:2–4, 20; 15:49; 16:34, 44
Widow

2 Esdras (a composite Jewish and Christian work of the first to third centuries C.E.) most often uses the term *widow* as a negative metaphor to represent the vulnerability and powerlessness of those bereft of the protection and support the paterfamilias accorded women as wives. In a listing of the evils that God will send against Asia, the third-century Christian editor lists widowhood as the first among punishments that also include "poverty, famine, sword, and pestilence, bring ruin to your houses, bringing destruction and death" (15:49).

In 2 Esdr 2:2–4, a second-century C.E. Christian editor presents a widowed mother, likely Zion (compare Bar 4:5–29), saying to her children that she is no longer able to do anything for them. Like them, the widow is forsaken and forlorn. The children have no recourse but to plead for mercy with their Lord. This widowed mother is clearly contrasted with and supplanted by the mother referred to in 2 Esdr 2:15–32, representing the church.

In 2:20, the editor counsels the Christian community to "guard the rights of the widow," just as it is to care for others in special need. The moral concerns are like those in the Book of Tobit and the Gospels of Mark and Luke. The spirit of this instruction is closely aligned with legal stipulations like those of Exod 22:22 and Deut 14:29.

2 Esdr 16:18–34, a third-century C.E. text, describes the trials that await sinners in the coming day of judgment from God. The judgment falls upon the foreign nations as well as upon the faithless among Israel. Women will mourn the loss of husbands, just as virgins will lament that they have no bridegroom (16:33). A community deprived of husbands and bridegrooms faces its impending end.

In 2 Esdr 16:44, the author warns the Christian

community to regard the present world as temporary. Those who marry are to understand themselves to be like those who are without children, just as those who do not marry are to be as those who are widowed. In the coming judgment, God's faithful ones will be spared and saved, while sinners will surely perish.

WALTER J. HARRELSON

SEE ALSO Part III: Jerusalem/Zion as Widow and Mother.

2 ESDR 2:15–32
Church as Mother and Wet Nurse
SEE Church as Mother and Wet Nurse (Part III).

2 ESDR 2:20   Widow
SEE ESDR 2:2–4, etc.   Widow (Part II).

2 ESDR 4:40–43; 5:35, 46–55; 6:21; 8:8–10; 16:38–39
Mother/Woman's Womb

The Book of 2 Esdras is a composite work, the earliest portions of which (chaps. 3–14) were written by an unknown Jewish author in the mid-90s C.E. Chaps. 1–2, dating from about a century later, and the closing two chapters, 15–16, from probably a century later still, are Christian additions. Images related to pregnancy as a nine-month process and to childbirth as an event that comes in its own time are of particular importance in 2 Esdras as metaphors for the impending end time and the current suffering of the faithful. Most appear in the Ezra apocalypse (chaps. 3–14, a special kind of revelatory literature disclosing future events, given by God through an otherworldly mediator to a human seer). Ezra seeks answers from the angel Uriel concerning the meaning of God's dealing with Israel and with the world. The dialogue between Ezra and the angel shows that, on the whole, the answers given by the angel to Ezra's questions fail to satisfy

Ezra. The author's own perspectives, therefore, are often to be found not in the answers given by the angel, but in the thought implicit in Ezra's questions.

It is noteworthy that 2 Esdras does not single out Eve, the mother of all human beings, as the instigator of sin in the world (as does Sir 25:24). On the contrary, Ezra notes several times that it was Adam (by which term he probably means humankind as such) who, "burdened with an evil heart" (2 Esdr 3:21; cf. 4:30), first sinned and brought ruin upon the earth (7:118 [or 7:48 in versions lacking vv. 36–105]). Ezra asks the angel if human sinfulness is impeding the coming of the new age, and in 4:40–43, the angel responds that, just as a pregnant woman cannot keep the fetus within her when her nine months are completed, so will the end arrive in its time.

In 5:35, Ezra cries out in pain and rage that, if he is to be denied any understanding of God's ways of directing life on earth, it would have been better not to have been born. Why could not his mother's womb have become his tomb? This theme is well known in the Hebrew Scriptures. Job 3 contains Job's curse of his birthday. Jeremiah 20 goes even further; the prophet curses the one who brought news to his father that a son had been born and wishes that his mother's womb could have been his tomb — an outcry that is a curse against his mother as well. It is one thing to wish that one had never been born; it is quite another to wish that one's mother had died in childbirth, as do Jer 20:17 and 2 Esdr 5:35.

Ezra presses the angel about the fate of those who have died before the arrival of the messianic age and those who will come after, questioning why all human generations could not have lived at the same time. In 2 Esdr 5:46–49, the angel explains that the generations must follow one another because such is the order of creation. The angel says, "Ask a woman's womb, and say to it, 'If you bear ten children, why one after another?' Request it therefore to produce ten at one time" (5:46). Ezra is quick to see that each birth must happen in its own time.

In 5:50–55, the angel responds to Ezra's question

concerning the age of Mother Earth by an analogy. The prophet should ask a human mother why the children she has borne in her older age are smaller in stature than those born in her youth. She will surely answer that in the bloom of youth, larger and stronger children are born; when the woman and the womb are old, smaller and frailer children are produced. The angel's answer, therefore, is that Mother Earth is indeed old, as one can see by the fact that today's children are much smaller and frailer than those born in years past. Is this a reference to the tradition that in ancient times, giants ruled the earth, the progeny of fallen angels and human mothers (Gen 6:4), most of whom disappeared in the cosmic flood in the days of Noah? It is difficult to believe that an author at the end of the first century C.E. actually thought that smaller and frailer children were being born than in earlier times.

Ezra is told by the angel that at the time of the end, many astonishing things will happen, including the birth of children after only a three-month or four-month pregnancy. Moreover, such children will enter the world rejoicing and leaping for joy. Many signs of the utter transformation of life and the world will accompany the day of consummation: "children a year old shall speak with their voices, and pregnant women shall give birth to premature children at three and four months, and these shall live and leap about" (2 Esdr 6:21).

In 7:102–103, Ezra asks the angel whether on the day of judgment the righteous will be able to intercede for the unrighteous. All along, this has been Ezra's chief concern: the fate of sinner in a world in which the number of sinners is massively larger than the number of righteous persons. Will God not find some way to bring deliverance for the unrighteous? Here, the question of the efficacy of intercessory prayer is put directly. It is noteworthy, however, that the author does not speak of mothers interceding for their daughters (or sons), daughters interceding in behalf of their parents, or sisters interceding for sisters (or brothers). The list is fathers for sons, sons for parents, brothers for brothers, relatives for their kinsfolk, and friends for friends

(7:103). The author seems to disclose, by this omission, the familiar evaluation of males over females. In this passage, the angel tells Ezra that on the decisive day of judgment, no prayers of intercession will avail.

In 8:8–10 Ezra praises God for having created all of life, including humankind, fashioned in the womb of the mother for nine months, nourished at the mother's breasts, while both the womb and the breasts are equally created by God and given their distinct functions in the bringing forth and the preserving of life.

In the book's last chapter, the third-century C.E. author uses the analogy of a pregnant woman to give assurance to the suffering Christian community. "Just as a pregnant woman, in the ninth month when the time of her delivery draws near, has great pains around her womb for two or three hours beforehand, but when the child comes forth from the womb, there will not be a moment's delay, so the calamities will not delay in coming upon the earth, and the world will groan, and pains will seize it on every side" (16:38–39). So it will be with the church: sufferings are a sign of the nearness of the end; the consummation, therefore, is close at hand.

Pregnancy and labor are understood as parts of a predictable process in 2 Esdras. The images serve as apocalyptic metaphors for the irrevocability of the end time and draw upon a fund of common knowledge regarding motherhood. God is credited as creator of wombs and women's breasts, as well as the nine-month process of pregnancy itself. The passages imply, though they do not say so explicitly, that Mother Earth's "nine months" are near to term.

WALTER J. HARRELSON

SEE ALSO Part I: Eve; Part II: Mother's Womb (Wis 7:1); (Sir 1:14, etc.); Part III: Earth as Mother.

FOR FURTHER READING: Johnson, Elizabeth E. "2 Esdras."

Metzger, Bruce M. "The Fourth Book of Ezra."

Stone, Michael. "Esdras, Second Book of."

2 ESDR 5:8
Menstruous Women

The reference in 2 Esdr 5:8 to women who shall give birth to monsters is from the Ezra apocalypse (chaps. 3–14, a special kind of revelatory literature disclosing future events, given by God through an otherworldly mediator to a human seer), written by an unknown Palestinian Jewish author of the first century C.E.

The angel Uriel tells Ezra about the signs that will occur during the age of tribulation that will precede the end of the world. Among these, the angel says, will be the birth of monsters to menstruous women (5:8). The Jewish author here aborts the usual nine-month gestation and birth process described frequently elsewhere in the apocalypse. In a purposeful confusion of the natural order, menstruating women are pregnant, and no fathers are even mentioned. This sign is a further indication of the topsy-turvy character of the time that precedes the end, a condition that the author's readers will recognize is even then evident in their world. The woes that are to precede the messianic age are well known from much Jewish and Christian literature; classic examples appear in the Gospels of Matthew (chap. 23) and Mark (chap. 13).

WALTER J. HARRELSON

SEE ALSO Part II: Women and Bodily Emissions (Lev 15:18–33, etc.); Menstruating Women (Ezek 18:6, etc.); Mother/Woman's Womb (2 Esdr 4:40–43, etc.).

2 ESDR 5:35, 46–55
Mother/Woman's Womb
SEE 2 ESDR 4:40–43, etc.
Mother/Woman's Womb (Part II).

2 ESDR 5:48–49   Earth as Mother
SEE Earth as Mother (Part III).

2 ESDR 6:21   Pregnant Women
SEE 2 ESDR 4:40–43, etc.
Mother/Woman's Womb (Part II).

2 ESDR 7:54–55, 62   Earth as Mother
SEE Earth as Mother (Part III).

2 ESDR 8:8–10   Womb
SEE 2 ESDR 4:40–43, etc.   Mother/Woman's Womb (Part II).

2 ESDR 8:8–12   God as Life-Giver
SEE Female Images of God in the Apocryphal/Deuterocanonical Books (Part III).

2 ESDR 9:38–10:59
Weeping Woman — Jerusalem/Zion as a City Being Built
SEE Weeping Woman — Jerusalem/Zion as a City Being Built (Part III).

2 ESDR 10:9–10   Earth as Mother
SEE Earth as Mother (Part III).

2 ESDR 10:22
Ravished Women

In 10:22, a late-first-century C.E. Jewish text, Ezra is addressing the grieving woman who has lost her beloved son. He insists that she should not be in utter despair over the death of one son. Rather, she should be grieving over the fate of God's people and the holy city of Jerusalem, now lying in ruins. The author describes vividly the calamities that have befallen the community of Israel, including the fact that "virgins have been defiled, and our wives have been ravished" (10:22). But Ezra's vision goes on to display God's intention to rebuild the city of Jerusalem as a place so large that it will accommodate all whom God will redeem.

WALTER J. HARRELSON

SEE ALSO Part III: Weeping Woman — Jerusalem/Zion as a City Being Built.

2 ESDR 13:54–55   Woman Wisdom
SEE Woman Wisdom in the Apocryphal/Deuterocanonical Books (Part III).

2 ESDR 15:46–63   Asia as a Prostitute
SEE Asia as a Prostitute (Part III).

2 ESDR 15:49   Widowhood

SEE 2 ESDR 2:2–4, etc.   Widow (Part II).

2 ESDR 16:1–2   Asia as a Prostitute

SEE Asia as a Prostitute (Part III).

2 ESDR 16:33
Mourning Women

2 Esdr 16:33 (a Christian composition of the third century C.E.) speaks of three age groups of women who will mourn because they will have no male help in the time of chaos and desolation before the End. "Virgins shall mourn because they have no bridegrooms; women shall mourn because they have no husbands; their daughters shall mourn, because they have no help." In other texts that employ gender pairs for brides and bridegrooms (Jer 7:34; 16:9; 25:10; 33:11; Bar 2:23; 1 Macc 1:26–27), devastation affects both females and males alike. Only in 2 Esdras will women survive to mourn, because "their bridegrooms shall be killed in war, and their husbands shall perish of famine" (16:34). This disruption of the natural order, in which women will live when their male counterparts are dead, is distinctive to 2 Esdras. Even in the New Testament apocalyptic text Rev 18:23, the fate of the bride and the bridegroom are the same: their voices will be heard no more when Babylon (meaning Rome) is destroyed before the marriage of the Lamb (19:6–19).

WALTER J. HARRELSON

SEE ALSO Part II: Bride (and Bridegroom) (Bar 2:23); Young Women (and Young Men); Brides (and Bridegrooms) (1 Macc 1:26–27); Part III: Great Whore; Weeping Woman — Jerusalem/Zion as a City Being Built.

2 ESDR 16:34   Widows

SEE 2 ESDR 2:2–4, etc.   Widow (Part II).

2 ESDR 16:38–39   Pregnant Woman

SEE 2 ESDR 4:40–43, etc.
Mother/Woman's Womb (Part II).

2 ESDR 16:44   Widows

SEE 2 ESDR 2:2–4, etc.   Widow (Part II).

2 ESDR 16:49
Virtuous Woman

Chap. 16 of 2 Esdras, a third-century C.E. Christian text, is addressed to Babylon, Asia, Egypt, Syria. Babylon stands for the Roman state, here and often in apocalyptic literature. Those suffering persecution within the Roman Empire — almost surely the Christian community — are urged to hold fast to their faith, to be "like strangers on the earth" (16:40), and to expect no normal life during the time of calamity in which they live. The community is to live a righteous and faithful life, despising iniquity "just as a respectable and virtuous woman abhors a prostitute" (16:49).

WALTER J. HARRELSON

2 ESDR 16:50–52
Righteousness and Iniquity as Females

SEE Righteousness and Iniquity as Females (Part III).

4 MACC 1:8, 10; 8:3–4, 20; 10:2; 12:6–7; 13:19; 14:11–18:24
Martyred Mother with Seven Sons

4 Maccabees, a first-century C.E. work of a loyalist Jew living perhaps at Antioch in Syria, draws upon the martyrology in 2 Macc 6:7–7:42 to construct its portrayal of the martyred mother and her seven sons. While 2 Maccabees is a lengthy and detailed report of the Seleucid persecution of Jerusalem and Judea, its martyrology is less than two chapters. By contrast, 4 Maccabees briefly summarizes 2 Maccabees in a historical preamble (4 Macc 3:20–4:26), with the martyrdoms occupying fourteen chapters (5–18). The aim of 4 Maccabees is to let the martyr stories inspire readers to accept the supremacy of

devout reason. 4 Maccabees is in no sense a history of the exploits of the Maccabean leaders; it is a philosophical exercise on the subject of devout reason's mastery over the emotions or passions (such as anger, envy, jealousy, grief, fear, love). It draws upon the Stoic philosophical tradition, wedding Greek philosophy to Jewish religion.

The author demonstrates the rule of religious reason over the emotions "from the noble bravery of those who died for the sake of virtue" (1:8), specifically Eleazar, the seven brothers, and the mother. His intention is to praise their virtue and call them blessed (1:10). Chaps. 8:1–9:9, an amplification of 2 Macc 7:1–2, set the stage for the seven brothers' defiance of Antiochus. The young men, "handsome, modest, noble, and accomplished in every way," come before the king "along with their aged mother" (4 Macc 8:3). Antiochus attempts to persuade the brothers to give up their ancestral traditions and adopt the Greek way of life by threatening them with severe tortures and death and promising them his friendship and benefaction if they will eat the defiling pork (8:12; an act prohibited by Lev 11:7–8). The brothers refuse, "for they were contemptuous of the emotions and sovereign over agonies" (8:28). One by one they undergo hideous torture, described in elaborate gruesome detail. Each endures for the sake of their law and tradition.

As the third is led in, many urge him to taste the meat and save himself, but he shouts, "Do you not know that the same father begot me as well as those who died, and the same mother bore me, and that I was brought up on the same teachings?" (10:2). Here, as in nearly every one of the eighteen Apocryphal/Deuterocanonical Books, Torah observance and instruction are important. Other women with roles in teaching Torah include Susanna's mother (Sus v. 3) and Tobit's grandmother, Deborah (Tob 1:8).

As in 2 Macc 7:25, the mother is summoned by the king to her youngest, seventh son, before he is tortured. But in 4 Macc 12:1–19, the king is supposedly showing compassion for this mother who had been bereaved of so many sons (12:6). After the mother exhorts her youngest, in Hebrew, he runs to

Married couple on a first-century B.C.E. tombstone found in Mysia (northwestern Asia Minor). Their clasped right hands are a well-documented ancient gesture of marital harmony, as in the description of the unnamed mother and her deceased husband in 4 Macc 18:9–19.

the braziers and gives a long speech that sums up the themes found in the other brothers' speeches, emphasizing that injustice and savagery will result in the king's eternal punishment (12:11–18), then he flings himself into the braziers and so ends his life (12:19).

Following a section praising the seven brothers' courage, piety, and endurance for the sake of religion (13:1–14:10), the death of the mother — told in one verse in 2 Macc 7:41 — artfully climaxes the oration (4 Macc 14:11–17:6). Written as a lengthy encomium, a tribute, the mother's martyrdom emphasizes her terrible torments and her mastery of her passions. "Sympathy for her children did not sway the mother of the young men; she was of the same mind as Abraham" (14:20). Intended as a high compliment, this verse raises serious problems for some contemporary readers. The stoic superiority of reason and its triumph over emotions is troubling, as is the exclusive association of reason with men and emotion with women. This "daughter of God-fearing Abraham" (15:28; compare 18:20) and mother of seven "sons of Abraham" (18:23) displays mastery over love of offspring and physical life. The promise of eternal life (15:3), not an angel's word (as in Gen 22:12), is the reward of her faith (4 Macc 15:24).

According to the book's logic, Antiochus violated physical bodies, but he could not touch the true life of the community or, in the end, this woman. By throwing herself into the flames (17:1), the mother's suicide prevents her being touched by a Gentile, and allows her to die with no violation of her chastity.

The most significant theological contribution of 4 Maccabees is its development of the idea that the suffering and death of the martyred righteous is an atoning sacrifice with redemptive efficacy for all Israel (17:20–22). This is particularly true of the mother's actions, which earn for her the very highest praise.

The mother's displaced last words to her sons (18:6–19; the seventh son died in 12:19) make of her — even in death (she died in 17:1) — the final spokeswoman for the supremacy of the Jewish religion and family values. She taught her sons through her example as a good wife while their father was alive (his death is mentioned in 4 Macc 18:9; he is absent in 2 Maccabees). She tells her sons that their father taught them the law, read to them about various male biblical figures, sang them songs, and saw to their proper education (see 18:10–19).

Virtue superseded love for family and life itself. Emotions were shared in common, but mothers "because of their birth pangs have a deeper sympathy toward their offspring than do the fathers" (15:4). Women, "the weaker sex," are by nature "more devoted to their children" (15:5). Affection and piety come together in the portrayal of this noble mother. Rational fear of God allows her to overcome her natural love of her children and encourage her sons' deaths. Their martyrdoms, and

hers, attained incorruption in eternal life for their family and all Israel.

In the end, earthly life means little in the light of life eternal. Temporal kingship means nothing when contrasted with God's eternal kingship. The passions of a mother are overshadowed by courage and "rational" behavior — if encouraging seven sons to die is so judged. For the author, she is the "mother of the nation, vindicator of the law, and champion of religion" (15:29). She is "more noble than males in steadfastness, and more courageous than men in endurance!" (15:30). This "guardian of the law," though flooded by emotion, withstood like "Noah's ark, carrying the world in the universal flood" (15:31–32). Later traditions accord the anonymous mother various names: Miriam bat Tanhum, Shamone, Maryam, and Hannah

TONI CRAVEN

SEE ALSO Part I: Deborah 3; Part II: Mother of Susanna/ Wife of Hilkiah (Sus v. 3, etc.); Martyred Mother with Seven Sons (2 Macc 7:1–42).

FOR FURTHER READING: Anderson, Hugh. "4 Maccabees."

Young, Robin Darling. "4 Maccabees."

———. "The 'Woman with the Soul of Abraham': Traditions about the Mother of the Maccabean Martyrs."

4 MACC 2:5, 11
Wife

Drawing together Greek philosophy and Jewish religion, 4 Macc 2:1–3:5 illustrates the compatibility of reason and the Mosaic law through a series of biblical examples. Reason rules a man's every desire, including that for a neighbor's wife (2:4–5; see Exod 20:17). Reason is equated to Jewish law in 2:9–10 in the author's claims that "reason rules the emotions" and "the law prevails even over affection." As illustration, this author holds that the law is "superior to love for one's wife, so that one rebukes her when she breaks the law" (2:11). The assumption here, as in Sirach, is that it is a man's role to oversee his household, including his wife. Unlike Sirach, however, 4 Maccabees envisions ways in which "goodness" is within a wife's reach if she, like the mother of the seven martyred sons, keeps her emotions (passions) in check through reason and observance of the law.

TONI CRAVEN

SEE ALSO Part II: Women in the Decalogue (Exod 20:8, etc.); Wife (Sir 7:19, etc.); Martyred Mother with Seven Sons (4 Macc 1:8, etc.).

4 MACC 4:9
Women Supplicants

This reference to women (and children) joining the priests in imploring God in the temple to shield the holy place recalls women's actions on behalf of the Jerusalem temple in 2 Macc 3:19 (when Heliodorus, a Seleucid official, purposed to dishonor the temple) and in 3 Macc 1:18–20 (when Ptolemy IV Philopater, king of Egypt, insisted on his right to enter the temple's Holy of Holies). The details here are greatly abbreviated and simplified from 2 Maccabees 3 where Heliodorus, not Apollonius (governor of Syria, Phoenicia, and Cilicia, 4 Macc 4:2), attempts to strip the temple's treasuries, because of Simon's misrepresentation that the temple is full of untold sums of money that could be taken by the king (2 Macc 3:6). The role of the women suppliants is more dramatically told in 2 Macc 3:19–20, where women rush into the streets and hold up their hands to heaven. In 4 Macc 4:9 women are more simply part of a list of supplicants in the temple.

TONI CRAVEN

SEE ALSO Part II: Widows (2 Macc 3:10, etc.); Women Supplicants (2 Macc 3:19); (3 Macc 1:18–20).

4 MACC 4:25
Women/Mothers with Circumcised Sons

One of the savage measures of the Seleucid king Antiochus IV (Epiphanes) against the Jews in Jeru-salem is the martyrdom of two mothers who, on account of having circumcised their sons, are executed with their dead infants hanging from their necks. This cruel action is told three times in the Maccabean literature. 1 Macc 1:60–61 illustrates the Seleucid attempt to destroy the tradition of the Jews. 2 Macc 6:10 places the story of the two mothers first in a series of martyr stories meant to encourage the faithful in oppression. 4 Macc 4:25 gives the story only passing notice as something Antiochus did to women to destroy respect for Jewish law.

TONI CRAVEN

SEE ALSO Part II: Women/Mothers with Circumcised Sons (1 Macc 1:60–61); (2 Macc 6:10).

4 MACC 8:3–4, 20; 10:2; 12:6–7; 13:19; 14:11–18:24
Martyred Mother with Seven Sons

SEE 4 MACC 1:8, etc.   Martyred Mother with Seven Sons (Part II).

4 MACC 18:7
Woman Made from Rib

The heroic mother martyred by Antiochus IV (Epiphanes) begins her last address to her seven sons (4 Macc 18:6–19) by telling them about her life before her marriage to their father: "I was a pure virgin and did not go outside my father's house; but I guarded the rib from which woman was made. No seducer corrupted me on a desert plain, nor did the destroyer, the deceitful serpent, defile the purity of my virginity" (18:7–8). The Greek has only "the rib that was build," not "the rib from which woman was made," but there is no doubt about the parallel to Gen 2:22 here. This passage is particularly interesting for the light it may shed on the practices of women's seclusion in some Jewish communities.

TONI CRAVEN

SEE ALSO Part I: Eve; Part II: Martyred Mother with Seven Sons (2 Macc 7:1–42); (4 Macc 1:8, etc.).

FOR FURTHER READING: Kraemer, Ross S., "Jewish Women in the Diaspora World of Late Antiquity."

The New Testament

MATT 1:6
Wife of Uriah

The identification of Bathsheba as "wife of Uriah" anticipates three Matthean themes: Uriah, a Hittite, foreshadows the entry of Gentiles into the church; as David's soldier, Uriah acts faithfully when the ruler of Israel does not; Bathsheba commits adultery with David and thereby foreshadows Jesus' unexpected and problematic conception.

AMY-JILL LEVINE

MATT 5:28
Woman Looked at Lustfully

In the Sermon on the Mount, Matthew's Jesus intensifies the commandment against adultery (Exod 20:14; Deut 5:18) by censuring lustful thoughts as well. Scholars have contrasted rabbinic views with Jesus' condemnation of those who treat women as objects, but similar equations appear in both Jewish and Gentile sources. The androcentrism of the verse, found also in parallel sources, emphasizes the man's possible sin more than the woman's dignity. The verse supports Matthew's demands for higher righteousness, preservation of marriage (5:23; 19:9), and emphasis on continence (19:10–12).

AMY-JILL LEVINE

MATT 5:31–32
Divorced Wife

The New Testament preserves several different ancient traditions about Jesus' teaching on divorce, including (1) Mark 10:2–12 and Matt 19:3–9, (2) 1 Cor 7:10–11, and (3) Matt 5:31–32 and Luke 16:18. Scholars often account for the duplication in Matthew (19:9 and 5:31–32) as evidence that the author

of this Gospel drew one version of Jesus' teaching about remarriage after divorce from Mark (10:11–12) and the other from a Q saying (Luke 18:16).

In Mark 10:11–12, Jesus teaches that a man who divorces his wife and then marries another woman commits adultery against the divorced wife; so, too, a wife who divorces her husband and remarries commits adultery against her husband. The implicit reasoning of this saying is that, since divorce countermands the divine creation, sex with the second spouse is by definition adultery.

Two elements of Mark 10:11–12 are significant. First, its view of adultery differs from that of both ancient Israelite and subsequent ancient Jewish law, which defined it as a man's having intercourse with another man's wife. Thus, a man cannot commit adultery against his own wife. In Mark 10:11, however, he clearly can. Second, the Markan saying implies that Jewish women could and did initiate divorce proceedings against their husbands, something usually assumed to have been prohibited in Jewish communities despite interesting evidence to the contrary (including this very passage).

Comparing Matt 5:31–32 (and Luke 16:18) with the Markan material is highly instructive. Luke's version, probably reflecting a tradition from the Sayings Source Q, has Jesus teach that a man who divorces his wife and then remarries commits adultery, an idea consistent with Mark 10:11. Instead, in Matt 5:32, Jesus teaches that a man who divorces his wife causes her to commit adultery. Matt 5:32 differs from the saying in 19:9, where a man who remarries commits adultery, although 19:9 does not contain the Markan phrase "against her." In 5:32, Matthew perhaps assumes that the divorced wife will remarry (because she needs to in order to survive?) and thereby commit adultery against the husband who divorced her. But both Matthean versions may be seen to resist a revision of the traditional definition of adultery: 5:32 by making the wife the adulterer, and 19:9 by omitting the Markan phrase "against her," thus making less explicit how a man's remarriage makes him guilty of adultery.

BERNADETTE J. BROOTEN

SEE ALSO Part II: Woman Being Divorced (Deut 24:1–4, etc.); Divorced Wife (Matt 19:3–9); (Mark 10:2–12); (Luke 16:18); Married Women (and Men), Unmarried Women (and Men), and Women (and Men) Married to Unbelievers (1 Corinthians 7).

MATT 8:14
Mother-in-Law of Peter (Simon)

Matthew's version of Jesus' healing of the mother-in-law of Simon (here called Peter) differs from the Markan narrative in several ways. It is no longer the first healing Jesus performs immediately after calling Simon and other disciples, but comes much later, after the Sermon on the Mount. In Matthew, the mother-in-law is one of many socially marginal persons whom Jesus cures to fulfill a prophecy in Isaiah (8:17), including a leper and the servant or slave of a Roman centurion.

In Mark, Jesus enters the house of Peter and Andrew with James and John; in Matthew, he is apparently alone. In Mark, it is the men who first inform Jesus of the woman's illness; in Matthew, Jesus sees her and cures her by touching her hand (although he does not lift her up). In Mark, the recovered woman serves (diakoneō) the men; in Matthew, she serves only Jesus.

It is difficult to know whether the author of Matthew eliminates the other men in the Markan (and Lukan) versions of this story because the presence of men who were not family members in the house of the stricken woman would have been considered inappropriate by the evangelist or his initial readers. Yet removing James and John does not materially affect the questions posed by the story, including whether the woman's service has a technical connotation of discipleship, whether her response alludes to her participation in the Jesus movement,

and what the passage may tell us about familial relationships in first-century Galilee.

ROSS S. KRAEMER

SEE ALSO Part II: Mother-in-Law of Simon (Peter) (Mark 1:30); (Luke 4:38).

MATT 9:18–19, 23–26
Daughter of Jairus

The shortest of the synoptic accounts of this story, Matthew's lacks the name Jairus, his identification as ruler of the synagogue, and reference to the girl's mother. The father's initial plea indicates that the child is already dead, her age is not given, and there is no mention of providing her with food. As in the other Synoptic Gospels, the daughter's tale is interrupted by the account of the hemorrhaging woman; its insertion here emphasizes faith in Jesus' healing powers and concern for women's health. It does not, however, indicate (as it is often argued) abrogation of Levitical injunctions concerning corpses or genital bleeding (Lev 15:25).

Matthew 9 is comparable to 14:1–12, the account of the daughter of Herodias and the tetrarch Herod Antipas. In the first, a "young girl" (korasion) motivates a ruler to humility and obtains life; her resurrection anticipates Jesus' resurrection. The second korasion reveals a ruler's abuse of power and motivates a death that anticipates both Jesus' death and the persecution of his followers (10:18).

AMY-JILL LEVINE

SEE ALSO Part II: Daughter of Jairus (Mark 5:22–23, etc.); (Luke 8:41–42a, etc.); Daughter of Herodias (Mark 6:22–29).

MATT 9:20–22
Woman with a Twelve-Year Hemorrhage

Interrupting Jesus' journey to raise a dead girl, a woman with a (probably uterine) hemorrhage touches his cloak's fringes (tzitzit) in hopes of gaining a cure. Jesus turns, sees the woman, and states, "Take heart, daughter; your faith has made you well" (or "has saved you"; v. 22). The conjoined healings both involve touching, mention "daughter," and depict faith (of the woman and of the girl's father) in Jesus' powers. Frequently contrasted to Levitical injunctions regarding vaginal bleeding (Lev 15:25) and interpreted as an ignoring or even an abrogation of Torah, Matthew's pericope neither mentions purity legislation nor depicts Jesus as deliberately touching the woman.

AMY-JILL LEVINE

SEE ALSO Part II: Woman with a Twelve-Year Hemorrhage (Mark 5:25–34); (Luke 8:43–48).

FOR FURTHER READING: Levine, Amy-Jill. "Discharging Responsibility: Matthean Jesus, Biblical Law and Hemorrhaging Women."

MATT 9:23–26   Daughter of Jairus
SEE MATT 9:18–19, etc.   Daughter of Jairus (Part II).

MATT 10:35
Daughters and Daughters-in-Law Against Mothers and Mothers-in-Law

This saying from Q, a reconstructed collection of sayings of Jesus, predicts household division created by Jesus' message. Similar division appears in contemporaneous eschatologically oriented Jewish texts, such as *Jubilees* (a reworking of much of the material in Genesis and Exodus), the Armenian version of 4 Ezra (2 Esdras 3–14 in the NRSV Apocryphal/Deuterocanonical Books), the Mishnah, and the Babylonian Talmud. The third part of a four-part recitation of domestic strife, Matt 10:35 emphasizes the Gospel's view that being part of Jesus' family takes precedence over biological ties and locates women among both the followers of Jesus and their opponents. The intergenerational component to the division disrupts the hierarchy of the family

unit. The absence of sons-in-law suggests patrilocal marriage and implies that the daughter is unmarried.

AMY-JILL LEVINE

SEE ALSO Part II: Daughters and Daughters-in-Law Against Mothers and Mothers-in-Law (Luke 12:53).

MATT 10:37
Mothers and Daughters (and Fathers and Sons) Not to Be Loved More Than Jesus

Matthew insists that primary love is to be directed not to parents or to children of either sex, but to Jesus. Like Matt 10:35 and its parallel, Luke 12:53, the verse emphasizes intergenerational rather than marital division. Matthew's Jesus elsewhere indicates that parents should treat their children well (7:9–11) and that children should honor and provide for their parents (15:4–5); there is not necessarily a contradiction between the biological family and the family of Jesus (compare 12:46–50). Luke's version intensifies the disruption by mandating the hatred of one's family.

AMY-JILL LEVINE

SEE ALSO Part II: Mother (and Father), Wife (and Children), and Sisters (and Brothers) to Be Hated by Jesus' Disciples (Luke 14:26).

MATT 11:19   Woman Wisdom
SEE Woman Wisdom in the New Testament (Part III).

MATT 12:42
Queen of the South

The queen of Sheba tested King Solomon (1 Kgs 10:1–13–2; Chr 9:1–12), just as the scribes and Pharisees test Jesus. This Q saying parallels the actions of the queen and the men from Nineveh (Matt 12:41):

foreign Gentiles, both women and men, recognize what local authorities cannot.

AMY-JILL LEVINE

SEE ALSO Part II: Queen of the South (Luke 11:31).

MATT 12:46–50   Mother of Jesus
SEE MARY 1 (Part I).

MATT 12:50   Sister of Jesus
SEE MARK 3:32–35, etc.   Sister(s) of Jesus (Part II).

MATT 13:33
Woman Mixing Flour with Leaven

This parable, paired with that of the mustard seed (Matt 13:31–32; Luke 13:18–19), indicates that the small and suspect can produce the great and valuable. In earlier times and in the cultural imagination of the first century C.E., yeast is usually negatively coded (see Exodus 12; Leviticus 2; 1 Cor 5:6–8; Gal 5:9): it operates by causing decay, is "hidden" (Matt 13:31), and is associated with Jesus' opponents (Matt 16:6). This parable's leaven, a negative symbol transformed into something of wondrous value, thus may represent the gospel message or the people, both men and women, who follow it.

The image of the woman may reinforce Matthew's frequent locating of women among the followers of Jesus, but this parable emphasizes the yeast, not the baker (compare 13:31–32, which focuses on the seed, not the sower). In contrast, the *Gospel of Thomas,* an early Coptic collection of sayings to Jesus, highlights the human actor: "Jesus says, 'The Kingdom of the Father is like a woman who has taken a little leaven and hidden it in dough and made large loaves of it.'" Matthew's sayings reinforce traditional gender roles; men sow, and women bake (compare Matt 24:40–41 — the men are in the field, and the women grind at the mill). They are not, however, placed in domestic roles as husband and wife, or parent and child, and this is consistent with Matthew's deemphasis of the biological family (10:35–37; 12:46–50).

The parable may have been originally preserved in Q (from the German *Quelle,* "source," a hypothetical document that many scholars believe underlies the traditions shared by Matthew and Luke but absent in Mark). Q material tends to pair female and male characters. The parable of the leaven may be seen as both complementary to and in contrast with Q's paternal image of God the father, who provides daily bread (Matt 6:11; Luke 11:3).

AMY-JILL LEVINE

SEE ALSO Part II: Woman with Leaven (Luke 13:20–21).

MATT 13:56
The Sisters of Jesus

In Matt 13:54–58, Jesus meets with skepticism when he preaches in his hometown synagogue at Nazareth. "Many" who hear him ask rhetorically: "Is not this the carpenter's son? Is not his mother called Mary? And are not his brothers James and Joseph and Simon and Judas? And are not all his sisters with us?" (vv. 55–56).

Matthew's narrative differs from the parallel account in Mark 6:1–6a in several ways. In Mark, Jesus himself is a carpenter; in Matthew, he is the son of a carpenter. Matthew specifies that "all" the sisters of Jesus are "with us," but lacks the specific "here." These changes do not affect the portrait of Jesus as having had many sisters and brothers. But the omission of the word *here* may possibly function, intentionally or not, to mute the implication of the Markan version that these sisters were present at the synagogue on the Sabbath. Since it is often claimed that Jewish women were excluded from synagogue participation, this is potentially quite significant. This suggestion may be strengthened by the fact that Matthew has Jesus preach in the synagogue, but without specifying the day on which he did so. Thus, even if the sisters are present, they are no longer there on the Sabbath.

ROSS S. KRAEMER

SEE ALSO Part II: Sister(s) of Jesus (Mark 3:32–35); Sisters of Jesus (Mark 6:3).

men, but the thesis lacks textual and even strong cultural support.

AMY-JILL LEVINE

MATT 14:6–11
Young Dancer Who Asks for the Head of John the Baptist

Virtually all ancient manuscripts of Matthew identify this dancer simply as the daughter of Herodias. Although some ancient manuscripts of Mark share this identification, others describe her as Herodias, the daughter of Herod (probably meaning Herod Antipas, tetrarch of Galilee and Perea, 4 B.C.E.–39 C.E.). Tradition has long identified the young dancer as Salome, but neither Mark nor Matthew (the only Gospels that narrate this famous tale) ever identifies her by this name. Rather, the name Salome is supplied from the first-century C.E. Jewish historian, Josephus, who tells us that Herod's wife, Herodias, had a daughter, Salóme, by her first husband (also named Herod).

ROSS S. KRAEMER

SEE ALSO Part I: Herodias 1; Herodias 2; Salome 2.

MATT 14:21
Women Fed by Jesus

Following the first miraculous feeding, Matthew alone among the Gospels notes that five thousand (men) ate, "besides women and children." The same addition appears in Matt 15:38. The reference complements Matthew's other recognitions of women's presence among Jesus' followers (for example, 9:20–22; 10:35; 24:41; 27:61; 28:1–10). It may also evoke the reading of "besides children" in the enumeration of the people in the wilderness (Exod 12:37; see also Philo, *Life of Moses*, book 1, section 147, and Josephus, *Antiquities of the Jews*, 1.317). Some scholars suggest that Matthew envisions the women and children as seated separately from the

MATT 15:4
Mother (and Father) to Be Honored

In a passage paralleling Mark 7:1–15, Matt 15:1–9 narrates a dispute between Jesus and some Pharisees and scribes over the custom of washing one's hands before eating. Jesus contends that his opponents honor human traditions, but violate divine commandments by allowing people to dedicate to God resources they would otherwise have provided for their parents, thus negating the commandment to honor father and mother (Exod 20:12; Deut 5:16). Jesus' response may suggest that, in the land of Israel in the first century C.E., mothers and fathers did not always receive the necessary financial support from their adult children, something that could easily have had a disparate impact on women.

ROSS S. KRAEMER

SEE ALSO Part II: Women in the Decalogue (Exod 20:8, etc.); Mother (and Father) to Be Honored (Matt 19:19); (Mark 7:10–13); (Mark 10:19); (Luke 18:20); (Eph 6:2–3).

MATT 15:21–28
Canaanite Woman

On the border of Tyre and Sidon, a Canaanite woman solicits Jesus' healing powers on behalf of her demon-possessed daughter. Jesus first ignores her, then rebuffs her by insisting his mission is only to the "lost sheep of the house of Israel" (Matt 15:24), and finally insults her by stating, "It is not fair to take the children's bread and throw it to the dogs" (15:26). Through her persistence, cleverness, and, as Jesus observes, her "faith" (15:28), the mother receives her request.

Matthew's account, the first instance in the Gospel of a woman's direct speech, significantly differs from its parallel in Mark 7:24–30. Mark's woman is a "Greek, a Syrophoenician by birth" (7:26) who approaches Jesus inside a house in gentile territory; her daughter has "an unclean spirit" (7:25), and Jesus performs the exorcism because of her words. In Matthew, the woman is a Canaanite; she comes out of the pagan area to meet Jesus in public space; no reference is made to anything unclean; and the healing, which occurs only after extensive conversation, transpires because of the woman's faith (whether only in Jesus' miraculous abilities or in his divine sonship as well is never made explicit).

Like Mark, Matthew omits the woman's name; rather than an indication of sexism, anonymity is characteristic of those for whom Jesus performs mighty works. For this story, it focuses attention on the woman's ethnicity. The term "Canaanite" is both a geographic indicator (see Jdt 5:9–10; Bar 3:22; 1 Macc 9:37) and a reference to the population of the land promised to Abraham and Sarah's descendants. Although the Book of Joshua emphasizes Canaan's conquest, it also records the account of the Canaanite woman Rahab, who protects Joshua's spies, misdirects Jericho's leaders, and recognizes Israelite theology and history. Matthew's mention of "Canaanite" in 15:22 recollects the Matthean genealogy (chap. 1), which lists Rahab (1:5) as well as another Canaanite woman, Tamar (1:3). All three Canaanite women overcome hesitancy or lack of initiative in Hebrew/Israelite/Jewish men; all three acknowledge, whether implicitly or explicitly, Israel's priority in salvation history; all three achieve their goals through clever speech and action.

These Canaanite women also foreshadow another gentile woman, Pilate's wife (27:19), as well as the Jewish woman who anoints Jesus (26:6–13) over the protests of the disciples (compare 15:23), and the Jewish women at the cross and the tomb, who, unlike Jesus' male followers, remain faithful.

The appearances of these gentile women reinforce rather than compromise Matthew's insistence on Israel's priority in salvation history. The Canaanite woman not only calls Jesus "Lord" (Greek *Kyrios*) three times, but also she concedes Israelite superiority by referring to him as "son of David" (Mark's Syrophoenician does not employ this epithet). The combination of titles highlights the political implications of her speech. Whereas Mark's Jesus states that the children must "first be fed" (Mark 7:27), Matthew avoids mention of a "first" (thereby eliminating indication of a second, gentile stage during Jesus' ministry). Mark's Syrophoenician notes that even the dogs eat the "children's crumbs" (Mark 7:28), while the Canaanite woman's response, "Yes, Lord, yet even the dogs eat the crumbs that fall from their masters' table" (Matt 15:27), reinforces the "mastery" of Jesus and so of Israel.

The Matthean account is even more jarring than Mark's: for Jesus to ignore a desperate parent is already problematic; to insist on the restricted nature of his mission is of little help to the woman in need; to call her a "dog" is offensive. Numerous explanations, many of them apologetic, have been proffered.

The story is frequently viewed as a remnant of Jewish-Christian exclusivity, which the evangelist felt constrained to repeat. However, the restricted mission is consistent with Matthew's presentation of Jesus' own behavior (he does not make a concerted effort to preach among Gentiles), and it echoes the missionary instructions in 10:5b–6:23. Therefore, it appears to be a Matthean theme. Confirming this theory, Matt 15:21–28 matches 8:5–13, the Gospel's other explicit healing of a Gentile. In each case, the ailing child (the centurion's *Pais* could be translated as either "son" or "servant") is absent; Jesus initially rebuffs the supplicant; both parental figures acknowledge Jesus' authority through detailed comment; and Jesus remarks on the faith of each. In neither story, finally, do the Gentiles follow Jesus.

On this last point, the woman provides a contrast to the Jewish blind men of 20:29–34. Like her, the men address Jesus as "son of David" and "Lord," they ask for "mercy," they are restrained by Jesus' disciples, and they have to make clear, in response to Jesus' question, what they desire. Unlike the woman, they follow him to Jerusalem.

Scholars have also proposed that Matt 15:21–28 is the evangelist's attempt to convince Jewish Christians that Gentiles are worthy of church membership; in this scenario, "dog" is viewed as an insult customarily directed by Jews at Gentiles. This theory again posits the story's origin in Jewish-Christian exclusivity, even though Jewish-Christian debates over the gentile mission were less a matter of whether it should happen than of the terms under which it should take place (for example, Torah observance). Moreover, "dog" is a term of disapprobation not only in Hebrew (1 Sam 17:43; Prov 26:11; Isa 56:10–11), but also in Greek thought; it is not ethnically coded (see Matt 7:6; 2 Pet 2:22; Rev 22:15).

The insult may suggest an aural connection between "Canaanite" (Greek *Xananaia*) and "dogs" (Greek *kynaria*); the latter is the origin of the name of the group of Greek philosophers called the Cynics; this name reflects, among other things, public presence, wit, and social criticism. Benevolent interpretations of Jesus' equating the woman with a dog — that he is "testing her faith," that he is speaking with a smile on his lips, and so on — do not account for either the lack of such insults elsewhere in the Gospel or the unseemliness of such cajoling when a child is ill. One argument holds that the use of the word for "household dogs" rather than "wild dogs" softens the insult, but this hardly makes a difference — "little bitch" is no improvement over "bitch."

Perhaps Matthew depicts Jesus as both reluctant to heal and debasing in attitude in order to highlight his change of heart. If so, the story would be consistent with both Jewish and pagan accounts of leaders called to task by their subordinates (often women). Matthew's main point would then be the excellence of Jesus' leadership: as "Lord" and "son of David," he listens well to his "subjects."

The conventionality of these scenes argues against another common interpretation of Matt 15:21–28: that the woman's appearance in public apart from her male protector and her addressing a strange man are actions that subvert propriety.

Also, Matthew elsewhere depicts unaccompanied women (such as the hemorrhaging woman in 9:20–22, the anointing woman in 26:6–13, women in parables, and the women at Golgotha in 27:55–56), but never suggests they are anomalous. Third, because the Canaanite woman's actions match those of the centurion in 8:5–13, any sense of indecorum is mitigated. Finally, the Canaanite matches a model established by Jeroboam's wife, who approaches the prophet Ahijah (1 Kgs 14:1–14), and the great woman of Shunem, who approaches the prophet Elisha (2 Kgs 4:18–37). A similar tale of "a little woman pleading for her boy . . . who had been possessed by a demon for the past two years" is found in the *Life of Apollonius of Tyana*. Apollonius was a philosopher and wonder worker of the first century C.E., whose life, miracles, and teachings are strikingly similar to those of Jesus in many ways.

AMY-JILL LEVINE

SEE ALSO Part I: Rahab; Tamar; Part II: Syrophoenician Woman (Mark 7:24–30); Daughter of the Syrophoenician Woman (Mark 7:24–30).

FOR FURTHER READING: Levine, Amy-Jill. "Matthew's Advice to a Divided Readership."

Ringe, Sharon H. "A Gentile Woman's Story, Revisited."

Wainwright, Elaine M. "Not Without My Daughter: Gender and Demon Possession in Matt 15:21–28."

MATT 15:21–28
Daughter of the Canaanite Woman

Unnamed, like most beneficiaries of Jesus' miracles, the daughter is "severely possessed" (15:22; contrast Mark 7:25's "unclean spirit"; Matthew avoids implications of impurity). Like the "ruler's" daughter (9:18–26) and epileptic boy (17:14–20), she requires parental intercession; a Gentile, like the centurion's son or servant (8:5–13), she is healed at a distance.

AMY-JILL LEVINE

SEE ALSO Part II: Canaanite Woman (Matt 15:21–28); Syrophoenician Woman (Mark 7:24–30); Daughter of the Syrophoenician Woman (Mark 7:24–30).

For further reading: Levine, Amy-Jill. "Matthew's
   Advice to a Divided Readership."
Ringe, Sharon H. "A Gentile Woman's Story, Revisited."

MATT 18:25
Wife (and Husband and Children) Sold to Pay Off Debt

Discussing forgiveness, Jesus tells of a king who orders his indebted slave to be sold "together with his wife and children." It is unlikely that the money accrued for the sale would cover the slave's debt of ten thousand talents. The practice of selling family members to creditors appears in Israelite (compare 2 Kgs 4:1) and Roman contexts. The Mishnah (c. 200 C.E.) prohibits selling a wife for debt. The early sources speak more frequently about selling children and even the debtor himself, rather than about selling wives. Evidence is scarce concerning the fates of these enslaved family members.

AMY-JILL LEVINE

MATT 19:3–9
Divorced Wife

Matthew's version of a dispute between Jesus and some Pharisees over the question of divorce follows the Markan narrative (10:2–12). The order of the discussion is different, and Jesus' private teaching to the disciples in Mark 10:10–12 becomes integrated into his response to the Pharisees. Two differences, though, are particularly significant.

First, in Matthew, Jesus allows for an exception in the general prohibition against divorce, in cases of *porneia*, a term usually translated as "unchastity," and often understood to mean that divorce was permissible when a wife had committed adultery. *Porneia* can also refer to marriages forbidden by the incest laws of Lev 18:6–18, and the use of an analogous term in one of the Dead Sea Scrolls suggests that *porneia* might also have referred to marriages

A first-century C.E. Jewish bill of divorce written in Aramaic on papyrus, found at the Wadi Murabba'at near the Dead Sea. See Divorced Wife (Matt 5:31–32; Matt 19:3-9, Mark 10:2–12; Luke 16:18).

with spouses outside the community (see also 1 Cor 7:12–16, which allows for divorce if the spouse is a nonbeliever and does not wish to continue the marriage, but recommends against it).

Second, in Mark, Jesus teaches that if either a woman or a man divorces the other and remarries, each has committed adultery. In Matthew, however, Jesus gives only the instance of the man who divorces his wife; the parallel instance of a wife who divorces her husband is absent. The same difference may be seen in Matthew's version of a Q saying on the same subject (Matt 5:31–32).

BERNADETTE J. BROOTEN

SEE ALSO Part II: Woman Being Divorced (Deut 24:1–4, etc.); Divorced Wife (Matt 5:31–32); (Mark 10:2–12); (Luke 16:18); Married Women (and Men), Unmarried Women (and Men), and Women (and Men) Married to Unbelievers (1 Corinthians 7).

MATT 19:19
Mother (and Father) to Be Honored

In Matthew (19:16–22), Mark (10:17–22), and Luke (18:18–23), a wealthy man asks Jesus what he must do to obtain eternal life. In Mark, on which Matthew based his version, and in Luke, Jesus responds that the man knows the commandments and then enumerates five of the Ten Commandments found in Exod 20:1–17 and Deut 5:6–21, including the commandment to honor one's mother and father. In Matthew, Jesus' response is slightly different: he tells the man, "If you wish to enter into life, keep the commandments" (v. 17). Only when the man asks which ones does Jesus specify these five.

Matthew's version of this story may thus be taken to imply that the other five (not to make or worship idols, not to misuse God's name, not to covet one's neighbor's possessions, and to observe the Sabbath) are not essential. Matthew's apparent revision of the scene may suggest that at least some of his intended audience were Gentiles who had not necessarily observed these commandments prior to their joining the movement. For such an audience, a commandment of filial piety would have been immediately comprehensible, as would commandments forbidding adultery, murder, theft, and false witness.

Unlike Matt 15:4 (and its parallel, Mark 7:10), where Jesus' invocation of the commandment to honor one's mother and father appears to reflect first-century disputes about how one honors one's parents, here the commandment is simply one of five required for eternal life.

Ross S. Kraemer

SEE ALSO Part II: Women in the Decalogue (Exod 20:8, etc.); Mother (and Father) to Be Honored (Mark 7:10–13); (Mark 10:19); (Luke 18:20); (Eph 6:2–3).

MATT 19:29
Mothers and Sisters Left for the Sake of Jesus' Name

In Matthew, as in Mark 10:29–30 (and Luke 18:29–30), Jesus follows his admonition to the rich man (to leave all his possessions and follow Jesus) with a private teaching to his disciples that those who leave families and households to follow him will receive back, many times over, what they have re-

nounced. Matthew's version of the saying follows Mark in listing houses, brothers, sisters, mother, father, children, and fields as the persons and possessions left, but lacks the lists of relationships and possessions to be restored.

In Matthew, as in Mark, it is possible to envision women and men equally as those who leave and are left behind. But the evangelists may not have given this impression intentionally. The version of this story in Luke specifies that those who follow Jesus leave wives to do so. Since *to leave* in Greek can also mean *to divorce,* the Lukan passage could have been understood, at least in antiquity, to mean that (male) followers of Jesus divorced their wives. By specifying mothers and sisters, but not explicitly wives, as those left behind, Matthew, with Mark, avoids attributing to Jesus a saying that might be read to condone divorce (something Matthew and Mark, but not Luke, have Jesus prohibit elsewhere).

Ross S. Kraemer

SEE ALSO Part II: Divorced Wife (Matt 5:31–32); (Matt 19:3–9); (Mark 10:2–12); (Luke 16:18); Sisters and Mothers Left for Jesus' Sake (Mark 10:29–30); Wife Left for the Sake of the Kingdom of God (Luke 18:29–30); Married Women (and Men), Unmarried Women (and Men), and Women (and Men) Married to Unbelievers (1 Corinthians 7).

MATT 20:20; 27:56
Mother of the Sons of Zebedee

In Matthew's version of Mark 10:35–45, the unnamed mother of two of the twelve, the sons of Zebedee, inappropriately asks Jesus that her sons might sit at his right and left hands in the kingdom. Replying that it is not his to grant such a request, Jesus uses the occasion to teach the other ten that "whoever wishes to be great among you must be your servant, and whoever wishes to first among you must be your slave" (Matt 20:26–27).

In Mark, it is the sons, explicitly identified as James and John, who ask for this honor and who do so without ceremony, unlike their mother as depicted in Matthew, who kneels (or prostrates herself, or worships) before Jesus, a gesture of submission, subservience, and reverence.

The substitution of the mother deflects responsibility from her sons for this inappropriate request, suggesting a desire to temper Jesus' rebuke of James and John in the Gospel of Mark. The result appears to be an unflattering representation of an ambitious mother who seeks improper prestige and honor for her sons. In a culture where a woman's own prestige and status depend primarily on that of her male relatives, such behavior may be presented as understandable, but nevertheless wrong.

Jesus' answer in Matt 20:22 (apparently taken directly from Mark 10:38), "you [plural] do not know what you are asking," makes clear that the sons are the true petitioners. It is directed primarily, if not exclusively, at them, rather than at the mother, who plays no further role in the scene. Matthew's Jesus may thus slight the mother by replying instead to her sons, but this aspect of the Matthean version may also be the unintended result of substituting the mother for James and John, while retaining most of the remainder of the Markan narrative. This particular story is absent in Luke (but compare 22:24–27).

Still identified only by her sons and their father, the unnamed mother appears again in Matt 27:56, watching the crucifixion from afar, along with Mary Magdalene and Mary the mother of James and Joses. Because Mark calls the third woman Salome, some interpreters have identified the two women, but it is unclear why Matthew would substitute an unnamed figure for a named one, and the identification is uncertain. Interestingly, she is absent from the subsequent scenes in Matthew where Mary Magdalene and "the other Mary" appear: at the tomb of Jesus in 27:57 on the day of his burial and, most importantly in 28:1–10, where the two women are the first to discover the empty tomb and the first to see the risen Jesus.

The Synoptic Gospels feature several mothers and their grown sons, while the husbands and fathers are conspicuous in their absence. This might reflect the demographics of ancient marriages: women who had married much older men regu-

larly found themselves widowed and dependent on, or closely allied with, their grown sons. Ironically, Zebedee appears alive and well in Matt 4:21–22 (parallel to Mark 1:19–20; compare Luke 5:10–11) when his sons leave him to follow Jesus. Since the mother is known only from Matthew, it is not impossible that she is a fictional character created specifically to absolve her sons and inserted in place of Salome at 27:56 (but not subsequently) to strengthen her identity.

Ross S. Kraemer

FOR FURTHER READING: D'Angelo, Mary Rose. "(Re)presentations of Women in the Gospel of Matthew and Luke-Acts."

MATT 21:5   Daughter of Zion
SEE Daughter of Zion (Part III).

MATT 21:31–32
Prostitutes

In the Gospel of Matthew alone, Jesus tells a parable of two sons to the chief priests and elders in the temple in Jerusalem. He compares the temple leaders to the son who promised his father that he would work in the vineyard, but did not. The son who truly did the will of his father was the one who at first refused his father's command, but then changed his mind and went. Jesus tells them that "the tax collectors and the prostitutes are going into the kingdom of God ahead of you" (v. 31), for they were the ones who believed John (the Baptist) while the priests and elders did not.

Corley points out that Jesus has long been assumed to have associated with prostitutes, based in part on the assumption that prostitutes are included under the more general rubric of "sinners" in traditions portraying Jesus as eating with "tax collectors and sinners." In fact, nowhere in the Gospels does Jesus ever eat with a woman identified explicitly as a prostitute. Further, contrary to ancient and popular tradition, nowhere in the Gospels is Mary Magdalene ever identified as a prostitute, nor for that matter any individual woman associated with the Jesus movement.

Does this passage point to the participation of prostitutes in either the Jesus movement or the circle around John the Baptist? Corley also observes that, in this passage, Jesus contrasts the superior faith of socially marginal and disreputable persons (tax collectors and prostitutes), who believed John the Baptist, with the faith of the religious elite — the chief priests and elders of the people. Although this might seem to point to their presence among the followers of John, it seems more likely that Matthew represents the tax collectors and prostitutes as believing John (21:32) when he preached the coming of Jesus, although the text is not explicit on this point.

Precisely because tax collectors and prostitutes are both stereotypical examples of marginal and despised persons, we should probably be cautious in taking this narrative as evidence for the actual presence of such persons. It is interesting that, whereas "tax collectors and sinners" is the more usual constellation (see Matt 9:10; 11:19; Mark 2:15–16; Luke 5:30), "tax collectors and prostitutes" appears to provide a gendered set of such persons: one largely male (tax collectors, although a female tax collector is attested in papyri from Egypt), the other largely female (the word *pornē*, "prostitute," is feminine, although men who sold their sexual services, mostly to other men, are known from antiquity; see, for example, 1 Cor 6:9 in the NRSV).

Whether or not the passage points to the presence of prostitutes in the Jesus movement, it certainly presupposes their presence in Jerusalem in the first century C.E. — prostitutes who, by their very representation as believers in the preaching of John the Baptist, however construed, almost certainly should be understood as Jewish women. Very little research has been done, however, on Jews as either prostitutes or purchasers of their services.

ROSS S. KRAEMER

SEE ALSO Part I: Mary 3; Part II: Prostitutes (Luke 15:30);
Prostitute (1 Cor 6:15–16).

FOR FURTHER READING: Corley, Kathleen. "Prostitute."

———. *Private Women, Public Meals.*

Matt 22:23–30
Woman Married to Seven Brothers in Succession

The woman with seven husbands in succession is a hypothetical character in a story told by the Sadducees, a Jewish priestly group who do not believe in the resurrection. Matthew's version follows Mark's fairly closely, with Jesus relativizing the marriage issue by claiming that resurrection surpasses the limits of such human institutions.

ELIZABETH STRUTHERS MALBON

SEE ALSO Part II: Woman Married to Seven Brothers in Succession (Mark 12:18–25); (Luke 20:27–36).

MATT 24:19
Women Pregnant or Nursing at the End of the Age

In all three Synoptic Gospels, following his prediction of the destruction of the temple in Jerusalem, Jesus is asked when this will happen and what signs will accompany it. As in Mark, the ushering in of the new age is envisioned as a birthing process, and the fall of the temple is one of the birth pangs that signal its onset (24:8). The coming desecration of the temple (24:15) will necessitate immediate flight, with no time to take any possessions. The text acknowledges that the distress of these days will be especially hard for pregnant women and nursing mothers (24:19).

Into the Markan apocalyptic description, Matthew weaves a Q saying: of two men in a field, one will be taken and the other left; of two women grinding at a mill, one will be taken and the other left (Matt 24:40–41; in Luke, a different version of this saying is part of an earlier discourse on the coming of the reign of God, 17:34–35). Levine observes that these combined images present women as equal participants in the events of the end while suggesting that traditional gendered roles will prevail in the interim.

ROSS S. KRAEMER

Detail from a second-century C.E. sarcophagus. An elite woman, her status signified in part by her high-backed chair, nurses a baby while the father looks on. See Women Pregnant or Nursing at the End of the Age (Matt 24:19; Mark 13:17; Luke 21:23).

SEE ALSO Part II: Two Women Grinding Meal (Matt 24:41); Women Pregnant or Nursing at the End of the Age (Mark 13:17); (Luke 21:23).

FOR FURTHER READING: Levine, Amy-Jill. "Matthew."

MATT 24:41
Two Women Grinding Meal

In Matthew 24:29–44, Jesus gives his disciples a preview of what will happen when the Son of Man comes. This statement, taken from Q, pairs two women at the mill (one of whom will be gathered among the elect, the other left behind) with two men in a field, thereby reinforcing traditional gender roles while indicating that gender is irrelevant to salvation.

AMY-JILL LEVINE

SEE ALSO Part II: Women Pregnant or Nursing at the End of the Age (Matt 24:19); Luke 21:23); Two Women Grinding Meal (Luke 17:35)

MATT 25:1–13
Ten Bridesmaids (Five Foolish and Five Wise)

This passage may be interpreted as a parable about self-responsibility and an allegory about the delayed coming of the messiah (the bridegroom), with its attendant final judgment. In context, the passage develops themes present in the parable of the faithful and unfaithful slaves (Matt 24:45–51): the delay of the master's return, faithful and unfaithful attendants, reward and punishment. Structurally similar, the two accounts differ in characterizations. Like several other sayings, Matt 25:1–13 locates women and men in traditional gender roles, implicitly addresses both women and men, and indicates that entry into and removal from the believing community is open to both. The master or groom remains male, but those who attend him, and those whom he condemns, may be women or men.

The ten bridesmaids, or virgins (Greek *parthenoi*, which can also be translated as "maidens" or "young women") may be the bride's attendants, although the bride is not mentioned in the majority of early manuscripts. Their task is to provide a lighted escort for the groom (or bride and groom, as some manuscripts attest). The groom being delayed, all ten virgins fall asleep. At midnight, the coming of the bridegroom is announced; the virgins awaken and trim their lamps. Realizing that they lack sufficient oil, five foolish virgins request supplies from their wise counterparts. The wise refuse, lest there not be enough for all, and they advise the foolish to purchase more.

When the foolish virgins return, they find the door to the wedding banquet locked. Calling "Lord, lord" (compare 7:21), they ask the groom to open the door. At this point, the story shifts from the culturally plausible to the shocking. The groom refuses, saying, "I do not know you" (v. 12). Although this harsh response appears elsewhere in the gospel tradition, only here is it addressed to women explicitly (compare Matt 7:21–23; Luke 13:25).

The refusal of the wise may be seen as an act not of selfishness, but of prudence. They are like the "wise man" who built his house on rock, whereas the "foolish man" built on sand (7:24–27); the adjectives in the two parables are the same. The parable of the wise and foolish bridesmaids may indicate that faithfulness and meritorious behavior are not transferable at the final judgment, although the story presents insufficient information to determine what the oil might represent, if anything.

On the allegorical level, the groom represents either God or Jesus. The deity appears as a bridegroom in the Hebrew Bible in Isa 54:4–6, Ezek 16:7–24, and Hos 2:19; and bridegroom metaphors are also attributed to Jesus (for example, Matt 9:15 and Rev 19:9). Bridegrooms and weddings usually suggest transient celebrations and moments of great joy. The parable suggests that the life of the community of faith can be considered analogous to preparation for and enjoyment of a permanent wedding celebration.

Although the parable is unique to Matthew, Luke speaks of the delayed return of a master from a wedding banquet, offers a warning that one must have lamps lit in readiness, and speaks of slaves who will "open the door for him as soon as he comes and knocks" (12:35–38). These sayings about watchfulness are juxtaposed with a parable concerning faithful and unfaithful slaves (12:41–48). Luke does not, however, explicitly identify the slaves or those who keep their lamps lit as either women or virgins.

AMY-JILL LEVINE

Judas settled (26:15). The woman is deliberately contrasted not only with the venal Judas, but also with the other disciples, identified as the diners who complain about the waste of ointment (26:8). Matthew omits the specific sum at which they assess the ointment, perhaps to soften the extravagance. As in Mark, the woman appears to act as a prophet, designating Jesus as Messiah; Jesus' response to the disciples' objection turns her deed into a work of mercy and a prediction of his death.

In Matthew 28, the ironic connection between this scene and the empty tomb story in Mark is effaced; the women do not bring spices to the tomb because the author either finds this an improbable excuse for their visit or wishes to present the women as recognizing the earlier anointing. To the prediction that the woman will be remembered wherever the gospel is preached, Matthew adds "this good news [gospel]" (26:13); thus in Matthew "gospel" may refer to the book itself.

Corley suggests that the woman was reclining with Jesus and the disciples; she sees this as a reflection of the more inclusive meal practices assumed by this particular Gospel. Deducing that the woman (unlike the male disciples) understood Jesus' predictions of his passion and therefore the true nature of his messiahship, Corley concludes that Matthew presents her as an example of true discipleship and service *(diakonia)*.

MARY ROSE D'ANGELO

SEE ALSO Part II: Woman Who Anoints Jesus (Mark 14:3–9).

FOR FURTHER READING: Corley, Kathleen. *Private Women, Public Meals: Social Conflict in the Synoptic Tradition.*

Levine, Amy-Jill. "Matthew."

Wainwright, Elaine. "The Gospel of Matthew."

MATT 26:6–13
Woman Who Anoints Jesus

Matthew's account of the woman who anoints Jesus follows Mark 14:1–11 very closely; Matt 26:1–5 and 14–16 elaborate Mark's betrayal narrative, adding a prediction of betrayal (26:2) and the sum for which

MATT 26:69–72
Two Servant-Girls Who Accuse Peter

Brief encounters between two servant-girls and Peter are part of a larger Matthean narrative segment,

A tombstone from ancient Smyrna (modern Izmir in Turkey) depicting the deceased as a seated woman with two female slaves. The spindle held by one slave is a common element in ancient funerary art, associating the deceased with those quintessential activities of virtuous married women, spinning and weaving. See Two Servant-Girls Who Accuse Peter *(Matt 26:69–72).*

three accusations (by two servant-girls and the bystanders) before the cock crows twice. Then Peter, admitting to himself that the servant-girls were as right as Jesus, goes out and weeps.

ELIZABETH STRUTHERS MALBON

SEE ALSO Part II: Servant-Girl, of the High Priest, Who Accuses Peter (Mark 14:66–69); Servant-Girl Who Accuses Peter (Luke 22:56–57); Woman Who Guards the Gate of the High Priest (John 18:15–17).

MATT 27:19
Wife of Pilate

Pilate's wife sends a message to interrupt the trial of Jesus: "Have nothing to do with that innocent man, for today I have suffered a great deal because of a dream about him." This Matthean detail complements the Gospel's consistent representation of both women and men in the Jesus movement as well as those outside it, and it highlights themes present elsewhere in the text: the use of dreams to communicate divine will (to the Jewish Joseph, the gentile magi, and now to the gentile wife of Pilate), a concern for "righteousness" (*dikaiosynē*), and a possible connection between suffering and discipleship.

In contrast to Joseph and the magi, however, the wife appears in a less direct manner; she is known only through her words sent by a messenger. The text's other elite women are presented similarly: Herodias does not appear herself but sends her message through her daughter (Matt 14:1–12), and the text states that the queen of the South will reappear only at the end-time (Matt 12:42). Her depiction is also consistent with Matthew's tendency to separate individuals by gender: other than the four women and their husbands mentioned in the genealogy, along with Mary and Joseph, married couples do not appear as characters in this Gospel. Even in these cases, no direct communication between wife and husband is reported.

Immediately juxtaposed with the wife's communiqué is a reference to the "chief priests and the elders" (v. 20) who had persuaded the crowds to

presumably based on Mark, that interweaves Jesus' appearance before the Jewish council and Peter's denial. Matthew's account of two servant-girls (rather than Mark's one) is consistent with other Matthean "inflations" (compare Matt 20:29–34 and Mark 10:46–52), but the change, along with the absence of Mark's specification that she was the servant-girl "of the high priest," weakens the ironic contrast between Jesus' accuser and Peter's. As prophesied by Jesus (26:33–35), Peter denies all demand the release of Barabbas and to have Jesus killed. Pilate acknowledges the leaders' request, even though it was not addressed directly to him but to the crowds. Conversely, his wife's urgent message goes unacknowledged by the characters depicted in the narrative, although it is implicitly echoed both by Pilate's hesitancy to condemn Jesus and by his later question, "What evil has he done?" (27:23).

In the *Acts of Pilate* (an anonymous Christian text dating to the fourth century or earlier), the wife's legend is extended. Here Pilate acknowledges his wife's communication and indicates that she is a Gentile who reveres the God of Israel: "And Pilate summoned all the Jews, and stood up and said to them, 'You know that my wife is pious and prefers to practice Judaism with you.'" When the Jews acknowledge his comment, Pilate then repeats his wife's message. The *Acts of Pilate* 11 reports that when Pilate and his wife heard that Jesus had died, they fasted and mourned. In later noncanonical texts, Pilate's wife, named Procla, becomes a disciple, and she dies after witnessing her husband's martyrdom.

AMY-JILL LEVINE

MATT 27:55
Unnamed Women at the Cross

Matthew follows Mark 15:41 in mentioning the presence of both named women and many unnamed women watching the crucifixion and death of Jesus from afar. In Matthew's version, the unnamed women are explicitly included in the description of the women as "following" Jesus and "ministering" to him. Some feminist scholars see these words as identifying the women at the cross as disciples and ministers, as they appear to do in Mark. Others view Matthew's Gospel as limiting discipleship to the twelve men named in 10:2–4, partly on the grounds of the Gospel's preference for the phrase "the twelve disciples" (Matt 10:1; 11:1;

20:17; 26:20; 28:16; the last scene speaks of eleven disciples because of the death of Judas).

MARY ROSE D'ANGELO

SEE ALSO Part I: Mary 3; Mary 4; Part II: Mother of the Sons of Zebedee (Matt 20:20, etc.); Unnamed Women at the Cross (Mark 15: 40–41).

FOR FURTHER READING: Wainwright, Elaine. "The Gospel of Matthew."

Wire, Antoinette Clark. "Gender Roles in a Scribal Community."

MATT 27:56
Mother of the Sons of Zebedee

SEE MATT 20:20, etc.   Mother of the Sons of Zebedee (Part II).

MARK 1:30
Mother-in-Law of Simon (Peter)

In Mark, Jesus' first exorcism of an unclean spirit (from a man in the synagogue) is quickly followed by his first healing miracle, involving the unnamed mother-in-law of his newly called disciple Simon (also known as Peter). Accompanied by James and John, Jesus enters the house of Simon and his brother, Andrew, where Jesus cures the woman of a fever by taking her hand and lifting her out of her sickbed. Although the story is brief, it contains the central elements of a healing story. The final scene provides concrete proof of the cure when the woman serves the men.

Found, with some differences, in all three Synoptic Gospels, the story raises questions about the participation of women in the Jesus movement. The Greek verb translated as "serve" (*diakoneō*) has technical meanings in many Roman-period religions, including later Christianity, and is the basis for the English word *deacon*.

Davies has suggested that, when the cured mother-in-law responds by "serving" Jesus and his newly appointed disciples, the story uses *diakoneō* in the sense of special discipleship manifest in close attendance. Others interpret *diakoneō* in an ordinary sense to mean merely that Simon's mother-in-law performs the appropriate gestures of hospitality (for example, the Scholars Version produced by the Jesus Seminar translates it: "Then she started looking after them"). Still others, arguing that it would have been unusual in first-century Galilee for a respectable free woman to wait on men who were not her immediate relatives, see this passage as evidence that the Jesus movement was characterized by egalitarian social practices (including meals) that conflicted with widespread (although not necessarily universal) ancient notions of propriety.

Does this story thus signal the unnamed mother-in-law's participation in the Jesus movement, or does it simply depict a woman whose miraculous return to health is demonstrated in her immediate ability to perform ordinary gendered tasks of hospitality? That she never reappears in the Gospel narratives might imply that she plays no significant role in the movement, yet cannot rule out the possibility.

The healing of the unnamed mother-in-law points to her absent daughter, Simon's similarly anonymous wife. By itself, the wife's absence from this story says nothing. The fact that she never appears in the Gospels, might be taken to mean that she is dead. However, 1 Cor 9:5 (Paul's claim that Cephas — usually taken to mean Simon Peter — was accompanied by a "sister-wife") is often taken as a reference to a wife of Peter's. Even if this is correct, that wife need not be the one implied here.

That the mother-in-law lives in the house of Simon and his brother, Andrew, suggests that she is a widow who has moved in with her daughter's marital family, although it is also possible that the house could be understood as hers. That she lives with her son-in-law makes it less likely that Simon and her daughter are divorced. Whereas other passages in the Synoptic Gospels (such as Matt 15:3–6; 19:19; Mark 7:10–13; 10:29–30) suggest that adult children do not always care for their parents properly, this story may represent Simon's family as fulfilling the commandment to honor one's mother and father.

ROSS S. KRAEMER

SEE ALSO Part II: Mother-in-Law of Peter (Simon) (Matt 8:14); Mother (and Father) to Be Honored (Mark 7:10–13); (Mark 10:19); Mother-in-Law of Simon (Peter) (Luke 4:38); Mother (and Father) to Be Honored (Luke 18:20); Sister/Wife Who Accompanies Apostles Other Than Paul (1 Cor 9:5).

FOR FURTHER READING: Corley, Kathleen. *Private Women, Public Meals: Social Conflict in the Synoptic Tradition.*

Davies, W. D. *The Setting of the Sermon on the Mount.*

MARK 3:32–35; MATT 12:50
Sister(s) of Jesus

Early in Mark, while surrounded by a crowd of followers in his native Galilee, Jesus is told that members of his family are outside, asking for him. Jesus responds that those around him are his true relatives; that whoever does the will of God is "my brother and sister and mother" (3:35). Similar versions occur in Matt 12:46–50 and Luke 8:19–21.

The reading of Mark 3:35 is uncontested, occurring in all significant early manuscripts. In 3:32, however, two important early Bible manuscripts, Alexandrinus (A) and Codex Bezae (D), have the crowd inform Jesus that "your mother and your *adelphoi* [masculine plural] and your *adelphai* [feminine plural]" are outside," whereas the majority of other ancient manuscripts read only "your mother and your *adelphoi* are outside."

Although the NRSV translates the reading of A and D for Mark 3:32, a reading attractive to modern audiences desirous of a gender-inclusive Bible, it may well be a later revision, produced by scribes who modified v. 32 to make it more consistent with Jesus' response in v. 35. A similar desire for consistency may account for the Lukan form of this story. There, Jesus' mother and brothers are outside, and Jesus replies, "My mother and my brothers are those who hear the word of God and do it" (8:21). Ancient attestations of Matthew follow the majority reading of Mark, which lacks the specific reference to the sisters outside, but includes "sister" in Jesus' saying. Mark and Matthew but not Luke, are thus unambiguous in their inclusion of "sister" and "brother" in the community of those who do the will of God.

Since the story privileges this community over blood relationships, it is unlikely that the revision in Mark should be taken as evidence of a desire to stress the presence of Jesus' sisters. Nor should the absence of sisters in Luke be taken as evidence of a desire to mute the presence of women in the Jesus movement, although both might fuel such interpretations in the absence of more careful consideration.

Ross S. Kraemer

See also Part II: The Sisters of Jesus (Matt 13:56); (Mark 6:3).

Mark 5:22–23, 35–43
Daughter of Jairus

Although she never acts or speaks, the daughter of Jairus plays a substantive role in considerations of Mark's Christology, depiction of social roles, and literary artistry. Her resuscitation anticipates the resurrection; the interruption of her story by the healing of the hemorrhaging woman adds to the miraculousness of her cure and insists that the two stories be treated in relation to each other; the daughter's relations to her parents and to the hemorrhaging woman have implications for family structures, gender categories, and economic issues.

The daughter is introduced in a series of deferred meetings, which both increase the tension regarding the extent of her illness and indicate the number of individuals drawn together by her condition. She is presented first through her father's description to Jesus, "My little daughter is at the point of death" (5:23); next through messengers from Jairus's house who announce her death; then through reference to the mourners at the house; and finally by means of the entry of Jesus, his three disciples, and her parents into her direct presence.

Her communal, domestic, and familial connections all contrast with the situation of the hemorrhaging woman, who appears without reference to family, home, or remaining economic resources; rather than gain Jesus' attention, she hopes to hide in the crowd.

By the time Jesus arrives at Jairus's home, the girl has died. Jesus nevertheless reassures Jairus: "Do not fear; only believe" (or "have faith"; 5:36). He tells the crowd that the girl is but sleeping, yet the mourners laugh at him (5:40). Their change of response, from "weeping and wailing loudly" (5:38) to laughter contrasts with the silence of the mother and the continuous concern of the father. Separating the child's parents and his three disciples (those who did not laugh) from the unbelievers, Jesus enters the place where the girl is and takes her by the hand. Commentators frequently see this gesture as indicating Jesus' abrogation of Levitical purity laws concerning corpse uncleanness. However, although contact with a corpse makes one ritually impure, it is neither illegal nor sinful, and the burying of the dead is an act of worthiness. It might be more appropriate to emphasize here Jesus' human compassion: he not only comforts her father and touches the girl, but also he addresses her directly in Aramaic, "*Talitha Koum,*" or, as Mark translates it, "Little girl, get up!" The child rises and walks, and Jesus commands then that she be provided with food.

The food confirms that the child is not a ghost. In Luke 24 and John 21, the resurrected Jesus demonstrates his corporeal nature by eating. Mark 16:14, an addition to the text, which originally ended at 16:8, also refers to the presence of Jesus in the context of a meal, but here Jesus himself is not depicted as eating.

Jairus's daughter may also be compared with other daughters in the Gospel. On one hand, her cure is more direct than that of the daughter of the Syrophoenician woman (Mark 7:24–30), although in both cases the parent seeks Jesus' miraculous power. On the other, she presents a contrast to the daughter of Herodias, who at a feast dances before another Jewish leader, Herod Antipas, bringing about a death rather than representing regained life.

AMY-JILL LEVINE

SEE ALSO Part I: Herodias 1; Herodias 2; Salome 2; Part II: Daughter of Jairus (Matt 9:18–19, etc.); (Luke 8:41–42a, etc.); Young Dancer Who Asks for the Head of John the Baptist (Matt 14:6–11); Daughter of the Syrophoenician Woman (Mark 7:24–30).

MARK 5:25–34
Woman with a Twelve-Year Hemorrhage

Mark interposes the account of a woman suffering from what is likely a uterine hemorrhage with the story of the request for the healing of a dead girl and the fulfillment of that request. The structure of the entwined stories, which suggests comparison of the woman to both the girl's father and to the girl herself, emphasizes several Markan themes: the former comparison evokes the themes of faith in Jesus, secrecy regarding his messianic status, Jesus' fidelity to the Law, gender and class issues, and family structures; the latter recollects interests in female sexuality, in the suffering of Jesus, and in his resurrection.

The hemorrhaging woman interrupts Jesus' journey to the home of the synagogue leader, Jairus. Contrasts immediately appear. The woman has no name; no family or home is mentioned; she has endured severe physical suffering for twelve years; she has become impoverished by spending all her resources on physicians; she approaches Jesus from behind. Jairus is named, makes a request on his daughter's behalf, brings Jesus to his home where the child's mother is also present, has status as a leader, is an official part of a synagogue community, and approaches Jesus directly. Yet the two figures share great faith in Jesus' healing power, and their faith is rewarded.

The woman's relationship to the girl is explicit in Mark's noting of the twelve-year illness and the

girl's age as "twelve years." The girl, at the transitional stage between childhood and womanhood, is comparable to the woman, who has an excess of vaginal bleeding. Both bleed, both are powerless, and both are healed (or "saved"). So too Jesus will bleed, become powerless, and finally be raised.

Although often read as indicating Jesus' rejection of Levitical purity laws, Mark shows no such interest here: the laws are not mentioned, the crowd does not part from the woman or ever show any surprise at her public presence, and even the synagogue leader shows no hesitancy in asking Jesus to touch his child. The woman's action has also been interpreted as violating expected female subservience, but this too may be extreme. On one hand, the woman does approach Jesus from behind; on the other, Mark on several occasions, without remark, depicts women in active and not necessarily subservient roles — for example, the Syrophoenician (Mark 7:24–30), the woman who anoints Jesus (Mark 14:3–9), and the servant who challenges Peter (Mark 14:66–69).

Indeed, the woman herself may be seen as having an active role: the money spent on physicians is identified as hers, and thus she was at one time economically independent. She is also self-directed and self-aware, as her internal monologue (5:28) and perception of healing (5:29) indicate. Finally, she comes forward to confess before Jesus and the crowd that she was the one who had touched him (5:30). Her story ends with the woman in a position of supplication before Jesus, and so it mirrors Jairus's initial position. Jesus addresses her as "daughter" — again evoking the narrative frame — and announces that her faith has made her well (or "saved" her). The final line anticipates the healing of the girl, but in this latter case, unlike his acceptance of the woman's public testimony, Jesus commands secrecy from those who witness the cure.

AMY-JILL LEVINE

SEE ALSO Part II: Women with a Twelve-Year Hemorrhage (Matt 9:20–22); (Luke 8:43–48).

FOR FURTHER READING: D'Angelo, Mary Rose. "(Re)Presentations of Women in the Gospels: Mark and John."

Levine, Amy-Jill. "Discharging Responsibility: Matthean Jesus, Biblical Law and Hemorrhaging Women."

MARK 5:35–43 Daughter of Jairus

SEE MARK 5:22–23, etc. Daughter of Jairus (Part II).

MARK 5:40–43
Wife of Jairus

In his narration of Jesus' healing of Jairus's daughter, Mark identifies Jairus's wife not in her marital role but as the child's mother. Jesus permits only her, his three disciples, and Jairus to witness the cure. The mother may be compared with other mothers in Mark. A woman who does Jesus' will becomes his metaphorical mother (3:34–35), whereas Jesus' own mother (3:31–33), unlike Jairus's wife, is not brought into the inner circle. Jairus's wife may also be contrasted with Herodias: the former is silent, her relationship to her husband is unquestioned, and she is present at the raising of a daughter; the latter is vocal, she is involved in an illegal relationship (6:18), and, with her daughter, she participates in bringing about the death of John the Baptist. Finally, the mother of James and Joses, like Jairus's wife, bears silent testimony to a death and resurrection (15:40, 47; 16:1).

AMY-JILL LEVINE

SEE ALSO Part I: Herodias 1; Part II: Daughter of Jairus (Matt 9:18–19, etc.); (Mark 5:22–23, etc.); (Luke 8:41–42a, etc.); Unnamed Women at the Cross (Matt 27:55); (Mark 15:40–41); Wife of Jairus (Luke 8:51–56).

MARK 6:3
Sisters of Jesus

In Mark 6:1–6a, when Jesus returns to Nazareth and preaches in the local synagogue, many who hear him question his wisdom and authority. They ask, is he not "the carpenter, the son of Mary and brother of James and Joses and Judas and Simon, and are not his sisters here with us?" Matt 13:53–58 reuses the Markan story, with some small but interesting revisions. It is absent in Luke, who thus never mentions any sisters of Jesus.

For the author of Mark, Jesus had at least four brothers and more than one sister. Unlike his brothers, the sisters of Jesus are never named. No members of Jesus' family are identified as participants in the Jesus movement. Mark 6:4 may be taken to suggest that the sisters of Jesus are among those of his relatives who do not honor him as a prophet.

The author of Mark does not specify where and when the "many" (a masculine plural that could grammatically include women as well as men, but equally well may not) who oppose Jesus do so, but it is reasonable to read their response as one made immediately on hearing Jesus, in the synagogue itself. If so, the description of the sisters as "here with us" places women in the synagogue on the Sabbath, in first-century Galilee. In light of claims that Jewish women were excluded from synagogue participation, this representation is significant counter-evidence, all the more so since the Gospel shows no interest in this question.

ROSS S. KRAEMER

SEE ALSO Part II: The Sisters of Jesus (Matt 13:56); Sister(s) of Jesus (Mark 3:32–35).

MARK 6:22–29
Daughter of Herodias

According to the NRSV, the preferred reading of v. 22 is "his [Herod's] daughter, Herodias." However, some ancient manuscripts read "the daughter of Herodias, herself."

ROSS S. KRAEMER

SEE ALSO Part I: Herodias 2; Salome 2; Part II: Young Dancer Who Asks for the Head of John the Baptist (Matt 14:6–11).

Mark 7:10–13
Mother (and Father) to Be Honored

In Mark 7:1–15, some Pharisees and scribes ask Jesus why his disciples eat without first washing their hands, ignoring the "tradition of the elders" (v. 3). Jesus counters that the Pharisees and scribes honor human tradition, but violate the divine commandment to honor mother and father (Exod 20:12; Deut 5:16) when they dedicate to God resources they would otherwise have provided for their parents. In so doing, Jesus suggests, they speak evil of their parents, an act deserving death (Lev 20:9).

Whose interpretation of the commandments is truly authoritative is cast as the heart of the debate. Why Jesus counters with the example of the commandment to honor one's parents is not immediately apparent. Conceivably, it is connected to the identification of the "tradition of the elders" with the traditions of "the fathers," a phrase common in ancient Jewish sources. It may also be that, in this particular instance of Markan anti-Pharisaic polemic, it is the author who has chosen to cast the Pharisees as violators of the most basic and common ancient moral principles of filial piety.

Once invoked, the injunction of Exodus and Deuteronomy dictates that the dispute be couched in terms of mothers as well as fathers. Jesus' response could be understood to suggest that, in the land of Israel in the first-century C.E., mothers and fathers did not always receive the necessary financial support from their adult children, something that could easily have had a disparate impact on women. If, however, the driving force here is anti-Pharisaic polemic that postdates Jesus himself, we should be cautious in drawing such specific conclusions about social conditions from the narrative.

ROSS S. KRAEMER

SEE ALSO Part II: Women in the Decalogue (Exod 20:8, etc.); Mother (and Father) to Be Honored (Matt 19:19); (Mark 10:19); (Luke 18:20); (Eph 6:2–3).

Mark 7:24–30
Syrophoenician Woman

By her bold faith and persistence, her courage and cleverness, the Syrophoenician woman effects not only the healing of her daughter by Jesus, but also a significant shift in Jesus' attitude toward Gentiles. In Mark, her story is part of a larger narrative segment (6:45–8:21) that recounts a "detour" through which Jesus leads his disciples after they fail to go on ahead of him to the other side of the Sea of Galilee, to gentile Bethsaida. During the "detour" the expansiveness of Jesus' teaching, feeding, and healing power not only for Jews, but also for Gentiles, is made manifest. Jesus' encounter with the Syrophoenician woman is presented as key to this transformation of boundaries.

The Markan narrator informs the audience that Jesus' intention in going north to the gentile city of Tyre is not to seek out more crowds to heal, but to escape public notice. The fact that the Syrophoenician woman seeks out the secluded Jesus is just the first indication of her persistence on behalf of her demon-possessed daughter. The Markan Jesus rebuffs her initial request, and he does so with a powerful and degrading metaphor: "Let the children be fed first, for it is not fair to take the children's food [bread] and throw it to the dogs" (7:27). The children are Israel. She is a dog, and she yaps right back! Two can play at metaphors. "Sir [or Lord], even the dogs under the table eat the children's crumbs (7:28)." She has him. She has risked a second rebuke and won her daughter's health. "For this saying ["word," *logos*]" (7:29, RSV), Jesus says, you may go home to a healed child, a healed gentile child. And Jesus, too, seems to have experienced healing in the widening of his initial view of God's power and care.

This story is bothersome in several ways. The fact that not the Syrophoenician demoniac, but the Gerasene demoniac (5:1–20), is the first Gentile healed in Mark's Gospel bothers biblical critics who want the text to be logical and consistent. Jesus has already moved beyond his Jewish community in exorcising a gentile demoniac in chap. 5, so what is the problem with healing a gentile child in chap. 7?, they ask. Such critics compensate by talking about Mark's compilation of oral sources. The fact that Jesus' initial response to the woman is rude and parochial bothers faithful readers who want Jesus to be a perfect model of morality and courtesy, untouched by his patriarchal culture and human nature. They compensate by talking about how Jesus, who always planned to heal the daughter, was "testing the faith" of her mother, or about how the diminutive form in the Greek (7:27, *kynariois*, "little dogs") minimizes the insult. But in the Markan narrative, it is first the woman who is bothered by Jesus' narrow view of God's power coming through him, and then Jesus who is bothered by the expansive truth of her observation. They continue by talking to each other, and healing is shared. The Markan narrator continues talking to the audience about the abundance of bread and healing through Jesus, proclaimer of God's ruling activity, until the disciples finally do reach gentile Bethsaida, where, although it takes two stages, even the blind can now see (8:22–26).

Like Jairus (5:21–24, 35–43), the Syrophoenician woman seeks healing not for herself, but for her daughter. Her non-Jewish status is as highly marked (7:24, Tyre; 7:26, Gentile, Syrophoenician) as the Jewish status of Jairus (5:21, "crossed again"; 5:22, "one of the leaders of the synagogue"). Both persevere in their faith: Jairus after his daughter dies, the woman after Jesus' initial rebuff. Together their stories portray a Jesus who listens to the pleas of both mothers and fathers and who heals both Jews and Gentiles.

The Syrophoenician woman knows when not to take "no" for an answer. In addition to her intense desire to be a channel of healing for her daughter, she senses the fuller implications of Jesus' ministry of healing: he heals what is broken — broken bodies, broken spirits, and broken relationships, including the broken relationships between Jews and Gentiles, insiders and outsiders. The Syrophoenician woman, an outsider as a Gentile (Greek) and as a woman, achieves her goal — and more — because of her "saying," not because of her faith alone

or her reasoning alone, but because of her speaking up and speaking out — because of her action. Jesus gracefully reacts with the maturity that empowers change and enables inclusivity.

ELIZABETH STRUTHERS MALBON

SEE ALSO Part II: Canaanite Woman (Matt 15:21–28); Daughter of the Canaanite Woman (Matt 15:21–28); Daughter of the Syrophoenician Woman (Mark 7:24–30).

FOR FURTHER READING: Malbon, Elizabeth Struthers. "Fallible Followers: Women and Men in the Gospel of Mark."

———. "Narrative Criticism: How Does the Story Mean?"

Tolbert, Mary Ann. "Mark."

MARK 7:24–30
Daughter of the Syrophoenician Woman

The demon-possessed "little daughter" of the Syrophoenician woman is healed at a distance by Jesus, who credits the bold and clever "saying" (RSV; Greek *logos*, 7:29) of her mother as she successfully challenges Jesus to include Gentiles as well as Jews in his healing power. In the patriarchal culture of the first century, it would be more usual for a girl's father to seek help for her from someone outside the family — as Jairus does for his "little daughter" (5:21–24, 35–43). But in the case of the daughter of the Syrophoenician woman, no father is mentioned. Whether the father is unwilling or unable to seek help for her is not known. The mother may be a widow, or she may be unwed. Her daughter may be her only family. The mother may simply be more willing to take the risk of presenting the request to this Jewish healer. As a woman, her status is already lower — lower if she is a widow, lower still if unwed. Thus she has less to lose — and her daughter's health to gain.

The mother does, however, seek out Jesus in a house, a more usual domain for a woman than the public space of a street or market area. Yet it is not her house, and she is not an invited guest but an intruder on Jesus' seclusion — as well as, it turns out, on Jesus' conviction about to whom his gift of healing should be extended. Her love for her daughter impels her to break with social norms that would not sanction her initial speech to Jesus, much less her snappy comeback. Following her lead, the Markan Jesus too breaks conventions, not only speaking to her, but also listening to her. The mother's bold love and faith are rewarded by Jesus' exorcism of the demon from her daughter, without his ever seeing the daughter, the only healing at a distance in Mark's Gospel.

Her story complements the raising of the "little daughter" of Jairus, a synagogue ruler (5:21–24, 35–43). As a Jewish father perseveres in pursuing Jesus' help for his daughter, despite an initial setback (her reported death!), so a gentile mother does the same for her daughter, despite an initial setback — Jesus' refusal to help. But while Jairus is encouraged by Jesus to resist fear and believe (5:36), the Syrophoenician woman has to overcome Jesus' resistance on the strength of her own fearlessness and wit. For Jairus, Jesus is always a helper; for the Syrophoenician woman, Jesus is at first an antagonist. Jairus must struggle with his fear; the Syrophoenician woman must struggle with Jesus. Both daughters benefit, and their stories, taken together, portray a Jesus who listens to mothers as well as fathers and heals and restores gentile as well as Jewish children.

ELIZABETH STRUTHERS MALBON

SEE ALSO Part II: Canaanite Woman (Matt 15:21–28); Daughter of the Canaanite Woman (Matt 15:21–28); Syrophoenician Woman (Mark 7:24–30).

MARK 10:2–12
Divorced Wife

Mark 10:2–12 combines two sayings of Jesus on divorce. In 10:2–9, Pharisees ask Jesus whether it is "lawful for a man to divorce his wife," paraphrasing Deut 24:1 as a biblical proof text for the permissibil-

ity of divorce (later rabbis based their divorce law on Deut 24:1–4). Jesus counters with Gen 1:27 ("God made them male and female") and 2:24 ("one flesh") as proof texts for his prohibition of divorce. In Mark 10:10–12, Jesus instructs his disciples privately that a man who divorces his wife and marries another woman commits adultery against the prior wife. So, too, a woman who divorces her husband and marries another commits adultery against the prior husband. The connection between divorce and remarriage is also found in Deut 24:1–4, which presumes the practice of divorce (effected through a written document) and is actually concerned with whether a man may remarry a wife he has divorced if she has remarried in the interim (the passage forbids it).

Jesus' prohibition of divorce changes the definition of adultery. According to ancient Israelite law, adultery was committed when an Israelite man had sex with the wife of another Israelite man (see Deut 22:22). A man did not commit adultery against his own wife by having sex with a prostitute, a foreigner, a slave, a divorced woman, a widow, or a virgin. Further, polygamy was allowed and did not constitute adultery. The wife of an Israelite man, in contrast, committed adultery against her husband by having sex with any other man. Jesus alters and equalizes the definition of adultery by claiming, "Whoever divorces his wife and marries another commits adultery against her" (Mark 10:11; compare Matt 19:9), as if a man could in fact commit adultery against his own wife. Jesus also extends the concept of adultery to include looking lustfully at a woman (Matt 5:27–30).

Mark, who presupposes women's power to initiate divorce, prohibits both women and men from initiating divorce, whereas Matthew's prohibition extends only to men. Some scholars believe that Mark adapted Jesus' prohibition to Greek and Roman law, according to which women had the power to divorce, whereas Matthew remained closer to Jesus' own formulation. We can, however, better explain the discrepancy between Matthew (and Luke) on the one hand and Mark (and Paul) on the other as reflecting the different strands of legal opinion within Judaism itself. In his own sermons, Jesus may have used either formulation, or perhaps both to different audiences.

The historical Jesus apparently prohibited divorce under all circumstances, which protected some women from unwanted divorces and prevented other women from obtaining desired divorces. We do not know why Jesus took such a strong stand against divorce. The tradition that Jesus prohibited divorce was widespread in the early church; the New Testament includes five formulations of Jesus' prohibition that probably derive from three different ancient traditions:

1. These verses in Mark, the earliest Gospel in the New Testament, used also in Matt 19:3–9;
2. A hypothetical sayings gospel that scholars call Q (mid–first century C.E., used in Luke 16:18 and in Matt 5:31–32); and
3. Paul, in 1 Cor 7:10–11.

These formulations differ in two major respects. First, Mark and Paul, who presuppose women's power to divorce (Mark 10:12; 1 Cor 7:11), prohibit both women and men from divorcing, whereas Matthew and Luke prohibit only men from so doing. Thus, according to Mark and Paul, Jesus wanted to prevent women from exercising a power that their society gave them, whereas according to Matthew and Luke, their society had apparently not granted them that power to start with. Second, only Matthew allows an exception to the strict prohibition: divorce is allowed if the wife has engaged in illicit sexual behavior or if the marriage was to a woman prohibited by the incest laws of Lev 18:6–18 (the word *porneia* can denote both kinds of illicit sexual acts). Perhaps Matthew added this exception clause to Jesus' prohibition because early Christian communities found it difficult to follow Jesus' strict teaching (see also 1 Cor 7:12–16, which allows for divorce if the spouse is a nonbeliever and does not wish to continue the marriage, but recommends against it).

The effect of Jesus' prohibition on married women varied greatly according to their circumstances. Within Jewish society, the marriage contract (Hebrew *kĕtûbâ*), with its guaranteed marriage settlement in the case of a divorce, was already a disincentive to husbands to divorce their wives and prevented divorced women from being destitute. But a wife who had married without a marriage contract might become destitute upon divorce, since without a written contract, she might not obtain a marriage settlement. Jesus' prohibition could protect such a woman from a life of abject poverty. Jesus' prohibition could also protect married women with or without a marriage contract from divorce on frivolous grounds. (One rabbinic school, that of the famous rabbi Hillel of the first century C.E., is said to have permitted a man to divorce his wife if she spoiled his food [*m. Gittin* 9:10]). On the other hand, Jesus' prohibition would have prevented his male followers from marrying divorced women. Women whose husbands had divorced them against their will (some of whom may have been destitute) were thereby prevented from gaining a higher standard of living through remarriage. The prohibition would have also kept these women from the hope of having children to support them in their old age.

Jesus' divorce prohibition would have also prevented women from divorcing or seeking a divorce from their husbands. Early Christian women living under Greek or Roman law, which allowed women to initiate divorce, would have relinquished this power if they followed Jesus' teaching. According to Jewish rabbinic law codified two centuries after Jesus, a man divorces a woman only of his own free will, but a woman can be divorced with or against her consent (*m. Yebamoth* 14:1). Jewish women at the time of Jesus, living under an early form of this school of Jewish law, would have experienced Jesus' prohibition as equalizing (if their husbands also abided by it): neither husband nor wife was allowed to divorce the other. According to later rabbinic law, however, a wife could appeal to a rabbinical court to make the husband write her a bill of divorce in certain cases. If this option existed for Jewish women at the time of Jesus, Jesus' teaching would have prevented them from appealing to the court for a divorce.

In some circles of ancient Judaism, however, women could initiate divorce, and Jesus' prohibition would have prevented them from exercising this option. Women's power to divorce was just one of many points of Jewish law on which ancient Jews disagreed. According to a strand of Jewish legal thought that is attested over a period of centuries, Jewish women could initiate divorce, whether orally or by means of a bill of divorce. Evidence for these practices comes from diverse sources: marriage contracts from Elephantine, Egypt (fifth century B.C.E.); a recently published document (dated to 134 or 135 C.E.) from a Judean woman named Shelamzion, found in the vicinity of the Dead Sea; Josephus's narratives about Herodian women (first century B.C.E.–first century C.E.), including Herodias, Drusilla, and Salome, sister of Herod the Great; and even a provision in the Jerusalem Talmud (but not the more authoritative Babylonian Talmud) for writing into a woman's marriage contract the power to initiate divorce (*y. Ketubboth* 30b, lines 56–57; *y. Baba Batra* 16c, lines 36–37). Female followers of Jesus from the groups within Judaism that allowed women to initiate divorce would have lost that power under Jesus' teaching. This could have included women who were being beaten, forced to have sex, or otherwise humiliated by their husbands (early rabbinic law also provided no recourse for such women).

BERNADETTE J. BROOTEN

SEE ALSO Part I: Drusilla; Herodias 1; Part II: Woman Being Divorced (Deut 24:1–4, etc.); Divorced Wife (Matt 5:31–32); (Matt 19:3–9); (Luke 16:18); Married Women (and Men), Unmarried Women (and Men), and Women (and Men) Married to Unbelievers (1 Corinthians 7).

FOR FURTHER READING: Dewey, Joanna. "The Gospel of Mark."

Ilan, Tal. "Notes and Observations on a Newly Published Divorce Bill from the Judaean Desert."

Levine, Amy-Jill. "Matthew."

Porten, Bezalal, and Ada Yardeni. *Textbook of Aramaic Documents from Ancient Egypt.*

Mark 10:19
Mother (and Father) to Be Honored

Mark (10:17–22), Matthew (19:16–22), and Luke (18:18–23) all narrate an encounter between Jesus and a wealthy man who asks what he must do to inherit eternal life. Jesus responds that the man must observe the commandments, specifically those forbidding murder, adultery, theft, and false witness, and the commandment to honor one's mother and father. When the man replies that he has done all this, Jesus tells him to sell all his possessions and give the proceeds to the poor, saddening the man greatly.

Unlike Mark 7:10 (and its parallel, Matt 15:4) where Jesus' invocation of the commandment to honor one's mother and father appears in the context of anti-Pharisaic polemic and might reflect first-century disputes about how one honors one's parents, here the commandment is simply one of five required for eternal life. Omitted from this list are the other five commandments found in Exod 20:1–17 and Deut 5:6–21 (not to have any other gods, not to make or worship idols, not to misuse God's name, not to covet one's neighbor's possessions, and to observe the Sabbath).

ROSS S. KRAEMER

SEE ALSO Part II: Women in the Decalogue (Exod 20:8, etc.); Mother (and Father) to Be Honored (Matt 19:19); (Mark 7:10–13); (Luke 18:20); (Eph 6:2–3).

MARK 10:29–30
Sisters and Mothers Left for Jesus' Sake

In Mark 10:28, on the heels of Jesus' admonition (Mark 10:17–22) to the rich man to sell all his possessions and follow Jesus — and in apparent contrast to the man's failure to comply — Peter tells Jesus that the disciples have left everything and followed him. Jesus responds that "there is no one who has left house or brothers or sisters or mother or father or children or fields for my sake and for the sake of the good news, who will not receive a hundredfold now in this age — houses, brothers and sisters, mothers and children, and fields, with persecutions — and in the age to come, eternal life." In Mark (and in Matthew), the implicit description of the person who leaves behind family and home to follow Jesus is gender-neutral, since both men and women would have had brothers and sisters (Greek *adelphos* and *adelphas*), mothers and fathers, children and fields. Similarly, those left behind appear equally to be female and male.

In Luke 18:29, however, the Greek word *gynē* ("wife, woman") appears where Mark (and Matthew) have *adelphas*: "there is no one who has left house or wife or brothers or parents or children." Has the author of Luke intentionally revised the Markan text, or does the Lukan text reflect instead an earlier version of the saying? Luke 18:29 appears to make the one who leaves to join the Jesus movement implicitly male. Theissen has argued precisely that Luke's version more accurately reflects the nature of the Jesus movement as consisting of male charismatics who left their wives.

Yet even if Luke has revised the saying, his choice of *gynē* may be less of a revision than might initially appear. Sibling terminology was often used in the ancient world for spousal relationships (see, for example, 1 Cor 7:14, where "husband" translates the Greek *adelphos*). Although the NRSV takes *adelphos* and *adelphē* in all three versions of this story to signify siblings, it is quite possible that spousal ties underlie all three versions, ties that are otherwise strikingly absent from the saying, and all the more strange given the explicit mention of children.

It is also possible that the author of Mark deliberately omitted wives (or "wife") from the list of those left. That author may also have understood the sibling vocabulary to have spousal connotations, and pluralized it to avoid the suggestion that (male) members of the early Jesus movement divorced their wives. The Greek verb translated as "leave" in all three Gospels can mean "to divorce." Both Mark and Matthew have Jesus expressly pro-

hibit divorce (Mark 10:2–9; compare Matt 19:2–9 and Matt 5:32) while Luke does not. This might suggest that Luke here preserves an earlier version of the saying before concerns about divorce affected its transmission or that Luke is untroubled by the implication of divorce.

Ross S. Kraemer

See also Part II: Divorced Wife (Matt 5:31–32); (Mark 10:2–12); (Luke 16:18); Mothers and Sisters Left for the Sake of Jesus' Name (Matt 19:29); Wife Left for the Sake of the Kingdom of God (Luke 18:29–30).

For further reading: D'Angelo, Mary Rose. "Remarriage and the Divorce Sayings Attributed to Jesus." Theissen, Gerd. *Sociology of Early Palestinian Christianity.*

Mark 12:18–25
Woman Married to Seven Brothers in Succession

This woman is not a character who acts in the Gospel, but a character within a story told by the Sadducees. Members of this priestly group are introduced as those "who say there is no resurrection" (12:18) and take part in a series of encounters with Jewish leaders who question Jesus in the Jerusalem temple. Their trick question, designed to show the foolishness of the idea of resurrection, presupposes the absolute nature of levirate law. This law provides that a surviving brother of a married man who dies with no children should marry the widow and raise up children for his brother. In the Sadducees' absurd story, seven brothers marry one woman in succession, and the point raised is not "How can a woman be asked to suffer so much?" but "In the resurrection, whose wife will she be?"

Jesus, in turn, questions their assumption of the timelessness of marriage. In the resurrection "they [men] neither marry nor are [they — women] given in marriage" (12:25). By "the power of God" (12:24) both women and men are free from the limits of such human (and patriarchal) institutions and are "like angels in heaven" (12:25), each responsible before God and all rejoicing together. The woman is marginalized by the issue of the resurrection; but in terms of the hypothetical woman, the Markan Jesus shifts concern from the question "to what man will she belong?" to "what is the God like who will be with her?"

ELIZABETH STRUTHERS MALBON

SEE ALSO Woman Married to Seven Brothers in Succession (Matt 22:23–30); (Luke 20:27–36).

FOR FURTHER READING: Wahlberg, Rachel Conrad. *Jesus According to a Woman.*

MARK 12:41–44
Poor Widow Giving Two Copper Coins

The story of the poor widow who puts two small copper coins, together worth a penny, into the temple treasury has often been retold as an exemplum for a stewardship campaign. After all, doesn't Jesus, who calls her action to the attention of his disciples in Mark's Gospel, tell them, "Truly I tell you, this poor widow has put in more than all those who are contributing to the treasury. For all of them have contributed out of their abundance; but she out of her poverty has put in everything she had, all she had to live on" (12:43–44)? It is not without significance, however, that the Markan Jesus does not, like some director of charitable giving, *encourage* the poor widow to give, but rather he *observes* her own moral action and points out its significance to his disciples.

Sensing the inappropriateness of interpreting the poor widow as a model of charity, Wright has argued that Jesus laments her misguided gift as an illustration of the ills of official devotion and, furthermore, since the temple will be destroyed, a waste. Wright insists that the proper interpretation of her story is "a matter of context," focusing on the immediate context of the preceding teaching against scribes who devour widows' houses (12:38–40) and the following prediction of the temple's destruction (13:1–2). A wider look at the multiple

contexts of the Markan story of the poor widow complicates, and enriches, interpretation.

Because widows in the ancient Israelite world were socially marginalized — having neither father nor husband to provide for and protect them — their vulnerability in the face of males with power was "guarded" by scriptural prescriptions for their care. The repetition of such pleas for Israel to show mercy to match God's mercy, however, betrays the continuing human failure to do so. Thus, to be a widow was to be poor, and to be poor was to be defenseless. But, in the story of the poor widow who gives all, the Markan Jesus calls attention not to her ordinary plight, but to her extraordinary action.

Certainly the poor widow who gives all, her whole means of living, presents a striking contrast to the scribes who take all, who "devour widows' houses" (12:40), that is, their means of living. The scribes who wear showy robes, solicit salutations in the marketplace, and claim the best seats in the synagogue are quite opposite to the unobtrusive widow whom only Jesus notices. The poor widow is unlike the self-centered scribes and instead like Jesus — one who gives all. The last words of her story could well be translated "but she from her need cast in all of whatever she had, her whole life [Greek *bios*]." Perhaps we *are* to assume that the poor widow has been victimized by the greedy scribes and by the authority of traditional religious teaching. But in this again she is like Jesus, who teaches with "authority, and not as the scribes" (1:22), yet is victimized by those who hold authority in the temple and in the broader religious tradition. If "blaming the victim" is inappropriate in the case of Jesus as he moves toward his death, it is inappropriate in the case of the poor widow who gives "her whole life."

In addition, the overall temple context of the poor widow's story serves not to suggest the absurdity of her gift but to add to the impressive irony of the Markan story of the crucified messiah. Jesus' first action in the temple is the driving out of the buyers and sellers (11:15–19), more a closing down of the temple than a cleansing of it. The narrating of this action is interwoven with an even more symbolic action: the withering of the fig tree (11:12–14, 20–26), an allusion to the temple's end. Jesus' final action in the temple is his reaction to the poor widow's action, an allusion to Jesus' own end in the gift of his "whole life." The temple's end and Jesus' end are not unrelated. Jesus' way of dealing with the one models for his disciples a way of dealing with the other. The poor widow's story is told on the boundary.

In fact, the story of the poor widow's gift of her last two coins serves, with the story of the unnamed woman's anointing of Jesus, as a frame around chap. 13, Jesus' discourse on the end time. (This is a uniquely Markan frame; Matthew does not include the story of the poor widow; Luke narrates in a different location a story of a sinful woman who anoints Jesus' *feet*.) Jesus' speech intrudes within the action of the passion narrative (chaps. 11–12; 14–15) and is framed by two stories of exemplary women in contrast with villainous men. Jesus' condemnation of the scribes' typical actions and his commendation of the poor widow's exceptional action immediately precede chap. 13; the accounts of the chief priests' and scribes' plot against Jesus and the woman's anointing of Jesus immediately succeed chap. 13. One woman gives what little she has, two copper coins; the other gives a great deal, ointment of pure nard worth more than three hundred denarii; but each gift is symbolically or metaphorically priceless. The irony that the poor widow's gift occurs in the doomed temple is matched by the irony that the anointing of Jesus Christ, Jesus Messiah, Jesus the anointed one, takes place not in the temple but in a leper's house (14:3), and not at the hands of the high priest but at the hands of an unnamed woman.

The story of the poor widow is part of the larger context of the stories of all the women characters in Mark's Gospel. The poor widow and the anointing woman, like the hemorrhaging woman (5:25–34) and the Syrophoenician woman (7:24–30), take decisive action to which Jesus makes a significant *re*action. Jesus is moved by their strong faith and self-giving service. Perhaps the historical reality of

women's lower status and the historical reality of women's discipleship together support in Mark's Gospel the surprising narrative reality of women characters who exemplify the demands of followership, from bold faith in Jesus' life-giving power to self-giving in parallel to, or in recognition of, his self-giving death. The poor widow is not a mere model for the charitable; she is a model of the Christ.

Elizabeth Struthers Malbon

See also Part II: Woman Who Anoints Jesus (Matt 26:6–13); (Mark 14:3–9); (Luke 7:36–50); Poor Widow Giving Two Copper Coins (Luke 21:1–4).

For further reading: Malbon, Elizabeth Struthers. "The Poor Widow in Mark and Her Poor Rich Readers."

Wright, Addison G. "The Widow's Mites: Praise or Lament? — A Matter of Context."

MARK 13:17
Women Pregnant or Nursing at the End of the Age

In all three Synoptic Gospels, following his prediction of the destruction of the temple in Jerusalem, Jesus is asked when this will happen and what signs will accompany it. The ushering in of the new age is envisioned as a birthing process, and the fall of the temple is one of the birth pangs (13:8) that signal its onset. Although predictions of cataclysmic disaster are typical motifs in ancient Jewish and Christian literature, many scholars think that Mark here alludes specifically to events in the late 60s C.E., perhaps including the sacrilegious entrance into the temple by the Roman general Titus in 70 C.E. (cited in *The Jewish War* by the Jewish historian Josephus).

Jesus instructs four of his male disciples that the coming desecration of the temple (13:14) will necessitate immediate flight, with no time to take any possessions. Mark 13:17 recognizes that the distress of these days will be especially hard for pregnant women and nursing mothers. This verse might thus be seen to reflect knowledge of the actual consequences of such events for pregnant and nursing women, or it could simply reflect a sensitivity to the special hardships that cataclysmic upheaval presents for such women.

Ross S. Kraemer

See also Part II: Women Pregnant or Nursing at the End of the Age (Matt 24:19); (Luke 21:23)

Mark 14:3–9
Woman Who Anoints Jesus

In Mark's Gospel, the passion opens with a dramatic anecdote in which an unnamed woman anoints Jesus' head. This striking narrative not only inspired many centuries of pious interpretation, but also supplied the title of the first book-length scholarly feminist treatment of the women in Christian origins, Elisabeth Schüssler Fiorenza's *In Memory of Her*. Much invoked in feminist theology, the passage carries considerable literary and theological weight in the Gospel.

Set two days before the Passover and the feast of unleavened bread, the story is intercalated (interwoven) with the narrative of the betrayal of Jesus; in vv. 1–2 the narrator describes the high priests and scribes plotting how they might take Jesus by stealth, since they fear that openly seizing Jesus during Passover might cause rioting. This implies that Jesus and the reign of God are connected with the festival of Passover and its theme of liberation. Mark 14:10–11 narrates Judas's agreement to hand over Jesus (vv. 10–11). Intercalation is a favored Markan compositional technique; here it allows events to unfold over a period of time while enhancing the impact of both narratives. The secret or inner character of these scenes is also characteristic of Mark; each gives the readers information not available to the characters in the Gospel.

The central narrative is classified as a pronouncement story, biographical apothegm, or *chreia*; it consists of an incident and a brief dialogue, culminating in two prophetic sayings of Jesus. Its setting

is a meal in Bethany (just outside Jerusalem) at the house of one "Simon the leper" (v. 3). An unnamed woman comes and, breaking a container of ointment, pours its contents over Jesus' head (14:3). The author notes the extraordinary value of the ointment; if Matt 20:2 reflects real economic conditions, the three hundred denarii mentioned in Mark 14:5 would amount to nearly a year's wage for a laborer. The woman's gesture reflects the anointing of kings in the Hebrew Bible: Samuel's anointing of Saul (1 Sam 10:1) and David (1 Sam 16:13) as well as Nathan's anointing of Solomon (1 Kgs 1:34–40). Although Tolbert suggests that having an anonymous woman servant designate Jesus as Messiah (meaning "anointed"; in Greek, *christos*) would fit well with Jesus' teaching on leadership in Mark (9:33–36; 10:41–45), the text does not identify her as a servant and implies that the expenditure is her own. More probably, she acts as a prophet designating Jesus as messianic king.

In the dialogue that follows, "some" object to the "waste" of ointment on the grounds that it could have been sold and the proceeds given to the poor (14:4–5). Their objection evokes a double response from Jesus; vv. 6–8 predict Jesus' imminent death, warning that they will not always have him with them and explaining what the woman has done as a good deed: not a "beautiful thing" (RSV) or even a "good service" (NRSV), but a work of mercy — preparing his body for burial. By interpreting her gesture this way, Jesus classifies it not as an act of love or worship, but as charity, a work of mercy, the equivalent of giving to the poor. Tob 1:16–17 lists feeding the hungry, clothing the naked, and burying the dead together as works of mercy, and the protagonist's courage in burying fellow Jews executed by Sennacherib is the chief evidence of his piety (Tob 1:17–20). In Mark, likewise, Jesus' body is hurriedly buried by the charitable and pious Joseph of Arimathea (15:42–45). Even more important for Mark's narrative, this interpretation changes the woman's prophetic designation of Jesus as Messiah into a prophetic prediction of his death. In keeping with the Gospel's concern to redirect all messianic imagery to his death and resurrection, Jesus is portrayed as accepting messianic status, but revising it to point to his death. The story also creates an ironic context for the women going to the tomb to anoint Jesus' body; the readers know that this has already been done — and probably also that the women will not find this body.

A final pronouncement by Jesus predicts that wherever the gospel is preached, the woman's deed will be told in her memory — another ironic touch that brings the readers or hearers into the text: Jesus' prophecy has come true once again in their presence. The anonymity of the woman produces an added irony: unlike the betrayer's, the woman's name is not commemorated by the Gospel or remembered by the readers.

All four of the canonical Gospels relate a story about a woman who anoints Jesus. The versions found in Mark 14:3–9 and Matthew 26:6–13 are nearly identical, so, since Mark is widely regarded as a source for both Matthew and Luke, Matthew's narrative is entirely explicable as a revision of Mark. But there are significant differences between John 12:1–8 and Mark 14:3–9, and the story of a woman anointing Jesus in Luke 7:36–50 diverges so substantially that it suggests a different story entirely. In Luke the story is located early in the narrative, there is no connection with Jesus' death, and the woman is identified as a sinner. She anoints Jesus' feet only after washing them with her tears and wiping them with her hair, and her deed is interpreted as a gesture of love and repentance rather than a work of mercy, a preparation for burial, or a proclamation of messiahship. John assigns the anointing to Mary, sister of Martha, who anoints Jesus' feet as does the woman in Luke, but whose deed is tied to Jesus' burial, as in Mark.

At least two explanations of these three versions are possible. According to one theory, the versions in Mark and Luke represent two different original stories; in one a woman anoints Jesus' head near his death, and in another a repentant sinner washes Jesus' feet. The affinities of John's narrative with both are then to be explained by John's use of the two preexisting stories or the dependence of John's Gospel upon both Mark and Luke. Another view posits one anecdote behind both Mark and Luke. A third, less likely option is that John 12:1–8 (or an early version of it) is the source of both Mark and Luke.

The question of the story's original form bears upon both the historical question of the status of this woman and other women companions of Jesus, and the literary and theological questions of Mark's purpose in revising the story. Corley has espoused the theory of a single original anecdote in which a woman anoints Jesus at a meal, is rebuked by others, and is then affirmed by Jesus. Reading the narrative in the context of the customs surrounding the symposium, the Greek-style all-male banquet, she suggests that the woman is presented as a "public" (sexually available) woman and that the anointing is sexual in connotation. Such a story presumably reflects a willingness within the Jesus movement to question social mores. Mark might have associated the anointing with Jesus' death in order to transform a scandalous episode, in which Jesus accepts the sexual ministrations of a woman "of luxury," into a preparation for burial, an irreproachable service usually assigned to women.

Postulating two original stories or a single original story closest to that of Mark casts a different light on both reconstruction of the movement in which Jesus preached God's reign and readings of Mark. For one thing, the narrative implies that Jesus is not always seen as the only prophet in the movement, which recognizes at least one woman prophet. If the association of the story with the death of Jesus precedes Mark, does the author see the political implications of the story? Accepting the anointing from the woman would amount to a tacit messianic claim, like the entry into Jerusalem (11:1–11) and Jesus' tacit acceptance of Peter's confession (8:27–31). Is the equation of messiahship and death meant to sanitize the incident by insisting that, far from revolting against Rome, Jesus never did accept a messianic claim? Or is the author's first concern rather to argue that Jesus' death was integral to his messiahship? Perhaps the intercalation with the betrayal implies that this messianic claim is actually what Judas betrayed, the basis of the accusation of sedition (15:2). If that is the case, the woman who was to be remembered is also the prophet who has been forgotten.

With the promise that the woman will be remembered "wherever the good news is preached," the Gospel uses the voice of Jesus to claim the presence of its audience: as they hear and read, they fulfill his prophecy. Recently Crossan has suggested that this promise may be the coy signature of the anonymous author — that is, in the case of the Gospel of Mark also, Anonymous was a woman. Although most scholars think it unlikely that the Gospel is the product of an eyewitness to the career of Jesus, this does not rule out Crossan's suggestion. A later author telling these stories assumes prophetic status and might well choose the persona of a woman prophet as her own representative in the narrative. Similarly, she might present herself as one of the women who close the Gospel with their flight from the empty tomb. They tell no one (16:8), but their silence is broken by the text itself. If they cannot prove the existence of a woman author, the dramatic function of these figures draws attention to the women readers and women hearers that the Gospel certainly had. Throughout the Gospel, anonymous women figures offer themselves as ways for the audience to place themselves within the narrative. The woman of 7:24–30 is especially striking, for like Mark's audience, she is a speaker of Greek and a Gentile (Syrophoenician). Whether or not such portrayals speak of a woman author, they certainly speak of and to the women readers and women hearers, for whom the woman prophet, with her named and unnamed companions, would be good news.

MARY ROSE D'ANGELO

SEE ALSO Part II: Woman Who Anoints Jesus (Matt 26:6–13); (Luke 7:36–50).

FOR FURTHER READING: Corley, Kathleen. *Private Women, Public Meals.*

Crossan, John Dominic. *The Historical Jesus: Life of Mediterranean Jewish Peasant.*

D'Angelo, Mary Rose. "(Re)Presentations of Women in the Gospels: John and Mark."

———. "(Re)Presentations of Women in the Gospel of Matthew and Luke-Acts."

Dewey, Johanna. "Gospel of Mark."

Schüssler Fiorenza, Elisabeth. *In Memory of Her: A Feminist Theological Reconstruction of Christian Origins.*

Tolbert, Mary Ann. "Mark."

MARK 14:66–69
Servant-Girl, of the High Priest, Who Accuses Peter

The brief encounter between one of the servant-girls of the high priest and the disciple Peter is part of a larger Markan narrative segment that ironically intercalates, or interweaves, the story of Jesus' appearance before the council (the Sanhedrin) and Peter's denial. Two contrasting scenes are set up in 14:53–54. Jesus is with the highest-ranking Jewish religious officials (male) inside a building and presumably upstairs. Peter is still following Jesus, although "at a distance" (compare 15:40), and is with lower-ranking characters (the guards, also male) outside and at ground level, that is, at the fire in the courtyard below (compare 14:66).

In the face of indirect false testimony before the higher-ups, Jesus remains silent. In the face of the high priest's direct question about his identity as the Christ (Messiah), Jesus responds affirmatively ("I am," 14:62), sealing his condemnation to death. The form of the mocking of the condemned Jesus (blindfolding, striking, saying "Prophesy"; 14:65) marks the transition back to Peter's story because earlier Jesus had prophesied Peter's threefold denial before the cock's twofold crow (14:29–31).

The triply lowly young female servant of the high priest first accuses Peter directly: "You also were with Jesus, the man from Nazareth (14:67)." Unlike Jesus, Peter answers the accusation with a cowardly equivalent of "I am not" (14:68), hoping to save his implicitly threatened life. Peter moves farther from Jesus, "out into the forecourt" (14:68). The cock crows once. Like the high priest, the servant-girl persists, accusing Peter indirectly in a more public statement to the bystanders: "This man is one of them" (14:69). When Peter denies Jesus a second time, the bystanders take up the servant-girl's accusation, emboldened perhaps by her daring, and giving, like her, true testimony. Peter's third denial, elaborated with cursing and an oath, is interrupted by the cock's second crow, which startles Peter first into remembrance and then into remorse. Yet Peter's remorse — and Jesus' promise (14:28) — suggest that Peter's story, like Jesus', is not yet over (see 16:7). Although the historicity of the incident is uncertain, the dramatic impact of the narrative is clear: as the high priest shows Jesus' resolve, so the high priest's servant-girl shows Jesus' follower's fallibility.

The social context behind the encounter of Peter and the servant-girl would give Peter a definite advantage. "Within the prevailing patriarchal-hierarchical structure of first-century Mediterranean households, servant-girls would clearly rank at the bottom of the ladder, subordinated by their gender and age as well as their slave class" (Spencer, 138). Thus servant-girls were easy for free adult males to dispute with and put down. This status disparity sharpens the contrast between the servant-girl's true observation about Peter's association with Jesus and Peter's self-serving lie. Although a servant-girl is likely to be disbelieved by characters in an early Christian text (compare Acts 12:12–17; as well as the Gospel parallels to the servant-girl who accuses Peter), the readers know what Peter is unable to say: she speaks the truth.

ELIZABETH STRUTHERS MALBON

SEE ALSO Part II: Two Servant-Girls Who Accuse Peter (Matt 26:69–72); Servant-Girl Who Accuses Peter (Luke 22:56–57); Woman Who Guards the Gate of the High Priest (John 18:15–17).

FOR FURTHER READING: Spencer, F. Scott. "Out of Mind, Out of Voice: Slave-Girls and Prophetic Daughters in Luke-Acts."

MARK 15:40–41
Unnamed Women at the Cross

The Gospel of Mark speaks of many women who had followed Jesus from Galilee to Jerusalem, who stand afar and watch the crucifixion and death of Jesus. Three specific witnesses are named (Mary Magdalene, Mary the mother of James the younger and of Joses, and Salome; 15:40). The text describes these women in terms that identify them as disciples and ministers of the movement. The terms *follow* and *come after* are technical language in Mark (1:16–20; 2:14; 8:34); the words "used to follow him" (v. 15:41) indicate that these women were disciples. The rest of v. 41 notes that many other (unnamed) women also accompanied Jesus up to Jerusalem. While it is possible these women did not have the same status as the named women, it is more likely that they fall into the same category, and the named women are singled out specifically as witnesses to the burial (15:47) and empty tomb (Mark 16:1); their ministry in Galilee enhances their testimony by underlining their long association with Jesus. In Mark, Jesus travels with those who were around him along with the "twelve" (4:10–12).

Mark 15:40–41 makes explicit that the larger group of disciples did include women. Although Mark's Gospel offers no account of a woman disciple being called, the new invitation to discipleship in 8:34 is directed to a large crowd (and to the readers or hearers of the gospel); 15:40–41 shows that the author assumes women to have been (and to be) among those addressed in 8:34 and wherever the term *disciples* is used. That discipleship includes "sisters" also emerges at 3:31–35 and 10:30.

The word that the NRSV translates "provide for him" (15:41) is *diēkonoun*, the basic meaning of which is "serve" and "wait on table"; it has a specialized function throughout the New Testament, where it draws upon uses of the word to refer to service to the city (as in magistracies) and to the temple service. In 2 Cor 3:6, the NRSV translates the noun *diakonous*, which refers to Paul and the apostles, as "ministers" (of a new covenant). In Mark, although the angels who serve or wait on Jesus in the wilderness may feed him (1:13), they are not waiters, but attendants to the divine (compare Heb 1:14). W. D. Davies has argued that the word group *diakon-* is used to denote the special disciples who are close personal attendants and heirs of the teacher, like Joshua to Moses. He attributes this meaning to the verb in Mark 15:41 and interprets the words that offer the proof of or response to the miraculous cure of Peter's mother-in-law ("she began to serve them" [Mark 1:31]) as indicating her new commitment to this role. Thus this second miracle of Jesus in Mark's Gospel can be read as narrating a woman's call to discipleship at the Gospel's very beginning (1:29–31). It may be this story that inspires Luke's comment that the women followers had been cured by Jesus (8:2). In Mark, the noun *servant* or *minister* applies to the ideal disciple and leader (9:35; 10:43); the verb is used as a metaphor for the redemptive function of Jesus' death (10:45).

The NRSV translation "provided for" appears to have been influenced by Luke 8:1–3, which, in speaking of the women who follow Jesus, changes "him" to "them" and adds the words "out of their resources." This revision depicts the women disciples not as ministers of Jesus, but as a sort of women's auxiliary to the "twelve," providing financial and material support for the men.

In Mark, the unnamed women at the cross serve a double narrative function: they provide witnesses to the reality of Jesus' death and underline the failure of the male disciples, who have all fled. Malbon notes that the named women, who follow Jesus to burial and discover the empty tomb, are, like the men, "failed followers"; they run away in fear and tell no one (16:8). This supposed failure is remedied by the appendix to Mark referred to as the "longer ending of Mark" and sometimes printed as Mark 16:9–20; in it, Jesus appears to Mary Magdalene, and she carries the news to the other disciples, who refuse to believe it. But it seems most probable that the author of Mark meant to leave the Gospel's readers and hearers with the terror of these women, who, with their unnamed companions, had withstood the horrors of the crucifixion, proffering the example for those whom the Gospel invites to follow Jesus to the cross (8:34).

MARY ROSE D'ANGELO

SEE ALSO Part II: Unnamed Women at the Cross (Matt 27:55); (Luke 23:49).

FOR FURTHER READING: Davies, W. D. *The Setting of the Sermon on the Mount.*

Dewey, Joanna. "The Gospel of Mark."

Malbon, Elisabeth Struthers. "Fallible Followers: Women and Men in the Gospel of Mark."

LUKE 4:25–26
Widow of Zarephath

In the Synoptic Gospels, a saying of Jesus that a prophet is without honor in his own country is addressed to Jesus' hometown synagogue in Nazareth (it is also found in a different setting in the Gospel of John 4:44 and the noncanonical *Gospel of Thomas* 31). Mark and Matthew contain fairly similar accounts in which the people of Nazareth are offended by what they perceive to be Jesus' pretentions to authority, and their unbelief renders him unable to perform many miracles. Where Mark and Matthew contrast Jesus' reception in his hometown with his reception in other Jewish villages, Luke's much longer version recasts the encounter as a prototype of Jesus' rejection by Jews and his acceptance by Gentiles.

In Luke alone, Jesus uses two examples from Jewish Scripture as proof that prophets are unacceptable in their own countries: the unnamed widow of Zarephath, in Sidon (whose only son is raised from the dead by the prophet Elijah: 1 Kgs 17:1–16) and Naaman the Syrian (whom the prophet Elisha cures of leprosy in 2 Kgs 5:1–14; Elisha also raises the only son of a widow in 2 Kgs 4:18–37). Jesus points out that in both cases, there were widows and lepers in Israel, yet God sent prophets only to these two: Gentiles who both believed in the God of Israel after a prophet performed a miracle on their behalf.

The pairing of the two stories, one about a woman, the other about a man, is a well-known feature of the Gospel of Luke, which frequently adds the story about a woman to a narrative featuring only a man. Here, however, the author is probably responsible for the choice of both examples. Narratives involving widows are particularly characteristic of Luke-Acts (for example, Anna, Luke 2:36–38, 7:11–17, 18:2–5, Acts 6:1; Tabitha/Dorcas, Acts 9:36–42).

ROSS S. KRAEMER

SEE ALSO Part II: Widow of Zarephath (1 Kgs 17:8–24).
FOR FURTHER READING: D'Angelo, Mary Rose. "Women and Luke-Acts: A Redactional View."

LUKE 4:38
Mother-in-Law of Simon (Peter)

Luke's version of Jesus' healing of the mother-in-law of Simon is closer to Mark's narrative than is Matthew's. In Luke, as in Mark, the cure follows immediately after Jesus' preaching in the synagogue at Capernaum and after his exorcism of a demon from a possessed man (4:31–37). Whereas in Mark, Jesus has entered Simon's house with James and John, in Luke, unnamed others appear present in the house: "they" ask Jesus about the woman, who suffers from a high fever. In Mark, Jesus cures the woman by taking her hand and lifting her up, but in Luke, Jesus rebukes the fever verbally, and it departs. The recovered woman then serves an unspecified "them," presumably, but not definitely, including Jesus.

If Matthew alludes to concerns about the presence of other men in the house (perhaps because they are not the woman's relatives), Luke's version of the story may be understood to address the potential discomfort differently, by retaining the presence of others, but failing to identify them. Rendering these others as anonymous, though, suggests that Luke does not understand the woman's service (*diakoneō*) as a form of discipleship, but rather as an ordinary gesture of household responsibility and hospitality. Alternatively, it could be read as an intentional effort on Luke's part to undermine the interpretation of the woman's service as a gesture of discipleship.

That Jesus here cures the woman through a spoken rebuke might be seen as the author's desire to closely parallel the exorcism of the demon in the preceding verses. But such an explanation seems less than likely, given that, in the verses that follow immediately (4:40–41), Jesus continues to exorcise demons verbally while curing the sick by laying hands on them. Although it is impossible to confirm, concerns about propriety may have led the evangelist to refashion this scene. In any case, the Lukan version of this story shares with Mark and with Matthew intriguing implications for familial relationships in first-century Galilee.

ROSS S. KRAEMER

SEE ALSO Part II: Mother-in-Law of Peter (Simon) (Matt 8:14); Mother-in-Law of Simon (Peter) (Mark 1:30)

LUKE 7:11–17
Widow of Nain

Nain was a small village in Galilee about seven miles southeast of Nazareth. Luke tells us that Jesus traveled to Nain from Capernaum, where he had cured the slave of a Roman centurion. Before Jesus enters the village gates, he encounters a funeral procession. Luke relates the circumstances to show how pitiful the situation is. "A man who had died was being carried out" (v. 12), accompanied by his mother, a widow.

When a woman's husband died in first-century C.E. Jewish communities, the wife was designated a widow, a term with strict social/economic meaning. A "widow" was a woman no longer under the authority of a male, either her father or her deceased husband. Although Jewish law recognized that widows lived legitimately by their own authority, this freedom from male authority could leave a woman in a vulnerable social position. Jewish widows did not automatically or ordinarily receive the estates of their husbands, although their dowries would be returned to them, as specified in the marriage contract (*kĕtûbâ*). Widows were often victims of injustice and exploitation because of their marginal societal position, their age, and — more often than not — their poverty.

Biblical law commanded all Israelites to protect and support widows. Most often, daughters and sons took care of their widowed mothers. In the Bible, God is the ultimate protector of all the poor, including widows (Ps 41:1–3; Prov 19:17; Isa 41:17). Jewish communities took the care of widows seriously as part of fulfillment of the Law, and this is still reflected in Luke's Gospel. Ilan has recently explored the variety of ways in which widows were taken care of by both the community and through creative interpretation of the Law.

All these social dynamics are implicit in Luke's story of a widow burying her only son. There is also a strong allusion to Elijah's raising of the widow's son in Zarephath (1 Kgs 17:8–24). Jesus, like the prophet Elijah, has compassion for the widow and can reverse death.

Then Jesus does a strange thing. He commands the woman not to weep. How can a widow not weep for her dead son? With this command, Jesus himself changes within the scene. Before this, Luke depicts Jesus as one of the large crowd that makes up the funeral procession. Like all those present, he shows empathy for the widow. At this point, however, Luke moves Jesus into the role of "divine man," the miracle worker. His divine identity begins to unfold with his impossible command to the widow, "Do not weep" (v. 13).

The reader would expect the widow to react to Jesus with anger at such inane words. But Luke does not give anyone — the widow or the audience — the chance to respond. Immediately Jesus touches the bier and commands the man to rise. The young man obeys Jesus and begins to talk. Unlike Elijah, who calls on God to perform the resuscitation, Jesus literally takes over the role of God as life giver and protector of widows in this text. In the end, Jesus gives back to the widow her son, and with him, according to Seim, "her social security and sources of sustenance" (p. 214).

VASILIKI LIMBERIS

FOR FURTHER READING: Ilan, Tal. *Jewish Women in Greco-Roman Palestine.*

Seim, Turid Karlsen. *The Double Message: Patterns of Gender in Luke-Acts.*

LUKE 7:35   Woman Wisdom

SEE Woman Wisdom in the New Testament (Part III).

LUKE 7:36–50
Woman Who Anoints Jesus

Luke's story of a woman anointing Jesus differs in substance, detail, and function from the anointings in Mark, Matthew, and John. But it has influenced and sometimes determined not only the interpretation of the other three versions, but also the image of the famous disciple and resurrection witness, Mary Magdalene.

In Luke the anointing takes place at a meal in the house of Simon, who is designated not as "the leper" (Mark 14:3), but as "the Pharisee" (Luke 7:36). The woman is identified as a sinner, and her gesture, which consists of washing Jesus' feet with her tears, wiping them with her hair, anointing them with ointment, and kissing them, is both highly erotic and abject; it appears to indicate penitence (7:37–38). The host silently impugns the woman's character and questions Jesus' prophetic knowledge (7:39), thus allowing Jesus to demonstrate his ability to know hearts and a complex instruction on forgiveness, love, and hospitality. Jesus initiates this teaching by asking Simon to compare the case of two debtors (7:40–42); when Simon answers correctly that one forgiven more will love more (v. 43), Jesus offers the woman's ministrations as a contrast to Simon's reception of him and proclaims that because of her great love, her many sins are forgiven (v. 44–47). He then announces this forgiveness to the woman (v. 48), causing the other guests to question themselves about his identity (v. 49); he then dismisses the woman (v. 50).

In Luke the story is located early in the narrative, in a structural unit in which material from Q is interspersed with special Lukan material (7:1–8:21). One principle that seems to be at work in the section's construction is the alternating of an anecdote involving a male figure with one about a female figure. The cure of the centurion's servant is followed by the raising of the widow's son; a debate inspired by John the Baptist is followed by one inspired by a sinful woman. For Seim, this text is the prime example of the author's use of women characters to contrast with Luke's "Pharisees" (compare 7:29–30). The story is followed by a list of women followers juxtaposed to the twelve (8:1–3); this list introduces Mary Magdalene as one "from whom seven demons had gone out" and may have begun her identification with the sinful woman of the preceding story.

Schaberg believes that Luke revised Mark 14:1–11 to produce this story. If that is the case, the author dropped the location in Bethany, disconnected the story from Jesus' death, changed the woman from a prophet to a sinner, moved the anointing from Jesus' head to his feet, added the washing with tears and the drying with hair and the kisses, replaced an objection to waste with an objection to impropriety, and transformed a prophecy of messiahship, a prediction of death, and a work of mercy into a gesture of love and repentance. The author of John must then be assumed to have selected and combined details from the two other Gospels into a narrative in which an anointing of Jesus' feet becomes an anticipation of burial.

Corley postulates a single original anecdote closer to Luke in which a "public" woman (prostitute) anoints Jesus at a meal, the bystanders object, and Jesus affirms her deed. She suggests that Luke may have used both Mark's revised version and an older version. If so, the story has been revised to articulate and then rebut the charge of impropriety inherent in accepting the erotic ministrations of the woman, and to extend Luke's presentation of Jesus' message as one of *aphesis* — both release and forgiveness (see 4:18–19).

Few would question that Luke knew Mark 14:1–11; the betrayal narrative in Luke 22:1–5 appears to revise Mark 14:1–2 and 10–11. The author of Luke must at least have suppressed Mark's narrative and had at least two strong motives for doing so. First, apologetic concerns probably led the author to avoid the implication that Jesus accepted messianic anointing, thus eliminating any grounds for the political charge that Jesus claimed to be the messianic king (Luke 23:1–2). Second, the Gospel's prophetic Christology is likely to have inspired the author to cast Jesus, rather than the woman, as a prophet.

MARY ROSE D'ANGELO

SEE ALSO Part I: Mary 2; Mary 3; Part II: Woman Who Anoints Jesus (Matt 26:6–13); (Mark 14:3–9); (John 12:1–8).

FOR FURTHER READING: Corley, Kathleen. *Private Women, Public Meals: Social Conflict in the Synoptic Tradition.*

D'Angelo, Mary Rose. "Women in Luke-Acts: A Redactional View."

Schaberg, Jane. "Luke."

Seim, Turid Karlsen. *The Double Message: Patterns of Gender in Luke-Acts.*

LUKE 8:2–3
Unnamed Women Who Provide for the Jesus Movement

Important followers of Jesus are listed in catalogues such as that of Mark 3:13–19 or as members of a "select" group, as in Mark 9:2. In Luke 8:1–3 the list of women disciples names the most prominent and indicates the presence of "many others." Modern readers may be tempted to see the anonymity of these women as the author's attempt to mask their identities or minimize their importance. Several alternative explanations are possible. The author might have been concerned with ancient notions of propriety and politeness (ancient classical Greek social convention, for instance, frowned on even mentioning the names of respectable women in public, although this practice does not seem to have been as widespread in the first century C.E.). Neither oral nor written traditions may have preserved the women's names. In Luke-Acts, anonymity is hardly restricted to women. Numerous persons throughout the two-part work are unnamed, from these women to elite persons who join the nascent movement (for example, Acts 14:1ff; 17:4, 12) to prophets (Acts 11:27), opponents of Paul (Acts 15:1), and many others. Thus, in Luke-Acts, anonymity may be a literary device that here, and probably elsewhere, intends to suggest that those who joined the movement were often too many to list by name. Nevertheless, strategies like this frequently render ancient women invisible to modern readers.

How is the place of the women in the movement to be understood? Luke 8:1–9:50 describes an itinerant ministry in Galilee. The (anonymous) evangelist here introduces from Mark 14:50–51 (where the retrospective information comes as a surprise) a group called "the women," who appear again in Luke 23–24 and are mentioned finally in Acts 1:14. The history of the New Testament text reveals efforts to obliterate references to their ministries. In some ancient manuscripts, references to the women are removed or changed to "wives and children" (of the male disciples).

A characteristic of these women, not shared with male disciples, is that they had been "healed" of demon possession or illness, conditions that would have prevented the fulfillment of expected social roles and, possibly, isolated them through ritual impurity. Pertinent examples from Luke include Simon's mother-in-law (4:38–39), the woman with a continuous flow (8:43–48), the cripple of 13:10–17, and the "sinner" of 7:36–50. In no case are these beneficiaries said to have "followed Jesus."

These women, named and unnamed, are stated to have "ministered to" or "served them" (Jesus and the twelve) from their resources. Several factors are to be considered. These women may have been marginalized, but they had money. They are depicted as benefactors. Wealthy people of the Greco-Roman world did not pay substantial taxes, but they were expected to use their riches for the public good. In antiquity many services now performed by governmental agencies were the responsibility of the rich. Dedications of benefactions "from one's own resources" (compare Luke 8:3) were so common that the formula was reduced to initials. Benefactors expected honor in return for their gifts, in-

cluding civic resolutions and statues. In addition, they served as patrons of their beneficiaries, who were called clients. Clients were obliged to provide their patrons with both honor and service. The women of Luke 8:1–3 were both beneficiaries, clients of Jesus, and patrons of the movement. Honor and service were due to each party. One important fact of ancient social history is that wealthy women could, as benefactors, receive power and prestige otherwise not available to them. Religion, including cults other than the traditional civic veneration of gods such as Zeus and Athena, was one sphere in which women made benefactions.

Since most Christian communities were, for over a century, based in house churches, a predictable development would have been for leadership to reside in the patrons of these households (see Rom 16:1–2). In the long run the church did not adopt this option. One element of the rise of episcopal leadership was a separation between wealth-based patronage and power. A quite possibly intentional aspect of this development was the limitation of female leadership.

The women of Luke 8:1–3 are described as "ministering" to Jesus and the twelve. This verb (*diakoneō*, "serve") is the key element of Christian ministry (Luke 22:26–27). Women provide most of the positive examples (Luke 4:38–39; 7:36–50). On the other hand, readers of the Gospel can understand this as no more than traditional "women's work": marketing, cooking, serving, and washing up (although one might ask whether truly wealthy women would not have deputized their slaves to perform such tasks).

Scholars have reason to suspect that the evangelist or earlier sources have covered up a less traditional mode of ministry. These wealthy women are also described as members of Jesus' entourage. Some philosophers, Cynics among them, were also itinerants who traveled about with disciples, including women. Behind Luke 8:1–3 appears to lie a somewhat scandalous but not unthinkable tradition that the followers of Jesus included some relatively well-off women. The evangelist has clouded this tradition in two ways. On the one hand, their ministry is reduced to the concrete activity of menial service; on the other hand, the later role of female benefactors of house churches has somewhat awkwardly been retrojected into the life of Jesus (see Luke 10:38–42). By this means the evangelist has provided models for the wealthy women of his own day. The ministry of women has not been eliminated, but it has been circumscribed. They are to be benefactors but not patrons, active but not leaders. The married Sapphira is their antithesis. Most important, they represent healing as empowerment for ministry to others.

RICHARD I. PERVO

SEE ALSO Part I: Joanna; Martha; Mary 2; Mary 3; Sapphira; Susanna 2.

FOR FURTHER READING: Corley, Kathleen E. *Private Women, Public Meals: Social Conflict in the Synoptic Tradition.*

Johnson, Luke T. *The Literary Function of Possessions in Luke-Acts.*

Seim, Turid Karlsen. *The Double Message: Patterns of Gender in Luke-Acts.*

———. "The Gospel of Luke."

LUKE 8:41–42A, 49–56
Daughter of Jairus

Alone of the accounts of Jesus' healing of Jairus's daughter in the Synoptic Gospels, Luke notes that the girl is an "only daughter"; this suggests a comparison to the widow of Nain (a figure unique to Luke), whose "only son" has died (7:11–17 and see also 9:37–43). Luke also informs readers at the outset of the story that the girl is twelve years old (Matthew lacks the notice, and Mark places it at the end), makes clear that the child is dead, adds Jesus' assurance to the girl's parents, "She will be saved," and presents the command "Little girl, get up" only in the Greek (in Mark, it is also given in Aramaic.) Luke's presentation of the girl's parents may be compared to the account of Jesus' own family (8:19–21), who are "outside"; the girl compares to other

presentations of children (9:37–43, 46–48) in this section of the Gospel.

AMY-JILL LEVINE

SEE ALSO Part II: Daughter of Jairus (Matt 9:18–19, etc.); (Mark 5: 22–23, etc.); Widow of Nain (Luke 7:11–17).

LUKE 8:43–48
Woman with a Twelve-Year Hemorrhage

Like Mark, Luke combines the accounts of a hemorrhaging woman and a dead girl, connecting the stories through these motifs: references to "daughter," saving or being made well, twelve years, the presence of crowds, and the concern for secrecy. They emphasize the connection of Jairus's daughter and the bleeding woman even as they highlight distinctions between them. The woman appears in public, outside of any family context, possessing no authority; she approaches Jesus from behind rather than, as does Jairus, directly. She has been bleeding for twelve years from what is probably a uterine hemorrhage; the condition may suggest that she has been unable to have children. The daughter is represented by a "synagogue leader," is connected with a house, and has two parents concerned with her well-being. She is identified as twelve years old, that is, at marriageable age or on the verge of sexual development.

Unlike Mark's, Luke's version lacks the woman's interior monologue, the disciples' questioning of Jesus' perception, and the report of the woman's knowledge of her healing. Added is her confession "before all the people." Omitted in several early manuscripts is the comment "She had spent all she had on physicians." The shifts create a comparably stronger Christological emphasis.

Although often read in light of Levitical (Lev 15:19–30) and rabbinic commentary on vaginal bleeding and ritual purity, Luke shows no such interest. To the contrary, by mentioning that "no one could cure her," Luke emphasizes her physical, not her ritual, situation. Nor does the crowd avoid the woman, which would be expected if they, or anyone in Luke's audience, were concerned with ritual purity.

AMY-JILL LEVINE

SEE ALSO Part II: Woman with a Twelve-Year Hemorrhage (Matt 9:20–22); (Mark 5:25–34).

FOR FURTHER READING: Levine, Amy-Jill. "Discharging Responsibility: Matthean Jesus, Biblical Law and Hemorrhaging Women."

LUKE 8:49–56　　Daughter of Jairus

SEE LUKE 8:41–42, etc.　Daughter of Jairus (Part II).

LUKE 8:51–56
Wife of Jairus

After being summoned to heal a sick girl who has in fact died before his arrival, Jesus permits Peter, John, and James, along with the dead girl's father and mother, to witness her resuscitation. At the miracle, her parents are astonished (Mark suggests instead that all those present are amazed), yet Jesus commands them to keep the incident secret.

The reference to the mother breaks the parallel with the story of the widow of Nain in Luke 7:11–17, where only one parent (no father) is mentioned. But it is consistent with Luke's depiction of faithful mothers (Elizabeth [1:5–25, 39–45], Jesus' own mother, Mary, the widow of Nain [7:11–17], the widow of Zarephath [4:25–26]). Although Luke does not always make the point explicit, each woman faces the horror of a dead child, and for Jairus's wife and all except for Elizabeth, the child returns to life.

AMY-JILL LEVINE

SEE ALSO Part I: Elizabeth; Mary 1; Part II: Wife of Jairus (Mark 5:40–43); Widow of Zarephath (Luke 4:25–26); Widow of Nain (Luke 7:11–17).

LUKE 11:27–28
Woman Who Praises the Womb and Breasts of Jesus' Mother

This short pericope depicts a brave woman in the crowd who bursts out with praise for Jesus' mother. One imagines that the exuberant woman has been overwhelmed by what Jesus has just done: he has exorcized a demon from a mute person (11:14–26) and then offered a wise answer to the charge that his authority derives from Beelzebub. Rather than bless Jesus himself, she blesses the woman who bore him.

Yet the woman does not bless Jesus himself nor, to be precise, the mother of Jesus. Rather, in graphic terms, she praises individual organs — unique to a female — that gestate a fetus and then sustain the child after the birth. Jesus is only indirectly praised by this saying.

Jesus replies to the woman quickly, contradicting the terms of her blessing rather rudely. He retorts that those who hear and obey the word of God are the blessed. His reply rejects her joyful outburst, and the exchange ends.

This pericope has only one parallel, in the noncanonical *Gospel of Thomas* 79. Jesus' reply there is longer; he continues by stating, "Blessed are the womb that has not conceived and the breasts that have not given milk." It is likely that Luke separated this last sentence from 7:27–28, because it is found later in 23:29.

On a literal level, Jesus' reply in both texts is antifemale. It reduces the female person to her gestating body parts. Couldn't a mother be recognized by the songs she sang to her children, or the values she imparted, or the stories she told them? Jesus' reply also denies his own humanity and declines to accept praise of his mother. In both Luke and the *Gospel of Thomas,* the pericope points to an eschatological reevaluation of what is worthwhile in the reign of God, and what is not. The last phrase heralds an apocalyptic reversal of values, when birth — and by implication death — will end. In the *Gospel of Thomas,* if not Luke, this may allude to an anticipated reversal of the conditions depicted in Genesis 1–3, where both death and procreation come to characterize human existence.

VASILIKI LIMBERIS

SEE ALSO Part II: Women Lamenting Jesus (Luke 23:27–29).

LUKE 11:31
Queen of the South

The queen of Sheba (1 Kgs 10:1–13; 2 Chr 9:1–12), a Gentile from southwest Arabia, tests Solomon, is convinced of his wisdom, and consequently blesses God. She thus serves as a foil for the people of Jesus' own country (compare Luke 10:13–16). By juxtaposing the Sayings Source Q tradition about the queen with the "men of Nineveh," Luke takes care to include female and male figures, a characteristic feature of this author. By placing the statement about the queen in the context of 11:27, the account of the woman who blesses the womb and breasts of Jesus' mother, Luke indicates that the community of faith functions irrespective of gender.

AMY-JILL LEVINE

SEE ALSO Part II: Queen of the South (Matt 12:42).

LUKE 11:49   Woman Wisdom
SEE Woman Wisdom in the New Testament (Part III).

LUKE 12:53
Daughters and Daughters-in-Law Against Mothers and Mothers-in-Law

In a saying assigned to the Q source, Jesus teaches that he has come to bring not peace, but rather division. Among those set against each other are daughters and mothers, daughters-in-law and mothers-in-law. According to Luke, this intergenerational conflict goes in both directions, whereas Matthew indicates that the younger members of the household separate from the elder (see also Mic 7:6). The saying presupposes a patriarchal, patrilocal family, and it focuses on generational rather than gender-based division; perhaps the specific issue is the denial of funerary rites to family members (compare Luke 9:59–60; Matt 8:21–22).

AMY-JILL LEVINE

SEE ALSO Part II: Daughters and Daughters-in-Law Against Mothers and Mothers-in-Law (Matt 10:35).

LUKE 13:11–16
Woman Bent Over for Eighteen Years

The setting for this story, unique to Luke, is a synagogue on the Sabbath, where there appears a woman bent over for eighteen years, crippled by a "spirit," though later this is said to be the work of "Satan" (13:16). Jesus heals her with a healing word (v. 12: "you are set free") and by laying his hands on her. She responds by praising God. In v. 14 this conventional miracle story involving healing and exorcism turns into a story of controversy about the Sabbath. It pits the indignant leader of the synagogue, arguing about the issue of work on the Sabbath, against Jesus, who argues that the real issue is the freeing from bondage (compare Luke 4:18–19). This reflects the rabbinical mode of arguing from the lesser (ox, donkey) to the greater (woman, a daughter of Abraham).

This story illustrates the Lukan ambivalence toward the position of women in the church: on the one hand, the author of Luke multiplies the numbers of stories about women in this Gospel; on the other hand, he significantly restricts the roles in which women appear. This tension may reflect the importance of educating women converts through stories about women while restricting their participation to conventions considered acceptable by the more conservative elements in the imperial world.

The tension is visible in three aspects of the story. First, Luke 13:11–16 is part of a Lukan "pair," two brief stories, one about a male (14:1–6, the man who had dropsy) and one about a female, both with a similar function. This pattern of genderspecified pairing multiplies stories about women and includes them in an explicit way. However, it also distances and segregates women; women and men belong to the same community, but they are grouped apart from each other by gender. Second, the bent-over woman demonstrates the appropriate response to her healing by praising God. But she is primarily a passive figure of inaction typical of the women in Luke, who receive healing and exorcism without any antecedent action of their own. Third, Luke here provides the only New Testament evidence for the term "daughter of Abraham" (for the more common "son of Abraham," see Luke 19:9). By affirming her as a daughter of Abraham, he is recognizing that she shares in the blessing that is promised to Abraham's children — thus her Sabbath liberation. On the other hand, the healing presupposes that she *is* Abraham's daughter — not that she becomes Abraham's daughter as a consequence of it. It is not a statement about her piety, nor is it used to suggest that her behavior is exemplary and like Abraham's (as compared to the heroic mother and children whose behavior is compared to Abraham in 4 Macc 14:20; 15:28; 17:6; 18:20).

SARAH J. TANZER

FOR FURTHER READING: D'Angelo, Mary Rose. "Women in Luke-Acts: A Redactional View."
Seim, Turid Karlsen. "The Gospel of Luke."

LUKE 13:20–21
Woman with Leaven

Luke's version of a parable from the Sayings Source Q comparing the kingdom of God to yeast mixed with flour by a woman is virtually identical to that in Matthew (except that Matthew, characteristically, has "kingdom of Heaven"). The import of the parable may differ slightly from Matthew's version:

Luke's juxtaposed account of the mustard seed emphasizes growth, rather than reversal. Yeast operates by the process of decay; as such, it has negative connotations in Luke's culture (see Luke 12:1; Mark 8:15; 1 Cor 5:7; Gal 5:9). The woman's "hiding" the yeast may suggest an underhanded action; the verb is not typically used for descriptions of breadmaking. Nor was her hiding successful: she has produced 50 pounds of dough, which can yield enough bread for 150 people. Both evangelists, however, focus on the yeast rather than on the baker. Conversely, the noncanonical *Gospel of Thomas* compares the kingdom to the woman. The comparison may be ironic, as the juxtaposed saying (*Gospel of Thomas* 97), which also compares the kingdom to a woman, describes that woman as unaware.

AMY-JILL LEVINE

SEE ALSO Part II: Women Mixing Flour with Leaven (Matt 13:33).

LUKE 14:26
Mother (and Father), Wife (and Children), and Sisters (and Brothers) to Be Hated by Jesus' Disciples

In a saying taken from the Sayings Source Q, Luke's Jesus tells large crowds traveling with him that his disciples must hate their blood relatives. Luke likely added "wife" to the list of those replaced by the kinship group gathered in Jesus' name, although it is possible that Matthew omitted it. Luke 18:29b also adds "wife" to Mark 10:29b. A reference to "wives" is consistent with 1 Cor 7:29. To forgo family ties, particularly in a culture in which the extended family is the primary social unit, would be a drastic action, but one not completely anomalous in either Jewish or Greek contexts.

AMY-JILL LEVINE

SEE ALSO Part II: Mothers and Daughters (and Fathers and Sons) Not to Be Loved More Than Jesus (Matt 10:37).

Luke 15:8–10
Woman Sweeping to Find a Lost Coin

The pericope of the woman and the lost coin comes in the middle of Luke's repentance chapter. It is sandwiched between the lost sheep and the prodigal son. Only the lost sheep parable also appears in Matthew; the other two are exclusive to Luke. This pericope teaches how precious each person is in God's eyes and how repentance requires human and divine synergistic participation. God searches for lost human beings, while they, in turn, find their way back to God.

The parable's unnamed woman possesses money — ten coins — so she could be either enslaved or free. We do not hear of her marital status. If a widow, she would have been entitled to the repayment of her dowry, as specified in her *kĕtûbâ* (marriage contract). It would also be likely that members of her family or the local community would be supporting her in some fashion. Her husband's estate probably would have gone to his sons, although Ilan's recent study has shown that there were a variety of ways to interpret ancient Jewish inheritance laws. If the woman is married, the ten coins may be under her authority, as it would be her responsibility to run the household. In either case, she may have earned the money herself, selling garden produce or textiles she has made.

The woman is careful. To find the lost coin, she expends time, energy, and money (in the form of oil for the lamp). Finally, we know that she lives in a community of friends and neighbors, on whom she can call and with whom she can rejoice.

Luke uses the pericope as an instructional wisdom saying. In Luke's Gospel, Jesus shows by analogy what God's role is in repentance. As such, the woman is analogous to God.

VASILIKI LIMBERIS

FOR FURTHER READING: Ilan, Tal. *Jewish Women in Greco-Roman Palestine.*

Seim, Turid Karlsen. *The Double Message: Patterns of Gender in Luke-Acts.*

LUKE 15:30
Prostitutes

In Luke 15:1–2, tax collectors and persons simply called "sinners" are drawn to Jesus, causing his Pharisaic opponents to complain that Jesus welcomes such persons and takes meals with them. In response, Jesus tells three parables, each illustrating that the repentance of a sinner is more highly valued than the righteousness of those who do not sin. In the second of these, the famous parable of the prodigal son (Luke 15:11–32), the formerly dissolute but now repentant younger son is accused by his older brother of having squandered his father's livelihood on prostitutes.

Although Christian traditions have long associated Jesus with prostitutes, this is the only explicit mention of prostitutes in the Gospel of Luke, and it is unconnected with the activities of Jesus himself. Corley points out that this traditional association is based in part on the assumption that prostitutes are included under the more general rubric of "sinners" in traditions portraying Jesus as eating with "tax collectors and sinners" (for example, Luke 15:1–2). In fact, nowhere in the Gospels does Jesus ever eat with a woman identified explicitly as a prostitute. Further, contrary to ancient and popular tradition, nowhere in the Gospels is Mary Magdalene ever identified as a prostitute, nor for that matter any individual woman associated with the Jesus movement.

Prostitutes figure nowhere in the Gospel of Mark. In the Gospel of Matthew, however, Jesus concludes a different parable of two sons with the observation that tax collectors and prostitutes, who believed John the Baptist, are going into the kingdom of God ahead of the chief priests and elders in the temple in Jerusalem, who did not (Matt 21:31–32). Such a tradition comes closer to associating Jesus with prostitutes, but as Corley observes, in Matthew, prostitutes and tax collectors are presented as exemplifying the superior faith of socially marginal and disreputable persons in contrast to that of the religious elite. The mention of prostitutes should not necessarily be taken as evidence for their actual presence in the Jesus movement.

Ross S. Kraemer

See also Part II: Prostitutes (Matt 21:31–32); Prostitute (1 Cor 6:15–16).

For further reading: Corley, Kathleen. "Prostitute."

LUKE 16:18
Divorced Wife

The New Testament appears to preserve several different ancient traditions about Jesus' teaching on divorce, including (1) Mark 10:2–12 and Matt 19:3–9, (2) 1 Cor 7:10–11, and (3) Matt 5:31–32 and Luke 16:18. Many scholars attribute this last tradition to the Sayings Source Q.

Both Mark and Matthew include traditions in which Jesus explicitly prohibits divorce: in Mark, the prohibition is absolute, whereas in Matthew, Jesus allows for an exception in cases of *porneia* (a term often understood to connote adultery that probably also encompasses marriages deemed incestuous according to Lev 18:6–18, and perhaps also marriages with persons outside of the community). Nowhere in the Gospel of Luke (nor in the Gospel of John, for that matter) does Jesus explicitly prohibit divorce per se.

Rather, Luke 16:18 presents Jesus as prohibiting divorce and remarriage together. Thus, a man who divorces his wife commits adultery against her by remarrying, although he presumably would not have committed adultery against her by simply marrying an additional wife (which Luke nowhere opposes). Divorced female followers of Jesus are not allowed to remarry, which may have caused them economic difficulty. If Luke knew the divorce prohibition in Mark, his omission of it, together with his representation of Jesus as forbidding remarriage but not explicitly divorce, may suggest that a rigid prohibition of divorce was not viewed as feasible in the community or communities for which the author wrote. Nevertheless, it is also

worth observing that the only explicitly legal passage in the Hebrew Bible that deals with divorce, Deut 24:1–4, is also concerned not with divorce per se, but with remarriage: it prohibits a man who has divorced his wife from remarrying her if she has married again after the divorce (regardless of whether her subsequent husband has died or divorced her).

Bernadette J. Brooten

See also Part II: Woman Being Divorced (Deut 24:1–4, etc.); Divorced Wife (Matt 5:31–32); (Matt 19:3–9); (Mark 10:2–12); Married Women (and Men), Unmarried Women (and Men), and Women (and Men) Married to Unbelievers (1 Corinthians 7).

LUKE 17:32
Wife of Lot

In a discourse on the coming of the reign of God (17:22–37), Jesus describes it as an instantaneous event that will overtake people by surprise, as did the destruction of Sodom in the days of Lot. Hence Jesus' followers should be indifferent to worldly pursuits, and there should be no looking back. "Remember Lot's wife!" (v. 32).

This warning, referring to Gen 19:26 (where Lot's wife did look back and became a pillar of salt), is found only in Luke; it is lacking in the parallel sections of Matthew and Mark and is, therefore, probably an addition by Luke. It is consistent with that author's tendency to include examples of women not found in other synoptic narratives. Other examples include Luke 7:11–17 (the widow of Nain), Luke 13:11–16 (the woman bent over for eighteen years), Luke 15:8–10, (the woman sweeping to find the lost coin), and Luke 18:25 (the widow pleading with the judge).

Pieter W. van der Horst

See also Part II: Wife of Lot (Gen 19:15–16, etc.).

LUKE 17:35
Two Women Grinding Meal

In Luke 17:22–37, Jesus gives his disciples numerous examples of what it will be like on the day the Son of Man is revealed. Luke pairs two men reclining to dine (probably on a dining couch, though the NRSV translates it "in a bed"; see *Gospel of Thomas* 61) with two women grinding meal; in Matt 24:42, the men are described as "in the field." This pairing, likely originating in the Sayings Source Q, is repeated in (Q) accounts of the man's lost sheep and the woman's lost coin (Luke 15:4–10); the man who plants a mustard seed and the woman who hides yeast in dough (Luke 13:19–21); and the "queen of the South" and the "people [men] of Nineveh" (Luke 11:31–32). In sayings on family construction, there are those (men) who marry and those (women) who are given in marriage (Luke 17:27). Also applicable is, perhaps, Luke (Q) 12:27; the (feminine) lilies that do not spin are compared to the (masculine) ravens, who neither "sow nor reap [and] have neither storehouse nor barn." Unique to Luke are the pairings of Naaman and the widow of Zarephath (4:25–27) and the couples in the infancy accounts.

These pairs may indicate an attempt to address both men and women. Conversely, they may reflect conventional legal formulations. If Luke 17:34–35 has social rather than simply illustrative implications, then it may indicate dismissal rather than enforcement of egalitarian meal practices even as it acknowledges women's contribution to the table.

AMY-JILL LEVINE

SEE ALSO Part II: Two Women Grinding Meal (Matt 24:41).

LUKE 18:2–5
Widow Pleading with a Judge

In a parable unique to Luke and startling for its candor, a widow pleads with a judge about a concern that is not specified. Rather than draw on the audience's empathy or good conscience, the parable makes its point through examples of injustice and annoyance.

Luke reverses audience expectations in this pericope. This judge is an arrogant misanthropist, not a wise man of beneficent power. By implication he jeers at the biblical prescription for judges: fairness and fear of God (Deut 1:16–17; 2 Chr 19:7). Twice the parable repeats the judge's words: "I have no fear of God and no respect for anyone" (v. 4).

Although we are not told if the widow is needy, given the fact that she has taken a case to court and, as Seim has pointed out, that there is so much concern for the care of widows in contemporaneous Jewish writings, it is not far-fetched to say that Luke is playing on the stereotype of the "poor widow." Her apparently vulnerable situation is exacerbated by such a horrible judge.

But the parable reverses the dynamics of power by pointing out the judge's vulnerability and the widow's strength: her persistence. She ignores his refusal, hounding him for the decision she desires. The judge cannot bear to be continually annoyed by her bothersome pleading. In the end he relents, and she wins.

VASILIKI LIMBERIS

FOR FURTHER READING: Ilan, Tal. *Jewish Women in Greco-Roman Palestine.*

Seim, Turid Karlsen. *The Double Message: Patterns of Gender in Luke-Acts.*

LUKE 18:20
Mother (and Father) to Be Honored

In Luke (18:18–23), Mark (10:17–22), and Matthew (19:16–22), a wealthy man asks Jesus what he must do to inherit eternal life. Jesus responds that the man must observe certain commandments, including the commandment to honor one's mother and father.

This is the only time in the Gospel of Luke that Jesus cites this commandment; the Gospels of Mark and Matthew also contain a dispute between Jesus and some of his opponents in which this commandment figures prominently. This disputational story is part of a larger collection of synoptic material sometimes known as the "Great Omission," since it is present in Mark (6:45–8:27, with parallels in Matthew), but absent in Luke. The author of Luke might have intentionally omitted it, but many scholars think it possible that he used a version of Mark differing from the subsequent, canonical manuscripts.

Ross S. Kraemer

SEE ALSO Part II: Women in the Decalogue (Exod 20:8, etc.); Mother (and Father) to Be Honored (Matt 19:19); (Mark 7:10–13); (Mark 10:19); (Eph 6:2–3).

LUKE 18:29–30
Wife Left for the Sake of the Kingdom of God

In Luke, as in Mark 10:29–30 (and Matt 19:29), Jesus follows his admonition to the rich man (to leave all his possessions and follow Jesus) with a private teaching to his disciples that those who leave families and households to follow him will receive back, many times over, what they have renounced. Where the list of those left in both Mark and Matthew includes brothers (*adelphous*) and sisters (*adelphas*), Luke's Jesus names instead wife (*gynaika*) and brothers (*adelphous*).

Whether this difference reflects an intentional revision on the part of the author or another version of the tradition is difficult to determine. As translated in the NRSV, Luke 18:29 strongly implies that those who join the Jesus movement are male, and further implies that such men might have divorced their wives in order to do so. Given the strong early traditions that Jesus opposed divorce (it appears already in 1 Cor 7:10–11, as well as in Mark and Matthew), Luke 18:29 may be understood in several ways. It might be a very early form of this saying of Jesus that itself suggests that the anti-divorce sayings do not originate with Jesus (emanating instead from early Christian prophets). Al-

ternatively, especially since Luke alone of the Synoptic Gospels does not explicitly have Jesus oppose divorce, Luke may have revised the Markan saying here without worrying about possible implications for Christian stances on divorce. If Luke's version of this saying is his own, its intention may well be to recast the early Jesus movement as one in which men, but not women, leave their homes, consistent with Luke's general representation of Christian women as conforming to ancient Greco-Roman norms of gender propriety.

Ross S. Kraemer

SEE ALSO Part II: Divorced Wife (Matt 5:31–32); (Matt 19:3–9); (Mark 10:2–12); (Luke 16:18); Mothers and Sisters Left for the Sake of Jesus' Name (Matt 19:29); Sisters and Mothers Left for Jesus' Sake (Mark 10:29–30).

FOR FURTHER READING: D'Angelo, Mary Rose. "Remarriage and the Divorce Sayings Attributed to Jesus."

LUKE 20:27–36
Woman Married to Seven Brothers in Succession

The woman with seven husbands in succession is a hypothetical character in a story told by the Sadducees, a Jewish priestly group who do not believe in the resurrection. Luke's version follows Mark's fairly closely, but the Lukan Jesus sets up more directly a contrast between "those who belong to this age" (v. 34) who marry and those who have "a place in that age" (v. 35) who don't.

Elizabeth Struthers Malbon

SEE ALSO Part II: Woman Married to Seven Brothers in Succession (Matt 22:23–30); (Mark 12:18–25).

LUKE 21:1–4
Poor Widow Giving Two Copper Coins

The story of the poor widow who puts two small copper coins in the temple treasury occurs in a somewhat similar narrative context in Luke and in Mark (and not at all in Matthew and John). As part of his teaching in the temple (Luke 19:47–21:4), Jesus observes the poor widow's action and calls it to the attention of his disciples. Her generosity contrasts not only with the behavior of the rich people giving donations (21:1) but also with that of the greedy scribes (19:45–47). Whereas Mark's Gospel gives end stress to the poor widow's giving of "her whole life" and thus opens up (and then develops narratively) a metaphorical parallel with Jesus' own self-giving death, Luke's Gospel ends more concretely with "she put in all she had to live on" (21:4). Since the value of the poor and the demand for generosity, especially among the rich, is a dominant theme in Luke, the poor widow who gives all is among both the blessed (like poor Lazarus, 16:19–31) and the exemplary (like Zacchaeus, who pledges to give to the poor, 19:1–10).

ELIZABETH STRUTHERS MALBON

SEE ALSO Part II: Poor Widow Giving Two Copper Coins (Mark 12:41–44).

LUKE 21:23
Women Pregnant or Nursing at the End of the Age

In all three Synoptic Gospels, following his prediction of the destruction of the temple in Jerusalem, Jesus is asked when this will happen and what signs will accompany it.

Luke's version of Jesus' reply differs significantly from the other two Synoptics, focusing on the destruction of Jerusalem itself rather than the broad apocalyptic scenarios of Mark and Matthew. Its prediction that the populace of Jerusalem will die or be taken into captivity is likely to be evidence that the Gospel was written after the actual enslavement of many Jews following the First Jewish Revolt of 66–73 C.E. Luke retains Jesus' saying that the distress of the fall of Jerusalem will be especially hard for pregnant women and nursing mothers. This Gospel lacks, however, the image shared by Mark (13:8) and Matthew (24:8) of the end as a

birthing process. Luke has also apparently moved the material in Mark 13:15–16 to an earlier discourse on the coming of the reign of God (17:31).

Both Mark and Matthew place Jesus' saying about pregnant and nursing women immediately following instructions to members of the nascent Christian movement, suggesting that such women are part of this community. Luke's reshaping of this material to focus on the destruction of Jerusalem makes it less likely that these women are to be understood as believers. Instead, they are simply among the inhabitants of Jerusalem slaughtered and enslaved as a result of the war.

The saying about pregnant and nursing women may illuminate a scene found only in Luke (23:27–31), where women beating their breasts and wailing in anticipated mourning follow Jesus on the way to his crucifixion. Jesus tells them to weep for themselves and their children, predicting that the day will soon come when "they will say, 'Blessed are the barren, and the wombs that never bore, and the breasts that never nursed'" (23:29), a prediction that refers to the fall of Jerusalem. Implicit in this second saying may be the same notion that the coming tribulation will be far easier on childless women.

ROSS S. KRAEMER

SEE ALSO Part II: Women Pregnant or Nursing at the End of the Age (Matt 24:19); (Mark 13:17); Women Lamenting Jesus (Luke 23:27–29)

LUKE 22:56–57
Servant-Girl Who Accuses Peter

A brief encounter between a servant-girl and Peter is part of a larger Lukan narrative segment, presumably adapted from Mark, that positions Peter's denial as a prelude to Jesus' appearance before the Jewish council. Luke shares the two contrasting scenes with Mark but does not interweave them. Oddly, the servant-girl (*whose* servant is not stated, although the setting is the high priest's house) stares at Peter but speaks more publicly to the bystanders. Predictably (see 22:31–34), Peter denies what she — and two nonspecific others — assert, ironically foreshadowing in his second negation ("Man, I am not"; 22:58) Jesus's affirmation to the high priest ("You say that I am"; 22:70). At cockcrow Jesus looks at Peter, eliciting from him a flood of remembrance and tears (22:61–62).

ELIZABETH STRUTHERS MALBON

SEE ALSO Part II: Two Servant-Girls Who Accuse Peter (Matt 26:69–72); Servant-Girl, of the High Priest, Who Accuses Peter (Mark 14:66–69); Woman Who Guards the Gate of the High Priest (John 18:15–17).

LUKE 23:27–29
Women Lamenting Jesus

As Jesus approaches Golgotha, Luke tells us that the women in the crowd begin the ritual lament. This kind of mourning, beating the breast and wailing, is reported in Zech 12:10 and Jer 9:19. Luke turns the lament into an occasion for Jesus to warn the women about the ensuing cataclysmic disaster. Throughout Luke, the city of Jerusalem is presented as a place of foreboding and trouble (11:49–50; 13:34–35; 19:41–44). Although he does not specifically say here that the city will be destroyed in the coming apocalypse, he calls the lamenting women, collectively, "daughters of Jerusalem," not daughters of Israel. He enjoins them to cry over their own lives and those of their children.

Next Luke recontextualizes this saying of Jesus, also found in the extracanonical *Gospel of Thomas*; in that text, it comes directly after the blessing of Jesus' mother. Luke has Jesus proclaim these words to the women at this moment, thereby particularizing the apocalyptic prophecy to their own situation as women in Jerusalem. By context the reader knows that Jerusalem's fate is to be so horrible that, by comparison, the curse of being childless will appear to be a blessing. These are potent, terrifying words.

Luke has made this saying of Jesus more focused and more powerful than it is in the *Gospel of Thomas*. He has used it to show Jesus addressing women in a most stressful situation — on the road to the crucifixion. Women play a major role in Luke's Gospel. Elizabeth and Mary open the Gospel of Luke with their cooperation in miraculously bearing sons. Now in the midst of Jesus' ignominious arrest, trial, and impending crucifixion, Luke has the women take center stage again.

VASILIKI LIMBERIS

SEE ALSO Part II: Woman Who Praises the Womb and Breasts of Jesus' Mother (Luke 11:27–28).

LUKE 23:49
Unnamed Women at the Cross

The Gospel of Luke follows Mark in mentioning a group of women at the cross. But unlike Mark, this author describes the women as accompanying "all his acquaintances." This appears to have a double effect. Whereas in Mark, all the male disciples flee when Jesus is arrested, Luke avoids mentioning their flight (see 22:53–54, 62) and in fact reverses it by bringing all Jesus' acquaintances to the cross. Introducing this note not only absolves the male disciples of the cowardice Mark attributes to them, but also supplements the women of Mark 15:40–41 with male witnesses. This is both an apologetic move, defending the community and the book against the charge of testimony based only on women, and a result of the author's literary and political preference for pairing references to women with references to men. None of the women are named, nor are they described as having been followers and ministers in Galilee (as at least some are in Mark 15:41), but as having followed along with him from Galilee. Presumably these women are to be identified with the women of 8:1–3, a list of famous women disciples that refers to many women who are described as benefactors.

Unnamed women also appear at the burial of Jesus (Luke 23:55–56), at the discovery of the empty tomb (24:1–3), and indeed after the ascension, praying for the coming of the spirit with the twelve and the mother and sisters of Jesus (Acts 1:14). Only after the discovery of the empty tomb (24:1–9) does the author give the names of three women (Mary Magdalene, Joanna, and Mary the mother of James 24:10–11); apparently their presence is implied not only at 24:1, but also in 23:55–56 and at the cross in 23:49. But in comparison with their source in Mark, the roles of the women at the cross whether as witnesses, as disciples, or as examples of endurance to the cross, have been diminished in Luke's account.

Mary Rose D'Angelo

SEE ALSO Part I: Joanna; Mary 3; Mary 4; Part II: Unnamed Women at the Cross (Matt 27:55); (Mark 15:40–41).

FOR FURTHER READING: D'Angelo, Mary R. "Women in Luke-Acts: A Redactional View".

Schaberg, Jane. "Luke."

LUKE 24:10; 22–24
Women at the Tomb of Jesus

> SEE LUKE 23:49 Unnamed Women at the Cross (Part II).

LUKE 24:13–35
Unnamed Companion of Cleopas

In this first resurrection appearance narrated in the Gospel of Luke, Jesus appears to two "of them" (v. 13) traveling to the village of Emmaus outside Jerusalem. The antecedent for *them* is ambiguous: clearly, followers of Jesus are intended, including the women who earlier discovered the empty tomb of Jesus (Luke 24:1–7, 22–23). Equally clearly, the group designated "the eleven" is not (see Luke 24:33–35, where these two relate their experience to the "eleven" and their companions). One of these two persons is a man named Cleopas. The gender and name of the other person are never specified. Although traditional interpretation has always taken this second person to be a man, some scholars have recently suggested that this unidentified person may be understood as the female half of a female-male missionary couple. Paul's letters attest to the existence of missionary pairs composed of a

woman and a man (see especially Romans 16 for examples). Such couples may have been married (such as Priscilla and Aquila, described in Acts 18:2 as married, although Paul, in Rom 16:3, is silent on their marital status) or perhaps represented themselves as such for reasons of propriety (this is one way to understand the term "sister-wife" of 1 Cor 9:5).

If this resurrection narrative, unique to Luke, is the author's own construction, asking about the unnamed person's gender is essentially asking why the author might intentionally mask the gender of this person in a resurrection appearance of his own creation — a difficult question to answer. If, however, Luke here incorporates (and undoubtedly shapes) older material, this story may reflect an early tradition of a resurrection appearance to a man named Cleopas and his female companion. Masking the female identity of the second person might then be seen as consistent with Luke's representation of resurrection appearances. Whereas the Gospels of both Matthew and John assign the first appearance of the resurrected Jesus to women (Mary Magdalene and "the other Mary" in Matt 28:9–10; Mary Magdalene alone in John 20:11–17), the Gospel of Luke presents a chronologically ambiguous narrative (does Jesus appear to Simon before or after the appearance to the two? — see Luke 24:33–34) that may intend to privilege the appearance to Simon. In any case it contains no explicit appearances to individual women. This may also have some connection with Luke's exclusion of women from the twelve in Acts 1:21.

Ross S. Kraemer

SEE ALSO Part I: Mary 3; Mary 5; Prisca/Priscilla; Part II: Sister/Wife Who Accompanies Apostles Other Than Paul (1 Cor 9:5).

JOHN 2:3–12
Mother of Jesus

Although the Gospels of Mark, Matthew, and Luke all name the mother of Jesus Mary, the author of the Gospel of John never identifies her by name.

She appears only twice in John, here and at the crucifixion (19:25–7) where Jesus entrusts her to the care of another famous anonymous figure, the beloved disciple; she is alluded to in 6:42, but not actually present in the narrative.

ROSS S. KRAEMER

SEE ALSO Part I: Mary 1.

JOHN 4:7–42
Samaritan Woman

John 4 describes the encounter between Jesus and a Samaritan woman. The setting is a well in the Samaritan city of Sychar, at which Jesus rests on his way from Jerusalem to Galilee. While his disciples go to the city to buy food (4:8), Jesus requests a drink of the Samaritan woman (4:7). This request initiates a lengthy theological dialogue concerning the contrast between well water, which must be drawn daily, and the living water of eternal life provided by Jesus (4:14). Also discussed is the nature of true worship, which, Jesus emphasizes, focuses neither on Jerusalem, as the Jews believe, nor on Mount Gerizim, as the Samaritans believe, but on the Father, who must be worshipped in spirit and truth. The Samaritan woman receives Jesus' words, requests the living water of which he speaks, and expresses her expectation that the messiah is coming, who "will proclaim all things to us" (4:25). In response, Jesus proclaims his identity: "I am he, the one who is speaking to you" (4:26).

After the disciples return, the woman leaves her water jar, for which she presumably has no further use, and returns to the city. There she urges the people to "Come and see" (4:29) Jesus, who may be the messiah. The people respond to her testimony, come to stay with Jesus for two days, and declare "this is truly the Savior of the world" (4:42).

Perhaps the most puzzling aspect of the story is Jesus' description of the woman's lifestyle: she has had five husbands, and her current mate is not her husband. Although some have interpreted this description symbolically, equating the five husbands

with the five books of the Torah, it may be more natural to read it as a reflection of the stereotype that Samaritan women are impure and immoral (compare 4:7, 27). Clearly, gender is not incidental to the story but central to it, as the disciples indicate when they marvel that Jesus is talking to a woman (4:27). The story may intend to stress that Jesus does not consider himself bound by traditional boundaries of gender, religion, and ethnicity, or, indeed, by related stereotypes. Such a reading would be consistent with the structure of the story itself, which recalls the biblical well-scene, in which the groom, or his substitute, meets the future bride at a well. The story frustrates the usual expectations by referring to her ambiguous marital status and by showing Jesus as offering a liaison of a divine sort, implicitly superior to the human betrothal central to Genesis 24 (Rebekah and Isaac), Genesis 29 (Rachel and Jacob), and Exodus 2 (Zipporah and Moses).

Interpreters suggest that the passage may allude to a Johannine mission to the Samaritans, to various aspects of Samaritan theology, or to the inclusion of Samaritan converts in the Johannine community. Some feminist historiographers read the Samaritan woman's active proclamation of her still tentative faith as evidence for women preachers and apostles in the early church.

ADELE REINHARTZ

SEE ALSO Part II: Samaritan Women (and Men) Baptized by Philip (Acts 8:12).

JOHN 8:3–11
Adulterous Woman

The stylistic features of this passage and its presence in some manuscripts of Luke indicate that it originally circulated separately from the Fourth Gospel. A confrontation between Jesus and the scribes and Pharisees over the stoning of a woman caught in the act of adultery (8:3) is resolved when Jesus challenges anyone who is without sin to throw the first stone (8:7). The crowd departs, leaving Jesus alone with the woman. Ascertaining that no one has condemned her, Jesus sends her on her way, asking only that she not sin again (8:11).

According to Lev 20:10 and Deut 22:22, stoning is the punishment for those convicted of adultery. It is unclear whether the woman has already been judged within a Jewish court, or whether such a court would have had the right to carry out capital punishment in the first century C.E. Also uncertain is whether the Jewish authorities are on the verge of taking the law into their own hands, or whether they are submitting the case to Jesus for decision. Absent from the story is her partner, who, if the woman is married, would also have been an adulterer.

The story focuses on the contrast between the judgmental behavior of the scribes and Pharisees and the compassion and mercy of Jesus. The former, who, like all human beings, are not without sin, were prepared to condemn the woman for *her* sin, whereas Jesus, who, in the subsequent view of the church, is the only sinless one, releases her with a word.

ADELE REINHARTZ

SEE ALSO Part II: Adulteress (and Adulterer) (Lev 20:10, etc.).

JOHN 9:2–3, 18–23
Mother of a Blind Son

In its story of Jesus' restoration of a man's eyesight, John 9 refers obliquely to the blind man's mother. In 9:2–3 Jesus' disciples wonder whether the man's blindness is a consequence of his sin or the sin of his parents. Jesus responds that his condition is not due to sin; rather, "he was born blind so that God's works might be revealed in him" (9:3).

John 9:18–23 describes the attempts of "the Jews" to cross-examine the parents as to the manner in which their son was healed. The parents resist this attempt, declaring that they know only that he was healed. They direct inquiries as to the manner of his healing to the man himself: "Ask him; he is of age. He will speak for himself" (9:21). The narrator at-

tributes their hesitation to their fear "of the Jews; for the Jews had already agreed that anyone who confessed Jesus to be the Messiah would be put out of the synagogue" (John 9:22). This passage is one of the bases of the current consensus that this Gospel should be read on two levels, as a story of Jesus and as the story of the Johannine community. Because expulsion from the synagogue is anachronistic to the time of Jesus, 9:22 is taken as evidence that Johannine Christians were expelled from the synagogue. This expulsion is seen to reflect the actual experience of the earliest readers of the Gospel and to provide at least part of the context for the negative portrayal of Jews in the Fourth Gospel.

The blind man's mother does not appear as a separate character but is included along with the man's father in the references to his parents. This mode of reference may stem from the story's source or the history of its transmission. In the Johannine context, this female parent, who fears the consequences of faith, contrasts with the other Johannine women, all of whom are believers in and followers of Jesus. The indirectness of her portrayal draws attention away from her specific identity and hence does not disturb the Johannine pattern of positive representation of women characters.

ADELE REINHARTZ

JOHN 12:1–8
Woman Who Anoints Jesus

The story of a woman anointing Jesus with expensive perfumed ointment occurs in all four gospels. In the Synoptic Gospels (Mark, Matthew, and Luke), the woman is anonymous, but in John, she is identified with Mary the sister of Martha and Lazarus.

ROSS S. KRAEMER

SEE ALSO Part I: Mary 2; Part II: Woman Who Anoints Jesus (Matt 26:6–13); (Mark 14:3–9); (Luke 7:36–50).

JOHN 12:15 Daughter of Zion
SEE Daughter of Zion (Part III).

Woman in Labor

The pain and subsequent joy of the birthing woman is used as a figure for the disciples' suffering at Jesus' death, followed by their joy at his resurrection. The eschatological meaning of the figure is indicated by its context, by the figurative usage of this motif in Rev 12:2–5 and Isa 66:7–10, and by the references to suffering as a prelude to the eschatological times in Dan 12:1 (Greek); Zeph 1:14–15; Hab 3:16, Mark 13:19,24; and Rom 2:9. Though it may be tempting to identify the woman with Jesus' mother Mary, this is not warranted by the context, in which the incarnation of Jesus does not appear.

ADELE REINHARTZ

SEE ALSO Part III: Woman in Labor Clothed with the Sun (Rev 12:2–5).

A terra-cotta midwife's sign from the port of Ostia, outside Rome, depicting two midwives assisting the delivery of a woman seated on a birthing chair. See Woman in Labor (John 16:21).

JOHN 18:15–17
Woman Who Guards the Gate of the High Priest

A brief encounter between a woman who guards the gate of the courtyard of the high priest and Peter is part of a larger Johannine narrative segment, generally parallel with the Synoptic Gospels, that interweaves Jesus' appearance before Annas and Caiaphas, the high priest, and Peter's denial. The woman questions Peter as she allows him in at the request of another disciple known to the high priest. Predictably (13:36–38), Peter denies that he is a disciple of Jesus, not only to her but to two others, ironically foreshadowing in his first and second negations ("I am not"; 18:17; 18:25) Jesus' affirmation to Caiaphas ("You say that I am a king"; 18:37).

Like the servant-girl Rhoda, who is stunned to find Peter at the door (having been freed from prison by an angel; Acts 12:6–17), the word of the woman who guards the gate of the high priest is disputed. The one gate guard is questioned by Peter when she accuses him of following Jesus; the other (Rhoda) is disbelieved by other followers of Jesus

when she announces Peter's presence. Their low social status makes them easy to dismiss — except by the readers, who know they speak the truth!

ELIZABETH STRUTHERS MALBON

SEE ALSO Part II: Two Servant-Girls Who Accuse Peter (Matt 26:69–72); Servant-Girl, of the High Priest, Who Accuses Peter (Mark 14:66–69); Servant-Girl Who Accuses Peter (Luke 22:56–57).

JOHN 19:25
Sister of Jesus' Mother

This verse is ambiguous about whether three or four women stand near Jesus' cross. The unnamed mother of Jesus is clearly present, as is Mary Magdalene. But the phrase "his mother's sister, Mary the wife of Clopas" (literally, just "of Clopas," which could also refer to the daughter, or even the mother, of Clopas) refers either to a maternal aunt of Jesus, named Mary, or to two separate women, an unnamed aunt, and Mary "of Clopas."

It seems unlikely that two Jewish sisters would have had the same name. The Gospel of John, however, never names the mother of Jesus: if the author did not know her name to be Mary, naming her sister Mary would pose little problem. The canonical Gospels nowhere else mention a sister of Jesus' mother, named or unnamed.

ROSS S. KRAEMER

SEE ALSO Part I: Mary 5.

JOHN 19:25–27   Mother of Jesus

SEE John 2:3–12, etc.   Mother of Jesus (Part II).

ACTS 1:14
Unnamed Women Who Stay with the Disciples After Jesus' Ascension

At the conclusion of the Gospel of Luke, Jesus ascends into heaven, having instructed his followers to remain in Jerusalem until they have been "clothed with power from on high" (Luke 24:49), foreshadowing the occurrence of this event on the Jewish festival of Shavuoth (Pentecost) in Acts 2:1–5. Acts 1:12–14 depicts the eleven apostles constantly praying in an upstairs room in Jerusalem. With them are Mary the mother of Jesus, Jesus' brothers, and unnamed and unnumbered women.

This passage must be read with Luke's prior descriptions of women in the Jesus movement. The women of Acts 1:14 should almost certainly be identified with the anonymous women who accompany Jesus from Galilee, provide financial support for the movement (Luke 8:3), witness the crucifixion (23:49) and burial (23:55), prepare spices and ointments for the body (23:56), and return to find the tomb empty and two angelic visitors announcing the resurrection (24:1–11).

Particularly noteworthy, then, is that the only woman named in 1:14 is Mary, the mother of Jesus. Absent (or at least unnamed) are the women explicitly named in Luke 8:2–3 (Mary Magdalene, Joanna, and Susanna) and in 23:10 (Mary Magdalene, Joanna, and Mary the mother of James).

Acts then chronicles the experiences of the male apostles and other prominent men, and these particular women never appear again in Luke's narrative.

It is difficult to draw historical conclusions from the absence of these women in Acts. It seems unlikely, although perhaps not impossible, that all these women would have abandoned the movement, or even died, between the death of Jesus and the Pentecostal experience. Their absence more likely reflects the author's intention. While emphasizing the gender-inclusiveness of the movement, he may minimize the presence of women whose claims to authoritative leadership could conceivably have been on a par with those men presented as apostles. Such an interpretation is strengthened by the prominence and authority of Mary Magdalene in many noncanonical gospels and traditions.

ROSS S. KRAEMER

SEE ALSO Part I: Joanna; Mary 1; Mary 3; Mary 4; Susanna 2; Part II: Unnamed Women Who Provide for the Jesus Movement (Luke 8:2–3, 24:10); Unnamed Women at the Cross (Luke 23:49).

FOR FURTHER READING: D'Angelo, Mary Rose. "(Re)Presentations of Women in the Gospel of Matthew and Luke-Acts."

ACTS 2:17–18
Prophesying Daughters and Female Slaves

Acts 2:1–4 relates that on the festival of Pentecost (Shavuot in the Jewish festal calendar) the followers of Jesus, gathered together in Jerusalem, experienced an outpouring of the Holy Spirit. Tongues of fire appeared on each of their heads, and all spoke in foreign languages. Acts 1:14 makes clear that this community included women and men.

In his so-called Pentecostal speech, Peter opposes the accusation that those newly filled with the Holy Spirit are drunk, by quoting by name the prophet Joel: "Your sons and your daughters shall prophesy . . . Even upon my slaves, both men and women, in those days I will pour out my spirit, and they shall prophesy." In both the Hebrew of Joel 2:28–29 and the Greek translation of Joel preserved in the Septuagint, the last phrase, "and they shall prophesy," is absent, although it is difficult to know whether the author of Acts has supplied it, or whether he already knew a version of Joel that included it.

In Joel, the prophecy envisions an eventual new world order where distinctions of gender and status (e.g. free versus slave) will be transcended. Its use in Acts affirms the inclusion not only of women and men in the community of those filled by the Spirit, but also of enslaved persons of both genders, and further implies that their inclusion signals the imminence of the "end."

PIETER W. VAN DER HORST AND ROSS S. KRAEMER

SEE ALSO Part II: Daughters (and Sons) Who Prophesy (Joel 2:28); Four Unmarried Daughters of Philip (Acts 21:9).

ACTS 5:14
Women (and Men) as New Believers

In Acts 5:12–16, the apostles heal sick persons and those possessed by spirits, causing large numbers of people in Jerusalem and the surrounding towns to become believers. Luke's description of the new believers as "men and women" *(andrōn te kai gynaikōn)* is typical (see also Acts 8:3; 8:12; 9:2; 13:50; 17:12).

For Seim, this phrase depicts the nascent Christian movement as gender-segregated, consisting of a group of women and a group of men. This representation may be the work of the author of Luke-Acts and should be used cautiously as evidence for the actual gender composition (and segregation) of the movement.

ROSS S. KRAEMER

FOR FURTHER READING: Seim, Turid Karlsen. *The Double Message: Patterns of Gender in Luke-Acts.*

ACTS 6:1
Widows of Hellenists and Hebrews

Acts 6 highlights the tension between the Hebrews (probably Aramaic-speaking, Palestinian-born Jewish believers) and the Hellenists (probably Greek-speaking, diaspora-born Jewish believers) within the Jerusalem church. The Hellenists' accusation that the Hebrews are neglecting the Hellenist widows provides the context for appointing the seven to oversee the church's ministry of service.

Throughout the ancient Near East, the term *widow* was an inclusive term, referring not only to once-married women whose husbands had died, but also to women who were divorced or otherwise without male protection and support.

Traditional interpretations of Acts 6 assume that the Hellenist widows lacked adequate economic resources and therefore were dependent upon the church's benevolence. Such interpretations place the Hellenist widows within the tradition of the Hebrew Scriptures, which mandate care of those without visible means of protection and support, namely, the widow, the fatherless, and the stranger. The daily distribution of food is thereby understood as part of the church's charitable activity of contributing to the care of the poor.

In the first century C.E., however, not all widows were economically disadvantaged and dependent upon the charity of others for their well-being. Within the Greco-Roman world, some widows were economically self-sufficient through the return of their dowries, the inheritance of property and wealth from their husbands, or their own economic activities. Further, no evidence in Acts 6 suggests that the Hellenist widows are among the needy of the community.

Schüssler Fiorenza has offered an alternative interpretation of the Hellenist widows' situation: the table service in Acts 6 referred to the church's eucharistic ministry, and the tension between the Hebrews and the Hellenists concerned the role and participation of women at the eucharistic meal. Acts 2:46 attests to the daily table ministry of the Jerusalem church, wherein believers shared meals together in their homes, praising God as a community. Further, descriptions of the financial welfare of the poor (see, for example, Acts 4:32–37) do not expressly mention table ministry as part of the church's charitable functions.

The accusation that the Hellenist widows were neglected in the daily distribution may well have meant that (1) they were not properly served during the eucharistic meal or (2) they were not assigned their proper turn in the table service. Schüssler Fiorenza suggests that the Hellenists were accustomed to female participation in the festive dinners of the Greco-Roman world and thus would have naturally assumed female participation in the eucharistic ministry of the church. Tension would have arisen as the Hellenists began to worship alongside the Hebrews, who had different cultural expectations regarding women's participation in community events.

The subsequent appointing of the seven would have served to mediate the cultural differences within the Jerusalem church as well as to differentiate the church's various emerging functions (preaching, teaching, liturgy, and service).

LUCINDA A. BROWN

FOR FURTHER READING: Schüssler Fiorenza, Elisabeth. *In Memory of Her: A Feminist Theological Reconstruction of Christian Origins.*

O'Day, Gail R. "Acts."

Richter Reimer, Ivoni. *Women in the Acts of the Apostles: A Feminist Liberation Perspective.*

ACTS 7:21; HEB 11:24–26
Daughter of Pharaoh

Pharaoh's daughter, who rescued Moses from exposure (Exod 2:5–10), appears in the historical summaries and example lists of Hebrews and Acts; in both, she is important for what she provided to Moses. Acts 7:21 reflects the widespread tradition that Pharaoh's daughter had not only rescued Moses from the Nile, but also adopted him as her own son and had him educated as a royal child. Heb 11:24–26 acclaims Moses' faith, judging that he rejected his status as "a son of Pharaoh's daughter," a status aligned with the "treasures of Egypt" and the "fleeting pleasures of sin," and instead preferred "abuse suffered for the Christ."

MARY ROSE D'ANGELO

ACTS 8:3
Women (and Men) Dragged Off and Imprisoned by Saul

Acts relates four times that, prior to Paul's conversion, he persecuted and imprisoned or sought to imprison the followers of Jesus. In Acts 8:3, 9:2, and 22:4, men and women (*andras te kai gynaikas*) are explicitly targeted: in Acts 26:10, Paul proclaims in a speech before King Agrippa and Bernice that he had previously imprisoned "many of the saints."

This gender-specific language appears characteristic of the author of Luke-Acts: in his own letters, Paul says only that "I was persecuting the assembly of God exceedingly and was trying to destroy it" (Gal 1:13; author's translation).

Taken at face value, these passages emphasize the presence of women among the early followers of Jesus, enduring persecution for their devotion in the same manner as men. Acts has Paul arrest people, punish them in the synagogues (usually taken to mean that he flogged them), and vote for their execution, presumably on charges of blasphemy (Acts 26:10–11). Modern readers may find it helpful to note that in ancient legal systems, imprisonment was not generally a form of punishment in and of itself, particularly for free persons. Rather, people were incarcerated while awaiting trial or punishment (such as public beatings, execution, exile, confiscation of property, and fines). Although some aspects of Luke's portrait are historically plausible, other aspects raise serious historical questions, among them whether Jewish authorities under Roman rule had the right to execute anyone, and whether free women would have been subject to arrest, imprisonment, flogging, and execution.

Apart from Acts, there is little evidence for women being subject to the kinds of sanctions and procedures envisioned here, whether under Roman law or under local Jewish law in the mid–first century C.E. Charges against free women under Roman law were generally expected to be handled within the family, rather than in public, and the same may well have been true for Jews in the land of Israel and environs in the first century C.E.

Luke's characterization of those persecuted and imprisoned by Paul as explicitly including women may be seen as consistent with that author's tendency to portray the earliest followers of Jesus as both women and men (for example, Acts 5:14; 8:12; 13:50; 17:4, 12). While Luke's presentation of Paul as detaining women, binding them, and placing them under guard may reflect the actual experiences of early followers of Jesus, it may also be the (perhaps unintended) consequence of Luke's repeated characterization of the movement as comprising both women and men. In addition, Roman prosecution of Christians in the late first and early second centuries may have influenced subsequent Christian representation of prior generations.

In Acts 8:3 only, the author explicitly states that in Jerusalem, Paul dragged members of "the Way" (NRSV, "church") out of their houses, a scenario that makes the detainment of women seem plausible. Finally, when Acts 8:3, 9:2, and 22:4 are read in conjunction with 26:10–11, they imply the presence of women in synagogues, for the term "saints" here clearly includes women as well as men, and there is no reason to read v. 10 inclusively but v. 11 exclusively. Given claims that Jewish women were excluded from synagogue participation, this implication may be significant evidence to the contrary.

ROSS S. KRAEMER

SEE ALSO Part II: Women (and Men) Persecuted by Saul (Acts 9:2).

Acts 8:12
Samaritan Women (and Men) Baptized by Philip

In the first century C.E., the region known as Samaria, between the Galilee and Judea, was inhabited especially by people whose worship of the God of Israel differed from that of their Jewish neighbors in several significant respects. In particular, they traced their descent to the ancient northern kingdom of Israel, read a different version of the Pentateuch, and denied the legitimacy and centrality of the temple in Jerusalem. Instead, they venerated the site of a temple on Mount Gerizim, which had been destroyed in 128 B.C.E. (Samaritan religion survives to the present in several communities in modern-day Israel.) The regularly tense relations between Jews and Samaritans may be evidenced in Matt 10:5–6, where Jesus instructs his disciples "to go nowhere among the Gentiles and enter no town of the Samaritans" (prohibitions lacking in the Markan and Lukan versions). In the Gospel of John, on the other hand, Jesus himself travels through Samaria and wins many followers there (4:7–42).

According to Acts, a pretender named Simon had dazzled Samaritans with his "magical" powers, proclaiming himself "the spirit of God that is called Great" (8:9–10). Many Samaritans, however, persuaded by the healings and exorcisms of the apostle Philip that Jesus was the Christ, were baptized by Philip, "both men and women" (andres te kai gynaikes).

Luke's representation of Samaritan believers as women and men is consistent with his regular portrait of early Christians and parallels his representation of new believers elsewhere in Acts, whether Jewish (5:14) or Gentile (17:12). Seim understands this phrase to depict the nascent Christian movement as gender-segregated, consisting of a group of women and a group of men. This representation may well be the work of the author of Luke-Acts and thus is best used cautiously as evidence for the actual gender composition (and segregation) of the movement. Interestingly, Samaritan women play a prominent role in other early Christian writings, most notably in the Fourth Gospel. In John 4:7–42, Jesus has a lengthy conversation with a Samaritan woman by a well, and many Samaritans become believers because of her report.

ROSS S. KRAEMER

SEE ALSO Part II: Samaritan Woman (John 4:7–42); Women (and Men) as New Believers (Acts 5:14); Devout Women of Pisidian Antioch (Acts 13:50); Greek Women (and Men) of High Standing in Beroea Who Became Believers (Acts 17:12).

FOR FURTHER READING: Anderson, Robert T. "Samaritans."

Seim, Turid Karlsen. *The Double Message: Patterns of Gender in Luke-Acts.*

ACTS 8:27
The Candace, Queen of the Ethiopians

Older English translations, most notably the KJV, treated the Greek *kandakē* as the name of the Ethiopian queen, calling her Candace. Newer translations, including the NRSV, recognize that Kandake is an Ethiopian title meaning either "queen" or "queen mother," and known to have been used for the queen of Meroë. It is impossible to identify the Kandake here with any particular Ethiopian queen. In any case, the queen herself is significant only for demonstrating the high status of the eunuch converted by Philip in this passage.

ROSS S. KRAEMER

ACTS 9:2
Women (and Men) Persecuted by Saul

In four passages, Acts relates that, prior to Saul's conversion, he persecuted the followers of Jesus. Three passages (Acts 8:3; 9:2; 22:4) explicitly identify men and women *(andras te kai gynaikas)* as Saul's

targets; the fourth passage (26:10) describes those oppressed as "the saints."

Acts 8:3 describes Paul's persecution of women and men in Jerusalem itself. The remaining instances occur as part of the three narratives of Saul's conversion (Acts 9:1–19; 22:3–21; 26:2–23). These narratives contain substantial differences and disagreements that have puzzled commentators since antiquity. All agree, though, that Saul was traveling to Damascus to seek out members of the movement and return them in chains to Jerusalem for punishment when Christ first appeared to him.

Luke's presentation of Paul as arresting, chaining, and placing women under guard may reflect the actual experiences of early followers of Jesus. But it is historically problematic and may also be the (perhaps unintended) consequence of Luke's repeated characterization of the Jesus movement as consisting both of women and of men (for example, Acts 5:14; 8:12; 13:50; 17:4; 17:12).

ROSS S. KRAEMER

SEE ALSO Part II: Women (and Men) Dragged Off and Imprisoned by Paul (Acts 8:3).

ACTS 13:50
Devout Women of Pisidian Antioch

In Acts 13:13–52, Paul preaches Jesus to Jews in Pisidian Antioch (in modern central Turkey) in the synagogue on the Sabbath, a message that is well received by "many Jews and devout converts" (13:43). The following Sabbath, however, when virtually the entire city shows up to hear Paul and his companion, Barnabas, Jews become jealous and oppose Paul's teachings.

Paul responds that God's word was to be preached first to Jews, but that when Jews reject it, the word of God is to be preached to Gentiles. Although many Gentiles become believers, Acts claims that the Jews "incited the devout women of high standing and the leading men of the city" to expel Paul and Barnabas (13:50).

This narrative exemplifies a recurring pattern in Acts (especially chaps. 13–14; 17–18). Paul preaches in diaspora synagogues to Jews, some of whom accept Jesus, most of whom do not. Once Jews reject Jesus, Paul turns his attention to the local gentile population, where he repeatedly succeeds in converting both women and men. At the same time, Paul is regularly persecuted by Jews who often incite local authorities against Paul and his companions, paralleling the Gospel depictions of Jews inciting Roman authorities to persecute Jesus. Paul's own letters often contradict the story in Acts (compare, for example, Acts 17:1–7 with 1 Thess 1:9 and 2:14), strengthening the likelihood that the pattern of these narratives is a Lukan construction.

In three of these episodes (Acts 13:50; 17:4; 17:12), elite women figure prominently. In Acts 13:50, Jews exert influence over women who are *sebomenas* (NRSV, "devout") and *euschēmonas* (of high standing or prominent). *Sebomenas,* which literally means "fearing/revering" (understanding God as the object of reverence), is understood by many scholars to designate non-Jewish devotees of the God of Israel. Ample evidence from the Roman period demonstrates that some Gentiles, women and men, attended Jewish synagogues and observed various Jewish practices, without necessarily undergoing a formal rite of conversion to Judaism. The phrase *sebomenē ton theon* ("fearing/revering God") appears to have this connotation in Acts 16:14, where it describes Lydia of Thyatira, whom Paul encounters at a prayer gathering on the Sabbath. Elsewhere in this same section (13:43), though, *sebomenōn* modifies *proselytes,* suggesting that, if it has a technical meaning in Acts, it may not have that meaning in every instance.

Perhaps the evangelist intends here to evoke an association between the women's affinity for Judaism and their willingness to persecute Paul and Barnabas. Interestingly, no such connection is suggested for the men, who are described here only as the "leading [literally: first] men" of the city, a title well attested for women and men, primarily in Roman-period Asia Minor. Alternatively, since Christians were regularly viewed as impious by pa-

gans, this passage might merely represent Jews exploiting gentile concerns about piety, without implying any specific interest in Judaism on the part of the women.

ROSS S. KRAEMER

SEE ALSO Part I: Lydia; Part II: Leading Women Converts of Thessalonica (Acts 17:4); Greek Women (and Men) of High Standing in Beroea Who Become Believers (Acts 17:12).

ACTS 16:1
Mother of Timothy

According to Acts 16:1–3, Paul circumcised his fellow missionary Timothy, the uncircumcised son of a Jewish mother, who was herself a "believer" *(pistēs),* and a gentile father. Timothy is well known from the undisputed letters of Paul, which confirm neither Timothy's parentage nor the story of his circumcision. Timothy's mother receives no further mention in Acts, but is found again, with the name Eunice, in the deutero-Pauline 2 Tim 1:5, where her own mother, called Lois, is also said to have been a believer.

Ancient and modern commentators alike have wondered how Paul, who did not have Titus circumcised (Gal 2:3) and who wrote against the necessity of circumcision for gentile (male) converts, in 1 Cor 7:18–20 ("Was anyone at the time of his call uncircumcised? Let him not seek circumcision") could possibly have required Timothy to be circumcised. Some scholars have suggested that the story of Timothy's gentile father and Jewish mother is a fictional device employed by the author of Acts to account for a tradition about Paul that was already troubling.

If Luke's description reflects reliable information about Timothy's family, and assuming that Timothy was the product of a licit marriage (something Acts does not specify), it constitutes important evidence for the existence of non-elite marriages between Jews and non-Jews. (Elite intermarriage is unquestionable — several members of the royal

Herodian family married non-Jews, including two women mentioned in Acts, Drusilla and Bernice.) Further, if Timothy's mother was a believer and became involved in the Christian movement while still married to Timothy's father, we might have a specific example of the situation addressed by Paul in 1 Cor 7:12–16, where he addresses the potential dilemmas encountered by believers married to nonbelievers (probably Gentiles, rather than non-Christian Jews). Unfortunately, Acts says nothing about whether Timothy's father was still alive when either Timothy or his mother became believers, nor whether he opposed the new religious affinities of his family.

Luke's claim that Timothy was the uncircumcised son of a Jewish mother and a Greek (gentile) father has often been seen as contrary to a rabbinic Jewish principle that the child of a Jewish mother is by definition a Jew. Cohen has shown that this "matrilineal" definition of Jewish identity is likely to have originated in the early rabbinic period and should not be assumed to have been known to or shared by Jews living in the diaspora in the first century C.E. On the contrary, Cohen argues that the author of Acts clearly understands Timothy as a Gentile, not a Jew: if Timothy was, indeed, the child of such a mixed marriage, prior to his circumcision, he would have been considered a Gentile by those around him, as well.

Ross S. Kraemer

See also Part I: Eunice; Lois.

For further reading: Cohen, Shaye J. D. "Was Timothy Jewish (Acts 16:1–3)? Patristic Exegesis, Rabbinic Law, and Matrilineal Descent."

Acts 16:13
Women at the Place of Prayer at Philippi

In examining the passage concerning women at the place of prayer in Acts 16:13, it is important to consider both the actuality of women's religious lives at Philippi in the mid–first century and Luke's pur-

pose in telling the story four or more decades later. There was no guarantee in Luke's time that the church as he knew it would endure without support from the ruling classes. A strong survival motive, then, underlies the writing of Acts. Early Christian writers like Luke attempted to convince people of power and high social standing that Christianity was a viable new cult, describing conversions of such people and portraying Christianity as non-threatening to the political establishment. Such an apologia was quite urgent, given the popularity of Christian groups who, among other things, ordained women and allowed them to preach and prophesy. In Acts, Luke promotes his understanding of the faith, which places more restrictions on the roles women may play.

Luke sets the stage for the conversion of a prosperous woman named Lydia by describing a group of women gathering for prayer on the Sabbath beside the river outside the gate at Philippi. The passage is perplexing for several reasons. First, some commentators have theorized that women were compelled to go outside the city to worship; however, evidence from the mid–second century shows that all of Philippi's major cults, including several with considerable female involvement, were housed in temples or shrines *within* city walls. Other commentators argue that the women gathered outside the gate for privacy; or that, in communities with insufficient numbers of men, the Jewish women were allowed to gather there in the absence of a synagogue; or that the term *proseuchē* meant "synagogue" at Philippi and that the women's presence there reflected their high social standing in Macedonia: they were allowed to gather as Jews despite the absence of men.

These explanations do not entirely consider the archaeological and historical data. From these, it is known that Philippi in the first century was heavily gentile; to date, no evidence has been found for a Jewish presence there, so Luke's inference of Judaism may have been theologically or structurally, not factually, motivated. Other details of Acts 16:13 can be verified, and Luke and his readers probably knew them. There was a river, the Gangites, and a creek, the Crenides, near the city; the latter was closer. There was also a city gate (most Roman cities had one). As attested by Paul's letter to the Philippians of about 50 C.E. and the epistle of Polycarp, bishop of Smyrna, of about 110 C.E., there was a Christian community in the city. As for women's presence and involvement, Paul's letter mentions two female leaders, Euodia and Syntyche (Philippians 4), and Polycarp addresses wives, widows, and virgins; both writings suggest that the women's strength and independence were causing some tension.

Roughly contemporaneous with Polycarp and Acts, other groups of Christians were circulating stories that often featured strong, celibate female heroines who evangelized, baptized, and administered the eucharist. These stories, later circulated in writing, are now known as apocryphal acts and noncanonical gospels. Later in the second century, strong women were featured at Philippi with the construction of twin temples to both the Roman emperor and empress and a colossal monument base on which stood seven statues — five of them female — honoring the deified Livia (wife of Augustus). Polycarp and Luke before him, therefore, did not write from positions of absolute Christian patriarchy; rather, the atmosphere at Philippi and elsewhere was heavily polytheistic, Christianity was far from a single united faith, and women were on the forefront of many of the groups that these writers opposed.

The women at prayer at Philippi in Acts, then, are Luke's examples to his audience. Luke paints a picture of Philippian women who, in the face of compelling competition from other groups, are drawn to the "right" Christianity and converted. By referring to the women's meeting occurring on the Sabbath, Luke implies that they are Jewish but leaves this point vague, since there were no compelling reasons to highlight Judaism at Philippi. *Proseuchē* in this passage most likely means "place of prayer," not "synagogue": he uses *synagōgē* elsewhere and apparently chose not to do so here.

Luke's main purpose in writing Acts was to convert Gentiles, or at least to present Christianity as nonthreatening to Greco-Roman society. The Philippian women in his stories are religious, upstanding, responsible, nonradical. They do not preach, baptize, evangelize, or administer the sacraments; rather, they provide financial resources to the church and fade safely into the background.

VALERIE ABRAHAMSEN

SEE ALSO Part I: Lydia.
FOR FURTHER READING: Fitzmyer, Joseph. "Acts of the Apostles."
O'Day, Gail R. "Acts of the Apostles."
Thomas, W. Derek. "The Place of Women in the Church at Philippi."

ACTS 16:16–18
Slave Girl Healed of a Spirit

This anonymous "slave girl" (Greek *paidiskē*, diminutive of *pais*, "girl") may be the most marginalized person in the New Testament: a demon-possessed, exploited, "pagan," female slave. Possibly because of a physical disorder that produced notable internal noises, her owners have presented this person as the source of oracles, which, the reader is to imagine, they alone can interpret. For the narrator this condition is neither disability nor divine gift, but demonic possession. As in the case of Jesus (Mark 1:21–28), the evil spirit begins to hail Paul (and Silas). Piqued by this apparently incessant, if free, advertising, Paul exorcises the demon, thus depriving the girl's owners of their revenue and precipitating his own incarceration. The segment is an important part of a literary complex: Acts 16:11–40. Whatever readers might desire or fantasize, the narrator reports nothing about the girl's fate after the exorcism. This slave would have been fortunate to escape with severe punishment for her owner's loss of income.

RICHARD I. PERVO

SEE ALSO Part I: Rhoda; Part II: Women (and Men) Slave Owners (Eph 6:7).
FOR FURTHER READING: Pervo, Richard I. *Luke's Story of Paul.*
———. *Profit with Delight.*

Acts 17:4
Leading Women Converts of Thessalonica

This narrative of Paul's preaching in the city of Thessalonica (modern Greece) exemplifies a recurring pattern in Acts (especially throughout Acts 14–19). Paul preaches in a diaspora synagogue on the Sabbath. While some Jews may become believers, others inevitably oppose Paul and incite the local populace against the apostle and his companions, forcing them to flee. In many of these accounts, Paul responds to Jewish rejection of his message by preaching instead to Gentiles. The repeated theme of these narratives is that, in the absence of Jewish opposition, Gentiles are regularly drawn to Paul's preaching of Jesus.

Previously, in Acts 13:50, "devout women of high standing and the leading men of the city" oppose Paul at the instigation of Jews in Pisidian Antioch. Here, however, "a great many of the devout [*sebomenōn*] Greeks [masculine plural] and not a few of the leading women" — more or less the reverse of the phrase in 13:50 — accept Paul's teachings, along with some Jews.

Sebomenōn, which literally means "fearing/revering" (and probably understands God as the object of reverence), is understood by many scholars as a technical designation for non-Jewish devotees of the God of Israel. Ample evidence from the Roman period demonstrates that some Gentiles, women and men, attended Jewish synagogues and observed various Jewish practices, without necessarily undergoing a formal rite of conversion to Judaism. The phrase *sebomenē ton theon* ("fearing/revering God") appears to have this connotation in Acts 16:14, where it describes Lydia of Thyatira, whom Paul encounters at a prayer gathering on the Sabbath. Other passages in Acts (such as 13:43 and 13:50) are more ambiguous.

Since Paul and his companion Silas have thus far preached only in the synagogue in Thessalonica, Acts 17:1–4 may imply that the Greeks (Gentiles) who join the movement heard Paul in that very synagogue, strengthening the possibility that their designation as "devout" refers to their attraction to Judaism. But if so, it is odd that, as at 13:50, only one gender is designated "devout," and a different one each time.

The phrase translated here as "leading women" (literally "first women") is well attested for elite women and men in inscriptions from imperial Asia Minor. *The Acts of (Paul and) Thecla,* a second-century tale of Paul and an elite woman from Iconium (Konya in modern Turkey), describes Thecla as "first [woman] of the Iconians."

Matthews has argued that the association of prominent Gentile women with Judaism in Acts 13:50, 17:4, and 17:12 is a topos common to apologetic Jewish literature of the same period, most notably the writings of the first-century c.e. Jewish historian Josephus. The affiliation of prominent Gentile women with the nascent Christian movement may thus also be seen as a similar rhetorical strategy. Coupled with the fact that Paul's own letters often contradict the version of his actions in Acts (compare, for example, Acts 17:1–7 with 1 Thess 1:9 and 2:14), it becomes more likely that the patterns in Acts are Lukan constructions that make it difficult to draw any historically reliable conclusions from these passages.

Apart from Acts itself, the evidence for the attraction of elite women and men to the nascent Christian movement is modest. Early (second-century) pagan polemics against Christianity portray it as a movement of slaves and free persons of lesser status. Yet the general image of elite women in Acts (particularly in Asia Minor) is reasonably consonant with the evidence, particularly from inscriptions honoring such women for their many public benefactions and their services as high-ranking religious officials. Such women had the resources and perhaps the necessary personal autonomy to join a new religious movement. Whether they did so, and certainly to the degree implied in Acts, cannot be verified. Matthews suggests that, by casting elite women as their benefactors and supporters, minority communities, including those of the Jews and Christians, sought to represent themselves as respectable communities modeled on Greek cities and communal associations *(collegia).*

A major textual variant exists for this passage, suggesting some of the difficulties it posed to ancient Christian readers. Codex Bezae, a famous manuscript dating to the fifth or sixth century C.E. reads instead, "And many of the 'fearers' joined the teaching, as well as a large number of Greeks [Gentiles] and not a few of the wives of the leading [first] men."

Ross S. Kraemer

See also Part II: Devout Women of Pisidian Antioch (Acts 13:50); Greek Women (and Men) of High Standing in Beroea Who Become Believers (Acts 17:12).

For further reading: Matthews, Shelly. "High-Standing Women and Mission and Conversion: A Rhetorical-Historical Analysis of the Antiquities and Acts."

Van Bremen, Riet. *The Limits of Participation: Women and Civic Life in the Greek East in the Hellenistic and Roman Periods.*

Witherington, Ben, III. "The Anti-feminist Tendencies of the 'Western' Text in Acts."

Acts 17:12
Greek Women (and Men) of High Standing in Beroea Who Become Believers

This relatively brief narrative of Paul's preaching in the city of Beroea in Greece conforms to a recurring pattern in Acts. Generally, Paul and a companion preach to Jews in the local synagogue: some find them persuasive, but many do not. Paul's preaching finds more success among Gentiles, frequently explicitly depicted as both women and men. Jews regularly incite Gentiles, prominent and otherwise, against the missionaries, forcing them to flee to another town, where similar events recur (see especially Paul's experiences in Pisidian Antioch, Acts 13:14–51; Iconium, 14:1–6; Thessalonica, 17:1–9; and Corinth, 18:1–17). Paul's persecution by Jews who incite the local authorities against him intentionally

parallels Gospel depictions of Jews inciting Roman authorities to persecute Jesus.

The narrative for Beroea has several interesting twists. Here, the Jewish opposition comes not from Beroea, whose Jews are quite receptive to Paul's message, but from the Jews of Thessalonica, who follow Paul to Beroea when they learn of his success. As at Thessalonica, Paul's new converts include elite women and men. In Acts 17:4, Luke refers to "devout Greeks [masculine plural] and not a few of the leading women." Here, in contrast to Luke's general tendency to mention men before women, the women precede the men: the new believers are "not a few Greek women and men of high standing." This translation from the NRSV in fact masks a possible ambiguity of the Greek, which more literally reads, "and (also believed) of the Greek women of high-standing, and men, not a few." *Euschēmonōn* ("high-standing or prominent") most likely here refers to both the women and the men, but if it only modifies one gender, it is the women, not the men. Later Christian scribes apparently found this passage troubling, revising it to read in Codex Bezae "and a sufficient number of Gentiles, and of high-standing men and women believed," a rearrangement that juxtaposes *high-standing* and *men,* making it ambiguous whether this adjective also modifies *women.*

Further, and again in contrast to 17:4 (and also 13:50, where the local elites side with the Jews against Paul), no one is called "devout" (or "fearing/revering" [God]) — a term that is frequently taken to signify Gentile adherents to Judaism. Since Paul and his companion Silas have preached only in the synagogue, the Gentile believers are still often understood to be "God-fearers."

Ross S. Kraemer

See also Part II: Leading Women Converts of Thessalonica (Acts 17:4).

ACTS 21:5

Wives of the Disciples at Tyre

Acts 19:21–21:16 narrates Paul's journey back to Jerusalem, after he has traveled through Asia Minor (modern Turkey) and Greece, visiting existing churches and establishing new ones. In Acts 21:4–5, after spending a week with disciples in the coastal city of Tyre (in present-day Syria), Paul and his traveling companions are sent on their way by "all of them [the disciples], with wives and children" (21:5).

This passage comes from one of four so-called "we" sections of Acts (16:10–17; 20:5–15; 21:1–18; 27:1–28:16). These first-person plural accounts were traditionally taken as evidence that the author of Acts had traveled with Paul for at least a portion of his journeys. Many contemporary scholars view these sections either as a literary artifice of the author's or as the author's incorporation of other narratives about Paul in diary form.

Here, as elsewhere in Acts, *disciples* is a term for members of the nascent Christian movement. Although Acts 9:36 explicitly identifies a woman, Tabitha (Dorcas), as a "disciple," 21:5 appears to use the term in a gender-specific way, distinguishing "all of them [the disciples]" from the wives and children. The disciples are therefore implicitly male, and the term appears not to include the wives (or perhaps women — *gynaikes* can mean both) and children. That the women and children are presented as sending off Paul and his companions would also seem to imply that they, too, are "Christians" (the term itself does not occur here; it occurs only once, in Acts 11:26).

The disciples at Tyre relay a prophecy they have received, that Paul should not continue on his journey to Jerusalem. By excluding women from the male disciples, the author of Acts also excludes them here from the group of prophets. Further, in the verses immediately following, which describe Paul's experience at Caesarea (a coastal town south of Tyre, in modern-day Israel), something similar may occur. Although four women prophets all live at Caesarea with their father, the evangelist Philip, it

is a male prophet, Agabus, who relates to Paul the same dire warning (one he continues to ignore). Thus, it is possible that this whole section reveals a concern on the part of the author of Acts to minimize the role of women prophets, grounded in broader early Christian conflicts about prophecy and gender.

ROSS S. KRAEMER

SEE ALSO Part I: Jezebel 2; Part II: Prophesying Daughters and Female Slaves (Acts 2:17–18); Four Unmarried Daughters of Philip (Acts 21:9); Women Praying and Prophesying (1 Cor 11:2–16); Women Commanded to Be "Silent" in the Assemblies (1 Cor 14:33b–36).

ACTS 21:9

Four Unmarried Daughters of Philip

Acts 21:1–16 is a first-person-plural narrative of Paul's final journey to Jerusalem. The party proceeded south along the coast of Syria and Palestine. At Caesarea Maritima, the coastal capital of the Roman government, they lodged with Philip, one of the seven (Acts 6:1–7), whose missions had brought him there (8:40). Acts 21:9 states that he had four unmarried daughters who engaged in prophecy. The author of Luke and Acts, in accordance with ancient religious tradition (for example, the priestesses of Apollo's oracle at Delphi), tends to associate female prophetic activity with virgins or celibate women, such as Mary of Nazareth and Anna of Jerusalem (Luke 1), although it is also true that he opposes marriage for believers (Luke 20:34–36) and includes "wife" among the renunciations made for the sake of discipleship (Luke 18:29), suggesting that all prophets and leaders were to be unmarried.

Except for Mary's, however, no prophecies of women are recorded (though in 16:16–18 a demon speaks through a slave girl). This is especially notable in 21:9, where, despite the presence of the four daughters, prophecy about Paul's fate comes from

Terra-cotta figure of a nurse holding an infant, from Myrina, circa 100 B.C.E. See Nurse Caring for Her Children *(1 Thess 2:7).*

Agabus of Jerusalem (21:10–14; compare 11:28). The writer of Acts is prepared to state that women will prophesy (2:17, from Joel 2:28), but chooses not to give specific examples. As in other instances, this writer both notes the ministry of women and represses it. In part the repression is due to an apologetic desire to show that Christianity is not threatening to the social order. In this instance the presence of Agabus also serves to show harmony between Paul and the Jerusalem church.

According to the fourth-century church historian Eusebius (*Ecclesiastical History* 3.31.3–4), late-second-century tradition claimed that these women removed to Hierapolis in Phrygia (in present-day Turkey), where they served as prophets. Other traditions report that one or more of these unnamed women later married.

RICHARD I. PERVO

ACTS 22:4
Women Persecuted by Paul
SEE ACTS 8:3, etc. Women (and Men) Dragged Off and Imprisoned by Saul (Part II).

ACTS 23:16
Sister of Paul

Acts 23:12–35 depicts a conspiracy planned by some Jews in Jerusalem to ambush and kill Paul while he is in Roman protective custody. Paul's unnamed nephew, son of his unnamed sister, learns about and reports the plot to the Roman tribune, thus thwarting it.

Nothing else is known about the nephew or Paul's sister. Neither one appears in Paul's letters, and there is no way to tell whether either is a historical figure. Their sympathies for the Christian movement cannot be inferred from this passage, and the nephew's actions could easily be attributed to familial devotion.

ROSS S. KRAEMER

ROM 1:26
Unnatural Intercourse of Women

In Rom 1:26 Paul states of idol worshippers: "Their women exchanged natural intercourse for unnatural." This most likely refers to sexual relations between women, because (1) in Rom 1:27, Paul states that "*in the same way* also the men . . . were consumed with passion for one another" (emphasis added); and (2) other ancient sources (Plato, Seneca the Elder, Martial, Ovid, Ptolemy, Artemidoros, and probably Dorotheos of Sidon) depict sexual relations between women as unnatural. Early Christians (for example Clement of Alexandria and John Chrysostom) interpreted Paul to have condemned such relations because by nature women are to be passive and subordinate to their husbands.

BERNADETTE J. BROOTEN

FOR FURTHER READING: Brooten, Bernadette J. *Love Between Women: Early Christian Responses to Female Homoeroticism.*

Martin, Dale. "Heterosexism and the Interpretation of Romans 1:18–32."

ROM 7:2–3
Married Woman

In this passage Paul makes an analogy between, on the one hand, marriage and its termination in the death of a husband and, on the other, the obligation to the Jewish law and the termination of this obligation (as Paul argues) by the death and resurrection of Christ. The perceived passivity of the married woman is the crux of the analogy. Paul's argument rests on the assumption that, according to Jewish law, a woman had no right to terminate her marriage through divorce. (Recent scholarship, though, suggests that Jewish women may sometimes have had the legal right to initiate divorce proceedings.) As Paul presents it, the married woman has no legal means to seek out another relationship while her husband lives, but can only commit adultery if she tries.

Paul appears to have chosen this analogy to address listeners among the audience of Romans who were knowledgeable about Jewish law because it underscores his argument about the helplessness of a person under Jewish law. It also indicates that Paul thought the *obvious* subjection of a wife to her husband would make a compelling vehicle for his theological argument.

SHEILA BRIGGS

SEE ALSO Part II: Divorced Wife (Matt 5:31–32); (Matt 19:3–9); (Mark 10:2–12); (Luke 16:18); Married Women (and Men), Unmarried Women (and Men), and Women (and Men) Married to Unbelievers (1 Corinthians 7).

FOR FURTHER READING: Castelli, Elizabeth. "Romans."

ROMANS 16:13
Mother of Rufus

We know little about this woman, other than Paul's fond regard for her. The son's (Latin) name was often given to slaves and freedmen, suggesting that he was of low status. But Paul identifies him by his special status in the Lord ("chosen"). She, however, is identified by her special relationship to Paul ("a mother to me also"). Paul uses the word *mother* figuratively here, but does not indicate how she mothered him. Elsewhere Paul claims to have "mothered" (1 Cor 3:2; Gal 4:19) or "fathered" (1 Cor 4:15) new converts. If this woman had some role in Paul's conversion, he does not acknowledge it anywhere else. More likely, she showed generous hospitality to Paul on one of his trips or, like Phoebe, served as his patron.

JOUETTE M. BASSLER

SEE ALSO Part I: Phoebe.

ROM 16:14
Sisters (and Brothers) Greeted by Paul

Among the many places where the NRSV has introduced the translation of the masculine plural *adelphoi* by the gender-inclusive "brothers and sisters" is Paul's greeting here to "Asyncritus, Phlegon, Hermes, Patrobas, Hermas, and the *adelphoi* who are with them." Although there are many places where *adelphoi* clearly designates women and men together, this passage is not necessarily one of them. All the other persons greeted here are men, and it is conceivable, although not verifiable, that Paul here refers to a small male community of Christians at Rome. Gender-inclusive translation here might inadvertently mask a reference to a single-sex community.

Ross S. Kraemer

ROMANS 16:15
Sister of Nereus

This unnamed woman probably belonged to a small Roman house church, whose members Paul greets in this verse. She was probably Nereus's natural sibling (and both may have been children of Julia and Philologus), though the term *sister* was sometimes used of Christian wives (1 Cor 9:5) and coworkers (Rom 16:1).

Jouette M. Bassler

See also Part I: Julia; Martha; Mary 2; Part II: Sister/Wife Who Accompanies Apostles Other Than Paul (1 Cor 9:5).

1 COR 1:24   Woman Wisdom
See Woman Wisdom in the New Testament (Part III).

1 COR 5:1
Woman Living with Her Husband's Son

Paul condemns a man "living with his father's wife," but the apostle does not say that the woman is the man's mother. Most likely the woman is the father's wife in a later marriage. Since men in the ancient world usually married women much younger than themselves in second and later marriages, the woman could be of the same age or even younger than her husband's son. The woman, if a slave (or perhaps a freedwoman), would be a concubine rather than a wife in the full legal sense. The word *gynē* literally means "woman" and, although translated here as "wife," also could denote a concubine. In such a case it is possible that the son began his liaison with the woman in his father's

household before she married his father, a predicament that informed the plots of Roman comedies. Whatever the circumstances, Paul feels justified in denouncing the liaison as forbidden not only in Jewish law (Lev 20:11), but also more generally in Greco-Roman law codes including Roman law, which prevailed in Corinth as a Roman colony.

Sheila Briggs

See also Part II: Married Women (and Men), Unmarried Women (and Men), and Women (and Men) Married to Unbelievers (1 Corinthians 7).

For further reading: Countryman, William L. *Dirt, Greed, and Sex: Sexual Ethics in the New Testament and Their Implications for Today.*

Gardner, Jane F. *Women in Roman Law and Society.*

Treggiari, Susan. *Roman Marriage: Iusti Coniuges from the Time of Cicero to the Time of Ulpian.*

1 COR 6:15–16
Prostitute

Much of the letter now known as 1 Corinthians comprises Paul's responses to the teachings and practices of some persons within the church at Corinth, labeled "the strong" (4:10), whose central slogan may have been "all things are lawful to me" (1 Cor 6:12). Although *porneia* (NRSV, "fornication") encompasses a wide range of illicit sexual activity, in 1 Cor 6:13–20, Paul targets sexual intercourse between male believers and female prostitutes. Because the ancient city of Corinth once had a reputation as a vice-ridden port, older interpretations of this passage tended to explain the behavior of Corinthian men within such a context. Recognizing the inaccuracy of these stereotypes for first-century C.E. Corinth, more recent scholarship has understood Paul's response as a critique of the position that, for the truly "spiritual," being "in Christ" meant that all bodily activity was irrelevant, and therefore also permissible. For such persons, engaging in transgressive acts, including illicit sex, might have been viewed as an expression of their true spiritual freedom and their dissociation from the body.

Paul vociferously opposes this view, quoting part of Gen 2:24 (that a husband and wife become one flesh) to ground his argument that any man who has sex with a prostitute becomes one with her (6:16). Because the Corinthians, having been baptized (6:11), are now part of Christ, their bodies are members of Christ: to unite those members with a prostitute is a sin against the body. Martin reads Paul as subscribing to a dualist view in which the cosmos has become alienated from God and Christ. Just as the believing male represents (and is part of) the body of Christ, the prostitute represents the alienated cosmos. What's wrong with sex between a believing man and a female prostitute is, for Paul, the joining of two fundamental (and here gendered) opposites: (masculine) Christ and the (feminine) cosmos. "In the face of such cosmic consequences . . . Paul insists on limiting the freedom of the Christian man" (Martin, 178).

Prostitution was widespread in the ancient world. In Greco-Roman legal systems (including those of Jews), married men who had sex with prostitutes committed no offense against their wives. Many, if not most, prostitutes were slaves whose owners sold their services or who sold themselves in order to earn the money to purchase their freedom. We cannot tell whether Corinthian "spiritual" men were patronizing female prostitutes any more than other Corinthian men of similar social standing. Men who did not share their wives' beliefs that those in Christ should abstain from sexual intercourse (an issue addressed by Paul in 1 Corinthians 7) may have sought the services of prostitutes. It seems more likely, though, that the underlying motivation was an intentional expression of beliefs about freedom from the body.

Such actions appear confined to male "spirituals." Paul nowhere upbraids women for consorting with male prostitutes (who, in antiquity, generally provided sexual services to other men) or for comparable acts of sexual transgression. Glancy points out that the passage may imply that it would have been difficult for women who worked as prosti-

tutes, whether under the compulsion of slavery or otherwise, to have been members of a Pauline congregation. Elsewhere in 1 Corinthians (11:3–16), Paul does chastise Corinthian spiritual women for different transgressions related to gender, namely their failure to cover their heads when praying and prophesying in the communal assembly. All can be seen as Paul's responses to certain Corinthian views of "being in Christ."

ROSS S. KRAEMER

SEE ALSO Part II: Prostitutes (Matt 21:31–32); (Luke 15:30).

FOR FURTHER READING: Glancy, Jennifer, A. "Obstacles to Slaves' Participation in the Corinthian Church." Martin, Dale B. *The Corinthian Body.*
McGinn, Thomas A. *Prostitutes, Sexuality, and the Law in Ancient Rome.*

1 CORINTHIANS 7

Married Women (and Men), Unmarried Women (and Men), and Women (and Men) Married to Unbelievers

In the Greco-Roman world, women were primarily defined by their marital status. In 1 Corinthians 7, Paul addresses women (and men) and places obligations on them according to marital status. Paul's advice is characterized by a far-reaching, though not complete, gender parity in his treatment of whether women and men should marry and the duties that one owes to one's spouse. Members of the believing community at Corinth had written to Paul, asking him to intervene in debates over marriage within their community. Thus, at a distance he is attempting to resolve a controversy that had sharply divided the Corinthians.

The social reality of marriage in the first-century Roman Empire was very diverse. Corinth was a Roman colony where Roman law prevailed, but the Roman law of marriage applied only to Roman citizens. Greek and Jewish residents of the city contracted marriages according to their own laws and customs. Roman marriage had recently been overhauled by the emperor Augustus to encourage childbearing, also providing legal benefits for women who proved themselves sufficiently fertile. A Roman marriage under Roman law came into effect when adult citizens began cohabiting as man and wife, although there were more formal ways of constituting marriage. In the first century, Roman citizens and other inhabitants of the empire often entered informally into marriage; this was especially common among those who did not belong to social elites. On the other hand, spouses (or their families) used individual contracts to arrange the disposal of property and the conditions under which they would conduct or terminate their marriage. Often these individual arrangements diverged from traditional law and custom and the marriage contracts, such as the Roman *stipulatio* and the Jewish *kĕtûbâ*, associated with them. So, for example, Jewish women obtained the right to initiate a divorce through individual contracts, a right that was not allowed them in Jewish law generally or in most known forms of the *kĕtûbâ*.

Divorce was relatively easy to obtain throughout the legal systems of the Greco-Roman world, and it frequently occurred. Under Roman law a woman or her father, if she were under his authority, could dissolve her marriage. Paul thus confronted a situation where women as well as men had the opportunity to leave their marriages. Furthermore, many residents of Corinth could not contract a legal marriage because they were slaves. However, many slaves entered into long-term relationships that they considered marriages, although these unions were not legally protected. Paul probably included this form of social monogamy within his use of the term *marriage,* which he does not define.

Marriage was not only controversial among the Corinthians. In the Greco-Roman world, widespread ideological debates took place concerning whether the wise (man) should marry or not. Best known to us is the disagreement between two groups of philosophers, the Stoics and the Cynics. Put simply, the Stoics defended marriage as an obligation that a male citizen owed to his community. Only through the existence of households could the city-states and the wider order of the cosmos, which embraced them, endure. Therefore nature decreed that men take on the burden of wives and families so that the species and civilized life might survive. The Cynics, on the other hand, argued that the wise held only one responsibility: to cultivate a life of philosophy. Household and civic affairs interfered with this effort and therefore should be shunned. These two attitudes were widely diffused through the ancient world, and some version of them underpinned the controversy in Corinth.

In 1 Corinthians 7, Paul addresses both married and unmarried women. Married women are exhorted (1) to continue sexual relations with their husbands (2) not to divorce a believing spouse, and (3) not to initiate divorce from a nonbelieving husband. In the first matter (vv. 1–6) Paul quotes a slogan presumably much heard in the Corinthian community, "It is well for a man not to touch a woman" (v. 1). In Paul's view, refusing a spouse sex encourages *porneia,* a word that has very broad meaning and is usually translated here as "sexual immorality" (v. 2). However, in the previous chapter the apostle has castigated male believers for visiting prostitutes, that is, for engaging in *porneia* in its narrowest sense. Although Paul carefully phrases his demands of wives and husbands in exactly the same terms, he may see wives as morally endangering their spouses more by withholding sex than vice versa, since men but not women had in antiquity the socially accepted option of frequenting brothels. Paul allows temporary sexual abstinence between spouses for religious purposes (v. 5), as was common in Judaism and other Greco-Roman religions, as long as this occurred by mutual consent.

Paul prohibits believers from divorcing each other, calling this stipulation the Lord's command (vv. 10–12) This may refer to Jesus' prohibition of divorce in the Synoptic Gospels (for example, Matt 19:3–9). Paul's ban differs markedly: the Gospel passages are directed at men, but Paul addresses women first and at most length in 1 Corinthians 7. The Gospels appear to reflect the situation under

Jewish law by which only husbands can initiate divorce (although recent scholarship suggests a diversity of Jewish thought and practice on this point). 1 Corinthians 7 acknowledges that, under Roman law, women could initiate divorce in Paul's day. In this chapter, the verbs often translated as "separating from" spouses (referring to women's actions) and "divorcing" spouses (referring to men's actions) should not be taken as distinguishing two distinct legal steps, as they do in English; they indicate equivalent terminations of a marriage. However, Paul stresses that divorced women are to remain unmarried or return to their former husbands, but does not explicitly place men under the same restrictions (though he may have desired men to exercise the same restraint).

Paul's third concern is that believers are divorcing nonbelieving spouses. He places injunctions equally on female and male believers not to initiate such a divorce. If the spouse insists on divorce, then the believing partner is not "bound," which seems to indicate that they are not obligated to remain unmarried after divorce, as they are in the case of divorcing a believing spouse. Again women are addressed first, which may indicate that women were more likely to seek divorce from unbelieving spouses than were men.

Paul clearly states that he prefers for both women and men to remain unmarried, a condition requiring that both women and men be capable of self-control. Such self-control does not mean repressing sexual desire, which Paul, with his Jewish contemporaries and the Greco-Roman philosophers, sees as part of the natural order. Instead, it involves detachment from worldly affairs, which the truly wise cultivate when they avoid marriage. Paul gives this common ancient view a distinctive Christian twist. Refraining from marriage allows both women and men to be "anxious about the affairs of the Lord, how to please the Lord" in contrast to the married, who must be "anxious about the affairs of the world, how to please [the spouse]" (vv. 32–33). This detachment from worldly affairs is especially urgent because of the "impending crisis" (v. 26), Christ's return and the final judgment of the world.

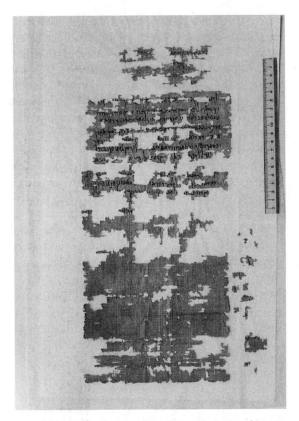

The marriage contract (kĕtûbâ) of Babatha of Ma'oza, from her husband, Judah, early second century C.E., found in the so-called Cave of the Letters near the Dead Sea. See Married Woman (Rom 7:2–3); Married Women (and Men) (1 Corinthians 7).

Gender parity diminishes in 1 Corinthians 7 when Paul concentrates on the initiation of a marriage. Paul's maxim is that the Corinthians should "remain as you are" (v. 26). Paul is responding, in 1 Cor 7:25–38, to a question from the Corinthians about what should happen to "virgins," meaning unmarried young women. Men are exhorted to stay married if they are so already and to remain unmarried if not. However, the decision to marry is not considered sinful, and Paul adds, "if a virgin marries, she does not sin" (v. 28). In vv. 36–38, Paul assumes the ancient understanding of betrothal as a state that confers on the betrothed and their families many of the obligations and benefits of marriage. Women were frequently betrothed when they were infants, and the virgin in this passage is a young betrothed woman who has now reached the age of marriage. Paul's address exclusively to the male fiancé reflects the disparity in age between bride and groom at the time of a woman's first marriage. Women normally married in their early teens (under Roman law women became marriageable at age twelve). Grooms were usually a decade or more older than their brides, having completed their education or military service or seeking a replacement for a dead or divorced wife. In such a situation, only the male fiancé had any control over whether the marriage took place or not. Paul encourages the betrothed male not to proceed to marriage if he is capable of controlling his sexual passions, but otherwise he should marry, incurring no sin through finding an outlet for his sexual desire in marriage.

Conversely, in vv. 39–40, Paul addresses only women among the widowed. In the ancient world widowers were more common than widows because of the high female death rate due to the risks of childbirth. However, when a woman survived her husband, she could attain independence, including control over whether and whom she married. Paul's advice parallels that given to the male betrothed earlier. The woman is morally free to remarry (as long as her spouse is a fellow believer), but she does better to remain unmarried. In contrast to his advice to men, Paul does not discuss a widow's ability to control her sexual desires.

This, and the lack of advice to the more numerous widowers, supports Wire's recent suggestion that, in 1 Corinthians 7, Paul's chief concern is women's independence and the effects it was having on *men's* sexual lives. Women, Wire argues, were more likely than men to embrace a celibate lifestyle since this afforded them independence and avoided the perils of childbirth. Paul seeks to persuade women to stay in marriage by placing on them the responsibility of containing male sexual desire. Despite the gender parity in this chapter, Paul's injunctions to the married would bear more heavily on wives than on husbands. Similarly, in his advice to the unmarried, the apostle's preference for celibacy (and women's independence) is constrained by his concern to contain male sexual desire.

SHEILA BRIGGS

SEE ALSO Part II: Divorced Wife (Matt 5:31–32); (Matt 19:3–9); (Mark 10:2–12); (Luke 16:18).

FOR FURTHER READING: Deming, William. *Paul on Marriage and Celibacy: The Hellenistic Background of 1 Corinthians 7.*

Martin, Dale B. *The Corinthian Body.*

Treggiari, Susan. *Roman Marriage: Iusti Coniuges from the Time of Cicero to the Time of Ulpian.*

Wire, Antoinette Clark. *The Corinthian Women Prophets: A Reconstruction Through Paul's Rhetoric.*

1 COR 9:5
Sister/Wife Who Accompanies Apostles Other Than Paul

The phrase "sister/wife" translates an awkward Greek phrase in one of Paul's letters, which apparently refers to the widespread presence of missionary couples in the early church. In 1 Corinthians 9, Paul presents himself as an example for the Corinthians to follow, since he has freely given up his deserved apostolic rights, which he names in three parallel rhetorical questions in 9:4–6. The middle question literally reads thus in Greek: Do we not have the right "to lead around a sister [as] a wife?" The NRSV translates it "to be accompanied by a believing wife." The other apostles and the brothers of the Lord and Cephas (Peter) were married, and their wives traveled with them as they spread the gospel. Paul could have done this, but chose not to, he insists.

Paul's phrasing here is unusual. The double object, "a sister, a wife/woman," is strange. From early on in the church, *sister* (*adelphē*) meant "Christian" or "fellow-believer", as in 1 Cor 7:15 and Rom 16:1. The second word, *gynē,* could mean either "woman" or "wife," but after *sister* would be redundant if it meant only "woman," so it must mean "wife." Further, the verb used can mean literally "to lead around" or "to have as one's constant companion" (as translated in the NRSV). It is not clear whether Paul is particularly emphasizing the right to be married, the right to have one's wife along on mission trips, or the right for the sister-missionary to receive material support from the churches along with her husband, though the immediate context suggests the last of these.

Traditionally, interpretation of this verse has assumed that these women accompanied their husbands in order to provide for their domestic needs while the men accomplished the important work of evangelization. Other, especially Catholic interpretation, worked hard to minimize the obvious implication of this verse, that the earliest apostles and leaders of the Jerusalem church were all married (for Peter this is confirmed also by Mark 1:30). Recent feminist analysis has insisted that, despite Paul's androcentric way of presenting this arrangement (given his argumentative focus on "apostolic rights"), the practice to which he refers was that of missionary couples, such as Prisca and Aquila (Rom 16:3; 1 Cor 16:19) and Junia and Andronicus (Rom 16:7). In these cases, which Paul mentions with lavish praise elsewhere, there is no indication that the women had roles of less significance than those of the men. Missionary pairs appear to have been a characteristic of the Christian movement from the beginning, initiated already by Jesus (Mark 6:7 and parallels; note also the pair on the road to Emmaus in Luke 24:13–32, of which the unnamed member could be a woman, perhaps the wife of Cleopas). Most scholars assume, with justification from Paul's phrasing, that the women were wives of the men, but Crossan has speculated that the pairs presented themselves to the outside world as married merely for the protection of the woman (if true, this would be an ironic reversal of the "wife/sister" motif found in the Hebrew Bible narratives of the patriarchs, such as Gen 12:10–20!). However, there is no concrete evidence to support this suggestion.

Though "sister/wife" was likely not a title in the early church, this Pauline locution indicates that women were active in missionary activity alongside their now better-known husbands in the earliest years of the spread of Christianity around the Mediterranean basin.

MARGARET M. MITCHELL

SEE ALSO Part I: Junia; Prisca/Priscilla; Part II: Unnamed Companion of Cleopas (Luke 24:13–35).

FOR FURTHER READING: Crossan, John Dominic. *Jesus: A Revolutionary Biography.*

Schüssler Fiorenza, Elisabeth. *In Memory of Her: A Feminist Theological Reconstruction of Christian Origins.*

Wire, Antoinette Clark. *The Corinthian Women Prophets: A Reconstruction Through Paul's Rhetoric.*

1 COR 11:2–16
Women Praying and Prophesying

This passage from 1 Corinthians — one of the most tortured in Paul's letters — is of crucial importance for women's history in the early church, both for the clues it gives about women's actual practices and beliefs, and for what it tells us of Paul's reactions to them. Its repercussions have extended from the time this letter was written through the centuries thereafter in which it has been read as authoritative Scripture.

Paul's argument responds to conflict in the church about appropriate costume during worship. Though it is unclear whether the issue is headwear or haircuts, and whether he regards only women's or both women's and men's current practice as problematic, it is certain that Paul attempts to put some constraints on the women prophets' freedom, both in practice and belief. His argument here begins with a reinscription of the hierarchy of heads: God, Christ, man, woman (11:3). Although there has been debate over whether the word *kephalē* means "head" as in "superior" or as in "source," nonetheless in Paul's argument the woman is head to no one, the inheritor of only second-hand divine glory through the man (11:7). Paul buttresses this thoroughly patriarchal disposition by appeals to Gen 1:27 (though he inserts a gender distinction about the divine image and glory not found in the original) and Gen 2:22 (11:7–9). On the practical level, the imperative "let her be covered" in 11:6 (author's translation; the NRSV is softer: "she should wear a veil") seems to be Paul's bottom-line injunction.

However, in v. 10, Paul's argument takes a sharp and unexpected turn. Just when we expect him to repeat the consequences of his interpretation of Genesis 2 as fixing the subordination of women to men ("For this reason . . ."), Paul turns the argument around to the opposite position. He stresses that a woman should have "authority" (*exousia*) over her own head "because of the angels" (an obscure reference that may refer simply to angels' attendance in the assembly at worship or to potential supernatural rapists). Paul further supports the woman's authority over her head in v. 11–12 with appeals to the new church order marked by mutual interdependence of men and women, and a reference to the matriarchal priority in childbirth through which all men once passed (a clear corrective to the reading of Genesis 2 in 11:9). Because v. 10 seems to contradict what the reader expects from the prior context, readers since antiquity have tried to account for it either by granting the word *exousia* here a meaning elsewhere unattested or by altering the text. The former strategy can still be seen in the NRSV rendering of *exousia* in this verse as "*a symbol of* authority," a translation that is not really warranted and that diverges from how they render the term in other places in this letter (for example, "control" in 7:37, "liberty" in 8:9, and "right" in 9:4–6, 12) and elsewhere in the New Testament. The latter strategy was employed by some early church fathers who replaced the (to them) problematic term *exousia* with *kalymma* ("a veil"), thus entirely subverting the women's freedom to decide how to adorn their heads in favor of a single command to be covered.

In the final verses of this argument (11:13–16), Paul abandons the uneasy task of adjudicating the relationship between women and men in the order of creation, and tosses the question to the Corinthians to decide on the basis of what he regards as clear guidelines from "nature" (11:14) and "custom" (11:16). Paul's vacillating approach is part of his overall strategy of mediation in 1 Corinthians, by which he seeks to unite a divided church by ending "contentiousness" (11:16). It is also likely due to his own ambiguous position as the bearer of the message of liberation who had not envisioned the consequences it might actually have.

From the point of view of historical reconstruction, this passage shows without a doubt that in the Corinthian church some women prayed and prophesied publicly in the worship assembly (see 11:5). These liturgical leadership roles for women are assumed to exist by the Corinthians and by Paul, who nowhere here curtails them. Women's prophetic activity in Corinth may perhaps go back to the example of Prisca, one of the founding missionaries of the Corinthian Christian community (Acts 18:2, 26; 1 Cor 16:19). Because the logic of this passage rests upon the assumption that women were leaders of liturgical speech, the apparent inconsistency with 14:33b–36 (the command to be silent in the assembly) must be resolved on that end (the arguments made by a few scholars that 11:2–16 is a later editorial insertion are not convincing and have not been generally accepted).

Paul's letters document the major importance of women in the church at Corinth. We know the names of one, and perhaps two, prominent Corinthian women leaders — Phoebe (Rom 16:1) and, if she was herself a believer, Chloe, whose "people" were believers — and there were surely many more. The role of these women in the life and disputes of that church was largely overlooked until feminist scholarship emphasized their crucial significance. Wire has attempted a full-scale reconstruction of the theology and behavior of the Corinthian women prophets in her important 1990 book. She regards them as adherents of the Sophia (wisdom) theology associated with Apollos of Alexandria, who saw in the Christ event the realization of the promises of the end time, and in their baptism their own incorporation into the ungendered life of the deity. The reason they refused to have their heads covered while engaged in worship is that they regarded the baptismal formula of Gal 3:28 celebrating incorporation into the androgynous God ("there is no longer male and female") as now essentially fulfilled. They sought to live out the implications of the spirit-infused life marked by freedom, which Paul taught was available in Christ. Like their contemporaries who were devotees of Isis and Dionysus, the Corinthian women prophets may have unbound their usually tight coiffures when enraptured in prophetic speech (a parallel that distressed Paul).

Paul's reactions to some of the Corinthian women's expressions of his gospel were mixed and ultimately ambiguous; traditionally, only the subordinationist side of his teaching was emphasized and ecclesially reinforced, while his accession of a woman's authority over her own head was suppressed. The garbled logical progression of this passage and our lack of full historical detail, have resulted in a barrage of exegetical studies, especially recently. Many argue for one of the two perspectives (subordinationist or liberationist) over against the other, rather than recognize the deliberate (though annoying!) two-sidedness of Paul's argumentation here.

MARGARET M. MITCHELL

FOR FURTHER READING: Mitchell, Margaret M. "Review Essay on A. C. Wire's *The Corinthian Women Prophets.*"

Schüssler Fiorenza, Elisabeth. *In Memory of Her: A Feminist Theological Recognition of Christian Origins.*

Thompson, Cynthia L. "Hairstyles, Head-coverings, and St. Paul: Portraits from Roman Corinth."

Wire, Antoinette Clark. *The Corinthian Women Prophets: A Reconstruction Through Paul's Rhetoric.*

1 Cor 14:33b–36
Women Commanded to Be "Silent" in the Assemblies

Embedded in 1 Corinthians 14, which contains Paul's appeal for proper exercise of spiritual gifts in the Corinthian worship assembly, are several verses that refer solely and pointedly to women. In the strongest possible language, the text issues the dual commands "let them be silent" and "let them be subordinated" in the assemblies (author's translation; the NRSV softens "let them be" to "should be"). Several supporting arguments are given for these blanket injunctions: an appeal to "what is permissible," to the authority of the Law, and to shame. An alternative plan is offered in v. 35: if they wish to learn something, women should ask their own husbands (literally: men) at home. The passage ends with a second-person censure in the form of two rhetorical questions (v. 36), though the addressee is unclear (the Greek word translated "the only ones" is masculine, so it cannot refer solely to the women). The upshot of the passage is that "[women] are not permitted to speak" in the assembly, "for it is shameful for a woman to speak in church" (NRSV, but note that the Greek word *ekklēsia* here does not refer to a building, but to the worship assembly).

This passage, together with its cousin in 1 Tim 2:11–15, has for most of Christian history been used to deny women participation and leadership in the Christian community. These verses have received an enormous amount of attention in recent years, spurred on by women's ordination debates and feminist investigations of early Christianity. Many contemporary New Testament scholars, both women and men, regard part or all of these verses to be a later editorial insertion into Paul's letter, likely by a subsequent follower of Paul, such as the one who penned the pseudepigraphical letter 1 Timothy. The impact of this scholarship can be seen in the interpretive parentheses supplied around the passage in the NRSV (lacking in the RSV). However, some feminist scholars argue that Paul did write these verses, because they can be readily accounted for, both historically and rhetorically, in their present setting.

The arguments for the inauthenticity of these verses are contextual, traditional, and text-critical. The strongest argument that Paul did not write these verses is the contradiction between them and 11:2–16 of this same letter, where Paul mentions women's praying and prophesying in the assembly without hesitation or hint of correction (his interest is in what they should have on their heads when they do so). Further, these verses are seen to interrupt the flow of the argument in chap. 14 on prophecy, for the immediate link between 14:32–33 and v. 37 is restored when these verses are omitted. Also, clear linguistic and thematic connections exist between these verses and 1 Tim 2:11–12, which presupposes a later stage of church organization and self-understanding, during which women were being systematically excluded from leadership in the church. Hence it is thought that the author of those words edited Paul's 1 Corinthians to claim his hero's authority for that later position — one contrary to Paul's own, which was to celebrate and affirm women's leadership in the church. The appeal to the Law in v. 34 is also regarded as strangely un-Pauline. A final argument refers to the history of the text of Paul's letters. Although these verses are not missing in any New Testament manuscripts, v. 34 and 35 are found after v. 40 in several bilingual Greek/Latin manuscripts. This fact suggests to some scholars that those words were originally added in the margin to a manuscript of Paul's letters and then were incorporated into the text in two different places. The extent of the proposed interpolation varies among these scholars, from v. 34–35 only, to vv. 33b–35 or vv. 33b–36 (one scholar even includes vv. 37–38). All arguments do not work equally well for each proposal (for instance, the text-critical argument concerns only vv. 34–35).

Those who think Paul wrote this passage argue that the varied placement of vv. 34–35 in the manuscript history is due simply to later corrections of an inadvertent scribal omission. They emphasize that no manuscript supports the omission of these verses entirely. Further, these scholars point to the many connections of the passage with its present context: silence (14:28, 30, and 34), subordination (14:32 [NRSV, "are subject to"], 34), and learning (14:31, 35). On that basis they regard this passage as another, though extreme, instance of Paul's calling for compromise in spiritual practice for the sake of "decency and order" (14:40). The parallel in 1 Timothy 2 indicates literary dependence in the other direction, this passage providing the prototype for that later author (as also for the roughly contemporary 1 Clement 21:6–7). The patriarchal conservatism of these verses, though in seeming contradiction to 11:5, is fully at home in an argument for unity and concord such as we find in this chapter (14:33) and throughout 1 Corinthians. The tension concerning 11:2–16 has then been explained by historical arguments that limit the apparent absoluteness of the command to silence: either Paul assumes the women prophets of 11:5 are single but here addresses only married women (14:35), or these verses are not concerned with liturgical speech, but with extracurricular chatter in the church, unrelated to the worship service proper. Feminist scholarship defending the Pauline authorship of these verses does not thereby condone their intent, but also critiques the ideologies of patriarchy and of compromise to ensure concord in the status quo that led Paul to single out the women for such categorical restrictions.

Recently a third position has emerged alongside the other two: that Paul did write these verses, but vv. 34–35 are a quotation from some Corinthians, which Paul himself subsequently refutes in vv. 36–38. Though possible, the length and complexity of the alleged quotation — which is not signaled in the text in any way — speak against this proposal.

The debate between these positions will surely continue. At any rate, it is doubtful whether a historical-critical judgment about the authorship of these verses can veto claims to their authority for some churches. The authority and role of time-conditioned biblical texts within contemporary Christian communities will still have to be addressed.

MARGARET M. MITCHELL

SEE ALSO Part II: Women Praying and Prophesying (1 Cor 11:2–16).

FOR FURTHER READING: MacDonald, Margaret. "Reading Real Women Through the Undisputed Letters of Paul."

Mitchell, Margaret M. *Paul and the Rhetoric of Reconciliation.*

Schüssler Fiorenza, Elisabeth. *In Memory of Her: A Feminist Theological Reconstruction of Christian Origins.*

Wire, Antoinette Clark. *The Corinthian Women Prophets.*

1 COR 15:6
Sisters (and Brothers) to Whom the Risen Jesus Appeared

Of the many places where the NRSV introduces the translation of the masculine plural *adelphoi* by the gender-inclusive "brothers and sisters," this passage may be the most significant and the most problematic. In 1 Cor 15:5–8, Paul lists, in apparent chronological order, those to whom the resurrected Christ appeared: to Cephas, then "the twelve"; to five hundred *adelphoi* at one time; to James, and then to "all the apostles"; and last of all, to Paul himself.

Although the canonical Gospels themselves differ significantly in their accounts of who saw the risen Jesus and in what order, none agrees with Paul's version. The shorter (and probably earliest) version of Mark contains no resurrection appearances. John 20:14–18 unambiguously states that Jesus appears first to Mary Magdalene, whereas according to Matt 28:9, Jesus appears first to Mary Magdalene and "the other" Mary (possibly, but by no means definitely, his mother). In Luke, Jesus appears first either to a man named Cleopas and his unidentified companion walking to the village of Emmaus (24:13–31) or to Simon (24:33–34). Subsequent to these appearances, Jesus appears again, to the eleven and their companions (24:36), among whom are almost certainly the women of the group who discovered the empty tomb earlier that same morning.

Paul, in short, relates a tradition of resurrection appearances in which no named women are said to have seen the risen Christ, although the masculine plural *apostoloi* might conceivably include women such as Junia (Rom 16:7). This tradition is seriously at odds with other early Christian traditions, including the narratives of Matthew and John. Accounting for these differences is difficult, especially since 1 Corinthians is one of the earliest Christian writings we have, earlier by as much as several decades than any of the Gospels. There are some possible explanations: Paul was ignorant of the tradi-

tions narrating an appearance to Mary (and other women); Paul intentionally omitted those traditions; those traditions had not yet been formulated or were not yet circulating among Christians.

For the translation of *adelphoi* in 1 Cor 15:6, we need not resolve these difficult questions. We need only recognize that the translation "brothers and sisters" makes this passage an unambiguous description of Christ appearing to a mixed group of five hundred women and men. The appeal of such a reading for many contemporary Christian communities is obvious. Nevertheless, given the discrepancies between Gospel narratives of appearances to women, including Mary, and Paul's otherwise men-only list of appearances, it seems appropriate to be cautious in concluding that Paul here uses *adelphoi* to designate women as well as men.

ROSS S. KRAEMER

SEE ALSO Part I: Junia; Mary 3; Mary 4; Part II: Unnamed Women at the Cross (Luke 23:49); Unnamed Companion of Cleopas (Luke 24:13–35).

2 COR 6:18
Believers as Daughters (and Sons) of God

In this passage, a pastiche of quotations from Jewish Scripture supports the argument of 2 Cor 6:14–7:1 that believers are the temple of the living God and God's people. The final quotation (6:18) comes from 2 Sam 7:14, where God promises David, through the prophet Nathan, that after David's death, God will establish the throne of David's son forever: "I will be a father to him, and he shall be a son to me." In 2 Cor 6:18, the addressee is altered to the second-person plural, interpreted with reference to believers in Christ, and revised to include women: "I will be your [plural] father, / and you shall be my sons and daughters."

The practice of stringing together quotations of scriptural materials occurs not only elsewhere in Paul (for example, Rom 3:10–18 and 15:9–12), but also in the Dead Sea Scrolls, Gospels, and later Jewish and Christian writings. Elsewhere, as here, the citations of Jewish Scripture (which Paul read in Greek) sometimes diverge from other ancient readings. While some scholars see this as evidence for otherwise unknown ancient versions of biblical texts, Hayes proposes that Paul's citations reflect his own interpretations of Scripture.

Whether the revision of 2 Sam 7:14 in 2 Cor 6:18 illuminates Paul's understanding of women in the Christian community remains unclear. Because 2 Cor 7:2 seems to follow naturally on 2 Cor 6:13, and because the nonscriptural vocabulary of this passage differs from the rest of the Pauline corpus, some scholars propose that 6:14–7:1 was originally part of another letter to the Corinthians, a non-Pauline composition borrowed by Paul, or perhaps even a later editorial insertion. But if the passage is authentic, whether Paul has revised it himself or merely adopted an existing form, he has chosen a citation that is explicitly gender-inclusive.

ROSS S. KRAEMER

FOR FURTHER READING: Hayes, Richard B. *Echoes of Scripture in the Letters of Paul.*

2 COR 11:2   Chaste Virgin
SEE   Chaste Bride (of Christ) (Part III).

GAL 3:28
No Male and Female in Christ Jesus
SEE   No "Male and Female" in Christ Jesus (Part III).

GAL 4:4
Born of a Woman

As part of a complex argument about the relationship of believers to the law, Paul explains that "God sent his Son, born of a woman, born under the law, in order to redeem those who were under the law" (4:4–5).

The phrase "born of a woman" simply means a mortal human being (compare Job 14:1 and Matt 11:11), grounded in the Genesis creation narrative

where, subsequent to the creation and actions of the primordial couple, all humans are mortal and born of women. Here it thus highlights the humanity (and mortality) of God's son. The passage is unlikely to be an intentional reference to the actual mother of Jesus.

ROSS S. KRAEMER

SEE ALSO Part I: Mary 1.

GAL 4:22
The Free Woman, Mother of a Son of Abraham

In Gal 4:21–31, Paul interprets the story of Abraham, Sarah, and Hagar (Gen 16:1–21:21) allegorically. He explicitly names the slave Hagar, whom he interprets as the present Jerusalem, enslaved with her children. He never names the free woman (Greek *eleuthera*), who corresponds to the heavenly Jerusalem and whom Paul designates "our mother." Interestingly, Paul names the son of the free woman, Isaac, but omits the name of Hagar's son, Ishmael. Precisely because Paul's ultimate argument in this passage depends on foregrounding the slave/free dichotomy, both the omission of Ishmael's name and the omission of Sarah's name (together with her designation as *eleuthera* — something never explicit in the Genesis narrative) may serve to heighten the opposition between the sons of the two women, one also free, the other also enslaved.

ROSS S. KRAEMER

SEE ALSO Part I: Hagar; Sarah 1/Sarai.

EPH 5:22–33
Wives (and Husbands) Exhorted

The Epistle to the Ephesians addresses the author's concerns about the alienation that characterizes human society, expressed as the division that previously existed between Jews and Gentiles but now is ended through Jesus Christ. Envisioning the church as the symbol of God's reconciliation at work on earth, Ephesians exhorts Christians to live the life to which they have been called in response to the revelation of God's plan for unity. Most biblical scholars doubt its claim to be written by Paul.

The household code in Eph 5:22–6:9 is part of this exhortation to unity and reconciliation. It is typical of other New Testament household codes written under the names of Paul or Peter. It casts relationships between wives and husbands, children and parents, and slaves and masters in the frame of subordinate relating to superior. Each party is exhorted to behave appropriately toward the other. In Ephesians the subordinate group is always addressed first. In Ephesians, the exhortation to wives and husbands is significantly longer than the exhortations to the other pairs, indicating a particular interest. Also typical is the inclusion of a specific Christological reference or a reference to some aspect of Jesus' ministry in order to motivate or theologically justify the prescribed behavior. Many scholars, noting the close literary relationship between Ephesians and Colossians, have argued that the Ephesians household code is dependent upon the much briefer one found in Col 3:18–4:1.

The philosophical provenance of these household codes can be traced back to Aristotle (fourth century B.C.E.), who emphasizes that nature determines the patriarchal social order. But studies of Roman society have found a variety of indicators about the status of women, and what was true about women in the eastern part of the empire was not necessarily true about women in the western empire. On the one hand, there was the household headed by the husband/father/master, a hierarchical order-obedience structure that included those who were economically dependent. On the other hand, there were emancipatory ideas about women that allowed them greater freedom and economic independence (some were even the heads of households). Many of the major tasks and needs that are addressed by government and society at large today were addressed by private households in Roman society: social services, education, work and eco-

nomic production, and numerous juridical functions.

The subordinate view of women preserved in Eph 5:22–33 could well be an outgrowth of Paul's ambiguity on the question of women (as observed in the corpus of Pauline letters) — on the one hand, acknowledging and respecting the work of women colleagues and advocating a certain degree of equality in social relations, but on the other hand, enforcing certain social and religious practices that clearly underscore the inferior position of women. The early Christian household codes are not inconsistent with this latter, patriarchal Pauline trajectory. The household was formative in shaping early Christianity, which began as a household movement: in the first two centuries C.E., believers relied exclusively on private households to provide the meeting spaces for Christian communities, or "house-churches." The private household served as a model for the local church and eventually for the universal church. The terminology used to describe the functions and relationships within the private household became the terminology used to describe the functions and relationships within the church and between Christians and God. In other words, the private household provided more than the physical meeting space for the early church; it provided the conceptual foundation as well — hence, the household code. The household codes idealize the Christian household as a hierarchically ordered social unity, and within them is found the self-understanding of the church as an interdependent household in relationship to Christ. In this sense, these household codes may prescribe an ideal (how the life in Christ is to be implemented) much more than they describe what actually existed. Clearly, they also seek to establish the authority of the ruler of the household (husband, father, master). The implications of this interest in authority are even more far-reaching, because these household codes are ultimately not only about household relationships, but also about the church understood on the model of the household, with Christ as ruler.

The exhortation to wives and husbands in Eph 5:22–33 includes instruction to wives (5:22–24), a longer set of instructions to the husbands (5:25–30), quotation from Gen 2:24 (5:31), an interpretation of that text (5:32), and a final command addressed to both wives and husbands that is influenced by the Genesis passage (5:33). Noteworthy throughout this exhortation is the phrase "as Christ" (5:23, 25, 29), which seems intended to motivate human behavior by comparing it to Christ's relationship with the church. Wives are exhorted to respond to their husbands as the church does to Christ; husbands are exhorted to respond to their wives as Christ does to the church.

Although 5:21 is not a part of the Ephesians household code (and is grammatically problematic in relationship to it), it nevertheless functions as a bridge between the general exhortations that precede it and the household code that follows it. It provides both the thematic ("Be subject" and "reverence for Christ") and syntactic (5:22 understands as its verb the participle of 5:21) links that may explain the placement of the household code following 5:21. Eph 5:22–24 forms the basic block of exhortations to wives to be subject to their husbands as the church is subject to Christ. The Christ/husband and church/wife analogies are meant to motivate each member of the wife/husband pair. In the various household codes, wives are consistently exhorted by some form of the verb *be subject* (see Col 3:18; 1 Pet 3:1; 1 Tim 2:11; Titus 2:4–5). There is no parallel consistency in the verbs used to exhort husbands. The exhortation to wives to be subject to their husbands is often understood as a request for voluntary subordination. However, the strength of the analogy with Christ and the church undercuts the "voluntary" quality of the exhortation. For how should a Christian wife resist this "voluntary" call when it is cast in terms that would make any other choice an apparent slight to Christ? The further qualification that the wives' subordination to their husbands is to be "in everything" (v. 24) also derives its force from this analogy, which cements the subordinate position of the wife in the marriage.

Eph 5:25–30 contains instructions to husbands and comprises two subsections: vv. 25–27 and vv. 28–30. Both subsections exhort husbands to love their wives (vv. 25, 28), and both use the analogy with Christ and the church as motivation. Eph 5:28–30 exhorts husbands to love their wives using the qualifying "as they do their own bodies." "Love" and "body" provide the linguistic touchstones for these verses, but the language is richer still, calling to mind the commandment of Lev 19:18 (to love one's neighbor as oneself) and anticipating the quotation of Gen 2:24 (stating that in marriage, a woman and man become one flesh) in 5:31. The object of love moves from "their wives" to "their own bodies" to "himself." In 5:30, with the shift to "we" and the addition of "members," the author dramatically draws himself and his audience in, reminding all concerned that they too are members of Christ's body, and the entire code pertains directly to them.

In 5:31–32, the writer quotes Gen 2:24 and then interprets the "mystery" of the relationship between Christ and the church as the model for human marriage. 5:33 concludes this part of the household code with summary exhortations. The husband is exhorted (here clearly echoing Lev 19:18) to "love his wife as himself," and the wife is told to "respect [literally, "fear"] her husband."

The irony of the household code is that, whereas the early chapters of Ephesians describe a new kind of equality, through Christ, of Jew and Gentile and the breaking down of the dividing wall, these exhortations are clearly not about equals but about hierarchy; they do not break down dividing walls, but rather establish them and teach one to live within hierarchical bounds in the name of Christian unity.

SARAH J. TANZER

SEE ALSO Part II: Wives (and Husbands) Exhorted (Col 3:18–19); Older and Younger Women Exhorted (Titus 2:3–5).

FOR FURTHER READING: Lampe, Peter. "'Family' in Church and Society of New Testament Times."

Schnackenburg, Rudolf. *Ephesians: A Commentary.*
Tanzer, Sarah J. "Ephesians."

EPH 5:25–27   Wife as Church
SEE Chaste Bride (of Christ) (Part III).

Eph 6:2–3
Mother (and Father) to Be Honored

In a letter claiming Pauline authorship, the author of Ephesians instructs Christians to adhere to a Greco-Roman household code that sets forth the appropriate hierarchical relationships between husbands and wives, parents and children, slaves and owners. In Christian household codes (found also in Col 3:18–4:1 and 1 Pet 2:18–3:7), these relationships are presented as analogous to the relationship of Christ with the church.

In 6:2–3, children are exhorted to love their parents, in fulfillment of the commandment to honor father and mother. The author also observes that this commandment is the first to be accompanied by a promise, that of well-being and long life. The much shorter exhortation to children in Col 3:20 lacks this reference to the scriptural commandment, while the household code in 1 Peter contains no exhortations for parents or children, giving only those for slaves, wives, and husbands.

ROSS S. KRAEMER

SEE ALSO Part II: Mother (and Father) to Be Honored (Matt 19:19); (Mark 10:19); (Luke 18:20); Wives (and Husbands) Exhorted (Eph 5:22–33); (Col 3:18–19); (1 Pet 3:1–7).

EPH 6:7
Women (and Men) Slave Owners

In Eph 5:21–6:9, the author (who uses the name of Paul, although the authenticity of the letter is highly disputed) offers a Christianized version of a Greco-Roman "household code" delineating the proper behaviors for persons in subordinate and superior relationships to one another. Eph 6:5–9 presumes that some Christians will be slaves, while other Christians will be slave owners. Offering no critique of ancient slavery itself, these verses nevertheless direct slaves to obey their owners as they obey Christ and tell owners to stop threatening their slaves.

In the NRSV translation of 6:7, slaves are directed to "render service with enthusiasm, as to the Lord and not to men and women." This explicitly inclusive phrase takes the grammatically masculine plural *anthrōpoi* to include persons of both genders. Given the sense of the verse, an alternative and perhaps better translation might have been "as to the Lord, and not to human beings." Even this translation conceals an ironic pun, for the Greek *kyrios* here designates Christ ("the Lord"), whereas in 6:5 and 6:7 the same Greek term, in the plural, designates slave owners.

The NRSV translation of 6:7 properly alerts us to the fact that in antiquity, women as well as men were part of the extensive slave economy, not only as enslaved persons, but also as owners of slaves, both female and male. Several women mentioned elsewhere in the New Testament appear to have been slave owners, including Chloe, who may or may not have been a believer herself (1 Cor 1:11), and Lydia of Thyatira (Acts 16:14–15). If the *paidiskē* Rhoda in Acts 12:13 is best understood as a slave (*paidiskē* can mean both "slave" and "servant"), her owner should most likely be understood as Mary, the mother of John Mark (Acts 12:12). Paul understands Hagar to have been the slave of Sarah (Gal 4:21–31).

This inclusive translation does not extend to 6:9, where the author addresses slave owners, *kyrioi*, which the NRSV translates with the more blatantly masculine "masters." Nor does the translation of the masculine plural *douloi* as "slaves" heighten our awareness that women were regularly enslaved. Interestingly, in the similar but briefer household code in Colossians (another disputed letter in the name of Paul), a phrase identical to that in Eph 6:7 is translated differently: "for the Lord and not for your masters" (Col 3:23). Here the NRSV eliminates the ambiguity of *anthrōpoi* and omits any reference to women slave owners. The small-print notes accompanying the NRSV do alert readers to the translation of *anthrōpoi* in Col 3:23, but not to that in Eph 6:7, leaving English readers with the impression that the underlying Greek differs in each verse.

Ross S. Kraemer

See also Part I: Chloe; Lydia; Mary 6; Sarah 1/Sarai.

For further reading: Bartchy, S. Scott. "Slavery (Greco-Roman)."

Bradley, Keith R. *Slavery and Society at Rome.*

————. *Slaves and Masters in the Roman Empire: A Study in Social Control.*

Glancy, Jennifer A. "Obstacles to Slaves' Participation in the Corinthian Church."

Martin, Dale J. *Slavery and Salvation: The Metaphor of Slavery in Pauline Christianity.*

Phil 4:3
Loyal Companion

In Phil 4:2–3, Paul entreats two women in the church at Philippi, Euodia and Syntyche, to be in accord. In v. 3, he appeals to a third person to assist them in this endeavor, a person referred to as "loyal *syzyge*."

The Greek *syzygos* (literally "yoke-sharer") has a variety of meanings, from "one of a pair of gladiators" to the more general "comrade" or "companion." Although the word is normally masculine, it is sometimes used with a feminine definite article to mean "wife." Several ancient interpreters took this as a reference to Paul's own spouse (supported in part by the ambiguous reference to a "sister-wife" in 1 Cor 9:5), but given Paul's apparent abstinence from marriage (1 Cor 7:7–8), this seems unlikely. It has also occasionally been suggested that the word should be read as a proper name, Syzygos (see, for example, the translation in the NIB), but this would be the only known instance of such usage.

The NRSV translation "loyal companion" is sufficiently subtle that ordinary readers are unlikely to recognize its ambiguity. It is perfectly possible that the "loyal *syzyge*" refers to a woman, although many interpreters have assumed that Paul is here addressing a man (perhaps even Epaphroditus, who carried the letter).

Ross S. Kraemer

See also Part I: Euodia; Syntyche.

For further reading: Osiek, Carolyn. "Philippians."

Col 3:18–19
Wives (and Husbands) Exhorted

The exhortation to wives and husbands forms the first part of the household code found in Col 3:18–4:1. It is shorter and less theologically complex than the closely related code found in Ephesians (5:22–6:9). Typical of such New Testament household codes written under the names of Paul or Peter, it treats three relationships — between wives and husbands, children and parents, and slaves and masters. The writer frames each relationship as that of subordinate to superior, exhorting each party within these pairs to behave appropriately toward the other. The subordinate group is always addressed first, being exhorted "to be subject" (wives) or "to obey" (children, slaves) their husbands, parents, or masters, and the text does not grant women authority as either mothers or the masters of slaves. Not all exhortations are symmetrical in the different codes. In Colossians, the exhortation to slaves is significantly longer, indicating a particular focus of that letter. As in other household codes, Colossians uses a Christological reference to motivate or theologically justify the prescribed behavior. Notably, it is used primarily to exhort the subordinate member of the pair (wives, children, slaves).

The overarching theme of the Colossians code is the universal lordship of Christ and is well summarized in 3:24: "serve the Lord [Master] Christ." The exhortation to wives is brief (3:18), and as in other household codes, wives are exhorted to "be subject" to their husbands. Here, the only justification for the command is that it is "fitting in the Lord" (3:18). The meaning of "Lord" is ambiguous and may refer both to Christ and to the husband as lord and master. Equally brief (3:19) is the exhortation to husbands "to love" their wives and "never treat them harshly" — literally, "do not be embittered against them." Perhaps this latter command refers to women as the target of anger aroused by others, as we find in Greek and Roman literature from this period.

The household codes of Colossians and other early Christian texts may trace their origins as far back as Aristotle, and they likely build upon the idealized, hierarchical Roman household, headed by the husband/father/master, which was current in some parts of the Roman Empire in New Testament times. One must keep in mind that early Christianity began as a household movement, and the private household served as a model for the local church and eventually the universal church, helping to shape relationships within the church and between Christians and God. But these codes also take their lead from Paul's ambivalence toward women as attested in the undisputed letters, in particular building on his enforcement of certain social and religious practices that underscore the inferior position of women (including his insistence that Corinthian women prophets cover their heads when they pray and prophesy in the communal assembly [1 Cor 11:3–16] and his prohibition of women speaking in the assembly [if this is authentically Pauline — 1 Cor 14:33b–36]).

Moreover, Colossians revises Pauline Christology, which compared Christ to a body with many members (compare 1 Cor 6:12–20; 12:12–21; Rom 12:3–8), instead of viewing Christ as the head over the body of the church, a change that lays the groundwork for 3:18–4:1, with its pattern of social domination.

Much of the rest of Colossians might have proved empowering to women: the resistance to the powers, rules, and authorities; the highlighting of the spiritual riches that the faithful enjoy; and the concern with wisdom. But this is undermined by the letter's proscription of ascetic and visionary practices (areas in which women and slaves were known to have been active) and by the emphasis on submission to the social order. As perhaps the earliest of the Christian canonical household codes, Colossians endorses social patterns of restricting and subordinating women, children, and slaves.

SARAH J. TANZER

SEE ALSO Part II: Wives (and Husbands) Exhorted (Eph 5:22–23); (1 Pet 3:1–7).
FOR FURTHER READING: D'Angelo, Mary Rose. "Colossians."
Schüssler Fiorenza, Elisabeth. *In Memory of Her.*

1 THESS 2:7
Nurse Caring for Her Children

In the letter known as 1 Thessalonians, apparently defending himself from detractors, Paul presents himself as far more concerned for his charges, the Thessalonians, than for his own welfare or reputation. Drawing on one feminine and one masculine simile, Paul says first that he and his coworkers had treated the Thessalonians as "a nurse tenderly caring for her own children" (2:7), then that "we dealt with each one of you like a father with his children, urging and encouraging you and pleading that you lead a life worthy of God" (2:11–12).

In the ancient Mediterranean, wet nurses were regularly engaged to nurse and raise children whose mothers had died in childbirth or infancy, a common occurrence, or whose mothers were otherwise unable to nurse. Elite women sometimes also apparently utilized wet nurses by choice rather than necessity. Literary sources and burial inscriptions alike suggest that ties between wet nurses and their charges were often strong.

Most wet nurses appear to have been slaves or poor free women who nursed children other than their own for financial compensation. Wet-nurse contracts surviving on papyrus from this period provide us details of the legal arrangements and glimpses of the social circumstances, as in the case of a contract from Egypt, in 13 B.C.E., wherein a free married woman (whose name suggests that she was Jewish) agrees to nurse an infant foundling slave (probably abandoned) and promises to do nothing to compromise her milk supply for a period of eighteen months.

ROSS S. KRAEMER

FOR FURTHER READING: Bradley, Keith R. "The Social Role of the Nurse in the Roman World."

1 THESS 5:3
Pregnant Woman in Labor

The section of 1 Thessalonians in which this verse occurs addresses itself to the coming "day of the Lord" (5:2). The author (probably Paul himself) reminds readers that the impending destruction will be sudden, the way labor comes upon a pregnant woman.

The "day of the Lord" is likened to labor pains in Isa 13:6–8, and this passage may well draw on that connection. But it also assumes that ancient audiences, women and men alike, had shared understandings of the experience of labor and childbirth and of their utility as an analogy or metaphor for various other experiences.

ROSS S. KRAEMER

SEE ALSO Part II: Woman in Labor (Isa 13:8, etc.); Woman/Women in Labor (Sir 19:11, etc.); Woman in Labor (John 16:21); Part III: Woman in Labor, Clothed with the Sun.

2 THESSALONIANS
No Women Mentioned

2 Thessalonians contains no references to named women; in most English translations, it also contains no references to unnamed women. As a consequence of the translators' decision to render the Greek masculine plural *adelphoi* (literally "brothers") with the inclusive phrase "brothers and sisters," in the NRSV, 2 Thessalonians appears to address both women and men six times (1:3; 2:1, 13, 15; 3:1, 15). Unaccountably, in 3:6 the translators use "beloved" instead. They also translate the masculine singular *adelphos* as "believers" in 3:6 and 3:15. In these two cases, they probably sought a gender-neutral term that would nevertheless differentiate

these cases from those instances where the Greek has the masculine plural *(adelphoi)*.

In the opening greeting, the writers of the letter are identified as Paul, Silvanus, and Timothy, although in the closing salutation only Paul is named. Many scholars doubt that the letter is authentic. The concerns of the letter are several. Chap. 1 indicates that the church at Thessalonica (in modern Greece) is experiencing persecution and affliction of an unspecified nature; chap. 2 refutes claims that the day of the Lord is already here, claims apparently made in the name of Paul and his associates (2:2). Much of chap. 3 is concerned with members of the church (NRSV, "believers"; Greek masculine singular *adelphos*) who abstain from productive labor, expecting support from other members of the church.

2 Thessalonians intentionally expands on the themes of 1 Thessalonians, including the fate of those who have died before the return of the Lord and the importance of productive labor. Much of 1 Thessalonians (whose Pauline authorship is undisputed and which, like 2 Thessalonians, names Paul, Silvanus, and Timothy as its authors) does not appear concerned with issues that, at least at first glance, are particularly susceptible to a gender-sensitive analysis (with the possible exception of 1 Thess 4:4–6, on the avoidance of lust). Were it not for the use of two gendered images, that of the tender nurse in 1 Thess 2:7, and the pregnant woman in labor in 1 Thess 5:3, 1 Thessalonians, too, would fall into the category of books with no named or unnamed women. Perhaps because it is derived from 1 Thessalonians, 2 Thessalonians, too, does not seem to speak to gendered issues.

Nevertheless, it seems reasonable to ask whether the problem of believers who fail to earn their own living is, in fact, gender-specific. In 1 Cor 9:1–18, Paul asserts the right of wandering preachers, including himself, to the support of the local community, while nevertheless making clear that he has refused such support. In 1 Thess 2:9, Paul reminds the Thessalonians that he, Timothy, and Silvanus "worked night and day, so that we might not burden any of you while we proclaimed to you the gospel of God"; in 4:11, he urges them to work with their hands, so as to be independent. In 2 Thess 3:9, the writers appear to assert their own right to support, but nevertheless contend that they have previously instructed the Thessalonians that "anyone unwilling to work should not eat" (3:10).

Does "anyone" include women as well as men? The answer may depend on whether there is a meaningful distinction between the language of 1 Thess 4:11, "working with your hands," and that of 2 Thess 3:10, "work" (without reference to hands). If by "work" the author(s) of 2 Thessalonians envision any productive labor, compensated or not, we may well expect that this injunction could easily be directed to both women and men. Many women in the Roman period engaged in commercial labor for which they received compensation, in varied occupational roles such as merchants, shopkeepers, and wet nurses, and occasionally as physicians and even scribes. In the New Testament itself, Lydia of Thyatira is described as a merchant dealing in purple-dyed goods (Acts 16:14); in Acts 18:3, Priscilla is said to be a tentmaker together with her husband, Aquila. Elite women are less likely to have labored for financial gain. Enslaved women could expect no financial compensation from their owners, but could, and sometimes did, earn money on their own, often through prostitution. Whether free non-elite women labored for financial compensation probably depended on whether they were married, widowed, or divorced, and on their access to financial support from husbands and male kin. Numerous early Christian communities appear to have provided financial support for widows (see, for example, 1 Tim 4:4–16).

But if labor that produces financial remuneration is at stake, as 2 Thess 3:8 suggests ("we did not eat anyone's bread without paying for it"), it becomes harder to imagine that 3:10 is directed equally to men and to women, many of whom would not have labored for direct financial compensation. In that case, 2 Thess 3:6–12 might be directed primarily, if not entirely, at men who now refrain from productive labor and expect support from the community.

ROSS S. KRAEMER

FOR FURTHER READING: Beavis, Mary Ann. "2 Thessalonians."

1 TIM 2:9–15
Women Who Profess Reverence for God

1 Tim 2:9–15 presents a set of rules governing the life of an early Christian community, perhaps the church at Ephesus, a cosmopolitan city in Asia Minor (modern-day Turkey) in which a variety of religious groups were active. Since these rules shift easily from an initial focus on worship to more general conduct, it is probable that they derive from first-century household codes — general regulations that governed, among other things, female behavior.

Although the Pastoral Epistles are written in the name of Paul, most scholars consider the theology and church development implied in all three (1, 2 Timothy, Titus) to support the idea that they were authored by one of Paul's followers. Commentators generally agree that the Pastorals were written to counteract the influence of "false teachers" within the community — most probably those espousing some form of Gnostic belief that denied the relevance to salvation of the physical aspects of human experience. The author's audience would thus have had contact with religious teachers who advocated both libertine and ascetic behaviors.

McDonald has suggested that the Pastoral Epistles also reflect the growing tension between the newly emerging church hierarchy and more charismatic forms of Christianity. It is not surprising to find here a conservative policy regulating theological, ethical, and social matters.

The instruction that women maintain a modest physical appearance during worship was not unusual for the times. Both Christian and Roman writers extolled modesty as a standard female virtue in the Greco-Roman world of late antiquity. Modesty was also emphasized as a womanly virtue in the honorary inscriptions of the period. By re-

Head of a young woman with braided hair, from a marble statue of the Roman period. Women are admonished to avoid such hairstyles in 1 Tim 2:9. See Women Who Profess Reverence for God (1 Tim 2:9–15).

Gold and pearl earrings, exact provenance unknown, from the second–third century C.E. Devout women are instructed to avoid wearing gold or pearls in 1 Tim 2:9. See Women Who Profess Reverence for God (Tim 2:9–15).

fraining from ostentation in dress, hairstyle, ornamentation, and use of cosmetics, the virtuous woman could exercise self-control and avoid tempting or otherwise offending the men around her.

The injunction that women must learn in silence shifts the focus even more specifically to female behavior in the church. Appealing to a rhetorical analysis of the rules, commentators such as Dewey argue that the author would not have spent so much time and effort instructing Christian women to remain silent unless the goal was to change already existing behavior. According to such an interpretation, the women in this church were active and vocal participants.

The injunction for women to remain silent is clarified by the further injunction that women not teach or have authority over men. Elsewhere, the Pastorals make clear that women did have a teaching function within the church, insofar as older women were to teach younger women (Titus 2:3–5). The problem at hand was thus relational rather than strictly functional.

Commentators have struggled to understand the precise meaning here of the Greek verb "to have authority over" (*authentein*). This is the only New Testament occurrence of this verb, which appears here in its infinitive form. The verb had a varied use in other early Christian writings.

Kroeger and Kroeger have offered a unique interpretation of this injunction, suggesting that *authentein* at one time denoted participation in religious fertility rites. According to such an interpretation, the author was admonishing the women of the Ephesian church not to teach or engage in fertility practices with men, evidently referring to the

Artemis cult at Ephesus and the role of courtesans as teachers. Kroeger and Kroeger stand alone in their interpretation. Other commentators tend to view the injunction within the context of power, suggesting that women were not to exercise authority over men in an abusive manner. Modern interpretations of this passage reveal the long-abiding tension within the Christian church regarding the role of women. Both Kroeger and Kroeger and their detractors offer interpretations they hope will be palatable to modern sensibilities without undermining the traditional authority of the Bible.

The relational nature of the injunction, and of the term *authentein,* seems to be substantiated by the author's appeal to the order of creation. Just as Adam was created first, and then Eve, so were men and women within the church to remain in proper relationship. The theological argument further anchored the popular notion that women were flighty and easily led astray by false teachers. Although women were not prohibited from teaching altogether, their relationship with men was clearly to remain a subservient one.

LUCINDA A. BROWN

FOR FURTHER READING: Dewey, Joanna. "1 Timothy."

Gritz, Sharon Hodgin. *Paul, Women Teachers, and the Mother Goddess at Ephesus: A Study of 1 Timothy 2:9–15 in Light of the Religious and Cultural Milieu of the First Century.*

Kroeger, Catherine C., and Richard Kroeger. *I Suffer Not a Woman: Rethinking First Timothy 2:11–15 in Light of Ancient Evidence.*

Schüssler Fiorenza, Elisabeth. *In Memory of Her: A Feminist Theological Reconstruction of Christian Origins.*

Witherington, Ben, III. *Women and the Genesis of Christianity.*

1 TIM 3:11
Women Deacons

1 Timothy 3 outlines the characteristics of those who could aspire to be bishops and deacons within a church, thought by many to have been at Ephesus in western Asia Minor (modern-day Turkey), the fourth largest city in the Roman Empire. Although the author claims to be Paul, most scholars think this unlikely. The description of women deacons is included as an aside within the more general description of deacons. These instructions concerning church leaders were given so that members of the church might know how to behave in the household of God until such time as the author was able to be with them personally.

The description of bishops and deacons focuses on the behavior that qualifies them for the positions, rather than on the beliefs they were to hold or the duties they were to perform. The author of the Pastoral Epistles clearly had in mind a set of beliefs that were to be understood as true and worthy of acceptance within the Christian community. These beliefs were not fully articulated in the Pastoral Epistles, but were referred to categorically as "the truth" and "the mystery of our religion."

The descriptions of deacons and bishops are presented in list form. Lists were a common literary device in the ancient world. Examples of lists are found throughout the Hebrew Scriptures and the New Testament. These and other New Testament lists are typical examples of the Greco-Roman catalogues of vices and virtues.

1 Tim 3:11 emphasizes certain virtues that are to characterize women deacons. The author is not, however, simply repeating virtues that have already been used to describe their male counterparts. Rather, in the Greco-Roman world, discussion of vices and virtues sometimes had different implications when applied to women than when applied to men. Both female and male deacons, for example, are to be temperate. For men, this would involve maintaining some measure of moderation and self-control — such as not indulging in much wine. For the women, however, it would refer more specifically to bodily chastity.

In other instances, characteristics that describe male deacons might have been applied to female deacons as well, even though they are not explicitly stated. The injunction that deacons are to be married only once, for example, might well apply to both women and men. Early Christian (patristic) writers such as Jerome and Tertullian later argued that both Christian men and women were not to remarry following divorce or the death of a spouse. Although the Pastoral Epistles probably predate the patristic era, they certainly reflect ideas that would be stated more fully at that time. Even the concession in 1 Tim 5:14 regarding the remarriage of widows — which could perhaps shed some light on the marital status of women deacons — applies only to widows of childbearing age.

The extent to which women deacons were to be good managers of their households, as were male deacons, is also open for speculation. The New Testament attests to female heads of household within the early Christian community (see, for example, Luke 10:38–42; Acts 12:12–17; 16:14–15), so certain expectations might well have existed regarding women's household management skills. Torjesen has further noted that, within the Greco-Roman household system, both female heads of household and married women would have had significant responsibilities for household management. Tension would have arisen in late antiquity as church leadership functions moved from the more private sphere of the household to the more public sphere of the city. So long as the church was based on a household model, however, women's contributions to household management would have been assumed.

Schüssler Fiorenza has described women deacons within the context of the patron-client relationship that predominated in the Greco-Roman world. Some women had achieved economic independence and accumulated their own wealth, but had not achieved corresponding political influence and power. By joining religious associations or becoming involved in the Christian movement, such women were able to derive some measure of authority not available to them elsewhere.

The reason for including the description of deacons in the Pastoral Epistles is not entirely clear. A probable explanation lies, however, in the author's overarching concern with the presence of false teachers within the audience's church. By demonstrating in both word and deed their adherence to what is "true" (as understood by the author of the Pastoral Epistles), both female and male deacons would show that they could stand strong in the face of false teachings and be faithful leaders of the audience's church. Describing women deacons as "serious, not slanderers" and "faithful in all things" would also set these women apart from the women who are led astray by the false teachers and who are described elsewhere in the Pastoral Epistles as the tellers of tales (1 Tim 4:7), idle women who gad about from house to house as gossips and busybodies (1 Tim 5:13), and silly women (2 Tim 3:6).

The description of deacons in terms of the household system also supports MacDonald's argument that the Pastoral Epistles seek to diminish the "legend tradition," as found in noncanonical *Acts* of the various apostles, wherein Paul is depicted as an itinerant, charismatic preacher. (The noncanonical *Apocryphal Acts of the Apostles*, written from the second century C.E. on, were very popular throughout Asia Minor. They represent a form of early Christian spirituality that authenticates the authoritative role of personal experience.) The growing tension between charismatic forms of Christianity and the emerging church hierarchy would certainly have raised questions about the locus of authority and the means by which God was known, whether through personal experience or through adherence to a set of beliefs and behaviors.

LUCINDA A. BROWN

SEE ALSO Part I: Phoebe.

FOR FURTHER READING: MacDonald, Dennis Ronald. *The Legend and the Apostle: The Battle for Paul in Story and Canon.*

MacDonald, Margaret Y. "Rereading Paul: Early Interpreters of Paul on Women and Gender."

Schüssler Fiorenza, Elisabeth. *In Memory of Her: A Feminist Theological Reconstruction of Christian Origins.*

Torjesen, Karen Jo. *When Women Were Priests: Women's Leadership in the Early Church and the Scandal of Their Subordination in the Rise of Christianity.*

1 Tim 4:7
Women Tale Tellers

The Pastoral Epistles (1, 2 Timothy; Titus) include a number of warnings about the last days. These warnings utilize standard apocalyptic rhetoric, denouncing those who do not hold fast to the true faith. In 1 Timothy 4, the recipient is warned particularly about teachers of an extreme form of asceticism that demands celibacy and fasting. The author, writing under the name of Paul, juxtaposes these "false teachings" with the sound teachings of the "true faith," and the physical training demanded by the false teachers with the training in godliness demanded by the church.

The "myths and old wives' tales" (1 Tim 4:7) that the audience is to avoid are clearly linked with those who are renouncing the "true faith." Such tales stand in opposition to emerging Christian doctrine, and the tellers of such tales threaten to undermine the authority of early church leaders.

It is not entirely clear who the tellers of the "old wives' tales" were. They were, perhaps, women who followed the proto-gnostic teachers (who endorsed various ascetic practices) condemned elsewhere in the Pastoral Epistles. They may have shared stories among themselves or passed stories along to the next generation.

MacDonald links the "old wives' tales" with the physical training denounced in 1 Tim 4:8. The women who adhered to the ascetic practices would have regarded the tales as sacred legends, whereas the author of the Pastorals regarded them as lies. The author's condemnation of the tales and the women who told them would have thus been part of the church's attempt to break the tie between prophecy and celibacy — an association that was taking root in prophetic movements such as New Prophecy/Montanism.

Schüssler Fiorenza links the "profane stories told by old women" with the young widows of 1 Tim 5:13, who are described as "gossips and busybodies." Such an association would be consistent with the author's concern with idle talk and people who do not know what they are saying (see, for example, 1 Tim 1:6–7; 4:2–3; 2 Tim 3:6–9; Titus 1:1–14).

It is also possible that the phrase "old wives' tales" was used derogatorily to refer to the false teachers themselves. To refer to men in terms of womanly nature would constitute a significant rhetorical put down. The author of the Pastoral Epistles and other Christian writers of the period understood women to be of secondary nature to men. Whereas men were associated with the mind and rationality, women were associated with the body and irrationality. The author of the Pastoral Epistles took the further step of differentiating between women and men on the basis of the order of creation (see 1 Tim 2:13–15).

The section concludes by noting that "this saying is sure and worthy of full acceptance" (1 Tim 4:9) — a common refrain in the Pastoral Epistles. The author drives the final wedge between the church and its opponents by asserting that the church sets its hope in the living God, the savior of all people, especially of those who believe. The tellers of "old wives' tales" are thus summarily dismissed.

LUCINDA A. BROWN

SEE ALSO Part II: Women Who Profess Reverence for God (1 Tim 2:9–15); "Silly" or Little Women (2 Tim 3:6).

FOR FURTHER READING: MacDonald, Dennis Ronald. *The Legend and the Apostle: The Battle for Paul in Story and Canon.*

Schüssler Fiorenza, Elisabeth. *In Memory of Her: A Feminist Theological Reconstruction of Christian Origins.*

1 Tim 5:2
Older and Younger Women

In 1 Tim 5:1–2, Timothy (the pseudonymous addressee named after Paul's fellow missionary) receives advice about how he should treat the various groups within the church by age and gender. The form of the advice assumes the existence of a patriarchal household structure, speaking first of men and then of women and moving from those who have authority over all who follow on the list (older men) to those who have authority over none (younger women). Older women have authority only over younger women. The advice given is conventional, and similar instructions can be found in popular Greek and Roman moral philosophy and in the wisdom literature of the Hebrew Bible.

Located where it is, it provides a smooth transition between the personal instructions to Timothy (4:6–16) and the extensive instructions (5:3–6:2) concerning three problematic groups within the church: widows, elders, and slaves. It also emphasizes a key theme in 1 Timothy, the church as the household of God (3:15). Timothy (as an example to other church members) is to speak to the various members of the household of God as he would to members of his own family.

SARAH J. TANZER

SEE ALSO Part II: Older and Younger Women Exhorted (Titus 2:3–5).

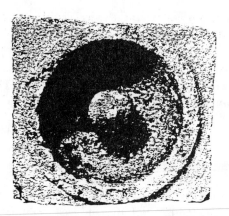

So-called footbath, found at the top of the steps to a bath thought to be a mikveh, or ritual bath, in the first-century B.C.E. complex of Herod the Great in Jerusalem. Foot washing was an act of hospitality in antiquity: in 1 Tim 5:10, women wishing to be enrolled as "real widows" must have washed the feet of the saints. See Widows (1 Tim 5:3–16).

1 TIM 5:3–16
Widows

1 Tim 5:3–16 is the longest New Testament passage concerning widows. In the ancient Mediterranean world, the term *widow* essentially referred to any woman who lacked the visible protection and economic support of a husband. Thus, a widow could be a woman whose husband had died, a divorced woman, or even a woman whose husband was simply away for an extended period of time (which was the case for women whose husbands were soldiers).

In the Hebrew tradition and in certain early Christian traditions, the widow was an object of charity. The widow, the fatherless, and the stranger symbolized those who were not otherwise spoken for within the patriarchal system and thus in need of special protection. By the period of formative Judaism and early Christianity, caring for the widow, the fatherless, and the stranger had had a long history as a symbol of faithfulness to God's commandments.

Although some widows within the early Christian community were no doubt economically disadvantaged, others were self-sufficient. Jewish-

Christian widows presumably could have followed the Jewish custom of reclaiming their *kětûbâ*, or marriage payment, upon the death of their husbands, rather than remain under the financial protection of their husbands' families. Other widows of the Greco-Roman world could have inherited property or other wealth from their husbands. Some widows presumably supported themselves by means of their own economic activities. The Pastoral Epistles (1, 2 Timothy; Titus) and other early Christian writings that associated widows with the practice of hospitality — which would have included activities such as the provision of meals and overnight accommodations to travelers — certainly assumed that widows had access to money and property. Care must, therefore, be taken in reading texts such as 1 Tim 5:3–16, in order to determine what was economically and socially descriptive and what was simply a rhetorical device.

A number of early Christian writings, including those of Tertullian and Hippolytus, attest to an order of widows within the early church that was responsible for prayer, instruction of younger women, hospitality, and services similar to those performed by deacons. Such widows came to be held in high esteem within the early church, perhaps even participating in pastoral and liturgical activities alongside members of the emerging clergy. Some commentators suggest that the widows of 1 Tim 5:3–16 belonged to an early form of such an order.

The proximity of 1 Tim 5:3–16 to the description of bishops in 1 Tim 3:1–7 and deacons in 1 Tim 3:8–13, as well as its similarity in content and style, would seem to confirm this suggestion. This would certainly be consistent with other early Christian writings in which widows are mentioned alongside presbyters, bishops, and deacons. An honored role for widows within the church could also underlie the author's concern with differentiating between those who are "real widows" (5:3) and those who are not.

The description of widows in 1 Tim 5:3–16 is, however, distinguished from the earlier description of bishops and deacons in some rather significant ways. Whereas bishops and deacons are described by the characteristics (such as temperance, sensibleness, and respectability) that they are to manifest *while* holding their respective offices, the widows must meet certain qualifications *before* they can be considered "real widows." Most notably, "real widows" have to be at least sixty years old. Nowhere is a corresponding age requirement imposed on bishops and deacons. Further, widows must have demonstrated their good works, hospitality, and devotion prior to being designated as "real widows."

The author of the Pastoral Epistles, who writes in the name of Paul, seems to be concerned with keeping the "real widows" from becoming too numerous and, presumably, too influential. This is most clearly demonstrated by the injunction that young widows are to remarry and bear children (5:14), even though this would violate the earlier injunction that "real widows" could be married only once. This would limit the number of women who could qualify as "real widows." It would also separate older from younger women, thus limiting the widows' sphere of influence within the church.

The stature of widows in this church is further diminished by the attempt to make them the objects of charity. The author of the Pastorals depicts widows without traditional family support as financially dependent on the church, in spite of the fact that these same women might well have had access to other resources. It is also possible that wealthy widows were among the church's principal financial contributors.

Torjesen suggests that the effort to keep these widows in their place reflected a growing tension between heads of household (including widows) and the titular heads of the church (the bishops). Torjesen has argued that "real widows" were those whose ministries kept them within the private sphere of their homes. Those who were not "real widows" were those whose activities — wandering about, teaching, and the like — led them into the public sphere.

By restricting the "real widows" to a life of prayer, the Pastorals appear to curtail the activities that had characterized the everyday lives of these women. In order to qualify as a "real widow," a woman had to have led a life, even when defined largely by the Greco-Roman household system, that was quite active; it included good works, hospitality, and caring for the afflicted. These achievements would have afforded women some measure of visibility within the community. The change to a life of prayer, by which "real widows" were to be known, was much less visible and much more socially restrictive. Such a redefining of function might well have been part of an organized attempt to strip influential women of their authority, contain their numbers, and diminish their influence.

LUCINDA A. BROWN

SEE ALSO Part I: Tabitha; Part II: Widows (Exod 22:22, etc.); Widow of Nain (Luke 7:11–17); Widow Pleading with a Judge (Luke 18:2–5); Widows of Hellenists and Hebrews (Acts 6:1).

FOR FURTHER READING: MacDonald, Margaret Y. "Rereading Paul: Early Interpreters of Paul on Women and Gender."

Torjesen, Karen Jo. *When Women Were Priests: Women's Leadership in the Early Church and the Scandal of Their Subordination in the Rise of Christianity.*

2 TIM 3:6
"Silly" or Little Women

Drawing on the apocalyptic tradition, which focuses on the end of the world, in 2 Tim 3:1–9 the author of the Pastoral Epistles (who writes in the name of Paul) warns about the distressing nature of the last days. The warning makes use of a vice list, a standard rhetorical device in the Greco-Roman world. Aside from monetary greed and disobedience of parents, the vice list does not mention specific behaviors, but rather consists of standard rhetorical putdowns. The list is undoubtedly a polemic against the "false teachers" mentioned elsewhere in the Pastoral Epistles.

The warning emphasizes the vulnerability of certain women whom the author denigrates as "silly" (literally "little" women — *gynaikaria*). Under the influence of false teachers, they have been "overwhelmed by their sins" and "swayed by all kinds of desires"; though they are "always being instructed," they never arrive "at a knowledge of the truth" (3:6). Although the author relies on standard rhetorical devices rather than citing specific behaviors, the women described are most likely being instructed in various ascetic disciplines.

The author relies on the tradition that considered women to be flighty by nature — not rational like men, and thus easily confused by false teachers. He appears to assume that if women possessed a rational nature, they would not be deceived by false instruction.

Like other material in the Pastoral Epistles, the warning here also reflects a continuing struggle over the issue of authority within the audience's church, thought by many scholars to have been at Ephesus, a large city on the western coast of modern Turkey.

LUCINDA A. BROWN

SEE ALSO Part II: Women Who Profess Reverence for God (1 Tim 2:9–15); Women Tale Tellers (1 Tim 4:7).

Titus 2:3–5
Older and Younger Women Exhorted

The instructions for "older" and "younger" women in Titus 2:3–5 is part of a series of exhortations to different groups within the church found in 2:2–10 and furthers the establishment of a particular church structure (a key purpose of the Epistle to Titus, written in the name of Paul by the writer of 1 and 2 Timothy). To give weight to the exhortations the Christian purposes underlying some of them are included (compare vv. 5, 8, and 10), and the doctrinal foundation follows in 2:11–14. Framing this section are two instructions to Titus: to "teach what is consistent with sound doctrine" (2:1) and to "exhort and reprove" concerning these things "with all authority" (2:15). Titus links authentic Christian behavior with sound doctrine and sees the two together as forming the way to avert moral and social chaos.

In form and content these exhortations reflect a transition point between the traditional pairings found in other New Testament household codes (wives/husbands, children/parents, and slaves/masters) and the stratification of groups within the church by age and gender. Age and gender determine the first four groups addressed, which are arranged chiastically: 2:2, older men; 2:3–5, older and younger women; 2:6, younger men. Possibly as an example to the younger men or to all, Titus is exhorted concerning his behavior in 2:7–8. The fifth group to be addressed, slaves (2:9–10), is found in the household codes (though masters are not reciprocally addressed here). Household codes typically use imperatives to exhort (compare Eph 5:22–6:9 and Col 3:18–4:1), whereas the exhortations in Titus are formulated primarily with adjectives and the verb *to be*. They are most reminiscent of the household codes in exhorting younger women to be submissive to their husbands and slaves to be submissive to their masters.

The exhortations to older and younger women in 2:3–5 have a unity of their own and are lengthier than the exhortations to older and younger men. Unlike the behavior urged upon older and younger men, the behavior impressed upon women is directly determined by their roles in relationships (older women as teachers of younger women; younger women as wives to their husbands and mothers to their children). The behavior urged upon older women draws heavily from the language of Greek and Roman moral discourse and contrasts with the behavior of the rebellious teachers envisioned in 1:10–16. Older women are exhorted to reverent behavior (unlike that of the corrupt teachers in 1:15–16); they must not be "slanderers" (the Greek *diabolous* recalls Satan's title as *the* Slanderer); and they must not be "slaves" to drink (calling to mind the less virtuous past of this community as "slaves to various passions" in 3:3, and contrasted with Paul's example as a "slave" of God in 1:1). Further, older women have a role to play within the community as those who "teach about what is good" — though not in the public sphere, but in the private domain and there only as teachers of domestic duties to younger women (2:3). Younger women are addressed only indirectly, in listing the qualities that older women are to teach them (2:4). The list of behaviors to be taught to younger women reflects patriarchal ideals for domestic behavior, beginning and ending the list with love and submission to their husbands. The self-control that younger women are to exhibit (a well-known Stoic virtue; here, it is also urged upon the younger men in 2:6) probably has a sexual connotation as sexual fidelity to their husbands. The term translated "good managers of the household" *(oikourgous)* does not actually imply authority, but only defines the household as the appropriate sphere for women's activities. Justifying the behavior to be taught to younger women is a purpose clause (a similar one is found in 2:10 to justify the exhortations to slaves), "so that the word of God may not be discredited" (2:5). This reflects the high value Titus places on the good opinion of society, with its emphasis on conformity to social norms and submission to appropriate authorities.

A disproportionate amount of space is given to exhorting older and younger women, prescribing behavior for them rather than describing their actual behavior. This suggests that, from the author's view, women's participation in the community needed to be circumscribed for several possible reasons: they were teaching beyond the domestic sphere; they were following Christian ascetic tendencies and upsetting the family household; they were asserting their leadership in the church over men as well as women; their active participation was giving Christianity a bad name in the larger society.

SARAH J. TANZER

SEE ALSO Part II: Wives (and Husbands) Exhorted (Eph 5:22–23); (Col 3:18–19); (1 Pet 3:1–7); Older and Younger Women (1 Tim 5:2).

FOR FURTHER READING: Bassler, Jouette M. *1 Timothy, 2 Timothy, Titus.*

Verner, David C. *The Household of God: The Social World of the Pastoral Epistles.*

PHILEMON

No Unnamed Women Mentioned

The briefest of the undisputed letters of Paul and one of the shortest writings of the New Testament, the letter to Philemon is the only one of Paul's undisputed letters addressed particularly to individuals, rather than to a community of believers in a specific geographic location. Considered by many scholars to be an exemplar of Greco-Roman rhetoric, the letter to Philemon, a Christian, concerns the fate of Philemon's slave, Onesimus, who had apparently become a Christian under Paul's tutelage.

The precise circumstances that occasion the letter are not entirely clear, and several scenarios have been proposed:

1. Onesimus had previously run away; Paul is now sending him back to his owner with the expectation that Philemon will free him and not punish him for having run away. Many

scholars now doubt this older interpretation.

2. Philemon had previously sent Onesimus to aid Paul in prison; Paul is now writing to request that Philemon manumit Onesimus and return him to work with Paul.

3. Onesimus, having committed some offense, had sought Paul's intervention with Philemon. Paul now writes to Philemon in the expectation that he will not only manumit Onesimus, but also return him to work with Paul. This most recent scenario accords well with what we know of relations between slaves, slave owners, and third-party advocates in the Roman period.

Whichever of these scenarios is correct, it is perhaps not surprising that Philemon contains no explicit references to unnamed women: it is, nevertheless, highly likely that women are among those unnamed persons understood by the phrase "the church in your house" (v. 2). It should not be overlooked, though, that the letter is in fact addressed to three individuals, as well as to a house church, and that the second of these is a woman named Apphia. Despite this, the body of the letter is written in the second-person singular, suggesting that the primary addressee of the letter is indeed Philemon.

ROSS S. KRAEMER

SEE ALSO Part I: Apphia.

FOR FURTHER READING: Bartchy, S. Scott. "Philemon, Epistle to."

Petersen, Norman. *Rediscovering Paul.*

Winter, S. C. "Philemon."

HEB 11:24–26   Daughter of Pharaoh
     SEE ACTS 7:21, etc.   Daughter of Pharaoh (Part II).

HEB 11:35–36
Women Who Received Their Dead by Resurrection

Women who "received their dead by resurrection" are commemorated among the examples of faith in

Hebrews 11. Their anonymity gives the impression that there were many instances of this phenomenon, but the primary references are to the widow of Zarephath, whose son Elijah raised, and the Shunammite, whose son Elisha raised. Hebrews may think also of Sarah (Heb 11:11, 19). Probably the mother of the seven martyrs (2 Maccabees 7; 4 Maccabees, especially 14:11–18:24) is remembered here among those who accepted torture, awaiting a future resurrection (11:36).

MARY ROSE D'ANGELO

JAS 1:27
Widows (and Orphans)

The Epistle of James emphasizes the importance not merely of hearing the word of God, but of doing it. It recalls the language of Deut 5:27, where Moses reminds all Israelites of their prior promise to hear everything God had told Moses and to do it.

In 1:27, the author argues that true worship of God (NRSV, "true religion") entails caring for orphans and widows as well as keeping "oneself unstained by the world." Responsibility for widows and orphans is emphasized in many books of the Hebrew Bible, and nothing in the passage suggests that singling them out for concern here points to specific circumstances in the author's community. Nevertheless, numerous early Christian writings suggest that widows made up a significant component of many communities and that such communities were concerned both with the financial support of widows and with the problems posed by the relative autonomy of adult women not under the authority of any male.

ROSS S. KRAEMER

SEE ALSO Part II: Widows (Exod 22:22, etc.); Poor Widow Giving Two Copper Coins (Mark 12:41–44); Widow at Zarephath (Luke 4:25–26); Widow of Nain (Luke 7:11–17); Widow Pleading with Judge (Luke 18:2–5); Widows of Hellenists and Hebrews (Acts 6:1); Widows (1 Tim 5:3–16).

JAS 2:15
Sister (or Brother) in Need

In this section of the Epistle of James, the author argues that faith requires commensurate works, offering the example that one should respond to a "brother or sister [who] is naked and lacks daily food" by providing for his or her physical needs.

Beyond affirming the presence of women in the author's community, this reference raises questions about how modern translators should render Greek masculine plurals in English. The author of James repeatedly uses the masculine plural *adelphoi* to address readers (1:2, 16, 19; 2:1, 5, 14; 3:1, 10, 12; 4:11; 5:7, 9–10, 12, 19) and the masculine singular *adelphos* to refer to a member of the community (1:9). Not all of these are immediately visible in the NRSV, which inconsistently translates *adelphoi* in James as "brothers and sisters," "beloved," or "my beloved," and *adelphos* in 1:9 as "believer."

Precisely because both the words *sister* and *brother* are used separately in 2:15, it might be argued that the author does not intend the plural inclusively, since then the words *adelphoi* and *adelphai* would have been chosen. On the other hand, one might suggest that here the author uses both singular forms to avoid the possibility that the masculine singular might mistakenly be understood exclusively. Then, however, the author's use of the masculine singular *adelphos* in 1:9 becomes somewhat troubling: if the author intends *adelphos* to designate a member of the community of either sex, why did the author find it necessary to use *adelphē* in 2:15?

These questions have no easy resolution, but remind us repeatedly of the interpretive nature of translation.

ROSS S. KRAEMER

JAS 3:1
Women Teachers

Of the many places where the NRSV has introduced the translation of the masculine plural *adelphoi* by the gender-inclusive "brothers and sisters," this passage is one of the most interesting and perhaps least noted. The author here warns his community: "Not many of you should become teachers, my *adelphoi*, for you know that we who teach will be judged with greater strictness."

The decision of the translators of the NRSV to render *adelphoi* as "brothers and sisters" puts the writer in the position of envisioning, if not endorsing, women as Christian teachers, at least implicitly. Yet the question of women as teachers was controversial among early churches, and the authority of Paul in particular was invoked both in opposition (1 Tim 2:12) and in support (the noncanonical *Acts of [Paul and] Thecla* 41). Whether this accurately represents the view of the author of James is impossible to know, but this example illustrates, as do several others, the ways in which contemporary gender-inclusive translation may affect our reconstruction of early Christian practices and ideas concerning women and gender.

ROSS S. KRAEMER

SEE ALSO Part II: Sisters (and Brothers) Greeted by Paul (Rom 16:14); Sisters (and Brothers) to Whom the Risen Jesus Appeared (1 Cor 15:6); Sister (or Brother) in Need (Jas 2:15).

1 PET 3:1–7
Wives (and Husbands) Exhorted

The exhortation to wives and husbands in 1 Peter is part of the household code (2:11–3:12) in which slaves and wives are exhorted to accept the authority of their masters and husbands, and husbands are encouraged to show consideration to their wives. Typical of other New Testament epistles with household codes, it has been written pseudonymously, claiming the name of the apostle Peter perhaps in part to help the community to whom it is addressed identify with his suffering and vision of hope. Unlike the Ephesians (5:22–6:9) and Colossians (3:18–4:1) household codes, 1 Peter presents an incomplete code in which only servants, wives, and husbands are specifically addressed. Further, the sequence of the other New Testament lists (wives/husbands, children/parents, slaves/masters) is not followed here: servants are exhorted first, and one of the pairs (children/parents) is completely absent. Reciprocity is also missing: servants are addressed, but not masters; wives (seemingly of gentile husbands) are addressed, as are Christian husbands (whose wives are also Christian).

The context for this household code in 1 Peter is the stressful experience for Christians in Asia Minor who find themselves "resident aliens" in an increasingly hostile environment toward the latter part of the first century C.E. The letter consoles, confirms, exhorts, and encourages these Christians to stand fast in the true grace of God (5:12). It attempts to counteract the erosive effect of their suffering by reminding them that their homelessness in society only points to their true home as the favored family of God. Dominant images of the letter also form part of the strategy of the exhortations of the household code: these Christians are called to be a holy people (3:5–6), their innocent suffering indicates their special union with Jesus and God (2:18–25), and they are the household of God — homeless in society, but at home with God. As a household they are called to certain responsibilities — to foster internal cohesion, to live up to their holy calling, and to set themselves apart from those outside the household. The language of the household dominates the letter and certainly the household code (for example, the typical New Testament terminology for servant/slave is deleted in favor of the rarely used terminology for household servants).

Christian wives are exhorted to subject themselves to their husbands to win them over to the faith through the purity and reverence of their lives (3:2). The context suggests that their husbands may be Gentiles (3:1, "some of them do not obey the word"). Wives are urged to adopt the inward adorning of "a gentle and quiet spirit" rather than fashionable outer adornments (3:4). Their examples are the "holy women," who adorned themselves likewise and subjected themselves to their husbands, such as Sarah, who "obeyed Abraham and called him lord." They will be Sarah's daughters (heirs) if they do right (3:5–6). Christian husbands are encouraged to recognize woman as the "weaker sex" and to treat their wives with consideration, recognizing that they are joint heirs in the inheritance of the grace of life. By doing so their prayers will not be hindered (3:7).

Much debated is the function of this household code in its original context. Was it apologetic, encouraging Christians not to corrupt the status quo of Roman household relationships (with the exception of religion) in order to contradict Roman slanders and create the potential for greater harmony? Or was this more in keeping with the strategy of 1 Peter as a whole, encouraging Christians toward distinctive Christian behavior and reminding them of the centrality of Christian household relationships in order to steel them against the disintegrative dangers of suffering as resident aliens?

Problematic from a feminist point of view is the way in which these exhortations in 1 Peter have been used historically as divine support for (1) the institution of slavery — in 2:18–25 the suffering of slaves at the hands of harsh masters gains them "God's approval" and is modeled after Christ's silent and noble suffering, suffering that frees believers from sins; (2) the view of women as the "weaker sex" (3:7); (3) the advocacy of modest and quiet behavior for women (3:3–5) — often a way of advocating more limited roles for women; (4) the subjection of wives to their husband's authority — obedience modeled after Sarah's obedience of Abraham gains for the wife her inheritance as a daughter of Sarah (3:1–6); (5) the rationale for staying in relationships characterized by suffering and abuse (drawing most heavily on the exhortation to slaves). This is perhaps the most problematic — through the glorification of the suffering Christ as a model and as a means of atonement for sin, the believer is presented with a lofty justification for victimization, violence, and abuse.

SARAH J. TANZER

SEE ALSO Part I: Sarah 1/Sarai; Part II: Wives (and Husbands) Exhorted (Eph 5:22–33); (Col 3:18–19).

FOR FURTHER READING: Balch, David L. *Let Wives Be Submissive: The Domestic Code in 1 Peter.*

Corley, Kathleen. "1 Peter."

Elliott, John H. *A Home For the Homeless.*

1 PET 3:5
Holy Women of the Past

The behavior of the holy women of the past (1 Pet 3:5) provides both the example and the rationale for 1 Peter's exhortation to Christian wives (3:1–6) to subject themselves to their husbands and to adorn themselves with a quiet spirit. This is illustrated in 3:6, when one holy woman's obedience (Sarah's) to her husband (Abraham) is held up as the way for Christian wives to do right. This verse interprets Gen 18:12 (focusing on Sarah's reference to Abraham as "my lord" — a simple convention of speech; in 1 Pet 3:6 this has been interpreted as a sign of submission) as evidence of Sarah's quiet obedience to her husband. As long as they follow Sarah's example of obedience to her husband and inward adornment, they are "her daughters." To be included among her daughters would not only have been high praise, but also likely refers to them as joint heirs to the promises made to Abraham and his offspring (compare 3:7; 3:8–12; Genesis 12).

SARAH J. TANZER

SEE ALSO Part I: Sarah 1/Sarai.

1 PET 5:13   Sister Church
SEE Sister Church (Part III).

2 PET 1:21
Women (and Men) Moved by the Holy Spirit

The letter known as 2 Peter appears to address the concerns of some early Christians that Jesus had not yet returned as expected and prophesied, focusing particularly on false prophets and false teachers.

In 1:20–21, the author warns readers that the interpretation of scriptural prophecy is not an individual matter, since no prophecy ever came because of human desire, "but men and women moved by the Holy Spirit spoke from God" (v. 21).

The NRSV decision to translate the Greek *anthrōpoi* here as "men and women" reflects an effort to produce a more explicitly gender-inclusive translation. The Greek word *anthrōpos* (masculine plural *anthrōpoi*) literally means "man," but is regularly used in a more generic sense to mean "humans" or "people." Because v. 21 emphasizes the divine, rather than human, origin of prophecy, the English translation of other recent versions, "human beings" or "people" (see the REB and the NJB), may better reflect the sense of the text, without specifying the gender of prophets. (Instead of *anthrōpoi*, some ancient manuscripts read *hoi hagioi*, "the saints" or "holy ones," another masculine plural that can certainly intend women and men, but, like *anthrōpoi*, need not.)

Women prophets are attested both in the Hebrew Bible (for example, Miriam, Deborah, and Huldah) and in early Christian writings (for example Anna and the unnamed women prophets in Corinth cited in 1 Cor 11:2–13), so that the author of 2 Peter might well have understood *anthrōpoi* to include both women and men. But the force of the verse appears to be elsewhere, and we should be cautious in interpreting this verse as a specific reference to women prophets.

ROSS S. KRAEMER

SEE ALSO Part I: Anna 2; Part II: Daughters (and Sons) Who Prophesy (Joel 2:28); Prophesying Daughters and Female Slaves (Acts 2:17–18); Women Praying and Prophesying (1 Cor 11:2–16); Woman Prophet Referred to as Jezebel (Rev 2:20).

1 JOHN
No Women Mentioned

Despite its title, 1 John is anonymous and lacks the characteristic features of ancient letters. Although its association with the author of the Gospel of John is ancient, it is more likely that 1 John was composed by a different author, one indebted to the Fourth Gospel. Although three books of the New Testament are titled as epistles of John, it is unlikely that the author of 1 John also wrote 2 and 3 John. Its actual genre is a matter of some dispute. It appears to have been occasioned by a split of some sort within a Christian community (2:19) over differing views of the identity and significance of Jesus.

1 John contains no references to any named persons, women or men. The audience is repeatedly addressed in masculine plural terms: *agapētoi* ("beloved ones"); *pateres* ("fathers"); and *neaniskoi* ("young men"). Yet of these, *agapētoi* and *neaniskoi* could be construed inclusively (as do the NRSV and the NJB), and the author also regularly employs neuter plurals, *teknia* and *paidia*, to address readers as "children." The use of these terms for children is common in antiquity and does not necessarily suggest that the "children" are to be construed as of both sexes, but it is also true that the author could have used the masculine plural *huioi* ("sons") and does not.

1 John also contains no references to unnamed women. The decision of the NRSV translators to introduce the inclusive translation of the masculine singular *adelphos* and the masculine plural *adelphoi* produces an English text that makes several references to "a brother or a sister" or to "brothers and sisters" (by which are meant a member or members of the community): for example, 1:9, 10; 3:10, 13, 15, 17; 4:20–21; 5:16 (in 1:11, the NRSV uses "believer" instead of "brother or sister"). Whether this accords well with the author's vision of the audience, the author's exhortations would seem to apply to women and men, and there is every reason to think that the communities behind this letter encompassed both women and men.

ROSS S. KRAEMER

FOR FURTHER READING: Kysar, Robert. "John, Epistles of."

2 JOHN VV. 1, 5
Elect Lady

The brief letter known as 2 John concerns itself principally with a warning about false teachers who should not be received into the house of the letter's recipient. The salutation in v. 1 reads, "The elder to the elect lady [*eklektē kyria*] and her children." V. 5 again addresses this "lady," and the letter concludes, "The children of your elect sister send you their greetings."

In antiquity, at least one prominent Christian writer, Clement of Alexandria (second–third centuries C.E.) appears to have understood 2 John to be written to a woman named Eklekta (a name he thought symbolic of the "election" of the church itself). Yet the majority of modern scholars have interpreted the term *kyria* (the feminine form of the Greek *kyrios* — "lord, master, sir") as a metaphor for a church and understood the phrase *eklektē kyria* to refer to some particular church, probably in ancient Asia Minor (modern Turkey). In support of this reading, they have pointed to the closing greeting of v. 13, understood as a reference to a sister church, and have argued that the term *eklektē* ("elect or chosen") is more likely to be applied to a Christian community than to an individual person.

Other scholars have recognized that these arguments do not resolve the question of whether 2 John is written to an actual woman or to a church personified as female. Rom 16:13 calls Paul's coworker Rufus *eklektos*, and Kyria is well documented as a personal name in this period, like Martha in Aramaic and Domna in Latin. If 2 John v. 1 were read as "the elder to the elect Kyria," its salutation would conform much more closely to that of 3 John (generally thought to be the work of the same author), "the elder to the beloved Gaius" (v. 1).

The interpretation of 2 John v. 1 is heavily affected by the apparent use of the term *tekna* ("offspring" or "children") for members of the church. The elder professes to love all the lady's children in the truth (v. 1), a somewhat ambiguous phrase, but in v. 4 he writes that he rejoiced to find some of her children following the truth, which seems to refer to members of the group. Since the children are metaphorical, scholars have concluded the lady must be as well. But the lady could be quite real, even though the term *tekna* would refer not to her biological offspring, but to the community she leads, probably in her house (v. 10).

Behind all the debate about the addressee of 2 John lies the implicit dilemma posed by a letter in the canon of the New Testament explicitly written to a woman as the head of a church. Such a letter could conceivably be understood to contradict the position of other canonical writings, such as 1 Tim 2:11, forbidding women to have authority over men, a contradiction avoided if the Kyria of 2 John is understood metaphorically.

We are unlikely ever to know for sure the true addressee of 2 John. If, however, it was written to a specific woman and to the church in her house, it would simply constitute additional evidence for a phenomenon already documented within the New Testament writings themselves (for example, Nympha in Col 4:15).

ROSS S. KRAEMER

SEE ALSO Part I: Nympha; Part II: 1 John; Elect Sister (2 John v. 13); 3 John.

FOR FURTHER READING: Bultmann, Rudolph. *The Johannine Epistles: A Commentary on the Johannine Epistles.*

Lieu, Judith. *The Second and Third Epistles of John.*

Strecker, Georg. *The Johannine Letters: A Commentary on 1, 2, and 3 John.*

2 JOHN V. 13
Elect Sister

The concluding verse of 2 John conveys the greetings of "the children of your elect sister" to the letter's recipient, described in v. 1 as "the elect lady and her children." Both references have traditionally been taken to refer metaphorically to Christian communities, imaging the church as a *kyria* (the

feminine form of the Greek *kyrios* — "lord, master, sir") and the members as her children. It is possible, although by no means certain, that the "elect lady" of 2 John v. 1 was an actual person. If so, it might strengthen the possibility that 2 John v. 13 also refers to a church led by a woman, but the two phrases need not be interpreted identically.

ROSS S. KRAEMER

SEE ALSO Part II: Elect Lady (2 John vv. 1, 5).

3 JOHN
No Women Mentioned

Addressed to a man named Gaius, 3 John is an anonymous letter from a writer who identifies himself only as "the elder" (v. 1) and who may also be the author of 2 John. Although the precise circumstances that prompt the letter are not clear, the elder is obviously concerned about the behavior of one Diotrephes, who disputes the elder's authority, has been spreading false accusations, has been refusing to welcome associates of the elder, and has been expelling those members of his own community who extend hospitality to these associates. In this letter, the elder seeks the support of Gaius on their behalf and on behalf of another man named Demetrius, who is clearly allied with the elder, but whose precise role in these circumstances is unknown.

If 2 John and 3 John are the work of the same author and reflect identical or similar disputes, central to the conflict may be whether "Jesus Christ has come in the flesh" (2 John v. 7). Christological disputes like this appear to be at the heart of 1 John as well, even though it seems unlikely that all three writings are the work of a single author.

For most of the letter, the elder calls his associates *adelphoi* ("brothers, brethren"). Only in v. 15 does he make reference to a group called *philoi* ("friends"): "the *philoi* send you [singular] their greetings. Greet the *philoi* there, each by name." Consistent with its introduction of inclusive translations, the NRSV does not translate *adelphoi* as "brothers" or "brethren." Whereas in most instances in the New Testament the NRSV renders *adelphoi* "brothers and sisters," here the translators instead use "friends," drawing obviously on the language of v. 15. In doing so, however, they equate the two terms, and perhaps mask an intentional discrimination of specific parties to the dispute. The *philoi* and the *adelphoi* may or may not be the same people.

No named women figure in 3 John, nor are there any explicit references to unnamed women. Whether women are among either the *adelphoi* or the *philoi* is difficult to say. That hospitality for travelers is a central issue does not resolve the matter: women travelers, Christian or otherwise, are well documented in ancient sources. The size of the communities involved in the disputes may be relevant: if they are sufficiently large, women should almost certainly be presumed to be among them. That the elder asks Gaius to greet the *philoi* there by name suggests that their number is relatively few, but whether we should imagine small cells of Christians consisting only of women or only of men is difficult to say.

If 2 and 3 John were composed by the same "elder," it may be of some relevance that 2 John is addressed to "the elect lady and her children." If, as many interpreters assume, this is a metaphorical description of a church, it is interesting that the communities in 3 John are not described in similarly gendered language. Whether this suggests something about the actual composition of any of these communities is uncertain, but certainly provocative.

ROSS S. KRAEMER

SEE ALSO Part II: Elect Lady (2 John vv. 1, 5).

FOR FURTHER READING: Kysar, Robert. "John, Epistles of."

JUDE
No Women Mentioned

One of the shortest Epistles in the New Testament is a letter written in the name of Jude (Judas), apparently a brother of Jesus who is here identified as a slave (NRSV, "servant") of Jesus Christ and brother of James. Like many letters of the New Testament (and other early Christian writings), Jude appears to be an effort on the part of its author to dissuade its audience from certain teachings and practices promulgated as the divine truth by others within the same community.

The author's central concern appears to be illicit sexual behaviors, which the author's opponents probably understood as consistent with the spiritual freedom they now had in Christ (a position comparable to that of Corinthian spirituals refuted by Paul particularly in the letter now known as 1 Corinthians). In this light, it is particularly interesting that the letter contains no explicit references to women, named or unnamed. No individual men are named as addressees of the letter or identified as the author's opponents. However, the letter is replete with examples of male figures from Jewish Scriptures (including but not limited to those canonized in the Hebrew Bible) who by virtue of their sinful behaviors constitute types for the false teachers in the author's community. Among these are Cain (Genesis 4), Balaam (especially Num 22:5–24:25) and Korah (Numbers 16), as well as the inhabitants of Sodom and Gomorrah (especially Gen 18:16–19:29). Just as these were judged by God, so will be the author's opponents. (It is noteworthy that the fate of the errant women of Sodom and Gomorrah is mixed: Lot's wife is punished by God for her disobedience in looking back, but his daughters are not punished for their incestuous intercourse with their father.)

It is certainly possible that women are among those whom the author addresses with the masculine plural "beloved," as well as among those teachers and spirituals who, relying on the authority of prophetic visions, engage in transgressive sex. In the better attested example of a community engaging in such practices, the spirituals or the "strong" in mid-first-century C.E. Corinth, women appear prominent among those who prophesy (and perhaps also teach). Nevertheless, the implicit framework of Jude appears to be masculine, from the male scriptural figures both negative and positive, to the invocation of the apostles (v. 17). It is also possible that the author envisions a conflict in which women are primarily, if not exclusively, the objects of illicit male sexuality, and not subjects and actors in their own right.

Ross S. Kraemer

See also Part II: Women Praying and Prophesying (1 Cor 11:2–16); Women Commanded to Be "Silent" in the Churches (1 Cor 14:33b–36).

For further reading: Rosenblatt, Marie-Eloise. "Jude."

Rev 2:20
Woman Prophet Referred to as Jezebel

The author of Revelation, called John of Patmos, does not provide us with the true name of the female prophet of the church at Thyatira (in ancient Asia Minor, now Turkey). Instead, he vilifies her by calling her "Jezebel," the name of an ancient Israelite queen herself vilified for her worship of Baal and her opposition to prophets of yhwh, especially Elijah.

Ross S. Kraemer

See also Part I: Jezebel 1; Jezebel 2.

Rev 12:1–6, 14–17
Woman in Labor, Clothed with the Sun
See Woman in Labor, Clothed with the Sun (Part III).

Rev 17:3–18:24 Great Whore
See Great Whore (Part III).

Rev 18:23
Bride (and Bridegroom)

Revelation 18 prophesies the coming destruction of the city of Babylon, a pseudonym for Rome, itself represented particularly as a prostitute. In vv. 21–23, an angel enumerates the things that will no longer be found in the destroyed city, including the sound of the voice of the bride and bridegroom (note that the NRSV reverses the order of the Greek, which reads bridegroom and bride). The same phrasing and imagery appear in Jer 7:34 (see also Jer 16:9 and 25:10), where the coming destruction of Jerusalem will be marked, among other things, by the absence of sounds of rejoicing, the voice of the bride and bridegroom (here again, the NRSV reverses the order of the original). The rejoicing of the newly married couple is by itself an appropriate symbol of joy and its absence an appropriate symbol of destruction and mourning. Yet the prophecy in Revelation may well draw deliberately on the passages in Jeremiah and their association with the destruction of Jerusalem, particularly since Revelation appears to have been written fairly close to the time of the destruction of the city of Jerusalem and the second temple by the Romans in 70 C.E.

Ross S. Kraemer

See also Part III: Great Whore.

Rev 19:7–8; 21:2, 9–11; 22:17
Bride of the Lamb
See Bride of the Lamb (Part III).

Female Deities and Personifications

Anath

meaning unknown

(Judg 3:31)

Anath (Anat) is a prominent figure in the Canaanite mythological texts, dating to c. 1400 B.C.E., discovered at Ugarit on the Syrian coast. She is a maiden/warrior goddess, the sister or consort of the fertility and storm god Baal. She plays a major role in the Ugaritic myths, rescuing Baal from the underworld and defeating Mot, the god of death. In the Hebrew Bible, however, Anath is barely visible. Her name appears only within the place names Beth-anath/anoth (Josh 15:59; 19:38; Judg 1:33) and Anathoth (Josh 21:18; 1 Kgs 2:26; Isa 10:30; Jer 1:1) and the personal names Shamgar ben Anath (son of Anath, in NRSV) (Judg 3:31; 5:6), Anthothijah (1 Chr 8:24), and Anathoth (1 Chr 7:8; Neh 10:19).

These names are generally taken to reflect the worship or veneration of the goddess Anath among Israelites. Beth-anath, for example, means "house or temple of Anath. Anathoth is the plural of the name Anath, just as Ashtaroth (compare Deut 1:4) is the plural of the divine name Ashtar (Astarte). The name Shamgar son of Anath, however, might not mean "Shamgar, son of [the goddess] Anath." The formula "[personal name], son of [personal name]," usually places one's father's name in the second position. Therefore the name Anath, in this instance, may be a shortened form of a masculine name such as Anathothijah or Anatyahu, which may simply mean "sign(s) of YHWH." If so, then Shamgar's name would have nothing to do with the goddess Anath. Yet because Shamgar was a warrior and Anath a warrior deity, and because place names such as Beth-anoth point to the veneration of the goddess among some Israelites, the label "son of Anath" following Shamgar's name may indeed connect him with the goddess. Extrabiblical data support such a possibility.

ELIZABETH C. LaRocca-Pitts

SEE ALSO Part III: Asherah/Asherim.

FOR FURTHER READING: Walls, Neal H. *The Goddess Anat in Ugaritic Myth.*

McCarter, P. Kyle, Jr. "Aspects of the Religion of the Israelite Monarchy: Biblical and Epigraphic Data."

Artemis

meaning uncertain; perhaps from Greek, *artameō,* "to cut in pieces" or "butcher," or *artemeō,* "to be safe and sound," and *artemia,* "soundness, health"

(Acts 19:24–41)

Artemis is the only Greco-Roman deity mentioned by name in the New Testament. Like most of the ancient pan-Hellenic deities, Artemis is more of a category name than a specific divine individual. Each specific place of worship honored its own unique form of a given deity, designated by the epithet, or surname, attached to the divine figure — in this case, Artemis Ephesia (of the Ephesian people).

Greco-Roman religion used sacred spaces and sacred images as focal points for worship. Artemis Ephesia was honored throughout the city, but possessed her own sanctuary a short distance away. The main temple of this sanctuary, the Artemision, was very famous (one of the Seven Wonders of the World) and a source of significant local pride. The Ephesian sacred image of Artemis, itself infused with the power of deity, was also a great source of pride and the subject of fierce devotion. Both temple and statue frequently appear on coins and in sculptured reliefs.

Artemis Ephesia functioned mainly as a city goddess, protecting the safety and wealth (based on trade and agriculture) of its people, as well as their social institutions of justice and democracy. As a city protector, Artemis Ephesia was remarkably successful — if the security, fame, and prosperity of

A colossal statue of Artemis of Ephesos, first century c.e. The identity of the objects on her torso continues to be a subject of debate. See Artemis.

Ephesus are a reliable measure. This led to the "adoption" of Artemis Ephesia by other cities and by Ephesian individuals living abroad, as both a personal and a collective protector. In this way, the originally local worship of Artemis of Ephesus achieved a fairly wide distribution.

The passage in Acts, commonly referred to as "the revolt of the silversmiths," takes place in Ephesus and clearly refers to this goddess and her image. A group of individuals who derive their income from the manufacture of sacred souvenirs (a lively business in antiquity as today) object to Christian preaching by Paul and his companions that images lack divine power; their anger erupts into a city-

wide pro–Artemis Ephesia demonstration, with significant bad feeling directed against Paul and his companions in particular and the Ephesian Jewish community in general. The disturbance is finally calmed by the Ephesian secretary of the city (Greek *grammateus,* translated as "town clerk" in the NRSV) on the grounds that the dispute is a private one between the silversmiths and the missionaries.

The secretary of the city was a real local office in Ephesus, and his statement that the city is the "temple keeper" (Greek *neōkoros*) of Artemis accurately reflects an ancient Ephesian title, though in this period it more usually reflects a city's possession of a temple to the imperial family. But the secretary's allusion to a statue that fell from heaven is strange. Although some worship centers did make this divine claim for their sacred images, Ephesians knew very well who had sculptured their central image, and when. Therefore, this account in Acts reflects some knowledge of local Ephesian life but may also conflate traditions about sacred images from other places, in order to make an overall point about Greco-Roman attachment to images.

Lynn LiDonnici

For further reading: LiDonnici, Lynn. "The Images of Artemis Ephesia and Greco-Roman Worship: A Reconsideration."

Oster, Richard. "The Ephesian Artemis as an Opponent of Early Christianity."

———. "Ephesus as a Religious Center Under the Principate I: Paganism Before Constantine."

Asherah/Asherim

from Hebrew *'ăšērâ/'ăšērîm,* to be associated with Ugaritic *'ṭr,* "to stride" or with Akkadian *aširtu,* Aramaic *'trt',* and Phoenician *'šrt,* "shrine"(?)

(Exod 34:13; Deut 7:5; 12:3; 16:21; Judg 3:7; 6:25–26, 28, 30; 1 Kgs 14:15, 23; 15:13; 16:33; 18:19; 2 Kgs 13:6; 17:10; 18:4; 21:3, 7; 23:4, 6–7, 14–15; 2 Chr 14:3; 15:16; 17:6; 19:3; 24:18; 31:1; 33:3, 19; 34:3–4, 7; Isa 17:8; 27:9; Jer 17:2; Mic 5:14)

Asherah, along with Astarte and Anath, was one of the three great goddesses of the Canaanite pantheon. In Canaanite religion her primary role was that of mother goddess. In mythological texts from the Late Bronze Age (c. 1550–1200 B.C.E.) city-state of Ugarit, she is called "the creatress of the gods"; her consort at Ugarit, the god El, is called "creator." El is also referred to as father and patriarch at Ugarit, as Asherah, likewise, is called mother. Their children form the pantheon of the gods, who are said to number seventy; a Hittite myth similarly mentions the seventy-seven and eighty-eight children of Asherah. On occasion in Ugaritic myth, Asherah performs the maternal role of wet nurse. Ugaritic and other Canaanite materials further associate Asherah with lions (indicating power), serpents (representing immortality or healing), and sacred trees (signifying fertility). Thus Asherah's children at Ugarit can be called her "pride of lions"; the goddess is called "lady of the serpent" in second-millennium B.C.E. inscriptions from the Sinai; the late-thirteenth-century B.C.E. Lachish ewer dedicated to Asherah is decorated with images of sacred trees.

The Canaanite association of Asherah with sacred trees is also found in Israelite tradition. For example, one of the Canaanite epithets of Asherah, *'ēlat*, "goddess," is etymologically identical to the Hebrew word for the terebinth tree (*'ēlâ*). Another word for "terebinth" (*'allâ*) and two words for "oak" (*'ēlôn* and *'allôn*) are also closely related. Gen 2:4b–3:24 may further suggest the association of Asherah with sacred trees, since the way that Eve, "the mother of all living" (3:20), is described in the Eden story mimics in certain respects the role of the Canaanite mother goddess Asherah. If a correspondence holds, then the trees of life and of knowledge in the Eden narrative may also reflect Asherah imagery.

Most significant, though, in demonstrating Israel's association of Asherah with sacred trees are biblical materials that describe the *asherah* (singular) or *asherim* (plural), the cult object(s) that are associated with the goddess Asherah more than thirty times in the Hebrew Bible. These cult objects are generally described as being in the shape of a pole or stylized tree. Like a pole or tree, they can be said to be planted, stood up, or erected. Conversely,

Enthroned female figure playing a lyre, drawn on a large eighth-century B.C.E. storage jar discovered at Kuntillet 'Ajrud, a site in the northeast Sinai desert. Because the jar bears an inscription referring to "YHWH . . . and his Asherah," many scholars believe that the enthroned female is meant to represent the goddess Asherah, perhaps considered a consort of YHWH by those who inscribed and decorated the vessel. See Asherah/Asherim.

when destroyed, these cult symbols can be described as being cut down, hewn down, or uprooted; they can also be said to be burned, overturned, or broken. Both the Greek and Latin translations of the Bible, moreover, render the words *asherah* and *asherim* as "grove" or "wood."

According to the biblical record, these sacred poles or stylized trees associated with Asherah were erected by the Israelites throughout most of their history, especially during the premonarchic (tribal) period (Judg 6:25–26, 28, 30) and during the period of the divided monarchy, both in the northern kingdom of Israel (1 Kgs 14:15; 16:33; 2 Kgs 13:6; 17:10, 16; 23:15; and parallel references in 2 Chronicles) and in Judah, in the south (1 Kgs 14:23, 15:13; 2 Kgs 18:4; 21:3, 7; 23:6, 14; and parallel references in 2 Chronicles). These sacred poles were situated in various locations. In Judges 6, a sacred pole of

Asherah is said to have stood beside the altar of the Canaanite storm god, Baal. The Bible also connects sacred poles with the "high places" (open-air cult sites?) and frequently mentions that they stood "on every high hill and under every green tree" (1 Kgs 14:23; 2 Kgs 17:10; 18:4; 21:3; 23:13–14; 2 Chr 14:3; 17:6; 31:1; 33:3, 19; 34:3; Jer 17:2). Both of these phrases are stereotypically used by the biblical writers to describe sites of idolatrous worship, implying, as does Judges 6, that the worship of Asherah was an apostate behavior in Israel and improper for followers of YHWH.

Yet despite these and other references associating Asherah with apostasy (for example, Exod 34:13; Deut 7:5; 12:3; Judg 3:7; 1 Kgs 18:19), and despite the fact that the Israelites are explicitly forbidden in Deut 16:21 to erect one of Asherah's sacred poles beside an altar of YHWH, there are multiple indications in biblical tradition that many in ancient Israel did regard Asherah's cult icon as an appropriate sacred symbol within the religion of YHWH. For example, one of Asherah's sacred poles stood next to YHWH's altar at Bethel, one of the two great cult sites of the northern kingdom of Israel (2 Kgs 23:15). Another of Asherah's sacred poles stood in that kingdom's capital city, Samaria. The sacred pole of Samaria, moreover, which was erected during the reign of King Ahab (reigned 873–852 B.C.E.), was allowed to remain standing by the reformer King Jehu (1 Kgs 16:33; 2 Kgs 13:6), even though Jehu was generally at pains to remove all non-Yahwistic cults and cult imagery from the land. This fact suggests that Jehu perceived the sacred pole as appropriate in the worship of YHWH.

Archaeological discoveries from the late 1970s and early 1980s have further indicated that, at least in the opinion of some ancient Israelites, YHWH and Asherah were appropriately worshipped as a pair. From the site of Kuntillet 'Ajrud, in the eastern Sinai, come three ninth- or eighth-century B.C.E. inscriptions that mention YHWH and "his Asherah" (meaning YHWH's companion [consort?], the goddess Asherah) or "his asherah" (meaning YHWH's sacred pole that represents the goddess Asherah and that sits in his temple or beside his altar). An eighth-century B.C.E. inscription from Khirbet el-Qom, about twenty-five miles southwest of Jerusalem, contains similar language. 1 Kgs 15:13 and 2 Kgs 18:4, 21:7, and 23:6 (with parallels in 2 Chronicles) indicate that at least during certain points in the ninth, eighth, and seventh centuries B.C.E., Asherah's sacred pole was perceived as an appropriate icon to erect in Jerusalem, even in YHWH's temple. Also, vessels in the temple were used to make sacrifices to Asherah (2 Kgs 23:4), and in a compound within the temple's walls, women cult functionaries wove garments used to clothe Asherah's cult statue (2 Kgs 23:7). Thus it appears that, although generally the biblical writers — especially certain prophets (Isa 17:8; 27:9; Jer 17:2; Mic 5:14) and the authors responsible for Deuteronomy, Judges, 1 and 2 Kings, and 2 Chronicles — regarded Asherah worship as inappropriate, at least some and possibly many in ancient Israel incorporated the goddess's cult imagery and ritual into the cult of YHWH.

Unfortunately, our sources do not provide enough information to identify definitively which Israelites were particularly attracted to the worship of Asherah or the reasons for this attraction. One possibility is that in royal circles, especially in the southern capital city of Jerusalem, the cult of Asherah was particularly attractive to the king's mother. Not only was the queen mother's position in the palace generally paralleled by Asherah's position as mother goddess in the heavens, but also the queen mother's status as the wife of the king's father suggests an affinity to Asherah's cult. This is because southern royal ideology typically described the king's metaphorical father as YHWH. For those ancient Israelites who saw Asherah as YHWH's consort, this should suggest a correspondence between the queen mother, the wife of the king's biological father on earth, and Asherah, the wife of YHWH, who was the king's metaphorical father in the heavens.

Whether women, more generally, were more likely to be devotees of Asherah's cult is unknown. There is some biblical evidence that does see women as particularly attracted to goddess cults (for example, women's role in the cult of the queen of heaven, according to Jer 7:18 and 44:17–19, 25), and the various female figurines found in domestic contexts at multiple Israelite sites might also suggest this, assuming, as many scholars do, that women played an especially important role in family-centered religious activities. Nevertheless, the presence of Asherah's cult in the Jerusalem temple and in the cult city of Bethel indicates that worship of the goddess was also appealing to men, given that it was an all-male clergy that officiated at these (and at every) Israelite religious site.

The presence of Asherah's cult in Israel also raises questions about the nature of the monotheistic confession that is often assumed to be a core principle in Israelite faith. Generally speaking, biblical scholars assume that full-blown, radical, or philosophical monotheism came to Israel fairly late in its history, during the time of the exile in the sixth century B.C.E. Prior to this, we have abundant evidence that other gods and goddesses were worshipped in Israel in addition to (or sometimes instead of) YHWH. Yet even in these earlier materials, we sometimes see evidence of a phenomenon that comes to dominate in the exilic period: the impulse to assimilate the attributes of the many gods and goddesses of older polytheistic systems to the one god, YHWH. Language that speaks of God as mother, for example (as in Deut 32:18; Num 11:12–13; Isa 45:9–10, 49:15; 66:13), probably represents the assimilation of Asherah's maternal characteristics to YHWH.

SUSAN ACKERMAN

SEE ALSO Part II: Weaving Women (2 Kgs 23:7); Part III: Anath; Astarte; Female (and Male) Idol; Female Images of God in the Hebrew Bible; Woman Wisdom.

FOR FURTHER READING: Ackerman, Susan. "The Queen Mother and the Cult in Ancient Israel."

———. *Under Every Green Tree: Popular Religion in Sixth-Century Judah.*

Day, John. "Asherah in the Hebrew Bible and Northwest Semitic Literature."

Olyan, Saul M. *Asherah and the Cult of Yahweh in Israel.*

Wiggins, Steve A. *A Reassessment of 'Asherah': A Study*

According to Textual Sources of the First Two Millennia B.C.E.

Ashima/Ashimah

meaning uncertain; probably from Aramaic *šĕmā*, "name"

(2 Kgs 17:30; Amos 8:14)

According to 2 Kgs 17:30, Ashima is a god or goddess worshipped by the people of Hamath, in northern Syria, who were settled in Samaria after the Assyrian destruction of Israel in 721 B.C.E. Amos 8:14 may also mention this deity, although the name is spelled differently ('ăšîmā' in 2 Kings; 'ašmâ in Amos). Some, therefore, read 'ašmâ in Amos as a common noun, "shame"; others emend the text to read 'ăšērâ, "Asherah," the name of the Canaanite mother goddess.

The most probable etymology derives Ashima/Ashimah from the Aramaic *šĕmā*, meaning "name." If this is correct, then it suggests that Ashima/Ashimah should be identified with Astarte, the Canaanite goddess of love and fertility, who is called by the epithet "name of Baal" in several texts from the Late Bronze Age city-state of Ugarit in Syria and from fifth-century B.C.E. Sidon in Phoenicia. Yet this epithet, whereby the "name" of Baal comes to stand for his presence, is equivalent to the epithet "face of Baal," which is borne by the Phoenician goddess Tannit. Moreover, although the identity of Tannit is debated, the most plausible hypothesis links her to Asherah. This suggests in turn an identification of Ashima/Ashimah with Asherah. The third of the great Canaanite goddesses, Anath, can also be called "face of Baal" (presuming the war goddess called by this epithet at Ashkelon in Israel is the war goddess Anath) and the "name of Bethel" (presuming we equate the deities Eshem-Bethel, "the name of Bethel," and Anat-Bethel from fifth-century B.C.E. Elephantine, a Judean colony in Egypt). Ashima/Ashimah, accordingly, could be identified as Anath.

SUSAN ACKERMAN

SEE ALSO Part II: Beautiful Young Women (and Men) (Amos 8:13); Part III: Anath; Asherah/Asherim.

FOR FURTHER READING: Cross, Frank M. *Canaanite Myth and Hebrew Epic: Essays in the History of the Religion of Israel.*

Fulco, William J. "Ashima."

Asia as a Prostitute

(2 Esdr 15:46–63; 16:1–2)

2 Esdras 15–16 (sometimes called 6 Ezra) is a Christian addition to the original Jewish work (2 Esdras 3–14) that claims God has rejected a faithless Jewish community in favor of a new people of God, the church. This third-century C.E. author speaks of Asia as a female prostitute who revels in her sins and flaunts her debauchery. The crimes of Asia, imitating those of "hateful" Babylon (15:48), include her mistreatment of the chosen people as well as her moral corruption. God will send seven evils upon her, including widowhood, poverty, famine, sword, pestilence, ruin to her houses, destruction, and death. Her fate is assured: "You shall be weakened like a wretched woman who is beaten and wounded, so that you cannot receive your mighty lovers" (15:51). The reference borrows especially from Ezekiel 16 (Jerusalem as a harlot) and 23 (Jerusalem and Samaria as harlots), as well as from Revelation 17 (Babylon, the mother of whores, meaning Rome). Asia probably stands for the Asia Minor portion of the Roman Empire.

In 2 Esdr 16:1–2, the author presents Asia and Babylon, along with Egypt and Syria, as mourners who are told to put on sackcloth and prepare for the coming destruction. The faithful within these four nations, that together represent the Roman Empire, have nothing to fear. The historical situation here is obscure. Some argue that Asia as a prostitute reflects political events that transpired in the reign of the Persian king Shapur I (240–273 C.E.), when he devastated a number of Syrian cities and defeated the Romans near Edessa, capturing the emperor Valerian and his troops. Odenathus, husband of the noble Zenobia, with his Syrian and Arab troops, liberated Valerian, defeating Shapur and gaining for himself the status of emperor of the

eastern provinces of the empire. If so, then the denunciation of Asia in 2 Esdras is a castigation of Odenathus for relying upon the power and luxuries characteristic of Babylon (meaning Rome). The association of Babylon, Asia, Egypt, and Syria in 2 Esdr 16:1–17 seems only to reflect a general judgment against the Roman Empire.

The scriptural tradition of depicting cities and nations as prostitutes raises troublesome issues. The metaphoric connection equating political oppression with female harlotry can easily mislead readers and hearers. They may come to view real women in a negative light that more properly belongs to the males within these cities and nations who are likely to be more responsible for the abuses. In addition, the passages legitimate violence and support physical abuse as ways to reclaim and maintain male control over females.

WALTER J. HARRELSON

SEE ALSO Part II: Widow (2 Esdr 2:2–4, etc.); Part III: Great Whore; Oholah, Woman Samaria; Oholibah, Woman/Whore Jerusalem.

FOR FURTHER READING: Johnson, Elizabeth E. "2 Esdras."

Metzger, Bruce M. "The Fourth Book of Ezra."

Stone, Michael. "Esdras, Second Book of."

Astarte

from Hebrew *'aštōret*, meaning "increase," "progeny"

(Judg 2:13; 10:6; 1 Sam 7:3–4; 12:10; 31:10; 1 Kgs 11:5, 33; 2 Kgs 23:13)

Astarte is the Greek form of the name Ashtart, who, along with Asherah and Anath, was one of the three great goddesses of the Canaanite pantheon. In Canaanite religion she was associated primarily with love and fertility, playing the role of divine courtesan, for example, in mythological texts from the Late Bronze Age (c. 1550–1200 B.C.E.) city-state of Ugarit (in western Syria). Texts from the middle and late first millennium B.C.E, by equating Astarte with the Greek goddess of love, Aphrodite, further indicate Astarte's character as a goddess of sexual love. In biblical Hebrew the noun 'aštārôt, derived from the divine name Ashtart/Astarte, means "increase, progeny," an indication of Astarte's fertility functions. Also, in Egypt Astarte is known as a goddess of fertility, as she, along with Anath, is called one of "the great goddesses who conceive but do not bear."

Although they are not as well known as her fertility characteristics, Astarte also has associations with war, shown in several Egyptian representations in which she carries weapons of war and in descriptions in both Egyptian and Ugaritic texts that characterize her as a warrior goddess. In 1 Sam 31:10, the armor of the dead King Saul is taken by the Philistines to the temple of Astarte, and this may further indicate the goddess's warrior characteristics. Moreover, Astarte, like both her Greek counterpart Aphrodite and her Mesopotamian equivalent, the goddess Ishtar, has astral features. She is labeled the "lady of heaven" in several second-millennium B.C.E. Egyptian texts, and in the first-millennium B.C.E. inscription of Eshmunazor, she is called "Astarte of the highest heavens." In Phoenician Sidon, the city most associated with the goddess's cult (see Judg 10:6; 1 Kgs 11:5, 33; 2 Kgs 23:13), her sacred precinct is called "highest heavens." Phoenician sources also report Astarte's identification with Venus, the morning and evening star.

In the Hebrew Bible the worship of Astarte is repeatedly condemned: twice in Judges the Israelites are punished for straying after the god Baal and "the Astartes" (Judg 2:13–14; 10:6–7); the people are similarly castigated for Astarte worship twice in 1 Samuel (7:3–4; 12:10); Solomon is thrice criticized for introducing the cult of Astarte into Jerusalem during his tenure as king (1 Kgs 11:5, 33; 2 Kgs 23:13); Jeremiah castigates the people for making offerings to the queen of heaven, a goddess who most probably represents a syncretism of Canaanite Astarte and Mesopotamian Ishtar (Jer 7:18; 44:17–19, 28). Nevertheless, the very fact of these multiple condemnations is evidence that, for at least some ancient Israelites, the cult of Astarte held great appeal. Although our sources do not provide enough information to identify definitively which Israelites were

particularly attracted to the worship of Astarte or the reasons for their attraction, it is possible that some devotees were compelled by the presence of a female divine figure in an otherwise male-dominated religious environment.

SUSAN ACKERMAN

SEE ALSO Part III: Anath; Asherah/Asherim; Queen of Heaven.

FOR FURTHER READING: Ackerman, Susan. *Under Every Green Tree: Popular Religion in Sixth-Century Judah.*

Day, John. "Ashtoreth."

Atargatis

meaning uncertain, Greek compound of Aramaic elements of 'tr (Astarte) and 't or 'nt (Anath)
(2 Macc 12:26)

Atargatis, a fertility deity often called the "Syrian goddess" (*Dea Syria*) in Greek and Roman times, was principally associated with the city of Hierapolis-Bambyke in Syria. Her cult as a fish and grain goddess, consort of Hadad, was popularized by Syrian merchants, slaves, soldiers, and mendicant eunuch priests, and spread throughout the Mediterranean world. Atargatis's name associates her with two great Canaanite deities, Astarte, goddess of sexual love and fertility, and Anath, a fierce invincible warrior. In Egypt she was identified with the cowhorned goddess Hathor. Her sanctuaries often contained sacred pools and sacred fish. According to a mid-second-century C.E. report of the satirist Lucian of Samosata, the priests of Atargatis ate sacred fish meals and bathed her image each year in a sacred pool.

In 2 Macc 12:26, the Greek *Atergateion* means a "temple of Atargatis" either in or near the Gileadite town of Carnaim (Ashteroth-karnaim, perhaps "Ashtaroth of the two horns," in Gen 14:5). Here Judas Maccabeus, the leader of the second-century B.C.E. Jewish revolt, put to death twenty-five thousand people, including the women and children of Timothy, a military officer of the Ammonites who joined forces with the Syrians to oppose Judas (see

2 Macc 12:21). The parallel story in 1 Macc 5:37–44 mentions only "the sacred precincts at Carnaim" (5:43) with no direct reference to Atargatis. In both accounts, the Gentiles who take refuge at this sacred site are killed and the town of Carnaim is utterly destroyed.

Ironically, female deities provide no protection in 2 Maccabees. Death is dealt in the temples of both Atargatis and Nanea (2 Macc 1: 13–17). Judas executes those who have sought refuge at the sanctuary in Carnaim (2 Macc 12:26); the priests of Nanea execute the Seleucid king Antiochus IV (Epiphanes) at Elymais (2 Macc 1: 13–14).

TONI CRAVEN

SEE ALSO Part II: Women/Wives as Victims of War (2 Macc 5:13, etc.); Part III: Anath; Astarte; Nanea.
FOR FURTHER READING: Carroll, Scott T. "Atargatis." Goldstein, Jonathan A. *I Maccabees: A New Translation with Introduction and Commentary.*
———. *II Maccabees: A New Translation with Introduction and Commentary.*

Azubah/Forsaken, Jerusalem

from Hebrew '*āzab,* "to forsake"
(Isa 62:4)

In a text that describes how Jerusalem, also called Zion, will be restored after suffering destruction at the hands of the Babylonians in 586 B.C.E., the city is told by God that although now called Azubah, "Forsaken," she will soon be called Hephzibah, "My Delight Is in Her"; likewise her land, now called Shemamah, "Desolate," will soon be called Beulah, "Married" (Isa 62:4). The next verse expands this marriage metaphor introduced by Beulah by promising the city that "as the bridegroom rejoices over the bride, so shall your God rejoice over you." Similar imagery of the restored Jerusalem as the bride of YHWH is found in Isa 49:7–26, 54:1–10, and also, possibly, 52:1.

This marriage imagery of Isa 62:4–5 and its kindred texts is remarkable in its sense of YHWH's unbounded and unconditional love for Jerusalem/Zion and in its statement that, whatever strains the

loving relationship between God and the city has endured in the past, YHWH now wishes the marriage to be fully restored. Isa 62:4, moreover, by describing Jerusalem as "Forsaken," may even suggest that it was YHWH's fault that the relationship encountered difficulties; this same notion is hinted at in Isa 54:1–10, which also describes Jerusalem as "forsaken" as well as "cast off" by her husband. Such an exalted notion of the city Jerusalem as the beloved, yet wronged, wife of God is unparalleled in the Hebrew Bible and is a strikingly positive use of female imagery in ancient Israel.

SUSAN ACKERMAN

SEE ALSO Part III: Beulah/Married, Jerusalem; Hephzibah/My Delight Is in Her, Jerusalem; Shemamah/Desolate, Jerusalem; Woman Jerusalem/Zion in Isaiah.
FOR FURTHER READING: Ackerman, Susan. "Isaiah." Sawyer, John. "Daughter of Zion and Servant of the Lord in Isaiah: A Comparison."

Beulah/Married, Jerusalem

from Hebrew *bā'al,* "to marry"
(Isa 62:4)

In a text that describes how Jerusalem will be restored after being destroyed by the Babylonians in 586 B.C.E., the city is told that, although she has been previously known as Azubah, "Forsaken," and Shemamah, "Desolate," her land will soon be called Beulah, "Married" (Isa 62:4). The next verse elaborates: "For as a young man marries a young woman, so shall your builder marry you" (reading "your builder," Hebrew *bōnēk,* for the received tradition's "your sons," Hebrew *bānāyik,* in accord with most modern translations and commentaries). The second line of 62:5 ("As the bridegroom rejoices over the bride, so shall God rejoice over you") makes clear that the "builder"/bridegroom in this passage is God (on God as builder, see also Ps 147:2). This imagery of YHWH as the spouse of Jerusalem and/or Israel appears elsewhere in the Hebrew Bible and is especially common in prophetic literature (for example, Ezekiel 16; Hosea 1–3). Generally, however, this imagery is negative, with Jerusalem/Israel being described as an adulterous wife who has strayed from exclusive devotion to YHWH. Oracles found in the second half of Isaiah (Isa 49:7–26; 52:1; 54:1–10; 62:4–5) offer a remarkable contrast through their unqualified portrayals of Jerusalem as God's beloved bride, who will be lavished with jewels (49:18) and beautiful garments (52:1) and who is assured of God's overwhelming compassion and everlasting love (54:7–10).

SUSAN ACKERMAN

SEE ALSO Part I: Gomer; Part III: Azubah/Forsaken, Jerusalem; Female Images for Nations in Ezekiel; Hephzibah/My Delight Is in Her, Jerusalem; Shemamah/Desolate, Jerusalem; Woman Jerusalem/Zion in Isaiah.

FOR FURTHER READING: Ackerman, Susan. "Isaiah." Weems, Renita J. "'Is She Not My Wife?' Prophets, Audiences, and Expectations."

Bride of the Lamb
(Rev 19:7–8; 21:2, 9–11; 22:17)

The bride of the Lamb appears in the last half of the Book of Revelation and is one of the central symbols in the utopian vision of God's heavenly realm. After the violent murder of the great whore, the scene shifts to the marriage banquet of the Lamb and his bride. The bride wears "fine linen, bright and pure," and this linen consists of "the righteous deeds of the saints" (Rev 19:8). Revelation describes only the banquet and not the wedding ceremony.

Traditional interpretations view the bride at this banquet as the church, and the church as bride. The bride is also synonymous with the new Jerusalem, the utopian city that comes down from heaven, described "as a bride adorned for her husband" (Rev 21:2). The bride becomes a city. When the angel shows the seer John "the bride, the wife of the Lamb," the city of the new Jerusalem appears (Rev 21:9). The bride has one speaking part in unison with the Spirit: "The Spirit and the bride say, 'Come'" (Rev 22:17).

This symbolism makes clear the role of the female in the future world. It is limited; the female presence in God's new realm is like a beautiful, submissive, and virginal bride whose bodily purity provides the material and landscape for the holy city. The female is passive, not active. All the evil females (Jezebel and the great whore) are destroyed, and in the end the pure bride of the Lamb remains, taking the form of the new Jerusalem.

The bride metaphor occurs in other places in the New Testament, in bride-and-bridegroom images (for example, John 3:29) and in descriptions likening the church to a chaste virgin. As in Revelation, a distinction is made between good and evil women. 2 Cor 11:2 sets the church as virgin against sinful Eve. Eph 5:25 reveals the hierarchical relationships that characterize Christ, husbands, and wives: husbands are to love their wives "just as Christ loved the church" and made her holy and pure through his sacrifice; wives should respect husbands. In Revelation the bride metaphor for the church is expanded into a symbolic geographic place where the saints of God will reside after the heavens and the earth are no more.

Many feminist scholars reject the bride metaphor as an appropriate one for the church, since this image emphasizes submissiveness and sacrifice from women.

TINA PIPPIN

SEE ALSO Part III: Chaste Bride (of Christ); Great Whore; Woman in Labor, Clothed with the Sun.

Chaste Bride (of Christ)
(2 Cor 11:2; Eph 5:25–27)

In 2 Cor 11:2–3, Paul uses marital and sexual imagery to express his concern for the errant beliefs of the Corinthians: "I promised you in marriage to one husband, to present you as a chaste virgin to Christ. But I am afraid that as the serpent deceived Eve by its cunning, your thoughts will be led astray from a sincere and pure devotion to Christ."

Paul here draws upon ancient Israelite associations of idolatry with the adultery committed by married women against their husbands. Although later Christian tradition regularly depicts the church in a marital relationship with Christ, often as the pure, virgin bride, Paul's image here is more complex and more critical. He casts himself as the father who has betrothed his virgin daughter to a prospective husband, only to learn that her virginity may in fact be threatened. Implicit in this image is the view that, once a virgin was formally betrothed, it was an act of adultery for her to have sex with any man other than her intended husband. (This concept underlies the description of the pregnant Mary's plight in Matt 1:18–19.)

In casting himself as the betrothing father, Paul draws upon a complex constellation of images found in the Hebrew Bible. The community of Israel, normally envisioned as masculine (for instance, Israel is at once the name of the community and an alternate name of the patriarch Jacob), is portrayed numerous times as the male God's adulterous wife, whose adultery actually consists of her devotion to other gods (for example, Jer 3:1–14; Ezekiel 23; Hosea 2–3; 9:1). In applying this image to Corinthian believers, Paul implicitly identifies them with Israel, an identification that quickly became central to early Christian self-understanding.

The potential adultery of the Corinthians is not so much the worship of false gods, as in the Hebrew Bible, but the acceptance of false teachings, which Paul here thus equates with idolatry. The competition, however, is not between two male gods, but between Paul and the so-called "super-apostles" (11:5), a competition cast in terms of another biblical image of a woman associated with sexuality. The misled Corinthians are analogous to Eve, vulnerable to the deceits of the serpent; thus Paul effectively but indirectly identifies the super-apostles with the snake of Genesis 2–3.

Although Paul regularly represents himself as a father to churches he has founded, rarely if ever does he elsewhere image the members of those churches as exclusively female. In 2 Cor 11:2, Paul's characterization of Corinthian error as adultery requires him to feminize them, for the image does not work in reverse. In antiquity, a man who had sex with a woman other than his lawful wife committed no offense against his wife. His action was unlawful only if he had sex with a woman whose sexuality was the rightful property of another man (meaning that man's legally married wife or his virgin daughter). In such a case, his offense was against the other man. The representation of idolatry, or false belief, as adultery requires that the idolater be female.

But to characterize a church as female, in the cultural context of the first century C.E., was to invoke pervasive ancient notions of hierarchical relationships in which female was subordinate to male, slave was subordinate to owner, and children were subordinate to parents. These hierarchical associations are more explicit in another image of the church as chaste bride of Christ. In Ephesians, a letter whose Pauline authorship is disputed, the image occurs within the context of a hierarchical household code (5:25–27) and differs from the image in 2 Corinthians. The church is not explicitly called a bride of Christ; rather, the association is subtler. Husbands are instructed to love their wives as Christ loved the church, thus implicitly imaging the church as a wife. These verses mingle the language of unblemished brides with that of umblemished sacrifices: the term *amōmos* occurs regularly in the Greek translation of the Hebrew Bible to describe the appropriate blemish-free state of animals to be sacrificed in the temple. Christ's death is seen as purifying the church bride, "so as to present the church to himself in splendor, without a spot or wrinkle or anything of the kind — yes, so that she may be holy and without blemish" (5:27).

Ross S. Kraemer

SEE ALSO Part II: Wives (and Husbands) Exhorted (Eph 5:22–23); Part III: Bride of the Lamb; Oholah, Woman Samaria; Oholibah, Women/Whore Jerusalem; Women in Imagery for Jerusalem, Judah, and Israel in Jeremiah.

Church as Mother and Wet Nurse
(2 Esdr 2:15–32)

Chaps. 1–2 of the Book of 2 Esdras (sometimes called 5 Ezra, second century C.E.) form a Christian introduction that radically alters the intent of the seven apocalyptic visions of the Jewish author of chaps. 3–14 (4 Ezra, first century C.E.) by interjecting God's transfer of the covenant from the Jews to the Christians.

In a long passage dealing with God's favor for the Christian community, the second century author portrays the Christian church as Mother (2:15–24, 30–32), probably the counterpart of Mother Zion in 2:2–7. The author is providing instruction to the church in the manner of the latter sections of some of Paul's Epistles and in the Pastoral Epistles (1–2 Timothy and Titus). The beautiful language is akin to that of Isaiah 40–55, where Zion is consoled and comforted by God (see Isaiah 54, for example). God has in store glorious blessings for the children of Mother Church; therefore, the church should bring up her children with gladness, like that of a dove (2:15). "Do not fear, mother of children, for I have chosen you, says the Lord" (2:17). God promises shortly to raise up the dead from their places (2:16, 31), shower good things upon the community in accordance with the counsel of the prophets Isaiah and Jeremiah, and lavish upon the church exotic fruits, springs flowing with milk and honey, and mountainsides covered with lilies and roses.

In 2 Esdr 2:25–29, God addresses the church as a good nurse, offering reassurance that in the times of trial and testing, God will be there to protect both the nurse and children. At the same time, the text is a strong reminder to the nurse (meaning the church) that God will hold her accountable for proper nourishment of the community's members. There seems not to be a real distinction drawn here between the use of the image of the church as mother (2:15–24, 30–32) and the church as nurse (2:25–29). Both are nurturing female figures associated with child rearing and care of the young. Through the portrayal of Mother-Nurse Church as God's chosen, caring for her children, the second-century author readdresses the traditional concerns of Mother Zion and the assurances addressed by the book — divine justice and the fate of Israel — to the Christian community.

WALTER J. HARRELSON

SEE ALSO Part III: Jerusalem/Zion as Widow and Mother; Weeping Woman — Jerusalem/Zion as a City Being Built.

FOR FURTHER READING: Johnson, Elizabeth E. "2 Esdras."

Metzger, Bruce M. "The Fourth Book of Ezra."

Stone, Michael. "Esdras, Second Book of."

Daughter

(see biblical references listed in entry)

Scattered throughout the poetic literature of the Hebrew Bible, the Hebrew term *bat* ("daughter, young woman") is found linked to the names of certain cities and countries, most commonly Zion (an alternative name for Jerusalem). The resulting expression (daughter Zion, daughter Babylon, and others) seems to function as a poetic personification of the named locality or its inhabitants. Here is a list showing where these expressions occur:

- **daughter Babylon/Chaldea** (Babylon: Ps 137:8; Isa 47:1, 5; Jer 50:42; 51:33; Zech 2:7) (Chaldea: Isa 47:1, 5)
- **daughter Dibon** (Jer 48:18)
- **daughter Edom** (Lam 4:21, 22)
- **daughter Egypt** (Jer 46:11, 19, 24)
- **daughter Gallim** (Isa 10:30)
- **daughter Jerusalem** (2 Kgs 19:21; Isa 37:22; Lam 2:13, 15; Mic 4:8; Zeph 3:14; Zech 9:9)
- **daughter Judah** (Lam 1:15; 2:2, 5)
- **daughter Sidon** (Isa 23:12)
- **daughter Tarshish** (Isa 23:10)
- **daughter Tyre** (Ps 45:12)
- **daughter Zion** (2 Kgs 19:21; Ps 9:14; Isa 1:8; 10:32; 16:1; 37:22; 52:2; 62:11; Jer 4:31; 6:2, 23; Lam 1:6; 2:1, 4, 8, 10, 13, 18; 4:22; Mic 1:13; 4:8, 10, 13; Zeph 3:14; Zech 2:10; 9:9)
- **maiden** (*bĕtûlat*) **Babylon** (Isa 47:1)
- **maiden** (*bĕtûlat*) **Israel/Jerusalem/Judah** (2 Kgs 19:21; Jer 18:13; 31:4, 21; Lam 1:15; Amos 5:2)

In the Hebrew this expression is structured grammatically by what is known as a construct chain, the juxtaposition of two or more words to constitute one compound idea. In the expression *bat* + Place Name, *bat* is known as the dependent word and appears in the construct state; it precedes the word appearing in the absolute state, which is said to be in the genitive. When a construct chain involves more than two words, a more complicated situation results. For example, in the phrase *bĕtûlat bat ṣiyyôn,* "the virgin daughter of Zion" (2 Kgs 19:21; Isa 37:11; Lam 2:13), the middle term *(bat)* functions both as a genitive to what precedes it *(bĕtûlat)* and a construct (dependent) to what follows *(ṣiyyôn).*

The genitive in a construct chain can express a wide variety of relationships to its preceding construct, such as possession, attribution, apposition, or explication. Hence, the precise meaning of the phrase *bat* + Place Name remains contested. Many English translations, including the NIV, the RSV, and the KJV, translate a phrase such as *bat ṣiyyôn* as "the daughter of Zion." This translation seemingly takes the Hebrew as a genitive of possession, which, in English idiom, conveys the notion that Zion *had* a daughter. The difficulty is that the literary contexts of this phrase — and others involving the term *bat* — denote a whole city or country and its inhabitants, not just one individual daughter. Hence, an alternative translation, "daughter Zion," has been suggested (compare the NRSV). This translation understands the Hebrew as a genitive of apposition, meaning that the two terms are taken as a reference to the same thing (that is, Zion *was* a daughter). Such a translation is akin to English phrases such as "the river Nile" or "the city Jerusalem." In these English examples, the terms *Nile* and *Jerusalem* are understood as more specific references to the same thing designated by the first term *(river, city).*

Grammatical and translational challenges accompany the problem of understanding the phrase's meaning and significance. What is to be made of linking the term *daughter* to the names of certain cities and countries? Part of the explanation comes from certain features of the Hebrew language. Hebrew has no neuter gender; all nouns are either masculine or feminine. And the feminine is especially affiliated with certain categories of

nouns. Many abstract concepts are feminine (for example, wisdom — *ḥokmâ;* love — *'ahăbâ;* truth — *'ĕmet),* as are most collective entities, (for example, inhabitants — *yôšebet;* caravan — *'ōrḥâ;* the poor — *dallâ).* The proper names of countries and cities are usually construed as feminine. This use of the feminine case for these noun categories may have encouraged the practice in poetic literature of portraying certain specific concepts and collective entities as feminine personifications. For instance, some texts in the wisdom literature personify wisdom and folly as figures of women (see Proverbs 8–9; Ben Sira 24). Certain prophetic texts depict the collective people of Israel, Judah, Jerusalem, or Samaria as YHWH's wife (see Jeremiah 2–3; Ezekiel 16, 23; Hosea 1–3). These examples should probably be placed on a continuum with the practice of personifying cities and countries as daughters.

Another possible factor derives from the cultural world of the Bible — especially with regard to the specific association of the feminine with cities, countries, or their inhabitants. Studies of Mesopotamian literature have identified a city-lament genre that includes a weeping goddess motif. This weeping goddess has, as her primary function, the mourning of the destruction of her city and its population. This function corresponds remarkably well with the passage in the Book of Lamentations (Lam 2:18) in which daughter Zion/daughter Jerusalem bewails the destruction of "her" city and its inhabitants. It also fits with the role of women, including daughters (see Jer 9:20), as professional mourners. Another correspondence with the Hellenistic world has recently been pointed out. Specifically, the Greek city of Athens was conceptualized as the holy city of the goddess Athena, who was the divine daughter of the great god Zeus. Hence, in a parallel fashion, Jerusalem — in her guise as daughter Zion/daughter Jerusalem — may have been understood as the daughter of YHWH, just as the king was understood to be the son of YHWH (2 Sam 7:14; Ps 2:7).

The Mesopotamian parallels are relevant to the idea of daughter Zion and others as female, but the Greek comparison — though farther afield geographically — relates more specifically to the city-as-daughter image. Yet it is difficult to establish that any extrabiblical parallels informed the biblical practice of personifying cities, countries, or their inhabitants as daughters. The idea of doing so may have originated independently in ancient Israel, in accord with the ways in which daughters were positioned socially.

In a patrilocal social structure like that of ancient Israel, a daughter's position in her natal household was temporary, since it was expected that she would leave at the time of her marriage, entering into and becoming a part of her husband's household. Hence, a daughter was a liminally positioned person. Many of the narratives involving daughters in the Hebrew Bible portray her in just this way, caught between the often competing demands of father and husband (see especially Michal, Rachel, and Leah).

One consequence of this liminal state is that daughters in biblical narratives are sometimes depicted in quite strong, positive, independent ways. At other times, though, their positioning leaves them exposed, vulnerable, and victimized. And both of these positionings are found also in the *bat* + Place Name expressions.

The positive image of a daughter is manifested especially in those instances in which the *bat* + Place Name expression denotes a figure who is rejoicing, militarily powerful, or the recipient of words of comfort or hope. Such rejoicing figures (as in Jer 31:4; Zeph 3:14; Zech 2:10; 9:9) have significant parallels with narrative instances of daughters celebrating, with song, instrumental music, and dance, the return of Israelites victorious in battle (for example, Jephthah's daughter, Miriam, Deborah). Militarily powerful figures (as in Isa 87:22; Mic 4:8, 13) depend on a close relationship to YHWH, since YHWH is the source of the military power demonstrated, or wielded by, the daughter figures. The recipient of hope (as in Isa 62:11) is also linked to YHWH, insofar as it is YHWH (as father) who comforts "his daughter."

The negative expressions almost always have a military connotation. The specific images express the threat of destruction (Isa 10:32; Jer 6:23), disaster currently taking place (Jer 4:31; Mic 4:10), or destruction that has already occurred (Lam 1:6; 2:15; Amos 5:2), with the aftermath calling forth expressions of mourning and lamentation.

Finally, the *bat* + Place Name expressions, taken collectively, demonstrate some particular political and cultural interests. All those with positive nuances (such as Ps 9:14; Isa 62:11; Jer 6:2) pertain only to Israelite cities or territories (that is, Jerusalem, Zion, Israel). The negative connotations are reserved exclusively for localities considered "other" vis-à-vis Israel, such as Babylon/Chaldea (Ps 137:8; Isa 47:1, 5), Egypt (Jer 46:24), and Edom (Lam 4:22). And yet, though these biblical daughters reflect the concerns of a specific people at a specific time and place, the phrase also resonates with all women, since all have experienced that familial role.

KARLA G. BOHMBACH

SEE ALSO Part II: Women with Hand-Drums, Dancing (Exod 15:20, etc.); Mourning Women (Jer 9:17–20, etc.); Part III: Mother/Daughter as Territory; Woman Wisdom.

FOR FURTHER READING: Dobbs-Allsopp, F. W. "The Syntagma of *bat* Followed by a Geographical Name in the Hebrew Bible: A Reconsideration of Its Meaning and Grammar."

Fitzgerald, Aloysius. "*BTWLT* and *BT* as Titles for Capital Cities."

Follis, Elaine R. "The Holy City as Daughter."

Stinespring, William F. "No Daughter of Zion: A Study of the Appositional Genitive in Hebrew Grammar."

Daughter of Zion

(Matt 21:5; John 12:15)

In the Gospel of John, Jesus enters Jerusalem for his final Passover sitting on a young donkey, in fulfillment of a partially quoted verse from the Hebrew Bible addressed to Israel personified as the "daughter [of] Zion."

John's unidentified verse, from Zech 9:9, differs from ancient Hebrew and Greek versions: they begin, "Rejoice greatly, O daughter Zion! / Shout aloud, O daughter Jerusalem," whereas John 12:15 reads, "Do not be afraid, daughter of Zion" (compare Matt 21:5, "Tell the daughter of Zion").

The same verse is cited also in the Gospel of Matthew (21:2–7), although not in either Mark or Luke. Whereas the author of the Gospel of John correctly understands the parallelism of Zechariah ("your king comes to you; / . . . humble and riding on a donkey, / on a colt, the foal of a donkey") to refer to one animal described twice, Matthew's Jesus enters Jerusalem riding on two animals, a donkey and a colt; apparently the author failed to see the common Hebrew use of parallelism in this verse.

The personification of Israel as feminine pervades the Hebrew Bible and is one of the many factors in the subsequent personification of the Christian church as female. Here, however, the use of feminine imagery is probably ancillary to the primary use of Zech 9:9 as evidence for Jesus' fulfillment of ancient Hebrew prophecies.

Ross S. Kraemer

See also Part III: Daughter.

Earth as Mother

(2 Esdr 5:48–49; 7:54–55, 62; 10:9–10)

Earth stands as a female representation in several texts, all of them in the portion of 2 Esdras known as 4 Ezra (chaps. 3–14), a Jewish apocalypse of the first century C.E. Indeed, all of them appear in the portion of 4 Ezra where the dialogue between the angel Uriel and Ezra is found (chaps. 3–10).

In 5:46–49, the angel responds to Ezra's query as to why the earth did not bear all the generations of mortals at once. The angel makes the point by saying that Ezra should ask a woman's womb why it did not bear all ten of her children at once. Just as that is impossible, so it would be impossible for earth to support all the generations at once. Rather, each generation comes in its appointed time. And just as a woman ceases to bear children in her old age, so also will the earth cease to produce the generations when it has grown old. When the angel

questions whether Ezra loves Israel more than his Maker, Ezra responds that he is striving to understand the way of the Most High. The angel declares that God's ways are inscrutable and, in the context of the dispute with Ezra, speaks of earth as both mother and tomb for humanity (5:48–49).

In 7:45–61, Ezra laments to the interpreting angel that the number of those whom God will save is terribly small. The angel makes the point that this only proves how precious in God's sight are the righteous, who will be saved. In 7:54–58, the angel uses the analogy of the rarity of precious metals within the earth. If Ezra should ask the earth which of her elements are most plentiful and which most precious and rare, earth would say that, of course, gold and silver and iron and lead and clay are, in descending order, most valuable. The analogy is also found in Daniel 2.

In 2 Esdr 7:62, Ezra cries out to earth personified, saying, "O earth, what have you brought forth?" For Ezra, earth would have done better to have brought forth no children at all. Human life is without meaning, if its members cannot know at least the basic meaning of life on earth, Ezra maintains. The angel insists that God rightly rejoices over the few human beings that will be saved, rather than grieves over the many sinners who must perish;

A Roman marble relief, from the second century C.E., *depicting an allegorical personification of the earth mother. See* Earth as Mother.

Ezra must do the same. But that is what Ezra cannot do. Earth should better have refused to bring forth children with the ability to think, to feel, to seek understanding, since — against all human reason, it would seem — God will not find a way to provide salvation for sinners.

The representation of earth as mother appears together with a remarkable set of female images in 2 Esdras, including passages dealing with earthly mothers and women's wombs, as well as portrayals of the church, righteousness and iniquity, the law, Jerusalem/Zion, and even God in female personifications. Earth is portrayed as a mother of animate and inanimate creation.

WALTER J. HARRELSON

SEE ALSO Part II: Mother/Woman's Womb (2 Esdr 4:40–43, etc.); Part III: Church as Mother and Wet Nurse; Female Images of God in the Apocryphal/Deuterocanonical Books; Righteousness and Iniquity as Females; Weeping Woman — Jerusalem/Zion as a City Being Built; Woman Wisdom.

FOR FURTHER READING: Johnson, Elizabeth E. "2 Esdras."

Metzger, Bruce M. "The Fourth Book of Ezra."

Stone, Michael. "Esdras, Second Book of."

Enemy Cities as Female

(Bar 4:32–35)

In a book that took shape sometime between 200 and 60 B.C.E., Baruch, Jeremiah's scribe, is pseudonymously credited with writing an edifying letter from Babylon to the priests and people of Jerusalem. Nowhere else in the Bible do the two female figures Torah Wisdom (3:9–4:4) and Widow Zion (4:5–5:9) appear side by side as they do in this book. According to the Book of Baruch, Israel will be restored through following the path of Torah Wisdom and through the intercession of Widow Zion. The present desolation is about to change: the enemies will be destroyed (4:5–5:9), and the people of Israel will return to Jerusalem (5:4).

The enemy cities, who had rejoiced in Jerusalem's fall and the exile of her people, are personified

as females who will be duly punished for their mistreatment of Israel. Jerusalem is assured of help: "Wretched will be the cities that your children served as slaves; / wretched will be the city that received your offspring. / For just as she rejoiced at your fall and was glad for your ruin, / so she will be grieved at her own desolation" (Bar 4:32–33).

In Greek and Hebrew, the most common words for "city" are feminine nouns (*polis* and *ʿîr*). In the imagery of the ancient Near East, a city is always spoken of as the mother of its inhabitants and so is personified as a female. As a mother, a city will inevitably share the fate of her children, that is, all the joys and sorrows of her population. Although not expressly mentioned by name, the great city of Babylon, capital city of the enemy Nebuchadnezzar, will (insists Bar 4:32–35, and earlier, Isa 47:8–11) suffer greatly for all the destruction, humiliation, and contempt she had heaped upon Jerusalem over the years. For her sins against Jerusalem, Babylon will reap all that she has sown — and then some!

Although in terms of literary imagery, an ancient city, whether Israelite or Babylonian, is characterized as a female, in reality, a city's "children" (that is, the ones who carry out the punishments mentioned in Baruch 4 — slaughtering, raping, torching, and looting) are most always males. War, as depicted in the Bible, was almost a uniquely male "sin" (but see Judg 4:4–10, 17–21; 2 Sam 11:21).

CAREY A. MOORE

SEE ALSO Part II: Daughters (and Sons) of Zion (Bar 4:10, etc.); Part III: Jerusalem/Zion as Widow and Mother; Mother/Daughter as Territory.

FOR FURTHER READING: Mendels, Doron. "Baruch."

Tull, Patricia K. "Baruch."

Female (and Male) Idol

(Deut 4:16)

The possibility of Israel's worshipping gods other than YHWH was a major problem for most biblical writers. Many injunctions against this practice appear in Israelite legal codes (Exod 20:4–6, 23; 34:17;

Female figurine (5 inches high) cast in solid bronze and partially coated in electrum. Of Syrian-Lebanese origin, it probably dates to the Late Bronze Age (thirteenth century B.C.E.). Depicted with a short wig and a decorated robe, the figure's hands are in a benedictory pose, perhaps indicating that the image represents a deity, although she lacks the headdress usually associated with the metal goddess figurines well known from this period. See Female (and Male) Idol.

Lev 19:4; 26:1; Deut 5:8; 9:16; 27:15), but one of the most complete is Deut 4:15–20, which enjoins the Israelites not to "act corruptly by making an idol for yourselves, in the form of any figure — the likeness of male or female" (v. 16) or animals, birds, or fish or by serving such idols.

Two issues are at stake in this injunction. The first is the commandment to aniconism, meaning

that YHWH does not wish any images to be made *at all,* even if YHWH is the subject of these images. The second issue is monolatry — worship of only one god — Israel's YHWH. This is not the same as radical monotheism, which contends that there is only one god in the universe. Various sources within the Hebrew Bible acknowledge the existence of the gods of other nations and state that other nations make images of their gods (for example, 1 Sam 31:9; 1 Kgs 11:5; 2 Kgs 23:13; Ps 106:36; Isa 46:1; Ezek 23:14; Amos 5:26). Israel, however, is not allowed to worship the gods that other nations worship, and neither are they allowed to worship YHWH in the same way in which the other nations worship their gods.

But if aniconism signifies a religious practice that uses no visual imagery whatsoever, then ancient Israel cannot be described as totally aniconic. Making images of YHWH's "person" was forbidden; symbolic or representational visual imagery related to YHWH, however, was used within Israelite religion. One such image is the cherub motif, which appears in descriptions of the tabernacle (Exod 36:8–9; 37:1–9), the Solomonic temple interior (1 Kgs 6:23–36), and various temple fixtures (1 Kgs 7:27–37). The cherub functioned as a "companion animal" on whose back YHWH was said to ride (Ps 18:10). The "golden calf" image also may have functioned in this way. Several poetic texts connect YHWH to the visual image of a bull through the divine title "Mighty One [literally, "Bull"] of Jacob/Israel" (Gen 49:24; Ps 132:2, 5; Isa 1:24; 49:26; 60:16).

Ancient Israel did not lack imagery related to the divine, but rather avoided attempts to represent God's person. Nonetheless, the extensive and emphatic language forbidding idols in Deut 4:15–20 and elsewhere probably means that ancient Israelites did produce cultic statuary and other images that violated the command to worship only YHWH.

Many biblical accounts refer to the use of such imagery within Israel. Israel and Judah (the northern and southern kingdoms, after 922 B.C.E.) periodically instituted state-level cults of the goddess Asherah, some of which appear to have included the production of statuary in her image and its installation in state sanctuaries (compare 1 Kgs 15:13; 16:33; 18:19; 2 Kgs 13:6; 21:7). Statuary representing other goddesses and gods, such as Astarte, Milcom, and Chemosh, may also have been features of the cultic installations erected for them by Solomon, though this is not explicitly stated (1 Kgs 11:4–7, 33; 2 Kgs 23:13). These passages demonstrate that, although the legal texts mandated the exclusive worship of YHWH as Israel's god, other gods were worshipped from time to time in Israel, and at least one other deity, namely Asherah, seems to have occupied a predominant place within the major state level cults of both the northern and southern kingdoms. Household practice likewise included worship of gods other than YHWH (see, for example, Jer 44:15–25).

In addition, archaeological remains illuminate the domestic religious practices of Israelites. Significantly, no images of YHWH's person have been found in the archaeological record, though images of divine female personages do occur. For instance, certain small ceramic images, frequently found in the remains of the period of the divided monarchy, may be depictions of Asherah as "mother goddess" that were kept in household shrines (not in state sanctuaries). However, it is also possible that these small statues served as personal devotional or votive objects, perhaps as charms intended to protect women and their children or to induce YHWH (or Asherah) to make women fertile.

Other images thought more certainly to represent female deities appear on metal charms and on ceramic cult vessels. A unique example of this last type appears on the lowest register of a cult stand found at Taanach. It is not certain whether this is an Israelite or a Canaanite artifact, but it is generally accepted that the female figure standing between two lions on the bottom register is Asherah. The goddess's close association with lions and lion imagery in extrabiblical texts and archaeological finds from other neighboring cultures makes the identification fairly sound. Clearly goddesses and goddess imagery were part of ancient Israelite culture before monotheism prevailed.

ELIZABETH C. LaRocca-Pitts

SEE ALSO Part II: Women Who Went to Egypt (Jer 43:6, etc.); Part III: Anath; Asherah/Asherim; Ashima/Ashimah; Astarte; Queen of Heaven.

FOR FURTHER READING: Frymer-Kensky, Tikva. *In the Wake of the Goddesses: Women, Culture, and the Biblical Transformation of Pagan Myth.*

Hestrin, Ruth. "Understanding Asherah — Exploring Semitic Iconography."

Female Images for Nations in Ezekiel

(Ezekiel 16)

The author of Ezekiel 16 (writing in the early sixth century B.C.E.) uses marriage as an extended metaphor to describe the relationship between God (YHWH) and God's people (Jerusalem). YHWH appears as the lover, husband, and lord of Jerusalem, his adulterous wife. Although the woman Jerusalem and the marriage metaphor dominate in this text, other cities and nations are also depicted as her female relatives. The use of feminine images to describe various cities or national entities is not unique to Ezekiel; however, because of the length and detailed nature of Ezekiel 16, this language is developed in a manner not typically seen in the prophets.

In describing cities and nations with feminine images, the prophets use "dead metaphors" — expressions that continue in the language even though their origins can no longer be determined. Theories as to how these metaphors developed nonetheless abound. Typically these theories center on the idea that ancient Near Eastern cities had protective patron goddesses. The identification of a city with a goddess led to the use of feminine pronouns and images for both the city and its inhabitants. Capital cities, by extension, could represent the nation, and thus nations were also often referred to in the feminine. The author of Ezekiel 16 uses this linguistic convention to create a metaphorical cast of female characters. However, these women are not merely figures of speech. They embody Ezekiel's understandings of women and ethnicity, and they make a theological point about the status of Jerusalem.

The author of Ezekiel 16 opens the story by describing the woman Jerusalem as a product of mixed ethnic heritage. Although both the mother and the father are mentioned, once the woman shows herself to be a whore, the author offers a simple proverb to describe her behavior — "like mother, like daughter" (v. 44). Just as the woman Jerusalem was initially neglected by her parents, so also does she, specifically following the ways of her Hittite mother, loathe and fail to take care of her husband and children. Indeed, the author of the text seems to indicate that her behavior can be seen as some kind of female genetic defect since it also extends to her sisters (Sodom and Samaria). The centrality of the mother's role in the woman Jerusalem's behavior receives further emphasis when the order of parentage, first given in v. 3 with the father mentioned first, is reversed in v. 45 to foreground the mother.

All of the female relatives mentioned in this text come from ethnic groupings or cities that are negatively valued in most biblical passages. From the "pagan" pre-Israelite inhabitants of the land (the Hittites), to some of the traditional enemies of Israel (the Philistines, and Aram or Edom), to the preeminent symbol of depravity (Sodom), to the apostate rival kingdom (Samaria), the author pulls together a collection of peoples traditionally seen in the Bible as far removed from God and the things of God. They are particularly problematic because they are not only foreign, but also women. The connection of depraved conduct with women follows with an emphasis in Ezekiel on women as the source of uncleanness, whether through menstrual blood or through sexual conduct outside of defined cultural boundaries. Women in Ezekiel are thus often unable to achieve purity or holiness and thereby to be in relationship to a holy God.

These women serve as points of comparison to the woman Jerusalem, illustrating how her conduct is even more corrupt than the worst of Israel's ideological enemies. Her worship of other gods or idolatry, here described as sexual immorality, will necessarily be punished. Recent feminist and womanist work on this text focuses on the problematic nature of this connection made between women and degeneracy as well as the use of violence against women to illustrate the fate of Jerusalem.

SANDRA L. GRAVETT

SEE ALSO Part III: Daughter; Mother/Daughter as Territory; Woman Wickedness.

FOR FURTHER READING: Darr, Katheryn Pfisterer. "Ezekiel."

Weems, Renita J. *Battered Love: Marriage, Sex, and Violence in the Hebrew Prophets.*

Female Images of God in the Apocryphal/ Deuterocanonical Books

(2 Esdr 1:15–30; 2:2–4; 8:8–12)

Explicit female representations for God in the Apocryphal/Deuterocanonical Books appear only in 2 Esdras, where in addition to God's law, divine wisdom, and Jerusalem/Zion, God's own self is so portrayed. The following discussion highlights these rich female images for the Holy One.

In 2 Esdr 1:30, the second-century C.E. Christian author uses a simile depicting God as mother hen to describe God's care and protection of Israel through the centuries. "I gathered you as a hen gathers her chicks under her wings. But now, what shall I do to you? I will cast you out from my presence" (1:30). Here, past protection gives way to God's rejection of Israel in favor of the Christian church. On the whole, animal imagery for God in the Bible is fairly limited. God is likened to a lion (Jer 49:19; 50:44; Hos 5:14; 11:10; 13:7–8; Amos 3:4, 8; Lam 3:10), a bear (Hos 13:8; Lam 3:10), and an eagle (Exod 19:4 and Deut 32:11). References to the sheltering protection of God's wings (Exod 19:4; Deut 32:11; Pss 17:8; 36:7; 57:1; 61:4; 63:7; 91:4) and to the Lord of hosts being "like birds hovering overhead" (Isa 31:5) also appear. Strikingly, only in 2 Esdr 1:30,

Matt 23:37, and Luke 13:34 do we find the maternal image of God as a mother hen.

Several important texts refer to the deity under the image of a human mother. The first are found in 2 Esdras 1–2. The author uses in turn the images of father, mother, and nurse to portray God's relation to the covenant people, Israel. "Thus says the Lord Almighty: Have I not entreated you as a father entreats his sons or a mother her daughters or a nurse her children" (1:28). God, under the image of mother, reminds Israel of the divine entreaty in times past that Israel, God's children, be faithful.

In 1:15–23, the Christian author, drawing upon incidents described in Exodus and Numbers, may be portraying the deity under the image of mother. God provided quails for food, camps for protection, manna (the very bread of angels), water from the rock, the leaves of trees for cover (an alternative reading: "for shade"), and land to support life. Instead of destroying Israel because of its faithlessness, God dispossessed the Canaanites and turned undrinkable water into sweet. The heaping up of biblical images of divine protection suggests the incessant care of the mother for her children.

In 2 Esdr 2:2, the author presents either God or (more probably) Zion as mother of Israel. The mother who bore Israel now sends the children away, for she is no longer able to do anything for them. The children are told to ask for mercy from the Lord. Since the text goes on to call on God to destroy the mother as well, the reference is much more likely to be to Zion as mother than to God as mother.

Another possible reference to God as mother comes in 2 Esdr 8:8–12. In one of the great meditations of the prophet Ezra on God's justice, or lack thereof, Ezra depicts God as the one who gives life to the newborn, fashions its members, preserves it for nine months in the womb, provides breasts to give the newborn food, and milk to the breasts. These references may, of course, be simply to God the provider of life in the womb (see Psalm 139), but they may be portraying God as mother/life-giver.

In 2 Esdr 1:28, the author refers to God's care over faithless Israel in times past as like that of a nurse — likely a wet nurse — caring for her children. The reference is parallel to references in the same place to God as father and as mother.

In 2:2 and 2:4, the author refers either to God or to Zion (Jerusalem) under the image of widow. It seems more likely that Zion is the intended reference, for the author goes on to speak of coming ruin to this mother/widow (2:6).

Just as Woman Wisdom, "a reflection of eternal light, a spotless mirror of the working of God," (Wis 7:26), is not quite God nor is she distinguishable from God, so some of the female images in 2 Esdras are not God, but neither is there a way in some of the references to sharply distinguish mother, nurse, and widow from God. This reflects the very nature of language depicting God: what is said is never quite clear, and words are never fully adequate to express God's reality. It is intriguing that the preponderance of these female representations appear in portions of 2 Esdras that are attributed to the second-century Christian author and that some of these representations are also found in the New Testament.

WALTER J. HARRELSON

SEE ALSO Part II: Mother/Woman's Womb (2 Esdr 4:40–43, etc.); Part III: Church as Mother and Wet Nurse; Earth as Mother; Female Images of God in the Hebrew Bible; Righteousness and Iniquity as Females; Weeping Woman — Jerusalem/Zion as a City Being Built; Woman Wisdom.

FOR FURTHER READING: Johnson, Elizabeth E. "2 Esdras."

Metzger, Bruce M. "The Fourth Book of Ezra."

Stone, Michael. "Esdras, Second Book of."

Female Images of God in the Hebrew Bible

(Exod 19:4; 34:6; Num 11:12; Deut 32:11, 18–19; Neh 9:20–21; Job 38:8, 29; Hos 11:3–4, 8–9; Isa 27:11; 42:14; 43:1; 45:10–11; 46:3–4; 49:15; 66:7–9, 12–13)

The Hebrew Bible does not provide a direct exposition of the nature of God. Indeed, because its texts derive from such an extended time period and from so many different authors, a systematic or dogmatic presentation in Hebrew Scriptures of its own "theology" would not be expected. Yet ideas about God are present throughout the Hebrew Bible, largely in the form of actions attributed to God, which are thought to reveal something of God's character, and in images, drawn from the human realm, depicting God's nature.

Many of the actions and images used to reveal God in relationship to Israel are andromorphic; they use the culturally determined behaviors and roles of males to indicate what God is like. For example, the power of YHWH in rescuing Israel from the bondage of Egypt or from exile in Babylon is conveyed by images of God as a divine warrior (as in Exod 15:3; Zech 9:13–14). And the sovereignty and justice of YHWH in dealing with Israel's iniquity are found in images of God as universal king and judge (as in Isa 33:22). The variety of such images and the frequency with which they are used (God is called king some forty-seven times in the Hebrew Bible) can produce the impression of God as exclusively male — the so-called patriarchal God of the Hebrew Bible. The nature of Hebrew as a gendered language also contributes strongly to the sense of a male deity. That is, all nouns in Hebrew must be either feminine or masculine; there is no neuter. Because the word for God ('ēl or 'ĕlōhîm) and the name of God (YHWH) are both masculine, God is always referred to as "he" in the Hebrew Bible and thus in English translations.

Biblical language and andromorphic imagery together have thus obscured the presence of images for God that are derived from roles associated with women in Israelite society. Gynomorphic images for God can in fact be identified throughout the Hebrew Bible. The most common of these are maternal ones; they express, in terms of birth and nurturance, the way God created and cares for Israel. But there are other portrayals of God — as provider of food and water, clothing, and even instruction — that can equally be considered female imagery. Many scholars link these maternal images to mother goddess figures in Near Eastern mythol-

ogy, especially to the influence of the cult of Asherah in ancient Israel. But these images can equally stem from the awareness of female biological functions.

Perhaps the most direct statement of God as the one who gave birth to and then suckled Israel appears in Moses' desperate rhetorical question to God in Num 11:12. Moses insists that God take responsibility for the Israelites when he cries "Did I conceive all this people? Did I give birth to them, that you should say to me, 'Carry them in your bosom, as a nurse carries a suckling child'?" Moses clearly attributes to God the birthing and suckling of Israel. A similar depiction appears in the ancient poem (chap. 32) at the end of Deuteronomy, where Moses chastises the Israelites — the daughters and sons of YHWH (32:19) — for abandoning their parent: "You were unmindful of the Rock that bore [begot] you; / you forgot the God who gave you birth" (32:18). That poem also uses animal imagery — an eagle hovering over its nest — to depict YHWH's maternal care for Israel (32:11; see also Exod 19:4). Such maternal imagery is pushed even farther in Job, where the cosmos itself comes from the "womb" of God the creator (38:8, 29).

The use of "womb" in relation to God may also allude to the feminine nature of God as the source of divine mercy or compassion. The adjective "compassionate" (raḥûm), the noun "compassion" (raḥămîm), and the verb "to love, have compassion" (rāḥam) are all related to the Hebrew word for "womb" (reḥem); and they are used for God more often than for humans in the Hebrew Bible. The oft-repeated creedal statement of Exod 34:6 (see Exod 33:19; Neh 9:17; Pss 78:38; 86:15; 103:8; 111:4; Joel 2:13; Jonah 4:2) proclaims the steadfast and unending nature of divine love as that of a "merciful" (raḥûm) God. Divine compassion thus evokes *uteral* imagery — of God having powerful maternal love for Israel.

Language depicting God as the mother of Israel appears in several prophetic books. In Hosea, for example, God asserts that "I have taught Ephraim [Israel] to walk" and also that God has carried the infant people, fed them, and healed them (11:3–4)

— all quintessentially maternal tasks. Several verses later (11:8–9), the prophet refers to divine "compassion" for Ephraim and also asserts that God is not a human ("I am God and no mortal"). Maternal imagery for God is probably present in Isa 27:11, where divine creation is linked with compassion. Female imagery for God is especially prominent in the second part of the Book of Isaiah (chaps. 40–66), which dates to the time after the Babylonian conquest in the sixth century B.C.E. Isa 42:14 uses images of childbirth to convey God's expected creation of a new Israel, and other oracles assert God's maternal parentage of Israel (45:10–11; 46:3–4; 49:15; 66:7–9). In addition, images of a mother's compassion are evoked to provide comfort to the devastated people. That a maternal God will never forget Zion (Jerusalem) is expressed in the poignant rhetorical questions "Can a woman forget her nursing child, / or show no compassion for the child of her womb?" (49:15; see also 43:1; 49:23; 66:9, 12–13).

Most of the gynomorphic imagery for God is fairly direct; it uses metaphors and similes to express God's maternal creativity, compassion, and caregiving. But other aspects of God's deeds are indirectly gynomorphic. For example, the household tasks of women in ancient Israel included fetching water, preparing and serving food, making clothing, and contributing to the instruction of small children. Unlike the biological functions of childbirth and breast-feeding, these activities could also be performed by men; yet they were largely a woman's domain. Therefore, biblical texts acclaiming God as provider of water and food, particularly in the narratives about the period after the exodus when the people struggle to survive in the wilderness (for example, Exod 16:4, 15; Num 11:18), evoke culturally specific images of women's tasks. If the exodus event itself is presented directly as the result of actions of an andromorphic warrior deity, the subsequent survival of Israel en route to the promised land is presented indirectly as the result of actions of a gynomorphic deity providing nourishment. A retrospective speech by Ezra in the postexilic Book of Nehemiah depicts a series of divine acts on behalf of Israel after the exodus, all of which

relate to female tasks: "You [YHWH] gave your good spirit [feminine *rûaḥ*] to instruct them, and did not withhold your manna from their mouths, and gave them water for their thirst. . . . they lacked nothing; their clothes did not wear out and their feet did not swell" (Neh 9:20–21).

The direct and indirect gynomorphic images for God do not, of course, necessarily indicate a belief in a female deity any more than the andromorphic images constitute evidence that the Israelites believed that YHWH was literally male. To be sure, postbiblical theological tradition, heavily influenced by the prominent "God the father" language of early Judaism and Christianity, has certainly asserted conviction that the deity is male. Yet the presence of both female and male images for God in the Hebrew Bible should open the question not so much of whether God is female and/or male, but rather about the nature of metaphoric language for God. Because God is so utterly Other, God's nature transcends the ability of humans to express it. The biblical writers used the language of human behavior, female or male as appropriate, to convey their ideas about YHWH. More often than not, such metaphoric language appears in biblical poetry, where it is meant to cause an emotional impact rather than depict a concrete reality.

Whether the sexual or gendered images of God had a literal meaning for the ancient authors and their audiences can probably never be known, although it is clear that the God of Israel does not have sexual relations with another deity to produce children as do the gods of Israel's neighbors. Most likely, all individuals had their own particular understanding of what the various images of God meant and of how they facilitated divine-human relationships. What seems certain is that the ancient Israelites would have not understood our contemporary interest in the sex or gender of God. The dominant male metaphors for God may seem sexist and even harmful today, when wrenched from their original cultural context; but it is worth considering that those images, and also the less visible but nonetheless vivid female ones, together allowed humans to grasp aspects of the fundamentally nonhuman character of God. For much of the period of the Hebrew Bible, images of a maternal YHWH helped people understand the intimate and abiding love, care, and compassion of their God.

CAROL MEYERS

SEE ALSO Part II: Woman (and Man) in the First Creation Story (Gen 1:26–28, etc.); Nurse (Num 11:12); Woman in Labor (Isa 13:8, etc.); Mother of the Servant (Isa 49:1, etc.); Nursing Mothers (Isa 49:15, etc.); Wife of One's Youth (Mal 2:14–16); Part III: Asherah/ Asherim; Female Images of God in the Apocryphal/ Deuterocanonical Books; Woman Wisdom.

FOR FURTHER READING: Benjamin, Don C. "Israel's God: Mother and Midwife."

Bronner, Leah. "Gynomorphic Imagery in Exilic Isaiah [40–66]."

Frymer-Kensky, Tikva. *In the Wake of the Goddesses: Women, Culture, and the Biblical Transformation of Pagan Myth.*

Gruber, Mayer I. "The Motherhood of God in Second Isaiah."

McFague, Sally. *Metaphorical Theology: Models of God in Religious Language.*

Meyers, Carol. "Gender and God in the Hebrew Bible — Some Reflections."

Trible, Phyllis. "God, Nature of, in the Old Testament."

Great Whore

(Rev 17:3–18:24)

The most notorious symbolic female in the New Testament is the great whore of Babylon, in the Book of Revelation. The whore is the symbol of the city and empire of Babylon; many scholars hold that this image represents the city of Rome and the Roman Empire in the late first century C.E. The whore symbolizes political power, and her reign is characterized by extreme political oppression, especially of the saints and believers in Jesus Christ. Thus her downfall and destruction are particularly graphic, and some scholars note the cathartic impact of this narrative for first-century Christians under Roman rule.

One of the seven angels with the seven bowls offers to show the narrator John "the judgment of the great whore who is seated on many waters" (Rev 17:1). As in the story of the woman prophet referred to as Jezebel in Rev 2:20, the accusations against the whore *(pornē)* include illicit sex or "fornication" *(porneia),* this time with the kings of the earth (17:2). The believers are warned against fornicating with her, and those who have are instructed to "come out of her" (18:4). The whore is also accused of being drunk with a wine that consists of the impurities of her fornication (17:2, 4) and also the blood of the saints and martyrs or witnesses of Jesus (17:6). She also associates with the beast/ dragon/devil, which she rides (17:3).

The whore is simultaneously a beautiful and horrifying figure. She wears regal clothing of "purple and scarlet . . . with gold and jewels and pearls" (17:4). On her forehead (in the manner of marking slaves) is her name: "'Babylon the great, mother of whores and of earth's abominations'" (17:5). The multiple characterizations of the whore have inspired much art; she is depicted as beautiful, drunk, seductive, and dangerous. The whore is evil incarnate, persecuting the saints and then drinking their blood from a golden cup. She is arrogant in her luxurious lifestyle and says to herself, "I will never see grief" (18:7).

John's response is one of great amazement (17:6). The powerful figure of the whore causes him to gaze at her wealth and oppressive actions. But the scene in Revelation is primarily one of judgment, and the whore is quickly brought down by the beast and its ten horns (kings), who turn on the whore with hate. The scene of her destruction is as follows: the ten horns and the beast "make her desolate and naked; they will devour her flesh and burn her up with fire" (17:16). The stripping, making desolate, eating, and burning of her flesh bring her to a grotesque, violent end. Her destruction is followed by rejoicing: "Hallelujah! / The smoke goes up from her forever and ever" (19:3). The scene of her death represents total vengeance on the ruling political power. As an angel throws a millstone into the sea, he says: "With such violence Babylon the great city will be thrown down, / and will be found no more" (18:21). Although the destruction of the whore takes only one hour (18:10, 17), she will burn forever (19:3). Her connections, not only with the kings of the earth but also the merchants and sailors, mourn for her as she burns because her destruction signals the end of their trade and wealth. These followers of the whore are in turn eaten by the birds of mid-heaven (19:17–18).

The three major scenes related to the end time share a central theme of eating: the destruction and eating of the whore, the marriage supper of the Lamb, and the "great supper of God" (19:17), in which the birds eat the kings and other enemies. Thus two anti-eucharistic scenes frame a eucharistic one. Corporate judgment falls on the whore and her followers, just as it did on Jezebel and her "children" in Rev 2:22–23. The whore, her followers, and the earth are destroyed to purify the space for the new earth and the new city, the new Jerusalem, symbolized as the opposite of a whore — as a virginal bride.

Biblical prophets often characterize cities as female. This tendency continues in Revelation, in the symbols of the whore and the bride. The fallen city is depicted as the fallen woman; when she falls, an authoritative angel sings the famous funeral dirge for the whore: "Fallen, fallen is Babylon the great! / It has become a dwelling place of demons . . ." (18:2). Many scholars focus on the downfall of the city as the destruction of an evil political power, ignoring the gender dimensions of the narrative. Some feminist scholars find a liberating message in this story of the destruction of the whore; the evil imperial system has fallen. Others note a more ambiguous reading by pointing out problems with symbolizing the evil political power as a woman and then destroying the woman.

TINA PIPPIN

SEE ALSO Part II: Woman Prophet Referred to as Jezebel (Rev 2:20); Part III: Bride of the Lamb; Woman in Labor, Clothed with the Sun.

FOR FURTHER READING: Carpenter, Mary Wilson. "Representing Apocalypse: Sexual Politics and the Violence of Revelation."

Collins, Adela Yarbro. *Crisis and Catharsis: The Power of the Apocalypse.*

Garrett, Susan R. "Revelation."

Pippin, Tina. *Death and Desire: The Rhetoric of Gender in the Apocalypse of John.*

Schüssler Fiorenza, Elisabeth. *The Book of Revelation: Justice and Judgment.*

Hephzibah/My Delight Is in Her, Jerusalem

from Hebrew *ḥepṣî*, "my delight," plus *bāh*, "in her"
(Isa 62:4)

In a text proclaiming how Jerusalem will be restored after being destroyed by the Babylonians in 586 B.C.E., the city is told that, although she has previously been known as Azubah, "Forsaken," and Shemamah, "Desolate," God will soon call her Hephzibah, meaning "My Delight is in Her," for "the Lord delights [*ḥāpēṣ*] in you" (Isa 62:4). Similar imagery describing Jerusalem as female is found elsewhere in Isaiah (1:21–23; 3:25–26; 51:17–52:2; 57:6–13; 66:7–13) and in Jeremiah (4:30–31; 6:2, 23; 13:20–27; 22:20–23), Lamentations (1:8–9), and Ezekiel (16:1–63; 23:1–4, 11–49). In almost all of these passages, however, the imagery is hostile, and Jerusalem is often equated with a female apostate or harlot who has strayed from the proper worship of YHWH. Yet in several other passages in Isaiah (49:7–26; 51:17–52:2; 54:1–10; 66:7–13), as in this one, the imagery is positive: Jerusalem is celebrated as both a loving mother and as God's beloved bride. Positive imagery is typical of the second half of the Book of Isaiah (chaps. 40–66), whose overall theme is to offer comfort to the people of Judah in the wake of the Babylonian exile. But even given the generally positive thrust of Isaiah 40–66, the positive female imagery of those chapters is remarkable, unparalleled elsewhere in the prophetic books and, indeed, almost anywhere else in the Hebrew Bible.

SUSAN ACKERMAN

FOR FURTHER READING: Ackerman, Susan. "Isaiah." Bronner, Leah. "Gynomorphic Imagery in Exilic Isaiah (40–66)."

Jerusalem/Zion as Widow and Mother

(Tob 13:9; Bar 4:5–5:9; 1 Macc 1:38–40; 2:8–11; 3:45)

Jerusalem/Zion (interchangeable terms for the great temple city) is poetically personified as a widow bereft of her children to form a powerful metaphor for various devastating historical events depicted in the Apocryphal/Deuterocanonical Books (Tob 13:9; Bar 4:5–5:9; 1 Macc 1:38–40; 2:8–11; 3:45). Drawing heavily from the imagery of the Hebrew Bible (see, for example, Isa 54:1–6) and appearing also in pseudepigraphical works (Psalms of Solomon 11:1–2), this maternal female figure reflects the lamentable conditions of real-life widowhood in ancient Israel. In this context, a "widow" (Hebrew 'almānâ, "the silent one"; the English word originates from Sanskrit vidhava, "to be void") is a married woman who finds herself without male support or protection either through the death of her husband or, more generally, because protection has been lost or is not available from husband, sons, or brothers.

Because of her vulnerability and precarious situation (she had no inheritance rights), the widow was often marginalized with the orphan (see Exod 22:22; Deut 14:29; Isa 1:17) and the alien, or foreigner of non-Israelite descent, who lived permanently in Israelite territory (Deut 16:11; Zech 7:10). Widowhood, like childlessness (see Gen 16:2; 30:1–2; 1 Sam 1:5), was often viewed as sent from God. Worst of all, widowhood was sometimes regarded as proof of a woman's sin or that of her deceased husband (see Isa 54:4). Yet according to Hebrew Scripture, the widow and her children were to be protected and accorded justice by God (Deut 10:18; Ps 68:5; Jer 49:11) and the community (Deut 24:19–21; 26:12).

In Tobit, Baruch, and 1 Maccabees, the city of Jerusalem is personified as a desolate mother, bereft of her children. Despite certain similarities in the three accounts, they refer to two quite different historical events. Tob 13:9 and Bar 4:5–5:9 speak of Jerusalem/Zion as destroyed by the Babylonian ruler Nebuchadnezzar in 587 B.C.E., although the accounts themselves were constructed between two and four hundred years later. 1 Maccabees (1:38–40; 2:8–11; 3:45) describes Jerusalem as mastered by the Seleucid king Antiochus IV Epiphanes in 167 B.C.E., and the text is almost contemporaneous with the events described.

Bar 4:9–29 movingly depicts Jerusalem/Zion as a long-suffering widow who addresses, first, her hostile neighbors (4:9b–16) and then her exiled children (4:17–29), assuring the latter of God's help. Jerusalem/Zion's phraseology and imagery are reminiscent of Second Isaiah (Isa 49:14–23; 54:1–6). The widow claims she "was left desolate because of the sins of my children" (Bar 4:12). "You were handed over to your enemies," she tells them, "because you angered God" (4:6). This mother instructs her children to go into exile (4:19), saying that she has taken off her "robe of peace and put on sackcloth," pledging she will "cry to the Everlasting all my days" (4:20). Zion encourages her children (4:21–29) and is herself encouraged with promises concerning the destruction of her enemy and the return of her children (4:30–5:9).

God's treatment of Widow Jerusalem/Zion contains disturbing images of spousal abuse. Jerusalem is punished and abandoned by her "spouse" YHWH for the sins of their children (though Baruch never specifically names God as husband or spouse). To couch it in more modern terms, "When the children turn out well, Dad claims the credit; when they don't, the mother is to blame." God's negative actions stand in sharp contrast to typical covenantal assurances to the marginalized from a God who "executes justice for the orphan and the widow, and who loves the strangers, providing them food and clothing" (Deut 10:18).

Given her experience, Widow Jerusalem/Zion's

instruction to her children is remarkable. She explicitly charges God with causing their predicament while at the same time acknowledging God as the source of salvation: "Take courage, my children, and cry to God, / for you will be remembered by the one who brought this upon you. . . . For the one who brought these calamities upon you / will bring you everlasting joy with your salvation" (Bar 4: 27–29).

The situation described in 1 Maccabees is quite different. Although Jerusalem is again personified as a mother bereft of her children, no mention is made of her widowhood nor of deserving such terrible treatment at the hands of their Seleucid masters. Describing the second Syrian attack of Jerusalem (in 167 B.C.E.) and the establishment of a Syrian garrison there, the author says that Jerusalem's "dishonor now grew as great as her glory; her exaltation was turned into mourning" (1 Macc 1:40). Mattathias, father of Judas Maccabeus and his four brothers, laments the ruin of the holy city whose infants and youths have been killed in her streets (1 Macc 2:8–9). "All her adornment has been taken away; no longer free, she has become a slave" (1 Macc 2:11).

Jerusalem/Zion personified as widow and mother movingly portrays the great temple city as a paradoxical symbol: bearer of the national disgrace of fallen Judah and special protector of those born for her, protected by her walls, and delivered through her intercession with God. This biblical figure counterbalances the more prevalent tradition that associates Zion with inviolability, justice, faithfulness, security, privilege, peace, and God's invincibility. Jerusalem/Zion as widow and mother tempers this largely triumphalist tradition.

CAREY A. MOORE

SEE ALSO Part II: Daughters (and Sons) of Zion (Bar 4:10, etc.); Part III: Weeping Woman — Jerusalem/Zion as a City Being Built.

FOR FURTHER READING: Fischer, Thomas. "Maccabees, Books of."

Mendels, Doron. "Baruch."

Moore, Carey A. *Daniel, Esther, and Jeremiah: The Additions.*

Tull, Patricia K. "Baruch."

Lilith

Hebrew *lîlît*, from Sumerian *lîl,* "wind"
(Isa 34:14)

A Sumerian storm demon of the third millennium B.C.E. (see the "Myth of Inanna, Gilgamesh, and the Huluppu Tree"), Lilith, by biblical times, had assimilated traits of the Babylonian demon Lamashtu, later associated with night by a false etymology with the Hebrew term *laylâ* ("night"). Lilith is mentioned only once in the Hebrew Bible: in a prophetic oracle (Isa 34:14) directed against Edom, which will be turned into a demon-haunted desert wilderness where even one such as she might be comfortable.

Lilith emerges in postbiblical Jewish and Islamic folklore as Adam's first wife. The most coherent form of the Lilith myth appears in a sophisticated Jewish story called *The Alphabet of Ben Sirah* (c. ninth century C.E.). In that legend, God creates her on the same day and of the same material as Adam. Considering herself the equal of her mate, she refuses Adam's male-dominant sexual advances. She will not let him lie above her, claiming that they are equal because both were made from earth. They come to an impasse, and she escapes by uttering God's ineffable name, which allows her to fly off safely into the desert (or the Red Sea).

Subsequent tradition, probably drawing on ancient Mesopotamian folklore, characterizes Lilith as a demon who especially threatens pregnant women, newborns, and men sleeping alone. This demonic Lilith, with strange sexual behaviors, overshadows the independent Lilith, equal to Adam, of earlier legend.

CAROLE L. FONTAINE

SEE ALSO Part I: Eve.

FOR FURTHER READING: Cantor, Aviva. "The Lilith Question."

Hutter, Manfred. "Lilith."

Lassner, Jacob. *Demonizing the Queen of Sheba: Boundaries of Gender and Culture in Postbiblical Judaism and Medieval Islam.*

Mistress Babylon

(Isa 47:5–7)

This mocking oracle against Babylon portrays the country as a woman who has fallen from her formerly high and respectable status. The prophet declares that this "mistress of kingdoms" (v. 5) will fall because she cruelly oppressed the Israelites, whom YHWH placed under her power, and arrogantly believed that she was beyond the deity's reproach.

Prophetic literature often uses woman as a metaphor for a country or a city. When used negatively, as it is here, the symbol carries connotations of vulnerability, infidelity, and powerlessness. A condemned country is portrayed as a woman sexually humiliated and deprived of her socially acceptable destiny as wife and mother. When used positively to describe Judah's restoration, the symbol abounds with images of female fertility. Thus, woman as a metaphor for a city or country both derives from and reinforces Israel's socially constructed gender patterns.

RHONDA BURNETTE-BLETSCH

SEE ALSO Part III: Daughter; Woman Jerusalem/Zion in Isaiah; Woman Nineveh.

Mother/Daughter (NRSV, Village) as Territory

(Num 21:25; 32:42; Josh 15:45, 47; Judg 1:27; 2 Sam 8:1; 20:19; 1 Chr 2:23; 18:1; Neh 11:25; Ps 48:11; Isa 14:2; Jer 49:2–3; Ezek 26:6, 8; 30:18)

In the Hebrew Bible, the most common word for "city" is the feminine noun ʿîr, which occurs more than one thousand times, in all genres of biblical literature. The word for "city" is feminine, corresponding to the characteristic gender of places in Hebrew. Hebrew grammarians typically list several classes of nouns that are feminine. The common reason given for the proper names of countries and towns being feminine is that they were thought of as the mothers and nurturers of their inhabitants. By extension, the common nouns for "land" and "city" are also feminine. Some scholars link Israelite notions of female cities to the fact that, in Mesopotamia, cities may have been considered female because their patron city deities were goddesses.

Suggesting the relationship between a city and its satellite villages, the expression "X and its daughters," meaning "the city X and its villages," occurs numerous times in the Hebrew Bible (for example, Num 21:25; Josh 15:45; Judg 1:27; 1 Chr 2:23; Neh 11:25; Jer 49:2–3). Most English translations obscure this expression by using villages rather than daughters. In Ezekiel (26:6, 8) there is the expression "her daughters which are in the fields," which the NRSV translates as "its daughter-towns in the country" (compare Ezek 30:18). In 2 Sam 20:19, the city of Abel is called a "mother in Israel"; and in Isa 14:2 the phrase "daughters of Moab" denotes Moabite settlements. Also Ps 48:11 anticipates the rejoicing of the "daughters of Judah," which the NRSV renders "towns of Judah."

In addition to the personification of a city and its villages as a mother and her daughters, there is the phrase "Metheg-ammah" in the account of David's conquest of the Philistines in 2 Sam 8:1: "David took Metheg-ammah out of the hand of the Philistines" (NRSV). Metheg-ammah is unknown as a place name anywhere else in the Bible. The Hebrew phrase it translates literally means "the bridle of a cubit." The ASV thus translates the phrase as "bridle of the mother city," and the NAS translation is "control of the chief city." The word meteg ("bridle"), however, is never used figuratively in all the Bible, nor is the word ʾammâ used for ʾēm ("mother") elsewhere in the Bible. The ASV and NAS translations of the phrase thus rest on a parallel text in 1 Chr 18:1: "David attacked the Philistines . . . ; he took Gath and its villages," wherein Gath is understood as one of the mother cities of the Philistines.

Female imagery is also employed in an extended metaphor illustrating the relationship between peoples and cities. In Ezek 16:44–63, Jerusalem is pictured as the "daughter" of two "peoples," the Amorites and the Hittites. Samaria and Sodom are called her "sisters." In the frequent references to Jerusalem as the "daughter of Zion," however, the intention is probably not that implied by the English translation. The phrase probably refers to Zion/

Jerusalem herself and should be understood as "daughter Zion." Jerusalem is once referred to as "daughter Jerusalem," (Lam 2:13, 15), where the translation "daughter of Jerusalem" would be nonsensical.

In speaking of cities and their villages as mothers and daughters, there are obvious analogies to the status and role of women in Israelite society. Both mother and daughter played socially critical roles in the Israelite family. Mothers had considerable authority over their daughters — hence the analogy of a walled mother-city exerting control over the unwalled, dependent daughter-villages. Just as a mother had major responsibilities in caring for her children, so the city provided protection for its people. Although the dominant image of protection in the Hebrew Bible may be that of military might, the fundamental awareness of maternal care permeates the concept of cities as female.

FRANK S. FRICK

SEE ALSO Part III: Daughter; Female Images for Nations in Ezekiel; Oholah, Woman Samaria; Oholibah, Woman/Whore Jerusalem; Women in Imagery for Jerusalem, Judah, and Israel in Jeremiah.

FOR FURTHER READING: Follis, Elaine R. "The Holy City as Daughter."

Frick, Frank S. *The City in Ancient Israel.*

Nanea

(2 Macc 1:13–17)

Nanea, originally a Sumerian goddess, who during the time of the Seleucids was the chief goddess of the Persian city of Susa, was identified with Artemis or Aphrodite in the Greek world, with Isis in Egypt, with Anahite in Iran, and with Venus in Rome. A female deity of love and war, Nanea was affiliated with the sun and moon. Reference to the temple of Nanea (likely located in Elymais, biblical Elam, the region between Babylonia and Persia of which Susa was the chief city) as the place where Antiochus IV (Epiphanes) dies during his eastern campaign (165–164 B.C.E.) appears in 2 Macc 1:13–17, in the second of two letters addressed to Alexandrian Jews.

The first part of the second letter (1:10–17) sends greetings from the Jews in Jerusalem-Judea and Judas (Maccabeus, the leader of the revolt against the Seleucids) to Aristobulus (a Jewish philosopher who dedicated a book on the Torah to Ptolemy VI Philometor) and the Jews in Egypt. The Jews in Jerusalem tell those in Egypt that their God has had a hand in the demise of Antiochus IV (Epiphanes). Ironically, and not likely accidental in a book dedicated to returning measure for measure, the powerful prime antagonist of the Jerusalem temple has been eliminated in the temple of Nanea by a mere handful of priests.

According to the story in 2 Macc 1:13–14, Antiochus had gone to contract a marriage with the goddess Nanea in Persia. Such a marriage is both a religious and an economic transaction, entitling Antiochus to claim the wealth of the temple. The sacred marriage of a reigning king to a goddess is a rite with a long history in Mesopotamia and the adjoining regions. Antiochus IV is also reported to have married the goddess Atargatis of Hierapolis-Bambyke in Syria and to have taken her temple treasures as dowry.

Other ancient sources (Polybius, Josephus, and Appian) confirm Antiochus's attack on a temple in Elymais, though they identify the goddess as either Artemis or Aphrodite. 1 Macc 6:1–4 describes Antiochus's unsuccessful attempt to take the rich treasure of a temple in Elymais, including golden shields, breastplates, and weapons left by Alexander, the great Macedonian king. The major difference in these accounts is that Nanea is not mentioned and Antiochus does not die.

The account of the death of Antiochus in the temple of Nanea differs from those found in all other sources. Only in 2 Macc 1:13–17 does Antiochus die before the purification of the temple. According to Polybius, the king makes an expedition against the temple of Artemis in Elymais, but is foiled by the local tribes, takes sick, and dies at Tabae (modern Isfahan). In 1 Macc 6:1–16, failure in Judea distresses the king to repentance of his misdeeds against the Jews (6:12–13) and causes him to die in the "strange land" of Persia, thus cutting him off from a proper burial place in his own homeland. In a second account of his death in 2 Macc 9:1–29, Antiochus, after unsuccessfully attempting to rob the temples in Persepolis (the old capital of the Persian Empire), receives news of Judas's victories against Nicanor and restoration of the Jerusalem temple (9:1–4) and decides to return to defeat the Jews, but God strikes him with illness and a mad rage (9:5–12). After repenting (9:13–27), Antiochus dies at Ecbatana in Media of an incurable disease (9:28–29).

2 Macc 1:15–16 offers a gruesome account of the death of Antiochus IV in the temple of Nanea. The priests of Nanea deceptively display the temple treasures and lure the king and a few of his men into the temple, which they then seal shut (1:15). From a concealed door in the ceiling, the priests stone Antiochus and his men, dismember and behead their bodies, and throw them to the people outside (1:16). Here, as in the Book of Judith, the powerful enemy is beheaded by the most unlikely of agents. Thinking to marry a goddess and plunder the riches of her treasuries, the great Antiochus IV meets his death at the hands of the servants of Nanea in her temple. In the end, the goddess of love and war proves stronger than the powerful Seleucid ruler, though the story in 2 Maccabees would not be told to make this point, but rather that the God of Israel "brought judgment on those who have behaved impiously" (1:17).

Toni Craven

See also Part III: Atargatis.

For further reading: Doran, Robert. "2 Maccabees."

Goldstein, Jonathan A. *II Maccabees: A New Translation with Introduction and Commentary.*

Pietersma, Albert. "Nanea."

No "Male and Female" in Christ Jesus

(Gal 3:28)

Paul's letter to the churches in Galatia (a region in ancient Asia Minor, now modern Turkey) contains a verse, Gal 3:28, that has become the focus of extensive contemporary feminist exegesis. "There is

no longer Jew or Greek, there is no longer slave or free, there is no longer male and female; for all of you are one in Christ Jesus."

Much of Galatians works out a complex argument which seeks to assure Paul's readers that gentile believers in Christ need not, in fact should not, be required to be circumcised or keep the Law (Torah) given by God to Moses. Much of this argument is based upon Genesis 15, when God promises Abram (as he is there called) that although he is presently childless, Abram will ultimately have descendants as numerous as the stars. According to Gen 15:6, Abram believes God, and his belief (or trust) is reckoned to him as righteousness. For Paul, because this belief (or faith, or trust: the Greek *pistis* can mean all of these) made Abram, who was still an uncircumcised Gentile, righteous before God, all those who now experience the same faith through Christ are reckoned as righteous, and as Abraham's heirs (3:29). Gal 3:26–28 adds to this argument an appeal to the readers' experience of baptism, reminding them that all those persons who have been baptized into Christ are now clothed with Christ (3:27) and arguing that their original status has been rendered irrelevant: "There is no longer Jew or Greek, there is no longer slave or free, there is no longer male and female; for all of you are one in Christ Jesus." Paul's only concern in Galatians appears to have been to show that gentile Christians were not disadvantaged and had no need of circumcision and the law. Thus the relevance of the phrase to the lives of ancient and contemporary women is primarily a matter of the way other Christian writers have used it.

In 1958, Stendahl made the verse a central issue in the argument for the ordination of women in the Lutheran church in Sweden. He argued that it was not original to Paul but rather an ancient formula that was recited over the newly baptized believer. Stendahl called attention not only to the baptismal context, but to a crucial distinction between the first two oppositional categories (Jew or Greek, slave or free) and the third, which uses two neuter adjectives, *male* and *female*, instead of the nouns *man* and *woman* (which would better parallel the earlier pairs), and which uses the conjunctive *and* rather than "[n]or." He concluded that the phrase "male and female" is a radical reinterpretation of the Greek version of Gen 1:27b, "male and female [God] created them." Together with Col 3:9–11, the formula testifies to a baptismal theology of the new creation. Stendahl thus argued that for early Christians (and consequently for later Christian churches), baptism abolished gender and social distinctions and restored the human being to the image of God.

In an influential article, Meeks argued that the utterance of the baptismal formula in Gal 3:28 both announced and actually brought about, through ritual speech, the restoration of the baptized person to the image of God in Gen 1:27a ("in the image of God he created him [NRSV, them])" an image they understood, based on Gen 1:27b to have been originally androgynous. MacDonald then suggested that Gal 3:28 was Paul's reworking of a saying attributed to Jesus that appears in somewhat different form in a number of second-century Christian sources, including the *Gospel of Thomas* 22, and that originally endorsed sexual abstinence.

Still more influential, particularly among feminists, has been Schüssler Fiorenza's interpretation of the passage, which gave Gal 3:26–28 a central place in her reconstruction of the early Christian movement before Paul, which she called the early Christian mission. She rejected the equating of "no male and female" with the idea of the androgyne, arguing that the verse enshrined the early Christian mission's abolition of patriarchal marriage, an abolition she also saw in a differing interpretation of Gen 1:27 in Mark 10:2–9, which she attributed to the Jesus movement. Other feminists have adopted the interpretation of the phrase as referring to androgyny. Fatum has argued that the verse, and all of Paul's views on women, spring from a conviction that the divine image, as androgynous, is an image of perfect maleness.

Like later interpreters, early Christians may not have agreed on the precise effect of uttering the baptismal formula at the time of baptism. The phrase "male and female" was used in a number of differing ways in ancient Judaism and Christianity. "Male and female" can be a merismus, a figure of speech that designates the whole by referring to its poles; then "no 'male and female'" could mean that all are included, as "Jew or Greek, slave or free" does in 1 Cor 12:12–13. This must be part of the meaning of the slogan in Gal 3:28, but doesn't explain why the text says "no 'male and female.'" "Male and female" also characterized a relationship of disadvantage. Thus "no 'male and female'" meant "no disadvantage." This meaning is clearly attested both by the other two dissolved pairs and by Paul's argument in Galatians. "Male and female" could also refer to sex and marriage; "no 'male and female'" could thus be a rejection of, or even a prohibition of, sex and marriage. This interpretation of the baptismal formula could have inspired both the Corinthians' conviction that "it is good for a man not to touch a woman" (1 Cor 7:1) and Paul's rejoinder that whether one is married or not makes no difference to salvation (1 Cor 7:7–24, 26–28). Thus it is possible that, as Schüssler Fiorenza has argued, some participants in the early Christian mission would indeed see the formula as abrogating "patriarchal marriage"; that is, as abolishing the social institution that regulates sexual roles and family structure. For instance, women like Junia or Prisca, who worked with male partners (Rom 16:3–5, 7) or Tryphaena, who worked with a woman (Rom 16:12) might have claimed this meaning. But it is also possible that such women invoked the baptismal formula primarily against gendered constrictions of their missionary labor, while other members of the community, for instance, male ascetics, saw it as repudiating sex, but insisted on the continuing validity of gender hierarchies. Thus, the formula may have been a source of the gender discord that surfaced in later first- and second-century Christianity rather than the product of early Christian sexual revolution.

Whether the formula referred to the androgyne is even more complex. "Androgyny" is a label that recent interpreters have applied to a wide variety of disparate ancient ideas about sexual dimorphism and sexual union. In antiquity, it was sometimes applied to hermaphrodites (that is, human beings born with both male and female sexual characteristics), to human beings who did not observe gender roles, or to divine or symbolic figures of this type; these were almost always viewed negatively. Plato's *Symposium* applies the term *androgyne* to a double-bodied, original human being, a complete male and a complete female joined together; this double-bodied being also appears in rabbinic Jewish traditions where it serves as a warrant for heterosexual union. Some interpreters see the divine male-and-female pairs called *syzygies* in Gnostic creation myths as androgynous. Others attribute androgyny to figures who are said to be neither male nor female, to transcend sexuality, like the divine *logos*, or word, described as the creator by Philo of Alexandria, the first-century C.E. Jewish philosopher. There thus was no coherent "image of the androgyne" that could provide a consistent meaning for "no . . . male and female."

The meaning of Gal 3:28 in its ancient context continues to be a matter of debate even as the text plays a role in contemporary struggles over Christian theology and communal organization. While the text still plays a role in feminist critique of gender-based restrictions, many feminists have become concerned that the erasure of difference is too often implemented as the erasure of the oppressed and the other.

MARY ROSE D'ANGELO

SEE ALSO Part I: Junia; Prisca/Priscilla; Tryphaena; Part II: Woman (and Man) in the First Creation Story (Gen 1:26–28, etc.); Divorced Wife (Mark 10: 2–12); Married Women (and Men), Unmarried Women (and Men), and Women (and Men) Married to Unbelievers (1 Corinthians 7).

FOR FURTHER READING: D'Angelo, Mary Rose. "Gender Refusers in the Early Christian Mission: Genesis 1:27 in Gal 3:28."

———. "Trans-scribing Sexual Politics: Images of the Androgyne in Discourses of Antique Religion."

Fatum, Lone. "Image of God and Glory of Man: Women in the Pauline Congregations."

MacDonald, Dennis Ronald. *There Is No Male and Female: The Fate of a Dominical Saying in Paul and Gnosticism.*

Meeks, Wayne A. "The Image of the Androgyne: Some Uses of a Symbol in Earliest Christianity."

Schüssler Fiorenza, Elisabeth. *In Memory of Her: A Feminist Theological Reconstruction of Christian Origins.*

Stendahl, Krister. *The Bible and the Role of Women.*

Oholah, Woman Samaria

meaning uncertain; perhaps "her tent," from Hebrew *'ōhel*, "tent"

(Ezekiel 23)

The name Oholah is derived from the Hebrew word meaning "tent." Although the exact meaning of the name is debated, it may be translated "her [own] tent." The tent is a traditional sign of God's presence among the people, specifically in the form of a sanctuary or place of worship (as in Ps 15:1). In this case, Oholah personifies the Northern Kingdom (Israel) — a nation that the author of Ezekiel 23 considers to be apostate. According to 1 Kgs 12:25–33, Jeroboam, the first ruler (reigned 928–907 B.C.E.) of the Northern Kingdom, discouraged his people from traveling to Jerusalem to worship by setting up two alternative sanctuaries. The name Oholah suggests that these religious centers do not have divine authorization, but rather emerge from the initiative of the people. This name contrasts with Oholibah ("my tent [is] in her"), woman Jerusalem and sister of Oholah.

The author of Ezekiel 23 uses the figures of these two sisters to tell the story of Israel and Judah, or the Northern and Southern Kingdoms. Specifically representing the cities of Samaria and Jerusalem, the capitals of the two kingdoms, these women are described as YHWH's lovers (vv. 4–5), the mothers of his children (vv. 4, 37), and, by implication only, his wives (vv. 37–39, 45). The story explicitly details the sexual conduct of both women (vv. 5–8, 11–21, 36–44), characterizing their behavior as "lewdness" and "whorings" (vv. 21, 29, 35, 48–49). A series of brutal punishments, at the behest of YHWH, results (vv. 9–10, 22–35, 45). The final section, vv. 46–49, restates the punishment as YHWH calls for a public execution — including stoning, mutilation, rape, the murder of the women's children, and the destruction of their homes — as punishment for adultery and so "that all women may take warning" (v. 48) not to act likewise.

Personification of the cities, and thus of the nations, as two women allows the author of Ezekiel 23 to draw on ancient Near Eastern traditions of referring to cities as women while also developing a marital metaphor to describe the history of covenant relationship between YHWH and YHWH's people. In the ancient Near East, it was common to refer to cities as women. Although the origins of this convention are not known, it most likely stems from identification of a city with a patron goddess. These goddesses were often consorts of male gods and associated with the temples built to those gods. The picture of YHWH as a male god "married" to female cities in Ezekiel 23 might thus be related to ancient Near Eastern traditions of a male god "married" to a goddess consort or to a city containing his temple. Further, describing the covenant between God and God's people as a marriage and, more frequently, the violations of this covenant as adultery is common both in the Pentateuch and the prophets. The author of Ezekiel 23, like the author of Ezekiel 16, merely develops this metaphor in unusual length and graphic detail. Cultural ideals about women's behavior and prescribed punishments for adulterous women provide a basis for these stories.

The metaphor in Ezekiel 23 is historical only in the broadest sense. It pictures the degeneracy of both Israel and Judah as beginning in Egypt, when covenants with YHWH were either new or still being established. For the Northern Kingdom, or Oholah, this conduct continued with the Assyrians until they destroyed her. The Southern Kingdom, or Oholibah, was unfaithful with the Assyrians, Chaldeans, Babylonians, and, for a second time, the Egyptians. In this text, the women's sexual infidelity represents two distinct types of behavior. First, these nations stand accused of worshipping other gods. Second, they are judged guilty of making political and military alliances with foreign nations. Both types of conduct violate the exclusivity of the covenant relationship with YHWH.

The punishment sequences in these texts are particularly problematic. They emerge, at least in part, from punishments such as stoning, stripping, and mutilation prescribed elsewhere in the Bible or in ancient Near Eastern law codes for persons caught in adultery. Adultery was a serious offense for both women and men in ancient Israel (dating before the kingdom split into Israel and Judah). A woman's sexuality was strictly controlled first by her father and then by her husband. Maintaining virginity prior to marriage and remaining faithful to a spouse following marriage served to ensure a child's paternity and thereby to guarantee proper lines of inheritance. Adultery had repercussions for the structure of the family and community, for it threatened the social and economic system. Execution was deemed an appropriate punishment for both female and male adulterers in ancient Israel.

The punishments described in Ezekiel 23, however, go beyond what the legal texts determined to be the consequences for adultery. For example, the woman's former lovers often serve as her executioners. No law code ever makes such a provision; indeed, according to biblical law, the man who commits adultery is also liable (Deut 22:22–27; Ezek 16:37, 39–41; 23:9–10, 22–26, 28–30). Furthermore, the texts describe actions such as the burning of homes, the capture or murder of children, the taking of booty, and rape. This extreme violence appears more in line with the destruction of a city by foreign invaders. Indeed, given that the metaphor uses women to represent cities and that both Samaria and Jerusalem were destroyed militarily, it makes sense to conclude that the metaphor slips between describing the punishment of an adulteress and the pillaging of a city. Nonetheless, the violence depicted against these figurative women cannot be easily dismissed as being merely a metaphor nor should it be explained away by saying that the metaphor slips. Without doubt, during wartime both women and men were subject to loss of property, loss of children, brutal execution, or capture and enslavement. However, women were often sought out as booty to serve as slaves or wives to the conquerors and were especially vulnerable to sexual violence. Women were also raped in war zones, as cities were captured. Therefore, although the punishment sequences may refer most directly to the destruction of cities at the hands of their enemies, the gang rape of these figurative women by their former lovers should also be read as expressing the sexually violent reality women faced in times of war.

Additionally, the violence in this text is set up to serve as a warning both to other cities and to women. Stories of the violent end of Oholah are said to circulate among other women (v. 10), and the violence done to both Oholah and Oholibah is said to function to prohibit similar conduct by other women (v. 48). Although most directly a warning to other cities and peoples who might choose to take on this God and to violate the standards of relationship as defined in covenants, the implications for women readers should not be overlooked. These presentations of sexual violence against women, seen as punishments for sexual conduct outside of societal norms, attempt to coerce women into idealized roles and particular behaviors and thus to maintain established social structures that subordinate women's sexuality to men.

SANDRA L. GRAVETT

SEE ALSO Part II: Adulteress (and Adulterer) (Lev 20:10, etc.); Part III: Mother/Daughter as Territory; Oholibah, Women/Whore Jerusalem.

FOR FURTHER READING: Darr, Katheryn Pfisterer. "Ezekiel."

Oholibah, Woman/Whore Jerusalem

> meaning uncertain; perhaps "my tent[is] in her," from Hebrew 'ōhel, "tent," and bâ, "in her"
> (Ezekiel 23)

Oholibah is derived from the Hebrew word for "tent," and although the exact meaning of the name is debated, it is most often translated "my tent is in her." The tent represents God's presence among the people, and since Oholibah represents Jerusalem,

this reference is probably to the temple. Oholibah is paired with Oholah. Together they symbolize the illegitimate (according to strict YHWH religion) northern sanctuary in Samaria and the apostate condition of the true YHWH temple in Jerusalem — and by extension the cities of Samaria and Jerusalem. They are discussed together in the entry on Oholah.

SANDRA L. GRAVETT

See also Part III: Oholah, Woman Samaria.

Princess Jerusalem

> (Lam 1:1)

The Book of Lamentations, which depicts the grief and suffering of Jerusalem (Zion) and Judah in the aftermath of the Babylonian conquest of 586 B.C.E., is full of female voices witnessing war's atrocities and the people's pain. In the opening verse, the radical reversal in Jerusalem's status, as capital of the nation, is indicated by the image of Jerusalem as a "princess among the provinces." In such a role, others were subject to her rule; but now she has taken on the role of "vassal" to others.

The word for princess, śārâ, usually denotes a woman who has royal status by virtue of her relationship to a man with political power (as Solomon's wives; 1 Kgs 11:3). In this case, however, as part of the personification of Jerusalem as a woman, a princess is a figure who would have exercised power in her own right. This political image differs from most other biblical personifications of Jerusalem as a woman, which portray the city using family images (daughter, bride, widow, wife, mother) or negatively depicted female figures (prostitute).

ANGELA BAUER

SEE ALSO Part III: Daughter; Woman Jerusalem/Zion in Isaiah.

Queen of Heaven

> (Jer 7:18; 44:17–19, 25)

According to the seventh- and sixth-century B.C.E. prophet Jeremiah, this goddess was worshipped first in Judah in the late seventh century B.C.E. and then by Judeans who fled to Egypt after the Babylonian destruction of Jerusalem in 586 B.C.E. Jeremiah's remarks associate the goddess especially with agricultural fertility: according to her devotees, when they worshipped the goddess, they had plenty of food, but when they abandoned the queen's cult, they suffered from famine (Jer 44:17–18). The goddess is also associated somewhat with war: again, the people claim that when the goddess was properly worshipped, they "saw no misfortune," but when her cult was abandoned, they "perished by the sword" (Jer 44:17–18). Moreover, as her title, queen of heaven, indicates, this deity has astral characteristics. Although Jer 44:17 identifies the kings and princes of Judah as among those who worshipped the queen, her cult seems primarily to be family centered; in it "the children gather wood, the fathers kindle fire, and the women knead dough, to make cakes for the queen of heaven" (Jer 7:18). Indeed, women seem particularly attracted to the cult of the queen, as they, in addition to baking offering cakes in the goddess's image (Jer 7:18; 44:19), are said to pour out libations and offer incense to her (Jer 44:15, 19). Perhaps the setting of her worship involved the leadership of women as household managers. In any case, Jeremiah's castigations of the cult single out women in his scorn of those who worship the queen of heaven (Jer 44:24–25).

The identity of the queen of heaven is a question that has long plagued biblical commentators. The most promising candidate from Israel's Canaanite heritage is Astarte. This goddess is called "lady of heaven" in several Egyptian texts and "queen" in multiple Phoenician sources. She plays the role of divine courtesan in mythological texts from the Late Bronze Age (c. 1550–1200 B.C.E.) city-state of Ugarit in western Syria, and the noun derived from her name in biblical Hebrew, 'aštārôt, means "increase, progeny." She can be depicted carrying weapons of war, and an inscription from Kition, Cyprus, identifies the baking of offering cakes as a crucial element of her cult.

Astarte's cult, however, is not known to be one in which women play a special role. Yet women do have a important place in the cult of Astarte's Mesopotamian counterpart, Ishtar, a young goddess of agricultural fertility whose consort, the god Tammuz, dies a premature and tragic death. As Ishtar, and also Tammuz's sister and mother, mourn the god in myth, so too do Ishtar's female devotees ritually weep in imitation (see Ezek 8:14). Ishtar's cult also involves the offering of cakes, which in Mesopotamian sources are called *kamānu*, a word cognate to the Hebrew term used for cakes in Jeremiah, *kawwānîm*. The queen of heaven is thus best identified as a syncretism of Canaanite-Phoenician Astarte and Mesopotamian Ishtar. The two cults probably began intermingling sometime during the last centuries of the second millennium B.C.E.; and this syncretism continued until Jeremiah's day.

SUSAN ACKERMAN

SEE ALSO Part II: Women Worshipping the Queen of Heaven (Jer 7:18, etc.); Women Weeping for Tammuz (Ezek 8:14); Book of Zephaniah (No Women Mentioned); Part III: Astarte.

FOR FURTHER READING: Ackerman, Susan. "'And the Women Knead Dough': The Worship of the Queen of Heaven in Sixth-Century Judah."

Olyan, Saul M. "Some Observations Concerning the Identity of the Queen of Heaven."

Rast, Walter E. "Cakes for the Queen of Heaven."

Righteousness and Iniquity as Females

(2 Esdr 16:49–52)

In 2 Esdr 16:49–52, the third-century Christian author presents two female figures: righteousness, who abhors iniquity, "as a respectable and virtuous woman abhors a prostitute" (16:49). There is no suggestion that iniquity is presented as female because Eve ate the forbidden fruit. In fact, in the main body of 2 Esdras, chaps. 3–14, the author traces human sin back to Adam, not Eve (see 3:21). The community is admonished not to be like her

— that is, iniquity. In a very short while, the author says, righteousness will reign and iniquity will be no more.

Iniquity, the one "who decks herself out" (16:50), is opposed by righteousness who "shall accuse her to her face when he comes who will defend the one who searches out every sin on earth" (16:50). Iniquity or human sinfulness will be overcome in the near future by God's saving action in righteousness. The Christian community would have understood the reference to the one who comes as Jesus. The poetic personifications of iniquity and righteousness are literary products of the wisdom tradition here employed to express apocalyptic expectations of impending disasters.

WALTER J. HARRELSON

SEE ALSO Part II: Virtuous Woman (2 Esdr 16:49); Part III: Asia as a Prostitute; Woman Wisdom.

this motif in Isa 54:1–10 and 62:4 is remarkable. Yet it is consistent with the generally positive use of gynomorphic imagery in the second half of the Book of Isaiah (chaps. 40–66). Indeed, in Isaiah 40–66, not only is Jerusalem portrayed as a beloved bride and a loving mother, but also God too can be imagined as female, especially as a mother, midwife, and nurse (Isa 42:14; 45:9–10; 45:15; 46:3–4; 66:12–13).

SUSAN ACKERMAN

SEE ALSO Part I: Gomer; Part III: Azubah/Forsaken, Jerusalem; Beulah/Married, Jerusalem; Female Images of God in the Hebrew Bible; Hephzibah/My Delight Is in Her, Jerusalem; Woman Jerusalem/Zion in Isaiah.

FOR FURTHER READING: Ackerman, Susan. "Isaiah." Gruber, Mayer. "The Motherhood of God in Second Isaiah."

Shemamah/Desolate, Jerusalem

from Hebrew *šāmēm*, "to be desolate"
(Isa 62:4)

In a text describing how Jerusalem will be restored after suffering destruction at the hands of the Babylonians in 586 B.C.E., the city is told that her land, although now called Azubah, "Forsaken," and Shemamah, "Desolate," will soon be called Hephzibah, "My Delight Is in Her," and Beulah, "Married" (Isa 62:4). In all these images, YHWH is the bridegroom of the restored Jerusalem; similar imagery is found elsewhere in Isaiah (Isa 49:7–26; 54:1–10; possibly, 52:1). Isa 54:1–10, which shares with Isa 62:4 the notion that Jerusalem before her restoration was desolate (54:1, 3) and forsaken (54:6), further describes Jerusalem as a wife "grieved in spirit," "cast off," and "abandoned" (54:6–7). Elsewhere in the Hebrew Bible, when God and Jerusalem are described using marital imagery (for example, Ezekiel 16; Hosea 1–3), it is typically YHWH who is described as the aggrieved marriage partner and Jerusalem who has cast off or abandoned her God in order to devote herself to some other deity. The reversal of

Sister Church

(1 Pet 5:13)

In the NRSV, the letter known as 1 Peter closes with greetings from "your sister church in Babylon, chosen together with you" (5:13). A small note indicates that the phrase "sister church" does not actually occur in Greek. Rendered more literally, 5:13 reads, "She in Babylon, also chosen [*syneklektē*], greets you."

The NRSV translators understand *syneklektē* as a reference to a church rather than to an individual woman, based particularly on the mention of Babylon (which is assumed to be a cryptic reference to Rome — a few late manuscripts actually even have Rome instead of Babylon). 1 Pet 5:13 appears to be the only known ancient usage of *syneklektē*, so if it does here refer to a particular church, such terminology was clearly not widespread. It is not impossible that *syneklektē* could designate a person, as *eklektē* may in 2 John 1:1 and 1:5, although the argument for 2 John is somewhat stronger.

Feminine imagery for the Christian church as a whole appears relatively early. Paul images the church at Corinth as a virgin bride of Christ (2 Cor

11:2). Revelation (which was probably composed in the first century C.E.) also represents "the saints" as the bride of the Lamb, while in the noncanonical *Shepherd of Hermas* (second-century C.E.), a man called Hermas has repeated visionary encounters with a woman who ultimately reveals herself to be the church itself.

ROSS S. KRAEMER

SEE ALSO Part II: Elect Lady (2 John vv. 1, 5); Part III: Bride of the Lamb; Chaste Bride (of Christ).

Sister Judah

(Jer 3:7–10)

The prophet Jeremiah condemns the faithlessness and subsequent destruction of the northern kingdom of Israel. He hopes that the southern kingdom of Judah will take the example of Israel's demise to heart; and he hopes that Judah will repent of her sins, which are expressed as whoredom and adultery in following other gods. The female imagery for transgressions is maintained in the prophet's depiction of the two kingdoms as sisters. The "false sister Judah" (7:7–8, 10) does not return to YHWH but proves herself to be even more faithless than Israel. Like the image of Samaria (Oholah) and Jerusalem (Oholibah) as sinful sisters in Ezekiel (see Ezek 16:46), the personification of political units as women is rooted in ancient conceptions of territory as female.

CAROL MEYERS

SEE ALSO Part III: Mother/Daughter as Territory; Oholah, Woman Samaria; Oholibah, Woman/Whore Jerusalem; Sister Sodom and Her Daughters.

Sister Sodom and Her Daughters

(Ezek 16:46–61)

The sixth-century B.C.E. prophet Ezekiel compares and contrasts the wantonness of Jerusalem, capital of the southern kingdom of Judah, with that of Samaria, capital of the northern kingdom of Israel.

In doing so, he uses female imagery: those two wicked cities are called sisters. In addition, he mentions a third city, Sodom, as a sister.

Sodom is an unusual addition to this kinship imagery. For one thing, that city was destroyed long before the kingdoms of Israel and Judah existed. Also, Samaria and Sodom are not equivalent political units. Although the NRSV calls Sodom the "younger sister" of Jerusalem, in contrast to Samaria as "elder sister" (16:46, 61), those antithetical descriptions are better translated as size rather than age designations. Samaria, as head of a sizable kingdom, is the "larger sister"; Sodom, a city with a few territorial dependencies or "daughters" (16:46, 49), is the "smaller sister." Finally, the sins of Sodom are those associated with prosperity (16:49) rather than the adultery and idolatry that are Samaria's transgressions.

Despite their differences, Ezekiel perhaps links Samaria with Sodom, presenting both as wicked sisters of Jerusalem, to represent the ways in which God can punish. Samaria's demise comes from human instrumentality, that is, the Assyrian army; natural disaster ("sulfur and fire from . . . heaven," Gen 19:24) brings an end to Sodom. The contrasting modes of destruction fit the way the prophet uses contrast and antithesis in this extended chapter on Jerusalem's wantonness. The ultimate contrast, however, is that Jerusalem is far more culpable than either of her sisters.

That ultimate contrast leads to a strange metamorphosis. Because YHWH cares for all three sisters, all three will be restored (46:53–54). The relationship of Jerusalem with Sodom and Samaria, however, will cease to be one of sisterhood; it will become one of parenthood. Sodom and Samaria will become Jerusalem's daughters, that is, her dependents. In giving eschatological supremacy to Jerusalem, the powerful family metaphors of Ezekiel 16 transform the roughly egalitarian sister relationship to the hierarchical one of mother-daughter.

CAROL MEYERS

SEE ALSO Part III: Daughter; Mother/Daughter as Territory; Oholah, Woman Samaria; Oholibah, Woman/Whore Jerusalem; Sister Judah.

Two Winged Women Carrying a Basket

(Zech 5:9)

In this "basket" or "ephah" vision (Zech 5:5–11) of the prophet Zechariah, whose series of visions has been dated to 519 B.C.E. during the reign of Darius I of Persia, two women with wings like those of the high-flying stork are detailed to remove a basket containing "Wickedness" (meaning idolatry) from Judah. Such composite creatures, like the biblical cherubim, were well known in the ancient Near East, often flanking a deity's shrine or providing transportation for divine beings.

The Hebrew word for stork (*ḥăsîdâ*) is closely related to the word *ḥesed,* meaning "goodness, kindness." Thus, the two storklike women, whose work at YHWH's behest has a cleansing effect on the postexilic Judahite community, serve as a vivid and positive counterbalance to the one woman "Wickedness" (idolatry), who represents a threat to or the destruction of God's sovereignty.

BETH GLAZIER-MCDONALD

SEE ALSO Part III: Woman Wickedness.

Weeping Woman — Jerusalem/Zion as a City Being Built

(2 Esdr 9:38–10:59)

The longest and most striking female representation in 2 Esdras is found in chaps. 9–10, the work of the first-century C.E. Jewish author responsible for the Ezra Apocalypse (chaps. 3–14), a special kind of revelatory literature in which Ezra seeks answers from the angel Uriel concerning the meaning of God's dealing with Israel and with the world. The personification of Jerusalem/Zion as a mother mourning the loss of her only son suddenly transformed into a glorious city is unparalleled in apocalyptic literature.

Preparation for Ezra's fourth of his seven visions begins in 2 Esdr 9:23, with instructions from the interpreting angel to Ezra to go to a field of flowers, which is entirely uninhabited. There he is to pray and to sustain himself by eating only the flowers that surround him. The prophet's prayer (9:29–37) is about the dreadful fate that awaits the wicked — the theme that has occupied him continuously since chap. 3. Ezra once more places himself among the wicked who are doomed to destruction, even though the angel had insisted earlier that Ezra should recognize that no such fate awaits him; Ezra belongs among the righteous (7:76–77).

While he is praying, Ezra suddenly sees a woman in deepest grief, crying aloud, her clothes in tatters and ashes on her head (traditional acts for mourning women; see Jer 9:17–22; Ezek 32:16). Ezra lays aside his own inquiry about the fate of the wicked and asks the woman why she weeps so bitterly. She tells him her story (2 Esdr 9:43–10:4). She and her husband waited for long years to have their first child, a son. When the child grew up, she found a wife for him (as did Hagar in Gen 21:21), they were married, and on their wedding night her son fell down dead (compare Tobit 7–8). She considers this calamity the very end of her life. She has come out into the field to mourn and fast until she dies.

Ezra rebukes the grieving woman (2 Esdr 10:5–17), reminding her that she weeps for the loss of only one son, while Zion, the mother of us all, is in deep mourning over the loss of her children. Indeed, Mother Earth herself rightly grieves, for her children, almost all of them, are marked for destruction because of their iniquity. The woman should keep her sorrow to herself, bear her troubles bravely, and await the day when she will receive her son back; that day will come in due time, Ezra assures her.

The woman will not be consoled (10:18), and Ezra then describes in fuller detail the calamities that have befallen Mother Zion (10:19–24). The catalogue includes the loss of temple, priesthood, Levites, altar, all that makes Jerusalem the glorious treasure that she is. Let Zion's grief assuage your grief, Ezra tells the woman. Lay aside your grief, he urges, and the Most High may give you rest and an easing of your burden.

In that very moment, the woman is transformed into a city being built (10:25–27, reading with the Latin text; other readings have "an established city";

also 10:42, 44), with massive foundations. The weeping woman with whom Ezra has been speaking is in fact Mother Jerusalem/Zion. Zion is soon to be restored as a city massive enough to provide for all those whom God has in mind to forgive and save. Is the prophet suggesting that only God knows the extent of the divine mercy for sinners?

Ezra is overwhelmed (10:28). The angel comes to his assistance and gives him a long allegorical interpretation of the vision of the grieving woman (10:29–59). But the author probably intends for readers to see in the vision something of an answer to Ezra's urgent concern about the fate of those who fail to do the will of God. Their fate rests with a Zion that God will restore, a city so vast that none can know who or how many will have a place in it. Ezra can be assured, in any event, that the number of those who will find mercy from God is by no means few; it is enormous.

The author draws here on those texts of the Hebrew Bible that also speak of the wideness of God's mercy — texts such as Exod 34:6–7, Isa 19:23–25, and especially Zech 2:5–12 (Hebrew Zech 2:9–16). Zechariah 2 is particularly important, for it gives a vision of a man sent to measure the length and breadth of the city of Zion. The man, however, is called back before he can do the measuring. Only God can know the extent of the Zion that is to come.

2 Esdras 3–10, accordingly, may be intended to offer a message of consolation to the Jewish community following the destruction of Jerusalem by the Romans in 66–70 C.E. The future of the people of Israel and of Mother Zion is by no means in jeopardy. That a grieving mother is transformed into a glorious city contrasts what is seen with what is actually taking place. The extent, the bounds of God's mercy, are known only to God.

WALTER J. HARRELSON

SEE ALSO Part II: Mourning Women (Jer 9:17–20, etc.); Part III: Earth as Mother; Jerusalem/Zion as Widow and Mother; Woman Jerusalem/Zion in Isaiah.

FOR FURTHER READING: Johnson, Elizabeth E. "2 Esdras."

Metzger, Bruce M. "The Fourth Book of Ezra."

Stone, Michael. "Esdras, Second Book of."

Woman Folly (Foolish Woman)

(Prov 9:13–18; 14:1)

This stock wisdom character is clearly contrasted with positive female figures in Proverbs, such as Woman Wisdom, and belongs to the complex of images designating the sage's view of women, who can bring chaos and death as well as life and order. Such themes are also common in the wisdom traditions of Israel's neighbors, since they aim to guide young men in proper conduct in their royal bureaucratic careers. The foolish woman, or Folly, presents another face of Woman Wisdom's "evil twin." An "evil twin" is the inversion of a character archetype, a reservoir of negative characteristics associated with the good character's opposite. The evil twin of Woman Wisdom is represented by Woman Stranger ("strange" [foreign] or loose woman), the prostitute, and the adulteress of the sages' warnings to young men in Proverbs 1–9.

Like her counterparts, she is known by her speech and behavior. She calls aggressively from the public areas of the town, defying the virtues of female docility and modesty. In a direct caricature of Wisdom's speech (9:4–6) and earlier warnings by the sages (compare 2:10; 5:15; 6:30 for specific wordplays), she suggests that adultery ("stolen water," "bread eaten in secret") holds much pleasure. She relates her longings in metaphors of appetite, terms that the sages use elsewhere to refer to the unseemly desires of women (5:3; 30:20).

Overtones of destruction resonate in these passages: though young men may think they are simply indulging in enjoyable acts, in fact, heeding her invitation brings ruin (2:18–19; 7:21–27). Like the strikingly "military" love goddesses of the ancient Near East (such as Inanna-Ishtar and Anath), she leads her human lovers to their deaths as the sages' punctuate their warnings with mythic allusions. Thus, Folly in female form tears down the family household, contrary to the wise, good wives of Proverbs who build up their families.

CAROLE R. FONTAINE

SEE ALSO Part II: Prostitute (Prov 6:26, etc.); Part III:

Woman Stranger (Loose Woman/Adulteress); Woman Wisdom.

FOR FURTHER READING: Fontaine, Carol R. "The Social Roles of Women in the World of Wisdom."

Yee, Gale A. "'I Have Perfumed My Bed with Myrrh': The Foreign Woman (*'iššâ zārâ*) in Proverbs 1–9."

Woman in Labor, Clothed with the Sun

(Rev 12:1–6, 14–17)

The woman in labor, clothed with the sun constitutes a central female presence in Revelation, though mention of her is brief. She appears in the heavens as an astrological figure, with a crown of twelve stars and the sun and moon under her feet (Rev 12:1). This woman is pregnant and experiences a painful birth. She appears miraculously, accompanied by the great red dragon (the devil) with seven heads, ten horns, and seven crowns. This dragon threatens to take her child, but as soon as she gives birth, God arranges for the child to be taken to the heavenly throne (12:5). The woman then flees to the wilderness (for 1,260 days) to a place that God has set up for her (12:6). The dragon wages war with the warrior angel Michael and his angel army; they throw the dragon and his angels out of heaven to earth. On earth the dragon pursues the woman. His attempts at capturing her are thwarted when she gains eagle wings that allow her to fly farther into the wilderness (12:14). When the dragon tries to drown her by vomiting water, the earth (Greek *Gē*) helps the woman by swallowing the flood (12:16). Angry at this outcome, the dragon leaves to wage war with "her children," all the believers (12:17). This woman does not appear again in Revelation.

Much speculation has been focused on the identity of the woman in labor, clothed with the sun. The most frequent reference is to Mary the mother of Jesus, and many works of art portray this woman as the Madonna with child. This image also brings to mind the Egyptian goddess Isis with her son, Horus. The astrological features of Revelation 12

also correspond to ancient Babylonian goddess symbolism — in particular, that of the goddess Inanna with the moon at her feet. The earth (perhaps to be understood as the goddess Gaia) is present, aiding the woman against the dragon. This text borrows much from ancient goddess traditions.

Other scholars find a broader symbolism in the woman clothed with the Sun. She represents Israel, the Christian church, or both. The messiah comes out of the woman, who is a symbol of Israel; the dragon persecutes the woman, who is a symbol of the church. Some interpreters link this woman to the bride of Christ, but this interpretation can be confusing, since the woman clothed with the sun gives birth to the messiah, and the bride marries him. Probably the bride and the woman in Revelation 12 represent two separate women.

The woman in labor, clothed with the sun forms a positive and powerful female image. She cries out when giving birth (12:2) — one of the few times women have voice in Revelation. Some works of art show the woman with two powerful wings, fighting off the dragon. Some medieval manuscripts depict her flying off into the wilderness while reading a book. These scenes show an independent, strong woman. Revelation does not tell the end of her story; she is left in the wilderness and is not explicitly named in the description of the new Jerusalem.

TINA PIPPIN

SEE ALSO Part III: Bride of the Lamb.

FOR FURTHER READING: Collins, Adela Yarbro. *The Combat Myth in the Book of Revelation.*

Pippin, Tina. *Death and Desire: The Rhetoric of Gender in the Apocalypse of John.*

Woman Jerusalem/Zion in Isaiah

(Isa 1:21–23; 3:25–26; 49:18; 51:17–52:2; 54:1–10; 57:3–13; 62:4–5; 66:7–13)

At multiple points in the Book of Isaiah, the city Jerusalem, also called Zion, is personified as a woman. Sometimes this identification castigates Jerusalem/Zion as a female apostate or harlot (Isa 1:21–23; 3:25–26; 57:3–13). More generally, though, the imagery, especially in the second half of the book (Isaiah 40–66), celebrates Jerusalem/Zion as a loving mother or as God's beloved bride.

As elsewhere in prophetic literature, the language of prostitution or whoredom can be used in Isaiah to describe those deemed particularly responsible for behaviors that are unacceptable in the prophet's eyes. Thus, in Isa 1:21, Isaiah labels Jerusalem a "whore" because he believes her citizens have so perverted righteousness within her walls that murder, rebellion, thieving, and bribery reign supreme. In 3:25–26, Isaiah further describes how the city will be left ravaged because of these offenses. Isa 57:3 has in mind these same images of Jerusalem's citizens as reprobates who must be punished, describing them as the whoring city's "offspring" and accusing them of transgression and deceit. The city herself, later in the same passage (57:7–8), is said to have set up a "bed" on which she, harlot-like, has offered herself to other gods.

With the exception of Isa 57:3–13, however, this negative image of Jerusalem as a prostitute is limited to the first half of Isaiah (Isaiah 1–39), most of which dates to the eighth century B.C.E. In the second half of the book (Isaiah 40–66), which dates to the time of the Babylonian exile in the sixth century B.C.E., more positive imagery is found. In Isa 66:7–13, for example, a poem that looks forward to the future restoration of the people of Israel after the end of the Babylonian exile, Jerusalem is described as the mother who will bring forth the renewed nation and, with her "consoling" and full-laden breast, will bring the Israelites satiation and "delight" (66:11). Maternal imagery for Jerusalem/Zion is further evoked in 51:17–52:2 and 54:1–10, especially in 51:18 and 20 and 54:1. In 54:1, for example, the prophet promises that the once-suffering city will be restored, proclaiming that Jerusalem, although she has been desolate and barren, shall now bear children, even more children than a woman who is married.

Elsewhere in these same poems, Jerusalem/Zion is depicted as a bride and wife. As a bride, she is to put on beautiful garments appropriate to a wedding day (52:1; see also 49:18). As a wife, she is told that, although she was previously abandoned by her husband, YHWH, she now will be reclaimed in a restored marriage in which the deity promises everlasting love (54:4–8). Isa 62:4 is also replete with marital imagery, as the city is promised that on the day of her redemption, she will no more be called "Forsaken" nor will her land be known as "Desolate," but instead God will call her "My Delight Is in Her" and the land will be known as "Married." The next verse expands the image by promising the city that, "as the bridegroom rejoices over the bride, / so shall your God rejoice over you." Such an exalted notion of the city Jerusalem as the beloved wife of YHWH is virtually unparalleled in the Hebrew Bible and shows how the originally negative imagery in Isaiah of Jerusalem/Zion as harlot has given way to an overwhelmingly positive portrayal.

SUSAN ACKERMAN

SEE ALSO Part II: Mother of the Servant (Isa 49:15, etc.); Part III: Azubah/Forsaken, Jerusalem; Beulah/Married, Jerusalem; Daughter; Hephzibah/My Delight Is in Her, Jerusalem; Oholibah, Woman/Whore Jerusalem; Shemamah/Desolate, Jerusalem.

Woman Nineveh
(Nah 3:4–7)

In this depiction of the destruction of Nineveh, the capital of Assyria, the city is likened to a prostitute who will be publicly humiliated by YHWH. Since cities and lands are grammatically feminine in Hebrew, they are metaphorically female throughout the Bible. Since YHWH was imaged almost exclusively as male, and since women's sexuality was considered dangerous, cities and lands were easily pictured as unfaithful wives or prostitutes (see, for example, Hosea 2 on Israel; Jeremiah 13 and Ezekiel 16 and 23 on Judah/Jerusalem; Isa 23:15–18 on Tyre). The seventh-century B.C.E. prophet Nahum depicts Nineveh as a prostitute with many lovers (political and military allies) whom "she" has seduced (see 2

Kgs 18:31–32) and then deceived (presumably by failing to deliver the aid promised or even betraying them; see 2 Chr 28:16–21). Part of her success, Nahum claims, is due to her witchcraft and magical powers ("mistress of sorcery," v. 4; compare Isa 47:9–15 against Babylon and 2 Kgs 9:22 against Jezebel), again revealing how dangerous female sexuality was considered to be.

YHWH is pictured as determined to punish this prostitute-sorcerer by publicly exposing her genitals and pelting her with filth. Thus the punishment will fit the crime: as she flaunted her sexuality, she will be humiliated sexually before the nations. None of her former lovers will come to her defense. The destructiveness of this imagery lies in two areas: YHWH is consistently depicted as both male and righteous while human communities are consistently both female and wicked; and YHWH (and therefore by extension, human males?) is perceived as justified in violating the sexuality of a woman as a form of richly deserved punishment.

JUDITH E. SANDERSON

SEE ALSO Part I: Gomer; Jezebel 1; Part III: Oholah, Woman Samaria; Oholibah, Woman/Whore Jerusalem; Sister Sodom and Her Daughters; Woman Thebes.

FOR FURTHER READING: Sanderson, Judith E. "Nahum."

Woman Stranger (Loose Woman/Adulteress)

(Prov 2:16–19; 5:3–8, 20; 6:24–26, 29, 32; 7:5–27; 22:14; 23:27–28; 30:20; 31:3)

Like the prostitute and the foolish woman found in Proverbs, the "loose woman" and the "adulteress" are major preoccupations of the sages. The symbolic and functional inversion of the good wife and nurturing mother, the loose woman embodies all that male culture finds objectionable in women. The terms referring to her, 'iššā zārâ, "foreign, strange woman" or "woman stranger," and nokriyyâ, "foreigner," betray a xenophobic fear. Such women are thought to be ripe for sexual misconduct, and their behavior threatens group norms concerning ethnicity, inheritance practices, and sexual standards.

The Hebrew Bible, which urges people not to let their own daughters be prostitutes (Lev 19:29), provides another association for the behavior of the "woman stranger." Sexual activity outside of marriage was seen as being provided primarily by encounters with out-group, foreign women whose lost "honor" presented no particular problem ("shame") for the in-group men who visited them. Because biblical texts often view foreigners as participants in loose sexual practices, perhaps cultic in nature, the foreign Woman Stranger becomes an apt image for illicit or adulterous activity.

The almost mythic description of the adulteress (měnā'āpet) highlights her relationship to Woman Wisdom, the paragon who is the "patron" of the sages and the true, divinely sanctioned female ideal for the wise. Like Wisdom, the adulteress's language skills are paramount: her words are sweet, but they bring death rather than life (5:3–6; 7:5, 21; 22:14). A man who falls into her trap harms himself and runs afoul of the laws of the covenant (6:24–35), whereas the one who turns to Wisdom receives wealth and long life. What may be seen here is both a transfer of motifs from goddess mythology of surrounding cultures and a subsequent bifurcation of those elements into "good" and "evil" categories. Although Sumerian, Egyptian, and Canaanite goddesses certainly have major contact with death and the underworld, their activities on behalf of their fertility partners turn out to be life-giving for the communities who worship them. The sages have taken these connections and split them in two: Woman Wisdom now embodies all the positive qualities of scribal and life-giving fertility goddesses, whereas Woman Stranger (loose woman/adulteress) has absorbed all of the negative aspects of that mythology. These include disloyalty to one's mate, death-dealing language and behavior, sexual promiscuity (especially when allied to insincere cultic practice; compare 7:14), ventures into the male-dominated public domain, failure to nurture, and excessive carnal appetites.

The sages' portrait contains not only allusions

to goddess mythology, but also a window into the condition of women — at least those in upper-class urban settings like those reflected in Proverbs — in societies where arranged marriages and male dominance are the rule. The adulteress speaks to the truth of her own situation when she says "I have done no wrong" (30:20) or "Stolen water is sweet, and bread eaten in secret is pleasant" (9:17). Given little choice in her selection of a mate, and perhaps even less attention to her own fulfillment in performance of "conjugal duties," she aggressively seeks her own pleasure as a desiring subject. If barren within her own marriage, she may even be seeking a remedy to her infertility by obtaining a different partner. Further, she even finds that the danger of her illicit behavior adds "spice" to appetites previously denied gratification. In her boldness, she invalidates the sages' worldview and serves as a temptation to women who might emulate her, as well as to the men who provide her pleasures.

CAROLE R. FONTAINE

SEE ALSO Part II: Prostitute (Lev 19:29, etc.); Adulteress (and Adulterer) (Lev 20:10, etc.); Prostitute (Prov 6:26, etc.); Part III: Woman Folly (Foolish Woman); Woman Wisdom.

FOR FURTHER READING: Bird, Phyllis A. "To Play the Harlot."

Camp, Claudia V. "What's So Strange about the Strange Woman?"

Fontaine, Carole R. "The Social Roles of Women in the World of Wisdom."

Washington, Harold C. "The Strange Woman (*'šh zrh/nkryh*) of Proverbs 1–9 and Post-Exilic Judean Society."

Yee, Gale A. "'I Have Perfumed My Bed with Myrrh': The Foreign Woman (*'iššâ zārâ*) in Proverbs 1–9."

Woman Thebes
(Nah 3:8–10)

In his vision of the destruction of Nineveh, the capital of the Assyrian Empire, the seventh-century B.C.E. prophet Nahum asks rhetorically if Nineveh is better than Thebes (*nō' 'āmôn*, or "the city of the god Amon," in Hebrew). Though it was one of Egypt's greatest and most ancient cities, protected by its position on the Nile River and its reliance on the might of four allied peoples (Ethiopia, Egypt, Put, and Libya), the city had been sacked and some of its inhabitants killed or taken into exile by Assyria in 663 B.C.E. Since cities are grammatically feminine in Hebrew and Greek, they are consistently personified as women throughout the Bible, as is Nineveh itself by this same prophet (see, for example, Nah 3:4–7). But whereas Nineveh has just been personified as a prostitute and sorcerer, Thebes is depicted as a queen sitting enthroned by the Nile, surrounded by her strong army and warriors, by her nobles and dignitaries, and by her children. Yet none of that availed her, Nahum states: she went from her throne into exile; her nobles and dignitaries were killed or captured, their various fates being determined by casting lots (compare Joel 3:3); and her infants were killed because they could not have withstood the long trip into exile in Assyria (compare, for example, 2 Kgs 8:12; Isa 13:16; Ps 137:8–9).

JUDITH E. SANDERSON

SEE ALSO Part III: Woman Nineveh.

Woman Wickedness
(Zech 5:6–11)

In one of the visions (dated to 519 B.C.E.) of the prophet Zechariah, a woman is seen trapped inside an ephah, or basket, by a heavy lid. Carried off to Babylon, her departure signals the removal of idolatrous worship from the postexilic province of Yehud, where it does not belong, to its rightful place in a foreign land.

The choice of the terms *ephah* and *wickedness* provide one key to understanding this vision. Not only is an ephah a barrel-shaped grain container, but it also designates a Mesopotamian cult room. Thus, the woman called "Wickedness" (*hāriš'â*, a technical term for idolatry) may represent a goddess in her shrine and so symbolize worship of other gods. It is interesting to note that Ishtar and Asherah, two prominent Semitic goddesses, are anagrams of *hāriš'â*. This suggests a wordplay on the real name of the deported goddess.

It is also possible to view the woman in the basket as a human figure. As such she would represent the foreign wives brought back from exile by returning Judahites. Indeed, a feature of postexilic literature is the depiction of foreign women as purveyors of alien culture, threatening the integrity of the restored community (Ezra 10; Mal 2:10–16). Thus, it is unnecessary to conclude that the identification of "Wickedness" as female is an example of an antifeminine bias on Zechariah's part. The woman "Wickedness" represents idolatry not because of any inherent female uncleanness, but rather because of the historical connection between intermarriage with foreign women and the contamination or weakening of the indigenous community.

Synthetically, the woman "Wickedness" may represent both foreign woman and goddess. As such, she denotes the explicit danger of foreign cultural integration and the result of that integration — idolatry.

As Zechariah's vision unfolds, two women with storklike wings advance toward the ephah, seize it, and carry it away to Shinar, an archaic reference to Babylon (Gen 11:2). There they will build a house (meaning temple) for it, setting the ephah (meaning cult room) in its proper place. There is irony in the suggestion that "Wickedness" (idolatry) is relegated to Babylon, the place from which it originated and the only place fit for it. The close relation of the Hebrew word for "stork" to the word meaning "devoted, faithful" suggests that the female winged creatures are "faithful" attendants of YHWH whose work has a cleansing effect on the postexilic community. Indeed, the removal of "Wickedness" to Babylon serves as the necessary counterpart to YHWH's return to the land and to the temple in Jerusalem.

BETH GLAZIER-MCDONALD

SEE ALSO Part II: Daughters of Judah and Foreign Daughters/Wives (Ezra 9:2, etc.); Part III: Asherah/ Asherim; Two Winged Women Carrying a Basket.

FOR FURTHER READING: Barker, Margaret. "The Evil in Zechariah."

Meyers, Carol L., and Eric M. Meyers. *Haggai, Zechariah 1–8*.

Woman Wisdom

Hebrew *hokmâ/hokmôt*, "wisdom"

WOMAN WISDOM IN THE HEBREW BIBLE

(Job 28:1–28; Prov 1:20–33; 3:13–18; 4:1–9; 7:1–5; 8:1–36; 9:1–6; 14:1)

The books of Proverbs and Job, along with Ecclesiastes and the Apocryphal/Deuterocanonical Books of Sirach and the Wisdom of Solomon, are classified by scholars as "wisdom literature" because of their interest in this fundamental human attribute and its relationship to the divine, and because of their similarities to other ancient Near Eastern literature with similar forms and concerns. Notable in Proverbs and the Wisdom of Solomon (and to a lesser degree in Job and Sirach) is the personification of the concept of wisdom as a woman (here referred to as Woman Wisdom to distinguish the personified figure from the more general use of the term). Why the *female* personification? Perhaps in part because, in Hebrew, *wisdom* is a grammatically feminine noun. Grammar does not fully explain, however, Proverbs' interest in repeated and varied development of the female persona, which contrasts with the only incipient personification in Job. The female imagery for Woman Wisdom is also closely connected to her negative counterpart in Proverbs, that embodiment of evil referred to as the "loose woman" ("strange woman," or "Woman Stranger").

Job 28, perhaps originally an independent poem, now serves as an interlude within Job's final discourse of self-defense. The poem begins with the image of mining — humans' difficult but successful search for precious things in earth's depths — to highlight by contrast the negative answer to its central question: "But where shall wisdom be found? / And where is the place of understanding?" (28:12; compare v. 20). Although the mythological entities Abaddon and Death have "heard a rumor of it," only God "understands the way to it" (vv. 22–23). Here, the NRSV appropriately translates the pronoun referring to wisdom as a neuter, because, although the concept is accorded a high degree of independent existence, it has yet to be personified. As in Proverbs, wisdom is associated with God's creative and ordering activities. Surprisingly, wisdom seems to be something even God has to "search out" (28:27; is there a hint of personification here?), though God's successful search concludes with a conventional instruction: "Truly, the fear of the Lord, that is wisdom" (28:28).

The female personification of wisdom in Proverbs is dramatic, exalted, and varied, leading scholars to draw correlations both to ancient Near Eastern goddesses and to the roles and literary portrayals of women of the time. It is particularly notable in a book that feminist scholars generally acknowledge as perhaps the most androcentric in the Bible, its instructions addressed clearly to a "son" or "sons" (the NRSV's efforts at the inclusive "child/ren" notwithstanding) from, presumably, a father-teacher (4:1–4). Brenner, however, argues for the possibility of a mother-teacher's voice and interests as well, patriarchally conditioned though these may be.

Reflections of traditional women's roles — especially aspects of the role of wife — may be seen in the characterizations of Woman Wisdom in Prov 3:13–18, 4:5–9, 7:4–5, and 9:1–6. Lest the modern reader think "*only* a wife," one must note the real, if behind-the-scenes, social power wielded by the wife as manager of an extended and productive family household and as counselor to husband and children (see Prov 31:10–31). Just as the husband of this capable wife "will have no lack of gain" (31:11), so also Woman Wisdom will exalt and honor the man who prizes and embraces her (3:13–18; 4:8). Both bring the trusting husband a "crown" (4:9; 12:4). Just as the wife provisions "her household" (31:21, 27) with both moral and material well-being, so also Woman Wisdom builds her house, sets her table, and teaches "the way of insight" (9:1–2, 6; 14:1). Both wife and Wisdom are, moreover, desirable sexual partners: Prov 5:15–19 urges husbandly faithfulness and satisfaction in his wife's body, while

7:4 tells the seeker of Wisdom to call her "sister," a term of endearment common in the Song of Solomon.

Public imagery and domestic imagery both appear in passages on Woman Wisdom. A variation on the human imagery occurs in Prov 1:20–33 and 8:1–21, where she appears as a prophet, calling out for followers in the most public places of human interaction: in the street and squares, at the busiest corner and the city gates (1:21–22), on the heights, beside the way, and at the crossroads (8:2). Her rhetoric of persuasion offers both carrot and stick. To one who chooses her way, she offers wealth and power, as well as "fruit . . . better than gold" (8:15–19). To those who ignore her counsel, she promises mockery when panic strikes and ultimately death (1:26, 32). Woman Wisdom's vocabulary, especially in chap. 1, is reminiscent of prophetic language (she "calls," is "refused," "stretches out her hand," needs to be "sought" and "found"; 1:24, 28; 8:17; compare 2 Chr 15:2; Isa 6:9–10; 65:1–2; Hos 5:6; Amos 8:12). The prophets, however, use such terminology to describe Israel's relationship to God; Wisdom speaks of relationship with herself!

This at first subtle shift from the prophet's role as speaker *for* God to more intimate identity *with* God takes a dramatic turn in Woman Wisdom's self-description in 8:22–36. Translation of the verb in 8:22a is debated. The NRSV's "The Lord created me" (from the Septuagint) is less likely correct than either "acquired" or "conceived" (in the biological sense; compare "I was brought forth" in vv. 24–25). A similar ambiguity occurs in 8:30a, where the NRSV's "master workman" could also be "darling child." In either case, Woman Wisdom is present with God before and during the process of creation, as a playful child (see 8:30b) or a wise architect, or, in the artful ambiguity of poetry, both! It is this primordial relationship that authorizes her claim in 8:35: "whoever finds me finds life / and obtains favor from the Lord."

This near-deification of Woman Wisdom in 8:22–36 cannot help but recall certain ancient goddesses, in this case especially Ma'at, the Egyptian goddess of justice, who was also understood both as the child of the creator god and (especially in Egyptian wisdom literature) as the ordering principle of creation. Allusions to Ma'at may also be seen in Wisdom's claim to establish just rule (8:15–16) and in the depiction of her with long life in her right hand and wealth in her left (3:16), for Ma'at also appears with the ankh, symbol of life, in one hand and a scepter in the other. Parallels may also be drawn to the Egyptian Isis, the Sumerian Inanna, and the (related) Babylonian Ishtar/Canaanite Astarte. Some of these parallels depend on a related analysis of Proverbs' strange woman (loose woman) as representative of the love and fertility practices of the Ishtar/Astarte cults. Lang has suggested that Wisdom was worshipped as a goddess of scribes, though this remains speculative. New archaeological evidence for the ongoing Israelite worship, well into the monarchic period, of the Canaanite goddess Asherah alongside YHWH has led McKinlay to argue that female-personified Wisdom is part of a complex dynamic of theological convergence, wherein YHWH took on attributes of Asherah as worship of the goddess was repressed. Asherah, associated symbolically with trees, was reduced, in effect, to the wisdom of YHWH personified, who is "a tree of life to those who lay hold of her" (Prov 3:18).

Attempts to understand the significance of Woman Wisdom in ancient Israelite life and in the canonical and deuterocanonical traditions underscore her deep ambiguity to feminist thought, whether historically or theologically inclined. At worst she represents the domestication of a powerful goddess into a good wife who supports her man and whose honor depends on his willingness to give her public recognition. Along with her counterpart, Woman Stranger, she may be seen as part of patriarchy's perennial classification of all women as either all-good or all-evil, and her apparent power but a mouthpiece for the voice of the fathers. On the other hand, it is difficult to read Proverbs' paeans to the power of both wisdom personified as woman (chaps. 1–9) and of woman as the ideal representative of wisdom (chap. 31) without imagining some related social reality at their base. One likely context for such open recognition of women's

contributions — as well as perceived danger from "loose women" — is the period after the Babylonian exile, as the Judeans struggled for a new definition of "Israel" as a people identified by family households rather than a monarchic polity. Especially notable is the editor's choice to open and close the Book of Proverbs with female imagery. Whatever one might make of it — whether ultimate co-optation or ultimate subversion — this quintessentially male book is framed with a woman's voice.

CLAUDIA V. CAMP

SEE ALSO Part III: Asherah/Asherim; Woman Stranger (Loose Woman/Adulteress).

FOR FURTHER READING: Brenner, Athalya. "Some Observations on the Figurations of Woman in Wisdom Literature."

Camp, Claudia V. *Wisdom and the Feminine in the Book of Proverbs.*

Fontaine, Carole. "Proverbs."

McKinlay, Judith E. *Gendering Wisdom the Host: Biblical Invitations to Eat and Drink.*

Newsom, Carol A. "Woman and the Discourse of Patriarchal Wisdom: A Study of Proverbs 1–9."

WOMAN WISDOM IN THE APOCRYPHAL/DEUTEROCANONICAL BOOKS

(Wis 6:12–11:1; Sir 1:1–20; 4:11–19; 6:18–37; 14:20–15:10; 24:1–34; 51:13–30; Bar 3:9–4:4; 2 Esdr 13:54–55) The poetic personification of wisdom as a woman, begun in Proverbs, continues in the later literary products of the wisdom tradition, the books of Sirach, the Wisdom of Solomon, Baruch, and 2 Esdras.

The Wisdom of Solomon, a pseudonymous work by an educated, Hellenized Jew, was most likely written for a similarly sophisticated Jewish audience in Alexandria. The tension of living in an adopted culture is evident, however, especially in the attacks on the "ungodly" in the first part of the book (Wis 1:1–6:21). The author makes free use of Greek philosophical style and terminology to convince his co-religionists to remain faithful to their traditions. This borrowing is quite evident in the second major section of the book (Wis 6:22–10:21), where the figure of Woman Wisdom is developed and elevated to an unparalleled degree.

Having introduced Wisdom in 6:12–21, the author begins a first-person discourse in Wis 6:22 in which his own assumed identity as King Solomon is gradually revealed. As this great and wise king of the past, he enters into relationship with a female Wisdom who both has her source in God (as a "pure emanation" of God's power and glory, Wis 7:25) and yet also at points takes over God's roles (as protector of the great heroes of Israel's past, Wis 10:1–11:1). Her characterization draws on several sources.

The Jewish tradition of female personification of wisdom (Proverbs 1; 8; Sirach 24) is complemented and intensified by borrowing from the traits and functions associated with the Hellenistic Egyptian goddess Isis. Isis, goddess of fertility, was important in Egyptian royal ideology, and Wisdom's mediation of relationship between God and "Solomon" appears to be patterned on Isis's relationship to the sun god Re and the earthly king Osiris. Thus, to take just one example, we find the striking representation of Woman Wisdom as lover and "throne partner" to both God and the king (Wis 8:2–4; 9:4, 10). At the same time, Greek philosophical style, vocabulary, and values appear in units like Wis 7:22–24, which uses twenty-one epithets to describe Wisdom's spirit, and in Wisdom's teaching of the four philosophical virtues: self-control, prudence, justice, and courage (Wis 8:7). If Woman Wisdom is not quite God ("she is a reflection of eternal light, a spotless mirror of the working of God, an image of his goodness," Wis 7:26), neither is there any way for the reader to distinguish her from God.

Sirach (also known by the Hebrew name of its author, Ben Sira, as well as by its Latin title, Ecclesiasticus) was written in Palestine in about 180 B.C.E. by a scribe closely associated with the Jerusalem temple. It was translated into Greek in Alexandria by Ben Sira's grandson sometime after 132 B.C.E. The book is made up mainly of instructional poems like those in Proverbs 1–9, but also includes hymns, prayers, and a long paean to Israel's ancestors. With respect to the figure of Wisdom, the author walks a line between simple objectification and true personification. Several poems use the term as the subject or object of active verbs, yet without distinctively human, much less female, attributes (Sir 1:1–20; 6:18–31; 51:13–30). Wisdom is from the Lord, created before all things, poured out on all his works. To fear the Lord is the beginning, fullness, crown, and root of wisdom. She (it?) will offer her produce to those who plow and sow, but be like a heavy stone to the undisciplined. Experienced at first as fetters and yoke, she will eventually be worn like a glorious robe and splendid crown. Elsewhere human metaphors — of teacher, bride, and mother — enhance the personification (Sir 4:11–19; 15:1–2). As a teacher, Wisdom is harsh, but, in the end, the source of joy. She is to be loved and held fast. Sir 14:20–27 captures this shifting characterization between the personal and the impersonal, moving from Wisdom as animal, to human, to tree. One who seeks wisdom will pursue her like a hunter, camp near her house, and be sheltered under her boughs.

Throughout Sirach, Wisdom is associated with following the Torah, most notably in chap. 24 where personified Wisdom "praises herself, and tells of her glory in the midst of her people" (v. 1). Reminiscent of Genesis 1 and 2, she says, "I came forth from the mouth of the Most High, and covered the earth like a mist" (Sir 24:3). She seeks a home, and God commands her to dwell in Israel. The poet concludes, "All this is the book of the covenant of the Most High God, / the law that Moses commanded us / as an inheritance for the congregations of Jacob" (Sir 24:23).

The date and provenance of the five chapters comprising the Book of Baruch are difficult to determine. It is ostensibly written to the people of Jerusalem by Jeremiah's scribe, Baruch, depicted as being in Babylonian exile during the early sixth century B.C.E. Many factors militate against accepting this as a historical account, however. The book is a pastiche of allusions to other biblical works, including Deuteronomy, Jeremiah, Ezra-Nehemiah, Proverbs, Daniel, Job, and Second Isaiah. The text moves from a confession of sin and a plea for divine deliverance from exile (1:15–3:8) to a wisdom poem (3:9–4:4) that is strongly reminiscent of Job 28 and the wisdom poems in Proverbs and Sirach. The exiles' failure to walk "in the way of God" and to "learn where there is wisdom" (Bar 3:13–14) has brought about their fate. Like the writer of Job 28, the poet asks who has found the place of wisdom and concludes that only God knows the way to her and gives her to Israel (Bar 3:36). She "appeared on earth and lived with humankind" in the form of the "book of the commandments of God, / the law that endures forever" (Bar 3:37–4:1). Baruch's understanding of the meaning of Woman Wisdom as explicitly identified with the Torah thus echoes Ben Sira's. Distinctive here is the presentation of Woman Wisdom as the gift of the Torah with little sexual innuendo and no evil counterpart.

The Jewish core of 2 Esdras, the first-century C.E. Ezra apocalypse (chaps. 3–14), is a special kind of revelatory literature in which Ezra seeks answers from the angel Uriel concerning the meaning of God's dealing with Israel and with the world. In the sixth of seven visions (13:1–58), Ezra dreams about a man who rises from the heart of the sea and, without spear or weapon, destroys all who have waged war with him by sending forth a stream of fire, wind, and tempest from his mouth (compare Daniel 7 and storm-god imagery). Greatly terrified by this dream, Ezra begs the Most High for an interpretation. He is told that before the end comes, "my Son will be revealed, whom you saw as a man coming up from the sea" (13:32; since this is God's chosen in a general sense, not specifically Jesus, it is better rendered as "son," with no capital). Following the destruction of the aggressor nations, this messianic figure will defend those who remain of the tribes of Israel and show them many wonders (13:39–40, 49–50).

Still troubled, Ezra prays for an explanation why he saw the man coming up from the heart of the sea (13:51). Ezra is told "you alone have been enlightened about this; because you have forsaken your own ways and have applied yourself to mine, and have searched out my law; for you have devoted your life to wisdom, and called understanding your

mother" (13:53–55). Sharing the tradition of texts like Sirach and Baruch that also link Torah with Wisdom, 2 Esdras alone portrays a human, Ezra, rewarded with special revelation for pursuing law and wisdom as mother. The text lacks the usual reciprocal pattern in which Torah/Wisdom seeks out humanity and speaks for herself.

CLAUDIA V. CAMP

FOR FURTHER READING: Cady, Susan, Marian Ronan, and Hal Taussig. *Sophia: The Future of Feminist Spirituality.*

Camp, Claudia V. "Honor and Shame in Ben Sira: Anthropological and Theological Reflections."

Kloppenborg, John S. "Isis and Sophia in the Book of Wisdom."

Reese, James M. *Hellenistic Influence on the Book of Wisdom and Its Consequences.*

Schroer, Silvia. "The Book of Sophia."

WOMAN WISDOM IN THE NEW TESTAMENT
(Matt 11:19; Luke 7:35; 11:49; 1 Cor 1:24)

The word *wisdom (sophia)* appears with several distinct meanings in the writings of the New Testament. It is most frequently used in a nonpersonified, and apparently non-gendered, sense. In several passages, wisdom refers to an aspect or attribute of the divine, without explicit personification (for example, Rom 11:33; 1 Cor 1:21; Eph 3:10). In others, it denotes an attribute of human beings bestowed upon them by the divine, as in "the wisdom of Solomon" (Matt 12:42; Luke 11:31; also used of Jesus in Matt 13:54; Mark 6:2; Luke 2:40; 2:52; and of the Christian community in 1 Cor 12:8; Eph 1:17; Col 1:9; Jas 3:13). Wisdom also appears in discourses on teaching, sometimes in the sense of a divine mystery (1 Cor 2:7) or in the negative sense of "the wisdom of this world" (1 Cor 3:19; Jas 3:15).

The clearest examples of the female personification of Wisdom are found in three sayings of Jesus that derive from the Sayings Source Q (Matt 11:19; its parallel in Luke 7:35; Luke 11:49). In these sayings, "Woman Wisdom" appears as one who is "vindicated" by "her deeds" (Matt 11:19), as a mother "vindicated by her children" (Luke 7:35), and as one who speaks of sending "prophets and apostles," some of whom will be persecuted and killed (Luke 11:49). Outside of these, there are no other explicit references to Woman Wisdom in the New Testament. The personification of Woman Wisdom or Sophia is, however, more fully developed in texts such as the *Gospel of Thomas,* a noncanonical collection of Jesus' sayings related to Q, and in the various versions of the Gnostic Sophia myth (*The Apocryphon of John, The Sophia of Jesus Christ,* and so on).

Most intriguing are those passages that relate Wisdom, personified or not, to the identity of Jesus of Nazareth (Matt 11:19; Luke 7:35; 11:49; also 1 Cor 1:24; 1:30). Yet equally important are those passages, such as John 1:1–18 and 1:15–20, that echo images of Woman Wisdom in Jewish wisdom literature, though neither the term nor the personified figure of Wisdom herself appears. Although the title Wisdom of God is rarely applied to Jesus in the New Testament and early Christian literature, recent scholarship has shown that early Christians drew heavily from motifs and images associated with Woman Wisdom, especially in framing and developing their conceptions of the identity and significance of Jesus. In the process, they radically transformed the symbolic significance of both the female personification of Woman Wisdom and the male Jesus of Nazareth. Unfortunately, many of the traces of Woman Wisdom in Christian Scripture have been ignored, underestimated, or "submerged" (as Schüssler Fiorenza describes it) in the history of Christian thought as indeed they were already downplayed in the ancient church.

In the Synoptic Gospels (Matthew, Mark, and Luke) and especially in Sayings Source Q, the source used by Matthew and Luke, Jesus may be described as a teacher of wisdom. Filled with "wisdom," he speaks in parables, aphorisms, and other literary forms familiar from wisdom literature to communicate his message and to call disciples. The sayings in which Jesus speaks directly of Woman Wisdom (Luke 7:35; 11:49; Matt 11:19) express two distinct views of the relationship between Wisdom and Jesus. The first, articulated in Luke 7:35 and

11:49, understands Jesus as a prophet, envoy, or representative of Woman Wisdom. The second, found in Matthew's version of the same passages as Matt 11:19 and 23:34, appears more directly to *identify* Jesus with Wisdom. The Lukan passages are thought more clearly to preserve traces of the Q traditions that circulated well before 70 c.e., while the Matthean passages reflect the later editorial work of the evangelist himself.

All three passages in which Jesus speaks of Woman Wisdom appear in a context of controversy, rejection, and judgment. In Luke 7:35, Jesus addresses the question of his relation to John the Baptist. What marks them both is rejection by "the people of this generation," whom Jesus compares to children in a marketplace. These children taunt one another: "We played the flute for you, and you did not dance; / we wailed, and you did not weep" (7:32). They demonize John for refusing to join in their dance; they call Jesus "a glutton and a drunkard, a friend of tax collectors and sinners" for refusing to join their game of lament (Luke 7:33–34). "Nevertheless," Jesus says, "Wisdom is vindicated by all her children" (7:35). Here the "children" of Wisdom clearly include both John and Jesus, and "all" suggests others who are rejected yet are among these children. Despite their rejection, all of Wisdom's children vindicate their mother.

Luke 11:49 continues to associate Wisdom with rejection, but adds a harsh warning of judgment. In Luke 11:45–52, Jesus critically addresses "lawyers" who "build the tombs of the prophets whom your ancestors killed." The Wisdom of God says, "'I will send them prophets and apostles, some of whom they will kill and persecute,' so that this generation may be charged with the blood of all the prophets" (Luke 11:48–50). Here Jesus is not identified with Wisdom, but delivers her oracle. He is a representative or envoy of Wisdom who will be killed and whose followers will be persecuted.

The two Wisdom sayings in Luke suggest a powerful connection between Woman Wisdom and the persecuted who speak in her name: the prophets, John the Baptist, Jesus, the apostles, and even, perhaps, the communities of Q. All have been rejected like Wisdom herself (Prov 1:20–33; 8:22–36), yet ultimately all are vindicated.

The Matthean versions of these sayings (Matt 11:19; 23:34) appear in similar settings of controversy and rejection. In Matthew, the saying about the vindication of Wisdom appears in a context identical to that of Luke 7:35, but with a significant difference of wording: "Yet Wisdom is vindicated by her deeds [*erga*]" (Matt 11:19). Matthew's repetition of the term "deeds" in 11:2 and 11:19 leads the attentive reader to identify "the deeds of the Christ" (11:2) — namely, the acts of healing, preaching good news to the poor, and table fellowship that Jesus performs — with "the deeds" of Wisdom herself. Here, as in Matt 23:34, the words of Wisdom become Jesus' own. Matthew explicitly identifies Jesus with Wisdom — not as one Wisdom's envoys, but Wisdom itself.

Scholars take varying views on the metaphorical conjunction of female Wisdom and male Jesus of Nazareth, as they do in interpreting all gendered language in early Christian texts. For some, identifying Jesus as Wisdom masculinizes Sophia or feminizes Jesus. For others, gender, or at least the femaleness of Sophia, is irrelevant to theological interpretation. But for many, the gendered representation of the divine in Christian Scripture opens valuable new possibilities for the rebuilding of Christian theological discourse.

The representation of Jesus and Wisdom in other writings of the New Testament, most notably in the letters of Paul, the prologue of John, and the Christological hymn of Colossians, has produced diverse scholarly interpretations. All these writings witness to a relinquishing of the fully personified figure of Woman Wisdom, even as they draw on Wisdom traditions to develop their conceptions of Jesus Christ.

In the first chapters of 1 Corinthians, written in about 55 C.E., the apostle Paul addresses the community after receiving reports that the community is divided into factions, and some in the community appear to be making claims about wisdom and other spiritual gifts. In response, Paul sets up a sharp antithesis between "the wisdom of God" and "the wisdom of the world." Paul reminds the

Corinthians that he did not preach the gospel "with eloquent wisdom, so that the cross of Christ might not be emptied of its power" (1:17). For Paul, the message of the cross centers on "Christ crucified" and reveals God's power to destroy the wisdom of the wise (1 Cor 1:19–20, citing Isa 29:14), bringing about a reversal of worldly values: "We proclaim Christ crucified . . . Christ the power of God and the wisdom of God. For God's foolishness is wiser than human wisdom" (1 Cor 1:23–24). Although this passage identifies Jesus as "the Wisdom of God" (1:24; see also 1:30) and draws on powerful images of status reversal (1 Cor 1:26–29), it does not explicitly point to the fully personified female Woman Wisdom that was available and undoubtedly known to Paul. This lack of female imagery parallels the absence of gender in the baptismal formula of 1 Cor 12:13 and the lack of female witnesses to the resurrection in 1 Corinthians 15. It is not implausible that Paul's non-gendered representation of Wisdom in 1 Corinthians reflects his overriding concern to establish "order" in a community that was challenging norms of class and gender relations. This seems especially likely if the Corinthian women were supporting their claims to be free from such norms by drawing on traditions that celebrated Woman Wisdom, Sophia, as their mother.

Traces of Wisdom imagery also appear in the Christological hymns of John 1:1–18 and Col 1:15–20. In both, Jesus is identified with a personified preexistent entity who is active in the creation and redemption of the world. The theological conception of the preexistent Christ in these passages is clearly drawn in part from the representation of Woman Wisdom as active in creation and redemption (Prov 8:22–36; Wis 7:25–28; Sir 24:3–22). Yet in their present form, distinctively female images are almost completely absent. In John, the preexistent entity is named Word (*logos*), a masculine noun that draws from Greek philosophical traditions as well as from Jewish notions of the redemptive power of God's word, Torah (compare Sir 24:23), and the text quickly adopts the language of Father and Son (John 1:14). In Colossians, the preexistent Christ is named Image, a feminine noun, but the letter as a whole adopts more exclusively masculine images for the divine. In Col 1:18, the preexistent Image is described as "the head of the body, the church" (1:18), language that echoes Paul's hierarchical argument in 1 Corinthians 11 and that appears again in Eph 5:23, this time to legitimate the patriarchal order of marriage in the household codes (Col 3:18–4:1; Eph 5:21–33). Clearly, the representation of the preexistent Christ in the prologue to John and the hymn of Col 1:15–20 draws from traditions of Woman Wisdom, but this representation, like much of the New Testament and the history of Christian theological discourse, leaves precious few traces of her imagery.

ANNE MCGUIRE

FOR FURTHER READING: Deutsch, Celia M. *Lady Wisdom, Jesus, and the Sages. Metaphor and Social Context in Matthew's Gospel.*

Levine, Amy-Jill. "Matthew."

———. "Women in the Q Communit(ies) and Traditions."

Schüssler Fiorenza, Elisabeth. *Jesus: Miriam's Child, Sophia's Prophet: Critical Issues in Feminist Christology.*

———. "Wisdom Mythology and the Christological Hymns of the New Testament."

Women in Imagery for Jerusalem, Judah, and Israel in Jeremiah

(Jer 2:2, 20, 23–28, 32–37; 3:1–3, 6–10, 19–20; 4:30–31; 5:7–9; 11:15; 12:7; 13:20–27)

The Book of Jeremiah contains a wide variety of female images: bride, prostitute, wife, promiscuous woman, woman in labor, woman raped, wise women mourners, musicians, teachers, daughter Zion, daughter My People lamenting, virgin Israel dancing, Rachel weeping for her children, and women worshipping the queen of heaven. These images clash and contend, helping to embody the literary-theological scope of the book, spanning calls to repentance in the face of impending death and destruction, remembrance in mourning, and an eschatological vision of redemption in exile. Some few refer to specific activities of women in the late seventh and early sixth centuries B.C.E.; most serve as metaphors for Jerusalem, Judah, and Israel in Jeremiah's prophetic oracles.

In the early chapters of Jeremiah, marital imagery represents YHWH's relationship with the people (as in the Book of Hosea, especially chaps. 1–3). Israel as the loving bride of cherished memory (Jer 2:2, 32) provides background contrast for the present picture of Israel (and Judah) as prostitute/whore, promiscuous woman, and faithless wife (Jer 2:20, 25–28; 3:1, 6–10, 19–20; 4:30–31; 5:7–9). "Woman glorified" is juxtaposed with its polar opposite, "woman vilified." Under judgment, Israel as female is compared to a cow-camel and a wild ass that are unable to control their sexual impulses (Jer 2:23–25). She is exposed, violated, and publicly humiliated (Jer 2:33–37). Her indictment results in divorce (Jer 3:1–8). The beloved who has done vile deeds no longer belongs to the household (Jer 11:15; 12:7). Her sexual activity is faulted for the pollution of the land (Jer 3:1–3). Images of sexual violence against the female underscore the severity of the judgment. Some have called these passages pornographic. Metaphoric woman's violated body functions as a metonym for society's body ravaged by war.

Images of sexual violence against Jerusalem-Judah-Israel as female continue in later sections of Jeremiah. The metaphor of woman violated, exposed, and raped, with the approval and involvement of the deity, while accused as prostitute/whore and promiscuous woman (Jer 13:20–27, especially 13:22, 26), confronts the cruelty of the people's fate in pornographic terms.

ANGELA BAUER

SEE ALSO Part I: Gomer; Part II: Wife/Wives (Jer 3:1, etc.); Woman in Labor (Jer 4:31, etc.); Part III: Daughter; Oholah, Woman Samaria.

FOR FURTHER READING: Bauer, Angela. *Gender in the Book of Jeremiah: A Feminist Literary Reading.*

Brenner, Athalya. "On Prophetic Propaganda and the Politics of 'Love': The Case of Jeremiah."

Keefe, Alice. "Rapes of Women/Wars of Men."

Weems, Renita J. *Battered Love: Marriage, Sex, and Violence in the Hebrew Prophets.*

Women Sidon and Tyre
(Isa 23: 4, 15–18)

Female imagery for geopolitical units and for God appears frequently in the Book of Isaiah, and personifications of Tyre and Sidon are two examples. In an oracle against Sidon (23:4), a Phoenician city on the Levantine coast to the north of ancient Israel, the city is personified as a mother and is condemned as barren, having neither reared young men nor brought up young women. This is an allusion to the city's depopulation in time of war and an indication that Sidon, without offspring, will have no future. Sidon's sister city Tyre on the Phoenician coast is also personified as a woman in Isaiah 23 (vv. 15–18). Tyre is labeled as a "prostitute" by the prophet because of her misdeeds. Tyre's prostitution, however, will ultimately come to some good, as it is said that she will dedicate the wages of her harlotry to God, something that Israelite prostitutes (female and male) are forbidden to do.

SUSAN ACKERMAN

SEE ALSO Part II: Prostitute (Lev 19:29, etc.); Young Women (and Men) of Sidon (Isa 23:4); Part III: Woman Jerusalem/Zion in Isaiah.

Additional Ancient Sources

ACTS OF (PAUL AND) THECLA Composed in Greek, probably in the second century C.E., perhaps in Asia Minor, the *Acts of (Paul and) Thecla* narrates the conversion of an elite unmarried young woman named Thecla to an ascetic form of Christianity, in response to the preaching of the apostle Paul in her native Iconium (Konya in modern Turkey). Part of a larger composite work known as the *Acts of Paul*, the story appears to have no demonstrable historical basis. It is particularly significant for its representation of Thecla as a missionary instructed by Paul to "go and teach the word of God."

ACTS OF PILATE This work narrates the trial of Jesus and its aftermath, foregrounding the role, actions, and speeches of Pontius Pilate. It was composed sometime during the second through fourth centuries C.E., almost certainly in Greek, and incorporated into a later work known as the *Gospel of Nicodemus.*

AMARNA LETTERS This archive of more than 350 letters, written in cuneiform Akkadian on clay tablets, was discovered at Amarna, the capital of Egypt in the fourteenth century B.C.E. The Amarna letters are part of a correspondence between the Egyptian pharaohs and the rulers of their vassal city-states — including Gezer, Jerusalem, Megiddo, and Shechem — in Syria and Palestine. The context of these texts reveals the unstable social and political conditions in the land of Canaan in the period just preceding Israelite beginnings. Some of the unrest among the city-states was apparently generated by a marginal group called the Habiru, who may have had some connection with the biblical Hebrews.

ANCIENT GNOSTIC SCRIPTURES (NAG HAMMADI LIBRARY) In 1945, approximately a dozen Coptic manuscripts in codex form (writing on both sides of sheets bound together at one edge), dating from the fourth century C.E., were discovered not far from Nag Hammadi in Egypt. These codices contain many writings believed to have been composed by gnostics, that is, by persons who thought they possessed special knowledge (from the Greek word *gnōsis*), only accessible to certain persons, including knowledge about the true nature of the universe, the divine, and human existence. Many of these works have an explicitly Christian cast, although not all ancient gnostics appear to have been Christians. Most of these writings, which were originally composed in Greek and translated into Coptic (a late form of Egyptian), were previously either unknown altogether or known only through quotations or ancient fragments.

Although collectively these works are often called the Nag Hammadi Library, they were actually found outside Nag Hammadi near an abandoned ancient monastery, and many scholars think it misleading to consider them a formal library. Together with the Dead Sea Scrolls, this archaeological discovery ranks as the most significant find of the twentieth century for the study of early Christianity and religion in Greco-Roman antiquity.

APOCALYPSE OF PETER One of the Coptic texts found near Nag Hammadi, the *Apocalypse of Peter* contains a revelation (apocalypse) of Peter as well as the Savior's interpretation of the vision. This revelation apparently relates to conflict between gnostic Christians and their opponents. It appears to date from the third century C.E. *See also* Ancient Gnostic Scriptures (Nag Hammadi Library).

APOCRYPHON OF JOHN The *Apocryphon of John* provides one of the most extensive presentations of a gnostic worldview, in the form of a revelatory dialogue between the Savior (Jesus, although the name isn't used within the text) and his disciples. It is extant in several ancient versions, including two in the Coptic manuscripts found near Nag Hammadi. The precise date of the work is difficult to determine, although Christian writers as early as the second century C.E. appear familiar with many of its basic ideas. *See also* Ancient Gnostic Scriptures (Nag Hammadi Library).

BABYLONIAN TALMUD *See* Talmud.

1 CLEMENT This letter concerning leadership debates presents itself as having been written by the church in Rome to the church in Corinth (Greece). It is usually dated to the end of the first century C.E. Although no individual author is named, it was attributed early to an author named Clement whom some ancient sources took to have been a leader in the Roman church. Together with a second Clementine epistle, it apparently had canonical status for Christians in Egypt and Syria, for both are included in several ancient biblical manuscripts.

2 CLEMENT This work, composed perhaps in the mid–second century C.E., came to be attributed to an author named Clement. Although ancient manuscripts call it an epistle, the work appears to be more of a sermon concerned with general themes of righteousness, repentance, and resurrection.

CODE OF HAMMURABI This collection of laws, inscribed on a stone stele, contains a series of 282 legal cases as well as a prologue and an epilogue. Although not strictly speaking a "code" — it is not systematic or comprehensive — it is

an invaluable record of the sophisticated legal thinking of the ancient Semitic world. Promulgated by Hammurabi, the most famous ruler (reigned 1792–1750 B.C.E.) of Babylon's First Dynasty, the casuistic (case) form of the laws as well as the content of many of them resemble features of biblical law collections, especially the Book of the Covenant (Exodus 21–23).

CODEX ALEXANDRINUS This fifth-century C.E. Greek manuscript contains all the books commonly found in the Septuagint as well as the New Testament, Psalms of Solomon, and *1 and 2 Clement.*

A codex is made of individual leaves or sheets of writing material, usually papyrus or parchment, inscribed on both sides and bound together along one edge. The ancient codex is the forerunner of the modern book.

CODEX BEZAE This bilingual (Greek and Latin) manuscript of the canonical Gospels and the Acts of the Apostles dates from the late fifth or early sixth century C.E. *See also* Codex Alexandrinus, paragraph 2.

CODEX SINAITICUS This fourth-century C.E. Greek manuscript contains most of the books commonly found in the Septuagint as well as the New Testament, the *Epistle of Barnabas,* and the *Shepherd of Hermas.* It was discovered in 1844 at St. Catherine Monastery on the Sinai Peninsula. *See also* Codex Alexandrinus, paragraph 2.

CODEX VATICANUS This exceptionally fine fourth-century C.E. Greek manuscript contains most of the books commonly found in the Septuagint, except the books of the Maccabees, as well as the New Testament. *See also* Codex Alexandrinus, paragraph 2.

DIALOGUE OF THE SAVIOR One of the texts found near Nag Hammadi, the *Dialogue of the Savior* contains sayings attributed to Jesus in the form of a discussion between Jesus and three disciples, Mariam, Judas, and Matthew. The Coptic manuscript translates a Greek original that dates perhaps to the middle or late second century C.E., although it appears to rely on an earlier (late first century C.E.?) sayings source. *See also*

Ancient Gnostic Scriptures (Nag Hammadi Library).

DIDACHE This early Christian handbook focuses on both individual and communal behavior. The first portion draws heavily on the tradition, common to a number of early Christian writings, of the "two ways," that of life and that of death. Known also as the *Teaching of the Lord to the Nations Through the Twelve [Apostles]*, in its present form, *Didache* is difficult to date. Much of the material it contains is considered to be quite early (perhaps late first or early second century C.E.).

ELEPHANTINE DOCUMENTS This collection of papyrus texts, written in Aramaic, was discovered at the site of Elephantine, an island in the Nile in upper Egypt. Dating to the fifth century B.C.E., the archive consists mainly of letters and contracts but also contains some literary and historical texts, as well as lists and accounts. These papyri are of great importance for late biblical and early Jewish history because they document the personal, religious, and commercial practices of the members of a Jewish colony established in the Persian-period garrison at Elephantine. The archive of one woman, named Mibtahiah, contains a marriage contract with language suggesting that women had the legal right to initiate the termination of marriage.

EPIC OF GILGAMESH Perhaps the best-known and oldest mythic poem of the ancient Near East, this epic describes the adventures of Gilgamesh, a legendary king of Uruk, which was a prominent city in southern Mesopotamia. Fragments of the clay tablets on which the epic was written date to as early as 3000 B.C.E. and have been found in Anatolia and ancient Israel as well as in Mesopotamia. One portion of the poem, which describes a great flood, is strikingly similar to the flood narrative in the Book of Genesis.

EPIC OF KIRTA See Ugaritic Texts.

EPISTLE OF POLYCARP This letter was written by one Polycarp of Smyrna (Izmir in modern Turkey) to the church in Philippi (in Greece), apparently at their behest. The letter is probably to be dated to the early or middle second century C.E. Polycarp died a martyr in the mid–second century C.E.

EUSEBIUS, ECCLESIASTICAL HISTORY This narrative of the birth and growth of Christianity was composed in the early fourth century C.E. by Eusebius of Caesarea (in modern Israel) shortly after Constantine legitimized Christianity. Although the work's obvious ideological cast compels us to be cautious in evaluating its historical reliablity, the *Ecclesiastical* [or *Church*] *History* continues to be invaluable for its presentation of contemporaneous events and its extensive quotation of ancient sources otherwise lost.

GOSPEL OF MARY One of the texts found near Nag Hammadi, the fragmentary *Gospel of Mary* contains a dialogue in which the risen Savior and his disciples discuss sin. It also contains a longer dialogue in which Mary (Magdalene, almost certainly) tells the male disciples what the Lord has revealed to her privately. Although Peter questions her authority (a contest found in several other early Christian writings), the other disciples side with Mary, recognizing that "[the Lord] loved her more than us" (18). Originally composed in Greek, it probably dates to the second century C.E. *See also* Ancient Gnostic Scriptures (Nag Hammadi Library).

GOSPEL OF PETER This fragmentary early Christian gospel contains traditions about the passion (suffering and death) of Jesus, the empty tomb, and the resurrection. Similar in some respects to the Synoptic Gospels (Matthew, Mark, and Luke), it is thought by some scholars to contain traditions about Jesus that are earlier than those preserved in the canonical Gospels. The *Gospel of Peter* could have been composed as early as the mid–first century C.E. and no later than the end of the second century C.E.

GOSPEL OF PHILIP This work is an eclectic discussion of various sacraments, all of which may be related to an initiation ritual centered on the image of the bridal chamber. Although it contains some materials about Jesus, it differs significantly from the many other ancient works designated as gospels. The title *Gospel of Philip* occurs in the Coptic manuscript found near Nag Hammadi; the original Greek text is thought to date to the second century C.E. *See also* Ancient Gnostic Scriptures (Nag Hammadi Library).

GOSPEL OF THOMAS   This collection of sayings attributed to Jesus is said to have been written down by Didymus Judas Thomas, who was known in some early Christian circles as the twin brother of Jesus. Some of these sayings are also found in the canonical Gospels, often worded somewhat differently. Only fragments of the original Greek survive, but the gospel is well known from translations into Coptic. Some form of the *Gospel of Thomas* is attested as early as the end of the second century C.E.; some scholars think it could have been written down as early as the mid–first century C.E., which would make it the oldest gospel known.

GOSPEL OF TRUTH   This ideas in this gnostic Christian homily link it to the teachings of one Valentinus. One of the texts found near Nag Hammadi, it may date to the middle or late second century C.E.. The Coptic manuscripts give no title for the work, which is taken instead from its opening line. *See also* Ancient Gnostic Scriptures (Nag Hammadi Library).

HITTITE LAWS   These legal materials, dating mainly to the mid–second millennium B.C.E., were produced by the Hittites, an Indo-European people occupying central Anatolia. Some two hundred laws from the Hittite Old Kingdom concern homicide, theft, assault, marriage, land tenure, and taxation; they resemble law collections of the Hebrew Bible as well as of Mesopotamia (such as those of Hammurabi and from the Middle Assyrian period).

INSTRUCTION OF PTAH-HOTEP   This compilation of wise sayings is purported to come from Ptah-hotep, a high official in the court of King Izezi of the fifth dynasty in Egypt (c. 2450 B.C.E.). The "Instruction" contains directives to Ptah-hotep's son, who will succeed him in his royal position. Some of his counsel for becoming a successful official is similar to advice given in the Book of Proverbs and Ecclesiastes.

JERUSALEM TALMUD   *See* Talmud.

JOSEPH AND ASENETH   This tale, composed in Greek, narrates how the biblical Joseph came to marry the beautiful eighteen-year-old daughter of an Egyptian priest. The text foregrounds Aseneth's transformation from an arrogant, man-hating idolator to a pious worshipper of the God of Israel and a devoted wife. The date, authorship, and place of composition are uncertain; often thought to be a Jewish composition from the late first or early second centuries C.E., it may well have been composed in the third or fourth century, perhaps by a Christian author.

JOSEPHUS, *ANTIQUITIES OF THE JEWS*   This history of the Jews was written in Greek by a Jewish man who served as a general in the first Jewish revolt against Rome (66–73 C.E.). Flavius Josephus wrote all his works in Rome after the revolt, under the patronage of the Flavian imperial family (hence the name Flavius). The title *Antiquities* illuminates Josephus's desire to demonstrate the ancient nature of the Jewish people, a quality greatly esteemed by the Romans. The twenty books of the work begin with the creation of the world and end just before the onset of the revolt.

JOSEPHUS, *JEWISH WAR*   This narrative of the first Jewish revolt against Rome and the events precipitating it was written in Greek around the last quarter of the first century C.E. by Flavius Josephus. *See also* Josephus, *Antiquities of the Jews*.

JUBILEES   This Greek work of the second century B.C.E., likely written by a Jewish priest, follows the story line of Genesis 1 through Exodus 20, using a chronology that divides time into seven "weeks of years," or forty-nine units of forty-nine years (hence the name "Jubilees," as in Lev 25:8). Ostensibly a revelation to Moses on Mount Sinai, the work celebrates the centrality of the law and the sabbath and uses a distinctive solar calendar. Sometimes known as "Little Genesis," *Jubilees* was lost to the Western world, except for a few quotations in the church fathers, until the nineteenth century, when it was found in usage in the Ethiopic Church.

JUSTIN MARTYR, *DIALOGUE WITH TRYPHO* This work is a lengthy critique of Judaism and defense of Christianity in the form of a philosophical debate between a Jewish man, named Trypho, and the author, a philosopher and convert to Christianity named Justin Martyr (second century C.E.). Trypho may well have been a fictional character created by Justin.

MASORETIC TEXT   The standard text of the Hebrew Bible was produced by the Masoretes of Tiberias (on the western shore of the Sea of Galilee). The Masoretes were Jewish scholars dedicated to the careful transmission of the biblical text (their name derives from the Hebrew *masorah*, "transmission"). The Masoretes added accents and vowel signs to the consonantal text, often with detailed marginal notes and annotations. The Masoretic system of vowels and accents is represented in numerous manuscripts dating from the ninth century C.E. and onward. The best available example is the unfortunately incomplete Aleppo Codex (c. 915 C.E.); the best complete example is the Leningrad Codex (c. 1009 C.E.). *See also* Codex Alexandrinus, paragraph 2.

MIDDLE ASSYRIAN LAWS   Inscribed on clay tablets, these legal materials date to the reign of Tiglath-pileser I (1114–1076 B.C.E.). Discovered at the ancient site of Ashur in northern Mesopotamia, the laws, some of which may date originally to as early as the fifteenth century B.C.E., consist of more than one hundred cases dealing with a variety of criminal and civil matters. Like the Code of Hammurabi, these laws are similar in form and content to some biblical laws.

MIDRASH RABBAH SONG OF SONGS   This rabbinic allegory interprets each of the eight chapters of the Song of Songs. It likely dates to the sixth through eighth centuries C.E.

MISHNAH   This collection of Jewish traditions, many concerned with legal matters, was probably compiled in the early third century C.E. at Sep-

phoris (in the Galilee, near Nazareth). The work became foundational to subsequent mainstream Judaism. The Mishnah (meaning "study" or "oral instruction") contains sixty-three tractates grouped into six divisions (*Seeds* [on agriculture], *Set Feasts, Women, Damages, Holy Things, Purities*). Mishnah tractates are usually abbreviated with the letter *m*, followed by the name of the individual tractate.

M(ISHNAH) GIṬṬIN   This tractate of the Mishnah deals with bills of divorce (plural *giṭṭin;* singular *get*). It falls within the larger division known as *Nashim, "Women." See also* Mishnah.

M(ISHNAH) NAZIR   This tractate of the Mishnah deals with a particular class of vows known as Nazirite vows, which both women and men could take. Although only a small portion of the tractate deals specifically with women, the tractate (as well as another, *Nedarim,* dealing with vows more generally) is considered part of the larger division of the Mishnah known as *Nashim, "Women." See also* Mishnah.

M(ISHNAH) NEDARIM   This tractate of the Mishnah deals with vows (*Nedarim*). Although only a small portion of the tractate deals with women's vows, the tractate (as well as another dealing with a specific category of vows called Nazirite) is considered part of the larger division of the Mishnah known as *Nashim, "Women." See also* Mishnah.

M(ISHNAH) YEBAMOT   A tractate of the Mishnah whose name means "Sisters-in-Law," *Yebamot* belongs to the larger division of the Mishnah known as *Nashim, "Women."* Many of its discussions treat problems arising from the biblical requirement that a woman whose husband dies without a male heir must marry her husband's brother and produce a legal heir for her deceased spouse. *See also* Mishnah.

MYTH OF INANNA, GILGAMESH, AND THE HULUPPU-TREE   One of the world's first recorded tales of cosmic beginnings, "The Huluppu-Tree" is part of a cycle of sacred stories dealing with the goddess Inanna and dates to the third millennium B.C.E. This masterpiece of

Sumerian literature is a spiritual exploration of the place of the gods and of humans in the universe.

PHILO OF ALEXANDRIA, *LIFE OF MOSES* This life of the biblical Moses was composed in Greek by the Jewish philosopher Philo of Alexandria. Writing in the first four decades of the first century C.E., Philo had both a classical Greek education and extensive knowledge of Jewish Scriptures and Jewish interpretive traditions (which he read in Greek). Many of Philo's works apply allegorical methods of interpretation to Jewish Scripture. His representation of Moses as the philosopher par excellence draws on prevailing ideas of ancient biography, which sought to demonstrate the essential character traits of exemplary public persons (generally men).

PHILOSTRATUS, *LIFE OF APOLLONIUS OF TYANA* This work tells of the life of a contemporary of Jesus, Apollonius of Tyana, a wandering ascetic sage and miracle worker whose career bears some fascinating resemblances to that of Jesus. Julia Domna, wife of the emperor Septimius Severus (193–211 C.E.), commissioned the work from its author, Philostratus.

PISTIS SOPHIA This collection of dialogues between the risen Jesus and his disciples, which foregrounds the role of Mary (Magdalene), is considered of the same genre as various revelation discourses found near Nag Hammadi. The only known copy of *Pistis Sophia*, a Coptic manuscript of unknown provenance, was acquired by the British Museum in 1785. Pistis Sophia (the Greek words mean, respectively, "faith" or "trust"; "wisdom") is the name of a female divine emanation, one of twenty-four such emanations paired into twelve male and female couples. It may have been written as early as the third century C.E.

PLATO, *SYMPOSIUM* This work is part of a trilogy of fictional prose dialogues of the fourth century B.C.E. written by the Greek philosopher Plato. In this dialogue, Phaedrus, Aristophanes, and Socrates, three guests at a drinking party (symposium), give a series of speeches in praise of Eros (love). The *Symposium* presents for the first time the non-Socratic idea of a platonic form.

PROTEVANGELIUM (INFANCY GOSPEL) OF JAMES This Christian account of Mary, the mother of Jesus, foregrounds her own conception and birth, the conception and birth of Jesus, and Mary's virginity. Composed in the name of James, sometime after the mid–second century C.E., it is the source of many popular traditions about Mary.

THE QUR'AN (KORAN) The sacred book, or scriptures, of Islam is written in Arabic. The Qur'an is believed to have been revealed by Allah to Muhammad during his twenty-two years as a prophet in the early sixth century C.E. According to Islam, the Qur'an has foundational status because it reveals, in 114 suras (chapters), God's intentions for human life, including gender relations.

SAYINGS SOURCE Q This collection of sayings attributed to Jesus has been hypothesized by modern scholars to explain the large number of similar (and sometimes identical) sayings of Jesus found in the Gospels of Matthew and Luke but not the Gospel of Mark, a Gospel that the authors of Matthew and Luke appear to have known in some form and incorporated into their own works. The designation Q comes from the German *Quelle*, meaning "source." No ancient copies of Q have ever been found, and some scholars remain skeptical that it ever existed, preferring to explain the similar material in Matthew and Luke as the result of one author's direct use of the work of the other.

SECRET GOSPEL OF MARK An ancient edition of the Gospel of Mark was partially quoted in Greek in a fragment of a letter written by Clement of Alexandria (late second century C.E.), which was discovered in an eighteenth-century copy in 1958. The designation "secret" comes from Clement, according to whom different versions of the *Secret Gospel of Mark* were used by different Christian churches in his time.

SEDER OLAM RABBAH A chronologically

comprehensive, two-part outline of time from Adam to the end of the Persian period, and from Alexander the Great to Bar Kokhba, *Seder Olam Rabbah* (the "Great Book of the World") is a rabbinic work of uncertain date, traditionally attributed to a second-century rabbi, Yose ben Halafta.

SEPTUAGINT   This is the general name given to an ancient collection of Greek translations of the Hebrew Bible that were first undertaken in the third century B.C.E. in Alexandria, Egypt. The name, which comes from the Latin word for "seventy" (LXX in Roman numerals), derives from a legend that seventy-two elders translated the Pentateuch into Greek. The Septuagint includes the Pentateuch (the first five books of the Bible) as well as diverse collections of other "Old Greek" translations of Jewish/Hebrew Scripture and related literature.

SHEPHERD OF HERMAS   This second-century C.E. Christian text narrates a series of revelations, received by one Hermas, from three separate figures: a woman who becomes younger and younger, and represents the church; a shepherd; and a great angel. Portions of the work are contained in one of the earliest and most important ancient biblical manuscripts, Codex Sinaiticus, suggesting that it had scriptural status for some early Christian communities.

SOPHIA OF JESUS CHRIST   This work is a Christian reworking of an earlier epistle, *Eugnostos the Blessed,* in the form of a dialogue between the Savior and several disciples, including Mary. Both *Eugnostos* and the *Sophia* [*Wisdom*] *of Jesus Christ* are among the texts found near Nag Hammadi, in two versions each. *Sophia* may be as early as the late first century C.E. *See also* Ancient Gnostic Scriptures (Nag Hammadi Library).

STORY OF AQHAT   *See* Ugaritic Texts.

TALE OF TWO BROTHERS   This Egyptian folktale, known from a papyrus manuscript of the late thirteenth century B.C.E., tells of how a young man of good character was wrongly accused of adultery by his older brother's wife, who had unsuccessfully tried to seduce him. Part of the narrative resembles the biblical story, in the Book of Genesis, of Potiphar's wife and Joseph.

TALMUD   The classic compilation of Jewish law, the Talmud (meaning "study" or "instruction") contains the Mishnah and commentary (known as Gemara) in Aramaic, on many, although not all, tractates of the Mishnah. The Babylonian Talmud, usually referred to as *the* Talmud, contains traditions attributed to rabbis living in Sassanid Babylonia (modern Iraq), while the less well known Jerusalem Talmud, or Talmud of the Land of Israel, contains traditions attributed to rabbis living in the land of Israel. Given the complex nature of both Talmuds, dating them is quite difficult. The Jerusalem Talmud is generally thought to have been redacted in the early fifth century C.E., while the Babylonian Talmud appears to be somewhat later, perhaps of the sixth century C.E. *See also* Mishnah.

TESTAMENT OF SOLOMON   This pseudonymous Greek legend tells how Solomon built the temple of Jerusalem with the aid of the demons under his control. Written in the first person and containing twenty-six chapters, this testament (last words) combines ancient lore about magic, astrology, angelology, demonology, and medicine. Explicit references to the virgin birth, the Son of God, the temptations of Jesus, Jesus' rule over the demons, and the crucifixion suggest Christian revision of an earlier Jewish legend. It dates anywhere from the first to the third century.

THUNDER, PERFECT MIND   This revelation discourse by a female figure is delivered in language and form highly reminiscent of Greco-Roman hymns and praises of the Egyptian goddess Isis. The discourse never identifies the speaker apart from the title phrases and contains nothing that is distinctive to a particular ancient religious tradition. Although it obviously originated no later than the fourth century (it was found near Nag Hammadi in a fourth-century Coptic manuscript), its date is difficult to determine. *See also* Ancient Gnostic Scriptures (Nag Hammadi Library).

Y(ERUSHALMI) KETUBBOTH This is the Jerusalem Talmud's version of the tractate concerning marriage contracts (*Ketubboth*). *See also* Talmud.

Y(ERUSHALMI) BABA BATRA This is the Jerusalem Talmud's version of the tractate concerning the ownership of movable property and related matters. *Baba Batra* (meaning "The Last Gate") is one of three tractates related to property damages; the other two are *Baba Kamma* ("The First Gate") and Baba Meṣi'a ("The Middle Gate").

UGARITIC TEXTS This large group of inscriptions, most of them inscribed on clay tablets, was discovered at the site of Ras Shamra (Ugarit) on the Mediterranean coast of Syria. Many of the texts, which date largely to the thirteenth and early twelfth centuries B.C.E., are in the local language, Ugaritic, a Northwest Semitic language related to Hebrew. Included among these documents are extensive religious texts, both mythological and ritual, that provide important evidence for Canaanite religion. The most prominent myths are the *Baal-Anath Cycle,* about the agricultural god Baal and his warrior/love goddess sister Anath; the *Epic of Kirta,* about the struggles of the legendary King Kirta; and the *Story of Aqhat,* a long narrative depicting human-divine interactions.

Abbreviations

—◦◦◦—

Hebrew Scripture

Gen	Genesis
Exod	Exodus
Lev	Leviticus
Num	Numbers
Deut	Deuteronomy
Josh	Joshua
Judg	Judges
Ruth	Ruth
1, 2 Sam	1, 2 Samuel
1, 2 Kgs	1, 2 Kings
1, 2 Chr	1, 2 Chronicles
Ezra	Ezra
Neh	Nehemiah
Esth	Esther
Job	Job
Ps[s]	Psalm[s]
Prov	Proverbs
Ecccl	Ecclesiastes
Song	Song of Solomon
Isa	Isaiah
Jer	Jeremiah
Lam	Lamentations
Ezek	Ezekiel
Dan	Daniel
Hos	Hosea
Joel	Joel
Amos	Amos
Obad	Obadiah
Jonah	Jonah
Mic	Micah
Nah	Nahum
Hab	Habakkuk
Zeph	Zephaniah
Hag	Haggai
Zech	Zechariah
Mal	Malachi

Apocryphal/Deuterocanonical Books

Tob	Tobit
Jdt	Judith
Add Esth	Greek Additions to Esther
Wis	Wisdom of Solomon
Sir	Sirach
Bar	Baruch
Ep Jer	Letter of Jeremiah
Pr Azar	Prayer of Azariah and the Song of the Three Jews
Sus	Susanna
Bel	Bel and the Dragon
1, 2 Macc	1, 2 Maccabees
1 Esdr	1 Esdras
Pr Man	Prayer of Manasseh
Ps 51	Psalm 51
3 Macc	3 Maccabees
2 Esdr	2 Esdras
4 Macc	4 Maccabees

The New Testament

Matt	Matthew
Mark	Mark
Luke	Luke
John	John
Acts	Acts
Rom	Romans
1, 2 Cor	1, 2 Corinthians
Gal	Galatians
Eph	Ephesians

Phil	Philippians	NAS	New American Standard
Col	Colossians	NEB	New English Bible
1, 2 Thess	1, 2 Thessalonians	NIV	New International Version
1, 2 Tim	1, 2 Timothy	NJB	New Jerusalem Bible
Titus	Titus	NJPS	New Jewish Publication
Phlm	Philemon		Society
Heb	Hebrews	NRSV	New Revised Standard
Jas	James		Version
1, 2 Pet	1, 2 Peter	REB	Revised English Bible
1, 2, 3 John	1, 2, 3 John	RSV	Revised Standard Version
Jude	Jude		
Rev	Revelation		

Translations of the Bible

ASV	American Standard Version
KJV	King James Version
NAB	New American Bible

Other Abbreviations

B.C.E.	before the common era (B.C.)
C.E.	common era (A.D.)
c.	circa
chap[s].	chapter[s]
v[v].	verse[s]

Bibliography

⟨⟨⟩⟩

Abbreviations

ABD	*Anchor Bible Dictionary,* ed. David Noel Freedman, 6 vols. New York: Doubleday, 1992.
AJP	*American Journal of Philology*
AJS	Association for Jewish Studies
AJSL	*American Journal of Semitic Languages and Literature*
BA	*Biblical Archaeologist*
BARev	*Biblical Archaeology Review*
BibRev	*Bible Review*
BR	*Biblical Research*
CBQ	*Catholic Biblical Quarterly*
HAR	*Hebrew Annual Review*
HTR	*Harvard Theological Review*
IEJ	*Israel Exploration Journal*
JAC	*Jahrbuch für Antike und Christentum*
JAOS	*Journal of the American Oriental Society*
JBL	*Journal of Biblical Literature*
JFSR	*Journal of Feminist Studies in Religion*
JPS	Jewish Publication Society
JJS	*Journal of Jewish Studies*
JSOT	*Journal for the Study of the Old Testament*
NovT	*Novum Testamentum*
NTS	*New Testament Studies*
PEQ	*Palestine Exploration Quarterly*
SBL	Society of Biblical Literature
STS	*Searching the Scriptures,* ed. Elisabeth Schüssler Fiorenza. Vol 1: *A Feminist Introduction.* 1993. Vol. 2: *A Feminist Commentary.* New York, Crossroad, 1994.
USQR	*Union Seminary Quarterly Review*
VT	*Vetus Testamentum*
WBC	*Women's Bible Commentary,* ed. Carol A. Newsom and Sharon H. Ringe. Louisville: Westminster/John Knox Press, 1992. Expanded edition, 1998.
ZAW	*Zeitschrift für die alttestamentliche Wissenschaft*

Abba, R. "Name." In *The Interpreter's Dictionary of the Bible,* ed. George A. Buttrick, 3:500–508. New York: Abingdon Press, 1962.

Abbott, Nabia. "Pre-Islamic Arab Queens." *AJSL* 58 (1941): 1–22.

Abrahamsen, Valerie. "Women at Philippi: The Pagan and Christian Evidence." *JFSR* 3 (1987): 17–30.

Ackerman, James S. "The Literary Context of the Moses Birth Story." In *Literary Interpretations of Biblical Narratives,* ed. Kenneth R. R. Gros Louis, with James S. Ackerman and Thayer S. Warshaw, 74–119. Nashville: Abingdon Press, 1974.

Ackerman, Susan. "'And the Women Knead Dough': The Worship of the Queen of Heaven in Sixth-Century Judah." In *Gender and Difference in Ancient Israel,* ed. Peggy L. Day, 109–24. Minneapolis: Fortress Press, 1989.

———. "Isaiah." *WBC,* 161–68.

———. "The Queen Mother and the Cult in Ancient Israel." *JBL* 112 (1993): 385–401.

———. *Under Every Green Tree: Popular Religion in Sixth-Century Judah.* Atlanta: Scholars Press, 1992.

———. *Warrior, Dancer, Seductress, Queen: Women in Judges and Biblical Israel.* New York: Doubleday, 1998.

Albright, William F. "The Lachish Cosmetic Burner and Esther 2:12." In *A Light unto My Path: Old Testament Studies in Honor of Jacob M. Myers*, ed. Howard N. Bream, Ralph D. Heim, and Carey A. Moore, 25–32. Philadelphia: Temple University Press, 1974.

———. "Northwest-Semitic Names in a List of Egyptian Slaves from the 18th Century B.C." *JAOS* 74 (1954): 222–33.

Alexander, T. Desmond. "Are the Wife/Sister Incidents of Genesis Literary Compositional Variants?" *VT* 42 (1992): 145–53.

Allen, Christine Garside. "Who Was Rebekah? 'On Me Be the Curse, My Son.'" In *Beyond Androcentrism: New Essays on Women and Religion*, ed. Rita M. Gross, 183–216. Missoula, Mont.: Scholars Press, 1977.

Alter, Robert. *The Art of Biblical Narrative*. New York: Basic Books, 1981.

Anderson, Hugh. "4 Maccabees (First Century A.D.)." In *The Old Testament Pseudepigrapha*, ed. James H. Charlesworth, 2: 531-64. Garden City, N.Y.: Doubleday, 1985.

———. "Third Maccabees." *ABD* 4: 450–52.

———. "3 Maccabees (First Century B.C.)." In *The Old Testament Pseudepigrapha*, ed. James H. Charlesworth, 2:509–29. Garden City, N.Y.: Doubleday, 1985.

Anderson, Janice Capel. "Mapping Feminist Biblical Criticism: The American Scene, 1983–1990." In *Critical Review of Books in Religion: 1991*, ed. Eldon Jay Epp, 21–44. Atlanta: Scholars Press, 1991.

Anderson, Robert T. "Samaritans." *ABD* 5: 940–47.

Andreasen, Niels-Erik. "The Role of the Queen Mother in Israelite Society." *CBQ* 45 (1983): 179–94.

Archer, Léonie J. "The Role of Jewish Women in the Religion, Ritual, and Cult of Graeco-Roman Palestine." In *Images of Women in Antiquity*, rev. ed., ed. Averil Cameron and Amélie Kuhrt, 273–87. Detroit: Wayne State University Press, 1993.

Ashby, Godfrey. "The Bloody Bridegroom: The Interpretation of Exodus 4:24–26." *Expository Times* 106 (1995): 203–5.

Avalos, Hector. *Illness and Health Care in the Ancient Near East: The Role of the Temple in Greece, Mesopotamia, and Israel*. Atlanta: Scholars Press, 1995.

Avigad, Nahman. *Bullae and Seals from a Post-Exilic Judean Archive*. Jerusalem: Hebrew University, Institute of Archaeology, 1976.

———. "The Seal of Jezebel." *IEJ* 14 (1964): 274–76.

Bailey, Randall C. *David in Love and War: The Pursuit of Power in 2 Samuel 10–12*. Sheffield, Eng.: JSOT Press, 1990.

———. "They're Nothing but Incestuous Bastards: The Polemical Use of Sex and Sexuality in Hebrew Canon Narratives." In *Reading from This Place*, ed. Fernando F. Segovia and Mary Ann Tolbert, 121–38. Minneapolis: Fortress Press, 1995.

Bal, Mieke. *Death and Dissymmetry: The Politics of Coherence in the Book of Judges*. Chicago: University of Chicago Press, 1988.

———. *Lethal Love: Feminist Literary Readings of Biblical Love Stories*. Bloomington: Indiana University Press, 1987.

———. *Murder and Difference: Gender, Genre, and Scholarship on Sisera's Death*. Bloomington: Indiana University Press, 1988.

———. "Sexuality, Sin, and Sorrow: The Emergence of the Female Character." In *Lethal Love: Feminist Literary Readings of Biblical Love Stories*, 104–30. Bloomington: Indiana University Press, 1987.

Balch, David L. *Let Wives Be Submissive: The Domestic Code in 1 Peter*. Chico, Calif.: Scholars Press, 1981.

Bar-Efrat, Shimeon. *Narrative Art in the Bible*. Sheffield, Eng.: Almond Press, 1989.

Barker, Margaret. "The Evil in Zechariah." *Heythrop Journal* 19 (1978): 12–27.

Bartchy, S. Scott. "Philemon, Epistle to." *ABD* 5: 305–10.

———. "Slavery (Greco-Roman)." *ABD* 6:65–73.

Bass, Dorothy C. "Women's Studies and Biblical Studies: An Historical Perspective." *JSOT* 22 (1982): 6–12.

Bassler, Jouette M. *1 Timothy, 2 Timothy, Titus*. Nashville: Abingdon Press, 1996.

Bauer, Angela. *Gender in the Book of Jeremiah: A Feminist Literary Reading.* New York: Peter Lang, 1999.

Bauman, A. "*ḥyl; chîl; chîlah; chalchālāh.*" In *Theological Dictionary of the Old Testament,* ed. G. Johannes Botterweck and Helmer Ringgren, 4: 344–47. Grand Rapids, Mich.: Eerdmans, 1980.

Beattie, D. R. G. "The Book of Ruth as Evidence for Israelite Legal Practice." *VT* 24 (1974): 251–67.

Beavis, Mary Ann. "2 Thessalonians." *STS* 2:263–71.

Bechtel, Lyn M. "A Feminist Reading of Genesis 19.1–11." In *Genesis,* ed. Athalya Brenner, 108–28. A Feminist Companion to the Bible, 2nd ser. Sheffield, Eng.: Sheffield Academic Press, 1998.

———. "What If Dinah Is Not Raped? (Genesis 34)." *JSOT* 62 (June 1994): 19–36.

Beck, David R. "The Narrative Function of Anonymity in Fourth Gospel Characterization." *Semeia* 63 (1993): 143–58.

Bellis, Alice Ogden. *Helpmates, Harlots, and Heroes: Women's Stories in the Hebrew Bible.* Louisville: Westminster/John Knox Press, 1994.

———. "The Story of Eve." In *Helpmates, Harlots, and Heroes: Women's Stories in the Hebrew Bible,* 45–66. Louisville: Westminster/John Knox Press, 1994.

Ben-Barak, Zafrira. "The Status and Right of the *gᵉbîrâ.*" *JBL* 110 (1991): 23–34.

Benjamin, Don C. "Israel's God: Mother and Midwife." *Biblical Theology Bulletin* 19 (1989): 115–20.

Berg, Sandra Beth. *The Book of Esther: Motifs, Themes and Structure.* Missoula, Mont.: Scholars Press, 1979.

Berlin, Adele. "Characterization in Biblical Narrative: David's Wives." *JSOT* 23 (1982): 69–85.

———. *Poetics and Interpretation of Biblical Narrative.* Sheffield, Eng.: Almond Press, 1983. Reprint: Winona Lake, Ind.: Eisenbrauns, 1994.

Berlyn, P. J. "The Great Ladies." *Jewish Bible Quarterly* 24 (1996): 26–35.

Berquist, Jon L. "Controlling Daughters' Bodies in Sirach." In *Parchments of Gender: Deciphering the Bodies of Antiquity,* ed. Maria Wyke, 95–120. Oxford: Clarendon Press, 1998.

Beyer, Klaus. *Die aramäischen Texte vom Toten Meer,* suppl. vol. Göttingen, Germany: Vandenhoeck & Ruprecht, 1994.

Bickerman, Elias J. "The Colophon of the Greek Book of Esther." *JBL* 63 (1944): 339–62.

Biddle, Mark E. "The 'Endangered Ancestress' and Blessing for the Nations." *JBL* 109 (1990): 599–611.

Bird, Phyllis A. "The Harlot as Heroine: Narrative Art and Social Presupposition in Three Old Testament Texts." *Semeia* 46 (1989): 119–39.

———. "Images of Women in the Old Testament." In *The Bible and Liberation: Political and Social Hermeneutics,* ed. Norman K. Gottwald, 252–88. Maryknoll, N.Y.: Orbis Books, 1983.

———. "Male and Female He Created Them: Genesis 1:27b in the Context of the Priestly Account of Genesis." In *Missing Persons and Mistaken Identities: Women and Gender in Ancient Israel,* 123–54. Minneapolis: Fortress Press, 1998.

———. "The Place of Women in the Israelite Cultus." In *Ancient Israelite Religion: Essays in Honor of Frank Moore Cross,* ed. Patrick D. Miller, Jr., Paul D. Hanson, and S. Dean McBride, 397–419. Philadelphia: Fortress Press, 1987.

———. "To Play the Harlot: An Inquiry into an Old Testament Metaphor." In *Gender and Difference in Ancient Israel,* ed. Peggy L. Day, 75–94. Minneapolis: Fortress Press, 1989.

———. "Translating Sexist Language as a Theological and Cultural Problem." *USQR* 42 (1988): 89–95.

Bledstein, Adrien Janis. "The Trials of Sarah." *Judaism* 30 (Fall 1981): 411–17.

———. "Was *Habbiryâ* a Healing Ritual Performed by a Woman in King David's House?" *BR* 37 (1992): 15–31.

Bloch, Ariel, and Chana Bloch. *The Song of Songs: A New Translation with an Introduction and Commentary.* New York: Random House, 1995.

Bloch-Smith, Elizabeth. *Judahite Burial Practices and Beliefs about the Dead.* Sheffield, Eng.: Sheffield Academic Press, 1992.

Bohak, Gideon. *"Joseph and Aseneth" and the Jewish Temple in Heliopolis.* Atlanta: Scholars Press, 1996.

Boling, Robert G., and G. Ernest Wright. *Joshua: A New Translation with Introduction and Commentary*. Garden City, N.Y.: Doubleday, 1982.

Bos, Johanna. "Out of the Shadows: Genesis 38; Judges 4:17–22; Ruth 3." *Semeia* 42 (1988): 37–67.

Bow, Beverly, and George W. E. Nickelsburg. "Patriarchy with a Twist: Men and Women in Tobit." In *"Women Like This": New Perspectives on Jewish Women in the Greco-Roman World*, ed. Amy-Jill Levine, 127–43. Atlanta: Scholars Press, 1991.

Bowen, Nancy. "The Daughters of Your People: Female Prophets in Ezekiel 13:17–23." *JBL* 118 (1999): 417–33.

Bozak, Barbara A. *Life 'Anew': A Literary-Theological Study of Jer. 30–31*. Rome: Editrice Pontificio Istituto Biblico, 1991.

Bradley, Keith R. *Slavery and Society at Rome*. New York: Cambridge University Press, 1994.

———. *Slaves and Masters in the Roman Empire: A Study in Social Control*. New York: Oxford University Press, 1987.

———. "The Social Role of the Nurse in the Roman World." In *Discovering the Roman Family: Studies in Roman Social History*, 13–36. New York: Oxford University Press, 1991.

Brenner, Athalya. "Athaliah." In *The Israelite Woman: Social Role and Literary Type in Biblical Narrative*, 28–31. Sheffield, Eng.: JSOT Press, 1985.

———. "Female Social Behaviour: Two Descriptive Patterns Within the 'Birth of the Hero' Paradigm." *VT* 36 (1986): 257–73.

———. *The Israelite Woman. Social Role and Literary Type in Biblical Narrative*. Sheffield, Eng.: JSOT Press, 1985.

———. "On Incest." In *A Feminist Companion to Exodus to Deuteronomy*, ed. Athalya Brenner, 113–38. Sheffield, Eng.: Sheffield Academic Press, 1994.

———. "On Prophetic Propaganda and the Politics of 'Love': The Case of Jeremiah." In *A Feminist Companion to the Latter Prophets*, ed. Athalya Brenner, 256–74. Sheffield, Eng.: Sheffield Academic Press, 1995.

———. "Some Observations on the Figurations of Woman in Wisdom Literature." In *Of Prophets' Visions and the Wisdom of Sages: Essays in Honour of R. Norman Whybray on His Seventieth Birthday*, ed. Heather A. McKay and David J. A. Clines, 192–208. Sheffield, Eng.: JSOT Press, 1993.

———. "A Triangle and a Rhombus in Narrative Structure: A Proposed Integrative Reading of Judges 4 and 5." *VT* 40 (1990): 129–38.

———, ed. *A Feminist Companion to the Latter Prophets*. Sheffield, Eng.: Sheffield Academic Press, 1995.

———, ed. *A Feminist Companion to Ruth*. Sheffield, Eng.: Sheffield Academic Press, 1993.

Brenner, Athalya, and Carole Fontaine, eds. *A Feminist Companion to Reading the Scriptures: Approaches, Methods, and Strategies*. Sheffield, Eng.: Sheffield Academic Press, 1997.

Brenner, Athalya, and Fokkelien van Dijk-Hemmes. *On Gendering Texts: Female and Male Voices in the Hebrew Bible*. Leiden, Netherlands: E. J. Brill, 1993.

Brettler, Marc Zvi. "Women and Psalms: Toward an Understanding of the Role of Women's Prayer in the Israelite Cult." In *Gender and Law in the Hebrew Bible and the Ancient Near East*, ed. Victor H. Matthews, Bernard M. Levinson, and Tykva Frymer-Kensky, 25–56. Sheffield, Eng.: Sheffield Academic Press, 1998.

Bronner, Leila Leah. *From Eve to Esther: Rabbinic Reconstructions of Biblical Women*. Louisville: Westminster/John Knox Press, 1994.

———. "Gynomorphic Imagery in Exilic Isaiah (40–66)." *Dor le Dor* 12 (1983–84): 71–83.

Brooten, Bernadette J. "'Junia . . . Outstanding among the Apostles' (Romans 16:7)." In *Women Priests: A Catholic Commentary on the Vatican Declaration*, ed. Leonard and Arlene Swidler, 141–44. New York: Paulist Press, 1977.

———. *Love Between Women: Early Christian Responses to Female Homoeroticism*. Chicago: University of Chicago Press, 1996.

Brosius, Maria. *Women in Ancient Persia: 559–331 B.C.* Oxford: Clarendon Press, 1996.

Brown, Raymond E., and Raymond F. Collins. "Canonicity." In *The New Jerome Biblical Commentary*, ed. Raymond E. Brown, Joseph A. Fitzmyer, and Roland E. Murphy, 1034–54. Englewood Cliffs, N.J.: Prentice Hall, 1990.

Brown, Raymond E., Karl P. Donfried, Joseph A. Fitzmyer, and John Reumann, eds. *Mary in the New Testament: A Collaborative Assessment by Protestant and Catholic Scholars.* Philadelphia: Fortress Press, 1978.

Brown-Gutoff, Susan E. "The Voice of Rachel in Jeremiah 31: A Calling to 'Something New.'" *USQR* 45 (1991): 177–90.

Brueggemann, Walter. *Genesis.* Atlanta: John Knox Press, 1982.

Bultmann, Rudolph. *The Johannine Epistles: A Commentary on the Johannine Epistles,* trans. R. Philip O'Hara with Lane McGaughy and Robert Funk. Philadelphia: Fortress Press, 1973.

Burns, Rita J. *Has the Lord Indeed Spoken Only Through Moses?: A Study of the Biblical Portrait of Miriam.* Atlanta: Scholars Press, 1987.

Cady, Susan, Marian Ronan, and Hal Taussig. *Sophia: The Future of Feminist Spirituality.* San Francisco: Harper & Row, 1986.

Camp, Claudia V. "The Female Sage in Ancient Israel and in the Biblical Wisdom Literature." In *The Sage in Israel and the Ancient Near East,* ed. John G. Gammie and Leo G. Perdue, 185–203. Winona Lake, Ind.: Eisenbrauns, 1990.

———. "Female Voice, Written Word: Women and Authority in Hebrew Scripture." In *Embodied Love: Sensuality and Relationship as Feminist Values,* ed. Paula M. Cooey, Sharon A. Farmer, and Mary Ellen Ross, 97–113. San Francisco: Harper and Row, 1987.

———. "Honor and Shame in Ben Sira: Anthropological and Theological Reflections." In *The Book of Ben Sira in Modern Research: Proceedings of the First International Ben Sira Conference,* ed. Pancratius C. Beentjes, 171-88. Berlin: Walter de Gruyter, 1997.

———. "1 and 2 Kings." *WBC,* 96–109.

———. "The Strange Woman of Proverbs: A Study of the Feminization and Divinization of Evil in Biblical Thought." In *Women and Goddess Traditions: In Antiquity and Today,* ed. Karen L. King, 310–29. Minneapolis: Fortress Press, 1997.

———. "Understanding a Patriarchy: Women in

Second Century Jerusalem Through the Eyes of Ben Sira." In *"Women Like This": New Perspectives on Jewish Women in the Greco-Roman World,* ed. Amy-Jill Levine, 1–39. Atlanta: Scholars Press, 1991.

———. "What's So Strange about the Strange Woman?" In *The Bible and the Politics of Exegesis: Essays in Honor of Norman K. Gottwald on His Sixty-Fifth Birthday,* ed. David Jobling, Peggy L. Day, and Gerald T. Sheppard, 17–31. Cleveland: Pilgrim Press, 1991.

———. *Wisdom and the Feminine in the Book of Proverbs.* Decatur, Ga.: Almond Press, 1985.

———. "The Wise Women of 2 Samuel: A Role Model for Women in Early Israel." *CBQ* 43 (1981): 14–29.

Cannon, Katie Geneva, and Elisabeth Schüssler Fiorenza, eds. "Interpretation for Liberation." *Semeia* 47 (1989).

Cantor, Aviva. "The Lilith Question." In *On Being a Jewish Feminist,* 2nd ed., ed. Susannah Heschel, 40–50. New York: Schocken Books, 1995.

Carasik, Michael. "Isolating a Contemporary Issue in the Bible." *Brandeis Review* 13 (1993): 22–27.

Carpenter, Mary Wilson. "Representing Apocalypse: Sexual Politics and the Violence of Revelation." In *Postmodern Apocalypse: Theory and Cultural Practice at the End,* ed. Richard Dellamora, 107–35. Philadelphia: University of Pennsylvania Press, 1995.

Carroll, Robert P. *Jeremiah: A Commentary.* Philadelphia: Westminster Press, 1986.

Carroll, Scott T. "Antiochis." *ABD* 1:269.

———. "Atargatis." *ABD* 1:509.

Cartledge, Tony W. *Vows in the Hebrew Bible and the Ancient Near East.* Sheffield, Eng.: JSOT Press, 1992.

———. "Were Nazirite Vows Unconditional?" *CBQ* 51 (1989): 409–22.

Cartlidge, David R., and David L. Dungan. *Documents for the Study of the Gospels.* Philadelphia: Fortress Press, 1980.

Cassuto, Umberto. *A Commentary on the Book of Genesis,* Part I, trans. Israel Abrahams. Jerusalem: Magnes Press, Hebrew University, 1961.

Castelli, Elizabeth A. "Heteroglossia, Hermeneutics

and History: A Review Essay of Recent Feminist Studies of Early Christianity." *JFSR* 10 (1994): 73–98.

———. "Romans." *STS* 2:272–300.

———, ed. *Reimagining Christian Origins: A Colloquium Honoring Burton L. Mack.* Valley Forge, Pa.: Trinity Press International, 1996.

Cervin, Richard S. "A Note Regarding the Name 'Junia(s)' in Romans 16.7." *NTS* 40 (1994): 464–70.

Charlesworth, James H. "Apocrypha." *ABD* 1:292–94.

———. "Manasseh, Prayer of." *ABD* 4:499–500.

Charlesworth, James H., with James A. Sanders. "Psalm 151." In *The Old Testament Pseudepigrapha*, ed. James H. Charlesworth, 2:612–15. Garden City, N.Y.: Doubleday, 1985.

Chesnutt, Randall D., and Judith Newman. "Prayers in the Apocrypha and Pseudepigrapha." In *Prayer from Alexander to Constantine: A Critical Anthology*, ed. Mark Kiley, 38–42. London: Routledge, 1997.

Chirichigno, Gregory C. *Debt-Slavery in Israel and the Ancient Near East.* Sheffield, Eng.: JSOT Press, 1993.

Clines, David J. A. "The Significance of the 'Sons of God' Episode (Genesis 6:1–4) in the Context of the 'Primeval History.'" *JSOT* 13 (1979): 33–46.

———. "What Does Eve Do to Help? And Other Irredeemably Androcentric Orientations in Genesis 1–3." In *What Does Eve Do to Help? And Other Readerly Questions to the Old Testament*, 25–48. Sheffield, Eng.: JSOT Press, 1990.

Clines, David J. A., and Tamara C. Eskenazi, eds. *Telling Queen Michal's Story: An Experiment in Comparative Interpretation.* Sheffield, Eng.: JSOT Press, 1991.

Cohen, Norman J., "Two That Are One: Sibling Rivalry in Genesis." *Judaism* 32 (1983): 331–42.

Cohen, Shaye J. D. "From the Bible to the Talmud: The Prohibition of Intermarriage." *HAR* 7 (1983): 23–39.

———. "Was Timothy Jewish (Acts 16:1–3)? Patristic Exegesis, Rabbinic Law and Matrilineal Descent." *JBL* 105 (1986): 251–68.

Collins, Adela Yarbro. *The Combat Myth in the Book of Revelation.* Missoula, Mont.: Scholars Press, 1976.

———. *Crisis and Catharsis: The Power of the Apocalypse.* Philadelphia: Westminster Press, 1984.

———, ed. *Feminist Perspectives on Biblical Scholarship.* Chico, Calif.: Scholars Press, 1985.

Collins, John J. *Daniel: A Commentary on the Book of Daniel.* Minneapolis: Fortress Press, 1993.

———. *Jewish Wisdom in the Hellenistic Age.* Louisville: Westminster/John Knox Press, 1997.

———. *The Sibylline Oracles of Egyptian Judaism.* Missoula, Mont.: Scholars Press, 1974.

Corley, Kathleen. "1 Peter." *STS* 2:349–60.

———. *Private Women, Public Meals: Social Conflict in the Synoptic Tradition.* Peabody, Mass.: Hendrickson Publishers, 1993.

———. "Prostitute." In *Dictionary of Jesus and the Gospels*, ed. Joel B. Green and Scot McKnight, 643. Downers Grove, Ill.: InterVarsity Press, 1992.

Countryman, L. William. *Dirt, Greed and Sex: Sexual Ethics in the New Testament and Their Implications for Today.* Philadelphia: Fortress Press, 1988.

Craven, Toni. *Artistry and Faith in the Book of Judith.* Chico, Calif.: Scholars Press, 1983.

———. "The Greek Book of Daniel." *WBC*, expanded ed., 311–15.

———. "Judith." In *The New Jerome Biblical Commentary*, ed. Raymond E. Brown, Joseph A. Fitzmyer, and Roland E. Murphy, 572–75. Englewood Cliffs, N.J.: Prentice Hall, 1990.

———. "Judith Prays for Help (Judith 9:1–14)." In *Prayer from Alexander to Constantine: A Critical Anthology*, ed. Mark Kiley, 59–64. London: Routledge, 1997.

———. "Women Who Lied for the Faith." In *Justice and the Holy: Essays in Honor of Walter Harrelson*, ed. Douglas A. Knight and Peter J. Paris, 35–49. Atlanta: Scholars Press, 1989.

Cross, Frank Moore. *Canaanite Myth and Hebrew Epic: Essays in the History of the Religion of Israel.* Cambridge, Mass.: Harvard University Press, 1973.

———. "A Phoenician Inscription from Idalion: Some Old and New Texts Relating to Child Sacrifice." In *Scripture and Other Artifacts: Essays on the Bible and Archaeology in Honor of Philip J. King*, ed. Michael D. Coogan, J. Cheryl Exum, and Lawrence E. Stager, 93–107. Louisville: Westminister/John Knox Press, 1994.

Crossan, John Dominic. *The Historical Jesus: The Life of a Mediterranean Jewish Peasant.* San Francisco: HarperSanFrancisco, 1991.

———. *Jesus: A Revolutionary Biography.* San Francisco: HarperSanFrancisco, 1994.

Cryer, Frederick H. *Divination in Ancient Israel and Its Near Eastern Environment: A Socio-Historical Investigation.* Sheffield, Eng.: JSOT Press, 1994.

D'Angelo, Mary Rose. "Colossians." *STS* 2:313–24.

———. "Hebrews." *WBC*, 364–67.

———. "Gender Refusers in the Early Christian Mission: Genesis 1:27 in Gal 3:28." In *Interpretation and (Early) Christian Identity: Essays in Honor of Rowan A. Greer,* ed. Charles A. Bobertz and David Brakke. Notre Dame, Ind.: University of Notre Dame Press, forthcoming.

———. "Remarriage and the Divorce Sayings Attributed to Jesus." In *Divorce and Remarriage,* ed. William P. Roberts, 78–106. Kansas City, Mo.: Sheed & Ward, 1990.

———. "(Re)Presentations of Women in the Gospels: John and Mark." In *Women and Christian Origins,* ed. Ross Shepard Kraemer and Mary Rose D'Angelo, 129–49. New York: Oxford University Press, 1999.

———. "(Re)presentations of Women in the Gospels of Matthew and Luke-Acts." In *Women and Christian Origins,* ed. Ross Shepard Kraemer and Mary Rose D'Angelo, 171-95. New York: Oxford University Press, 1999.

———. "Trans-scribing Sexual Politics: Images of the Androgyne in Discourses of Antique Religion." In *Descrizioni e Iscrizioni: Politiche del Discorso,* ed. Carla Locatelli and Giovanna Covi, 1–32. Trento, Italy: Editrice Università degli Studi di Trento, 1998.

———. "Women in Luke-Acts: A Redactional View." *JBL* 109 (1990)3: 441–61.

———. "Women Partners in the New Testament." *JFSR* 6 (1990): 65–86.

Daniels, Jon B. "Clopas." *ABD* 1:1066.

Darr, Katheryn Pfisterer. "Ezekiel." *WBC*, 183–90.

———. *Far More Precious Than Jewels: Perspectives on Biblical Women.* Louisville: Westminster/John Knox Press, 1991.

Davies, Eryl W. "Inheritance Rights and the Hebrew Levirate Marriage." *VT* 31 (1981): 138–44.

Davies, Graham I. "Hosea's Marriage." In *Hosea,* 79–92. Sheffield, Eng.: JSOT Press, 1993.

Davies, W. D. *The Setting of the Sermon on the Mount.* Cambridge: Cambridge University Press, 1964.

Day, John. "Asherah in the Hebrew Bible and Northwest Semitic Literature." *JBL* 105 (1986): 385–408.

———. "Ashtoreth." *ABD* 1:491–94.

Day, Peggy L. "From the Child Is Born the Woman: The Story of Jephthah's Daughter." In *Gender and Difference in Ancient Israel,* ed. Peggy L. Day, 58–74. Minneapolis: Fortress Press, 1989.

Deming, Will. *Paul on Marriage and Celibacy: The Hellenistic Background of 1 Corinthians 7.* New York: Cambridge University Press, 1995.

Deutsch, Celia M. *Lady Wisdom, Jesus and the Sages: Metaphor and Social Context in Matthew's Gospel.* Valley Forge, Pa.: Trinity Press International, 1996.

de Vaux, Roland. *Ancient Israel: Its Life and Institutions,* trans. John McHugh. New York: McGraw Hill, 1961.

———. "The Name." In *Ancient Israel: Its Life and Institutions,* trans. John McHugh, 43–46. New York: McGraw Hill, 1961.

Dewey, Joanna. "The Gospel of Mark." *STS* 2:470–509.

———. "1 Timothy." *WBC*, 353–58.

Di Lella, Alexander A. "Women in the Wisdom of Ben Sira and the Book of Judith: A Study in Contrasts and Reversals." In *Congress Volume: Paris 1962,* ed. John A. Emerton, 39–52. Leiden, Netherlands: E. J. Brill, 1991.

Dillard, Raymond B. *2 Chronicles.* Waco, Tex.: Word Books, 1987.

Dobbs-Allsopp, F. W. "The Syntagma of *bat* Followed by a Geographical Name in the Hebrew Bible: A Reconsideration of Its Meaning and Grammar." *CBQ* 57 (1995): 451–70.

Doran, Robert. "1 Maccabees." In *The New Interpreter's Bible*, ed. Leander E. Keck, 4:1–178. Nashville: Abingdon Press, 1996.

———. "2 Maccabees." In *The New Interpreter's Bible*, ed. Leander E. Keck, 4:179–299. Nashville: Abingdon Press, 1996.

Douglas, Mary. "Couvade and Menstruation: The Relevance of Tribal Studies." In *Implicit Meanings: Essays in Anthropology*, ed. Mary Douglas, 60–72. London: Routledge & Kegan Paul, 1975.

———. *Purity and Danger: An Analysis of Concepts of Pollution and Taboo*. London: Routledge & Kegan Paul, 1966. Reprint, 1988.

Driver, Godfrey Rolles. "Hebrew Mothers." *ZAW* 67 (1955): 246–48.

Driver, Godfrey Rolles, and John C. Miles. *The Babylonian Laws*, 2 vols. Oxford: Clarendon Press, 1952, 1955.

Duling, D. C. "Testament of Solomon." In *The Old Testament Pseudepigrapha*, ed. James H. Charlesworth, 1:935–87. Garden City, N.Y.: Doubleday, 1983.

Edelman, Diana Vikander. *King Saul in the Historiography of Judah*. Sheffield, Eng.: JSOT Press, 1991.

Eichler, Barry L. "On Reading Genesis 12:10–20." In *Tehillah Le-Moshe: Biblical and Judaic Studies in Honor of Moshe Greenberg*, 23–38. Winona Lake, Ind.: Eisenbrauns, 1997.

Eisenbaum, Pamela M. "Sirach." *WBC*, expanded ed., 298–304.

Elgood, Percival George. *The Ptolemies of Egypt*. Bristol, Eng.: Arrowsmith, 1938.

Elliott, John H. *A Home for the Homeless: A Sociological Exegesis of 1 Peter, Its Situation and Strategy*. Philadelphia: Fortress Press, 1981.

Emmet, C. W. "The Third Book of Maccabees." In *The Apocrypha and Pseudepigrapha of the Old Testament* ed. R. H. Charles, 1:155–73. Oxford: Clarendon Press, 1913.

Eskenazi, Tamara Cohn. "Ezra-Nehemiah." *WBC*, 116–23.

———. *In an Age of Prose: A Literary Approach to Ezra-Nehemiah*. Atlanta: Scholars Press, 1988.

———. "Out of the Shadows: Biblical Women in the Postexilic Era." *JSOT* 54 (1992): 25–43.

Eslinger, Lyle. "A Contextual Identification of the bene ha'elohim and benoth ha'adam in Genesis 6:1–4." *JSOT* 13 (1979): 65–73.

Exum, J. Cheryl. *Fragmented Women: Feminist (Sub)versions of Biblical Narratives*. Sheffield, Eng.: JSOT Press, 1993.

———. "Mother in Israel: A Familiar Story Reconsidered." In *Feminist Interpretation of the Bible*, ed. Letty M. Russell, 73–85. Philadelphia: Westminster Press, 1985.

———. "Murder They Wrote." In *Fragmented Women: Feminist (Sub)versions of Biblical Narratives*, 16–41. Valley Forge, Pa.: Trinity Press International, 1993.

———. *Plotted, Shot, and Painted: Cultural Representations of Biblical Women*. Sheffield, Eng.: Sheffield Academic Press, 1996.

———. "Second Thoughts about Secondary Characters: Women in Exodus 1.8–2.10." In *A Feminist Companion to Exodus to Deuteronomy*, ed. Athalya Brenner, 75–87. Sheffield, Eng.: Sheffield Academic Press, 1994.

———. *Tragedy and Biblical Narrative: Arrows of the Almighty*. Cambridge: Cambridge University Press, 1992.

———. "Who's Afraid of 'The Endangered Ancestress'?" In *The New Literary Criticism and the Hebrew Bible*, ed. J. Cheryl Exum and David J. A. Clines, 91–113. Sheffield, Eng.: JSOT Press, 1993.

———. "'You Shall Let Every Daughter Live': A Study of Exodus 1:8–2:10." *Semeia* 28 (1993): 63–82.

Fatum, Lone. "Image of God and Glory of Man: Women in the Pauline Congregations." In *The Image of God: Gender Models in Judaeo-Christian Traditions*, ed. Kari Elisabeth Borresen, 50–133. Minneapolis: Fortress Press, 1995.

Faulkner, Raymond O. "The Maxims of Ptahhotpe." In *The Literature of Ancient Egypt: An Anthology of Stories, Instructions and Poetry*, ed. William Kelly Simpson, 159–76. New Haven: Yale University Press, 1972.

Fee, Gordon D. *The First Epistle to the Corinthians*. Grand Rapids, Mich.: Eerdmans, 1987.

———. "Judges." *WBC*, 67–77.

Fewell, Danna Nolan. "Deconstructive Criticism:

Achsah and the (E)razed City of Writing." In *Judges and Method: New Approaches in Biblical Studies*, ed. Gale A. Yee, 119–45. Minneapolis: Fortress Press, 1995.

———. "Joshua." *WBC*, 69–72.

———. "Judges." *WBC*, 73–83.

Fewell, Danna Nolan, and David M. Gunn. *Gender, Power, and Promise: The Subject of the Bible's First Story*. Nashville: Abingdon Press, 1993.

Fischer, Thomas. "Maccabees, Books of." *ABD* 4:439–50, trans. Frederick Cryer.

Fishbane, Michael. "Accusations of Adultery: A Study of Law and Scribal Practice in Numbers 5:11–31." *Hebrew Union College Annual* 45 (1974): 25–45.

Fitzgerald, Aloysius. "*BTWLT* and *BT* as Titles for Capital Cities." *CBQ* 37 (1975): 167–83.

Fitzmyer, Joseph. "Acts of the Apostles." In *The Jerome Biblical Commentary*, ed. Raymond E. Brown, Joseph A. Fitzmyer, and Roland E. Murphy, 2:165–214. Englewood Cliffs, N.J.: Prentice Hall, 1968.

———. *Romans: A New Translation with Introduction and Commentary*. New York: Doubleday, 1993.

Follis, Elaine R. "The Holy City as Daughter." In *Directions in Biblical Poetry*, 173–84. Sheffield, Eng.: JSOT Press, 1987.

Fontaine, Carole R. "Ecclesiastes." *WBC*, 153–55.

———. "More Queenly Proverb Performance: The Queen of Sheba in the Targum Esther Sheni." In *Wisdom, You Are My Sister: Studies in Honor of Roland E. Murphy, O. Carm., on the Occasion of His Eightieth Birthday*, ed. Michael L. Barré, 216–33. Washington, D. C.: Catholic Biblical Association of America, 1997.

———. "Proverbs." In *Harper's Bible Commentary*, ed. James L. Mays, 495–517. San Francisco: Harper & Row, 1988.

———. "Proverbs." *WBC*, 145–52.

———. "The Sage in Family and Tribe." In *The Sage in Israel and the Ancient Near East*, ed. John G. Gammie and Leo G. Perdue, 155–64. Winona Lake, Ind.: Eisenbrauns, 1990.

———. "The Social Roles of Women in the World of Wisdom." In *A Feminist Companion to Wisdom Literature*, ed. Athalya Brenner, 24–49. Sheffield, Eng.: Sheffield Academic Press, 1995.

Forster, Brenda. "The Biblical *'omēn* and Evidence for the Nurturance of Children by Hebrew Males." *Judaism* 42 (1993):321–31.

Fowler, Jeaneane D. *Theophoric Personal Names in Ancient Hebrew: A Comparative Study*. Sheffield, Eng.: JSOT Press, 1988.

Fox, Michael V. *Character and Ideology in the Book of Esther*. Columbia: University of South Carolina Press, 1991.

———. *The Song of Songs and the Ancient Egyptian Love Songs*. Madison: University of Wisconsin Press, 1985.

Freedman, R. David. "Woman, a Power Equal to Man: Translation of Woman as a 'Fit Helpmate' for Man Is Questioned." *BARev* 9 (1983): 56–58.

Freund, Richard A. "Naming Names: Some Observations on 'Nameless Women' Traditions in the MT, LXX and Hellenistic Literature." *Scandinavian Journal of the Old Testament* 6 (1992): 213–32.

Frick, Frank S. *The City in Ancient Israel*. Missoula, Mont.: Scholars Press, 1977.

———. "Widows in The Hebrew Bible: A Transactional Approach." In *A Feminist Companion to Exodus to Deuteronomy*, ed. Athalya Brenner, 139–51. Sheffield, Eng.: Sheffield Academic Press 1994.

Friedman, Mordechai. "Tamar, a Symbol of Life: The 'Killer Wife' Superstition in the Bible and Jewish Tradition." *AJS Review* 15 (1990): 23–61.

Frymer-Kensky, Tikva. "Deuteronomy." *WBC*, 52–62.

———. *In the Wake of the Goddesses: Women, Culture, and the Biblical Transformation of Pagan Myth*. New York: Free Press, 1992.

———. *Motherprayer: The Pregnant Woman's Spiritual Companion*. New York: Riverhead Books, 1996.

———. "Patriarchal Family Relationships and Near Eastern Law." *BA* 44 (1981): 209–14.

——— "Reading Rahab." In *Tehillah Lemoshe: Biblical and Judaic Studies in Honor of Moshe Greenberg*, ed. Mordechai Cogan, Barry Eichler, and Jeffrey Tigay, 57–72. Winona Lake, Ind.: Eisenbrauns, 1997.

———. "Sarah and Hagar." In *Talking about Gene-*

sis: A Resource Guide, 94–97. New York: Main Street Books/Doubleday, 1996.

———. "Sex and Sexuality." *ABD* 5:1144–46.

———. "The Strange Case of the Suspected Sota (Numbers 5:11–31)." *VT* 34 (1984): 11–26.

———. *Victors, Victims, Virgins, and Voice: Rereading the Women of the Bible*. New York: Schocken Books, forthcoming.

———. "Virginity in the Bible." In *Gender and Law in the Hebrew Bible and the Ancient Near East*, ed. Victor H. Matthews, Bernard M. Levinson, and Tikva Frymer-Kensky, 79–96. Sheffield, Eng.: Sheffield Academic Press, 1998.

Fuchs, Esther. "The Literary Characterization of Mothers and Sexual Politics in the Hebrew Bible." In *Feminist Perspectives on Biblical Scholarship*, ed. Adela Yarbro Collins, 117–36. Chico, Calif.: Scholars Press, 1985.

Fulco, William J. "Ashima." *ABD* 1:487.

Furnish, Victor Paul. *II Corinthians: A New Translation with Introduction and Commentary*. Garden City, N.Y.: Doubleday, 1984.

Gardner, Jane F. *Women in Roman Law and Society*. Bloomington: University of Indiana Press, 1986.

Garrett, Susan R. "Revelation." *WBC*, 377–82.

Gaventa, Beverly Roberts. *Mary: Glimpses of the Mother of Jesus*. Columbia: University of South Carolina Press, 1995.

Ghalioungui, Paul. *The House of Life: Per Ankh: Magic and Medical Science in Ancient Egypt*, 2nd ed. Amsterdam: B. M. Israel, 1973.

Gillman, Florence Morgan, "Apphia." *ABD* 1:317–18.

———. "Chloe." *ABD* 1:911.

———. "Euodia." *ABD* 2:670–71.

———. "Syntyche." *ABD* 6:270.

Ginsberg, H. L. "The Quintessence of Koheleth." In *Biblical and Other Studies*, ed. Alexander Altmann, 47–59. Cambridge, Mass.: Harvard University Press, 1963.

Ginzberg, Louis. *The Legends of the Jews*. 7 vols. Philadelphia: Jewish Publication Society, 1908–1938.

Glancy, Jennifer A. "The Accused: Susanna and Her Readers." *JSOT* 58 (1993): 103–16.

———. "The Mistress-Slave Dialectic: Paradoxes of

Slavery in Three LXX Narratives." *JSOT* 72 (1996): 71–87.

———. "Obstacles to Slaves' Participation in the Corinthian Church." *JBL* 117 (1998): 481–501.

Glazier-McDonald, Beth. "Obadiah." *WBC*, 210–11.

Goitein, S. D. "Women as Creators of Biblical Genres." *Prooftexts* 8 (1988): 1–33.

Goldstein, Jonathan A. *I Maccabees: A New Translation with Introduction and Commentary*. Garden City, N.Y.: Doubleday, 1976.

———. *II Maccabees: A New Translation with Introduction and Commentary*. Garden City, N.Y.: Doubleday, 1983.

Goodfriend, Elaine Adler. "Adultery." *ABD* 1:82–86.

———. "Prostitution (Old Testament)." *ABD* 5:505–10.

Goodman, William R. "Esdras, First Book of." *ABD* 2:609–11.

———. "A Study of I Esdras 3:1–5:6." Duke University, Ph.D. dissertation, 1972.

Goody, Jack. *Cooking, Cuisine, and Class: A Study in Comparative Sociology*. Cambridge: Cambridge University Press, 1982.

Gordon, Pamela, and Harold Washington. "Rape as a Military Metaphor in the Hebrew Bible." In *A Feminist Companion to the Latter Prophets*, ed. Athalya Brenner, 308–25. Sheffield, Eng.: Sheffield Academic Press, 1995.

Gossai, Hemchand. *Power and Marginality in the Abraham Narrative*. Lanham, Md.: University Press of America, 1995.

Gottwald, Norman K. "Immanuel as the Prophet's Son." *VT* 8 (1958): 36–47.

Graef, Hilda C. *Mary: A History of Doctrine and Devotion*. Westminster, Md.: Christian Classics, 1985.

Graham, M. Patrick. "A Connection Proposed Between 2 Chr 24:26 and Ezra 9–10." *ZAW* 97 (1985): 256–58.

———. "Mahlah." *ABD* 4:475–76.

Gray, George Buchanan. *Studies in Hebrew Proper Names*. London: Adam and Charles Black, 1896.

Gray, John. *I & II Kings: A Commentary*, 3rd ed. London: SCM, 1977.

Green, Alberto R. W. *The Role of Human Sacrifice in*

the Ancient Near East. Missoula, Mont.: Scholars Press, 1975.

Greenberg, Moshe. "Another Look at Rachel's Theft of the Teraphim." *JBL* 81 (1962): 239–48.

———. "Job." In *The Literary Guide to the Bible*, ed. Robert Alter and Frank Kermode, 283–304. Cambridge, Mass.: Belknap Press of Harvard University Press, 1987.

———. "Some Postulates of Biblical Criminal Law." In *Yehezkel Kaufmann Jubilee Volume: Studies in Bible and Jewish Religion: Dedicated to Yehezkel Kaufmann on the Occasion of His Seventieth Birthday*, ed. Menaham Haran, 5–28. Jerusalem: Magnes Press, Hebrew University, 1960.

Greenstein, Edward L. "The Riddle of Samson." *Prooftexts* 1 (1981): 237–60.

Griffith, Frederick. "Home Before Lunch: The Emancipated Women in Theocritus." In *Reflections of Women in Antiquity*, ed. Helen P. Foley, 247–73. New York: Gordon and Breach, 1986.

Gritz, Sharon Hodgin. *Paul, Women Teachers, and the Mother Goddess at Ephesus: A Study of 1 Timothy 2:9–15 in Light of the Religious and Cultural Milieu of the First Century*. Lanham, Md.: University Press of America, 1991.

Gruber, Mayer I. "Breast-Feeding Practices in Biblical Israel and in Old Babylonian Mesopotamia." In *The Motherhood of God and Other Studies*, 69–107. Atlanta: Scholars Press, 1992.

———. "The Motherhood of God in Second Isaiah." *Revue Biblique* 90 (1983): 351–59.

———. "Women in the Cult According to the Priestly Code." In *The Motherhood of God and Other Studies*, 49–68. Atlanta: Scholars Press, 1992.

Gunn, David M. *The Story of King David: Genre and Interpretation*. Sheffield, Eng.: Department of Biblical Studies, University of Sheffield, 1978.

Hackett, Jo Ann. "In the Days of Jael: Reclaiming the History of Women in Ancient Israel." In *Immaculate and Powerful: The Female in Sacred Image and Social Reality*, ed. Clarissa Atkinson, Constance H. Buchanan, and Margaret R. Miles, 15–38. Boston: Beacon Press, 1985.

———. "1 and 2 Samuel," *WBC*, 85–95.

———. "Women's Studies and the Hebrew Bible." In *The Future of Biblical Studies: The Hebrew Scriptures*, ed. Richard Elliott Friedman and H. G. M. Williamson, 141–64. Atlanta: Scholars Press, 1987.

Hamilton, Victor P. "Marriage: Old Testament and Ancient Near East." *ABD* 4:559–69.

Handy, Lowell K. "The Role of Huldah in Josiah's Cult Reform." *ZAW* 106 (1994): 40–53.

Haran, Menahem. "The Non-Priestly Image of the Tent of *MÔ'ÊD*." In *Temples and Temple-Service in Ancient Israel: An Inquiry into the Character of Cult Phenomena and the Historical Setting of the Priestly School*, 260–75. Oxford: Clarendon Press, 1978.

Harrington, Daniel J. "Introduction to the Canon." In *The New Interpreter's Bible* 1: 7–21. Nashville: Abingdon Press, 1994.

Haskins, Susan. *Mary Magdalen: Myth and Metaphor*. New York: Harcourt Brace, 1993.

Hayes, John H. *Amos, The Eighth-Century Prophet: His Times and His Preaching*. Nashville: Abingdon Press, 1988.

Hayes, Richard B. *Echoes of Scripture in the Letters of Paul*. New Haven: Yale University Press, 1989.

Heider, George C. "Molech." *ABD* 4:895–98.

Hendel, Ronald S. "Of Demigods and the Deluge: Toward an Interpretation of Genesis 6:1–4." *JBL* 106 (1987): 13–26.

Henshaw, Richard A. *Female and Male: The Cultic Personnel: The Bible and the Rest of the Ancient Near East*. Allison Park, Pa.: Pickwick Publications, 1994.

Hess, Richard S. "Getting Personal: What Names in the Bible Teach Us." *BibRev* 13 (1997): 31–37.

Hestrin, Ruth. "The Lachish Ewer and the 'Asherah," *IEJ* 37 (1987): 212–23.

———. "Understanding Asherah: Exploring Semitic Iconography." *BARev* 17 (1991): 50–59.

Hiebert, Paula S. "'Whence Shall Help Come to Me?' The Biblical Widow." In *Gender and Difference in Ancient Israel*, ed. Peggy L. Day, 125–41. Minneapolis: Fortress Press, 1989.

Hillers, Delbert R. *Lamentations: A New Translation*

with Introduction and Commentary. Garden City, N.Y.: Doubleday, 1972.

Holladay, William L. *Jeremiah 1: A Commentary on the Book of the Prophet Jeremiah, Chapters 1–25.* Philadelphia: Fortress Press, 1986.

———. *Jeremiah 2: A Commentary on the Book of the Prophet Jeremiah, Chapters 26–52.* Philadelphia: Fortress Press, 1989.

Hollis, Susan Tower. *The Ancient Egyptian "Tale of Two Brothers": The Oldest Fairy Tale in the World.* Norman: University of Oklahoma Press, 1990.

———. "The Woman in Ancient Examples of the Potiphar's Wife Motif, K2111." In *Gender and Difference in Ancient Israel,* ed. Peggy L. Day, 28–42. Minneapolis: Fortress Press, 1989.

Hopkins, Denise Dombkowski. "Judith." *WBC,* expanded ed., 279–85.

Horsley, G. H. R. "Names, Double." *ABD* 4: 1011–17.

Hostetter, Edwin C. "Puti-el." *ABD* 5:561.

Houlden, J. Leslie. *The Pastoral Epistles: I and II Timothy.* Philadelphia: Trinity Press International, 1989.

Hudson, Don Michael. "Living in a Land of Epithets: Anonymity in Judges 19–21." *JSOT* 62 (1994): 49–66.

Hutter, M. "Lilith." In *Dictionary of Deities and Demons in the Bible,* ed. Karel van der Toorn, Bob Becking, and Pieter W. van der Horst, 973–76. Leiden, Netherlands: E. J. Brill, 1995.

Ilan, Tal. *Jewish Women in Greco-Roman Palestine: An Inquiry into Image and Status.* Peabody, Mass.: Hendrickson, 1996.

———. "Notes and Observations on a Newly Published Divorce Bill from the Judaean Desert." *HTR* 89 (1996): 195–202.

Jackson, Bernards. "Reflections on Biblical Criminal Law." *JJS* 24 (1973): 8–38.

Jacobsen, Thorkild. *Toward the Image of Tammuz and Other Essays on Mesopotamian History and Culture.* Cambridge, Mass.: Harvard University Press, 1970.

Jagendorf, Zvi. "'In the Morning, Behold, It was Leah': Genesis and the Reversal of Sexual Knowledge." *Prooftexts* 4 (1984): 187–92.

Japhet, Sara. *I & II Chronicles: A Commentary.* Louisville: Westminster/John Knox Press, 1993.

Jewett, Robert. "Paul, Phoebe, and the Spanish Mission." In *The Social World of Formative Christianity and Judaism: Essays in Tribute to Howard Clark Kee,* ed. Jacob Neusner, Peder Borgen, Ernest S. Frerichs, and Richard Horsley, 142–61. Philadelphia: Fortress Press, 1988.

Johnson, E. Elizabeth. "2 Esdras." *WBC,* expanded ed., 267–71.

Johnson, Luke Timothy. *The Literary Function of Possessions in Luke-Acts.* Missoula, Mont.: Scholars Press, 1977.

Justi, Ferdinand. *Iranisches Namenbuch.* Hildesheim: Georg Olms Verlagsbuchhandlung, 1963.

Kahn, Jack H. *Job's Illness: Loss, Grief and Integration: A Psychological Interpretation.* Oxford: Pergamon Press, 1975.

Kaiser, Barbara Bakke. "Poet as 'Female Impersonator': The Image of Daughter Zion as Speaker in Biblical Poems of Suffering." *Journal of Religion* 67 (1987): 164–82.

Kaiser, Otto. *Isaiah 13–39: A Commentary.* Philadelphia: Westminster Press, 1974.

Kasher, Aryeh. *The Jews in Hellenistic and Roman Egypt: The Struggle for Equal Rights.* Tübingen, Germany: J. C. B. Mohr, 1985.

Kates, Judith A., and Gail Twersky Reimer, eds. *Reading Ruth: Contemporary Jewish Women Reclaim a Sacred Story.* New York: Ballantine, 1994.

Katzenstein, H. Jacob. "Who Were the Parents of Athaliah?" *IEJ* 5 (1955): 194–97.

Keck, Brian E. "Raphia." *ABD* 5:622.

Keefe, Alice A. "The Female Body, the Body Politic, and the Land: A Sociopolitical Reading of Hosea 1–2." In *A Feminist Companion to the Latter Prophets,* ed. Athalya Brenner, 70–100. Sheffield, Eng.: Sheffield Academic Press, 1995.

———. "Rapes of Women/Wars of Men." *Semeia* 61 (1993): 79–97.

Kelber, Werner H. *The Oral and the Written Gospel: The Hermeneutics of Speaking and Writing in the Synoptic Tradition, Mark, Paul, and Q.* Philadelphia: Fortress Press, 1983.

Kitchen, Kenneth A. *The Third Intermediate Period*

in Egypt (1100–650 B.C.*).* Warminster, Eng.: Aris & Phillips, 1973.

Kittredge, Cynthia Briggs. "Hebrews." STS 2:428–52.

Klein, Jacob. "The Bane of Humanity: A Lifespan of One Hundred and Twenty Years." *Acta Sumerologica* 12 (1990): 57–70.

Klein, Lillian R. "Hannah: Marginalized Victim and Social Redeemer." In *A Feminist Companion to Samuel and Kings,* ed. Athalya Brenner, 77–92. Sheffield, Eng.: Sheffield Academic Press, 1994.

Klein, Ralph W. "1 Esdras." In *The Books of the Bible,* ed. Bernhard W. Anderson, 2:13–19. New York: Charles Scribner's Sons, 1989.

Kloppenberg, John S. "Isis and Sophia in the Book of Wisdom." *HTR* 75 (1982): 57–84.

Kokkinos, Nikos. *The Herodian Dynasty: Origins, Role in Society and Eclipse.* Sheffield, Eng.: Sheffield Academic Press, 1998.

———. "Which Salome Did Aristobulus Marry?" *PEQ* 118 (1986): 33–50.

Kraemer, Ross Shepard. "The Book of Aseneth." STS 2: 859–88.

———. *Her Share of the Blessings: Women's Religions among Pagans, Jews, and Christians in the Greco-Roman World.* New York: Oxford University Press, 1992.

———. "Jewish Women in the Diaspora World of Late Antiquity." In *Jewish Women in Historical Perspective,* ed. Judith R. Baskin, 2nd ed., 46–72. Detroit: Wayne State University Press, 1998.

———. *When Aseneth Met Joseph: A Late Antique Tale of the Biblical Patriarch and His Egyptian Wife.* New York: Oxford University Press, 1998.

———. "Women's Devotion to Adonis." In *Her Share of the Blessings,* 30-35. New York: Oxford University Press, 1992.

Kroeger, Catherine C., and Richard Kroeger. *I Suffer Not a Woman: Rethinking First Timothy 2:11–15 in Light of Ancient Evidence.* Grand Rapids, Mich.: Baker Book House, 1992.

Kvam, Kristen E., Linda S. Schearing, and Valarie H. Ziegler, eds. *Eve and Adam: Jewish, Christian, and Muslim Readings on Genesis and Gender.* Bloomington: Indiana University Press, 1999.

Kysar, Robert. "John, Epistles of." *ABD* 3:900–912.

La Cocque, André. "Ruth." In *The Feminine Unconventional: Four Subversive Figures in Biblical Tradition* 84–116. Minneapolis: Fortress Press, 1990.

Lampe, Peter. "'Family' in Church and Society of New Testament Times." *Affirmation* 5 (1992): 1–20.

———. "Prisca." *ABD* 5:467–68.

———. "Tryphaena and Tryphosa." *ABD* 6:669.

Lasine, Stuart. "Jehoram and the Cannibal Mothers (2 Kings 6.24–33): Solomon's Judgment in an Inverted World." *JSOT* 50 (1991): 27–53.

———. "The Riddle of Solomon's Judgment and the Riddle of Human Nature in the Hebrew Bible." *JSOT* 45 (1989): 61–86.

———. "Solomon, Daniel, and the Detective Story: The Social Functions of a Literary Genre." *HAR* 11 (1987): 247–66.

Lassner, Jacob. *Demonizing the Queen of Sheba: Boundaries of Gender and Culture in Postbiblical Judaism and Medieval Islam.* Chicago: University of Chicago Press, 1993.

Layton, Scott C. "Remarks on the Canaanite Origin of Eve." *CBQ* 59 (1997): 22–32.

Lefkowitz, Mary R. "Influential Women." In *Images of Women in Antiquity,* ed. Averil Cameron and Amélie Kuhrt, 49–64. Detroit: Wayne State University Press, 1983.

Levenson, Jon D. *Esther: A Commentary.* Louisville: Westminster/John Knox Press, 1997.

———. "1 Samuel 25 as Literature and History." *CBQ* 40 (1978): 11–28.

Levenson, Jon D., and Baruch Halpern. "The Political Import of David's Marriages." *JBL* 99 (1980): 507–18.

Levine, Amy-Jill. "Discharging Responsibility: Matthean Jesus, Biblical Law, and Hemorrhaging Women." In *Treasures New and Old: New Essays in Matthean Studies,* ed. Mark Allan Powell and David Bauer, 379–97. Atlanta: Scholars Press, 1996.

———. "'Hemmed in on Every Side': Jews and Women in the Book of Susanna." In *Reading from This Place.* Vol. 1: *Social Location and Biblical Interpretation in the United States,* ed. Fernando

F. Segovia and Mary Ann Tolbert, 175–90. Minneapolis: Fortress Press, 1995.

———. "Matthew." *WBC*, 252–62.

———. "Matthew's Advice to a Divided Readership." In *The Gospel of Matthew in Current Study: In Memoriam Wm. G. Thompson*, ed. David Aune. Grand Rapids, Mich.: Eerdmans, 2000.

———. "Ruth." *WBC*, 78–84.

———. "Women in the Q Communit(ies) and Traditions." In *Women and Christian Origins*, ed. Ross Shepard Kraemer and Mary Rose D'Angelo, 150-70. New York: Oxford University Press, 1999.

Levine, Baruch A. *Leviticus-Va-yikra: The Traditional Hebrew Text with the New JPS Translation*. Philadelphia: Jewish Publication Society, 1989.

Levison, Jack. "Is Eve to Blame? A Contextual Analysis of Sirach 25:24." *CBQ* 47 (1985): 617–23.

Lichtheim, Miriam. *Ancient Egyptian Literature: A Book of Readings*. Vol. 1: *The Old and Middle Kingdoms*. Berkeley: University of California Press, 1973.

LiDonnici, Lynn R. "The Images of Artemis Ephesia and Greco-Roman Worship: A Reconsideration." *HTR* 85 (1992): 389–415.

Lieu, Judith. *The Second and Third Epistles of John: History and Background*. Edinburgh: T & T Clark, 1986.

Limberis, Vasiliki. *Divine Heiress: The Virgin Mary and the Creation of Christian Constantinople*. London: Routledge, 1994.

Liverani, Mario. *Prestige and Interest: International Relations in the Near East ca. 1600–1100 B.C.* Padova, Italy: Sargon, 1990.

Ljung, Inger. *Silence or Suppression: Attitudes Towards Women in the Old Testament*. Stockholm, Sweden: Almqvist & Wiksell International, 1989.

Lo, H. C. "Bithiah." *ABD* 1:750.

Locher, C. "*ṭap*." In *Theological Dictionary of the Old Testament*, ed. G. Johannes Botterweck and Helmer Ringgren, 5:347–50. Grand Rapids, Mich.: Eerdmans, 1986.

Long, Burke. "The Shunammite Woman: In the Shadow of the Prophet?" *BibRev* 7 (1991): 12–19, 42.

MacDonald, Dennis Ronald. *The Legend and the Apostle: The Battle for Paul in Story and Canon*. Philadelphia: Westminster Press, 1983.

———. *"There Is No Male and Female": The Fate of a Dominical Saying in Paul and Gnosticism*. Philadelphia: Fortress Press, 1987.

MacDonald, Margaret Y. "Reading Real Women Through the Undisputed Letters of Paul." In *Women and Christian Origins*, ed. Ross Shepard Kraemer and Mary Rose D'Angelo, 199–220. New York: Oxford University Press, 1999.

———. "Rereading Paul: Early Interpreters of Paul on Women and Gender." In *Women and Christian Origins*, ed. Ross Shepard Kraemer and Mary Rose D'Angelo, 236–53. New York: Oxford University Press, 1999.

Macurdy, Grace H. *Hellenistic Queens: A Study of Woman Power in Macedonia, Seleucid Syria, and Ptolemaic Egypt*. Baltimore: Johns Hopkins University Press, 1932.

———. "Julia Berenice." *AJP* 56 (1935): 246–53.

———. "Royal Women in Judea." In *Vassal Queens and Some Contemporary Women in the Roman Empire*, 63–91. Baltimore: Johns Hopkins University Press, 1937.

Maier, Walter A. *ʾAšerah: Extrabiblical Evidence*. Atlanta: Scholars Press, 1986.

Malbon, Elizabeth Struthers. "Fallible Followers: Women and Men in the Gospel of Mark." *Semeia* 28 (1983): 29–48.

———. "Narrative Criticism: How Does the Story Mean?" In *Mark & Method: New Approaches in Biblical Studies*, ed. Janice Capel Anderson and Stephen D. Moore, 23–49. Minneapolis: Fortress Press, 1992.

———. "The Poor Widow in Mark and Her Poor Rich Readers." *CBQ* 53 (1991): 589–604.

Margalit, Baruch. *The Ugaritic Poem of Aqht: Text, Translation, Commentary*. New York: Walter de Gruyter, 1989.

Martin, Clarice J. "The Acts of the Apostles." *STS* 2: 763–99.

Martin, Dale B. *The Corinthian Body*. New Haven: Yale University Press, 1995.

———. "Heterosexism and the Interpretation of

Romans 1:18–32." *Biblical Interpretation* 3 (1995): 332–55.

———. *Slavery as Salvation: The Metaphor of Slavery in Pauline Christianity*. New Haven: Yale University Press, 1990.

Matthews, Shelly. "High-Standing Women and Mission and Conversion: A Rhetorical-Historical Analysis of the Antiquities and Acts." Harvard University, Th.D. dissertation, 1997.

———. "2 Corinthians." *STS* 2:196–217.

Matthews, Victor H., and Don C. Benjamin. *Social World of Ancient Israel 1250–587 BCE*. Peabody, Mass.: Hendrickson, 1993.

McCarter, P. Kyle, Jr. "Aspects of the Religion of the Israelite Monarchy: Biblical and Epigraphic Data." In *Ancient Israelite Religion: Essays in Honor of Frank Moore Cross*, ed. Patrick D. Miller, Jr., Paul D. Hanson, and S. Dean McBride, 137–55. Philadelphia: Fortress Press, 1987.

McFague, Sally. *Metaphorical Theology: Models of God in Religious Language*. Philadelphia: Fortress Press, 1982.

McGinn, Thomas A. *Prostitutes, Sexuality, and the Law in Ancient Rome*. New York: Oxford University Press, 1998.

McKinlay, Judith E. *Gendering Wisdom the Host: Biblical Invitations to Eat and Drink*. Sheffield, Eng.: Sheffield Academic Press, 1996.

Meeks, Wayne A. "The Image of the Androgyne: Some Uses of a Symbol in Earliest Christianity." *History of Religions* 13 (1974): 165–208.

Mendels, Doron. "Baruch." *ABD* 1:618–20.

Metzger, Bruce M. "The Fourth Book of Ezra." In *The Old Testament Pseudepigrapha*, ed. James H. Charlesworth, 1:514–59. Garden City, N.Y.: Doubleday, 1983.

———. "Introduction to the Apocryphal/Deuterocanonical Books." In *The New Oxford Annotated Bible*, ed. Bruce M. Metzger and Roland E. Murphy, iii–xv. New York: Oxford University Press, 1991.

———. "Names for the Nameless in the New Testament: A Study in the Growth of Christian Tradition." In *Kyriakon: Festschrift Johannes Quasten*, ed. Patrick Granfield and Josef A. Jung-

mann, 1:79–99. Münster, Germany: Verlag Aschendorff, 1970.

Meurer, Siegfried, ed. *The Apocrypha in Ecumenical Perspective*. New York: United Bible Societies, 1991.

Meyers, Carol L. *Discovering Eve: Ancient Israelite Women in Context*. New York: Oxford University Press, 1988.

———. "Everyday Life: Women in the Period of the Hebrew Bible." *WBC*, 244–51.

———. "The Family in Early Israel." In *Families in Ancient Israel*, by Leo G. Perdue, Joseph Blenkinsopp, John J. Collins, and Carol Meyers, 1–47. Louisville: Westminster/John Knox Press, 1997.

———. "Gender and God in the Hebrew Bible — Some Reflections." In *"Ihr Völker alle, klatscht in die Hände!" Festschrift für Erhard S. Gerstenberger Zum 65. Geburtstag*, ed. Rainer Kessler et al., 256–68. Münster, Germany: Lit Verlag, 1997.

———. "Guilds and Gatherings: Women's Groups in Ancient Israel." In *Realia Dei: Essays in Archaeology and Biblical Interpretation in Honor of Edward F. Campbell, Jr. at His Retirement*, ed. Prescott H. Williams, Jr., and Theodore Hiebert, 154–84. Atlanta: Scholars Press, 1999.

———. "Hannah and Her Sacrifice: Reclaiming Female Agency." In *A Feminist Companion to Samuel and Kings*, ed. Athalya Brenner, 93–104. Sheffield, Eng.: Sheffield Academic Press, 1994.

———. "The Hannah Narrative in Feminist Perspective." In *Go to the Land I Will Show You: Studies in Honor of Dwight W. Young*, ed. Joseph Coleson and Victor Matthews, 117–26. Winona Lake, Ind.: Eisenbrauns, 1996.

———. "Illness and Health in the Hebrew Bible." In *Thoughts from Our Tradition: Illness and Recovery in Jewish Writings*, ed. David L. Freeman and Judith Z. Abrams, 129–33. Philadelphia: Jewish Publication Society, 1999.

———. "Of Drums and Damsels: Women's Performance in Ancient Israel." *BA* 54 (1991): 16–27.

———. "Mother to Muse: An Archaeomusicological Study of Women's Performance in Ancient Israel." In *Recycling Biblical Figures: NOSTER Conference 1997*, ed. Athalya Brenner and Jan

Willem van Henten. Leiden, Netherlands: Deo, 1998.

———. "Parashat Ḥayyei Sarah (Genesis 23.1–25.18)." In *Learn Torah with . . .: 1994–1995 Torah Annual*. Los Angeles: Alef Design Group, 1996.

———. "Procreation, Production, and Protection: Male-Female Balance in Early Israel." *Journal of the American Academy of Religion* 51 (1983): 569–93.

———. "Returning Home: Ruth 1.8 and the Gendering of the Book of Ruth." In *A Feminist Companion to Ruth*, ed. Athalya Brenner, 85–114. Sheffield, Eng.: Sheffield Academic Press, 1993.

———. "'To Her Mother's House': Considering a Counterpart to the Israelite *Bêt 'āb*." In *The Bible and the Politics of Exegesis: Essays in Honor of Norman K. Gottwald on His Sixty-Fifth Birthday*, ed. David Jobling, Peggy L. Day, and Gerald T. Sheppard, 39–51. Cleveland: Pilgrim Press, 1991.

———. "'Women of the Neighborhood' (Ruth 4.17) — Informal Female Networks in Ancient Israel." In *A Feminist Companion to Ruth and Esther*, ed. Athalya Brenner. A Feminist Companion to the Bible, 2nd ser. Sheffield, Eng.: Sheffield Academic Press, 1999.

Meyers, Carol L., and Eric M. Meyers. "Haggai, Book of." *ABD* 3:20–23.

———. *Haggai, Zechariah 1–8: A New Translation with Introduction and Commentary*. Garden City, N.Y.: Doubleday, 1987.

Meyers, E. M. "The Shelomith Seal and the Judean Restoration, Some Additional Considerations." *Eretz Israel* 18 (1985): 33–38.

Milgrom, Jacob. "Adultery in the Bible and the Ancient Near East." In *Numbers-Ba-midbar: The Traditional Hebrew Text with the New JPS Translation, Excursus 9*, 348–50. Philadelphia: Jewish Publication Society, 1990.

———. "The Case of the Suspected Adulteress, Numbers 5:11–31: Redaction and Meaning." In *The Creation of Sacred Literature*, ed. Richard F. Friedman, 69–75. Berkeley: University of California Press, 1981.

Miller, J. Maxwell. "Moab." *ABD* 4:882–93.

Miller, J. Maxwell, and John H. Hayes. *A History of Ancient Israel and Judah*. Philadelphia: Westminster Press, 1986.

Miller, Patrick D. *They Cried to the Lord: The Form and Theology of Biblical Prayer*. Minneapolis: Fortress Press, 1994.

Milne, Pamela J. "Feminist Interpretations of the Bible: Then and Now." *BibRev* 8 (1992): 38–43, 52–55.

Mitchell, Margaret M. *Paul and the Rhetoric of Reconciliation: An Exegetical Investigation of the Language and Composition of 1 Corinthians*. Louisville: Westminster/John Knox Press, 1993.

———. "Review Essay on A. C. Wire's *The Corinthian Women Prophets*." *Religious Studies Review* 19 (1993): 308–11.

Moltmann-Wendel, Elisabeth. "Mary Magdalene." In *The Women Around Jesus*, trans. John Bowden, 61–90. New York: Crossroad, 1982.

Moore, Carey A. *Daniel, Esther, and Jeremiah: The Additions: A New Translation with Introduction and Commentary*. Garden City, N.Y.: Doubleday, 1977.

———. "Epistle of Jeremiah." In *Daniel, Esther, and Jeremiah: The Additions*, 317–58. Garden City, N.Y.: Doubleday, 1977.

———. *Esther*. Garden City, N.Y.: Doubleday, 1971.

———. "Esther, Additions to." *ABD* 2:626–33.

———. "Esther, Book of." *ABD* 2:633–43.

———. "Jeremiah, Additions to." In *ABD* 3:698–706.

———. *Judith: A New Translation with Introduction and Commentary*. Garden City, N.Y.: Doubleday, 1985.

———. "I Baruch." In *Daniel, Esther, and Jeremiah: The Additions: A New Translation with Introduction and Commentary*, 255–316. Garden City, N.Y.: Doubleday, 1977.

———. "Tobit, Book of." *ABD* 6:585–94.

Morris, Paul, and Deborah Sawyer, eds. *A Walk in the Garden: Biblical, Iconographical and Literary Images of Eden*. Sheffield, Eng.: JSOT Press, 1992.

Mosca, Paul G. "Child Sacrifice in Canaanite and Israelite Religion: A Study in *Mulk* and *mlk*." Harvard University, Th.D dissertation, 1975.

Murphy, Roland Edmund. *Ecclesiastes.* Dallas: Word Books, 1992.

Myers, Jacob M. *I & II Esdras: A New Translation with Introduction and Commentary.* Garden City, N.Y.: Doubleday, 1974.

Newsom, Carol A. "Psalm 151." *WBC,* expanded ed., 335–36.

———. "Women and the Discourse of Patriarchal Wisdom: A Study of Proverbs 1–9." In Gender and Difference in Ancient Israel, ed. Peggy L. Day, 142–60. Minneapolis: Fortress Press, 1989.

Nickelsburg, George W. E. *Jewish Literature Between the Bible and the Mishnah.* Philadelphia: Fortress Press, 1981.

Niditch, Susan. "Eroticism and Death in the Tale of Jael." In *Gender and Difference in Ancient Israel,* ed. Peggy L. Day, 43–57. Minneapolis: Fortress Press 1989.

———. "Genesis." *WBC,* 10–25.

———. *Underdogs and Tricksters: A Prelude to Biblical Folklore.* San Francisco: Harper & Row, 1987.

———. *War in the Hebrew Bible: A Study in the Ethics of Violence.* New York: Oxford University Press, 1993.

———. "The Wronged Woman Righted: An Analysis of Genesis 38." *HTR* 72 (1979): 143–49.

Nolland, John. *Luke.* Vol. 2: *Luke 9:21–18:34.* Dallas: Word Books, 1993.

Noth, Martin. *Die israelitischen Personennamen im Rahmen der gemeinsemitischen Namengebung.* Stuttgart, Germany: W. Kohlhammer, 1928.

Nowell, Irene. "Tobit." In *The New Jerome Biblical Commentary,* ed. Raymond E. Brown, Joseph A. Fitzmyer, and Roland E. Murphy, 568–71. Englewood Cliffs, N.J.: Prentice Hall, 1990.

O'Brien, Julia M. "Judah as Wife and Husband: Deconstructing Gender in Malachi." *JBL* 115 (1996): 241–50.

O'Connor, Kathleen M. "Jeremiah." *WBC,* 169–77.

———. "Lamentations." *WBC,* 178–82.

O'Day, Gail R. "Acts." *WBC,* 305–12.

———. "John." *WBC,* 293–304.

Odelain, O., and R. Séguineau. *Dictionary of Proper Names and Places in the Bible,* preface by Raymond Tournay, trans. Matthew J. O'Connell. Garden City, N.Y.: Doubleday, 1981.

Oden, Robert A. *Studies in Lucian's De Syria dea.* Missoula, Mont.: Scholars Press, 1977.

Olson, Mark J. "Lydia." In *Mercer Dictionary of the Bible,* ed. Watson E. Mills, 531–32. Macon, Ga.: Mercer University Press, 1990.

Olyan, Saul M. *Asherah and the Cult of Yahweh in Israel.* Atlanta: Scholars Press, 1988.

———. "Some Observations Concerning the Identity of the Queen of Heaven." *Ugarit-Forschungen* 19 (1987): 161–74.

Osiek, Carolyn, "Philippians." *STS* 2:237–49.

Oster, Richard E. "The Ephesian Artemis as an Opponent of Early Christianity." *JAC* 19 (1976): 24–44.

———. "Ephesus as a Religious Center under the Principate. I: Paganism Before Constantine." *Aufstieg und Niedergang der römischen Welt,* ed. W. Haase and H. Temporini, ser. 2, vol. 18, no. 3: 1661–1728. Berlin: Walter de Gruyter, 1990.

Otto, Eckart. "False Weights in the Scale of Biblical Justice? Different Views of Women from Patriarchal Hierarchy to Religious Equality in the Book of Deuteronomy." In *Gender and Law in the Hebrew Bible and the Ancient Near East,* ed. Victor H. Matthews, Bernard M. Levinson, and Tikva Frymer-Kensky, 128–46. Sheffield, Eng.: Sheffield Academic Press, 1998.

Overholt, Thomas W. *Cultural Anthropology and the Old Testament.* Minneapolis: Fortress Press, 1996.

Pardes, Ilana. "Beyond Genesis 3: The Politics of Maternal Naming." In *Countertraditions in the Bible: A Feminist Approach,* 39–59, 162–65. Cambridge, Mass.: Harvard University Press, 1992.

———. *Countertraditions in the Bible: A Feminist Approach.* Cambridge, Mass.: Harvard University Press. 1992.

———. "Creation According to Eve." In *Countertraditions in the Bible: A Feminist Approach,* 13–38. Cambridge, Mass.: Harvard University Press, 1992.

Patai, Raphael. *The Hebrew Goddess.* 3rd ed. Detroit: Wayne State University Press, 1978.

———. *Sex and Family in the Bible and the Middle East.* Garden City, N.Y.: Doubleday, 1959.

Paul, Shalom M. *Amos: A Commentary on the Book of Amos.* Minneapolis: Fortress Press, 1991.

———. "Exodus 1:21: 'To Found a Family,' a Biblical and Akkadian Idiom." *Maarav* 8 (1992): 139–42.

Perdue, Leo G., Joseph Blenkinsopp, John J. Collins, and Carol Meyers. *Families in Ancient Israel.* Louisville: Westminster/John Knox Press, 1997.

Pervo, Richard I. *Luke's Story of Paul.* Minneapolis: Fortress Press, 1990.

———. *Profit with Delight: The Literary Genre of the Acts of the Apostles.* Philadelphia: Fortress Press, 1987.

———. "Social and Religious Aspects of the Western Text." In *The Living Text: Essays in Honor of Ernest W. Saunders,* ed. Dennis E. Groh and Robert Jewett, 229–41. Lanham, Md.: University Press of America, 1985.

Petersen, David L. *Zechariah 9–14 and Malachi: A Commentary.* Louisville: Westminster/John Knox Press, 1995.

Petersen, Norman R. *Rediscovering Paul: Philemon and the Sociology of Paul's Narrative World.* Philadelphia: Fortress Press, 1985.

Petter, Gerald J. "Barzillai." *ABD* 1:623.

Phillips, John A. *Eve: The History of an Idea.* San Francisco: Harper & Row, 1984.

Phipps, William E. *Assertive Biblical Women.* Westport, Conn.: Greenwood Press, 1992.

Pietersma, Albert. "Nanea." *ABD* 4:1019–20.

Pike, Dana M. "Names, Hypocoristic." *ABD* 4:1017–18.

———. "Names, Theophoric." *ABD* 4:1018–19.

Pilch, John J. "'Beat His Ribs While He Is Young' (Sirach 30:12): A Window on the Mediterranean World." *Biblical Theology Bulletin* 23 (1993): 101–13.

Pippin, Tina. "'And I Will Strike Her Children Dead': Death and the Deconstruction of Social Location." In *Reading from This Place.* Vol. 1: *Social Location and Biblical Interpretation in the United States,* ed. Fernando F. Segovia and Mary Ann Tolbert, 191–98. Minneapolis: Fortress Press, 1995.

———. *Death and Desire: The Rhetoric of Gender in the Apocalypse of John.* Louisville: Westminster/John Knox Press, 1992.

———. "Jezebel Re-Vamped." In *A Feminist Companion to Samuel and Kings,* ed. Athalya Brenner, 196–206. Sheffield, Eng.: Sheffield Academic Press, 1994.

Plaskow, Judith. *Standing Again at Sinai: Judaism from a Feminist Perspective.* San Francisco: Harper & Row, 1990.

Platt, Elizabeth E. "Jewelry, Ancient Israelite." *ABD* 3:823–34.

Pomeroy, Sarah B. *Women in Hellenistic Egypt: From Alexander to Cleopatra.* New York: Schocken Books, 1984.

Pope, Marvin H. *Song of Songs: A New Translation with Introduction and Commentary.* Garden City, N.Y.: Doubleday, 1977.

Porten, Bezalel, and Ada Yardeni, trans. *Textbook of Aramaic Documents from Ancient Egypt.* Vol. 2: *Contracts.* Jerusalem: Akademon, 1989.

Pressler, Carolyn. *The View of Women Found in the Deuteronomic Family Laws.* New York: Walter de Gruyter, 1993.

———. "Wives and Daughters, Bond and Free: Women in the Slave Laws of Ex 21:2–11." In *Gender and Biblical Law,* ed. Victor Matthews, Bernard Levinson, and Tikva Frymer-Kensky. Sheffield, Eng.: Sheffield Academic Press, 1998.

Price, James L. "Widow." In *Harper's Bible Dictionary,* ed. Paul J. Achtemeier, 1132. San Francisco: Harper & Row, 1971.

Pritchard, James B., ed. *Ancient Near Eastern Texts Relating to the Old Testament.* 3rd ed. with suppl. Princeton: Princeton University Press, 1969.

———, ed. *Solomon and Sheba.* London: Phaidon, 1974.

Propp, William H. "That Bloody Bridegroom (Exodus iv 24–6)." *VT* 43 (1993): 495–518.

Purnbam, Timothy John. "Male and Female Slaves in the Sabbath Year Laws of Exodus 21:2–11." In *SBL Seminar Papers,* 1987, 549–59.

Rast, Walter E. "Cakes for the Queen of Heaven." In *Scripture in History & Theology: Essays in Honor of J. Coert Rylaarsdam,* ed. Arthur L. Merrill and Thomas W. Overholt, 167–80. Pittsburgh: Pickwick, 1977.

Redmond, Layne. *When the Drummers Were Women: A Spiritual History of Rhythm.* New York: Three Rivers Press, 1997.

Reed, William LaForest. *The Asherah in the Old Testament.* Fort Worth, Tex.: Texas Christian University Press, 1949.

Reese, James M. *Hellenistic Influence on the Book of Wisdom and Its Consequences.* Rome: Pontifical Biblical Institute, 1970.

Reinhartz, Adele. "Anonymity and Character in the Books of Samuel." *Semeia* 63 (1993): 117–41.

———. "Anonymous Women and the Collapse of the Monarchy: A Study in Narrative Technique." In *A Feminist Companion to Samuel and Kings,* ed. Athalya Brenner, 43–65. Sheffield, Eng.: Sheffield Academic Press, 1994.

———. "From Narrative to History: The Resurrection of Mary and Martha." In *"Women Like This": New Perspectives on Jewish Women in the Greco-Roman World,* ed. Amy-Jill Levine, 161–84. Atlanta: Scholars Press, 1991.

———. "The Gospel of John." *STS* 2:561–600.

———. "The Greek Book of Esther." *WBC,* expanded ed., 286–92.

———. "Samson's Mother: An Unnamed Protagonist." *JSOT* 55 (1992): 25–37.

———. *"Why Ask My Name?": Anonymity and Identity in Biblical Narrative.* New York: Oxford University Press, 1998.

Ricci, Carla. *Mary Magdalene and Many Others: Women Who Followed Jesus,* trans. Paul Burns. Minneapolis: Fortress Press, 1994.

Rice, Gene. "Africans and the Origin of the Worship of Yahweh." *JRT* 50 (1993–1994): 27–44.

Richter Reimer, Ivoni. *Women in the Acts of the Apostles: A Feminist Liberation Perspective,* trans. Linda M. Maloney. Minneapolis: Fortress Press, 1995.

Ringe, Sharon H. "A Gentile Woman's Story, Revisited." In *A Feminist Companion to Mark and Matthew,* ed. Amy-Jill Levine. Sheffield, Eng.: Sheffield Academic Press, forthcoming.

Robbins, Tom. *Skinny Legs and All.* New York: Bantam Books, 1990.

Roberts, Jimmy J. M. "Isaiah and His Children." In *Biblical and Related Studies Presented to Samuel Iwry,* ed. Ann Kort and Scott Morschauser, 193–203. Winona Lake, Ind.: Eisenbrauns, 1985.

Robins, Gay. *Women in Ancient Egypt.* Cambridge, Mass.: Harvard University Press, 1993.

Robinson, Bernard P. "Zipporah to the Rescue: A Contextual Study of Exodus 4:24–6." *VT* 36 (1986): 447–61.

Rosenblatt, Marie-Eloise. "Jude." *STS* 2:392–98.

Ross-Burstall, Joan. "Leah and Rachel: A Tale of Two Sisters [Gen 29:31–30:24]." *Word & World* 14 (1994): 162–70.

Rostovtzeff, M. "Ptolemaic Egypt." In *The Cambridge Ancient History* 7:109–54. Cambridge: Cambridge University Press, 1963.

Rowley, Harold Henry. "The Marriage of Hosea." In *Men of God: Studies in Old Testament History and Prophecy,* 66–97. London: Nelson, 1963.

Russell, Letty, ed. *Feminist Interpretation of the Bible.* Philadelphia: Westminster Press, 1985.

Sakenfeld, Katharine Doob. "Feminist Biblical Interpretation." *Theology Today* 46 (1989): 154–68.

———. "Old Testament Perspectives: Methodological Issues." *JSOT* 22 (1982): 13–20.

Sanday, Peggy R. "Female Status in the Public Domain." In *Woman, Culture, and Society,* ed. Michelle Zimbalist Rosaldo and Louise Lamphere, 189–206. Stanford, Calif.: Stanford University Press, 1974.

Sanderson, Judith E. "Amos." *WBC,* 205–9.

———. "Habakkuk." *WBC,* 222–24.

———. "Nahum." *WBC,* 217–21.

———. "Zephaniah." *WBC,* 225–27.

Sasson, Jack M. "Who Cut Samson's Hair? (And Other Trifling Issues Raised by Judges 16)." *Prooftexts* 8 (1988): 333–39.

Sawyer, John F. A. "Daughter of Zion and Servant of the Lord in Isaiah: A Comparison." *JSOT* 44 (1989): 89–107.

Schaberg, Jane. "How Mary Magdalene Became a Whore." *BibRev* 8 (1992): 30–37, 51–52.

———. *The Illegitimacy of Jesus: A Feminist Theological Interpretation of the Infancy Narratives.* San Francisco: Harper & Row, 1987.

———. "Luke." *WBC,* 275–92.

Schearing, Linda S. "Queen." *ABD* 5:583–86.

Schiffman, Lawrence H. "Priests." In *Harper's Bible*

Dictionary, ed. Paul J. Achtemeier, 821–23. San Francisco: Harper & Row, 1985.

Schilling, O. "*bśr*." In *Theological Dictionary of the Old Testament*, ed. G. Johannes Botterweck and Helmer Ringgren, 2:313–16. Grand Rapids, Mich.: Eerdmans, 1975.

Schnackenburg, Rudolf. *Ephesians: A Commentary*, trans. Helen Heron. Edinburgh: T. & T. Clark, 1991.

Schneider, Jane, and Annette B. Weiner. "Cloth and the Organization of Human Experience." *Current Anthropology* 27 (1986): 178–84.

Schroer, Silvia. "The Book of Sophia." *STS* 2:17–38.

Schuller, Eileen M. "The Apocrypha." In *WBC*, 235–43.

———. "Introduction to the Apocrypha." *WBC*, expanded ed., 263–64.

———. "1 Esdras." *WBC*, expanded ed., 265–66.

———. "Tobit." *WBC*, expanded ed., 272–78.

Schulman, Alan R. "Diplomatic Marriage in the Egyptian New Kingdom." *Journal of Near Eastern Studies* 38 (1979): 177–93.

Schüssler Fiorenza, Elisabeth. *The Book of Revelation — Justice and Judgment*. Philadelphia: Fortress Press, 1985.

———. *But She Said: Feminist Practices of Biblical Interpretation*. Boston: Beacon Press, 1992.

———."The Ethics of Interpretation: De-centering Biblical Scholarship." *JBL* 107 (1988): 3–17.

———. "A Feminist Critical Interpretation for Liberation: Martha and Mary: Luke 10:38–42." *Religion and Intellectual Life* 3 (1986): 21–36.

———. *In Memory of Her: A Feminist Theological Reconstruction of Christian Origins*. New York: Crossroad, 1983.

———. *Jesus: Miriam's Child, Sophia's Prophet: Critical Issues in Feminist Christology*. New York: Continuum, 1994.

———. "Missionaries, Apostles, Coworkers: Romans 16 and the Reconstruction of Women's Early Christian History." *Word and World* 6 (1986): 420–33.

———. "The 'Quilting' of Women's History: Phoebe of Cenchreae." In *Embodied Love: Sensuality and Relationship as Feminist Values*, ed. Paula M. Cooey, Sharon A. Farmer, and Mary

Ellen Ross, 35–49. San Francisco: Harper & Row, 1987.

———. "Wisdom Mythology and the Christological Hymns of the New Testament." In *Aspects of Wisdom in Judaism and Early Christianity*, ed. Robert L. Wilken, 17–41. Notre Dame, Ind.: University of Notre Dame Press, 1975.

Seim, Turid Karlsen. *The Double Message: Patterns of Gender in Luke-Acts*. Nashville: Abingdon Press, 1994.

———. "The Gospel of Luke." *STS* 2:728–62.

Seipel, Wilfried. "Heiratspolitik." In *Lexikon der Ägyptologie*, ed. Wolfgang Helck and Eberhard Otto, 2:1104–7. Wiesbaden, Germany: Otto Harrassowitz, 1979.

Selvidge, Marla. *Notorious Voices: Feminist Biblical Interpretation, 1550–1920*. New York: Paragon, 1975.

Setel, Drorah O'Donnel. "Exodus." *WBC*, 26–35.

Sheres, Ita. *Dinah's Rebellion: A Biblical Parable for Our Time*. New York: Crossroad, 1990.

Shields, Mary E. "Subverting a Man of God, Elevating a Woman: Role and Power Reversals in 2 Kings 4." *JSOT* 58 (1993): 59–69.

Siebert-Hommes, Jopie. "But If She Be a Daughter . . . She May Live! 'Daughters' and 'Sons' in Exodus 1–2." In *A Feminist Companion to Exodus to Deuteronomy*, ed. Athalaya Brenner, 62–74. Sheffield, Eng.: Sheffield Academic Press, 1994.

Skehan, Patrick W., and Alexander A. Di Lella. *The Wisdom of Ben Sira: A New Translation with Notes, Introduction, and Commentary*. Garden City, N.Y.: Doubleday, 1987.

Spanier, Kitziah. "The Queen Mother in the Judaean Royal Court: Maacah — A Case Study." In *A Feminist Companion to Samuel and Kings*, ed. Athalya Brenner, 186–95. Sheffield, Eng.: Sheffield Academic Press, 1994.

———. "Rachel's Theft of the Teraphim: Her Struggle for Family Primacy [Gen 31]." *VT* 42 (1992): 404–12.

Spencer, F. Scott. "Out of Mind, Out of Voice: Slavegirls and Prophetic Daughters in Luke-Acts." *Biblical Interpretation* 7 (1999): 133–55.

Stager, Lawrence E. "Archaeology, Ecology, and Social History: Background Themes to the Song of

Deborah." In *Jerusalem Congress Volume, 1986,* ed. J. A. Emerton, 221–34. Leiden, Netherlands: E. J. Brill, 1988.

Stager, Lawrence E., and Samuel R. Wolff. "Child Sacrifice at Carthage — Religious Rite or Population Control?: Archaeological Evidence Provides Basis for New Analysis." *BARev* 10 (1984): 31–51.

Stansell, Gary. "Mothers and Sons in Ancient Israel." In *"Ihr Völker alle, klatscht in die Hände!" Festschrift für Erhard S. Gerstenberger Zum 65. Geburtstag,* ed. Rainer Kessler et al., 269–90. Münster, Germany: Lit Verlag, 1997.

Steinberg, Naomi. "Kinship and Gender in Genesis." *BR* 39 (1994): 46–56.

———. *Kinship and Marriage in Genesis: A Household Economics Perspective.* Minneapolis: Fortress Press, 1993.

Stendahl, Krister. *The Bible and Role of Women: A Case of Hermeneutics,* trans. Emilie T. Sander. Philadelphia: Fortress Press, 1966.

Sternberg, Meir. *The Poetics of Biblical Narrative: Ideological Literature and the Drama of Reading.* Bloomington: Indiana University Press, 1985.

Stinespring, William F. "No Daughter of Zion: A Study of the Appositional Genitive in Hebrew Grammar." *Encounter* 26 (1965): 133–41.

Stone, Kenneth Alan. "Gender and Homosexuality in Judges 19: Subject-Honor, Object-Shame?" *JSOT* 67 (1995): 87–107.

———. *Sex, Honor, and Power in the Deuteronomistic History.* Sheffield, Eng.: Sheffield Academic Press, 1996.

———. "Sexual Power and Political Prestige: The Case of the Disputed Concubines." *BibRev* 10 (1994): 28–31, 52–53.

Stone, Michael E. "Esdras, Second Book of." *ABD* 2:611–614.

Strecker, Georg. *The Johannine Letters: A Commentary on 1, 2, and 3 John,* trans. Linda M. Maloney. Minneapolis: Fortress Press, 1996.

Stricker, B. H. "Trois études de phonétique et de morphologie coptes." *Acta Orientalia* 15 (1937): 1–20.

Swidler, Arlene. "In Search of Huldah." *Bible Today* 98 (1978): 1780–85.

Tanzer, Sarah J. "Ephesians." *STS* 2: 325–48.

———. "The Wisdom of Solomon." *WBC,* expanded ed., 293–97.

Teugels, Lieve. "'A Strong Woman Who Can Find?' A Study of Characterization in Genesis 24 with Some Perspectives on the General Presentation of Isaac and Rebekah in the Genesis Narrative." *JSOT* 63 (1994): 89–104.

Theissen, Gerd. *Sociology of Early Palestinian Christianity,* trans. John Bowden. Philadelphia: Fortress Press, 1978.

Thomas, W. Derek. "The Place of Women in the Church at Philippi." *Expository Times* 83 (1972): 117–20.

Thompson, Cynthia L. "Hairstyles, Head-coverings, and St. Paul: Portraits from Roman Corinth." *BA* 51 (1988): 99–115.

Thompson, Mary R. *Mary of Magdala: Apostle and Leader.* New York: Paulist Press, 1995.

Thorley, John, "Junia, a Woman Apostle," *NovT* 38 (1996): 18–29.

Tigay, Jeffrey H. "Israelite Religion: The Onomastic and Epigraphic Evidence." In *Ancient Israelite Religion: Essays in Honor of Frank Moore Cross,* ed. Patrick D. Miller, Jr., Paul D. Hanson, and S. Dean McBride, 157–94. Philadelphia: Fortress Press, 1987.

———. *You Shall Have No Other Gods: Israelite Religion in the Light of Hebrew Inscriptions.* Atlanta: Scholars Press, 1986.

Tolbert, Mary Ann. *The Bible and Feminist Hermeneutics. Semeia* 28 (1983).

———. "Mark." *WBC,* 263–74.

Torjesen, Karen Jo. *When Women Were Priests: Women's Leadership in the Early Church and the Scandal of Their Subordination in the Rise of Christianity.* San Francisco: HarperSanFrancisco, 1993.

Towler, Jean, and Joan Bramall. *Midwives in History and Society.* London: Croom Helm, 1986.

Treggiari, Susan. *Roman Marriage: Iusti Coniuges from the Time of Cicero to the Time of Ulpian.* Oxford: Clarendon Press, 1991.

Trenchard, Warren C. *Ben Sira's View of Women: A Literary Analysis.* Chico, Calif.: Scholars Press, 1982.

Trible, Phyllis. "Bringing Miriam Out of the Shadows." *BibRev* 5 (1989): 14–25, 34.

———. "The Daughter of Jephthah: An Inhuman Sacrifice." In *Texts of Terror: Literary-Feminist Readings of Biblical Narratives*, 92–116. Philadelphia: Fortress Press, 1984.

———. "Genesis 22: The Sacrifice of Sarah." In *Not in Heaven: Coherence and Complexity in Biblical Narrative*, ed. Jason P. Rosenblatt and Joseph C. Sitterson, 170–91. Bloomington: Indiana University Press, 1991.

———. *God and the Rhetoric of Sexuality*. Philadelphia: Fortress Press, 1978.

———. "God, Nature of, in the Old Testament." In *Interpreter's Dictionary of the Bible*, suppl. vol., ed. Keith Crim, 368–69. Nashville: Abingdon Press, 1976.

———. "Hagar: The Desolation of Rejection." In *Texts of Terror: Literary-Feminist Readings of Biblical Narratives*, 9–35. Philadelphia: Fortress Press, 1984.

———. "A Human Comedy." In *God and the Rhetoric of Sexuality*, 166–99. Philadelphia: Fortress Press, 1978.

———. "Journey of a Metaphor." In *God and the Rhetoric of Sexuality*, 31–59. Philadelphia: Fortress Press, 1978.

———. "A Love Story Gone Awry." In *God and the Rhetoric of Sexuality*, 72–143. Philadelphia: Fortress Press, 1978.

———. "The Odd Couple: Elijah and Jezebel." In *Out of the Garden: Women Writers on the Bible*, ed. Christina Büchmann and Celina Spiegel, 166–79, 340–41. New York: Fawcett Columbine, 1994.

———. *Texts of Terror: Literary-Feminist Readings of Biblical Narratives*. Philadelphia: Fortress Press, 1984.

———. "Two Women in a Man's World: A Reading of the Book of Ruth." *Soundings* 59 (1976): 251–79.

Troy, Lana. *Patterns of Queenship in Ancient Egyptian Myth and History*. Uppsala, Sweden: Almqvist & Wiksell International, 1986.

Tucker, Gordon. "Jacob's Terrible Burden: In the Shadow of the Text." *BibRev* 10 (1994): 20–28, 54.

Tull, Patricia K. "Baruch." *WBC*, expanded ed., 305–8.

———. "The Letter of Jeremiah." *WBC*, expanded ed., 309–10.

———. "The Prayer of Manasseh." *WBC*, expanded ed., 316.

Turnbaum, Timothy John. "Male and Female Slaves in the Sabbath Year Laws of Exodus 21:2–11." In *SBL Seminar Papers, 1987*, 549–59. Decatur, Ga.: Scholars Press, 1989.

van Bremen, Riet. *The Limits of Participation: Women and Civic Life in the Greek East in the Hellenistic and Roman Periods*. Amsterdam: J. C. Gieben, 1996.

van der Toorn, Karel. "The Nature of the Biblical Teraphim in the Light of the Cuneiform Evidence." *CBQ* 52 (1990): 203–22.

———. "Prostitution (Cultic)." *ABD* 5:510–13.

van Dijk-Hemmes, Fokkelien. "The Great Woman of Shunem and the Man of God: A Dual Interpretation of 2 Kings 4:8–37." In *A Feminist Companion to Samuel and Kings*, ed. Athalya Brenner, 218–30. Sheffield, Eng.: Sheffield Academic Press, 1994.

———. "Tamar and the Limits of Patriarchy: Between Rape and Seduction." In *Anti-Covenant: Counter-Reading Women's Lives in the Hebrew Bible*, ed. Mieke Bal, 135–56. Sheffield, Eng.: Almond Press, 1989.

van Wolde, Ellen. "Deborah and Ya'el in Judges 4." In *On Reading Prophetic Texts: Gender-Specific and Related Studies in Memory of Fokkelien van Dijk-Hemmes*, 283–95. Leiden, Netherlands: E. J. Brill, 1996.

———. "Who Guides Whom? Embeddedness and Perspective in Biblical Hebrew and in 1 Kings 3:16–28." *JBL* 114 (1995): 623–42.

———. "Ya'el in Judges 4." *ZAW* 107 (1995): 240–46.

Verner, David C. *The Household of God: The Social World of the Pastoral Epistles*. Chico, Calif.: Scholars Press, 1983.

Wahlberg, Rachel Conrad. *Jesus According to a Woman*, rev. ed. New York: Paulist Press, 1986.

Wainwright, Elaine M. "The Gospel of Matthew." *STS* 2:634–77.

————. "Not Without My Daughter: Gender and Demon Possession in Matt 15.21–28." In *A Feminist Companion to Mark and Matthew*, ed. Amy-Jill Levine. Sheffield, Eng.: Sheffield Academic Press, forthcoming.

Wallace, Howard N. *The Eden Narrative*. Atlanta: Scholars Press, 1985.

Walls, Neal H. *The Goddess Anat in Ugaritic Myth*. Atlanta: Scholars Press, 1992.

Washington, Harold C. "'Lest He Die in the Battle and Another Man Take Her': Violence and the Construction of Gender in the Laws of Deuteronomy." In *Gender and Law in the Bible and the Ancient Near East*, ed. Victor H. Matthews, Bernard M. Levinson, and Tikva Frymer-Kensky, 185–213. Sheffield, Eng.: Sheffield Academic Press, 1998.

————. "The Strange Woman (*'šh zrh/nkryh*) of Proverbs 1–9 and Post-Exilic Judaean Society." In *A Feminist Companion to Wisdom Literature*, ed. Athalya Brenner, 157–85. Sheffield, Eng.: Sheffield Academic Press, 1995.

Wassen, Cecilia. "The Story of Judah and Tamar in the Eyes of the Earliest Interpreters." *Literature & Theology* 8 (1994): 354–66.

Watty, William W. "The Significance of Anonymity in the Fourth Gospel." *Expository Times* 90 (1979): 209–12.

Weems, Renita J. *Battered Love: Marriage, Sex, and Violence in the Hebrew Prophets*. Minneapolis: Fortress Press, 1995.

————. "'Is She Not My Wife?' Prophets, Audiences, and Expectations." In *Battered Love: Marriage, Sex, and Violence in the Hebrew Prophets*, 35–67. Minneapolis: Fortress Press, 1995.

————. *Just a Sister Away: A Womanist Vision of Women's Relationships in the Bible*. San Diego, Calif.: LuraMedia, 1988.

————. "Song of Songs." *WBC*, 156–60.

Wegner, Judith Romney. *Chattel or Person? The Status of Women in the Mishnah*. New York: Oxford University Press, 1988.

————. "Leviticus." *WBC*, 36–44.

Weinfeld, Moshe. *Deuteronomy and the Deuteronomic School*. Oxford: Clarendon Press, 1972.

————. "Sarah and Abimelech (Genesis 20) Against the Background of an Assyrian Law and the Genesis Apocryphon." In *Mélanges bibliques et orientaux en l'honneur de M Mathias Delcor*, ed. A. Caquot, S. Légasse, and M. Tardieu, 431–36. Kevelaer, Germany: Butzon und Bercker, 1985.

Wenham, David. "Abomination of Desolation." *ABD* 1:28–31.

Wenham, Gordon J. "Divorce." In *The Oxford Companion to the Bible*, ed. Bruce M. Metzger and Michael D. Coogan, 169–71. Oxford: Oxford University Press, 1993.

————. "Why Does Sexual Intercourse Defile (Lev 15:18)?" *ZAW* 95 (1983): 432–34.

Westbrook, Raymond. "Cuneiform Law Codes and the Origins of Legislation." *Zeitschrift für Assyriologie und Vorderasiatische Archäologie* 79 (1989): 201–22.

————. "The Prohibition on Restoration of Marriage in Deuteronomy 24:1–4." In *Studies in Bible 1986*, ed. Sara Japhet, 387–405. Jerusalem: Magnes Press, Hebrew University, 1986.

————. *Property and the Family in Biblical Law*. Sheffield, Eng.: Sheffield Academic Press, 1991.

Westenholz, Joan Goodnick. "Tamar, *Qedesa, Qadistu*, and Sacred Prostitution in Mesopotamia." *HTR* 82 (1989): 245–65.

White, Marsha C. "Jonah." *WBC*, 212–14.

White, Sidnie A. "Esther." *WBC*, 124–29.

————. "Esther: A Feminine Model for Jewish Diaspora." In *Gender and Difference in Ancient Israel*, ed. Peggy L. Day, 161–77. Minneapolis: Fortress Press, 1989.

Whitehorne, John. "Cleopatra." *ABD* 1:1064.

Wiggins, Steve A. *A Reassessment of 'Asherah': A Study According to the Textual Sources of the First Two Millennia* B.C.E. Kevelaer, Germany: Butzon & Bercker, 1993.

Willey, Patricia K. "The Importunate Woman of Tekoa and How She Got Her Way." In *Reading Between Texts: Intertextuality and the Bible*, ed. Danna Nolan Fewell, 115–31. Louisville: Westminster/John Knox Press, 1992.

Williamson, H. G. M. *Ezra, Nehemiah*. Waco, Tex.: Word Books, 1985.

————. "Source and Redaction in the Chronicler's Genealogy of Judah." *JBL* 98 (1979): 351–59.

Wilson, Robert R. *Genealogy and History in the Biblical World.* New Haven: Yale University Press, 1977.

Winston, David. *The Wisdom of Solomon: A New Translation with Introduction and Commentary.* Garden City, N.Y.: Doubleday, 1979

Winter, Miriam Therese. *WomanWitness: A Feminist Lectionary and Psalter. Women of the Hebrew Scriptures,* part 2. New York: Crossroad, 1992.

Winter, S. C. "Philemon." *STS* 2:301–312.

Wire, Antoinette Clark. *The Corinthian Women Prophets: A Reconstruction Through Paul's Rhetoric.* Minneapolis: Fortress Press, 1990.

————. "Gender Roles in a Scribal Community." In *Social History of the Matthean Community: Cross Disciplinary Approaches,* ed. David L. Balch, 87–121. Minneapolis: Fortress Press, 1991.

Witherington, Ben, III. "The Anti-Feminist Tendencies of the 'Western' Text in Acts." *JBL* 103 (1984): 82–84.

————. "Dorcas." *ABD* 2:225–26.

————. *Women and the Genesis of Christianity.* Cambridge: Cambridge University Press, 1990.

Wright, Addison G. "The Widow's Mites: Praise or Lament? — a Matter of Context." *CBQ* 44 (1982): 256–65.

Wright, David P., and Richard N. Jones. "Discharge." *ABD* 2:204–7.

Yardeni, Ada. *'Nahal Se'elim' Documents.* Jerusalem: Ben-Gurion University of the Negev Press and the Israel Exploration Society, 1995 (Hebrew).

Yee, Gale A. "Asenath." *ABD* 1:476.

————. "By the Hand of a Woman: The Metaphor of the Woman Warrior in Judges 4." *Semeia* 61 (1993): 99–132.

————. "Hosea." *WBC,* 195–202.

————. "Ideological Criticism: Judges 17–21 and the Dismembered Body." In *Judges and Method: New Approaches in Biblical Studies,* ed. Gale Yee, 146–70. Minneapolis: Fortress Press, 1995.

————. "Jezebel." *ABD* 3:848–49.

————. "'I Have Perfumed My Bed with Myrrh': The Foreign Woman (*'iššâ zārâ*) in Proverbs 1–9." In *A Feminist Companion to Wisdom Literature,* ed. Athalya Brenner, 110–26. Sheffield, Eng.: Sheffield Academic Press, 1995.

Yohannan, John D, compiler. *Joseph and Potiphar's Wife in World Literature: An Anthology of the Story of the Chaste Youth and the Lustful Stepmother.* New York: New Directions, 1968.

Young, Robin Darling. "1 Maccabees." *WBC,* expanded ed., 318–21.

————. "2 Maccabees." *WBC,* expanded ed., 322–25.

————. "3 Maccabees." *WBC,* expanded ed., 326–29.

————. "4 Maccabees." *WBC,* expanded ed., 330–34.

————. "The 'Woman with the Soul of Abraham': Traditions about the Mother of the Maccabean Martyrs." In *"Women Like This": New Perspectives on Jewish Women in the Greco-Roman World,* ed. Amy-Jill Levine, 67–81. Atlanta: Scholars Press, 1991.

Zadok, Ran. *The Pre-Hellenistic Israelite Anthroponymy and Prosopography.* Leuven, Belgium: Uitgeverij Peeters, 1988.

Zlotowitz, Meir, trans. and ed. *The Megillah: The Book of Esther: A New Translation with a Commentary Anthologized from Talmudic, Midrashic and Rabbinic Sources.* 2nd ed. Brooklyn: Mesorah Publications, 1981.

Zonabend, Françoise. "An Anthropological Perspective on Kinship and the Family." In *A History of the Family.* Vol. 1, *Distant Worlds, Ancient Worlds,* ed. André Burguière et al., 8–70. Trans. Sarah Hanbury Tenison, Rosemary Morris, and Andrew Wilson. Cambridge, Mass.: Belknap Press of Harvard University Press, 1996.

Illustration Credits

Acknowledgments

Women in Scripture proved to be more complex in its organization, design, and production than any of us had anticipated. We are indebted in countless ways to those at our own institutions and at Houghton Mifflin Company for the expertise and energy necessary to make our vision for this book a reality. We hope that the quality of this work will be some measure of reward for everyone who contributed to the project. And we would like to add to that our profound gratitude for the enthusiasm as well as the skill with which they helped us bring this work to fruition.

At Houghton Mifflin, a number of editors — Elizabeth Buckley Kubik, Chris Coffin, Borgna Brunner, and Holly Hartman — facilitated the early stages of our work, and Susan Canavan saw us through to completion with extraordinary patience and unfailing good cheer. We are grateful to all of them and also to Becky Saikia-Wilson (managing editor), Jaquelin Pelzer (production coordinator), Peg Anderson (manuscript editor), Gordon Brumm (blind entry compiler), Dorothy Henderson (proofreading coordinator), Sherri Dietrich (proofreader), Heather Downey (manuscript editing assistant), Anne Chalmers (designer), Martha Kennedy (cover designer), Billie Porter (photo researcher), Suzanne Cope (marketing), and Maya Baran (publicist). Kevin and Kenneth Krugh of Technologies 'N Typography provided essential and careful service as compositors. Above all, we want to express our amazement and pleasure at the way manuscript editor Susanna Brougham brought the disparate styles of so many contributors into a coherent and comprehensible manuscript with her superb copyediting skills.

The assistance of Rhonda Burnette-Bletsch, Karla G. Bohmbach, Lynda Harrison, John Jackson, and Madeline McClenney-Sadler at Duke University was invaluable, as was that of Mary Colvin Hill at Texas Christian University and Debra B. Bucher at the University of Pennsylvania. Likewise, many of our colleagues at these institutions, and also Mary Rose D'Angelo at Notre Dame University, were generous with their encouragement and advice.

Finally, our deepest thanks must go to our families. They supported us fully in this project even when our attention and time were diverted, more than we would have liked, from our loved ones.

CAROL MEYERS
TONI CRAVEN
ROSS S. KRAEMER

November 1999